Peter Löhr

Computer-Supported Cooperative Work: A Book of Readings

Edited by Irene Greif
Lotus Development Corporation
Cambridge, Massachusetts

Morgan Kaufmann Publishers, Inc.
San Mateo, California

Editor and President *Michael B. Morgan*
Production Manager *Jennifer M. Ballentine*
Text and Cover Design *Michael Rogondino*
Composition *Rosenlaui Publishing Services, Inc.*
Copy Editor *Adam Cornford*
Proofreader *Catherine Cambron*

Library of Congress Cataloging-in-Publication Data

Computer-supported cooperative work.

   Includes bibliographies and index.
   1. Work groups--Data processing. 2. Microcomputers.
3. Microcomputer workstations. I. Greif, Irene.
HD66.C554 1988   658.4'036'0285416   88-9147
ISBN 0-934613-57-5

Morgan Kaufmann Publishers, Inc.
2929 Campus Drive, Suite 260
San Mateo, CA 94403
©1988 by Morgan Kaufmann Publishers, Inc.
All rights reserved.
Printed in the United States of America
ISBN 0-934613-57-5

93 92 91 90 89 5 4 3 2 1

Preface

This collection of papers grows out of two meetings on Computer-Supported Cooperative Work (CSCW). It includes several background papers—reports of the original visionary works, early research projects, and related technologies. Many of the more recent papers are in widely disseminated journals, but have never appeared together in final form. Together, they constitute a set that will have continuing value as a basic reference for both researchers and practitioners in the CSCW field. Although this is not a "how to" book for "groupware," it can also serve as valuable background reading for developers, designers and users of computer systems.

An overview of the research field precedes the papers, which are divided into three parts. Within each part of the book, papers are grouped into sections of three or four papers each. The introductions to those sections contain more detailed summaries of the individual papers. The main themes of the collection are:

Part I—Visions and First Steps toward CSCW. The early visions of Vannevar Bush and Doug Engelbart are presented in the first two papers (Readings 1 and 2). The other papers in this section (Readings 3–9) report on some of the first research projects inspired by those visions. Early technologies that first opened channels of communication for meetings at a distance—e-mail, teleconferencing, and office information systems—are also reviewed in this part of the book.

Part II—New Technologies for CSCW. Included in this section are reports on group-work support systems and their underlying technologies. These systems are prototypes being used to support different kinds of cooperative work: work at a distance, work spread over time as well as distance (asynchronous meetings), and work among a group in a conference room. A set of papers on underlying technologies emphasizes data-sharing issues. Hypertext and other database technologies for information sharing are highlighted, and several aspects of multimedia conferencing are also examined.

Part III—CSCW Design Theories. New approaches to system design and evaluation are being formulated for CSCW. The papers in this section report on some recent theoretical perspectives and on methodologies now being created that will allow us to study the complex interactions between computer systems and people systems.

I have not included an additional bibliography. The reference sections of the papers in this volume provide many clues to the reader who wants to learn more. New research results will continue to be published in journals such as *ACM Transactions on Office Information Systems, Communications of the ACM,* and *Human Computer Interaction.* The proceedings of the Second Conference on Computer-Supported Cooperative Work will be available through ACM after September 1988.

Acknowledgments

Tom Malone, Ben Shneiderman, Marilyn Mantei, Skip Ellis, and Lucy Suchman helped with the initial selection of papers. Also, my thanks to the anonymous reviewers who refined the selection and made valuable suggestions regarding the organization of the book. I am sincerely grateful for their thoughtful help.

I'm equally grateful to Julie Kling, Albert R. Meyer, Peter Orbeton, and Sunil Sarin for reviewing my own contributions. They took time from busy schedules on short notice to read the drafts and to discuss the material. Their support cheered me on, and their editing improved the text in many ways.

The collection is also based on the work of people who organized and funded the early meetings on CSCW. Paul Cashman co-chaired with me the first workshop on CSCW and helped coin the descriptive phrase "Computer-Supported Cooperative Work." Herb Krasner was the entrepreneur who initiated, found funding for, and chaired the first CSCW conference. DEC, MIT, MCC, ACM SIGCHI and SIGOIS, Lotus, and Xerox have been organizational sponsors and financial backers of the meetings. I am happy to acknowledge their help in making this volume possible.

The editor would also like to acknowledge the publishers and authors who graciously granted permission to reprint material in this volume.

Attewell, Paul, and Rule, James, "Computing and Organizations: What We Know and What We Don't Know," *CACM* **27**(12):1184–1192, 1984. Copyright ©1984 by Association for Computing Machinery. Reprinted with permission of the publisher and authors.

Bush, V., "As We May Think," *Atlantic Monthly* **176**(1):101–108, June 1945. As first published in THE ATLANTIC MONTHLY, June

Kedzierski, B., "Communication and Management Support in System Development Environments," *Proceedings of the Conference on Human Factors in Computer Systems*, Gaithersburg, MD, March 15–17, 1982. Copyright ©1982 by Association for Computing Machinery. Reprinted with permission of the publisher and author.

Keisler, S., Siegel, J., and McGuire, T. W., "Social Psychological Aspects of Computer-Mediated Communication," *American Psychologist* **39**:1123–1134, 1984. Copyright ©1984 by the American Psychological Association. Reprinted by permission of the publisher and authors.

Kraut, R., Galegher, J., Egido, C., "Relationships and Tasks in Scientific Research Collaborations," *Human Computer Interaction* **3**(1): 31–58, 1988. Copyright ©1988 by Lawrence Erlbaum Associates. Reprinted with permission of the publishr and authors.

Licklider, J. C. R., and Vezza, A., "Applications of Information Networks," *Proceedings of the IEEE* **66**(11):1330–1346, 1978. Copyright ©1978 IEEE. Reprinted, with permission, from *Proceedings of the IEEE*, 1978, pp. 1330–1346.

Malone, T., Benjamin, R. I., and Yates, J., "Electronic Markets and Electronic Hierarchies," *CACM* **30**(6):484–497, 1987. Copyright ©1987 by Association for Computing Machinery. Reprinted with permission of the publisher and authors.

Malone, T. W., Grant, K. R., Lai, K-Y., Rao, R., and Rosenblitt, D., "Semi-Structured Messages Are Surprisingly Useful for Computer-Supported Coordination," *TOOIS* **5**(2):115–131, April 1987. Copyright ©1987 by Association for Computing Machinery. Reprinted with permission of the publisher and authors.

Sarin, S., and Greif, I., "Computer-based Real-Time Conferencing Systems," *IEEE Computer* **18**(10):33–45, 1985. Copyright ©1985 IEEE. Reprinted, with permission, from *IEEE Computer*.

Sathi, A., Morton, T. E., and Roth, S. F., "Callisto: An Intelligent Project Management System," *AI Magazine*, Winter 1986, pp. 34–52. Reprinted with permission from the AI MAGAZINE, published by the American Association for Artificial Intelligence.

Sproull, L., and Kiesler, S., "Reducing Social Context Cues: Electronic Mail in Organizational Communication," *Management Science* **32**(11):1492–1512, 1986. Copyright ©1986 by Institute of Management Sciences. Reprinted with permission of the publisher and authors.

Stefik, M., Foster, G., Bobrow, D., Kahn, K., Lanning, S., and Suchman, L., "Beyond the Chalkboard: Computer Support for Collaboration and Problem Solving in Meetings," *CACM* **30**(1):32–47, 1987. Copyright ©1987 by Association for Computing Machinery. Reprinted with permission of the publisher and authors.

Thomas, R. H., Forsdick, H. C., Crowley, T. R., Schaaf, R. W., Tomlinson, R. S., Travers, V. M., and Robertson, G. G., "Diamond: A Multimedia Message System Built on a Distributed Architecture," *IEEE Computer* **18**(12):65–78, 1985. Copyright ©1985 IEEE. Reprinted, with permission, from *IEEE Computer*.

Winograd, T., "A Language/Action Perspective on the Design of Cooperative Work," *Human Computer Interaction* **3**(1):3–30, 1988. Copyright ©1988 by Lawrence Erlbaum Associates. Reprinted with permission of the publisher and author.

Contents

PART II: NEW TECHNOLOGIES FOR CSCW

Domain-Specific Coordination Support

Support for Meetings

Technology

PART III: CSCW DESIGN THEORIES

Recent Theoretical Approaches

Overview

Personal computers have penetrated large segments of our population at work and at home, making us aware of their value as well as their current limitations. But in our enthusiasm for this absorbing technical artifact, we must not lose sight of the end goal of working with *each other*, using computers to facilitate, mediate, and enhance our skills and capabilities. At the boundary between individual and group work the limits of current technology are most visible. Today, the computer that amplifies an individual's ability to calculate or to write cannot usually be brought to a meeting. For most of us, toting our computer to a meeting is cumbersome if not impossible. We revert to paper and pencil for note taking and to our own memory for facts. But with "lap-tops" here and more powerful miniature machines on the horizon, it is easy to anticipate everyone at a meeting having their own workstation and private files. CSCW is based on the expectation that far more than better note taking can accrue from bringing workstations into group settings.

Over the last half-dozen years, Computer-Supported Cooperative Work has emerged as an identifiable research field focused on the role of the computer in group work. The questions being asked relate to all aspects of how large and small groups can collaborate using computer technology: How should people plan to work together to take advantage of this powerful medium? What kinds of software should be developed? How will group work be defined and redefined to tap the potential of people and technology? The answers will come from research across a range of disciplines including computer science, artificial intelligence, psychology, sociology, organizational theory, and anthropology. CSCW is the rubric for this interdisciplinary research.

Researchers from these different intellectual communities started to recognize their shared interest in group work in the early 1980s. The first workshop, at MIT, was sponsored by DEC in August 1984. An open meeting in December 1986, this time sponsored by MCC, attracted 300 people. Since then, CSCW has gotten increased coverage in scholarly journals, as well as in the popular press.

The papers for this collection have been selected to be representative of the range of issues that make up CSCW research. Early visions of the relationship between people and information resources, mediated by the computer, are the foundation of the field. They inspired a number of technological innovations, some represented in the first set of papers—First Steps toward CSCW. A number of meeting-support systems and underlying technologies that are now considered central to CSCW are reported in papers in the second part of the book. Recently there has been increasing focus on design theories and on new methodologies for studying the impact of technology on groups. Those contributions are represented by the papers in the third section of the book. Throughout this book you will find more attention given to people—to individual and group needs—than is typical in technical papers. That focus on helping people work together is the unifying theme of CSCW, and of this collection.

CSCW research is examining ways of designing systems—people and computer systems—that will have profound implications for the way we work. It is a young field, drawing on a diverse set of more established disciplines. It has a history going back at least forty years—a history of visionaries, of advances in communications technologies, and of applying communications technologies to problem solving and decision making. The predictions of the early visionaries are being borne out today. As Vannevar Bush foresaw, it is not possible to manage all the information we collect. As Engelbart hoped, people are now more willing to master a new technology or change the way they work in order to gain the needed aid. Perhaps most important, the computer is less and less a novelty that distracts us from our real business. It is simply a device, a communications medium, a part of the process. Already, we are taking the computer into account in planning buildings that allow for network cables. We must start to take it into consideration also as we set out our work plans, organizational goals, and organizational structures.

The technology of CSCW has some distinctive characteristics resulting from its focus on people and their working relationships. We can start by saying what CSCW is not. It is not simply electronic mail. Electronic mail is a useful general-purpose communication medium, designed for person-to-person messaging, adaptable through mailing-list capabilities to some group situations, but not really tuned (or tunable) to the needs of the work group. Computer conferencing systems come closer, because of the use of shared databases of messages, with access based on the roles of people in a group. Transaction-oriented database systems rely on "coordination technologies" for concurrency and access control, and coordination is indeed fundamental to group work. However, database coordination tools are in the hands of a database administrator rather than of the end-user, and are used more to keep people from inadvertently corrupting data than for the positive goal of having a workgroup build something together.

In most CSCW systems, application software and group software are closely coupled. The papers on domain-specific CSCW software in Part 2 describe systems in which information about group processes—speech acts, roles, and working relationships—is embedded in the application support tools. The features of the systems reflect the ways in which coordination and collaboration are managed. In addition to common data formats for information exchange, and common user-interface abstractions for general-purpose operations such as cut-and-paste, another dimension is added to the integrated workstation: there will now have to be common ways for users to deal with people-related aspects of their work across all their application systems.

These mechanisms, in part, can be seen in the evolution of electronic mail into computer conferencing systems that make roles, access control, and conversational structure available to the user. Computer conferencing was first designed for certain kinds of meetings. In consensus-building meetings, for example, the Delphi technique suggests an interactive process by which participants express their opinions, review other opinions, and revise their own contributions. This sort of process can be accomplished asynchronously; the group may never be working all at the same time or in the same place. It's a natural for organized messaging, the beginning of conferencing. Messages are placed in one shared database, as opposed to the individual mailboxes of an electronic mail system. All participants can see new messages and respond to them. A moderator can step in and start new topics of discussion to shift the group from one stage of the process to the next.

Computer conferencing has since been expanded to support a wide range of "many-to-many communication" patterns. However, when computer conferencing is applied to some tasks, the model breaks down. The unstructured body of messages is suitable for the free-flowing text of natural language, but does not let us set the computer to work on our problems. Designers who draw pictures, software developers who jointly write code, financial analysts who collaborate on a budget—they all need coordination capabilities as an integral part of their work tools. That means coordination support within the CAD engineer's graphics package, within the programmer's source-code editor, within the budget writer's spreadsheet program. It means support for managing multiple versions of objects, be they pictures, programs, or spreadsheets. It means ways to distribute parts of the object for work by contributing group members, ways to track the status of those distributed parts, ways to pull completed objects back together again. The limit of electronic mail and computer conferencing is that they have such features for managing messages only. CSCW widens the technology's scope of application to all the objects we deal with.

Ideally these coordination tools should be implemented as reusable software modules that may not stand alone, but can be used by developers as components of other domain-specific products. One way to understand this is in terms of integrated workstations that provide the user with certain standard capabilities in standard ways. When products are installed, users expect to be able to tailor them to their particular hardware configuration and to their personal preferences. They expect to be able to extend the functionality of many systems through end-user programming capabilities such as macro languages. They expect to exchange information uniformly between applications through conventions like cut-and-paste. Users will soon be expecting similar levels of consistent support across products for their collaborative work needs. They will expect similar ways of tailoring a product to their organizational structures and to their immediate workgroup conventions.

Once users expect this kind of consistency, developers will need software tools—libraries of programs—that will let them provide such features in many different contexts. Just as user-interface management tools, databases, and operating-system utilities all exist to provide programmers with common services that they invoke time and again in building applications, there will have to be group-work tools—role-definition facilities, distributed-database tools, meeting-support packages—that will facilitate a similar integration of common group-work features into all products.

The necessary abstractions are beginning to emerge because many different applications have been, in *ad hoc* ways, incorporating group-work features. Areas for such applications include software engineering, CAD/CAM, office systems, co-authorship, and project management. All these applications share the same need for version management, for definition of group members' roles, for status reporting and tracking, and for connections to electronic mail. Many of the requirements are summarized in the Greif and Sarin paper in this volume (Reading 17).

The issue of anticipating group usage in individual support systems is going to become more important as people realize the limits of their current software and try to use it in group settings. The extent to which group awareness is considered in the early design of a product will affect its functionality in future conferencing settings.

Keith Lantz's paper in (Reading 19) suggests techniques to add meeting support to existing applications. For example, this could make your favorite word processor usable in a meeting with a co-author: you could work at different sites, see the same document, and take turns typing into it. However, you could not maintain a history of the alternating authors' versions of a single paragraph unless the original word processor supported versioning. Today's application programs have limited use in meetings. As designers begin to anticipate multi-user situations, even in software for individuals, their products will have wider applicability in group settings.

A new class of commercial software has been named "groupware." It is software designed to take group work into account in an integral way. Groupware products range from the electronic-mail–like coordination tools to forms-tracking systems and document-commenting process managers. They have in common that they put coordination technology into the hands of the group members, giving them access to the positive aspects of coordination—not just preventing collisions, but enabling collaboration. Groupware will be made commonplace by the evolving understanding of what the key coordination technologies are, how they should appear to end-users, and what the software libraries are that embody this understanding.

As a research field, CSCW is distinct from any of the fields on which it draws. These fields from which we borrow methodologies—sociology, anthropology, and organizational design—have specialties for studying computer-related phenomena, but are certainly not primarily interested in the interaction of computers and people. Some fields that do focus on computer technology (various subfields of Computer Science, Human Factors in Computing, and Office Information Systems) are more closely related, and have significant overlap.

This overlap has historical precedence. In 1968, at the IFIP Fall Joint Computer Conference in San Francisco, Engelbart demonstrated a prototype system for collaborative work (see Reading 4). This early system was built from scratch, without the benefit of software tools that most developers now take for granted. The system architecture was based on many now common principles. The way the user interface was supported, through separable code, anticipated today's User Interface Management Systems (UIMS). The structured documents, linked text, and archival databases of documents were precursors of hypertext; network access and remote procedure calls were also used. If Engelbart's system were taken as the measure of CSCW's overlap with other computer science fields, it would be almost all-inclusive.

Today CSCW continues to incorporate computer science research that facilitates the building of collaboration tools. Most of the technologies—programming language, operating system, database—are covered in other research communities. CSCW seems to require a particularly rich platform for systems development. Problems having to do with integrating these technologies remain a topic of special interest to CSCW researchers.

Engelbart's system was also the first to incorporate features such as windows, mixed text and graphics, pop-up menus, and mouse input. His concern for how people would work together naturally led him to focus on the user interface and to invent tools such as the mouse that make the computer easier to use. Today, the human-computer interface aspects of his work might more properly be labelled research in Human Factors in Computing Systems; only those aspects explicitly related to group work would appear in CSCW. The Computer-Human Interaction (CHI) community now studies group work because it does affect the interface, and because the sociotechnical issues that arise are of interest.

The Human Factors in Computing community has a similar interdisciplinary mix, although until recently, probably not as broad a base in organizational systems and management. A challenge is to find ways to test and evaluate technological impacts on groups. It's difficult enough to get meaningful results that take into account differences in experience and individual differences of users in their reactions to user interfaces. But at least it's possible to get volunteers to sit down with word processing systems or spreadsheet programs for relatively self-contained tasks. It is more difficult to "stage" a realistic group-work setting in a lab and have volunteers use the system in a way that provides meaningful data. Methodologies for testing individual user interfaces don't apply as well to group support systems. As a result, CSCW is looking more to anthropology to find methodologies for studying groups at work in their natural settings.

There are many CSCW projects in which the research group itself served as the user community and the evaluation site. This is a risky business: the validity of conclusions drawn from such specialized communities of experts remains to be validated against less-biased samples in other kinds of organizations. However, there are technical barriers to these studies. The research labs have equipment that may eventually be in the hands of the general population, but that today is expensive and not sufficiently available to permit broadbased, naturalistic testing. For example, exciting prototypes such as Colab or Lens (reported in Readings 12 and 13 in Part 2), run on expensive networked workstations that are not generally available. Incremental changes will come from both ends of the cost spectrum: groupware will be developed for lower-cost PCs, and the higher-cost platforms will slowly lower in price and become accessible.

One question about this kind of research project is whether we can generalize about the impact of the computer on meeting behavior from the experiences of a research group using its own technology. The paper on the Colab meeting room (Reading 13) shows that the effects of the technology can be surprising. We should not miss the opportunity to record meeting behavior for further analysis. Colab decided after the fact to start videotaping meetings. New rooms at other sites are being built with such equipment available from the outset. When we can compare results from observing contrasting kinds of groups—engineers versus managers, for example—we will begin to know which of the phenomena observed in Colab can be anticipated in other settings.

As research fields, Office Information Systems and CSCW have very similar descriptions. Both are interdisciplinary and strongly concerned with social as well as technical issues. The Ellis and Nutt survey of OIS (Reading 9) has a section on future trends that reads like a description of the CSCW research field. The differences are subtle: the office is a particular type of workplace, with its own particular needs both technical and social. For example, in OIS attention is paid to providing appropriate tools for different classes of people—clerical worker, knowledge worker, manager. The principle of modifying workstation design and user interface to suit classes of people applies generally. However, the specific classes seen in the office may not exhaust all the kinds of differences and interactions that can be found among classes of people working together in other settings. The classroom, the engineering division, the research lab, the design team, the software development group also deserve the same attention given the office. While the group-work issues are similar, they are looked at across applications in CSCW, but in specialized form in OIS. To the extent that OIS focuses on the special needs of the office, it can also focus on specialized approaches to group work that arise in that environment. Other specialized group-work applications—group decision support systems, management information systems, and the like—have similar relationships to CSCW.

Both sorts of research are important: we form hypotheses on the basis of special cases and test the generalizations in the larger context. The fields are thus complementary and intertwined. OIS journals will continue to feature CSCW articles with special relevance to offices; CSCW researchers will continue to value case studies and systems-design experiences originating in office settings.

Such close relationships to other fields might lead one to question the need for a new field. However, it is clear to all who attended the first CSCW conference that there is a need—a need met by CSCW's central focus on issues that are peripheral to the other fields. Although overlaps exist, CSCW is distinct from even the most closely related fields. Each of these also has its own special slant on group work as a specialization, within its broader set of issues. Only CSCW has the specific focus on groups of people and groups of computer systems that both requires and enables the kinds of theoretical research on design and organizational structures illustrated in the papers in Part 3 of this book.

One of the most exciting aspects of CSCW research is that its results are tantalizingly close to realizability. Commercial groupware products are being offered on all hardware platforms, from micros to mainframes. There remains a wealth of deep unanswered questions about group work and computer impacts, but research will have much practical experience from which to benefit as the industry runs ahead. We are approaching a level of awareness and usage in the commercial world that will provide researchers with unprecedented opportunities for observing—and influencing—the way people work together.

Engelbart may have underestimated how strong people's resistance to change would be, but he did *not* expect that simply placing equipment in front of people would solve any problem. He also knew that as the new technology is understood and people adjust their ways of working, the problems they attempt to address will also change. In part, he was creating opportunities for people to dare to define bigger problems as they acquired the augmentation tools that would allow them to work on such problems.

This opportunity was originally offered only to the select few in the research lab who had access to large, expensive customized systems not easily reproduced for general use. In the workplace, network computing will enhance information gathering and dissemination. And as campuswide computing is implemented at major universities, computer-supported collaborative teaching and learning will be part of the educational experience for all students. On graduating, they will arrive at the workplace with expectations of similarly enhanced work environments. The opportunities will be there and people will be ready to take advantage of them.

I have recently moved from a research laboratory to a software company. As a result, I have learned a lot about the practical barriers to successful commercialization of groupware products: the hardware, networking, and data management facilities are not yet in place. As those barriers break down—and they are breaking down—groupware as a news item will recede from the limelight. *All* software will be groupware. But CSCW as a research field will still be addressing the larger questions of how to design and refine good groupware—software that will allow people to work together with the best help they can get from the computer.

I

VISIONS AND FIRST STEPS TOWARD CSCW

Early Visions

The inspiration for this field comes from the "memex" first described by Vannevar Bush in his 1945 *Atlantic Monthly* article "As We May Think" (Reading 1, this volume). Bush anticipated technologies for information storage that would lead to unmanageably large information bases and then proposed an organizing structure of associative memory and trails through data. He was wrong about the technology that would drive this change: he thought it would be microfilm. But he was right in asserting that eventually technology would bring us more information than we could manage. That idea of a large, shared, structured information base inspired many researchers. Most notable among the early system developers who elaborated on this theme is Doug Engelbart and his team of researchers at SRI in the early 1960s. Engelbart bases his system for *A Conceptual Framework for Augmentation of Man's Intellect* (Reading 2, this volume) largely on high-performance workstations for accessing shared, structured information.

The papers in this section contain the seminal ideas for CSCW, as well as for much of the rest of modern computer science and many successful products. Some of these ideas—the use of the mouse, the menu, and the windows, the software architecture, the structured document, for example—are widely accepted, and many are integral parts of commercial products. Others, such as shared-screen concurrency, role hierarchies for defining user capabilities, and (most notably) the social issues affecting the adoption of skills that allow new artifacts to become everyday tools, remain the open issues of CSCW research.

The first Engelbart paper (Reading 2) sets out his framework for understanding how human capabilities can be augmented through use of artifacts, language, and training. One way to enlarge one's powers is to develop and master new skills. He points out that people who operate in a culture are in fact augmented: anyone who is effective in a society is using language tools and other artifacts to communicate with and interact with others who share his/her background and some comparable level of training. To understand how to improve people's effectiveness, he proposes taking a systems-engineering approach to this whole complex of hierarchies. The people and the computer systems must be designed together, as suggested by the framework he labels "Humans using Language, Artifact and Methodologies in which they are Trained." His process hierarchy models a way in which people can incrementally master new skills that allow them to take advantage of augmentation means. Much of what he does points to uses of hierarchy and structuring of information; the realization of these ideas can be seen in the computer systems he built (see Readings 4 and 5, this volume).

The 1982 Engelbart paper (Reading 3, this volume) provides an updated restatement of that vision, including an architectural overview of its implementation in modern networked workstations. He lists the categories of system elements, including tools, methods, skills, and the organization itself. The coevolution of the system elements points to the need for flexible systems; this motivated the very modular architecture of the systems built in his labs. However, the architecture described in this paper was not so surprising by the time of its publication (1982). The description of their research lab by Engelbart and English (Reading 4, this volume), written in 1968, presents the pioneering versions of such now-common architectural concepts as User Interface Management System (UIMS) and Remote Procedure Call (RPC).

This second paper may also give some insight into a major difference between Engelbart's approach and current expectations. His system was designed for high-performance teams whose members are trained collectively in new skills aimed at enhancing their ability to work together. The assumption was that group-work tools required skills that might be mastered only by an elite, highly trained team. CSCW looks at bringing group work support to a broad range of users, from high-performance teams to casual e-mail readers.

1

As We May Think

Vannevar Bush[1]

This has not been a scientist's war; it has been a war in which all have had a part. The scientists, burying their old professional competition in the demand of a common cause, have shared greatly and learned much. It has been exhilarating to work in effective partnership. Now, for many, this appears to be approaching an end. What are the scientists to do next?

For the biologists, and particularly for the medical scientists, there can be little indecision, for their war work has hardly required them to leave the old paths. Many indeed have been able to carry on their war research in their familiar peacetime laboratories. Their objectives remain much the same.

It is the physicists who have been thrown most violently off stride, who have left academic pursuits for the making of strange destructive

---

[1] As Director of the Office of Scientific Research and Development, Dr. Vannevar Bush has coördinated the activities of some six thousand leading American scientists in the applications of science to warfare. In this significant article he holds up an incentive for scientists when the fighting has ceased. He urges that men of science should then turn to the massive task of making more accessible our bewildering store of knowledge. For years inventions have extended man's physical powers rather than the powers of his mind. Trip hammers that multiply the fists, microscopes that sharpen the eye, and engines of destruction and detection are new results, but not the end results, of modern science. Now, says Dr. Bush, instruments are at hand which, if properly developed, will give man access to and command over the inherited knowledge of the ages. The perfection of these pacific instruments should be the first objective of our scientists as they emerge from their war work. Like Emerson's famous address of 1837 on "The American Scholar," this paper by Dr. Bush calls for a new relationship between thinking man and the sum of our knowledge.

gadgets, who have had to devise new methods for their unanticipated assignments. They have done their part on the devices that made it possible to turn back the enemy. They have worked in combined effort with the physicists of our allies. They have felt within themselves the stir of achievement. They have been part of a great team. Now, as peace approaches, one asks where they will find objectives worthy of their best.

1

Of what lasting benefit has been man's use of science and of the new instruments which his research brought into existence? First, they have increased his control of his material environment. They have improved his food, his clothing, his shelter; they have increased his security and released him partly from the bondage of bare existence. They have given him increased knowledge of his own biological processes so that he has had a progressive freedom from disease and an increased span of life. They are illuminating the interactions of his physiological and psychological functions, giving the promise of an improved mental health.

Science has provided the swiftest communication between individuals; it has provided a record of ideas and has enabled man to manipulate and to make extracts from that record so that knowledge evolves and endures throughout the life of a race rather than that of an individual.

There is a growing mountain of research. But there is increased evidence that we are being bogged down today as specialization extends. The investigator is staggered by the findings and conclusions of thousands of other workers—conclusions which he cannot find time to grasp, much less to remember, as they appear. Yet specialization becomes increasingly necessary for progress, and the effort to bridge between disciplines is correspondingly superficial.

Professionally, our methods of transmitting and reviewing the results of research are generations old and by now are totally inadequate for their purpose. If the aggregate time spent in writing scholarly works and in reading them could be evaluated, the ratio between these amounts of time might well be startling. Those who conscientiously attempt to keep abreast of current thought, even in restricted fields, by close and continuous reading might well shy away from an examination calculated to show how much of the previous month's efforts could be produced on call. Mendel's concept of the laws of genetics was lost to the world for a generation because his publication did not reach the few who were capable of grasping and extending it; and this sort of catastrophe is undoubtedly being repeated all about us, as truly significant attainments become lost in the mass of the inconsequential.

The difficulty seems to be not so much that we publish unduly in view of the extent and variety of present-day interests, but rather that publication has been extended far beyond our present ability to make real use of the record. The summation of human experience is being expanded at a prodigious rate, and the means we use for threading through the consequent maze to the momentarily important item is the same as was used in the days of square-rigged ships.

But there are signs of a change as new and powerful instrumentalities come into use. Photocells capable of seeing things in a physical sense, advanced photography which can record what is seen or even what is not, thermionic tubes capable of controlling potent forces under the guidance of less power than a mosquito uses to vibrate his wings, cathode ray tubes rendering visible an occurrence so brief that by comparison a microsecond is a long time, relay combinations which will carry out involved sequences of movements more reliably than any human operator and thousands of times as fast—there are plenty of mechanical aids with which to effect a transformation in scientific records.

Two centuries ago Leibnitz invented a calculating machine which embodied most of the essential features of recent keyboard devices, but it could not then come into use. The economics of the situation were against it: the labor involved in constructing it, before the days of mass production, exceeded the labor to be saved by its use, since all it could accomplish could be duplicated by sufficient use of pencil and paper. Moreover, it would have been subject to frequent breakdown, so that it could not have been depended upon; for at that time and long after, complexity and unreliability were synonymous.

Babbage, even with remarkably generous support for his time, could not produce his great arithmetical machine. His idea was sound enough, but construction and maintenance costs were then too heavy. Had a Pharaoh been given detailed and explicit designs of an automobile, and had he understood them completely, it would have taxed the resources of his kingdom to have fashioned the thousands of parts for a single car, and that car would have broken down on the first trip to Giza.

Machines with interchangeable parts can now be constructed with great economy of effort. In spite of much complexity, they perform reliably. Witness the humble typewriter, or the movie camera, or the automobile. Electrical contacts have ceased to stick—note the automatic telephone exchange, which has hundreds of thousands of such contacts, and yet is reliable. A spider web of metal, sealed in a thin glass container, a wire heated to a brilliant glow, in short, the thermionic tube of radio sets, is made by the hundred million, tossed about in packages, plugged into sockets—and it works! Its gossamer parts, the precise location and alignment involved in its construction, would have occupied a master craftsman of the guild for months; now it is built for thirty cents. The world has arrived at an age of cheap complex devices of great reliability; and something is bound to come of it.

2

A record, if it is to be useful to science, must be continuously extended, it must be stored, and above all it must be consulted. Today we make the record conventionally by writing and photography, followed by printing; but we also record on film, on wax disks, and on magnetic wires. Even if utterly new recording procedures do not appear, these present ones are certainly in the process of modification and extension.

Certainly progress in photography is not going to stop. Faster material and lenses, more automatic cameras, finer-grained sensitive compounds to allow an extension of the minicamera idea, are all imminent. Let us project this trend ahead to a logical, if not inevitable, outcome. The camera hound of the future wears on his forehead a lump a little larger than a walnut. It takes pictures 3 millimeters square, later to be projected or enlarged, which after all involves only a factor of 10 beyond present practice. The lens is of universal focus, down to any distance accommodated by the unaided eye, simply because it is of short focal length. There is a built-in photocell on the walnut such as we now have on at least one camera, which automatically adjusts exposure for a wide range of illumination. There is film in the walnut for a hundred exposures, and the spring for operating its shutter and shifting its film is wound once and for all when the film clip is inserted. It produces its result in full color. It may well be stereoscopic, and record with two spaced glass eyes, for striking improvements in stereoscopic techniques are just around the corner.

The cord which trips its shutter may reach down a man's sleeve within easy reach of his fingers. A quick squeeze, and the picture is taken. On a pair of ordinary glasses is a square of fine lines near the top of one lens, where it is out of the way of ordinary vision. When an object appears in that square, it is lined up for its picture. As the scientist of the future moves about the laboratory or the field, every time he looks at something worthy of the record, he trips the shutter and in it goes, without even an audible click. Is this all fantastic? The only fantastic thing about it is the idea of making as many pictures as would result from its use.

Will there be dry photography? It is already here in two forms. When Brady made his Civil War pictures, the plate had to be wet at the time of exposure. Now it has to be wet during development instead.

In the future, perhaps it need not be wetted at all. There have long been films impregnated with diazo dyes which form a picture without development, so that it is already there as soon as the camera has been operated. An exposure to ammonia gas destroys the unexposed dye, and the picture can then be taken out into the light and examined. The process is now slow, but someone may speed it up, and it has no grain difficulties such as now keep photographic researchers busy. Often it would be advantageous to be able to snap the camera and to look at the picture immediately.

Another process now in use is also slow, and more or less clumsy. For fifty years impregnated papers have been used which turn dark at every point where an electrical contact touches them, by reason of the chemical change thus produced in an iodine compound included in the paper. They have been used to make records, for a pointer moving across them can leave a trail behind. If the electrical potential on the pointer is varied as it moves, the line becomes light or dark in accordance with the potential.

This scheme is now used in facsimile transmission. The pointer draws a set of closely spaced lines across the paper one after another. As it moves, its potential is varied in accordance with a varying current received over wires from a distant station, where these variations are produced by a photocell which is similarly scanning a picture. At every instant the darkness of the line being drawn is made equal to the darkness of the point on the picture being observed by the photocell. Thus, when the whole picture has been covered, a replica appears at the receiving end.

A scene itself can be just as well looked over line-by-line by the photocell in this way as can a photograph of the scene. This whole apparatus constitutes a camera, with the added feature, which can be dispensed with if desired, of making its picture at a distance. It is slow, and the picture is poor in detail. Still, it does give another process of dry photography, in which the picture is finished as soon as it is taken.

It would be a brave man who would predict that such a process will always remain clumsy, slow, and faulty in detail. Television equipment today transmits sixteen reasonably good pictures a second, and it involves only two essential differences from the process described above. For one, the record is made by a moving beam of electrons rather than a moving pointer, for the reason that an electron beam can sweep across the picture very rapidly indeed. The other difference involves merely the use of a screen which glows momentarily when the electrons hit, rather than a chemically treated paper or film which is permanently altered. This speed is necessary in television, for motion pictures rather than stills are the object.

Use chemically treated film in place of the glowing screen, allow the apparatus to transmit one picture only rather than a succession, and use a rapid camera for dry photography. The treated film needs to be far faster in action than present examples, but it probably could be. More serious is the objection that this scheme would involve putting the film inside a vacuum chamber, for electron beams behave normally only in such a rarefied environment. This difficulty could be avoided by allowing the electron beam to play on one side of a partition, and by pressing the film against the other side, if this partition were such as to allow the electrons to go through perpendicular to its surface, and to prevent them from spreading out sideways. Such partitions, in crude form, could certainly be constructed, and they will hardly hold up the general development.

Like dry photography, microphotography still has a long way to go. The basic scheme of reducing the size of the record, and examining it by projection rather than directly, has possibilities too great to be ignored. The combination of optical projection and photographic reduction is already producing some results in microfilm for scholarly purposes, and the potentialities are highly suggestive. Today with microfilm, reductions by a linear factor of 20 can be employed and still produce full clarity when the material is re-enlarged for examination. The limits are set by the graininess of the film, the excellence of the optical system, and the efficiency of the light sources employed. All of these are rapidly improving.

Assume a linear ratio of 100 for future use. Consider film of the same thickness as paper, although thinner film will certainly be usable. Even under these conditions there would be a total factor of 10,000 between the bulk of the ordinary record in books and its microfilm replica. The *Encyclopaedia Britannica* could be reduced to the volume of a matchbox. A library of a million volumes could be compressed into one end of a desk. If the human race has produced since the invention of movable type a total record, in the form of magazines, newspapers, books, tracts, advertising blurbs, correspondence, having a volume corresponding to a billion books, the whole affair, assembled and compressed, could be lugged off in a moving van. Mere compression, of course, is not enough; one needs not only to make and store a record but also be able to consult it, and this aspect of the matter comes later. Even the modern great library is not generally consulted; it is nibbled at by a few.

Compression is important, however, when it comes to costs. The material for the microfilm *Britannica* would cost a nickel, and it could be mailed anywhere for a cent. What would it cost to print a million copies? To print a sheet of newspaper, in a large edition, costs a small fraction of a cent. The entire material of the *Britannica* in reduced microfilm form would go on a sheet eight and one-half by eleven inches. Once it is available, with the photographic reproduction methods of the future, duplicates in large quantities could probably be turned out for a cent apiece beyond the cost of materials. The preparation of the original copy? That introduces the next aspect of the subject.

3

To make the record, we now push a pencil or tap a typewriter. Then comes the process of digestion and correction, followed by an intricate process of typesetting, printing, and distribution. To consider the first stage of the procedure, will the author of the future cease writing by hand or typewriter and talk directly to the record? He does so indirectly, by talking to a stenographer or a wax cylinder; but the elements are all present if he wishes to have his talk directly produce a typed record. All he needs to do is to take advantage of existing mechanisms and to alter his language.

At a recent World Fair a machine called a Voder was shown. A girl stroked its keys and it emitted recognizable speech. No human vocal cords entered into the procedure at any point; the keys simply combined some electrically produced vibrations and passed these on to a loudspeaker. In the Bell Laboratories there is the converse of this machine, called a Vocoder. The loudspeaker is replaced by a microphone, which picks up sound. Speak to it, and the corresponding keys move. This may be one element of the postulated system.

The other element is found in the stenotype, that somewhat disconcerting device encountered usually at public meetings. A girl strokes its keys languidly and looks about the room and sometimes at the speaker with a disquieting gaze. From it emerges a typed strip which records in a phonetically simplified language a record of what the speaker is supposed to have said. Later this strip is retyped into ordinary language, for in its nascent form it is intelligible only to the initiated. Combine these two elements, let the Vocoder run the stenotype, and the result is a machine which types when talked to.

Our present languages are not especially adapted to this sort of mechanization, it is true. It is strange that the inventors of universal languages have not seized upon the idea of producing one which better fitted the technique for transmitting and recording speech. Mechanization may yet force the issue, especially in the scientific field; whereupon scientific jargon would become still less intelligible to the layman.

One can now picture a future investigator in his laboratory. His hands are free, and he is not anchored. As he moves about and observes, he photographs and comments. Time is automatically recorded to tie the two records together. If he goes into the field, he may be connected by radio to his recorder. As he ponders over his notes in the evening, he again talks his comments into the record. His typed record, as well as his photographs, may both be in miniature, so that he projects them for examination.

Much needs to occur, however, between the collection of data and observations, the extraction of parallel material from the existing record, and the final insertion of new material into the general body of the common record. For mature thought there is no mechanical substitute. But creative thought and essentially repetitive thought are very different things. For the latter there are, and may be, powerful mechanical aids.

Adding a column of figures is a repetitive thought process, and it was long ago properly relegated to the machine. True, the machine is sometimes controlled by a keyboard, and thought of a sort enters in reading the figures and poking the corresponding keys, but even this is avoidable. Machines have been made which will read typed figures by photocells and then depress the corresponding keys; these are combinations of photocells for scanning the type, electric circuits for sorting the consequent variations, and relay circuits for interpreting the result into the action of solenoids to pull the keys down.

All this complication is needed because of the clumsy way in which we have learned to write figures. If we recorded them positionally, simply by the configuration of a set of dots on a card, the automatic reading mechanism would become comparatively simple. In fact, if the dots are holes, we have the punched-card machine long ago produced by Hollorith for the purposes of the census, and now used throughout business. Some types of complex businesses could hardly operate without these machines.

Adding is only one operation. To perform arithmetical computation involves also subtraction, multiplication, and division, and in addition some method for temporary storage of results, removal from storage for further manipulation, and recording of final results by printing. Machines for these purposes are now of two types: keyboard machines for accounting and the like, manually controlled for the insertion of data, and usually automatically controlled as far as the sequence of operations is concerned; and punched-card machines in which separate operations are usually delegated to a series of machines, and the cards then transferred bodily from one to another. Both forms are very useful; but as far as complex computations are concerned, both are still in embryo.

Rapid electrical counting appeared soon after the physicists found it desirable to count cosmic rays. For their own purposes the physicists promptly constructed thermionic-tube equipment capable of counting electrical impulses at the rate of 100,000 a second. The advanced arithmetical machines of the future will be electrical in nature, and they will perform at 100 times present speeds, or more.

Moreover, they will be far more versatile than present commercial machines, so that they may readily be adapted for a wide variety of operations. They will be controlled by a control card or film, they will select their own data and manipulate it in accordance with the instructions thus inserted, they will perform complex arithmetical computations at exceedingly high speed, and they will record results in such form as to be readily available for distribution or for later further manipulation. Such machines will have enormous appetites. One of them will take instructions and data from a whole roomful of people armed with simple keyboard punches, and will deliver sheets of computed results every few minutes. There will always be plenty of things to compute in the detailed affairs of millions of people doing complicated things.

4

The repetitive processes of thought are not confined, however, to matters of arithmetic and statistics. In fact, every time one combines and records facts in accordance with established logical processes, the creative aspect of thinking is concerned only with the selection of the data and the process to be employed, and the manipulation thereafter is repetitive in nature and hence a fit matter to be relegated to the machines. Not so much has been done along these lines, beyond the bounds of arithmetic, as might be done, primarily because of the economics of the situation. The needs of business, and the extensive market obviously waiting, assured the advent of mass-produced arithmetical machines just as soon as production methods were sufficiently advanced.

With machines for advanced analysis, no such situation existed; for there was and is no extensive market; the users of advanced methods of manipulating data are a very small part of the population. There are, however, machines for solving differential equations—and functional and integral equations, for that matter. There are many special machines, such as the harmonic synthesizer which predicts the tides. There will be many more, appearing certainly first in the hands of the scientist and in small numbers.

If scientific reasoning were limited to the logical processes of arithmetic, we should not get far in our understanding of the physical world.

One might as well attempt to grasp the game of poker entirely by the use of the mathematics of probability. The abacus, with its beads strung on parallel wires, led the Arabs to positional numeration and the concept of zero many centuries before the rest of the world; and it was a useful tool—so useful that it still exists.

It is a far cry from the abacus to the modern keyboard accounting machine. It will be an equal step to the arithmetical machine of the future. But even this new machine will not take the scientist where he needs to go. Relief must be secured from laborious detailed manipulations of higher mathematics as well, if the users of it are to free their brains for something more than repetitive detailed transformations in accordance with established rules. A mathematician is not a man who can readily manipulate figures; often he cannot. He is not even a man who can readily perform the transformations of equations by the use of calculus. He is primarily an individual who is skilled in the use of symbolic logic on a high plane, and especially he is a man of intuitive judgment in the choice of the manipulative processes he employs.

All else he should be able to turn over to his mechanic, just as confidently as he turns over the propelling of his car to the intricate mechanism under the hood. Only then will mathematics be practically effective in bringing the growing knowledge of atomistics to the useful solution of the advanced problems of chemistry, metallurgy, and biology. For this reason there will come more machines to handle advanced mathematics for the scientist. Some of them will be sufficiently bizarre to suit the most fastidious connoisseur of the present artifacts of civilization.

5

The scientist, however, is not the only person who manipulates data and examines the world about him for the use of logical processes, although he sometimes preserves this appearance by adopting into the fold anyone who becomes logical, much in the manner in which a British labor leader is elevated to knighthood. Whenever logical processes of thought are employed—that is, whenever thought for a time runs along an accepted groove—there is an opportunity for the machine. Formal logic used to be a keen instrument in the hands of the teacher in his trying of students' souls. It is readily possible to construct a machine which will manipulate premises in accordance with formal logic, simply by the clever use of relay circuits. Put a set of premises into such a device and turn the crank, and it will readily pass out conclusion after conclusion, all in accordance with logical law, and with no more slips than would be expected of a keyboard adding machine.

Logic can become enormously difficult, and it would undoubtedly be well to produce more assurance in its use. The machines for higher analysis have usually been equation solvers. Ideas are beginning to appear for equation transformers, which will rearrange the relationship expressed by an equation in accordance with strict and rather advanced logic. Progress is inhibited by the exceedingly crude way in which mathematicians express their relationships. They employ a symbolism which grew like Topsy and has little consistency; a strange fact in that most logical field.

A new symbolism, probably positional, must apparently precede the reduction of mathematical transformations to machine processes. Then, on beyond the strict logic of the mathematician, lies the application of logic in everyday affairs. We may some day click off arguments on a machine with the same assurance that we now enter sales on a cash register. But the machine of logic will not look like a cash register, even of the streamlined model.

So much for the manipulation of ideas and their insertion into the record. Thus far we seem to be worse off than before—for we can enormously extend the record; yet even in its present bulk we can hardly consult it. This is a much larger matter than merely the extraction of data for the purposes of scientific research; it involves the entire process by which man profits by his inheritance of acquired knowledge. The prime action of use is selection, and here we are halting indeed. There may be millions of fine thoughts, and the account of the experience on which they are based, all encased within stone walls of acceptable architectural form; but if the scholar can get at only one a week by diligent search, his syntheses are not likely to keep up with the current scene.

Selection, in this broad sense, is a stone adze in the hands of a cabinetmaker. Yet, in a narrow sense and in other areas, something has already been done mechanically on selection. The personnel officer of a factory drops a stack of a few thousand employee cards into a selecting machine, sets a code in accordance with an established convention, and produces in a short time a list of all employees who live in Trenton and know Spanish. Even such devices are much too slow when it comes, for example, to matching a set of fingerprints with one of five million on file. Selection devices of this sort will soon be speeded up from their present rate of reviewing data at a few hundred a minute. By the use of photocells and microfilm they will survey items at the rate of a thousand a second, and will print out duplicates of those selected.

This process, however, is simple selection: it proceeds by examining in turn every one of a large set of items, and by picking out those which have certain specified characteristics. There is another form of selection best illustrated by the automatic telephone exchange. You dial a number and the machine selects and connects just one of a million possible stations. It does not run over them all. It pays attention only to a class given by a first digit, then only to a subclass of this given by the second digit, and so on; and thus proceeds rapidly and almost unerringly to the selected station. It requires a few seconds to make the selection, although the process could be speeded up if increased speed were economically warranted. If necessary, it could be made extremely fast by substituting thermionic-tube switching for mechanical switching, so that the full selection could be made in one one-hundredth of a second. No one would wish to spend the money necessary to make this change in the telephone system, but the general idea is applicable elsewhere.

Take the prosaic problem of the great department store. Every time a charge sale is made, there are a number of things to be done. The inventory needs to be revised, the salesman needs to be given credit for the sale, the general accounts need an entry, and, most important, the customer needs to be charged. A central records device has been developed in which much of this work is done conveniently. The salesman places on a stand the customer's identification card, his own card, and the card taken from the article sold—all punched cards. When he pulls a lever, contacts are made through the holes, machinery at a central point makes the necessary computations and entries, and the proper receipt is printed for the salesman to pass to the customer.

But there may be 10,000 charge customers doing business with the store, and before the full operation can be completed someone has to select the right card and insert it at the central office. Now rapid selection can slide just the proper card into position in an instant or two, and return it afterward. Another difficulty occurs, however. Someone must read a total on the card, so that the machine can add its computed item to it. Conceivably the cards might be of the dry photography type I have described. Existing totals could then be read by photocell, and the new total entered by an electron beam.

The cards may be in miniature, so that they occupy little space. They must move quickly. They need not be transferred far, but merely into position so that the photocell and recorder can operate on them. Positional dots can enter the data. At the end of the month a machine can readily be made to read these and to print an ordinary bill. With tube selection, in which no mechanical parts are involved in the switches, little time need be occupied in bringing the correct card into use—a second should suffice for the entire operation. The whole record on the card may be made by magnetic dots on a steel sheet if desired, instead of dots to be observed optically, following the scheme by which Poulsen long ago put speech on a magnetic wire. This method has the advantage of simplicity and ease of erasure. By using photography, however, one can arrange to project the record in enlarged form, and at a distance by using the process common in television equipment.

One can consider rapid selection of this form and distant projection for other purposes. To be able to key one sheet of a million before an operator in a second or two, with the possibility of then adding notes thereto, is suggestive in many ways. It might even be of use in libraries, but that is another story. At any rate, there are now some interesting combinations possible. One might, for example, speak to a microphone, in the manner described in connection with the speech-controlled typewriter, and thus make his selections. It would certainly beat the usual file clerk.

6

The real heart of the matter of selection, however, goes deeper than a lag in the adoption of mechanisms by libraries, or a lack of development of devices for their use. Our ineptitude in getting at the record is largely caused by the artificiality of systems of indexing. When data of any sort are placed in storage, they are filed alphabetically or numerically, and information is found (when it is) by tracing it down from subclass to subclass. It can be in only one place, unless duplicates are used; one has to have rules as to which path will locate it, and the rules are cumbersome. Having found one item, moreover, one has to emerge from the system and re-enter on a new path.

The human mind does not work that way. It operates by association. With one item in its grasp, it snaps instantly to the next that is suggested by the association of thoughts, in accordance with some intricate web of trails carried by the cells of the brain. It has other characteristics, of course; trails that are not frequently followed are prone to fade, items are not fully permanent, memory is transitory. Yet the speed of action, the intricacy of trails, the detail of mental pictures, is awe-inspiring beyond all else in nature.

Man cannot hope fully to duplicate this mental process artificially, but he certainly ought to be able to learn from it. In minor ways he may even improve, for his records have relative permanency. The first idea, however, to be drawn from the analogy concerns selection. Selection by association, rather than by indexing, may yet be mechanized. One cannot hope thus to equal the speed and flexibility with which the mind follows an associative trail, but it should be possible to beat the mind decisively in regard to the permanence and clarity of the items resurrected from storage.

Consider a future device for individual use, which is a sort of mechanized private file and library. It needs a name, and, to coin one at random, "memex" will do. A memex is a device in which an individual stores his books, records, and communications, and which is mechanized so that it may be consulted with exceeding speed and flexibility. It is an enlarged intimate supplement to his memory.

It consists of a desk, and while it can presumably be operated from a distance, it is primarily the piece of furniture at which he works. On the top are slanting translucent screens, on which material can be projected for convenient reading. There is a keyboard, and sets of buttons and levers. Otherwise it looks like an ordinary desk.

In one end is the stored material. The matter of bulk is well taken care of by improved microfilm. Only a small part of the interior of the memex is devoted to storage, the rest to mechanism. Yet if the user inserted 5000 pages of material a day it would take him hundreds of years to fill the repository, so he can be profligate and enter material freely.

Most of the memex contents are purchased on microfilm ready for insertion. Books of all sorts, pictures, current periodicals, newspapers, are thus obtained and dropped into place. Business correspondence takes the same path. And there is provision for direct entry. On the top of the memex is a transparent platen. On this are placed longhand notes, photographs, memoranda, all sorts of things. When one is in place, the depression of a lever causes it to be photographed onto the next blank space in a section of the memex film, dry photography being employed.

There is, of course, provision for consultation of the record by the usual scheme of indexing. If the user wishes to consult a certain book, he taps its code on the keyboard, and the title page of the book promptly appears before him, projected onto one of his viewing positions. Frequently used codes are mnemonic, so that he seldom consults his code book; but when he does, a single tap of a key projects it for his use. Moreover, he has supplemental levers. On deflecting one of these levers to the right he runs through the book before him, each paper in turn being projected at a speed which just allows a recognizing glance at each. If he deflects it further to the right, he steps through the book 10 pages at a time; still further at 100 pages at a time. Deflection to the left gives him the same control backwards.

A special button transfers him immediately to the first page of the index. Any given book of his library can thus be called up and consulted with far greater facility than if it were taken from a shelf. As he has several projection positions, he can leave one item in position while he calls up another. He can add marginal notes and comments, taking advantage of one possible type of dry photography, and it could even be arranged so that he can do this by a stylus scheme, such as is now employed in the telautograph seen in railroad waiting rooms, just as though he had the physical page before him.

7

All this is conventional, except for the projection forward of present-day mechanisms and gadgetry. It affords an immediate step, however, to associative indexing, the basic idea of which is a provision whereby any item may be caused at will to select immediately and automatically another. This is the essential feature of the memex. The process of tying two items together is the important thing.

When the user is building a trail, he names it, inserts the name in his code book, and taps it out on his keyboard. Before him are the two items to be joined, projected onto adjacent viewing positions. At the bottom of each there are a number of blank code spaces, and a pointer is set to indicate one of these on each item. The user taps a single key, and the items are permanently joined. In each code space appears the code word. Out of view, but also in the code space, is inserted a set of dots for photocell viewing; and on each item these dots by their positions designate the index number of the other item.

Thereafter, at any time, when one of these items is in view, the other can be instantly recalled merely by tapping a button below the corresponding code space. Moreover, when numerous items have been thus joined together to form a trail, they can be reviewed in turn, rapidly or slowly, by deflecting a lever like that used for turning the pages of a book. It is exactly as though the physical items had been gathered together from widely separated sources and bound together to form a new book. It is more than this, for any item can be joined into numerous trails.

The owner of the memex, let us say, is interested in the origin and properties of the bow and arrow. Specifically he is studying why the short Turkish bow was apparently superior to the English long bow in the skirmishes of the Crusades. He has dozens of possibly pertinent books and articles in his memex. First he runs through an encyclopedia, finds an interesting but sketchy article, leaves it projected. Next, in a history, he finds another pertinent item, and ties the two together. Thus he goes, building a trail of many items. Occasionally he inserts a comment of his own, either linking it into the main trail or joining it by a side trail to a particular item. When it becomes evident that the elastic properties of available materials had a great deal to do with the bow, he branches off on a side trail which takes him through textbooks on elasticity and tables of physical constants. He inserts a page of longhand analysis of his own. Thus he builds a trail of his interest through the maze of materials available to him.

And his trails do not fade. Several years later, his talk with a friend turns to the queer ways in which a people resist innovations, even of vital interest. He has an example, in the fact that the outranged Europeans still failed to adopt the Turkish bow. In fact, he has a trail on it. A touch brings up the code book. Tapping a few keys projects the head of the trail. A lever runs through it at will, stopping at intersecting items, going off on side excursions. It is an interesting trail, pertinent to the discussion. So he sets a reproducer in action, photographs the whole trail out, and passes it to his friend for insertion in his own memex, there to be linked into the more general trail.

8

Wholly new forms of encyclopedias will appear, ready-made with a mesh of associative trails running through them, ready to be dropped into the memex and there amplified. The lawyer has at his touch the associated opinions and decisions of his whole experience and of the experience of friends and authorities. The patent attorney has on call the millions of issued patents, with familiar trails to every point of his client's interest. The physician, puzzled by a patient's reactions, strikes the trail established in studying an earlier similar case, and runs rapidly through analogous case histories, with side references to the classics for the pertinent anatomy and histology. The chemist, struggling with the synthesis of an organic compound, has all the chemical literature before him in his laboratory, with trails following the analogies of compounds, the side trails to their physical and chemical behavior.

The historian, with a vast chronological account of a people, parallels it with a skip trail which stops only on the salient items, and can follow at any time contemporary trails which lead him all over civilization at a particular epoch. There is a new profession of trail blazers, those who find delight in the task of establishing useful trails through the enormous mass of the common record. The inheritance from the master becomes not only his additions to the world's record, but for his disciples the entire scaffolding by which they were erected.

Thus science may implement the ways in which man produces, stores, and consults the record of the race. It might be striking to outline the instrumentalities of the future more spectacularly, rather than to stick closely to methods and elements now known and undergoing rapid development, as has been done here. Technical difficulties of all sorts have been ignored, certainly, but also ignored are means as yet unknown which may come any day to accelerate technical progress as violently as did the advent of the thermionic tube. In order that the picture may not be too commonplace, by reason of sticking to present-day patterns, it may be well to mention one such possibility, not to prophesy but merely to suggest, for prophecy based on extension of the known has substance, while prophecy founded on the unknown is only a doubly involved guess.

All our steps in creating or absorbing material of the record proceed through one of the senses—the tactile when we touch keys, the oral when we speak or listen, the visual when we read. Is it not possible that some day the path may be established more directly?

We know that when the eye sees, all the consequent information is transmitted to the brain by means of electrical vibrations in the channel of the optic nerve. This is an exact analogy with the electrical vibrations which occur in the cable of a television set: they convey the picture from the photocells which see it to the radio transmitter from which it is broadcast. We know further that if we can approach that cable with the proper instruments, we do not need to touch it; we can pick up those vibrations by electrical induction and thus discover and reproduce the scene which is being transmitted, just as a telephone wire may be tapped for its message.

The impulses which flow in the arm nerves of a typist convey to her fingers the translated information which reaches her eye or ear, in order that the fingers may be caused to strike the proper keys. Might not these currents be intercepted, either in the original form in which information is conveyed to the brain, or in the marvelously metamorphosed form in which they then proceed to the hand?

By bone conduction we already introduce sounds into the nerve channels of the deaf in order that they may hear. Is it not possible that we may learn to introduce them without the present cumbersomeness of first transforming electrical vibrations to mechanical ones, which the human mechanism promptly transforms back to the electrical form? With a couple of electrodes on the skull the encephalograph now produces pen-and-ink traces which bear some relation to the electrical phenomena going on in the brain itself. True, the record is unintelligible, except as it points out certain gross misfunctioning of the cerebral mechanism; but who would now place bounds on where such a thing may lead?

In the outside world, all forms of intelligence, whether of sound or sight, have been reduced to the form of varying currents in an electric circuit in order that they may be transmitted. Inside the human frame exactly the same sort of process occurs. Must we always transform to mechanical movements in order to proceed from one electrical phenomenon to another? It is a suggestive thought, but it hardly warrants prediction without losing touch with reality and immediateness.

Presumably man's spirit should be elevated if he can better review his shady past and analyze more completely and objectively his present problems. He has built a civilization so complex that he needs to mechanize his records more fully if he is to push his experiment to its logical conclusion and not merely become bogged down part way there by overtaxing his limited memory. His excursions may be more enjoyable if he can reacquire the privilege of forgetting the manifold things he does not need to have immediately at hand, with some assurance that he can find them again if they prove important.

The applications of science have built man a well-supplied house, and are teaching him to live healthily therein. They have enabled him to throw masses of people against one another with cruel weapons. They may yet allow him truly to encompass the great record and to grow in the wisdom of race experience. He may perish in conflict before he learns to wield that record for his true good. Yet, in the application of science to the needs and desires of man, it would seem to be a singularly unfortunate stage at which to terminate the process, or to lose hope as to the outcome.

2

A Conceptual Framework for the Augmentation of Man's Intellect[1]

Douglas C. Engelbart
SRI International
Menlo Park CA

1 *Introduction*

By "augmenting man's intellect" we mean increasing the capability of a man to approach a complex problem situation, gain comprehension to suit his particular needs, and to derive solutions to problems. Increased capability in this respect is taken to mean a mixture of the following: that comprehension can be gained; that a useful degree of comprehension can be gained more quickly; that better comprehension can be gained where previously the situation was too complex; that solutions can be produced more quickly; that better solutions can be produced; that solutions can be found where previously the human could find none. And by "complex situations" we include the professional problems of diplomats, executives, social scientists, life scientists, physical scientists, attorneys,

[1]Partial support of this work was received from the Air Force Office of Scientific Research, Directorate of Information Sciences, under Contract AF 49(638)-1024. This paper is an excerpt from a summary report (AFOSR-3223) which also includes a discussion of background material, a hypothetical description of a computer-based augmentation system, and research recommendations. The paper could never have been written without the considerable effort of Mrs. Rowena Swanson of the AFOSR, who extracted and organized the material upon which this chapter is based.

designers—whether the problem situation exists for twenty minutes or twenty years. We do not speak of isolated clever tricks that help in particular situations. We refer to a way of life in an integrated domain where hunches, cut-and-try, intangibles, and the human "feel for a situation" usefully coexist with powerful concepts, streamlined terminology and notation, sophisticated methods, and high-powered electronic aids.

This paper covers the first phase of a program aimed at developing means to augment the human intellect. These methods or devices can include many things, all of which appear to be but extensions of those developed and used in the past to help man apply his native sensory, mental, and motor capabilities. We consider the total system of a human plus his augmentation devices and techniques as a proper field of search for practical possibilities. This field constitutes a very important system in our society; like most systems its performance can best be improved by considering the whole as a set of interacting elements rather than a number of isolated components.

This kind of system approach to human intellectual effectiveness does not find a ready-made conceptual framework such as exists for established disciplines. Before a research program can pursue such an approach intelligently, so as to derive practical benefits within a reasonable time in addition to results of long-range significance, a conceptual framework must be searched out—a framework that provides orientations as to the important factors of the system, the relationships among these factors, the types of change among the system factors that offer likely improvements in performance, and the kind of research goals and methodology that seem promising.

Man's population and gross product are increasing at a considerable rate, but the *complexity* of his problems grows even faster. And the *urgency* with which solutions must be found becomes steadily greater in response to the increased rate of activity and the increasingly global nature of that activity. Augmenting man's intellect, in the sense defined above, would warrant the full-time efforts of an enlightened society if its leaders could be shown a reasonable approach and some plausible benefits.

2 Objective of the Study

The objective of this study is to develop a conceptual framework for a coordinated research and development program whose goals would be the following: (1) to find the factors that limit the effectiveness of the individual's basic information-handling capabilities in meeting the various needs of society for problem solving in its most general sense; and

(2) to develop new techniques, procedures, and systems that will better adapt these basic capabilities to the needs, problems, and progress of society. We have established the following specifications for this framework:

1. It must provide perspective for both long-range basic research and research that will yield immediate practical results.

2. It must indicate what this augmentation will actually involve in the way of changes in working environment, thinking, skills, and methods of work.

3. It must be a basis for evaluating and assimilating the possibly relevant work and knowledge of existing fields.

4. It must reveal areas where research is possible and indicate ways to assess the research; must be a basis for choosing starting points and developing appropriate methodologies for the needed research.

Two points need emphasis here. First, although a conceptual framework has been constructed, it is still rudimentary. Further search and actual research are needed for the evolution of the framework. Second, even with a basic framework, an apparently small modification can significantly alter the results of the framework. The framework must therefore be viewed as tentative, and considered as a detailed prediction or a collection of factual statements.

3 Conceptual Framework

3.1 General

The conceptual framework we seek must orient us toward the real possibilities and problems associated with using modern technology to give direct aid to an individual in comprehending complex situations, isolating the significant factors, and solving problems. To gain this orientation, we examine how individuals achieve their present level of effectiveness, and expect that this examination will reveal possibilities for improvement.

The entire effect of an individual on the world stems essentially from what he can communicate to the world through his limited motor channels. This communication, in turn, is based on information received from the outside world through his limited sensory channels; on information, drives, and needs generated within him; and on his processing of that information. His processing is of two kinds: that which he is generally conscious of (recognizing patterns, remembering, visualizing, abstracting, deducing, inducing, etc.), and that involving self-generated information, unconscious processing and mediating of received information, and mediating of conscious processing itself.

The individual does not use this information or processing to grapple directly with the sort of complex situation in which we seek to give him help. He uses his innate capabilities in a rather indirect fashion, since the situation is generally too complex to yield directly to his motor actions, and always too complex to yield comprehensions and solutions from direct sensory inspection and use of basic cognitive capabilities. For instance, an aborigine who possesses all of our *basic* sensory-mental-motor capabilities but does not possess our background of indirect knowledge and procedure cannot organize the proper direct actions necessary to drive a car through traffic, request a book from the library, call a committee meeting to discuss a tentative plan, call someone on the telephone, or compose a letter on the typewriter.

Our culture has evolved means for us to organize and utilize our basic capabilities so that we can comprehend truly complex situations and accomplish the processes of devising and implementing problem solutions. The ways in which human capabilities are thus extended are here called *augmentation means,* and we define four basic classes of them:

1. *Artifacts*—physical objects designed to provide for human comfort, the manipulation of things or materials, and the manipulation of symbols.

2. *Language*—the way in which the individual classifies the picture of his world into the concepts that his mind uses to model that world, and the symbols that he attaches to those concepts and uses in consciously manipulating the concepts ("thinking").

3. *Methodology*—the methods, procedures, and strategies with which an individual organizes his *goal-centered* (problem-solving) activity.

4. *Training*—the conditioning needed by the individual to bring his skills in using augmentation means 1, 2, and 3 to the point where they are operationally effective.

The system we wish to improve can thus be visualized as comprising a trained human being together with his artifacts, language, and methodology. The explicit new system we contemplate will involve as artifacts computers and computer-controlled information-storage, information-handling, and information-display devices. The aspects of the conceptual framework that are discussed here are primarily those relating to the individual's ability to make significant use of such equipment in an integrated system.

Pervading all of the augmentation means is a particular structure or organization. While an untrained aborigine cannot drive a car through traffic because he cannot leap the gap between his cultural background and the kind of world that contains cars and traffic, it is possible for him to move step by step through an organized training program that will enable him to drive effectively and safely. In other words, the human mind neither learns nor acts by large leaps, but by a series of small steps so organized or structured that each one depends upon previous steps.

Although the size of the step a human being can take in comprehension, innovation, or execution is small in comparison to the over-all size of the step needed to solve a complex problem, human beings nevertheless do solve complex problems. It is the augmentation means that serve to subdivide a large problem in such a way that the human being can walk through it in little steps. The structure or organization of these little steps or actions we designate as *process hierarchies.*

Every thought process or action is composed of subprocesses. Such subprocesses include making a pencil stroke, writing a memo, or devising a plan. An appreciable number of discrete muscle movements must be coordinated to make a pencil stroke. Similarly, making particular pencil strokes and composing a memo are complex processes in themselves which are subprocesses to the over-all writing of the memo.

Although every subprocess is a process in its own right in that it consists of further subprocesses, there is no advantage here in isolating the ultimate "bottom" of the process-hierarchical structure. There may be no way of determining whether the apparent "bottom" (processes that cannot be further subdivided) exists in the physical world or in the limitations of human understanding. In any case, it is not necessary to begin from the "bottom" in discussing particular process hierarchies. No person uses a completely unique process every time he performs a new task. Instead, he begins from a group of basic, sensory-mental-motor process capabilities, and adds to these certain of the process capabilities of his artifacts. There are only a finite number of such basic human and artifact capabilities from which to draw. Moreover, even quite different higher-order processes may have in common relatively high-order subprocesses.

When a person writes a memo (a reasonably high-order process), he makes use of many processes as subprocesses that are common to other high-order processes. For example, he makes use of planning, composing, dictating. The process of writing a memo is utilized as a subprocess within many different processes of a still higher order, such as organizing a committee, changing a policy, and so on.

It is likely that each individual develops a certain repertory of process capabilities from which he selects and adapts those that will compose the processes that he executes. This repertory is like a tool kit. Just as the mechanic must know what his tools can do and how to use them, so the intellectual worker must know the capabilities of his tools and have suitable methods, strategies, and rules of thumb for making use of them. All of the process capabilities in the individual's repertory rest ultimately on basic capabilities within him or his artifacts, and the entire repertory represents an integrated, hierarchical structure (which we often call the *repertory hierarchy*).

We find three general categories of process capabilities within a typical individual's repertory: (1) those executed completely within the human integument, which we call *explicit-human* process capabilities; (2) those possessed by artifacts for executing processes without human intervention, which we call *explicit-artifact* process capabilities; and (3) those we call the *composite* process capabilities, which are derived from hierarchies containing both of the other kinds.

We assume that it is our H-LAM/T system (Human using Language, Artifacts, and Methodology, in which he is Trained) that performs a process in any instance of use of this repertory. Let us consider the process of issuing a memorandum. There is a particular concept associated with this process—that of putting information into a formal package and distributing it to a set of people for a certain kind of consideration. That the type of information package associated with this concept has been given the special name of *memorandum* shows the denominating effect of this process on the system language.

The memo-writing process may be executed by using a set of process capabilities (intermixed or repetitive form) such as planning, developing subject matter, compromising text, producing hard copy, and distributing. There is a definite way in which these subprocesses are organized that represents part of the system methodology. Each of these subprocesses represents a functional concept that must be a part of the system language if it is to be organized effectively into the human's way of doing things, and the symbolic portrayal of each concept must be such that the human can work with it and remember it.

If a memo is short and simple, the first three processes may be of the explicit-human type (i.e., the memo may be planned, developed and composed within the mind), and the last two of the composite type. If it is complex, involving a good deal of careful planning and development, then all of the subprocesses may be of the composite type (at least including the use of pencil and paper artifacts), and there may be many different applications of some of the process capabilities within the total process (successive drafts, revised plans).

Executing the above-listed set of subprocesses in proper sequence represents an execution of the memo-writing process. However, the very process of organizing and supervising the utilization of these subprocess capabilities is itself a most important subprocess of the memo-writing process. Hence the subprocess capabilities as listed would not be complete without the addition of a seventh, which we call the *executive* capability. This is the capability stemming from habit, strategy, rules of thumb, prejudice, learned method, intuition, unconscious dictates, or combinations thereof, to utilize the appropriate subprocess capabilities in a particular sequence and timing. An executive process (i.e., the exercise of an executive capability) involves such subprocesses as planning, selecting, and supervising; it is within the executive processes that the methodology in the H-LAM/T system is embodied.

To illustrate the capability-hierarchy features of our conceptual framework, let the reader consider an artifact innovation appearing directly within the relatively low-order capability for composing and modifying written text, and see how this can affect his hierarchy of capabilities. Suppose you had a new writing machine—a high-speed electric typewriter with some very special features. You can operate its keyboard to cause it to write text much as with a conventional typewriter. But the printing mechanism is more complicated; besides printing a visible character at every stroke, it adds special encoding features by means of invisible selective components in the ink and special shaping of the character.

As an auxiliary device, there is a gadget that is held like a pencil and, instead of a point, has a special sensing mechanism which can be moved along a line of the special printing from your writing machine (or one like it). The signals which this reading stylus sends through the flexible connecting wire to the writing machine are used to determine which characters are being sensed, thus causing the automatic typing of a duplicated string of characters. An information-storage mechanism in the writing machine permits you to sweep the reading stylus over the characters much faster than the writer can type; the writer will catch up with you when you stop to think about what word or string of words should be duplicated next, or while you reposition the straightedge guide along which you run the stylus.

This hypothetical writing machine thus permits you to use a new process of composing text. For instance, trial drafts can rapidly be composed from rearranged excerpts of old drafts, together with new words or passages which you insert by hand typing. Your first draft may represent a free outpouring of thoughts in any order, with the inspection of foregoing thoughts continuously stimulating new considerations and ideas to be entered. If the tangle of thoughts represented by the draft becomes too complex, you can compile a reordered draft quickly. It would be practical for you to accommodate more complexity in the trails of thought you might build in search of the path that suits your needs.

You can integrate your new ideas more easily, and thus harness your creativity more continuously, if you can quickly and flexibly change your working record. If it is easier to update any part of your working record to accommodate new developments in thought or circumstance, you will find it easier to incorporate more complex procedures in your way of doing things. This will probably allow you, for example, to accommodate the extra burden associated with keeping and using special files whose contents are both contributed to and utilized by any current work in a flexible manner—which in turn enables you to devise and use even more complex procedures to better harness your talents in your particular working situation.

The important thing to appreciate here is that a direct new innovation in one particular capability can have far-reaching effects throughout the rest of your capability hierarchy. A change can propagate *up* through the capability hierarchy, higher-order capabilities that can utilize the initially changed capability can now reorganize to take special advantage of this change and of the intermediate higher-capability changes. A change can propagate *down* through the hierarchy as a result of new capabilities at the high level and modification possibilities latent in lower levels. These latent capabilities may have been previously unusable in the hierarchy and become usable because of the new capability at the higher level.

The writing machine and its flexible copying capability would occupy you for a long time if you tried to exhaust the reverberating chain of associated possibilities for making useful innovations within your capability hierarchy. This one innovation could trigger a rather extensive redesign of this hierarchy; your method of accomplishing many of your tasks would change considerably. Indeed, this process characterizes the sort of evolution that our intellect-augmentation means have been undergoing since the first human brain appeared.

For our objective of deriving orientation about possibilities for actively pursuing an increase in human intellectual effectiveness, it is important to realize that we must be prepared to pursue such new-possibility chains throughout the *entire* capability hierarchy (calling for a "system" approach). It is also important to realize that we must be oriented to the *synthesis* of new capabilities from reorganization of other capabilities, both old and new, that exist throughout the hierarchy (a "system-engineering" approach).

3.2 *The Basic Perspective*

Individuals who operate effectively in our culture have already been considerably "augmented." Basic human capabilities for sensing stimuli, performing numerous mental operations, and communicating with the outside world are put to work in our society within a system—an H-LAM/T system—the individual augmented by the language, artifacts, and methodology in which he is trained. Furthermore, we suspect that improving the effectiveness of the individual as he operates in our society should be approached as a system-engineering problem—that is, the H-LAM/T system should be studied as an interacting whole from a synthesis-oriented approach.

This view of the system as an interacting whole is strongly bolstered by considering the repertory hierarchy of process capabilities that is structured from the basic ingredients within the H-LAM/T system. The realization that any potential change in language, artifact, or methodology has importance only relative to its use within a process, and that a new process capability appearing anywhere within that hierarchy can make practical a new consideration of latent change possibilities in many other parts of the hierarchy—possibilities in either language, artifacts, or methodology—brings out the strong interrelationship of these three augmentation means.

Increasing the effectiveness of the individual's use of his basic capabilities is a problem in redesigning the changeable parts of a system. The system is actively engaged in the continuous processes (among others) of developing comprehension within the individual and of solving problems; both processes are subject to human motivation, purpose, and will. Redesigning the system's capability for performing these processes means redesigning all or part of the repertory hierarchy. To redesign a structure we must learn as much as we can about the basic materials and components as they are utilized within the structure; beyond that, we must learn how to view, measure, analyze, and evaluate in terms of the functional whole and its purpose. In this particular case, no existing analytic theory is by itself adequate for the purpose of analyzing and evaluating over-all system performance; pursuit of an improved system thus demands the use of *experimental* methods.

It need not be solely the sophisticated or formal process capabilities that are added or modified in the redesign. Even so apparently minor an advance as artifacts for rapid mechanical duplication and rearrangement of text during the course of creative thought process could yield changes in an individual's repertory hierarchy that would represent a great increase in over-all effectiveness. Normally we might expect such equipment to appear slowly on the market; changes from old procedures would be small, and only gradually would the accumulated changes create markets for more radical versions of the equipment. Such an evolutionary process has been typical of the way our repertory hierarchies have formed and grown.

But an active research effort, aimed at exploring and evaluating possible integrated changes throughout the repertory hierarchy, could greatly accelerate this evolutionary process. The research effort could guide the product development of new artifacts toward taking long-range meaningful steps; simultaneously, competitively minded individuals who would respond to demonstrated methods for achieving greater personal effectiveness would create a market for the more radical equipment innovations. The guided evolutionary process could be expected to be considerably more rapid than the traditional one.

The category of "more radical innovations" includes the digital computer as a tool for the personal use of an individual. Here there is not only promise of great flexibility in the composing and rearranging of text and diagrams before the individual's eyes, but also promise of many other process capabilities that can be integrated into the H-LAM/T system's repertoire hierarchy.

3.3 *Details of the H-LAM/T System*

3.3.1 *Synergism*[2] *as the Source of Intelligence*   If we ask ourselves where human intelligence is embodied, our present state of knowledge forces us to concede that it appears to be elusively distributed throughout a hierarchy of functional processes—a hierarchy whose foundations extend into natural processes beyond the level of present definition. Intelligence, however, seems primarily to be associated with *organization*. All of the social, biological, and physical phenomena we observe about us seem to derive from a supporting hierarchy of organized functions (or processes), in which the principle of synergism applies to give increased phenomenological sophistication to each succeedingly higher level of organization. In particular, the intelligence of a human being, which appears to be derived ultimately from the signal-response characteristics of individual nerve cells, is a synergistic phenomenon.

---

[2]Synergism is a term used by biologists and physiologists to designate (from *Webster's New International Dictionary*, 2d ed.) the "... cooperative action of discrete agencies such that the total effect is greater than the sum of the two effects taken independently ...".

3.3.2 *Intelligence Amplification* During the course of this study, we had originally rejected the term *intelligence amplification*, (initially used by W. Ross Ashby [1, 2]) to characterize our objectives. Instead, we characterized them as the attempt to make a better match between existing human intelligence and problems to be solved. But we have come to accept the foregoing term in a special sense that does not imply any attempt to increase native human intelligence. *Intelligence amplification* seems applicable to our goal (of augmenting the human intellect) in that the entity to be produced will exhibit more of what can be called intelligence than an unaided human could demonstrate. That which possesses the amplified intelligence is the resulting H-LAM/T system, in which the LAM/T augmentation means represent the amplifier of the individual's intelligence.

In amplifying human intelligence we are applying the principle of synergistic structuring that pertains in the natural evolution of basic human capabilities. What our culture has done in the development of our means of augmentation is to construct a superstructure that is a synthetic extension of the biologically derived sensory-mental-motor structure on which it is built. In a very real sense, the development of "artificial intelligence" has been going on for centuries.

3.3.3 *Two-Domain System* The human together with his artifacts comprise the only physical components in the H-LAM/T system. It is upon their combined capabilities that the ultimate capability of the system will depend. This conclusion was implied in the earlier statement that every composite process of the system decomposes ultimately into explicit-human and explicit-artifact processes. There are thus two separate domains of activity within the H-LAM/T system: that represented by the human, in which all explicit-human processes occur, and that represented by the artifacts, in which all explicit-artifact processes occur. In any composite process there is cooperative interaction between the two domains, requiring interchange of energy (much of it for information exchange purposes only). Figure 2.1 depicts this two-domain concept and embodies other concepts discussed below.

Where a complex machine represents the principal artifact with which a human being cooperates, the term *man–machine interface* has been used for some years to represent the boundary across which energy is exchanged between the two domains. However, the *man–artifact interface* has existed for centuries, ever since humans began using artifacts and executing composite processes.

Exchange across this "interface" occurs when an explicit-human process is coupled to an explicit-artifact process. Quite often these coupled processes are designed for just this exchange purpose, to provide

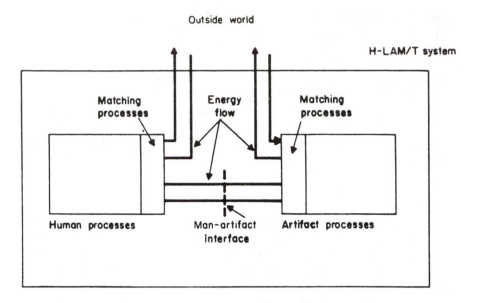

Figure 2.1   Representation of the two active domains within the H-LAM/T System.

a functional match between other explicit-human and explicit-artifact processes buried within their respective domains that do the more significant things. For instance, the finger and hand motions (explicit-human processes) activate key-linkage motions in the typewriter (coupled to explicit-artifact processes). But these are only part of the matching processes between the deeper human processes that direct a given word to be typed and the more involved artifact processes that actually imprint the ink marked on the paper.

The outside world interacts with our H-LAM/T system by the exchange of energy with either the individual or his artifact. Again, special processes are often designed to accommodate this exchange. However, the direct concern of our present study lies within the system, with the internal processes that are and can be significantly involved in the effectiveness of the *system* in developing the human's comprehension and pursuing the human's goals.

3.3.4 Concepts, Symbols, and a Hypothesis   Before we pursue further direct discussion of the H-LAM/T system, let us examine some background material. There is a certain progression in the development of our intellectual capabilities— not necessarily historical—that can shed light on the human part of the system:

Concept manipulation: Humans have the biological capability for developing abstractions and concepts. They can mentally manipulate these concepts to a certain extent, and "think" about situations in the abstract. Their mental capabilities allow them to develop general concepts from specific instances, predict specific instances from general concepts, associate concepts, remember them, etc. We speak here of concepts in their raw, unverbalized form. For example, a person letting a door swing shut behind him suddenly visualizes a person behind him carrying a cup of hot coffee and some sticky pastries. Of all the aspects of the impending event, the spilling of the coffee and the squashing of the pastry somehow are abstracted immediately and associated with a concept of personal responsibility combined with a fear of the consequences. But a solution comes to mind immediately as an image of a quick stop and an arm extended back toward the door, with motion and timing that could prevent the collision, and the solution is accepted and enacted. With only non-verbal concept manipulation, we could probably build primitive shelter, evolve strategies of war, hunt, play games, and make practical jokes. But further powers of intellectual effectiveness are implicit in this stage of biological evolution (the same stage we are in today).

Symbol manipulation: Humans made another great step forward when they learned to represent particular concepts in their minds with specific symbols. Here we temporarily disregard communicative speech and writing and consider only the direct value to the *individual* of being able to do his heavy thinking by mentally manipulating *symbols* instead of the more unwieldy concepts which they represent. Consider, for instance, the mental difficulty involved in herding twenty-seven sheep if, instead of remembering one cardinal number and occasionally counting, we had to remember what each sheep looked like, so that if the flock seemed too small we could visualize each one and check whether or not it was there.

Manual, external, symbol manipulation: Another significant step toward harnessing the biologically evolved mental capabilities in pursuit of comprehension and problem solutions came with the development of the means for externalizing some of the symbol-manipulation activity—particularly in graphic representation, which supplements the individual's memory and ability to visualize. (We are not concerned here with the value derived from human cooperation made possible by speech and writing, both forms of external symbol manipulation, but with the manual means of making graphic representations of symbols—a stick and sand, pencil and paper and eraser, straightedge or compass, and so on.) It is principally this kind of means for external symbol manipulation that has been associated with the evolution of the individual's present way of manipulating his concepts (thinking).

It is undoubtedly true that concepts which people found useful became incorporated as symbols in their language. However, Korzybski [3] and Whorf [4] (among others) have argued that the language we use affects our thinking to a considerable extent. They say that a lack of words for some types of concepts makes it difficult to express those concepts, and thus decreases the likelihood that we will learn much about them. If this is so, once a language has begun to grow and be used it would seem reasonable to suspect that the language also affects the evolution of the new concepts to be expressed in that language.

Apparently there are counter-arguments to this; e.g., if a concept needs to be used often but its expression is difficult, then the language will evolve to ease the situation. However, the studies of the past decade into what are called *self-organizing systems* seem to reveal that subtle relationships among interacting elements can significantly influence the course of evolution of such a system. If this is true, and if language is (as it seems to be) a part of a self-organizing system, then it appears probable that the state of a language at a given time strongly affects its own evolution to a succeeding state.

For our conceptual framework, we tend to favor the view that a language does exert a force in its own evolution. We observe that the shift over the last few centuries in matters that are of daily concern to the individual has necessarily been forced into the framework of the language existing at the time, with alterations generally limited to new uses for old words, or to the coining of new words. The English language since Shakespeare has undergone no alteration comparable to the alteration in the cultural environment; if it had, Shakespeare would no longer be accessible to us. Under such evolutionary conditions, it would seem *unlikely* that the language we now use provides the best possible service to our minds in pursuing comprehension and solving problems. It seems very likely that a more useful language form can be devised.

The Whorfian hypothesis states that "the world view of a culture is limited by the structure of the language which the culture uses." But there seems to be another factor to consider in the evolution of language and human reasoning ability. We offer the following hypothesis, which is related to the Whorfian hypothesis: Both the language used by a culture, and the capability for effective intellectual activity, are directly affected during their evolution by the means by which individuals control the external manipulation of symbols. (For identification, we will refer to this later on as the Neo-Whorfian hypothesis.) If the Neo-Whorfian hypothesis could be proved readily, and if we could see how our means of externally manipulating symbols influence both our language and our way of thinking, then we would have a valuable instrument for studying human-augmentation possibilities. For the sake of discussion, let us assume the Neo-Whorfian hypothesis to be true, and see what relevant deductions can be made.

If the means evolved for an individual's external manipulation of his thinking-aid symbols indeed directly affect the way in which he thinks, then the original Whorfian hypothesis would offer an added effect. The direct effect of the external-symbol-manipulation means on language would produce an indirect effect on the way of thinking via the Whorfian-hypothesis linkage. There would then be two ways for our external symbol manipulation to affect our thinking.

One way of viewing the H-LAM/T system changes that we contemplate—specifically, integrating the capabilities of a digital computer into the intellectual activity of humans—is that we are introducing new and extremely advanced means for externally manipulating symbols. We then want to determine the useful modifications in the language and in the way of thinking that could result. This suggests a fourth stage to the evolution of our human intellectual capability.

Automated external symbol manipulation: In this stage, the symbols with which the human represents the concepts he is manipulating can be arranged before his eyes, moved, stored, recalled, operated upon according to extremely complex rules—all in very rapid response to a minimum amount of information supplied by the human, by means of special cooperative technological devices. In the limit of what we might now imagine, this could be a computer, with which individuals could communicate rapidly and easily, coupled to a three-dimensional color display within which *extremely sophisticated images* could be constructed on parts or all of these images in automatic response to human direction. The displays and processes could provide helpful services and could involve concepts not hitherto imagined (e.g., the pregraphic thinker would have been unable to predict the bar graph, the process of long division, or card file system).

In searching for some simple ways to determine what the Neo-Whorfian hypothesis might imply, we might imagine some relatively straightforward means of increasing our external symbol-manipulation capability and try to picture the consequent changes that could evolve in our language and methods of thinking. For instance, imagine that our budding technology of a few generations ago had developed an artifact cheap enough for almost everyone to afford and small and light enough to be carried on the person. Assume that individual cartridges sold by manufacturers (publishers) contained the lookup information, that one cartridge could hold the equivalent of an unabridged dictionary, and that a one-paragraph definition could always be located and displayed on the face of the device by the average practiced individual in less than three seconds. What changes in language and methodology might not result? If it were so easy to look things up, how would our vocabulary develop, how would our habits of exploring the intellectual domains of others shift, how might the sophistication of practical organization mature (if each person could so quickly and easily look up applicable rules), how would our education system change to take advantage of this external symbol-manipulation capability of students and teachers and administrators?

The significance to our study of this discussion lies in the perspective it gives to the ways in which human intellectual effectiveness can be altered by the particular device used by individuals for their external symbol manipulation. These hypotheses imply great richness in the new evolutionary spaces opened by progressing from Stage 3 to Stage 4. We would like to study the hypotheses further, examining their possible manifestations in our experience, ways of demonstrating their validity, and possible deductions relative to going to Stage 4.

3.3.5 *Capability Repertory Hierarchy*   The concept of our H-LAM/T system possessing a repertory of capabilities that is structured in the form of a hierarchy is most useful in our study. We shall use it below to tie together a number of considerations and concepts.

There are two points of focus in considering the design of new repertory hierarchies: the materials with which we have to work, and the principles by which new capability is constructed from these basic materials.

Basic capabilities: *Materials* in this context are those capabilities in the human and artifact domains from which all other capabilities in the repertory hierarchy must be constructed. Each such basic capability represents a type of functional component with which the system can be built. Thorough redesigning of the system requires making an inventory of the basic capabilities available. Because we are exploring for perspective, and are not yet recommending research activities, we are free to discuss and define in more detail what we mean by "basic capability" without regard to the amount of research involved in making an actual inventory.

The two domains, human and artifact, can be explored separately for their basic capabilities. In each we can isolate two classes of basic capability—those classes distinguished according to whether or not the capability has been put to use within our augmentation means. The first class (those in use) can be found in a methodical manner by analyzing present capability hierarchies. For example, select a given capability at any level in the hierarchy and determine whether it can be usefully changed by any means that can be given consideration in the augmentation research contemplated. If it can, then it is not basic but can be decomposed into an eventual set of basic capabilities. Proceed through the hierarchy; capabilities encountered which cannot be usefully changed compose the basic capability inventory. Ultimately, for every such recursive decomposition of a given capability in the hierarchy, every one of the branching paths will terminate in basic capabilities. Many of the branching paths in the decomposition of a given higher-order capability will terminate in the same basic capability, since a given basic capability will often be used within many different higher-order capabilities.

Determining the class of basic capabilities not already utilized within existing augmentation systems requires a different exploration method. Examples of this method occur in technological research, where analytically oriented researchers search for new understandings of phenomena that can add to the research engineer's list of things to be used in the synthesis of better artifacts.

Before this inventorying task can be pursued in any specific instance, some criteria must be established as to what possible changes within the H-LAM/T system can be given serious consideration. For instance, some research situations might have to disallow changes which require extensive retraining, or which require undignified behavior by the human. Other situations might admit changes requiring years of special training, very expensive equipment, or the use of special drugs.

The capability for performing a certain finger action, for example, may not be basic in our sense of the word. Being able to extend the finger a certain distance would be basic, but the strength and speed of a particular finger motion and its coordination with higher actions generally are usefully changeable and therefore do not represent basic capabilities. What would be basic in this case would perhaps be the processes whereby strength could be increased and coordinated movement patterns learned, as well as the basic movement range established by the mechanical-limit loci of the muscle-tendon-bone system. Similar capability breakdowns will occur for sensory and cognitive capabilities.

Structure types: The fundamental principle used in building sophisticated capabilities from basic capabilities is structuring—the special type of structuring (which we have termed synergistic) in which the organization of a group of elements produces an effect greater than the mere addition of their individual effects. Perhaps *purposeful* structuring (or organization) would best express the need, but how the structuring concept must mature is uncertain. We are developing growing awareness of the significant and pervasive nature of structuring within every physical and conceptual element we inspect, where the hierarchical form seems almost universally present as stemming from successive levels of organization.

The fundamental entity which is being structured in each and every case seems to be what we could call a process, where the most basic of physical processes (involving fields, charges, and moments associated with the dynamics of fundamental particles) appear in every case as the hierarchical base. Dynamic electro-optical-mechanical processes associated with the function of our artifacts, and metabolic, sensory, motor, and cognitive processes of the human, which we view as relatively fundamental components within the structure of our H-LAM/T system, each seems to be ultimately based (to our degree of understanding) on the above-mentioned basic physical processes. The elements that are organized to give fixed structural form to our physical objects (e.g., the "element" of tensile strength of a material) are also derived from what we could call synergistic structuring of the most basic physical processes.

. At the level of the capability hierarchy where we wish to work, it seems useful to distinguish different types of structuring, even though each type is fundamentally a structuring of the basic physical processes. Tentatively we have isolated five such types, although we are not sure how many we shall ultimately want to use in considering the problem of augmenting the human intellect, nor how we might divide and subdivide these different manifestations of physical-process structuring. We use the terms *mental structuring, concept structuring, symbol structuring, process structuring*, and *physical structuring*.

Mental structuring: *Mental structuring* we apply to the internal organization of conscious and unconscious mental images, associations, or concepts which somehow manage to provide the human with understanding and the basis for judgment, intuition, inference, and meaningful action with respect to his environment. (The psychologist's "cognitive structure" may be very near to what we need in our concept of mental structure.)

We do not now try to specify the fundamental mental "things" being structured, not the mechanisms that accomplish the structuring or the use of that which has been structured. We feel reasonably safe in assuming that learning involves some kind of meaningful organization within the brain, and that whatever is so organized or structured represents the operating model of the individual's universe to the mental mechanisms that derive his behavior. Further, our assumption is that when the human in our H-LAM/T system makes the key decision or action that leads to the solution of a complex problem, this action will stem from the state of his mental structure at that time; the basic purpose of most of the system's activity on that problem up to that point was in developing his mental structure to permit the mental mechanisms to derive a solution from it.

We don't know whether a structure is developed in a manner analogous to (a) the development of a garden, where one provides a good environment, plants the seeds, keeps competing weeds and injurious pests out, but otherwise lets natural processes take their course, or (b) the development of a basketball team, where much exercise of skills, patterns, and strategies must be provided so that natural processes can slowly knit together an integration, of (c) the development of a machine, where carefully formed elements are assembled in a precise, planned manner so that natural phenomena can immediately yield planned function. We do not know the processes, but we can develop and have developed empirical relationships between the experiences given a human and the associated manifestations of developing comprehension and capability; we see the near-future course of the research toward augmenting the human intellect as depending entirely on empirical findings (past and future) for the development of better means to serve the development and use of mental structuring in the human.

We do not mean to imply by this that we renounce theories of mental processes. What we mean to emphasize is that the pursuit of our objective does not have to wait on understanding the mental processes that accomplish what we call mental structuring and that derive behavior therefrom. Not to make the fullest use of any theory that provided a working explanation for a group of empirical data would be to ignore the emphases of our own conceptual framework.

Concept structuring: Within our framework we have developed the working assumption that the manner in which formal experiences favor the development of mental structures is based largely on *concepts* as "media of exchange." We view a concept to be a tool that can be grasped and used by the mental mechanisms, that can be composed, interpreted, and used by natural mental substances and processes. The grasping and processing done by these mechanisms can often be accomplished more easily if the concept is explicitly represented by a symbol. Somehow the mental mechanisms can learn to manipulate images (or something) of symbols in a meaningful way and remain calmly confident that the associated concepts are within call.

Concepts seem to be structurable in that a new concept can be composed of an organization of established concepts. For present purposes we can view a concept structure as something which we might try to develop on paper for ourselves or work with by conscious thought processes, or as something which we try to communicate to one another in serious discussion. We assume that for a given unit of comprehension to be imparted there is a concept structure (which can be consciously developed and displayed) that can be presented to an individual in such a way that it is mapped into a corresponding mental structure which provides the basis for that individual's "comprehending" behavior. Our working assumption also considers that some concept structures would be better for this purpose than others in that they would be more easily mapped by the individual into workable mental structures, or in that the resulting mental structures enable a higher degree of comprehension and better solutions to problems, or both.

A concept structure often grows as part of a cultural evolution—either on a large scale within a large segment of society, or on a small scale within the activity domain of an individual. But it is also something that can be directly designed or modified, and a basic hypothesis of our study is that better concept structures can be developed—structures that when mapped into a human's mental structure will significantly improve his capability to comprehend and to find solutions within his complex-problem situations. A natural language provides its user with a ready-made structure of concepts that establishes a basic mental structure, and that allows relatively flexible, general-purpose concept structuring. Our concept of "language" as one of the basic means for augmenting the human intellect embraces all of the concept structuring which the human may make use of.

Symbol structuring: The other important part of our "language" concerns the way in which concepts are represented—the symbols and symbol structures: by means of which words as structured into phrases, sentences, paragraphs, monographs, or charts, lists, diagrams, and tables. A given structure of concepts can be represented by any one of an infinite number of different symbol structures, some of which would be much better than others for enabling the human perceptual and cognitive apparatus to search out and comprehend the conceptual matter of significance and/or interest. A concept structure involving many numerical data, for example, would generally be better represented with Arabic than Roman numerals; quite likely, a graphic structure would be better than a tabular structure.

In our special framework, it is worth noting that a given concept structure can be represented with a symbol structure that is completely compatible with the way a computer handles symbols. Such structuring has immensely greater potential for accurately mapping a complex concept structure than does the structure which an individual might practically construct and use on paper. A computer can transform back and forth between some limited view of the total structure as represented by a two-dimensional portrayal on a screen, and an aspect of the n-dimensional internal image that represents this "view." If the human adds to or modifies such a "view," the computer integrates the change into the internal-image symbol structure (in terms of the computer's favored symbols and structuring), and thereby can automatically detect a certain proportion of his possible conceptual inconsistencies. The human need no longer work on rigid and limited symbol structures, where much of the conceptual content can only be implicitly designated in an indirect and distributed fashion.

Many radical new ways of matching the dynamics of our symbol structuring to those of our concept structuring are basically available with today's technology. Their exploration would be most stimulating, and potentially very rewarding.

Process structuring: Essentially everything that goes on within the H-LAM/T system (in relation to our direct interest here) involves the manipulation of concept and symbol structures in service to the human's mental structure. Therefore the processes within the H-LAM/T system what we are most interested in developing are those that provide for the manipulation of all three types of structure. This brings us to the fourth category of structuring, namely, *process structuring*.

As we currently use it, the term process structuring includes the organization, study, modification, and execution of processes and process structures. Whereas concept structuring and symbol structuring together represent the language component of our augmentation means, process structuring represents primarily the methodology component.

Many of the process structures are applied to the task of organizing, executing, supervising, and evaluating other process structures. Others are applied to the formation and manipulation of symbol structures (the purpose of which will often be to support the conceptual labor involved in process structuring).

Physical structuring: Physical structuring, the last of the five types which we currently use in our conceptual framework, is nearly self-explanatory. It represents the artifact component of our augmentation means, insofar as the actual manifestation and organization of physical devices are concerned.

Interdependence and regeneration: An important feature to be noted from the foregoing discussion is the interdependence among the various types of structuring which are involved in the H-LAM/T system, where the capabilities for doing each type of structuring is dependent upon the capability of achieving one or more of the other types of structuring. (Assuming that the physical structuring of the system remains basically unchanged during the system's operation, we exclude its dependence on other factors in this discussion.) This interdependence has a cyclic, regenerative nature which is very significant. A good portion of the capability for mental structuring is finally dependent on the process structuring (human, artifact, composite) that enables symbol-structure manipulation. But it is also evident that this process structuring is dependent not only on basic human and artifact process capabilities but also on the ability of the human to learn how to execute processes and— no less important—on the ability of the human to select, organize, and modify processes from his repertory to structure a higher-order process that he can execute. Thus capability for structuring and executing processes is partially dependent on the human's mental structuring, which, in turn, is partially dependent on his process structuring (through concept and symbol structuring), which is partially dependent on his mental structuring, etc.

This means that a significant improvement in symbol-structure manipulation through better process structuring (initially perhaps through much better artifacts) should enable us to develop improvements in concept and mental-structure manipulations that can in turn enable us to organize and execute symbol-manipulation processes of increased power.

When considering the possibilities of computerlike devices for augmenting human capabilities, often only the one-pass improvement is visualized. This presents a relatively barren picture in comparison with that which emerges on consideration of regenerative interaction.

Roles and levels: In the repertory hierarchy of capabilities possessed by the H-LAM/T system, the human contributes many types of capability that represent a wide variety of roles. At one time or another he will be the policy maker, the goal setter, the performance supervisor, the work scheduler, the professional specialist, the clerk, the janitor, the entrepreneur and the proprietor (or at least a major stockholder) of the system. In the midst of some complex process, in fact, he may well be in several roles concurrently—or at least have the responsibility of the roles. For example, usually he must be aware of his progress toward a goal (supervisor), he must be alert to the possibilities for changing the goal (policy maker, planner), and he must keep records for these and other roles (clerk).

A given capability at some level in the repertory hierarchy seems to include standard grouping of lower-order capabilities which can be viewed as existing in two classes—an *executive* class and a *direct-contrib-*

utive class. In the executive class are capabilities for comprehending, planning, and executing the process. In the direct-contributive class are the capabilities organized by the executive class toward the direct realization of the higher-order capability. For example, when the telephone rings, direct-contributive processes are picking up the receiver and saying "hello." The executive processes comprehended the situation, directed a lower-order executive-process that the receiver be picked up and, when the receiver was in place (first process accomplished), directed the next process—the saying "hello." This represents the composition of the capability for answering the telephone.

At a little higher level of capability, more of the conscious conceptual and executive capabilities become involved. To telephone someone, there must be conscious comprehension of the need for this process and how it can be executed.

At a still higher level of capability, the executive capabilities must have a degree of power that cannot be provided by unaided mental capabilities. In such a case, a sequence of steps might be drafted and checked off as each is executed. For an even more complex process, comprehending the situation in which the process is to be executed—before even beginning to plan the execution—may take months of labor and a very complex organization of the system's capabilities.

At any particular moment the H-LAM/T system is usually in the middle of executing a great number of processes. For example, the human in the process of making a telephone call may be in the middle of the process of estimating manpower needs, and so on.

Not only does the human need to play various roles (sometimes concurrently) in the execution of any given process, but he is playing these roles for the many concurrent processes that are being executed at different levels. This situation is typical for individuals engaged in reasonably demanding types of professional pursuits, and yet they have never received explicit training in optimum ways of performing any but a very few of the roles at a very few of the levels. A well-designed H-LAM/T system would provide explicit and effective concepts, terms, equipment, and methods for all these roles, and for their dynamic coordination.

Model of executive superstructure: It is repertory hierarchy of process capabilities upon which the ultimate capability of the H-LAM/T system rests. This repertory hierarchy is rather like a mountain of white-collar talent that sits atop and controls the talents of the "workers." We can illustrate executive superstructure by considering it as though it were a network of contractors and subcontractors in which each capability in the repertory hierarchy is represented by an independent contractor whose mode of operation is to do the planning, make up specifications, subcontract the actual work, and supervise the performance of his sub-contractors. This means that each subcontractor does the same thing in his turn. At the bottom of this hierarchy are those independent contrac-tors who do actual "production work."

If by some magical process the production workers could still know just what to do and when to do it even though the superstructure of contractors was removed from above them, no one would know the difference. The executive superstructure is there because humans do not operate by magic, but even a necessary superstructure is a burden. We can readily recognize that there are many ways to organize and manage such a superstructure, resulting in vastly different degrees of efficiency in the application of the workers' talents.

Suppose that the applicable talent available to the total system is limited. The problem is one of distributing that talent between super-structure and workers for maximum total production and efficiency. This situation has close parallel to the H-LAM/T system in its pursuit of comprehension and problem solutions. Closer parallel exists by postu-lating for the contractor model that the thinking, planning, supervising, record keeping, etc., for each contractor is done by a single individual who time-shares his attention and talents over the various tasks of the entire superstructure.

Today's individual does not have special training for many of the roles he plays, and he is likely to learn them by cut-and-try and indirect imitation processes. The H-LAM/T system also often executes a complex process in multipass fashion (i.e., cut-and-try). This approach permits freedom of action which is important to the effectiveness of the system with respect to the outside world. We could expect significant gains from automating the H-LAM/T system if a computer did no more than in-crease the effectiveness of the executive processes. More human time, energy, and productive thought could be allocated to direct-contributive processes, which could be coordinated in a more sophisticated, flexible and efficient manner. But there is every reason to believe that the pos-sibilities for much-improved process structuring that would stem from this automation could in turn provide significant improvements in both the executive and direct-contributive processes in the system.

Symbol structures: The executive superstructure is a necessary com-ponent in the H-LAM/T system, and there is finite human capability which must be divided between executive and direct-contributive ac-tivities. An important aspect of the multirole activity of the human in the system is the development and manipulation of the symbol struc-tures associated with *both* his direct-contributive roles and his executive roles.

When the system encounters a complex situation in which comprehension and problem solutions are being pursued, the direct-contributive roles require the development of symbol structures that portray the concepts involved within the situation. But executive roles in a complex problem situation also require conceptual activity—e.g., comprehension, selection, supervision—that can benefit from well-designed symbol structures and fast, flexible means for manipulating and displaying them. For complex processes, the executive problem posed to the human (of gaining the necessary comprehension and making a good plan) may be more difficult intellectually than the problem faced in the role of direct-contributive worker. If the flexibility desired for the process hierarchies (to make room for human cut-and-try methods) is not to be degraded or abandoned, the executive activity will have to be provided with fast and flexible symbol structuring techniques.

The means available to humans today for developing and manipulating symbol structures are both laborious and inflexible. To develop an initial structure of diagrams and text is difficult, but because the cost of frequent changes is often prohibitive, one settles for inflexibility. Also, the flexibility that would be truly helpful requires added symbols structuring just to keep track of the trials, branches, and reasoning thereto that are involved in the development of the subject structure. Present symbol-manipulation means would soon bog down completely among the complexities that are involved in being more than just a little bit flexible.

In H-LAM/T systems, individuals work essentially continuously within a symbol structure of some sort, shifting their attention from one structure to another as they guide and execute the processes that ultimately provide them with the comprehension and the problem solutions they seek. This view emphasizes the essential importance of the basic capability of composing and modifying efficient symbol structures. Such a capability depends heavily on the particular concepts isolated and manipulated as entities, on the symbology used to represent them, on the artifacts that help to manipulate and display the symbols, and on the methodology for developing and using symbol structures. In other words, this capability depends heavily on proper language, artifacts, and methodology, our basic augmentation means.

The course of action which must respond to new comprehension, new insights, and new intuitive flashes of possible explanations or solutions is not an orderly process. Existing means of composing and working with symbol structures penalize disorderly processes heavily. It is part of the real promise of the automated H-LAM/T systems of tomorrow that the human can have the freedom and power of disorderly processes.

Compound effect: Since processes in many levels of the hierarchy are involved in the execution of a single higher-level process of the system, any factor that influences process execution in general will have a highly compounded total effect on the system's performance. There are several such factors that merit special attention.

Basic human cognitive powers, such as memory, intelligence, or pattern perception can have such a compounded effect. The augmentation means employed today have generally evolved among large statistical populations, and no attempt has been made to fit them to individual needs and abilities. Each individual tends to evolve his own variations, but there is not enough mutation and selection activity, nor enough selection feedback, to permit very significant changes. A good, automated H-LAM/T system should provide the opportunity for a significant adaptation of the augmentation means to individual characteristics. The compounding effect of fundamental human cognitive powers suggests further that systems designed for maximum effectiveness would require that these powers be developed as fully as possible—by training, special mental tricks, improved language, new methodology.

In the automated system contemplated here, the human should be able to draw on the explicit-artifact process capability at many levels in the repertory hierarchy. Today, artifacts are involved explicitly in only the lower-order capabilities. In future systems it should be possible for computer processes to provide direct manipulative service in the executive symbol structures at all the higher levels, which promises a compounding of the effect a computer may have.

Another factor capable of exerting a compound effect on overall system performance is the human's unconscious processes. Clinical psychology seems to provide clear evidence that a large proportion of a human's everyday activity is significantly mediated or basically prompted by unconscious mental processes that, although "natural" in a functional sense, are not rational. Observable mechanisms of these processes (observable by a trained person) include an individual's masking of the irrationality of his actions, and the construction of self-satisfying rationales for any action that could be challenged. Anything that might have so general an effect on our mental actions as implied here is a candidate for ultimate consideration in the continuing development of our intellectual effectiveness. It may be that the first stages of research on augmenting the human intellect will have to proceed without coping with this problem except to accommodate to it as well as possible. This may be one of the significant problems whose solution awaits our development of increased intellectual effectiveness.

4 Other Related Thought and Work

When we began our search, we found much literature of general significance to our objective—frankly, one is tempted to say too much. Without a conceptual framework we could not efficiently filter out the significant kernels of fact and concept from the huge mass which we initially collected as a "natural first step" in our search. We feel rather unscholarly not to have buttressed our conceptual framework with plentiful reference to supporting work, but in truth it was too difficult to do. Developing the conceptual structure represented a sweeping synthesis job full of personal constructs from smatterings picked up in many places. Under these conditions, giving reference to a back-up source would usually entail qualifying footnotes reflecting an unusual interpretation or exonerating the cited author from the implications we derived from his work. We look forward to a stronger, more comprehensive, and more scholarly presentation evolving out of future work.

However, we do want to acknowledge thoughts and work we have come across that bear most directly upon the possibilities of using a computer in real-time working association with a human to improve his working effectiveness. These findings fall into two categories. The first, which would include the present report, offers speculations and possibilities but does not include reporting of significant experimental results. Of these, Bush [5] is the earliest and one of the most directly stimulating. Licklider [6], who provides the most general clear case for the modern computer, coined the expression *man–computer symbiosis* to refer to the close interaction relationship between the man and computer in mutually beneficially relationship cooperation. Ulam [7] has specifically recommended close man–computer interaction in a chapter entitled "Synergesis," where he points out in considerable detail the types of mathematical work which could be aided. Good [8] includes some conjecture about the possibilities of intellectual aid to the human by close cooperation with a computer in a rather general way, and also presents a few interesting thoughts about a network model for structuring the conceptual kernels of information to facilitate a sort of self-organizing retrieval system. Ramo has given a number of talks dealing with the future possibilities of computers for "extending man's intellect," and wrote several articles [9, 10]. His projections seem slanted more toward larger bodies of humans interacting with computers, in less of an intimate personal sense than the above papers or than our initial goal. Fein [11], in making a comprehensive projection of the growth and dynamics interrelatedness of "computer-related sciences," includes specific mention of the enhancement of human intellect by cooperative activity of men, mechanisms, and automata. Fein coined the term *synnoetics* as applicable generally to the cooperative interaction of people, mechanisms, plant or animal organisms, and automata into a system whose mental power is greater than that of its components; he presents a good picture of the integrated way in which many currently separate disciplines should be developed and taught in the future to do justice to their mutual roles in the important discipline defined as "synnoetics."

In the second category, there have been a few papers published recently describing actual work that bears directly upon our topic. Licklider and Clark [12], and Culler and Huff [13], at the 1962 Spring Joint Computer Conference, gave what are essentially progress reports of work going on now in exactly this sort of thing—a human with a computer-backed display getting minute-by-minute help in solving problems. Teager [14, 15] reports on the plans and current development of a large time-sharing system at M.I.T., which is planned to provide direct computer access for a number of outlying stations located in scientists' offices, giving each of these users a chance for real-time utilization of the computer.

There are several efforts we have heard about but for which there are either no publications or for which none have been discovered by us. Just before the deadline date, we have received two publications from the M.I.T. Electronic Systems Laboratory; an Interim Engineering Report (of work done over two years ago), "Investigations In Computer-Aided Design," appears to contain much detailed analysis of applied work in close man–computer cooperation. A Technical Memorandum, "Method for Computer Visualization," by A. F. Smith, apparently elaborates on Chapter VII of the Interim Report. These documents seem extremely relevant. Mr. Douglas Ross, of the M.I.T. Electronic Systems Laboratory has, we have recently learned, been thinking and working on real-time man–machine interaction problems for some years. In addition, an M.I.T. graduate student, Glenn Randa [16], developed the design of a remote display console under Ross for his graduate thesis project. We understand that another M.I.T. graduate student, Ivan Sutherland, is currently using the display-computer facility on the TX-2 computer at Lincoln Laboratory to develop cooperative techniques for engeineering design problems. At the RAND Corporation, Cliff Shaw, Tom Ellis, and Keith Uncapher have been involved in implementing a multistation time-sharing system built around their JOHNNIAC computer. Termed the JOHNNIAC Open-Shop System (JOSS for short), it apparently is near completion, and will use remote typewriter stations.

Undoubtedly there are other efforts falling into either or both categories that have been overlooked. Such oversight has not been intentional, and it is hoped that these researchers will make their pertinent work known to the present writer.

5 *Summary and Recommendations*

This paper states the hypothesis that the intellectual effectiveness of an individual is dependent on factors which are subject to direct redesign in pursuit of an increase in that effectiveness. A conceptual framework is offered to help in giving consideration to this hypothesis. The framework in part derives from recognition that human intellect is already "augmented," and incorporates the following attributes:

1. As principal elements, the language, artifacts, and methodology which man has learned to use.

2. Dynamic interdependence of the elements within an operating system.

3. A hierarchical system structure, best considered a hierarchy of process capabilities whose primitive components are the basic human capabilities and the functional capabilities of the artifacts, organized into increasingly sophisticated capabilities.

4. As capabilities of primary interest, those associated with manipulating symbols and concepts in support of organizing and executing processes from which are ultimately derived human comprehension and problem solutions.

The framework also pictures the development of automated symbol manipulation to accommodate minute-by-minute mental processes as a significant means of increasing intellectual capability. This can be a logical next step in the cultural evolution of the means by which humans can match their mental capabilities against their problems. This approach pertains to any problem area in which the human does his thinking with concepts that he can express in words, charts, or any other explicit symbol form.

If the hypothesis and extrapolations discussed here and elsewhere (AFOSR 3223) are substantiated in future developments, the consequences will be exciting and assumedly beneficial to a problem-laden world. What is needed now is a test of this hypothesis and a calibration on the gains, if any, that might be realized by giving total-system design attention to human intellectual effectiveness. If the test and calibration prove favorable, then better and better augmentation systems could be developed for our problem solvers.

In this light, a research program is recommended aimed at (*a*) testing the hypothesis, (*b*) developing the tools and techniques for designing better augmentation systems, and (*c*) providing real-world augmentation systems. These goals are idealized, but results in these directions are nonetheless valuable. The approach should be on an empirical, total-system basis, i.e., coordinated study and innovation among all the factors admitted to the problem in conjunction with experiments that provide realistic action and interplay among the variables. The recommended environment for this approach is a laboratory with a computer-backed display and communication system. The experimental work of deriving, testing, and integrating innovations into a growing system of augmentation means is helped by having a specific type of human task on which to operate. From a long-range research-program point of view, characteristics of the task of computer programming make it particularly attractive as the initial such specific task.

In our view, we do *not* have to suspend such research until we learn how human mental processes work. We do *not* have to wait until we learn how to make computers more "intelligent." We *can* begin developing powerful and economically feasible augmentation systems on the basis of what we now know and have. We will want to integrate further basic knowledge and improved machines into existing augmentation systems. However, getting started now will provide not only orientation and stimulation for these pursuits, but also better problem-solving effectiveness with which to carry out such pursuits.

References

1.   Ashby, W. Ross, *Design for a Brain*, 2d ed., John Wiley & Sons, Inc., New York, 1960.

2.   _____, *Design for an Intelligence Amplified*, Automatic Studies, C. E. Shannon and J. McCarthy, Princeton Univ. Press, Princeton, N.J., 1956, pp. 215–234.

3.   Korzybski, A., *Science and Sanity*, International Non-Aristotelian Library Publishing Company, Lancaster, Pa., 1933.

4.   Whorf, B. L., *Language, Thought, and Reality*, M.I.T. and John Wiley & Sons, Inc., New York, 1956.

5.   Bush, Vannevar, "As We May Think," *The Atlantic Monthly* July, 1945.

6.   Licklider, J. C. R., "Man–Computer Symbiosis," *IRE Transactions on Human Factors in Electronics*, March, 1960.

7.   Ulam, S. M., *A Collection of Mathematical Problems*, Interscience Publishers, Inc., New York, 1960, p. 135.

8.   Good, I. J., "How Much Science Can You Have at Your Fingertips?" *IBM Journal of Research and Development*, October, 1958.

9. Ramo, Simon, "A New Technique of Education," *IRE Transactions on Education*, June, 1958.

10. _____, "The Scientific Extension of the Human Intellect," *Computers and Automation*, February, 1961.

11. Fein, Louis, "The Computer-Related Science (Synnoetics) at a University in the Year 1975," unpublished paper, December, 1960.

12. Licklider, J. C. R., and W. E. Clark, "On-Line Man–Computer Communication," *Proceedings Spring Joint Computer Conference*, National Press, Palo Alto, Calif., May, 1962.

13. Culler, G. J., and R. W. Huff, "Solution of Non-Linear Integral Equations Using On-Line Computer Control," paper for presentation at S.J.C.C., San Francisco, Ramo-Wooldridge, Canoga Park, Calif., May, 1962.

14. Teager, H. M., "Real-Time, Time-Shared Computer Project," report, M.I.T. Contract #Nonr–1841(69) DSR #8644, July 1, 1961.

15. _____, "Systems Considerations in Real-Time Computer Usage," paper presented at ONR Symposium on Automated Teaching, Oct. 12, 1961.

16. Randa, Glenn C., "Design of a Remote Display Console," Report ESL–R–132, M.I.T. Cambridge, Mass., February, 1962, available through ASTIA.

Toward High-Performance Knowledge Workers

Douglas C. Engelbart
Tymshare, Inc.
Cupertino, CA

Introduction

Among the on-line knowledge workers of tomorrow, there will be found as always a wide distribution both in personal motivation and flexibility, and in organizational roles and responsibility levels. In this view of the future, two things stand out for me: the workstations and work products of all of the workers must be interconnected; and special roles for high-performance knowledge workers within this interlinked organizational and informational network will be extremely important. This paper outlines a framework stemming from this perception toward developing high-performance knowledge workers as part of the evolutionary strategy of a knowledge organization.

In the early 60's when I began active, funded research in this area, well before the term "Office Automation" had emerged, I referred to my work as "Augmenting the Human Intellect." (References [1] , [2] summarize events and results for me and my co-workers over the intervening years.)

About ten years ago I re-named our pursuit, after reading Peter Drucker's discussions [3] about "knowledge workers," "knowledge organizations," and "knowledge industries." It seemed that a better term for the work would be "Augmenting the Knowledge Worker." From this

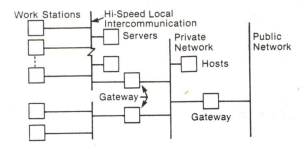

Figure 3.1 The workstations, computers and data bases for most large organizations will look something like this, and will connect to the outside world via at least one public network.

new perspective, a natural image emerged of a "Knowledge Workshop" as the place where a knowledge worker does his work and where, if we extended his tools, his means of collaborative communication, his working methods and his organizational roles, we could speak of an"Augmented Knowledge Workshop."

Workshop Architecture

General Features

It seems inevitable that, as depicted in Figure 3.1, there will be a combination of local, high-speed networking (Electronic PBX and Local-Area Network) together with higher-level networks (private and public) which will interconnect workstations and the many tools and services within an organization's "whole workshop." The effect will be as though there is a giant communication bus, where some elements seem far away (i.e., a slow or expensive communication path) and some seem very close (i.e., a fast and cheap communication path).

For the purposes of this discussion, let us put aside concerns for how much processing power and storage capacity should be built into the workstation, or where any particular problems or data should reside.

Let us instead consider the following principles, relative to supporting high-performance workers and integrating their capabilities into the larger organization:

- Their workstations should have access to many tools and services, assumedly provided by a number of distributed sources around this network, including both those newly implemented and those that have long existed and will be slow to disappear.

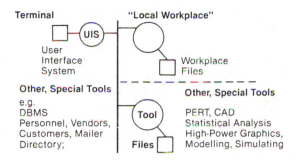

Figure 3.2   A user at a given terminal will "see" this kind of connection, looking "through" his UIS at his "local workplace" and beyond to the other, special tools that may be located anywhere on a connected network.

- The collection of tools and services for each worker must be integrated into a coherent whole into his "augmented knowledge workshop."

- Each worker should have access to his full complement of tools, services and personal working files from other workstations away from home base, even across the country so he can carry on with his work wherever he happens to be. (It would be a silly rejection of available communication technology to do otherwise.)

- This whole arrangement must provide pragmatically for continuing evolution of command language, tool and service functions, terminal hardware, processor horsepower, application packages and their support computers, etc. (See Reference [4] for a full development of such principles, and for the foundations for the architecture described below.)

Basic Organization of the Architecture

The overall architectural approach that we adopted has four major components, as shown in Figure 3.2 and summarized below. They are all operational today as part of Tymshare's AUGMENT system.

1.   A User Interface System (UIS) to handle the interface between the user's terminal and the interactive programs. (References [5] and [6] provide a detailed description of the implementation and utilization of the UIS.)

   The UIS takes care of all command-language dialog and all connection protocols. It also provides a uniform interface between the tool and the terminal to ensure that the user will (as nearly as possible) get the same treatment on a variety of terminals.

It interacts with an individual's user-profile file, to provide interface styles tailored to the needs and preferences of that individual.

It provides a reach-through service to non-AUGMENT systems, and can optionally translate between the command language of foreign-program modules and a command language designed to meet the user's particular needs. The user's command languages as translated for a number of different "foreign" systems can be designed for mutual consistency, to provide an important coherence in language and function.

It provides an adaptation to different terminal characteristics, allowing users to access their work from different terminals, and enabling application programmers to develop their software as though it were to serve a virtual terminal.

2.   A Procedure-Call Protocol (PCP) to provide for effective communication between processes on the network. (Reference [7] gives a thorough, detailed treatment of this "PCP approach.")

This protocol makes possible the implementation in each host of an application-independent, network run-time environment making remote resources accessible at the functional level essentially as though via a procedure call within a one-host application system. It greatly enhances the application programmer's flexibility; makes remote resources usefully accessible to other programs (not just to human users); significantly eases the problems of evolutionary changes within the network; and immensely improves the flexibility with which tools and services can be provided to the user.

3.   A Core Workshop, the user's own "Local Workplace," a basic collection of tools and services that a knowledge worker generally needs, regardless of his professional specialty.

The user feels that this is his "office," where in a similar, consistent and effective environment he can do most of his editing, studying, information management, mail management, etc. The AUGMENT Backend was designed to provide these core functions (and in addition has many features which reward a practiced user with significant gains in speed and flexibility).

The model in the user's mind is that he does most of his work here, and will "reach through" this "home workshop" to access other tools and services. There is special payoff for effective, flexible capabilities in this core workshop, where the user will spend a large proportion of his on-line time and can steadily acquire more of the available techniques toward higher performance.

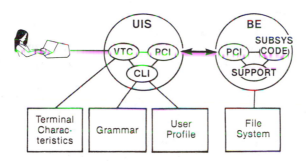

Figure 3.3   When using the Procedure Call Protocol to interact with a backend tool, the User Interface System (UIS) will employ three special software modules and three special control files.

4.   Other Special Tools with their own file conventions, operating systems, etc. A rich and ever-growing mix of data bases, application programs and special services will want to be "reachable" in a coherent manner by ever more of the knowledge workers in a larger organization, especially the higher-performance workers.

It is important to support the evolutionary integration of these services into coherent, composite tools systems. AUGMENT's implementation enables application-support programmers easily to provide customized mixes of function and command terminology for special classes of users, even for an individual user.

The general case, to be expected and probably encouraged, will find a variety of different hardware elements (terminals, personal computers, minis and large main frames, etc.) and a mix of software (different vintages, vendors, file conventions, terminology, user languages, help conventions, etc.).

Elements of the User Interface System

In Figure 3.3 are shown the main software modules (circles, ellipses) and support-file items (rectangles) involved when the User Interface System supports a user's access to a tool that is adapted for direct, "procedure call" service. The AUGMENT Backend is designed this way, and can work with full capability when the UIS and the Backend are separated by a network connection. This is true for any application system that has a procedure-call interface, regardless of the programming language and run-time environment, providing a suitable PCI module is implemented in its host computer to translate between the PCP and the particular procedure-call protocol for that application system.

The main UIS module is the Command Language Interpreter (CLI), interpreting each action by the user and responding with screen-action feedback or calls to the Backend tools for service, according to the particular Command Language in effect.

There are likely to be many UIS-Grammar files lying around, each being a compact, specially coded specification of a particular Command Language. When attached to the CLI, a particular Grammar file determines the command terms and the feedback on the terminal screen, as well as the service-call and data-transfer interaction with the Backend tools.

For any given user, there will be one User Profile file attached to the UIS to specify the particular set of options which that user desires in the action of the CLI, e.g., style of command recognition, amount and type of feedback, formatting defaults, initialization status, escape-code assignments to particular keys, etc.

It is an administrative decision whether or not a particular user is provided with commands for changing his profile file.

The Virtual Terminal Controller (VTC) module lets the rest of the UIS operate as though service a standard, "virtual" terminal, translating back and forth to/from the signals of whatever "actual" terminal is connected.

The characteristics of the particular terminal are packed into the special "Terminal Characteristic" file, one such for each different type of terminal that may be interfaced. For most of the modern terminals, this file is selected and installed automatically from interactions between the UIS and the terminal.

The UIS Process Communication Interface (PCI) allows the CLI to interact with the Backend tools making service requests and receiving the results as though it were making sub-routine calls in a "virtual" application-system environment.

In the general case, the UIS PCI would translate the UIS signals back and forth to/from a "universal procedure-call protocol" suitable for network interchange; a particular Backend tool (application system) would employ a version of the PCI that translates in turn back and forth to/from that tool's internally employed procedure-call protocol.

Foreign-System Reach-Through

Figure 3.4 shows the special provision for reaching through to "foreign" systems that do not provide a procedure-call interface, i.e., systems that can only be utilized by character-stream I/O as from a terminal. The Reach-Through Interface is a special module that can be programmed for the specific character-stream interactions of a given tool for eliciting from the tool the equivalent results as expected by each procedure call sent to that tool by the CLI.

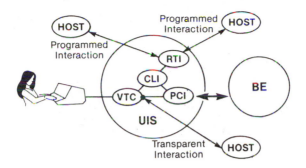

Figure 3.4   When interacting with a backend tool not equipped for procedure-call inter-action, the UIS can either employ programmed interaction via its Reach-Through Interface (RTI), or provide the user with direct, transparent connection.

In such a case, the UIS can interact with the Backend tool as though it (the UIS) were a terminal effectively translating between the CLI and the flow of characters back and forth to/from the tool, to call for service and to receive the results.

Seemingly inefficient, yet this "programmed-interaction" reach-through mode provides for an effective translation between the command language of that foreign tool and the UIS Command Language where the latter may be designed with verbs and nouns, etc., to fit the special usage and to be compatible with the rest of the grammar, vocabulary, and conceptual-model characteristics designed to serve this class of users as their coherent knowledge workshop.

This enables the coherent integration of many older systems, many of which will live on for years.

As an alternative mode of interacting with a foreign system through its terminal I/O, the UIS can connect the foreign-system link directly to the Virtual Terminal Controller (VTC) to provide interaction as though the UIS were "transparent."

Shared-Screen Conferencing

Figure 3.5 shows an interconnection mode, between two instances of UIS modules, whereby both terminals can share the screen content of one of them. Each VTC module converts the virtual-terminal screen image to the correct form for its connected terminal, so that shared-screen conferencing will work for dissimilar terminals.

This mode is established in response to a suitable set of commands by the participants, and in principle any number of users can have such a connection made to their UIS modules so that User A can in real time

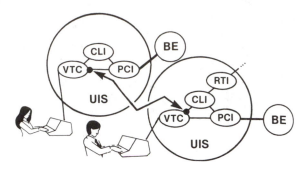

Figure 3.5 When employing their respective UISs in the shared-screen conferencing connection, two or more users can collaborate closely on whatever job the "showing user" has going.

show the dynamic workings of his screen to them all—no matter what command language and tool system he is using.

At his option, User A can pass control to User B; thereafter what everyone watches are the effects of commands from User B's terminal and VTC acting through User A's CLI upon A's active jobs and files.

In its usual employment, this conferencing mode is used in conjunction with simultaneous telephone dialog. It will work between any two users connected by a network path. (Reference [8] gives a fairly complete description of an earlier form of this "shared-screen teleconferencing.")

The Over-All Augmentation System

The Categories of System Elements

Here, from my framework, are the major elements involved in "augmenting" our knowledge workers and their organizations. For this purpose, a "craftsman" metaphor seems directly applicable—considering that our knowledge workers must be very much the professional craftsmen.

A. Tools: Craftsmen benefit from balanced collections of well-designed tools

B. Methods: To be effective, tools must be used with well-polished work methods

C. Skills: It takes practised skill to exercise a competent blend of tool and method

D.   Knowledge: True craftsmen depend upon much integrated "shop" knowledge

E.   Language OF THE CRAFT: Craftsmen need an effective language to discuss, teach, plan and collaborate among themselves (i.e., to do their "shop talk").

F.   Training: To develop an effective group of craftsmen in a planned way requires explicit training, in all of the above elements

G.   Organization: Role differentiation and organizational structure are necessary for integrating craftsmen effectively into an organization.

Tool System and Human System

For discussion's sake, call Category A the "Tool System" and the aggregate of Categories B through G the "Human System." We can immediately note that new technology, no matter how dramatic, contributes directly only to the Tool System.

Over the centuries there has been an immense amount of invention involved in the cultural evolution that brought the Human System to its present state. But its evolution took place with what will have to be described as a very primitive Tool System.

To take advantage of the absolutely radical, emerging Tool-System inventions, it is inevitable that evolution of the Human-System will begin to accelerate. In my view, this is strongly to be encouraged, since the power derived from the Tool System can only come from the way it is harnessed to human endeavors via the Human System.

Co-Evolution

The optimum design for either the Tool System or the Human System is dependent upon the match it must make with the other. There is a high degree of mutual dependence. But it seems that the Tool System is or soon will be "out of control" in the sense of our being able to design its target state, say for five years hence. And we possibly never will know how to "design" this Human System. So to be pragmatic about it, we can at best work in a "guided-evolution" mode for each of the sub-systems.

So, the ultimate capability of the larger "Augmentation System," and therefore the performance level of the knowledge workers and knowledge organizations of the future, will improve only through the co-evolution of these two sub-systems. A disastrous default mode would be for the perceptions of the technologists and the market-oriented product planners to steer the evolution of the Tool System, and leave the

Human System to adapt in its trail. There is no practical worry that the evolution of the Human System will drive that of the Tool System; it is inconceivable that the Human System could be served by analysts, inventors and intrepreneurs with the same fierce intensity as for the Tool System.

The practical worry is that there won't be enough perception of payoff from investing in explicit, conscious invention and evolution in the Human System, and that we will drift toward the above default mode.

It is something of a bind—our culture hasn't really developed an acceptance for cultural progress to anywhere near the extent it has for progress in the technological and material sense—and without a solid perception and acceptance that conscious evolution of such as this Human System (primarily a cultural matter) will pay off, we are not likely to become particularly effective at it. So it would seem that we need to invest an extra degree of attention and resource toward developing the perception that this Human System is not only acceptable but has a very high payoff. *Then* we probably could get moving toward a balanced co-evolution.

So, Why Talk About High-Performance Knowledge Workers

There is a first-order answer to this question. It makes sense, at least from my viewpoint, to aim for a balanced distribution among the knowledge workers in an organization, in terms of the level of knowledge-work performance targeted for different roles. In this view then, a certain proportion of research, development and implementation investment should be made toward making really significant improvements. This would involve special attention for such roles, over both the Tool System and the Human System.

And there is also a very important, second-order answer. The most effective strategy that I can think of, toward developing the perception and acceptance of "progress" in the Human System, is to invest in pursuit of truly high-performance for selected knowledge-work roles. The best roles for this pupose would be those that would expose important stakeholders to the EXPERIENCE of truly high performance, by BEING THERE when that high performance is being exercised on activities relevant to their workaday world.

As a general strategy then, we would aim for specially equipped and trained teams to be connected into the workshop networks of large organizations, to perform roles that lend themselves best to early pursuit of especially high performance, and where there would be an appropriate visibility, identification, and sense of relevance for the organization's trend setters.

Conclusions

We can reasonably hypothesize that a startling degree of improvement may be obtained in the performance level of knowledge organizations and their individual knowledge workers. And further, that in order to obtain this we must attend to changes in both the Tool System and the Human System.

If this hypothesis were to be proven valid, it would be of immense importance for a problem-laden society to have acted on it. It doesn't seem that we would have to risk much to test it out over the next decade. A very small proportion of what is being invested in the "easy to learn" level of Office Automation, if explicitly directed toward pursuing high augmented-human performance, would have a notable effect.

Architectural features such as described above seem necessary anyway to support the natural evolution of Office Automation, even without any special emphasis upon high-performance workers. A salient point is that these features also can support the accelerated evolution of individuals and groups, who can still work effectively with the rest of the organization, but where through their own efforts or through planned investment by the larger organization they have extended more rapidly than the rest the development of their augmentation categories—tools, methods, skills, etc.

And what is also important about these features is that they provide for the harmonious co-existence, within the same organizational environment, of knowledge workers of all levels of performance. The high-performance organization of the next decade must make do with many degrees of aspiration, talent and training, and must accommodate a wide spectrum in its workers' performance levels.

And it is also important to note that architectural characteristics of the organization's knowledge workshop will have a notable effect upon the co-evolution rate that can be achieved.

Acknowledgments

The concepts and the system described above have evolved over more than two decades, greatly aided by the research sponsorship of a number of organizations. Until 1978, at SRI International, research sponsorship by The Air Force Office of Scientific Research provided three years of critical conceptualization and planning support, from '59 through '62; DARPA's Information Processing Techniques Office, NASA, and the Air Force RADC contributed significantly until 1978, when SRI sold its rights to the system to Tymshare, Inc. There, while bringing it into the commercial market, the company has supported further conceptual and development work. During this more than two decades, probably a hundred different people have contributed directly, very significantly affecting the architecture and its implementation, and probably even affecting the way I see these things.

References

1.   Engelbart, D. C., "Toward Integrated, Evolutionary Office Automation Systems," Proceedings of the 26th Joint Engineering Management Conference, Denver, CO, 1978, pp. 63–68.

2.   Engelbart, D. C., "Evolving the Organization of the Future: A Point of View," published in the book, "Emerging Office Systems Issues," ed. Robert Landau, Ablex, 1982 (Proceedings of the Stanford International Conference on Office Automation, March 1980).

3.   Drucker, Peter F., "The Age of Discontinuity: Guidelines to Our Changing Society," Harper and Row, New York, 1968.

4.   Engelbart, D. C., Watson, R. W., and Norton, J. C., "The Augmented Knowledge Workshop," AFIPS Conference Proceedings, Volume 42, pp. 9–21, National Computer Conference, June 4–8, 1973.

5.   Irby, C. H., "The Command Meta Language System," AFIPS Conference Proceedings, NCC, Vol. 45, 1976.

6.   Watson, R. W., "User Interface Design Issues for a Large Interactive System," AFIPS Conference Proceedings, NCC, Vol. 45, 1976, pp. 357–364.

7.   White, J. E., "A High-Level Framework for Network-Based Resource Sharing," AFIPS Conference Proceedings, 1976, NCC, Vol. 45.

8.   Engelbart, D. C., "NLS Teleconferencing Features: The Journal, and Shared-Screen Telephoning," Proceedings of 1975 COMPCON, Washington, D.C., September 1975.

Early Research Projects

This section focuses on two major research projects in collaborative work that predate the renewed interest in CSCW. Engelbart's NLS system, designed and built first at Stanford Research Institute and then commercialized as the AUGMENT system, was a development effort founded on principles articulated in the early Conceptual Framework (Reading 2, this volume). Alphonse Chapanis's laboratory at Johns Hopkins University was for many years the site for some of the most serious testing of alternative modes of communication in group work.

The first two papers in this section describe the system Engelbart's group built: the Engelbart and English paper (Reading 4, this volume) is about NLS and the research lab environment in which it was developed; authorship provisions of AUGMENT are the subject of the second paper (Reading 5). This paper also makes explicit mention of several of the group-work support tools in NLS and AUGMENT. These "multiparty collaboration" tools include electronic mail, recorded mail, and shared-screen teleconferencing.

Recorded mail refers to items kept in a permanent and public journal. The reader may notice strange numbers in citations and in the reference list of this paper: they are journal numbers referring to articles and messages written by AUGMENT users over the years and permanently archived for future reference.

Journal-like textual databases with cross-references and citations are now regaining popularity as part of the renewed interest in hypertext (see Reading 16, this volume). Shared-screen conferencing has not taken off as much as have e-mail and structured documents, but it is being revisited both in research labs (see Reading 15, this volume) and in a number of commercial products for remote debugging.

The 1975 Chapanis paper (Reading 6) summarizes a long and thorough research program that set out to distinguish the relative values of three classes of communication media: text, voice, and video. The basic results indicated that productivity substantially increased when a group could use voice communication as well as text; not nearly as notable an effect was felt when video was added. This remains an important fundamental result. There are kinds of work where, as long as the object of interest is visible to all on the screen, a voice connection is as good as video. This is not universally true but tends to be the case with large classes of work that are already well supported by computer tools: software development, authoring, and design drawing. Types of meetings where shared-screen and voice connection might be less effective are those where the focal object is less clear—where people want to chat face to face and get to know each other. Without underestimating the importance of such meetings, it's important to realize that there are other kinds that can be enhanced by computer support without the expense of video.

4

A Research Center for Augmenting Human Intellect[1]

Douglas C. Engelbart
William K. English
SRI International
Menlo Park, CA

1 Summary

This paper describes a multisponsor research center at Stanford Research Institute in man–computer interaction.

For its laboratory facility, the Center has a time-sharing computer (65K, 24-bit core) with a 4.5 megabyte swapping drum and a 96 megabyte file-storage disk. This serves twelve CRT work stations simultaneously.

Special hardware completely removes from the CPU the burden of display refreshing and input sampling, even though these are done directly out of and into core.

The display in a user's office appears on a high-resolution (875-line) commercial television monitor, and provides both character and vector portrayals. A relatively standard typewriter keyboard is supplemented by a five-key handset used (optionally) for entry of control codes and brief literals. An SRI cursor device called the "mouse" is used for screen pointing and selection.

---

[1] Principal sponsors are: Advanced Research Projects Agency and National Aeronautics and Space Agency (NAS1–7897) and Rome Air Development Center F30602–68–C–0286.

The "mouse" is a hand-held X-Y transducer usable on any flat surface; it is described in greater detail further on.

Special-purpose high-level languages and associated compilers provide rapid, flexible development and modification of the repertoire of service functions and of their control procedures (the latter being the detailed user actions and computer feedback involved in controlling the application of these service functions).

User files are organized as hierarchical structures of data entities, each composed of arbitrary combinations of text and figures. A repertoire of coordinated service features enables a skilled user to compose, study, and modify these files with great speed and flexibility, and to have searches, analyses, data manipulation, etc. executed. In particular, special sets of conventions, functions, and working methods have been developed to air programming, logical design, documentation, retrieval, project management, team interaction, and hard-copy production.

2 Introduction

In the Augmented Human Intellect (AHI) Research Center at Stanford Research Institute a group of researchers is developing an experimental laboratory around an interactive, multiconsole computer-display system, and is working to learn the principles by which interactive computer aids can augment their intellectual capability.

The research objective is to develop principles and techniques for designing an "augmentation system."

This includes concern not only for the technology of providing interactive computer service, but also for changes both in ways of conceptualizing, visualizing, and organizing working material, and in procedures and methods for working individually and cooperatively.

The research approach is strongly empirical. At the workplace of each member of the subject group we aim to provide nearly full-time availability of a CRT work station, and then to work continuously to improve both the service available at the stations and the aggregate value derived therefrom by the group over the entire range of its roles and activities.

Thus the research group is also the subject group in the experiment.

Among the special activities of the group are the evolutionary development of a complex hardware-software system, the design of new task procedures for the system's users, and careful documentation of the evolving system designs and user procedures.

The group also has the usual activities of managing its activities, keeping up with outside developments, publishing reports, etc.

Hence, the particulars of the augmentation system evolving here will reflect the nature of these tasks—i.e., the system is aimed at augmenting a system-development project team. Though the primary research goal is to develop principles of analysis and design so as to understand how to augment human capability, choosing the researchers themselves as subjects yields as a valuable secondary benefit a system tailored to help develop complex computer-based systems.

This "bootstrap" group has the interesting (recursive) assignment of developing tools and techniques to make it more effective at carrying out its assignment.

Its tangible product is a developing augmentation system to provide increased capability for developing and studying augmentation systems.

This system can hopefully be transferred, as a whole or by pieces of concept, principle and technique, to help others develop augmentation systems for aiding many other disciplines and activities.

In other words we are concentrating fully upon reaching the point where we can do all of our work on line—placing in computer store all of our specifications, plans, designs, programs, documentation, reports, memos, bibliography and reference notes, etc., and doing all of our scratch work, planning, designing, debugging, etc., and a good deal of our intercommunication, via the consoles.

We are trying to maximize the coverage of our documentation, using it as a dynamic and plastic structure that we continually develop and alter to represent the current state of our evolving goals, plans, progress, knowledge, designs, procedures, and data.

The display-computer system to support this experiment is just (at this writing) becoming operational. Its functional features serve a basic display-oriented user system that we have evolved over five years and through three other computers. Below are described the principal features of these systems.

3 The User System

3.1 Basic Facility

As "seen" by the user, the basic facility has the following characteristics:

1.   Twelve CRT consoles, of which 10 are normally located in offices of AHI research staff.

2.   The consoles are served by an SDS 940 time-sharing computer dedicated to full-time service for this staff, and each console may operate entirely independently of the others.

Figure 4.1   Underside of mouse

3.   Each individual has private file space, and the group has community space, on a high-speed disc with a capacity of 96 million characters.

The system is not intended to serve a general community of time-sharing users, but is being shaped in its entire design toward the special needs of the "bootstrapping" experiment.

3.2 Work Stations

As noted above, each work station is equipped with a display, an alphanumeric keyboard, a mouse, and a five-key handset.

The display at each of the work stations is provided on a high-resolution, closed-circuit television monitor.

The alphanumeric keyboard is similar to a Teletype keyboard. It has 96 normal characters in two cases. A third-case shift key provides for future expansion, and two special keys are used for system control.

The mouse produces two analog voltages as the two wheels (see Figure 4.1) rotate, each changing in proportion to the X or Y movements over the table top.

The voltages control—via an A/D converter, the computer's memory, and the display generator—the coordinates of a tracking spot with which the user may "point" to positions on the screen.

Three buttons on top of the mouse are used for special control.

A set of experiments, comparing (within our techniques of interaction) the relative speed and accuracy obtained with this and other selection devices showed the mouse to be better than a light pen or a joystick (see Refs. English1 and English2).

Compared to a light pen, it is generally less awkward and fatiguing to use, and it has a decided advantage for uses with raster-scan, write-through storage tube, projection, or multiviewer display systems.

The five-key handset has 31 chords or unique key-stroke combinations, in five "cases."

The first four cases contain lower- and upper-case letters and punctuation, digits, and special characters. (The chords for the letters correspond to the binary numbers from 1 to 26.)

The fifth case is "control case." A particular chord (the same chord in each case) will always transfer subsequent input-chord interpretations to control case.

In control case, one can "backspace" through recent input, specify underlining for subsequent input, transfer to another case, visit another case for one character or one word, etc.

One-handed typing with the handset is slower than two-handed typing with the standard keyboard. However, when the user works with one hand on the handset and one on the mouse, the coordinated interspersion of control characters and short literal strings from one hand with mouse-control actions from the other yields considerable advantage in speed and smoothness of operation.

For literal strings longer than about ten characters, one tends to transfer from the handset to the normal keyboard.

Both from general experience and from specific experiment, it seems that enough handset skill to make its use worthwhile can generally be achieved with about five hours of practice. Beyond this, skill grows with usage.

3.3 *Structure of Files*

Our working information is organized into files, with flexible means for users to set up indices and directories, and to hop from file to file by display-selection or by typed-in file-name designations. Each file is highly structured in its internal organization.

The specific structure of a given file is determined by the user, and is an important part of his conceptual and "study-manipulate" treatment of the file.

The introduction of explicit "structuring" to our working information stems from a very basic feature of our conceptual framework (see Refs. Engelbart1 and Engelbart2) regarding means for augmenting human intellect.

With the view that the symbols one works with are supposed to represent a mapping of one's associated concepts, and further that one's concepts exist in a "network" of relationships as opposed to the essentially linear form of actual printed records, it was decided that the concept-manipulation aids derivable from real-time computer support could be appreciably enhanced by structuring conventions that would make explicit (for both the user and the computer) the various types of network relationships among concepts.

As an experiment with this concept, we adopted some years ago the convention of organizing all information into explicit hierarchical structures, with provisions for arbitrary cross-referencing among the elements of a hierarchy.

The principal manifestation of this hierarchical structure is the breaking up of text into arbitrary segments called "statements," each of which bears a number showing its serial location in the text and its "level" in an "outline" of the text. This paper is an example of hierarchical text structure.

To set up a reference link from Statement A to Statement B, one may refer in Statement A either to the location number of B or to the "name" of B. The difference is that the number is vulnerable to subsequent structural change, whereas the name stays with the statement through changes in the structure around it.

By convention, the first word of a statement is treated as the name of the statement, if it is enclosed in parentheses.

References to these names may be embedded anywhere in other statements, for instance as "see (AFI)," where special format informs the viewer explicitly that this refers to a statement named "AFI," or merely as a string of characters in a context such that the viewer can infer the referencing.

This naming and linking, when added to the basic hierarchical form, yields a highly flexible general structuring capability. These structuring conventions are expected to evolve relatively rapidly as our research progresses.

For some material, the structured-statement form may be undesirable. In these cases, there are means for suppressing the special formatting in the final printout of the structured text.

The basic validity of the structured text approach has been established by our subsequent experience.

We have found that in both off-line and on-line computer aids, the conception, stipulation, and execution of significant manipulations are made much easier by the structuring conventions.

Also, in working on line at a CRT console, not only is manipulation made much easier and more powerful by the structure, but a user's ability to get about very quickly within his data, and to have special "views" of it generated to suit his need, are significantly aided by the structure.

We have come to write all of our documentation, notes, reports, and proposals according to these conventions, because of the resulting increase in our ability to study and manipulate them during composition, modification, and usage. Our programming systems also incorporate the conventions. We have found it to be fairly universal that after an initial period of negative reaction in reading explicitly structured material, one comes to prefer it to material printed in the normal form.

3.4 *File Studying*

The computer aids are used for two principal "studying" operations, both concerned with construction of the user's "views," i.e., the portion of his working text that he sees on the screen at a given moment.

3.4.1 *Display Start* The first operation is finding a particular statement in the file (called the "display start"); the view will then begin with that statement. This is equivalent to finding the beginning of a particular passage in a hard-copy document.

3.4.2 *Form of View* The second operation is the specification of a "form" of view—it may simply consist of a screenful of text which sequentially follows the point specified as the display start, or it may be constructed in other ways, frequently so as to give the effect of an outline.

In normal, off-line document studying, one often does the first type of operation, but the second is like a scissors-and-staple job and is rarely done just to aid one's studying.

(A third type of service operation that will undoubtedly be of significant aid to studying is question answering. We do not have this type of service.)

3.4.3 *Specification of Display Start* The display start may be specified in several ways:

By direct selection of a statement which is on the display—the user simply points to any character in the statement, using the mouse.

If the desired display start is not on the display, it may be selected indirectly if it bears a "marker."

Markers are normally invisible. A marker has a name of up to five characters, and is attached to a character of the text. Referring to the marker by name (while holding down a special button) is exactly equivalent to pointing to the character with the mouse.

The control procedures make it extremely quick and easy to fix and call markers.

By furnishing either the name or the location number of the statement, which can be done in either of two basic ways:

- Typing from the keyboard

- Selecting an occurrence of the name or number in the text. This may be done either directly or via an indirect marker selection.

After identifying a statement by one of the above means, the user may request to be taken directly there for his next view. Alternately, he may request instead that he be taken to some statement bearing a specified structure relationship to the one specifically identified. For instance, when the user identifies Statement 3E4 by one of the above means (assume it to be a member of the list 3E1 through 3E7), he may ask to be taken to

- Its successor, i.e., Statement 3E5

- Its predecessor, i.e., Statement 3E3

- Its list tail, i.e., Statement 3E7

- Its list head, i.e., Statement 3E1

- Its list source, i.e., Statement 3E

- Its subhead, i.e., Statement 3E4A

Besides being taken to an explicitly identified statement, a user may ask to go to the first statement in the file (or the next after the current location) that contains a specified word or string of characters.

He may specify the search string by typing it in, by direct (mouse) selection, or by indirect (marker) selection.

3.4.4 Specification of Form of View　The "normal" view beginning at a given location is like a frame cut out from a long scroll upon which the hierarchical set of statements is printed in sequential order.

Otherwise, three independently variable view-specification conditions may be applied to the construction of the displayed view: level clipping, line truncation, and content filtering. The view is simultaneously affected by all three of these.

Level: Given a specified level parameter, L(L = 1, 2, ..., ALL), the view generator will display only those statements whose "depth" is less than or equal to L. (For example, Statement 3E4 is third level, 3E second, 4B2C1 fifth, etc.) Thus it is possible to see only first-level statements, or only first-, second-, and third-level statements, for example.

Truncation: Given a specified truncation parameter, T(T = 1, 2, ..., ALL), the view generator will show only the first T lines of each statement being displayed.

Content: Given a specification for desired content (written in a special high-level content-analysis language) the view generator optionally can be directed to display only those statements that have the specified content.

One can specify simple strings, or logical combinations thereof, or such things as having the word "memory" within four words of the word "allocation."

Content specifications are written as text, anywhere in the file. Thus the full power of the system may be used for composing and modifying them.

Any one content specification can then be chosen for application (by selecting it directly or indirectly). It is compiled immediately to produce a machine-code content-analysis routine, which is then ready to "filter" statements for the view generator.

In addition, the following format features of the display may be independently varied: indentation of statements according to level, suppression of location numbers and/or names of statements, and separation of statements by blank lines.

The user controls these view specifications by means of brief, mnemonic character codes. A skilled user will readjust his view to suit immediate needs very quickly and frequently; for example, he may change level and truncation settings several times in as many seconds.

3.4.5 "Freezing" Statements One may also preempt an arbitrary amount of the upper portion of the screen for holding a collection of "frozen" statements. The remaining lower portion is treated as a reduced-size scanning frame, and the view generator follows the same rules for filling it as described above.

The frozen statements may be independently chosen or dismissed, each may have line truncation independent of the rest, and the order in which they are displayed is arbitrary and readily changed. Any screen-select operand for any command may be selected from any portion of the display (including the frozen statement).

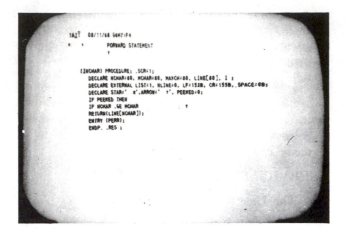

Figure 4.2 View of an MOL program, with level parameter set to 3 and truncation to 1

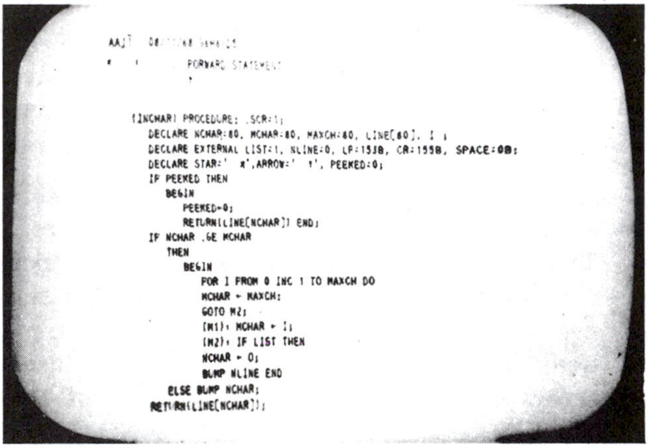

Figure 4.3 Same program as Figure 4.2, but with level parameter changed to 6 (several levels still remain hidden from view)

Examples

Figures 4.2 and 4.3 show views generated from the same starting point with different level-clipping parameters. This example happens to be of a program written in our Machine-Oriented language (MOL, see below).

Figure 4.4 demonstrates the freezing feature with a view of a program (the same one shown in Figure 4.7) written in our Control Metalanguage (CML, see below). Statements 3C, 3C2, 2B, 2B1, 2B2, 2B3, and 2B4 are frozen, and statements from 2J on are shown normally with L = 3, T = 1.

Figure 4.4 View of CML program, showing six frozen statements and illustrating use of reference hopping

The freezing here was used to hold for simultaneous view four different functionally related process descriptions. The subroutines (+ BUG1SPEC) and (+ WAIT) were located by use of the hop-to-name feature described above.

3.5 *File Modification*

Here we use a standard set of editing operations, specifying with each operation a particular type of text entity.

Operations: Delete, Insert, Replace, Move, Copy.

Entities (within text statements): Character, Text (arbitrary strings), Word, Visible (print string), Invisible (gap string).

Entities (for structure manipulation): Statement, Branch (statement plus all substructure), Group (sublist of branches), Plex (complete list of branches).

Structure may also be modified by joining statements, or breaking a statement into two at a specified point.

Generally, an operation and an entity make up a command, such as "Delete Word." To specify the command, the user types the first letter of each word in the command: thus "DW" specifies "Delete Word." There are occasional cases where a third word is used or where the first letter cannot be used because of ambiguities.

3.6 *File Output*

Files may be sent to any of a number of different output devices to produce hard copy—an upper/lower-case line printer, an on-line high-quality typewriter, or paper tape to drive various typewriters.

In future it will be possible to send files via magnetic tape to an off-line CRT-to-film system from which we can produce Xerox prints, Multilith masters, or microform records.

Flexible format control may be exercised in this process by means of specially coded directives embedded in the files—running headers, page numbering, line lengths, line centering, suppression of location numbers, indenting, right justification (hyphenless), etc., are controllable features.

3.7 *Compiling and Debugging*

Source-code files written in any of our compiler languages (see below), or in the SDS 940 assembly language (ARPAS, in which our compiler output is produced) may be compiled under on-line control. For debugging, we have made a trivial addition to the SDS 940's DDT loader-debugger so as to operate it from the CRT displays. Though it was designed to operate from a Teletype terminal, this system gains a great deal speed and power by merely showing with a display the last 26 lines of what would have been on the Teletype output.

3.8 *Calculating*

The same small innovation as mentioned above for DDT enables us to use the CAL system from a display terminal.

3.9 *Conferencing*

We have set up a room specially equipped for on-line conferencing. Six displays are arranged in the center of a square table (see Figure 4.5) so that each of twenty participants has good visibility. One participant controls the system, and all displays show the same view. The other participants have mice that control a large arrow on the screen, for use as a pointer (with no control function).

As a quick means of finding and displaying (with appropriate forms of view) any desired material from a very large collection, this system is a powerful aid to presentation and review conferences.

We are also experimenting with it in project meetings, using it not only to keep track of agenda items and changes but also to log progress notes, action notes, etc. The review aid is of course highly useful here also.

Figure 4.5   On-line conference arrangement

We are anxious to see what special conventions and procedures will evolve to allow us to harness a number of independent consoles within a conference group. This obviously has considerable potential.

4 Service-System Software

4.1 *The User's Control Language*

Consider the service a user gets from the computer to be in the form of discrete operations—i.e., the execution of individual "service functions" from a repertoire comprising a "service system."

Examples of service functions are deleting a word, replacing a character, hopping to a name, etc.

Associated with each function of this repertoire is a "control-dialogue procedure." This procedure involves selecting a service function from the repertoire, setting up the necessary parameter designations for a particular application, recovering from user errors, and calling for the execution of the function.

The procedure is made up of the sequence of keystrokes, select actions, etc. made by the user, together with the interspersed feedback messages from the computer.

The repertoire of service functions, together with their control-dialogue procedures, constitutes the user's "control language." This is a language for a "master-slave" dialogue, enabling the user to control application of the computer's capabilities to his own service.

It seems clear that significant augmentation of one's intellectual effectiveness from the harnessing of computer services will require development of a broad and sophisticated control-language vocabulary.

It follows that the evolution of such a control language is a very important part of augmentation-system research.

For the designer of user systems, it is important to have good means for specifying the nature of the functions and their respective control-dialogue procedures, so that a design specification will be

- Concise, so that its essential features are easily seen

- Unambiguous, so that questions about the design may be answered clearly

- Canonical, so that information is easily located

- Natural, so that the form of the description fits the conceptual frame of the design

- Easy to compose, study, and modify, so that the process of evolutionary design can be facilitated.

It is also important for the user to have a description of the service functions and their control-dialogue procedures.

The description must again be concise, unambiguous, canonical, and natural; furthermore, it must be accurate, in that everything relevant to the user about the service functions and their control-dialogue procedures is described, and everything described actually works as indicated.

4.2 State-Chart Representation of Control-Language Design

Figure 4.6 shows a charting method that was used in earlier stages of our work for designing and specifying the control procedure portions of the control language. Even though limited to describing only the control-dialogue procedures, this representation nonetheless served very well and led us to develop the successive techniques described below.

Figure 4.6 shows actual control procedures for four service functions from the repertoire of an interactive system: Delete Word, Delete Text, Place Up Statement, and Forward Statement.

The boxes contain abbreviated descriptions of relevant display-feedback conditions, representing the intermediate states between successive user actions. Both to illustrate how the charting conventions are

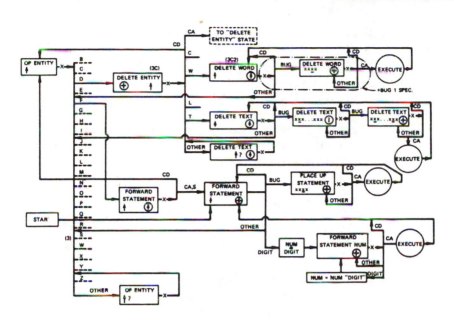

Figure 4.6   State-chart portrayal of part of the text-manipulation control language

used and to give some feeling for the dynamics of our user-system control procedures, we describe briefly below both the chart symbols and the associated display-feedback conventions that we have developed.

The writing at the top of each box indicates what is to be shown as "command feedback" at the top of the display (see Figures 4.2, 4.3, and 4.4).

An uparrow sometimes appears under the first character of one of the words of Command Feedback.

This indicates to the user that the next character he types will be interpreted as designating a new term to replace that being pointed to; no uparrow under Command Feedback signifies that keyboard action will not affect the command designation.

"Entity" represents the entity word (i.e., "character," "word," "statement," etc.) that was last used as part of a fully specified command.

The computer often "offers" the user an entity option.

The circle in the box indicated the character to be used for the "bug" (the tracking spot), which alternates between the characters uparrow and plus.

The uparrow indicates that a select action is appropriate, and the plus indicates that a select action is inappropriate.

The string of X's, with underlines, indicates that the selected characters are to be underlined as a means of showing the user what the computer thinks he has selected.

There is frequently an X on the output line from a box on the chart. This indicates that the computer is to wait until the user has made another action.

After this next action, the computer follows a branching path, depending upon what the action was (as indicated on the chart) to reach another state-description box or one of the function-execution processes.

4.3 *The Control Metalanguage*

In searching for an improvement over the state chart, we looked for the following special features, as well as the general features listed above:

- A representational form using structural text so as to harness the power of our on-line text-manipulation techniques for composing, studying, and modifying our designs.

- A form that would allow us to specify the service functions as well as the control-dialogue procedures.

- A form such that a design-description file could be translated by a computer program into the actual implementation of the control language.

Using our Tree Meta compiler-compiler (described below), we have developed a next step forward in our means of designing, specifying, implementing and documenting our on-line control languages. The result is called "Control Metalanguage" (CML).

Figure 4.7 shows a portion of the description for the current control language, written in Control Metalanguage.

This language is the means for describing both the service functions and their control-dialogue procedures.

The Control Metalanguage Translator (CMLT) can process a file containing such a description, to produce a corresponding version of an interactive system which responds to user actions exactly as described in the file.

There is a strong correspondence between the conventions for representing the control procedures in Control Metalanguage and in the state chart, as a comparison of Figures 4.7 and 4.6 will reveal.

The particular example printed out for Figure 4.7 was chosen because it specifies some of the same procedures as in Figure 4.6.

```
3 (wc:) zap case

  3A (b) [edit dsp (backward ↑es*) . case
   .
   .
   .

  3B (c) [edit] dsp (copy ↑es*) :s true => <am>adj1:.case
    3B1 (c) s*=cc dsp(↑copy character)
      e*=c,character +bug2spec
    +cdlim(b1,p1,p2,p3,p4) +cdlim(b2,p5,p6,p7,p8)
    +cpchtx(b1,p2,p4,p5,p6) ;

    3B2 (w) s*=cw dsp(↑copy word) e*=w,word +bug2spec
    +wdr2(b1,p1,p2,p3,p4) +wdr2(b2,p5,p6,p7,p8)
    +cpwdvs(b1,p2,p4,p5,p6) ;

    3B3 (1) s*=cl dsp(↑copy line) e*=1,line +bug2spec
    +ldlim(b1,p1,p2,p3,p4) +ldlim(b2,p5,p6,p7,p8) :c st
      b1← sf(b1) p2,
    rif :p p2>p1 cr: then (cr) else (null) , p5 p6, p4
      se(b1) : goto [s]

    3B4 (v) s*=cv dsp(↑copy visible) e*=v,
      visible +bug2spec
    +vdr2(b1,p1,p2,p3,p4) +vdr2(b2,p5,p6,p7,p8)
    +cpwdvs(b1,p2,p4,p5,p6) ;
   .
   .
   .

    3b10 endcase +caqm ;
  3C (d) [edit] dsp(delete | es*) . case
    3C1 (c) s*=dc dsp(↑delete character) e*=c,
      character +bug1spec
    +cdlim(b1,p1,p2,p3,p4) +del;

    3C2 (w) s*=dw dsp(↑delete word) e*=w,word
      +bug1spec +wdr
    (b1,p1,p2,p3,p4) +del ;

    3C3 (1) s*=dl dsp(↑delete line) e*=1, line +bug1spec...
   .
   .
   .
```

Figure 4.7 Metalanguage description of part of control language

For instance, the steps of display-feedback states, leading to execution of the "Delete Word" function, can readily be followed in the state chart.

The steps are produced by the user typing "D," then "W," then selecting a character in a given word, and then hitting "command accept" (the CA key).

The corresponding steps are outlined below for the control Metalanguage description of Figure 4.7, processing from Statement 3, to Statement 3c, to Statement 3c2, to Subroutine + BUGSPEC, etc.

The points or regions in Figure 4.6 corresponding to these statements and subroutines are marked by (3), (3C), (3C2), and (+ BUG1SPEC), to help compare the two representations.

These same steps are indicted in Figure 4.7, starting from Statement 3:

"D" sets up the state described in Statement 3C.

"W" sets up the state described in Statement 3C2.

The subroutine + BUG1SPEC waits for the select-word (1) and CA (2) actions leading to the execution of the delete-word function.

Then the TWDR subroutine takes the bug-position parameter and sets pointers P1 through P4 to delimit the word in the text data.

Finally, the + DEL subroutine deletes what the pointers delimit, and then returns to the last-defined state (i.e., to where $S^* = DW$).

4.4 *Basic Organization of the On-Line System (NLS)*

Figure 4.8 shows the relationships among the major components of NLS.

The Tree Meta Translator is a processor specially designed to produce new translators.

There is a special language—the Tree Meta Language—for use in describing the translator to be produced.

A special Tree Meta library of subroutines must be used, along with the output of the Tree Meta Translator, to produce a functioning new translator. The same library serves for every translator it produces.

For programming the various subroutines used in our 940 systems, we have developed a special Machine-Oriented Language (MOL), together with an MOL Translator to convert MOL program descriptions into machine code (see Ref. Hay1 for a complete description).

The MOL is designed to facilitate system programming, by providing a high-level language for interactive, conditional, and arithmetic operations, etc., along with a block structure and conventions for labeling that fit our structured-statement on-line manipulation aids.

These permit sophisticated computer aid where suitable, and also allow the programmer to switch to machine-level coding (with full access

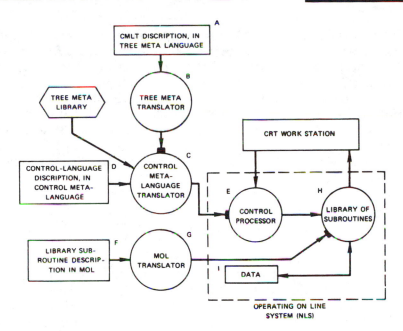

Figure 4.8 Basic organization of NLS showing use of compilers and compiler-compiler to implement it

to variables, labels, etc.) where core space, speed, timing, core-mapping arrangements, etc., are critical.

The NLS is organized as follows (letters refer to Figure 4.8):

The Control Processor (E) receives and processes successive user actions, and calls upon subroutines in the library (H) to provide it such services as the following:

- Putting display feedback on the screen

- Locating certain data in the file

- Manipulating certain working data

- Constructing a display view of specified data according to given viewing parameters, etc.

The NLS library subroutines (H) are produced from MOL programs (F), as translated by the MOL Translator (G).

The Control Processor is produced from the control-language description (D), written in Control Metalanguage, as translated by the CMLT (C).

The CMLT, in turn, is produced from a description (A) written in Tree Meta, as translated by the Tree Meta Translator (B).

4.4.1 *Advantages of Metalanguage Approach to NLS Implementation*

The metalanguage approach gives us improved means for control-language specification, in terms of being unambiguous, concise, canonical, natural, and easy to compose, study, and modify.

Moreover, the Control Metalanguage specification promises to provide in itself a users' documentation that is completely accurate, and also has the above desirable characteristics to facilitate study and reference.

Modifying the control-dialogue procedures for existing functions, or making a reasonable range of changes or additions to these functions, can often be accomplished solely by additions or changes to the control-language record (in CML).

With our on-line studying, manipulating and compiling techniques, system additions or changes at this level can be thought out and implemented (and automatically documented) very quickly.

New functions that require basic operations not available through existing subroutines in the NLS library will need to have new subroutines specified and programmed (in MOL), and then will need new terms in CML to permit these new functions to be called upon. This latter requires a change in the record (A), and a new compilation of CMLT by means of the Tree Meta Translator.

On-line techniques for writing and modifying the MOL source code (F), for executing the compilations, and for debugging the routines, greatly reduce the effort involved in this process.

5 Service-System Hardware (other than SDS 940)

In addition to the SDS 940, the facility includes peripheral equipment made by other manufacturers and equipment designed and constructed at SRI.

All of the non-SDS equipment is interfaced through the special devices channel which connects to the second memory buss through the SDS memory interface connection (MIC).

This equipment, together with the RAD, is a significant load on the second memory buss. Not including the proposed "special operations" equipment, the maximum expected data rate is approximately 264,000 words per second or one out of every 2.1 memory cycles. However, with the 940 variable priority scheme for memory access (see Pirtle1), we expect less than 1 percent degradation in CPU efficiency due to this load.

This channel and the controllers (with the exception of the disc controller) were designed and constructed at SRI.

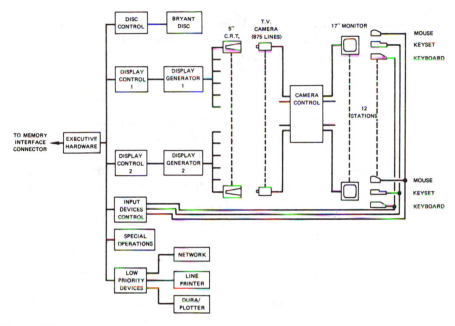

Figure 4.9   Special devices channel

In the design of the hardware serving the work stations, we have attempted to minimize the CPU burden by making the system as automatic as possible in its access to memory and by formatting the data in memory so as to minimize the executive time necessary to process it for the users.

Figure 4.9 is a block diagram of the special-devices channel and associated equipment. The major components are as follows.

5.1 Executive Control

This is essentially a sophisticated multiplexer that allows independent, asynchronous access to core from any of the 6 controllers connected to it. Its functions are the following:

1.   Decoding instructions from the computer and passing them along as signals to the controllers.

2.   Accepting addresses and requests for memory access (input or output) from the controllers, determining relative priority among the controllers, synchronizing to the computer clock, and passing the requests along to memory via the MIC.

The executive control includes a comprehensive debugging panel that allows any of the 6 controllers to be operated off-line without interfering with the operation of other controllers.

5.2 *Disc File*

This is a Model 4061 Bryant disc, selected for compatibility with the continued 940-system development by Berkeley's Project GENIE, where extensive file-handling software was developed.

As formatted for our use, the disc will have a storage capacity of approximately 32 million words, with a data-transfer rate of roughly 40,000 words per second and average access time of 85 milliseconds.

The disc controller was designed by Bryant in close cooperation with SRI and Project GENIE.

5.3 *Display System*

The display systems consist of two identical subsystems, each with display controller, display generator, 6 CRT's, and 6 closed-circuit television systems.

The display controllers process display-command tables and display lists that are resident in core, and pas along display-buffer contents to the display generators.

The display generators and CRT's were developed by Tasker Industries to our specifications. Each has general character-vector plotting capability. They will accept display buffers consisting of instructions (beam motion, character writing, etc.) from the controller. Each will drive six 5-inch high-resolution CRT's on which the display pictures are produced.

Character writing time is approximately 8 microseconds, allowing an average of 1000 characters on each of the six monitors when regenerating at 20 cps.

A high-resolution (875-line) closed-circuit television system transmits display pictures from each CRT to a television monitor at the corresponding work-station console.

This system was developed as a "best solution" to our experimental-laboratory needs, but it turned out to have properties which seem valuable for more widespread use:

1. Since only all-black or all-white signal levels are being treated, the scan-beam current on the cameras can be reduced to achieve a short-term image-storage effect that yields flicker-free TV output even when the display refresh rate is as low as 15 cps. This allows

a display generator to sustain about four times more displayed material than if the users were viewing direct-view refreshed tubes.

2. The total cost of small CRT, TV camera, amplifier-controller, and monitor came to about $5500 per work station—where a random-deflection, display-quality CRT of similar size would cost considerably more and would be harder to drive remotely.

3. Another cost feature which is very important in some system environments favors this TV approach: The expensive part is centrally located; each outlying monitor costs only about $600, so terminals can be set up even where usage will be low, with some video switching in the central establishment to take one terminal down and put another up.

4. An interesting feature of the video system is that with the flick of a switch the video signal can be inverted, so that the image picked up as bright lines on dim background may be viewed as black lines on a light background. There is a definite user preference for this inverted form of display.

In addition to the advantages noted above, the television display also invites the use of such commercially available devices as extra cameras, scan converters, video switches, and video mixers to enrich system service.

For example, the video image of a user's computer-generated display could be mixed with the image from a camera focused on a collaborator at another terminal; the two users could communicate through both the computer and a voice intercom. Each user would then see the other's face superimposed on the display of data under discussion.

Superimposed views from cameras focused on film images or drawings, or on the computer hardware, might also be useful.

We have experimented with these techniques (see Figure 4.10) and found them to be very effective. They promise to add a great deal to the value of remote display terminals.

5.4 Input-Device Controller

In addition to the television monitor, each work-station console has a keyboard, binary keyset, and mouse.

The controller reads the state of these devices at a preset interval (about 30 milliseconds) and writes it into a fixed location table in core.

Bits are added to information from the keyboards, keysets and mouse switches to indicate when a new character has been received or a

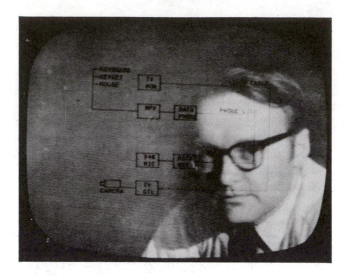

Figure 4.10   Television display obtained by mixing the video signal from a remote camera with that from the computer-generated display

switch has changed state since the last sample. If there is a new character or switch change, an interrupt is issued after the sample period.

The mouse coordinates are formatted as a beam-positioning instruction to the display generator. Provisions are made in the display controller for including an entry in the mouse-position table as a display buffer. This allows the mouse position to be continuously displayed without any attention from the CPU.

5.5 *Special Operations*

The box with this label in Figure 4.9 is at this time only a provision in the executive control for the addition of a high-speed device. We have tentative plans for adding special hardware here to provide operations not available in the 940 instruction set, such as character-string moves and string-pattern matching.

Low-Priority Devices   This controller accommodates three devices with relatively low data-transfer rates. At this time only the line printer is implemented, with provisions for adding an on-line typewriter (Dura), a plotter, and a terminal for the proposed ARPA computer network.

The line printer is a Potter Model HSP-3502 chain printer with 96 printing characters and a speed of about 230 lines per minute.

References

(English1) W. K. English, D. C. Engelbart, B. Huddart, *Computer-aided display control*. Final Report Contract NAS 1-3988 SRI Project 5061, Stanford Research Institute, Menlo Park, California, July 1965.

(English2) W. K. English, D. C. Engelbart, M. L. Berman, Display-selection technique for text manipulation. *IEEE Trans. on Human Factors in Electronics*, Vol. HFE-8, No. 1, 1967.

(Engelbart1) D. C. Engelbart, *Augmenting human intellect: A conceptual framework*. Summary Report Contract AF 49 638 1024 SRI Project 3578, Stanford Research Institute, Menlo Park, California, October 1962.

(Engelbart2) D. C. Engelbart, A conceptual framework for the augmentation of man's intellect. In *Vistas in Information Handling*, Vol. 1, D. W. Howerton and D. C. Weeks, eds. Spartan Books, Washington, D.C. 1963.

(Hay1) R. E. Hay, J. F. Rulifson, *MOL940 Preliminary speciffcations for an ALGOL-like machine-oriented language for the SDS 940*. Interim Technical Report Contract NAS1-5940 SRI Project 5890, Stanford Research Institute, Menlo Park, California, March 1968.

(Pirtle1) M. Pirtle, Intercommunication of processors and memory. *Proc. Fall Joint Computer Conference*, Anaheim, California, November, 1967.

5

Authorship Provisions in AUGMENT

Douglas C. Engelbart

Tymshare, Inc.
Cupertino, CA

Abstract

AUGMENT is a text processing system marketed by Tymshare for a multi-user, network environment. In AUGMENT's frontend is a User Interface System that facilitates flexible evolution of command languages and provides optional command recognition features. Exceptionally fast and flexible control of interactive operations is enabled by concurrent action of mouse and optional one-handed chord keyset. Files are hierarchically structured, and textual address expressions can flexibly specify any text entity in any file. The screen may be divided into arbitrary, rectangular windows, allowing cross-file editing between windows. Many options exist for controlling the "view" of a file's test in a window, e.g., level clipping, paragraph truncation, and content filtering. Structural study and modification of on-line documents are especially facilitated. A Journal system and "Shared Screen Teleconferencing" support collaboration among authors and their colleagues. Graphic illustrations may be embedded in the same file with text.

Introduction

AUGMENT was designed for augmenting human intellectual capabilities. It was targeted particularly toward the core work of professionals engaged in "tough knowledge work"—e.g., planning, analyzing, and designing in complex problem domains. And special attention was paid to augmenting group collaboration among workers pursuing common goals.

Authorship has received a great deal of attention in AUGMENT's evolution, as one of the central human activities to be augmented. An important set of provisions within AUGMENT—in its architecture, design principles, and specific features—is directly aimed toward bringing high performance to the authorship activities of knowledge workers. For the purposes of this paper, we thus speak interchangeably of "knowledge worker" and "author."

We recognize explicitly that highly skilled workers in any field, and knowledge work is no exception, are those with good command of their tools. Our basic design goal was to provide a set of tools that would not themselves limit the capabilities of the people using them. A system designed to encourage more skilled workers will always enable higher human performance than one designed to support less skilled workers.

In this regard, our design goal was to provide as much capability as possible for each level of system usage skill, and a continuous evolution path between skill levels. We believe firmly that knowledge workers are motivated to grow in knowledge and skill and that provisions in system design should support this. As the rest of the paper reveals, this approach translates into a rich set of AUGMENT provisions, aimed at providing speed and flexibility for skilled workers in organizing and pursuing their core knowledge work—in which "authorship" is a primary activity.

An explicit sub-goal in AUGMENT's development was to "augment" the development, production and control of complex technical documentation—through the whole cycle of gathering information, planning, creating, collaborating, reviewing, editing, controlling versions, designing layout, and producing the final documents.

This paper concentrates upon the development phase of this cycle. AUGMENT has well-developed tools to support the later, production phase, but their discussion is not included here.

Studying another's work provides a well-recognized challenge, but one of the toughest jobs is to study one's own work during its development: to see what it really says about Issue X; to see if it does provide for Concept Y; to see if it is reasonably organized and structured—and to do these over a body of material before it is "polished," i.e., before it is well structured, coherently worded, non-redundant and consistently termed.

Some Background

History

AUGMENT is an integrated system of knowledge-worker tools that is marketed by Tymshare's Office Automation Division. The system was developed at SRI International over an extended period under the sponsorship of NASA, DARPA, and RADC. Commercial rights were transferred to Tymshare in 1978 (where the system has since been renamed from NLS to AUGMENT) and its evolution continued. A short history of AUGMENT's development may be found in [1] along with a summary of system characteristics and features. The general R&D philosophy and the design principles behind AUGMENT's development are laid out in [2].

The system evolved on time-shared, mainframe computers, and in a packet-switched network environment. In 1970 our computer was the second to be attached to the ARPANET, and since 1978 we have also operated extensively in the TYMNET environment. We have benefited directly from both the time-sharing and the network environments in matters that are important to the authorship process—especially in dealing with large documents and multi-party documentation activities. In 1976–77 we conducted some applied studies for the Air Force, as reported in [3] and [4], which concentrated upon this latter application.

Relevant Architectural Features

Perhaps AUGMENT's most unique architectural feature is its User Interface System (UIS), a special software module, which handles the human/computer interfaces to all interactive programs. It takes care of all command-language dialog and connection protocols, and provides a framework for building a coherent and integrated user environment while supporting flexible evolution on both sides: on the user's side, with evolution of command function and terminology; and on the technology side, with evolving hardware and software. (Design details are outlined in [5]; rationale and utilization in [6].)

The UIS provides a reach-through service to non-AUGMENT systems, and can optionally translate back and forth to a foreign program's command language. It also supports the shared-screen, remote collaboration capability discussed below.

AUGMENT's architecture provides for open-ended expansion and flexible evolution of system functionality and worker command languages.

It is assumed that for any class of knowledge workers, specialized application systems developed by other parties, perhaps running on other computers, will provide services worth integrating. The "author class" of worker should be no exception. Continuing evolution toward the "author workshop of the future" will certainly depend upon some such features in workshop architecture.

It provides adaptation for different terminal characteristics, enabling application programmers to work as though with a virtual terminal.

File Characteristics

AUGMENT employs explicitly structured files, with hierarchically organized nodes; each node can contain either or all of: up to 2,000 characters of text, a graphic structure, or other forms of useful data (e.g., digitized speech). The worker has a definite model in mind for the structuring of any file that he works with; in composing and modifying it he can organize and modify structure using the same verbs as for working with text strings (e.g., Insert, Replace, Move, Copy, Delete), with appropriate structural-entity nouns (e.g., Statement, Branch, Group, Plex). For any existing hierarchical structure he has many flexible alternatives for addressing its entities, modifying its organization, jumping around within it, and viewing it in a most beneficial manner.

(Note: AUGMENT workers generally use the term "statement" to refer to a file node, which is natural enough since the terminology became established before we added the graphic capability. Now an AUGMENT "statement" can contain either or both a text statement and a graphic diagram.)

Controlling the Tools

Many of AUGMENT's unique author-support provisions address basic operations common to almost every task, things done over and over again. These operations, executed with speed and flexibility, provide for composing and modifying one's working material, and for studying what is there over a wide range of substantive levels—from a single text passage to a collection of end-product draft documents and their associated set of working notes, reference material, and recorded-message dialog (assuming all to be on line).

In the early stages of our program at SRI, we did a great deal of detailed work on what we called the "control interface"—how users control the functional application of their tools. These details can be very important to "low-level" interactions which are done hundreds of times during a working day. Some of these details are quite relevant to bringing high performance to the authorship process.

AUGMENT commands are expressed with verbs, nouns, and appropriate qualifier words; every command word is designated by entering one or more characters. The UIS recognizes the command word from these characters according to the command-recognition options designated in each individual's "profile file." Users seem to migrate fairly rapidly to "expert" recognition modes, where a minimum number of characters will elicit recognition of command words. The fully spelled-out command words are presented in the Command Feedback Window as soon as they are recognized. The Backspace Key will cause backup, one command word at a time.

Of the system requirements behind our choice of this noun-verb command form, two are particularly relevant here: (1) The "vocabulary" of the functions of the tools, and of the entities they operate upon, must be as extensible as is a natural language; (2) Textual lists of commands must conveniently lend themselves to writing, documenting, and executing as "macro" commands.

Screen selection is done with a mouse. If the command's noun is a single, defined text or structure entity, e.g., a "word," then there is only one selection needed (e.g., to pick any character in the designated word).

Besides using a standard keyboard for character entry, an AUGMENT user may optionally use a five-key, one-hand, chord keyset. Remarkably little practice is required in order to enter alphabetic characters, one hand-stroke per character. With less than five hours practice, a person can begin profitably working in a two-handed, concurrent mode—operating the mouse with one hand and simultaneously entering command characters and short literal strings with the other hand.

Here is an example of a low-level action which reveals some basic characteristics of high-performance execution. It is a very simple situation, but representative of what is met over and over and over again in doing hard knowledge work. The worker is composing or modifying something in one area of the screen, when his eye catches a one-character typo in another area. For a skilled AUGMENT worker, the typo could be corrected in less time than it would take someone to point it out to him—with three quick strokes of the keyset hand during a casual flick of the mouse hand, and an absolute minimum of visual and mental attention taken from the other ongoing task.

Fast, flexible, graceful, low effort—these are important to all high-frequency, low-level, knowledge-work action. This same kind of speed and flexibility are achieved by skilled AUGMENT workers in executing all of the other functional features described below. Description of mouse and keyset, and their concurrent employment, may be found in [7].

Addressing the Working Materials

There is a consistent set of addressing features that a worker may use in any command to designate a particular structural node or some element of text or graphics attached to that node. It adds appreciably to the power and flexibility of the system commands to have a rich, universally applicable vocabulary for directly addressing particular entities within the working files. Below are some examples.

Explicit Statement Addresses

There are four "handles" by which a given statement may be directly addressed:

Structural statement number: This designates the current "structural location" of the statement. It is assigned by the system, depending upon where the worker installs or moves a statement within an existing structure, or how that structure might have been re-organized subsequently. It is usually expressed as an alternating sequence of number-letter fields— e.g. "1", "1a", "1a1", "1a2", and "1b". At a worker's option, these same statement numbers could be shown as "1", "1.1", "1.1.1", "1.1.2", or "1.2", but this bulkier alternative is seldom chosen.

Statement identifier, or SID: This is a unique integer, assigned in sequential order by the system as each statement is first inserted, and which stays with a statement no matter how much its content may be altered or where it may be moved in its file structure. To make it uniquely recognizable for what it is, a SID is always displayed, printed, or designated with a prefixed "0"—e.g., "012", "0417", etc. SIDs are particularly useful for referencing passages in a document while it is evolving.

A worker-assigned statement name (or label): For any statement or part of the file structure, an author can designate as "name delimiters" a pair of characters that indicate to the system when the first word of a statement is to be treated as a name for that statement. For instance, if "(" and ")" are set by the author as name delimiters for a specified part of the file, any parenthesized first word in a statement would be recognized by the system as that statement's name. (Note: it is optional whether to have any of the above three identifiers displayed or printed with the statements' text.)

A direct screen selection: When a statement to be designated is displayed in a window, usually the best way to "address" it is to use the mouse to position the cursor anywhere on the statement and depress the mouse's "Select" key (indicated below by "<Select>"). This mode is generally used for text manipulation—selecting characters, words, numbers, visibles, invisibles, etc. (any of the text entities which have been made system recognizable).

Markers

As one "holds a place" in a book by leaving a temporary place marker in it, an author can place "markers" at arbitrary locations within an AUGMENT file. When placing a marker, he attaches it to a specific character in the text and gives it a name or label. Marker names are local to each file. Simple commands provide for displaying where one's markers are located and what their names are, for deleting or moving a marker, or for installing a new one.

A marker name may be included in an address expression, to provide another way of designating an address. A marker name can designate not only a particular statement, but a specific character within that statement. For example, "Copy Word #x to follow word) <Select>" would designate that a word located somewhere in the file and marked with an "x" is to be copied to follow the cursor-selected word. There are many unique ways in which markers may be employed by an author who has integrated their artful use into her working methodology.

As a comparative example of some of the foregoing addressing forms, consider a statement whose SID is "069", whose statement number is "3b5", that has statement-name delimiters designated for it as "NULL" and ":", that starts with the text "Capacity: For every ...", and that has a marker names "x" positioned on one of its characters. A command to move this statement could optionally be expressed as:

"Move Statement <Select> ... ",

"Move Statement 3b5... ",

"Move Statement 069... ",

"Move Statement Capacity... ", or

"Move Statement #x... ".

Relative-Address Extensions

A sequence of characters may be appended to the address of a given statement to specify an address of a position "relative" to that statement. A major class of these designations deals with relative structural location, such as: Up a level, Down a level, Successor at same level, Predecessor at same level, Head at this level, Tail at this level, and End statement at last and lowest position in this branch. A period (".") in the address string indicates that relative addressing is beginning, and each of these relative-location designators is indicated with a directly mnemonic, one-letter designation.

For example, "Move Statement 0609 (to follow statement) 4b.dt" would move Statement 0609 to follow the tail statement of the substructure one level down from Statement 4b—or, to conceptualize the associated address-location pathway, "go to 4b, then Down a level and to the Tail".

Embedded Citation Links

A special use of address expressions is within an explicit text entity that we call a "Citation Link" (or "Link" for short). Links are used as textual citations to some specific file item within the workshop domain. A link is delimited by parentheses or angle brackets and contains a valid address string whose path leads to the cited file entity. For example, "(0306)" or "(4b.dt)" are valid links. Also, the reference items at the end of this paper are statements named "Ref-1", "Ref-2", etc., and as such can be cited with links "<Ref-1>", "<Ref-2>, etc. An AUGMENT reader may travel via such a link directly to the referenced bibliographic citation.

A special feature in AUGMENT's link provisions is the use of "indirect link referencing." In path-following terms, including ".1" in an address string stipulates "scan forward from this point to the next link, and follow that link to its target." For example, to follow the path prescribed by link "(4b.1)", one would "go to 4b, then find the first link in that statement and follow the path that it specifies." This latter path in turn could prescribe use of another link, etc. There is no intrinsic limit to the number of these indirect links that may be employed in a given path—only a natural caution against such a path looping back upon itself.

As an example, note that "<Ref-1>" is a link to the statement named "Ref-1", a bibliographic citation at the end of this paper. In that citation, there is a link to the original source document of the referenced publication, permanently stored in the AUGMENT Journal as Item 71279 (the Journal is described below). The point to be made here is that with the link "<Ref-1.1>", I can reference the original source document—and a Jump Link command would "take me there."

Text and Content Addressing

Other addressing options include scanning for a content match, and/or stepping backward and forward a given number of characters or words (or other text entities). For instance, the foregoing link could have involved a bit more smarts in designating which link to follow: e.g., the path for '(4b "*D".1)' would be "to 4b, scan for first occurrence of "*D", then follow the next link found in that statement."

Other-File Addressing

By preceding an in-file address string with a file address, and separating the two strings with a comma, one obtains a composite address designating a given entity within a given file. Extending this principle lets one prefix the file name with a directory name in which the file is to be found; and further, one can prefix this with a host-computer name.

For example, '(Office-5, Program-Documentation, Sequence-Doc, Specifications "Journal")' specifies the path: to the Office-5 host computer, to its Program-Documentation file directory, to its Sequence-Doc file, to its statement named "Specifications", and then scan to the location of the text "Journal".

If a person were working on the Office-5 host, he would only have to specify '(Program-Documentation, Sequence-Doc, Specifications "Journal")'. If he were already working within a file with its "link default" set to the Program-Documentation directory, he would only have to specify '(Sequence-Doc, Specifications "Journal")'. And if he were already working within the Sequence-Doc file, he would only have to specify '(Specifications "Journal")'. And if he were planning to reference items relative to the Statement named "Specifications" very often, he could affix a marker (e.g., named "s") to its front and would then only have to specify '(#s "Journal")'.

Or, suppose he were working in another file in a different directory on Office-5 and wanted to reference items relative to that same "far-off" statement with special ease: in some temporary place in that file he could install a statement named "Ref" (for example) containing the textual link, "(Program-Documentation, Sequence-Doc, Specifications)". He could then cite the above reference with the link '(Ref.1 "Journal")'. This path description is: go to the statement in the file named "Ref", take the first link that you find there (traveling across intervening directories and files and statements), and beginning in the statement on the other end of that link, scan forward to the string "Journal".

This is only a cursory treatment, but should illustrate well enough what is meant by "a rich and flexible addressing vocabulary." As with other high-performance features in AUGMENT, a beginner is not forced to become involved in the larger vocabulary in order to do useful work (with productivity on at least a par with some other, restricted-vocabulary system). But an AUGMENT worker interested in higher performance can steadily pick up more of the optional vocabulary and skills in a smooth, upward-compatible progression.

Controlling the Views

A user of a book, or of most on-line text systems, is constrained to viewing the test as though he had a window through which he sees a fixed, formatted document. But as described below, our worker can view a section of text in many ways, depending upon his need of the moment.

Multiple Windows

For whatever total screen area is available to the worker, his general performance will be improved significantly if he can flexibly allocate that area into arbitrary-sized windows whose contents can be independently controlled. AUGMENT has long provided this basic capability, along with the provision that material from any accessible file may be shown in any window, and also that screen-select copying or moving can be done across the different windows.

(Note: Cross-file editing can be done at any time, between any two legally accessible files. If one or the other file's material or destination is not being displayed in any of the windows, one may always opt to employ a textual address expression instead of a <Select> within any editing command.)

User-adjustable parameters are used to control the view presented on the display. Adjusting one's view parameters is a constantly used AUGMENT feature that has solidly proved its value. To facilitate their quick and flexible use, the view-specification actions evolved into cryptic, single-character codes, called "view specs." The syntax of all Jump commands (used for traveling) includes the option of designating new viewspecs, and a special combination of mouse buttons enables quick, concurrent, keyset action to change the viewspecs for a given window. Here are a few of the frequently used view controls:

Window Views

Structure cutoff: Show only the statements that lie "below" this statement in the structure (i.e., this "branch"); or show only those following statements that are at this level or deeper; or show all of the following statements that will fit in this window.

Level clipping: For the designated structure cutoff, show only the statements down to a specified level. Lower-level statements are "clipped" from the view; the worker can thus view just a selected number of the upper levels of his document/file.

Statement truncation: For those statements brought into view (as selected by other view specifications) show only their first n lines. Truncation to one line is often used, along with level clipping, in order to get an effective overview.

Inter-statement separation: For viewing ease—blank lines can be optionally installed between statements. (Note: The foregoing view controls are extremely helpful when studying and modifying a document's structural organization.)

Statement numbers and names: Optionally, for a given window, show the Statement Number (or the SID) of each statement—with an option for showing them at either the right or at the left margin. Independently, the showing of statement names may be turned on or off.

Frozen statements: A worker may select a number of statements, in random order, and designate them as "frozen." One of the view-specification options is to have the frozen statements appear at the top of the frame, with the rest of that window left for normal viewing and editing. The frozen statements may be edited, or even cross-edited between any other displayed (or addressable) statements.

User-specified content filters: A simple content-analysis language may be used in a "Set Content Pattern" command, which compiles a little content-checking program. One of the view-specification options will cause the system to display only those statements which satisfy both the structure and level conditions imposed by other viewspecs, and which also pass the content-analysis test applied by this program. Where desired, very sophisticated content-analysis programs may be written, using a full-blown programming language, and placed on call for any user.

User-specified Sequence Generators

In the foregoing, a "view" is created by beginning at a designated location in a document (file) and selecting certain of the "following" statements for display, according to the viewing parameters—possibly suppressing statements that don't pass the test of a content-analysis program. This is essentially a "parametrized sequence generator," and provides very useful options for selectively viewing statements within a document; however, it works only by selectively discarding statements from a sequence provided in standard order.

Application programmers can provide alternate sequence-generator programs, which any user can invoke in a straightforward manner. In such a case, the apparent structure being presented to the user could be generated from a sequence of candidate statements according to any rules one may invent—and the actual views could be further controlled by the above-described viewspecs for level clipping, truncation, content filtering, etc.

Perhaps the most commonly used, special sequence generator is one that provides an "Include" feature, where specially tagged links embedded in the text will cause their cited passages to be "included" in place of the Include-Link statements, as though they were part of this file. This provision enables arbitrary assemblage of text and formatting directives, from a wide collection of files, to represent a virtual, one-document, super file. For instance, the whole assemblage could be passed to the formatter, by means of a single user action, to generate a composite, photo-typeset document.

Traveling through the Working Files

An important provision in AUGMENT enables an author to freely "travel around" in his on-line file space to reach a particular "viewpoint" of his choice—i.e., the position within a file from which the system develops the desired form of "view" according to the currently invoked view specifications.

Traveling from one view point to another is accomplished by Jump commands, of which the simplest perhaps is a direct Jump to a statement designated by a screen selection. Then, for a worker grown used to employing address strings, a next form would be a Jump on an embedded link, or to a statement designated by a typed-in address string— using any combination of the addressing elements and viewspecs described above. For example, the line "<4b:mI>" points to the Statement 4b, while invoking viewspecs "m" and "I" which cause the statements' SIDs to be displayed. The line "<Ref-1.l:i,LL>" points to the document referenced by the link in the statement named "Ref-1", invoking viewspec "i" for user content filtering, and sets the filter to "LL" to show only those statements beginning with a lower-case letter. The applications are effectively endless.

Modifying the Document Structures

Given the array of capabilities described above, it is very simple also to provide for very flexible manipulation of the file structure. For operating on a small, basic set of structure-entity nouns, essentially the same basic verbs may be used as for text manipulation—i.e. Insert, Delete, Move, Copy, Replace, and Transpose are quite sufficient for most cases. For instance, "Move Branch 2b (to follow) 3c" immediately moves Statement 2b and all of its substatements to follow Statement 3c—and their statement numbers are automatically changed from 2b, 2b1, etc., to 3d, 3d1, etc.

A few extra verbs are useful for structure manipulation. For instance, a "Break" command will break a given statement off at a designated point in its text string, and establish the rest of the text as a new, separate statement. And an "Append" command does the reverse—i.e., it appends the text of one or more existing statements to the end of a designated statement.

A major source of structure-modification capability derives from the associated "studying" capabilities. For example, if an author can view a file (document) with specifications that show him only one line each of just those statements in the top two levels, he gets an overview of the high-level organization that helps immensely to study his current structure or outline.

Concurrent use of mouse and keyset also provides considerable gains in speed and flexibility for studying and modifying document structure. For example, if when studying the overview described in the previous paragraph, the author perceives that Statement 2b really belongs in Section 3, following Statement 3c, he can execute the necessary move command in a very quick, deft manner:

Keyset hand strikes "m" and "b" (for Move Branch), while the mouse hand is positioning the cursor anywhere in the text line of Statement 2b. [Two chord strokes.]

The mouse hand depresses the <Select> button on the mouse while the cursor is on Statement 2b, then moves to Statement 3c and depresses it again, and then depresses it again to say, "OK, do it." [Three button pushes, synchronized with the mouse movement as it made two selections on easy, window-wide, whole-line targets.]

(Note: I just had myself timed for this above operation—an unhurried 2.5 seconds.)

In our view, interactive computer support offers an author a priceless opportunity to get away from the geometric bondage inflicted by pages, margins, and lines—things which have very little if any bearing upon the content and organization of one's text. In terms of value to the authoring process, we differ sharply from those who advocate a "What you see is what you get" working mode during the development of a document's content and organization. For this kind of work, experienced users of the foregoing kind of flexible facility for addressing, viewing, and manipulating structured documents, would consider a "What you see ..." mode as a relative handicap.

Supporting Multi-Party Collaboration

The support that advanced technology can provide for close collaboration among knowledge workers is a very important and much underrated possibility. For multiple-author activities, collaborative support is an important aspect of system capability. Some years ago, we introduced the following provisions into AUGMENT. (A more complete, overview treatment of these is given in [8].)

Electronic mail: Its primary attributes of speed, automatic distribution, and computer-to-computer directness are well recognized—and are generally accepted now as important to the effectiveness of knowledge workers. AUGMENT Mail has features that are beyond what most electronic mail systems offer, and which provide unique benefit to the authorship process.

AUGMENT's mail system allows one to "send" complete, structured documents as well as small messages. In an authorship environment, an important role for "electronic mail" is for the control and distribution of documents—where small, throw-away messages are considered to be but a special class of document. An author should be able to bundle up any combination of text and graphics, in the forms that he has been using for studying and manipulating them—and send the bundle to other workers. In AUGMENT, such a bundle is just like any other file structure, and can be studied and manipulated, incorporated into other files (documents), saved or deleted.

Recorded mail—AUGMENT's Journal system: When mailing a document, an AUGMENT worker may optionally specify that it be installed as a "recorded" item. In this case, before distributing the item, the system will make a permanent record of it, as a file in a specified Journal collection. And, just as though it had been published, this recorded Journal item cannot later be changed. The system assigns a straightforward accession identifier (a simple number), and any authorized worker is henceforth guaranteed access to that Journal item by specifying the name of the Journal-collection and the Journal-item number—e.g., as specified in the link "<OAD,2237,>".

A given journal may be set up to serve multiple hosts and is much like a special library. It has its collection of documents, and AUGMENT provides associated support processes for entry, cataloging, retrieval, and access.

Together with the linking capability described above, a Journal system provides an extremely effective form of "recorded dialog." Cross-reference links between a succession of Journal items produces an interlinked network of collaborative contributions—plans, outlines, document drafts, schedules, short comments, detailed critiques, reference material, etc. The on-line worker can follow these links very easily and, using multiple windows and flexible viewing options, can make very effective use of such records.

For instance, consider a detailed commentary directed toward a "preliminary design" document recorded in a given Journal collection. The author writing the commentary could view the design document in one window and his developing commentary document in another. He can easily establish links in his commentary to cite any passage in the design document—e.g., a statement, a term in the statement, or a diagram. Then this author would submit his commentary into the Journal, perhaps specifying a list of colleagues for "distribution." Each listed user would automatically receive a mail item announcing this new Journal entry, giving subject, author, date, etc., and the all-important link to the new Journal file containing the commentary. Any such recipient can subsequently study both the commentary and its cited planning document in a similar, multi-window, link-assisted manner.

Furthermore, this second reader could develop and submit his own recorded commentary, which because of the citation power of AUGMENT links could be as short and to the point as: "Frankly, John, I think your comment in (DDD,xxx,aa) is a mistake! Didn't you notice the earlier assumption in (DDD,xxx,bb)? Maybe you should go back to Tom's earlier requirements document 25-Oct-83 12:07 PDT OAD,2221,—especially at (EEE,yy,cc)." (Here, "DDD" and "EEE" represent Journal names, "xxx", "yyy", and "zzz" represent Journal item numbers, and "aa", "bb", and "cc" represent addresses pointing to specific passages in those Journal files.)

In official parlance, "retrieval" is the finding out about the existence of a relevant piece of information, whereas "access" is the subsequent process of gaining possession of the information. For users of AUGMENT's Journal system, retrieval is immensely facilitated by the widespread use of citation links. When one can follow them as easily as can a practiced AUGMENT worker, these links provide extremely effective retrieval support. We have supplemented this with some simple, automatically generated catalog files, which made a rather nice balance. Access is provided by direct Jump on a reference link if the file is on line; if it isn't, AUGMENT asks the worker if she wants it retrieved, and a simple affirmative response automatically launches a request for the system operator to retrieve the file from its archive tape, after which the worker is notified of its availability via electronic mail.

A private document can be submitted into a Journal. In this case, only those workers listed at Journal-entry time can get access to the central copy. Such a private item would not be listed or indexed in the "public" catalogs.

We have used the Journal system very heavily since 1970 to support AUGMENT's development activity; many customers have employed it heavily since 1975. There are about 100,000 entries recorded in the original Journal now (I don't know about other, newer AUGMENT Journal collections). We found that as workers became at home in this environment, they were increasingly free about submitting their items to the "public." It became evident that the scientific tradition of active and open interchange has some solid relevance to the collaborative processes in our smaller, "colleague communities." Time and again a worker would come across others' dialog and be able to contribute some valuable information (sometimes a one-sentence comment with a critical citation link). Often the payoff went the other way: the new party found immediate value in an old piece of recorded dialog.

Shared-screen teleconferencing: Consider a case where two people sit down to work together at a terminal, where they can both see the screen(s), and where either one can take over the controls. This is being done countless times every day throughout the country, in different combinations of expert–expert, expert–novice, novice–coach, etc. When talking together on their telephones, two or more distantly separated AUGMENT users can collaborate in a manner very similar to this.

Suppose that two workers, Smith and Jones, want to set up and operate in a Shared-Screen Conferencing mode. Smith is in Princeton, working on host Office-4, and Jones is in San Francisco, working on host

Office-12—and both of these host computers are connected to the same network. Assumedly they are in telephone contact when they decide to work in this shared-screen mode to collaborate on Smith's current job.

Jones will enter the command "Share (display with user) SMITH! On host OF12! Viewing (other display)!!"

Smith will enter the command "Share (display with user) JONES! On host OF4! Showing (this display)!!"

To give these commands, each person only entered the characters shown in upper case (entry case actually irrelevant), plus the digits, plus an "OK Key" action where each exclamation point is shown.

Whatever tool that Jones is currently using will continue responding to his controlling actions, as evidenced by various feedback and portrayal actions in the windows on his screen. Smith's screen image will clear, and be replaced with a replica of Jones's screen image—multiple windows and all. For the duration of the shared-screen session, Smith's screen image will continue to replicate what is shown on Jones's screen.

There are provisions for passing control back and forth between workers. For instance, Jones can pass control to Smith so that Smith can show him some material or method of work. There are also provisions for the subsequent entry and departure of other conference participants.

Embedding the Graphic Illustrations

For complete support of document development, it is important to provide integrated means for developing, viewing, and manipulating graphical portrayals. These portrayals should be part of the working files from the very start, to be studied, passed about in mail, shared in Conferencing mode, edited, captioned, labelled, and moved about within the document structure. Furthermore, active, relevant citation links pointing to these graphical constructs would be installed in and followed from textual passages throughout the associated set of documents (including Mail and Journal documents).

AUGMENT's architecture and file structure were designed for this end, and a good bit of the associated implementation is in place.

A graphical data structure can be attached to any given file node, and there are basic capabilities for composing, studying, and modifying graphical diagrams. When formatting for a suitably equipped phototypesetting device, there are formatting directives to designate the position and scale for placing these diagrams on a page. An AUGMENT file with integrated text and graphics can thus be mapped automatically onto a high-quality document whose pages contain both text and line drawings.

Our goal here was for what we call an "illustrative graphics" capability—basic to which is a command that, when directed toward any conventional "plotter" file, will translate it into a diagram attached to a designated node. In this way we can make use of graphic constructs developed within almost any applications system, most of which have provision for outputting "conventional" plotter files.

The most important next step is to adapt a bit-mapped display as an AUGMENT workstation, so the integrated text and graphics can be viewed and manipulated on the same screen. Heretofore, to do graphic work, an author has had to attach a Tektronix 4014 storage-tube display to the special printer/graphic port of her AUGMENT workstation. This has made use of AUGMENT graphics slow and expensive enough to limit the number of user groups who have developed the integrated use of mixed text and graphics.

Conclusion

AUGMENT's unique provisions stemmed for the most part from the conceptual framework within which AUGMENT was developed. For instance, consider the pervasive and significant changes in the environment in which humans will be doing their knowledge work. Note that the habits, methods, conventions, intuitions, etc., that comprise the "ways" in which we think, work and collaborate, are for the most part products of many centuries of cultural evolution—in a radically different environment. With a radically different environment, this constant process of cultural evolution can be expected to take some radical turns.

The AUGMENT developmental framework assumed that many of these "ways" are candidates now for change in directions that heretofore would not have been beneficial. The AUGMENT system emerged as a first step in considering a few such changes, which perhaps can improve human capability for doing knowledge work because their new "ways" will enable us more effectively to harness the new tools toward more effective basic capability. (This is very different from trying to "automate" our old "ways" of doing things.)

As an example, consider the "What You See Is What You Get" (WYSIWYG) syndrome. It is a highly touted feature for many vendors. It provides a definite advantage for the final process of converting a computer-held document to a nicely formatted hard copy. But what does it do for authorship? Well, in our framework, it has a negative impact. We were happy to abandon those constraints of lines and pages and other formatting geometry which did not contribute to matters of content and structure. We have chosen instead to provide the authorship process with structured files, flexible addressing, flexible window-size viewing, level and truncation viewspecs, etc.—things that would be awkward or impossible to provide in a WYSIWYG environment. This provides the authorship phase with flexibility and power for studying and manipulating content and structure that we wouldn't consider trading off for WYSIWYG. Save it for the production phase.

Here is another bit of culture that deserves re-examination. Consider the dictum "Easy to learn, and natural to use." Or, "User friendly." The question is, for whom are you judging that things will be easy, or natural, or friendly? For designers of craft-work tool systems, very different perceptions of this issue are warranted between a system for the occasional, weekend do-it-yourself person and a system to be heavily used day after day by professionals. The AUGMENT User Interface System enables us easily to configure either kind of a tool collection.

This paper describes part of what is provided to professional knowledge workers who do a significant amount of authorship work. We observe no more difficulty in their learning how to employ this relatively large collection of tools than one would expect for professional woodworkers in their learning about the relatively large collection of chisels and other tools of their trade.

It is a basic part of our framework that, to augment human knowledge workers, attention must be given not only to tools, but to methods and skills as well. Because of space limitations, the scope of this paper was restricted to a summary of those tool provisions within AUGMENT that especially facilitate the authorship process. A full description of "How to use AUGMENT to ..." would definitely need to include methods of work that effectively harness these tool provisions, and the special kinds of skills that yield unique payoff in executing these methods. This is true for every tool system, of course, but it seems especially true in this case because many AUGMENT provisions do not fit into the general cultural background of our authorship process.

Perhaps the best way for very brief summarization of what AUGMENT's users feel about its unique features is simply to say that those who leave its working environment really miss them.

References

Ref-1: Engelbart, D. C., "Toward Integrated, Evolutionary Office Automation Systems," Proceedings of the 26th Joint Engineering Management Conference, Denver, CO, Oct. 16–18, 1978, pp. 63–68. (AUGMENT,71279,)

Ref-2: Engelbart, D. C., R. W. Watson, and J. C. Norton, "The Augmented Knowledge Workshop," AFIPS Conference Proceedings, Volume 42, pp. 9–21, National Computer Conference, June 4–8, 1973. (AUGMENT, 14724,)

Ref-3: Michael, Elizabeth K., Dirk H. van Nouhuys, Beverly R. Boli, Raphael Rom, and Ann C. Weinberg, "Document Production and Control Systems," Phase One report of Document Production and Control Systems Design Study, by the Augmentation Research Center, SRI International, for AF Rome Air Development Center, Contract F30602-76-C-003, March 1, 1977. (AUGMENT,37730,)

Ref-4: Boli, Beverly R., Harvey G. Lehtman, Elizabeth K. Michael, Raphael Rom, Dirk H. van Nouhuys, and Nina Zolotow, "A Model Document Production System," Phase Two report of Document Production and Control Systems Design Study, by the Augmentation Research Center, SRI International, for AF Rome Air Development Center, Contract F30602-76-C-003, July 30, 1977. (AUGMENT,29000,)

Ref-5: Engelbart, D. C., "Toward High-Performancce Knowledge Workers," OAC '82 Digest (Proceedings of the 1982 AFIPS Office Automation Conference, San Francisco, CA, April 5–7), pp. 279–290. (AUGMENT,81010,)

Ref-6: Watson, Richard W., "User Interface Design Issues for a Large Interactive System," AFIPS Conference Proceedings, Volume 45, AFIPS Press, 1976, Montvale, NJ, pp. 357–364. (AUGMENT,27171,)

Ref-7: Engelbart, D. C., "Design Considerations for Knowledge Workshop Terminals," AFIPS Conference Proceedings, Volume 42, pp. 221–227, National Computer Conference, June 4–8, 1973. (AUGMENT,14851,)

Ref-8: Engelbart, D. C., "Collaboration Support Provisions in AUGMENT," OAC '84 Digest (Proceedings of the 1984 AFIPS Office Automation Conference, Los Angeles, CA, February 20–22). (OAD,2221.)

6

Interactive Human Communication

Alphonse Chapanis
Johns Hopkins University
Baltimore, MD

Modern computers touch the life of every citizen in varied and often unexpected ways. Not only do computers prepare our utility bills, credit-card bills and bank statements, but also they control our traffic, assist us in making travel and theater reservations, keep tabs on the weather for us and help to diagnose our bodily ills. For all that, most of us still have little direct contact with computers. Most computers still require an intermediary between the ultimate user and the computer, someone who is familiar with the way the computer works and with the special language that is needed to address it.

A goal toward which many people have been working is the design and construction of conversational computers: computers that can interact with people in such familiar and humanlike ways that they require little or no special instruction. If such conversational computers are ever to come into existence, however, their designers and programmers will need to know more about how people interact in communicating with each other. With this rationale in mind my colleagues and I at Johns Hopkins University have been working to describe human communication in precise terms and to define its rules.

We have been concerned with three main questions. How do people naturally communicate with each other when they exchange factual information in the solution of problems? How is interactive human communication affected by the devices through which people converse? What other significant variables affect interactive communication?

Let me digress briefly to distinguish between unidirectional and interactive communication. For years psychologists have been concerned with the effectiveness of unidirectional modes of communication such as highway signs, books, lectures and television programs. In unidirectional communication the person to whom the message is addressed is a passive recipient of information. Nothing that he says or does affects the communicator, the communication process or the content of the message.

Interactive communication involves at least two participants. The content of any particular message is determined in part by the content of the prior messages from all participants and so cannot be predicted from the content of the message from any one of them. Conferences, arguments, seminars and telephone conversations are examples of interactive communication. This is the kind of communication that has been the focus of our investigation.

Our experiments are designed to model interactions between man and computer rather than to simulate any existing or planned interactive computer systems. We set up two-person teams and ask them to solve credible problems for which computer assistance has been or could be useful. The exchanges that result represent a limited class of conversations, to be sure, but it is an important class, and we have to start somewhere.

One of our primary interests is the channels and the modes through which people converse. Although the channels of communication that link man and computer are being broadened, most interactions of this kind involve a typewriter or a similar device. Our experiments examine four different channels: voice, handwriting, typewriting and video, the last being the picture part of television without the voice. Three of these four basic channels have been tested singly, and all of them have been tested in various communicative combinations that we call modes. We have tested as many as 10 different modes in a single experiment. As a standard of comparison we typically rely on normal, unrestricted, face-to-face communication, which we call a communication-rich mode.

When we have set up a team, we designate one member as the source (of information) and the other as the seeker. One can think of the source as an ideal computer, that is, a computer communicating in such a human way that a person who did not know he was dealing with a computer might readily believe he was communicating with another person. The seeker can be regarded as the user of the computer.

To continue the analogy, our different channels and modes of communication model various input and output channels between the computer and its human user.

The setting for a typical experiment consists of two adjoining rooms connected by a soundproof double door (see Figure 6.1). The wall between the rooms also has in it a large double-glass panel, which can be covered with an opaque screen so that the source and the seeker cannot see each other. When the panel is not covered, the participants can see each other and can converse freely through a microphone and loudspeaker, but they are still separated physically. Some of our experiments also have test conditions in which the two people can neither see each other nor communicate by voice; instead they use writing machines linked in such a way that anything typed or written in longhand on one machine is reproduced on the other.

Our problem-solving tasks differ significantly from the kind usually found in the problem-solving literature of psychology because they were designed to meet certain special criteria. They sample such psychological functions as verbal skill and psychomotor skill. They are representative of tasks for which interactive computer systems are or could sometimes be employed. Instead of being abstract or artificial puzzles of the kind often devised to measure hypothetical psychological processes, they are of recognizable and practical importance in everyday life. They have definite, recognizable solutions, which can usually be reached within approximately an hour. Finally, their solution requires no special skills or specialized knowledge.

The tasks are formulated in such a way that solving them requires the seeker and the source to work together as a team. The seeker is given a problem for which he has to find the solution. His information folio consists of certain parts of the problem. The source has a folio with the remainder of the information needed to solve the problem. Neither person can solve the problem by himself, but together they have all the information needed for doing so. Remember, however, that our problems are designed to elicit communication between the two members of a team. They do not necessarily represent the way tasks would be assigned to man and computer in any real system.

All together we have constructed 10 problems that meet our needs. The following brief descriptions of three of them will convey their flavor.

In the "equipment-assembly problem" the task of the seeker is to assemble a common household article: a trash-can carrier. His information folio consists of all the disassembled parts of that article exactly as it comes from the mail-order house from which it was bought. He is not

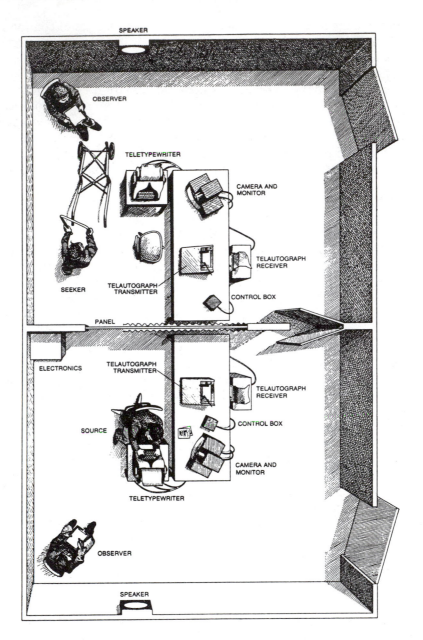

Figure 6.1 Laboratory setting for a typical experiment. The seeker has been given a trash-can carrier to assemble but has not been told its name or function. The source has the information for assembly. The experiment is designed to elicit communication in the hope of assisting in the design of a computer that would be analogous to the source in communicating much as a person communicates.

told either the name or the function of the device. The source's folio consists of the set of diagrams and instructions for assembly that came with the parts.

In the "information-retrieval problem" the seeker has to find the citation of every newspaper article relevant to an assigned topic that appeared in *The New York Times* during a given year. Usually he is told not to count editorials, reports of public speeches or letters to the editor. The source's information folio consists of *The New York Times Index* for the same year.

In the "geographic-orientation problem" (see Figure 6.2) the seeker's task is to find the office or residence address of the physician closest to a hypothetical home address. He is supplied with an index of streets, a gridded street map of Washington, D.C., and a card on which the home address is typed. His hypothetical home address is also marked on the map. The source is supplied with one page of the list of physicians in the yellow pages of the Washington telephone directory.

Our subjects have varied from experiment to experiment. We have relied heavily on that mainstay of psychological experiments, the college student. In one experiment, however, we enlisted high school boys, in another girls from a parochial high school and in a third a mixture of college and high school students.

We began with a series of tests involving four types of communication with less sophisticated equipment and procedures than have characterized our later experiments. In the communication-rich mode the subjects sat side by side at a table with no barrier between them. In the voice mode they were in separate rooms and communicated through a cloth panel that could be heard through but not seen through. In the handwriting mode they wrote messages in a notebook they passed through a slot in the wall between the two rooms. In the typewriter mode we had both experienced and inexperienced typists.

The results show large differences among the several modes of communication (see Figure 6.5). The inexperienced typists, for example, took almost two and a half times as long to solve problems as subjects in the communication-rich mode did. Differences of the same order have turned up repeatedly in other experiments.

An unexpected finding was the notably small difference in performance between the experienced and the inexperienced typists. This finding seemed so implausible that we later checked it in another experiment with different subjects and more elaborate procedures to help us figure out what was going on. We now think the explanation has at least two different components.

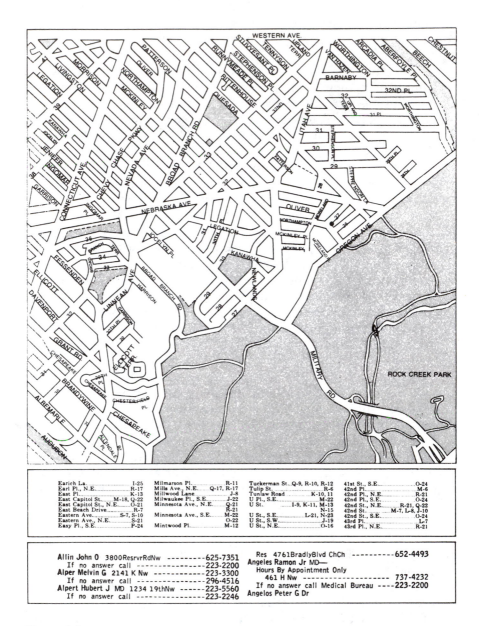

Earich La.	I-25	Milmarson Pl.	R-11	Tuckerman St.	Q-9, R-10, R-12	41st St., S.E.	O-24
Earl Pl., N.E.	R-17	Mills Ave., N.E.	Q-17, R-17	Tulip St.	R-6	42nd Pl.	M-6
East Pl.	K-13	Millwood Lane	J-8	Tunlaw Road	K-10, 11	42nd Pl., N.E.	R-21
East Capitol St.	M-18, Q-22	Milwaukee Pl., S.E.	J-22	U Pl., S.E.	M-22	42nd Pl., S.E.	O-24
East Capitol St., N.E.	O-21	Minnesota Ave., N.E.	Q-21	U St.	I-9, K-11, M-13	42nd St., N.E.	R-21, Q-22
East Beach Drive	R-7		R-21		N-15	42nd St.	M-7, L-8, J-10
Eastern Ave.	S-7, S-10	Minnesota Ave., S.E.	M-22	U St., S.E.	L-21, N-23	42nd St., S.E.	O-24
Eastern Ave., N.E.	S-21		O-22	U St., S.W.	J-19	43rd Pl.	L-7
Easy Pl., S.E.	P-24	Mintwood Pl.	M-12	U St., N.E.	O-16	43rd Pl., N.E.	R-21

Allin John O 3800ResrvrRdNw -------- 625-7351
 If no answer call ---------------- 223-2200
Alper Melvin G 2141 K Nw ------------ 223-3300
 If no answer call ---------------- 296-4516
Alpert Hubert J MD 1234 19thNw ------ 223-5560
 If no answer call ---------------- 223-2246

 Res 4761BradlyBlvd ChCh ---------- 652-4493
Angeles Ramon Jr MD—
 Hours By Appointment Only
 461 H Nw ------------------- 737-4232
 If no answer call Medical Bureau ---- 223-2200
Angelos Peter G Dr

Figure 6.2 Orientation problem imposes on the seeker the task of finding the address of the physician closest to seeker's hypothetical home. Seeker is given a street map of Washington, D.C., with the address marked as shown by black dot. He also receives a street index (*middle*) keyed to the map. The source receives one page from the listing of physicians in the yellow pages of the Washington telephone directory (*bottom*). Subjects occupy separate rooms and must solve the problem by one or more modes of communication.

```
goaheaddoyouknowhowto put this togher
ill tryits a trash toter   ill type you  the  directions  ok
put  axle  thru  38th holes  from  outside
38th holes/  ??yes
put 1 handlebar on back of  each  outer  frame  line  up  bolt  holes
what does outer frame look like ? its  like  a  (W)
put  bottom  frame to outer frames on  front + rear of outer  frames
ok use  1+12  bolts
are  your parts  labled  by  lettrs  ???
nookthe  thing  looks  like a cart with  room  for 2 trash cans the part
that looks like this(XX)goes on the bottom +the 2(W)parts go on the sids
put  male ends  ?  into  female  ends
what does that mean?  i dont  no
it  looks  like  3(u)s
what? 2(u)s   go  into  each  other  then  theyare  put on other u +put
on  W  put  top  frame  to  front  of  outer  fr.+to  handlbar  2 1/4
bolts  put  center  support  fr.  inside  topfr.  use 2 1/4  bo.  thru
center  of  top fr.  put 2  1/12  bolts thrub  center  of  side  fr.,
bottomfr. 2 bottom of center  support  fr.
okput  on wheels  3 spoks  on  outside put on  hubcap  with  hammer
put oh handgrips   DO  ALL  THESE  STEPS  FOR  BOTH  SIDES     ok?????
```

Figure 6.3   Typed exchange between a seeker and a source engaged in solving the equipment-assembly problem is reproduced in part, with messages by the seeker underlined. In spite of such confusing messages as "38th holes" in the third line, where the source intended to say 3/8th-inch holes, the two members of the team solved the problem in less than an hour. Both were inexperienced at typing.

First, by means of detailed measurements of what the subjects were actually doing when they solved problems we found that the average subject spends somewhat less than a third of his time in communication. In interactive problem solving subjects do a great many other things, such as make notes, think about what to say, handle objects and search for information in their respective folios. As a result the advantages one might expect to come from superior typing skill are diluted by the relatively small fraction of time in which the skill can be exercised.

Second, the kind of typing called for in interactive communication is unusual. Typing skill is normally measured by having subjects copy text material. In communication by typewriter, however, the communicator has to decide what to say, compose his thoughts into a message (often fragmented and incomplete) and then type out the message. The transmissions are characterized by hesitations, mistakes, changes of thought and irregular tempos that may at various times be indirect expressions of doubt, amusement or anger. In short, typing skill is usually measured as a strictly mechanical or psychomotor activity, whereas communication by teletypewriter is a much more intellectual process. It is small wonder that the two techniques seem to have so little in common.

```
SO:  Okay.  And but it's, all it is, is a frame.
SK:  All it is, is a frame.  And what's supposed to fit inside the frame?
     Do you fit, do you put, you know, a pan like in a wheel barrel or/
SO:  No, there's no pan.
⌈SO: Okay, now.
⌊SK: Or is it [Message continues below.]
SK:  like a wagon or what?
SO:  Now let, now let me read this for a second..It's like a wheel bar-
     rel like I said, there's a handle, there's two wheels..and all it
     is is like it's a frame wheel barrel like. But there is no, y'know,
     water will go through it in other words.
SK:  Do wheels go in the front?
SO:  I'm gonna, I'm gonna [Message continues below.]
⌈SO: read this.
⌊SK: Or do the [Message continues below.]
SK:  wheels go in the back?
SO:  I'm gonna read the direction now.  I'm gonna, give you, the, you
     know..Let me read it..oh, trash toter. Oh, is that what it is?
```

Figure 6.4   Voice exchanges between a seeker and a source working on the equipment-assembly problem are reproduced in a partial transcript in which *SO* is the source and *SK* the seeker. A bracket linking *SO* and *SK* indicates that both were talking simultaneously.

From the voluminous literature on kinesics, gestures and "body language" I had been led to predict a large difference between face-to-face communication and communication by voice alone. The voice channel by itself seems impoverished in comparison with the variety and richness of the information-bearing clues available in face-to-face communication. The data did not conform at all to my expectations. The average amount of time taken to solve problems by voice alone was only slightly more than it was in face-to-face communication.

If this were an isolated result, one might well question its validity. It has appeared, however, in other experiments that we have done with different subjects and different problems. One of these experiments, carried out by a former student of mine, Robert B. Ochsman, tested 10 different modes of communication. Arranging them according to richness, one finds that here too the mean problem-solving time is only slightly longer in the voice mode than in the communication-rich mode (see Figure 6.6).

Although solution times tend to increase as the channels of communication become more impoverished, the most striking feature of our data on the 10 modes is that they tend to fall into two fairly distinct groups. The faster five all have a voice link, whereas the slower ones do not. Statistical tests confirm that this one comparison is the only statistically significant one among the 10 communication modes.

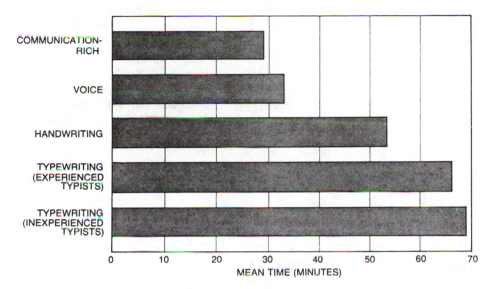

Figure 6.5 Solving time of problems is averaged for several modes of communication. In the communication-rich mode, for example, where the two members of a team were in the same room and could communicate freely, the average time for a solution was 29 minutes.

However interesting the data on problem-solving time are by themselves, they become even more interesting when they are related to the linguistic output of the communicators. The problems of measuring and quantifying that output have in turn been almost as interesting as the results. Most psycholinguistic research has been done on what I call immaculate prose. Such prose consists of grammatically correct sentences with nouns, verbs and other parts of speech in their proper place. Words are spelled correctly and rules of punctuation are observed. All computer programs based on what is called natural language require immaculate prose because the sentences that are fed into the computer are parsed in one way or another so that the meaning of the ensemble can be inferred from conventional rules of syntax.

The trouble is that people do not naturally speak in sentences. Most of us realize this in an intuitive way, but I suspect that few of us appreciate just how untidy normal human conversations really are. In our experiments recordings are made of conversations in all communication modes having a voice channel, and the recordings are then transcribed into typewritten protocols. Subjects generate their own protocols when they converse in the handwriting and typing modes.

Looking at the transcripts of conversations by voice or writing, one readily sees the untidiness I have mentioned. An example is the record produced by two inexperienced typists who were solving the equipment-assembly problem (see Figure 6.3). The first impression is one of complete unruliness. Not one grammatically correct sentence appears in the entire protocol. Words are continually misspelled and run together. Abbreviations, both conventional and unconventional, are common, and violation of the rules of punctuation is commoner than their observance.

The record even includes serious errors of fact. For example, at one point the source gives the seeker an instruction about "38th holes." The seeker queries the source on this point, and the source replies that his original statement was correct. Actually what the assembly instructions stated and the source meant to say was that the seeker should put the axle through the 3/8th-inch holes.

Perhaps the most remarkable thing is that in spite of all this apparent unruliness, the information got through. The two team members who generated the protocol completed their task successfully in less than the average time required by teams for the equipment-assembly problem. Equally remarkable is that the protocols of the experienced typists were also characterized by many of the same kinds of error and ungrammatical feature. Evidently unruliness tends to creep in when the emphasis is on natural communication rather than on precision of typing.

Transcripts of voice conversations have their own special idiosyncrasies that are no less perplexing and difficult to deal with (see Figure 6.4). It is clear that if truly interactive computer systems are ever to be created, they will somehow have to cope with the mispronunciations, errors and violations of format that are the rule rather than the exception in normal human communication. Discovering the rules and characteristics of normal communication is a problem that has been ignored by linguists for too long.

Measuring and counting such characteristics of the protocols as words, sentences and messages had seemed simple in prospect but proved difficult in execution. In the end, however, we were able to formulate sets of rules that enabled us to count the linguistic units. Next came the task of trying to decide what measures of linguistic performance to apply to our linguistic units.

On the basis of hunches, hypotheses and what we could find in the psychological literature we came up with 136 linguistic measures. A number of them turned out to be trivial, and many others were so highly intercorrelated that they were redundant. In the end we were left with only nine meaningful measures of linguistic performance that describe

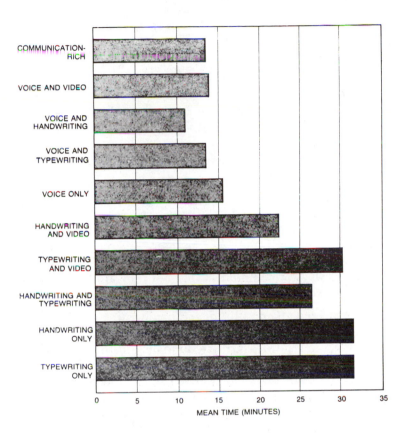

Figure 6.6 Mode of communication influenced the time required to solve problems. Here the average time taken by teams to solve problems is charted for 10 different modes of communication. The data fall into two fairly distinct groups. The faster five all involve the use of the voice in communication, whereas the voice is excluded in the five slower modes.

our data. To a certain extent the discarded measures are as interesting as the useful ones because they reveal where it would be fruitless to expend time and effort in the future. To list them here, however, would consume too much space.

The productive measures are: (1 and 2) The number of messages generated by each subject and, closely correlated, the number of sentences. (3 and 4) The number of words per message and, closely correlated, the number of words per sentence. (5) The percentage of sentences that were questions. (6) The total number of words employed by a subject. (7) The total number of different words employed by a subject. (8) The ratio of different words to total words, called the type-token ratio. (9) The communication rate, which is the number of words communicated per minute of time actually spent communicating.

In one sense our findings are disappointing, since there appears to be so little to show for so much effort. In another sense, however, they are gratifying. The linguistic performance of people who communicate naturally can be described by a rather small number of quantitative measures.

When the data are summarized (see Figure 6.7), the most striking thing about them is that the two fast modes of communication (the two that have a voice channel) are also extremely wordy. Subjects using the two voice modes, as compared with handwriting and typing, delivered about eight times as many messages, eight times as many sentences, five times as many words and twice as many different words; they also communicated words at a rate nearly 10 times as fast. In sum, the voice modes are fast ways of communicating, but they are extremely wordy, no matter how wordiness is measured.

The higher type-token ratio for the handwriting and typing modes confirms that they tend to be more parsimonious and less redundant than the voice modes. (Measuring redundancy in these experiments is extremely difficult because the data do not lend themselves to the conventional measures of redundancy relied on by information theorists. By making certain plausible assumptions, however, we concluded that in the voice modes subjects employ about 13 times as many words and four times as many unique words as are really required to solve problems.)

Interruptions in normal conversations are so common and apparently so important that we have tested their effects in a separate experiment. In brief, we found that if subjects do not have freedom to interrupt, they use fewer messages and more words per message. They also maintain a relatively constant number of messages in both speaking and typing.

Allowing subjects freedom to interrupt does not shorten the time needed to solve problems, nor does it result in any reduction in the number of words needed to reach solutions. What does happen is that when subjects have the freedom to interrupt, they package their words differently. They use more messages and fewer words per message, and they maintain a relatively constant message length whether they speak or communicate by typewriter. A final point of interest is that a subject is much more likely to take control of a voice channel than of a channel or any combination of channels lacking the voice.

	COMMUNICATION-RICH	VOICE	HANDWRITING	TYPEWRITING	
				EXPERIENCED TYPISTS	INEXPERIENCED TYPISTS
SOLUTION TIME IN MINUTES	29	33	53.3	66.2	69
NUMBER OF MESSAGES	230.4	163.8	15.9	27.2	31.5
NUMBER OF SENTENCES	372.6	275.9	24.9	45.8	44.1
TOTAL NUMBER OF WORDS	1,563.8	1,374.8	224.8	322.9	257.4
TOTAL NUMBER OF DIFFERENT WORDS	397.5	305.9	118.5	150.5	133.4
TYPE-TOKEN RATIO	.3	.3	.6	.5	.6
NUMBER OF WORDS PER MINUTE	190.3	171.2	17.3	18.1	10.2

Figure 6.7 Experimental results are enumerated for the solution of problems by various modes of communication. "Type-token ratio" is the ratio of different words to total words. Problem solving by voice takes the least time but is wordier than the other modes are.

In considering the generality of our findings one might ask whether we have found certain general principles of human communication or have merely found out about the ways in which particular pieces of equipment are employed. We think we have found general principles. In our experiments we tested some of the various channels of communication in distinctly different ways. For example, in one experiment the voice channel was tested by having subjects converse through a cloth panel that was visually opaque but acoustically transparent. In another they conversed through a microphone and loudspeaker. In a third experiment each subject wore a microphone positioned a fraction of an inch in front of his lips. Similar variations were devised for handwriting tests. The most gratifying thing to me is that the results and the comparisons are almost identical under all variations of a given mode. In short, I believe we have been discovering general principles of communication (by voice, typing or handwriting) that are largely independent of the particular devices employed in mediating the communications. Another kind of evidence bearing on the generality of our findings is that the results obtained with our different modes of communication hold for all the different problems we have tested and for both job roles assigned to the communicators: source and seeker.

As so often happens in research, the questions our findings have raised are more numerous than the answers they have supplied. Every reader will have his own list of questions. Four in particular intrigue me.

First, how do communication patterns vary among different nationalities? Anthropologists and sociologists tell us (and our own experience seems to confirm) that communication patterns differ markedly among different cultural groups. Would we have obtained results of the same kind if we had studied people who speak a language other than English? What kind of concessions will telecommunication systems in general and computers in particular have to make for national and cultural differences?

Second, how do communication patterns vary according to the purpose of the communication? All our experiments so far have involved factual problems. The problems all had single answers, and the information needed to solve them was directed toward that one goal. Interactive communication, even with computers, may serve many different functions. A communicator may browse through masses of data for items that he needs or that merely excite his interest and curiosity. He may want to have briefings and status reports that will help him to anticipate weather conditions for the next few hours or days, review the state of the economy or update his information about the condition of patients in a hospital. Communications can also provide information necessary for reaching decisions among conflicting alternatives and can serve in argumentation, bargaining and persuasion. Virtually nothing is known about how communication patterns vary according to these diverse purposes.

Third, what happens to communication patterns as the number of communicators increases? Our experiments were all done with teams of two people, but communications often involve a group of people and perhaps a computer. The full implications of this kind of communication are not known.

Finally, what are the rules that govern normal human communication? Perhaps the most interesting question of all concerns the grammatical, syntactical and semantic rules that apply to such communication. In spite of the apparent unruliness of natural communication, it obviously follows some rules, because problems do get solved, often with surprising speed. How are meanings conveyed in natural conversations? How can we even go about investigating this problem?

This brief introduction to our program of research has conveyed only a few of the many interesting findings we have made. Still, it may be enough to excite the interest of others to try to understand what happens when people communicate. If enough people work on these problems, who knows? Perhaps at some future time you and I shall be able to find out about the latest developments in science not by reading articles such as the ones in this magazine[1] but by conversing in ordinary English with a computer.

---

[1] *Editor's note:* Reference is to the issue of *Scientific American* in which this article originally appeared.

Related Technologies

The papers in this section provide background in three areas that once might have defined CSCW, but are now somewhat outside the main focus: electronic mail, teleconferencing, and office systems.

The ARPANET has been the enabling technology for large communities of researchers working together at a distance using electronic mail, file sharing, and file transfer. The Licklider and Vezza paper (Reading 7, this volume) is an early overview and analysis of the types of applications that might be developed for this technology. The authors review thirty applications and the network capabilities that each requires. The technology permits new kinds of communication, but also raises new issues—political, social, and economic—that the authors also address, anticipating accurately many of the concerns that we face today in dealing with the ARPANET and other commercial networks.

The Johansen and Bullen paper (Reading 8, this volume) reviews teleconferencing installations through the early 1980s. Several technologies are reviewed: audio, still video, computer conferencing, full-motion video, and live video. All can be used to substitute for travel and for face-to-face meetings. The authors point out that there are situations in which the alternative medium can be actually preferable to meeting in person. One example is the time and space independence afforded by computer conference systems. Participants can work whenever they like, without synchronizing or co-locating. These systems provide an e-mail-like medium in which messages in a conference are structured by topic and response, and can be accessed by large groups of people. Overall, the impact of such conferencing technologies has probably not been as great as these authors anticipated. However, various electronically mediated meeting experiments continue. They provide another route by which people will become more aware of the potential for meeting at a distance. With this awareness will come new ideas for meeting technology, including increased demand for the integration of the computer with other electronic media.

The Ellis and Nutt paper (Reading 9, this volume) surveys computer science research on Office Information Systems through 1980. The paper serves two purposes in this volume. One was referred to in the introduction: to give some perspective on the relationship between the OIS and CSCW research fields. The second purpose is that as part of this section on related technologies, it contains descriptions of several office systems that also illustrate the close relationship between the technologies of interest in both fields.

Applications of Information Networks

J. C. R. Licklider
Albert Vezza

Abstract

The present and projected applications of computer-communication networks or information networks include electronic mail, teleconferencing, "the office of the future," management information systems, modeling, "computerized commerce," monitoring of patients, military command and control, home security, education, and news. This paper briefly examines 30 such applications and the network capabilities they require. It presents a way of estimating the relative importance of various network characteristics and of predicting the suitability of a network or network architecture for a given set of applications. The paper then considers several issues that relate to the political, social, and economic impacts of networks. Among the issues are privacy, security, compatibility, impact on productivity, the roles of networks in international technology transfer and economic competition, and the confluence or collision of the fields of computers and telecommunications.

1 Introduction

The subject of this paper is applications of networks. The networks involve the use of computers, but computation in the narrow sense does not necessarily dominate the applications. The scope of the paper includes, no less than computation, computer-based applications in which

143

the main emphasis is on communication among people, on access to information, or on control of systems, organizations, or—to mention early one of the deepest though least imminent concerns—societies. The applications of networks that we shall examine include electronic message communication [1]–[4], electronic funds transfer [5], access to information, computer-based office work and "telework," management of organizations and command and control of operations, education, entertainment and recreation, reservations and ticketing, and several others.

Some of the problems and issues in network applications are mainly technical and some are mainly nontechnical, but almost all are mixtures of the two, and in most of them the technical and nontechnical factors interact strongly. For example, the relative merits of circuit switching and packet switching are mainly a technical matter, but the fact that the electronic switching stations of the existing telecommunications "plant" are circuit switches surely is an economic factor in the circuit-switching/packet-switching issue. The determination of what should be the individual citizen's right to informational privacy is mainly a nontechnical matter, but the pragmatics of providing informational security, the technical basis for assurance of privacy, must enter the decision process. The national telecommunications plant-in-being of the U.S. figures strongly in many of these problems and issues and forces them to involve both technical and nontechnical factors. The plant is valued at something like $120 billion, and most of it was designed to carry analog voice signals, which are quite different in their spectral and temporal parameters and in their requirements for error handling and security, from digital computer signals of the kinds that will flow through the networks of the future. Because of its inherent redundancy, speech remains intelligible even when mixed with considerable amounts of noise, but even a single undetected error—a single bit—can have extremely serious consequences in electronic funds transfer (EFT) or seriously degrade the performances of a network carrying enciphered information.

One of the major motivations for networking is the need to share resources. The main resources that are often advantageous to share are communications facilities, computer facilities, and information itself. The design of a network can make it easier or more difficult to share resources and thus directly influence the amount of resource sharing that will occur. The amount of communication facilities sharing depends upon many design factors, all of which influence how well the network is able to allocate resources dynamically in response to changing needs and availabilities. Though the need for sharing certain types of computational facilities may diminish with the arrival of the age of the personal computer, it is not at all likely that the need to share resources will disappear altogether. Geographically distributed users can share, through a computer network, the costly high-performance computers that are required to solve certain large computational problems. Even those using personal computers to satisfy the bulk of their computing needs may wish to avail themselves through a network of special software services provided by vendors—and they will certainly wish to communicate with one another.

The sharing of information is the most important type of resource sharing. The term "information sharing" immediately conjures up the thought of sharing large data banks of information among many users, but that is only one aspect of information sharing. All the applications discussed in this paper have aspects of information sharing. Applications concerned with communications, management, commerce, government, protection, education, and awareness all involve sharing. The convenience and effectiveness with which sharing can be accomplished and the facility with which information can flow across the boundaries of individual application programs will have profound effects on how the applications serve their intended purposes.

Many problems and issues arise from the interaction of information sharing with information security. For example, should EFT have a network of its own to simplify the problem of providing secure transmission, processing, and storage of funds data, or should EFT messages be carried over a general-purpose network so that a reservations and ticketing operation can be completed in a single transaction involving the traveler's organization, the airline, and the bank.

2 Applications

In the context of information networks, just as in the context of computer systems, an application is essentially the implementation of a purpose. Applications, like purposes, may be defined narrowly or broadly. When the airlines began to develop computer-based reservations systems and formed a consortium, ARINC, to interconnect several of their systems, the application was narrow: airline reservations. Now, after years of growth and augmentation, one can rent a car, reserve a hotel room, and arrange to be greeted with flowers and mariachi music. The broadened application might be defined as reservations and ticketing for almost anything that flies to or can be purchased at a distant place. One can project the broader definition into the future and envision a general reservations and ticketing application, operating in a nationwide or worldwide common-carrier network, through which anyone could examine the availability of, and reserve or buy a ticket to, almost anything in the broad class to which reservations and tickets apply. But, of course, there is no reason to stop at that particular class. One can expand the scope further and arrive at "computerized commerce," dealing with the whole gamut of things that can be bought and sold. The very broadly defined application would include advertising, dynamic pricing, and computer-based purchasing strategies. It might even make a place for cartels of suppliers and cooperatives of consumers. No doubt there would be vigorous competition among several or many offerers of the application, and perhaps one can imagine even a "meta-market," an over-arching system that interconnects and integrates the competing "computerized commerce applications."

In any event, that introduces the notion of applications of information networks. It might serve to introduce, also, the notion of issues, which involve the interplay of the opportunity and the threat aspects of applications. It is not difficult to imagine the mischief that could be played by pranksters or dissidents in a poorly protected, publicly accessible, nationwide reservations system.

2.1 *Basic Applications*

Computer-communication networks perform three basic classes of operations upon information: transmission, processing, and storage. The earliest recognized applications of networks were essentially separate exploitations of the three basis classes of operation. Transmission of information through a network from a program in one computer to a program in another, of course, requires some processing and some storage (memory), but in simple message communication and file transfer interest is focused sharply on transmission. In every practical computer, processing requires storage (memory or registers), but in early time-sharing services such as Quiktran [6]–[8], which when introduced did not provide intersession file storage, the (dial telephone) network application was essentially access to processing. In the Datacomputer [9] service available through the ARPANET [10]–[12], although processing is involved in both storage and retrieval, one of the main applications is essentially access to storage in and of itself: the Datacomputer is a place to park bits.

A fourth essential network function combines the basic transmission, processing, and storage operations to provide access to information—with the focus of interest on the information itself, rather than on any of the three basic elementary operations.

Simple message communication and file transfer, access to time-shared processing, access to storage, and access to information are important as well as fundamental network functions, but they are no longer typical of the activities or services we associate with the term "application." In present-day parlance, "application" suggests something more highly differentiated and specialized and closer to some specific task or mission.

2.2 Communication Applications

In the developmental history of the ARPANET, electronic message service was a sleeper. Even before the network included a dozen computers, several message programs were written as natural extensions of the "mail" systems that had arisen in individual time-sharing systems in the early 1960's. By the Fall of 1973, the great effectiveness and convenience of such fast, informal message services as SNDMSG [13] had been discovered by almost everyone who had worked on the development of the ARPANET—and especially by the then Director of ARPA, S. J. Lukasik, who soon had most of his office directors and program managers communicating with him and with their colleagues and their contractors via the network. Thereafter, both the number of (intercommunicating) electronic mail systems and the number of users of them on the ARPANET increased rapidly.

Electronic mail, electronic message systems: It soon became obvious that the ARPANET was becoming a human-communication medium with very important advantages over normal U.S. mail and over telephone calls. One of the advantages of the message systems over letter mail was that, in an ARPANET message, one could write tersely and type imperfectly, even to an older person in a superior position and even to a person one did not know very well, and the recipient took no offense. The formality and perfection that most people expect in a typed letter did not become associated with network messages, probably because the network was so much faster, so much more like the telephone. Indeed, tolerance for informality and imperfect typing was even more evident when the users of the ARPANET linked their consoles together and typed back and forth to each other in an alphanumeric conversation. Among the advantages of the network message services over the telephone were the fact that one could proceed immediately to the point without having to engage in small talk first, that the message services produced a preservable record, and that the sender and receiver did not have to be available at the same time. A typical electronic mail system now provides a rudimentary editor to facilitate preparation of messages, a multiple-addressee feature to make it easy to send the same message to several people, a file-inclusion scheme to incorporate already prepared text files into a message, an alerting mechanism to tell the user that he has new mail in his mailbox, facilities for reading received messages, and a "help" subsystem. The prospects of electronic mail appear to have caught the attention of computer manufacturers and software and time-sharing firms as well as telephone companies, national telecommunication authorities, and the U.S. Post Office—and most of them now seem to be planning, developing, or even offering some kind of electronic mail service.

Even before electronic mail was well established, it had become apparent that users would need computer aids for scanning, indexing, filing, retrieving, summarizing, and responding to messages. Indeed, messages are usually not isolated documents but documents prepared and transmitted in the course of performing complex activities often called "tasks." Within task contexts, messages are related to other messages and to documents of other kinds, such as forms and reports. It seems likely that we shall see a progressive escalation of the functionality and comprehensiveness of computer systems that deal with messages. If "electronic mail" refers to an early stage in the progression, "electronic message system" is appropriate for a later stage and "computer-based office system" or some comparable term for the stage of full integration. At some intermediate point, message service will no doubt be blended with direct user-to-user linking to provide for delay-free conversation whenever both sender and receiver are on-line at the same time and prefer conversation to sequential exchange of messages.

Duologue and teleconferencing: Although there has not been, thus far, very much use of networks for one-on-one interaction between users, it seems likely that some kind of computer-augmented two-person telephone communication will one day be one of the main modes of networking. In order to displace the conventional telephone, "teleduologue" will probably have to offer speech, writing, drawing, typing, and possibly some approximation to television, all integrated into a synergic pattern with several kinds of computer support and facilitation. The two communicators (and their supporting programs) will then be able to control displays in certain areas of each other's display screens and processes in certain sectors of each other's computers. Throughout a duologue, each communicator will be advised by his own programs and will use information from his own data bases and other sources accessible to him. The effect will be to provide each communicator with a wide choice of media for each component of his communication and with a very fast and competent supporting staff.

A teleconference [14]–[17] is an organized interaction, through a communication system or network, of geographically separated members of a group. The term "teleconference" has been used recently mainly to refer to interactions organized or presided over by or with the aid of programmed computers. In some teleconferences, the members of the group participate concurrently; in others, each member logs in when it is convenient for him to do so, reviews what has happened in his absence, makes his contribution, and logs out, perhaps to return later in the day or later in the week.

During the last five years, a considerable amount of experience has been gained with computer-facilitated teleconferencing, but it is evidently a complex and subtle art, and teleconference programs still have a long way to go before teleconferences approach the naturalness of face-to-face interaction. On the other hand, we note the inefficiency of traveling to meetings and the inefficiency of letting one participant take up the time of $n - 1$ participants when only $m < n - 1$ are interested in what he is saying. As teleconferencing is perfected (especially nonconcurrent teleconferencing), it will become an extremely important technique.

2.3 Neopaperwork

"Office automation," "computer-based office work," "the high-technology office," and a few other such phrases refer to the aggregation and integration of several applications of computers and networks in office work. ("Automation" is intended in its weak sense, which includes computer "aiding" and "semi-automation.") Office automation includes everything presently called "word processing" (dictation, document preparation, etc.) plus computer-based filing (information storage and retrieval), communication (electronic mail, electronic message services, duologue, teleconferencing), and modeling (simulation), and it connects with electronic funds transfer, management information systems, and parts—if not all—of computerized commerce.

Office automation is expected to make heavy use of networks, both local and geographically distributed. Much office work is organized in an approximately hierarchical manner, with component desk functions such as transcription, editing, filing, retrieval, scheduling, and telephone answering at low echelons and corporate or divisional functions such as planning, marketing, operations, and public relations at high echelons. Low-echelon functions typically are carried out locally, within a single office or suite of offices, and, when low-echelon functions are supported by minicomputers or microcomputers, local networks will be required in their integration. In geographically distributed organizations, of course, geographically distributed networks will be required as higher level functions are integrated.

Telework: Networks will make it possible for people to do informational work effectively at locations remote from their managers, their co-workers, the people who report to them, and, indeed, even from customers and clients with whom they must interact. Such telework will require facilities for duologue, teleconferencing, and all the other aspects of office automation—but little beyond what automation of a nondispersed office will require.

Telework will offer the possibility of saving the hours and the energy spent in commuting. It may burden some families with more togetherness than was contracted for through the marriage vows ("for richer or poorer, but not for lunch"). But its strongest impact on individual lives will surely be felt by persons immobilized by prolonged illness, physical handicap, or children. For many of them, networks will open many doors—including the door to gainful employment.

Augmentation of the intellect: The at-a-distance aspect of computer-based work that is emphasized by the term "telework" will be overshadowed, in the opinion of many, by what Engelbart [18]–[21] has called "augmentation of the intellect." Computers will help people do informational work faster and better by providing fast and accurate tools to supplement such slow and fallible human functions as looking up words in dictionaries, copying references for citation, stepping through checklists, and searching for matching patterns. Augmentation is needed at levels that range from A) helping poor typists who cannot spell to put out neat and accurate reports, to Z) improving the content and style of top-level policy statements. Expectations differ concerning the prospect for significant early contributions from artificial intelligence, but it is clear that relatively unsophisticated augmentation systems can make major contributions. Consider the help provided by descriptor-based and citation-index-based information retrieval systems to a person looking for references pertinent to a particular fact or concept. Or consider the impact that would be made, on writing such as this, by a text editor that automatically displayed the Flesch Count [22] of every paragraph it helped compose.

Task management and coordination: In addition to helping the individual worker, computers will facilitate teamwork. Each office task will have its planned course of actions, involving particular workers at particular projected times. A computer-based task management system will monitor the task as it moves along the course, checking the actions as they are taken, arranging that planned coordinations and approvals are obtained, and revising the plan (or calling for human help) when the schedule slips. In the early days of office automation, the task management process will be mainly a matter of maintaining orderly work queues for the office workers and displaying for them at each moment

1) what needs to be done and 2) the information needed in doing it. What will need to be done will usually be, of course, to solve a problem or to make a decision—most of the preliminary work will have been performed automatically by computers. With the passage of time, as people come to understand the problem-solving and decision-making processes and the supporting information in programmers' terms, computers will chip away at the problem-solving and decision-making substance of office work, but we expect the now-rising wave of office automation to succeed or fail on the measure of its help to human workers and to human teamwork.

2.4 Management Applications

Office automation will have its impact upon management, of course, as well as upon the office workers. Management deals almost exclusively with information. (Money is essentially information, of course.) The comptroller's department was computerized early. Electronic funds transfer will be a major application of special-purpose, limited-purpose, or general-purpose networks. On-line financial services may burgeon. Inventory, ordering, production, pricing, and planning will all be interrelated with the aid of networks and computer modeling.

Management information systems: The widespread feeling of disappointment in the management information systems (MIS's) [23]–[26] of the 1960's and early 1970's had, we believe, a simple basis: the activities that generated the information required to support management decision making had not yet been brought on line to computers, and, therefore, the required information was not available to the management information systems. To some extent, information important to the manager is so global in scope that capturing it all on line is still not possible. (It was not worthwhile to keypunch all the basic operating data just to feed them into the management information system, for only a small fraction of the totality would ever be used. It was impossible to anticipate just what subsets or aggregations of the basic operating data would be required.) As soon as all the informational activities involved in operating an organization are on line, however, the basis for an effective management information system will exist. A few organizations are already approaching that state, but most are just entering—or just beginning to contemplate—office automation.

Local and geographically distributed networks will make it possible, at a cost, for top management to access all the facts and figures involved in the minute-to-minute operations of a business. Top management should resist the temptation to convert that possibility into actuality. The principle that looks best at present is to let the data of a corporation reside where the managers most conversant with them reside ("keep the data near the truth points") and to have conversant managers "sign off" on the release of data upwards in the corporate tree. Certain data should be abstracted and moved upward according to preset schedules; other data may be queried from above—but queried through an authenticating release process. Of course, the release process may in some instances be mediated by programs operating on behalf of the human conversant manager rather than by the human conversant manager himself or herself.

The foregoing discussion pertains, indeed, to most of the data management functions in office automation. In distributed organizations, data will be distributed, and one of the main uses of networks will be to move data from points of residence to points of use.

Modeling and simulation: Computer-based modeling and simulation are applicable to essentially all problem solving and decision making. At present, however, modeling and simulation are computer applications much more than they are network applications—and they are far from ubiquitous even as computer applications.

The trouble at present is that most kinds of modeling and simulation are much more difficult, expensive, and time consuming than intuitive judgment and are cost-effective only under special conditions that can justify and pay for facilities and expertise. But those are prime conditions for resource sharing and, hence, networking. Whereas very large organizations will be able to afford their own concentrations of facilities and expertise, small organizations will not. As management grows tighter and more sophisticated, therefore, there may come to be a place for management consultation and service firms that specialize in modeling and simulation and offer very large or special facilities—and deliver their products through networks. Perhaps a glimpse of such a future has been given by the large array-processing computer, Illiac IV [27], [28], which has been used through the ARPANET in modeling the world climate and the space shuttle. Similarly, MIND [29], a system accessible through a value added packet network, is being used to design communication networks.

2.5 Commerce

Shifting our attention from activities within an organization, such as a business firm, to interactions among organizations, we can see another kind of application for networks.

Electronic markets: Networks will serve as marketplaces, providing meeting grounds for buyers and sellers. At first, networks will displace telephone and mail, which now serve the marketplace function for most businesses. Later, networks will begin to displace stock exchanges and commodity markets. Ordinary office automation and funds transfer facilities will adequately support negotiations and transactions when the "commodities" bought and sold are purely informational or sufficiently specifiable by words and figures. Wide-band facilities for examining products at the time of purchase ("squeezing the grapefruit") may extend the scope of the electronic marketplace to commodities that must be selected or approved individually by prospective purchasers. We can expect networks to go beyond the role of the mere place or medium for transactions and, with the aid of sophisticated programs, actively to "make a market" in the sense that certain stock brokers make markets in certain stocks.

Computerized commerce: Computerized commerce [30] is based on the idea of electronic markets. It goes beyond providing a marketplace and making a market—and back into the primary motivation of the business firm—by using computers to develop and carry out strategies and tactics of buying and selling. The concept of computerized commerce is applicable to both the wholesale and retail levels. At the wholesale level, a company's buying algorithms, using data from its inventory data base and from its model of its market and its use of supplies and equipment to produce goods for sale in that market, will try to optimize procurement with respect to operational effectiveness and cost—while its selling algorithms, using parts of the same model, will try to optimize sales with respect to profit. Obviously, a high degree of integration of the whole process from input through output will be advantageous. At the retail level, consumers will need the aid of computers to contend effectively against the computer-based sales procedures of merchants. Unless or until personal computers can provide that aid, there may be a place within networks for shoppers' advisory services and shoppers' cooperatives.

It is evident that a buyer, at either the wholesale or retail level, will often wish to screen the offerings and prices of several or many alternative sellers. To make extensive "comparison shopping" economic, either there must be a market data base that is integrated over sellers or the cost of establishing network connections with many separate sellers must be low.

Employment services: As suggested in the section on telework, networking may change considerably the conditions and dimensions of employment in the informational occupations. Because networking will for some eliminate the time now spent in travel between home and office, it will make it feasible in certain cases for a worker to work on several different tasks for several different employers or clients in a single day. The new flexibility will create a need for employment services that function essentially as electronic markets in human information processing. Such services would use indexing, abstracting, and retrieval techniques as though workers were books or journal articles. They might create a new mobility in employment, favoring free lancers over workers of constant fealty, and the effect might spill over into conventional employment.

2.6 *Professional Services*

The major professions deal heavily if not exclusively with information. The law *is* information, and the indexing and retrieval of legal information represents an already very important application of computers and networks. Engineering abounds in potential network applications. We shall deal with teaching shortly under the heading Education. Here, let us examine briefly a few medical applications.

Telecommunications have been used to let a physician at the hospital direct the work of paramedics at the scene of an accident and link a specialist consultant to an emergency operating room a thousand miles away. Networks may serve such applications a bit more effectively or economically than the presently available communication channels do, but the most significant impacts of networks will probably be made in other areas such as the monitoring of patients, the monitoring of (the health of) nonpatients, and access to medical data bases and knowledge bases.

Monitoring of patients: Microcomputers and networks will make it possible to monitor continually all the indicators that contribute significantly to the determination of a patient's condition—and to do so for the patient in the home almost as well as for the patient in the hospital. It may, therefore, be safe to send certain convalescent patients home from the hospital earlier than is now the practice and to care at home for certain chronic patients who now have to live in hospitals [31]. For the patients who must remain in hospitals, one can envisage intramural networks far more communicative than the typical present-day call button and signal light—but perhaps a patient with a wide-band channel to someone else's attention would demand more attention.

Monitoring of nonpatients: It is interesting to speculate upon the application of networks to the monitoring of the health of the entire population. One can imagine future situations in which epidemiological control might be much more crucial than it is now to the maintenance of public health. In order to determine the cause of a rapid increase in the incidence of some deadly new disease, birth defect, or form of cancer, for example, it might be necessary to monitor in detail everyone's dietary intake, exposure to radiation, or even contact with other people. The practical and philosophical difficulties inherent in such an undertaking are too profound to address here, but it is easy to imagine the network, together with the millions of input stations and the massive (distributed) data base, as *sine qua non*. Less easy to imagine, perhaps, but quite as vital, would be the medical detective work—based on the day-and-night scouring of the data base by analytical and hypothesis-testing programs—required to figure out the cause and to project the cure. But such speculation does not define an application of networks that is probable during the remainder of this century. More attuned to our chosen time scale is the prospect that batteries of routine physical and medical tests might be administered by computer via a network at frequent intervals to many people. Computer feedback from the resulting collections of data might be more effective than the chart beside the bathroom scale in motivating people to exercise, watch their calories, and take their vitamins.

Medical records: Networking promises to make medical records available wherever needed, even if the patient has an emergency far away from his regular physician and local hospital. The medical records application imposes strong requirements for informational privacy and security and for data management on a nationwide or even international basis, but the factor that will probably inhibit the development of a medical records network is the poor quality of most medical records. As long as a patient's record is kept in longhand (or shorthand) by his physician, there is not much pressure for comprehensiveness; many patients go from one doctor to another, and many records are therefore fragmentary. But the computer is bringing, or can bring, a new approach to the creation of medical records [32], [33] (data direct to record from clinical tests, prompting by computers on the basis of check lists, entry of patient histories by patients, and contribution to medical records by paramedics), and if it does so, it will make sense for networks to bring a new approach to storage and retrieval of medical records.

Medical knowledge bases: If the technology of knowledge develops in the way that can be projected from recent work in artificial intelligence, medical knowledge bases will probably become the foci of very significant network applications.

The application that will doubtless be considered most significant will be to make available to every physician, no matter how remote from the centers of medicine, the vast and carefully organized bodies of medical knowledge that will constitute the medical knowledge bases. Knowledge bases will be used as sources in medical education (especially including continuing education) and as consultants or assistants in medical practice [34], [35]. Human expert consultation will, of course, be available to supplement the computer knowledge bases, but considerations of cost and availability will almost surely favor the computer. Difficult problems of legal responsibility and liability may have to be solved: advice from a knowledge base may be similar to advice from a book, but a knowledge-based program that controls the administration of an anesthetic would appear to introduce a new factor.

Possibly even more far reaching in its implications than access to medical knowledge bases by physicians is access to medical knowledge bases by laymen. Knowledge bases for laymen would have to be quite different in content and packaging from knowledge bases for physicians, and ideally the two applications would complement each other. The layman-oriented application might deal mainly with the complaints not ordinarily taken to a doctor or with the decision process that determines whether or not to seek a physician's help. In either case, if the knowledge-base program had access to the individual's medical record, and if it could make simple observations such as temperature and pulse rate through the network, it could go rather far beyond the limits of the conventional book of medicine for the layman. Society should examine such incursions by the computer into medicine or even paramedicine very carefully before making up its collective mind about them. They obviously mix benefits with dangers. Unfortunately, they tend to be approached with prejudice.

2.7 Government Applications

Actual and potential government applications of networks include military command and control, communications, logistics, acquisition and interpretation of intelligence data, dissemination of intelligence, law enforcement, delivery of government services such as Social Security benefits to citizens, and converting the paperwork of the bureaucracy into bits. Paperwork in the government is rather like paperwork in the private sector, but carried a step or two further into detail. The other government applications, on the other hand, seem rather special. Military command and control, communications, intelligence, and to a considerable extent logistics systems must be able to operate fast, move fast or hide, and function in the presence of physical (as well as other) countermeasures. Law enforcement information systems are in some ways like highly amplified credit reference systems: derogatory information seems especially crucial, for to be forewarned is to be forearmed, and action must often be taken on the basis of whatever data can be assembled in a few seconds. Serving all the citizens and collecting taxes from most of them requires that certain personal data be held about almost everyone—enough in sum to make a several-trillion-character data base that at least conceivably could be subverted to political or economic exploitation. There are strong lessons about government applications of networks in the recent rejection by the Office of Management and the Budget (OMB), at the well-timed suggestion of several members of Congress, of the proposed new Tax Administration System of the Internal Revenue Service.

Military command and control and military communications: Military command and control and military communications are prime network applications. Both interactive computing and networking had their origins in the SAGE system (Semi-Automatic Ground Environment for air defense), and many of the military systems used to command forces and control weapons are essentially computer-communications networks. For reasons we do not fully understand—since fast response to a changing situation is the essence of command and control—the World-Wide Military Command and Control System (WWMCCS) is actually not very interactive, and its computers, which use the GECOS operating system [36] designed for batch processing, are not interconnected by an electronic network. But surely WWMCCS will in due course be upgraded. Autodin II is under development and will supplement or replace Autodin I [37], the Department of Defense's present store-and-forward digital telecommunications network, with a modern packet-switching network based on modified and secured ARPANET technology. Networking is being pursued actively, also, in the intelligence community. One of the most significant possibilities for the military that is opened up by advances in information technology is the achievement of a much tighter coupling between intelligence and command and control. One can envision a reduction in the time required for the distribution of intelligence information from days or hours to minutes or seconds. Such an advance would, of course, put pressure on intelligence gathering and processing to operate on faster time scales.

Military logistics: There is less progress, but also less pressure, in the logistics area, where more than 20 large batch inventory systems can be counted, diverse in respect of hardware, programming language, and data management system. Over the coming years, however, even the logistics situation will probably be brought under control and onto a network. The overall objective is to make the entire operation of a military effort responsive to coherent hierarchical command in the light of valid and current intelligence—with security against enemy actions and countermeasures.

The network of the National Crime Information Center (NCIC):   The NCIC is operated by the FBI and connects with state and local police units in most of the states. The NCIC contains, among other things, data on stolen cars and stolen license plates and the police histories of convicted criminals. The case of the NCIC network is an interesting study because, in it, the informational needs of the police and the information-providing capabilities of computers and telecommunications run head-on into Congressional concern for the right of informational privacy. When a police officer stops a speeding car and approaches it to make an arrest, he would like to know something about the car and driver. Is the car stolen? Does the owner have a history of resisting arrest? Forewarned is forearmed. About two years ago, however, an innocent man was killed by an arresting officer forearmed by forewarning with incorrect information. In the most recent chapter, the Senate Committee on Government Operations caused to be rejected the NCIC's request for permission to acquire a message-switched network to speed up communication with state and local police.

Social Security: In the U.S., the Social Security Administration (SSA) distributes more than $100 billion a year to more than 20 million people and interacts with millions of clients each year through about 1300 offices manned full-time and 3000 manned part-time. The set of computer processible data bases that support SSA operations contains more than a trillion characters, and it is estimated that in those operations each year several trillions of characters flow from one location to another, about a tenth of a trillion by a network and processing system called the "SSADARS system," and the rest mainly by mail.

In 1976, the SSA began planning the modernization of the process through which it discharges its massive responsibilities [38]. The new process will make even heavier use of computers than does the present one and there will be much consultation and updating of central or regional data bases from local offices. (The present process requires several computer areas, each with multiple mainframes, more than a hundred disk drives, and more than a hundred tape drives—and, in all, approximately 400,000 magnetic tapes.) The new communication subsystem will, therefore, be a network of very major proportions, probably a dedicated SSA network operated by the General Services Administration or (improbably in the near term) a part of an even larger and more comprehensive network. Most technologically developed countries will sooner or later have social security networks.

2.8 Protection

If military, intelligence, and police networks are reckoned as networks for protection, then protection is a very large category of network applications. There is another member of the class that deserves mention.

Home and neighborhood security: Several of the projected applications of computers in the home relate to security: sentry against intrusion, fire, and gas and water leakage, monitoring the well-being of the elderly and infirm, and "electronic babysitting." In most of these applications, computers will be better at detecting trouble than in correcting it, and there will be a strong requirement for communication with remote persons or agencies. At present, some burglar alarms are connected by dedicated lines to central security offices or police stations and some "dial up" in the event of trouble. If a packet network were available, it would probably be less expensive and it would provide a wider range of options, including absent members of the family, friends, and neighbors as well as security companies and public agencies.

It seems possible that a neighborhood communication medium (with a broader fan-out or faster sequencing of calls than the telephone) might be just what is required for the elderly to help one another achieve a higher level of security and peace of mind. CB radio or house-to-house (or apartment-to-apartment) wiring or a multipurpose packet network could provide the medium.

Probably just conversation of the kind that prevails on CB radio interconnections would go a long way, but it could be reinforced by slightly higher technology. Home computers could be programmed to interpret a variety of indicators of trouble—the sound of a fall, too long a flow of water, the refrigerator door open, prolonged quiescence—and to ask for an "all's well" report whenever there was cause for concern. Failing to be satisfied that all was indeed well, the computer could call for help. It would have a list of participating neighbors and a schedule of probable availability for each, and—by communicating with their home computers—it could quickly find someone to look in and check, or provide assistance. It has been suggested that a neighborhood net could monitor its clients while they were walking on the sidewalks as well as while they were at home, and a small device has been demonstrated that sends out a radio signal when its wearer falls down—or for some other reason becomes horizontal [31]. If neighborhood networks existed, there would probably be no end of inventions to exploit them in the interest of security: heartbeat monitors, breathing monitors, footstep sensors, and so on. And if the present trend of population statistics continues, security applications might constitute a significant sector of the network application pie.

2.9 Education and Awareness

Beginning with the last section and continuing now into this one, the focus of interest has moved from the organization—or the individual as a member of an organization—to the individual as an individual in the primary family group in the home. Probably the most important network prospects for the individual in this century lie in education and training.

Computer-based education and training: We assume that advances in computer representation of knowledge and in computer mediation of interactions between people and knowledge bases will advance computer-based education and training far beyond the "expensive page turners" and drill and practice routines that are associated in many minds with the term "computer assisted instruction." We assume that knowledge bases accessible through networks will eventually accumulate more knowledge, in each of many fields of learning, than typical teachers are able to master and retain, and that the knowledge in the knowledge bases will be well organized (by experts in each field) and effectively accessible to students at all levels of mastery and aptitude. However, computer-based techniques for the representation, organization, and exploration of knowledge are at present still topics of research—and even if they were fully developed today, it would still take a decade or two to translate the content of the many fields of learning into computer-processible knowledge bases. During the coming years, therefore, application of networks in the area of computer-based education and training will be preliminary and propaedeutic. Perhaps toward the end of the century it will approach its ultimate volume and significance— and be among the top three or four uses of networks.

News: At present, most people gain their awareness of what is going on in the world mainly through mass media that report on events rather than processes, that select a few news items instead of covering the news, and that give everyone, regardless of his or her interest pattern, the same few selections. Networking has the potential of changing the news into a multidimensional dynamic model of the world that each individual can explore in his own way, selecting for himself the topics, the time scales, the levels of depth and detail, and the modes of interrogation and presentation. Interest profiles and other techniques of selective dissemination may play important roles, but networking in principle removes the necessity of disseminating (with its implication that the initiative lies mainly with the transmitter) and opens the door to self-directed exploration and investigation by the receiver of the news. To provide the multidimensional dynamic model for exploration and investigation would, of course, be a demanding responsibility for the gatherers and organizers of news, but they gather and organize much more even now than they print or (especially) broadcast. There will probably be a long slow evolution from the newspaper/newsmagazine format and the nightly news format through increasing levels of user initiative toward truly user-dominated interaction with a whole-world knowledge base.

3 Requirements Imposed upon Networks by Applications

Now that we have sketched out several applications, we should examine briefly the network characteristics they require. The applications do not all require the same network characteristics, of course. One application may require one pattern of characteristics, while another application may require another pattern. Some of the frequently required characteristics are the following:

1. *Bidirectional Transmission:* Most applications require two-way communication—if not the capability of sending and receiving simultaneously (full duplex), then at least the capability of alternating between sending and receiving (half duplex).

2. *Freedom from Error:* One wrong bait may completely change the meaning, especially if numerical data are represented nonredundantly. In such cases, even though the basic communication channel itself is not error free, the end-to-end communications must be made error free through the use of adequate error handling mechanisms.

3. *Efficiency Despite Burstiness:* A source that transmits short bursts of information and is quiescent between bursts typically does not wish to pay for channel time while it is quiescent. Both human beings and computers are bursty sources.

4. *Low Cost per Bit:* The cost of network service depends, of course, upon many nontechnical factors as well as upon the technical effi-

ciency of the network in converting its resources into services. But technical efficiency is a very strong and basic factor. This characteristic refers to the cost of transmitting one bit from source to destination. The relation of cost to distance is considered separately.

5. *High Connectivity:* A source may need to transmit to any one or more of many destinations. A destination (i.e., user) may need to examine many sources.

6. *High Information Rate:* Wide-band channels are capable of transmitting many bits per second. The criteria for "high," "wide," and "many" vary widely with type of signal and level of expectation. The 50,000-bits/s information rate of most of the ARPANET channels seems like a high information rate for ordinary interactive computing, but it is too low for convenient transmission of large files (e.g., high-resolution photographs) and far too low for moving pictures, even low-resolution television pictures.

7. *Security:* Security is a complex of characteristics, some of which provide the technical basis for the protection of privacy. Others have to do with preventing disruption of service and protecting against fraud and theft.

8. *Privacy:* In the U.S., this complex of informational rights, including but by no means limited to protection against eavesdropping, has been formulated by the President's Commission on Privacy and, to a considerable extent, expressed in legislation in the Privacy Act of 1977. Other nations also have privacy laws, of course, some of them in some respects more stringent than ours.

9. *Authentication:* A good authentication scheme provides the electronic equivalent of a signature. Ideally, authentication identifies the author of a document and makes it impossible for him to escape responsibility for the authorship. Ideally, also, authentication makes it impossible for anyone to change even one character or bit of the document without destroying the "signature."

10. *High Reliability:* Low probability that network service, as seen by the application, will be impaired by macroscopic malfunctions. For present purposes, we distinguish between macroscopic malfunctions and microscopic errors in bit transmission.

11. *Full-Duplex Transmission:* Some applications require, and most are favored by, the capability of sending to another station and receiving from it at the same time.

12. *Priority Service:* Guaranteed or preferential service, especially when the network is congested, is widely regarded as essential for certain very important functions or for certain very important persons.

13. *Speech Capability:* Present speech circuits transmit alphanumeric information inefficiently, and most present data networks were not designed to transmit speech. It will be advantageous, however, to integrate speech with data.

14. *Pictures:* It will be advantageous to integrate pictures, also, into the repertoire. Graphs, charts, diagrams, and simple sketches fit readily into the pattern of data transmission, but high-resolution pictures and, especially, moving pictures require high information transmission rates. This characteristic is essentially a second "information rate"—but scaled in such a way as to be more demanding of very-wide-band capabilities.

15. *Insensitivity to Distance:* Synchronous satellites and packet switching both tend to make the difficulty and cost of transmission less dependent on distance than they are in traditional communication systems. Rarely is it an absolute requirement that difficulty and cost be independent of distance, but often it is desirable.

16. *Short Transit Time Delay:* If the sum of the signal-transit time and the signal-waiting-in-buffer time is too great, an application may be slowed down too much or disrupted. The 0.2-s delay introduced by transmission via a synchronous satellite somewhat disturbs two-way speech communication. The delay introduced by transmission from one processor to another may slow down the operation of a multiprocessor that is a network of microcomputers or microcomputers.

17. *Uniform Time Delay:* In some applications, successive segments of the signal must reach the destination in sequence (or be put back into sequence if they arrive in scrambled order). Note that reordering may cause all the segments to be delayed as much as the most-delayed segment.

18. *Broadcast Capabilities:* Some applications require, and some are favored by, the capability of transmitting to many or all destinations concurrently.

19. *Mobility:* Some or all of the stations may need to move from place to place and may need to communicate in transit.

To obtain rough measures of the requirements imposed upon networks by the several applications, we filled in the body of (an early version of) Table I.[1]   Into each cell we entered a number to indicate our intuitive rating of the importance of the characteristic for the application. The rating scale we used runs from 0 (lowest) to 5 (highest). For example, we considered connnectivity to rate at 4 in importance for mail and message systems because mail and messages typically fan out widely from senders to receivers and fan in to receivers from a wide distribution of senders. We did not assign a 5 because mail and message systems would still be valuable (cf., the plans of Satellite Business Systems) if connectivity were limited to within organizations. In the case of column 6, information rate, we used a somewhat special scheme. The numbers from 1 through 5 encode five class intervals of information rate in bits/s: 1) 75–300, 2) 300–1000, 3)1000–10,000, 4) 10,000–1,000,000, and 5) above 1,000,000. For the rough purposes of our analysis, nevertheless, we shall interpret the entries in column 6, as all the other entries, to be estimates of the importance of the (columnar) characteristics for the (row) application.

Figure 7.1 shows the relative importance of the 19 network characteristics. As one examines the average ratings of the characteristics, it comes as no surprise that bidirectionality is very important. It is the "co" in "communication."

It may be slightly surprising, however, that freedom from error is so important. It is freedom from error as seen by the application, of course. There are bound to be errors in the raw network channels, but they may be detected and eliminated by error-correcting circuits or by retransmission. "Error-free" may in practice mean one bit error in 10^{12} or 10^{14} bits, on the average. The importance of achieving an extremely low error rate stems in part from the fact that many of the applications involve information, such as financial data, in which changing a single character could make a great difference. Freedom from error is required, also, by most cryptographic schemes. Where freedom from error is not required by an application, one can usually find error detecting and correcting mechanisms within the application itself. Such mechanisms are quite evident, for example, in human conversation. But it greatly simplifies most network applications if the network can be counted on to do the error handling.

---

[1]   In order to obtain a broader basis on which to think about, and possibly model, the relations between networks and applications, we suggest that you (the reader) photocopy Table I and fill in some rows with your estimates of the importance of the characteristics to the applications. We have also provided room for you to define additional applications or characteristics.

Table I Importance coefficients of network characteristics for various classes of network applications (each cell entry should be subjective rating of importance on a scale from 0 (low) to 5 (high)).

NETWORK APPLICATIONS	1 Bi-Directionality	2 Freedom from Error	3 Efficiency Despite Burstiness	4 Low Cost Per Bit	5 Connectivity	6 Information Rate	7 Security	8 Privacy	9 Authentication	10 Reliability	11 Full-Duplex	12 Priority	13 Speech Capability	14 Picture Capability	15 Insensitivity to Distance	16 Shortness of Delay	17 Uniformity of Delay	18 Broadcast Capability	19 Mobility	SPACE FOR ADDITIONAL CHARACTERISTICS	SUBJECTIVE RATING OF IMPORTANCE OF APPLICATION
BASIC																					
Transmission																					
Storage																					
Processing																					
Information																					
COMMUNICATION																					
Mail, Messages																					
Duologue																					
Teleconferencing																					
Speech																					
Encrypted Speech																					
Still Pictures																					
Moving Pictures																					
NEOPAPERWORK																					
Telework																					
Augmentation																					
Task Management																					
MANAGEMENT																					
M.I.S.																					
Modeling																					
COMMERCE																					
Electronic Markets																					
Computerized Commerce																					
Employment Services																					
PROFESSIONAL																					
Monitoring Patients																					
Monitoring Non-Patients																					
Medical Records																					
Medical Knowledge Bases																					
GOVERNMENT																					
Military C³																					
Logistics																					
NCIC																					
Social Security																					
PROTECTION																					
Home Security																					
EDUCATION AND AWARENESS																					
Computer Based Education																					
News																					
SPACE FOR ADDITIONAL APPLICATIONS																					

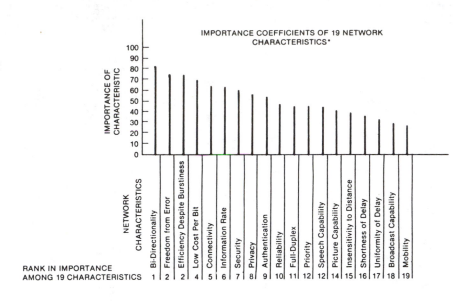

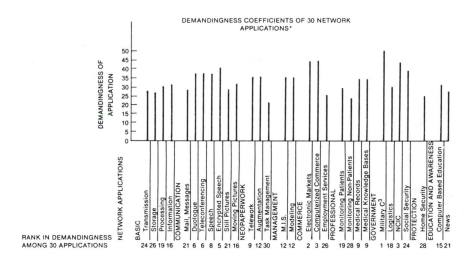

Figure 7.1 Importance coefficients of 19 network characteristics and demandingness coefficients of 30 network applications. (*Divide each number by 1000 to scale the sum to unity.)

Ability to handle bursty transmissions efficiently ranks third. The advantage provided by this characteristic translates directly into a cost advantage.

Low cost ranks fourth in importance. It did not rank higher because we recognized that certain of the applications, such as military command, control, and communication, are relatively insensitive to cost. Also, other network applications such as mail and messages are already quite cost competitive with their conventional counterparts and do not demand very-low-cost facilities.

Connectivity ranks fifth in importance. The reason connectivity does not rank higher is that we assigned only a medium score for connectivity to applications that required only connectivity within an organization or within a region, and many applications could function—though perhaps at some disadvantage—with such limited connectivity.

Information rate ranks sixth. We interpret that to mean that very wide-band transmission is not vital to most of the applications and that most of them could be satisfied with an information rate in the range 1000–10,000 bits/s. However, that is the information rate seen by the application. To handle heavy traffic, and to handle a few of the applications, a network should have channels of considerably greater bandwidth than that.

Security, the complex that includes assurance of service when required and protection against fraud and theft, ranks seventh.

Privacy, the complex that includes protection against disclosure of personal information and unauthorized use of it, ranks eighth.

Authentication, a characteristic closely associated with security, ranks ninth.

At the other end of the ranking, mobility (19th) is not required by most of the classes of applications we considered—but, of course, is essential for some applications.

Broadcast capability (18th) was scored low because it is not needed at all in many applications and is needed only occasionally in others such as mail and message systems—and, when needed, usually can be simulated adequately by repeated point-to-point transmissions.

Uniformity of time delay (17th) is important mainly for speech transmission. If speech had been given a weighting proportional to its probable eventual importance in networking, uniformity of time delay would have ranked higher.

The capability of giving preferential treatment to high priority traffic (12th) ranks as high as it does because we viewed priority in the context of present-day systems that may introduce considerable delays into the delivery of some or all of their messages. In the context of future systems in which a whole transmission will take less than a second, priority may be much less important. However, the need for priority is unlikely to vanish. Priority classes are useful in queuing messages for processing by people and in indicating the prioritizer's sense of urgency or importance to the recipient. Moreover, even very wide-band systems tend to be designed just barely to handle expected peak loads, and even such systems can be overloaded—in which case, prioritization might be helpful. On the other hand, it is conceivable that the processing of priorities might slow a system down more than eliminating low priority traffic could speed it up.

We do not want to attribute too much value to our no-doubt-idiosyncratic subjective estimates of the importance of network characteristics to applications, but we would like to carry the analysis another step to illustrate what we think might be a valuable method. It attempts to deal with the relative merits of various networks or network architectures.

The method begins with a table of applications versus characteristics similar to Table I except that each application has an importance weight and all its cell values are multiplied by that weight before the columns are totaled. The method assumes, also, a table of networks or network architectures versus network characteristics such as Table II. The entries in Table II represent our very subjective impressions of the degrees to which the characteristics at the top characterize the networks at the left-hand side. The values are certainly not definitive. In the case of the hypothetical augmentation of the ARPANET, they assume major increases in number of subscribers and in information rate, and they assume that advanced provisions are made for security, privacy, authentication, and priority service. They assume, also, that satellite relays are incorporated into the network along with wide-band surface channels and that there is a packet-radio subsystem to serve mobile applications.

In the case of the projected SBS service, indeed, they are based only on the most informal information, and they make rather optimistic estimates about the characteristics of the hypothetical networks that would be developed on the basis of the SBS facilities. The reader is invited to substitute his or her own estimates.

To determine the suitability of a network or network architecture to a set of applications, one simply multiplies each cell value in its row in (the table like) Table II by the importance of the corresponding characteristic at the bottom of (the table like) Table I—and then finds the sum (across the row) of the products.

To illustrate the use of the method, we worked with the four networks of Table II and with four sets of applications. Application set 1 was the set shown in Table I. Sets 2, 3, and 4 were subsets consisting of— set 2: speech and encrypted speech, set 3: still and moving pictures, and set 4: duologue and augmentation. (We gave equal or uniform weighting

Table II Estimated degrees to which four selected networks possess the 19 network characteristics. (The ratings are the authors' intuitive estimates on a scale from 0 (low) to 5 (high).)

NETWORK CHARACTERISTICS / NETWORKS	1 Bi-Directionality	2 Freedom from Error	3 Efficiency Despite Burstiness	4 Low Cost Per Bit	5 Connectivity	6 Information Rate	7 Security	8 Privacy	9 Authentication	10 Reliability	11 Full-Duplex	12 Priority	13 Speech Capability	14 Picture Capability	15 Insensitivity to Distance	16 Shortness of Delay	17 Uniformity of Delay	18 Broadcast Capability	19 Mobility
Dial Telephone	5	2	0	2	5	3	2	2	1	3	2	1	4	2	0	4	4	2	2
ARPANET	5	4	4	3	3	3	1	2	1	4	4	0	2	2	4	3	3	1	1
Hypothetical Augmented ARPANET*	5	4	4	4	5	5	4	4	4	4	4	3	4	4	4	4	4	3	4
Hypothetical Corporate Network Using SBS**	5	4	4	4	2	5	4	4	4	4	4	3	4	5	4	2	4	3	0

*A hypothetical network based on ARPANET technology but with very wide-band ground and satellite channels, very many subscribers, advanced provisions for security, an authentication scheme, arrangements for priority, and a mobile/portable radio adjunct based on the ARPA Radio Net.

**A hypothetical network of the kind that might be based on the projected facilities of the Satellite Business Systems Corporation and used by a large corporation with geographically distributed branches. It is assumed that this network is used only within the corporation and therefore has restricted connectivity.

to the applications in each set—to all 30 in the first set and to both of the two in each of sets 2, 3, and 4.)

We obtained the 16 appropriateness indexes shown in Table III. The dial telephone network performs best in the speech applications, of course, but it does not appear to do badly in the others. (Giving more weight to cost tends to reduce its scores.) The experimental ARPANET appears to perform well on speech, which surprised us despite the fact that experiments on the transmission of compressed speech over the ARPANET have been very successful, but best on duologue and augmentation, which we expected. In the scoring, the ARPANET suffers because, being experimental, it was not developed in respect to some of the important network characteristics. Assuming such development (Hypothetical Augmented ARPANET) yields the appropriateness scores

Table III Appropriateness scores for four selected networks, each rated on four different sets of applications. (The appropriateness scores are based on a scale from 0 (low) to 5 (high). The way they were determined is described in the text.)

NETWORKS / APPLICATION SETS	1 30 Applications of Table I	2 Speech and Encrypted Speech	3 Still and Moving Pictures	4 Duologue and Augmentation
Dial Telephone	2.5	2.8	2.4	2.6
Experimental ARPANET	2.8	2.8	2.5	3.0
Hypothetical Augmented ARPANET	4.1	3.9	4.0	3.8
Hypothetical Corporate Net Based on SBS Service	3.8	3.5	3.9	3.8

in the third row of Table III, which are all toward the upper end of the five-point scale. The hypothetical corporate network based on the projected SBS service appears to perform almost as well as the hypothetically augmented ARPANET, suffering in the comparison only because we assumed for it limited connectivity (intercorporate communication only), no surface channels (and therefore always the 0.2-s satellite delay), and no mobility. Those lacks showed up only in the average over the 30 applications and in the speech applications.

Obviously, the result obtained with the method is no better than the ratings it processes, and we do not make any claims for our ratings. We believe, nonetheless, that the scheme puts into an orderly array some of the basic factors that determine the relative appropriatenesses of various networks for various sets of applications, and that it leads the users of the method—or at least it led us, as we used it—to consider the factors carefully and to think about how they act and interact. Upon examining the interactions, it soon becomes clear that the linear weighting scheme smooths over many nonlinear logical interactions, and that a more advanced model would have to be more like a computer program than three tables and a pocket calculator. Nevertheless, the first step has to be to survey the variables that are active in networking, and the simple scheme provides a start on that.

4 Issues

4.1 Brittleness

Brittleness is approximately the inverse of the lauded complex of system attributes: flexibility, robustness, and gracefulness of degradation. Brittleness often arises from a quest for efficiency or economy. If you space the pony express posts as far apart as a fresh pony can run, then the mail does not get through when an emergency forces you to use a tired pony. A socioeconomic unit with a minimum-capacitance supply system avoids the waste inherent in having products stagnate in the pipeline but crumbles in a siege. Networks will almost surely be more efficient than the systems they supplant. Should not that expectation prompt us to ask whether they will also be more brittle?

From an engineering point of view, the preferred approach is to avoid brittleness through judicious choices in the architecture and design of networks. The dynamic routing feature of the ARPANET, for example, permits the network to continue to operate, as far as two functionally connected host computers are concerned, as long as there is some path left intact between them. Indeed, just as it is to reliability, redundancy is the main engineering antidote to brittleness in networks—redundancy of interconnection, redundancy of power supply, and redundancy of information storage. Moreover, sophisticated uses of redundancy, as in restructurable logic and error-detecting codes, provide much greater returns in robustness than do brute force applications that cost the same.

4.2 Electronic Imperialism or Technology Transfer to the World

Aviation may have had more impact in technologically not-yet-developed but developing countries with poor roads and few rails than in technologically developed countries that already had working transportation systems before airmail routes and airlines came upon the scene. Brazilia, for example, would not have been feasible without the DC-3. Analogously, networks may have their most dramatic effects where there are few critical masses of knowledge and few self-reinforcing centers of intellectual activity. Networks may link the geographically separated subcritical foci of cognition in the developing world with the concentrated supercritical centers of the developed world, bringing the former deeply into the interaction patterns of the latter and making it much easier for the former to grow and advance. If networks do turn out to have such an effect, it may represent a new dimension of imperialism, or it may open up broad new avenues of technology transfer, or, as seems most likely, it may look one way to some and the other way to others.

Although technology transfer to the developing world is often viewed as a matter of delivering journals, reports, and books and of transmitting data to third-world countries, truly effective transfer is a transfer not of data or of information but of knowledge and it flows through human interaction. Perhaps the most effective pattern involves graduate study by promising young people from developing countries in leading graduate schools in developed countries—followed by work experience in the developed countries and then return to form foci of advanced technology in the developing countries. But the difficulties with even that pattern are well known: reluctance to return resulting in the "brain drain," or isolation after return resulting in unhappiness and ineffectuality. What is needed is a way to return without breaking the ties of interaction with teachers, fellow students, managers, and coworkers in the centers of technology that, thanks to their highly developed intellectual and motivational supports, made possible the transfer of knowledge in the first place. Networks can fill that need. The ARPANET has provided several instances, albeit just in the U.S., in which students have remained functionally and motivationally in the research groups in which they worked for their degrees until they could build up self-sustaining foci of their own in their postdoctoral locations. It seems very likely that the postdoctoral locations could as well be in foreign countries, even countries with little technology, if only they had network connections and sufficient funding to keep local terminals in reliable operation and to pay for computing time and storage somewhere on the net. Indeed, it seems likely that technology transfer to developing countries could become real and effective through no more than informal extension of patterns of interaction that have become well established in the ARPANET community. But there is no reason to keep the patterns entirely informal. Formal associations between universities, not-for-profit organizations, and business firms in the have-technology and the have-not-technology countries would surely increase the productiveness of the technology-transfer enterprise [39].

We do not want to try to take sides with respect to, and we cannot hope to offer a solution to the problem suggested by the juxtaposition of "electronic imperialism" and 'technology transfer." We do suggest, however, that the prospect of networking between the developed and the developing worlds deserves very serious study. From the point of view of the imperialist, it may well be that packet networks will be to the not-far-distant future what clipper ships (or were they packet ships?) and clipper aircraft were to the not-far-distant past. From the point of view of the countries that need and want technology transfer, packet links to technologically developed countries may be by far the best way to get it if they can figure out how to keep the electronic colonialism from coming with it.

4.3 *Unity, Federation, or Fragmentation*

If we could look in on the future at, say, the year 2000, would we see a unity, a federation, or a fragmentation? That is: would we see a single multipurpose network encompassing all applications and serving everyone? Or a more or less coherent system of intercommunicating networks? Or an incoherent assortment of isolated noncommunicating networks, most of them dedicated to single functions or serving single organizations? The first alternative—the strongly unified network—seems improbable: of almost zero probability if the scope is taken as worldwide and still of very low probability even if the scope is taken to be the U.S., which seems to engender pluralistic solutions to most problems. The third alternative—many separate noninterconnecting networks—is what would be reached by proceeding with a plan and, therefore, may be judged rather probable, but it would be very disappointing to all those who hope that the whole will be much greater than the sum of the parts, i.e., that many of the projected applications will facilitate and contribute to one another to such an extent that the overall value will grow combinatorially. The middle alternative—the more or less coherent network of networks—appears to have a fair probability and also to be desirable, but it brings with it the problem of how to achieve enough coherence to support fast and facile intercommunications among the subnetworks when required, and that may be a difficult problem. Let us consider first why coherence is desirable and then turn to the difficulty of achieving it.

"Coherence" characterizes a system in which all the parts articulate well and function in synergy and in which the subsystems are compatible and cooperative. In an information network, coherence is desirable partly for the same reason it is desirable in a telephone system: the value to a typical user increases as the number of other accessible users increases. This is true no matter whether the users are people or computers. The importance of coherence is amplified, however, by the fact that some of the applications of computer networks will involve several functions operating on common information. Planning a trip, for example, will require interaction among: your calendar program and the calendar programs of people you will visit, the reservations programs of airlines, car rental services, and hotels, the funds transfer systems of your bank and several other banks, your company's travel office, and perhaps data basses pertinent to business to be transacted on the trip. The computers could not be of much help in the planning if each function or service had its own separate network or if their network were physically inter-connectable but incompatible at various levels of protocol. Indeed, co-herent interconnection of diverse functions will be essential if networks are to live up to expectations in electronic message services, computer-ized commerce, delivery of social services that involve both federal and state governments, and many military and intelligence applications.

Coherence, however, is a condition that has to be planned and striven for. It does not arise in a short time through evolution—at least not through evolution that conforms to the spontaneous-variation-plus-natural-selection model. Will the forces that are operating in the present network situation foster a sufficient degree of coherence for networks to fulfill their promise? On the positive side is the fact that a standard packet-switching interface protocol X.25 [40] was formulated and agreed upon in an unusually short time and that the interconnection of such dissimilar networks as Telenet [3] and the Canadian data network has already occurred. Also on the positive side is the possibility that one or two commercial networks, such as the one being developed by AT&T and the one being developed by Satellite Business Systems, will domi-nate the network market and thereby create the kind of coherence that IBM has created in a large part of the computer software field.

However, the other factors seem to work against coherent intercon-nection. First, the network situation is evolving without any national policy. (Within the U.S. government, it is evolving without any federal policy.) Several countries are building networks independently. Many companies are building networks independently. Second, although the lines may be leased from the same telephone company that leases lines to everyone else, there is some security in having one's own dedicated network. The need for security in such areas as EFT may be stronger than the need for interconnection. Third, wherever personal informa-tion is concerned, and especially in the federal government, privacy has become a major issue, and a simplistic interpretation of the privacy problem sets interconnection into opposition with privacy. Fourth, re-search and development in the area of network security and privacy assurance have not been and are not being supported at a high enough level to create—soon enough—a technology that will let one say: "You can have both interconnection and security, both interconnection and privacy; you can have your cake and eat it, too." Actually, the technology of communications security is rather well developed [41]-[44]—except for uncertainties arising from the "56-bit controversy" [45]—as a result of many years of work in the military intelligence area, but the tech-nology of computer security is less well developed [46], and nontechno-logical aspects—plant, personnel, and operational aspects—of network security are not in good condition at all.

The conclusion with respect to unification, federation, or fragmentation must be: we should strive for the kind of federation of networks that will provide coherent interconnection where needed and justified and, at the same time, provide informational privacy and security. That will require planning at national and international levels. It will require intensified research and development in network security and in internetting. And it will require an elevation of the ongoing discourse about privacy—to a level on which legislative and administrative policies can be defined clearly and networks can be designed responsibly.

4.4 Privacy

It is now very widely understood that the collection of large amounts of personal information in computer processible data banks tends to jeopardize personal privacy. The main reason, of course, is that aggregation and computerization open up the possibility of invading privacy efficiently and on a massive scale. At the same time, they open up the possibility of protecting privacy tirelessly and algorithmically and of using the personal data effectively in the effort to accomplish the legitimate purposes for which the data were collected. Indeed, the stage is set for a battle between the forces of good and evil.

The stage is, however, not set in reasonable balance. The things required for the protection of privacy in information networks are policy and technology: legislative and administrative policy to define what is to be achieved and a technological basis for achieving it. In the U.S., the legislation is the Privacy Act of 1974 and the administrative policy is an OMB Circular [47]. Both are cast in terms of absolutes. The technological basis, as mentioned in the preceding section, is a combination of communications security and computer security. Because computer security is a relatively new and neglected subject, it is difficult to provide convincing assurance to an intelligent skeptic that any proposed interconnection of personal data, transmission channels, information processors, and interrogation-and-display facilities will not jeopardize privacy. Repeatedly, indeed, the advocates of proposed federal data networks have failed to present convincing analyses of the threats to privacy and of the trade-offs between privacy and mission effectiveness—and, repeatedly, their request for permission to procure such networks (e.g., FEDNET, NCIC upgrade, IRS Tax Administrative System) have been sidetracked or denied with good reason.

At least in government circles, therefore, the issue of privacy is a very real and central network issue. Before it can be solved, three things have to be done. 1) The technology of information security has to be improved to the point at which reasonable analyses can be made and assurances can be given. 2) Network advocates have to develop plans and justifications that take privacy into account and provide strong assurances that it will be protected. And 3) the members of the oversight committees and their staffs have to face the fact that to protect privacy by precluding interconnection is not a very satisfactory solution for the long term. They should support and foster the accomplishment of steps 1) and 2) with the aim of receiving plans and proposals that they would not have to kill.

4.5 *Other Issues*

Space limitation precludes substantial discussion of other issues, but there are several that should be discussed. We shall discuss only a few of them, and those only very briefly.

Transborder data flow: Several European countries are beginning to restrict the flow of personal (or personnel) data across their borders on the ground that they must protect the informational privacy of their citizens against threats implicit in data processing in countries with less stringent privacy laws. Some of the countries have laws or regulations that preclude the transmission of encrypted information through their public communication facilities. Many believe that such restrictions may be used to discriminate against foreign (e.g., American) data processing firms and against multinational corporations.

Technology export and import: International networks can be expected to facilitate greatly the transfer of scientific and technical information and know-how among the technologically developed nations. From a nationalistic point of view, one can see both advantages and disadvantages in such transfer to ideological, military, and economic competitors. The advantages are mainly humanistic and short-term economic. The disadvantages are mainly security-related and long-term economic. The interplay of advantages and disadvantages is giving rise to issues that will probably intensify.

Competition versus monopoly and free enterprise versus regulation: These are the issues of the "Bell Bill" (Consumer Communications Reform Act), Computer Inquiry II, and several recent decisions of the Federal Communications Commission that have favored competition in the telecommunications industry. How these issues are settled will to a large extent determine who operates the networks of the future in the U.S. and how such applications as electronic message service and "the office of the future" are implemented.

Nature of office work and workforce: Some of the network applications we have discussed would tend to alter markedly the nature of white-collar work and the knowledge and skills required of members of workforce. That fact will give rise to issues involving reeducation and retraining, pay commensurate with responsibility, and displacement of labor by automation.

Impact on productivity: Many people are expecting that applications such as electronic mail and office automation will significantly increase productivity, but there are as yet few if any definitive experiences with such applications or quantitative models of them that will convince skeptics. Impact-on-productivity may become a major issue in and of itself.

Educational applications of networks: Packet-switched and satellite networks, together with the great advances being made in computers, appear to open the door to revolutionary improvements in education, but much more than mere access and mere hardware will be required to achieve truly significant results. The issue that is arising is whether the society values education enough to support the long and difficult effort that will be required to develop effective computer- and network-based methods—or whether there will be another wave of premature exploitation followed by disappointment as there was in the computer-assisted-instruction "revolution" of the early 1960's.

Networks versus stand-alone systems: Why do we need time sharing when everyone can have his or her own microcomputer? What good is a network when one can have a whole library on a video disk? Those questions have answers, of course, in such applications as electronic message systems, distributed but cooperating "offices of the future," and computerized commerce, but the questions will nevertheless constitute a major issue. Microcomputers and inexpensive digital storage devices have significantly changed the network concept. Less than a decade ago, a computer network was something that provided access to a time-sharing system. Now it is a facility to support communication among spatially distributed people and computers and to supply people and computers with common information bases and supplementary storage and processing capabilities.

World leadership: An important latent issue is implicit in the fact that different people have quite different perceptions of the importance of networking. A significant fraction of the people who have had experience as developers or intensive users of a packet-switching network believe they have been in on the beginning of a new era and that descendants of the ARPANET will constitute the nervous system of the world. On the other hand, most of the people who now determine the kind of national policy that earlier fostered the merchant marine, the railroads, the airlines, and the interstates seem not to be aware that any significant new potential exists or that there may be any reason to move rapidly to take advantage of it. And, of course, if it is meaningful at all to the man in the street, the term "information network" still suggests the telephone system, the radio, or a television network. In that situation, it is difficult to project as an issue the importance of networks to world economic leadership. We believe, nevertheless, that it is such an issue, and we hope that it will soon be recognized as such an issue.

Totalitarian control: If almost all the telecommunications in an area were based on computerized networks controlled by an organization— say by a government—then, in the absence of effective safeguards, that organization could map the life space of every individual and record the business transactions of every company. The notion of telecommunications in the hands of a "big brother with computers" goes beyond the bounds of what is usually called "invasion of privacy" into the realm of totalitarian control. One can detect at least a trace of the "big brother" issue in the coldness of certain members of Congress toward, and the rejection by the OMB of, the plans (mentioned earlier) of the IRS to develop a computer- and network-based Tax Administration System. The mere possibility of subversion was enough to kill the system. It is of the utmost importance, of course, to develop truly effective safeguards against misuse of networks for purposes of social control. But such safeguards will be more difficult to devise than safeguards against ordinary invasion of privacy or against fraud and theft. Networks will have to be designed in such a way that representatives of diverse interests can satisfy themselves that there is no subversion and that the audit trails are not dossiers. And the arrangements will have to be dictator-proof. We think that is a very great task and that it is being neglected.

5 Conclusions

Shakespeare could have been foreseeing the present situation in information networking when he said, "...What's past is prologue; what to come, in yours and my discharge" [48]. Most of the applications that will shape the future of networking are now in the stage of conceptualization or in the stage of early development. But it seems possible that a "network of networks" will, even in this century, become the nervous system of the world and that its applications will significantly change the way we live and work. The degree to which the potentials of networking will be realized will depend upon how we resolve some of the issues that have been discussed.

The value of information networks will depend critically upon their connectivity and their ability to connect any one of many sources to any one or more of many destinations. High connectivity will be precluded if conditions force the development of many separate, independent, incompatible networks. One condition that would force such an incoherent development is the combination of 1) a need for security against loss of "electronic funds" and (other) proprietary information and 2) the lack of a technology capable of providing security in an interconnected network or network of networks. That would lead to what we have called "fragmentation." Another such condition is based in a similar way on a combination of need for informational privacy and lack of the technology necessary to protect it except by isolating the privacy-sensitive data. The rapid and intensive development of computer and network security technology is vital to many network applications.

Many forces are fostering the development of networks to interconnect organizations or branches of organizations and the development of applications to serve organizations, but there are few forces that foster networks to interconnect individuals or network applications to serve individuals. Perhaps the main hope for the provision of network services to individuals—especially network services to individuals at home—is that the Bell System will move (as obviously it would like to do) into the processing, storage, and information-commodity parts of the overall information business. But the telephone companies will be very slow to provide high-information-rate services because they have such large investments in narrow-band facilities. To get inexpensive wide-band channels into homes at an early date, we need a new departure in cable (or fiber-optics) communication, taking off from cable television, or something truly revolutionary like a nation-wide network of aerostationary platforms: microwave platforms at 70,000 ft, supported by helium plus helicopter vanes, and relaying signals from housetop "dishes" a meter in diameter.

Examination of 30 actual and potential applications of networks suggest that the following network characteristics or capabilities are especially important: bidirectionality, freedom from undetected errors, efficiency despite "burstiness" in the transmission pattern, inherently low cost, high connectivity, high information transmission rate, security, privacy, authentication, and reliability. Mobility and broadcast capability turned out to be of the lowest priority in our analysis. Packet-switching and time-division-multiple-access networks, especially such networks with satellite relays, were suggested by the analysis to have the patterns of characteristics required to serve best the full range of applications. The analysis suggests an approach to the selection of the best network to serve any specified application or set of applications.

References

[1] T. H. Myer and C. D. Mooers, *HERMES User's Guide.* Cambridge, MA: Bolt Beranek and Newman, Inc., June 1976.

[2] A. Vezza and M. S. Broos, "An electronic message system: Where does it fit?" in *Proc. IEEE Conf. Trends and Applications 1976: Computer Networks,* New York, Nov. 1976.

[3] A. Vezza, "A model for an electronic postal system, " in *Telecommunications Policy Research Conf. Proc.*, Bruce M. Owen, Ed. Palo Alto, CA: Aspen Institute Program on Communications and Society, Apr. 1975, pp. 146–153.

[4] *SIGMA Message Service: Reference Manual,* Information Sciences Inst., Univ. Southern California, Marina Del Rey, CA, ISI/TM-78-11.

[5] J. B. Rule, "Value choices in electronic funds transfer policy," Office of Telecommunications Policy, Executive Office of the President, Washington, DC, Rep. Domestic Council Committee on the Right of Privacy, Oct. 1975.

[6] T. M. Dunn and J. H. Mirrissey, "Remote computing—An experimental system. Part 1: External specifications," in *Proc., Spring Joint Computer Conf.*, 1974.

[7] J. M. Keller, E. C. Strum, and G. H. Yang, "Remote computing—An experimental system. Part 2: Internal design," in *Proc., Spring Joint Computer Conf.*, 1974.

[8] J. E. Sammet, *Programming Languages: History and Fundamentals.* Englewood Cliffs, NJ: Prentice-Hall, 1969, pp. 226–229.

[9] T. Marill and D. Stern, "The datacomputer—A network data utility," in *AFIPS Conf. Proc.*, Montvale, NJ: AFIPS Press, May 1975.

[10] L. G. Roberts and B. D. Wessler, "Computer network development to achieve resource sharing," *AFIPS Conf. Proc.*, May 1970.

[11] L. G. Roberts, "ARPA network implications," ARPA Network Information Center Doc., 12 982, 1972.

[12] R. M. Metcalfe, "Packet communication," M.I.T. Lab. for Computer Science, MAC/TR-114, Dec. 1973.

[13] "SNDMSG," Tenex User's Guide, Bolt Beranek and Newman, Inc., Cambridge, MA, Oct. 1977.

[14] J. Vallee, "The forum project: Network conferencing and its future applications," *Comput. Networks (Netherlands)*, vol. 1, no. 1, pp. 39–52, June 1976.

[15] M. Turoff, "Party-line and discussion: Computerized conference systems," Office of Emergency Preparedness, Washington, DC, Rep., Apr. 1972.

[16] _____, "Delphi conferencing. Computer-based conferencing with anonymity," in *Technological Forecasting and Social Change*. Washington, DC: National Resource Analysis Center, 1972, vol. 3, no. 2, pp. 159–204.

[17] M. Turoff and J. Scher, "Computerized conferencing and its impact on engineering management," in *Proc. 23rd Annu. Engineering Management Conf. on E–ective Management of Engineering Resources*, Washington, DC, Oct. 1975.

[18] D. C. Engelbart, "Coordinated information services for a discipline- or mission-oriented community," in *Computer Communication Networks*, R. L. Grimsdale and F. F. Kuo, Eds. The Netherlands: Noordhoff International, 1975, pp. 89–99.

[19] D. C. Engelbart, R. W. Watson, and J. C. Norton, "The augmented knowledge workshop," in *AFIPS Conf. Proc.*, vol. 42, New York, June 1973.

[20] _____, *Advanced Intellect-Augmentation Techniques*. Menlo Park, CA: Stanford Research Institute, Feb. 1972.

[21] _____, "Human intellect augmentation techniques," Stanford Research Institute, Menlo Park, CA, Final Rep., 1969.

[22] R. Flesch. *The Art of Plain Talk*. New York: Harper & Brothers, 1946.

[23] J. O. Mason, Jr., "Management-information-systems—the auditor's role," *The International Auditor*, vol. 32, no. 5, pp. 40–48, Sept./Oct. 1975.

[24] S. J. Pokemper, "Management information-systems—A pragmatic survey," *Conf. Board Rec.*, vol. 10, no. 5, pp. 49–54, May 1973.

[25] R. G. Schroeder, "A survey of management science in university operations," *Manage. Sci.—Appl.*, vol. 19, no. 8, pp. 895–906, Apr. 1973.

[26] P. A. Strassman, "Managing the costs of information," *Harvard Bus. Rev.*, vol. 54, no. 5, pp. 133–142, Sept.–Oct. 1976.

[27] G. H. Barnes, R. M. Brown, M. Kato, D. J. Kuck, D. L. Slotnick, and R. A. Stoker, "The Illiac IV computer," *IEEE Trans. Comput.*, vol. C-17, pp. 746–757, 1968.

[28] W. J. Bouknight, S. A. Denenberg, D. E. McIntyre, J. M. Randall, A. H. Sameh, and D. L. Slotnick, "The Illiac IV system," *Proc. IEEE*, vol. 60, pp. 369–388, 1972.

[29] "Self-teaching design and analysis tools offered on timeshared basis," *Comput. Des.*, vol. 17, no. 2, pp. 18–20, Feb. 1978.

[30] I. E. Sutherland, *Computerized Commerce*. Santa Monica, CA: The Rand Paper Series, Rand Corp., Sept. 1975.

[31] National Research Council, Telecommunication for metropolitan areas: Near-term needs and opportunities. Washington, DC: Nat. Acad. Sci., 1977.

[32] L. L. Weed, "Technology is a link, not a barrier, for doctor and patient," *Modern Hospital*, vol. 114, pp. 80–83, Feb. 1970.

[33] ———, *Medical Records, Medical Education, and Patient Care. The Problem-Oriented Record as a Basic Tool*. Chicago, IL: Year Book Medical Publishers, Inc., 1970.

[34] R. Davis, B. Buchanan, and E. Shortliffe, "Production rules as a representation for a knowledge-based consultation program," Stanford Univ. Artificial Intelligence Lab., Stanford, CA, Memo AIM-266, Oct. 1975.

[35] H. Silverman, "A digitalis therapy advisor," M.I.T. Lab. for Computer Science, MAC/TR-143, Jan. 1975.

[36] "GECOS: General Comprehensive Operating Supervisor," Honeywell Information Systems, Waltham, MA, Rep. DD19.

[37] A. Stathopoulos and H. F. Caley, "The Autodin II network," in *EASCON-77 Rec. Proc. IEEE Electronics and Aerospace Systems Convention* (Arlington, VA), Sept. 1977.

[38] Social Security Administration, Office of Advanced Systems, *Recommended Design Concept for the Future SSA Process*, Washington, DC, OAS Pub. No. 005, Apr. 1977.

[39] V. Slamenka, private communication, May 1978.

[40] CCITT, "Recommendation X.25: Interface between data terminal equipment (DTE) and data circuit-terminating equipment (DCE) for terminals operating in the packet mode on public data networks," in *Public Data Networks, Orange Book* (vol. VII.2). Geneva, Switzerland: Sixth Plenary Assembly, International Telecommunications Union, 1977, pp. 70–108.

[41] W. Diffie and M. Hellman, "New directions in cryptography," *IEEE Trans. Inform. Theory*, pp. 644–654, Nov. 1976.

[42] R. Rivest, A. Shamir, and L. Adleman, "A method for obtaining digital signatures and public-key cryptosystems," M.I.T. Lab. for Computer Science, LCS/TM-82, Apr. 1977.

[43] *Federal Register*, vol. 40, no. 52, Mar. 17, 1975.

[44] *Federal Register*, vol. 40, no. 149, Aug. 1, 1975.

[45] W. Diffie and M. Hellman, "Exhaustive cryptanalysis of the NBS data encryption standard," *Computer*, vol. 10, no. 6, pp. 74–84, June 1977.

[46] J. H. Saltzer and M. D. Schroeder, "The protection of information in computer systems," *Proc. IEEE*, vol. 63, pp. 1278–1308, Sept. 1975.

[47] Office of Management and the Budget, OMB Circular A-108, Washington, DC, July 1975.

[48] William Shakespeare, *The Tempest*, act II, scene I.

8

Thinking Ahead: What to Expect from Teleconferencing

Robert Johansen
Christine Bullen

- Since 1968, Bank of America executives in San Francisco and Los Angeles have met regularly without subjecting themselves to the pressures of commuter flights. Using handsome conference rooms decorated with oil paintings of the company's founding fathers, the users flip a single switch and are immediately connected to each other via a high-quality audio conferencing system that allows them to converse.

- Since 1975, IBM has had its own in-house system for still video conferencing. This system displays snapshot-like images on television monitors, accompanied by audio conferencing. Most of the participants have technical backgrounds and find the system useful for discussions that draw on charts, viewgraphs, or diagrams.

- Since 1978, Procter & Gamble employees have had access to Confer—their own computer-based conferencing system. They can use the system directly, by typing their comments on computer terminals and checking periodically for new messages, or indirectly, through secretaries or the company's mail system. These text-based teleconferences are carried out over periods of weeks or months and involve managers from most divisions in the company.

- Since 1981, Aetna Life and Casualty Company has used full-motion video teleconferencing to link its offices in downtown Hartford and in suburban Windsor, Connecticut. The full-color system requires virtually no training to use. The data processing staff at these locations uses the system constantly. Aetna is now expanding the capability beyond the Hartford area to sites in other parts of the country.

- Since 1981, Hewlett-Packard has been using live video presentations by senior executives to introduce new products to its national sales force. participants gather at their local offices, receive the product information from people who developed the item, and ask questions through an audio call-back

Such success stories are sparking the interest of managers throughout the country. The idea of linking corporate offices around the world by some form of teleconferencing for easy—and economical—business communication is certainly attractive to a CEO, a controller, or a harried middle manager with a job to get done. The cost of moving people from place to place is escalating, as is the discomfort of the people being moved. While travel is still a perk for some, it's a pain for many, and managers grumble that there must be a better way. Teleconferencing is an answer to their pleas, but it is not a simple one.

Although a rigid definition of teleconferencing would be premature because the technology is changing so quickly, we use the term to mean interactive group communication through any electronic medium. Audio and full-motion video are probably the best-known forms. Still video snapshots also can be exchanged (often called "slow-scan" or "freeze-frame" teleconferencing), as can keyboarded messages ("computer conferencing" or "electronic mail"), drawings (for example, "electronic blackboard"), or page copies ("fax"). There are also options for large-group gatherings, in which hundreds of viewers watch a live video presentation and have the chance for question-and-answer follow-ups—usually via an audio network. These events are often more like television productions than business meetings but are part of the wide generic class of meetings called teleconferences.

One important difference among various forms of teleconferencing is the time element. If all participants are present simultaneously—regardless of location or time zone—the conference is synchronous, or "real time." Presently, most audio and video conferences are synchronous. If participants can check into the conference when they wish, it is an asynchronous, or "store and forward," conference. The use of voice message systems approaches the concept of asynchronous audio

Full-motion video

Consider using only when you can afford it.

Use when a task requires motion displays (for example, to screen TV ads or moving mechanical parts).

Use when more social presence is needed (for example, for executive sessions).

Don't forget about good audio.

Still video

Use when focus is on flip charts, overheads, or other simple graphics.

Use for technically oriented discussions.

Don't forget about good audio.

Audio-graphics

Use when the focus is on drawing or documents.

Select a graphics system carefully, based on your needs.

Consider personal computer graphics as well as systems marketed for teleconferencing.

Don't forget about good audio.

Audio

Use when visual communication is unimportant.

Use when you can't afford visual aids.

Don't forget about good audio.

Text

Use when participants have trouble scheduling meetings.

Use when participants are comfortable using keyboards.

Use when tasks are adaptable to text-only communication or when computer-based resources are important.

Exhibit I   Rules of thumb for using various media

conferencing, and electronic mail is introducing store-and-forward text communication. Exhibit I outlines rules of thumb for the various types of telecommunications systems.

Common Misconceptions

Teleconferencing is not yet a developed industry, but it could soon become one, or perhaps part of several industries. The range of products is increasing, as is their quality. It is becoming easier to find an appropriate system and to purchase or lease it. Still, it is an infant industry that is easily misconceived by potential users, who are likely to fall prey to come common misconceptions, as follows.

High Level of Use

At present, the teleconferencing industry is busy holding conferences (usually face to face) about teleconferencing. The resulting flurry of brochures, speeches, and demonstrations creates the impression of more activity than really exists.

The 1983 Teleconferencing Directory lists 204 organizations that have some form of permanent teleconferencing facilities [1]. That number has been growing slowly. We estimate that there are now about 75 organizations with permanently installed audio systems in North America, 20 full video, and perhaps 100 still video or audiographic systems. Boeing, Allstate, Arco, and Liberty Mutual, for example, have private video systems; Ford, IBM, and Hughes have slow-scan video systems; and Kellogg (Littleton, Colorado), Darome Connection (Harvard, Illinois), and Comex International (Danbury, Connecticut) have intercompany audio systems. There are many more semipermanent or portable systems, especially for conference calling. These numbers, however, include private telephone companies and systems vendors that have a built-in interest in the field. Also, finding systems in daily use is difficult. There are many experimenters but far fewer steady users, even today. Most users are what Elliot Gold, publisher of the most widespread newsletter on teleconferencing, describes as "tire kickers."

A study of full-motion and slow-scan video teleconferencing users supports this point. The study surveyed U.S. domestic business users whose systems had been in place for at least six months during 1981, were in use a minimum of 20 hours per month, and were used primarily for business meetings. Telephone operating companies were excluded. Even by these rather broad criteria, only ten systems qualified [2]. That number grew in 1982 and 1983, but not rapidly.

The teleconferencing industry is concentrating on promotion of the concept, as is appropriate for the early stages of new product marketing. Potential users should not assume, however, that its portrayal of actual use is accurate.

Best for Travel Substitution

Even though it is mostly a mirage, travel substitution is still the commonest justification for teleconferencing. New entrants in the field are almost always drawn to this idea. Then years of experience, however, yield few convincing examples of direct travel substitution. Indeed, in some cases travel increased with use of teleconferencing.

We do not mean to say that teleconferencing cannot help reduce travel or eliminate certain types of undesirable travel. But there is more to it than unlocking the door to the teleconferencing room and adding up the travel savings. Teleconferencing, if it works, will change the way business communicates. Travel patterns may change but probably not predictably, and almost certainly, teleconferencing will not substitute directly for travel. Nevertheless, travel statistics are the easiest and the safest quantitative justification for acquisition of the equipment.

Audio is Simple

One surprise for new users is that audio systems are the most technically difficult of any component—even in a video conferencing facility. However, high-quality audio systems have been used successfully for many tasks that users were convinced would require video. Furthermore, audio is improving with the development of high-quality microphones that do not require elaborate acoustical treatment.

The acceptable range in video quality is usually much broader than that of audio. Slightly fuzzy pictures of participants or less crisp letters in viewgraphs will not ruin a meeting; but the inability to hear clearly what is being said will. Unfortunately, new users often learn this the hard way. After companies have invested a great deal in the latest video equipment, some new teleconferencing rooms fail because of poor audio. This is often viewed (incorrectly) as a failure of users to accept the new technology.

Substitution for Face-to-Face Meetings

Many users fail to grasp the full potential of the new technology and try to create teleconferencing systems in the image of face-to-face communication. This sort of horseless-carriage thinking is limits. Though personal meetings are the most familiar, they are not always best for business communications. At times, an electronic meeting is preferable.

The computer conferencing systems now used by several thousand employees at Procter & Gamble illustrate the main advantages of meetings at which participants are not present simultaneously. Reading entries from others and making their own comments, users come and go according to their own schedules. They remain in their normal work environment, with access to resource materials and time to consider their responses. thus, the meeting becomes extended over time and (in some cases) time zones. Trying to schedule a face-to-face meeting of the same participants would be frustrating at best.

Favorable occasions for electronic meetings are just beginning to come to light. Imagine a manufacturing assembly line that malfunctions during the night shift. A full-motion video recording of the line could be made immediately and sent electronically to engineers in three distant cities, along with a verbal description of the problem and perhaps some sketches showing what the on-site engineer thinks might be wrong. When the engineers at the three remote sites arrive at work, the messages are waiting for them. After studying these reports, they are ready for a synchronous electronic meeting to troubleshoot the problem.

Business meetings make up an incredibly large fraction of many managers' time, anywhere from 30% to 70%. Teleconferencing implies changes in this critical aspect of the business day. So organizational change is the main event when teleconferencing is implemented— whether or not the implementers recognize this process.

Teleconferencing has the potential to change not just meetings but business communication in general. The guiding question should be: What might the medium allow us to do that we cannot do now? The companies that take this question seriously will be the ones that exploit its great promise. Potential users must determine their requirements, understand their needs, and design a system to suit those needs. So far, the teleconferencing industry has been driven by the technology producers, which is not unusual in an infant business. Until users begin pressing for capabilities to meet their needs and wants, the industry will remain technology driven and confused about what teleconferencing is and can become.

Critical Success Factors

The concept of critical success factors (CSFs) is normally used when identifying "things that must go right" for an individual to succeed in his or her job or a company to succeed in its industry. We think the concept is useful to examine what is critical for successful teleconferencing. Here we discuss four major factors.

Clear Business Requirement

A teleconferencing system cannot be introduced successfully to a corporate environment as the latest panacea for office productivity; nor does it work to introduce the procedure as an experimental toy. Such approaches lead to only passing interest and use, rendering systems expensive failures and leaving users disappointed if not angry. The technology must address a specific task or area of need. Managers must be convinced that they are getting value, that they are gaining support in accomplishing an important task, and that they are helping productivity.

Some business needs are obvious, and teleconferencing adds value by answering those needs. In other cases, teleconferencing adds value only subtly. Hoffman-LaRoche Laboratories, for example, uses audio teleconferencing with remote slide projection to conduct new product training for its large, scattered sales force. Teleconferencing improves coordination among the various salespeople so that information about new products reaches customers quickly. Other pharmaceutical companies are using teleconferencing to encourage communication among their scientists engaged in upstream R&D activities. Here the value added is even harder to measure, but it may be at least as important.

Accurate Needs Assessment

As important as identifying a clear business requirement is understanding the nature of the work involved.

Managers can use the CSF interview technique to elicit from potential users the chief tasks teleconferencing could facilitate. Because the CSF interview emphasizes critical tasks, it also clarifies what *form* the technological support needs to take. For example, if the showing of documents or drawings is a key element (as opposed to seeing participants face-to-face and reading body language), then slow-scan video technology can support the meeting well and full-motion video is unnecessary. For example, a major personal computer vendor found that immediate access to current product information was critical for regional sales representatives. the company installed a computer conferencing system to provide this.

For many companies, assessing needs has meant browsing through vendor brochures or assigning a junior staff person to develop a questionnaire overnight. Clearly, the process is too important to receive such perfunctory treatment. It is key to the successful use of teleconferencing.

Just asking people as they file out of a conference room, "Could you have conducted that meeting with slow-scan video plus audio and fax?" does not work either. People need to try various teleconferencing options before they know what they need, which often makes introducing teleconferencing an adventurous process.

Learning from experience. Many teleconferencing failures can be traced to an inability to learn from experience. It should be possible to transfer to teleconferencing the positive experience and the intelligence gained from successful information systems and office systems project. But such a transfer of learning is not easy.

The newcomer to teleconferencing who tries to learn through reading must sift through a bewildering array of articles, products, case studies, and vendor claims. Then years have generated a lot of information along with a lot of noise. The first synthesis of teleconference evaluations found over 200 studies of audio, video, and computer-based teleconferencing in 1979. There are perhaps twice that number now. About half of the studies have never been published formally or distributed broadly, making it difficult to dig out candid information.

While it is true that companies in some industries (for example, energy and telecommunications) can benefit from publicizing their use of teleconferencing, incentives are low for user organizations to publicize their teleconferencing experiences, either successes or failures. Although a small support network exists of people concerned, important experiences with teleconferencing often go undocumented and are lost to a company when key people move on to something else.

Importance of culture. A further complication is that each company —or group within the company—has a culture that sets the tone for business meetings. By culture we mean the unspoken clues that guide behavior within a group: the shape of the conference table, the type of chairs, the thickness of the carpeting, the location of the system in relation to other parts of the office building, and so on. Bank of America's executive teleconference room, for example, has a tone very different from the Stanford Linear Accelerator Center's (SLAC) teleconference room for research physicists. The bank's executives would not feel at home amid the chalk dust of the SLAC room, and SLAC's scientists would not be at home sitting around a mahogany table. Unfortunately, many teleconference rooms are more consistent with the culture of telecommunication departments that built them than with that of the intended users.

Of course, the people who can best understand the needs and culture of the users will be the users themselves—or at least people who are sensitive to the users. Many failures in teleconferencing can be traced to situations in which the momentum, and thus the cultural influence, is never transferred from the system builders to the system users. At Procter & Gamble, for instance, the R&D and engineering divisions introduced teleconferencing. The telecommunications and systems group played an important support and service role, but the momentum came from the users.

One of the most successful video teleconferencing systems illustrates the importance of culture. The private, four-city system at Ohio Bell was originally assembled from surplus videotape equipment. It is not a flashy system, and therefore telecommunications experts tend to ignore it. Yet it works. Indeed, when frequency of use is taken as the measure of success, it is much more successful than most high-tech systems.

Ohio Bell's system is accepted because it matches the culture of the user organizations. The arrangement of the room, the table, the chairs, and the colors on the walls all reflect the typical tone of an Ohio Bell work environment. It is an attractive alternative to a very uncomfortable drive across Ohio. The low-tech appearance of the Ohio Bell system is much more the state of the art (and has been for several years) than is an elaborate high-tech image—at least in settings where the primary users are nontechnical.

Somewhat different is the example of Digital Equipment Corporation, which has its own helicopter fleet for transporting employees among the numerous Massachusetts and New Hampshire company sites. But bad weather can ground helicopters, and some employees don't like to fly in them. So DEC built full-motion color video conferencing "transporter" rooms in its locations in these two states. In addition to the clear business need, the DEC culture, which readily accepts new technology, has contributed to the system's success. The rooms—more high-tech than Ohio Bell's—are designed to fit the diverse needs and the culture of the users.

Likely Effects

Teleconferencing has evolved independently from other electronic technologies used in offices. Although viewed more as an extension of the telephone than as a companion to the office computer or word processor, it is indeed an information system that will fit into the office of the future.

Experience with other information systems is similar to that of teleconferencing. Information systems have evolved from the early data processing days, in which applications developed mainly in the accounting and operations areas. The line manager benefitted only indirectly from these information systems (if in fact the printed reports churned out so regularly could be viewed as a benefit) since for most managers, and virtually all top executives, the information was not timely or crucial.

In the past few years, information systems have moved dramatically away from narrow accounting-oriented applications to applications for managerial support. Through advances in computers, communications, and software, managers and executives now have the potential for direct access to timely, useful information—both internal and external to their organizations. As more sources of data are integrated through the use of these systems, we are moving toward the office of the future.

Teleconferencing should be viewed as a branch in the family of office systems technologies. The ability to get information from people directly—regardless of their physical location—is critical. Most people —scientists, managers, secretaries—seek information from colleagues before searching written sources. In this sense, a teleconferencing system is also a "managerial support system." Indeed, a better name for emphasizing its role in supporting individuals in the task of business communication might be a "communication support system."

Some organizations are integrating traditional data and text processing systems with teleconferencing technologies and creating elaborate new systems. Already, there are examples of teleconferencing supported by computer access to data and modeling tools. During a meeting, participants can consult a computer-based model to evaluate alternative proposals. "What if?" questions can be asked of the model as inputs to the discussion and decision-making process. Computer-generated graphics can be used to present the results of these analyses to the teleconference participants. reports on file in text processing systems can be accessed, updated, and transmitted as well. Integrating these technologies for effective support of managers and executives is a big challenge for the present.

Face-to-face meetings and electronic meetings will become less and less alike as we move beyond the current "horseless carriage" stage. It will become easier to gather the right people at meetings, to have better preparation before and during meetings, to coordinate better with decentralized sites, and to spread human expertise within the company.

The tone of the meetings will change as the requirements of business communication, rather than the protocol of face-to-face meetings, become the driving force. In particular, computers will play increasingly important roles in electronic meetings. The emerging capabilities of electronic media will be used to pursue business goals in aggressive new ways, rather than to imitate the characteristics of face-to-face meetings. There will be new opportunities to make informed choices among various types of meetings, including, of course, the option of meeting in person.

Teleconferencing, when mixed with computing, will provide the building blocks for new forms of organization. For example, since the physical location of employees will become less important in selecting the best person to do a given job, companies may not have to sacrifice valuable employees when a spouse's career change requires relocation. Control Data Corporation (CDC) has used variants of teleconferencing to retain such employees. Although CDC is one of the few companies involved in this form of "telecommuting," its action represents longer-term trends and business opportunities for aggressive companies [8].

The incentives to use teleconferencing ought to be at least as attractive as travel. For example, each use of teleconferencing could earn credits toward benefits that were valued by the particular users—perhaps a personal computer or even a free vacation. The challenge is to create attractive incentives for potential user groups, incentives that benefit both the company and the employee.

Other cost reductions result from avoiding problems. For example, the Boeing Corporation says that the greatest saving from its teleconfer-

Cost advantages	Opportunity enhancement	Negative e—ects
Reduces travel expense.	Allows communication not practical before teleconferencing.	Increases unproductive time spent in unnecessary but easily arranged meetings.
Reduces unproductive time while traveling as well as travel fatigue.	Allows more people to attend a meeting, especially on short notice.	Decreases freedom of operation for remote field sites because of too much control by management.
Reduces mistakes made because the "right person" was not at meeting.	Improves opportunities to prepare for and follow up on face-to-face meetings.	Lowers morale because of decreased personal contact.
Lessens duplication of effort by geographically separated sites.	Increases flexibility in frequency and timing of communication.	Encourages overspecialization and narrowness.
Shortens business cycles and facilitates important decisions.	Improves managerial control over field sites and decentralized offices.	Fosters dependance on technology, creating vulnerability to breakdowns or even sabotage.
Reduces need to update people not at face-to-face meetings and improves accuracy of information at the update.	Improves ability to share geographically separate "people resources."	
Reduces equipment downtime when repair person is at another site.	Provides better personnel relations by keeping lines of communication open.	
Reduces effects of disruption such as fuel unavailability or political unrest.	Makes job assignments less dependent on where an employee happens to live.	
	Provides faster and better responses to emergencies when key people are geographically separated.	
	Allows new opportunities for chance meetings among people who could benefit from working together.	
	Encourages consideration of alternative solutions to given problems.	
	Increases potential for improved computer programs to contribute to the work of teleconference participants.	
	Alters how employees think about their roles and their relation to organizations.	

Exhibit II   Potential effects of teleconferencing

encing system comes from the ability of engineers at remote locations to catch problems that might otherwise go unnoticed. These Boeing engineers rely on audio and still photographs of drawings and charts, both sent easily over the system, and use motion video for special situations, such as interviewing test pilots immediately after test flights. In all these cases, teleconferencing has dramatically lowered the costs and removed the difficulty of frequent travel among sites in the Seattle–Tacoma area.

A pharmaceutical R&D group can use teleconferencing to coordinate and thus speed up the effort needed to move a new drug from the laboratory to the market. The focus here is on simplifying the often awkward logistics of bringing together people from various parts of the company who must play a role in the introduction of a drug. Because this industry often is subject to time pressures due to great competition, the necessary safety experts, legal advisers, and others need to have quick and easy ways to communicate.

Often, a company finds that teleconferencing has brought about unexpected changes in the organizational structure and communication network. For example, teleconferencing, particularly via computers, has often opened new channels of communication that tend to flatten—or at least change—corporate hierarchies. The new system provides the means for junior staff or staff in remote locations to communicate directly with those in power.

Teleconferencing can have both negative and positive aspects; for example, the ability of managers to keep closer contact and control, which is an advantage to them, may make workers feel restricted. Also, a lack of face-to-face meetings could narrow contacts and professional development. All the effects cannot be cataloged yet, but some can be anticipated. Exhibit II presents our summary of likely impacts.

Making it Work

There is no cookbook for successful teleconferencing, but it is important for managers to choose a proper configuration of the technology for their needs. Exhibit III presents a framework for making choices. It is organized around four basic functions.

Each option is described functionally to emphasize the action the user perceives, not the technology involved. The wanted action points to the type of equipment needed. For example, if drawing is a necessary input, the next question is, what form of output is wanted? Graphic documents may be desired, as well as still visuals to display work in progress. Next, would some form of computer graphics be useful to assist in free-hand drawing? Finally, must there be interaction among

Select one or more items from each column

Inputs	Computer aids	Transmission	Outputs
Talk	Text Processing	Two-point	Hear
Write	Data base manipulation	Multipoint	Text documents
Type	Graphics	Synchronous	Still visual display
Draw	Numerical processing	Asynchronous (store-and-forward)	Motion visual
Output from instruments or computers			Prerecorded video
			Computer inputs

Exhibit III   User's guide to basic teleconferencing functions

participants (which would require a shared drawing space) or is one-way sending sufficient? Would all the participants be present simultaneously, or would they want to work in an asynchronous mode? And so on.

Once such basic choices are made, integration becomes crucial: How many of these functions must work together in a single system? What other inputs, outputs, or computer aids should be added?

Cost factors are also bound to play a role, and possible systems are likely to give way to practical systems. This process will be an iterative one, resulting in one or more teleconferencing configurations described by function. Some hardware issues and many software issues are involved in designing functional systems, but the designers of such systems must have an accurate sense of how the systems will actually be used.

Because teleconferencing changes one of the most basic business activities, business communication, the manager trying to introduce it plays a delicate role. But if handled carefully, teleconferencing can become an important part of the growing array of office information systems.

References

1. (Madison, Wis.: Center for Interaction Programs, 1983).

2. See Kathleen J. Hansell, David Green, and Lutz Erbing, "Videoconferencing in American Business," (McLean, Va.: Satellite Business Systems. May 31, 1982).

3. For a summary of research on managers' use of time, see Raymond R. Panki, "Serving Managers and Professionals" in *Office Automation Conference Digest* (Arlington, Va.: AFIPS Press, April 1982).

4. For a description of this method, see John F. Rockart, "Chief Executives Define Their Own Data Needs," HBR March–April 1979, p. 81. A guide for use of CSFs is C. V. Bullen and J. F. Rockart, "A Primer in Critical Success Factors," Sloan School of Management, MIT, Center for Information Systems Research, working paper no. 69, June 1981.

5. For a more detailed discussion of needs assessment techniques, see Robert Johansen and Ellen Baker, "Needs Assessment Workshops," *Office Technology and People.* November 1983.

6. See Robert Johansen, Jacques Vallee and Kathleen Spangler, *Electronic Meetings* (Reading, Mass.: Addison-Wesley, 1979).

7. The International Teleconferencing Association (McLean, Va) was formed in 1982 as a professional exchange medium.

8. See Margrethe Olson "Remote Work: Changing Work Patterns in Space and Time," *Communications of the ACM.* March 1983, p. 182.

9

Office Information Systems and Computer Science

Clarence A. Ellis
Gary J. Nutt
Xerox, Palo Alto Research Center
Palo Alto, CA

Introduction

The automated office of the future is quickly becoming the topic of much important computer science research. The office machine industry, led by AT&T, Burroughs, Eastman Kodak, Exxon, IBM, 3M, and Xerox, is actively working on automating the information processing that takes place in an office [Burn77, Crea78, Weni78]. And most of these companies are investing significant sums of money in research programs for the automated office as well. Active research programs also exist in universities, for example, at M.I.T. [Hewi79a, Hamm79], the University of Pennsylvania's Wharton School [Ness78, Morg76a, Morg79, Zism77], the University of Toronto [Tsic79a, Tsic79b], and the Harvard Business School [Buch79].

The focus of most of this attention is not on traditional business data processing, nor is it on management information systems; rather, it is on systems and facilities to aid the office worker in the more basic aspects of his or her job. The worker must manage information by text editing, forms editing, and organizing, filing, copying, transforming, analyzing, and transmitting that information effectively. Although these tasks can be automated individually, the challenge of an office information system is to *integrate the components* in order to reduce the complexity of the user's interface to the system, control the flow of information and enhance the overall efficiency of the office. For example, an office information system might handle internal forms by incorporating a single interface that allows the user to create, copy, send, and file a form. The user might exercise control over information transmitted in a form by tracing the form in order to determine its progress through a predetermined route. The integration increases efficiency here by reducing the potential number of medium transformations as the form is processed at different stations.

A primary premise of this paper is that the integration of office tasks is difficult; the desire for office information systems creates a new area for applying results, techniques, and methodologies of computer science research. Solutions to a large number of difficult problems must be obtained before such office systems can become a reality. In particular, solutions are needed to the following three general problems: the complexities of distributed systems that implement the automated office; the necessity for simple, yet complete, interfaces between the machine and the human user; and the need for knowledge-based systems to aid the user.

The purpose of this paper is to introduce the computer scientist to the office automation research area. To do this we first describe the scope of office information systems, primarily by presenting state-of-the-art prototypes; then we discuss the intersection of the field with computer science. This intersection can be partitioned into subtopics in several different ways; the partition chosen here has been influenced by the ACM Special Interest Group taxonomy. We mention several of the appropriate topics, while providing a more complete discussion of only a few of them: programming languages, software engineering, operating systems and databases, measurement and evaluation, and communications. These detailed discussions tend to reflect the areas of research with which we are most comfortable, but one should not necessarily conclude that these are the most important areas of research in office automation. Our discussion of computer science and office information systems excludes many topics from management science that are appropriately a part of the research needed to solve office information systems problems. For a broader treatment of these related topics, see Aron69 and Tagg77.

This paper comprises three major sections: some example implementations of office information systems, a discussion of some problems from the standpoint of traditional computer science, and future trends in office automation research. This organization allows the reader to gain an overview from the introduction of each major section. Additional information is provided in each subsection introduction, and finally, several subsections are refined to contain detailed discussions.

1 *What is an Office Information System?*

The *office* is that part of a business that handles the information dealing with operations such as accounting, payroll, and billing. In particular, *office work* consists of information-handling activities such as text editing, forms editing, filing documents, performing simple computations, verifying information, and communicating within the office and between offices. Processing within the office is usually stimulated by the arrival of a request for service, such as an order, a bill, a complaint, or a message to order more materials. Processing, such as the preparation of weekly summaries, may even be stimulated by the passage of time. The office processes requests for service by causing the business to react to these inputs, including maintaining a record of its reactions.

The computer scientist can use a number of different models to describe office activity, such as

- a set of activities resulting from requests for service, each with a specific precedence, and with each activity requiring a supporting file system;

- a set of people "executing their procedures" ("carrying out tasks"), communicating with and referencing a supporting file system;

- a set of communication media (a telephone, a file, or an electronic message system) with its corresponding communications (a telephone call, a filled-in form, or a file system query);

- a very large database with users accessing and manipulating data.

An *automated office information system* (OIS) attempts to perform the functions of the ordinary office by means of a computer system. Automation in the office particularly aids the office worker in document preparation, information management, and decision making [Zism78]. Such systems may be as modest as a group of independent word processors or as complex as a distributed set of large, communicating computers. Within this spectrum is either a central computer with several interactive terminals or a set of small interconnected computers. In many of these systems the office worker interacts with a *work station* which is capable of electronically communicating with other work stations.

In this paper we distinguish office information systems from data processing systems, both by the autonomy of the system's parts and by the function of those parts. A data processing system is used to implement algorithms with a single locus of control in which there ordinarily are no collections of autonomous parts; the algorithm ordinarily proceeds without the need for human interaction. Typical data processing systems compute payrolls, implement accounting systems, and manage inventories. An OIS is made up of a collection of highly interactive autonomous tasks that execute in parallel, as stated earlier, including forms, document preparation and management, communication, and decision-making aids.

The terms "office of the future," "automated office," "office information system," and "integrated office system" have been frequently applied to small business computer and time-sharing systems. In this paper we take a narrower view of office information systems; hence, in order to describe our views more exactly, we cite some examples.

Officetalk-Zero: A Prototype OIS

Officetalk-Zero is a prototype "first-generation" office information system, designed and implemented by William Newman, Tim Mott, and others from the Office Research Group at Xerox Palo Alto Research Center (PARC). The Officetalk-Zero effort began in late 1976 as a study of languages for expressing office procedures, and subsequently evolved into an OIS emphasizing the interface between human users and automation. The prototype—operational by June 1977—was introduced into a clerical user environment the following year.

Goals of Officetalk-Zero   Officetalk-Zero, or Officetalk for short, is implemented in an environment of multiple minicomputers interconnected by a high-speed communication network [Metc76]. It is expected that many future automated office systems will be designed around a similar physical environment [Crea78]. Each minicomputer, a Xerox Alto, is a 128K 16-bit-word minicomputer with a 2.5-megabyte disk and a sophisticated cathode-ray-tube (CRT) display [Thac79]. Areas on the screen are pointed to by a cursor under the control of an x-y coordinate input device called a *mouse*. The mouse is operated by a button, which is depressed, then released. Software can determine the state of the button as well as the x-y coordinate addressed by the mouse.

The Officetalk designers took the position that the new OIS should be based on the data objects of single page forms and files of forms; intercommunication is accomplished by electronically passing forms among the work stations. The user's model of the Officetalk system is merely an electronic aid for carrying out his or her normal tasks. A primary difference between the user's Officetalk model and the user's pre-OIS model is the substitution of electronic forms for paper at the work station. Each work station provides a graphical window onto a worker's desk, allowing the worker to manipulate electronic forms by employing the pointing device and the keyboard.

Officetalk is not a decision support tool, nor is it a management information system. It is intended to be used by office workers to aid in document management, preparation, and communication. Part of the reason for focusing on clerical work was to investigate office procedure specification and interpretation. Officetalk designers recognized that the procedural specification of "routine clerical work" was an unsolved problem, and that its solution would be a step toward solving the more general OIS problem.

Many of the individual facilities needed to implement Officetalk already existed as separate programs on several computer systems. Some useful subsystems include a text editor, graphics package, communications facility, filing facility, and forms data entry capability. However, an OIS should offer all of these facilities to the user via a *simple, uniform interface*. Officetalk combines all of these facilities, plus a few others, into a single integrated system. This system is currently being used on an experimental basis in offices outside of PARC.

Another experimental study is the Citibank project [Whit77]. At Citibank, management work stations have been interconnected to implement electronic mail, distributed calendar maintenance, forms development and manipulation, and cost/benefit analysis.

Capabilities and Functions Officetalk is a distributed program that executes on at least one minicomputer in conjunction with the communication network and a second minicomputer system for file storage (called a *file server*). Ordinarily, there will be several minicomputers, each acting as a work station for an individual user of Officetalk. The file server maintains a database describing all pending electronic transactions, such as electronic mail, information about each authenticated user of the system, or a set of tailored blank forms to be used in the particular application. Officetalk is designed to save the major portion of the user's information state in the file server and as little as possible in the local minicomputer.

To implement a particular Officetalk application, a tailored set of blank forms must be designed and entered into the database. Officetalk provides a forms editor which allows one to specify the graphical design of a form and the style of each field on the form. The forms editor requires that the newly designed forms satisfy certain conditions, such as no overlapping fields. It also permits certain fields to be designated as signature fields.

Upon starting Officetalk, the user is shown an image of a desktop containing parts of forms, similar to Figure 9.1. The user employs the mouse to manipulate the forms on the desktop. Each form is displayed in a rectangular *window* on the CRT device, as originally conceived within

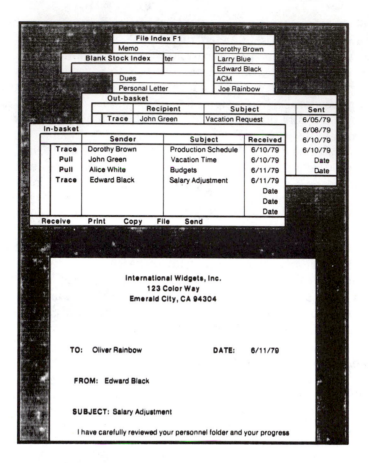

Figure 9.1

the Smalltalk system [Gold79]. The form may be larger than the window; hence the user is allowed to enlarge or shrink the window by pointing the cursor to appropriate parts of the window frame. The user can also move the window around on the display screen by using the cursor to "pick up" the window and move it. If the new window position overlaps another window already on the screen, Officetalk treats the two windows as simulated pieces of paper. The last window "laid down" is wholly visible, whereas intersecting windows are at least partially "covered up." Each window includes a menu of Officetalk commands which can be applied to the form that is visible in the window. The particular menu used is a function of the type of form showing in the window. The mouse is used to point at, and thereby invoke, commands.

An Officetalk desktop contains the following four forms, which are called *file indexes*:

1. the *in-basket*—an index of incoming mail,

2. the *out-basket*—an index of mail to be sent and mail that has been recently sent,

3. the *forms index*—forms that the user has saved,

4. the *blank stock index*—the set of available forms.

Each file index entry contains several fields: One field names the file, an *action field* specifies a command which can be applied to that file entry, while other fields list other information. A file index form is special in the sense that it contains a field on the form itself which allows command invocation. Ordinary forms do not contain an action field (instead, all commands are invoked from the window menu).

A user who wishes to generate a document selects a blank form from the blank stock index by pointing at the action field of the appropriate entry. The form is then drawn in a new, fully visible window. The user may enter information into the form by pointing at a field and typing a character string (or causing a signature to be entered). The editor restricts the data types to match the form's field definitions; for example, a signature field can contain only a signature. Officetalk also allows the user to draw freehand on a form; the mouse is used as a "brush" which can take on several different styles. Freehand illustrations can be removed later without harming the form's layout or previously typed information. This capability is particularly useful for marking a draft or appending a signature. Once prepared, a document can be filed in the user's personal file and thus be listed in the personal form index mentioned above. It can also be copied, the original filed, and the copy placed in the out-basket for mailing. The contents of the out-basket are actually mailed (placed on the file server) when the user points to a *transmit* selection in the out-basket menu.

The user can work on an existing document by retrieving a previously filed form from any index, including the in-basket. Electronic mail is routed from the sender to a mailbox on the file server; the user moves the mail to the local in-basket by pointing to a menu selection. Forms that have been mailed can be traced by the user. When the trace option is chosen, Officetalk opens a window on the electronic desk and then describes the current location of the form and an audit trail describing its route to that location.

Some Implementation Issues in Officetalk   Officetalk integrates a number of ideas and facilities that exist in many different systems into a single interface. The interface takes full advantage of the interactive graphics capability of the Alto. For example, the user can visually manipulate forms, read mail, or read previously filed documents [Teit77]. (Some of these functions are also implemented in the HP300 Computer System using the concepts of windows and means [Hewl78].) There are several other interesting aspects to the Officetalk design: the memory management of the file server, a work station's local disk, and the work station's complex primary memory. The primary memory can be used more effectively if parts of a form are "demand paged" from the local disc [Coff73]. Similarly, in form storage there are trade-offs of network traffic versus local disk space utilization. The network communication mechanism has been the subject of careful study; Bogg80, for example, discusses the trade-off between reliability and program size in choice of protocol level. The production of hardcopy documents from graphical images requires more than brute force algorithms. (Several of these parts of the Officetalk implementation were adapted from OIS-independent packages that already existed at PARC; e.g., see Swin79 and Inga78.)

The basic software under the graphics package implements some portions of Level 4 of the Core System developed by the ACM SIG-GRAPH Graphics Standard Committee [ACM78, ACM79]. The Alto environment provides low-level implementation of the *pick, locator*, and *keyboard* input devices. The *viewing transformation* is defined by a bit map for a 606×808 point screen; to place an image on the screen, it is necessary only to set the appropriate bits in the bit map. Officetalk designers implemented the two-dimensional notions of *windows* and *view ports*, so that clipping, scrolling, and moving windows can be handled efficiently. The techniques used in the display maintenance are described in Newm79.

Designing an editor for electronic forms involves issues beyond those encountered in most text editors [More76b]. In addition to the usual low-level interface problems, such as text selection and replacement, the field types must be checked for proper values. Some fields may be unalterable once written into (e.g., the "amount" field of a pay voucher); if the form is a copy, then none of its fields can be altered. (One important problem that arose here was how visually to identify a copy from the original. The approach taken was to provide a different set of capabilities for manipulating a copy than an original; hence the menus for the two types of forms differ.)

Limitations   Officetalk is a prototype office information system that integrates a set of common facilities into a single system with a simple user interface. Although the study was intended to provide a means of defining procedural specifications of office activities, the user interface turned out to be a problem that was difficult enough to absorb the full energies of its designers. In order to increase the reliability of a distributed OIS, production systems are likely to incorporate more sophisticated database systems than the one used in Officetalk. The designers chose to use an existing facility which does not allow a distributed database, which supports no query system, and which uses overly simplistic forms of locks for data consistency. (See Paxt79 for subsequent development of the file system.)

Even with these limitations, Officetalk-Zero is a unique prototype that illustrates the power and utility of the integration of a set of information manipulation facilities into a single office information system.

SCOOP: Another Prototype OIS

Whereas Officetalk-Zero emphasizes the user interface Michael Zisman's SCOOP (System for Computerization of Office Processing) emphasizes the specification, representation, and automation of office procedures [Zism77]. Zisman has developed a system based on Petri nets augmented by production rules for modeling offices as asynchronous concurrent processes. This model, called the *Internal Representation*, is a conceptualization of how the machine represents the problem to itself. In addition, an *External Representation* describes office procedures as activities and documents in a nonprocedural programming language for the office analyst. A prototype system for computerization of office procedures was implemented at the University of Pennsylvania's Wharton School. The system, driven by an internal representation as input, tracks instances of procedures and automatically executes portions of them. Throughout his thesis, Zisman focuses on automating office procedures rather than simply automating devices in the office.

The Approach   The augmented Petri nets Zisman uses to describe office procedures can also be used to represent asynchronous processes in general. The notation specifies a process representation as a Petri net [Pete77] and a knowledge representation as sets of productions [Newe72] associated with the Petri net transitions. For any given situation it is necessary to consider only those productions associated with the Petri net transitions that are enabled at the time. Thus the model partitions the total knowledge set into useful, not necessarily disjoint, subsets.

We shall consider the order entry process in an office as an example of the model. For the purposes of this paper, the office that performs the

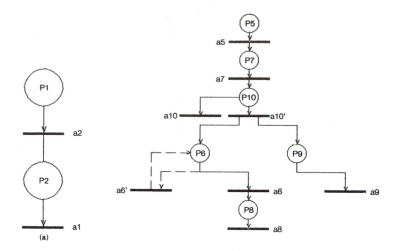

Figure 9.2   (a) Receptionist agent; (b) order administrator agent.

order processing function consists of a receptionist and an order administrator. The receptionist records the arrival of each customer request for goods in a log book, types the required information onto an order form, and then sends the form to the order administrator. Upon receipt of the order form, the order administrator processes the order, using the customer file. He or she next uses information from the billing file to validate the fact that this customer is not delinquent in previous payments. Then a decision is made whether to ship the goods C.O.D. or to bill the customer for later payment. In the case of C.O.D., a single form, f3, is completed; in the bill-later case, two forms, f1 and f2, are filled out. This fragment of an office procedure, although simplified, will serve as an expository aid throughout the remainder of the paper.

One Petri net must be constructed for each *agent*, who is frequently, but not always, human. Thus the *receptionist agent* is described by the Petri net of Figure 9.2a, and the *order administrator agent* is described by the Petri net of Figure 9.2b. The semantics of the actions that occur at the nodes of the net are presented as sets of productions in Tables 1a and 1b, respectively.

Let us consider what happens within the model when a customer's request for a product arrives. Customer request arrivals are modeled by a token arriving at the place P1 of the Petri net presented in Figure 9.2a. Note that P1 is the initial place specified for this net. The token appearing at P1 enables transition a1. Some unspecified time after this enabling, the action specified by transition a1 will actually occur; that is, the transaction will "fire." Note that we do not know exactly when this activity will take place because the receptionist may be busy doing something else or may not even be working at the time of arrival. This nondeterministic timing notion is captured nicely within the Petri net formalism because Petri net transitions are defined to fire at some finite but indefinite time after the transition is enabled. One variation from the standard Petri net definition that occurs in this model is that transition firing is not instantaneous. This instantaneity could be accomplished by associating transitions with the termination of transactions, but there are advantages to associating times with transactions in order to separate execution time from wait time and to perform analysis. Because a Petri net is an uninterpreted model, we must look at the associated productions in order to find out what is really happening within any transition. Table 1a implies that transition a1 results in the writing of an entry into the log book. This action enables the next step in the Petri net (transition a2): the keying of a customer request into the system. Transition a2 also has the side effect of enabling an instance of the order administrator agent to begin by placing a token on the initial place P5 of the Petri net in Figure 9.2b.

Methods for modeling decision making (location p10) and parallel processing (transition a10′) are illustrated in Figure 9.2b. Note that a single token on place P10 can cause either transition a10 or transition a10′ to fire, thus removing the token from place p10. However, both transitions cannot fire since removal of the token by one disables the other. Firing of a transition also depends on the production rules associated with the transition. If the condition portion of all associated productions is "true," then the transition can fire (see Patil's coordination sets [Pati70]). In this case it depends on the value of the variable "shipping mode," which was set by the previous transition a7. When transition a10′ fires, it places tokens onto both P6 and P9, thus enabling transitions a6 and a9. Again, these enabled transitions cannot fire until their associated production predicates are true. In this case, as in many cases of parallel asynchronous processing, productions associated with different independent transitions are in the *active production rule set.* In the SCOOP system implementation, each production consists of a list of predicates followed by a list of actions to be performed if all predicates are true. In Table 1b, after transition a7 has fired, if "shipping mode" equals "C.O.D.," then a10 can fire; if "shipping mode" equals "pay later," then a10′ can fire. The dashed lines to and from the new transition a6′ in Figure 9.2b have been added to illustrate the mechanism for modeling time-outs on a transition such as a6 in this example. If activity a6 is not completed within the time limit specified, then (and not before) transition a6′ will fire and cause some reminder to be generated. The enabled a6′ predicate performs this triggering function (Table 1b).

Table 1a   Productions for Receptionist Agent

INITIAL MARKING: (P1)	
TRANSITION a1-	TRANSITION a2-
Conditions:	Conditions:
[exists log-book]	Actions:
Actions:	[filem write sys-scratch this-order]
[filem write log-entry this-order]	[instantiate order-administrator this-order]

Table 1b   Productions for Order Administrator Agent

INITIAL MARKING: (P5)	
TRANSITION a5-	TRANSITION a8-
Conditions:	Conditions
[exists customer-file]	Actions:
Actions:	[assign f1 v]
[filem read customer-file this-order]	TRANSITION a9-
[assign u activity-output]	Conditions:
TRANSITION a6-	Actions:
Conditions:	[assign f2 u]
[exists billing-file]	TRANSITION a10-
Actions:	Conditions:
[filem read billing-file this-order]	[compeq shipping-mode cod]
[assign v activity-output]	Actions:
TRANSITION a6'-	[assign f3 u]
Conditions:	TRANSITION a10'
[enabledsince 6'5]	Conditions:
Actions:	[compeq shipping-mode bill-later]
[doc reminder order-administrator]	Actions:
TRANSITION a7-	
Conditions:	
[exists customer-file]	
Actions:	
[assign shipping-mode cust-type]	

The rule associated with transition a6' states that if this transition has been enabled for five or more days, then a document entitled "reminder" should be sent to the order administrator. Then the timer is reset and transitions a6 and a6' are reenabled. One generalization of the augmented Petri net formalism that is not visible in this example is the ability of one net to cause a variable number of initiations of another net. This notion of spawning a variable number of processes is useful for representing systems in which the number of concurrent activities is determined by dynamic conditions.

The SCOOP Implementation   The system implementation contains an execution monitor that is driven by the internal representation of a set of augmented Petri nets; as a transition T fires, the execution monitor removes the productions associated with T from the active productions rule set and enters productions of any transitions which are enabled by the firing of T. The execution monitor starts some processes which can be implemented as automatic procedures and other processes which are interactive cooperative ventures between person and machine. At a lower level, special-purpose hardware and software systems exist to carry out various office tasks that receive messages from SCOOP. The special-purpose systems used by SCOOP are document generators, electronic mail senders and receivers, file services, and media schedulers.

Although the complexity and number of the special-purpose systems may increase as the office automation area grows, the monitor (or office operating system supervisor) can remain a relatively constant size. Zisman provides guidelines and frameworks for a high-level nonprocedural specifications language containing a document definition section for declaring all documents needed, an activity initiation section for describing when each activity can be performed, and an activity detail section. The activity detail section describes the tasks to be done when the activity is initiated by a few basic operations. Procedure descriptions in this language could then be translated into an augmented Petri net and run, using the execution monitor SCOOP. By considering the specification language, the internal representation, and the design of a prototype system using one unified model, Zisman has been able to study the office as a system rather than simply as a collection of isolated tasks and pieces of equipment. Although he does suggest that the language and the model need refinement, his basic notions will probably have great impact on the office of the future.

2 OIS Research Problems

In this section we describe a number of problems in the field of computer science that relate directly to OIS research. In some cases, a particular topic is discussed in detail in order to give the reader a better understanding of the nature of that problem. A special attempt has been made to emphasize two kinds of problems: those that might reveal new and/or interesting facets owing to the context of OIS research, and those that may yield to specialized techniques within a subdiscipline. The emphasis in this section is on languages and systems; detailed discussions cover topics in programming languages, modeling, consistency, and simulation.

Programming Languages

Programming language design is an important area of OIS research, partially because of the potential desire for very-high-level programming languages that can be used by the clerical worker. The implementation of OISs on distributed systems will also affect programming languages, since a large OIS will likely require the ability to recompile parts of the system dynamically while other parts are running. Programming language design will be influenced both by the need to support the clerical user and by the need to handle parallelism. After mentioning a variety of such problems, this section presents a more lengthy discussion of IBM's Business Definition Language developed for clerical users to implement data processing algorithms.

Because of the dynamic nature of office procedures, the clerk is likely to find it necessary to write and modify problems. Such programs might execute at the work station, yet affect the global environment. In the past, the end user of a batch system could be given an English description of the input to a program and some instructions about interpreting the output. The user model of the system became more complex when the user was expected to interact with a terminal, although that too could be explained by another set of instructions. Because of the potential need to create and alter procedures, the description of the OIS that is presented to the clerical programmer/user will have to depart significantly from the machine models to which that user has grown accustomed. We expect that the average clerical worker will not be willing to learn very sophisticated notations in order to understand the operation of the OIS; nor will he or she be willing to learn drastically different approaches to the solutions of familiar problems.

Traditionally, in order to use a programming language, the user has had to understand the notions of compile time, load time, and run time. A simpler metaphor is used to describe an interpreter to the user: Encode an algorithm into symbolic form, then "run" the program. One alternative is to provide the clerical worker with a skeletal program which can be filled in with appropriate parameters (as in query-by-example systems [Zloo75]). Various other aspects of the user model may profit from new abstract machines; for example, should the user be concerned with I/O devices other than, perhaps, a mailbox, keyboard, and display? (The clerk could ignore the existence of hierarchical file systems if file access messages could be sent to a file server.) A natural question that arises from this area relates to the computational completeness of OIS programming languages. Is it necessary to be able to encode any algorithm into the user's language? If the language is restricted, can one (more easily) test for certain consistency features such as decidability of a program, correctness, or deadlock? What should be the nature of such "restrictions" to the language? Should there be unorthodox control structures (e.g., no explicit loops) or very limited data structures? Answers to these questions depend on the user's application requirements.

Future OIS languages may reduce the amount of information needed to program the system. It may also be necessary to expand the abstract machine model over conventional languages. A model of a distributed OIS might emphasize, rather than disguise, the network aspect of the system. For example, the model may be that of a communication network with server nodes, with each work station's view of the system being that there will be request for service, and that services can be requested from other nodes in the network by sending a request to the appropriate server. Work on such a communal system is accomplished by cooperation among a set of servers in the network. An extension of this idea is that of sending procedures to other work stations rather than sending messages (allowing procedures to run in different physical domains). Other features that are not ordinarily in a programming language model may have to be added to simplify the human interface. How can a distributed OIS be updated by multiple clerical workers in a systematic manner? Can any work station dynamically recompile its own procedures (or those passed into it from another work station) without some global form of communication? Should there be a central compiler/consistency-checker which each work station must use if it wishes to recompile a procedure? Since it has been shown that there is a significant amount of parallelism in an office [Elli79], should OIS procedural specifications explicitly denote parallelism or should it be detected by a compiler? The answers to these questions can strongly affect the structure of a cooperative system.

BDL: A Very-High-Level Business Language BDL, a Business Definition Language developed at IBM's Thomas J. Watson Research Center, is a very-high-level programming language constructed for the clerical user. Although the specific application area of the BDL work is business data processing, the work corresponds closely to that of programming language development for OIS users. BDL has been designed to simplify the translation of concepts and algorithms of business data processing into instructions which implement those ideas on a computer. Quite generally, the approach has been "to apply the design philosophy of structured programming and very high level languages to a particular application area, namely business data processing" [Hamm77, p. 833].

There has been no claim that BDL is a general-purpose language; the trade-off between generality and simplicity of use has purposely been biased toward simplicity. This does not mean that BDL is simply a parametrized program, nor is it even built on an existing programming language foundation. BDL is a new approach that incorporates a number of assumptions from business data processing such as the kinds of problems that will be encountered and the common methods for solving them. The language is intended to be sufficiently expressive that it can also serve as formal documentation of the application. One result of this bias toward simplicity in BDL has been the decision to build as much structure as possible into the language. The result is that the language does not allow for alternative ways to accomplish a given function. Instead, only one method per function is provided. BDL syntactic program segments have a common style and structure; each program is constructed from the common schema.

The extensive use of structured programming concepts in the BDL design becomes apparent in the expression of control flow and information transformation. BDL recognizes *documents, steps, paths*, and *files* as objects for describing a business data processing algorithm. A *document*, the fundamental data item in BDL, can be thought of as an organized set of primitive values. Each *step* can read documents, perform some computations, and then produce new documents. *Composite* steps can be hierarchically decomposed into more primitive steps. *Irreducible* steps define the derivation of output documents from input documents; they can be defined only in terms of a program segment. A *path* connects steps together, indicating the flow of documents in the program; it defines an output document for one step and an input document for another step. (Several paths may enter and exit any step.) Documents can be saved for distinct program activations by placing them in *files* in one activation, then retrieving them in a later activation.

A BDL program is defined by three distinct components: *A Form Definition Component (FDC)* defines the forms which will contain documents; the *Document Flow Component (DFC)* graphically represents steps, paths, and files; and the *Document Translation Component (DTC)* specifies the procedural interpretation of the irreducible steps.

A BDL form, a template for documents, is comparable to the notion of an Officetalk blank form in that the form definition includes a physical graphic image specification similar to a traditional paper form. The electronic form tends to be more "intelligent" than paper since it can be made to respond to varying conditions; for example, fields in BDL forms can align themselves depending on the contents of the document. The FDC is implemented at an interactive graphics terminal which allows the forms specialist to define the form by drawing rectangles and filling in sample field contents. The physical layout of the form is first described by specifying its size and its preprinted information, fields, and field headings. Detailed form information is also defined by using the FDC to specify field names, data types, data formats, names for groups of fields, and key fields for sorting groups of fields, as well as explicit error-handling instructions.

The Document Flow Component describes the data flow by means of a directed graph; the components of the graph are steps and files (nodes) interconnected by path segments (edges). The DFC is similar to a number of other methods for specifying the hierarchical design of computer programs and systems. The reader of BDL literature will recognize ideas and constructs similar to those used in the TELL system [Heba79], LOGOS [Rose72], the Information Control Networks discussed in a later section of this paper, and many others.

The node set in a DFC graph is made up of rectangles, representing steps, and of circles, representing files. The edge set is made up of solid directed edges, which interconnect steps, and of dashed directed edges, which interconnect steps and files. Each edge is labeled to define the document type that flows over the corresponding path (a file is assumed to contain only one kind of document). A document is said to be an *output* (*input*) *document* of step α if the path from (to) step α is labeled with the document's name. Figure 9.3 shows a DFC graph for the order-processing example used in the discussion of SCOOP. In the figure, the solid arc connecting the "Verify order" rectangle to the "Procedure invoice" rectangle represents a path of "Verification" documents that are output from the first step and input to the second.

A DFC graph is produced by the BDL programmer using an interactive system. The DFC graph is constructed as a set of hierarchical graphs in which each intermediate level in the hierarchy is made up of one or more composite nodes. A BDL program is defined by first specifying a graph made up of composite steps, paths, and files, each of which illustrates the organizational units of the business and the flow of documents among those units. Top-down refinements are made by decomposing steps into constituent steps until each step is irreducible. Once a computer step has been refined into an irreducible step, the function of the step can be defined by the DTC. If the irreducible step is a complex unit of computation, its interpretation reflects that complexity. An executable BDL program is defined by a DFC graph over a set of irreducible steps and a set of functional definitions for each step.

Figure 9.3 illustrates two levels in the hierarchical construction of a DFC graph for the order-processing example. The two large boxes

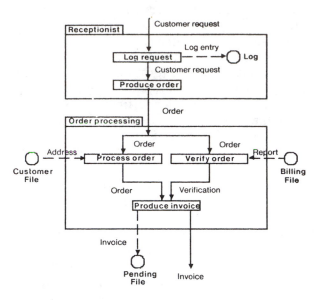

Figure 9.3 Order processing.

labeled "Receptionist" and "Order processing" are composite steps interconnected by the path for the "Order" document. The high-level graph indicates that the receptionist receives a "Customer request" document and produces an "Order" document on its single output path. The "Order processing" step uses the document to produce an "Invoice" document. During this processing it receives documents from the "Customer file" and the "Billing file" and places a document on the "Pending file." The "Receptionist" step is refined into the steps "Log request" and "Produce order," saving customer request information on a "Log entry" document in the internal "Log" file. The figure also illustrates a decomposition of the "Order processing" step into steps to "Process order," "Verify order," and "Produce invoice." This BDL program of the order processing office assumes that the billing decision is internal to the "Produce invoice" step, and that the result of the decision produces invoices for the shipment and the "Pending file," with appropriate entries to reflect the method of billing.

At run time, a step in a BDL program can be executed whenever there is a document on each input path of the step. The step is assumed to execute instantaneously, destroying each input document and creating new output documents on each output path (similar to Petri net tokens [Pete77]). For information to be passed from an input document to an output document, the step definition must explicitly copy that information from the input document(s) to the output document(s). The BDL run-time support system provides an implicit queue of documents on each edge of the DFC graph. BDL also allows a step definition to process a group of documents from the input path set and to create a group of documents for the output set (as in parallel program schemata [Karp69]).

The Document Transformation Component could, in principle, be any arbitrary programming language. Each DTC procedure is invoked when the DFC execution enables a step with input documents. The DFC run-time system could merely provide a mechanism for calling the corresponding step procedure and for passing to it the arguments that exist as input documents in the DFC graph. In BDL, DTC is a very-high-level language directed toward business data processing of aggregates of data. The DTC programmer uses this framework to define the particular transformations of information from the input document onto the output document. (Although the innate algorithm framework handles single-input-single-output steps, multiple inputs/outputs are handled by using the document-grouping feature of the DFC.) The step interpretation must specify an expression for each value field on the output document. The expressions are made up of ordinary arithmetic operators, conditional expressions over logical and relational operators (such as summation) to handle groups of data.

In the order processing example, the DTC for the "Produce order" step in Figure 9.3 might specify that a name field on the "Order" document be copied from the name field of the "Customer request" document; similarly, the items and quantity fields of the "Order" document are derived from the input document, while a unit price field might be determined from information internal to the "Produce order" DTC. The item price, tax, and total price fields on the output document can then be computed within the step as a function of unit price and quantity.

BDL Capabilities and Limitations This discussion of the Business Definition Language and the previous discussions of the Officetalk-Zero and SCOOP systems have introduced the notion of expressing information flow in the business application by casting information into modules—documents and forms. The need for sophisticated mechanisms to create templates for the data structures is apparent from the effort spent in developing forms editors; all of these efforts appear to be leading to the "intelligent form." The notions of a trace facility in Officetalk and the form error-handling mechanism in BDL can both be thought of as procedures to be executed in the context of the form rather than in the context of a work station or DTC procedure. Although there are many similarities between Officetalk and BDL, the emphasis in the

Officetalk-Zero work is on the graphical interface to system facilities, whereas the BDL effort is aimed at creating a logical programming environment for the clerical user. One can also distinguish among the three systems by considering the degree of user programming. Officetalk-Zero users are not expected to construct programs; BDL users can construct simple programs from templates; sophisticated SCOOP users must be versed in algorithm generation.

One facet of the BDL approach is that it does not explicitly differentiate between control flow and data flow. The whole question of conditions under which a model should represent control and/or data flow, and to what extent they should be separated, is still open; the data flow representation in the business data processing environment may be exactly right. Only experience with BDL and other data flow languages [Denn74] can resolve this debate.

However the office information system environment is different from the data processing environment of BDL. BDL models explicitly orient the description around the flow of documents through various steps which might be executed on arbitrary processors, ignoring the assignment of steps to processors. For example, the document flow through five steps implemented at two different locations could require as few as one or as many as four communications over a network, depending on the assignment of steps to processors; a document-oriented model may not distinguish between these two cases. One alternative representation is to orient the model around processors; that is, work stations and people. In this case, network internode communication may be apparent, but the path of the document may be difficult to discern. Document-oriented descriptions of information processing tend to be useful for ascertaining information about the data flow, for example, the temporal ordering of processing that takes place on the information. Processor-oriented models of the computation often tend to be easier to use for analyzing resources in the system.

Capturing the information content of informal conversation is neither trivial nor well understood. One criticism of the BDL's application as an OIS programming language is the stance of the designers on the problem of informal communication. Although some applications do not use forms for communication, BDL assumes that communications are accomplished only by forms: "For example, it is possible to represent a telephone call as a stylized document carrying certain information" [Hamm77, p. 833].

The DTC language is intentionally constraining when compared with general-purpose programming languages or other structured programming systems. However it is definitely a programming language and not a parameterization of a previously written program. The BDL effort is one of the few published works that adequately addresses the problem of programming languages for business users (see Teic72 and Rohl79). It is only through these and similar efforts that programming languages that can be utilized by the clerical worker in the automated office will be made available.

Software Engineering

In this section we discuss some topics of software engineering, particularly an office modeling scheme (Information Control Nets) that has been used both to describe offices to managers and to analyze the office for consistency and performance. The scheme can also be extended into a simulation model or a requirements specification for the OIS design.

At the heart of many software engineering methodologies lies a model of the design; for example, see Ross77, Camp78, and Heba79. The goals of these methodologies are usually as general as possible within the scope of software development. The methodologies are intended to specify requirements before implementation, to check the correctness of a design, and/or to be used as a design system. The model itself is molded to reflect the particular part of the methodology that is important to that system.

In considering the development of office information systems, there are compelling arguments in favor of analytic modeling: (1) The technology of the systems is still in the formative stage; (2) these systems are quite dynamic (changes in office procedures, office personnel, or office requirements are frequent); and (3) there is no comprehensive theory of office information systems. Indeed, there is reason to believe that the office of the future will need to lean heavily on modeling and theoretical analysis. And since the office can be viewed as a network of highly interactive parallel processes, models and analyses used in studies of computer systems are highly applicable. However, as the level of detail increases, analytic models may need to be augmented by simulation techniques.

Information Control Nets We next present one particular model developed over the last few years by researchers at Xerox PARC to describe and analyze information flow within offices. (Other models with similar goals have been described by Baum80, Tilb79, and Tsic79a.) This model, called an *Information Control Net*, has been used within actual as well as hypothetical automated offices to yield a comprehensive description of activities, to test the underlying office description for certain flaws and inconsistencies, to quantify certain aspects of office information flow, and to suggest possible office restructuring permutations.

Examples of office analyses that can be performed via this model include detection of deadlock, analysis of data synchronization, and detection of communication bottlenecks. Restructuring permutations that can be performed via this model include parallelism transformations, streamlining, and automation. Thus one requirement for the model is mathematical tractability; another is simplicity, allowing clerical workers to comprehend and manipulate the model; and a third is extensibility so that one model is equally applicable to theoretical analysis, simulation, and implementation.

The Informational Control Net model [Elli79] defines an *office* as a set of related procedures. Each *procedure* consists of a set of *activities* connected by temporal orderings called *precedence constraints*. In order for an activity to be accomplished, it may need information from *repositories*, such as files and forms. An information control net (ICN) captures these notions of procedures, activities, precedence, and repositories in graphical form. ICN diagrams in their simplest form use circles to denote activities and squares to denote repositories, as in Figure 9.4. A solid line from activity A to another activity, B, is a precedence arc and denotes that activity A must be completed before activity B can begin. Dashed lines to and from repositories denote, respectively, the storing of information into and the reading of information out of repositories.

An ICN describes the activities or tasks that make up an office procedure. This section presents a formal definition of a basic ICNB as a set of activities, a set of repositories, and the various functional mappings between these elements. One set of mappings, δ, describes precedence constraints among activities, and another, γ, describes repository input-output requirements of activities. A great deal of information can be attached to a basic ICN—information concerning, for example (1) the particular data items transferred to or from repositories, (2) who performs the activity, (3) the amount of time the activity takes, and (4) the amount of data transferred by an activity.

Definition A basic ICN is a 4-tuple $\Gamma = (\delta, \gamma, I, O)$ over a set A of activities and a set R of repositories, where

1. I is a finite set of initial input repositories, assumed to be loaded with information by some external process before execution of the ICN;

2. O is a finite set of final output repositories, perhaps containing information used by some external process after execution of the ICN;

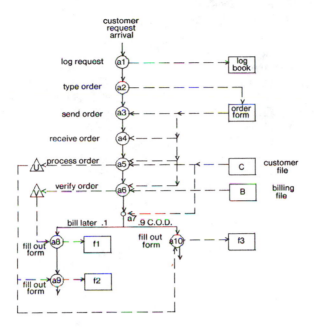

Figure 9.4   Order processing.

3. $\delta = \delta_i \cup \delta_o$

where $\delta_o : A \to P(A)$ is a multivalued mapping of an activity to its sets of (immediate) successors, and $\delta_i : A \to P(A)$ is a multivalued mapping of an activity to its sets of (immediate) predecessors. (For any given set S, $P(S)$ denotes the power set of S.)

4. $\gamma = \gamma_i \cup \gamma_o$

where $\gamma_o : A \to P(R)$ is a single-valued mapping (function) of an activity to its set of output repositories, and $\gamma_i : A \to P(R)$ is a single-valued mapping (function) of an activity to its set of input repositories.

In mapping ICN diagrams into formal definitions, solid lines into an activity node correspond to the δ_i function, and solid lines out of a node correspond to δ_o. Similarly, dashed lines into an activity node correspond to the γ_i function, and dashed lines out correspond to γ_o. As an example, the formal definition corresponding to Figure 9.4 is shown in Table 2. Given a formal definition, the execution of an ICN can be

Table 2   Order Processing—Formal ICN Specification

$A = \{$ a1, a2, a3, a4, a5, a6, a7, a8, a9, a10$\}$	
$R = \{$ B, C, f1, f2, f3, U, V, log book, order form$\}$	
$I = \{$B, C$\}$	
$O = \{$f1, f2, f3, log book, order form$\}$	
$\delta_i(\text{a1}) = ((\lambda)), \delta_o(\text{a1}) = ((\text{a2}));$	$\gamma_i(\text{a1}) = (\lambda), \gamma_o(\text{a1}) = (\text{log book})$
$\delta_i(\text{a2}) = ((\text{a1})), \delta_o(\text{a2}) = ((\text{a3}));$	$\gamma_i(\text{a2}) = (\lambda), \delta_o(\text{a2}) = (\text{order form}, \emptyset)$
$\delta_i(\text{a3}) = ((\text{a2})), \delta_o(\text{a3}) = ((\text{a4}));$	$\gamma_i(\text{a3}) = (\emptyset), \gamma_o(\text{a3}) = (\lambda)$
$\delta_i(\text{a4}) = ((\text{a3})), \delta_o(\text{a4}) = ((\text{a5}));$	$\gamma_i(\text{a4}) = (\emptyset), \gamma_o(\text{a4}) = (\lambda)$
$\delta_i(\text{a5}) = ((\text{a4})), \delta_o(\text{a5}) = ((\text{a6}));$	$\gamma_i(\text{a5}) = (C, \emptyset), \gamma_o(\text{a5}) = (\text{U})$
$\delta_i(\text{a6}) = ((\text{a5})), \delta_o(\text{a6}) = ((\text{a7}));$	$\gamma_i(\text{a6}) = (B, \emptyset), \gamma_o(\text{a6}) = (\text{V})$
$\delta_i(\text{a7}) = ((\text{a6})), \delta_o(\text{a7}) = ((\text{a8}));$	$\gamma_i(\text{a7}) = (C), \gamma_o(\text{a7}) = (\lambda)$
$\delta_i(\text{a8}) = ((\text{a7})), \delta_o(\text{a8}) = ((\text{a9}));$	$\gamma_i(\text{a8}) = (V), \gamma_o(\text{a8}) = (\text{f1})$
$\delta_i(\text{a9}) = ((\text{a8})), \delta_o(\text{a9}) = ((\lambda));$	$\gamma_i(\text{a9}) = (U), \gamma_o(\text{a9}) = (\text{f2})$
$\delta_i(\text{a10}) = ((\text{a7})), \delta_o(\text{a10}) = ((\lambda));$	$\gamma_i(\text{a10}) = (U), \gamma_o(\text{a10}) = (\text{f3})$

interpreted as follows: For any activity α, in general,

$$\delta_o(\alpha) = \{\{\beta_{11}, \beta_{12}, \ldots, \beta_{1,m(1)}\},$$
$$\{\beta_{21}, \beta_{22}, \ldots, \beta_{2,m(2)}\}, \ldots,$$
$$\{\beta_{n1}, \beta_{n,2}, \ldots, \beta_{n,m(n)}\}\},$$

meaning that upon completion of activity α, a transition which simultaneously initiates all of the activities β_{i1} through $\beta_{i,m(i)}$ occurs. Only one value of i ($1 \leq i \leq n$) is selected as the result of a decision made within activity α. (Note that if $n = 1$, then no decision is needed and α is not a decision node.) In general, if $m(i) = 1$ for all i, then no parallel processing is initiated by completion of α. One complication to the above discussion is that $\delta_i(a)$ must also be taken into account for each α because synchronization is frequently needed within offices.

For example, if α or β will execute, and one or the other must finish before η can begin, then this can be modeled by utilizing a hollow dot with two incoming arcs from α and β and one outgoing arc to η. If α and β execute in parallel, and both must finish, then the solid dot with two incoming arcs can be used. Our formalism using δ_i and δ_o handles the description of all of these cases unambiguously.

The execution of an ICN commences by a single λ transition. We always assume without loss of generality that there is a single starting node:

$$\exists! \, \alpha_1 \in A \ni \{\{\lambda\}\} \in \delta_i(\alpha_1).$$

At the commencement, it is assumed that all repositories in the set $I \subseteq R$ have been initialized with data by the external system. The execution is terminated by any one λ output transition. The single-input-node assumption allows any complex procedure to be viewed as a single node. If there are many λ output nodes, the procedure shrunken to a single node is a decision activity. If this decision making at a detailed modeling level is superfluous at a higher modeling level, then a hollow dot can be used to join output arcs to a single terminal node within this procedure. This implies that data arcs show information repositories that *may* be used, rather than those that *must* be used. The set of output repositories are data holders that may be used after termination by the external system.

An ICN Example   Figure 9.4 shows the order processing example, introduced earlier, in terms of the ICN diagram. For clarity, triangles are used instead of rectangles to denote those repositories that are temporary (analogous to local variables within procedural programming languages). The initial incoming arc is labeled by a comment ("customer request arrival") to specify startup semantics. Order processing then proceeds by logging the customer's request into the log book (activity a1), typing and sending the order (activities a2 and a3), and receiving the order (activity a4). Decision nodes, or choice nodes (drawn as small, hollow circles), are activities with multiple immediate successors. When a decision node terminates, one of the successors is selected to be activated next. The decision node a7 is labeled by information indicating the semantics of the decision; that is, a decision is made to send the goods C.O.D. or to bill later. In the case of a bill-later decision, two forms, f1 and f2, are filled out in activities a8 and a9, respectively. In the case of C.O.D., only form f3 is filled out. The arcs emanating from a7 are labeled by numbers to indicate the probability that any given transaction will next be processed by a8 or a9. In the example, 90 percent of the transactions result in C.O.D. billing. This important branching probability implies that a mapping should be added to our basic definition. Unlabeled branches in this mapping have a probability of 1.0 associated with them. Another mapping that could be added to our basic information is a mapping from each activity to a person (or people) performing that activity (compare with Zisman's agents).

Each activity in a diagram such as Figure 9.4 can be described as a macro activity by an ICN diagram. Similarly, it is possible to envision that the order processing procedure specified in Figure 9.4 may be one node in a higher level diagram. For example, one could have a diagram showing an order processing node followed by a credit department processing node followed by an accounting node followed by billing and shipping in parallel. Figure 9.5 shows this same order processing example after some standard automated ICN transformations for office restructuring have been applied to it. In Figure 9.5 the activities *send*

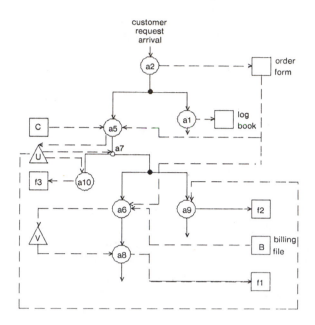

Figure 9.5 Order processing restructured.

order and *receive order* do not appear because in an automated system the typing-in activity would automatically cause the information to appear on the screen or be available to all of the people involved in the process. Activity a1, logging; and activity a2, typing, can be freely interchanged, and so are termed *Abelian* activities; such activities form the basis for a number of parallelism transformations [Elli79]. In Figure 9.5 we notice that the typing activity precedes the logging activity. Once the typing activity is done, and the information is available to all the workers involved in this process, it is possible to do activities in parallel. Thus, after activity a2 is completed, both the logging activity (a1) and the order processing activity (a5) can begin. This is shown in the ICN diagram by small, solid dots with lines pointing to activities a1 and a5. The omission of a3 and a4 is an automation transformation; the performance of activities in a different order or in parallel is a reorganization transformation.

In this example there is a streamlining of procedure in that activity a7 no longer requires access to customer file C; instead, this information is available locally in temporary repository U. This is an example of a transformation called *data rollback*, in which data are accessed at an earlier time in the process, thereby rendering future accesses unnecessary. *Data rollforward* is also exemplified in Figure 9.5. Activity a6, which accesses the billing file, has now been "rolled forward" so that it is performed after activity a7. Thus, access to the billing file is limited to those cases in which it is really necessary (when the customer will be billed later). Also in this case, parallelism is now obtained between the order processing activity a6 and the forms fill-out activity a9, although it is not possible for activity a8 to be performed before activity a6 has completed. Notice that, in general, these transformations involve what can be described as probabilistic parallelism and are predicated on branching probabilities associated with decision nodes. If all the activities in this procedure have reasonably similar execution times, then these transformations will speed up the average processing time by approximately 50 percent.

Operating Systems and Databases

The office information system is commonly defined as "a distributed operating system with a highly refined user interface and database facility." As such, operating systems present challenging problems with regard to a number of issues: distribution versus centralization, functionality, reliability, distribution of operating systems kernel, parallelism, consistency, and security, to name a few. For example, one of the areas of high concern to office managers is security of sensitive data (data which may now be displayed on terminals at multiple locations within an office). Similarly, they are very concerned about reliability and the ability to continue processing transactions in the face of component failures.

Other problems are involved in the servicing, organization, and management of an office. In the typical office there exists a conglomeration of unstructured tasks [Elli79]. How to group, couple, and uncouple these tasks is a very important question. Dynamic links, such as those incorporated into the DEMOS Operating System [Bask77], may offer a solution to the problem. The concept of the intelligent form, a process that may travel from one work station process to another in order to fulfill its goals, is another possible solution.

Distributed synchronization in the form of efficient distributed implementations of network synchronization primitives is yet another problem in the design of an OIS [Reed78]. Possible solutions might include distributed implementation of even counts or some other type of distributed monitor system [Reed79], and primitive serializers [Hewi79b].

These problems and their solutions are relevant even if the OIS is viewed solely as a database management system. The design and implementation of effective office information systems require solution of a number of additional research problems on the database, involving personal filing systems, office database schema organization, specialized languages for office databases, duplicate database update algorithms, distributed-query processing, and other issues regarding organization of distributed databases.

In the office, information is highly diffuse and dispersed; there are strong implications that the redundant storage of data at multiple sites is desirable. If, at each side, the frequently accessed data are local, then reading the data requires no overhead from network transmission. A yet-unsolved OIS research problem is the minimization of the cost of updating this information at all relevant nodes. If users at several sites were to attempt to update simultaneously, the result could be inconsistent copies, and so yet more research has been centered around efficient maintenance of multiple-copy databases. Possible solutions might include a centralized controller scheme [Garc79] in which all nodes must ask permission from the primary controller, although this scheme generally tends to create performance bottlenecks at the primary site. A variant of this scheme employs one or more centralized controllers for various segments of the database with distributed crash recovery [Mena80]. One algorithm allowing totally distributed control is the ring-structured scheme of Elli77, in which messages circulate around all relevant nodes in a prescribed order and return to the sender afterward as permission to update. This technique, however, tends to be slow because of low utilization of parallelism. It is also possible to implement a "primary update token" that moves around the network and symbolizes control. A node that holds the token can freely update the database. A less cumbersome scheme employing distributed control is the voting algorithm of Thom79: If a node wants to update, it can do so by asking its neighbors to perform local consistency checks and to vote "yes" or "no" to the update. Each neighbor, in turn, asks its neighbors to vote. After getting a positive vote from a majority of the nodes, the node may update. In fact, the update may be performed even before voting is complete if transaction restart or rollback is available. This scheme allows the system to continue gracefully even if a minority of the nodes are not functioning. The complexity of this algorithm and others indicates the strong need for formal proofs of correctness [Elli77]. Also, experience is still needed with implementations. At the Computer Corporation of America, an ambitious project is being considered that will implement a duplicated database facility for the Arpanet community that utilizes different update protocols for different classes of update transactions [Bern77].

All of these schemes have the common objectives of efficiency, consistency, robustness in the face of partial failures, and formal correctness. Some additional techniques that might be used include *time-stamps*, which are attached to transactions so that such problems as out-of-order updates can be avoided; *node IDs* and *transaction IDs*, which break dead-locks in an unbiased fashion; *locking* of records or pages of a database, which can ensure that several users will not access the same data at the same time; *two-phase commit protocol*, which locks multiple resources in a safe (i.e., robust) manner; and *time-outs*, which detect transmission problems and malfunctioning nodes. These techniques are all directly relevant to the design and implementation of office information systems.

Office Systems Consistency   Suppose that in the previously explained order processing example (Figure 9.4), a count must be maintained of the number of customers per week; however a count at activity a10 yields 90 customers (the number leaving the system), whereas a count at activity a2 yields 100 customers (number entering). This type of inconsistency can be detected automatically by using formal models such as ICNs. Such automatic detection can alert the office administrator to an error (in this case, the administrator forgot to count those customers who exited via path a6). In a typical large office with many paths of communication, such inconsistencies can be readily detected and corrected by the OIS. Consistence takes on an even more important role within the automated office. Clerical users' interaction with the automated system, the frequency of change within the office, and highly complex communications and control all necessitate rigorous verification of consistency.

Within this paper we define consistency broadly to mean "a collection of specifications or rules that are not contradictory." A distinction is made between internal and external consistency: Internal consistency is defined as the impossibility, given a set of axioms and inference rules, of generating contradictory theorems, whereas external consistency is defined as the absence of discrepancy between two sets of specifications of a system, between a system and assertions about that system, or between two "equivalent" systems.

Some classes of consistency, if breached, leave the system in an illegal or undesirable state. This occurs in the following four classes:

1. *Security Violation.* For example, displaying sensitive private information on a terminal in a public area is an undesirable state.

2. *Improper Responsibility Delegation.* Although it may be feasible for an automated system to take over assigned mundane tasks at a work station while that clerk is out of the room or on vacation, some person or process should have responsibility for each transaction that enters the system. If too few (or too many) parties have responsibility, this may be detectable as an undesirable state.

3. *Contradictory Information State.* If an order form indicates that 100 widgets were ordered today but the log book says no orders were placed today, then we have another example of inconsistency. This type of inconsistency frequently occurs with respect to monetary figures. In some cases, if the discrepancy is small, then the office may ignore it; if the discrepancy is large, then it becomes an undesirable state.

4. *Contradictory Database State.* If an office manager, after finishing both business and the processing of all transactions for the day, discovers that two copies of the primary database (which are automatically maintained by the OIS) have different values, then the bad database state shows that this is a case of inconsistency.

Violation of the following classes of consistency, however, cannot always be so readily detected.

5. *Message Transmission Semantics.* Inconsistencies could occur when A sends, B never receives; A sends form F, B does not understand F; A sends to a nonexistent receiver; or B waits to receive, but A never sends.

6. *Data semantics.* Consistency can be demanded in terms of field types (e.g., that no letter of the alphabet be in a salary field, or that the field value for the number of customers during a specific month not be negative).

7. *Procedure Semantics* (correctness of programs). If specifications or assertions are provided in addition to the system documentation, then correctness of implementation with respect to the specifications can be checked [Hant76]. One would like to have version consistency over dynamic re-calculation; that is, although the system is constantly changing and it is not possible to stop the system in the sense of restarting all transactions, it is nevertheless desirable to maintain consistency with respect to which version of each subsystem everybody is using.

8. *Synchronization.* Deadlock, starvation, and time-erratic service are examples of violation of interprocess consistency. These problems occur when multiple processes need to synchronize.

Having previously given a definition of ICNs, we are able to build on this mathematical framework to formally carry out external consistency analyses. For this purpose it is useful to distinguish between ICNs (Table 2) and ICN diagrams (Figure 9.4). Completeness and consistency of ICNs can then be defined with respect to ICN diagrams. Intuitively, these answer the following two questions.

1. *Completeness.* Does the mathematical notation suffice to describe all office procedures? The working meaning of "office procedure" would be any office procedure describable by an ICN diagram. To ensure completeness, we insist that any two black dots (AND nodes) in a diagram be separated by at least one activity node.

2. *Consistency.* Given one of our mathematical descriptions, does it always describe an office procedure? The working meaning of this is that the mathematical description has some ICN diagram that corresponds to it. If the mathematical description says that activity α is a predecessor of activity β but β is not a successor of α, then the consistency constraint is violated. Thus we impose the following criterion.

$$\forall \alpha \in A, \forall \{\beta_1, \beta_2, \ldots, \beta_n\} \in \delta_k(\alpha), \exists \Upsilon \ni \alpha \in \Upsilon \in (\cap \delta_k(\beta_i))$$

where k can take on the value i or 0 implying, respectively, that $k' = 0$ or i. This criterion states that if $\{\beta_1, \beta_2, \ldots, \beta_n\}$ is one of the possible successor sets of α, then all β_i must agree that α is in one of their common predecessor sets.

Questions of uniqueness of the above correspondence can be rigorously investigated by defining structural and functional equivalence among models (see Nutt79b). These notions of equivalence imply that any reorganization transformations performed on a model ought to yield an alternative office structure that meets certain consistency constraints with respect to the original structure.

Measurement and Evaluation

Computer system measurement and evaluation might easily be included under a different topic heading such as software engineering or operating systems. It appears as a separate topic primarily because the measurement and evaluation subjects include human users as well as computer systems. Performance tools, such as queuing models, operational analysis models, simulation models, and performance monitors, all are used to test an OIS, measure its performance, or predict its performance from specifications. Many of these same tools can be used to measure the *user* of the system as well as the system itself. After briefly surveying the area, we include a more complete discussion of a facility that was used to test Officetalk during its final stages of development.

Many of the more pragmatic motivations for so measuring and/or predicting the performance of an OIS are the same as those in any computer system: the need to choose between alternative systems or approaches, to project performance in order to evaluate the power of a system or configuration, and to make better use of existing facilities through tuning [Luca71]. Because of the complexity of interactive loads placed on an OIS, it has become important to better characterize the user of such systems. It is also useful to measure the user in order to design better user interfaces. Such user performance measures may be based on either the time a user takes to react to the system output or the time a user takes to correct a line of text.

Tuning studies in the OIS include traditional matters such as locating files in some part of the system such that access time is a function of the amount of traffic between the file and the user. Tuning a work station for a particular user may require more flexibility, since each user may wish to tailor the station to his or her own needs on any given day. For example, the user may wish to configure the station such that it always presents a standard initial display or perhaps have the same initial display that existed when the user last used the system.

OIS Simulation   Simulation in the study of an office information system helps both to predict the performance and to test the operation of the OIS. It is also useful in OIS testing in that it can establish a controlled environment in which a segment of a distributed system can be exercised. Simulation in the network environment of the office system also naturally leads to notions of distributed simulation, particularly when, as in the controlled environment case, a detailed simulator needs to execute in real time.

Testing a distributed OIS requires that one simulate the various possible interactions that may take place in a network of work stations. Ordinarily, these nodes have relative autonomy and are not directly controlled by their neighbors. Whenever a system is subjected to testing, it is important to establish causal relationships between the observed performance of the system and the stimulus (in this case, work load) that is applied to the system, in order to determine the events causing unusual behavior. In traditional computer systems, much is known about controlling the work load during periods of observation. A benchmark program is used to drive a system with a well-known, fixed amount of work; the synthetic program is useful for establishing a benchmark that can be systematically increased [Ferr72]. Similarly, in time-sharing systems, scripts have been used to provide a well-defined fixed load on a system (see Hold73). For the OIS, however, it is more difficult to apply a well-understood work load, since requests for service that are directed to a work station may be interactive. For example, clerk A may request that clerk B prepare a bill from a shipping list, but if the shipping list is incomplete, B will return it to A and request more information or clarification.

The *Backtalk* facility was designed to provide just such a controlled environment for testing Officetalk-Zero [Nutt79a]. Establishing this controlled environment for the system makes it possible to

1. repeat a sequence of events in an experiment so that system errors can be studied more carefully;

2. determine a standard, or canonical, load for a distributed system so that relative performances of two versions of the system can be compared;

3. increase the load on the distributed system in a controlled manner so that system bottlenecks can be observed.

Within this controlled environment, a subset of the nodes can also be used as a personnel training tool; each work station in the subset interacts with a model of the complementary subset of nodes rather than the remaining real nodes. Even a single work station can be used within this environment to measure the performance of the individual human user.

Each instance of Officetalk executes at a node in a local network; other nodes of the network implement other Officetalk instances, hardcopy devices, or a filing system. Several diverse facilities can be used by making appropriate requests at the network interface; if results are to be returned, they will arrive at the network interface. Thus the system environment of any single node corresponds to the information sent and received at the network interface. In order to provide a controlled environment for one node, it is necessary to model the network and all other nodes within the network by generating the information input to the node and by acting upon the information exiting the node. The format of the information passed into the work station must be consistent with that work station's facilities; for example, if the station is expecting a complex description of a CRT image of a form with certain fields filled in, the environment must provide information in exactly that format. In simulating an interactive conversation, the environment becomes even more complex. As information is received from the subject node, the environment model must absorb that information and respond accordingly. More complex interactions can be modeled by constructing procedural definitions of the facilities provided to the subject node. The controlled environment facility then simply replaces the network and all other nodes. Thus a controlled environment for the single node can be derived by using procedures to model the activity of all other work stations and servers. The accuracy of the model of the environment is determined by its ability to simulate the interacting work stations by procedural definitions.

A simulation of the environment in a distributed system will always depend on the particular function of that system; that is, the algorithmic description of the tasks performed at a work station is unique to that organization and work station type. Therefore, a specified facility to model a user and his or her function is necessary. The primitive operations provided by this facility should correspond to the set of functions made available to the user of the work station. For example, if a user has the ability to create a new report, fill in certain fields, and send the report to another user/work station, then the simulation facility ought to incorporate these capabilities as primitive operators. Hence the user interface portion of Officetalk is replaced by Backtalk, which appears as a series of procedures to the user of Backtalk/Officetalk and appears as a user to the remainder of Officetalk. It is still necessary to implement a model of the human user. If procedures have not been defined to automate the user's functions, then appropriate models of those functions must be constructed to interact with Officetalk through Backtalk.

The Backtalk facility allows implementation of real-time models of work stations at various nodes by using Officetalk facilities driven by models of the human user. In this manner one can specify a sporadic load on some work stations by modeling the corresponding interacting work stations with Backtalk. The level of detail in the Backtalk models is determined for the purpose of controlling the network environment of a particular (set of) Officetalk work station(s). This facility allows the designers of Officetalk to set the load on experimental versions systematically in order to compare different versions, increase the load to determine location of bottlenecks, and repeat any tests, if necessary.

Distributed Simulation   Simulation models have frequently been used to investigate concurrent systems. Building models that are exercised on a single processor is relatively straightforward since the distributed aspects of the system are modeled rather than implemented; for example, a simulation of a network of machines can cause the machines to execute in quasi-parallel while the entire internode communication is simulated. A more interesting problem arises if the simulation is actually to execute in real time, which would be required if it were necessary to simulate some, but not all, of the nodes in a network. One such application is that of training employees on a new OIS. For certain high-level, low-detail models, a single node in the network could simulate the input/output behavior of several nodes. However, as the detail increases, the real-time constraints on the simulator become more difficult to meet, and at some point it would become necessary to distribute the simulator itself over two or more nodes of the network.

An individual work station could be used to model the activity of different work stations simultaneously. There are limiting factors to the implementation of *virtual work stations* on a single work station: real-time response of human users, complexity of the model of their activity, and computational power of the work station. Carefully designed models of virtual work stations will not depend on the mapping of virtual work stations to real work stations. Instead, a single module of the model will completely implement the mapping, obscuring it from all other parts of the model. Whenever a simulation mode of multiple virtual work stations is implemented on more than one real work station, the model is termed a *distributed simulator*. Other forms of distributed simulators have been used to investigate queuing networks [Chan79, Peac79], packet communication architectures [Brya77], and air traffic control systems [Thom72].

Distinguishing between virtual and real work stations, in particular those driven by Backtalk, makes it possible to distribute the controlled environment model. Logically, the system may contain N distinct work stations, whereas physically the configuration may contain one real work station per user, and some undetermined number of virtual Backtalk work stations per real work station. If the number of virtual Backtalk work stations is the same as the number of real Backtalk work stations, then control is implemented by the operating system for the distributed system itself. If the number of virtual Backtalk work stations exceeds the number of real Backtalk work stations, then the distributed simulation must perform the mapping into real machines. A better modularization of the simulation model might be realized by simulating N different work stations on M different nodes, where M varies from experiment to experiment (or perhaps even from moment to moment). To implement such a simulator, it is necessary to construct a careful mapping of virtual work stations to real work stations and to build some good synchronization mechanisms into the simulator itself.

Distributed systems force the designer to deal with added complexity in the implementation and testing of a system; therefore the user may require more complex training in order to use the system. Each node in the distributed system takes on the complexity of a traditional computer system, yet the designer must still cope with interactions among the nodes of a set. The techniques implemented and described above are some initial attempts at providing a set of tools to aid the distributed system designer by controlling the environment in which individual components of the overall system are tested. A properly designed controlled-environment subsystem should be flexible enough to allow one to model various kinds of user loads, yet specific enough to make those loads applicable to a particular situation. The Backtalk approach is to incorporate basic commands of the office information system into the basic subsystem so that specific modeling procedures can be constructed from these facilities.

Communications

The area of communications encompasses many diverse topics of both direct and indirect interest to the office researcher/computer scientist. This spectrum covers such topics as optical communication, telecommunication, packet radio techniques, satellite communications, digital signal processing, and the regulation of communication facilities. In addition, there is a sociological discipline concerned with the linguistic culture of the office. In this section the diversity (rather than technical detail) of communications topics is emphasized. Finally, we discuss informal communication in the office.

The aspect of communications that has been studied most intensively by the computer science community is computer communication networks [Kimb75]. There has been a recent emphasis on the same area with respect to local computer networks (see the annotated bibliography by Shoch [Shoc79]). Much of this work has been directed toward improving the performance, reliability and flexibility of the communication over a data network. In the process of investigating ways to accomplish these improvements, researchers have concentrated on network structures and network protocols. For example, researchers have considered structures ranging from fully interconnected nodes, as might be found in a multiprocessor system, to central switching facilities, which rely on a switching center to pass information among the nodes. Between these extremes lie partially connected systems, star organizations, and ring organizations. In the area of transmission protocols, investigators have concentrated on mechanisms to increase reliability, communication unit sizes, and protocols offered to the end user of the communication facility.

The bandwidth of a communication medium dictates the use of that medium. Voice-grade transmission media ($\sim$2.4 kilobits per second) have commonly been used for interconnecting computers and are used in the Citibank system. A higher bandwidth, of the order of 3 megabits per second, is frequently used for facsimile transmission and is employed by Officetalk. In order to support color facsimile transmission, the communication bandwidth may need to be 25 megabits per second. Some applications, such as video teleconferencing, require a bandwidth of 1 gigabit per second.

The distance of the communication will influence the choice of a particular transmission technology. Intraoffice communication systems can utilize voice-grade telephone lines, leased lines, coaxial cable, or fiber optics. Within a city, the choice is more limited; telephone lines, leased lines, or packet radio. Notice that such applications may take advantage of *gateway* technology to combine intraoffice techniques with other short- and long-haul media (see Bogg80). Intercontinental communication may be limited to such media as satellite transmission systems. These satellite systems provide a bandwidth approaching 1 gigabit per second and can be used to transmit information anywhere in the world [Whit78]. The Satellite Business Systems and the Xerox XTEN communication systems, among others, rely on satellites for transmission.

Communication network technologies have led to the idea of *value-added networks*, which may incorporate various useful features into the mechanism that implements the basic protocol; for example, the network may provide teleconferencing, electronic mail, node management, or accounting as basic utilities. The AT&T Advanced Communications Service (ACS) provides several functions in addition to basic communication [Roch79]. This additional functionality results from the use of modern communication technologies; since computers are already used for switching, they can also be used to provide other services to the customer.

Although the idea of electronic mail is now common in network environments, further developments are likely to take place with respect to designs. For example, the Arpanet mail service uses a scheme by which anyone can establish a mailbox at certain stations in the network, and any other user of the net can deposit mail into that mailbox [Hend77]. It is possible to construct facilities that can effectively broadcast information as well as direct a copy to a given mailbox. Some variations on this scheme, especially for local networks, might provide "intelligent mailboxes" which filter incoming mail, prepare stock answers, maintain a calendar, or systematically query information repositories.

It can be seen that the area of network communications, in all of its technical and political breadth, is critical to the development of the OIS discipline. Furthermore, it is necessary to take a wider point of view toward communications, including the sociological aspects.

Informal Communications in the Office   An office is an information processing and transforming mechanism. Within the office, people communicate through gestures and informal communications, as well as through more formal channels. The formal communications are usually well formulated and can often be algorithmically specified; the informal communications are ordinarily not well enough understood to specify their effect by an algorithm. As a consequence, automation of an office is likely to upset the informal communication mechanisms, possibly causing the office information system to fail.

It is well known that many offices function in an informal atmosphere in which the office workers exchange banter and often discuss business in lighthearted terms. The first observation that might be made about such office environments is that they merely reflect the personalities of the workers or their managers. One might also assume that it is necessary to allow such an informal atmosphere to exist in order to keep the morale of the workers at a productive level. Studies have shown that informal communication is much more important than any of these theories might suggest. Browner et al. point out that the office is full of structural dependencies in which groups of people depend on each other in order to accomplish their own work [Brow78]. Their study showed that salespeople who maintained a good relationship with the accountant tended to be promptly reimbursed for expenses; in turn, the accountant required complete information from the salespeople in order to keep accurate books. As a result, each made some effort to create a friendly atmosphere through informal communication, thus optimizing the situation for both.

Wynn has made an extensive study of the nature of informal communication in offices in an effort to aid the computer scientist in confronting some human factors of office system designs [Wynn79]. She has concluded that not only is conversation useful in maintaining a cooperative atmosphere among co-workers, but that such conversation is *necessary* in order to implement the normal distributed problem solving that takes place in the day-to-day activity of many offices. Typically, the function of the office is defined by an informal, intuitive specification of the tasks rather than by a formal document that specifies the exact procedures to be followed. As a result, the actual office procedures frequently do not exist in a manual or in any one person's knowledge; they are distributed over the set of people who work in the office. A simple example of these interactive conversations might be the experienced worker's explanations to the novice. Typically, the capable experienced worker corrects and guides the novice in the guise of informal conversation, frequently casting the information in the form of a joke or parenthetical remark of social comment. Workers of equivalent experience level also make use of informal conversations to solve an office problem cooperatively. For example, two customer service workers may enter into informal negotiations in order to decide which has more of the information required to handle a customer's particular problem;

such negotiations are frequently not explicit but are embedded in social conversation. One result of this communal approach to problem solving is that the group of workers maintains a constant conversational framework for interpreting remarks and transmitting and transforming information. It is this complex social environment that provides a medium for exchange of information that would be absent in a formal, vigorous specification of processing. The environment is conducive to carrying out distributed work, implementing error handling, and implementing the constant education of the office workers.

The problem of retaining social contact among office workers is yet unsolved; the trend toward automation works against the goal of maintaining a social structure. If the communication medium emphasizes structured business transactions, there is the danger that the informal conversation will be destroyed. One partial solution is to encourage the use of a mail system for casual as well as formal communication, as in the Arpanet mail system. Future communications systems might also incorporate audio and visual transmission technologies. An appropriate physical design of the office can also help prevent isolation of workers.

With the possible exception of some word processing centers, most current automated office facilities have not developed to the point where they have endangered channels of social conversation. However, the next steps in such automation will probably require more effort toward maintaining informal communication channels.

Other Related Areas

OIS research is interdisciplinary in nature and encompasses a number of other relevant areas such as sociology, psychology, economics, operations research, management science, legislation, and regulation. Within computer science there are areas other than those we have discussed, including information retrieval, graphics, text editing, architecture, and artificial intelligence. In this section we discuss a few of these briefly.

Social Implications   New systems may be marketed that will allow an office to operate with a relatively small number of people or to increase the functionality of each worker. There are indications that the increase in administrative work load is outracing the current capabilities of the office; hence added functionality will be necessary to handle this work load without an increase in the work force [Crea78]. Since technology is producing more and more compact work stations, the physical organization of the office may soon decentralize to the point that workers will perform some of their duties in their own homes. The possible impact of such a radical strategy is yet unknown, but such disturbance of the logical and physical organization of the office will probably have a great effect on office procedures owing to the potential decrease in informal communication, as discussed in the previous section. Sociology has become an integral part of system design. See Klin80 for a more comprehensive treatment of the topic. In our opinion, the technology in and of itself is neither good nor bad; it is the use of the technology that determines the effect on the office worker and on society.

Psychology   Psychology is the study of emotional and behavioral characteristics of individuals. Some of the relevant topics include human factors, the person-machine interface, and user conceptualization of systems. The study of person-machine interfaces addresses the type of work station display, the applicability of color graphics, the layout of a keyboard, and the convenience of alternative pointing devices. Models of users include microlevel representations of the human memory, keystroke models for time and motion studies, and models that represent a set of editing tasks. User conceptualization was mentioned in the section on programming languages; OIS systems ought to provide a conceptual model that does not conflict with the informal model held by the individual within the office. (A forthcoming special issue of *Computing Surveys* will elaborate on psychology and computing systems.)

Computing Architecture   Hardware technology has developed much further than software technology, and software system designers, aware of the problem, have increasingly relied on computer architects to incorporate more traditional software functionality into specialized hardware designs. Computer architecture and integrated circuit design have made the concept of the intelligent work station a reality through the development of such devices as word processors, small business computers, and intelligent terminals. Recent work in computer architecture has included novel designs for office systems, as well as more well-known architectures for integration of software functions into software or hardware [ACM80].

Fixed-instruction sets and bit-slice microprocessors have both contributed to the current trend toward preference for local networks of small computers. Intelligent terminals and communicating word processors frequently employ byte-oriented microprocessors as small computational units that can execute complex programs in reasonable times. The declining costs of such machines have made them especially suitable as work stations in an OIS network. Bit-slice microprocessors are chip sets that can be composed to form machines of extended word width.

They have been used in small microprogrammed machines for wider word sizes. Such machines are inexpensive enough to serve as common nodes in a network.

The increasing density of integrated circuit design is also drastically influencing computer architecture. The most obvious impact has come from the chip connection restrictions that are pushing designers into bit serial designs, resulting in new ways of thinking about machines. One trend has been toward data flow machines with many processors [Scha78; Denn74]. An example is Wilner's Recursive Machine [Wiln78], which rejects the basic notions of the von Neumann machine in favor of an architecture composed of logically regular elements, each of which can store, process, and transmit information. The basic idea behind the design is that such a collection of regular elements can take on the same interface specifications as the individual elements. The design is ideally suited for VLSI technology. The elements can be logically structured to represent a recursively defined hierarchy of variable-length cells, allowing the presentation of hierarchical data structures. As a result of this generality of logical interconnection, and of the ability of the architecture to mold itself to represent the logical interconnection, Wilner argues that his machine is especially well adapted to handling "a growing, adaptive set of flexible structures." In particular, he claims that "office procedures are a growing, adaptive set of loosely interconnected, event-driven activities" for which the Recursive Machine is especially well suited.

Artificial Intelligence Designers of the automated office can profit from many solutions to pending artificial intelligence problems. In particular, the research areas of natural-language understanding, speech understanding, knowledge representation and description, and knowledge-based systems can all provide useful results to the OIS researchers. Natural-language understanding is a powerful aid to clerical workers and managers in directing their machines to perform work. This area begins to overlap the study of programming languages for clerical users, although the philosophical underpinnings of the two groups are different. Speech understanding, even isolated utterance recognition, can drastically improve the acceptance of automated equipment in the office. Managers have traditionally avoided keyboards, and they may also tend to avoid other mechanical input devices such as a joystick or mouse. If an OIS can recognize even a limited form of speech, the probability of its acceptance in the traditional office will increase. Knowledge representation and knowledge-based systems can be utilized in a number of ways to aid the office worker. An intelligent "Help" system can greatly aid the user during the initial stages of use of the OIS; it can also be useful after the system has been used for a while if the worker uses certain facilities infrequently. Forms manipulation can be improved by applying learning techniques. Suppose that a clerk always fills in his or her name in the originator field of a blank form. The system might be put into a "learning mode" during which it attempts to recognize a consistent set of actions that take place from one transaction to the next. Subsequently, the system would fill in the originator field of the blank form with the clerk's name whenever necessary. Knowledge engineering has been successfully applied to a number of other application areas such as chemistry [Buch69] and geology [Duda78]. Although it seems clear that one cannot immediately derive similar systems for an entire office, portions of the office may be amenable to such techniques.

3 *Future Trends in OIS Research*

A number of research topics in computer science have been introduced in the new interdisciplinary field of office information systems. In this paper we have articulated several problems that much be solved in order for office information systems to be successful in the modern business world. In some cases we have also speculated on solutions to these problems, while in others we have simply described the problem. We believe that the areas that we have described, even those for which we discussed some approaches, are open for research.

The state of the art in office information systems is built upon the ideal of Officetalk-Zero, BDL, and Zisman's system (although there are probably unpublished advanced systems being developed within the various corporations). Each of these approaches to OIS work has addressed a subset of the problems mentioned in this article, yet none of them has provided a universal OIS: Officetalk emphasizes the user interface, BDL emphasizes the structured programming environment for the clerical user, and Zisman concentrates on the automation of office procedures.

Future research in the area of computer science and office automation will probably fall into two distinct subfields. The first subfield includes the set of familiar technical problems on which computer scientists can immediately begin to work; the second subfield includes problems that are less familiar and more dependent on future research.

One second-domain problem is the need for integration to take place on at least three fronts: functional integration, system integration, and interdisciplinary integration. Functional integration refers to the need for the user's model of a system to be complete and consistent. The clerical user must be able to work in an environment that provides all of the facilities he or she will need in order to perform the work without having to learn several different command languages or subsystem models. System integration refers to the need for operating systems, programming languages, architecture, databases, and artificial intelligence systems that converge into a single, uniform environment; for example, researchers at PARC have experimented with the Smalltalk environment as an integration of operating system, programming language, debugger, and text editor [Kay77, Inga78]. Interdisciplinary integration refers to the need for researchers in computer science to interact with workers in management science, political science, psychology, sociology, and perhaps law. Wynn's work [Wynn79] is a good example of such interdisciplinary integration.

Although we have directed much of our discussion toward office information systems for clerical workers, future OIS work must also address the problem of designing systems for management. For example, an OIS might support successively higher levels of management by offering

1.   the office manager the ability to change the structure of individual clerks' tasks,

2.   the administrative vice-president the ability to change the structure of the entire system, and

3.   the chief executive officer the ability to control and audit corporate resources.

Such systems will need the ability to control and audit corporate information rather than manipulate characters. Interdisciplinary work involving computer scientists and management scientists is especially evident in the design of management systems.

As a result of particular constraints on OIS application, we may see several new and radical system designs emerge. For example, local networks of minicomputers provide a physical medium for the design of exotic systems of work stations that share compilers, consistency-checkers, and databases, while autonomously performing other tasks with private facilities. The notion of the intelligent form, as mentioned in the Officetalk and BDL discussions, could be extended to allow a forms process to guide itself through various work stations and measure its own progress, utilizing the facilities of particular work stations within their own domains.

Research on office information systems intersects with research in many other disciplines, particularly in computer science. Many unsolved problems of OIS research can be addressed wholly within computer science; many others invite the computer scientist to extend into other disciplines.

Acknowledgments

We wish to thank the computer scientists, designers, and implementers at Xerox PARC for the years of labor that form the foundation of this paper. We especially thank our colleagues in the Office and Analysis Research Groups for their work, which provided direction and motivation for this paper.

References

ACM78 ACM. Special Issue: Graphics Standards, *ACM Comput. Surv.*, **10**, 4(Dec. 1978), 363–502.

ACM79 ACM. Status report of the Graphics Standards Planning Committee, *Comput. Graphics*, **13**, 3(Aug. 1979).

ACM80 ACM Workshop on Computer Architecture for Non-Numeric Processing, Pacific Grove, Calif., Mar. 1980.

Aron69 Aron, J. D., "Information systems in perspective," *ACM Comput. Surv.*, **1**, 4(Dec., 1969), 213–236.

Bask77 Baskett, F., Howard, J. H., and Montague, J. T. "Task communication in DEMOX," *Proc. 6th Symp. Operating Systems Principles*, 1977, pp. 23–31.

Baum80 Baumann, L. S., and Coop, R. D. "Automated workflow control: A key to office productivity," *Proc. AFIPS Office Automation Conf.*, Mar. 1980.

Bern77 Bernstein, P. A., Shipman, D. W., Rothnie, J. B., and Goodman, N. "The concurrent control mechanism of SDD-1: A system for distributed databases (the general case)," Tech. Rep. CCA-77-09, Computer Corporation of America, Cambridge, Mass., Dec. 1977.

Bogg80 Boggs, D., Shoch, J., Taft, E., and Metcalfe, R. "Pup: An internetwork architecture," *IEEE Trans. Commun.*, (to appear).

Brow78 Browner, C., Chibnik, M., Crawley, C., Newman, K., and Sonafrank, A. "Report on a summer research project: A behavioral view of office work," Xerox PARC ORG Rep., Xerox Palo Alto Research Center, Palo Alto, Calif., Jan. 1978.

Brya77 Bryant, R. E., "Simulation of packet communication architecture computer systems," M.S. thesis, MIT/LCS/TR-188, M.I.T. Laboratory for Computer Science, Cambridge, Mass., 1977.

Buch69 Buchanan, B., Sutherland, G., and Feigenbaum, E. A. "HEURISTIC DENDRAL: A program for generating explanatory hypotheses in organic chemistry," in *Machine intelligence 4*, B. Meltzer, D. Michie, and M. Swann (Eds.), American Elsevier, New York, 1969, pp. 209–254.

Buch79 Buchanan, J. R. "Office scheduling and the production of documents," M.I.T.–I.A.P. Course on Electronic Office of the Future, Jan. 1979.

Burn77 Burns, J. C. "The evolution of office information systems," *Datamation*, **23**, 4(Apr. 1977), 60–64.

Camp78 Campos, I. M., and Estrin, G. "Concurrent software system design supported by SARA at the age of one," *Proc. 3rd Int. Conf. Software Engineering*, 1978, pp. 230–242.

Chan79 Chandy, K. M., and Misra, J. "Distributed simulation: A case study in design and verification of distributed programs," *IEEE Trans. Softw. Eng.*, **SE-5**, 5(Sept. 1979), 440–452.

Coff73 Coffman, E. G., Jr., and Denning, P. J. *Operating systems theory*, Prentice-Hall, Englewood Cliffs, N. J., 1973.

Crea78 Creative Strategies International. "Office automation," Rep. no. 27804, San Jose, Calif., July 1978.

Denn74 Dennis, J. B., and Misunas, D. P. "A computer architecture for highly parallel signal processing," *Proc. ACM Annual Conf.*, San Diego, Calif., Nov. 1974, pp. 402–409.

Duda78 Duda, R. O., Hart, P. E., Barrett, P., Gaschnig, J. G., Konolige, K., Reboh, R., and Slocum, J. "Development of the prospector consultation system for mineral exploration." Projs. 5821 and 6414, SRI International, Menlo Park, Calif., Oct. 1978.

Elli77 Ellis, C. A. "Consistency and correctness of duplicate database systems," 1977, pp. 67–84.

Elli79 Ellis, C. A. "Information control nets: A mathematical model of office information flow," *ACM Proc. Conf. Simulation, Modeling and Measurement of Computer Systems*, Aug. 1979, 225–240.

Ferr72 Ferrari, D. "Wordload characterization and selection in computer performance measurement," *Computer* (IEEE), **5**, 4(July–Aug. 1972), 18–24.

Garc79 Garcia, H. *Performance of update algorithms for replicated data in a distributed database*, Ph. D. dissertation, Dep. Computer Science, Stanford Univ., Stanford, Calif. 1979.

Gold79 Goldberg, A. J., and Robson, D. J. "A metaphor for user interface design," *Proc. Systems Sciences Conf.*, Univ. Hawaii, Jan. 1979, pp. 148–157.

Hamm77 Hammer, M., Howe, W. G., Kruskal, V. J., and Wladawsky, I. "A very high level programming language for data processing applications," *Commun. ACM*, **20**, 11(Nov. 1977), 832–840.

Hamm79 Hammer, M., and Zisman, M. D. "Design and implementation of office information systems," *Proc. N.Y.U. Symp. Automated Office Systems*, May 1979.

Hant76 Hantler, S. L., and King, J. C. "An introduction to proving the correctness of programs," *ACM Comput. Surv.*, **8**, 3(Sept. 1976), 331–353.

Heba79 Hebalkar, P. G., and Zilles, S. N. "TELL: A system for graphically representing software designs," *Proc. IEEE Spring CompCon79*, 1979, San Francisco, Calif., pp. 244–249.

Hend77 Henderson, D. H., Jr., and Myer, T. H. "Issues in message technology," *Proc. 5th Data Communications Symp.*, 1977, pp. 6-1–6-9.

Hewi79a Hewitt, C. "Behavioral characteristics of office systems," M.I.T.-I.A.P Course on Electronic Office of the Future, Jan. 1979.

Hewi79b Hewitt, C., Attardi, G., and Lieberman, H. "Specifying and proving properties of guardians for distributed systems," working paper, M.I.T. Artificial Intelligence Lab., Cambridge, Mass., Feb. 1979.

Hewl78 Hewlett-Packard Company. *HP 300 Computer System General Information Manual*, Santa Clara, Calif., Sept. 1978.

Hold73 Holdsworth, D., Robinson, G. W., and Wells, M. "A multi-terminal benchmark," *Software—Practice and Experience*, **3**, 1(Jan.–Mar. 1973), 43–59.

Inga78 Ingalls, D. H. "The Smalltalk-76 programming system: design and implementation," *Proc. 5th Annual Symp. Principles of Programming Languages*, Jan. 1978.

Karp69 Karp, R. M., and Miller, R. E. "Parallel program schemata," *J. Comput. Sys. Sci.*, **3** (1969), 147–195.

Kay77 Kay, A. C. "Microelectronics and the personal computer," *Sci. Am.*, **237**, 3(Sept. 1977), 231–244.

Kimb75 Kimbleton, S. R., and Schneider, G. M. "Computer communications networks: Approaches, objectives, and performance considerations, " *ACM Comput. Surv.*, **7**, 3(Sept. 1975), 129–173.

Klin80 Kling, R. W. "Social analyses of computing: Theoretical perspectives in recent empirical research," *ACM Comput. Surv.*, **12**, 1(Mar. 1980), 61–110.

Luca71 Lucas, H. C., Jr. "Performance evaluation and monitoring," *ACM Comput. Surv.*, **3**, 3(Sept. 1971), 79–91.

Mena80 Menasce, D. A., Popek, G. J., and Muntz, R. R. "A locking protocol for resource coordination in distributed databases," *ACM Trans. Database Syst.* (to appear).

Metc76 Metcalfe, R. M., and Boggs, D. R. "Ethernet: distributed packet switching for local computer networks," *Commun. ACM*, **19**, 7(July 1976), 395–404.

Morg76a Morgan, H. L. "Office automation project: A research perspective," *Proc. AFIPS 1976 Nat. Computer Conf.*, Vol. 45, AFIPS Press, Arlington, Va., pp. 605–610.

Morg76b Morgan, H. L. "DAISY: An applications perspective," *Proc. Wharton/ONR Conf. Decision Support Systems*, 1976.

Morg79 Morgan, H. L. "Database alerting and corporate memory," M.I.T.–I.A.P Course on Electronic Office of the Future, Jan. 1979.

Ness78 Ness, D. Office Automation Project, Decision Sciences working papers, Wharton School, Univ. Pennsylvania, Philadelphia, Pa., 1976–1978.

Newe72 Newell, A., and Simon, H. *Human problem solving*, Prentice-Hall, Englewood Cliffs, N.J., 1972.

Newm79 Newman, W. M., and Sproull, R. F. *Principles of interactive computer graphics* (2 ed.), McGraw-Hill, New York, 1979.

Nutt79a Nutt, G. J., and Ellis, C. A. "Backtalk: an office environment simulator," *Proc. 1979 Int. Conf. Communications*, vol. 2, June 1979, pp. 22.3.1–22.3.5.

Nutt79b Nutt, G. J., and Ellis, C. A. "On the equivalence of office models," Rep. SSL-79-8 Xerox Palo Alto Research Center, Palo Alto, Calif., Dec. 1979.

Pati70 Patil, S. S. "Coordination of asynchronous events," Ph.D. dissertation, Dep. Electrical Engineering, Project MAC, M.I.T., Cambridge, Mass, 1970.

Paxt79 Paxton, W. H. "A client-based transaction system to maintain data integrity," *Proc. 7th Symp. Operating Systems Principles*, Dec. 1979, pp. 18–23.

Peac79 Peacock, J. W. "Synchronization of distributed simulation using broadcast algorithms," *Proc. 4th Berkeley Conf. Distributed Data Management and Computer Networks*, Aug. 1979, pp. 237–259.

Pete77 Peterson, J. L. "Petri nets," *ACM Comput. Surv.*, **9**, 3(Sept. 1977), 223–252.

Reed78 Reed, D. P. "Naming and synchronization in a decentralized computer system," Ph.D. dissertation, MIT/LCS/TR-205, M.I.T. Lab. for Computer Science, Cambridge, Mass., 1978.

Reed79 Reed, D. P., and Kanodia, R. K. "Synchronization with eventcounts and sequencers," *Commun. ACM*, **22**, 2(Feb. 1979), 115–122.

Roch79 Rochkind, M. M. "Service concepts underlying ACS," *Proc. 1979 Int. Conf. Communications*, vol. 3, June, 1979, pp. 38.1.1–38.1.6.

Rohl79 Rohlfs, S. "Linguistic considerations for user interface design," *Proc. Int. Workshop Integrated Office Systems*, Nov. 1979.

Rose72 Rose, C. W. "LOGOS and the software engineer," *Proc. AFIPS 1972 Fall Jt. Computer Conf.*, vol. 41, pt. I, AFIPS Press, Arlington, Va., pp. 311–323.

Ross77 Ross, D. T. "Structured analysis (SA): A language for communicating ideas," *IEEE Trans. Softw. Eng.*, **SE-3**, 1(Jan. 1977), 16–34.

Scha78 Schaffner, M. R. "Processing by data and program blocks," *IEEE Trans. Comput.*, **C-27**, 11(Nov. 1978), 1015–1028.

Shoc79 Shoch, J. F. "An annotated bibliography on local computer networks (preliminary edition)," Rep. SSL-79-5, Xerox Palo Alto Research Center, Palo Alto, Calif., May 1979.

Swin79 Swinehart, D., McDaniel, G., and Boggs, D. "WFS: A simple centralized file system for a distributed environment," *Proc. 7th Symp. Operating Systems Principles*, Dec. 1979, pp. 9–17.

Tagg77 Taggart, W. M., Jr., and Tharp, M. O. "A survey of information requirements analysis techniques," *ACM Comput. Surv.*, **9**, 4(Dec 1977), 273–290.

Teic72 Teichroew, D. "A survey of languages for stating requirements for computer-based information systems," *Proc. AFIPS 1972 Fall Jt. Computer Conf.*, vol. 41, AFIPS Press, Arlington, Va., pp. 1203–1224.

Teit77 Teitelman, W. "A display oriented programmer's assistant," *Proc. 5th Int. Jt. Conf. Artificial Intelligence*, 1977, pp. 905–915.

Thac79 Thacker, C. P., McCreight, F. M., Lampson, B. W., Sproull, R. F., and Boggs, D. R. "ALTO: A personal computer," to appear in *Computer structures: Readings and examples*, D. Siewiorek, C. G. Bell, and A. Newell (Eds.).

Thom72 Thomas, R. H., and Henderson, D. A., Jr. "McRoss—A multi-computer programming system," *Proc. AFIPS 1972 Spring Jt. Computer Conf.*, vol. 40, AFIPS Press, Arlington, Va., pp. 281–293.

Thom79 Thomas, R. H. "A majority consensus approach to concurrency control for multiple copy databases," *ACM Trans. Database Syst.*, **4**, 2(June 1979), 180–209.

Tilb79 Tilbrook, D. "Information systems primitives," *Proc Int. Workshop Integrated Office Systems*, Nov. 1979.

Tsic79a Tsichritzis, D. "Form flow models," working paper, Univ. Toronto, Toronto, Ont., Canada, 1979.

Tsic79b Tsichritzis, D. "A form manipulation system," *Proc. N.Y.U. Symp. Automated Office Systems*, May 1979.

Weni78 Wenig, R. P., and Pardoe, T. D. *Oflce Automation Systems: A Management Guidebook to Advanced Integrated Oflce Systems*, International Management Services, Inc., Natick, Mass., Apr. 1978.

Whit77 White, R. B. "A prototype for the automated office," *Datamation*, **23**, 4(Apr. 1977), 83–90.

Whit78 White, W., and Holmes, M. "The future of commercial satellite telecommunications," *Datamation*, **24**, 7(July 1978), 94–102.

Wiln78 Wilner, W. T. "Recursive machines," Internal LSI Group Rep. Xerox Palo Alto Research Center, Palo Alto, Calif., Aug. 1978.

Wynn79 Wynn, E. "Office conversation as an information medium," Ph.D. dissertation, Dep. Anthropology, Univ. California, Berkeley, Calif., 1979.

Zism77 Zisman, M. D. "Representation, specification and automation of office procedures," Ph.D. dissertation, Wharton School, Univ. Pennsylvania, Philadelphia, Pa., 1977.

Zism78 Zisman, M. D. "Office automation: Revolution or evolution," *Sloan Management Review* (M.I.T.), **19**, 3(Spring 1978), 1–16.

Zloo75 Zloof, M. M. "Query by example," *Proc. AFIPS 1975 Nat. Computer Conf.*, vol. 44, AFIPS Press, Arlington, Va., pp. 431–437.

II

NEW TECHNOLOGIES FOR CSCW

Domain-Specific Coordination Support

CSCW has been driven by applications: people need to work together on specific tasks such as co-authorship, project management, and software development. In the overview to this collection, we contrasted CSCW systems with the generic communication support provided by electronic mail and computer conferencing. The latter are playing a less central role in CSCW system design, although they are still the focus of many user studies (see Readings 24 and 25). The papers in this section are about some group work systems in which the communications support is tightly integrated into the domain-specific functionality of the system.

Software development is one domain in which the importance of coordination technology has been apparent for some time. The paper by Kedzierski included here (Reading 10) is about a system to support this process. The communication primitives are based on a theory of Communication Acts related to Searle's work on speech acts. The communication acts supported by the system are those whose meaning is specialized to the business at hand, that of developing and maintaining a software system.

The second paper (Reading 11) describes Callisto, a project management system for the kind of large engineering project typical of prototype development for a large computer system. The tools in Callisto facilitate the documentation of project management expertise related to the prototyping effort so that it can be transferred to future projects.

The final paper (Reading 12), on Semistructured Messages as a basis for computer-supported coordination, takes a contrasting approach by starting with a very sophisticated mail system, the Information Lens, and proposing ways of tuning it to domain-specific tasks. In Lens, semistructured message templates highlight domain-specific information that can be used in sorting and prioritizing information. The set of templates can be easily extended and tailored to domain-specific uses.

It is interesting to note that these systems all make some use of artificial intelligence techniques. While CSCW systems are not necessarily dependent on artificial intelligence breakthroughs for successful implementation, the coordination-technology parts of these domain-specific CSCW systems make heavy use of well-understood artificial intelligence technology. These systems are rule-based, and represent information about the tasks by means of data structures tuned to supporting reasoning about such things as user roles and routing of information.

10

Communication and Management Support in System Development Environments

Beverly I. Kedzierski

Kestrel Institute, Palo Alto, CA

The Computer Science Department

University of Southwestern Louisiana

Lafayette, LA

1 Introduction

A System Development Support Environment that assists in communication and management tasks of software project members should aid the development of large, evolutionary computer systems. The environment proposed in this paper will include integrated capabilities for project management, system evaluation, documentation/help, and intelligent communication between designers/users, and either the system or other designers. The goal is to have the environment help collect, organize and disseminate information about a project, using a model of the underlying system. The work is based on the idea that people perform "Communication Acts"(ACTs) such as: questioning, griping, planning, requesting or informing, while interacting with a system, and that processing of these ACTs can be automated. A Taxonomy of "simple" ACTs has been created from initial, informal studies of system/user interaction. A knowledge-based synthesis approach is used to create an experimental environment to support a program synthesis (software) project [Phillips-81]. The environment design and framework, which is part of the author's Ph.D. thesis work in progress [Kedzierski-80], is discussed.

2 Motivation

Two intriguing questions concerning the development and application of complex interactive software systems are:

1.   What kind of activity do people engage in while working on a software system?

2.   What causes most problems during system evolution or development?

The answer to both of these questions can be stated in a single word: *Communication.*

Better software environments can be developed by studying and understanding the way people actually behave while interacting with a computer system, and using knowledge about the causes and solutions of problems they encounter.

An informal study of designer behavior during development of an evolutionary computer system, later described as the Target System, showed that the designers spent most of their time communicating among themselves or with the system (see chart below). The study was based on a small sample of data and a simple evaluation. Every action designers made during a period of time they were using the system was recorded. Then the data was reviewed and the actions were classified. The results gave rise to the Taxonomy described in Section 3, where example data are presented.

Interaction Type	Percent of Designer Time
Questioning	27%
Informing	25%
Complaining	13%
Planning and discussion	14%
Trying existing commands	21%

The results show that designers only spent 1/5 of their time working with the existing system, and that much communication activity was not being handled by the system.

Problems arise when so much activity involved in software development must be performed exclusively by humans. Breakdowns in communication are the cause of major problems in software development, or evolution, because communication plays such a large part in the programming process. An article by Keider [Keider-74] gives a list of reasons for project failure. Most of these reasons involve communication breakdown, which leads to ineffective project management.

Another problem of software designers, namely *slow progress* in building systems, occurs when designers (particularly new project members) do not have tools to aid them in communication. Communication and management activities occur during the "life cycle" of a software system. A software life cycle cost distribution from a study by Zelkowitz [Zelkowitz-78] and reported by Ledbetter [Ledbetter-80] shows that 67% of software cost is attributed to *maintenance*. Maintenance (or evolution) costs have been reduced up to 70% when design tools, with allowances for growth and management techniques, are used. Similarly, capabilities planned for the experimental environment, described in this paper, should contribute to cutting software life cycle costs.

Creating an environment to enhance communication among designers is particularly important when the details and implications of a complex system are not understood. There will be an even greater need for communication tools in the future, particularly in large, complex research environments. Therefore, this work is both cost effective and a valid endeavor.

3 System/User Interactions

This section will concentrate on the problems of handling communication information that results from user interaction with a large, complex evolutionary system.

In evolutionary system design, a small version of a large system is implemented, used, evaluated and then expanded. The final version is not determined before the building takes place. This process, called *structured growth* [Sandewall-78], relies on communication among the designers/users. Structured growth can be facilitated by determining, through interaction with the user, what information should be recorded. This recorded information, resulting from designer plans, gripes, questions, responses, etc., must then be properly organized and disseminated.

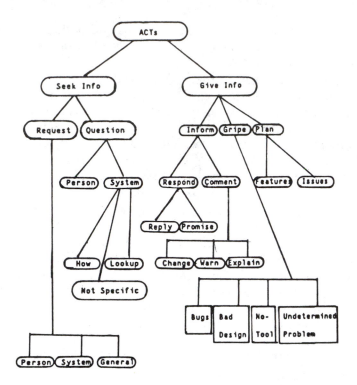

Figure 10.1

As a system is growing, breakdowns or secondary subgoals that arise during designer/user interaction with a system can impede progress toward the user's initial goal. For example, a user might have to solve a particular problem as a result of an error or might need a schedule of what to do after a task is completed. In this work, such a subgoal is called a communication "ACT," in accordance with the *Speech Act* theory of linguistics [Searle-78]. To "process" an ACT, the user's intentions are synthesized into elementary actions, including some suggested by the environment. This synthesis will be described later in more detail in Section 5.

ACTs are processed by recording, organizing, and disseminating information, thereby aiding the user, as well as the structured growth of the system. These activities form the basis of system-aided developer communication. An ACT Taxonomy, created by analyzing data of user/system interactions, gives examples of simple ACTs (see Figure 10.1). These form the major components of complex ACTs.

Examples of complex ACTs, collected in the informal designer behavior studies described above, are presented (in non-edited form). They are classified according to the ACT Taxonomy. This data was collected from various sources, including:

1. Comments written by users during sessions with an evolutionary system,

2. Notes taken from demonstrations of this system, and

3. Information recorded on "gripe and change" files for other large systems (e.g., INTERLISP).

Question

- *Tom, when will you have the new version ready?*

- *How do I delete nodes?*

- *Why is it sprouting a context?*

- *What is proto-setup?*

Inform

- *Try di—erent LISP version (as person tries to solve the problem and notices that a new version of LISP is running).*

- *I will have a version of the rule compiler ready by Friday.*

- *A new version has been created.*

- *Watch for changes in this part.*

- *The purpose of this function is to print prototypes in a nicer way.*

Gripe

- *PR.PROTS won't read my rules.*

- *There are two ways of doing the same thing.*

- *Need space to make it work.*

- *Tried to print compiled rules with no result.*

Plan

- *We need a printer for debugging.*

- *When should this be done?*

Request

- *Steve, please change the print prototypes in this way.*

- *What are my current jobs?*

Each datum does not suggest a unique simple ACT, but is actually a complex composition of many simple ACTs and related processing. The reason is that the processing of one ACT involves others (e.g., a question of the system may entail a complaint about a problem and a possible request or promise to fix it).

This data gave rise to the idea of communication ACTs. The results helped to determine what ACTs are usually performed when users interact with a system and how the ACTs are handled, so that an environment to automate the process could be designed.

The studies demonstrated that frequency, implementors recorded communication and management information in an unstructured, untimely manner, without the help of the system to handle related tasks. The system also did not help in organizing and disseminating information, or lists of problems, schedules, and plans. As usual, the users were expected to perform these tasks by hand, without a consistent or integrated method. Some of the disadvantages of recording information by hand (i.e., using a notebook) during or after a session with a system are described below, followed by a proposed solution.

Only a certain kind of ACT, such as a gripe about a definite bug, is captured using hand-written notebooks. An ACT which requires discussion or results from a previous ACT, such as a design decision or a response, is usually not recorded. When hand methods are used, the processing of ACTs is usually deferred, causing information to be forgotten, and is often haphazard. Tasks (other ACTs) related to a specified ACT (such as recording the state of the system when a problem occurs and adding the problem to a "bug" list) are not performed. The biggest disadvantage of processing ACTs by hand is that information becomes unavailable. Notebooks and manuals are lost or misplaced; blackboards are erased.

Many of the problems in processing ACTs can be eliminated by using knowledge about ACTs to guide the interaction between the environment and the user. The environment can also make suggestions so that all relevant information is recorded properly, organized immediately and disseminated when needed. For example, the environment should ask for relevant facts when a designer states a warning or a plan, and the users should be given the option of what should be displayed when warning or schedules appear.

A support environment which would help process the ACT:

- *Function PR needs to be changed to be PRINT instead of MAPC*

could try to:

1. determine if PR was known function, (and if so) →

2. figure out who wrote PR;

3. ask the user if a message should be sent to the person (along with other information);

4. list the problem as a current *bug* (if it was not already listed), and

5. warn other users of the problem.

To summarize: this work consists of structuring communication tasks necessary for organization and management of evolutionary computer systems as ACTs. Structuring includes analyzing user/system interactions, classifying communication ACTs according to a taxonomy and codifying the knowledge necessary to process them.

4 Target System

A programming project in which programmers are developing a large system, referred to as a "Target System," was needed to test the ideas presented here. The project associated with the evolutionary knowledge-based program synthesis system, CHI [Phillips-81], was chosen to gain development support by having an environment built for it. The major function of CHI will be reviewed to demonstrate the support needed for CHI, and how CHI tools can be used.

CHI can be described as an extremely smart compiler which transforms high-level program specifications into executable code. CHI may also be thought of as a set of tools that manipulates all components of the compilation process, including the smart compiler. From another point of view, CHI is a set of rules about how to carry out the translation process, how to use the tools, and how to apply the rules themselves to these tasks. All the programming knowledge, tools, and even the smart compiler can operate on each other. For example, the compiler can compile rules that tell the compiler how to compile rules, etc. The support environment can take advantage of this self-knowledge and referentiality [Phillips-80].

CHI consists of a very high-level language called V and an objectbase of knowledge. V is capable of expressing programming constructs, such as sets, mappings, etc., as well as rules for expressing knowledge. The objectbase consists of descriptions of the constructs and other knowledge.

The support environment for CHI will be integrated into the CHI system, and will make use of its features. The goal is to make the support environment consistent with the CHI design philosophy, convenient to use and based on actual designer/user behavior.

5 *Support Interface and Processing Issues*

A natural system/user interface was needed for the environment. Possibilities included natural language, database query languages and system command languages. Graphics, speech and other advanced technology methods were not considered.

Since the problem domain of CHI is "programming," and a language for specifying programs already exists in CHI, this very high-level extendible language, V, was chosen as the interface language. Several factors support this choice:

- The data of CHI, namely programs and knowledge of programming, is written in V.

- The users of CHI should be experienced programmers who will have already learned the V language.

- Existing tools and capabilities of CHI involving V can be used.

- CHI would remain a "closed" system [Phillips-80].

Existing features of CHI which can be used in building its support environment are shown below.

1. CHI's object-oriented description base can be extended to include descriptions for ACTs and related support data.

2. Knowledge about ACTs, the project and the system can be distributed throughout the system, just as programming knowledge is currently distributed.

3. ACTs can be represented as V programs, allowing a natural user interface, by adding interaction constructs to CHI's own very high level specification language, V.

4. Rules for processing ACTs can be added to CHI's rule base.

5. Plans can be constructed for communication between a user and the system, or a designer. These plans are similar to CHI's high level plans for synthesis and algorithm design.

In order to understand how V can be used as a support interface and representation language, we must review the use of V in CHI. CHI uses the language V to describe systems. Transformation rules then refine V constructs into constructs in an executable language. The extendible constructs are represented in CHI's objectbase. Questions about the objectbase can be expressed as V programs which calculate the answers. Then CHI can synthesize the programs using the objectbase and other CHI objects called rules.

This same process of accessing the objectbase can be used to perform ACTs. V programs representing ACTs can be formed from very high level constructs for recording, searching and disseminating information, and the V description of the support environment objectbase (project information, etc., which is part of the CHI objectbase). Rules can then refine these ACTs into executable code. The results of processing the ACTs will depend upon the database, user interaction and the existing state of the system. Alternative ACT programs can be created.

Initially, we can extend V and write one-step transformation rules which refine our constructs to executable routines. These transformation steps later can be developed further, or the ACT programs can be rewritten in some kernel of V. The effect will be to let properties, objects (V constructs) and rules (knowledge) aid CHI users in representing facts about the *environment* and the *project*, just as they have done for facts about *programming*.

The way ACTs are handled depends on various factors. The experience of the user will determine the way an ACT is specified. A designer should be able to perform an ACT by synthesizing a V expression on the spot. A less experienced user could access a library of V programs (ACTs), which handle project management and communication tasks. The V programs, represented as CHI objects, would function as commands. Techniques, such as a menu of commands, would further simplify the user's task.

When ACTs are synthesized, custom tailoring will be allowed. For example, the amount, type, form and timing of the information handled should be optional and vary according to the particular situation of how and when it is needed. Some ACTs should be performed automatically. The ACT to "Print all (overdue) tasks" could be performed whenever a user enters CHI. Also, certain users should be able to have priority to perform particular ACTs. For example, a manager may be the only one who can give out tasks and delete them.

6 *Approach and Framework*

This section covers the dynamic, evolutionary approach of CHI's support environment. Its capabilities are described and a work plan is given, along with a user scenario.

Passive interface systems, such as typical documentation assistance systems, do not include a "model" of the process of interaction. Some user help systems, or apprentice-like projects, are *dynamic* in that they do incorporate a model of the user [Rich-79 and Genesereth-78]. The user's *plan* can be matched against a set of known plans to explain or infer actions. However, the domain of actions is *programming*, rather than *communication of system design*. These systems lack sufficient knowledge about communication.

The environment proposed here will be dynamic, but not in the sense of "modeling" the user's plan to solve the initial problem of creating a program [McCune-79]. The ACTs which will be processed are initiated when interruptions of the user's initial plan occur. Therefore, it is the user's *"implicit" plan* within a particular ACT that the system models, using knowledge about ACTS and interaction with the user. The term *"implicit"* is used because the system can make suggestions to handle tasks that the user might not be aware of having wanted to perform. A "model" of the target system (CHI) and the environment itself, including its structure and description, will also be used.

The environment will be *"evolutionary"* as well as dynamic. This means that the initial version of the support environment can be used to assist in its own growth, as well as CHI's. Feedback from users can help the designers make proper changes and additions. This includes information about features that users prefer or dislike. The actual knowledge about processing ACTs could also be modified in this fashion so that an extended environment could *"learn"* (i.e., the developers could add the knowledge that promises usually follow requests).

Such performance evaluation can be extended to the target system. Information collected about which features and tools people use, as well as which components and objects the system uses, could enhance the system's structured growth. Consider the implications, for example, of knowing that a certain *rule* in CHI is never referenced; perhaps it is stated incorrectly or is irrelevant. Therefore, just as CHI has aided in the development of algorithms, the support environment will help in the development of CHI itself.

The support environment will provide the target system with various capabilities in a consistent and effective way. The capabilities include: project management, system evaluation, documentation/help and intelligent message sending. It is important that support be readily available without the user having to change environments. Therefore, these are not separate subsystems; they are integrated domains of knowledge represented as rules.

ACT knowledge will be added to the environment in the form of rules which (1) handle input, access, and display of the support database, (2) perform other related ACTs and (3) interact with the user. The environment can process ACTs by using CHI, along with this new knowledge, to create executable programs which will differ depending upon the domain.

The growth of the environment will be incremental. The initial version of the support environment has Project Management Support (PMS) including a PMS database and knowledge for displaying PMS data and performing questioning and planning ACTs. The support environment can be extended by considering a new domain, e.g. Critiquing (CS). Existing knowledge can then be specialized. For example, questioning of Critique data may differ from questioning PMS data. New ACT knowledge will be created, e.g. for Griping. Also, knowledge on *how* to critique existing knowledge, e.g. CHI, PMS and CS, is needed. The database will also be expanded for new domain data. Finally, this process is repeated for each domain, and knowledge of existing domains is modified and enhanced. This process will be facilitated by the rule-based form of knowledge. The power of the environment comes from the interrelationship of knowledge from all the domains. Therefore, complex ACTs can be processed intelligently only after enough knowledge is included in the environment.

An early version of the environment will have a minimal amount of knowledge to handle simple ACTs having different capabilities. The following scenario segments, presented in English for convenience of reading, demonstrate how the environment should perform (see Figure 10.2). The interaction is between a user (u) and the environment (e).

7 Project Management Support

Project management support has been added to CHI's support environment. The initial version includes a project management data base, access routines and ACT knowledge. This capability was developed first, because it forms the core of the support environment, and could be used by the support environment project itself.

Project Management

u: "What tasks of CHI have not been started?"

e: (1.) Implement module X   (2.) Write an "instance dumper"

u: "Do anyone else's tasks depend upon these getting done?"

e: Yes, both Tom and Sue can't finish their work until you write an instance dumper.

Intelligent Messages

u: "Who can I talk to that is working on the problem area which includes the instance dumper task?"

e: Steve

u: "Request Steve to complete the instance dumper and ask for an estimated completion date."

e: OK ... (giving link to task, user name, date, etc.) (creating a promise ...)

System Evaluation

u: "I don't like how dependency among tasks is handled by the system."

e: OK ... (creating gripe of dependency links of tasks ... by u, today, while referencing: instance dumper task)

Documentation/Project Management

u: "What is the instance dumper?"

e: There is no documentation on it, but it is a part of saving data in CHI.

(Here, since no documentation existed about the task, project management support was able to give useful information)

u: "Take down my ideas for a project management scenario."

e: Where should the scenario go?

u: "Create a task in the project management database called *scenario*, and add to its documentation!"

Figure 10.2   Scenario segments

Some of the major factors that interfere with the success of a project involve management of design, scheduling, planning, etc. A designer could plan more effectively if Project Management Support (PMS) helped record new ideas and represent them as tasks of the project. These tasks could then be divided and organized using the PMS to help in design. Project scheduling would be enforced by the PMS prompting managers or designers to specify *who* should do *what*, *how much* and *when*. The task structure would reflect the development of the system. Tasks completed and tasks remaining would be explicitly listed, and available for study when the project is reviewed. Finally, the task information would help in reporting the accomplishments, milestones and bottlenecks of the project.

Information on current and future tasks of the CHI designers was needed for project management support. The information was collected by determining the structure of CHI's major components, which could only be determined by having some initial data. Other information relevant to project management or communication support (such as people, time, etc.) was also needed. The ACTs that utilize the project management data were formed by studying how the information collected could be used and what knowledge could be gained from it.

The underlying structure, or abstraction of CHI, which is used to organize the PMS information, can be viewed in two ways: (1) as a structure to support annotations, such as documentation or bugs, associated with a part of CHI and (2) as a task hierarchy with high-level tasks, such as the "CHI Project" itself, as well as low-level tasks such as "write function x," which have identical internal structure. This task structure, which is the major part of the project management system, can be used to organize or index other data.

Currently, the support environment data forms a subgraph of CHI's original objectbase. There are other support structures, including one which accounts for non-CHI tasks of CHI designers, such as those related to the computer facility or administration. They are necessary for purposes of effective management. The power of this representation comes from the meaningful interconnection of the data these structures represent.

An example of a *Request of System Information ACT*:

"List all tasks,"

which queries the project management database (performed perhaps by a manager), is given to illustrate the PMS. It can be expressed in V as:

```
FORM the SET of {*|*.CLASS = PMTASK}
```

and is read as:

> "return all objects (*) such that the object's class is a project management task."

The phrase:

```
"*.CLASS = PMTASK,"
```

can be replaced by any unary logical predicate P, containing possible quantifiers and relational operators, to form other queries. For instance, to ask the question:

> "List all of Tom's tasks,"

the predicate P might be expressed as:

```
*.CLASS = PMTASK & *.HEAD = TOM.
```

Many forms of queries, as well as other ACTs, can be clearly stated this way.

8 Concluding Remarks

Knowledge about simple ACTs has been easy to formulate and express; some complex ACTs have been analyzed on paper. Further study of designer/user behavior is needed. Project information was represented without much difficulty in most cases. With a few hours of work, enough rules were added to CHI so that some simple project management ACTs, expressed in V, could be processed.

The effectiveness of the experimental support environment is not yet known. However, informal studies are planned to determine if the designers of the target system, CHI, choose to use the environment capabilities, and if they work more efficiently with the features. The experimental implementation should determine whether the approaches for classification, structuring, and processing communication and management information are valuable. Smaller projects can be formed along the way to enhance particular support capabilities. Future plans include support for program maintenance and for other software engineering tasks.

The ideas presented here should apply to development support environments for systems other than CHI. Of course, the task could be more difficult without the features and self-knowledge of CHI. The claim is that determining the knowledge needed to process ACTs is a valid endeavor in itself, and that this knowledge could be useful in building other intelligent system aids.

Given that such aids are desirable, we must not forget that effective communication, using a computer system, ultimately serves human beings. A support environment can only hope to serve as a *mediator* in such communication. The controversy between handling problems by "always using the system" vs. "doing everything by hand" is important to consider. We must determine when and how the computer is most useful.

9 Acknowledgments

The following people have provided useful discussion and ideas for this work: Tom Pressburger, Jorge Phillips, Cordell Green, Susan Angebranndt, Allen Goldberg and Dr. William R. Edwards, Jr.

This paper describes research done at Kestrel Institute and Systems Control, Inc., using the SCI-ICS, ISIC and the Stanford SAIL Systems. The research was supported by the Defense Advanced Research Projects Agency under DARPA Order 3687, Contract N00014-79-C-0127, which is monitored by the Office of Naval Research. The views and conclusions contained in this paper are those of the author and should not be interpreted as necessarily representing the official policies, either expressed or implied, of any of the organizations mentioned above.

References

[Genesereth-78] Genesereth, M. R., *Automated Consultation for Complex Computer Systems*, Ph.D. thesis, Harvard University, September 1978.

[Green et al.-79] Cordell Green, Richard P. Gabriel, Elaine Kant, Beverly I. Kedzierski, Brian P. McCune, Jorge V. Phillips, Steve T. Tappel, and Stephen J. Westfold, "Results in Knowledge-based Program Synthesis," *IJCAI-79: Proceedings of the Sixth International Joint Conference on Artificial Intelligence*, Volume 1, Computer Science Department, Stanford University, Stanford, CA, August 1979, pages 342–344.

[Hayes-81] Hayes, P., Ball, E., and Reddy, R., "Breaking the Man–Machine Communication Barrier," IEEE Computer, March 1981.

[Kedzierski-76] Kedzierski, B. I., *A Structured Paper on Large Project Management*, Special Projects in Computer Software, University of Southwestern Louisiana, December 1976.

[Kedzierski-80] Kedzierski, B. I., "Codification of Communication Knowledge for Extending Evolutionary System Environments," Ph.D. thesis proposal, Systems Control Technical Report, SCI-ICS.I.81, April 1980.

[Kedzierski-81] Kedzierski, B. I., "Communication Support in a System Development Environment," Systems Control Technical Report, SCI-ICS.L.81.4, 1981.

[Keider-74] Keider, Stephen P., "Why Projects Fail," Datamation, December 1974, pp. 53–55.

[Ledbetter-80] Ledbetter, L. E., "The Software Life Cycle Model: Implications for Program Development Support Systems," Schlumberger-Doll Research, Schlumberger Technology Corporation, Ridgefield, CT, May 1980.

[McCune-79] Brian P. McCune, *Building Program Models Incrementally from Informal Descriptions*, Ph.D. thesis, Memo AIM-333, Report STAN-CS-79-772, Artificial Intelligence Laboratory, Computer Science Department, Stanford University, Stanford, California, Technical Report SCI.ICS.U.79.2, Computer Science Department, Systems Control, Inc., Palo Alto, CA, October 1979.

[Moran-81] Moran, Thomas (Ed.), "The Psychology of Human–Computer Interaction," ACM Surveys Special Issue, 1981.

[Phillips-80] Phillips, J., Green, C., "Towards Self-Described Programming Environments", SCI Tech Report SCI.ICS.L.81.3, June 1980.

[Phillips-81] Phillips, J., *Self-Described Program Synthesis Environments: An Application of a Theory of Design to Programming Systems*, Ph.D. thesis, Computer Science and Electrical Engineering Department, Stanford University [forthcoming].

[PgmEnv-81] "Programming Environments," IEEE Computer, Vol. 14, No. 4, April 1981.

[Rich-79] Rich, C., Shrobe, H., and Waters, R., "Programmer's Apprentice Project," MIT, Outline of Research, 1979–80.

[Sandewall-78] Sandewall, E., "Programming in an Interactive Environment: The LISP Experience," *ACM Computing Surveys*, 10, 1 (March 1978), 35–72.

[Searle-78] Searle, J. R., *Speech Acts: An Essay in the Philosophy of Language*, Cambridge University Press, New York, NY, 1978.

[Zelkowitz-78] Zelkowitz, M. V., "Perspectives on Software Engineering," *ACM Computing Surveys*, June 1978.

11

Callisto: An Intelligent Project Management System

Arvind Sathi
Thomas E. Morton
Steven F. Roth

Introduction

In the following two subsections, we present a brief discussion of the project management problem and how the Callisto project began.

The Project Management Problem

Innovation is important to the continued vitality of industry. New products and changes in existing products are occurring at an increasing rate, causing product lives to decrease. In order to maintain market share, companies are forced to reduce product development time and bring their products to the market as early as possible.

A major portion of development involves performing and managing many activities. For example, in high-technology industries such as the computer industry, thousands of activities must be performed to design and build the prototype of a new product. Poor performance or management of an activity can result in critical delays. If product development time is to be reduced, better management and technical support are crucial.

The Callisto project was started at the initiative of Digital Equipment Corporation (DEC) with the goal of studying and supporting the management of large projects. The focus has been on large system development *programs* (collections of several projects geared toward the design of a new computer). The following points illustrate the complexity of project management tasks in such programs:

- A large number of activities (possibly greater than 10,000) make it impossible for a manager to acquire current information about all activities.

- A number of departments are involved with different foci, attitudes, and goals.

- A program requires significant cooperation. The engineering department cannot use components that are short in supply and has to interact with the purchasing department to ascertain the supply position. The engineering department also has to interact with the manufacturing department for prototype development. Any changes made by any of these departments have an impact on the entire program.

- The developmental and technological nature of these programs makes it difficult to plan accurately. Changes are frequent and need to be approved by a large number of managerial personnel.

Related project management tasks can be decomposed into three areas: (1) activity management, (2) product-configuration management, and (3) resource management. Each of these areas can, in turn, be further delineated. **Activity management** involves four elements: (1) *planning*, which involves definition of activities, specification of precedence, resource requirements, durations, due dates, milestones, and responsibilities; (2) *scheduling*, which is the selection of activities to be performed (if more than one way exists) and the assignment of actual times and resources; (3) *chronicling*, which is the monitoring of project performance, detection of deviations from the schedule, and analysis of deviations for changes to plan (possibly resulting in renewed planning and scheduling); and (4) *analysis*, which is the evaluation of plans, schedules, and chronicled activities for normal reporting and extraordinary situations and involves the study of durations, budgets, and risk projections.

Product configuration management involves two elements: (1) *product management*, which is the management of various versions and variations of the product being designed, and (2) *change management*, which is the management of change proposals and impact evaluations, assignment of personnel for making changes, and installation of product versions.

Finally, **resource management** involves three elements: (1) the projection and acquisition of resources for project needs; (2) the assignment of responsibilities to ensure proper utilization of resources; and (3) the storage, maintenance, and repair of critical resources to minimize bottlenecks.

Deficiencies in past approaches can be attributed to inadequate modeling techniques, poor scheduling algorithms, and limited analytical tools. Our first and foremost research effort concentrated on modeling how good managers deal with the size, complexity, and changes in large projects and how they foster cooperation given the organizational diversity and loose coupling. The first leg dealt with using rule-based models to build quick prototypes of project expertise. This understanding of point solutions was then used to capture the underlying models of project expertise in the areas of project negotiations and computer-generated explanation of change using comparative analysis. The article describes our exploration into project management needs and the evolution of the resulting models of project management.

The Callisto Project

An initial investigation was encouraged by the vice-president of engineering at Digital Equipment Corporation during Fall 1981. It was observed that in many ways the problems encountered in managing large development projects were similar to those associated with managing job shop activities, which was the focus of the Intelligent Scheduling and Information Systems (ISIS) project at CMU. The focus of the initial investigation was to determine the feasibility of developing an expert system to aid in the management of large system development projects.

It was concluded that a significant improvement could be realized in project scheduling, monitoring, and control through the inclusion of resources and other project management constraints in the project-scheduling algorithms. It was also expected that a knowledge-based project management tool would facilitate the documentation of project management expertise and its reuse from one project to another. The engineering prototype development for large systems was selected as the representative application. No tools existed to monitor and control these projects. Their nature—engineering oriented, volatile, ill structured—was ideal for a test case.

Research goals were established in the following four areas for the Callisto project: In the area of activity modeling, the goal was to generate a model of the activities and the constraints related to these activities. It was hoped that the model would facilitate the manager's ability to create activities and identify problems at creation time. In the area of configuration management, the goals were to generate a hierarchical product representation for various versions and prototypes and a way of representing the changes of these products and to develop a system to support the management of change. In the area of activity scheduling, the goal was to schedule with various hard and soft constraints and goals, which involve dynamic rescheduling and what-if simulation during project monitoring and heuristics to guard against "bad" schedules. Finally, in the area of project control, the goal was to study and model the status updating and activity-tracking procedures and the use of managerial heuristics for reporting, focusing, and diagnosing problems.

A number of factors make engineering prototype development a difficult domain for experimentation with intelligent project management systems. First, building rule-based prototypes for large and dynamic environments is a resource-intensive activity and cannot be justified on its own. Second, such projects involve a mix of economic, engineering, and manufacturing considerations. It is not possible to appreciate the problem-solving process without an understanding of all these areas. Finally, such projects involve a large number of important, yet specialized project management problems. It is difficult to understand all of these problems, isolate important ones, or develop systems that solve everyone's problems. Figure 11.1 traces the phases of the Callisto project.

The first phase of the project lasted about two years. Its purpose was to develop the first Callisto prototype, which consisted of a model of project knowledge and a rule-based prototype of project expertise to formulate hard-wired solutions to specific problems using production rules. Although the prototype was found to be operationally usable for configuration tracking, a useful subset of the program management problem, its usability was restricted. The information was to be funneled through a group whose responsibility was to maintain the project model. The existence of a committee inevitably causes a reduction in the information recorded, delays in the incorporation of information in the model, and the cleansing of information (for example, project reports might be too optimistic). Another problem was the level of analysis provided by Callisto. Although the model used a set of hard-wired procedures for pattern matching of typical comparisons, it could not intelligently configure the procedures together to decipher real problems.

A toy example project that engineered a fictitious computer named Micro-84 was fabricated for demonstration purposes. All the examples and scenarios in this article refer to this fictitious computer. The following test cases were used for the experiments: the developmental plans (40 activities) and configuration of Micro 84 (9 parts), the project network for Callisto itself (80 activities), a portion of the activity network for an ongoing system development project (125 activities), a random

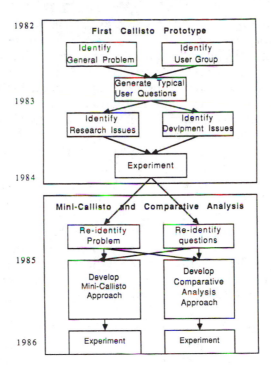

Figure 11.1 Callisto development path.

set of activity networks (776 networks with a range of 10 to 200 activities), and the system configuration and changes for a system under development (17 layers of hierarchy with 5000 parts).

The development of the configuration-tracking system (currently under way) uses as a test case a configuration with seven layers of hierarchy and about 10,000 schemata (Lynch, Marshall, and O'Connor 1986). The earlier versions of Callisto used the scheme representation language (SRL) (Wright and Fox 1983; Wright, Fox, and Adam 1984), and the current work is being done using Knowledge Craft™ (Carnegie Group 1986).

Two models of project expertise emerged from the experiments. The first model attempts to capture the expertise used by good project managers in developing cooperation among project participants. In distributed project management situations, project participants often carry divergent and possibly conflicting goals and constraints. The plan specification and revision involves considerable negotiation around the constraints in order to formulate contracts to ensure cooperation. The constraint-directed negotiation model captures the expertise used by project managers in specification and revision of plans that satisfy individual constraints and foster cooperation on project goals (see Mini-Callisto for a description of the theory). These negotiations occur iteratively during plan generation, scheduling, monitoring, and repair. This model resulted in explorations with Mini-Callisto,[1] a distributed problem-solving approach. Constraint-directed negotiations are examined in this article by exploring a number of negotiation situations.

A second model captures the expertise in comparative analysis of project knowledge. This analysis includes understanding the quantitative, qualitative, and causal relations among activities, people, and resources (for example, the impact of a delay in resource procurement on the risk of meeting a follow-on milestone); how these properties change; how they can be classified, aggregated, abstracted (for example, a common project member responsible for all the delayed activities); and how the result of analysis can be explained using verbal and pictorial means. The purpose of this model is to support automated explanation by providing search and comparison, computation, significance testing, and verbal descriptions of change in project models. The work in this area is still in the formative state and is the primary focus of current Callisto research.

Section 2 provides a summary of past approaches. Section 3 describes the first Callisto prototype. The experiments and related observations are described in Section 4. Section 5 describes the distributed problem-solving architecture and its application to resource, activity, and configuration management. Section 6 summarizes the ongoing experiments with the distributed problem-solving architecture. Section 7 describes the current work on comparative analysis. Finally, Section 8 summarizes the achievements and unexplored areas for research.

Past Approaches

The origin of computer-based network analysis for project management dates back to 1959 when two separate but essentially similar procedures were developed: Program Evaluation and Review Technique (PERT) (Malcolm, Rosenboom, and Clark 1959) and Critical Path Method (CPM) (Kelley and Walker 1959; Kelley 1961). PERT involved the use of three separate time estimates for each activity and statistical procedures to produce probability estimates of project completion. CPM used a one-time estimate. Today, both terms are interchangeably used to refer to the common approach of (1) representing the project in the form of

---

[1] The word Mini-Callisto was coined to signify that the new Callisto system locally contained a "mini" knowledge base and "mini" problem-solving capabilities which were owned by a suborganization or project member.

a network diagram and (2) performing the necessary calculations on the diagram to determine the "critical path" and start and finish times for each activity.

PERT/CPM was limited to precedence constraints and single project. A number of researchers in management science were drawn toward the project-scheduling problem. Notable among them are Turban (1976), Pritsker et al. (1966), Crowston (1970), Weist (1967), Lambourn (1963), Davis (1973), and Talbot (1982). Their main agenda for research was the inclusion of resource considerations in the scheduling of project activities. Work has also been conducted in the project measurement area, where the emphasis has been on measuring, forecasting, and reporting project information, for example, cost (DeCoster 1964; Saitow 1969). For a detailed review of project management techniques, refer to Davis (1973, 1976) and Elmaghraby (1977). Despite their versatility, most of these techniques have gained little popularity. In a study of research and development (R&D) projects, Liberatore and Titus (1983) found that managers used very few sophisticated techniques to manage their projects. Gantt charts and project network diagrams were the only notable exceptions. Clearly, real-world project management problems were either different or too complex.

The human planning process has often been scrutinized by researchers in artificial intelligence (AI); their findings are applicable to project management problems. There are three major streams of research efforts that apply to project management: (1) plan representation; (2) plan generation and scheduling; and (3) plan measurement, diagnostics, and explanation.

Research in plan representation explores the semantics of various concepts associated with human planning, such as time (Smith 1983; Allen 1984; Allen and Hayes 1985), process or activity (Hayes 1979; Georgeff, Lansky, and Besseire 1985; Sathi, Fox and Greenberg 1985), causality (Rieger and Grinberg 1977), and possession (Fox 1983). The research in this area has led to the development of semantic models of projects that can be used for intelligent reasoning and problem solving.

Research in plan generation and scheduling uses the knowledge about activities and goals to generate a sequence of steps for a plan (Tate 1977; Sacerdoti 1974; Fox 1983). A number of planning techniques have evolved, such as hierarchical planning (Sacerdoti 1974), least commitment (wait and see) approaches (Sacerdoti 1977), script-based planning (Stefik 1981; Wilensky 1983), blackboard architecture (Hayes-Roth 1985), constraint-directed search (Fox 1983), and distributed planning (Corkill 1983).

Research in plan measurement, diagnostics, and explanation interprets the project progress and diagnoses the delays to find problem areas. Many types of research touch this area including model explanation (Kosy and Wise 1984; Wise and Kosy 1985; Weiner 1980), plan recognition (Schmidt 1978), reactive scheduling (Fox and Smith 1984), vehicle monitoring (Lesser and Corkill 1983), speech interpretation (Erman et al. 1980), and simulation analysis (Reddy 1985).

Hierarchical descriptions of products are common to computer-aided design (CAD) (Freeman and Newell 1971; Latombe 1976; Preiss 1976; Stallman and Sussman 1977; Barbuceanu 1984) and software management systems (Tichy 1980) and draw upon the hierarchical modeling of objects (Winston 1975; Brachman 1979; Hendrix 1979). Refinement and change processes, however, are found less frequently (Tichy 1980; Zdonik 1984).

Tichy designed a software development and maintenance environment with three aspects: representation, interface control, and version control. His model supports multiple versions and configurations. A module family can have three kinds of members: parallel versions, revisions or sequential versions, and derived versions. A system family includes compositions or configurations and derived compositions (Tichy 1980).

The distributed constraint-directed negotiation approach is based on work in three research areas: (1) economic literature, (2) organizational behavior literature, and (3) distributed AI literature. Economic literature contains modeled agents in n-player game situations. Each player makes a choice whose outcomes (gains) are dependent upon the actions taken by the other agents, and the joint benefits depend upon the level of cooperation (Nash 1950; Luce and Raiffa 1957). The extensions to Nash's model include syndicate theory (Wilson 1968; Demski and Swieringa 1974; Demski 1976), team theory (Marschak and Radner 1972), the demand revelation model (Loeb 1975; Groves 1975; Groves and Loeb 1979), and agency theory (Fama 1980; Harris and Townsend 1981; Baiman 1982).

The work in agency theory deals with a principal and an agent. The principal forms a contract with the agent. Any returns from this contract are shared so as to maximize the returns to the principal, while subject to the constraints imposed by the agent. Agency theory model has been used by economists to study the optimal contract formulation (which would maximize cooperation between the principal and the agent subject to self-interests), admissible action rules for the agents, and the information asymmetry between principal and agent (Baiman 1982).

Organizational behavior literature provides studies in human organizations on the human negotiation process (Pruitt 1981) and on the formation of matrix management in project organization (Galbraith 1973). Although this research is closely linked with project management, we have not yet encountered its impact on project management techniques.

In distributed AI literature, the distributed problem-solving approach conceptualizes a network of intelligent agents or actors (Greif and Hewitt 1975) capable of generating and executing plans and negotiating with other agents (Davis and Smith 1981). These problem-solving agents can be organized in an organizational hierarchy (Fox 1979; Fox 1981a; Fox 1981b) and can dynamically refine their roles (Durfee, Lesser, and Corkill 1985). This problem-solving approach decentralizes the problem solving with a limited communication sufficient for functionally accurate cooperation (Lesser and Corkill 1981) and makes solution generation feasible for large problems (Fox 1979). The approach also provides models of the contract formation process (Smith 1978) and organization designs for optimal flexibility and efficiency (Malone and Smith 1984). It theorizes distributed problem solvers with different beliefs (Fagin and Halpern 1985) negotiating on contracts (Smith 1980) and proposes a calculus of resource ownership (Lee 1980; McCarty and Sridharan 1981).

First Callisto Prototype

This section describes the various components of the first Callisto prototype which was developed to experiment with the emerging semantic model of project management.

Introduction

Consider the following scenario: *The engineering development activity for a central processing unit (CPU) typically involves the development of specifications, design on a CAD tool, and verification of the board on test cases. A committee of hardware engineers develops the specifications and assigns an engineer to design and verify the board specifications. Hence, specification is followed by design and verification. If verification is successful, the CPU is released for prototype development. Otherwise, the bug is located, the board is revised, and the design is performed again.*

Mr. Jones, a project manager in the engineering department, has been assigned the responsibility of designing the Micro-84 CPU board. Because it is not possible to cover all design aspects together, two milestones have been set for developing versions 1 and 2 of the board, respectively, and it is expected that the second version of the board will conform to project goals. The expected duration of the design activity depends heavily on whether a new technology is used for the design. Because the decision on whether to go with the new technology has not yet been made, two schedules need to be developed, one with the assumption that the design durations will be reduced using the new technology and the other without the new technology.

Although this scenario sounds simplistic from a project management viewpoint, it raises a number of project management system engineering issues that are nontrivial. For an intelligent system that supports the management of such projects, we need to identify the critical components of the project management expertise and project knowledge representation. We need to define how this expertise and knowledge is acquired, maintained, and extended from one domain to another and how it supports the project managers.

The project representation should be complete. That is, the project knowledge should span the application domain and include all the relevant project elements used by expert project managers. For example, it should include activities (such as CPU specification); the durations of the activities; logical and temporal precedence; aggregation and abstraction (for example, how engineering development of the CPU is linked to the three activities of specification, design, and verification); individuation of schedules for the two versions of the board; representation of the two alternate schedules, one with and the other without the new technology; representation of Micro-84 and its component hierarchy, versions, and variations; representation of changes in the product; changes in the start or end dates; and resources required for each of these activities (for example, engineers, CAD tools, simulation software, and test examples). For each resource, one needs to define their availability, capabilities, and ownership. Finally, the project representation should include the representation of constraints that restrict the usage of the resources, for example, the maintenance schedule and previous reservations by other users on the CAD machine and the use of engineers for the next project.

An arbitrary set of data structures cannot be used to capture this knowledge, especially if completeness implies extensibility to include new concepts. The knowledge architecture should have clarity. That is, one and only one representation exists for a given situation. For example, if a new situation involves a new type of resource, say suppliers, there should be a semantic rationale for how this new element is represented in the project knowledge base.

In addition, the knowledge representation should be precise. That is, the project descriptions should be at the appropriate granularity of knowledge. For example, depending upon the type of retrieval, the system should be able either to state that CPU verification is the next activity of CPU design or to specify all the conditions under which one activity can follow another.

The architecture for the first Callisto prototype was comprised of two major components: the knowledge architecture and the interface architecture.

Knowledge Architecture   The project knowledge is organized into layers of representation. For details of the layers and their rationale, refer to Sathi, Fox, and Greenberg (1985). The *domain layer* provides concepts, words, and expressions specific to a domain of application. The *semantic layer* is composed of models of the common primitives, such as the concepts of time, activity, state, possession, agent, ownership, and so on. These concepts are common across domains and can, therefore, be used as building blocks for modeling the domain-specific concepts. The *epistemological layer* provides a way of regulating the flow of information through inheritance. It includes the concepts of set, prototype, and individuals as well as the structural relationships such as classification and aggregation. The *logical layer* defines the blocks or chunks of knowledge, such as concepts, assertions, and relations. Finally, the *implementation layer* provides primitives for machine interpretation of knowledge, such as schema, slot, relation, value, metaschema, and so on. Their specification depends on the knowledge engineering tool used.

Interface Architecture   Callisto was interfaced as a single-writer, multiple-reader system with user-directed commands for activity management, configuration management, and resource management (inventory only) and supported a common (centralized) knowledge base. Through a hierarchical menu, it provided the user with the capability of interactively generating plans, scheduling the project in a simulated world to analyze the project progress under several what-if scenarios (one or more of these schedules could be stored and compared to actual progress), posting project progress, and reviewing project progress. Product configurations could be developed or changed. The user could post inventory transactions or seek status reports. Various expert critics could be activated to analyze plans, schedules, inventory status, and configuration changes. Some functional details of this system are described in the following subsections.

Resource Management

Resource management is concerned with the specification and allocation of resources to support activities. Resources in this context include personnel, work centers, tools, parts, and so on. Semantic and domain layers include the following concepts that relate to resource representation: At the domain layer exist calendars and shifts of work, stocks, vendors, stockrooms, kits, work centers, supervisors, and managers with responsibility for various resources. At the semantic layer exist resources, the time line, temporal relations, possession of resources, agents, objects and their transactions from one agent to another, aggregation of objects, resources, and associated inheritance of ownership and status.

The project-scheduling system included considerations of resource availabilities and capacities. Our initial resource-management system had three components: an inventory management component tracking resource consumption; a resource adjudication component dealing with decision making in resource allocation; and a resource critic documenting managerial heuristics for isolating problems in the utilization of resources.

The inventory management component was a discrete event-based inventory transaction system that was developed to support the activity scheduling and chronicling tasks. For example, "arrival event" increases the quantity of a given part. Events were defined for the loading and unloading of resources and for changes in the inventory. All machines and personnel were treated as resources that were possessed for the execution of activities.

The second component, resource adjudication, was an automated manager that could operate under any of three modes: the mail notification mode, the interactive mode, and the heuristic mode. In the mail notification mode, concerned responsibility centers were informed of conflicts by electronic mail, which were, in turn, resolved manually. In interactive mode, the user was given the conflicts on the screen and resolved them interactively by initiating the important activities. In heuristic mode, conflicts were resolved using a set of predefined managerial rules. A large number (56) of scheduling heuristics were collected from the management science literature, and experiments were conducted to determine their comparative performance (Lawrence 1984).

The third component, the resource critic, was a rule base constructed by acquiring and encoding a number of managerial heuristics related to resources and suppliers. These rules criticized schedules and monitored performance. The rule base was assembled for concept demonstration. No experiments were performed to measure the adequacy or the impact of the criticisms.

Activity Management

Activity management deals with the generation, scheduling, and chronicling of project activities. The three phases are considered distinctly. The knowledge architecture supports these three phases using specific project knowledge at the domain and semantic levels. At the domain level exist knowledge of project activities, associated durations, risks, milestones, average (default) durations, aggregate activities for specification, design,

Concept	Definition	Illustration
State	Fact which holds as of some point in time	*Cpu-specification is complete* *Possess CAD tool during cpu-design*
Activity	Basic unit of action Transforms states	*Specification of cpu*
Aggregation	Combine parts to make a whole	*Cpu-engg-network has three* *activities, spec, design and verification.*
Abstraction	Process of reducing specific information	*Cpu-engg abstracts cpu-engg-network* *as a single activity*
Instances	Development of individual from universal	*Micro-84-design is an instance of* *cpu-design activity*
Manifestation	State specific description of individual	*M-cpu-design-1 specifies the schedule* *for Micro-84-design*
Temporal Relations	Relations to describe relative time	*Cpu-design is after cpu-specification*
Causality	Specifies an order of occurance	*Start-cpu-design (an aggregate state)* *enables cpu-design*
Relational Abstraction	Abstract relations to summarize complex relationships	cpu-design is the next activity-of cpu-verification (abstract) It occurs when verification fails (detail)

Figure 11.2   Activity representation definitions.

verification, project members, mailing addresses, and responsibilities. At the semantic level exist representation of activities, states, the time line, causal and temporal relations, possession of resources, and agents and their relation to activities (see Figure 11.2) (Sathi, Fox, and Greenberg 1985).

The three phases activity management is comprised of, are: (1) plan generation, (2) scheduling, and (3) chronicling. In the plan generation phase, an activity editor was developed to create and edit hierarchical activity networks. Interaction with the editor was through an English-like interface based on dynamic parser (DYPAR) (Carbonell et al. 1983). A rule-based activity critic was used to criticize the plans generated by the manager using structural (for example, missing precedence constraints) and heuristic (for example, duration estimates) project rules.

We perceived a major difference between the project scheduling of large engineering projects and the job shop scheduling being attempted in ISIS. Such projects involve a large degree of uncertainty and many changes. The accuracy or optimality of scheduling in such an environment is not as important as the development of a rough schedule that can be used for assessing and managing risk. In addition, the plan is typically too big to be developed or scheduled by one individual. Various organizational techniques, such as mutual agreements, internal pricing, and slacks, are used to distribute the scheduling problem and to solve it independently at multiple responsibility centers. A typical schedule might consist of a detailed three-month plan. Every week, or as often as needed, the project managers create a revised plan, implementing only its first week. This type of a procedure is widely used in industry and is termed a *rolling horizon procedure*; it involves scheduling far ahead of time to be sure what to do this week.

There are basically two ways of scheduling: forward or "dispatch" and backward or "reservation." The *dispatch approach* basically simulates the activities working forward in time. At each time point in the simulation, activities whose preconditions have been met are considered for scheduling. When two or more activities require the same resource, priority rules are applied to resolve the conflicts. The strength of the dispatch method is that it gives good control over the schedule in the near future. Compact schedules that make full use of resources are produced. The disadvantage is that there is less control over what happens in the distant future, for example, meeting due dates.

In contrast, the *reservation approach* works backward from the due date, reserving starting and ending times for each activity. First, a reservation is made for the last subactivity of the most important activity, then the next to the last, and so forth. Then the second most important activity is scheduled from its due date, and so forth. The strength of the reservation method is that the distant future is well controlled. Due dates for the most important projects are considered first. The disadvantage is that it provides poor control of scheduling in the near future. Gaps are often left in the schedule, and all activities of a project might not be reservable. These problems must be resolved in a second pass working forward. The reservation approach is typically useful in situations where the environment is stable, and there is a need to push work close to the deadline (for example, to reduce the cost of work-in-process inventory).

Given the level of risk and unforeseen changes, we decided to use a version of the dispatch approach. We simulated forward in time and forecast which projects create the most difficulties. These forecasts were then used to correct the current priorities so that the project with the maximum difficulties was given current priority over other projects.

Now, our principal problem was that slacks and lead times are unknown but must be included in forecasting priority. We recognized four distinct methods: (1) estimate the slacks using simple PERT/CPM; (2) use a historically estimated lead time for each resource to augment the duration of an activity; (3) repeatedly use the actual lead-time results instead of the historical estimates, and input these actual results for a second run, repeating the process until convergence is obtained; and (4) use regression to estimate the lead time for each resource from a set of critical factors, which might include shop dynamic load factor, load composition, and so on.

For multiple projects and multiple resource constraints, the algorithm can be extended by weighting the lead time on each resource by its price. The proper way to calculate prices is an interesting and complex subject. In general, one would have to solve a simpler, aggregate version of the problem with a method that would produce dual prices. These prices could be used in the detailed scheduling procedure. We found the computation of dual prices to be a cumbersome and unstable process and used the following approximation (which is similar to the way expert project managers would schedule): If a resource is, on an average, less than fully utilized, the price is 0. If a large number of activities demand the resource in the near future, the price is the ratio of resource demand to the supply available. For example, if given two engineers, one is required for two full-time activities and the other for two half-time activities, their respective prices are 2.0 and 1.0. Expensive resources are avoided during resource conflict resolution, resulting in less bottlenecking of those higher in demand.

Project chronicling is comprised of three components: progress recording, reporting, and repairing. The first Callisto prototype was restricted to the first two. It provided capabilities of propagating the progress along the activity hierarchy and for generating rate charts, which combines progress from different levels to compute scheduled or actual performance. The structured reports and query system are used for passive reporting, and monitoring rules are used for proactive reporting, such as reporting all the pending activities at least once a week.

Configuration Management

Product configuration management involves maintenance of the configuration status, impact analysis, and installation of changes. The primary emphasis in the first Callisto prototype was on representing the configuration and change knowledge (including their relationship to the resources and the activities).

At the domain layer exist components, versions, variations, basic parts, systems and prototypes, a configuration editor, configuration reports, and the change management system. Micro-84 is composed of hardware and software. The hardware contains two circuit boards: board-h1, which consists of the CPU and the I/O, and board-h2, which contains the memory. There are two versions of board-h1. The first version is composed of a workable CPU with all the proper interfaces; the second version is a speed enhancement of version 1. Variations consist of different specifications for power supply in the U.S. and European models, requiring 60 Hz and 50Hz power supply, respectively. Basic parts represent generic parts. Each part is defined conceptually; the parts are not connected hierarchically, for example, Micro-84 hardware. Finally, systems and prototypes represent actual physical products as instances of versions. For example, prototype 1 is an instance of Micro-84 version 1.

At the semantic layer exist the physical description, the behavioral description, and the links to activities. The physical description is derived from the work by Hayes (1979): Objects have a number of physical properties, such as mass, volume, momentum, and so on. In addition to the physical description, objects carry a description of how they behave under given conditions. The behavioral description is also the functional view of the object description.

Links to activities refers to objects in the project world that are produced, consumed, and transformed by project activities. Thus, the Micro-84 CPU behavior is defined through specifications, although its structure is defined by the design activity, and is released to the rest of the project organization by the verification activity. The specific activities, such as *revise part definitions*, are called *change orders*.

The configuration description in Callisto is hierarchical (that is, defined at multiple levels of detail). At its highest level of abstraction, Micro-84 is composed of hardware, software, and peripherals. At a detailed level, the hardware can be expanded into board-h1 and board-h2, and so on. Figure 11.3 is an illustration of the product representation. It shows the relationship between the two versions of Micro-84 and how one is generated from the other. The scope of the activity that acts on Micro-84-50Hz-v1 to produce Micro-84-50Hz-v2 can be reduced or increased by redefining the two versions.

The configuration editor is a semantic editor for specification and revision of product configuration. It can be used for adding or deleting basic parts, revisions, variations, and engineering change orders. The configuration reports can be used for reporting the configuration status or for comparatively analyzing at arbitrary levels of detail. Comparative analysis reports the changes from one version or revision to another and the associated causes for changes.

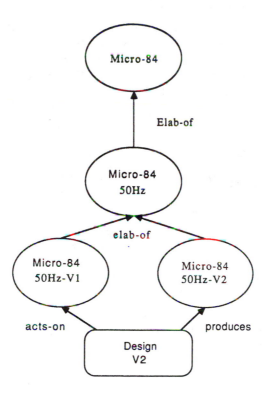

Figure 11.3   The Micro-84 and changes.

Finally, the change management system can be used for entering a change. The changes can be grouped and used for creating a new version of the configuration. At any level, the system interactively chooses three optional procedures for installing a change: destructive change (the new option supersedes the old), disjunctive (both new and old coexist) or release version (a new version is created for the part, and the procedure is repeated at the next higher level). A rule base is then used to analyze the impact of the change on the existing and scheduled prototypes.

Conclusion

The primary objective of the first Callisto prototype was to explore the knowledge architecture and the rule base prototypes of project management expertise. Although the knowledge architecture addressed some of the issues listed at the beginning of this section, the rule base prototype was inadequate for documenting or utilizing project management expertise. Although the rules matched the point solutions to the problems, they could not be extended to other problems. The project-scheduling approach required tolerance to incompleteness of project knowledge, appreciation for distribution of the plans and resources to various project managers, and the use of change orders in schedule revisions. The next section describes in detail the experiments with the first Callisto prototype and the associated observations.

Observations

The single user system was developed to the proof-of-concept level (that is, having enough functionality to demonstrate concepts but not really usable) and extended for the purpose of experimentation into the areas of activity scheduling and product-configuration management. The Callisto prototype was used in test cases for activity networks with up to 776 activities. The system was augmented with a subroutine written in C for faster number crunching. Our observations developed from the following activities:

- Interviewing key scheduling personnel: Interviews help to determine tasks and information-acquisition strategies.

- Observing review meetings to augment descriptions given by scheduling managers: The observations provided snapshots of actual project progress and problem-solving strategies used by program management personnel.

- Ascertaining commonly asked activity management questions from the project managers: These questions were the primary data points in understanding the difference between needs and available tools.

- Modeling of activities for two test cases using Callisto: These networks involved 80 and 125 activities, respectively, at multiple levels of detail. The modeling experiments were used to refine the expressiveness of the initial model.

- Interactively developing the next set of ideas: Continuous discussions, presentations, and concept demonstrations were used to foster idea development.

- Experimenting with scheduling: The purpose of the experimentation was to study and compare project-scheduling heuristics based on knowledge used, time taken for scheduling, and the quality of schedule generated. A random set of activity networks (776 networks with a range of 10 to 200 activities) was created. Fifty-six scheduling heuristics were used individually to schedule the networks using the dispatch approach and the knowledge available for the scheduling (Lawrence 1984).

- Experimenting with product configurations: Callisto was used to model configurations and associated changes for a product under development. The system was used experimentally to assess its interface and problem-solving abilities compared to existing systems being used. The system contained two versions of the configuration, with 17 layers of hierarchy and about 5000 parts. Nearly 15,000 schemata were needed to store the above configuration.

Numerous observations were made in regard to the various aspects of system development. In relation to planning, it was noted that plans evolve through negotiations and are not prespecified. For example, negotiations are often used to allocate slack time. The project support system should model and support negotiations on slack time and associated revisions in the plan rather than assume fixed durations and generate slack time as in PERT/CPM-based models.

Obvious organizational distances in communications were observed. Typically, the activities are not executed in the same department, office, or plant. The lack of face-to-face contact makes it difficult to maintain or analyze activity information in networks of the order of 10,000 activities. The critical paths generated by the PERT/CPM models lose their meaning in such situations because they do not carry or support the justifications and assumptions made during negotiations on the allocation of slack time.

Incomplete plans must be allowed for. Because networks of the order of 10,000 activities cannot be fully specified or maintained, we need tools for planning, scheduling, and monitoring that tolerate incompleteness in specification and trigger revisions when more knowledge is made available.

Project knowledge should be used for scheduling. Although a number of scheduling heuristics have been developed, they take a narrow view of constraints as applied to activity scheduling. As the knowledge is increased, the scheduling results improve; however, the time needed for scheduling increases (Lawrence 1984).

In regard to organizational ownership, it was noted that program management brings together a number of plants, divisions, and departments. The program manager seldom has overall control over the resources used by these organizations, and each of these organizations is a fairly autonomous unit with goals (that might not be identical to the program goals), management structure, and resources owned.

In regard to resource commitments, it was observed that these organizations commit some portion of their resources to the product development program. The commitments might have to coexist with other commitments made elsewhere. Very often, the commitments might be relaxed or renegotiated due to unforeseen changes, such as breakdowns, emergency needs, or changes in organizational structures.

Product descriptions need to be diverse. Various project personnel need different descriptions of the product. The perspectives of the supply department person counting the number of chips needed and the CAD simulation expert looking into behavioral modeling are very different. It should be possible for each one of them to maintain local definitions that are not necessarily tightly coupled with others' definitions.

Change needs to be managed. A large number of changes are made to the product at various stages of development. These changes are circulated to the other engineers, the field service staff supporting the product at Beta test sites, the manufacturing personnel building the prototypes, the supply department involved in the purchase of parts, and so on. One needs to identify whether a given change, such as the formation of the two subversions, needs to be communicated outside the negotiating entities and, if so, to whom and when. For example, for a change introduced by the design engineers, the supply department might need to be informed that some of the integrated circuits would be needed earlier than originally specified.

Product configurations are generated for diverse needs. As the needs change, they result in new definitions. The project management system should track the negotiation on definitions and the resulting product configuration.

Mini-Callisto

In this section, we describe the Mini-Callisto approach and illustrate it with resource activity and configuration management applications.

Problem-Solving Architecture

Consider the following scenario: *A new integrated circuits technology was introduced in the engineering design of Micro-84, a new supermicro. While the CAD engineers started designing the CPU using the new technology, the materials department was asked to procure the chips. The materials department informed the program manager that they could not come up with a definite plan unless they knew which chips would be included in the bill of materials. When the program manager asked the CAD group about the exact specifications of the chips, he was informed that they would be ready in about one year when the design was fully finalized. A detailed negotiation mediated by the program manager resulted in a revised plan with a predesign activity: The CAD team would develop rough specifications using high-level designs, and the materials department would purchase the chips using the rough specifications. From the first communication, the entire negotiation took about five months. Project management tools were then used to specify the resulting plan.*

In situations such as this, organizations or individuals initiate negotiations when faced with inconsistent or incomplete project knowledge. Constraints are shared, relaxed, and strengthened among all individuals involved in the negotiations. The negotiations result in plans which satisfy everyone and which, possibly, are much more detailed than the original plans. Existing support systems help the managers in storing the plans but only after the negotiations are complete.

Many project management systems, including the first Callisto prototype, are based on a fundamental assumption. They focus their attention on a plan, which is generated, stored, scheduled, and monitored, for proper project management. Such support systems are likely to fare well in situations involving stable or small project models. In contrast, engineering program management involves a large number of changes that are initiated and cooperatively agreed upon by a large number of participating project members or organizations. The support system in such an environment requires additional emphasis on the specification and revision processes and the need for cooperation, which leads to the concept of Mini-Callisto.

Mini-Callisto is a system capable of supporting the specialized needs of an organizational unit and of communicating with other such systems in a network during specification and revision processes. This system draws upon past research in distributed problem solving. A description of the design of the Mini-Callisto architecture follows.

It is assumed that the project is distributed across a number of organizational entitles, such as the program manager, the CAD group, and the materials department, with overlapping, but not necessarily common, goals and associated specialized knowledge. These organizational entities hold agreements with one another to facilitate cooperation on the project. Each organizational entity has a Mini-Callisto that provides a portion of the project management capabilities. Thus, a Mini-Callisto attached to the program manager is capable of working as a scheduling assistant with procedures for critical-path and risk analyses. Each Mini-Callisto has its own local knowledge base that reflects the beliefs of the organizational entity it supports.

These Mini-Callistos are connected together. They use messages to communicate with each other. Each message has an associated action. Messages are used for generating proposals, communicating constraints, proposing constraint relaxations, committing to plans, and querying others' knowledge. The messages are grouped into protocols that describe how a specification or change can be made.

A *constraint* expresses an impediment to plan variables. It can be interpreted in three ways: (1) an elimination rule from the perspective of object selection; (2) a partial description and commitment from the perspective of plan refinement; and (3) a communications medium for expressing interactions among organizational entities, each of which solves a subproblem. A constraint is not only a restriction but also the aggregation of a variety of knowledge used in the reasoning process. In particular, it includes the relative importance of multiple constraints; the possible relaxations and their relative utilities; the obligation to satisfy constraints according to time, context, and source; the interactions among constraints; and the dynamic generation of constraints (Stefik 1981; Fox 1983).

Negotiation is a form of decision making in which two or more parties communicate with one another in an effort to resolve nonoverlapping interests (Pruitt 1981). In the context of project management, the nonoverlapping interests are in the form of constraints faced by each party. A negotiation is initiated if and when an organizational entity faces an inconsistency or an incompleteness in the project knowledge base that can only be resolved with the help of other organizational entities. Negotiation is the process of isolating the constraints, communicating them to the other organizational entities, and jointly relaxing or strengthening them in order to resolve the inconsistency or incompleteness. A variety of negotiation operators, such as cost cutting, trading, arbitration, and mediation, are used for selecting the direction and magnitude of the strengthening or relaxing (see Figure 11.4).

In a centralized algorithm, the constraint-directed search uses global importance for each constraint and global utility for each relaxation. In the distributed case, such global measures are extremely expensive (if not impossible) to compute. Instead, the negotiation needs to accommodate multiple agents, each with a set of constraints and their evaluations. A number of techniques are used by expert negotiators to reach an agreement (Pruitt 1981). The techniques that can be chosen to manipulate constraints in an automated negotiation situation are cost cutting; trade, substitution, and compensation; log rolling; bridging; unlinking; mediation; and arbitration.

Cost cutting involves reducing the cost of a relaxation for the other party by manipulating other parameters, such as the context. For exam-

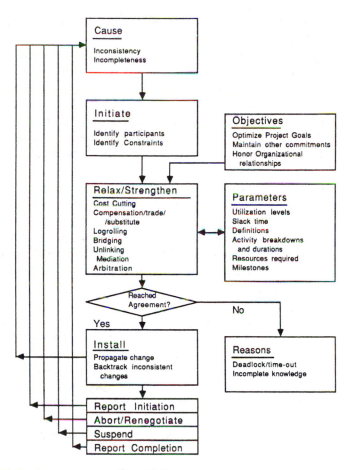

Figure 11.4 Constraint directed negotiation.

ple, an overutilization of a resource for a short duration of time can be made to look like normal utilization by extending the time horizon.

Trade, substitution, and compensation involves the exchange of project objects, such as resource reservations, to reduce the cost of relaxation for all the negotiating parties. The sharing of the losses, if any, should be according to goals shared.

Log rolling involves an exchange of concessions through selective violation of a portion of the constraints. For example two agents, each contributing three constraints to the negotiation, might decide to violate one constraint each, in order to reach an agreement. Log rolling involves prioritizing constraints by their importance and selectively violating those which are low in priority. Although trading involves bargaining on relative losses, log rolling focuses on the relative importance of the competing constraints.

Bridging occurs when a new option is developed that satisfies both parties' most significant constraints. Such a relaxation is selected even though it violates all the other constraints.

Unlinking occurs when selective concessions are necessary to reach a solution and bridging or log rolling has not worked. It involves removing weak interactions among constraints for the purpose of negotiation (for example, relaxation of a due date that affects organizational stability).

Mediation occurs when the negotiating parties reach a deadlock (that is, are unable to relax any more constraints to reach an agreement). Mediation involves reassessment of the relaxations and the important constraints by a third party with, hopefully, a global perspective.

Arbitration occurs when the negotiation reaches a deadlock and even a third party cannot mediate. In such cases, if the need is critical, a third party assigns losses and forces relaxations to the constraints posed by each of the negotiating parties.

Each Mini-Callisto is managed by a program module called an R-object (R stands for responsible). *R-objects* maintain the organizational structure of the project and have mechanisms for generating, filtering, and archiving messages for communicating with other modules as well as mechanisms for generating procedures for solving problems. The R-objects are comprised of ports, views, plans, and local and shared knowledge.

Ports provide the mechanism for communication across R-objects. Messages can be generated by an R-object and directed to the out port where they are preprocessed before the communication. Then the messages arrive at the in port of the receiving R-object where auxiliary communication can take place to resolve any inconsistency and incompleteness before their assimilation into the rest of the local knowledge.

Each R-object carries *views* specifying the other R-objects and their organizational relationships. The views use the organizational information to process a message for inconsistency and incompleteness. For example, in a given incomplete message, a Mini-Callisto can automatically fill in the name of the project if this is the only project common to the Mini-Callisto sending the message.

R-objects also carry *plans* associated with each protocol or message. Given a message in the in port, an R-object executes the associated plan. For example, the plan associated with a query message involves checking whether the query is understandable and whether the source has the authority to make the query and then responding to it (Kedzierski 1983).

Each Mini-Callisto carries two types of objects: those objects which are local to the Mini-Callisto and are thereby owned by the local R-object (*local knowledge*) and those objects which have been moving from one Mini-Callisto to another and are possibly owned by another R-object residing in another Mini-Callisto (*shared knowledge*). Any revisions to an object owned by another Mini-Callisto use *revision protocol*, which involves negotiation and approval before the revision is finalized.

A test bed of the Mini-Callisto network has been created using knowledge craft and its context (alternate world) mechanism (Carnegie Group 1986) in a simulated distributed environment. This network facilitates modeling of distributed knowledge and problem solving on local knowledge. The choice of simulating rather than actually using a distributed environment was made entirely for convenience (a real distributed version was also created but was found too difficult to experiment with). The test bed has provisions for creating several Mini-Callisto nodes; switching from one node to another; sending messages from one node to another; negotiating on project management problems; and gathering associated statistics on the number of messages, the processing load, and the associated changes for each negotiation. The test bed is currently being used for the experiments described under Mini-Callisto experiments. The next three subsections discuss the evolution of constraint-directed negotiation for resource, activity, and configuration management, respectively.

Resource Management

Consider the following scenario: *The printed circuit lab to be used for the design of the Micro-84 CPU belongs to the manufacturing department. The manufacturing department has agreed to the engineering department's use of 40% of the throughput. Jack, the supervisor of the printed circuit lab, schedules its use for the engineering department along with the preventive maintenance requirements and ongoing manufacturing department needs. The engineering department requested from Jack specific reservations for lab use for the next month. A round of negotiation was conducted, ending with a mediation by the plant manager, to provide the needed throughput.*

Although project-scheduling systems have been extended to include considerations of resource availability and capacity (Talbot 1982; Project/2 1981), we have not yet come across any approaches that include resource negotiations based on ownership and commitments in project scheduling. Large projects involve resource sharing between resource owners and project-activity owners (for example, sharing of the printed circuit lab between engineering and manufacturing departments). The sharing is finalized through negotiations, which involve complex agreements resulting from trading, log rolling, or arbitration.

The Mini-Callisto model explicitly brings resource ownership and commitment into the resource-allocation process. Each resource is owned by an agent. Resource sharing needs to be negotiated with the agent owning the resource. Agents are interdependent through organizational links. These organizational links are used for delegating of resource ownership from one agent to another and for adjudicating conflicts at lower levels of the organization. Contracts are formed across two or more agents for the use of a resource. The contracts specify the resource, the contracting parties, and the duration of use. No changes can be made to a contract without the approval of the contracting agents.

The steps for constraint-directed resource negotiation begin with the cause: A Mini-Callisto locates an incompleteness or an inconsistency in the project knowledge that needs to be resolved. As an example, a Mini-Callisto supporting the plan generation for the engineering team recognizes the absence of a contract for the use of the printed circuit lab in the design and verification activities. (Every resource reservation that requires a resource outside the engineering department should be in the form of a contract).

Next, it is necessary for the initiating Mini-Callisto to identify the negotiation participants (that is, those agents whose input or approval is necessary for resolving the inconsistency or incompleteness). Thus, our Mini-Callisto supporting the engineering department locates Jack as the owner of the printed circuit lab.

The third step is to identify the constraints. The agent requiring the resource shares the constraints with the agent owning the resource. The Mini-Callisto that supports our engineering department communicates to Jack's Mini-Callisto of the need to use 40% of the printed circuit lab over the next month.

Jack's Mini-Callisto then searches through the existing reservations for the lab and recognizes that the available capacity is less than 40%. It communicates the constraint to the Mini-Callisto supporting the engineering department. The Mini-Callisto supporting the engineering department responds back, informing Jack's Mini-Callisto that the reservations cannot be made in any other time period (because of a due-date constraint).

Any of the negotiation operators can be used to relax the constraints. This negotiation takes into account the importance of the agents, their organizational relationship, and the past contracts. If conflicts cannot be resolved, the negotiation is passed to a higher level for mediation. If mediation at a higher level fails, the proposal is aborted or revised.

Thus, in our example, Jack's Mini-Callisto searches through the existing reservations to find that the contracts are with the manufacturing department and that Jack is unable to assess their importance. In the absence of any other local ways of relaxation, Jack's Mini-Callisto informs the engineering department that the PC lab is not available. The engineering department communicates the negotiation situation to the plant manager (request for mediation). The Mini-Callisto supporting the plant manager searches and finds a contract specifying an overall 40% throughput for the engineering department and decides to trade the reservations (by moving or bumping manufacturing reservations into the future).

Finally, if no conflicts remain, the contract is formalized. The formalization can result in auxiliary proposals for associated changes in contracts with other organizations. For example, the Mini-Callisto supporting the plant manager communicates the changes in existing reservations to the Mini-Callisto supporting Jack. Jack's Mini-Callisto reevaluates the constraints associated with the utilizations and recognizes that the proposed reservations can be granted to the engineering department. It informs the Mini-Callisto supporting the engineering department of the agreement to use the printed circuit lab. The Mini-Callisto supporting the engineering department responds with an acknowledgement, thereby signaling the contract formation. New negotiations are initiated within the manufacturing department to decide when the manufacturing reservations should be scheduled.

The test bed is being used for experiments with the Mini-Callisto model of resource management in various allocation specification and revision situations. In the next two subsections, we explore other types of negotiations and how they are used if and when the resource negotiations fail (or take too long).

Activity Management

Consider the following scenario: *The design engineers were falling behind in their work because of the unavailability of CAD machines. The negotiations between the CAD machine owners and the design engineers resulted in the realization that verification of the first version of the CPU was competing (in the CAD machine utilization) with the design of version 2. It was decided to trade some slack time available in the verification of version 2 to version 1, thereby pushing the design of version 2 into the future.*

Resource management dealt with the specification of resource schedules through negotiations based on ownership and commitment levels. Activity management tasks extend the negotiation to include the constraints related to the activities, such as activity criticality and available slack time. These negotiations often repeat, with the focus changing from resource to activity constraints and back again. In the scenario just described, each of the two versions of the Micro-84 CPU design carry slack time meant to be used in unforeseen situations. The contention for resources, which could not be adequately addressed through resource-commitment negotiations, was retried and resolved through negotiations on the activity slack, thereby "substituting" or "trading" some time available for version 2 to version 1.

The activity negotiation support system involves three activities. The first is the distribution of problem and activity knowledge, which assumes that the project organization is divided into a large number of groups, each possessing the capability to execute a subtask and each having the knowledge of the prototypical activity networks for the subtask. The project goals are divided accordingly and distributed to each group. These goals are translated by each group into a set of activities to meet the goals.

The second activity is a negotiation on plan specification and revision. The groups begin to share a portion of their local plans to define the durations and the performance in accordance with the project objectives or milestones. Extending activities beyond the due dates (as assigned in the milestones) implies additional costs to be incurred. The most common way to eliminate these additional costs is to trade slack time available from one activity to the activity requiring more time. Another strategy, one that is often technically infeasible, is to compensate by providing more resources (that is, activity crashing). Sometimes, it is possible to reduce the costs of delaying the activity beyond the due date. Mini-Callisto supports the sharing of plans as well as the relaxation of constraints (for example, changes to activity durations and related slack times). It provides the support by computing constraint utilities (for example, using critical-path evaluation for the local network) or by using automated interactions for simpler negotiations.

The third activity is the completion of incomplete specifications. The local plans might not be complete for the negotiation with others. Completion of the incomplete portions initiates new negotiations at a future time.

Figure 11.5 illustrates the negotiation process for the CPU engineering activity. The test bed experiments with the use of activity negotiations to augment resource negotiations and to improve the quality of the final plans (that is, the level to which they satisfy all of the constraints). The experiments simulate a set of engineers negotiating on the completion of the overall project using commitments, resource substitutes, and activity slack times.

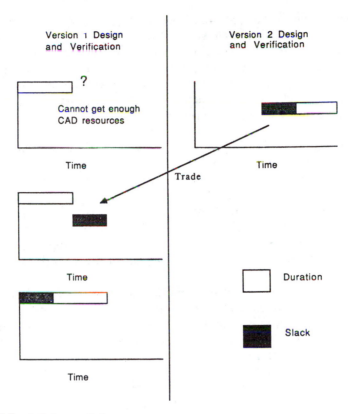

Figure 11.5   Activity negotiation.

Often negotiations on resources or activities require consistent understanding of the plan or product definitions, which is especially true when the negotiations fail at the resource or activity level. The next subsection extends the negotiations to include the definitional constraints.

Configuration Management

Consider the following scenario: *Each of the CPU design and verification activities for Micro-84 will take a year. The engineers were told that the engineering development needs to be completed in 1 1/2 years. It became apparent to the engineers that some verification had to take place while design was still being done. Detailed negotiations on the design elements and technological precedence constraints resulted in a plan for verification of a portion of the instruction set while other portions were still being designed. The supply department was informed about the change so that the related purchases were made six months earlier.*

Such negotiations require a good understanding of the components of the CPU and their design, verification, and associated purchase activities. Any changes to the components of the CPU can affect or initiate such negotiations. Also, multiple versions of the CPU can exist, and negotiations can focus on one or more of these versions.

Definitional negotiations use product definitions and generate new definitions in order to resolve project conflicts. These changes have far-reaching consequences for previously negotiated resource allocations or activity networks. The biggest deficiency in conventional project management tools for use in engineering program management is their exclusion of configuration and change management and their inability to propagate these changes to the rest of the project activities. For example, if a change made to the design activities is not communicated to the supply department, it nullifies the intended effect of finishing the design early. In order to model negotiations and related changes, one needs to model the diverse descriptions, their relationships, and the impact of one specification or revision on another.

The Mini-Callisto approach models product definition and change negotiations as an integral part of the negotiation process. It supports user-initiated change negotiations and identifies and initiates the associated activity management or resource-allocation negotiations. A typical scenario begins with the generation of a change requirement. The design team detects the need for a change in the plan for Micro-84 CPU design. A goal of reducing the engineering time by six months is established.

Change negotiation is the next step. A number of negotiations are attempted to meet the goal. Let us assume that the goal cannot be met through increased resource commitments because they are already 100%. Also, available slack time cannot be decreased any more because no slack time is left. Each of these negotiations involves sharing of knowledge, such as resource commitment, capacities, and slack time available for the entire activity network. Finally, the negotiation is turned toward product definitions. A possible relaxation is found in dividing the CPU into two parts, each complete in itself (that is, no design dependence). The cost of delaying a part of the design is thereby reduced.

Change installation is the final step. The changes lead to two subversions of Micro-84. A search among other activities related to the Micro-84 CPU reveals that the supply department needs to be informed. A subsequent negotiation is initiated with the supply department and results in changes to the project activities.

Figure 11.6 shows the activity and product knowledge before and after the negotiations. The part definition negotiations are the most difficult to implement and support. As can be seen from this scenario, the

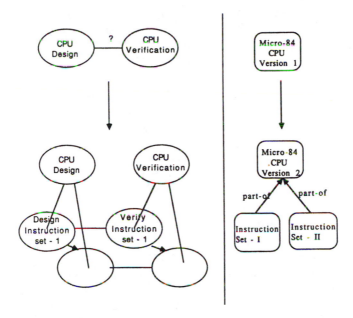

Figure 11.6   Product definition negotiations.

negotiations cannot be done unless the model includes design descriptions. A miniature design expert was developed to explore the design knowledge and its use in project negotiations (Glackemeyer 1984), although the related experiments are yet to be designed or conducted.

To summarize, the three components of project management—activity, resource, and configuration management—are interconnected both at the project knowledge and negotiation levels. Negotiations begin with one type of constraint and are either resolved or continued to include relaxations of other constraints, with possible back-tracking if the negotiations fail. The Mini-Callisto system can be used for modeling, supporting, or automating these negotiations.

Mini-Callisto Experiments

We need to validate the constraint-directed negotiation approach on real project situations. The Mini-Callisto experiments initiate the validation process in three ways.

First, Does it work? The constraint-directed negotiation should be able to model various project management situations within activity, resource, or configuration management. Also, the approach should converge to a solution wherever a solution exists. This article demonstrates the applicability of the approach. The experiments involve a number of random situations for each of the three types of negotiation situations. The solutions are tracked for quality (that is, the number of successful negotiations) and negotiation effort (that is, the number and size of communication messages).

Second, How good is it? A centralized project-scheduling or change installation algorithm can provide an ideal solution to a cooperative problem, that is, the performance of the systems when the goals are identical and when the information is completely available to all the project members. A series of experimental runs compare the distributed project negotiation-based solutions to the upper limit generated by the centralized solution under different distributions of goals to the project members.

Third, Does it use negotiation expertise? Choosing the right goals and constraints for negotiation is important. Choosing incorrect constraints involves additional sharing of information, expensive trade-offs, and additional time spent searching and backtracking.

The third set of experiments will probably be the most difficult and will take the longest time. At the same time, the comparisons and adequacy of the approach (as in the first two experiments) will be affected by the level of negotiation expertise, thereby requiring a reasonable level of negotiation expertise to be captured in the Mini-Callisto test bed. The details of experiments and their results will be the subject of a follow-on article.

The Mini-Callisto concept is being developed with the goal of fulfilling any of the following roles, depending on the objectives, the complexity of the situation, and the negotiation expertise embedded in the system: a support system which documents human negotiations, such as that developed by Marca and Cashman (1985); an enhancement to existing tools, providing minimal negotiation and change management support; an expert system that automatically negotiates in simpler (yet large and dynamic) situations, especially those involving automation of the activities (for example, flexible manufacturing systems (FMS) scheduling); and a test bed for understanding and exploring project management practices. The extension to these areas will trigger a set of experiments to assess the adequacy of the Mini-Callisto approach to problem solving.

Model of Explanation Using Comparative Analysis

We observed that it is inherently difficult to interpret and analyze complex, resource-constrained activity networks (even when graphically illustrated). For example, it requires tremendous effort to identify and understand the effects of changes to some areas of a schedule on other areas. Project managers regularly study project schedules and status information to analyze progress and its effect on related activities. Very often, such analysis is done using unfamiliar tools and graphic aids that offer virtually no assistance other than fancy documentation. Such utilities usually allow users to peruse a project schedule at a single phase of completion and never support comparison of multiple schedules.

By "explanation," we mean the analysis, interpretation, clarification, and report presentation of plans, schedule information, and conclusions produced by activity management systems. The motivation for our work is based on several observations about the task of project management and our attempts to build tools to support it. First, managers must be able to maintain, access, interpret, and act upon information from large and diverse project knowledge bases. Monitoring and managing change in project plans and the status of project activities requires frequent comparisons of lengthy schedules and networks. Managers must know what information is needed, where to locate it, and how to interpret and use it. Equally important is that they be able to do so without great effort.

Our second observation is that with advances in project management research, this task has become more difficult rather than easier. AI and operations research (OR) techniques for project management are increasing the quantity and complexity of knowledge about projects that can be represented and maintained. Decision support systems are using this knowledge to assist or automate many aspects of management decision making. As a result, advances in knowledge representation and inference-making capabilities will greatly expand the need for managers to access and interpret project knowledge and procedures and justifications behind system decision making. Although the process of monitoring the evolution of project plans was complex enough when only activity precedences and durations were represented (for example, with critical path method (CPM) approaches), this process becomes an even greater bottleneck as plans become more knowledge intensive.

Our approach to explanation extends a technique called *comparative analysis* (Kosy and Roth 1986), that has been used successfully in the explanation of change in financial modeling (Kosy and Wise 1984). Although previous work was limited to explaining change in quantitative models, our approach involves identification and interpretation at many levels of understanding, depending on the depth required by the user or the knowledge that is available to the system. These levels include (1) understanding the quantitative relations among the temporal properties of activities and resources contained in PERT networks (for example, knowing statistically how the change in risk in a milestone was produced by changes in delays of prior activities); (2) understanding the qualitative properties of activities, resources, and other project entities and the ways they can be classified, aggregated, abstracted, and summarized in order th help managers find reasons for changes beyond quantitative relations (for example, recognizing that a set of activities contributing to the increased risk for the milestone of a large project is the responsibility of a single subproject); (3) understanding the methods by which changes to a plan are made, including who makes the changes (people or software agents), the types of changes made (for example, precedence, time estimates, detailed breakdowns, or addition of new activities), and (when possible) awareness of other information that might provide the rationale for changes (for example, recognizing the existence of new precedence links and realizing their creation is the result of a Mini-Callisto in response to new commitment information); and (4) understanding other events in a project environment which explain the causes of changes (for example, the process and results of commitment negotiation among people or software agents in a project).

A series of experiments were performed to implement components of comparative analysis within Callisto (Roth et al. 1986). CPM was chosen as the first application because it involves only a single dimension (time) and a single quantifiable constraint (technological precedence) and is therefore analogous to financial spread sheets (costs and algebraic equations) (Kosy and Wise 1984). Although this restriction limits explanation to the identification of change based on quantitative relations (the first level of understanding), it serves as a starting point for explaining complex models of projects.

Explanation is one of the important future areas of research in project management. We intend to expand the necessary expertise in the following ways: (1) to increase the complexity of quantitative models that can be explained (for example, resource-constrained schedules and probabilistic time estimates), (2) to expand comparative analysis to deal with qualitative changes and integrate with quantitative changes, (3) to develop explanatory capabilities for the results of distributed processes for negotiation, (4) to develop an approach to knowledge-based graphics for creating and coordinating multiple text and graphic displays to satisfy the needs of explanation, and (5) to develop a discourse model of human explanations in project management both to support and test our approach to computer-generated explanation.

Conclusions and Future Plans

The Callisto project has made a number of significant research contributions. It has successfully modeled the specification and revision process of project management as a series of constraint-directed negotiations. This model enhances the capabilities of project management tools in dealing with large, complex, and dynamic projects. It has also contributed toward the development of knowledge-based models for project management and similar planning tasks. This model has subsequently been applied to a number of diverse situations ranging from software engineering to manufacturing planning. A configuration-tracking system has been developed out of the first Callisto prototype to be used by Digital Equipment Corporation for the tracking of product configurations. The system is currently being field tested.

The successful implementation of Mini-Callisto requires a set of user interface capabilities that facilitate the use of mixed-mode negotiations. The interfaces are critical for intelligent assistants because the users need to share assumptions, defaults, and decisions with the system. The capabilities include methods for displaying and reporting information contained in various Mini-Callistos as well as tools for their specification and revision. Our efforts in the comparative analysis area need to be extended to include other interface tools required to support mixed-mode project negotiations.

Callisto provides an excellent opportunity for studying distributed problem solving and validating the constraint-directed negotiation approach. We foresee a large number of experiments to validate and extend the Callisto model in project management and similar domains. The approach can be used to solve large real-world problems. The successful applications, though, require a maturing of technologies in the areas of communications, hardware for workstations, and system software for distributed problem solving.

Acknowledgments

This research was conducted at the Intelligent Systems Laboratory at CMU and was partially supported by Digital Equipment Corporation and Carnegie Group Inc. The views and conclusions contained in this document are those of the authors and should not be interpreted as representing the official policies, either expressed or implied, of Digital Equipment Corporation or Carnegie Group Inc.

We would like to acknowledge Mark Fox, Mike Greenberg, and LeRoy C. Smith who contributed to earlier versions of this article. Also, we would like to acknowledge the helpful suggestions of John McDermott, William Sears, Robert Murphy, Mark Olsen, Richard Glackemeyer, Ray Ross, Pam Gage, Jean Kauffmann, and two anonymous referees.

References

Allen, J. F. 1984. General Theory of Action and Time. *Artificial Intelligence* 23(2): 123–159.

Allen, J. F., and Hayes, P. J. 1985. A Common-Sense Theory of Time. In Proceedings of the Ninth International Joint Conference on Artificial Intelligence, 528–531.

Baiman, S. 1982. Agency Research in Managerial Accounting: A Survey. *Journal of Accounting Literature* 1: 154–213.

Barbuceanu, M. 1984. Object-Centered Representation and Reasoning: An Application to Computer-Aided Design. In SIGART Newsletter, January, 33–39.

Brachman, R. J. 1979. On the Epistemological Status of Semantic Networks. In *Associative Networks: Representation and Use of Knowledge by Computers*, ed. N. V. Findler, 3–50. New York: Academic.

Carbonell, J.; Boggs, M.; and Monarch, I. 1984. DYPAR User's Manual, Computer Science Dept., Carnegie-Mellon Univ.

Carnegie Group. 1986. Knowledge Craft User's Manual, Version 3.1, Carnegie Group.

Corkill, D. D. 1983. A Framework for Organizational Self-Design in Distributed Problem Solving. Ph.D. diss., Computer and Information Science Dept., Univ. of Massachusetts.

Crowston, W. B. S. 1970. Decision CPM: Network Reduction and Solution. *OR Quarterly* 21(4): 435–452.

Davis, E. W. 1976. *Project Management: Techniques, Applications, and Managerial Issues*. Atlanta, Ga.: American Institute of Industrial Engineers, Inc.

Davis, E. W. 1973. Project Scheduling under Resource Constraints: Historical Review and Categorization of Procedures. American Institute of Industrial Engineering Transactions 5: 297–313.

Davis, R., and Smith, R. G. 1981. Negotiation as a Metaphor for Distributed Problem Solving, Technical Report, AI Memo 624, Artificial Intelligence Laboratory, Massachusetts Institute of Technology.

DeCoster, D. T. 1964. PERT/Cost—The Challenge. *Management Services*, May–June.

Demski, J. S. 1976. Uncertainty and Evaluation Based on Controllable Performance. *Accounting Research*, Autumn: 230–245.

Demski, J. S., and Swieringa, R. J. 1974. A Cooperative Formulation of the Audit Choice Problem. *Accounting Review* 49(3): 506–513.

Durfee, E. H.; Lesser, V. R.; and Corkill, D. D. 1985. Increasing Coherence in a Distributed Problem Solving Network. In Proceedings of the Ninth International Joint Conference on Artificial Intelligence, 1025–1030.

Elmaghraby, S. E. 1977. *Activity Networks: Project Planning and Control by Network Models*. New York: Wiley.

Erman, L. D.; Hayes-Roth, F.; Lesser, V. R.; and Reddy, D. R. 1980. The Hearsay-II Speech Understanding System: Integrating Knowledge to Resolve Uncertainty. *Computing Surveys* 12(2): 213–253.

Fagin, R.; and Halpern, J. Y. 1985. Belief, Awareness, and Limited Reasoning: Preliminary Report. In Proceedings of the Ninth International Joint Conference on Artificial Intelligence, 491–501.

Fama, E. F. 1980. Agency Problems and the Theory of Firm. *Journal of Political Economy* 88(2): 299–307.

Fox, M. S. 1983. Constraint-Directed Search: A Case Study of Job-Shop Scheduling. Ph.D. diss., Computer Science Dept., Carnegie-Mellon Univ.

Fox, M. S. 1981a. The Intelligent Management System.: An Overview. In *Processes and Tools for Decision Support*, ed. H. G. Sol. Amsterdam, The Netherlands: North Holland.

Fox, M. S. 1081b. An Organizational View of Distributed Systems. In *IEEE Transactions on Systems, Man, and Cybernetics 11*(1): 70–80.

Fox, M. S. 1979. Organization Structuring: Designing Large Complex Software, Technical Report, CMU-CS-79-155, Computer Science Dept., Carnegie-Mellon Univ.

Fox, M. S., and Smith, S. 1984. The Role of Intelligent Reactive Processing in Production Management. In Proceedings of the Thirteenth Annual Computer Aided Manufacturing International Incorporated Technical Conference, 6-13–6-17.

Freeman, P., and Newell, A. 1971. A Model for Functional Reasoning in Design. In Proceedings of the First International Joint Conference on Artificial Intelligence, 621–640.

Galbraith, J. 1973. *Designing Complex Organizations*. Reading, Mass.: Addison-Wesley.

Georgeff, M. P.; Lansky, A. L.; and Bessiere, P. 1985. A Procedural Logic. In Proceedings of the Ninth International Joint Conference on Artificial Intelligence, 516–523.

Glackmeyer, R. 1984. Behavioral Simulation of Electronic Design, Technical Report, Intelligent Systems Laboratory, The Robotics Institute, Carnegie-Mellon Univ.

Greif, I., and Hewitt, C. E. 1975. Actor Semantics of PLANNER-73. In Proceedings of Association of Computing Machinery, Special Interest Group in

Programming Languages–Special Interest Group in Automata and Computability Theory Conference, Palo Alto, Calif.: ACM.

Groves, T. 1975. Information, Incentives, and the Internalization of Production Externalities. In *Theory and Measurement of Economic Externalities*, ed. S. Lin. New York: Academic.

Groves, T., and Loeb, M. 1979. Incentives in Divisionalized Firms. *Management Science* 25: 221–230.

Harris, M., and Townsend, R. M. 1981. Resource Allocation under Asymmetric Information. *Econometrica* 49(91): 33–64.

Hayes, P. J. 1979. The Naive Physics Manifesto. In *Expert Systems in the Micro Electronics Age*, ed. D. Michie, 243–270. Edinburgh, United Kingdom: Edinburgh.

Hayes-Roth, B. 1985. A Blackboard Architecture for Control. *Artificial Intelligence* 26(3): 251–321.

Hendrix, G. G. 1979. Encoding Knowledge in Partial Networks. In *Associative Networks, Representation and Use of Knowledge by Computers*, ed. N. V. Findler. New York: Academic.

Kedzierski, B. I. (1983). Knowledge-Based Communication and Management and Support in a System Development Environment. Ph.D. diss., Computer Science Dept., Univ. of Southwestern Louisiana.

Kelley, J. E., Jr. 1961. Critical-Path Planning and Scheduling: Mathematical Basis. *Operations Research* 9(3): 296–320.

Kelley, J. E., Jr., and Walter, M. R. 1959. Critical-Path Planning and Scheduling. In Proceedings of Eastern Joint Computer Conference, 160–173.

Kosy, D. W., and Roth, S. F. 1986. Applications of Explanation to the Analysis of Schedules and Budgets, Technical Report, Intelligent Systems Laboratory, The Robotics Institute, Carnegie-Mellon Univ.

Kosy, D. W., and Wise, B. P. 1984. Self-Explanatory Financial Planning Models. In Proceedings of the Fourth National Conference on Artificial Intelligence, 176–181. Menlo Park, Calif.: American Association of Artificial Intelligence.

Lambourn, S. 1963. Resource Allocation and Multi-Project Scheduling (RAMPS)—A New Tool in Planning and Control. *Computer J.* 6: 300–303.

Latombe, J. C. 1976. Artificial Intelligence in Computer-Aided Design: The TROPIC System, Technical Report, Tech Note 125, Artificial Intelligence Center, Stanford Research Institute.

Lawrence, S. R. 1984. Resource-Constrained Project Scheduling: An Experimental Investigation of Heuristic Scheduling Techniques, Technical Report, GSIA, Carnegie-Mellon Univ.

Lee, R. M. 1980. CANDID: A Logical Calculus for Describing Financial Contracts. Ph.D. diss., Dept. of Decision Sciences, The Wharton School, Univ. of Pennsylvania.

Lessr, V. R., and Corkill, D. D. 1983. The Distributed Vehicle-Monitoring Testbed: A Tool for Investigating Distributed Problem-Solving Networks. *AI Magazine* 4: 15–33.

Lesser, V. R., and Corkill, D. D. 1981. Functionally Accurate, Cooperative Distributed Systems. In *IEEE Transactions on Systems, Man, and Cybernetics* 11(1): 81–96.

Liberatore, M. J., and Titus, G. J. 1983. Management Science Practice in R&D Project Management. *Management Science* 29, 962–974.

Loeb, M. 1975. Coordination and Informational Incentive Problems in the Multidivisional Firm. Ph.D. diss., Graduate School of Management, Northwestern Univ.

Luce, R. D., and Raiffa, H. 1957. *Games and Decisions*. New York: Wiley & Sons.

Lynch, F.; Marshall, C.; and O'Connor, D. 1986. AI in Manufacturing Start-Up. Paper presented at Computer and Automated Systems Association, Society of Mechanical Engineers Untratech Conference on AI in Manufacturing.

McCarty, L. T., and Sridharan, N. S. 1981. The Representation of an Evolving System of Legal Concepts. In Proceedings of the Seventh International Joint Conference on Artificial Intelligence, 246–253.

Malcolm, D. G.; Rosenboom, J. H.; Clark, C. E.; and Fazar, W. 1959. Application of a Technique for Research and Development Program Evaluation. *Operations Research* 7(5).

Malone, T. W., and Smith, S. A. 1984. Tradeoffs in Designing Organizations: Implications for New Forms of Human Organizations and Computer Systems, Technical Report, CISR WP #112, Sloan WP# 1541–84, Center for Information Systems Research, Sloan School of Management, Massachusetts Institute of Technoogy.

Marca, D., and Cashman, P. 1985. Toward Specifying Procedural Aspects of Cooperative Work. In IEEE Proceedings of Third International Workshop on Software Specification and Design, 151–154.

Marschak, J., and Radner, R. 1972. Economic Theory of Games, Monograph 22 Cowles Foundation, Yale Univ.

Nash, J. F. 1950. The Bargaining Problem. *Econometrics* 18: 155–162.

National Air and Space Administration. 1979. Voyager Encounters Jupiter.

Preiss, K. 1976. Engineering Design Viewed as an Activity in Artificial Intelligence, Technical Report SRIN-167, Stanford Research Institute (SRI).

Pritsker, A. A. B.; Watters, L. J.; Wolfe, P. M.; and Happ, W. 1966. GERT: Graphical Evaluation and Review Technique, Part 1. *The Journal of Industrial Engineering* 17(5): 267–274.

Project/2 User's Manual, Sixth Edition. 1981. Project Software & Development, Inc., Cambridge, MA.

Pruitt, D. G. 1981. *Negotiation Behavior*. New York: Academic.

Reddy, Y. V.; Fox, M. S.; and Hussain, N. 1985. Automating the Analysis of Simulations in KBS. In Proceedings of Summer Computer Simulation Multiconference, 34–40.

Rieger, C., and Grinberg, M. 1977. The Declarative Representation and Procedural Simulation of Causality in Physical Mechanisms. In Proceedings of the Fifth International Joint Conference on Artificial Intelligence, 250–255.

Roth, S. F.; Mesnard, X.; Mattis, J. A.; Kosy, D. W.; and Sathi, A. 1986. Experiments with Explanation of Project Management Models, Technical Report, Intelligent Systems Laboratory, The Robotics Institute, Carnegie-Mellon Univ.

Sacerdoti, E. D. 1977. *A Structure for Plans and Behavior*. New York: American Elsevier.

Sacerdoti, E. D. 1974. Planning in a Hierarchy of Abstract Spaces. *Artificial Intelligence* 5(2): 115–135.

Saitow, A. R. 1969. CSPC: Reporting Project Progress to the Top. *Harvard Business Review* 47(1): 88–97.

Sathi, A.; Fox, M. S.; and Greenberg, M. 1985. Representation of Activity Knowledge for Project Management. In *IEEE Transactions on Pattern Analysis and Machine Intelligence* 7 (5): 531–552.

Schmidt, C. F.; Sridharan, N. S.; and Goodson, J. L. 1978. The Plan Recognition Problem: An Intersection of Psychology and Artificial Intelligence. *Artificial Intelligence* 11(1–2): 45–83.

Smith, R. G. 1980. The Contract Net Protocol: High-Level Communication and Control in a Distributed Problem Solver. In *IEEE Transactions on Computers* C-29(12): 1104–1113.

Smith, R. G. 1978. A Framework for Problem Solving in a Distributed Processing Environment. Ph.D. diss., Computer Science Dept., Stanford Univ.

Smith, S. F. 1983. Exploiting Temporal Knowledge to Organize Constraints, Technical Report, CMU-RI-TR-83-12, Intelligent Systems Laboratory, The Robotics Institute, Carnegie-Mellon Univ.

Stallman, R. M., and Sussman, G. J. 1977. Forward Reasoning and Dependency-Directed Backtracking in a System for Computer-Aided Circuit Analysis. *Artificial Intelligence* 9(2): 135–196.

Stefik, M. 1981. Planning with Constraints (MOLGEN: Part 1), 111–139; and Planning and Meta-Planning (MOLGEN: Part 2), 141–169. *Artificial Intelligence* 16(2).

Talbot, F. B. 1982. Resource-Constrained Project Scheduling with Time Resource Tradeoffs, The Nonpreemptive Case. *Management Science* 28(10): 1197–1210.

Tate, A. 1977. Generating Project Networks. In Proceedings of the Fifth International Joint Conference on Artificial Intelligence, 888–893.

Tichy, W. F. 1980. Software Development Control Based on System Structure Description. Ph.D. diss., Computer Science Dept., Carnegie-Mellon Univ.

Turban, E. 1976. The Line of Balance—A Management by Exception Tool. In *Project Management: Techniques, Applications, and Managerial Issues*, 39–47. Atlanta, Ga.: American Institute of Industrial Engineers, Inc.

Weiner, J. L. 1980. BLAH, A System That Explains Its Reasoning. *Artificial Intelligence* 15(1–2): 19–48.

Wiest, J. D. 1967. A Heuristic Model for Scheduling Large Projects with Limited Resources. *Management Science*, 13(6): 359–377.

Wilensky, R. 1983. *Planning and Understanding*. Reading, Mass.: Addison-Wesley.

Wilson, R. B. 1968. The Theory of Syndicates. *Econometrica* 36(1): 119–132.

Winston, P. H. 1975. *The Psychology of Computer Vision*. New York: McGraw-Hill.

Wise, B. P., and Kosy, D. W. 1985. Model-Based Evaluation of Long-Range Resource Allocation Plans. Technical Report, CMU-RI-TR-85-22, The Robotics Institute, Carnegie-Mellon Univ.

Wright, J. M., and Fox, M. S. 1983. SRL: Schema Representation Language, Technical Report, The Robotics Institute, Carnegie-Mellon Univ.

Wright, J. M.; Fox, M. S.; and Adam, D. 1984. SRL/2 User's Manual. Technical Report, The Robotics Institute, Carnegie-Mellon Univ.

Zdonik, S. B. 1984. Object Management System Concepts. In Second Association of Computing Machinery–Special Interest Group in Office Automation Conference on Office Information Systems, 113–19. Toronto, Canada: ACM.

12

Semistructured Messages are Surprisingly Useful for Computer-Supported Coordination[1]

Thomas W. Malone
Kenneth R. Grant
Kum-Yew Lai
Ramana Rao
David Rosenblitt
Massachusetts Institute of Technology
Cambridge, MA

1 *Introduction*

The goal of this paper is to articulate one of the major lessons learned so far from our design and use of the Information Lens, an intelligent system for information sharing in organizations [16]. The simple idea of using semistructured message templates turns out to be surprisingly powerful, with implications for designing a variety of group communi-

[1]A previous version of this paper appeared in the *Proceedings of the Conference on Computer-Supported Cooperative Work* (Austin, Tex., Dec. 3–5, 1986).This research was supported by the Xerox Corporation, Wang Laboratories, Inc., Bankers Trust Co., the Management in the 1990s Program at the Sloan School of Management, MIT, and the Center for Information Systems Research, MIT.

cation and coordination systems. We first describe how this idea simplifies the design of general capabilities for composing and processing messages. Then we show how these general capabilities have helped us develop not only our original information sharing application, but also simple applications for a variety of other purposes such as task tracking, calendar management, and computer conferencing. Finally, we discuss several general issues about how a community defines its message types.

Most previous systems for supporting group work can be thought of as belonging to one of two categories. In one category are forms processing, calendar management, and other systems that contain a great deal of formalized knowledge about the application domains they are intended to support (e.g., [3, 6, 9, 20]). In the other category are electronic mail, computer conferencing, and hypertext systems that provide some very general representational tools (such as topic structures in computer conferences or embedded links between documents) and very little other formal knowledge about their domains (e.g., [4, 11, 23]). By using semistructured message templates, we are able to achieve an intermediate, but variable, level of formalization that can flexibly accommodate as much or as little structure as is useful for a particular kind of communication.

2 Semistructured Messages

We define *semistructured messages* as messages of identifiable types, with each type containing a known set of fields, but with some of the fields containing unstructured text or other information. For example, seminar announcements can be structured as templates that include fields for "time," "place," "speaker," and "topic," along with the usual header fields of messages and any additional text describing the content of the talk (e.g., [8]). There are several reasons why this idea is important:

1. *Semistructured messages enable computers to process automatically a much wider range of information than would otherwise be possible.* By letting people compose messages that already have much of their essential information structured in fields, we eliminate the need for any kind of automatic parsing or understanding of free text while still representing enough information to allow quite sophisticated processing of the messages.

2. *Semistructured messages allow people to communicate nonroutine information without the constraints of a rigid structure.* By letting people include unstructured text in some fields and use other fields

in nonstandard ways, we greatly increase the flexibility and usefulness of our systems. Unusual situations do not bring the system to a halt, as they do in rigid forms-based systems. Instead, such situations merely reduce the usefulness of the automated support and depend, for their resolution, on the attention of human users.

3. *Much of the processing people already do reflects a set of semistructured message types.* It is a common observation that routine information processing in organizations is often based on structured forms. Even when structured forms are not used, we found in our informal studies [16] that people often describe their processes for filtering information according to categories of documents being filtered (e.g., *This is a brochure advertising a seminar. I usually throw these away unless the title intrigues me or unless it looks like a brochure I could use as a model for the ones I write.* [paraphrased comments of a research center administrator in our informal study]).

4. *Even if no automatic processing of messages were involved, providing a set of semistructured message templates to the authors of messages would often be helpful.* Two of the people in our informal interviews mentioned simple examples of this phenomenon: One remarked about how helpful it would be if any memo requesting some kind of action included, in a prominent place, the deadline by which the action needed to be taken; a second commented about how wonderful it would be if all the meeting invitations he received included a field about why he was supposed to be there. We shall later see how message templates can be provided in a flexible way that encourages, but does not require, their use.

5. *Semistructured messages simplify the design of systems that can be incrementally enhanced and adopted.* The initial introduction and later evolution of a group communication system can be much easier if the process occurs as a series of small changes, each of which has the following properties: (a) individual users can continue to use their existing system with no change if they so desire, (b) individual users who make small changes receive some immediate benefit, and (c) groups of users who adopt the changes receive additional benefits beyond the individual benefits. Although semistructured messages are not necessary for building such incrementally expandable systems, we shall see how they facilitate this process.

In addition to these general reasons why semistructured messages are desirable, we shall also see how their use can be simplified by (a) *arranging the message types in a frame inheritance network* so that specific message types can "inherit" properties from more general types they resemble, and (b) *using a consistent set of display-oriented editors* for composing messages, constructing message-processing rules, and defining new message templates.

Even though we will emphasize the use of these ideas in message-based systems, many of the same concepts are also directly applicable to systems based on shared databases (e.g., [10]). As we note in several places below, the addition of shared databases to the message-based facilities we have now seems likely to provide even further benefits.

3 *Example: The Information Lens System*

In order to illustrate our discussion of features made possible by semistructured messages, we first briefly describe our implementation of the Information Lens, an intelligent system for information sharing in organizations [15, 16]. We define the information sharing problem as one of disseminating information to the people who will find it useful, without distracting others who will find no value in its contents. This problem is likely to become increasingly important as it becomes both technically and economically feasible to send electronic messages and other documents to large numbers of possible recipients. Firs, it is already a common experience in mature computer-based messaging communities for people to feel flooded with large quantities of electronic junk mail (e.g., [2, 12]). At the same time, it is also a common experience for people to be ignorant of facts that would facilitate their work and that are known elsewhere in their organization. The Information Lens helps people solve both problems: It helps people filter, sort, and prioritize messages that are already addressed to them, and it also helps them find useful messages they would not otherwise have received.

More specifically, the Lens system enhances the usual capabilities of an electronic mail system with four important optional capabilities, which individual users may or may not choose to use: (1) senders can compose their messages using structured templates that suggest the kinds of information to be included in the message and likely alternatives for each kind of information; (2) receivers can specify rules to filter and classify their incoming messages automatically into folders on the basis of the same dimensions used by senders in constructing messages; (3) senders can include as an addressee of a message, in addition to specific individuals or distribution lists, a special mailbox (currently named

"Anyone") to indicate that the sender is willing to have this message automatically redistributed to anyone else who might be interested; and (4) receivers can specify rules for finding and showing messages addressed to Anyone that the receiver would not otherwise have seen.

Messages that include "Anyone" as an addressee are delivered by the existing mail server directly to the explicit addressees, as well as to an automatic mail sorter that runs on a workstation and periodically retrieves messages from the special mailbox. This automatic mail sorter then, in turn, sends the messages to any additional recipients whose rules select them. Messages can thus be selectively disseminated only to people who are likely to be interested in them. When, for reasons of confidentiality, it is necessary to restrict the potential recipients, messages can be addressed to "Anyone-in-(distribution list name)," and the messages will then be distributed only to members of the distribution list whose rules select them.

This framework supports many kinds of information sharing, in addition to straightforward electronic mail. For example, we have recently begun receiving a daily on-line feed of *New York Times* articles (via the system described by Gifford et al. [7]). These articles already contain fields such as subject, priority, and author, and the users of our system can specify rules based on these fields for selecting and sorting news articles that are just like the rules for sorting any other kind of message.

All the applications we describe are written in the Interlisp-D programming environment for Xerox 1100 series workstations using Loops, an object-oriented extension of LISP. In order to provide a natural integration of these applications with the capabilities that people already use, our system is built on top of the existing electronic mail system (called Lafite). Users can continue to send and receive their mail as usual, including using centrally maintained distribution lists and manually classifying messages into folders. As of this writing, the Lens system has been in regular use by about five members of our research group for over a year, and a larger scale test in a corporate research laboratory has just begun.

4 Features Made Possible by Semistructured Messages

As noted above, the use of a set of semistructured message templates simplifies the original composition and subsequent processing of messages. In this section, we list several general features of this type and illustrate them with examples from our original implementation of the Information Lens system [16] and our subsequent enhancements to it.

Some of the features we will describe (such as automatic processing of incoming messages) might, in principle, be provided without using structured messages, if robust and general natural language processing capabilities were available. The required capabilities, however, still appear to be significantly beyond the current state of the art. As natural language parsers improve, they can be used to parse more and more kinds of unstructured documents into templates like those we describe. Then the kinds of knowledge represented in our system will still be necessary, and it will become useful for a much wider range of documents. In a few cases, such as automatic aids for constructing messages, the simple user interfaces that are possible with structured messages appear to be "cleaner" and probably easier and more efficient to use than natural language interfaces with unstructured text.

4.1 *Automatic Aids for Constructing Messages*

The presence of a set of structured message types makes possible a variety of automatic aids for constructing messages. For example, the templates provided by the Information Lens system for each message type include specialized information about each field. Figure 12.1 illustrates the highly graphical interaction through which users can construct messages using these templates. After selecting a field of a message by pointing with a mouse, the user can point with the mouse again to see the field's default value, an explanation of the field's purpose, or a list of likely alternatives for filling in the field. If the user selects one of these alternatives, that value is automatically inserted in the message text.

By providing a wealth of domain-specific knowledge about the default and alternative values for particular types of messages, the system can make the construction of some messages much easier. For example, Figure 12.2 shows a regular weekly meeting announcement with default values already filled in for most of their fields. As we shall see, these default, explanation, and alternative values can be tailored by individual users to match their own communication habits and preferences. System developers can also write special functions to compute these values on the basis of other information in the system (e.g., the alternatives for the "To" field might be computed from a list of people to whom other recent messages have been addressed).

In the current system, all message types include a particular field called "Topic" which is intended to contain one or more keywords indicating the general topics of the message. The alternatives presented for this field are arranged, not as a simple list, but as a network (similar to the network of message types described below) with more specific topics shown below the general topics to which they pertain. This "topic

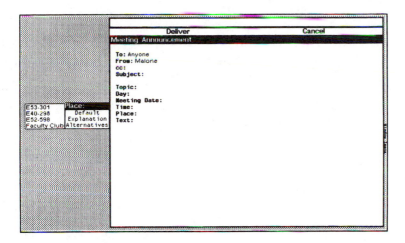

Figure 12.1 Messages are composed with a display-oriented editor and templates that have pop-up menus associated with the template fields.

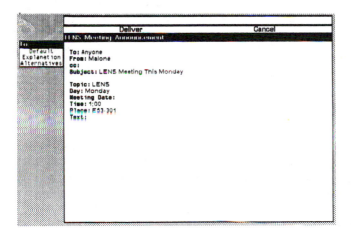

Figure 12.2 Some templates already have a number of default values filled in for different fields.

network" is, in a sense, "orthogonal" to the network of message types. For instance, users might send meeting announcements or requests for information about any of a variety of topics. The fact that the alternatives shown in this topic network are shared by all users in a group encourages (but does not, of course, require) different users to use the same keywords for the same topics.

Users who do not want to take advantage of any of these message construction aids can always select the most general message type (*message*) and they can always edit any fields directly at any time using the built-in, display-oriented text editor. For example, the user can add as much free text as desired in the text field of the message. We expect, however, that the added convenience provided to the senders by semistructured templates will be a significant incentive for senders to use templates in constructing their messages.

4.2 Rules for Automatically Processing Messages

Just as the structure of messages simplifies the process of composing messages, it also simplifies the process of constructing rules for processing messages. For instance, Figure 12.3 shows an example of the display-oriented editor used to construct rules in the Information Lens system. This editor uses rule templates that are based on the same message types as those used for message construction, and it uses a similar interaction style with menus available for defaults, alternatives, and explanations. We expect that this template-based graphical rule construction will be much easier for inexperienced computer users than more conventional rule or query languages. For example, the users of most typical database retrieval systems must already know the structure of the database fields and their plausible values in order to construct queries. Users of our system have all this information immediately available and integrated into the rule-construction tools [22].

4.2.1 Local Rules   There are currently two kinds of rules in the Lens system: *local rules* and *central rules*. Local rules are applied when messages are retrieved from the mail server to a user's local workstation. Typical rule actions possible here include moving messages to specific folders (Figure 12.4a), deleting messages (Figure 12.4b), and automatically resending messages to someone else (Figure 12.4c). Both "move" and "delete" mark a message as deleted, but do not physically expunge it. Thus, subsequent rules can move different copies of the same message to different folders. "Resending" a message is similar to "forwarding" it, except that, instead of copying the entire original message into the body of a new message, the new message preserves the type and all but the "To" and "cc" fields of the original message. The new value of the "To" field is a parameter the user specifies for the automatic rule action, and the user whose rule does the resending is added as the "Sender" of the new message.

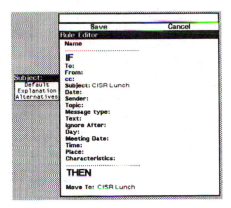

Figure 12.3 Rules for processing messages are composed using the same kind of editor and the same templates as those used for composing messages in the first place.

When the local rules have finished processing all incoming messages, the numbers of new messages that have been automatically moved into different folders since the last time the folder was viewed are shown on a hierarchical display of the folder names. Messages that were not moved anywhere remain in the "root" folder.

By combining conditions within and between fields, users can construct arbitrary Boolean queries. More interesting is the fact that users can also construct elaborate multistep reasoning chains by having some rules set *characteristics* of messages and then having other rules test these characteristics (Figure 12.4d; see [16] for details).

As an indication that we expect the set of possible rule actions to grow, we include a rule action called "LISP code" that takes as a parameter the name of an arbitrary LISP function to be called if the rule fires. It is also possible to have different kinds of actions available for different kinds of messages. For example, rules for "meeting proposal" messages have an automatic action available to "accept" a meeting.

4.2.2 Central Rules In addition to the local rules applied when messages are brought to a user's workstation, an individual user can also specify central rules for selecting messages addressed to "anyone" that the user wants to see. Only two kinds of rule action are possible for central rules: "show" (Figure 12.4e) and "set characteristic." "Show" causes a message to be sent to the user, unless the user would have already received it as one of the original recipients. When these messages arrive

```
(a)  If    Message type: Action request
           Action deadline: Today, tomorrow
     THEN  Move to: Urgent
(b)  IF    Message type: Meeting announcement
           Day: Not Tuesday
     THEN  Delete
(c)  IF    Message type: Meeting proposal
           Sender: Not Axsom
     THEN  Resend: Axsom
(d)  IF    From: Silk, Siegel
     THEN  Set Characteristic: VIP

     IF    Message type: Action request
           Characteristics: VIP
     THEN  Move to: Urgent
(e)  IF    Message type: Request for information
           Subject: AI, LISP
     THEN  Show
(f)  IF    Message type: NYT Article
           Subject: Computer
     THEN  Move to: Computers

     IF    Message type: NYT Article
           Subject: Movies
     THEN  Move to: Movies

     IF    Message type: NYT Article
           Article date:<Today
           Characteristics: Not MOVED
     THEN  Delete

     IF    Message type: NYT Article
           Characteristics: Not MOVED and not DELETED
     THEN  Move to: NYT Articles
```

Figure 12.4 Sample rules.

at the user's workstation they are processed, along with all the other messages, by the user's local rules.

4.2.3 *Rule Interactions* Our early experience with the system suggested the importance of being able to give users some control over the interactions between local rules (e.g., having certain rules fire only if no other rules have fired on a message) and of being able to explain to users why certain messages were processed as they were. Accordingly, we have recently added several simple features to the rule system. First, the rules

Original Message	*Suggested Reply Types*
Message	Message
Action request	Commitment, Request for information, Action request, Message
Notice	Request for information, Action request, Message
Bug fix request	Bug fix commitment, Bug fix announcement, Request for information
Meeting proposal	Meeting proposal, Meeting acceptance
Meeting announcement	Request for information

Figure 12.5   Sample of message types automatically suggested as replies.

for a given message type are applied in the order they appear in the "rule set editor" for that message type, and the rules pertaining to a specific message type are always applied before the rules inherited from more general message types. Also, rules that take actions (such as moving or deleting a message) always set a characteristic of the message (such as MOVED or DELETED). Thus subsequent rules can include conditions such as "the message has not yet been moved or deleted" (see Figure 12.4f). Finally, in order to help users understand and modify their rules, a simple explanation capability allows users to see a history of the rules that fired on a given message.

4.3 Intelligent Suggestions for Responding to Messages

The presence of recognizable types of semistructured messages also simplifies the task of having the system intelligently present options for what a user might want to do after seeing a message. Almost all electronic mail systems provide standard actions (such as "answer" and "forward") that can be taken after seeing a message. We have recently generalized this capability in two ways:

1. *Suggested reply types.* First, since either answering or forwarding a message creates a new message, our system suggests options for the type of new message to be created. For instance, when a user selects the "answer" option for a "bug fix request," a pop-up menu appears with three choices: "bug fix commitment," "request for information," and "other." Selecting commitment results in the construction of a new "commitment" message to answer the message. Figure 12.5 shows a selection of message types and their default reply types.

2. *Suggested response actions.* Even more important than suggesting reply types, our system is also able to suggest other actions

a user might want to take after seeing a message of a given type. For example, when a user reads a message of type "meeting announcement" another option, "add to calendar," is automatically presented, in addition to the standard options like "answer" and "forward." If the user selects the calendar option, the information already present in the message in structured form (e.g., date, time, and meeting topic) are used to add an appropriate entry to the user's on-line calendar.[2] As another example, when a user reads a message of type "software release" (or any of its subtypes such as "bug fix announcement"), an option called "load file" is automatically presented, and if this option is chosen, the file specified in the message is automatically loaded into the user's system.

5 *Inheritance of Message Type Characteristics*

The construction and use of message templates can be greatly simplified if the templates are arranged in a network with some templates designated as subtypes of others. Then the subtypes of a given template can automatically *inherit* from the *parent* template the field names and other properties (such as defaults and alternatives for field values, rules for processing incoming messages, suggested reply types, and suggested response actions).[3] Any subtype may also, in turn, add new fields or override any of the property values inherited from the parent (e.g., see [5]). For example, Figure 12.6 shows the simple network of message types in use in our prototype system. The *seminar notice* template adds a field for "speaker" that is not present in its parent template *meeting announcement*, and the *LENS meeting announcement* (Figure 12.2) adds a number of default values that are not present in its parent. The inheritance network eliminates the need to continually reenter redundant information when adding new templates that resemble old ones, and it provides a natural way of organizing templates, thus making it easier for senders to select the right template.

6 *Applications*

Our first, and most fully developed, application of these ideas is the intelligent information sharing system described above. In order to demon-

---

[2] The on-line calendar program we use was written by Michel Denber and is part of the user-contributed library of the Interlisp-D system.

[3] Though we have not yet found it useful, the *multiple inheritance* capabilities of the underlying knowledge representation system that we use (Loops, see below) also allow one message type to inherit properties from more than one parent

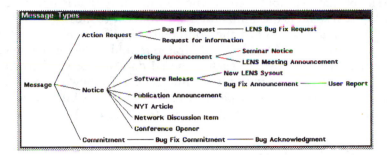

Figure 12.6 The message templates are arranged in a network with more general types at the "top" (shown at the left) and more specific types at the "bottom" (shown at the right).

strate the generality of the ideas, we now describe several other simple applications we have implemented in the same framework. The most important point here is not that it is possible to implement these other applications—in fact, we have chosen applications that have already been implemented in other systems. Instead the point is that a wide variety of applications for supporting cooperative work can all be implemented in a way that (1) is smoothly integrated from the user's point of view, and (2) is much easier to implement because it takes advantage of the basic capabilities for supporting structured messages.

6.1 Computer Conferencing

Many of the capabilities of a computer conferencing system (e.g., [11]) can be easily incorporated in the Information Lens system. We have recently done this by (1) adding a new message type called "conference opener" that includes the name of the conference and (optionally) its parent conference, and (2) adding a response option called "join" for this type of message that, if chosen, will automatically (a) create a new folder by this name, (b) create a new rule to select messages, addressed to "Anyone," that contain this name in the topic field, and (c) create a new rule to move all messages received about this topic to the new folder.

Our system thus includes the capability that computer conferencing systems have for structuring communication on the basis of flexibly defined sets of topics and subtopics. It is also easy to see how our system goes beyond these customary capabilities of a computer conferencing system by allowing, for example, more sophisticated rules that filter not only on topic but also on other characteristics such as sender.

The primary computer conferencing capability that is not included in our system so far is the ability for a user to retrieve messages that were sent before that user joined the conference. This capability is clearly important, and it would be quite desirable to add a shared database to our system. The addition of such a shared database of semistructured messages could be done within the same general framework and would make possible much more sophisticated retrieval possibilities than are possible with only unstructured messages (e.g., see [22]).

6.2 *Calendar Management*

We have already seen how a very simple form of calendar management is included in the system by providing users with a response option that will automatically insert incoming meeting announcements into the user's on-line calendar. We have also implemented a more sophisticated protocol for semiautomated meeting scheduling. This protocol uses several new message types, including "meeting proposals" and "meeting acceptances." Proposals and acceptances both include all the fields that "meeting announcements" do, but the values may often be nonspecific (e.g., "sometime this week" for the date field). People can schedule meetings by sending a sequence of proposals (and possibly counterproposals) until a proposal is accepted.

Our system provides automated support for this process in several ways. First, some people may want to automatically resend all messages of certain types (e.g., meeting proposals) to other people (e.g., their secretaries) for a response. Second, the system helps people construct replies to these messages. For instance, users can choose to reply to a "meeting proposal" with a "meeting acceptance," and all the information (such as time, place, and topic) will be automatically copied from the proposal to the acceptance. When a meeting acceptance is received, one of the action options presented is to "confirm" the meeting. Selecting this option automatically adds the meeting to the user's calendar and sends a meeting announcement to the other participant(s), confirming the scheduled time.

Though we have not done so yet, this general framework also makes it possible to have some meetings scheduled completely automatically (e.g., see[9]). For example, meeting proposals from certain people (e.g., members of one's own work group) might be automatically accepted if they fall within regular working hours and do not conflict with other meetings already scheduled. Any messages that are exceptional (e.g., a request to meet outside of regular working hours or a request to meet at a time when a conflicting meeting is already scheduled) will then be brought to the attention of the human user for special handling.

These systems are, by no means, a complete solution to the meeting scheduling problem. For instance, since people can find out about each other's schedules only through messages, the system may require a number of iterations just to eliminate times in which they have conflicts due to publicly scheduled meetings. Adding shared databases might help solve this problem, but it brings up other problems about who has access to which parts of other people's calendars. Even in a system with partially shared databases, the semistructured approach we have described has the desirable property that some cases (e.g., some meeting requests) are handled automatically, while others are handled by human users in a smoothly integrated way. We believe this "graceful degradation" property will be especially important to the acceptance of systems, like those for calendar management, that involve subtle interpersonal and political issues about which people are reluctant or unable to be explicit.

6.3 *Project Management and Task Tracking*

Systems based on structured messages can support project management and other coordination processes by helping to keep track of what tasks have been assigned to whom (e.g., see [19, 20, 25]). One simple way for users to do this in the current system is simply to set up rules that move copies of all action requests and commitments into special folders. For example, action requests a user receives might be categorized in folders by the project to which they relate, whereas action requests a user sends might be categorized by the people to whom they are sent.

To illustrate how more elaborate capabilities can be built up within the same framework, we have implemented a simple task-tracking system for software maintenance activities similar to the example described by Sluizer and Cashman [20]. In this application, "users" of a software system send "problem reports" to a "work assigner." The work assigner first sends an "acknowledgement" to the user and then sends the problem report to a "developer." When the developer fixes the problem, the developer sends the "fix report" to the work assigner who, in turn, sends a "user report" to the original user noting that the problem has been fixed.

This application was implemented in our system by defining the three message types (two of which already existed under different names) and adding several new response options. Users who play the role of work assigners have two possible response actions suggested when they view problem reports. If the problem report has not been acknowledged, the option presented is to acknowledge it. Selecting this option prepares a standard acknowledgment message with the appropriate fields filled in from the information on the original problem report. When the acknowledgment message is sent, the token "acknowledged" is added to the "characteristics" field in the problem report message. Whenever a problem report that includes "acknowledged" in its "characteristics" field is displayed, a response action of "assign" is suggested. Selecting this option prepares the problem report message for forwarding to a developer whose name the work assigner selects from a list of alternatives.

Clearly this task-tracking system is quite limited. The original XCP system, for example, used a set of primitive actions to define protocols involving a number of roles, message types, and actions. A similar capability would be desirable in our system. Another obviously desirable capability would be more elaborate database facilities for sorting, displaying, and modifying the status of tasks. For example, the current system can sort messages into folders according to various criteria, and it can display the header information (e.g., date, sender, and subject) for the messages in a folder. But it would also be quite useful to be able to display the tasks one had committed to do in a report format, sorted by due date, that summarized the task names and the task requestors. If these database capabilities are implemented in a general way for structured objects, then they should be useful for developing many other coordination-supporting applications as well.

7 Defining the Network of Message Types

Because of the prominent role we are advocating for structured message types, the definition of these types becomes especially important. The network shown in Figure 12.4 includes some message types that we believe will be useful in almost all organizations (e.g., meeting announcements) and some that are important only in our environment (e.g., LENS meeting announcement). Different groups and different applications can develop detailed structures to represent the information of specific concern to them. For example, a product design team might have an elaborate network of message types describing different aspects of the product (e.g., market size estimates, response time estimates, alternative power supply vendors).

One of the attractive features of this approach is that it is easy to incrementally increase both the number of message types defined and the number of people who use these message types. For example, individuals who begin using the information sharing system before most other people do can get some immediate benefit from constructing rules using only the fields present in all messages (To, From, Subject, Date). Groups of individuals who begin to use a set of common message types can get much greater benefits from constructing more sophisticated rules for dealing with more specialized message types. For example, individuals in a work group may initially use unstructured electronic mail for scheduling many of their meetings. When this use of the system is recognized as a common and important one, special message types (such as meeting announcements and proposals) might be defined to facilitate sorting and prioritizing these messages appropriately. Eventually, automatic capabilities for scheduling certain kinds of meetings might be added as well. From the viewpoint of organization theory, we know that *internal codes* are among the most important productive assets of an organization [1, 17]. In effect, the Lens system provides a medium in which this collective language of an organization can be defined and redefined.

7.1 *Principles for Defining Message Types*

In our current system, we have used three principles for defining message types. First, we have based our highest level classification of messages on the *purpose* of the message. The taxonomies of *speech acts* derived by linguists (e.g., [18]) appear to be quite useful for making these distinctions (see [13] and [25]). For example, messages whose purpose is to *request information* should be routed to people who know about the topic of the message, whereas messages whose purpose is to *provide information* should be routed to people who are interested in the topic of the message. Distinctions at this level of generality appear to be quite useful for many kinds of more specific messages. We have also used two more pragmatic principles: (1) Add a specialized message type when a new field would be useful (e.g., the speaker field in "seminar announcements"), and (2) add a specialized message type when a new set of defaults would be useful (e.g., the regular weekly time and place in "Lens meeting announcements").

We do not believe that these principles are either necessary or sufficient as a basis for defining message types. We also do not know whether the most useful number of message types will turn out to be relatively small (e.g., a few dozen) or large (e.g., hundreds or thousands). Presumably the answers to these questions depend on the community using the system and the application for which it is being used. One of the important research directions we intend to pursue involves observing how communities evolve a useful set of message types and developing principles (and possibly software) to aid in such a process. For example, we are beginning to explore how the number of message types might be substantially reduced by developing representations for other types of objects that can be included in messages. A single message type called "announcement," for instance, might be used to convey descriptions of many different types of objects, such as meetings, publications, and projects.

7.2 Message Type Editor

We have already developed a display-oriented editor, like the message and rule editors discussed previously, for creating and modifying the message type definitions themselves. As shown in Figure 12.7, this editor allows people to create new message types, change the fields and field names of existing message types, and change the properties (such as defaults and alternatives) of existing fields. We expect that in some (e.g., rarely used) regions of the network anyone should be able to use this "template editor" to modify an existing message type or define a new one, whereas in other regions, only specifically designated people should have access to this capability. In the current version of the system, anyone can use a simple version of this editor to personalize the *default*, *explanation*, and *alternatives* properties of the fields in existing message types, and the "network administrator" can use the full version of the editor to change the definitions shared by the whole group.

8 Conclusion

In this paper, we have seen how the use of semistructured messages can simplify designing systems that (1) help people formulate information they wish to communicate, (2) automatically select, classify, and prioritize information people receive, (3) automatically respond to certain kinds of information, and (4) suggest actions people may wish to take on receiving certain other kinds of information. We believe that systems like this illustrate important, and not yet widely recognized, possibilities for collaboration between people and their machines.

As Stefik has noted, "The most widely understood goal of artificial intelligence is to understand and build autonomous, intelligent, thinking machines" [21, p. 34]. Recently, however, there have been a number of suggestions for other goals in this field. Stefik, for example, suggests the goal of building an "interactive knowledge medium" [21]; Winograd and Flores suggest possibilities for designing "tools for conversation" [25]; Luconi, Malone, and Scott Morton advocate designing "expert support systems" as well as "expert systems" [14]; and Waters notes the im-

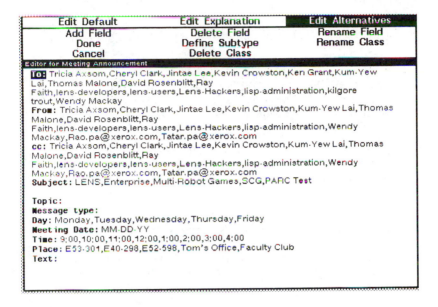

Figure 12.7 Another graphical editor is used to edit the definitions of message types.

portance of the "assistant" approach in building useful artificial intelligence systems [24].

We have seen in this paper how a combination of ideas from artificial intelligence and user interface design can provide the basis for powerful computer-based communication and coordination systems. We believe that the power of this approach is partly due to the fact that it does not emphasize building intelligent, autonomous computers but instead focuses on using computers to gradually support more and more of the knowledge and processing involved when humans work together.

Acknowledgments

The authors would like to thank Jin Lee for implementing the display mechanism for alternative topics in messages and Kevin Crowston, Jin Lee, Irene Greif, and an anonymous referee for helpful comments.

References

1. Arrow, K. *Limits of Organization*. Norton, New York, 1974.

2. Denning, P. Electronic junk. *Commun. ACM 23*, 3 (1982), 163–165.

3. Ellis, C., and Bernal, M. OFFICETALK-D: An experimental office information system. In *Proceedings of the ACM Conference on Office Information Systems* (Philadelphia, Pa., June 21–23). ACM, New York, 1982, pp. 131–140.

4. Engelbart, D. C., and English, W. K. Research center for augmenting human intellect. In *Proceedings of Fall Joint Computing Congress*, vol. 33 (San Francisco, Calif., Dec. 9–11). AFIPS Press, Reston, Va., 1968, pp. 395–410.

5. Fikes, R., and Kehler, T. The role of frame-based representation in reasoning. *Commun. ACM 28*, 9 (Sept. 1985), 904–920.

6. Fox, M., Greenberg, M., Sathi, A., Mattis, J., and Rychener, M. Callisto: An intelligent project management system. *AI Magazine* (Winter 1986), 34–52.

7. Gifford, D. K., Baldwin, R. W., Berlin, S. T., and Lucassen, J. T. An architecture for large scale information systems. In *Proceedings of the 10th ACM Symposium on Operating Systems Principles* (Orcas Island, Wash., Dec. 1–4). ACM, New York, 1985, pp. 161–170.

8. Goldstein, I. P., and Bobrow, D. An experimental description-based programming environment: Four reports. Tech Rep. CSL-81-3, Xerox Palo Alto Research Center, Palo Alto, Calif., Mar. 1981.

9. Greif, I. Cooperative office work, teleconferencing, and calendar management: A collection of papers. Unpublished Tech. Memo, Laboratory for Computer Science, Massachusetts Institute of Technology, Cambridge, Mass., May 1982.

10. Greif, I., and Sarin, S. Data sharing in group work. *ACM Trans. Off. Inf. Syst. 5*, 2 (Apr. 1987), 187–211.

11. Hiltz, S. R., and Turoff, M. *The Network Nation: Human Communication Via Computer*. Addison-Wesley, Reading, Mass., 1978.

12. Hiltz, S. R., and Turoff, M. Structuring computer-mediated communication systems to avoid information overload. *Commun. ACM 28*, 7 (July 1985), 680–689.

13. Kedzierski, B. Communication and management support in system development environments. In *Proceedings of the National Bureau of Standards Conference on Human Factors in Computer Systems* (Gaithersburg, Md., Mar. 15–17), 1982.

14. Luconi, F., Malone, T. W., Scott Morton, M. S. Expert systems: The next challenge for managers. *Sloan Manage. Rev. 27* (Summer 1986), 3–14.

15. Malone, T. W., Grant, K. R., and Turbak, F. A. The Information Lens: An intelligent system for information sharing in organizations. In *Proceedings of the CHI '86 Conference on Human Factors in Computing Systems* (Boston, Mass., Apr. 13–17). ACM, New York, 1986, pp. 1–8.

16. Malone, T. W., Grant, K. R., Turbak, F. A., Brobst, S. A., and Cohen, M. D. Intelligent information-sharing systems. *Commun. ACM 30*, 5 (May 1987), 390–402.

17. March, J. G., and Simon, H. A. *Organizations*. Wiley, New York, 1958.

18. Searle, J. A taxonomy of illocutionary acts. In *Minnesota Studies in the Philosophy of Language*, K. Gunderson, Ed. University of Minnesota Press, Minneapolis, Minn., 1975.

19. Sathi, A., Fox, M. S., and Greenberg, M. Representation of activity knowledge for project management. *IEEE Trans. Pattern Analysis and Machine Intelligence PAMI-7*, 5 (1985), 531–552.

20. Sluizer, S., and Cashman, P. XCP: An experimental tool for managing cooperative activity. In *Proceedings of the ACM Computer Science Conference* (New Orleans, La., Mar. 14–15). ACM, New York, 1985, pp. 251–258.

21. Stefik, M. The next knowledge medium. *The AI Magazine*, Spring, 1986, 34–46.

22. Tou, F. N., Williams, M. D., Fikes, R. E., Henderson, D. A., and Malone, T. W. RABBIT: An intelligent database assistant. In *Proceedings of the National Conference of the American Association for Artificial Intelligence* (Pittsburgh, Pa., Aug. 18–20), 1982.

23. Trigg, R. H., Suchman, L. A., and Halasz, F. G. Supporting collaboration in NoteCards. In *Proceedings of the Conference on Computer-Supported Cooperative Work* (Austin, Tex., Dec. 3–5).

24. Waters, R. C. KBEmacs: Where's the AI? *The AI Magazine*, Spring, 1986, 47–56.

25. Winograd, T., and Flores, F. *Understanding Computers and Cognition: A New Foundation for Design*. Ablex Publishing Corp., Norwood, N.J., 1986.

Support for Meetings

The papers in the section on domain-specific coordination support focused on coordination and collaboration between people who probably would not be working simultaneously. When people do need to work together at the same time, they are more likely to meet face to face than at a distance, but in either case they should still have the full support of their computer tools. This mode of interaction is closer to a conventional "meeting." As computer usage at meetings becomes more widespread, new meeting conventions may be established, so that our notions of what can be accomplished in meetings will be expanded. This section contains three papers that examine different aspects of working together simultaneously with computer support.

The paper on Colab (Reading 13) is about a system designed by and for Artificial Intelligence researchers at Xerox PARC. Colab is a meeting room that includes a computer for each participant as well as an "electern" at the front of the room. Large-screen projection makes a shared workspace visible to all. The same workspace can also be viewed on each individual workstation. Colab has several different types of tools for different types of meetings: Cognoter, for instance, is a brainstorming session tool; Argnoter supports sessions in which specific proposals are being presented and evaluated. The paper analyzes ways in which the group's meetings have changed compared to earlier meetings in ordinary conference rooms. It also compares the observed to the expected changes; interestingly enough, the changes were not exactly those foreseen.

The paper by Lakin (Reading 14) analyzes the role in a meeting of text-graphics displays—not necessarily computer-supported ones. He develops a notion of text-graphic performance to capture the changes over time of the images on the chalkboard. His view of performed text-graphics provides a framework for designing computer support based on criteria of the agility and generality of the medium. Using this framework, he outlines the design of a graphics editor that would provide the features required to support some of the meetings described in the paper. The appendix on measures of agility suggests another way to analyze the effectiveness and impact of computer-support tools. Measures of cursor movements, groupings of objects, and so on may be taken through program instrumenting: the computer can supply the data as well as being the medium of the meeting.

The final paper looks at real-time meetings that do not happen in a conference room. Simultaneous collaboration without face-to-face contact raises a different set of technical issues, as well as social ones. In line with the Chapanis results, the MIT research reported in the Sarin and Greif paper (Reading 15) assumes that a voice channel will be available in any meeting. The computer provides shared workspaces for presenting the object of the meeting—whether a calendar, a drawing, or a document—so that changes to it are communicated visually. The primary medium for exchanging unstructured information (conversation) is the voice line. (Real-time messaging—the use of typed text that appears simultaneously on all screens—as the only medium may be an interesting technology to support emergency situations. Real-time shared workspaces supporting voice conferencing, however, can have much wider application and can facilitate ongoing work at a distance.) The paper focuses on design tradeoffs that must be evaluated in building a real-time conferencing system in an application area for which good individual support tools already exist.

13

Beyond the Chalkboard: Computer Support for Collaboration and Problem Solving in Meetings

Mark Stefik
Gregg Foster
Daniel G. Bobrow
Kenneth Kahn
Stan Lanning
Lucy Suchman

Meetings are used for virtually any intellectual task that requires the coordination or agreement of several people. Statistical studies suggest that office workers spend as much as 30–70 percent of their time in meetings [26]. Paradoxically, even with the widespread distribution of computers, most computer systems in use aid the work of separate individuals rather than their work in groups. In meetings, computers are typically left behind in favor of more passive media like chalkboards[1] and flip charts.

---

[1]The term *chalkboard* in this article refers to any of the wall-mounted erasable writing surfaces commonly used in meeting rooms, whether they are white, black, or some other color and whether the marks are made with chalk, crayon, or ink. We use this term to avoid misunderstandings about the work *blackboard*, which, among other things, can mean a commercially available teleconferencing product, or a programming organization for artificial-intelligence systems. We also avoid the term *whiteboard*, which can mean a white metal writing surface on which colored pens are used, or a specific graphical database tool developed at Xerox PARC [9].

Media influence the course of a meeting because they interact strongly with participants' resources for communication and memory. Chalkboards, for example, provide a shared and focused memory for a meeting, allowing flexible placement of text and figures, which complements our human capabilities for manipulating spatial memories. However, space is limited and items disappear when that space is needed for something else, and rearranging items is inconvenient when they much be manually redrawn and then erased. Handwriting on a chalkboard can be illegible. Chalkboards are also unreliable for information storage: They are used in rooms shared by many groups, and text and figures created in one meeting may be erased during the next. If an issue requires several meetings, some other means must be found to save information in the interim.

Many of the functions that are awkward or impossible with chalkboards are implemented easily with computers. Window systems and drawing aids, for example, provide flexibility for rearranging text and figures, and text can be displayed in fonts that are crisp and reproducible. File systems make it possible to retrieve information generated from previous meetings, to revisit old arguments, to show the history of a series of arguments, and to resume discussions. Independent workstations allow meeting participants to share views, point to objects under discussion, and work on different aspects of a problem simultaneously, with the result that participation can feel less like being a member of a committee, and more like acting as a collaborator at a barn raising.

To explore these ideas, an experimental meeting room known as the Colab has been set up at Xerox PARC. In the Colab, computers support collaborative processes in face-to-face meetings. The Colab is designed for small working groups of two to six persons using personal computers connected over a local-area network (Figure 13.1). In our design, we have drawn on familiar elements from conventional meeting rooms. The focus of the Colab project is to make our own meetings among computer scientists more effective and to provide an opportunity for conducting more general research on how computer tools affect meeting processes.[2]

Much prior research has focused on the use of computer and communication technology to support teleconferencing [18, 19] and what is known as computer conferencing [16, 17], which emphasizes the use of computers to support asynchronous communication and discussion over a computer network. The Colab, on the other hand, focuses on problem solving in face-to-face meetings—the most common kind of meeting in our research group and our starting point.

---

[2]Lucy Suchman, the last author of the present article, is an anthropologist for whom the Colab represents part of a larger study of face-to-face collaboration and its technology.

Figure 13.1   A view of the Colab. The Colab is an experimental meeting room designed for typical use by two to six persons. Each person has a workstation connected to a personal computer. The computers are linked together over a local-area network (ethernet) that supports a distributed database. Besides the workstations, the room is equipped with a large touch-sensitive screen and a stand-up keyboard.

In this article, we describe the meeting tools we have built so far as well as the computational underpinnings and language support we have developed for creating distributed software. Finally, we present some preliminary observations from our first Colab meetings and some of the research questions we are now pursuing.

Tools for Collaboration

An office worker using a computer will choose different programs to achieve different purposes. Completing a single project may involve the use of several different tools: a spreadsheet program, a text editor, and a sketching program. In a similar vein, activities arise in the course of a meeting that require different supporting programs. In this article, we use the term *meeting tools* to refer to programs that support group interaction and problem solving in meetings, and the term *Colab tools* to refer to meeting tools developed specifically for use in the Colab.

A fundamental requirement for meeting tools is that they provide a coordinated interface for all participants. Such a *multiuser* interface is intended to let meeting participants interact with each other easily and immediately through a computer medium.

The term *WYSIWYG* (what you see is what you get) is generally used to describe text editors in which text appears the same during editing as it will during printing. To describe an important abstraction for meeting tools, we have defined an analogous term: *WYSIWIS* (what you see is what I see—pronounced "whizzy whiz"), which refers to the presentation of consistent images of shared information to all participants. A meeting tool is *strictly* WYSIWIS if all meeting participants see exactly the same thing and where the others are pointing.

WYSIWIS creates the impression that members of a group are interacting with shared and tangible objects. It extends to a group conversation the kind of shared access to information that is experienced by two people sitting together over a sketch. WYSIWIS is the critical idea that makes possible the sense of teamwork illustrated in the barn-raising metaphor. It recognizes the importance of being able to see what work the other members have done and what work is in progress: to "see where their hands are." With meeting tools, this visual cue can be approximated by providing pointers to work in progress and by graying out objects that are being worked on.

Although *strict* WYSIWIS would give everyone the same image on their displays, in practice we have found this too limiting and instead use relaxed versions of WYSIWIS [32]. For example, it can be useful to differentiate between *public* interactive windows that are accessible to the entire group, and private windows with limited access (e.g., for personal electronic mail). Private windows violate the concept of strict WYSIWIS, as does relaxation of pointer displays. Although pointing is an efficient way to refer to things in conversation, displaying the cursors of all active participants is usually too distracting. Making pointers visible only on request becomes an effective compromise. Another WYSIWIS relaxation permits public windows to appear at different places on different screens so that public pointers can be translated into window-relative coordinates. This sacrifices some ability to refer to things by screen position, but it does permit personalized screen layouts.

Meetings, like other processes, can be more efficient when several things are done at once. Since Colab tools support simultaneous action, a key issue in tool design is recognizing and supporting those activities that can be decomposed for parallel action. For parallel action, a task must be broken up into appropriately sized operations that can be executed more or less independently by different members of the group. If the operations are too small, they will be too interdependent, and interference will preclude any substantial parallelism. For example, to create a shared text, interactions should not be at the level of individual keystrokes. On the other hand, if operations are needlessly large, opportunities for synergy are lost.

The ability to act in parallel on shared objects also brings with it potential for conflict. Conflict resolution strategies will become necessary in some cases, but often we can rely on social constraints. A conflict detection system or "busy signal" graphically warns users that someone else is already editing or otherwise using an item; a busy item is grayed out on all screens.

Our initial goal was to create tools to support the kinds of meetings that our group has, which range from the informal to the formal. One of the informal meeting tools we have developed, Boardnoter, closely imitates the functionality of a chalkboard (Figure 13.2). It is intended for informal meetings that rely heavily on informal freestyle sketching. To draw with Boardnoter, one uses the "chalk," to erase one uses the "eraser," to type one uses the miniature "typewriter," and to point one uses the "pointer." To sketch a square with Boardnoter, one simply "picks up the chalk" and makes four strokes. A subsequent version of Boardnoter will go beyond the chalkboard by adding capabilities for copying, moving, resizing, linking with rubber band lines, grouping, and smoothing (neatening), and for using and scaling selections from a set of predrawn images.

Other Colab tools are based on much more formal models of the meeting process. In this article, we focus our attention on two such tools: *Cognoter*, a tool for organizing ideas to plan a presentation; and *Argnoter*, a tool for considering and evaluating alternate proposals. Although both tools are intended to bring appropriate computational support to structured meeting processes, the contrast between the two processes will highlight the range of opportunities that exist for applying computer technology in this medium.

Organizing Ideas for a Presentation Using Cognoter

Cognoter[3] is a Colab tool used to prepare presentations collectively. Its output is an annotated outline of ideas and associated text. We have

---

[3]The name *Cognoter* comes from both *cog-noter* (a cognition noter) or *co-gno-ter* (knowing together).

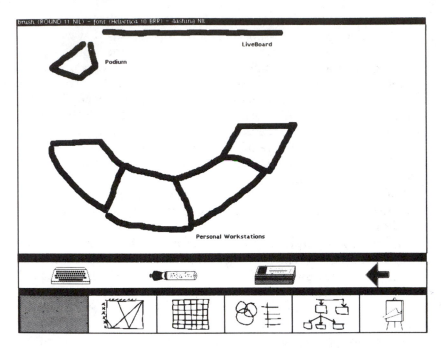

Figure 13.2   Screen image of Boardnoter. The Boardnoter meeting tool in the Colab is operational but still in the early stages of development. A key feature is that it provides a large area for freestyle sketching. Below the writing area is a "chalk tray" containing several implements: a piece of chalk, an eraser, a miniature typewriter, and a pointer. To draw on the board, one picks up the chalk by clicking the mouse or pen over the chalk icon; to erase one picks up the eraser; to point one picks up the pointer. Since more than one boardful of information may be needed in the course of a meeting, the "stampsheet" of shrunken stamp-sized boards at the bottom makes it possible to obtain a fresh board or to switch back to a board created earlier.

used Cognoter to prepare outlines for talks and papers, including this one. In some ways, it is similar to the Think-Tank, Freestyle [25], and NoteCards [34] programs. All are used to organize ideas, but Cognoter is unique in that it is intended for collective use by a group of people.

The Cognoter process imitates a meeting style for collaborative writing that we have used at Xerox PARC without computational support for several years. Usually, we begin with a clear slate: The ideas are in our heads and nothing is written down. The problem at this point is how to get started: It is not very helpful to begin by asking, "Well, we need an outline. What should we put in I.A.1?" Rather, planning a presentation requires that the group decide what the ideas are, which ideas go together, which ideas come first, the order of presentation, and, finally, which ideas warrant elimination.

Cognoter organizes a meeting into three distinct phases—*brainstorming, organizing,* and *evaluation*—each of which emphasizes a different set of activities. As the group advances through the respective phases, the set of possible actions is expanded: For instance, brainstorming, which is emphasized in the first phase, is still possible in the last phase. Groups that find the rigid enforcement of phases too prescriptive can skip immediately to the last phase where all the operations are possible. Our intention is to experiment with methods for encouraging particular meeting processes and styles of behavior without making the tools too inflexible and prescriptive.

Brainstorming

Since the brainstorming phase involves the initial generation of ideas used in the presentation, it is important to encourage synergy in group interactions and to not interfere with or inhibit the flow of ideas [10]. In Cognoter, therefore, ideas are not evaluated or eliminated in this phase, and little attention is given to their organization (see Figure 13.3). Instead, there is one basic operation: A participant selects a free space in a public window and types in a catchword or catchphrase characterizing an idea. Participants may act simultaneously, adding idea items and supporting text at any time, but may not delete an item (even their own), although they can move them around. Supporting text is used to clarify the meaning of an item and to establish terminology for the presentation. Once entered, it can be publicly displayed or further edited by any participant. As the window fills up to encompass what appears to be a jumble of ideas on different levels, begging for organization, pressure to move on the next phase begins to mount.

Organizing

In the organizing phase, the group attempts to establish an order for the ideas generated in the brainstorming phase. With Cognoter, the order of ideas can be established incrementally by using two basic operations: linking ideas into presentation order and grouping ideas into subgroups. In addition, the item-moving operation allows these operations to be discussed prior to actually executing them by moving items near each other before clustering or linking.

The basic operation is to simply assert that one idea should come before another. Linking is usually accompanied by some verbal discussion: For example, a participant may say, "I'm putting *Colab tools* before *open issues* because you need to understand what we have done before

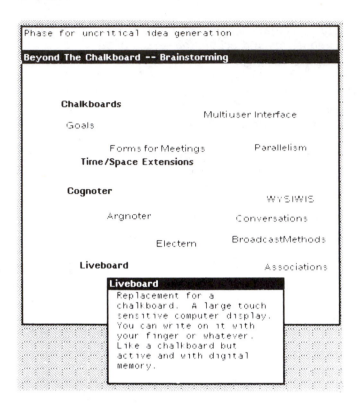

Figure 13.3 Brainstorming with Cognoter. In the brainstorming phase, participants may add ideas and supporting text. Criticism or deletion of ideas is discouraged. Ideas are entered into the window by clicking the mouse in the background of the window and typing in a short title or phrase that stands for the idea. Text explaining the ideas in more detail is entered by selecting the item with a mouse and then using a text editor in a separate window.

you can understand what comes next." The ordering is indicated visually by directed links between items as shown in Figure 13.4. The meaning of the links is transitive, meaning that, if X comes before Y, and Y comes before Z, then X must come before Z. The links are used collectively to determine a complete order of presentation. Items can also be clustered into groups and moved to their own windows as shown in Figure 13.5. When a group is formed, a bracketed item standing for the whole group is displayed in the window; the grouped items themselves are displayed in an associated window. Links are distributive across groups; a link to or from a bracketed item is treated like a link to or from the whole group. By these transitive and distributive operations, a small number of explicit links can highly constrain the total order of ideas.

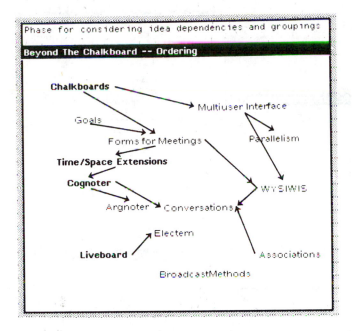

Figure 13.4 Establishing the order of ideas. In Cognoter, the order of ideas is established incrementally. The basic operation is determining that one idea should come before
another, which is indicated visually by directed links between items. The meaning is transitive, meaning that, if X comes before Y, and Y comes before Z, then X must come before Z. Collectively, the links determine the order of idea presentation. Links are added or
removed by clicking the mouse on the desired items. Items will usually have one or more
links to other items.

Evaluation

The third phase, evaluation, determines the final form of the presentation. Participants review the overall structure to reorganize ideas, fill in
missing details, and eliminate peripheral and irrelevant ideas.

In Cognoter, the various decision-making processes are separate and
distinct operations. Delaying deletion until the last phase, for example,
provides a more visible basis for argument in the sense that an argument
for deleting an idea because it is not relevant may be more convincing
when that idea is not visibly linked with any others; or arguing the unim-
portance of an idea may be more convincing when the competing ideas
are available for comparison. In the same sense, an argument that there
is an excess of material may be more compelling when all the material
can be seen, or a charge that an idea is vague may be more convincing
in the presence of other ideas that are more fully substantiated.

Delaying deletion also has some beneficial effects on group dynam-

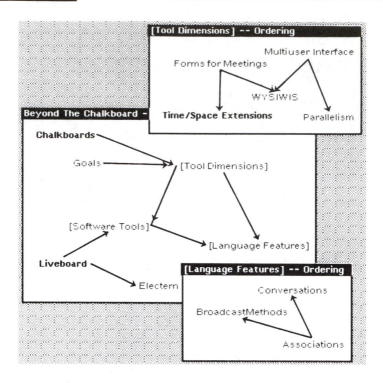

Figure 13.5   Grouping items. Items can be clustered into groups representing ideas that will be worked on together. Each group has an associated window for displaying its items. A group is named when it is formed, and that name appears as a bracketed item in the original window.

ics: Deleting an idea during the brainstorming phase could easily be interpreted as criticism and might either inhibit certain participants or provoke tangential argument, whereas arguing that an idea does not fit or is insubstantial in the evaluation phase may have the beneficial effect of prodding other group members to clarify or extend the idea.

Other operations besides deletion are also appropriately delayed until the evaluation phase. For example, arguing that an idea is misplaced is more compelling when alternate places to put it are visible; this is a good time to consider the reordering of ideas. Since the linking operation that takes place in the organizing phase is usually based on considerations local to two ideas, seeing the entire presentation, with most of the links in place, allows the user to appraise the overall structure and consider more global concerns, such as balance.

Cognoter provides a systematic process for answering the question, "What should we put in I.A.1?" Starting points for a presentation can be identified systematically: These are the items with no incoming links.

Cognoter then helps in the final ordering of ideas by preparing an outline and indicating which ideas are ordered arbitrarily. By traversing the item graph, an outline is generated, with or without the attached text.

In many respects, Cognoter supports a process that is quite different from that underlying tools like ThinkTank. Beyond the most obvious difference, which is that Cognoter is designed for simultaneous use by multiple participants (although the process it embodies is also useful for single users), Cognoter also divides the thinking process into smaller and different kinds of steps that are incremental and efficient. In Think-Tank, ideas are always organized in an outline—there is no other place to put them—whereas Cognoter separates the tasks of idea generation and ordering. Cognoter also provides for incremental ordering through a link-forming operation whereby a partial ordering of ideas is refined step-wise toward a complete ordering. Transitivity and grouping operations make it possible to organize the ideas efficiently with a small number of links.

Some important parts of the presentation planning process are not explicit in Cognoter: For example, Cognoter does not inquire as to the audience, the appropriate technical level, the goals of the paper, or arguments for deleting or ordering ideas. Modifications to Cognoter could make such questions explicit, but they are now outside the scope of the current tool.

Cognoter is the first useful Colab tool developed and is still evolving. We are now experimenting with various relaxations of the WYSIWIS concept. In the current version of Cognoter, for example, windows showing links and items are public, but outline and item editing windows are private. The absence of visual cues indicating which are public and which private can be confusing for the first-time users. With several months experience using Cognoter's multiuser interface, we are actively exploring trade-offs in the design of the next generation of the tool [32].

An Argumentation Spreadsheet for Proposals (Argnoter)

Argnoter,[4] the Colab tool being developed for presenting and evaluating proposals, is now in the early stages of design and implementation and is presented here chiefly as a contrast to Cognoter. Implementing and experimenting with Argnoter are now major focuses of the Colab project. As with Cognoter, the basic meeting process supported by Argnoter has been used by our group without computational aid for several years.

---

[4]The name *Argnoter* is intended to suggest *argument noter*, that is, a tool to help organize and evaluate arguments.

Proposal meetings start when one or more members of the group have a proposal for something to be done, typically a design for a program or a plan for a course of research. The goal of the meeting then becomes to pick the best proposal. The proposals are at least partially worked out before the meeting, as opposed to Cognoter meetings, which begin with a blank slate. Since Argnoter participants have already invested some energy in the creation of these proposals, the meetings have a greater potential for dispute and disagreement. Discovering, understanding, and evaluating disagreement are therefore essential parts of informed decision making in these meetings.

In developing a design—which is essentially a dialectic between goals and possibilities—designers usually begin without knowing exactly what is wanted or what is possible. They explore parts of the design space as driven by their current goals, and sharpen their goals as they learn what is possible. In collaborative design tasks, this interaction and tension between goals and alternatives must play itself out in the communications among collaborators. At the beginning, design goals are not necessarily shared; the elaboration of a common set of goals is part of the collaborative process and includes the incremental development and selection of design alternatives.

The intuition guiding the Argnoter process is the recognition that much of the dispute and misunderstanding that arise in meetings about design proposals is due to three major causes: *owned positions*, that is, personal attachment to certain positions; *unstated assumptions;* and *unstated criteria*. Hence, a major theme of Argnoter design is that alternatives be made explicit: Proposals themselves are explicit, as are assumptions and evaluation criteria.

In essence, the Argnoter meeting comprises three distinct phases—*proposing, arguing*, and *evaluating*—which in some respects are similar to the respective phases in Cognoter, but different enough to warrant description.

Proposing

In the proposal phase, the proposals are stated explicitly: Each proposal is given a short text description, and perhaps a sketch, and is named according to its features or functions. In Argnoter, a proposal will be created in, and displayed by, a set of connected windows called proposal "forms," which can be either private or public. Public proposal forms are WYSIWIS, whereas a private form appears only on the machine of the participant who controls it. Private forms ensure that every participant can view or create a new proposal without having to share its use. Other windows will allow viewing any of the proposals under consideration in the meeting. New proposals are created by modifying an existing one or combining features from two or more different ones. A new proposal automatically inherits text, sketches, and statements from its parent proposals.

Even with the high-resolution, wide-format displays used in the Colab, space for windows is limited: A proposal displayed with its text, sketch, and arguments occupies about one-fourth of the screen. The default configuration allows enough viewing space for two public proposal forms, one private form, and a variety of other forms. However, displays of the kind available on most personal computers would be inadequate for viewing even a single proposal and would not work well for most Colab tools.

Arguing

The next phase consists of presenting reasons for choosing or not choosing individual proposals. Reasons must be written down. On the chalkboard, the reasons are written as statements underneath the respective proposals. Each statement is identified as either pro or con and consists of a short text description like "very expensive" or "can't be done in less than six months." The structure of Argnoter encourages participants to write pro and con statements about all proposals, not just pro statements for the ones they are in favor of and con statements for the rest. Since the pro and con statements are there for all to see and contemplate, participants tend to take the time to formulate them carefully. Insubstantial statements like "I just don't like proposal X" will carry less weight than ones that are specific and focused.

This shared use of a chalkboard to present proposals and arguments has been used habitually and successfully by other groups that we know about. The following anecdote about another laboratory illustrates this:

> On any given morning at the Laboratory of Molecular Biology in Cambridge, England, the blackboard of Francis Crick or Sidney Brenner will commonly be found covered with logical trees. On the top line will be the hot new result just up from the laboratory or just in by letter or rumor. On the next line will be two or three alternative explanations, or a little list of "what he did wrong". Underneath will be a series of suggested experiments or controls that can reduce the number of possibilities. And so on. The tree grows during the day as one man or another comes in and argues about why one of the experiments wouldn't work, or how it should be changed. [27]

For comparative purposes, it is possible in the argument phase to categorize pro or con statements across proposals in terms of categories like compatibility, cost, development time, efficiency, feasibility, simplicity, and utility. With computational support, it is possible to automatically create auxiliary tables that compare proposals on the basis of these categories.

In the argument stage, participants can add statements or modify existing proposals. This tends to foster a synergy among ideas, joint contributions to proposals and reasons, and the systematic development of parallel reasoning across proposals. According to Platt [27], this kind of group participation in the articulation of *multiple* proposals and arguments often leads to a very productive decision-making process:

> The conflict and exclusion of alternatives that is necessary for sharp inductive inference has been all too often a conflict between men, each with his single Ruling Theory. But whenever each man begins to have multiple working hypotheses, it becomes purely a conflict between ideas. ... In fact, when there are multiple hypotheses which are not anyone's "personal property" and when there are crucial experiments to test them, the daily life in the laboratory takes on an interest and excitement it never had, and the students can hardly wait to get to work to see how the detective story will come out.

The articulation of multiple proposals and their arguments leads naturally into the next phase—evaluation—in the sense that proposals are being evaluated *indirectly* by analyzing the reasons behind them. Moreover, this articulation encourages a style of decision making that separates arguments about evaluation criteria from arguments about the proposals themselves.

Evaluating

First, the evaluation considers the assumptions behind individual arguments. Assumptions in Argnoter are expressed as statements about statements: For example, the statement "this assumes that labor costs can be ignored" could refer to the statement "this proposal is inexpensive." Whereas historically we might have written such assumptions on the chalkboard next to the corresponding arguments, with Argnoter, we will ultimately provide facilities for viewing the structure of arguments in terms of the connections between these statements.

Meeting participants often disagree about the validity of statements: One person might believe that "'sixteen million bit memory chips will be readily available in six months" and another may not. In Argnoter, we will try to model these differences with explicit "belief sets," a belief set being a mapping of a set of statements into valid (believed) or invalid (not believed) categories. This kind of modeling is something that cannot effectively be done on chalkboards.

The act of making belief sets explicit enables Argnoter to act as a kind of *argumentation spreadsheet* where a proposal is viewed and evaluated in relation to a specified set of beliefs. The proposal display is generated by stepping through the arguments about the proposal, looking up the assumptions, and then displaying those arguments that are supported in the specified belief set. Multiple belief sets may coexist, and any participant is able to create (or specialize) belief sets. The belief sets are intended to characterize different generic points of view (e.g., liberal versus conservative, marketing versus development).

Just as a numerical spreadsheet program provides a way of exploring entailments of hypothetical numerical relationships, an argumentation spreadsheet like Argnoter provides a way of exploring belief entailments. A numerical spreadsheet program provides no in-depth understanding of the meanings of interest rate, tax rate, or monthly income, but it does compute the necessary sums and display changes in the derived values when the input values are changed. In the same way, Argnoter need not understand the meanings of design proposals: It need only differentiate between proposals, arguments, assumptions, and belief sets, and compute the relevant logical support relationships. One should be able to change a belief assignment and then immediately see the relevant changes in the proposal display. Differences in point of view can also be highlighted (e.g., by displaying a proposal under different belief sets). Other evaluations, like sensitivity analyses, can be done using the same information.

Next, evaluation criteria are selected and ranked. The values of specific criteria are often ranked differently by different participants: Feasibility, for example, is usually considered important, but there may be disagreements about trade-offs between cost versus utility or space versus time.

Evaluation criteria and beliefs represent different dimensions of the evaluation process. Two participants may agree that cost is a primary criterion, but disagree about whether a specific proposal is expensive; conversely, they might agree on the costs of different proposals, but disagree about the significance of cost as a criterion. Using Argnoter, we can experiment with different ways of ranking criteria and provide mechanisms for viewing proposals according to these rankings.

A major working hypothesis behind the design of Argnoter is that making the structure of arguments explicit facilitates consensus by reducing disagreement that arises from uncommunicated differences. Since participants using Argnoter first agree on criteria and then systematically apply those criteria to proposals, experiments suggest themselves as to whether in fact such behavior actually speeds consensus and to what extent Argnoter actually encourages such behavior.

In the process of making particular kinds of statements explicit and leaving other kinds implicit, Colab tool designers may inadvertently bias the meeting processes. In both Cognoter and Argnoter, the lack of an explicit representation of goals for the meetings may prejudice the discussion at particular times. Designers of Colab tools are therefore necessarily creating more than just tools: They are also designing and enforcing meeting processes. We see the Colab as a working laboratory for increasing our understanding of meeting processes and examining the effects of computational support tools on these processes.

Programming Issues and Concepts

Two primary assumptions about the Colab's computing architecture were made: (1) Each meeting participant was to have a personal computer, and all the computers were to be connected together through a local-area network; and (2) all the computers were to run the same software. In retrospect, this approach has been workable and appears reasonable: It is also open-ended to the extent that processors can be added to the network to carry out special functions, and special software can be added to some of the computers.

Programs distributed over several machines are notoriously difficult to write and debug. This, combined with our need to experiment and change code frequently, motivated us to develop programming tools to simplify developing, testing, and revising. In the balance of this section, we describe certain extensions to a programming language and environment we developed for the Colab, and how we have used them.

Colab tools enable people to share and jointly revise information presented in meeting situations. For this discussion, it is useful to think of this information as residing in a computer database that has certain properties. To this end, we leave the granularity of logical data items unspecified, although, in practice, grain size is determined by our intentions about the independence of the data items. The design of the database is a starting point for understanding the issues and programming techniques used in designing and executing Colab tools. The following goals arise naturally out of the Colab application and reflect as well general expectations about the use of personal computers:

- The delay in getting information should be very short. To generate complex information displays, the average retrieval time should be on the order of a few microseconds.

- The delay in changing information should be short. To avoid a feeling of sluggishness, it should usually be possible to change information in a fraction of a second.

- The database should converge quickly to a consistent state.

- The database should not be vulnerable to either the accidental actions of one participant or the failure in one participant's machine.

Maintaining the Database

To maintain the Colab database, we experimented with several control regimes: the centralized model, the centralized-lock model, the cooperative model, the dependency-detection model, and the roving-locks model.

Centralized Model   The straightforward centralized approach, which has been used successfully in other similar applications (e.g., [29, 30]), ensures that all participants use the same data: There is only one copy of the database, and concurrency control is straightforward. To coordinate simultaneous changes, database transaction mechanisms must be used. The centralized model was rejected out of hand for Colab purposes because we could not use these mechanisms to retrieve data fast enough to update our displays. Moreover, given our plan to use networked personal computers, we would incur the additional delay of network communication.

Centralized-Lock Model   The distributed model corrects the slow retrieval problem of the centralized model by caching data on each of the workstations. Data for the visual display are always fetched directly from the cache and are updated whenever changes are received. Several variations on this approach are described in [2].

In this model, each computer has a copy of the database, but cannot make changes to an item until it obtains ownership of that item. To secure ownership of data means obtaining a lock from a centralized lock server. There can be one lock for the whole database, or separate locks for different parts of it. With multiple locks, changes to different parts of the database can proceed in parallel. When there is just one lock, only one participant at a time can make changes since any change requires locking the entire database. Another extreme is to have a separate lock for every datum.

Locks provide mutual exclusion for processes that write data, and changes to the database are serialized by the numbered sequences of lock owners. This ensures that machines will converge to the same state. If some transactions require ownership of more than one lock, the usual cautions and techniques for avoiding deadlock apply [7, 15] (e.g., transactions that require multiple locks must acquire them all at once).

Unfortunately, our implementation of this model has so far yielded unacceptable delays for obtaining locks; these delays can be traced to a limitation of the process scheduler in our programming environment, namely, that it is not preemptive. There is no way to guarantee limits on delays in our system since processes are not prioritized and can run an arbitrary amount of time without yielding.

Cooperative Model   In the cooperative model, the approach we are currently using, each machine has a copy of the database, and changes are installed by broadcasting the change without any synchronization. By itself, this approach entails the following inherent race conditions: If two participants make changes to the same data simultaneously, there is a race to see which change will take effect first, and the results can be different on different machines.

Two factors mitigate against these apparent shortcomings. The first is that most sequences of changes to our databases yield results that are independent of the order in which they are done. Moreover, Colab participants are aware of the problem and use verbal cues ("voice locks") to coordinate their behavior; it is therefore rare that participants will change the same data at the same time.

The second factor is that, quite apart from the mechanisms for ensuring integrity of the distributed database, in the Colab we need to provide mechanisms that coordinate the activities of the participants and support the social mechanisms for both partitioning work and reaching agreement that meetings by their nature rely on. One such mechanism is the busy signal described earlier. By graying out screen items that are in use, the signal warns other collaborators not to change them (see Figure 13.6). But, because there is an inherent delay between the moment that someone starts working on an item and the time that the busy signal is propagated to others, it is possible that a second participant will begin an incompatible revision. In this case, the busy signal ensures that two participants will *quickly discover* that they are working in a conflicting way.

In total, we are not satisfied with the properties of the cooperative model and are planning to investigate several alternatives presented in [2] for using two-phased locking and time stamps. Since the immediate users of our database are all people in visual and verbal contact, we

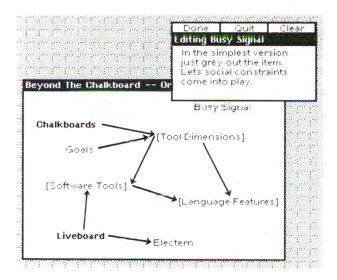

Figure 13.6 A busy item. When multiple users interact with a shared object, conflicts can occur. An early conflict detection system—a busy signal—quickly warns users that someone else is already editing an item, and brings social constraints into play; one way to indicate a busy item is to gray it out.

are willing to consider the need for manual intervention in occasional cases of synchronization failure (i.e., to make some sacrifices to achieve the desired performance levels). Two specific approaches that we are considering are the last two discussed here: the dependency-detection model and the roving-locks model.

Dependency-Detection Model The dependency-detection model corrects some of the shortcomings of the cooperative model by annotating data with a stamp describing the author and time of the change. Every request to change data broadcasts several things: the new data, its stamp, and the stamp of the previous version of the data on the originating machine. When a machine receives a message requesting a change, it first checks whether the previous stamp in the request is the same as the stamp in its database. If they are different, a "dependency conflict" is signaled. The conflict is then resolved by a process that involves human intervention (at least to temporarily suspend activity), followed by propagation of the resolved values for data or the creation of multiple versions of the data.

The advantage of the dependency-detection approach is responsiveness. Changes to data do not first require serialization or the delay of obtaining a lock. The system assumes that a change can always be made, but it may have to fix things later if a conflict is detected.

Like the cooperative model, the dependency-detection model contains inherent race conditions, but it is able to detect them after the fact. If two participants change data at the same time, at least one of the machines will detect a dependency conflict as described above. However, it is possible to get "false alarms" if messages about changes to data from different sources arrive out of order; a dependency conflict would then be incorrectly signaled. Similarly, if two participants made a series of nearly simultaneous changes to a datum, multiple false alarms might be signaled. The ability to distinguish false alarms can be enhanced by keeping a longer history of changes. We do not yet have enough experience to decide whether the dependency-detection model (which is closely related to an approach called *certification* [2]) is necessary or practical.

Roving-Locks Model The roving-locks model tries to reduce the delay in obtaining locks that is incurred with the centralized-lock model by distributing the lock-granting processes along with lock ownership. This is different than simply locating locks with the data; the intention here is to distribute control over specific data items to their last user, leading to a sort of "working set" [8] for locks. In this scenario, a participant's machine would tend to acquire the set of locks for that subset of the database on which it is actively working. Most lock requests would require no communication with other machines. After the first access, delay in getting a lock would be significant only in those cases where the lock is on a remote machine, that is, when two or more participants are actually competing for the same parts of the database.

Even if the working-set model is valid for locks, we suspect that the success of this model may depend on its having a preemptive scheduler to bound the delays in obtaining remote locks. More experience with the model is needed to determine whether roving locks are a practical solution.

Language Support

Colab software is built on Xerox Lisp Machines connected by an Ethernet [23]. The software is written in Loops [4], an object-oriented extension of Lisp [28] that resembles Smalltalk-80 [14] in that programs are organized in terms of objects that can hold data. Computation proceeds as objects send messages to each other. Loops supports the notion of permanent objects whose identity is specified by a unique identifier that is guaranteed to be unique across machines. Versions of these permanent objects can exist on several machines simultaneously. An *association* is a set of representations on multiple machines that stand for the same object; the individual representations are called *associates* and have the same unique identifier.

In the Colab, we use the term *conversation* to refer to the combination of a set of machines, Colab tools, and participants working together to solve a problem. When a new participant is added to a conversation, all participants find out about the newcomer, and the newcomer finds out about the other participants; the newcomer's machine gets copies of the object that represent the database.

In a conversation, communication is implemented by a combination of system facilities and programming abstractions and is supported over the Ethernet by several layers of protocols. Our implementation rests on a protocol for remote procedure calls [3]. On top of this, we have added a mechanism for sending messages to an object on a remote machine, and another for sending messages to all the associates of an object in a conversation.

Colab tools communicate via a programming abstraction that we call *broadcast methods*. Broadcast methods extend the object-oriented notion of methods from a single machine to multiple machines in a conversation. When a method is annotated as being a broadcast method, invoking it on one machine means that it will be run on all machines in the conversation. For example, if *Move* is a broadcast method in a Cognoter window for moving an item in the window, and *item37* receives a *Move* message on one of the machines, then *item37*'s associates on all the other machines will also receive the same message. All the details of queuing and transmitting the message to the relevant machines are handled automatically without further specification by the programmer.

Broadcast methods provide a simple abstraction for organizing communication, and a mechanism for efficient communication about changes to the database. Colab tools assume that the software is loaded on the machines of all participants. In most cases, the bandwidth of network communication can be reduced by sending instructions rather than data.

Ideally, one should be able to take a program written for a single machine and change it into a distributed program by annotating some of the methods so that they will broadcast. In practice, this has worked out rather well. To support this facility, we have found it useful to establish a discipline for deciding which methods should be broadcast.

Methods are categorized roughly into three different sets that are treated differently with respect to conversion to broadcast methods: *user input, semantic actions,* and *display actions.* User-input methods control user interaction that specifies a change to be made to the database; they are run at the user's request (e.g., caused by mouse action) and are used to determine the nature and scope of a change. User-input methods are not made into broadcast methods because only the user initiating the change wants to engage in the interaction. The actual changes to the database are made by the semantic-action methods, which are broadcast so that the changes to the database will propagate to all machines containing the meeting database. Display-action methods update the displays and are not broadcast because the display is updated as a side effect of changing the database. If the image in more than one window depends on the value of a datum, then multiple display-action methods should be triggered by a single semantic-action method.

In some cases, the appropriate partitioning of methods into these categories can be subtle. For example, windows for displaying data can be parametrized (as in the case of proposal forms for Argnoter), thereby altering their display according to display parameters that specify belief sets or rankings of evaluation criteria. Maintaining WYSIWIS for these windows requires that changes to these parameters be considered part of the database and be broadcast as semantic actions; the subtlety arises to the extent that "display parameters" might be confused with display-action methods, which are not broadcast. Furthermore, when semantic actions can be derived from more primitive ones, only the primitive ones need be broadcast.

Support for Debugging

To make the debugging process more manageable, we have created tools for tracing and intercepting messages on the network. To monitor message transmission between machines, we use a conversation viewer. It works for all Colab tools, letting us monitor the broadcast queues and processes used to send messages between machines. The viewer shows when messages are queued, sent, and received, as well as the identity of the other machines. Using the viewer, we can often detect cases of unnecessary or incorrect message sending.

We have also developed tools for propagating program changes between machines. In debugging sessions, we have found it useful to make program changes on one machine and then to broadcast the changes to the other machine.

Preliminary Observations and Research Questions

If computers are to provide more effective meeting tools, we need a commensurately more adequate understanding of meeting processes. Although meetings are something that most of us know well, they come under the heading of those everyday activities that, because we know them so well, remain largely unexamined. Designing the Colab has required that we look again at the organization of meetings and meeting technology; at the same time, the Colab currently in place provides an experimental setting for pursuing these lines of research. In this section we present our preliminary observations about the Colab and describe the research issues that have been raised by these observations.

In their current form, Colab tools reflect our experience of, and ideas about, our own work processes, in particular those aimed at collaborative writing and argumentation. Our research strategy is to draw upon familiar practices first, and then to locate those practices within a wider range of face-to-face meetings in different settings and with different participants. The Colab was used early on to produce the present article, and even though the Colab was not yet fitted with audiovisual recording equipment or documenting software, these early sessions did provide a set of preliminary observations about the relationship between Cognoter tools and the writing process, and their relation to the process of collaborative writing.

The Structure of the Writing Process

The current Cognoter design reflects a set of conjectures regarding the writing process, from the early stage of idea generation and development through the generation of a path or outline for a final presentation. The actual use of Cognoter revealed not only the points of fit between design and process, but some subtle disjunctures as well.

For example, the design premise for Cognoter was that the brainstorming window be an unstructured repository for ideas. The availability of a public window, into which people could easily and spontaneously enter new text, would allow the group to put a large number of ideas "onto the table" without a great deal of discussion or negotiation. Ideally, this initial brainstorming phase is followed by an organizing phase, in which group members elaborate the relationships between ideas and debate their cogency. However, in early sessions with Cognoter, we found that even before moving on to the organizing phase, members began using spatial grouping in the brainstorming window to display relationships between ideas. Even after items were explicitly linked, the spatial cues helped to display the relationships between items; these spatial cues, in turn, were important to the elaboration of meaning.

The process of organizing and evaluation made it easier to see whether or not the set of ideas generated during brainstorming was complete. Although our initial design assumption was that use of the outlining tool would follow completion of the evaluation phase, in practice, participants found the outlining tool useful for displaying intermediate states of the emerging structure as well. These observations suggest slightly different "joints" in the process than we had originally assumed.

In future sessions, we will look carefully at the natural organization of the group writing process, the way people use the available tools to see the developing structure of their collective argument, and the relationship between the initial design assumptions and the actual uses people make of the tools.

Maintaining the Collaboration

The Colab's starting premise was that serial access to problem-solving technology obstructs the kind of equal participation that ideally characterizes collaboration, particularly for an activity like writing, where collaboration seems ideally not to involve any predetermined or fixed division of labor among participants. The multiuser interface was designed to overcome this obstacle by letting participants act simultaneously, write independently, and enter new text into a shared database—virtually at the same time. By equalizing access of all participants to displays and shared data, the Colab's interface enhances flexibility as to roles and discourages control over the activity by any one participant.

However, our early sessions demonstrated that the constraints imposed by current technologies are not just a limitation on collaboration but in some ways a resource as well. In particular, the fact that a writing technology allows only one person to enter text at a time enforces a kind of shared focus (i.e., a focus on that person's actions) that maintains a common context for the group. Where only one person at a time has access to the writing technology, roles are in a very real sense visible at a glance; moreover, what is being done to the text is transparent in the actions of whomever controls the writing technology. Many of the accompanying practices—rising to go to the chalkboard, taking over the keyboard—can also be viewed as resources for the participants in the sense of seeing what is going on and providing a basis for the smooth exchange of roles. The possibility of independent writing activity and simultaneous entry of new text brings new demands on participants to stay informed about what others are doing. Relaxing the requirements on turn taking by allowing parallel actions necessitates alternative ways of accomplishing what the turn-taking system accomplishes: namely, an orderly transition from one participant to the next, and an incremental, sequentially coherent development of the joint activity.

In early Cognoter meetings, the work of maintaining a shared focus was evident in the ebb and flow of meeting activity. During the ordering phase particularly, where ideas are elaborated, participants tended to interact verbally for a few minutes, explaining immediate goals and making short-term plans of action, after which the group settled into their "assignments," typing intently for a while. After a few minutes of parallel editing, people would lose track of what the others were doing and, therefore, of what to do next. The group would then stop interacting with the system and again discuss where they were and what they should do. These transitions between parallel and convergent activity sometimes required negotiation. In particular, individuals engaged in different activities might not arrive at transition places simultaneously and might not be equally interruptable at any given time. The early Cognoter sessions encompassed several such cycles of regrouping, summarization, joint planning, and then parallel action.

Along with personal interaction, shared focus is achieved by means of reference to common objects. Cognoter's goal, as with a chalkboard, is to enable participants to refer to common objects through various kinds of efficient reference such as deixis[5] and pointing. Although the WYSIWIS idealization recognizes that efficient reference depends on a common view of the work at hand, a distinctive problem arises in computer-based environments in that the boundary between logical and physical objects is blurred. This represents a tremendous advantage, on one level, in that relaxations of WYSIWIS allow participants to tailor their individual display of the shared view to their own specifications. However, it also means that, although people may be referring to the "same" piece of text, the text may be in an entirely different location on their respective displays. With the use of windows that can be moved, reshaped, and scrolled, conventions are required to avoid situations in which one person tries to see some text at the top of a long passage while another tries to see text at the bottom, or one member of the group puts up a very large public window, obscuring everyone else's view (situations that we have informally dubbed "Scroll Wars" and "Window Wars").

As well as confirming the usefulness of a single view of the public record, our early experience with Cognoter identified a more subtle element of shared focus. With a single display device (e.g., a chalkboard or workstation), it is common for one person to be assigned the task of actually entering new text into the record; typically, not only the new text, but the writing activity itself, is visible to the other participants. In the current design of Cognoter, however, the actual editing is done in private windows, with only the finished text broadcast to coparticipants. This design decision, while encouraging parallel activity, poses some interesting new problems for the collaborative process. In particular, participants in the early sessions expressed frustration at not being able to see what the others were doing; specifically, at not being able to watch when others were engaged in writing. To an important

---

[5]*Deixis* means referring to something either verbally (e.g., "the gray house across the street") or by pointing.

degree, it seems that participants need access not only to the product of each other's writing, but to the writing process itself. The unanticipated usefulness of the video switch, which allows one to switch between displays,[6] underscores the importance of a shared view for maintaining the joint focus. User frustrations in this regard reopen the question as to the ideal grain size at which individual and group transactions take place, and the relationship between private and public views.

In general, these early observations were confirmed by a small set of controlled experiments run at UC Berkeley. In the trials, several pairs of student collaborators unfamiliar with the Colab used either Cognoter or a chalkboard to plan article outlines. The outcomes showed that the interface of Cognoter is complicated enough to require practice to be used effectively [13]. More extensive trials with larger groups will await the completion of video recording and meeting analysis tools that are now being created.

Research Questions

Our guiding question has been, What are the processes of collaboration for which the computer is an appropriate tool, and what particular Colab tools could be designed to support these processes? As a first approximation, Cognoter and Argnoter have assumed two contrasting processes of collaborative writing and argumentation, both drawn from our own experience. Cognoter takes a joint presentation as its object and encourages consensus by supporting a single viewpoint, whereas Argnoter encourages competing proposals and delayed consensus by allowing the display and comparison of multiple views.

Having identified the collaborative processes and refined the associated tools, we need next to question the generality of our assumptions. To what extent do our work practices compare and contrast with other settings and other participants? Does a tool, by reifying a process and making it explicit, thereby also make it portable across groups? Or do we need a set of tools that can be customized to different users in different settings? Under what circumstances are explicit structures desirable, and under what circumstances do we want to minimize the amount of structure we build into our tools? These questions and others will be explored as we extend the design and experiment with its use.

---

[6]The Colab video switch allows the content of any screen to be directed to another screen; it was originally designed to aid in debugging across multiple machines.

Related Work

The possibility that computers might be used to support group problem solving was appreciated by early visionaries long before it was practically feasible. In 1945, Bush presented a hypothetical system called a "Memex" that included an interactive database [6] by which associative "trails" of exploration could be saved to be recalled and retraced at a later time. Bush believed that a common encyclopedic database of information integrated from many areas of human activity would enhance the quality of societal problem solving.

In the 1960s, experimental systems like the NLS/AUGMENT [11, 12] began to use computers to support collaboration. The NLS/AUGMENT supported terminal linking, electronic mail, sharing of files, and "televiewing"—the ability to "pass the gavel" among several people working together at separate terminals. Engelbart saw machines as providing an important medium for communication and was known for his development of novel user interfaces like the mouse. Engelbart was also an early worker in hypertext, systems that organize fragments of text in annotated networks. This work has been pursued in several other systems including TEXTNET [33], Xanadu [24], NoteCards [34], and Annoland.

At a time when time-shared systems like TENEX [5] popularized electronic mail and shared files, some observers (e.g., Lederberg [21]) reported a qualitative difference in the ways they were interacting with colleagues. In the mid 1970s, researchers at the Stanford AI Lab built a video, audio, and keyboard crossbar switch to allow users at multiple workstations to collaborate from separate workstations. At the same time, another line of work pursued the use of communications facilities to tie together people working at different locations. Known as *teleconferencing* [18, 19], this work eschewed much use of computers and has developed slowly, due largely to high communication costs for video images. Meanwhile, others have developed systems for remote conferencing that rely mostly on computers rather than video: Known as *computer conferencing*, these systems include electronic mail, editors, voting mechanisms, shared files, and archiving, but do not provide structure for the conferences based on any models of group problem-solving processes. In [16], Hiltz and Turoff review some of these systems and provide an extensive bibliography; prime examples are EIES [17] and some parts of NLS/AUGMENT [11].

Although computers have been used experimentally in meetings to support specialized problem-solving processes since at least 1972 [35], the impact has been much less dramatic than with other computer applications (see [20]). Most of these systems are organized around formal and mathematical models of decision making like multiattribute utility models and cost–benefit analyses. The Delphi method [22] and the Nominal Group method [20], for example, are techniques for structuring group problem solving that have been used with and without computer support. The Delphi model considered by Turoff [35] is designed for technological forecasting by a geographically dispersed group, while the Nominal Group represents a consensus-forming process for face-to-face meetings; both have been characterized as "rational but naive" [20]. Since we have little experience with them, we offer no independent assessment; however, we note that the meeting processes used in the Colab are similar to the meeting methods commonly taught in corporate training programs.

RTCAL/IOLC, a somewhat analogous system to the Colab that was developed at MIT by Sunil Sarin [30], allows a group of users to synchronously exchange information from personal calendar databases to schedule a future meeting. It differs from the Colab in particular trade-offs of computer communication (e.g., RTCAL has a centralized database management scheme) and the absence of process models for problem solving, but is similar in that it uses personal computers, works in real time, and maintains consistent views by message passing over a local network [29]. Another research project reported by Applegate, Konsynski, and Nunamaker [1] also resembles the Colab in that it provides personal computers to meeting participants around a conference table and uses a video projector to provide large public views; it also provides tools for brainstorming and analysis. However, unlike the Colab, it is oriented around decision support models for planning and quantitative analysis. Also, since it is built using microcomputers with very limited display space, there has been little opportunity to experiment with private and public windows or multiuser interfaces.

Kraemer and King [20] observe that there are very few successful computer conference rooms, if any, and that even these systems have been plagued by hardware difficulties. As the primary obstacles to success, they cite inaccessibility of computing resources, unreliable video projectors, and limited graphics capabilities. However, they quite rightly note that in recent years computing and projection technology have become much more reliable and also less expensive. We agree with them that most of the activity with computer-supported conferences over the next three to four years will center on research and development.

In terms of technology, there have been several advances that will enable this work to proceed at a much more rapid pace: among them, more powerful personal workstations, local-area networks, advanced programming environments [31], distributed programming, and interface technology. These advances will make it possible to develop prototype systems quite rapidly and thus to experiment readily with new tools.

Conclusions

Focusing on developing and understanding "team computers" (i.e., collaborative systems for group meetings), the Colab project has produced a usable meeting room and several operational tools. The liveboard is operational but not fully integrated with our software. As we begin to use the Colab on a regular basis, it will afford a laboratory for studying the effects of the tools on collaborative meetings. The Colab meeting room is now being fitted with the video equipment necessary to record working Colab sessions. We will use the Colab to try to understand why collaborative problem solving is organized as it is, the relationship of that organization to existing technology, and the trade-offs involved in displacing old practices with new technology.

Upon hearing about the Colab, a manager from a large American corporation whose job it is to introduce appropriate computing technology at the executive staff level told us an interesting story. After working diligently for several months to bring things up-to-date and to revitalize operations with tools like electronic mail, document processing, databases, and automatic spreadsheets, he remained unsure about the degree of success he had achieved. One day, in a burst of frank evaluation, one of his charges told him that, despite the best intentions, he felt the computer was not making a difference and did not expect it to save him more than 30 minutes a day, even if he did learn how to use it. The reason was that this individual was not in his office for more than 30 minutes; he spent almost his entire day in meetings! *Moral: Office automation simply does not reach people who are away from their offices*, which brings us back to the premise of the Colab project: Meetings are important. They are at the core of the way most organizations do business. As such, tools like the Colab touch fundamentally the ways we meet and make decisions collectively.

Acknowledgments

This article has benefited greatly from the suggestions and criticisms of Agustin Araya, John Seely Brown, Richard Fateman, John Florentin, Mark D. Hill, Bernardo Huberman, Randy Katz, Mark Miller, Sanjay Mittal, Ted Selker, Jeff Shrager, and Mike Stonebraker.

Many thanks to Bill Volkers for creating the liveboard, and to Stu Card and Jeff Shrager for early ideas for the liveboard. We wish to acknowledge Ted Selker for his suggestions about many aspects of the Colab and for designing electronic chalk for the liveboard; Steve Osburn, Joan Osburn, Gene Hall, and Lee Anderson for creating the Colab physical setting; and Steven Levy for his contributions to the first implementations of Colab software.

Special thanks to John Seely Brown for his ideas, criticisms, and encouragement on the Colab project. Without his support, the project could never have been launched nor could the initial momentum have been sustained. Thanks also to Bill Spencer and George Pake for creating an environment at Xerox PARC that makes projects like this possible.

References

1. Applegate, L. M., Konsynski, B. R., and Nunamaker, J. F. A group decision support system for idea generation and issue analysis in organizational planning. In *Proceedings of the Conference on Computer-Supported Cooperative Work* (Austin, Tex., Dec.). ACM, New York. To be published.

2. Bernstein, P. A., and Goodman, N. Concurrency control in distributed database systems. *ACM Comput. Surv. 13*, 2(June 1981), 185–221.

3. Birrell, A. D., and Nelson, B. J. Implementing remote procedure calls. Tech. Note CSL-83-7, Xerox PARC, Palo Alto, Calif., Dec. 1983.

4. Bobrow, D. G., and Stefik, M. J. *The Loops Manual.* Xerox PARC, Palo Alto, Calif., 1983.

5. Bobrow, D. G., Burchfiel, J. D., Murphy, D. L., and Tomlinson, R. S. TENEX, a paged time-sharing system for the PDP-10. *Commun. ACM 15*, 3(Mar. 1972), 135–143.

6. Bush, V. As we may think. *Atlantic Mon. 176*, 1(June 1945), 101–108.

7. Coffman, E. G., Elphick, M. J., and Shoshani, A. System deadlocks. *ACM Comput. Surv. 3*, 2(June 1971), 67–78.

8. Denning, P. J. Virtual memory. *ACM Comput. Surv. 2*, 3(Sept 1970), 153–189.

9. Donahue, J., and Widom, J. Whiteboards: A graphical database tool. *ACM Trans. O–. Inf. Syst. 4.* 1(Jan. 1986), 24–41.

10. Doyle, M., and Straus, D. *How to Make Meetings Work.* Berkeley Publishing Group, New York, 1984.

11. Engelbart, D. C. Collaboration support provisions in AUGMENT, OAC 84 digest. In *Proceedings of the 1984 AFIPS Oflce Automation Conference* (Los Angeles, Calif., Feb 20–22). AFIPS, Reston, Va., 1984, pp. 51–58.

12. Engelbart, D. C., and English, W. K. Research center for augmenting human intellect. In *Proceedings of the Fall Joint Computing Conference* (San Francisco, Calif., Dec. 9–11). AFIPS, Reston, Va., 1968, pp. 395–410.

13. Foster, G. Collaborative systems and multi-user interfaces: Computer-based tools for cooperative work. Doctoral dissertation, Computer Science Division, Univ. of California at Berkeley, Dec. 1986. To be published.

14. Goldberg, A., and Robson, D. *Smalltalk-80: The Language and Its Implementation.* Addison-Wesley, Reading, Mass., 1983.

15. Hansen, P. B. *Operating System Principles.* Prentice-Hall, Englewood Cliffs, N.J., 1973.

16. Hiltz, S. R., and Turoff, M. *The Network Nation: Human Communication via Computer.* Addison-Wesley, Reading, Mass., 1978.

17. Hiltz, S. R., and Turoff, M. The evolution of user behavior in a computerized conferencing system. *Commun. ACM 24*, 11(Nov. 1981), 739–752.

18. Johansen, R. *Teleconferencing and Beyond: Communications in the Oflce of the Future.* McGraw-Hill, New York, 1984.

19. Johansen, R., Vallee, J., and Spangler, K. *Electronic Meetings: Technical Alternatives and Social Choices.* Addison-Wesley, Reading, Mass., 1979.

20. Kraemer, K. L., and King, J. L. Computer supported conference rooms: Final report of a state of the art study. Dept. of Information and Computer Science, Univ. of California, Irvine, Dec. 1983.

21. Lederberg, J. Digital communications and the conduct of science: The new literacy. *Proc. IEEE 66*, 11(Nov. 1978), 1313–1319.

22. Linstone, H. A., and Turoff, M. *The Delphi Method: Techniques and Applications.* Addison-Wesley, Reading, Mass., 1975.

23. Metcalfe, R. M., and Boggs, D. R. Ethernet: Distributed packet switching for local computer networks. *Commun. ACM 19*, 7(July 1976), 395–404.

24. Nelson, T. *Literary Machines.* Ted Nelson, Swarthmore, Pa., 1981.

25. O'Connor, R. J. Outline processors catch on. *InfoWorld* (July 2, 1984), 30–31.

26. Panko, R. R. Office work. *O–. Technol. People* 2(1964), 205–353.

27. Platt, J. R. Strong Inference. *Science 146*, 3642 (oct. 1964), 347–353.

28. Sanella, M., et al. *Interlisp Reference Manual.* Xerox PARC, Palo Alto, Calif., 1983.

29.   Sarin, S. K. Interactive on-line conferences. Ph.D. thesis MIT/LCS/TR-330, MIT, Cambridge, Mass., Dec. 1984.

30.   Sarin, S., and Greif, I. Computer-based real-time conferencing systems. *Computer 18*, 10(Oct. 1985), 33-45.

31.   Sheil, B. Power tools for programmers. *Datamation* (Feb. 1983), 131–144.

32.   Stefik, M., Foster, G., Lanning, S., and Tatar, D. The scope of WYSIWIS: Early experiences with multi-user interfaces. In *Proceedings of the Conference on Computer-Supported Cooperative Work* (Austin, Tex., Dec.). ACM, New York. To be published.

33.   Trigg, R., and Weiser, M. TEXTNET: A network-based approach to text handling. *ACM Trans. O–. Inf. Syst. 4*, 1(Jan. 1986), 1–23.

34.   Trigg, R., Suchman, L., and Halasz, F. Supporting collaboration in Note-Cards. In *Proceedings of the Conference on Computer-Supported Cooperative Work* (Austin, Tex., Dec.). ACM, New York. To be published.

35.   Turoff, M. Delphi conferencing: Computer-based conferencing with anonymity. *Technol. Forecasting Soc. Change 3* (1972), 159–204.

A Performing Medium for Working Group Graphics

Fred Lakin

Center for the Study of Language and Information
Center for Design Research
Stanford University
Rehabilitation R&D Center
Palo Alto Veterans Hospital
Palo Alto, CA

Abstract

Writing and drawing together on a common display often assist a working group in a task. For example, face-to-face groups have long enjoyed the richness of graphic communication found on blackboards. The spontaneous image manipulations which take place over time on a blackboard can be viewed as a *text-graphic performance*. A human performer generates and manipulates text and graphics for the purpose of assisting the working group in their task.

The phenomenon of performed text-graphics presents opportunities for research in the area of computer-supported cooperative work. 1] Spontaneous generation demands a *performing medium* where the focus is on *live* manipulation of text and graphics. Design of a computer-based medium with enough agility and generality to support blackboard-like activity is a challenge for interface design. 2] Agility and generality must not be achieved at the expense of specializability. After a group has initially sketched an idea in text and graphics, then that same

Figure 14.1   Engineers in the early sixties doing "Panoramic Design" on a blackboard.

medium should also support refining the sketch according to formal schema. 3] The performing medium can also be used as a recording medium for studying image manipulation as part of the working group process.

This paper presents a stepwise approach to the design of a performing medium for working group graphics. First, examples of non-computer text-graphics for groups are examined to get a preliminary idea of the underlying phenomenon: the *performing* of text-graphic manipulation to assist working groups. Next, key features of that kind of text-graphic manipulation are isolated. Then, third, the architecture and behavior of a graphics editor providing those features is described.

1 Introduction: Working Group Graphics on Non-computer Media

1.1 Examples

Blackboard   Figure 14.1: engineers in the early sixties working together on a common display for the entire design process, taking projects all the way from brainstorming to machine drawings which were then sent to the shop as polaroid prints [TAB62]. Duration: unknown. Operator: multiple. Style: "Panoramic Design."

Large Sheet Paper Graphics   Figure 14.2: concept exploration session for interdisciplinary mix of computer scientists and cognitive rehabilita-

Figure 14.2 Concept exploration on a large sheet of paper operated by professional facilitator.

tion engineers; text and graphics manipulated by professional facilitator [Sibbet84]. Recorded on video tape and also in 35mm slides. Duration: 40 minutes. Operator: single. Style: "Mapping state of the art."

Manipulable Card Paper Graphics   Figure 14.3: problem definition session with working group from U.S. Geological Survey; group generates key phrases in brainstorm, organizes them using spatial juxtaposition and movable line networks [Lakin74].[1]   Recorded in 35mm slides. Duration: 90 minutes. Operator: multiple. Style: "Group Concept Growth."

1.2 The Phenomenon

First, the subjective impression after ten years of observing working groups is what we might call *text-graphic dance*: chunks of text and graphics created at one location on the display, lingering there for a while, and then moved or changed or erased; continually shifting patterns forming and reforming as the group goes about developing and displaying their concepts. An expressive performing art, the meaning of which is in all of the intermediate imagery, where the final frame may not be any more meaningful than the final position in a ballet. And finally, the impression is also of a performing art so horribly artifact-bound that text-graphic dance as it was "meant" to be is only glimpsed

---

[1]   Use of waxed cards for manipulable group display was first developed by Porter and Verger [Porter74]; then extended by Lakin with movable line networks and color overlays. A similar technique involving (less agile) cards pinned to cork boards arose independently in Europe [Jacobs73].

Figure 14.3   Problem definition session using manipulable cards to brainstorm, then organize.

now and then through the clumsy media that circumstances force the performers to employ.

Next, to more objectively characterize the phenomenon underlying the three examples: a text-graphic performance to serve a task-oriented group. The performance is text-graphic in that it involves manipulating text and graphics over a set period of time. The performance serves the working group in that the images displayed during the performance relate to their task (present, represent, express, explain, diagram, show the structure of, mean). The performance is by an operator (or operators) whose purpose it is to insure that the performance serves the group.

We will call this kind of text-graphic performance "working group graphics." There are many other kinds of possible text-graphic performances that we won't discuss in this paper (a single operator for his own consumption, multiple operators for a play oriented group, etc.). There are many different possible styles of text-graphic performing within the kind we have designated working group graphics. The use of the blackboard described above was called "Panoramic Design" by the practitioners; that style can be described in more detail as brainstorm-and-then-do-machine-drawing [TAB62]. Styles will be discussed below.

There is various theoretical work which either deals directly with the phenomenon of working group graphics, or can shed some light on it. Having a common display often aids face-to-face task groups. Ball and Gilkey coined the term "explicit group memory" to point out the fact that the display provides a lingering representation of the task state

[Ball72]. Graphical imagery seems to tap a powerful kind of conceptionalizing: "visual thinking" [Arnheim69, McKim72]. The social dynamics of the working group may change for the better. Professional display operators like Brunon, Doyle, Sibbet and Straus point out that more of the group's members tend to participate in idea generation, rather than the concepts being controlled by the verbally and/or politically dominant [Brunon71, Doyle76, Sibbet76].

1.3 *Methodological Assumption*

It is a major premise of this paper that text-graphics performed for working groups have spatial and temporal structure. First, the images themselves are spatial, and arranged spatially. Second, the manipulation of these images takes place over time and so has temporal arrangement. And third, both kinds of arrangement are orderly and patterns can be discovered.

The more radical extension to this premise is that the text-graphics themselves can be studied separate from their context. That is, the social situation of working group graphics is a group in a room together with a common display; in conjunction with the text-graphic performance the group members talk to each other and use their bodies to gesture and point. Without question, the concomitant aural and gestural annotations are crucial to the overall meaning of the performance (probably best studied through video taping). But the premise here is that the manipulation of the text-graphics *themselves* constitutes an orderly phenomenon that can be supported and studied: in a sense, the text graphics have a life of their own. The study of this aspect of text-graphic performances, in isolation, is much like linguistics: a quest for temporal and spatial structures of the expressions themselves.[2]   It is also like an odd kind of dance choreography which attempts to notate improvised dances.

In terms of the text-graphics themselves, then, the notion of *style* is one way of labelling certain spatial/temporal structures. There are many different ways (styles) of operating displays in order to help a face-to-face group. Styles can be characterized by, among other features, distinctive static images (charts, diagrams, matrices, lists) and distinctive dynamics (sequences of images and manipulations). Skilled practitioners (like Ball, Brunon, Doyle, Sibbet, Straus) provide a good reference for styles; they each have defined many distinct ones. Part of an operator's skill is matching a style to a group and a task.

---

[2]   Actually, this method of study is akin to old-style linguistics, which should be seen in contrast to newer approaches like the study of *situated* language at the Center for the Study of Language and Information at Stanford.

In conclusion, we note that de-situating the text-graphics from the working group situation must be done carefully and under advisement. It is a methodological move, and in the long run may lead to problems. In the short run, however, it has two payoffs. First, it allows us to focus on the text-graphics themselves to see what structure is there.[3] Second, it is a direct way to describe the specifications for a computer-based medium to support this kind of text-graphic manipulation.

2 Features of Text-Graphic Manipulation for Working Groups

This section strives for a delicate balance, attempting to characterize the phenomenon of text-graphic manipulation which lies "behind" the examples while at the same time aware that our view is admittedly constrained by their limited technology. Yet the examples are also liberating in their own way, demanding capabilities not easily attained on computer graphics systems. What is ultimately at stake is supporting the "heir" to blackboard activity. We want to include all the features of text-graphic manipulation found in earlier instances of that activity without being restrained to them.

2.1 *Chronological*

If we were to come upon a text-graphic performance cold and unprepared, what might strike us first is that it is a dynamic phenomenon, unfolding over time: *something's moving*. What's moving is the text-graphics, described below. The state of the text-graphics at any one time can be captured in a static image or frame. Yet the performance as a whole cannot be captured in any one frame, but instead must be represented as a dynamic sequencing of the frames over time.

2.2 *Text-Graphic*

The fact that text-graphic manipulation unfolds over time allows us to observe how objects precipitate out of the activity (why chronology was introduced first). That is, a flurry of activity is observed and then there is a pause—the difference in the image state before and after the flurry

---

[3] In fact, an early study comparing telemediated groups with face-to-face groups provided writing and drawing media in each case, but failed to record or measure its use [Weston73].

is a new object (or a manipulation of an old object). Sometimes new objects are text, sometimes graphics, sometimes both.

Static frames from the examples show the kind of images that are being manipulated: text and graphics in spatial arrangement. As a general policy, we don't want to say whether any particular object is text or graphics until we need to. Often times the distinction between text and graphics is dubious at best—perhaps the group will be using Chinese characters or circuit diagram symbology.

2.3 Manipulatory

Now that in the course of describing this phenomenon we have time, and text-graphics, then just an eye-blink later we have manipulation. It's thanks to manipulation that the text-graphics change over time (and in changing, we can see what the pieces of text-graphics *are*). Manipulation includes generating, moving, modifying, and erasing text-graphic objects. We observe that sometimes operators want to manipulate just little pieces, whereas other times they want to manipulate groups of objects as a unit (most apparent in the manipulable cards).

2.4 Performed

Working group graphics is performed *by* an operator *for* a group. This fact helps characterize the operation of the medium, and the nature of the medium being operated. There is a performer, and there are consumers of the performance. The consumers are there to watch the images, using them as explicit group memory. The display can be easily seen by all members of the group.

2.5 Fast

What is fast? It is manipulation of text-graphic objects in time. In working group graphics, the agility of text-graphic manipulation is paramount. Leisurely illustration will *not* do—the group will get bored or lose their train of thought. Loss of a minute may mean loss of an idea. Figure 14.4 is the final frame from the large sheet paper graphics performance in Figure 14.2; it took the operator 20 minutes to make this image. Figure 14.5 shows generation times for selected images in Figure 14.4 as timed from the video tape of the performance. The images are being put up there very quickly. In addition to initial image generation, agile manipulation of images observed in the examples includes erasability (blackboard) and shuffling (manipulable cards).

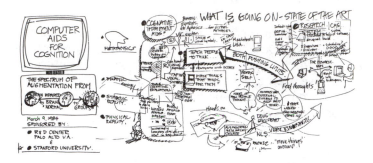

Figure 14.4   Final frame in large sheet paper graphics performance depicted in Figure 14.2.

2.6 *Unstructured*

The media in the three examples do not restrict the kind of objects that can be written or drawn;[4] nor do they restrict the temporal order in which images are created. The point is, any kind of image can be created—from diagrams to paragraphs to LISP code to cartoons to matrices—regulated only by the purpose and style of the operator.

2.7 *Structured*

Both spatial and temporal structures can be observed in the text-graphic manipulation found in the examples. A formal spatial schema called "mechanical drawing," for instance, is during the blackboard activity in example one. Mechanical drawing is a system which limits the kind of text-graphics one may create and their arrangement; in fact, it could be called a kind of visual language.

Likewise, temporal pattern can be observed in the examples. In the case of the manipulable cards several temporal trends became obvious during the 90 minute performance. Cards were put up on the display space in the upper-middle area first. As more cards appeared, columns began to form. Thirty minutes into the session, colored overlays appeared on top of some of the cards. Then at 45 minutes, the line networks showed up. During the course of the performance, 106 cards were generated; as many as 88 were on the display at one time but only 73 were present in the final frame.

---

4   The manipulable card system does impose a size limitation on images.

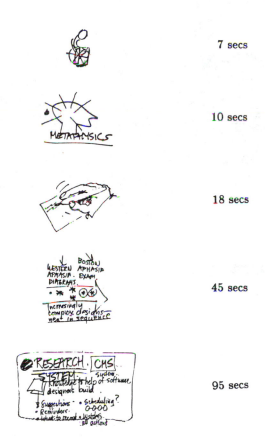

7 secs

10 secs

18 secs

45 secs

95 secs

Figure 14.5   Generation times for subimages from Figure 14.4.

2.8 Reflective

Text-graphic manipulation for working groups can be reflective: that is, using a piece of text-graphics which refers to some aspect of a text-graphic performance. The engineers in example one are taking an instant photograph of the final frame on the blackboard (Figure 14.1). Each member of the group in example two was provided with an image of the final frame (Figure 14.4). And the performers in example three made competing *plans* for the reorganization of the display as part of their performance (Figure 14.6). The plans were themselves pieces of text-graphics, each of which diagrammed a possible way to reorganize the display (as it turned out, the final development of the display was guided by a merger of two plans, the one in the lower left and the one in the upper right of Figure 14.6).

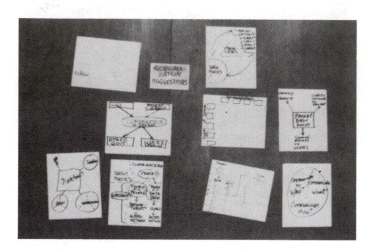

Figure 14.6   Plans, themselves pieces of text-graphics, each of which diagram a possible reorganization for the display in Figure 14.3.

The reflecting on performances characteristic of working group graphics can take place both during the act and afterwards. Reflection serves a variety of purposes. During the act, it can be used to guide the performing. And after the fact, reflecting at leisure has more academic uses. Medium designers might want to delineate the manipulation capabilities of equipment. Psychologists might want to study that aspect of the cognitive behavior of the group explicitly displayed in the sequence of image manipulations. And members of a working group want a record of conclusions reached and how they came about.

Reflection manifests itself in two concrete features of text-graphic manipulation. The first is simply the storage and retrieval of static images and image dynamics from performances. The second feature is measurement (one way academics like to reflect on performing). Measurement is embodied in "soft" instruments for uncovering and delineating temporal/spatial patterns in performances. For instance, a more detailed account of the card movements in example three could easily be represented in a table or a chart. In fact, in a sense measurement itself can be described as a kind of text-graphic manipulation: measurement is a transformation on a performance into a text-graphic object in some formal visual language (designed to perspicuously present some structures in the performance and leave out others).

3 *A Computer Medium for Performing Text-Graphics*

The computer medium designed to provide the capability for the features in Section 2 is a graphics editor called **vmacs**™.[5] **vmacs** combines the generality and agility of **emacs** with LISP-like processing of visual objects.

The name **vmacs** indicates that it was inspired by **emacs** [Stallman81]; is meant to co-exist with **emacs**; can be thought of as a collection of visual macros bound to keys and mouse buttons; and is basically a general purpose editor which can then be specialized for particular applications (like LISP mode in **emacs**). **vmacs** is for people who spend a lot of time in their graphics editor. The primary functions are *not* invoked by menu to avoid visual clutter. **vmacs** is written partly in the **PAM** graphics language, which provides text-graphic objects, manipulations on them, and computing with text-graphic forms [Lakin80a, 80b, 80c].

vmacs and **PAM** are implemented in ZetaLISP on a Symbolics 3645. The display is approximately 1000 by 800 lines and can be used by small groups of 3–4 around a single terminal. Video projection will support larger groups. For the time being **vmacs** is intended to be operated by a single skilled individual.

The following sections describe **vmacs** in more detail as a text-graphic manipulator for group graphics. Each section discusses **vmacs** in terms of one of the key features from Section 2 (Chronological, Text-Graphic, Manipulatory, Performed, Fast, Unstructured, Structured, Reflective).

4 Chronological

The notion of a **vmacs** *event* gives us image frames—statics—and then dynamics are event and image sequences. This comes about in the following way. The mouse and keyboard handler determines when a user event has taken place (i.e., when the mouse has been moved or buttons or keys pushed). An event is a 4-tuple consisting of a time, a cursor location, a user input, and a parameter to the input. Each event changes the appearance of the display. Cursor moving is considered the "minimal" event with user input equal to (MOVE-CURSOR). Each tuple in an event is textual symbolic expression (in LISP); there are no visual objects in event slots.

A history is a sequence of events. **vmacs** keeps a history list at all times. Histories can be replayed. A static frame is the state of the display

---

[5] **vmacs** is a trademark of Fred Lakin.

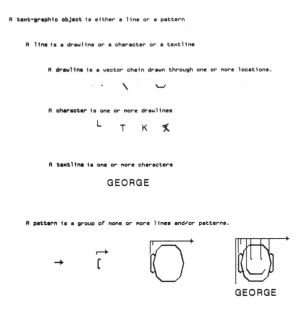

A text-graphic object is either a line or a pattern

A line is a drawline or a character or a textline

A drawline is a vector chain drawn through one or more locations.

A character is one or more drawlines

A textline is one or more characters

GEORGE

A pattern is a group of none or more lines and/or patterns.

GEORGE

Figure 14.7　Taxonomy for graphic objects in the **vmacs** graphics editor.

between events. "Statics" deal with matters in one frame. "Dynamics" deal with matters across frames—i.e., with histories (event sequences) and the corresponding image sequences.

5 *Text-Graphic*

Figure 14.7 shows the taxonomy for manipulable objects in the **vmacs** graphics editor. The aim is for text and graphics to be so completely integrated that the very distinction is secondary: initially we have raw, undifferentiated text-graphic objects, and then text is just a *kind* of graphics. To speak of text-graphic objects is to delay making the distinction between text and graphics for as long as possible: first, because the distinction is only useful in certain situations and inappropriate in others; and second, because we may want to use the **PAM** language to redefine just what text is (i.e., **textp** can have different definitions). Chinese characters are a good example of objects for which the traditional distinction between text and graphics is inappropriate. The taxonomy in Figure 14.7 was designed from the start to include Chinese characters (see that the character examples are L, T, K, and *tien*). The taxonomy provides a way of describing the appearance of objects in a single frame from a performance.

6 Manipulations

vmacs is organized around manipulations on the currently selected object. Manipulations include dragging, erasing and scaling. Atomic objects (the drawlines and textlines in Figure 14.7) can be grouped into patterns; patterns can contain other patterns. The tree structure of patterns is indicated by the spider webs in Figure 14.7.

Any object can be selected, from the smallest visual atom up to the largest pattern (everything on the screen). Since any selected object can be manipulated, the operator's experience of grouping objects into patterns is simply the determination of "what moves with what." The pattern structures allow support of the hierarchical manipulations observed on media like blackboards.[6] Structural manipulation is very important for agility in handling complex images. Erasure and shuffling (moving more than one object at a time) are two important moves supported by pattern structures.

7 Performing Medium

Group Display **vmacs** currently supports small groups of 3–4 around a single terminal. Larger groups will be supported with projection; Figure 14.8 shows the layout for a room with a 6 ft projection screen and the operator console to one side.

Skilled Single User **vmacs** is currently designed for a single operator (a co-operated version is planned). Skill level required is equivalent to touch typing **emacs:** someone who doesn't have to look at his/her hands in order to input text and type the control keys. In addition to the manual skills of image manipulation, some skill at group facilitation is also required of the operator. For beginners, this can be simply the ability to listen and put what the group says up on the screen. At more expert levels, facilitation involves knowing many styles of text-graphic performing and when each is appropriate.[7] The long-term goal of this research is for

---

[6] **PAM** and **vmacs** are both based on the SAM (*Structure-Arises-out-of-Manipulation*) model of text-graphic activity [Lakin83].

[7] Facilitation skills—what they are and how to acquire them—have for the most part been ignored in this paper. This is in part due to the methodological focus on the text-graphics themselves, and in part due to lack of space. However, three comments about the facilitation skills of operators need to be made. First, the facilitory expertise of the operator may well be *more important* than the power of the performing medium in determining the overall productivity of a meeting for a task-oriented group. A well facilitated group on a poor medium will probably out-perform a poorly facilitated group on a powerful medium. Other eras may have been more aware of this. There is a possibly apocryphal report that

Figure 14.8   Room layout for **vmacs** on 6 ft projection screen.

the system to act as an assistant during performance, taking the burden off the human operator by supplying both manipulatory and facilitory expertise through graphic intervention.

Imagery Reserved for Content   The content of the display is being continually viewed by the group for cognitive purposes. Therefore we don't want it obscured by menus popping up or other visual clutter solely for the purpose of controlling image manipulation. Skilled **vmacs** operators can use control keys for all primary functions (changing selection, erasing, etc.) so no menus appear during performing.

6 Agility

Agility is measured in text-graphic manipulations per second. Right off, we must acknowledge the problem with mice for generating freehand graphics. Optical mice are definitely an improvement; styluses are better yet.

---

around the turn of the century training in blackboard use was part of every school teacher's professional preparation. Second, one issue is simply consciousness raising: it is easier to get good performance out of a group which is meeting literate, i.e., which has used text-graphic media and expects to do so. Third, the focus on the text-graphics themselves provides a good framework for studying facilitation skills and teaching them.

Your Usual Editor for Text   There is a lot of text entry/editing in most performances, and so it's important that the operator's customary text editing reflexes invoke the appropriate functions. Since **vmacs** is designed for the **emacs** community, the text entry interface happens to be a sub-set of **emacs** (it could be any other text editor used by the operator).

Touch Typing in a Graphic Editor   **vmacs** employs the NLS control organization paradigm: operator's eyes on the display, one hand on the mouse for spatial input and the other hand on a keyboard for inputting additional control information [Engelbart62, English67]. The hypothesis is that *agility in a graphics editor requires touch typing* (controlling). The operator can't take time to look away from the images being manipulated, either to his hands or to menus. Menus might be OK for cross-country skiing, but not for slalom [Engelbart85].

Agility Measures   A big deal has been made of agility. Does **vmacs** have it? Test results so far are mixed. At this point in development, **vmacs** is fast enough to be successfully used in improvisational, blackboard-type image manipulation for small working groups. However, the clumsiness of mouse drawing is holding back performance on blackboard transcription tests for image *generation*. Figure 14.9a is the final frame of the large sheet paper graphics example; Figure 14.9b is a **vmacs** transcription of that image. The overall generation time for the image in Figure 14.9a was 20 minutes (operator: professional facilitator/cartoonist) as opposed to 120 minutes for the **vmacs** version in Figure 14.9b (operator: amateur and not particularly fast cartoonist). Clearly it's hard to draw with a mouse; dry marker on newsprint is six times faster! For a different perspective on agility, Figure 14.10 compares the generation times for selected sub-images from the video tape of the performance with the generation times for their **vmacs** counterparts. Here we notice the same factor of six time differentials for the first three images, which are drawing-intensive. However, **vmacs** is only three times slower on the last two images, which are predominantly textual.

The real issue is not whether the professional facilitator with dry marker is faster than the **vmacs** operator, but how much generative agility is necessary to support working group graphics. We *know* the speed of generation in the video tape is fast enough because it was taken from a successful performance. For this reason, the comparisons are presented. However, as mentioned, **vmacs** is used to facilitate small groups; **vmacs** has other manipulative strengths which compensate. When considering agility, we must remember that image generation is only part of the story, albeit an important part. Since computer media have

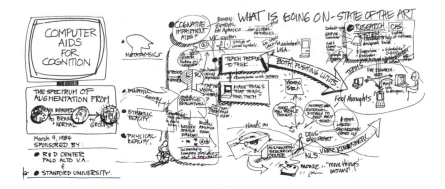

Figure 14.9a   Final frame in large sheet paper graphics performance depicted in Figure 14.2.

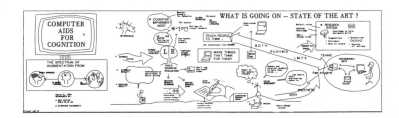

Figure 14.9b   **vmacs** transcription of image from Figure 14.9a.

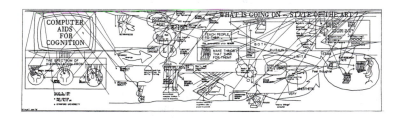

Figure 14.9c   Grouping structures for manipulation created by operator in making Figure 14.9b.

traditionally been weak in this capability, it was chosen for the focus here. But the media differential favors computer graphics for other kinds of agility: for example, when it comes to erasure and shuffling, **vmacs** the computer medium is clearly superior. Precise measures for agility of this kind will be a goal of future work.

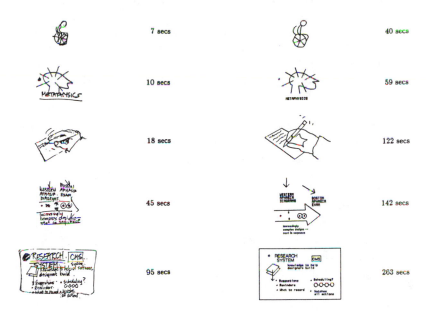

Figure 14.10 Comparisons of the generation times for selected sub-images from Figure 14.9a with the generation times for their **vmacs** counterparts.

The Most Agility Imaginable In order to get a better feeling for all aspects of agility working in concert, let's see if we can imagine the most responsive possible medium for text-graphic dance. This imaginary performing instrument will represent the limits of agility which the present medium tries to approach. We might describe this medium in operation as *hand-powered performance animation*. Not only are text and graphics moving as fast as the operator desires, but even the very quality of their movement is under his or her complete control. Admittedly such a medium is hard to imagine—complete animation of text-graphics generated live in performance—but perhaps part of the problem lies with our ability to imagine...

Consider the following parable. A cargo plane is flying over the jungle enroute to a very remote Club Med. Through a freak accident, the player piano meant for the night club accidentally falls out of the cargo bay along with hundreds of paper rolls, some with music and some blank. Miraculously the piano survives intact, the only damage being the total destruction of the keyboard. Discovered by a local tribe, one of their musicians figures out how the player piano can be operated in order to make music. It takes about two days to punch a roll which then produces two minutes of music. Years later an explorer happens upon the tribe and they demonstrate piano music for him. He listens politely and thinks somebody ought to tune the thing. Then he tries to explain the concept of a *keyboard* and its use in jazz improvisation. The tribe listens politely and thinks he is crazy. They explain patiently that his idea would never work: piano music is far too complex for human beings to make up and control in real time—and even if they could, no interface could possibly handle the bandwidth.

Now it is true that the operator may *later* choose to have the system process some of those objects under particular systems of interpretation (next section). But then again, he or she may *not* choose to do so; in fact, there may not be any particular, specifiable system of interpretation for objects nevertheless perfectly useful in working group graphics.

The point is, there will always be this tension in text-graphic performing between specifiable formal structure and the lack of it—images may start out looking like one thing and end up being another. And the change may have been the performer's intention, or he may have changed his mind. **vmacs** supports this feature of working group graphics by being general purpose; this is in contrast to other systems which allow processing of visual objects, but at the expense of syntax-directed editing, forcing the user to choose a single system of interpretation for the images before they can be created. In **vmacs**, every graphic act which is not prohibited is permitted.

A consequence of the **vmacs** approach is the freedom to use different visual languages in the same image, as is typical of blackboard use. Equally important, as mentioned above, is the flexibility to create objects in no particular visual language. **vmacs** supports new and different styles of performance *before* we understand them well enough to build special tools.

One general purpose manipulation important across many different styles of text-graphic performance is *shuffling*. Shuffling is the organized moving of image groups. "Take these pieces in the middle and put them over at the right-hand edge." Shuffling is supported in **vmacs** by the generalized grouping structures mentioned in Section 6; these structures can be created very rapidly, on the fly in the course of a performance.

10 *Specializable*

vmacs is an experiment. Fundamentally it is *first* an agile, general purpose graphics editor which can *then* be extended (we hypothesize) to handle different special purpose graphics applications. Generality means that objects can be created in any spatial pattern in any temporal order. Specialization lies in recognizing certain spatial or temporal structures and then acting to assist the user. The necessary prerequisite for this specializability is the programmatic processing of both statics and dynamics. This will be clearer if we consider the specifics of the static and dynamic cases.

10.1 *Formal Visual Languages (Statics)*

vmacs supplies the basic primitives with which to construct images for many different applications. But for any particular application, certain patterns of visual objects, distinguished by definable static criteria, have special significance. For the person employing those text-graphic objects in communication, they have meaning under a system of interpretation or "visual language." In such cases, based on their spatial arrangement, an appropriate structure representing a syntactic grouping of the objects can be found; this underlying structure can then be used in processing the objects semantically. Recovering underlying structure based on spatial structure for use in interpretation is a way of specializing **vmacs**. The recovery can be called spatial parsing; if successful it then facilitates programmatic manipulation and interpretation of images, including: *assistance*-like functions for manipulating visual forms, including `viz-first`, `viz-rest`, `viz-equal`, `viz-assoc` and `viz-eval` [Lakin80c].

Procedurally Specified   Figure 14.11 shows the result of parsing four visual communication objects in **vmacs** using procedurally directed processing; the resulting objects can then be processed semantically by the system [Lakin87]. *VennLISP:* A visual programming language based on lisp. *VIC:* A visual communication system for aphasics. *SIBTRAN:* Graphic devices for organizing textual sentence fragments; this is a first attempt to formalize some of the structures found in blackboard activity like Figure 14.2. *FSA:* Finite state automaton diagrams.

Grammar Driven   Spatial parsing is quite complex; it is advantageous to simplify programming by embedding the parsing knowledge explicitly in grammars rather than implicitly in procedures. Figure 14.12 shows a grammar for bar charts represented in Visual Grammar Notation

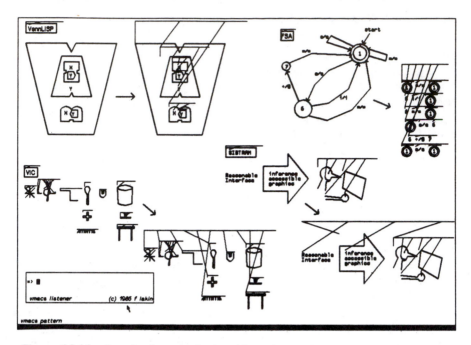

Figure 14.11 Four visual communication objects that can be procedurally parsed for interpretation in **vmacs**.

[Lakin87]. The Visual Grammar Notation is well suited for dealing with the patterning of elements in visual communication objects. The whole enterprise is made possible by the fact that visual objects created in **vmacs** can be computed with by **PAM** functions—including both the visual objects representing the grammars and the elements in the visual communication objects to be parsed.

Figure 14.13 shows grammar directed parsing for objects from four visual languages. *Bar Charts:* A simple family of bar charts. *DAGS:* Directed acyclic graph notation as used by linguists. *SIBTRAN:* The grammar directed parser for this language is more powerful than the procedurally directed one, handling recursive forms. *Visual Grammar Notation:* Itself a visual language, with the bar grammar as an example.

Work is underway on two other grammars for visual languages of use to working groups. *10-page manuscript with figures (*future*):* Useful for groups massaging working images into presentable form. *Machine drawing (*future*):* To support groups like those in Figure 14.1 who want to move from brainstorming into dimensioned drawings.

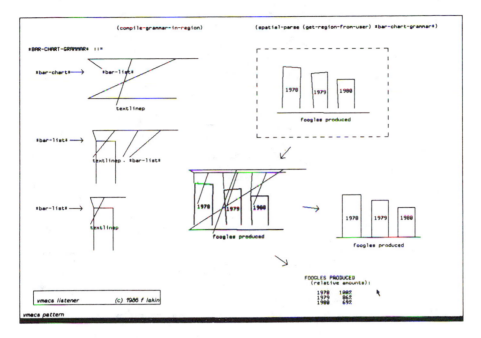

Figure 14.12 A visual grammar for a very simple family of bar charts, the input region, the resulting parsed object; and then, based on the parse, textual interpretation and automatic "prettifying."

10.2 Formal Visual Dynamics

The dynamics of text-graphic manipulation in vmacs can be temporally structured according to formal schema. This is accomplished through software modules called *performance administrators* which guide the course of user interaction. A performance administrator examines each event before it takes place, and also the state of images on the display [Lakin87]. It may intervene with graphic actions of its own when appropriate to a predefined goal. Performance administrators have been created to assist people in using two of the visual languages, VIC and SIBTRAN. Both of these administrators utilize spatial parsing as an integral part of assistance. Other performance administrators have been created which train brain damaged users in basic mouse skills, and teach full **vmacs** to brain normals.

Procedurally Specified *VIC:* The administrated environment provides a training facility for the VIC language, continually parsing phrases

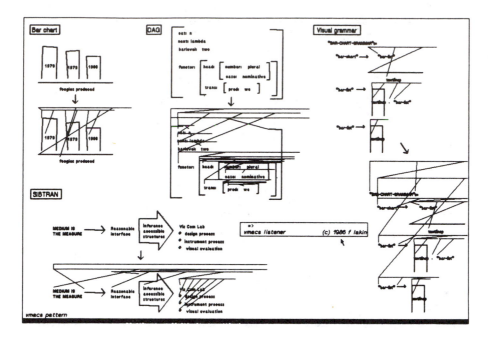

Figure 14.13 Examples of grammar directed parses for visual objects.

as they are assembled and undoing ungrammatical constructions. *SIB-TRAN:* The SIBTRAN assistant uses the grammar directed parser to intervene when it recognizes certain spatial constructions. *Trainers:* Low-level performance administrators teach basic skills like tracking a target with the mouse (see Figure 14.14) and making marks. *Administrated replay:* User interacts with images as they are replayed, and *that* interaction is administrated. This technique is utilized for a **vmacs** tutorial.

Grammar Driven (*future*)   A language for visually specifying the dynamics of visual interaction is the next logical step. Paul Haeberli has already implemented such a system based on the data flow formalism [Haeberli86].

11 Reflection

In **vmacs** a performance is a sequence of text-graphic to capture a performance so that we may reflect upon it. **vmacs** supports the capture for reflection of many aspects of a text-graphic performance—both statics and dynamics can be stored and measured. Some of the techniques are literally reflective, transforming an aspect of a performance into a piece of text-graphics which refers to it.

11.1 *Storing and Retrieving Performances*

Statics vmacs has emacs-style files and buffers for on-line storage of images. Figures 14.7, 14.8, 14.9b, 14.9c, 14.11, 14.12, 14.13, 14.14, and 14.15 are images from **vmacs** buffers. For paper hard copy there is only a screen dump facility at present, but a **vmacs** image to page description language translator is planned. Hardcopy could be formatted for various purposes, under either procedure or grammar direction.

Dynamics *Actual dynamics:* Recorded live from performance; then stored, retrieved and replayed on-line. *Composed dynamics:* Created "synthetically" through score compilers or history editors. Passive dynamics are viewed in replay like an animated cartoon. Interactive dynamics are participatory, where the user interacts with the replaying images, and *that* performance is administrated. We might imagine a group creating an interactive graphic tutorial for the final presentation of their concept.

11.2 *Measuring Performance*

Measuring some aspect of a performance implies a level of interpretation or filtering beyond merely recording it. For instance, an audio tape of a working group session is a record; while a transcription of that tape into speakers and their phrases is an interpretation, albeit a very low-level one.[8] In this sense, a **vmacs** history is already a low-level measurement because the mouse and keyboard handler has interpreted the dynamics in terms of events. However, it's a funny kind of interpretation—first, because some of the interpretation was done at the time when the medium was designed (when the handler was coded); and second, because the performance couldn't even take place without some kind of artifact for text-graphic manipulation. The result is that **vmacs** has shaped the performance into nicely chunked events about nicely computable-with text-graphic objects. In so far as **vmacs** is a good medium, the performers will not complain, since they benefit from the power of the system. And at the same time, those who want to measure performances benefit greatly: *the medium is the measure.*

---

[8] Transcribing a video tape of a performance seems inherently trickier (into what notation would it be transcribed? a storyboard?). Is this because any cinematographic documentary is already interpretative in a way that just putting a microphone in a room is not?

More detailed thoughts on measurement can be found in the Appendix, Section 14. The discussion there uses measurement to explore intuitions about the richness of the text-graphic dance that **vmacs** is designed to support. In addition, the discussion indicates how measurement may provide a bootstrap for improving **vmacs** as a better medium for that dance.

However generated, one result of any measurement will finally be a piece of text-graphics for human consumption. An algorithm has transformed an image or a history and obtained data which then needs to be presented clearly and effectively. For this purpose there exist formal visual languages (or notations) designed to emphasize aspects of interest in the data while leaving out the non-essential. Here **PAM** and **vmacs** can assist the measurers as well as the measurees. First, after the data has been generated, **PAM** programs can automatically translate it into a form in the appropriate visual language. And once displayed as a visual object, then the power of **vmacs** is available for manipulating these images too. The result of all of the measurements described below can be automatically displayed as graphs or charts; Figures 14.14 and 14.15 are examples.

Statics (Measuring Things in One Frame) *Spatiality:* Parsing is one way of measuring the spatial arrangement of objects—indicating whether they fall into specified patterns, Figures 14.11 and 14.13. **vmacs** also keeps track of spatial details like cursor position and the defining points in drawlines. *Grouping Structure:* Explicit user-built tree structures can be recorded. Figure 14.9c shows the grouping structures for manipulation created by the operator in the course of making Figure 14.9b.

Dynamics (Measuring Things that Change over Time) In **vmacs**, histories are amenable not only to replaying but also to analysis. Because a history list is symbolic, it can be processed symbolically and various tabulations made of the events comprising it. Or a history can be replayed, with analysis performed on each of the image frames as they are generated. In either case—history with or without the spatial image context—as with the other measures, the result will be some text-graphic object: a table, chart, or graph.

Spatiality: **vmacs** keeps track of spatial dynamics during performances. One such dynamic is cursor position; Figure 14.14 shows the results of an aphasic patient's performance in the tracking task for cursor movement control. Expressed in Figure 14.14 are the location and seconds elapsed for each hit (boxed numbers), and the distance between cursor position and target for each cursor movement (the comet-like tails

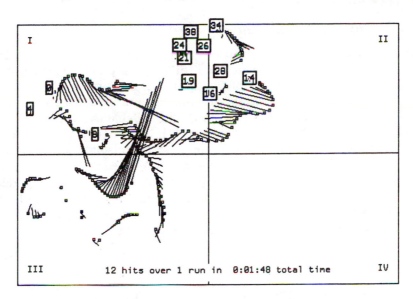

Figure 14.14 Plot of target hits during aphasic patient's tracking task for cursor movement control.

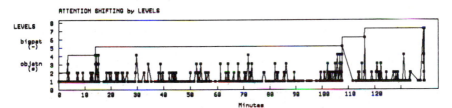

Figure 14.15 Depth of tree structure in each object selected during creation of Figure 14.9b.

along the cursor path). Other spatial dynamics are monitored in **vmacs**, such as the drag vectors for each move operation. *Grouping Structure:* The unmodified tree structure of the whole image reflects the temporal order in which objects were created. For example, Figure 14.15 shows the depth of tree structure (the little squares) in each object selected during the creation of Figure 14.9b. Remember that an object must be selected before it can be manipulated, so that selection behavior indicates where the operator was spending his manipulation time. Out of 464 selection acts made during the performance, atomic objects (level 1) were selected about 70% of the time. Simple patterns with only atomic members (level 2) were selected about 22% of the time; and patterns with simple patterns as members (level 3) 5% of the time. More complex patterns were targets for the remaining 3% of the selection acts.

11.3 *On What Can't Be Measured*

The part of a text-graphic performance most important may finally be the hardest to measure. Text-graphics for working groups is important at all because it is expressive of the group's task. Some of the expression takes place in the static image content, and is relatively easy to measure. And yet finally, to return to the initial characterization of the phenomenon of working group graphics, it is like a dance, and the most effective expressive quality may be the hardest to isolate scientifically: *the quality of movement of the text-graphics.*[9]   If each visual event is under full expressive control of the performer, then nuances of phrasing and timing may strike the audience very forcibly, but be very hard to measure. To algorithmically measure the full effect of a performance may be like trying to write a program to measure the effectiveness of a piece of music.

12 *Conclusion*

Manipulating text-graphics for working groups is a performing art similar to dance. To support such performances on a computer requires a performing medium.

Examining examples of non-computer text-graphics for groups gives a preliminary idea of the underlying phenomenon: the *performing* of text-graphic manipulation to assist working groups. Among key features of this kind of text-graphic manipulation are: *agility* (speed in creation, moving and modifying images); *generality* (freedom to create any kind of image at any time and place); *structure* (definable spatial patterns of text and graphics are often used); and *dynamics* (manipulation of text-graphics unfolding over time).

The **vmacs**™ graphics editor is a computer medium designed to provide these features. **vmacs** achieves *agility* through a touch-typing interface with no waiting for menus. The features of *generality* and *structure* are tied together. **vmacs** is basically a general purpose editor which can then be specialized to support manipulations of the specific spatial patterns found in particular applications. LISP-like processing of text-graphic objects is available for spatial parsing and interpretation according to formal schema. And finally, the *dynamics* of text-graphic manipulation for working groups are represented in **vmacs** by symbolic history lists, which allows live performances to be assisted by performance-administrator software modules, and also allows the recorded history

---

[9]   This point is directly due to conversations with Gayle Curtis and Margo Apostolos on robot ballet.

of a performance to be replayed, or analyzed according to various measurement algorithms.

Acknowledgments

The development of **vmacs** as a performing medium has profited from contributions by Harlyn Baker, John Baer, Gayle Curtis, Scott Kim, Larry Leifer, Mike Lowry, Paul Martin, Rob Myers, Alex Pentland, Fernando Pereira, Warren Robinett, Ted Selker, Stuart Shieber, Josh Singer, Dick Steele, Hans Uszkoreit, Mabry Tyson, and Machiel Van der Loos.

Appendix: On the Measurement of Working Group Graphics

What kind of measures can be made of **vmacs** performances, and why would we want to? Measurement of simple parameters of performance—like cursor position over time, results of selection attempts on visual objects, size of drawline marks made, distance objects were dragged, grouping structures created—are used in representing and teaching basic manipulation skills (Figures 14.14 and 14.15). Measures for more complex parameters are in working prototype stage. As an example, one program replays histories in order to search for occurrences of "drag-grouping"; the idea behind this measure is that simple conceptual groupings of visual objects can be inferred by finding spatial juxtaposition relations that the operator preserves during dragging.[10] Measures of drag-grouping use temporal and spatial patternings to discover how people are "thinking about" (in a primitive sense) the visual objects. Another approach to getting at underlying cognitive issues is the spatial parsing described in Section 10.1, which is a tool for looking at static spatial patternings during visual communication. Each of the visual languages analyzed is, in part, a set of rules used by humans for collecting a set of visual elements into conceptual groups—visual phrases—for interpretation in that language. And Visual Grammar Notation is a perspicuous way of representing those rules, with each grammar *visually* displaying the patterns of human spatial arrangement for a well-defined subset of visual communication activity.

---

[10] Of course, this is only when the human himself has *not* constructed explicit grouping structures in order to drag groups of objects as a unit.

One promising avenue for future work lies in examining the explicit creation of grouping structures for manipulation which are easy to measure in **vmacs**. For example, in Figure 14.9c we might try to find the relation between the manipulative groupings indicated by the tree networks and conceptual groupings (how people see the images together). Now these two kinds of grouping can't be *unrelated* (unless the operator is trying to trick us), but nor does it seem likely that the relation is one-to-one. Specifying exactly *how* they are related will take careful research.

But the measures described above only scratch the surface in examining working group graphics; this phenomenon seems to offer fundamental leverage for measuring cognitive behavior. In comparison with protocols taken from a single individual during a cognitive task, working group graphics is *explicit, synoptic* and *graphic*. The text-graphics on the group display are explicit and complete in that the group itself monitors to make sure nothing important is left off the display. And at the same time, there is neither room nor time to put up irrelevant material, so the group itself performs synopsis, distilling the salient points from their own verbalizing. In addition, working group graphics uses rich yet easy to process graphic devices of gross texture (line networks, spatial arrangements and juxtaposition, variation in text case) to show semantic connections among smaller text-graphic pieces.

However, the cognitive aspects of the current research are still in the fledgling stage, unable to do much with all this leverage. The display of concept development on **vmacs** may be so rich yet so easy to measure, but the phenomenon of interest seems just out of reach. During the performance, we can see the text-graphics shifting and measure their coursings precisely, so what does that tell us about the coursing of ideas?

Assuming progress can be made on these problems, then in the future perhaps heuristics about text-graphic patternings during concept development can be discovered which could be used by assistive software modules. Under the guidance of such performance-administrators, the group's text-graphic medium might finally become a "rational external device." A. R. Luria coined this term to describe a card system he deigned to help a brain-damaged soldier tell a story. The problem was not unlike one often faced by working groups: when telling a story orally, the patient could either generate the pieces or order them, but he couldn't do both. "Replacement of the defective internal schemes by a system of rational external aids provided a practical means of overcoming the patient's defect ... " [Luria66].

References

Arnheim69 Arnheim, Rudolph, *Visual Thinking*, University of California Press, 1969.

Ball71 Ball, Geoffry H., and Gilkey, James Y., "Facilitation and Explicit Group Memory—Their Application in Education," SRI International IR&D No. 183531-409, Menlo Park, CA, Dec 1971.

Brunon71 Brunon, Joseph, "Group Dynamics and Visual Thinking," Journal of Architectural Education, No. 3, 1971.

Doyle76 Doyle, Michael, and Straus, David, *How to Make Meetings Work*, Wyden Books, 1976.

Engelbart62 Engelbart, D. C., *Augmenting Human Intellect: A Conceptual Framework*, SRI International, Menlo Park, CA, Oct 1962.

Engelbart85 Engelbart, D. C., remark made in keynote address at SIGCHI85, San Francisco, CA, April 1985.

English67 English, W. K., Engelbart, D. C., and Berman, M. L., "Display-Selection Techniques for Text Manipulation," IEEE Trans. on Human Factors in Electronics, Vol. HFE-8, No. 1, March 1967.

Haeberli86 Haeberli, Paul, "A Data-Flow Manager for an Interactive Programming Environment," USENIX Summer Proceedings, 1986.

Jacob73 Jacob, Heiner, *Team Teaching*, unpublished manuscript, 107 Carroll Place, New Brunswick, New Jersey 08901, 1973.

Lakin74 Lakin, Fred, facilitation at the U.S. Geological Survey, Menlo Park, CA, May 3, 1974.

Lakin80a Lakin, Fred, "A Structure from Manipulation for Text-Graphic Objects," published in the proceedings of SIGGRAPH '80, Seattle, WA, July 1980.

Lakin80b Lakin, Fred, "Diagramming a Project on the Electric Blackboard," video tape for SIGGRAPH '80, July 1980.

Lakin80c Lakin, Fred, "Computing with Text-Graphic Forms," published in the proceedings of the LISP Conference at Stanford University, August 1980.

Lakin83 Lakin, Fred, "Measuring Text-Graphics Activity," published in the proceedings of GRAPHICS INTERFACE '83, Edmonton, Alberta, May 1983.

Lakin87   Lakin, Fred, "Spatial Parsing for Visual Languages," to appear in *Visual Languages*, edited by Shi-Kuo Chang, Plenum Press, New York, NY, Spring 1987.

Luria66   Luria, A. R., *Human Brain and Psychological Processes*. New York, Harper & Row, 1966.

McKim72   McKim, Robert H., *Experiences in Visual Thinking*, Wadsworth Publishing Co., Inc., Belmont, CA, 1972.

Porter74   Porter, Elias H., and Verger, Morris D., "Interactive Planning System," unpublished manuscript, Los Angeles, CA, 1974.

Sibbet76   Sibbet, David, "Introduction to Group Graphics," The Correspondent, CORO Foundation Northern California Public Affairs Quarterly, Summer 1976.

Sibbet84   Sibbet, David, facilitation at Stanford University, March 9, 1984.

Stallman81   Stallman, Richard, "EMACS, the Extensible, Customizable Self-Documenting Display Editor," MIT AI Memo 519a, March 1981.

TAB62   TAB Engineers, Inc., "Training Course in Panoramic Design," reprinted from METALFAX Magazine for April 1962.

Weston73   Weston, J. R., and Kristen, C., *Teleconferencing: A Comparison of Attitudes, Uncertainty and Interpersonal Atmospheres in Mediated and Face-to-Face Group Interaction*, prepared for the Social Policy and Programs Branch, the Dept. of Communications, Ottawa, Canada, December 1973.

15

Computer-based Real-Time Conferencing Systems

Sunil Sarin
Computer Corporation of America
Cambridge, MA

Irene Greif
MIT
Cambridge, MA

Computer support for group work, including electronic mail, computer conferencing [1], form management [2], and coordination support [3,4] primarily addresses *asynchronous* interaction among users. These systems are most useful when each user can work at times of his own choosing. However, although relatively little work has been done on computer support for people working together simultaneously, for certain group tasks, such as crisis handling, simultaneous (or *real-time*) interaction is essential. In a *real-time conference*, for example, each participant can be seated in his own office at a workstation that might include a high-resolution screen for computer output, a keyboard and a pointing device, a microphone and a speaker, and possibly a camera and video monitor. Parts of each participant's screen can be dedicated to displaying a *shared space* in which everyone sees the same information. The voice communication equipment can be used by the conference participants for discussion and negotiation; video communication can add an illusion of physical presence by simulating a face-to-face meeting; and conversational references ("this number" or "that sentence") can be clarified by pointing at displayed information. The displayed information can be dynamically edited and processed, permanent records can be saved, and new information that is relevant to the discussion can be retrieved for display at any time. Participants can, in addition, have *private spaces* on their screens that allow them to view relevant private data or to compose and review information before submitting it to the shared space.

Systems that provide some of the above features already exist. As early as 1968, the NLS system [5] provided a *shared-screen mode* for simultaneous collaborative authoring of structured documents. This facility, which can be used to access any interactive program from multiple terminals, is now available in many time-shared operating systems in the form of *terminal linking*. Terminal linking on most systems does not work correctly unless all linked terminals are of the same type. A notable exception to this is Tymshare's Augment [6] system (the commercial successor to NLS), which supports "virtual" terminal linking across dissimilar terminal types.

Real-time conferencing can be used to support joint work in many different applications. For example: (1) A fairly common use of terminal linking is joint debugging of programs from remote terminals, often accompanied by a telephone conversation. (2) The Balsa algorithm animation system at Brown University [7] supports programming tutorials and demonstrations. (3) Bell Laboratories' TOPES system, which supports the design and engineering analysis of complex building plans, has a *graphics teleconferencing* feature [8] that allows a group of engineers to hold a design meeting on-line while conducting a conversation over the phone.

Real-time-conferencing software is also beginning to appear on the personal-computer market. At the American Society of Civil Engineers Annual Conference in October 1982, Structural Programming, Inc., demonstrated a teleconferencing enhancement to its Palette computer-aided drafting system. This feature allows two users at personal computers connected by a telephone line to edit the same design-drawing jointly by making use of independent cursors that are visible to both users. At the Federal Computer Conference in September 1984, Teneron Corp. demonstrated the Tango-writer Interactive Word Processor, which allows a telephone link between two PCs to be switched alternately between voice communication and data communication, the latter allowing either user to edit a document while the other user watches.

Each of the above systems was built on an *ad hoc* basis to meet a particular need. Our research into real-time conferencing [9] identified general principles underlying the design and implementation of real-time conferences, which are summarized in this article.

Other Conferencing Media

For people who have already established a working relationship and who use shared, on-line information as an integral component of their work, a real-time conference is an ideal way of holding a problem-solving meeting. The emphasis in the kind of real-time conference we describe is somewhat different from *teleconferencing* that uses video communication to provide some simulation of face-to-face contact among participants. [10] Video teleconferencing is valuable when nonverbal communication, in the form of gestures and facial expressions, is an important part of the discussion and negotiation that takes place. Video communication may be a useful enhancement to the kinds of real-time conferences we are describing, but is less critical than voice communication and the ability to share information and software.

Computer-based information-sharing tools have an advantage over informational aids typically included in teleconferencing systems, such as *facsimile transmission* and *telewriting* (which transmits hand-drawn sketches in highly compressed form): Such aids do not allow information that originated from one location to be modified by participants at other locations. *Electronic blackboards* do allow joint manipulation of a shared image, but are subject to the same limitations as a physical blackboard. That is, the only manipulations possible on a real or simulated blackboard are writing, drawing, and erasing; It is not possible to move and rearrange text or the components of a drawing easily, or to change an entry in a spreadsheet and have the totals automatically recomputed, or to run a complex simulation model in order to evaluate a proposed plan. Furthermore, the only information that can be shared by means of these aids at a face-to-face meeting or a teleconference is that which was brought to the meeting or composed during the meeting. Participants cannot access the increasing multitude of private, corporate, and public databases to satisfy unanticipated information needs. The participants' ability to access and manipulate information dynamically by making use of powerful computer-based tools is the distinguishing characteristic of the real-time conferences we discuss in this article. (It should be noted that the ability to access information for which one had not foreseen a need, as well as the ability to process and analyze information, also makes the computer useful for meetings held within a single room.)

Two Prototype Systems

This section describes two prototype real-time conferencing systems, developed at the MIT Laboratory for Computer Science, that illustrate two ends of the spectrum of possible implementation strategies. With either system, voice communication must be set up by outside means, such as the telephone system.

Real-time Meeting Scheduling

The first prototype, RTCAL, supports meeting scheduling by building a shared workspace of information from participants' on-line calendars. RTCAL provides users with information and tools for decision support; it does not automate the selection of a meeting time. We chose meeting scheduling as an application area partly because many users on our system used the personal calendar system PCAL [11] to maintain on-line calendars. This gave RTCAL a realistic database from which to read relevant calendar information, and in which to record decisions made during a conference. The salient features of RTCAL, which are illustrated in Figures 15.1 and 15.2, are

- *Shared and private spaces.* Shared spaces (such as the shared calendar window and the summary window in Figure 15.1) present information that is visible to all participants, while the private calendar window presents appointment details visible only to the individual participants.

- *Alignment of related information.* Whenever the shared-calendar window is scrolled, the private window is also scrolled so that the two always show the same date and time range side by side. The participant can thus always see relevant private details about his own appointments for the date and time range that is visible in the shared space.

- *Voting.* Voting on-line is more efficient than voting in a voice-only conference (where each participant must be polled in turn) because participants can vote in parallel (and are not influenced by each other's votes). When a meeting time is proposed, each participant is prompted and asked to vote yes or no. Votes are collected and tabulated on the shared display (as shown in Figure 15.2) until all participants have voted. If some participants take a very long time to vote, the chairperson can "time out" the voting procedure and allow the conference to continue. The vote status of proposals (alternative proposals are allowed) can be examined later, in which case a participant's vote that arrived late will be reflected in the display.

- *Participant autonomy.* A participant is free to leave a conference at any time and to return when he pleases; when he notifies the system of his return, his display of the shared space is automatically brought up to date. A participant can choose to ignore the decision of the group as to the committed meeting time and not have the committed time entered into his private calendar. Further autonomy in manipulating the private space could have been provided (but was not implemented), by giving participants the option to scroll the private windows at any time to dates and time ranges independent of the shared window and to return to automatic alignment of the windows.

- *Separation of application and conference-control commands.* Calendar-specific commands (such as scrolling the shared window and proposing or committing a meeting time), are "echoed" in every participant's command window as typed, and only one participant at a time (the *controller*) can enter such commands. A separate set of control commands, invoked by typing a special character (CTRL-↑, as shown in the informational window), is used for conference-specific actions such as requesting and passing control, and leaving and terminating the conference. A participant may enter a control command at any time.

- *Conference roles.* The *chairperson* oversees all activity in the conference. He determines who has control (permission to enter calendar commands) at any given time, and is the only participant who can terminate the conference. The other participants have power only when they are given control of the shared space by the chairperson, who may take it away.

- *Presentation of status information.* A small summary window indicates what the conference is about, which participants are present (and which were invited and are unavailable or have not yet responded), who the chairperson is, and who currently has control. In addition, a one-line events window displays important changes in status, such as when a participant is leaving or joining or the passing of control.

RTCAL supports a specific application activity in a real-time conference. The next prototype system is an example of a generic facility, albeit a limited one, that can be used for multiple applications.

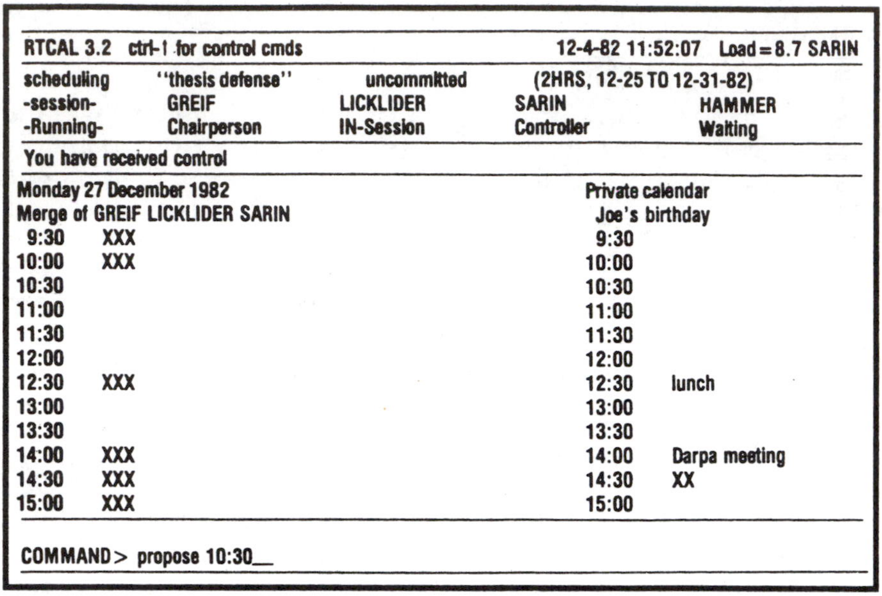

RTCAL 3.2 ctrl-1 for control cmds			12-4-82 11:52:07 Load = 8.7 SARIN	
scheduling -session- -Running-	"thesis defense" GREIF Chairperson	uncommitted LICKLIDER IN-Session	(2HRS, 12-25 TO 12-31-82) SARIN Controller	HAMMER Waiting
You have received control				
Monday 27 December 1982			Private calendar	
Merge of GREIF LICKLIDER SARIN			Joe's birthday	
9:30	XXX		9:30	
10:00	XXX		10:00	
10:30			10:30	
11:00			11:00	
11:30			11:30	
12:00			12:00	
12:30	XXX		12:30	lunch
13:00			13:00	
13:30			13:30	
14:00	XXX		14:00	Darpa meeting
14:30	XXX		14:30	XX
15:00	XXX		15:00	
COMMAND> propose 10:30__				

Figure 15.1   An RTCAL display screen for a participant in a real-time conference. The following windows are shown (from top to bottom): the informational window; the summary window; the events window; the main calendar windows, shared (left) and private (right); and the command window.

Shared Bit-Map System

Our shared bit-map system, *MBlink*, extends an existing experimental protocol, *Blink*,[1] which supports remote bit-mapped graphics output from a host to a workstation and graphical input from the workstation's pointing device (a mouse). MBlink allows a given bit map to be displayed identically on multiple workstations rather than just one. In addition, MBlink can track every workstation's mouse and show its position on the shared bit map, thus allowing participants in a real-time conference to point at information under discussion.

MBlink, like Blink, is implemented with the application program running on a DEC VAX mainframe and with the participants viewing a shared bit map on Xerox Palo Alto workstations; the machines are connected by local area networks and gateways with the DoD Internet Protocol. The shared bit map is implemented on the mainframe as an

---

[1]   Designed by David Reed at MIT.

```
RTCAL 3.2   ctrl-↑ for control cmds                    12-4-82 11:53:21   Load = 8.8 SARIN

scheduling      "thesis defense"      uncommitted     (2HRS, 12-25 TO 12-31-82)
-session-       GREIF                 LICKLIDER       SARIN              HAMMER
-Voting-        Chairperson           IN-Session      Controller         Waiting

12-27-82 10:30am-12:30pm PROPOSED

Monday 27 December 1982                         Private calendar
Prop#1: 12-27-82 10:30am-12:30pm                  Joe's birthday
  GREIF:   N   LICKLIDER:   -                   9:30
  SARIN:   Y   HAMMER:      -                   10:00
                                                10:30
                                                11:00
                                                11:30
                                                12:00
                                                12:30     lunch
                                                13:00
                                                13:30
                                                14:00     Darpa meeting
                                                No conflicts, 10:30am-12:30pm
                                                Accept proposal?   y_

No participant conflicts
COMMAND > propose 10:30
```

Figure 15.2 Voting on a proposal in RTCAL.

abstract-data-type module that is linked to an application program. The application program manipulates the bit map as if it were the bit map of a memory-mapped screen; in other words, the program can read and write arbitrary pixels or regions, perform "RasterOps" (bit-wise Boolean operations) on rectangles, and so on. The shared bit-map module transmits bit-map changes to the remote workstations on which the bit map is actually displayed.

Each workstation reports the position of its mouse and the state (up or down) of the buttons on the mouse to the bit-map module on the mainframe. Each workstation is assigned a 16×16-pixel pointer "shape" (bit pattern) that is superimposed on the bit map at the reported mouse position. Each participant can thus see on his workstation screen the position of every participant's mouse. In addition, the hardware at each workstation tracks its own mouse and displays a distinguishing pattern on the screen; each participant can therefore easily see the location of his own mouse. A participant actually sees two cursors showing his own mouse position, one "locally tracked" by his workstation's hardware and the other remotely tracked, or "echoed," by the mainframe.

When the mouse is moving, the remote echo lags behind the locally tracked position by about half a second; when the mouse stops moving, the participants can judge approximately when the other workstations will catch up and can see his pointer at the correct position.

The shared bit-map module provides procedure calls for adding and removing workstations to and from a conference in which a given bit map is shared. In addition, the application program can synchronize the module with the workstations, regaining control when all workstations are known to have received all bit map updates or when a specified time-out period has expired. This can be useful if, for example, the application program must display an important prompt before reading input. The application program can at any time check the status of any workstation in order to determine whether it is displaying the bit map (a workstation that was added may never have responded) and, if it is, whether the workstation's bit map display is up to date.

To demonstrate MBlink, we took an existing single-user application program[2] and linked it with the MBlink version of the bit-map module in place of the Blink version. This application program uses the bit map to present a graphical view of an internetwork being simulated, together with dynamically updated information describing the state (for example, the packet queue lengths) of the hosts, networks, and gateways. About a dozen lines of code were added to the application program's command input loop to allow workstations to be added to and removed from the conference; this was the only change to the existing application code.

Conference Design Issues

Our model of a real-time conference is that participants are interested in manipulating some collection of abstract *objects* of various types (for instance, a collection of electronic circuit designs, or documents, or spreadsheets) that is relevant to the problem they wish to solve. Some kind of *editor* may be provided for displaying and modifying the state of an object, and various application tools (such as circuit simulators and spelling correctors) may be invoked to analyze and process the objects in some useful way. This abstract model readily extends to multimedia conferencing systems in that either a shared voice channel or video image can be treated as an abstract object that supports an interface peculiar to its object type. The design principles that we have formulated suggest ways of making such objects accessible to conference participants.

---

[2] The application program, written by Lixia Zhang of MIT, is used for experimenting with different internetwork congestion-control algorithms.

User Interface

Many contemporary interactive systems emphasize the principle of *uniformity* across multiple applications: Similar commands do similar things, so the number of commands a user must learn for a new application is minimized. For real-time conferencing, this principle can be extended in two important ways:

- Real-time conferencing systems developed for different applications should have similar commands for conference control.

- When participants wish to view or modify an application object, this should be accomplished with commands similar to those available when working alone.

Achieving the above objectives will depend largely on having reusable software, both for applications and for conference control. Modern trends in software engineering, such as *object-oriented programming*, which allows new information types to be defined as incremental extensions of existing types, and user interface *toolkits*, which allow construction of uniform interfaces to different applications, are likely to be useful in developing such software.

Shared Versus Individual Views

If all participants in a real-time conference have identical views of shared information, they can make conversational references to the data with the assurance of being understood, just as if they were viewing a common blackboard in a face-to-face meeting. There are occasions, however, when participants with different interests and viewpoints (or with different display capabilities on their workstations) may wish to see the same data presented in different ways. Conversational references can be more difficult to interpret in this case, but need not be if there is sufficient similarity between the different participants' views (for example, if the same text is formatted differently) and if the references are made in logical terms (for example, one could refer to "the second sentence of the first paragraph") rather than in terms of the displayed view.

When participants do wish to see identical views of the shared space, it is important to allow some variation in the individual views so that each participant knows which displayed objects have special meaning to him and not to the others. In MBlink, for example, each participant can not only distinguish the different participants' cursors, but can also tell which is his own. Similarly, messages about important changes of status should be specially tailored to the participant that they pertain to. When participant Smith is given the floor in RTCAL, the other participants see the message "Smith has received control," but Smith himself sees "YOU have received control."

In some situations, conference participants may want to view different parts of a large shared space, such as different documents or drawings, or different sections of a large document. Since conversational references are ineffective when participants are looking at different parts of the shared space, it is useful for participants to know who is looking at what part of the shared space. Participants can then choose whether to align their views or to allow them to diverge; they can also tell when others are looking at the same data and will understand conversational references to the data.

Access Control

It is convenient to think of a real-time conference as an abstract object that contains other objects, which the conference participants will work on. Existing access control techniques can then be applied to specify which users will be allowed to participate in a conference. Such a specification will typically take the form of a short "access control list" of user names, which may in certain cases include the names of user "groups," or even allow any user ("the public") to join. A possibly useful extension, not available with most object-access-control schemes, is to allow users to find out about a conference, but to be given permission only to submit requests to join. Such requests are approved or denied by a participant who is authorized to do so. A conference should permit new participants to join at any time (and join in as many times as) they wish, although in certain circumstances a conference may be permanently or temporarily closed to new participants.

A participant can leave a conference at any time. A conference can be terminated by a command from an authorized participant (in RT-CAL, this participant is the chairperson). In real life, meetings do not end so abruptly, and it is desirable to permit a smoother phasing out. A few participants may wish to linger and hold follow-up discussions, or some participant may wish to review and possibly edit the "minutes" of the conference before committing them to permanent storage. In general, unless revocation of access to the conference seems necessary, a conference should not terminate until all participants leave of their own accord.

Within a conference, it is possible to give different participants different access rights to objects in the shared space, tailoring these rights to match their "roles" (such as moderator or note-taker) in the conference. However, participants in a real-time conference change roles quite frequently, and complex access controls may be a hindrance. It will usually be better to give all participants equal power to read and update shared data. At most, it may be useful to designate one participant as chairperson, as is done in RTCAL. There may also be conferences in which update permission is restricted to one or a few participants, with the other participants acting only as observers.

Concurrency Control

If more than one participant has permission to update the shared space, problems may arise if participants concurrently enter update commands. This has been observed in terminal linking (in which characters typed concurrently by the participants are interleaved arbitrarily, probably in order of arrival at some process in the system).

The problem with interleaving of commands (or characters typed) is that the effect of a given command may be different from what the participant expected because some other participant's concurrent command may have been processed between the time that this participant entered his command and the time that the system executed it. This can be avoided by using a floor-passing strategy, such as RTCAL's, which allows only one participant at a time to update the shared space. Floor-passing can be generalized by having participants set *reservations* on different parts of the shared space. This will allow participants to work concurrently on different documents or on different sections of a document; in a multimedia conference, one participant may be speaking while another is working on shared data. Two key issues that must be addressed are the granularity at which reservations are set on the shared space, and the policy (automatic or manual, for instance) for passing a reservation from one participant to another.

Participants may find it a burden to request and release reservations explicitly, especially if reservations must be set on many small subparts of the shared space. Participants might instead wish to dispense with reservations altogether and informally negotiate (perhaps using voice communication) who should work in the shared space and when. Such negotiation will not always work perfectly, and we can expect that interference caused by conflicting concurrent commands will occasionally happen. However, if all participants are looking at the same displayed information, they are likely to notice when interference does happen and take action to recover from it. The extent to which this approach is workable is yet to be determined; it may be quite reasonable with two or three participants. With a large number of participants, the voice channel itself becomes an object of contention, making it less likely that voice negotiation will successfully prevent concurrent interference.

Getting Data In and Out

A real-time conference does not exist in isolation. Participants typically access information that had an independent existence prior to the conference and generate information that will continue to exist after the conference. The data being read in or written out may have significance to users other than the actual participants in the conference. For example, some other user may have prepared a draft design or position statement but be unable to attend, or a follow-up task assignment may need to be communicated to a user who was not present at the conference. Such transfer of information into and out of the conference raises some new access-control questions that do not arise when an individual user is reading and updating shared information:

- Whose access rights are checked before allowing an object, such as a file, to be read into the shared space and displayed? Is it sufficient for the participant invoking the read operation to have read access, even if some of the others do not?

- When data from the shared space is written to a file, is it sufficient for the invoking participant to have write access to the file or must every participant have write access? What if the writing of the file was not explicitly invoked by any participant but was automatically activated by the system, as is the case with periodic "auto-saving" of an edited file; whose access rights must be checked in order for such write operations to be approved by the file system?

- When a new file, or new version of a file, is successfully written from the conference shared space, who gets permission to access the file in the future? Who "owns" the file? (That is, who has the ability to grant and possibly revoke access permissions in the future?) Should the file somehow be "jointly owned" by the participants who contributed to its content, rather than individually owned by the participant (if there was one) who happened to invoke the command to write the file?

The answers to these questions will vary from one user community to the next, and will also depend on the ability of the underlying operating system to perform sophisticated access checking for groups of users.

Constraints on Real-Time Conference Design

The extent to which the desired functionality can be achieved in a real-time conference depends on the available hardware and software (the workstation, communication network, and operating systems). Thus, it will not be feasible to display high-resolution bit-mapped images if participants only have alphanumeric terminals. (Even when participants can display bit-mapped images, transmission may take too long if the available communication channel is an ordinary telephone line, as opposed to a local area network or a satellite.) Communication and processing delays may influence the choice of concurrency control policy. Existing operating-system facilities may also constrain access-control policies.

We expect that at least for the immediate future, each real-time conferencing system will be tailored to a particular communication environment and class of workstations. If a flexible system that can adapt itself to different kinds of equipment is desired, the designer will have to consider the possibility of participants in the same conference having workstations with widely differing capabilities or workstations that are connected by communication lines of different delay and bandwidth. In such a situation, the following choices are available:

- All participants' interfaces could be degraded to the "least common denominator" supported by all workstations.

- A minimum requirement could be established, and only workstations that meet the requirement be allowed to participate.

- Sophisticated features could be exploited at the more powerful workstations only, at the expense of no longer having a common, shared image on all participants' displays.

How these decisions should be made (by a chairperson, by voting, or automatically by the system), and how they affect the quality of a conference, remains to be seen.

The number of participants in a conference influences the nature of the interaction among participants and also constrains the achievable functionality because of the communication and processing load that is imposed. A given real-time conferencing system will probably have to be tailored to a given range of conference sizes; within this range, it might provide special support based on the actual conference size (for example, it might be equipped for changing its "mode" when a third participant is added to a two-person conference).

Software Organization

We next turn to the practical problem of realizing some of the above conferencing functions in a real system. We assume a *logically distributed* system consisting of a collection of interconnected *nodes*. Nodes do not share memory; they communicate by message-passing only. A node will typically be a host on a network, but could be a process on a time-shared host. Each participant in a real-time conference is represented by a node called a *workstation*. Other nodes might be involved in a conference to provide services such as user name look-up or permanent storage.

Sharing Existing Programs

If participants already have a particular application program (say, a document editor or a circuit simulator) that they use as part of their work, they will be most comfortable using the same program during real-time conferences. Then the only learning overhead is that of mastering a few simple commands for conference control. Given that existing application programs typically interact with a single user's terminal via an input-and-output character stream, such programs can be shared without modification in a real-time conference as follows:

- Instead of interacting directly with a user's terminal, the program interacts via a *virtual terminal* channel with a *controller* node (or process) that reads the output of the program and sends input to the program.

- The controller node communicates with the participants' workstations and multiplexes the program's input and output in such a way as to realize the functionality desired in the conference. That is, output from the program can be sent by the controller to every workstation, and the controller can selectively feed input from the workstations to the program, based on which workstation has the floor.

This *virtual terminal approach*, illustrated in Figure 15.3(a), has several advantages: Constructing the controller program is not difficult or time-consuming, and once the controller code is available, other programs can be connected up in a real-time conference. It is also possible to share more than one program by making use of multiple windows, and individual participants can run private programs in separate windows on their workstation screens. Other

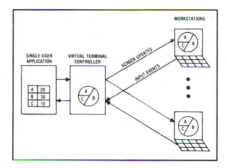

Figure 15.3(a)   When participants share a single-user application program, each participant's workstation holds only a screen image of the application data; it does not have access to the application objects.

convenience features can also be provided, such as copying of output from one window to be fed as input into any window, and recording of input and output "scripts," which can be replayed or reviewed.

When using the virtual terminal approach, it is necessary to choose a virtual terminal protocol that the controller will support and that the application program and workstations must adhere to. Many kinds of virtual terminal protocols are available, such as

- alphanumeric screen protocols that allow positioning of the cursor at arbitrary locations and selective erasing of parts of the screen, and

- graphics terminal protocols (such as Stanford's VGTP [12]) that allow drawing lines and arcs, filling regions that have specified patterns, and various operations (and, exclusive-or, and so on) on rectangular subsets of the screen bit map.

Because application programs that do not follow the chosen protocol will not be accessible during a real-time conference, the protocol used by the conference controller should be chosen based on the terminal functions used by existing programs. Workstations that can interact directly with an application program by making use of the given protocol will then be able to access the same program through the conference controller as well.

While sharing existing programs has the virtues of simplicity and low cost (of implementation and of user training), this is offset by the following limitations in functionality that arise because the application program is designed for interaction with a single, fixed user:

- Multiple concurrent contexts (such as editing cursors) in the same shared space cannot be supported.

- Private views of shared information cannot be supported. (Private windows into separate application programs can be supported, but that is not the same thing.)

- Transfer of application information between shared and private windows can be done only at a very low level. The shared space consists of arrays of characters or bits, which a receiving program may not be able to parse.

- Participants cannot be given different access privileges or environments for resolving filenames. All operations executed by the shared program will be based on the privileges and naming environment of a specified user (the chairperson, say), which will in general be different from those of the other participants. Thus a participant may attempt to read or write a file that he normally has access to, only to fail because the chairperson does not have the required access. Or, a participant may inadvertently write a file into the chairperson's directory rather than his own.

A variant of the virtual terminal approach that has slightly different characteristics but shares many of the same limitations is the sharing of terminal input rather than output. Each participant's workstation runs an identical instance of the program, and identical input (from whichever participant has the floor) is sent to all workstations for processing by the program. Sending program input, rather than the output generated by a single program instance, can save considerable transmission bandwidth. This approach, which is used in Brown University's Balsa system [7], is useful when the workstations can run the program in parallel; it is wasteful and slow if the workstations share a processor on a host machine. Some care is needed to ensure that the program instances on the workstations actually do the same thing when presented with identical input. This will entail some modifications to the application code to trap commands that interact with the program's environment, such as the command to write a file. Such commands should usually be executed by one workstation (the one that issued the command) rather than by all in order to avoid anomalous results.

Multiuser Applications

The alternative to using existing single-user programs is to write new application programs that can interact with multiple users simultaneously. What distinguishes a multiuser application program from a single-user application program is that it explicitly takes into account the identity of different participants in a conference. The use of multiple editing cursors on shared data can be supported, and shared application data (such as a structured document with sections and paragraphs) can have associated ownership and access information that determines who can perform what operations. This access information can be derived from the access controls on external data objects that were brought into the conference.

In this approach, a participant's workstation (which may be a process on a host machine, if the participant has an ordinary terminal) is supplied with high-level application information rather than a screen image so that it can provide the participant with whatever view of the shared space he desires; this is illustrated in Figure 15.3(b). This approach requires defining a protocol for application-level communication between the controller and workstations in a conference. Different applications require different application-level protocols, so this approach has some cost (relative to the virtual terminal approach) in that each new conferencing application may require significant programming effort to construct. This was one of the limitations of the RTCAL implementation. As more experience with different applications is gained, it should be possible to factor out software for common functions (such as conference initiation, floor-passing, and voting) into a conferencing toolkit that can be used in multiple applications. The cost of implementing the toolkit will be incurred only once: The code for each new conferencing application will only have to implement application-specific data types and operations, and interface them with the toolkit functions.

Improving Response Time

A multiuser application program with a centralized architecture (such as that shown in Figure 15.3(b)) suffers from the same performance limitation found in virtual-terminal systems: A command issued by a participant must undergo two message-transmission delays (from the originating workstation to the controller, and then from the controller to the workstations) before its effects can be displayed on participants' screens. This delay can sometimes be reduced to the time required for a single message transmission by permitting direct communication of application commands between workstations. Some care must be taken to ensure that if commands issued concurrently by two or more workstations arrive at different workstations in different orders, the receiving workstations' copies of

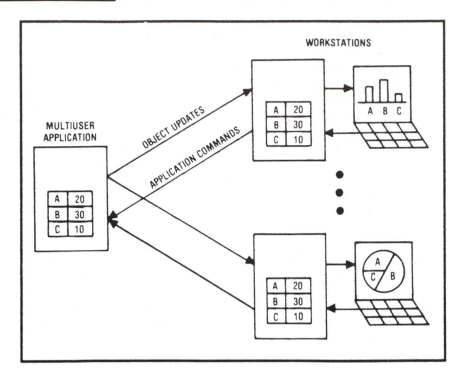

Figure 15.3(b)   When a multiuser application program is used, a participant's workstation holds copies of application objects and derives the screen image locally.

shared data do not become inconsistent. We have identified two main approaches to ensuring this:

1.   At any given time, one workstation is the sole source of update commands to a given object or collection of objects in the shared space. This workstation (the *controller* for the given object or objects) can transmit commands directly to the other workstations, and the workstations (including the controller) can process commands immediately with no danger of inconsistency. Control of a given part of the shared space can be passed dynamically from one workstation to another by a resynchronization protocol that ensures that all workstations have processed all commands from the first workstation before they begin receiving commands from the second workstation. A few special objects, such as a participant's pointer position, can be updated only by a specific workstation; no passing of control and resynchronization is needed for these.

2. Any workstation can issue an update command to any object at any time by transmitting the command directly to all work stations. A workstation receiving a command (including one issued by itself) executes it immediately in a *reversible* way (one that allows its effects to be undone). Some synchronization mechanism, either a central sequencer or timestamps, is used to define the correct order in which commands from different workstations should be processed. A workstation that received and processed conflicting commands in other than the defined order will undo their effects and reexecute the commands in the correct order. Thus, while workstations may temporarily hold (and display) inconsistent copies of data, such inconsistencies are quickly rectified.

While passing control of an object among workstations is very similar to passing reservations among participants, the idea can be applied independently at the system level and the user interface level. That is, either of the above methods can be used within the system, whether or not participants use reservations for concurrency control.

The first approach would appear to be simpler to implement, especially if one workstation at a time controls the entire shared space. However, each change of control involves the exchange of a large number of messages and a delay of at least the time it takes to transmit two messages. If the activity in the conference is such that the same participant performs many commands in a row, then this overhead will have minimal impact because (1) changes of control will be infrequent, and (2) once a given workstation gains control, each subsequent command will be processed after one message transmission delay. However, if control must be passed frequently, the overhead will be significant and will probably cause response time to increase as the conference goes on.

The second approach never requires any resynchronization, and every command is processed after undergoing one message-transmission delay. While undoing and reexecuting commands may seem complicated, many modern interactive programs already have this capability. This technique does affect the user interface in that a participant may see inconsistent states that no other participant sees and that could not have occurred if command execution were delayed until the correct order were known. The application designers must consider whether temporarily inconsistent states are an acceptable price to pay for the improved response time. For simple editing and display commands, users may well find it acceptable to see inconsistent states if the inconsistency is quickly corrected (which it is) and if this happens infrequently. The frequency with which participants issue concurrent conflicting commands can be minimized if participants negotiate externally by voice or use reservations on objects in the shared space.

Implementation Protocols

Initiation and Negotiation

In order for users to participate in a real-time conference, their workstations must be able to establish appropriate network connections with the conference controller node. Establishing a connection requires that either party be able to determine the network address of the other, which may be done by accessing a name server or conference registration server. Conference architectures in which all workstations communicate directly with each other will require that more network connections be set up. A workstation need only determine the address of any other workstation, from which it can then obtain the addresses of the other workstations in order to establish its connections.

For a given real-time conference, some collection of *parameters* that governs the communication and user interfaces will need to be determined. Examples of such parameters are the size of the virtual terminal screen or windows, the maximum data-transmission rate, and whether particular response time optimizations will be used. This can be done by *negotiation* among the controller and the workstations: the controller proposes a set of parameter values and then makes a selection based on the replies received from the workstations. Such negotiations can be performed at any time in a conference.

Message Transport

We assume that the abstract operations and arguments that the workstations exchange can be encoded in linear messages suitable for communication over a network, and that these messages can be decoded at the receiving end. (In RTCAL, we used M. Herlihy's algorithm for transmitting abstract data values [13], which saved considerable programming effort by relieving us of the need to deal with low-level encodings.) The messages themselves can be transmitted over a *virtual circuit* that masks communication errors in order to provide reliable, sequenced delivery. For certain types of messages, such reliable sequencing is not really needed; for these, the application can make use of *datagram communication*, which is less reliable but gets new messages delivered faster because they are not held up by earlier messages awaiting retransmission. Datagram communication is used in packet voice communication, and may be useful for transmitting certain special kinds of information in a conference, such as the position of a participant's pointer. Updates to such information can be sent in "absolute" form (for example, one can send the actual coordinates of the pointer rather than an offset from the previous value) so that they do not depend on previous updates. There is no need for such updates to be acknowledged or retransmitted because new ones will be issued very quickly. Sequence numbers or timestamps can be used to ensure that delayed or duplicated old updates are correctly discarded by the receiver. (This method was used in MBlink, based on David Reed's original Blink protocol.)

The number of connections that must be established in a conference with N workstations will depend on the communication architecture being used. If all communication goes through a central controller, the number of virtual circuits needed is linear ($N - 1$, assuming the controller is itself a workstation) and depends on the number of workstations. If workstations need to communicate directly, however, the number of virtual circuits, $N*(N - 1)/2$, grows as the square of the number of nodes. While we have argued that direct workstation-to-workstation communication can be useful in improving response time, it may instead have a detrimental effect on response time if the overhead of a large number of virtual circuits causes the message transmission delay to increase; this may well happen for large values of N, say greater than four or five.

For large conferences, an alternative to having a large number of virtual circuits is to exploit *multicast communication*, on networks (such as Ethernet, token-ring, token-bus, and satellite) that allow a single transmitted packet to be received by all or a specified subset of the machines they serve. This will not be useful when the workstations are scattered among different networks in an internetwork. This may be remedied in the future, as evidenced by recent proposals [14], and at least one operational protocol [15], for multicast across multiple interconnected networks.

Because of the unreliability of transmission, multicast datagrams are useful mainly for special kinds of data, such as voice or pointers. For other kinds of data, real-time conferences need reliable, sequenced delivery, which should be provided by a transport-level protocol that builds on any network-level multicast datagram service that is available. Currently, no general-purpose, reliable multicast transport protocols are available that application programs can use with the same ease as virtual circuit protocols. Until such protocols are defined, real-time conferencing applications will either have to use multiple virtual circuits, or use unreliable multicast datagrams and implement an acknowledgment and retransmission scheme that is tailored to their needs.

Integrating Data and Voice

The real-time conferencing systems we have mentioned are meant to be used in multimedia conferences that include voice communication as well as on-line data communication. Since these systems (including ours) actually implement only the on-line data component of such a multimedia conference, voice communication must be established by a separate mechanism.

Given that voice conferencing can be implemented on a packet computer network [16], it may well be feasible to transmit both voice and data over a single communication channel or network. Not only would the participants be relieved of the multiple connection setup (as are users of automatic phone number look-up and dialing), but the system would also be able to provide additional feedback, such as indicating which participant was speaking. It would also be possible to address a subgroup of participants on the voice channel, should that be desired.

The transmission characteristics and requirements of voice and data are quite different, and not all computer networks are able to provide the desired level of service for both. Voice transmission requires short, bounded transmission delays and low variation in delay, and can tolerate small amounts of data loss or corruption, whereas on-line data transmission typically requires reliable delivery, which can only be achieved by accepting longer and more variable delays. Nonetheless, to whatever extent is feasible, using a single communication channel is more economical than transmitting voice and data separately. In some situations (for example, in remote field locations or with personal computers communicating over a single telephone line) there may be only one communication channel available. The design guidelines and implementation techniques we have described can be adapted to integrated systems that perform both voice and data conferencing over a single network.

Conclusion

This article examined some prototype real-time conferencing systems and presented guidelines for the design and implementation of future real-time conferencing systems. Access to and manipulation of on-line information can enhance the effectiveness of meetings, both remote and face to face. However, further research is needed in evaluating which of the available functions are useful and when, and what the long-term impact of this new mode of communication will be on the effectiveness and morale of groups of people working together.

We have identified two contrasting approaches to constructing real-time conferencing systems: (1) sharing existing single-user interactive programs by means of virtual terminals, and (2) writing new application programs that interact with multiple users and can treat each one differently (in terms of command context and access control). The former approach is easy to implement but limited in functionality, while the latter can provide better functionality and performance, but requires more work to implement. Some systems may be able to use a mixture of the two approaches.

For the immediate future, it is probably more important to build some real-time conferencing systems quickly than to ensure that they have broad-based functionality; that way users will have an opportunity to experiment with this new technology. Rapid development and deployment will require (1) reusing existing application software with little or no modification and (2) using simple communication architectures that can be trusted to work correctly rather than extremely efficiently. As experience is gained with the use of real-time conferencing systems, it will become clear which kinds of more advanced functions users need and where the performance enhancement techniques we have outlined can be fruitfully applied. It will then be appropriate to construct more powerful systems that remove the limitations of existing systems. In the meantime, we expect to ee continued development of software-engineering toolkits and communication protocol standards. We hope that real-time conferencing requirements will be recognized early and incorporated into these tools so that they can be used for building the next generation of conferencing systems.

Acknowledgments

We would like to thank Michael Greenwald, Maurice Herlihy, David Reed, Larry Rosenstein, and Lixia Zhang for their voluntary and involuntary contributions to the prototype systems described; Harry Forsdick for providing information about existing conferencing systems; and the quest editors and reviewers for their constructive suggestions for improvement.

This research was sponsored by the Defense Advanced Research Projects Agency and was monitored by the Office of Naval Research under Contract Number N00014-83-K-0125.

References

1. S. R. Hiltz and M. Turoff, "The Evolution of User Behavior in a Computerized Conferencing System," *Comm. ACM*, Vol. 24, No. 11, Nov. 1981, pp. 739–751.

2. D. Tsichritzis, "Form Management," *Comm. ACM*, Vol. 25, No. 7, July 1982, pp. 453–478.

3. S. Sluizer and P. M. Cashman, "XCP: An Experimental Tool for Supporting Office Procedures," *Proc. First Int'l Conf. Office Automation*, IEEE-CS Press, Silver Spring, Md., Dec. 1984, pp. 73–80.

4. B. I. Kedziersky, "Knowledge-Based Project Management and Communication Support in a System Development Environment," *Proc. Fourth Jerusalem Conf. Information Technology*, IEEE-CS Press, Silver Spring, Md., May 1984, pp. 444–451.

5. D. C. Engelbart and W. K. English, "A Research Center for Augmenting Human Intellect," *Proc. Fall Joint Computing Conf.*, Thompson Book Co., Washington, D.C., Dec. 1968, pp. 395–410.

6. D. C. Engelbart, "Toward High-Performance Knowledge Workers," *Office Automation Conf. Digest*, AFIPS Press, Arlington, Va., April 1982, pp. 279–290.

7. M. H. Brown and R. Sedgewick, "Techniques for Algorithm Animation," *IEEE Software*, Vol. 2, No. 1, Jan. 1985, pp. 28–39.

8. W. Pferd, L. A. Peralta, and F. X. Prendergast, "Interactive Graphics Teleconferencing," *Computer*, Vol. 12, No. 11, Nov. 1979, pp. 62–72.

9. S. K. Sarin, "Interactive On-Line Conferences," tech. report TR-330, MIT Laboratory for Computer Science, Dec. 1984. (Available from LCS Publications, 545 Technology Square, Cambridge, Mass. 02139.)

10. G. Heffron, "Teleconferencing Comes of Age," *IEEE Spectrum*, Vol. 21, No. 10, Oct. 1984, pp. 61–66.

11. I. Greif, "PCAL: A Personal Calendar," tech. memo TM-213, MIT Laboratory for Computer Science, Cambridge, Mass., Jan. 1982.

12. K. A. Lantz and W. I. Nowicki, "Structured Graphics for Distributed Systems," *ACM Trans. Graphics*, Vol. 3, No. 1, Jan. 1984, pp. 23–51.

13. M. Herlihy and B. Liskov, "A Value Transmission Method for Abstract Data Types," *ACM Trans. Programming Languages and Systems*, Vol. 4, No. 4, Oct. 1982, pp. 527–551.

14. L. Aguilar, "Datagram Routing for Internet Multicasting," *Proc. Symp. Communications Architectures and Protocols*, ACM, New York, June 1984, pp. 58–63.

15. J. W. Forgie, "ST—A Proposed Internet Stream Protocol," Internet Experimental Note IEN-119, MIT Lincoln Laboratory, Lexington, Mass., Sept. 1979.

16. C. J. Weinstein and J. W. Forgie, "Experience with Speech Communication in Packet Networks, *IEEE J. Selected Areas in Communications*, Vol. SAC-1, No. 6, Dec. 1983, pp. 963–980.

Technology

Data sharing is fundamental to computer-supported cooperative work: people share information through explicit communication channels and through their coordinated use of shared databases. The papers in this section cover some of the data-sharing technologies that underlie communication through shared information.

Information bases, as envisioned by Bush and Engelbart (see Readings 1–5), formed the basis for sharing information in large organizations. Later Ted Nelson coined the term "hypertext" to refer to the kinds of databases that Bush and Engelbart had begun to invent. Hypertext has come to refer to a wide range of textual database systems, most containing small chunks of text linked in complex ways. The paper reprinted here (Reading 16) is a survey of existing hypertext systems and open design issues. Many of the systems mentioned in the article do support collaboration (see Table 1, Reading 16). At the 1987 Hypertext meeting at the University of North Carolina, it was already clear that this survey paper is destined to be one of the most heavily cited papers in that field.

Hypertext databases are used primarily to link unstructured textual information. Conventional database technology, such as the relational database, is used for very regular, structured information. The data-sharing paper examines the data management requirements of group-work applications on the basis of experience with three prototype systems. Relevant support technologies range from conventional DBMSs for very regular information to "object management systems" aimed at storing very irregular, unstructured entities. The paper contains a survey of requirements and covers, in some depth, the unresolved issues of access control and concurrency control.

The Diamond system (Reading 18, this volume) is a computer-based message system that provides the means to create, send, receive, display, and file documents. The documents are multimedia, structured objects in a document store that integrates e-mail and other working documents. Diamond illustrates the full complexity of building a distributed system in the internet environments. The paper explains how the developers handled interfaces with other mail systems, authentication for access control, and naming of objects. The barriers to commercializing this kind of system are still serious: the high cost of the full-functioned workstations, new operating-system features, and the need for interconnectivity between local area networks.

The final paper (Reading 19) deals with the integration of multimedia conferencing facilities into an existing software environment. Assuming that the meeting-management capabilities are defined and are to be implemented independently of the pre-existing application software, Lantz presents the basic architectural approaches to adding conferencing capabilities. He puts forward some architectural recommendations that would make it easy to add conferencing. However, the paper does not deal with the issue of making the application itself aware of multiple users. Although this approach may limit the kinds of functionality that the conferencing system can have (some of the tradeoffs are discussed in Sarin and Greif, Reading 15, on meeting-support tools), it does allow the *ad hoc* addition of conferencing to a wide range of systems with which users are already familiar in their individual work settings.

16

Hypertext: An Introduction and Survey

Jeff Conklin
Microelectronics and Computer Technology Corp.

Most modern computer systems share a foundation which is built of directories containing files. The files consist of text which is composed of characters. The text that is stored within this hierarchy is linear. For much of our current way of doing business, this linear organization is sufficient. However, for more and more applications, a linear organization is not adequate. For example, the documentation of a computer program[1] is usually either squeezed into the margins of the program, in which case it is generally too terse to be useful, or it is interleaved with the text of the program, a practice which breaks up the flow of both program and documentation.

As workstations grow cheaper, more powerful, and more available, new possibilities emerge for extending the traditional notion of "flat" text files by allowing more complex organizations of the material. Mechanisms are being devised which allow direct machine-supported references from one textual chunk to another; new interfaces provide the user with the ability to interact directly with these chunks and to establish new relationships between them. These extensions of the traditional text fall under the general category of *hypertext* (also known as *nonlinear text*). Ted Nelson, one of the pioneers of hypertext, once defined it as "a

---

[1] *Documentation* is the unexecutable English text which explains the logic of the program which it accompanies.

combination of natural language text with the computer's capacity for interactive branching, or dynamic display...of a nonlinear text...which cannot be printed conveniently on a conventional page." [1]

This article is a survey of existing hypertext systems, their applications, and their design. It is both an introduction to the world of hypertext and, at a deeper cut, a survey of some of the most important design issues that go into fashioning a hypertext environment.

The concept of hypertext is quite simple: Windows on the screen are associated with objects in a database, and links are provided between these objects, both graphically (as labelled tokens) and in the database (as pointers). (See Figure 16.1.)

But this simple idea is creating much excitement. Several universities have created laboratories for research on hypertext, many articles have been written about the concept just within the last year, and the Smithsonian Institute has created a demonstration laboratory to develop and display hypertext technologies. What is all the fuss about? Why are some people willing to make extravagant claims for hypertext, calling it "idea processing" and "the basis for global scientific literature"?

In this article I will attempt to get at the essence of hypertext. I will discuss its advantages and disadvantages. I will show that this new technology opens some very exciting possibilities, particularly for new uses of the computer as a communication and thinking tool. However, the reader who has not used hypertext should expect that at best he will gain a perception of hypertext as a collection of interesting features. Just as a description of electronic spreadsheets will not get across the real elegance of that tool, this article can only hint at the potentials of hypertext. In fact, one must work in current hypertext environments for a while for the collection of features to coalesce into a useful tool.

One problem with identifying the essential aspects of hypertext is that the term "hypertext" has been used quite loosely in the past 20 years for many different collections of features. Such tools as window systems, electronic mail, and teleconferencing share features with hypertext. This article focuses on machine-supported *links* (both within and between documents) as the essential feature of hypertext systems and treats other aspects as extensions of this basic concept.[2]   It is this linking capability which allows a nonlinear organization of text. An additional feature that is common to many hypertext systems is the heavy use of windows that have a one-to-one correspondence with nodes in the database. I consider this feature to be of secondary importance.

---

[2]   While this article seeks to establish the criterion of machine-supported links as the primary criterion of hypertext, this is by no means an accepted definition. Therefore I will also review and discuss some systems which have a weaker notion of links.

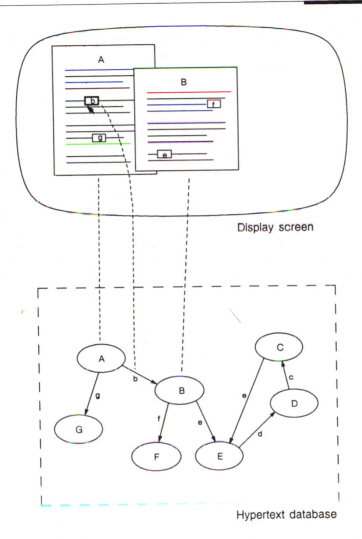

Figure 16.1   The correspondence between windows and links in the display, and nodes and links in the database. In this example, each node in the hypertext database is displayed in a separate window on the screen when requested. The link named "b" in window A has been activated by a pointing device, causing a new window named "B" to be created on the screen and filled with the text from node B in the database. (Generally, links can have names that are different from the name of the node they point to.)

One way to delimit hypertext is to point out what it is not. Briefly, several systems have some of the attributes of hypertext but do not qualify. Window systems fall into this category; while window systems do have some of the interface functionality, and therefore some of the "feel" of hypertext, window systems have no single underlying database, and therefore lack the database aspect of hypertext. File systems also do not qualify as hypertext; one could claim that a file system is a database, and that one moves among *nodes* (files) by simply invoking an editor with their names. However, to qualify as hypertext, a system must use a more sophisticated notion of links and must provide more machine support for its links than merely typing file names after a text editor prompt. Similarly, most outline processors (such as ThinkTank) do not qualify. They provide little or no support for references between outline entries, although their integrated hierarchical database and interface do approximate hypertext better than the other systems that I have mentioned. Text formatting systems (such as troff and Scribe) do not qualify. They allow a tree of text fragments in separate files to be gathered into one large document; however, this structure is hierarchical and provides no interface for on-line navigation within the (essentially linear) document. Similarly, database management systems (DBMSs) have links of various kinds (for example, relational and object-oriented links), but lack the single coherent interface to the database which is the hallmark of hypertext.

As videodisc technology comes of age, there is growing interest in the extension of hypertext to the more general concept of *hypermedia*, in which the elements which are networked together can be text, graphics, digitized speech, audio recordings, pictures, animation, film clips, and presumably tastes, odors, and tactile sensations. At this point, little has been done to explore the design and engineering issues of these additional modalities, although many of the high-level design issues are likely to be shared with hypertext. Therefore, this survey will primarily address the more conservative text-based systems.

A Glimpse of Using Hypertext

It is useful to have a sense of the central aspects of using a hypertext system, particularly if you have never seen one. Below is a list of the features of a somewhat idealized hypertext system. Some existing systems have more features than these, and some have fewer or different ones.

- The database is a network of textual (and perhaps graphical) nodes which can be thought of as a kind of *hyperdocument*.

- Windows on the screen correspond to nodes in the database on a one-to-one basis, and each has a name or title which is always displayed in the window. However, only a small number of nodes are ever "open" (as windows) on the screen at the same time.

- Standard window system operations are supported: Windows can be repositioned, resized, closed, and put aside as small window icons. The position and size of a window or icon (and perhaps also its color and shape) are cues to remembering the contents of the window. Closing a window causes the window to disappear after any changes that have been made are saved to the database node. Clicking with the mouse on the icon of a closed window causes the window to open instantly.

- Windows can contain any number of *link icons*[3] which represent pointers to other nodes in the database. The link icon contains a short textual field which suggests the contents of the node it points to. Clicking on a link icon with the mouse causes the system to find the referenced node and to immediately open a new window for it on the screen.

- The user can easily create new nodes and new links to new nodes (for annotation, comment, elaboration, etc.) or to existing nodes (for establishing new connections).

- The database can be browsed in three ways: (1) by following links and opening windows successively to examine their contents, (2) by searching the network (or part of it) for some string,[4] keyword, or attribute value, and (3) by navigating around the hyperdocument using a *browser* that displays the network graphically. The user can select whether the nodes and links display their labels or not.

The browser is an important component of hypertext systems. As the hyperdocument grows more complex, it becomes distressingly easy for a user to become lost or disoriented. A browser displays some or all of the hyperdocument as a graph, providing an important measure of contextual and spatial cues to supplement the user's model of which nodes he is viewing and how they are related to each other and their neighbors in the graph. (See Figure 16.2.) Using a browser can be likened to using visual and tactile cues when looking for a certain page in a book. Sometimes we remember the general way the page looked and about how far it was through the book, although we

---

[3] Note that I am describing two uses of icons: those that function as placeholders for windows that have been temporarily put aside, and those within windows that represent links to other nodes.

[4] A *string* is a series of alphabetic and numeric characters of any length, for example "listening" or "G00274."

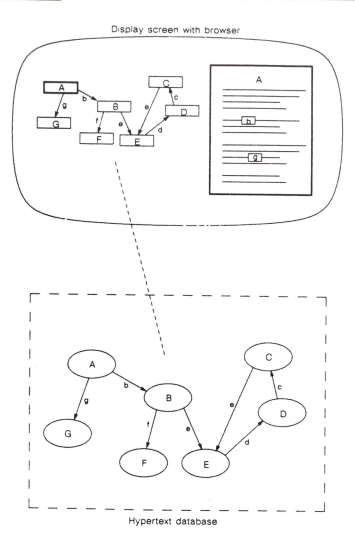

Figure 16.2   The screen at the top illustrates how a hypertext browser provides a direct two-dimensional graphic view of the underlying database. In this illustration, the node "A" has been selected for full display of its contents. Notice that in the browser view you can tell not only which nodes are linked to A but also how the subnetwork fits into the larger hyperdocument. (Of course, hyperdocuments of any size cannot be shown all at once in a browser—only portions can be displayed.)

don't recall the page number or even which keyword terms would help us find it by using the index or table of contents. The browser display can be similarly scanned and scrolled when the user has forgotten all but the appearance or location of a node.

Hypertext Implementations

The history of hypertext is rich and varied because hypertext is not so much a new idea as an evolving conception of the possible applications of the computer. Many people have contributed to the idea, and each of them seems to have had something different in mind. In this section, I will review these theorists and their ideas in an effort to present a historical perspective as well as to sketch some of the hypertext applications that have been devised to date. I do not describe the individual systems and ideas reviewed here in any detail. For more detailed information, the reader is invited to consult the literature directly.

One kind of manual hypertext is the traditional use of 3 × 5 index cards for note taking. Note cards are often referenced to each other, as well as arranged hierarchically (for example, in a shoebox or in rubber-banded bundles). A particular advantage of note cards is that their small size modularizes the notes into small chunks. The user can easily reorganize a set of cards when new information suggests a restructuring of the notes. Of course, a problem with note cards is that the user can have difficulty finding a specific card if he has many of them.

Another kind of manual hypertext is the reference book, exemplified by the dictionary and the encyclopedia. In the sense that each of these can be viewed as a graph of textual nodes joined by referential links, they are very old forms of hypertext. As one reads an article or definition, explicit references to related items indicate where to get more information about those items. The majority of people's transactions with a dictionary make use of the linear (alphabetic) ordering of its elements (definitions) for accessing a desired element. An encyclopedia, on the other hand, can best be used to explore the local nodes in the "network," once one has found the desired entry through the alphabetic index.

There are also many documents in which references to other parts of the document, or to other documents, constitute a major portion of the work. Both the Talmud, with its heavy use of annotations and nested commentary, and Aristotle's writings, with their reliance on references to other sources, are ancient prototypes of hypertextual representation.

But if one insists, as most modern proponents of hypertext do, that navigation through hypertextual space must be computer-supported in order to qualify as true hypertext, then the field is narrowed considerably, and the history likewise shortened.

In some ways, the people who first described hypertext—Bush, Engelbart, Nelson—all had the same vision for hypertext as a path to ultimate human-computer interaction, a vision which is still alive today among hypertext researchers. Thus the historical review below stresses the early development of ideas about hypertext as much as the more contemporary implementation efforts.

Because of the difficulty of precisely classifying hypertext systems according to their features, my description will list systems according to application. There are four broad application areas for which hypertext systems have been developed:

- *macro literary systems:* the study of technologies to support large on-line libraries in which interdocument links are machine-supported (that is, all publishing, reading, collaboration, and criticism takes place within the network);

- *problem exploration tools:* tools to support early unstructured thinking on a problem when many disconnected ideas come to mind (for example, during early authoring and outlining, problem solving, and programming and design);

- *browsing systems:* systems similar to macro literary systems, but smaller in scale (for teaching, reference, and public information, where ease of use is crucial);

- *general hypertext technology:* general purpose systems designed to allow experimentation with a range of hypertext applications (for reading, writing, collaboration, etc.)

These categories are somewhat informal. Often the single application to which a system has been applied to date determines which category it is described in. Bear in mind that some of the systems mentioned below are full-scale environments, while others are still only conceptual sketches. Some systems have focused more on the development of the *front end* (the user interface aspects), while others have focused on the database issues of the *back end* (the database server). Table 1 identifies various features of the different hypertext systems which have been implemented.

Macro Literary Systems

The earliest visions of hypertext focus on the integration of colossal volumes of information to make them readily accessible via a simple and consistent interface. The whole network publishing system constitutes a dynamic corpus to be enriched by readers without defacing the original documents; thus, the difference between authors and readers is diminished. The advent of the computer has brought this vision closer to reality, but it has also revealed the monumental problems inherent in this application area.

Table 1 Hypertext systems and their features

Hypertext Systems	Hierarchy	Graph-based	Link Types	Attri-butes	Paths	Ver-sions	Procedural Attachment	Keyword or String Search	Text Editor	Concurrent Multi-users	Pictures or Graphics	Graphical Browser
Boxer	Yes	Yes	Fixed¹	No¹	No	No	Yes	Yes	Emacs	No	Yes	Yes
CREF	Yes	Yes	Yes	No	No	By link	No	Yes	Zmacs	No	Yes	No
Emacs INFO	Yes	No	No	No	No	No	No	Yes	Emacs	No	No	No
IBIS	Yes	Yes	Yes	No	No	By link	No	No	A basic text editor	Yes	No	No
Intermedia	Yes	Yes	Yes	Yes	No²	No	No²	Yes	Custom	Yes	Yes	Yes
KMS	Multiple	Yes	Fixed	No	No¹	Yes	Yes	Yes	Text/ graph. WYSIWYG	Yes	Yes	No
Neptune	Yes	Yes	Yes	Yes	No	Yes	Yes	Yes	Smalltalk-80 editor	Yes	Yes	Yes
NLS/Augment	Yes	Yes	Yes	Yes	Yes	Yes	Yes	Yes	Custom	Yes	Yes	No
NoteCards	Multiple	Yes	Yes	Nodes	No	No	Yes	Yes	Interlisp	Yes	Yes	Yes
Outline Processors	Yes	No	No	No	No	No	No	Yes	Various	No	No	No
PlaneText	Unix file sys.	Yes	No	No	No	No	No	Unix/ grep	SunView text ed.	Yes	Yes	Yes
Symbolics Document Examiner	Yes	Yes	No	No	Yes	No	No	Yes	None	No	No	No
SYNVIEW	Yes	No	No	No	No	No	No	No	line ed./ Unix	No	No	No
Textnet	Multiple	Yes	Yes	Yes	Yes	No	No	Keyword	Any	No	No	No
Hyperties	No	Ye.	No	No	No	No	No	No²	A basic text editor	No	Yes	No
WE	Yes	Yes	No	Fixed	No²	No²	No²	No	Smalltalk-80 editor	No²	Yes	Yes
Xanadu	No	Yes	Yes	Yes	Yes	Yes	No	No	Any	No	Yes	No
ZOG	Yes	No	No	No	No	No	Yes	Full text	Spec. Pur.	Yes	No	No

¹Can be user programmed.
²Planned for next version

In this table, each column represents one possible feature or ability that a hypertext system can provide. The negative or affirmative entries in the table indicate whether the corresponding hypertext system meets the standard criteria for a specified feature. These criteria are listed below.

Hierarchy: Is there specific support for hierarchical structures?
Graph-based: Does the system support nonhierarchical (cross-reference) links?
Link types: Can links have types?
Attributes: Can user-designated attribute/value pairs be associated with nodes or links?
Paths: Can many links be strung together into a single persistent object?
Versions: Can nodes or links have more than a single version?
Procedural attachment: Can arbitrary executable procedures be attached to events (such as mousing) at nodes or links?
String search: Can the hyperdocument be searched for strings (including keywords)?
Text editor: What editor is used to create and modify the contents of nodes?
Concurrent multiusers: Can several users edit the hyperdocument at the same time?
Pictures or graphics: Is some form of pictorial or graphical information supported in addition to text?
Graphics browser: Is there a browser which graphically presents the nodes and links in the hyperdocument?

Bush's Memex Vannevar Bush, President Roosevelt's Science Advisor, is credited with first describing hypertext in his 1945 article "As We May Think" [2], in which he calls for a major postwar effort to mechanize the scientific literature system. In the article, he introduces a machine for browsing and making notes in an extensive on-line text and graphics system. This *memex* contained a very large library as well as personal notes, photographs, and sketches. It had several screens and a facility for establishing a labelled link between any two points in the entire library. Although the article is remarkably foresightful, Bush did not anticipate the power of the digital computer; thus his memex uses microfilm and photocells to do its magic. But Bush did anticipate the information explosion and was motivated in developing his ideas by the need to support more natural forms of indexing and retrieval:

> The human mind ... operates by association. Man cannot hope fully to duplicate this mental process artificially, but he certainly ought to be able to learn from it. One cannot hope to equal the speed and flexibility with which the mind follows an associative trail, but it should be possible to beat the mind decisively in regard to the permanence and clarity of the items resurrected from storage. [2]

Bush described the essential feature of the memex as the ability to tie two items together. The mechanism is complex, but clever. The user has two documents that he wishes to join into a *trail* he is building, each document in its own viewer; he taps in the name of the link, and that name appears in a code space at the bottom of each viewer; out of view, the code space is also filled with a photocell-readable dot code that names the other document and the current position in that document. Thereafter, when one of these items is in view, the other can be instantly recalled merely by taping a button below the corresponding code space. Bush admitted that many technological breakthroughs would be needed to make his memex practical, but he felt that it was a technological achievement worthy of major expenditure.

Engelbart's NLS/Augment Just less than two decades later Douglas Engelbart, at Stanford Research Institute, was influenced by Bush's ideas. In 1963, Engelbart wrote "A Conceptual Framework for the Augmentation of Man's Intellect" [3]. Engelbart envisioned that computers would usher in a new state of human evolution, characterized by "automated external symbol manipulation":

> In this stage, the symbols with which the human represents the concepts he is manipulating can be arranged before his eyes, moved, stored, recalled,

operated upon according to extremely complex rules—all in very rapid response to a minimum amount of information supplied by the human, by means of special cooperative technological devices. In the limit of what we might now imagine, this could be a computer, with which individuals could communicate rapidly and easily, coupled to a three-dimensional color display with which extremely sophisticated images could be constructed ... [3]

His proposed system, H-LAM/T (Human using Language, Artifacts, and Methodology, in which he is Trained), included the human user as an essential element: The user and the computer were dynamically changing components in a symbiosis which had the effect of "amplifying" the native intelligence of the user. This is still a common vision among developers of hypertext systems.

Five years later, in 1968, Engelbart's ideas about augmentation had become more specific, and had been implemented as NLS (oN Line System) by the Augmented Human Intellect Research Center at SRI. NLS was designed as an experimental tool on which the research group developed a system that would be adequate to all of their work needs, by

placing in computer store all of our specifications, plans, designs, programs, documentation, reports, memos, bibliography and reference notes, etc., and doing all of our scratch work, planning, designing, debugging, etc., and a good deal of our intercommunication, via the consoles [4].

These consoles were very sophisticated by the standards of the day and included television images and a variety of input devices, including one of Engelbart's best known inventions, the mouse.[5]

Files in NLS were structured into a hierarchy of segments[6] called *statements,* each of which bore an identifier of its level within the file. For example, a document might have statements "1," "1a," "1a1," "1a2," "1b," etc., though these identifiers did not need to be displayed. Any number of reference links could be established between statements within files and between files. Note that this is a structure which is primarily hierarchical, but which allows nonhierarchical links as well. The importance of supporting both kinds of structures is a point to which I will return later. The system provided several ways to traverse the statements in files.

---

[5] Engelbart also introduced a five-key handset—a one-handed keyboard. The operator enters alphanumeric text by "chording" the five keys. Although this method is slower than two-handed typing, it has a considerable advantage for short commands when used with a mouse in the other hand.

[6] Segments were limited to 3000 characters in length.

NLS, like other early hypertext systems, emphasized three aspects: a database of nonlinear text, *view filters* which selected information from this database, and *views* which structured the display of this information for the terminal. The availability of workstations with high resolution displays has shifted the emphasis to more graphical depictions of nodes, links, and networks, such as using one window for each node.

NLS provided viewing filters for the file structure: One could clip the level (depth) of hierarchy displayed, truncate the number of items displayed at any level, and write customized filters (in a "high-level content analysis language") that displayed only statements having the specified content. NLS also introduced the concept of multiperson distributed conferencing/editing.

NLS has evolved over the years. It is now called Augment (or NLS/Augment) and is marketed as a commercial network system by McDonnell Douglas. In developing NLS, the emphasis has been on creating a consistent environment for "knowledge workers" (that is, office automation for software engineers). The system now includes many forms of computer-supported communication, both asynchronous (email with links to all documents, journaling of ideas and exchanges, bulletin boards, etc.) and synchronous (several terminals sharing the same display, teleconferencing, etc.). It includes facilities for document production and control, organizational and project information management, and software engineering. (See Figures 16.3 and 16.4.)

Nelson's Xanadu Project During Engelbart's development of Augment, another hypertext visionary, Ted Nelson, was developing his own ideas about augmentation, but with an emphasis on creating a unified literary environment on a global scale. Nelson coined the term "hypertext." His thinking and writing are the most extravagant of any of the early workers. He named his hypertext system Xanadu, after the "magic place of literary memory" in Samuel Taylor Coleridge's poem "Kubla Khan." In Xanadu, storage space is saved by the heavy use of links. Only the original document and the changes made to it are saved. The system easily reconstructs previous versions of documents. Nelson describes his objectives as follows:

> Under guiding ideas which are not technical but literary, we are implementing a system for storage and retrieval of linked and windowing text. The *document*, our fundamental unit, can have windows to any other documents. The evolving corpus is continually expandable without fundamental change. New links and windows can continually add new access pathways to old material. Fast proprietary algorithms render the extreme data fragmentation tolerable in the planned back-end service facility [5].

Figure 16.3 Engelbart at the NLS/Augment workstation. Note the chord key set under Engelbart's left hand. The chord key set is optional for Augment. It is a remarkable accelerator for character-driven commands and mouse-select screen operands.

The long range goal of the Xanadu project has been facilitating the revolutionary process of placing the entire world's literary corpus on line. In fact, Xanadu's design makes a strong separation between the user interface and the database server, with most of the emphasis placed on the latter. In particular, great care has been taken that copyright protection is maintainable, and that a system for the electronic accounting and distribution of royalties is in place. Nelson predicts that the advent of on-line libraries will create a whole new market for the organization and indexing of this immense information store.

The back end of the Xanadu system has been implemented in Unix and is available in several forms, including as an on-line service (much like Engelbart's Augment). A crude front end for the Xanadu system is also available which runs on Sun workstations.

Trigg's Textnet Randall Trigg wrote the first and to date the only Ph.D. thesis on hypertext. In his thesis, he describes his Textnet system as supporting *nonlinear text*—text in which documents are organized as "primitive pieces of text connected with typed links to form a network

```
Journal Document                                              2   1
                                                            gJuCP
BASE Jump (to) Link ! OK:

   WINDOW-1: IN JOHN'S MAIL FILE        WINDOW-3: IN DOCUMENT B, OF USER X

                                          "... AUGMENT's Addressing and Links,
  John, we should consider some new      described in <Ref-6.1*6 :ebtzgm>..."
  viewspecs for the list of             [JUMP NAME: CLICK ON "Ref-6" IN W-3:
  <OAD,2250,7c :ebtzgm>, ... Frank       CLICK IN WINDOW-4 BELOW: RESULT IN W-4.]
                                         Ref-6:  "Authorship Provisions in
                                         AUGMENT," Douglas C.Engelbart, COMPCON
                                          '84 Digest, ..., COMPCON Conference,
 ["JUMP LINK" RESULTS BELOW, IN WINDOW 2]San Francisco, (OAD,2250,)
   7C WINDOW VIEWS                       WINDOW-5: IN ITEM 2250 OF OAD JOURNAL,
     7C1 STRUCTURE CUTOFF. Show only     AFTER JUMP ON INDIRECT LINK OF WINDOW 3
     7C2 LEVEL CLIPPING. For the
     7C3 STATEMENT TRUNCATION. For       6 ADDRESSING THE WORKING MATERIALS
     7C4 INTER-STATEMENT SEPARATION.      6A There is a consistent set of
     7C5 (Note: The foregoing view       6B EXPLICIT STATEMENT ADDRESSES
     7C6 STATEMENT NUMBERS AND NAMES.     6C MARKERS
     7C7 FROZEN STATEMENTS.  A worker     6D RELATIVE-ADDRESS EXTENSIONS
     7C8 USER-SPECIFIED CONTENT           6E EMBEDDED CITATION LINKS
                                          6F TEXT AND CONTENT ADDRESSING
```

Figure 16.4 Augment display showing five windows. Window 1 (W-1) has a passage as if embedded in a message, showing a link to Branch 7c of Document 2250 in the OAD Journal. A ViewSpec ("ebtzgm") provides the following specifications: target level plus one, truncate to one line per statement, no blank lines between statements, show only that branch (e.g., not Branch 7d), and turn on Location Numbers. Window 2 (W-2) shows the view obtained with a jump link command. To perform a jump link command, the operator clicks on the link in W-1, then moves the cursor into W-2 for the final click. The very top-left system message announces that the desired Journal Item has been accessed, and the cluster at the top left of the screen verifies that the view is clipped to three levels and the statements truncated to one line each. Window 3 (W-3) shows an indirect link that specifies the linkage path. In effect, this link says "go to the statement in the file named 'Ref-6,' follow the link found there to its target file, and in that file find Location Number 6." Note that the same View Spec is specified here as for the link in W-1. Window 4 (W-4) identifies Ref-6 and provides its general reference source as the reference section at the end of the document; a user can jump from the link citation in W-3 to see this statement by using the jump name command. To perform this command, he clicks on "Ref-6" in W-3 then clicks on W-4. Window 5 (W-5) shows a view in the OAD-Journal Item 2250. The user can obtain this view by performing a jump link command on the indirect link of W-3. To perform this command, the user clicks on the indirect link of W-3 and then clicks in W-5.

similar in many ways to a semantic net." The thesis focuses on specific link types that support literary criticism.

In the tradition of the field, Trigg's system is just a first step in the direction of his vision:

> In our view, the logical and inevitable result [of the computer revolution]
> will be the transfer of all such [text handling] activities to the computer,
> transforming communication within the scientific community. All paper
> writing, critiquing, and refereeing will be performed on line. Rather than
> having to track down little-known proceedings, journals or unpublished
> technical reports from distant universities, users will find them stored in
> one large distributed computerized national paper network. New papers
> will be written using the network, often collaborated on by multiple au-
> thors, and submitted to on-line electronic journals [6].

Textnet implements two basic types of nodes: those which have
textual content (*chunks*) and those which hierarchically organize other
nodes (*tocs*, for "table of contents"). Thus Textnet supports both hierarchical trees (via the toc nodes) and nonhierarchical graphs (via the
typed links).

Trigg further proposes a specific taxonomy of link types for use by
collaborators and critics in Textnet. He argues that there is generally
a specific set of types of comments, and that there is a link type for
each comment. For example, there are *refutation* and *support* links, and,
more specifically, there are links to say that a point is irrelevant ("Pt-
irrelevant"), that data cited is inadequate ("D-inadequate"), or that the
style is rambling ("S-rambling"). Trigg describes over 80 such link types
and argues that the disadvantage of having a limited set of link types
is outweighed by the possibility of specialized processing on the hyperdocument afforded by a definite and fixed set of primitives.

In addition, Textnet supports the definition of *paths*—ordered lists
of nodes used to browse linear concatenations of text and to dump such
scans to hard copy. The path facility relieves the hypertext reader from
having to make an *n-way* decision at each link; rather, the reader is
provided a default pathway through the network (or part of the network),
and can simply read the material in the suggested order as if he were
reading a linear document.

Trigg joined Xerox PARC after completing his thesis and was one
of the principal architects of the Xerox NoteCards system.

Problem Exploration Systems

These are highly interactive systems which provide rapid response to
a small collection of specialized commands for the manipulation of information. They can be thought of as the early prototypes of electronic
spreadsheets for text and symbolic processing. One important feature of
most of these tools is a facility for suppressing detail at various levels
specified by the user. For example, the outline processors all have single
keystroke commands for turning on and off the display of subsections of

a section. This is an unusual but natural facility. Hypertext and similar tools excel at the collection of large amounts of relatively unstructured information. But such collections are of little use unless adequate mechanisms exist for filtering, organizing, and browsing. These are the primary desiderata of these authoring/thinking/programming systems.

Issue-Based Information Systems   Horst Rittel and his students have introduced the notion of Issue-Based Information Systems (IBIS)[7] to handle systems analysis in the face of "wicked problems." Rittel describes wicked problems (as opposed to "tame" ones) as problems which cannot be solved by the traditional systems analysis approach (that is, (1) define the problem, (2) collect data, (3) analyze the data, (4) construct a solution). Wicked problems lack a definitive formulation; their problem space cannot be mapped out without understanding the solution elements; in short, the only way to really understand a wicked problem is to solve it. Wicked problems have no stopping rule. The design or planning activity stops for considerations that are external to the problem (for example, lack of time, money, or patience). Solutions to wicked problems are not "right" or "wrong"; they just have degrees of sufficiency. Rittel argues that solving wicked problems requires all those involved to exchange and argue their many viewpoints, ideas, values, and concerns. By coming to understand other viewpoints better, each participant is able to understand the whole problem better. This process enables a common understanding of the major issues and their implications to emerge. IBIS is designed to support this design/planning conversation.

IBIS systems are thus a marriage of (1) teleconferencing systems which enable many people to participate in one conversation, and (2) hypertext, which allows participants to move easily between different issues and the different threads of argument on the same issue. The current version of Rittel's IBIS runs on an Apple PC and is being ported to Sun workstations.[7]   IBIS has three types of nodes (*issues, positions,* and *arguments*), and uses nine types of relations to link these nodes. In a typical application, someone posts an issue; then that person or others post positions about that issue; and then the positions are argued using argument nodes. Of course, any of the three types of nodes can be the seed of a new issue. (See Figure 16.5.) The current set of relationships between nodes is: *responds-to, questions, supports, objects-to, specializes, generalizes, refers-to,* and *replaces*. The research on IBIS concentrates on ways to summarize and present the issue network, both for participants and decision makers.

---

[7]   A graphical Sun version, called gIBIS, is also being developed at the MCC/Software Technology Program.

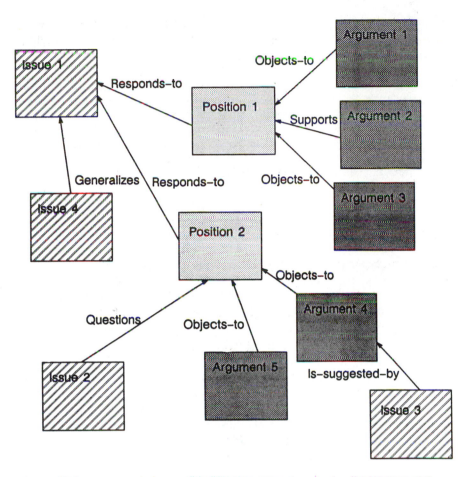

Figure 16.5 A segment of a possible IBIS-style discussion showing the topology of the IBIS network. Each node contains information on the type of the node, the time and date of creation, the author, a short phrase describing the content, a longer body of text with the text of the comment, a list of keywords, and a list of the incoming and outgoing links.

Lowe's SYNVIEW David Lowe's SYNVIEW system is similar in concept to Rittel's IBIS but goes in a different direction. It proposes that the participants, in addition to posting their own issues and arguments, assess previous postings as to their validity and relevance. The assessment is done by a kind of quantitative voting. For example, if you think that Joe's response to Sam makes a good point but is not really a direct response to Sam's posting, you might grade it "5,1" (where 5 is a high validity rating and 1 is a low relevance rating). These values are averaged into the existing values for that posting. The various displays of the argument structure show the values for each posting, allowing readers to focus, if they choose to, on those argument trails having the highest voted validity.

> Through debates on the accuracy of information and on aspects of the structures themselves, a large number of users can cooperatively rank all available items of information in terms of significance and relevance to each topic. Individual users can then choose the depth to which they wish to examine these structures for the purposes at hand. The function of this debate is not to arrive at specific conclusions, but rather to collect and order the best available evidence on each topic [8].

UNC's WE   A group at the University of North Carolina at Chapel Hill has been developing a *writing environment* called WE [9]. Their research is based on a cognitive model of the communication process which explains reading as the process of taking the *linear* stream of text, comprehending it by structuring the concepts hierarchically, and absorbing it into long-term memory as a *network*. Writing is seen as the reverse process: A loosely structured network of internal ideas and external sources is first organized into an appropriate hierarchy (an outline) which is then "encoded" into a linear stream of words, sentences, etc.

WE is designed to support the upstream part of writing. It contains two major view windows, one graphical and one hierarchical, and many specialized commands for moving and structuring material (nodes and links with attached text) between these two views. Normally a writer will begin by creating nodes in the graph view, where he can place them anywhere within the window. At this stage, little or no structure is imposed on the conceptual material. The writer can place nodes in "piles" if they seem to be related, or he can place individual nodes between two piles if they are somewhat related to both. As some conceptual structure begins to emerge from this process, the writer can copy nodes into the hierarchy window, which has specialized commands for tree operations. The hierarchy window has four different display modes: (1) the tree can be laid out on its side, with the root node on the left; (2) the tree can be hung vertically with the root at the top; (3) child nodes can be displayed inside their parent node; and, (4) the hierarchy can be shown in the traditional outline view.

WE uses a relational database for the storage of the nodes and links in the network. The user points with a mouse to select a node. A third window is an editor for the material within the currently selected node. A fourth window on the screen is for queries to the database. A fifth window is used to control system modes and the current working set of nodes.

WE is designed to be an experimental platform to study what tools and facilities will be useful in a writer's environment. The real validation of these ideas, as with so many of the systems described here, will come with further experiments and analysis.

Outline Processors   An *outline processor* is a word processing program which is specialized for processing outlines, in that its main commands deal with movement among, creation of, and modification of outline entries. In this respect, these programs commercialize many ideas from Engelbart's NLS/Augment. Outline processors also have at least simple text editors and do some text formatting, so that the user can use the same tool to go from outline to finished document. One of the most powerful features of outline processing is the ability to suppress lower levels of detail in the outline. As with Engelbart's NLS/Augment, the user can view just the top level of the outline, or the top n levels, or he can "walk the tree," opening up just those entries that are relevant or useful to the idea that he is working on. In addition, each outline entry can have a textual body of any length associated with it, and the user can make this body appear or disappear with a single keystroke. This feature is a real boon to the writing process, because it allows the user to have a view of both the immediate text that he is composing and the global context for it. It also facilitates rapid movement between sections, particularly in large documents, because in outline mode a remote section is never more than a few keystrokes away.

Most outline processors are personal computer programs, and they have done much to bring some of the concepts underlying hypertext into popularity. The first of these was called ThinkTank. It was released in 1984. It has since been joined by a host of others, with names like MaxThink, Executive Writer/Executive Filer, Thor, Framework, Kamas, Fact Cruncher, Freestyle, Idea!, and PC-Outline [10]. There are two very recent additions to the field: Houdini is an extension of MaxThink that supports rich nonhierarchical internode references; and ForComment is a word processor that allows up to 15 people to apply hypertext-like annotations to a document (and can operate over a Local Area Network (LAN) in real time).

Aside from Houdini, most outline processors do not support inter-entry references, except by "cloning" the whole entry and displaying it in the new location. Only a few others provide windows for nodes. None of them provide explicit "mousable" link icons. For these reasons, one could argue whether they qualify as hypertext as I have defined it here. However, ThinkTank was the first program to be billed—somewhat pretentiously—as an "idea processor," and all of these programs treat sections of text as first-class objects and support manipulations that coincide with the way one manages ideas. They share these features with hypertext, and in this sense, they anticipate the inevitable proliferation of hypertext features within the mainstream of computer applications.

Structured Browsing Systems

The systems reviewed in this section were designed primarily for applications involving large amounts of existing information or requiring easy access to information. These systems pose different problems for their designers. Ease of learning and ease of use are paramount, and great care goes into crafting the interface. On the other hand, writing (adding new information)is usually either not allowed to the casual user or not particularly well supported.

CMU's ZOG and Knowledge Systems' KMS   ZOG is a menu-based display system developed in 1972 at Carnegie-Mellon University [11]. It consists of a potentially large database of small (screen-sized) segments which are viewed one at a time. ZOG was developed with the particular goal of serving a large simultaneous user community, and thus was designed to operate on standard terminals on a large timesharing system. In 1981 two of the principals on the ZOG Project, Donald McCracken and Robert Akscyn, started the company Knowledge Systems and developed a commercial successor to ZOG called Knowledge Management System (KMS).

Each segment of the ZOG/KMS database is called a *frame*. A frame has, by convention, a one-line title at the top of the screen, a few lines of text below the title stating the issue or topic of the frame, a set of numbered (or lettered) menu items of text called *selections*, and a line of standard ZOG commands called *global pads* at the bottom of the screen. (Some of these commands are: *edit, help, back, next, mark, return,* and *comment.*) The selections interconnect the frames. When a user selects an item by typing its number or letter at the terminal keyboard, the selected frame appears on the screen, replacing the previous frame. The structure is generally hierarchical, though cross-referencing links can be included. In addition, an item in a frame can be used to activate a process.

In 1982 ZOG was installed and used as a computer-based information management system on the nuclear-powered aircraft carrier USS CARL VINSON. This system is probably the largest and most thoroughly tested hypertext system in service in the field. ZOG has also been used for more interactive process applications such as policy analysis, authoring, communications, and code management. Historically, however, ZOG made its name more as a bulletin board/textual database/CAI tool than as an interactive system. Hence it is included in this section on browsing. A drawback of the ZOG/KMS style of viewing a single frame at a time is that users may become disoriented, since no spatial event corresponds to the process of moving from frame to frame. In the KMS system, this tendency has been offset by minimizing system response time, so that frame-to-frame transition takes about half a second. The possibility of user disorientation is greatly reduced by the fact that the user can move very quickly among frames and thus become reoriented with very little effort. Creating text and graphics is also fast in KMS.

Emacs INFO Subsystem   The help system in the widely used text editor, Emacs, is called INFO, and is much like ZOG. It has a simpler set of standard commands, and its control input is done by single letters or short commands typed at the keyboard. It is primarily hierarchical, but a user can jump to a different place in the hierarchy by typing in the name of the destination node. It is used as an on-line help system in Emacs. INFO has the same potential for user disorientation which is shared by all of the systems which display only a single frame at a time and have no browser.

Schneiderman's Hyperties   The University of Maryland Hyperties project[8] has been developed in two directions—as a practical and easy-to-learn tool for browsing in instructional databases and as an experimental platform for studies on the design of hypertext interfaces. As a practical tool, it has already seen some use in the field at a Washington, D.C. museum exhibit about Austria and the Holocaust. (See Figure 16.6.) Designers of the exhibit emphasized making the system easy and fun for users who have never used a computer before. As an experimental platform, it has been used in five experimental studies involving over 220 subjects [12].

In Hyperties the basic units are short articles (50–1000 words typically), which are interconnected by any number of links. The links are highlighted words or phrases in the article text. The user activates the links by touching them with a finger (on a touch-sensitive screen) or using the arrow keys to jump to them.[9]   Activating a link causes the article about that topic to appear in its own window on the screen. The system keeps track of the user's path through the network of articles, allowing easy return from exploratory side paths.

---

[8]   The "ties" in "Hyperties" stands for "The Interactive Encyclopedia System."

[9]   The Hyperties system uses a different convention than the mouse to select links. In the Hyperties system, some link is always selected. When the user pushes one of the arrow keys, the system responds by selecting the nearest link in the direction of the arrow. Studies showed this to be a faster and easier technique for selecting arbitrary highlighted fields on the screen.

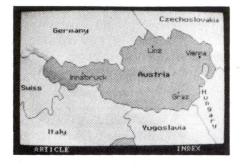

Figure 16.6 The Hyperties Browser enables users to traverse a database of articles and pictures by selecting from highlighted items embedded in the text of the articles. The photos show the IBM PC version of Hyperties. The upper node shows a map of Austria. The lower node shows double-spaced text with link terms highlighted. Either a touchscreen or jump-arrow keys are used for selection of brief definitions, full articles, or pictures. The Hyperties Author permits people with only word processing skills to create and maintain databases. Research versions of Hyperties run on the Enhanced Graphics Adapter to give more lines and multiple windows and on the Sun 3 workstation to show two full pages of text at a time. Current development efforts will enable readers to point at pictures and videodisc images to retrieve further information.

In addition to a title and a body of text, each article has a short (5- to 25-word) description which the program can display very quickly. This feature allows the user an intermediate position between bringing up the full article and trying to guess from the link name precisely what the article is about.

Hyperties runs on the IBM PC. Recently graphics capabilities have been added to the system. Current implementation efforts focus on support for videodisc images. Also, a browser is being developed which will provide string search, bookmarks, multiple windows, and user annotation.

Symbolics Document Examiner The most advanced of the on-line help systems, this tool displays the pages from the entire twelve-volume manual set on the Symbolics Lisp machine screen [13]. Certain textual fields in the document (printed in bold) are mouse-sensitive. Touching one of these fields with the mouse causes the relevant section of the manual to be added to the current working set of manual pages. The system allows the reader to place *bookmarks* on any topic and to move swiftly between bookmarked topics. The protocol for link following is tailored to browsing in a reference manual or encyclopedia. Mousing a link only causes it to be placed on a list of current topics. Then, mousing an entry in this list causes that link to be followed, bringing up the referenced topic in the main viewing window.

The system also supports on-line string search of preidentified keywords, including the search for whole words, leading substrings, and embedded substrings. The system is thus well designed for the specific task of browsing through a technical manual and pursuing several aspects of a technical question or several levels of detail simultaneously. The user cannot make any changes or additions to the manual set (although it is possible to save personalized collections of bookmarks).

General Hypertext Technology

So far I have discussed hypertext systems that have particular practical applications. The following systems also have one or more applications, but their primary purpose is experimentation with hypertext itself as a technology. For example, while NoteCards has been used for authoring, programming, personal information management, project management, legal research, engineering design, and CAI, its developers view it primarily as a research vehicle for the study of hypertext.

Xerox PARC's NoteCards   Perhaps the best known version of full hypertext is the *NoteCards* system developed at Xerox PARC [14]. The original motivation in building NoteCards was to develop an information analyst's support tool, one that would help gather information about a topic and produce analytic reports. The designers of NoteCards observed that an information analyst usually follows a general procedure that consists of a series of steps: (1) reading sources (news reports, scholarly articles, etc.), (2) collecting clippings and filing them (in actual shoeboxes!), and (3) writing analytic reports. The designers also observed that throughout the process, the analyst forms analyses and conceptual models in his head. The research goal of the PARC team was to develop technology to aid the analyst in forming better conceptual models and analyses, and to find better expressions of these models and analyses.

A programmer's interface makes NoteCards an open architecture that allows users to build (in Lisp) new applications on top of NoteCards. Using this interface, the user can easily customize the browser. NoteCards allows easy creation of new types of nodes. Forty or fifty such specialized node types have been created to date, including text, video,

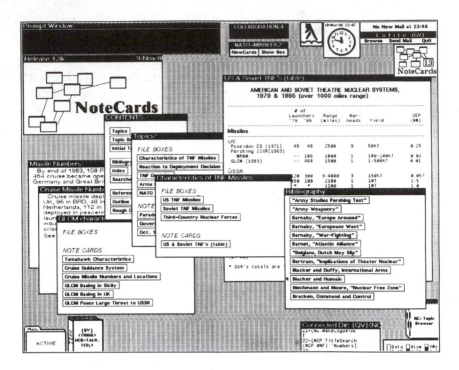

Figure 16.7 A typical NoteCards screen with five FileBox cards, two unformatted Text cards, and one Text card formatted as a table. Links between cards are represented by the boxed text inside the cards. The two menus at the top/middle of the screen control two different note files. The remainder of the icons on the screen belong to non-NoteCard applications running in the Xerox Lisp environment.

animation, graphics, and actions.[10]   The new version also allows several users to work in the same Notefile at the same time.

Part of NoteCards' success is due to the fact that it was developed on Xerox D-series Lisp machines, which are powerful workstations that have high resolution screens allowing windows and link and node icons to be displayed in very high resolution. (See Figure 16.7.) Currently between 50 and 100 users use NoteCards, many of them outside of Xerox (even though it is not a supported product). Several of these users have constructed very large databases in the system (for example, 1600 nodes with 3500 links between them).

Brown University's Intermedia   One of the oldest and largest hypertext research groups exists at Brown University, at the Institute for

---

[10]   An *action node* contains Lisp code which gets evaluated when a link to the node is activated.

Research in Information and Scholarship (IRIS) [15]. The Intermedia project builds on two decades of work and three prior generations of hypertext systems [16].

The first system was the Hypertext Editing System designed by Ted Nelson, Andy van Dam, and several Brown students for the IBM 2250 display in 1968. This system was used by the Houston Manned Spacecraft Center to produce Apollo documentation.

The second system was the File Retrieval and Editing System (FRESS). FRESS was a greatly enhanced multiterminal timesharing version designed by van Dam and his students. It became available in 1969 and was commercially reimplemented by Phillips in the early 1970's. FRESS was used in production by hundreds of faculty and students over more than a decade. Its users included an English poetry class that did all of its reading and writing on a communal hypertext document. Like NLS, FRESS featured both dynamic hierarchy and bidirectional reference links, and keyworded links and nodes. Unlike NLS, it imposed no limits on the sizes of nodes. On graphics terminals, multiple windows and vector graphics were supported.

The third project, the Electronic Document system, was a hypermedia system emphasizing color raster graphics and navigation aids.

As part of Brown's overall effort to bring graphics-based workstations into effective use within the classroom, the Intermedia system is being developed as a framework for a collection of tools that allow authors to create links to documents of various media such as text, timelines, diagrams and other computer-generated images, video documentaries, and music. Two courses, one on cell biology and one on English literature, have been taught using the system. Current applications include InterText, a text processor; InterDraw, a graphics editor; InterVal, a timeline editor that allows users interactively to organize information in time and date sequences; InterSpec, a viewer for sections of 3D objects; and InterPix, a scanned-image viewer. Under development are a video editor, a 2D animation editor, and more complex methods for filtering the corpus and creating and traversing trails.

Intermedia is being developed both as a tool for professors to organize and present their lesson material via computer and as an interactive medium for students to study the materials and add their own annotations and reports.

> For example, in the English literature course the first time a student is searching for background information on Alexander Pope, he or she may be interested in Pope's life and the political events that prompted his satiric criticism. To pursue this line of thought the student might retrieve the biography of Pope and a timeline summarizing political events taking

place in England during Pope's life. Subsequently, the student may want to compare Pope's use of satire with other later authors' satiric techniques. This time the student may look at the same information about Pope but juxtapose it with information about other satiricists instead of a time line. The instructor (and other students, if permitted) could read the student's paper, examine the reference material, and add personal annotation links such as comments, criticism, and suggestions for revision. While revising the document, the student could see all of the instructor's comments and examine the sources containing the counter-arguments.

Like most of the serious workers on hypertext, the Intermedia team is especially concerned with providing the user with ways of managing the increased complexity of the hypertext environment. For example, they contend that multiple links emanating from the same point in a document may confuse the reader. Their alternative is to have a single link icon in the material (text or graphics) which can be quickly queried via the mouse to show the specific outgoing links, their names, and their destination nodes [15]. They also propose a construct called a *web* to implement context-dependent link display. Every link belongs to one or more webs and is only visible when one of those webs is active. To view documents with the links that belong to a particular web, a user opens a web and then opens one or more of its documents. Although other webs may also reference the document, only the links which were made in the current web are displayed. As a result, the user does not have to sift through the connections made in many different contexts.

The Intermedia project is also studying ways of providing an effective browser for a network that can include hundreds or even thousands of nodes. The Intermedia browser has two kinds of displays: a *global map*, which shows the entire hyperdocument and allows navigation within it; and a *local map*, which presents a view centered on a single document and displaying its links and nearest neighbors in the web. In addition, a display can show nodes and links at several levels of detail. For example, it can show whole documents and the links between them, or each link and its approximate location within its documents. (See Figure 16.8.)

The Intermedia project has a long history, many participants, and a serious institutional commitment to long-term objectives. It conducts creative hypertext experiments and uses the classroom as a proving ground. Although this project is still in its early stages, we can expect it to contribute signficantly to the development of effective cooperative work environments based on hypertext.

Tektronix Neptune   Tektronix Neptune is one hypertext system that has been particularly designed as an open, layered architecture [17]. Nep-

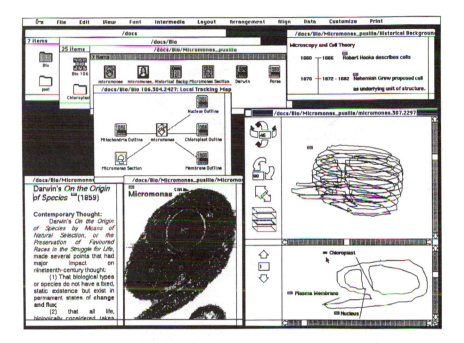

Figure 16.8   The Intermedia System. This figure illustrates materials from an Intermedia corpus called "Bio 106: Cell Biology in Context." Three folder windows containing hierarchically organized documents of different types are open in the upper left side of the display. An InterText document (lower left side) and an InterVal document (upper right side) are currently open, as well as an InterDraw document containing a scanned electronmicrograph (lower middle). This image has been linked to a corresponding three-dimensional image displayed in an InterSpect document (lower right). The "lower tracking map" (center) shows the links emanating from the current document. Authors or browsers can manipulate the three-dimensional image, edit text and graphics, follow links or create links at any time in this environment. (The electronmicrograph of *Micromonas* was published in the *Journal of Phycology* and is reprinted with the permission of the Editor.)

tune strongly separates the front end, a Smalltalk-based user interface, from the back end, a transaction-based server called the Hypertext Abstract Machine (HAM). The HAM is a generic hypertext model which provides operations for creating, modifying, and accessing nodes and links. It maintains a complete version history of each node in the hyperdocument, and provides rapid access to any version of a hyperdocument. It provides distributed access over a computer network, synchronization for multiuser access, a complex network versioning scheme, and transaction-based crash recovery.

The interface layer provides several browsers: A *graph browser* provides a pictorial view of a subgraph of nodes and links; a *document browser* supports the browsing of hierarchical structures of nodes and

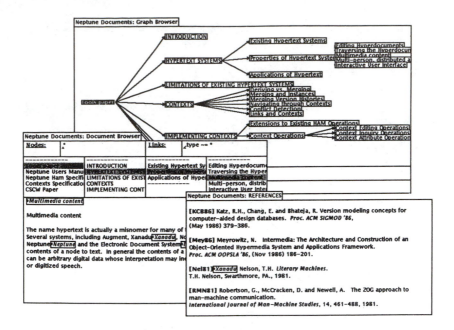

Figure 16.9   Neptune browsers. Three browsers from Neptune are illustrated. A pictorial view of a network of nodes and links is shown in the Graph Browser (the upper window). The lower right window and the lower pane of the Document Browser are viewers for text nodes. Icons representing link attachments are shown embedded within the text in each of the nodes.

links; and a *node browser* accesses an individual node in a hyperdocument. Other browsers include *attribute browsers*, *version browsers*, *node di–erences browsers*, and *demon browsers*. (See Figure 16.9.)

In Neptune, each end of a link has an offset within its node, whether that node is textual or graphical.[11]   The link attachment may refer to a particular version of a node, or it may refer to the current version. The HAM provides two mechanisms that are useful for building application layers: Nodes and links may have an unlimited number of attribute/value pairs; and special high-speed predicates are included for querying the values of these pairs in the entire hyperdocument, allowing higher level applications to define their own accessing mechanisms on the graph. The HAM also provides a demon mechanism that invokes arbitrary code when a specific HAM event occurs.

diSessa's Boxer   Boxer [18] is a highly interactive programming language specifically tailored to be easy for noncomputer specialists to

---

[11]   Unlike in most hypertext systems, the destination end of a Neptune link is an iconic point in the text of the destination node rather than the whole node.

learn. Boxer uses a *box* to represent a unit of information in the system. In Boxer, one box can contain other boxes, or data such as text or graphics. For example, a program is a box that contains some boxes that provide input and output variables, and other boxes that specify behavior. The system also supports alternate views of some boxes: A box which specifies a graphics routine can also show that graphic display.

Since Boxer is a programming language, it treats cross-reference links in a special way. Rather than using mousable icons as links, Boxer uses a specialized box, called a "port," which gives a direct view into the destination. For example, a port from box A to box B appears within A as a box which shows B. But a part is more than just a view of the destination box, because the destination box can be changed through any of the ports which lead to it, and the changes will be reflected in all of these ports.

Hierarchy is more naturally expressed in Boxer than in many of the other hypertext systems. Boxes are nested within each other two-dimensionally, and are filtered to reduce the level of clutter on the screen. This system of representation has the advantage of showing a natural hierarchy of nodes: The windows of lower-level nodes are nested directly within their parents. In most hypertext systems, no attempt is made to display the parent-child relationship once the nodes are opened as windows.

Pitman's CREF   The Cross-Referenced Editing Facility (CREF) is a prototype of a specialized text and graphics editor which was developed originally as a tool for use in analyzing the transcripts from psychological experiments (known as *protocols*), but which was also used to investigate more general hypertext design issues [19]. Much of the interactive feel of CREF reflects the style of use and programming of the Symbolics Lisp machine, on which it was built. Chunks of text, called *segments*, constitute the nodes in the system. Segments are arranged in linear series, and can have keywords and various kinds of links to other segments. The notion of a linear set of segments is natural to the protocol analysis problem, since the first step with such protocols is to segment them into the episodes of the experimental session.

CREF organizes segments into *collections*, which can be defined implicitly by a predicate (called an *abstract collection*) or explicitly by a list (called a *static collection*). At any time, the selected collection appears as a continuous length of text with the segment boundaries marked by named horizontal lines (such as "Segment 1," "Segment 2," etc.). This view can be edited as if it were a single document.

One way of forming an abstract collection is by selecting segments using a boolean predicate over keywords. To extend the power of this keyword facility, CREF allows the user to define a type hierarchy on the keywords. For example, if "card 105" is defined as a type of (i.e., a *child* of) "card," then collections based on the keyword "card" will also contain segments which have only "card 105" as a keyword.

CREF supports four kinds of links: *references links* cross-referencing among segments; *summarizes links* impose hierarchy (a *summary* is a segment which has one or more summarizes links to other segments); *supersedes links* implement versioning by copying the superseded segment and freezing it; and *precedes links* place a linear ordering on segments.

Finally, CREF allows multiple analysts to compose different *theories* about a protocol, using the same segmented data. Each theory imposes its own structure on the data, and has its own collections, diagrams, keywords, and annotations. This mode of selection is similar to the notion of contexts or webs used in other systems.

Hypertext on the Macintosh   At least two programs have been written for the Apple Macintosh that provide hypertext facilities: FileVision and Guide.

FileVision is primarily oriented to graphics nodes and to applications which can exploit visual indexing. The advertising for FileVision describes applications that encourage visual indexing. For example, in the database for a travel agency, the map of a region may contain icons for the main cities in that region. The user clicks on the icon for a city to obtain a display of a map of that city. The map of the city may have icons for the major landmarks in the city. The user clicks on one of these icons to obtain a display of data about the landmark, or perhaps even to obtain a picture of the landmark itself.

Guide is a more recent program which is based on an earlier Unix version developed in England [20]. It does not provide the graphics capabilities of FileVision (graphics are supported but cannot contain links), but it does support textual hypertext data very well. Guide uses three kinds of links: *replacement links*, which cause the text in the current window to be completely replaced by the text pointed to by the link; *note links*, which display the destination text in a pop-up window; and *reference links*, which bring up a new window with the destination text. Guide is now available for PCs as well.

As this article goes to press, there is news that Apple will soon have its own hypertext system, called HyperCards. HyperCards will be similar in some ways to Xerox PARC's NoteCards. It will provide special support for *executable links*, which will give it the flavor of a programming language. HyperCards will be bundled with the system software in new Macintoshes.

MCC's Plane Text   PlaneText, developed in the MCC Software Technology Program (STP), is a very recent addition to the family of general hypertext systems.[12]   Plane Text is based on the Unix file system and the Sun SunView window manager. Each node is a Unix file. Links appear as names in curly brackets ({}) whose display can be turned on and off. Links are implemented as pointers saved in separate files, so that the linked files themselves are not changed by creating hypertext references between them. This design allows for the smooth integration of hypertext into the rest of the Unix-based computational environment, including such tools as Mail and News. It allows for the hypertext annotation of standard source code files. In addition, the Unix file directory system serves as a "free" mechanism for creating hierarchical structures among nodes.[13]

PlaneText supports color graphics nodes which can be freely linked into a hyperdocument.

Summary   The systems in this section were presented in terms of four broad categories: macro literary systems, problem exploration systems, structured browsing systems, and general hypertext technology. Table 1 summarizes this discussion and provides a breakdown of the various features which current hypertext systems can include.

One additional area of research currently is the development of systems which aid the entire process of design, particularly the informal upstream aspects. Such systems require the features of hypertext problem exploration and structured browsing systems as well as the advanced features of the experimental hypertext technologies. Indeed, this area of investigation may become an important fifth category for hypertext systems of the future.

This history of hypertext presented here suggests that the concept and the advantages of hypertext were clear several decades ago, but that widespread interest in hypertext was delayed until the supporting technology was cheap and readily available. This suggestion may be misleading. Many of the "elders" of the field feel that something else has changed as well. They feel that today computer users easily accept the role of the computer as a tool for processing ideas, words, and symbols (in addition to numbers and mere data), and as a vehicle of interhuman communication. Those theorists who gave presentations of their hyper-

---

[12]   It is perhaps too early to say, however, how PlaneText will rank in the world of hypertext, since it will only be publicly available from the participant companies in the MCC/Software Technology Program.

[13]   The use of an existing tree-structuring mechanism limits any hypertext system to only being able to handle a single hierarchical structure. Single hierarchical organizations may be too limited for some advanced applications.

text systems 20 years ago, using expensive state of the art hardware, report that the computer science community showed little interest. This lack of interest seemed to stem as much from a lack of understanding of the basic concepts of hypertext as from a lack of hardware resources.

If this is so, then the recent upsurge in interest in hypertext may signal that the computer community is now ready to consider its technology as much a tool for communication and augmenting the human intellect as for analysis and information processing. Hypertext is certainly a large step in that direction.

The Essence of Hypertext

It is tempting to describe the essence of hypertext as its ability to perform high-speed, branching transactions on textual chunks. But this is a little like describing the essence of a great meal by listing its ingredients. Perhaps a better description would focus on hypertext as a computer-based medium for thinking and communication.

The thinking process does not build new ideas one at a time, starting with nothing and turning out each idea as a finished pearl. Thinking seems rather to proceed on several fronts at once, developing and rejecting ideas at different levels and on different points in parallel, each idea depending on and contributing to the others.

The recording and communication of such entwined lines of thought is challenging because communication is in practice a serial process and is, in any case, limited by the bandwidth of human linguistic processing. Spoken communication of parallel themes must mark items with stresses, pauses, and intonations which the listener must remember as the speaker develops other lines of argument. Graphical forms can use lists, figures, and tables to present ideas in a less than strictly linear form. These visual props allow the reader/viewer to monitor the items which he must understand together. One of the challenges of good writing, especially good technical writing, is to present several parallel lines of a story or an argument in a way that weaves them together coherently.

Traditional flat text binds us to writing and reading paragraphs in a mostly linear succession. There are tricks for signalling branching in the flow of thought when necessary: Parenthetical comments, footnotes, intersectional references (such as "see Chapter 4"), bibliographic references, and sidebars all allow the author to say "here is a related thought, in case you are interested." There are also many rhetorical devices for indicating that ideas belong together as a set but are being presented in linear sequence. But these are rough tools at best, and often do not provide the degree of precision or the speed and convenience of access that we would like.

Hypertext allows and even encourages the writer to make such references, and allows the readers to make their own decisions about which links to follow and in what order. In this sense, hypertext eases the restrictions on the thinker and writer. It does not force a strict decision about whether any given idea is either within the flow of a paper's stream of thought or outside of it. Hypertext also allows annotations on a text to be saved separately from the reference document, yet still be tightly bound to the referent. In this sense, the "linked-ness" of hypertext provides much of its power: It is the machine processible links which extend the text beyond the single dimension of linear flow.

At the same time, some applications demonstrate that the "node-ness" of hypertext is also very powerful. Particularly when hypertext is used as a thinking, writing, or design tool, a natural correspondence can emerge between the objects in the world and the nodes in the hypertext database. By taking advantage of this object-oriented aspect, a hypertext user can build flexible networks which model his problem (or solution). In this application the links are less important than the nodes. The links form the "glue" that holds the nodes together, but the emphasis is on the contents of the nodes.

From a computer science viewpoint, the essence of hypertext is precisely that it is a hybrid that cuts across traditional boundaries. Hypertext is a *database method*, providing a novel way of directly accessing data. This method is quite different from the traditional use of queries. At the same time, hypertext is a *representation scheme*, a kind of semantic network which mixes informal textual material with more formal and mechanized operations and processes. Finally, hypertext is an *interface modality* that features "control buttons" (link icons) which can be arbitrarily embedded within the content material by the user. These are not separate applications of hypertext: They are metaphors for a functionality that is an essential union of all three.

The Power of Linking

In the next two sections of this article, I will explore links and nodes in more detail as the basic building blocks of hypertext.

Link Following   The most distinguishing characteristic of hypertext is its machine support for the tracing of references. But what qualifies a particular reference-tracing device as a link? How much effort is permissible on the part of a user who is attempting to trace a reference?

The accepted lower limit of referencing support can be specified as follows: To qualify as hypertext, a system should require no more than a couple of keystrokes (or mouse movements) from the user to follow a single link. In other words, the interface must provide links which act like "magic buttons" to transport the user quickly and easily to a new place in the hyperdocument.

Another essential characteristic of hypertext is the speed with which the system responds to referencing requests. Only the briefest delay should occur (one or two seconds at most). Much design work goes into this feature in most systems. One reason for this concern is that the reader often does not know if he wants to pursue a link reference until he has had a cursory look at the referenced node. If making this judgement takes too long, the user may become frustrated and not bother with the hypertext links.

However, not all link traversals can be instantaneous. Perhaps as important as rapid response is providing cues to the user about the possible delay that a given query or traversal might entail. For example, some visual feature of the link icon could indicate whether the destination node is in memory, on the disk, somewhere else on the network, or archived off line.

Properties of Links   Links can be used for several functions. These include the following:

- They can connect a document reference to the document itself.

- They can connect a comment or annotation to the text about which it is written.

- They can provide organizational information (for instance, establish the relationship between two pieces of text or between a table of contents entry and its section).

- They can connect two successive pieces of text, or a piece of text and all of its immediate successors.

- They can connect entries in a table or figure to longer descriptions, or to other tables or figures.

Links can have names and types. They can have rich set of properties. Some systems allow the display of links to be turned on and off (that is, removed from the display so that the document appears as ordinary text).

The introduction of links into a text system means that an additional set of mechanisms must be added for creating new links, deleting links,[14] changing link names or attributes, listing links, etc.

Referential Links   There are two methods for explicitly linking two points in hypertext—by reference and by organization. The reference method is a nonhierarchical method. It uses referential links that connect points or regions in the text.

Referential links are the kind of link that most clearly distinguishes hypertext. They generally have two ends, and are usually directed, although most systems support "backward" movement along the link. The origination of the link is called the "link source," and usually acts as the *reference*. The source can logically be either a single point or a region of text. At the other end, the "destination" of the link usually functions as the *referent*, and can also be either a point or a region. (See Figure 16.10.)

A *link point* is some icon indicating the presence of the link. It usually shows the link's name and perhaps also its type. Or it may show the name and/or type of the destination node. In systems such as Neptune which support links with both point source and point destination, the icon also indicates which type of link is indicated. In some systems, the display of links can be suppressed, so that the documents appear linear.

A *link region* is a set of contiguous characters which is displayed as a single unit. In Figure 16.10, the link destination is a link region, namely, an entire node. Figure 16.10 illustrates the most common form of hypertext link, in which the source is a point and the destination is a region. This example typifies many of the link applications listed above, because it shows how a chunk of text—a region—is written about or referenced by some smaller chunk of text, often a sentence. Since most readers are accustomed to single point references to sentences (i.e., footnotes), they have no problem accepting a link with a point source. There can be regions in graphics as well—either bordered regions or collections of graphic objects in a figure.

Link regions can pose difficult design problems. They are easiest to implement as whole nodes, since setting a region off from its neighboring material within the same node raises a tough implementation issue—how to display the selected region to the user. It must be highlighted somehow, using reverse video, fonts, or color, but each of these options poses difficulties in keeping overlapping regions clearly highlighted. The Intermedia designers propose to draw a light box around

---

[14]   Link deletion is problematical. For example, what should the policy be for nodes which are stranded when all their links have been deleted? Should they be placed in "node limbo" until the user decides what to do with them?

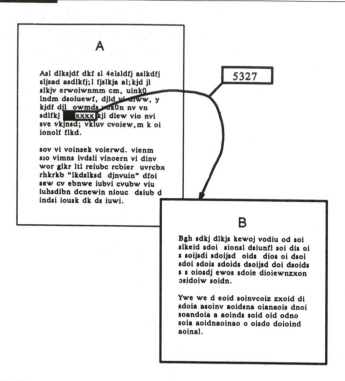

Figure 16.10 An example of a link with a point source and a region destination. The source of the link is a token in the text of document A which contains a textual identifier ("xxxx"). The identifier may be (1) the name of the destination node (in this case it would be "B"), (2) the name of the link, or (3) an arbitrary string which is neither the name of the link nor the destination node. The destination of this link is node B which is a region. The link has an internal name (5327) which is normally visible to the user.

regions and a darker box around region/region overlaps, thus showing a single level of overlapping [15]; however, this technique is not effective if there are more than two overlapping regions.

Another difficulty posed by link regions is how to show the name of the link. Unlike a link point, a link region has no obvious position for a title, unless it is placed arbitrarily at the beginning or end of the region.

Link regions can also be difficult to manipulate. Designers must devise a system for copying, moving, modifying, and deleting the region and the substrings within it. The movement of regions involves logistical dilemmas which are not easy to resolve: For example, when one moves a major portion of the text in a destination region to someplace else in the node, should the link destination move with it or stay with what remains? Also, designers must make special provisions for deleting, moving, or copying the defining end points of a region.

Organizational Links   Like reference links, organizational links establish explicit links between points in hypertext. Organizational links differ from referential links in that they implement hierarchical information.

Organizational links connect a parent node with its children and thus form a strict tree subgraph within the hypertext network graph. They correspond to the *ISA* (or *superconcept*) links of semantic net theory, and thus operate quite differently than referential links.[15]   For example, rather than appearing as explicit highlighted tokens in each node, organizational links are often traversed by a separate mechanism at the node control level (i.e., special *goto-parent*, *goto-first-child*, and *goto-next-sibling* commands). In other cases, there are organizational nodes (such as toc nodes in Textnet and FileBoxes in NoteCards) which record the organizational structure.

Keyword Links   In addition to the explicit linking performed by referential and organizational links, there is a kind of implicit linking that occurs through the use of keywords. This type of linking is yet to be fully explored.

One of the chief advantages of text storage on a computer is the ability to search large and complex documents and sets of documents for substrings and keywords.[16]   Naturally, this ability is also a valuable aspect of hypertext. Indeed, most users of large hyperdocuments insist on having some mechanism for scanning their content, either for selected keywords (which can apply to nodes, links, or regions) or for arbitrary embedded strings.

From a functional standpoint, link following and search are similar: Each is a way to access destination nodes that are of possible interest. Link following usually yields a single node, whereas search can yield many; hence, a keyword is a kind of implicit computed link. The value of this insight is that it may allow design of a hypertext interface which is consistent across all link-tracing activities.

To Tree or Not to Tree   Some hypertext systems (for example, Emacs INFO) support only hierarchical structures, others (such as Xanadu and

---

[15]   Note that organizational links are distinct from the class hierarchy links that would be used (in the object-oriented programming paradigm) to define types and subtypes of nodes in the hypertext system.

[16]   There is some controversy over the relative merits of keyword retrieval as opposed to full text search. On the one hand, keyword retrieval is only as good as the skill and thoroughness of the person selecting the keywords. On the other hand, full text search does not find all the relevant documents, nor does it always find only the relevant documents. Its shortcomings are due in part to the commonness of synonyms in English. In addition, full text search can be computationally prohibitive in large networks.

Hyperties) provide no specific support for hierarchical structures, and others (such as Textnet and NoteCards) support both kinds of structures.

One could question just how sufficient strictly hierarchical structures are, and for which applications they are sufficient and for which they are not. One the one hand, abstraction is a fundamental cognitive process, and hierarchical structures are the most natural structures for organizing levels of abstraction. On the other hand, cases obviously exist where cross-hierarchical links are required. Frank Halasz, one of the developers of NoteCards, has gathered statistics on the *hyperspace* of a single representative NoteCards user; this person had 1577 nodes (cards) in all, 502 of which were FileBoxes (hierarchical nodes). Connecting these nodes were a total of 3460 links, 2521 (73 percent) of which connected FileBoxes to each other or to individual notecards, 261 (7.5 percent) of which were nonhierarchical referential links, and the remainder of which were mail links (used by the system to tie mail messages to other nodes). This example, for what it is worth, suggests that hierarchical structure is very important in organizing a hypertext network, and that referential links are important but less common.

One advantage of a strictly tree-oriented system is that the command language for navigation is very simple: From any node, the most one can do is go to the parent, a sibling, or a child. This simplicity also diminishes the disorientation problem, since a simpler cognitive model of the information space will suffice.

Of course, the great disadvantage of any hierarchy is that its structure is a function of the few specific criteria that were used in creating it. For example, if one wishes to investigate what sea-based life forms have in common with land-based life forms, one may find that the traditional classification of life forms into the plant and animal kingdoms breaks up the information in the wrong way. The creator of a hierarchical organization must anticipate the most important criteria for later access to the information. One solution to this dilemma is to allow the information elements to be structured into multiple hierarchies, thus allowing the world to be "sliced up" into several orthogonal decompositions. Any hypertext system which has hierarchy nodes, such as Textnet (toc nodes) and NoteCards (FileBox nodes), can perform this operation quite easily. These are the only systems which explicitly claim to support multiple hierarchies. Indeed, one early user of NoteCards used the system in doing the research and writing for a major project paper; he imposed one organization on the data and his writings while doing the research, and then quite a different (yet coexistent) organization on the same material to produce his paper. As a generalization, it seems that engineering-oriented hypertext users prefer hierarchical organizations, whereas arts- or humanities-oriented users prefer cross-referencing organizations.

Extensions to Basic Links   Certain features of the link enable it to be extended in several ways. Links can connect more than two nodes to form *cluster links*. Such cluster links can be useful for referring to several annotations with a single link, and for providing specialized organizational structures among nodes. Indeed, the toc nodes of Textnet and the FileBoxes of NoteCards are both forms of cluster links.

One useful way to extend the basic link is to place attribute/value pairs on links and to query the network for them. The Neptune system, for example, has an architecture that is optimized for this function. Coupled with specialized routines in the database interpreter (the HAM), these attribute lists allow users to customize links in several ways, including devising their own type system for links and performing high-speed queries on the types.

It is also possible to perform procedural attachments on a link so that traversing the link also performs some user-specified side effect, such as customizing the appearance of the destination node. This ability is provided in Neptune and Boxer.

Hypertext Nodes

Although the essence of hypertext is its machine-supported linking, the nodes contribute significantly to defining the operations that a hypertext system can perform. Most users of hypertext favor using nodes which express a single concept or idea, and are thus much smaller than traditional files. When nodes are used in this fashion, hypertext introduces an intermediate level of machine support between characters and files, a level which has the vaguely semantic aspect of being oriented to the expression of ideas. But this sizing is completely at the discretion of the hypertext writer, and the process of determining how to modularize a document into nodes is an art, because its impact on the reader is not well understood [21].

The Modularization of Ideas   Hypertext invites the writer to modularize ideas into units in a way that allows (1) an individual idea to be referenced elsewhere, and (2) alternative successors of a unit to be offered to the reader (for instance, more detail, an example, bibliographic references, or the logical successor). But the writer must also reckon with the fact that a hypertext node, unlike a textual paragraph, tends to be a strict unit which does not blend seamlessly with its neighbors. Some hypertext systems (NoteCards, CREF, Boxer, FRES, NLS) allow nodes to be viewed together as if they were one big node, and this option is essential for some applications (for example, writing and reading prose). But the boundaries around nodes are always discrete and require sometimes difficult judgements about how to cleave the subject matter into suitable chunks.

The process of identifying a semantically based unit, such as an idea or concept, with a syntactic unit, such as a paragraph or hypertext node, is not unique to hypertext. Manuals of style notwithstanding, traditional text has rather loose conventions for modularizing text into paragraphs. This looseness is acceptable because paragraph boundaries have relatively minor effect on the flow of the reading. Paragraph boundaries are sometimes provided just to break up the text and give the eye a reference point. Thus, decisions about the distribution of sentences among paragraphs is not always critical.

Hypertext, on the other hand, can enforce a rather stern information hiding. In some systems, the only clue a user has as to the contents of a destination node is the name of the link (or the name of the node, if that is provided instead). The writer is no longer making all the decisions about the flow of the text. The reader can and must constantly decide which links to pursue. In this sense, hypertext imposes on both the writer and the reader the need for more process awareness, since either one has the option of *branching* in the flow of the text. Thus hypertext is best suited for applications which require these kinds of judgements anyway, and hypertext merely offers a way to act directly on these judgements and see the results quickly and graphically.

Ideas as Objects   While difficult to document, there is something very compelling about reifying the expression of ideas into discrete objects to be linked, moved, and changed as independent entities. Alan Kay and Adele Goldberg [22] observed of Smalltalk that it is able to give objects a perceptual dimension by allocating to them a rectangular piece of screen real estate. This feature offers enhanced retrieval and recognition over computer-processed flat documents, because to a much greater degree abstract objects are directly associated with perceptual objects—the windows and icons on the screen.

Paragraphs, sections, and chapters in a book, viewed through a standard text editor or word processor, don't stand out as first-class entities. This is particularly apparent when one can view one's document hierarchically (i.e., as an outline) at the same time that one adds new sections and embellishes existing ones. People don't think in terms of "screenfulls"; they think in terms of ideas, facts, and evidence. Hypertext, via the notion of nodes as individual expressions of ideas, provides a vehicle which respects this way of thinking and working.

Typed Nodes   Some hypertext systems sort nodes into different types. These *typed nodes* can be extremely useful, particularly if one is considering giving them some internal structure, since the types can be used to differentiate the various structural forms.

For example, in our research in the MCC Software Technology Program, we have been implementing a hypertext interface for a design environment called the Design Journal. The Design Journal is intended to provide an active scratchpad in which the designer can deliberate about design decisions and rationale, both individually and in on-line design meetings, and in which he can integrate the design itself with this less formal kind of information. For this purpose we have provided a set of four typed nodes for the designer to use—*notes, goals/constraints, artifacts*, and *decisions*. Notes are used for everything from reminders, such as "Ask Bill for advice on Module X," to specific problems and ideas relating to the design. Goals/constraints are for the initial requirements as well as discovered constraints within the design. Artifacts are for the elements of the output: The Design. And decisions are for capturing the branch points in the design process, the alternatives considered by the designer, and some of the rationale for any commitment (however tentative) that has been made. The designer captures assumptions in the form of decisions with only one alternative. Our prototype of the Design Journal uses color to distinguish between note types in the browser, and we have found this to be a very effective interface.

Hypertext systems that use typed nodes generally provide a specialized color, size, or iconic form for each node type. The distinguishing features help the user differentiate at a glance the broad classes of typed nodes that he is working with. Systems such as NoteCards, Intermedia, and IBIS make extensive use of typed nodes.

Semistructured Nodes   So far I have spoken of the hypertext node as a structureless "blank slate" into which one might put a work or a whole document. For some applications, there is growing interest in *semistructured nodes*—typed nodes which contain labelled fields and spaces for field values. The purpose of providing a template for node contents is to assist the user in being complete and to assist the computer in processing the nodes. The less that the content of a node is undifferentiated natural language (for example, English) text, the more likely that the computer can do some kinds of limited processing and inference on the textual subchunks. This notion is closely related to Malone's notion of semistructured information systems [23].

To continue with the example of the Design Journal, we have developed a model for the internal structure of decisions. The model is named ISAAC. It assumes that there are four major components to a design decision:

1.   an *issue*, including a short name for the issue and a short paragraph describing it in general terms;

2.   a set of *alternatives*, each of which resolves the issue in a different way, each having a name and short description, and each potentially linked to the design documents or elements that implement the alternative;

3.   an *analysis* of the competing alternatives, including the specific criteria being used to evaluate them, the trade-off analysis among these alternatives, and links to any data that the analysis draws upon; and

4.   a *commitment* to one of the alternatives (however tentatively) or to a vector of preferences over the alternatives, and a subjective rating about the correctness or confidence of this commitment.

Without getting into the details of the underlying theory, I merely wish to stress here that the internal structure of ISAAC suggests that the author of an ISAAC decision is engaged in a much more structured activity than just "writing down the decision," and the reader is likewise guided by the regularity of the ISAAC structure.

Of course, it may not be clear why we do not treat each of the elements listed above as its own typed hypertext node. The reason is that the parts of an ISAAC frame are much more tightly bound together than ISAAC frames are bound to each other. For example, we could not have an analysis part without an alternatives part; yet if we treat them as separate hypertext nodes, we have failed to build this constraint into the structure. The general issue here is that some information elements must always occur together, while others may occur together or not, depending on how related they are in a given context and how important it is to present them as a cluster distinct from "surrounding" information elements. This problem is recursive: An element that is atomic at one level may turn out on closer inspection to contain many components, some of which are clustered together.

In hypertext this tension presents itself as the twin notions of semi-structured nodes and composite nodes.

Composite Nodes   Another mechanism for aggregating related information in hypertext is the *composite node*. Several related hypertext nodes are "glued" together and the collection is treated as a single node, with its own name, types, versions, etc. Composite nodes are most useful for situations in which the separate items in a bulleted list or the entries in a table are distinct nodes but also cohere into a higher level structure (such as the list or table). This practice can, however, undermine the fundamental association of one interface object (window) per database object (node), and thus must be managed well to avoid complicating the hypertext idiom unduly.

A composite node facility allows a group of nodes to be treated as a single node. The composite node can be moved and resized, and closes up to a suitable icon reflecting its contents. The subnodes are separable and rearrangeable through a subedit mode. The most flexible means of displaying a composite node is to use a constraint language (such as that developed by Symbolics for Constraint Frames) which describes the sub-nodes as *panes* in the composite node window and specifies the interpane relationships as dynamic constraints on size and configuration.

Composite nodes can be an effective means of managing the problem of having a large number of named objects in one's environment. Pitman described the problem this way:

> In this sort of system, there is a never-ending tension between trying to name everything (in which case, the number of named things can grow quickly and the set can become quickly unmanageable) or to name as little as possible (in which case, things that took a lot of trouble to construct can be hard to retrieve if one accidentally drops the pointers to them)[19].

One problem with composite nodes is that as the member nodes grow and change the aggregation can become misleading or incorrect. A user who encounters this problem is in the same predicament as a writer who has rewritten a section of a paper so thoroughly that the section title is no longer accurate. This "semantic drift" can be difficult to catch.

Analogy to Semantic Networks

The idea of building a directed graph of informal textual elements is similar to the AI concept of *semantic networks*. A semantic network is a knowledge representation scheme consisting of a directed graph in which concepts are represented as nodes, and the relationships between concepts are represented as the links between them. What distinguishes a semantic network as an AI representation scheme is that concepts in the representation are indexed by their semantic content rather than by some arbitrary (for example, alphabetical) ordering. One benefit of semantic networks is that they are natural to use, since related concepts tend to cluster together in the network. Similarly, an incompletely or inconsistently defined concept is easy to spot since a meaningful context is provided by those neighboring concepts to which it is already linked.

The analogy to hypertext is straightforward: Hypertext nodes can be thought of as representing single concepts or ideas, internode links as representing the semantic interdependencies among these ideas, and the process of building a hypertext network as a kind of informal knowledge engineering. The difference is that AI knowledge engineers are usually striving to build representations which can be mechanically interpreted, whereas the goal of the hypertext writer is often to capture an interwoven collection of ideas without regard to their machine interpretability. The work on semantic networks also suggests some natural extensions to hypertext, such as typed nodes, semistructured nodes (frames), and inheritance hierarchies of node and link types.

The Advantages and Uses of Hypertext

Intertextual references are not new. The importance of hypertext is simply that references are machine-supported. Like hypertext, traditional literature is richly interlinked and is hierarchically organized. In traditional literature, the medium of print for the most part restricts the flow of reading to follow the flow of linearly arranged passages. However, the process of following side links is fundamental even in the medium of print. In fact, library and information science consist principally of the investigation of side links. Anyone who has done research knows that a considerable portion of that effort lies in obtaining referenced works, looking up cross-references, looking up terms in a dictionary or glossary, checking tables and figures, and making notes on notecards. Even in simple reading one is constantly negotiating references to other chapters or sections (via the table of contents or references embedded in the text), index entries, footnotes, bibliographic references, sidebars, figures, and tables. Often a text invites the reader to skip a section if he is not interested in greater technical detail.

But there are problems with the traditional methods.

- Most references can't be traced backwards: A reader cannot easily find where a specific book or article is referenced in a document, nor can the author of a paper find out who has referenced the paper.

- As the reader winds his way down various reference trails, he must keep track of which documents he has visited and which he is done with.

- The reader must squeeze annotations into the margins or place them in a separate document.

- Finally, following a referential trail among paper documents requires substantial physical effort and delays, even if the reader is working at a well-stocked library. If the documents are on line, the job is easier and faster, but no less tedious.

New Possibilities for Authoring and Design

Hypertext may offer new ways for authors and designers to work. Authoring is usually viewed as a word- and sentence-level activity. Clearly the word processor[17] is a good tool for authoring at this level. However, authoring obviously has much to do with structuring of ideas, order of presentation, and conceptual exploration. Few authors simply sit down and pour out a finished text, and not all editing is just "wordsmithing" and polishing. In a broad sense, authoring is the *design of a document*. The unit of this level of authoring is the idea or concept, and this level or work can be effectively supported by hypertext, since the idea can be expressed in a node. As the writer thinks of new ideas, he can develop them in their own nodes, and then link them to existing ideas, or leave them isolated if it is too early to make such associations. The specialized refinements of a hypertext environment assist the movement from an unstructured network to the final polished document.

New Possibilities for Reading and Retrieval

Hypertext may also offer new possibilities for accessing large or complex information sources. A linear (nonhypertext) document can only be easily read in the order in which the text flows in the book. The essential advantage of non-linear text is the ability to organize text in different ways depending on differing viewpoints. Shasha provides the following description of this advantage:

> Suppose you are a tourist interested in visiting museums in a foreign city. You may be interested in visual arts. You may want to see museums in

---

[17]   Actually, the term "word processor" is quite misleading. Most such tools accept input only at the character level, and manipulate characters, words, sentences, and paragraphs with equal facility. So these tools manipulate units of text, not words. But do they "process" these units? "Processing" implies that the computer performs some additional work, such as changing the verb form if the subject was changed from singular to plural, or performing real-time spelling and grammar correction. Since this is not the case, we really should return to the original term for these tools: "text editors."

your local area. You may only be interested in inexpensive museums. You certainly want to make sure the museums you consider are open when you want to visit them. Now your guidebook may be arranged by subject, by name of museum, by location, and so on. The trouble is: if you are interested in any arrangement other than the one it uses, you may have to do a lot of searching. You are not likely to find all the visual arts museums in one section of a guidebook that has been organized by district. You may carry several guidebooks, each organized by a criterion you may be interested in. The number of such guidebooks is a measure of the need for a nonlinear text system [21].

Another advantage is that it is quite natural in a hypertext environment to suspend reading temporarily along one line of investigation while one looks into some detail, example, or related topic. Bush described an appealing scenario in his 1945 article:

> The owner of the memex, let us say, is interested in the origin and properties of the bow and arrow. Specifically he is studying why the short Turkish bow was apparently superior to the English long bow in the skirmishes of the Crusades. He has dozens of possibly pertinent books and articles in his memex. First he runs through an encyclopedia, finds an interesting but sketchy article, leaves it projected. Next, in a history, he finds another pertinent item, and ties the two together. Thus he goes, building a trail of many items. Occasionally he inserts a comment of his own, either linking it into the main trail or joining it by a side trail to a particular item. When it becomes evident that the elastic properties of available materials had a great deal to do with the bow, he branches off on a side trail which takes him through textbooks on elasticity and tables of physical constants. He inserts a page of longhand analysis of his own. Thus he builds a [permanent] trail of his interest through the maze of materials available to him [2].

As we have seen, Bush's notion of the "trail" was a feature of Trigg's Textnet [6], allowing the hypertext author to establish a mostly linear path through the document(s). The main (default) trail is well marked, and the casual reader can read the text in that order without troubling with the side trails.

Summary

We can summarize the operational advantages of hypertext as:

- *ease of tracing references:* machine support for link tracing means that all references are equally easy to follow forward to their referent, or backward to their reference;

- *ease of creating new references:* users can grow their own networks, or simply annotate someone else's document with a comment (without changing the referenced document);

- *information structuring:* both hierarchical and nonhierarchical organizations can be imposed on unstructured information; even multiple hierarchies can organize the same material;

- *global views:* browsers provide table-of-contents style views, supporting easier restructuring of large or complex documents; global and local (node or page) views can be mixed effectively;

- *customized documents:* text segments can be threaded together in many ways, allowing the same document to serve multiple functions;

- *modularity of information:* since the same text segment can be referenced from several places, ideas can be expressed with less overlap and duplication;

- *consistency of information:* references are embedded in their text, and if the text is moved, even to another document, the link information still provides direct access to the reference;

- *task stacking:* the user is supported in having several paths of inquiry active and displayed on the screen at the same time, such that any given path can be unwound to the original task;

- *collaboration:* several authors can collaborate, with the document and comments about the document being tightly interwoven (the exploration of this feature has just begun).

The Disadvantages of Hypertext

There are two classes of problems with hypertext: problems with the current implementations and problems that seem to be endemic to hypertext. The problems in the first class include delays in the display of referenced material, restrictions on names and other properties of links, lack of browsers or deficiencies in browsers, etc. The following section outlines two problems that are more challenging than these implementation shortcomings, and that may in fact ultimately limit the usefulness of hypertext: *disorientation* and *cognitive overhead*.

Getting "Lost in Space"

Along with the power to organize information much more complexly comes the problem of having to know (1) where you are in the network and (2) how to get to some other place that you know (or think) exists in the network. I call this the "disorientation problem." Of course, one also has a disorientation problem in traditional linear text documents, but in a linear text, the reader has only two options: He can search for the desired text earlier in the text or later in the text. Hypertext offers more degrees of freedom, more dimensions in which one can move, and hence a greater potential for the user to become lost or disoriented. In a network of 1000 nodes, information can easily become hard to find or even forgotten altogether. (See Figure 16.11.)

There are two major technological solutions for coping with disorientation—graphical browsers and query/search mechanisms. Browsers rely on the extremely highly developed visuospatial processing of the human visual system. By placing nodes and links in a two- or three-dimensional space, providing them with properties useful in visual differentiation (color, size, shape, texture), and maintaining certain similarities to our physical environment (for example, no two objects occupy the same space, things only move if moved, etc.), browser designers are able to create quite viable virtual spatial environments. Users orient themselves by visual cues, just as when they are walking or driving through a familiar city. However, there is no natural topology for an information space, except perhaps that higher level concepts go at the top or on the left side, so until one is familiar with a given large hyperdocument, one is by definition disoriented. In addition, an adequate virtuality is very difficult to maintain for a large or complex hypertext network. Such parameters as (1) large numbers of nodes, (2) large numbers of links, (3) frequent changes in the network, (4) slow or awkward response to user control inputs, (5) insufficient visual differentiation among nodes and/or links, and (6) nonvisually oriented users combine to make it practically impossible to abolish the disorientation problem with a browser alone.

One solution to this dilemma is to apply standard database search and query techniques to locating the node or nodes which the user is seeking. This is usually done by using boolean operations to apply some combination of keyword search, full string search, and logical predicates on other attributes (such as author, time of creation, type, etc.) of nodes or links. Similarly, one can filter (or *ellide*) information so that the user is presented with a manageable level of

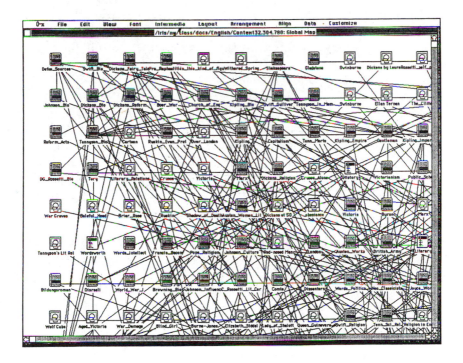

Figure 16.11 Tangled web of links. This experimental implementation of a global map in the Intermedia system shows the difficulty of providing users with spatial cues once a linked corpus contains more than a few dozen documents. This global map only represents about one tenth of the documents in a corpus designed for a survey of English literature course.

complexity and detail, and can shift the view or the detail suppression while navigating through the network. However, much research remains to be done on effective and standardized methods for ellision.

The Cognitive Task Scheduling Problem

The other fundamental problem with using hypertext is that it is difficult to become accustomed to the additional mental overhead required to create, name, and keep track of links. I call this "cognitive overhead." Suppose you are writing about X, and a related thought about Y comes to mind and seems important enough to capture. Ideally, hypertext allows you to simply "press a button" (using some mouse or keyboard action) and a new, empty hypertext window pops onto the screen. You record Y in this new window, then you press another button, the Y window disappears, and you are in the X window right where you were when Y occurred to you.

Unfortunately, the situation is a bit more complex than this scenario implies. If Y has just occurred to you, it may still be hazy and tentative; the smallest interruption could cause you to lose it. Coming up with a good word or short phrase to summarize Y may not be easy. You have to consider not just what is descriptive but also what will be suggestive for the reader when he encounters the link to Y within X. In addition, you must determine whether you should name the link to Y to suggest the contents of Y or to show Y's relationship to X. Some systems (for example, NoteCards) provide that links can have both a *type* (such as "idea") and a *label* (such as "subsume A in B"). Coming up with good names for both can impose even more load on an author struggling with an uncertain point. (One way to reduce this problem is for the authoring system to support immediate recording of the substance of the idea, deferring the creation and labeling of the link and/or the node until after the thought has been captured.)

Beyond that, you must also consider if you have provided sufficient links to Y before returning to work on X. Perhaps there are better ways to link Y to the network of thoughts than at the point in X where Y came to mind.

The problem of cognitive overhead also occurs in the process of reading hypertext, which tends to present the reader with a large number of choices about which links to follow and which to leave alone. These choices engender a certain overhead of metalevel decision making, an overhead that is absent when the author has already made many of these choices for you. At the moment that you encounter a link, how do you decide if following the side path is worth the distraction? Does the label appearing in the link tell you enough to decide? This dilemma could be called "informational myopia." The problem is that, even if the system response time is instantaneous (which it rarely is), you experience a definite distraction, a "cognitive loading," when you pause to consider whether to pursue the side path. This problem can be eased by (1) having the cross-referenced node appear very rapidly (which is the approach of KMS), (2) providing an instantaneous one- to three-line explanation of the side reference in a pop-up window (which is the approach of Intemedia), and (3) having a graphical browser which shows the local subnetwork into which the link leads.

These problems are not new with hypertext, nor are they mere byproducts of computer-supported work. People who think for a living—writers, scientists, artists, designers, etc.—must contend with the fact that the brain can create ideas faster than the hand can write them or the mouth can speak them. There is always a balance between refining the current idea, returning to a previous idea to refine it, and attending to any of the vague "proto-ideas" which are hovering at the edge of consciousness. Hypertext simply offers a sufficiently sophisticated "pencil" to begin to engage the richness, variety, and interrelatedness of creative thought. This aspect of hypertext has advantages when this richness is needed and drawbacks when it is not.

To summarize, then, the problems with hypertext are

- *disorientation:* the tendency to lose one's sense of location and direction in a nonlinear document; and

- *cognitive overhead:* the additional effort and concentration necessary to maintain several tasks or trails at one time.

These problems may be at least partially resolvable through improvements in performance and interface design of hypertext systems, and through research on information filtering techniques.

In this article, I have reviewed existing hypertext systems, the opportunities and problems of hypertext, and some of the top-level design issues of building hypertext systems. It has been my intention to give the reader a clear sense of what hypertext is, what its strengths and weaknesses are, and what it can be used for. But I also intended something more: that the reader come away from this article excited, eager to try using hypertext for himself, and aware that he is at the beginning of something big, something like the invention of the wheel, but something that still has enough rough edges that no one is really sure that it will fulfill its promise.

To that end, I mention one more book that night be considered to belong to the literature on hypertext. *Neuromancer* [24] is a novel about a time in the distant future when the ultimate computer interface has been perfected: One simply plugs one's brain into the machine and experiences the computer data directly as perceptual entities. Other computers look like boxes floating in three-dimensional space, and passwords appear as various kinds of doors and locks. The user is completely immersed in a virtual world, the "operating system," and can move around and take different forms simply by willing it.

This is the ultimate hypertext system. The basic idea of hypertext, after all, is that ideas correspond to perceptual objects, and one manipulates ideas and their relationships by directly manipulating windows and icons. Current technology limits the representation of these objects to static boxes on a CRT screen, but one can easily predict that advances in animation, color, 3D displays, sound, etc.—in short, Nelson's *hypermedia*—will keep making the display more active and realistic, the data represented richer and more detailed, and the input more natural and direct. Thus, hypertext, far from being an end in itself, is just a crude first step toward the time when the computer is a direct and powerful extension of the human mind, just as Vannevar Bush envisioned when he introduced his Memex four decades ago.

Acknowledgments

I wish to thank Les Belady, Bill Curtis, Susan Gerhart, Raymonde Guindon, Eric Gullichsen, Frank Halasz, Peter Marks, and Andy van Dam for their thoughtful reading of previous drafts.

References

1. T. H. Nelson, "Getting It Out of Our System," *Information Retrieval: A Critical Review*, G. Schechter, ed., Thompson Books, Wash., D.C., 1967.

2. V. Bush, "As We May Think," *Atlantic Monthly*, July 1945, pp. 101–108.

3. D. C. Engelbart, "A Conceptual Framework for the Augmentation of Man's Intellect," in *Vistas in Information Handling*, Vol. 1, Spartan Books, London, 1963.

4. D. C. Engelbart and W. K. English, "A Research Center for Augmenting Human Intellect," *AFIPS Conf. Proc.*, Vol. 33, Part 1, The Thompson Book Company, Washington, D.C., 1968.

5. T. H. Nelson, "Replacing the Printed Word: A Complete Literary System," *IFIP Proc.*, October 1980, pp. 1013–1023.

6. R. H. Trigg, *A Network-based Approach to Text Handling for the Online Scientific Community*, Ph.D. Thesis, University of Maryland, 1983.

7. H. Rittel and M. Webber, "Dilemmas in a General Theory of Planning," *Policy Sciences*, Vol. 4, 1973.

8. D. G. Lowe, "Cooperative Structuring of Information: The Representation of Reasoning and Debate," in *Int'l. J. of Man-Machine Studies*, Vol. 23, 1985, pp. 97–111.

9. J. B. Smith et al., "WE: A Writing Environment for Professionals," Technical Report 86-025, Department of Computer Science, University of North Carolina at Chapel Hill, August 1986.

10. W. Hershey, "Idea Processors," *BYTE*, June 1985, p. 337.

11. D. McCracken and R. M. Akscyn, "Experience with the ZOG Human-computer Interface System," *Int'l J. of Man-Machine Studies*, Vol. 21, 1984, pp. 293–310.

12. B. Schneiderman and J. Morariu, "The Interactive Encyclopedia System (TIES)," Department of Computer Science, University of Maryland, College Park, MD 20742, June 1986.

13. J. H. Walker, "The Document Examiner," *SIGGRAPH Video Review*, Edited Compilation from *CHI'85: Human Factors in Computing System*, 1985.

14. F. G. Halasz, T. P. Moran, and T. H. Trigg, "NoteCards in a Nutshell," *Proc. of the ACM Conf. on Human Factors in Computing Systems*, Toronto, Canada, April 1987.

15. N. L. Garrett, K. E. Smith, and N. Meyrowitz, "Intermedia: Issues, Strategies, and Tactics in the Design of a Hypermedia Document System," in *Proc. Conf. on Computer-Supported Cooperative Work*, MCC Software Technology Program, Austin, Texas, 1986.

16. N. Yankelovich, N. Meyrowitz, and A. van Dam, "Reading and Writing the Electronic Book," *Computer*, October 1985.

17. N. Delisle and M. Schwartz, "Neptune: A Hypertext System for CAD Applications," *Proc. of ACM SIGMOD Int'l Conf. on Management of Data*, Washington, D.C., May 28–30, 1986, pp. 132–143. (Also available as SIGMOD Record Vol. 15, No. 2, June 1986).

18. A. diSessa, "A Principled Design for an Integrated Computational Environment," *Human-Computer Interaction*, Vol. 1, Lawrence Erlbaum, 1985, pp. 1–47.

19. K. M. Pitman, "CREF: An Editing Facility for Managing Structured Text," A.I. Memo No. 829, M.I.T. A.I. Laboratory, Cambridge, Mass., February 1985.

20. P. J. Brown, "Interactive Documentation," in *Software: Practice and Experience*, March 1986, pp. 291–299.

21. D. Shasha, "When Does Non-Linear Text Help?" *Expert Database Systems, Proc. of the First Int'l Conf.*, April 1986, pp. 109–121.

22. A. Kay and A. Goldberg, "Personal Dyamic Media," *Computer*, March 1977, pp. 31–41.

23. T. W. Malone et al., "Intelligent Information-Sharing Systems," *Communications of the SCM*, May 1987, pp. 390–402.

24. W. Gibson, *Neuromancer*, Ace Science Fiction, 1984.

Reading

17

Data Sharing in Group Work[1]

Irene Greif
MIT Laboratory for Computer Science
Cambridge, MA

Sunil Sarin
Computer Corporation of America
Cambridge, MA

1 Introduction

A central concern in computer-supported cooperative work (CSCW) is coordinated access to shared information. Database management system (DBMS) technology provides data modeling and transaction management well suited to business data processing but not adequate for applications such as computer-aided design or software development. Group design applications deal with structured sets of data objects, such as design drawings and software modules, and complex relationships among data, people, and schedules. Advanced programming languages

---

[1] An earlier version of this paper appeared in the *Proceedings of the Conference on Computer-Supported Cooperative Work* (Austin, Tex., Dec. 1986). This research was supported in part by the Defense Advanced Research Projects Agency and was monitored by the Office of Naval Research under contract number N00014-83-K-0125. Authors' present addresses: I. Greif, Lotus Development Corporation, Cambridge, Mass. 02142; S. Sarin, Computer Corporation of America, Cambridge, Mass. 02142.

do provide excellent abstraction facilities for these classes of data but provide little support for data storage and sharing. Typically, application programmers have to write their own data management functions in terms of files and operating system calls.

The objective of this paper is to establish the scope of data management requirements of CSCW applications and to identify specific areas requiring further development. We begin by describing three cooperative work systems and their data sharing requirements. The limits of techniques used in the implementations of these systems are described in Section 3, which leads into an overview of new facilities becoming available in programming languages and database systems. CSCW application builders require support for object linking, inheritance, associative access, versions, and triggers to manage communication through shared data and to plan for data sharing between CSCW and single user applications. Our CSCW applications also include new features for defining and modifying roles and working relationships among people and new kinds of locking mechanisms to support users in long transactions and in transactions for which consistency constraints cannot be maintained automatically by the system. Section 4, on access control and concurrency control, describes our application level approach and suggests topics for research on generic data management support for these kinds of CSCW requirements.

The example systems we describe in Section 2 are drawn from different application areas—calendar management and document preparation—and span two modes of cooperative work, that of real-time and asynchronous meetings. Because of this diversity, we are confident that the requirements of these programs are representative of a wide range of cooperative work applications. Our conclusions are supported as well by reports of similar experiences in other research groups.

2 Three Cooperative Work Systems

The systems described in this section were developed at the MIT Laboratory for Computer Science from 1982 through 1985. These systems are research prototypes and were used mainly by the developers and their colleagues. Our objective was not only to develop useful functionality for supporting group work but also to explore the problems of implementing such functionality.

The two systems that deal with calendar management (MPCAL and RTCAL) both derive from the personal calendar system PCAL [20]. PCAL provides some multiuser functionality but is mainly intended for personal use by individuals. MPCAL is an extension of PCAL that provides controlled sharing and delegation of authority for calendar management on the basis of roles. MPCAL incorporates several new ideas that had previously been developed in student projects as separate extensions to PCAL. Some of the problems of extending the PCAL implementation, especially "migrating" data from PCAL to MPCAL, are discussed in Section 3.1.

RTCAL provides real-time conferencing functionality to users of PCAL and allows them to hold an on-line meeting in which they share information from their PCAL calendars in order to schedule a future meeting. The RTCAL implementation provided one test of a particular software organization for real-time conferencing; this organization and other alternatives are discussed in [43].

The collaborative document editing system CES was implemented in a distributed workstation environment; RTCAL and MPCAL only "simulated" distribution on a time-shared system. CES also provided the first major test of the distributed programming language Argus [29], reported in more detail in [21].

2.1 *Calendar Management*

MPCAL [7] is a *multiperson* calendar system for meeting scheduling and resource management. Each calendar has a set of *role* definitions and a specification of which roles can be assumed by different users. The system provides a default set of role definitions so that owners do not have to describe all roles from scratch. These defaults reflect some reasonable expectation about how individuals might wish to control access to their calendars. Owners can modify the defaults and define new roles to reflect different preferences or a different use of the calendar.

There are several types of calendars representing the schedules of a person, of a common resource (such as a conference room), or of open events such as seminars. The interfaces to all calendars are similar but they differ in their role definitions. For example, a conference room reserved by a sign-up sheet is built by using a *public* role that allows anyone to write a confirmed appointment but that allows no conflicting appointments. (Requests for appointments that conflict with existing confirmed ones may still be entered.) In contrast, with a personal calendar owners may choose to overbook themselves with conflicting appointments. Calendar owners may have secretary, team, and public roles that enforce the following:

- a *secretary* can confirm and cancel appointments on their behalf,

```
+---------------------------------------------------------------+
|  GREIF'S CALENDAR: VIEWED FROM SARIN'S SECRETARY ROLE         |
|  LAST COMMAND: SHOW DAY                                        |
+---------------------------------+-----------------------------+
|MONDAY     2 May 1983            |       PROPOSALS             |
|  9:00   MPCAL DEMO [New]        |                             |
|  9:30   XX                      | MPCAL DEMO [New]            |
|10:00    XX                      | 5-2-83    9:00 12:00        |
|10:30    XX                      |                             |
|11:00    XX                      | Test Appt [Canceled]        |
|11:30    XX                      | 5-2-83   12:00 14:00        |
|  NOON   *** [Can]               |                             |
|12:30    **                      | Another [Changed]           |
|  1:00   **                      | 5-3-83   10:00 11:00        |
|  1:30   **                      +-----------------------------+
|  2:00                           |       REMINDERS             |
|  2:30                           |                             |
|  3:00                           |                             |
|  3:30                           |                             |
|  4:00                           |                             |
|  4:30                           |                             |
|  5:00                           |                             |
+---------------------------------+-----------------------------+
|MPCAL> confirm 9:00_                                           |
+---------------------------------------------------------------+
```

Figure 17.1   Example MPCAL screen.

- members of the *public* can only make proposals for appointments; these appointments must be confirmed (or rejected) by either the manager or secretary,

- the public can see only blocks of time marked BUSY,

- members of the manager's *team* can see details of individual appointments.

Meetings can be scheduled through MPCAL by creating a *proposal* in a calendar. The proposal is written as an unconfirmed meeting into calendars of participants. (For each participating calendar, callers must be able to assume roles that permit them to add proposals.) Participants receiving a proposal will be notified when they next look at their calendars. (Figure 17.1 shows how these and other changes to a calendar are displayed. MPCAL and the other systems described in this section were designed for character-oriented terminals and do not take advantage of the graphics capabilities of modern workstations.) Participants are expected to accept or reject the proposal (which sets the meeting as confirmed in their calendars or deletes it) or can put it on hold and their responses are returned to the meeting callers' calendar. Callers may check the status of participants' responses at any time.

2.2 *Real-Time Conferencing*

RTCAL is a *real-time* conferencing system in which users share information from their personal calendars in order to schedule a future meeting. Participants speak to each other over a telephone connection and use the computer display as a shared blackboard. A *chairperson* invites participants and controls conference activity. The shared workspace of the conference includes a description of the meeting to be scheduled, and a filtered view of participants' calendars that shows only blocks of free and busy time. Individual participants can see more detailed information from their private calendars in a private window. Only one participant at a time, designated by the chairperson, can enter commands on the shared workspace for browsing in the calendar and proposing specific meeting times. Alternative proposals may be made: Participants vote on the alternatives and can review the result. If one of the proposals is confirmed, it is permanently installed in participants' private calendars.

As shown in Figure 17.2, the displays of the private and shared workspaces are next to each other on the screen so that as participants browse in the shared space, their private calendar displays change to show the same time period. Participants may leave and rejoin the conference at any time and may update their private calendars (using PCAL) while away from the conference. When they rejoin the conference, participants' displays are brought up-to-date with the other participants, and the shared workspace is updated to reflect changes made to participants' private calendars.

2.3 *Collaborative Document Editing*

CES [44] is a Collaborative Editing System for a group of co-authors working asynchronously on a shared document. As shown in Figure 17.3, a document contains a hierarchy of items or sections in which each section has a caption and a body. Each section is assigned a numeric label in accordance with its position in the hierarchy, as well as an internal, immutable unique identifier. A user edits one section of a document (in window "Document-Node") at a time but can see a view ("Text-Image") of the entire document and its structure ("Outline"). The document structure can also be edited to add and remove sections or to rearrange the order and hierarchical position of sections.

Each document has a set of coauthors with specified access (edit or read-only) to the document outline and sections. Separate privileges for each section are not supported; however, individual sections are stored at the workstations of their creating authors, so that primary authors

```
+----------------------------------------------------------------+
|RTCAL 3.2              12-4-82 11:52:07   Load=8.7    SARIN|
+----------------------------------------------------------------+
|scheduling "thesis"  uncommitted (2hrs, 12-25 to 12-31-82)|
|-session-   GREIF      LICKLIDER   SARIN       HAMMER    |
|-Running-   Chairperson IN-Session Controller  Waiting   |
+----------------------------------------------------------------+
| YOU have received control                                |
+--------------------------------+-------------------------------+
|Monday 27 December 1982         |Private calendar          |
|Merge of GREIF LICKLIDER SARIN  | Joe's birthday           |
| 9:00    XXX                    | 9:00                     |
| 9:30    XXX                    | 9:30                     |
|10:00                           |10:00                     |
|10:30                           |10:30                     |
|11:00                           |11:00                     |
|11:30                           |11:30                     |
|12:00                           |12:00                     |
|12:30    XXX                    |12:30     lunch           |
|13:00                           |13:00                     |
|13:30                           |13:30                     |
|14:00    XXX                    |14:00     Arpa meeting    |
|14:30    XXX                    |14:30     xx              |
|15:00    XXX                    |15:00                     |
+--------------------------------+-------------------------------+
| COMMAND> propose 10:30_                                  |
+----------------------------------------------------------------+
```

Figure 17.2   Example RTCAL screen.

have good response time and are assured of availability. The text of a section is accessible to other authors of the document, except when the creator disconnects the workstation to make that section inaccessible to others. The document outline is replicated and is accessible to all authors, even when individual sections are not.

Authors may work independently on separate sections of the document. If two or more authors try to write in the same section at the same time, one of them will be granted a *lock* and the others will be informed of who holds the lock. The lock is obtained implicitly when an author starts editing and is held as long as some editing activity continues: The lock will be released to a new coauthor after an idle period. These *tickle* locks are most useful in applications in which a user, when stopping work, may forget to release a lock. If a coauthor tries to edit while the current lock holder is idle, the lock will be released. In anticipation of this event, small editing changes are recorded in permanent storage on

```
+------------------------------------------------------------+
|                                                            |
| document: thesis/example   author: seliger    priv: edit |
+--[Outline]-------------------------------------------------+
|Version: 1  by: seliger  last cursor: 1/11    from: -       |
|[1@oa]   1.    CES Features                                 |
|[2@oa]      1.1.    One installation                        |
|[3@oa]      1.2.    Simultaneous views                      |
|[4@oa]      1.3.    Real-time screen editor                 |
|[5@oa]      1.4.    Locality of ownership                   |
+--[Document-Node]-------------------------------------------+
|[2@oa]      1.1.    One installation                        |
|Version: 2   by: greif  last cursor: 2/21   from: seliger |
|                                                            |
|One CES installation can support an unrestricted number of|
|editing sessions on an unrestricted number of documents.   |
|                                                            |
+--[Text-Image]---------------------------------------------+
|[1@oa]   1.    CES Features                                 |
|CES is a document editor which supports the collaboration |
|of authors on a shared document.  The system provides the |
|following features:                                        |
|[2@oa]      1.1.    One installation                        |
|One CES installation can support an unrestricted number of|
|editing sessions on an unrestricted number of documents.   |
|[3@oa]      1.2.    Simultaneous views                      |
|Each author participating in a CES session can simul-      |
|taneously view a shared document while editing a portion   |
+------------------------------------------------------------+
```

Figure 17.3   Example CES screen

a regular basis while the document is locked; if the lock is released without the explicit consent of the author, the committed changes will still be incorporated in the document.

CES allows users to read text that is being modified. If someone else is writing a section, the reader's view will be refreshed periodically as the section is updated. Although CES does not explicitly support real-time conferencing, a degraded form of real-time interaction (with longer delays in propagating changes) can be achieved by having multiple users view the same section and take turns updating.

3 *Data Abstraction Requirements*

This section provides an overview of data management features and their uses in CSCW application development. Our intention here is to touch briefly on a wide range of features to indicate the heavy demands placed on data management support by CSCW development. In Section 4 we cover access control and concurrency in more depth.

3.1 *Shared Data Management in the Prototypes*

MPCAL and RTCAL were both implemented in CLU [30], a language in which users can define new data abstractions. CES was implemented in Argus [29], which supports distributed programming using atomic transactions and retains the data abstraction facilities of CLU. The ability to define application-specific abstract object types and operations on them contributed to the rapid and reliable development of all three systems. However, a major bottleneck in the development process (and sometimes in performance as well) was the need to manage data outside of the address space of an executing program; this includes both long-lived data that persist between program invocations and, in the case of RTCAL, data that are communicated between program address spaces in real time.

Many high-level programming languages provide routines for automatic translation of internal object structures (including pointers) to and from an external representation. Languages like PS-Algol [2] and LISP support this translation for all objects that can be manipulated within a program; CLU and Argus support a more limited (but still useful) form of this translation that does not allow procedure objects to be represented externally [24]. If a single object within a program is designated as the internal database and all data that need to be externally stored are reachable by pointer from this object, then the application program only needs to invoke a single procedure to write this database to a file (or read it in from a file). This is how data were stored in MPCAL. This approach breaks down in several ways:

1. *Granularity.* Translating an entire large database to a single file, as in MPCAL, incurs significant overhead. When reading data, the entire file must be read in before any work can be done. To install even a small change, an entire new copy of the file must be written. The application programmer may partition the internal database into smaller files to reduce this overhead but incurs the additional cost of writing code to handle and translate cross-references between partitions. Argus does provide some support

for such partitioning: "Atomic" subcomponents of an object are stored separately and pointer translation is done automatically. This partitioning is useful in controlling the cost of update since only those atomic objects that have changed are written out. However, the programmer does not have as much control over this as might be desired because the decision as to whether a given object will be stored separately is fixed in the type definition for all objects of a given type.

2. *Extensibility.* As we extended PCAL with group support functions, we needed to extend the types of entries in a calendar and the types of information associated with calendar entries. With most programming languages, changes to type definitions usually make it impossible for a program to access data that were written to a file using the old type definition. This problem is usually dealt with by application programmers who define their own extensible representations for persistent data. For example, calendar entries in PCAL were implemented using a generic record object type with an extensible set of fields (field codes were explicitly stored with the object). The PCAL data structure also included an extensible set of indexes, so that new kinds of associative access (such as all changes not yet seen by the calendar owner) could be supported. This was important in supporting experiments with new calendar features and eventually in developing MPCAL. MPCAL could read data written by PCAL (it would see "nulls" in the new fields and its routines were prepared to deal with that), and PCAL could read data written by MPCAL (it would simply ignore the new fields and indexes, which would be preserved when PCAL wrote back the calendar file after modification).

3. *Persistence and Transience.* Sharing of data is usually only supported on secondary long-term storage such as a file system or DBMS. In RTCAL, where fast communication of changes to all participants is important, but recovery from failures is secondary, copies of the shared workspace of a conference are maintained only in the address spaces of the participants' programs. A similar approach is taken in other systems for meeting support, such as Colab [48]. The sharing of such data needs to be supported with database-style features, such as locking, and suggests that designers of shared data management software should decouple features for recovery or permanence of data from those for sharing and coordination.

4. *Access Rights*. All of our prototypes had access rights requirements that were implemented by the programs independently of the operating system access mechanisms for files. We discuss in Section 4.1 the problems with this approach.

Database management systems solve some of the problems of extensibility and access rights but not at the right level of abstraction. Since current DBMSs do not provide the data abstraction capabilities available in modern programming languages, programmers who use programming language data abstraction facilities and who also want to use DBMS technology must first translate their programming language structures into linked collections of records or tuples that can be handled by the DBMS.

3.2 *Abstract Objects*

Some of the features we describe below, such as abstract data types and inheritance, were originally designed for data internal to a single program but are now being developed in object-oriented database systems for management of external data [5, 32, 34, 49]. Other features, such as associative access, views, versions, and triggers, were developed mainly in applications and database systems that manage external data. However, they are now also appearing in programs that deal with internal data: history information in interactive programs that support "undoing" of operations [1], DBMS-like associative access in many knowledge-based systems, triggers in access-oriented programming [47], and recomputation of derived data in systems that present graphical views of structured data [39].

A common thread in these converging technologies is that of data abstraction. In the following, we assume that an application deals with abstract structured objects with associated *components* (e.g., named fields) or *attributes* (properties). Component and attribute values may be of simple data types (numbers, character strings, dates, times) or large unstructured types (document text or images) or may be other structured objects. A set of operations that are meaningful for a given object can be defined; programs that use the object will do so only via these operations rather than performing unconstrained manipulations on the object structure. Objects are created as instances of abstract *types* (or classes), in which all objects of a given type have a common structural format and support a common set of abstract operations.

3.3 *Inheritance*

Inheritance is a concept supported by object-oriented systems and artificial intelligence that allows an object type to inherit the structure and operations of its parent type(s) in a type hierarchy or lattice. Common structure and behavior can be specified once, in the parent type, and only the differences among subtypes are specified for each subtype. Presentation of the object type hierarchy, graphically or as an indented list, allows a user to browse without having to know in advance which types of objects he is looking for. Inheritance can also be used for smooth integration of structured and unstructured information, as in the LENS message system [33]. Applications that are not provided with an explicit inheritance mechanism often have to simulate it in the code. For example, MPCAL has both *appointments* that have date and time as well as *reminders* that have a date but no time; both are indexed and retrieved by date, but the reminders are displayed separately. This was implemented using a single data type in the programming language, with an explicit type field and a number of required and optional fields.

Many group work applications, including MPCAL, need to associate additional coordination-related attributes with objects, such as whether designated users have seen or responded to a given object. An inheritance scheme would allow the definition of a *coordination object type* hierarchy that specifies progressively more detailed collections of such attributes. A system that supports multiple inheritance would then allow an application to use any desired set of coordination attributes, and the associated code for manipulating these attributes, with application objects from a separate application object-type hierarchy.

3.4 *Links and Relationships*

The ability to *link* related objects is a fundamental feature of hypertext systems and their derivatives [12]. MPCAL supported certain specialized links between objects in a calendar, such as between the old and new versions of an appointment, that were interpreted in a fixed way by the system. It did not, however, allow users to create links and supply their own interpretations, to create a meeting object, link it to a proposal, and label that link as a *counterproposal* link. RTCAL did have the notion of alternative times for a proposed meeting but this again was a fixed structure that did not allow users to construct their own links.

Message-based communication systems that do not support links among messages are similarly limited: the sender of a message has to duplicate text referred to; when the text is not duplicated, the readers may have difficulty finding the referenced information. This limitation has been removed in computer conferencing systems such as EIES [25], which maintain links or threads among related messages in a conversation. It is also useful to allow linking of objects across different applications, that is, to send a mail message that refers to a given meeting object. In MPCAL, unstructured mail-like communication about a meeting could only be done in the comments field of the meeting or outside the calendar system. Links between mail messages and meetings would have integrated the full power of the mail system and the calendar system. Some support for linking objects across different applications is provided by systems such as Intermedia [53].

Typed links, organized in an inheritance hierarchy of link types, provide a framework in which users can choose which kinds of links to follow. For example, in TEXTNET [51] the class of *Argument* links is used to relate a piece of text to a piece of supporting text. Depending on the nature of the supportive argument, an Argument link can be further classified as A-deduction, A-induction, A-analogy, or A-intuition. A user browsing a text network can then ask to see general support by following all Argument links, or one specific kind of reasoning by following, say, A-deduction links only.

3.5 *Naming and Associative Access*

Most computer-based systems support selection of objects (e.g., files) by their unique names within a directly or from a displayed list (e.g., of newly received messages). However, users and application programs often need *associative* access to objects on the basis of their properties (type, structure, and relationships), such as all appointments on a given day, all messages not yet read, or all changes made since a given time. In general, an application can provide a set of associative access operations and implement the desired indexing structures. For example, MPCAL maintains indexes for all appointments on each day for changes not yet seen by the calendar owner, and so on. The costs of doing this in the application are

- Users are restricted to only those associative access paths implemented by the application. There is little flexibility compared with database query languages in which anticipated accesses are fast but others are still possible. Extending this set requires writing additional code, for example, for indexing a new field.

- Application code is responsible for keeping redundant information (such as indexes) consistent with the information from which it is derived.

Database management systems relieve application programmers of the above burdens by implementing the index access and maintenance code once (the application only needs to specify which fields it wants indexed and can add and drop indexes dynamically) and by translating predicate-based queries into accesses on the indexes and stored data.

The class of associative queries supported by a database system (such as a relational system) is much more powerful than the fixed set typically supported in application code. This power comes at a cost, in that the system's query optimizer must be invoked for each access. Many recent database systems provide significant performance improvements, comparable to implementing associative accesses directly in application code, by allowing the optimized execution plan of a query to be saved and used repeatedly without incurring the query optimization overhead each time [6].

Current DBMSs are limited to a small fixed set of data types and operations. This limitation is being addressed by research in object-oriented database systems that supports both abstract data types (as in programming languages) and associative access (as in database systems). The integration of the two introduces some challenges, in that the predicate in an associative query may involve an application-supplied abstract operation. Processing such queries in an efficient manner requires that the application specify properties of the abstract operations that can be exploited by an extensible query optimizer [5, 49]. These systems are also adding support for recursive queries [40]. Such a capability, not present in current DBMSs, would be useful in traversing all links, satisfying some criterion, that originate from a given object or collection of objects or in finding all access control groups to which a user directly or indirectly belongs.

3.6 *Views and Derived Data*

A view mechanism simplifies the process of displaying information that is computed from other information. A view specifies a computation (a formula, as in a spreadsheet, or a database query) that should be performed each time the user asks to see the view; the user need only use the name of the view and need not repeat the specification of the computation. A view mechanism also provides a means for achieving extensibility: A translation procedure can be associated with objects of one type that will let them be viewed as objects of a new type.

Views can be implemented in a variety of ways. At one extreme, the view specification can be recomputed from scratch each time the view is accessed. At the other extreme, a copy of the result can be maintained for fast access and kept up-to-date by recomputing it whenever any data on which it depends are changed. This requires maintaining dependency information so that all affected views can be identified when a given object is updated [49]. A variety of approaches between these extremes are available, such as

1.   *Caching* the result of computing a view and retaining version identifiers for the underlying information from which it is derived, so that recomputation at the next access can be avoided if it is found that none of the underlying information has been changed.

2.   Marking affected views out-of-date when an underlying object changes, and deferring the recomputation either until the view is accessed [41] or until the system has the resources to do the computation in background.

In some cases a user may also wish to control recomputation of derived information being looked at and ask to see changes only when he or she is ready.

Views can have many uses in group work. They provide a mechanism for users to specify what subsets of the available shared information they are interested in [19, 33], and what constitutes an interesting change to a user. For example, a participant in a meeting may be interested in any discussion about the meeting, whereas an aide who is scheduling a room and equipment will only be interested in date and time changes. Views can also be used as a unit of access control [22]: A given user can be supplied with a view that filters a subset or computes a summary of the underlying information, to which that user is not given direct access.

3.7 *Histories and Versions*

Access to past states of objects allows users to explore alternatives and to undo operations. Historical information is even more important when multiple users work on common information: The danger of accidental modification is higher, and a user may want to see objects in a stable state even though other users may be modifying them. Many file systems automatically maintain linear sequences of versions for each individual file; other systems for document revision control also allow multiple alternative branches [50].

In engineering design and software design environments, versions of objects are constructed by applying operations and transformations to other object versions, and this dependency information must be recorded as part of the object's *history*. Although a variety of such version control and configuration control models have been developed [26, 28], they all ultimately rely on the ability to define relationships or links among object versions. This appears to be the primitive form of support that is needed for historical information, rather than any particular built-in form of individual object histories. Once a particular configuration of objects has been constructed, it should remain stable, that is, the object versions it refers to should be *immutable*: it would not be possible to diagnose a bug in a particular software product if the exact source code from which it was produced could not be found. Typically, only the versions of objects and configurations currently under design should be allowed to change.

In some cases, such as message and conferencing systems, users can explicitly manipulate links to provide various kinds of versioning. For example, a *supersedes* link may declare one message to be a new version of another message or even of multiple messages that were merged before editing; the latter is hard to do in systems that support disjoint histories for each object. Other useful historical information can also be implemented using links. Dragonmail [8] records for each message submitted by users what other messages users have seen. This allows the messages in a conversation (an extended on-line discussion) to be presented in a meaningful order, so that a user's reply to an older message does not appear after a later message that the user did not see. This kind of information can also be useful in detecting conflicts resulting from concurrent activity (see Section 4.2.3).

In a multiuser system, it is important to record more than the content of object versions: Contextual information, such as who created an object version, and when, will allow object versions to be selected on the basis of properties of group interaction. Most file systems and DBMSs record only a fixed set of such attributes for a fixed set of operations. However, different applications may need different historical attributes, and the needs may change over time. Computer conferencing systems need to record what objects (or messages) a user has read. Similarly, MPCAL keeps track of whether the calendar owner has seen changes made by other users (e.g., a secretary) to a given appointment. Other contextual information that may need to be recorded include what a user saw at the time of performing an action (as in Dragonmail, above) and what role (Section 4.1.3) that user was playing at the time. The ability to define triggers (used in MPCAL) can provide the desired flexibility and extensibility in recording historical information.

The main drawback with recording historical information is its storage cost. This can be partly alleviated by sharing common substructure among object versions rather than by duplicating it (as in version management systems [26, 50] and in object-oriented database systems such as EXODUS [5]). It is also necessary to delete old information or migrate it to tertiary or off-line storage. Again, a flexible set of properties is needed to provide proper control over this process. Naive policies such as "keep the last N versions" are seldom useful and can even be dangerous: This one allows a single user to cause everybody else's changes to disappear. (In other words, giving users seemingly innocuous "create-new-version" privileges also implicitly gives them more powerful "delete-version" privileges.) An intelligent version migration policy should take into account not only the age of a version but also other criteria, such as what other objects contain references to a given object version and how important these other objects are, whether particular users who need to know about a given object version have seen it, and so on.

3.8 *Triggers*

In its simplest form, a *trigger* specifies additional computation to be invoked when a particular operation is performed on a particular object. (This is also referred to as an *active value* in access-oriented programming [47].) A trigger specification may apply to a single object instance or to a collection of objects; MPCAL associates a trigger with every operation, such as CHANGE, on every object type (e.g., APPOINTMENT). The triggered action in MPCAL can, in addition, do different things depending on the role of the user performing the operation.

Triggers can be useful for notifying users of changes to objects, detecting inconsistent states, and automatically initiating a step in a design or planning procedure. A more general form of trigger allows the association of an action with the occurrence of some specified condition on the database [13]. The condition may be a database query and may involve built-in system objects such as the current time. An example use of time in triggers is watching for deadlines. In MPCAL, a calendar owner's secretary may be informed if the owner has not responded to a proposed appointment by some specified interval before the time of the appointment. These triggers are similar to the condition-action rules of expert systems and have appeared in some experimental database systems [49].

4 *Control over Sharing*

Two critical issues in managing shared data for CSCW are access control and synchronization of concurrent actions. Our discussions in Sections 4.1 and 4.2 focus on issues that are independent of whether the information being shared is located on a single machine or is physically distributed; we do not cover communications protocols for transmitting operations and data across machines.

4.1 *Access Control*

In this subsection, we discuss access control in the absence of concurrency, that is, assuming users perform actions on the shared information one at a time. The rights of users to perform an operation on an object may depend on how contextual attributes of the users' computations match the access rights associated with the object and operation. A common approach in many operating systems is to have read, write, and execute permissions set for the owner of a file, and user group(s) associated with the file, and the general public; these are matched against the requesting user's identifier and groups. In some systems, this is extended to allow explicit access control lists (of users and other lists) to be associated with operations on a file.

A few operating systems provide a richer set of operations for which access can be controlled separately. For example, appending to a file is less dangerous than modifying the existing contents of a file, and it is therefore useful to allow some users who do not have write permission to perform this operation. Similarly, deleting a file may be considered more drastic than modifying it and could be controlled separately from creating new files and modifying files.

4.1.1 *Controlling Abstract Operations*   Although extensions such as the above are clearly useful, they are almost never sufficient for an application that has a more abstract model of information than files and wishes to control access to abstract operations on its object types. For example, MPCAL controls access to the operations of creating, viewing, and modifying appointments in a calendar, and of viewing time periods (days and weeks). (It is also possible to deny access to a calendar as a whole.) Similarly, although CES implemented a fairly traditional access control policy (distinguishing read-only from edit access to a document), it could have also distinguished and separately controlled *critique* access, that is, the ability to add annotations to a document.

The problem with attempting to control access in terms of abstract operations on shared information is that the underlying operating system may provide a more primitive form of access control, usually based on reading and writing of files. (A few object-oriented and capability-based systems directly support access control on abstract operations, but these are not yet in widespread use.) This limitation implies that an application's access control policy must be implemented by the application program itself, and that the access controls on the files used to store the information must be weak enough not to preclude any of the operations allowed by the application to different users. The latter usually means that files must be left completely unprotected at the operating system level because it is difficult, if not impossible, to use stronger protection and keep it consistent with the application's more complex requirements. This was done in MPCAL, which leaves all calendar files publicly modifiable. This approach is dangerous in that files are vulnerable to accidental or malicious modification and destruction by users who bypass the application program that exercises control. In some systems, this is alleviated by giving certain trusted programs *setuid* privilege. That is, the application program can temporarily change its user ID from that of the actual user to a special user ID allocated for this purpose, and the files in question can be made accessible and modifiable only by this special user ID. Or, in a logically distributed system, the desired access policy can be enforced by a *manager* or guardian that supports a given set of abstract operations via a message-passing or remote procedure-call protocol.

4.1.2 *Properties Determining Access* Even with the ability to control access to abstract operations, the use of conventional access criteria based on owner, group, and public is rarely sufficient to implement the rich policy desired in a cooperative application. It is here that MPCAL provides some novel features that are likely to be useful in other kinds of cooperative applications. These center around the use of the following properties to determine access:

1. *Roles.* A role (discussed further below) is an attribute of the user's computation that enters into the determination of whether or not to allow a given operation. This reflects the idea that the same users may have different privileges depending on what roles they are currently playing. A very primitive form of this idea is supported by operating systems that allow users to change the user IDs under which they are logged in or to explicitly enable or disable certain privileges that they hold. The role concept has appeared in other CSCW applications, such as XCP [46].

2. *Extensible user-valued attributes.* An MPCAL calendar that allows users in the public role (or some other role) to create new meeting objects may allow only the creator of that meeting to subsequently modify or cancel the meeting. That is, the access check for a modify or cancel operation must examine the created-by attribute of the meeting.

3. *Constraints on database content.* Rather than treating all integrity
    constraints as equal and always inviolate, different users can be
    allowed to violate particular constraints. Thus, calendar owners
    may allow colleagues to enter meetings into the owners' calendars
    that conflict with existing meetings but may choose not to let the
    public do so.

In addition MPCAL allows different variants of the attempted operation to be presented on the basis of access criteria such as the above.
For example, users in some roles may be allowed to see the detailed
descriptions of the appointments in a calendar, whereas users in other
roles may only see time slots marked FREE and BUSY. Similarly, when
a user attempts to enter a new appointment (or change an existing one)
in a calendar, it may be entered as a confirmed appointment or only
as a request awaiting confirmation, depending on the role definition in
effect. Different triggers or side effects may also be invoked for different
users or roles, for example, in MPCAL a new appointment entered in a
calendar may generate a notification to the owner of the calendar, except
when the owner enters the new appointment.

4.1.3 *Roles* Roles are also used in MPCAL as a means of abstracting
and packaging defined patterns of behavior. Roles provide the structure
for encapsulating access specifications, as follows:

- Each calendar has a collection of *role definitions* (whose structure
  is described below), a set of *user definitions* (listing the names of
  roles that each named user is allowed to assume), and a *default role*
  to be assumed by users who are not explicitly named.

- Each role has a *name* and a *description* and a set of *rules* determining access to each type of operation on each type of MPCAL
  object (e.g., SHOW DAY or CHANGE APPOINTMENT).

- Each rule, for a given role and a given operation, is a specification
  of whether or not a user in the given role can perform the operation
  in question, and if so, what variant of the operation (including
  triggers). This specification includes all of the criteria discussed
  above but in a restricted language that MPCAL interprets (rather
  than a general database query language).

This particular structure allows new roles to be defined easily by
copying the specification of an existing role and then modifying the
copy. MPCAL does not support all the different variations that might
be needed in a cooperative system. We expect the following refinements
to appear in next generation CSCW applications:

1. The ability to perform operations "on behalf" of someone else, with appropriate authorization. In the example above, in which modification of an appointment is restricted to the creating user, it is not possible for the creator's designated secretary to make such a modification. (Or, if the creator was a secretary acting on behalf of a manager, the manager would not be able to modify or cancel the appointment.) An MPCAL calendar specifies (via role definitions) only which users can perform which operations on the given calendar; it does not specify which users can act on behalf of this calendar's owner in performing operations on other calendars.

2. Support for requesting permission to perform some operation. For example, the federated architecture of [23] supports *negotiation* protocols whereby one component of a federation may ask another for permission to perform an operation advertised by the latter in the federation directory.

3. The ability to override access restrictions in emergency situations, for example, when the only user authorized to do something is in the hospital. This usually requires the help of a superuser or administrator with the power to override access controls. Alternative access definitions could allow most or all users to perform weaker variants of operations rather than denying access. An example is the ability to enter requests in MPCAL. Requests are a weaker form of appointment that users will see as not yet confirmed by an officially authorized user.

Although the individual role definitions of MPCAL are useful as a mechanism for learning and understanding what actions a role is permitted to perform, it is also important to know how different roles interact. This was not addressed in MPCAL; for example, there is no mechanism for ensuring or verifying that after a user in a given role performs some action on an object, there is some role that can perform further actions on the objects. Systems based on office procedures or coordination protocols support the definition of sequences (or partial orders) of actions for a collection of interacting roles [46]. Although these provide a more structured framework for defining and using roles, they do not currently provide sophisticated concurrency control mechanisms, which we describe next.

4.2 Concurrency Control

The conventional approach to ensuring database consistency in the face of concurrent access is to ensure that each transaction on its own preserves consistency, and that the effect of running multiple transactions must be the same as if they had been executed one at a time. The latter property is referred to as transaction *serializability* [14]. Transaction serializability can be ensured using concurrency control methods such as locking and timestamps. An underlying premise is that transactions will be short and conflicts resolved quickly. If long user interactions are managed in the same way, they can impose severe limits on concurrency. For example, a user who holds locks during an editing session might prevent other users from accessing the same data for hours. This problem can be particularly severe if there is a crash or network partition, making it impossible to determine whether a transaction committed or aborted. In this case, it is not possible to release the transaction's locks.

Concurrency can in some cases be improved by exploiting the semantics of the data and abstract operations [52]. However, even these methods face the same problems when transactions are long. In the discussion that follows, we will speak in terms of read and write operations for simplicity, with the understanding that similar arguments apply for other kinds of operations on shared data.

4.2.1 *Long-Lived Transactions*   If serializability is to be enforced for long interactive transactions, concurrency cannot in general be increased without incurring a higher probability of transaction abort. For example, *optimistic* concurrency control methods do not lock out transactions but instead check at the end of a transaction whether it saw a consistent state; if not, the transaction is aborted [27]. The checking can be done in any of several ways: by analyzing the conflicts among transactions that read and wrote the same data items, by recording the version identifiers of data read and checking that they have not changed, or by checking the assumptions (e.g., numeric value in a given range) made by a transaction about the data that it read. Whatever the test, it must be made atomically at transaction commit time, using locks or some other appropriate mechanism for that brief duration. The amount of work lost can be reduced somewhat by informing and aborting a transaction, before it attempts to commit, when its read set is modified. This is done in systems, such as Violet [17], that support read locks that can be broken when another transaction modifies the same data item.

Long transactions are also more vulnerable to aborting because of system failures. This can be alleviated by supporting *save points* within a transaction such that the effects of the transaction up to the save point are made permanent even if the transaction subsequently aborts. If save points are not built into the underlying transaction mechanism, they can often be supported on top. In the Alpine file system [4], for example, the transaction commit command has a *continue* option which, after committing the changes of the current transaction, creates a new transaction with the same state, holding the same locks. CES provides a similar mechanism by periodically saving small sets of changes made by an author, until such time as the author terminates his editing session or loses his lock to another author.

The CES locking mechanism also illustrates a different approach to resolving transaction conflicts in a cooperative work context. Most concurrency control algorithms have a fixed and inflexible way of deciding which transaction should wait (or abort) when a conflict occurs. More flexible policies are needed for interactive transactions controlled by users. The CES lock timeout (cf. Section 2.3) provides a measure of fairness to the coauthors of a document; various degrees of unfairness could have been introduced if the conditions for taking away a lock depended on the relative privileges of the users involved.

In a cooperative environment, it is also useful to inform a user which other user has the lock; the users may then informally negotiate and perhaps agree to take turns. We have proposed this concept for real-time conferencing, using the name *reservations* [43]; RTCAL's *floor-passing* Mechanism is a simple form of this. Reservations can be useful for concurrent activity outside a conference as well. The *self locks* of GORDION [11] appear to offer similar functionality: The user who set such a lock can later inspect an associated log to see if other users have accessed or modified the object and may enter into a negotiation (outside the system) with the other users. Such support for user-controlled coordination is analogous to some recent systems that support file sharing among cooperating rather than competing processes. For example, the Mesa file system, on receiving a lock request that cannot immediately be granted, will inform the process currently holding the lock; the process can release the lock, or refuse to do so, or specify that it will release the lock in a short period of time after completing necessary internal cleanup operations [38].

A long transaction or activity against shared data need not be limited to a single user session. It may be interrupted by a crash, or the user may leave his work unfinished at the end of the day with the intention of continuing at some later time. By saving the necessary state information, such activities can be made to last days or weeks or longer. This has been proposed for design database systems, which may also allow multiple users to cooperate in a design transaction [26]. In these systems, it is up to the users to pick up where they left off and continue the design transaction. In other scenarios, the actions that need to be performed may be known in advance and can be recorded in a *script* so as to provide a guarantee of execution; the system performs the actions in the background as and when the affected data become available. In

MPCAL, when a user issues a command to write a meeting proposal into the participants' calendars, the operation may fail on one or more calendars that are not immediately accessible; a queueing mechanism for automatic retrying of these operations would have been very useful. Tandem's ENCOMPASS distributed database has a suspense file that allows transactions to be queued for execution as soon as possible [35]. Gifford and Donahue's persistent actions [18] are another example of this idea. These mechanisms can also be extended by associating compensating actions (discussed below), in case a sequence of operations needs to be backed out [16].

4.2.2 *Relaxing Consistency Requirements* In order to increase concurrency among interactive or long-lived transactions, without increasing the frequency of aborts due to conflicts, it is necessary to examine closely the consistency constraints that the transactions are intended to preserve. The basic premise underlying most concurrency control mechanisms is that if a transaction saw a different value for a data item that it read, it would have performed a different update or external action. This may often be too strong an assumption. For interactive transactions involving a user decision, there may not be a very strong link between what data users see and what actions they perform as a result. It may therefore be acceptable to present users with data that are not guaranteed to be up-to-date. This approach is used in Grapevine [3] and other systems, in which a weak read operation may not see all of the effects of update transactions already executed (because of communication delays).

Some transaction-based systems that support strong read locks (that lock out concurrent updates until commit time) also give the application the option of reading a data item without locking out changes. With *notify locks* changes are not locked out, but the system informs the reading transaction when the data item is changed [45]. When users learn that the data they are looking at has changed, they can *compensate* for their actions, for example, by bringing back old versions or performing further changes. Some simple operations can be automatically compensated for (e.g., allocated resources, such as an airline seat, or a time slot in a calendar through simple release); in others, user intervention will be needed to determine the right course of action. Since users might often not need to compensate even when the data have changed, this is preferable to forcing users' transactions to abort when their readsets are modified. Compensation is a useful mechanism even in single user applications in which users can make mistakes or change their minds and undo prior actions.

Some data consistency constraints represent invariants that must always be true in order for operations on the data to work correctly. On the other hand, many constraints may simply be desirable but need not be required to hold at all times. In planning or design applications that involve constructing hypothetical future states, the enforcement of constraints on these future states may often be deferred. A simple example is presented by MPCAL, which allows multiple overlapping appointments to appear in a calendar. The constraint is known to MPCAL, but instead of refusing to violate the constraint, MPCAL informs users when a conflicting appointment is recorded.

Since individuals can overbook themselves in MPCAL, we did not try to prevent multiple users from concurrently entering conflicting appointments. A user may see a given time slot free on a given day and enter a new appointment, while another user (perhaps the secretary) sees the same time slot free and enters another, conflicting, appointment. Neither user has the time slot (or any larger granule, such as the date or calendar) locked while entering the new appointment. Instead, MPCAL, at the time of committing a user's update, applies the operation to the version of the calendar that exists at the time (which may be different from the version the user is currently seeing; a simple version check is used to determine whether this is the case). Thus, both new appointments will be entered into the calendar. This is not unreasonable, provided the users are made aware of the conflict so that they know that they may have to eventually compensate for it. MPCAL always informs a user when a new appointment (or one that was moved) conflicts with an existing one; and, a user will also clearly see the conflicts whenever the appointments for a given date are displayed on a time-of-day axis.

Similar forms of weak consistency constraints arise in applications such as design of software or circuits, where inconsistent states (incomplete or unverified designs) can be allowed to persist until a time of the users' choosing. Because individual transactions do not have to enforce consistency, the checking of constraints need not get in the way of concurrent activity or cause conflicting transactions to block or abort. Rather, the inconsistency (whether accidental or deliberate) can be detected and compensated for after the fact.

The relaxation of consistency as described above reduces conflicts among activities that read and update the same data item. It is also possible to reduce conflicts among update operations if these are treated as creating new versions rather than actually modifying an object. If the constraint that there always be a unique latest version of an object can be relaxed, users can concurrently work from a given version of an object, perform editing changes, and write back competing alternative versions. (They might choose to do so deliberately or may be forced to do so because of failure of the communication network.) The conflict can be detected and resolved after the fact, for example, by an authorized user who views the alternative versions and merges their changes in some meaningful way. Until this is done, a user who wishes to see "the" latest version may get an exception and may look at both versions (or neither, if access control is defined that way). Or, users may see the alternative that is designated by the system as being the latest (e.g., based on time stamp); this is not dangerous, provided users are aware of the existence of the other alternative(s) and can still retrieve it (them).

4.2.3 *Detecting Inconsistencies*   Since users acting concurrently may not be aware of conflicting actions, some mechanism is needed for recognizing situations that require compensation; appropriate users or programs can then be notified. The *version vector* approach of LOCUS [36] is an example that treats updates to a given object as being dependent on the previous version of that object only; it does not take into account other objects read by the activity updating the given object. This can be extended on the basis of serializability theory. That is, the activities are treated as if they were transactions, and a test is made to see whether the concurrent execution that occurred is equivalent to a serial one. This can be done by any of several methods:

1. Preassigning an ordering (e.g., timestamps) and seeing if any activity read an object version older than the one most recently written.

2. Constructing a conflict graph on the basis of readsets and writesets, and checking for cycles of certain kinds [10].

3. Retaining information with each object as to what other objects were read when this object was updated, and propagating this information when this object is read by an activity that updates other objects [37].

Although these are all tests for serializability, the testing is performed after the fact, and an activity is not made to abort if nonserializable execution is detected. Rather, compensation as needed is invoked by the application, which might determine that no compensation is needed even through an apparent problem exists. When the problem has been corrected, the dependency information that triggered the notification should be erased or overridden.

4.2.4 *Reducing the Probability of Inconsistency*   Although object locking and serializability are too restrictive of concurrency, and it is therefore necessary to accept the risk of inconsistency, it still seems useful to try to reduce the likelihood of inconsistencies. One approach is the use of a *warning* mechanism, such as the checkout command provided with many design databases. Users will typically be warned not to concurrently update the data checked out. In many systems of this kind, users do have the option of ignoring the warning and working concurrently, but they will do so with the full knowledge that they will have to deal with concurrent changes at some later time.

The probability of inconsistency can also be controlled using optional locks with automatic timeouts, as has been proposed for high availability distributed databases [42]. An activity (controlled by a user or program) attempts to set a lock at all affected objects (and sites holding copies of objects) within some reasonable period of time. If it is unable to do so, the activity must decide whether it wishes to perform the action that was planned; it may proceed anyway, or not perform the action, or perform a weaker variant (e.g., creating an alternative version of a document that cannot be locked). In addition, any locks that were successfully set automatically expire after a certain period of time, rather than remaining set indefinitely while waiting for the activity to complete its action (or abort) and release the locks. Although this technique resembles some of the time-based and reservation mechanisms described earlier, such as CES's tickle locks, there are some subtle differences. In CES, if the node of the user currently holding a given lock fails or is disconnected while writing a new version, the lock cannot be released until the node recovers; this may take much longer than the lock timeout period that CES attempts to achieve.

With the above *probabilistic* locks, on the other hand, it is possible that, because of communication delays and failures, two or more activities could believe they hold the same or conflicting locks. This is acceptable in an application model that allows for inconsistencies and supports compensation. It is not necessary for the locking policy to provide a guarantee of success, only a reasonably high probability. This is analogous to the coordination of distributed actions in the real world, where atomicity can never be guaranteed but time delays can be used to control the probability of inconsistency.

4.2.5 *Integration with Access Control*   So far, we have discussed access control and concurrency control in isolation; the two are, however, closely related. Consider the choices available when an operation on an object is invoked as part of some larger activity:

1.   The operation may immediately release results and resources on completion; the higher level activity may later need to perform a compensating operation.

2. The operation holds locks and other resources until the higher level activity commits or aborts.

3. The operation holds weaker locks that are automatically released after a timeout period.

The choice depends on users performing the operations *and* on their roles. When the larger activity is long running, concurrency control serves purposes in many ways similar to the use of coordination procedures or protocols for access control based on interacting roles. There is an opportunity for integrating the two into a single framework by combining both access control and concurrency control specifications. A specification for a coordination activity would include information as to

1. the operations allowed in the activity, at each of possibly several levels of nesting;

2. which roles are allowed to perform which operations, and which users can fill these roles;

3. the ordering of relationships among the operations. In some cases, an activity may simply go through a predefined script or protocol. In other cases, this may be too restrictive. A knowledge-based *task support* system [9] can recommend one or more operations on the basis of the goals and current state, while allowing users to perform some other operation if they wish;

4. the integrity constraints that must hold at each level of nesting, and triggers and notifications that apply at each level. For example, designers may not enforce strict constraints on information that they are working on privately; information that they pass to their co-workers may have to pass some minimal consistency criteria, whereas designs released outside the group may have to pass fairly strict tests.

5. the concurrency control method that applies to the operations at each level of nesting and which may allow nonserializable interleavings [15, 31].

5 Conclusion

Our experiences with prototype systems for cooperative work reveal a diverse set of requirements for managing data that is shared across programs. Many of the individual requirements are supported by features in one or more advanced programming languages, object-oriented systems, or database systems. The features include inheritance, object linking, associative access, views, and triggers. CSCW applications require a particularly rich mix of these features, which are not yet available in a single programming environment. Some specific features for access control and concurrency control are not yet fully addressed in any existing systems or applications. Our experiments with role definitions in MPCAL offer just a few of the kinds of fine control of access that will be required by end users of CSCW applications. Similarly, the tickle locks and support for concurrent reading and writing of documents in CES are indicative of the need for more flexible concurrency control in the context of long-running concurrent activities on shared data.

The set of features found in a given data management approach usually reflects the requirements of a particular application. When developing a new CSCW application, features not available in existing data sharing tools must be implemented in application code. As larger sets of these features are integrated into unified data modeling and management environments, this coding burden will be lifted from CSCW application development. We also expect this unified data management approach to play an important role in paving the way for acceptance of CSCW applications by providing the data sharing base for integration of CSCW applications more familiar individual work tools and electronic mail. CSCW applications can have significant impact on organization structure and work styles; their smooth introduction into the work place should be based on a gradual extension and augmentation to current work tools, not unlike the relationship among our personal calendar, PCAL, and the two CSCW calendars, MPCAL and RTCAL.

Acknowledgments

We would like to thank John Cimral and Robert Seliger, who designed and implemented MPCAL and CES, respectively, and Marvin Sirbu who helped to clarify the abstraction of roles.

References

1.   Archer, J. E., Conway, R., and Schneider, F. B. User recovery and reversal in interactive systems. *ACM Trans. Program. Lang. Syst. 6*, 1(Jan. 1984), 1–19.

2. Atkinson, M. P., and Morrison, R. Procedures as persistent data objects. *ACM Trans. Program. Lang. Syst. 4*, 7(Oct. 1985), 539–559.

3. Birrell, A. D., Levin, R., Needham, R. M., and Schroeder, M. D. Grapevine: An exercise in distributed computing. *Commun. ACM 25*, 4(Apr. 1982), 260–274.

4. Brown, M. R., Kolling, K. N., and Taft, E. A. The Alpine file system. *ACM Trans. Comput. Syst. 3*, 4(Nov. 1985), 261–293.

5. Carey, M. J., DeWitt, D. J., Frank, D., Graefe, G., Muralikrishna, M., Richardson, J. E., and Shekita, E. J. The architecture of the EXODUS extensible DBMS. In *Proceedings of the International Workshop on Object-Oriented Database Systems*. (Sept.). IEEE, New York, 1986, pp. 52–65.

6. Chamberlin, D. D., Astrahan, M. M., King, W. F., Lorie, R. A., Mehl, J. W., Price, T. G., Schkolnick, M., Selinger, P. G., Slutz, D. R., Wade, B. W., and Yost, R. A. Support for repetitive transactions and ad hoc queries in system R. *ACM Trans. Database Syst. 6*, 1(Mar. 1981), 70–94.

7. Cimral, J. J. Integrating coordination support into automated information systems. Master's thesis, Dept. of Electrical Engineering and Computer Science, Massachusetts Institute of Technology, Cambridge, Mass., May 1983.

8. Comer, D. E., and Peterson, L. L. Conversation-based mail. *ACM Trans. Comput. Syst. 4*, 4(Nov. 1986), 299–319.

9. Croft, W. B., and Lefkowitz, L. S. Task support in an office system. *ACM Trans. O–. Inf. Syst. 2*, 3(July 1984), 197–212.

10. Davidson, S. B. Optimism and consistency in partitioned distributed database systems. *ACM Trans. Database Syst. 9*, 3(Sept. 1984), 456–482.

11. Ego, A., and Ellis, C. A. Design and implementation of GORDION, an object base management system. In *Proceedings of 3d International Conference on Data Engineering* (Feb.). IEEE, New York, 1987, pp. 226–234.

12. Engelbart, D. C. Authorship provisions in Augment. IEEE COMPCON Digest of Papers, IEEE, New York (Feb. 1984).

13. Eswaran, K. P. Aspects of a trigger subsystem in integrated database systems. In *Proceedings of 2d International Conference on Software Engineering* (Oct.). IEEE, New York, 1976.

14. Eswaran, K. P., Gray, J. N., Lorie, R. A., and Traiger, I. L. The notions of consistency and predicate locking in a database system. *Commun. ACM 19*, 11(Nov. 1976), 624–633.

15. Garcia-Molina, H. Using semantic knowledge for transaction processing in a distributed database. *ACM Trans. Database Syst. 8*, 2 (June 1983), 186–213.

16. Garcia-Molina, H., and Salem, K. Sagas. In *Proceedings of SIGMOD International Conference on Management of Data* (May). ACM, New York, 1987.

17. Gifford, D. K. Violet, an experimental decentralized system. *Comput. Networks 5*, 6(Dec. 1981), 423–433. Also available as Xerox PARC Tech. Rep. CSL-79-12.

18. Gifford, D. K., and Donahue, J. E. Coordinating independent atomic actions. *IEEE COMPCON Digest of Papers* (Feb.). IEEE, New York, 1985, pp. 92–94.

19. Gifford, D., Baldwin, R., Berlin, S., and Lucassen, J. An architecture for large scale information systems. In *Proceedings of 10th Symposium on Operating Systems Principles* (Orcas Island, Wash., Dec. 1–4). ACM New York, 1985, pp. 161–170.

20. Greif, I. The user interface of a personal calendar program. In *Human Factors and Interactive Computer Systems—Proceedings of the NYU Symposium on User Interfaces* (May 1982), Y. Vassiliou, Ed. Ablex Publishing Corp., Norwood, N.J., 1984, pp. 207–222.

21. Greif, I., Seliger, R., and Weihl, W. Atomic data abstractions in a distributed collaborative editing sytem. In *Proceedings of the 13th Annual Symposium on Principles of Programming Languages* (St. Petersburg, Fla., Jan. 13–15). ACM, New York, 1986, pp. 160–172.

22. Griffiths, P. P., and Wade, B. W. An authorization mechanism for a relational database system. *ACM Trans. Database Syst. 1*, 3(Sept. 1976), 242–255.

23. Heimbigner, D., and McLeod, D. A federated architecture for information management. *ACM Trans. O–. Inf. Syst. 3*, 3(July 1985), 253–278.

24. Herlihy, M., and Liskov, B. A value transmission method for abstract data types. *ACM Trans. Program. Lang. Syst. 4*, 4(Oct. 1982), 527–551.

25. Hiltz, S. R., and Turoff, M. The evolution of user behavior in a computerized conferencing system. *Commun. ACM 24*, 11(Nov. 1981), 739–751.

26. Katz, R. H., Anwarrudin, M., and Chang, E. A version server for computer-aided-design data. In *Proceedings of 23d ACM/IEEE Design Automation Conference* (Las Vegas, Nev., June 29–July 2). ACM, New York, 1986, pp. 27–33.

27. Kung, H. T., and Robinson, J. T. On optimistic methods for concurrency control. *ACM Trans. Database Syst. 6*, 2(June 1981), 213–226.

28. Lampson, B. W., and Schmidt, E. E. Organizing software in a distributed environment. In *Proceedings of SIGPLAN 1983 Symposium on Programming Language Issues in Software Systems* (San Francisco, June 27–29). ACM, New York, 1983, pp. 1–13.

29. Liskov, B., and Scheifler, R. Guardians and actions: Linguistic support for robust, distributed programs. *ACM Trans. Program. Lang. Syst. 5*, 3(July 1983), 381–404.

30. Liskov, B., Atkinson, R., Bloom, T., Moss, E., Schaffert, J. C., Scheifler, R., and Snyder, A. *CLU Reference Manual*. Lecture Notes on Computer Science, vol. 114. Springer-Verlag, New York, 1981.

31. Lynch, N. A. Multilevel atomicity—A new correctness condition for database concurrency control. *ACM Trans. Database Syst. 8*, 4(Dec. 1983), 484–502.

32. Maier, D., and Stein, J. Indexing in an object-oriented DBMS. In *Proceedings of International Workshop on Object-Oriented Database Systems* (Sept.). IEEE, New York, 1986, pp. 171–182.

33. Malone, T. W., Grant, K. R., Lai, K.-Y., Rao, R., and Rosenblitt, D. Semi-structured messages are surprisingly useful for computer-supported coordination. *ACM Trans. O–. Inf. Syst. 5*, 2(Apr. 1987).

34. Manola, F., and Dayal, U. PDM: An object-oriented data model. In *Proceedings of International Workshop on Object-Oriented Database Systems* (Sept.). IEEE, New York, 1986, pp. 18–25.

35. Norman, A., and Anderton, M. EMPACT: A distributed database application. In *Proceedings of the National Computer Conference*. AFIPS Press, Reston, Va., 1983, pp. 203–217.

36. Parker, D. S., Popek, G. J., Rudisin, G., Stoughton, A., Walker, B. J., Walton, E., Chow, J. M., Edwards, D., Kiser, S., and Kline, C. Detection of mutual inconsistency in distributed systems. *IEEE Trans. Softw. Eng. SE-9*, 3(May 1983), 240–246.

37. Ramarao, K. V. S. Detection of mutual consistency in distributed databases. In *Proceedings of 3d International Conference on Data Engineering* (Feb.). IEEE, New York, 1987.

38. Reid, L. G., and Karlton, P. L. A file system supporting cooperation between programs. In *Proceedings of the 9th Symposium on Operating System Principles* (Bretton Woods, N.H., Oct. 11–13). ACM, New York, 1983, pp. 20–29.

39. Reiss, S. P. PECAN: Program development systems that support multiple views. *IEEE Trans. Softw. Eng. SE-11*, 3(Mar. 1985), 276–285.

40. Rosenthal, A., Heiler, S., Dayal, U., and Manola, F. Traversal recursion: A practical approach to supporting recursive applications. In *Proceedings of the 1986 ACM-SIGMOD International Conference on Management of Data* (Washington, D.C., May 28–30). ACM, New York, 1986, pp. 166–176.

41. Roussopoulos, N., and Kang, H. Principles and techniques in the design of ADMS+ − . *IEEE Comput. 19*, 12(Dec. 1986), 19–25.

42. Sarin, S. K. Robust application design in highly available distributed data-bases. In *Proceedings of the 5th Symposium on Reliability in Distributed Software and Database Systems* (Jan.). IEEE, New York, 1986, pp. 87–94.

43. Sarin, S., and Greif, I. Computer-based real-time conferences. *IEEE Comput. 18*, 10(Oct. 1985), 33–45.

44. Seliger, R. The design and implementation of a distributed program for collaborative editing. Master's thesis, Massachusetts Institute of Technology, Cambridge, Mass., Sept. 1985. Also available as Laboratory for Computer Science Tech. Rep. TR-350.

45. Skarra, A. H., Zdonik, S. B., and Reiss, S. P. An object server for an object-oriented database system. In *Proceedings of International Workshop on Object-Oriented Database Systems* (Sept.). 1986, pp. 196–204.

46. Sluizer, S., and Cashman, P. XCP: An experimental tool for managing cooperative activity. In *Proceedings of the 1985 ACM Computer Science Conference* (New Orleans, La., Mar. 12–14). ACM, New York, 1985, pp. 251–258.

47. Stefik, M. J., Bobrow, D. G., and Kahn, K. M. Integrating access-oriented programming into a multiparadigm environment. *IEEE Softw. 3*, 1(Jan. 1986), 10–18.

48. Stefik, M., Foster, G., Bobrow, D. G., Kahn, K., Lanning, S., and Suchman, L. Beyond the chalkboard: Computer support for collaboration and problem solving in meetings. *Commun. ACM 30*, 1(Jan. 1987), 32–47.

49. Stonebraker, M., and Rowe, L. A. The design of POSTGRES. In *Proceedings of the 1986 ACM-SIGMOD International Conference on Management of Data* (Washington, D.C., May 28–30). ACM, New York, 1986, pp. 340–355.

50. Tichy, W. F. Design, implementation and evaluation of a revision control system. In *Proceedings of 6th International Conference on Software Engineering* (Sept.). IEEE, New York, 1982, pp. 58–67.

51. Trigg, R. H., and Weiser, M. TEXTNET: A network-based approach to text handling. *ACM Trans. O–. Inf. Syst. 4*, 1(Jan. 1986), 1–23.

52. Weihl, W., and Liskov, B. Implementation of resilient, atomic data types. *ACM Trans. Program. Lang. Syst. 7*, 2(Apr. 1985), 244–269.

53. Yankelovich, N., Meyrowitz, N., and van Dam, A. Reading and writing the electronic book. *IEEE Comput. 18*, 10(Oct. 1985), 15–30.

Diamond: A Multimedia Message System Built on a Distributed Architecture

Robert H. Thomas
Harry C. Forsdick
Terrence R. Crowley
Richard W. Schaaf
Raymond S. Tomlinson
Virginia M. Travers
BBN Laboratories
Cambridge, MA

George G. Robertson
Thinking Machines, Inc.
Cambridge, MA

Diamond is a computer-based system for creating, editing, transmitting, and managing multimedia documents. A Diamond document might contain text, graphics, images, and speech as well as such other types of features as electronic spread sheets. A single Diamond document can contain, for example, a map in the form of a drawing combined with directions described in text or voice. Diamond documents can be used for a variety of purposes, including messages, memos, and forms.

Throughout this article we speak of Diamond as a system that handles "documents" rather than as a system that handles only "messages." In our view, a message is a document that has been sent from one user to another. The term "document" has been chosen because only part of what a modern message system does is concerned with message transmission; much of such a system is concerned with the preparation, storage, management, and processing of documents that might or might not be sent as messages.

Diamond is implemented as a distributed system. Documents and folders, which hold collections of documents and other folders, are stored in a distributed database. Information about users, such as the identity of the folder in which newly received messages will be filed (the *inbox*) and usage preferences, is maintained in a registry database managed by Diamond. Users access Diamond through user interface components. The user interface components, which typically run on powerful single-user workstations, interact with other distributed components of Diamond to make the services they provide accessible to users.

The development of Diamond was undertaken as part of a research project in the areas of multimedia and distributed systems. From the outset, a primary project objective was to produce a system that could be used by people other than the system developers. There were several reasons for this. As do others, we hold the view that in the systems area the validity of new ideas and approaches is best established through working systems that embody the ideas and approaches. One of the long-term project objectives is to understand how multimedia capabilities change the way computer-based person-to-person communication systems are used, and the extent to which the multimedia capability improves the quality and effectiveness of such systems. A widely used system is required to begin to answer these questions.

The objective of developing an operational system has, at times, limited the extent to which promising ideas could be explored. For example, in order to ensure that Diamond was a complete and usable system, the development of new mechanisms for handling various media types and for improving Diamond's performance and survivability characteristics as a distributed system were postponed until capabilities considered essential in modern message systems, such as *reply* and *forward* operations, were provided.

A discussion of Diamond should present the model of multimedia documents supported by Diamond, the characteristics of Diamond as a message system, the user interface currently provided by Diamond, and the distributed architecture on which Diamond is built.

Design Considerations

From the outset, we felt that the user interface to Diamond would be key to the system's success. It was important that the interface be responsive, easy to use, and helpful. Because substantial computing power must be dedicated to each user to provide adequate interactive responsiveness and to support important user interface features, such as multiple windows and graphical pointing devices, we decided that the primary user access to Diamond would be through powerful single-user workstation computers. Workstations in this class would include a powerful processor, high-resolution graphics, a substantial amount of main memory (1 to 2M bytes), an interface to a high-performance local area network, and possibly secondary storage; in addition, machines in this class are configured with graphical pointing devices and have the ability to interface a variety of devices, such as voice I/O equipment.

A consequence of using single-user computers for user access points was that Diamond would be built upon a distributed architecture. A Diamond configuration includes single-user access point workstations and a collection of shared computers that support the workstations by providing services, such as message delivery and long-term document storage. Two major benefits of this type of architecture are that it can be expanded incrementally to support a growing user community, and it can be structured to provide services in a highly reliable fashion by replicating key hardware, software, and database elements.

Although the primary access to Diamond is through powerful single-user workstations, not every Diamond user will have such a workstation, and those who do may need to access Diamond when they are away from their workstations. Consequently, we felt that Diamond should be able to accommodate a wide variety of types of user access points and user interfaces. Users who access Diamond without the complement of devices required to support all of the media will not be able to exercise Diamond's full multimedia capabilities. However, a user with an alphanumeric display and access to a telephone should, at a minimum, be able to create messages that contain text, electronic spread sheets, and voice. He should be able to "read" all messages; of course, the system would not faithfully present parts of messages that are in media beyond the capabilities of the access point, although it could provide an indication of the presence of those parts and their data type. Furthermore, different users may prefer very different styles of interacting with Diamond. To satisfy these users, it is important that Diamond be able to support different user interfaces.

Users will create documents that contain sensitive information and will rely upon Diamond to protect them from unauthorized disclosure. Therefore, Diamond should ensure the security and privacy of user messages and documents. In particular, all user access to documents should be subject to access control.

Like earlier generation text-only systems [1–3], Diamond operates in an environment that includes many interconnected computer networks and a variety of other message systems. The Department of Defense Internetwork is an example of such an environment [4]. A Diamond system should be able to interoperate with other Diamond systems as well as with other multimedia and text-only message systems. Interoperability requires adherence to a set of protocol conventions that govern the manner in which interactions occur between multimedia systems and the way in which multimedia documents are represented for transport between systems.

Diamond will outlive the hardware base used initially to support it; and as newer, more powerful hardware becomes available, there will be a desire to run Diamond on it. Consequently, it is important that the implementation be relatively easy to transport from one hardware base to another.

Multimedia Documents

A multimedia document might include elements of text, graphics, images, voice, and such other computer-originated features as electronic spread sheets. These elements are combined into a single, coherent entity. A typical text-only document of the type supported by most electronic mail systems is shown in Figure 18.1; in contract, a typical Diamond document is shown in Figure 18.2. As the example suggests, Diamond documents are integrated compound documents that can be displayed on a single display surface such as a computer display or a piece of paper. With the exception of voice, all multimedia objects are displayed directly as part of a composite document. Voice is represented by an icon and a caption. To hear a voice passage, the user must invoke an operation to play the passage.

A Diamond multimedia document is a structured object. It contains a collection of elements of various media types along with information about the individual elements, about how the elements in the document are related to one another, and about how the elements are to be presented. Figure 18.3 illustrates the data structure corresponding to the document in Figure 18.2.

Diamond currently supports a model for multimedia documents where a document consists of a collection of boxes that can be laid out on a quarter-plane in a nonoverlapping fashion [5]. Although boxes may be positioned anywhere in the quarter-plane, normally the horizontal dimension is limited to the standard width for hardcopy pages. Each box represents a document element of a particular media type. The following media are supported in the current implementation:

```
11-May-84 16:38.25---EDT,1142;
000000000001
Return-path: <Frankel@SRI-KL>
Date: 11 May 1984 10:23---PDT
Sender: FRANKEL@SRI---KL
Subject: Directions to Ft. Monmouth
From: FRANKEL@SRI---KL
To: ADDCOMPE Technical Working
Group
Cc: Frankel@SRI---KL
Message---ID:<[SRI---KL]11-May-84
10:23:36.Frankel>
```

Folks:
    Herewith are directions from Newark
Airport to Ft Monmouth where the ADD-
Compe meeting will be held next week.

Mike

Take the NJ Turnpike south to exit
11--Garden State Parkway. Take the
Garden State Parkway south to exit 105
--EatonTown/Ft. Monmouth.

    After the tollbooth, stay to the right and
continue past the traffic light and go
around the "left-hand turn" access
road. You are now on Hope Road.

    Cross the highway and continue past
the traffic light. Cross the railroad tracks
and continue until the 2nd street on your
left (Corrigador Road).
Turn left onto Corrigador and go straight
for about 1/4 mile. The hexagon building
will be on your left. It is the largest
building in the area so you can't miss it.

Figure 18.1.   Example of a text-only document.

From: Forsdick@BBN-Diamond
Date: 29 Oct 84 10:12-EST
To: Message-Meeting-People
Subject: Directions to BBN

To get to BBN from Hartford, Ct., take I91 North until you reach I90. Head east on I90 to the Allston/Cambridge exit:

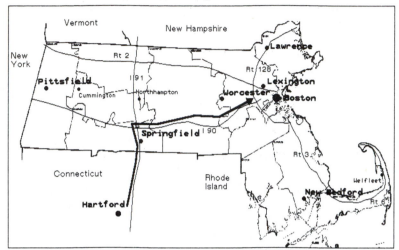

◁◁ Warning: Construction on Mass Turnpike

At the Allston/Cambridge exit:
   o Cross the Charles River and turn left onto Memorial Drive.

   o Follow Memorial Drive past Brattle St. and Huron Ave. until you reach Concord Ave. at the first of two traffic circles.

   o Continue on Concord Ave. through the second traffic circle.

   o BBN is on the right on the corner of Moulton St. and Corcord Ave., just after the Arco Station:

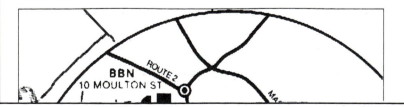

Figure 18.2   Example of a multimedia document.

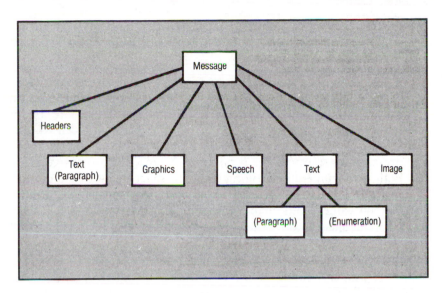

Figure 18.3 A multimedia document is a structured object.

- **Text.** Text elements may have a substructure. Different parts of a text element may be formatted according to a variety of styles. The formatting styles include a number of predefined basic styles, such as paragraph, itemization (marked lists of paragraphs), enumeration (numbered lists of paragraphs), and verbatim (as entered by the user), and the system allows users to define their own formatting styles from the basic predefined ones. In addition, multiple text fonts may be used in text elements.

- **Graphics.** A graphics element is a drawing that may include lines, geometric figures (polygons, circles, ellipses), text, and bit-map images. Closed regions (such as polygons) may be shaded with textures (regular bit patterns that fill the region), and the individual objects within a drawing may overlap one another.

- **Images.** An image element is a bit-map representation (digitized image) of a drawing, map, photograph, or other picture. Images can be entered into the system by an image scanner, such as a digital facsimile machine or a digitizing camera, or directly by use of the multimedia editor to "paint" an image. Black-and-white, color, and grey-scale images are supported.

- **Voice.** A voice element is a digitized speech passage entered into a document by means of a vocoder device. Diamond uses LPC vocoding devices to digitize and compress spoken speech. In a document, each voice element is represented graphically by an icon and a text caption. Selecting the icon will cause the voice to be played through a vocoder.

- **Electronic spread sheets.** A spread sheet element is a table that can be represented as a two-dimensional array where each element or cell may be empty or may contain a number, label, date, or formula. A formula serves to relate the contents of the cell to other cells in the table. A spread sheet element may be represented for presentation purposes as a table, as a type of business graph, or both. A document containing a spread sheet includes the underlying model (i.e., the formulas that interrelate cells) in addition to the cell values. This enables the recipient of a message containing a spread sheet to do "what if" experiments with the spread sheet.

It is easy to invent extensions to the relatively simple document model of nonoverlapping boxes Diamond currently supports. Boxes could be permitted to overlap; this would provide an "overlay" capability similar to overlapping transparencies. The multimedia editor supports the notions of "cutting" and "pasting," and it is possible to cut and paste across media types. The notion of time also could be incorporated into the presentation of documents. This would permit "slide shows" where a document could be grouped into collections of elements (slides); each slide would be presented in sequence, and the elements of each slide would be presented simultaneously. Although they are interesting, we have refrained from exploring these extensions in order to develop a fully functional and robust Diamond system. We expect that extensions to the Diamond document model will be made in the future.

Diamond as a Message System

As a computer-based message system, Diamond provides the means to create, send, receive, display, and file documents.

Users compose documents with a multimedia editor. The editor provides the means to combine input from various I/O devices, including the keyboard, mouse pointing device, vocoder, and image scanner, into a single integrated document. In addition, users can cut elements or parts of elements from one document and paste them into another and can include files prepared by other means in a document.

A user can send a multimedia document as a message by means of a *send* operation. When a user reads a document received as a message, the document is presented by the multimedia editor in the "read-only" mode. *Forward* and *reply* operations are available for routine message processing.

Documents and messages are stored in the Diamond Document Store, which is a hierarchical storage system organized much like a hierarchical file system [6]. A document store component holds documents belonging to users of a Diamond *cluster*, which is a set of computer systems that can communicate with each other at local area network speeds. The Document Store contains documents and folders. Folders may "hold" documents and other folders. The Document Store is citation-based [7, 8]; that is, folders hold references to documents and folders, which are called *citations*, rather than the documents and folders themselves. Citations for the same document can appear in more than one folder. Folders have symbolic names; documents may have symbolic names, but need not.

Each user has a folder, called his *office* folder, which is the root of the user's subtree in the Document Store hierarchy. In addition, each has an *inbox* folder, which is inferior to the office folder and is the location where citations for messages addressed to the user are delivered. Since the Document Store is citation-based, when a message is sent to a number of users, only a single copy of the message is held in the Document Store, and citations for the message are placed in each addressee's inbox folder. This is in contract with some message systems [2, 3] that deliver each recipient a copy of the message. The ability to share documents in this way is an important means for reducing the storage resources required by Diamond. This is especially important because message system users tend to keep a large number of documents on line, and multimedia documents can be expected to be significantly larger than text-only documents. To get a sense of document sizes, consider one page (8.5 by 11 inches) of text. A full page contains about 60 lines of 80 characters, or 38,400 bits. It would take about two minutes to read aloud. With a vocoder that compresses speech to 2400 bits per second, the page would require 288,000 bits if represented as speech. With one that operates at 64,000 bits per second, the page would require 7,680,000 bits. As an image, the page of text would require 786,000 bits if a display screen with a resolution of 100 dots per inch were used. This could be reduced by a factor of about six, to 131,000 bits, using standard facsimile compression techniques. Depending on the media and the amount of data compression used, an expansion by a factor from three to 200 over text can be expected as the media used to represent the information on the page is varied.

As previously mentioned, multimedia documents are structured objects. A multimedia document is stored within the Document Store as an object called a *DocStruc* along with objects for each of the individual media elements that make it up. The DocStruc for a document contains references to the individual media elements and information about their relation to one another in the document. The media elements themselves are each stored separately as objects within the Document Store. Because of the sharing this organization for the Document Store permits, a single element, for example, a map represented as a bit-map image, can be referenced in several documents.

Diamond includes a Registry database that is used in a manner similar to the registry in the Grapevine message transport system [9]. The Registry supports message addressing and delivery as well as user log-in and access control. There is an entry in the Registry for each authorized Diamond user. The user entries implement a mapping from user names to user inboxes that is used in message delivery. Messages are addressed to users by name. To deliver a message, Diamond uses the Registry to locate the addressed user's inbox folder. Each entry also contains the user's password and various "preference" settings, which are user-settable parameters that control aspects of Diamond's operation. Before being granted access to Diamond, a user must supply a name and password, which are checked against the Registry for validity.

The Registry also implements the notion of groups. A group is a collection of users and, possibly, other groups. Groups are used for message distribution lists and for access control.

Diamond operates in the DoD Internet environment [4]. Messages sent to users outside a cluster are sent to their destination through the Internet. Similarly, messages that originate outside of a cluster are transported to Diamond through the Internet.

The DoD Internet message system architecture [10] specifies how Diamond must interface to external message systems. The architecture includes Message Processing Modules (MPMs) that reside on various Internet host computers. MPMs are responsible for implementing an Internet message transport facility using lower-level Internet data transport mechanisms. They use a message transport protocol that specifies interaction patterns between MPMs. The protocol specification addresses control issues, such as how one MPM contacts another and requests message transmission, and data representation issues, such as how multimedia message data structures are encoded for transmission.

Both text-only and multimedia message systems exist within the DoD Internet. At present, the transport mechanisms and data representation mechanisms for text-only and multimedia messages are different. Diamond is capable of dealing with both the text-only and multimedia mechanisms, permitting it to exchange messages with both kinds of systems. When it receives a text-only message, Diamond translates it into a "multimedia" message with one text element. When it must send a multimedia message to a text-only destination, Diamond creates a text-only message that contains all the text elements of the original message and includes text descriptions of elements of other media types (e.g., "There was a voice passage here.").

The Diamond User Interface

The Diamond user interface was designed to satisfy several criteria:

- A user should be able to have more than one activity in progress at a time. For example, a user should be able to have several documents and folders "open" at a time and should be able to switch back and forth among them, scrolling through each independently. Similarly, it should be possible to interact with the Registry in order to add or remove users from groups while documents and folders are open. Concurrent activity is supported by multiple processes and multiple display windows. Roughly speaking, there is a process and a display window for each activity. For example, if there are three documents and two folders open, three windows are used by three processes acting as document editor/presenters to display the documents, and two windows are used by two processes acting as folder presenters to display the folders.

- A highly graphical mode of interaction should be supported. For the most part, the objects Diamond manages are highly visual in nature. Furthermore, the access point workstations have sophisticated graphics capabilities and are equipped with mouse pointing devices. Where appropriate, users should be able to specify operations by selection from pop-up menus and should be able to specify operands by pointing. For example, a user should be able to open (read) a document by pointing to its folder citation and selecting the open operation from a pop-up menu. In other situations, pop-up forms and dialog windows are more efficient ways of gathering information from the user. Of course, in some situations, such as text entry and editing, the conventional keyboard mode of interaction is more appropriate. Furthermore, since some users prefer keyboard interaction for most, if not all, situations, it should be supported for them.

- It should be possible to initiate any operation supported by Diamond regardless of what else is currently going on. For example, a user editing a document should be able to open another document, open a folder, or terminate the Diamond session without having to switch to another window.

- Users should be able to tailor Diamond to support their preferred style of interaction and usage. Where appropriate, the operation of the user interface should be parametric in nature. A user should be able to specify characteristics, such as the initial shape and placement of windows used to display documents and folders, the amount of the user's display surface Diamond can use, the text fonts used in various windows, etc. These preference settings are stored in the user's entry in the Registry and read by the user interface when the user invokes Diamond.

The access point user interface is structured to include a *coordinator process* and a collection of *tools* for various tasks, such as displaying documents. The Coordinator is responsible for allocating the display surface to the access point tools as they are started by the user and for managing their execution. The Coordinator has its own window that lists the tools and windows currently in use.

One of the key access point tools is the Diamond multimedia editor. It is used for creating and editing documents, and for displaying documents received as messages. As far as possible, the editor displays the document being edited directly on the display surface. For example, a document that contains a text element, a spread sheet element, and a graphics element has its elements displayed directly on the screen; to edit the graphics element, the user simply moves the pointing device over the graphics drawing and invokes graphics editing operations.

The editor supports three kinds of editing operations:

- **Document layout.** The user can specify how the various media elements of the document are laid out upon the document's quarterplane. The initial placement for an element can be specified. In addition, a media box can be moved from its current position by using the pointing device to "grab" the box and move it to the desired location. Similarly, a media box may be shaped by grabbing an edge or corner and moving it to the desired position.

- **Modiffcation of various media elements.** Reasonably complete editing capabilities for each of the media types are supported. Text elements are edited directly. The editing operations are similar to those found in many modern screen-oriented text editors [11]. As noted earlier, Diamond supports formatted text, and a particular text element or box may have substructure with respect to various format styles and type fonts. The editor formats text dynamically as it is entered and edited, and provides means for specifying and changing the format style for a text element or parts of it. The editing operations supported for drawings in graphics boxes are similar to those provided by programs like LisaDraw [12]. The graphical objects (lines, polygons, etc.) that make up a drawing can be moved and reshaped. The width of lines can be changed, and the interiors of closed figures, such as circles, can be filled with various shadings or can be made transparent. The manner in which the objects in a drawing overlap one another can be changed by moving objects to the front or back of the drawing. A variety of editing operations are supported for image elements. Images can be cropped like photographs. They can be scaled or rotated by arbitrary amounts, and it is possible to "paint" on the image using a variety of brush shapes and textures. Editing operations can be performed on the entire image or on a selected part of the image.

A voice passage in a document may be edited by pointing to the icon that represents it and invoking the editing operation. This results in the creation of a new window containing a graphical representation of the voice passage. Concurrently a waveform representation of the passage is used. An important editing operation is playback, which outputs the voice through a vocoder as a cursor moves from left to right under the graphical representation for the passage. This "what you see is what you hear" feature enables users to correlate features of the visual representation of the passage with words and phrases in the passage well enough to perform simple editing operations. With the editor it is possible to delete a segment of a voice passage, to delete silence from the passage, and to insert a speech fragment at a specified point in the passage. The inserted speech fragment may be new speech spoken into a vocoder, a speech passage that was previously stored in a file, or the last fragment that was deleted. A complete set of editing functions is provided for spread sheet elements. In addition to the standard spread sheet operations supported by programs such as VisiCalc [13], the editor permits the user to obtain multiple views of the spread sheet by splitting the spread sheet box into separate rectangular regions. Each region may contain a view of part of the sheet, or it may contain a chart or graph generated from values in the spread sheet table. A variety of chart types are supported. A spread sheet and its various chart views are tightly coupled, in the sense that when a value in the spread sheet changes, the change is reflected immediately in all of the charts.

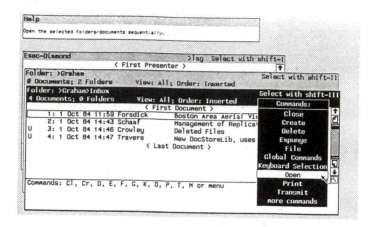

Figure 18.4 Windows for the Access Point Coordinator and the user office and inbox folders. The user is about to open a window to read a message.

- **Cutting and pasting.** Part of a document may be cut out and then pasted into another document or into the same document at another spot. It is possible to cut and paste between most of the different media types. This typically involves a type conversion. For example, when a text fragment is cut from a text box and pasted into an image, the fragment is converted from the representation used for text into bit map form before combining it with the image.

In addition to the multimedia editor, the other frequently used access point tools are the Folder Presenter, which is used to display and edit citations in folders, and the Registry Presenter, which is used to create, inspect, and modify Registry entries for users and groups.

A sense of which it is like to use Diamond can perhaps be best conveyed by briefly describing part of a typical Diamond session. When a user first invokes Diamond, she is asked to supply her name and password. After the password is verified, a window for the Coordinator is created and her office folder is opened in a second window. If the user has new mail, her inbox folder is also opened in a third window with the citation for the first unseen message in view (see Figure 18.4). To read a message the user simply points to the message citation, clicks a mouse button to pop up a menu, and selects the open operation from it (see Figure 18.4). This results in the creation of a new window where the message is displayed after being retrieved from the Document Store (see Figure 18.5). The user can send a document created with the multimedia editor by invoking the send operation (see Figure 18.6).

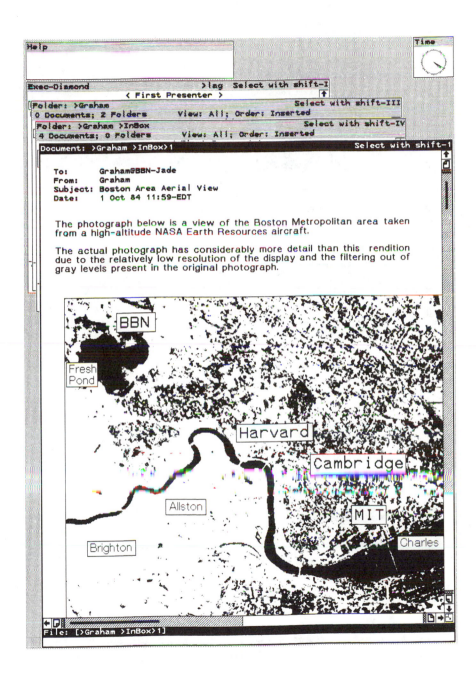

Figure 18.5   The message is displayed in a newly created window.

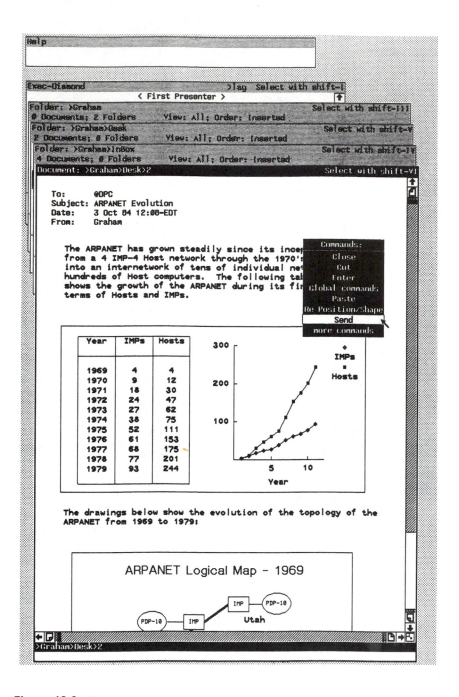

Figure 18.6   Sending a message.

The Diamond Distributed Architecture

Diamond operates in an environment made up of interconnected computer communication networks [4]. This internet environment includes both geographically distributed networks that span tens to thousands of miles and local area networks that span distances of up to a mile or two. From an architectural point of view, it is useful to think of this environment as being composed of clusters of host computers. Diamond runs within a cluster. Other systems, supporting other applications, may coexist with Diamond in a cluster.

A cluster is defined by its host components. The configuration of a cluster may change over time by the addition and removal of hosts. These changes are expected to occur relatively slowly. A cluster, in effect, acts to define the boundaries of a system.

A cluster may include hosts on several networks, and several clusters may exist on the same network. Performance considerations for systems such as Diamond generally lead to clusters that consist of a single local area network or a few local networks interconnected by means of high-performance gateways. Therefore, although *cluster* is a logical rather than a physical concept, clusters will tend to be aligned with local area networks.

The principal elements in a Diamond cluster include:

- **High-speed local area network.** The distributed nature of the Diamond design is feasible only when intercluster interhost communication with low delay and high throughput is possible. Acceptable performance requires that the local network operate in the multimegabit per second range.

- **Personal workstations.** Most users access Diamond from personal workstations that must have sufficient hardware resources, in terms of computing power and I/O devices, to provide the interface to the Diamond document and message services.

- **Shared server hosts.** Shared hosts provide a variety of data storage and device controlling services.

- **Internet gateway.** The gateway acts to make the cluster part of the Internet by supporting communication between cluster hosts and hosts external to the cluster.

Multimedia systems, such as Diamond, require specialized I/O equipment: vocoders for voice I/O, image scanners for image input, and high-resolution printers for image and document hard copy. Some

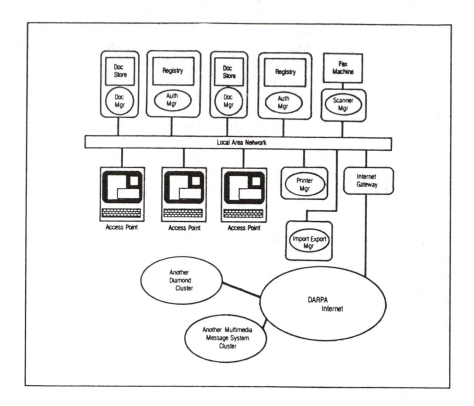

Figure 18.7 The Diamond Software Architecture.

equipment can be dedicated to single users and directly connected to the multimedia workstations used as user access points. Diamond workstations are configured with high-resolution bit-map graphics terminals and with mouse graphical pointing devices. In addition, some are equipped with microphones, vocoders, and speakers for voice I/O.

Other equipment is shared within a Diamond cluster. Shared equipment is typically too expensive to dedicate to a single user (e.g., laser printers) or too noisy or too bulky to place in a user's office (e.g., digital facsimile machines, printers).

The software that implements Diamond is partitioned into several components (see Figure 18.7), some of which have already been mentioned.

- User access to Diamond is supported by the Diamond *Access Point* software that runs on workstation computers. When the Access

Point needs services from other Diamond components, it interacts with them by means of interprocess communication (IPC).

- The Diamond Document Store is managed by a collection of *Document Manager* processes. A Document Manager runs on each server host that stores part of the Document Store. The design of the Document Store was based on a number of considerations:

  1. Users should be able to access their documents from any system access point.

  2. Multimedia documents will tend to be much larger than text documents.

  3. A substantial number of documents will have a relatively large fanout (number of recipients).

  4. The Document Store should be highly available.

  5. The Document Store should be scalable over a wide range of user populations.

  These considerations led to a design in which

  1. The Document Store is not on the user's workstation;

  2. The Document Store supports a high degree of sharing to minimize the storage required to support a cluster of hosts. Sharing is accomplished by the citation-based nature of the Document Store and DocStruct; and

  3. The Document Store is implemented in a distributed fashion.

  Allocation and deallocation of shared objects within the Document Store is managed by a reference count mechanism.[1]

- The Registry database is managed by a component called the *Authentication Manager*. In addition to supporting access to user and group entries in the Registry, the Authentication Manager is responsible for user authentication and supports access control. The names and passwords users supply when initiating Diamond sessions are verified by the Authentication Manager. After a user is authenticated in this way, the Authentication Manager makes an

---

[1]   Currently, the Document Store is purely hierarchical. If, in the future, the ability to move or to make copies of citations to folders is added, the possibility of circular structures that cannot be deallocated by the reference count mechanism will exist. A "mark and sweep" garbage collector to supplement the reference count mechanism has been designed for Diamond but not yet implemented [14].

entry in a local Authentication database, which is used to support access control (see below).

- *The Import/Export Manager* is responsible for exchanging messages with other message systems. It interacts with the Document Store and an Internet Message Processing Module (MPM) that takes responsibility for routing messages to their destination. It also performs protocol conversions between Diamond's internal format and the interchange format used for Internet message transport.

- The *Scanner* and *Printer Managers* act to make image scanning and printing services available to Diamond users. They interact between a CCITT-compatible digital facsimile machine and the Document Store to do image input and output.

- The Diamond development cluster also includes a *Vocoder Manager* that uses telephone lines to allow users to (serially) share vocoders. However, we feel that for voice to be used effectively and spontaneously each workstation should have its own vocoder.

Interprocess Communication

The key element of the distributed architecture is the IPC facility used to support interactions among Diamond's components. The IPC mechanism used by Diamond is also used by the Cronus Distributed Operating System [15]. As a result, Diamond is compatible with Cronus and can run as a Cronus utility.

The IPC was designed to support an abstract object model as the basic system organizing principle. With this model, all system activity can be thought of as operations on a collection of objects managed by the system and organized into classes called types. Examples of object types are documents, processes, and folders. In its simplest terms, the IPC provides the communication primitives and mechanisms for delivering operations to objects and delivering the results, if any, of operations back to invoking clients. Some processes, called object managers, play a special role in implementing objects. The Document Manager and Authentication Manager are examples of managers. Generally, when an operation is invoked on an object, it is delivered to a manager for the object that performs the operation.

Every object has a Unique Identifier (UID) that is a fixed-length, structured bit string. It includes fields that specify the object type and the host upon which the object was created, as well as fields that serve to ensure its uniqueness. Although, ultimately, all references to objects are through UIDs, some managers also support symbolic naming. For example, the folder hierarchy of the Document Store implements a symbolic name space by providing a mapping between user-defined symbolic names and object UIDs in order to facilitate user references to objects.

The IPC is message oriented, and it supports object-oriented addressing. Operations invoked on objects are sent as messages addressed to the objects. That is, addresses for messages are object UIDs. The object addressed is the operand, and the message data contains the operation and any additional parameters necessary to specify the operation. The role of the IPC is to deliver the message to the manager for the object (a process), which can perform the operation requested. Responses are sent as messages from object managers to requesting clients.

When sending a message, a process need not specify the host where the addressed object resides. To deliver the message, the IPC must determine the host. Certain object types are such that the objects never move from the host upon which they were created. These are called *primal* types. The important thing about primal objects is that, given the UID of a primal object, the IPC always knows where to find it, since the host where it resides is the one contained in its UID. A process is an example of a primal object. Nonprimal objects may move from host to host or may be replicated at several hosts. Diamond folders, Diamond documents, and the individual objects of various media are nonprimal. The IPC uses an *object location* procedure to find nonprimal objects. This procedure locates an object by means of a mechanism that broadcasts the generic operation *Locate* (as a message addressed to the object) to all managers for the object's type. This ensures that every manager for the object's type receives the Locate operation message. Because Locate is generic, it is defined for all object types and implemented by all object managers. Any manager that manages the object will reply, thereby locating the object for the IPC.

The object model implies a *client/manager* paradigm where a client invokes an operation performed by a manager by sending a message to the manager, and the manager responds by performing the operation and replying to the client with a message. To perform an operation for a client process, a process acting as a manager may itself need to act as a client with respect to some other manager. Client/manager interactions are governed by an Operation Protocol (OP) that specifies the details of how operations are invoked and responses are generated. IPC is used to transport data expressed in the OP representation scheme between clients and managers. Mechanisms defined by OP provide means for structuring data in messages and for associating transaction identifiers with messages so that clients and managers can keep track of operations in progress.

Access Control

All user access to folders, documents, and parts of documents is subject to access control through an access control list mechanism. The basis of access control in Diamond is the ability of the IPC to reliably deliver the identity of a sender of a message (or invoker of an operation) to the receiver of the message. The recipient can decide on the basis of the sending client's identity whether or not to perform the operation.

The Authentication Manager maintains a volatile database of bindings between client processes and user UIDs. These UIDs are typically obtained from the Registry database when the user logs in. To perform an access-controlled operation, a component, such as a Document Manager, contacts the Authentication Manager to obtain the user UID bound to the invoking process and the UIDs of the groups to which the user belongs. These UIDs can then be checked against the access control list for the requested operation. In order to increase its availability, the Authentication Manager is designed to be replicated on several hosts.

A prototype version of Diamond has been running since January 1984, and has been used since then as the electronic mail system for the project staff. Although Diamond has been operational for some time, it is undergoing development and improvement. The thrust of this work is to improve its usability and utility as a multimedia system, and to improve its performance and survivability as a distributed system.

Diamond was developed on a cluster configuration that includes BBN Jericho workstation computers [16] interconnected by means of a fiber-optic-based local network. The Jericho computer is not available commercially. Diamond has been ported from the Jericho hardware used for system development to the Sun Workstation [17], which is commercially available.

In the section on design considerations a number of objectives that have influenced the form Diamond has taken were discussed. With the exception of providing access for users without workstations, the design objectives have been met in Diamond.

The current implementation supports user access only from workstations. However, Diamond's hardware and software architecture is an *open* one capable of supporting alternative access points. In particular, the implementation is structured into two parts: a *core*, which provides basic document and message-handling services, and a collection of processes, including workstation access point processes, which make use of core services. The core services, which are implemented by various managers, are accessible through IPC by well-defined interfaces. This makes it reasonably straightforward to build alternative Diamond user interfaces.

Recently, a multimedia conferencing system [18] was developed using parts of the Diamond implementation. This new system explores the use of multimedia material in real-time conferences.

Systems like Diamond raise a number of interesting questions, such as what impact multimedia capability will have on person-to-person communication, which media will prove to be most useful, and what features will make multimedia systems easily usable. Questions like these will probably not be answered until systems such as Diamond become widely used.

One major impediment to widespread use is the current high cost of user access. For example, the workstations used in Diamond are in the $20,000 to $30,000 price range. Low-cost access points are required, and they appear to be within the state of the art. Diamond's architecture is capable of supporting alternative low-cost access points, and some of the newer personal computers appear to provide the resources required to support multimedia at costs that are in the acceptable range.

Acknowledgments

This work was sponsored by the Defense Advanced Research Projects Agency (DARPA) under Contract No. F30602-81-C-0256, which is monitored by the Rome Air Development Center (RADC). Views and conclusions contained in this report are the authors' and should not be interpreted as representing the official opinion or policy of DARPA, the U.S. Government, or any agency connected with them. This paper has been approved for public release and distribution is unlimited.

References

1. D. Crocker, E. Szurkowski, and D. J. Farber, "An Internet Memo Distribution Facility—MMDF," *Proc. Sixth IEEE Data Communications Symp.*, Nov. 1979.

2. T. H. Myer, "Future Message System Design: Lessons from the Hermes Experience," *Proc. CompCon Fall 1980*, IEEE, Sept. 1980, pp. 76–84.

3. J. Vittal, "MSG: A Simple Message System," *Proc. IFIP TC-6 Int'l Symp. Computer Message Systems*, North-Holland, April 1981.

4. B. M. Leiner et al., "The DARPA Internet Protocol Suite," *IEEE Communications Magazine*, Vol. 23, No. 3, March 1985.

5. H. C. Forsdick et al., "Initial Experience with Multimedia Documents in Diamond," *Computer Message Service, Proc. IFIP 6.5 Working Conf.*, IFIP, 1984, pp. 97–112.

6. E. I. Organick, *The Multics System: An Examination of Its Structure*, The MIT Press, 1972.

7. D. C. Engelbart, "NLS Teleconferencing Features: The Journal, and Shared-Screen Telephoning," *Proc. CompCon Fall 1975*, Sept. 1975.

8. D. C. Engelbart, "Authorizing Provisions in Augment," *Proc. CompCon 1984*, Feb. 1984.

9. A. D. Birrell et al., "Grapevine: An Exercise in Distributed Computing," *CACM*, Vol. 25, No. 4, April 1982, pp. 260–273.

10. J. Postel, *Internet Multimedia Mail Transport Protocol*, Tech. Report RFC 759, DARPA Network Working Group, March 1982.

11. R. M. Stallman, "EMACS: The Extensible, Customizable, Self-Documenting Display Editor," *Proc. ACM SIGPLAN Notices/SIGOA Conf. Text Manipulation*, ACM, Portland, Ore., June 1981, pp. 147–156.

12. *LisaDraw*, Apple Computer Inc., Cupertino, Calif., 1983.

13. D. Bricklin and R. Frankston, *VisiCalc (TM) Computer Software Program*, Personal Software, 1979.

14. H. C. Forsdick and R. H. Thomas, *The Design of Diamond: A Distributed Multimedia Document System*, Tech. Report 5402, Bolt Beranek and Newman, Inc., Oct. 1982.

15. R. Schantz et al., *Cronus, A Distributed Operating System*, Tech. Report 5086, Bolt Beranek and Newman, Inc., Nov. 1983.

16. N. R. Greenfeld, "The Jericho Professional Workstation," *Proc. Eighth Int'l Conf. Computer Architecture*, May 1981.

17. *Sun Workstation Architecture*, Sun Microsystems Inc., Mountain View, Calif., 1983.

18. H. C. Forsdick, "Explorations into Real-time Multimedia Conferencing," *Proc. Second Int'l Symp. Computer Message Systems*, Sept. 1985.

19

An Experiment in Integrated Multimedia Conferencing

Keith A. Lantz
Department of Computer Science
Stanford University
Stanford, CA

1 Introduction

Until recently, computer-based collaboration between geographically dispersed users has been limited primarily to electronic mail. Indeed, due to the lack of standards for the interchange of machine-processable multimedia information, "mail" has all too often meant postal rather than electronic mail. While ongoing work in document representation and interchange standards promises increased use of electronic mail, the asynchronous nature of electronic mail will still, at times, inhibit the collaborative process.

Electronic mail, like postal mail, imposes significant delays on any dialogue. While most advocates of contemporary asynchronous computer conferencing systems have argued that such delays allow "time for reflection" before responding, the evidence suggests that few users do so. Indeed, most users reply to new messages quickly, if at all, for one of three reasons:

1. They (have been led to) believe that not responding quickly reflects bad manners [2].

2. They do not wish to risk being "left behind" in a discussion on a topic in which they are deeply interested.

533

3.   They simply regard a message as if someone was talking to them in person, and reply immediately [5].

The last reason best reflects how accustomed humans are to real-time interaction. Unfortunately, in the environment of electronic mail, "real-time" responses are often generated in reply to messages that were ambiguous to begin with, leading to many additional message exchanges (frequently over many days) before the matter is cleared up. While misunderstandings also arise in real-time face-to-face communication, they are much more easily and expeditiously resolved.

As a result of these problems, and inspired by the proliferation of high-performance workstations and computer networks, several research groups are experimenting with computer-based teleconferencing systems that provide for the real-time exchange of multimedia information.[1] The first of these systems were the *audiographics conferencing* systems, which combine voice conferencing with the transmission of facsimile information or the use of telewriters, electronic blackboards, or slow-scan television. However, contemporary audiographics systems do not permit all conferees to interactively manipulate the images so transmitted. (See [10] for an introduction to the available systems.)

More recently, several systems have been developed which do not permit conferees to interactively edit their "shared space." These systems include AT&T's TOPES [19], Sarin and Greif's work at MIT [21, 22], Xerox's CoLab [7], BBN's MMConf [6], and SRI's EMCE [1]. Unfortunately, these and similar systems share one major limitation: They are not integrated with the existing software environment. That is, each *system* is actually a separate *application*, from which it is not generally possible to invoke other applications. Consequently, a conferee cannot invoke pre-existing design aids or editors within a conference. Rather, these facilities have had to be reimplemented for each conferencing system. Due to the usual time and manpower constraints, however, relatively few of these facilities have been reimplemented. Moreover, those that have been are often incompatible with each other and with the existing application base on their respective computer systems.[2]

In order for multimedia conferencing facilities to be widely accepted, they must be integrated with the users' existing computing

---

[1]   These systems should not be confused with so-called "computer conferencing" systems such as Planet, Forum, Com, and EIES—all of which belie the term "conference" by being concerned almost exclusively with non-real-time interaction—nor with the "shared screen" facilities of many timesharing systems—most of which are limited to a single medium, namely, fixed-width single-font text.

[2]   The developers of several of the existing conferencing systems have explicitly mentioned these disadvantages in their respective papers [6, 20, 21, 22].

environment—yielding *integrated multimedia conferencing*. Of course, there are several plausible uses of the term "integrated," including:

1. integrated with the user's conceptual model: The conferencing facilities support interaction that is "natural" for the user. At best, a conference should "feel" like a face-to-face meeting.

2. integrated with existing applications: Users can invoke (almost) any pre-existing application from within the framework of a conference.

3. integrated with existing programming methodology: Programmers can develop typical applications without having to deal explicitly with conferencing issues.[3]

4. integrated with existing systems software: Incorporation of the conferencing facilities required minimal changes to existing systems software, such as window systems.

This paper documents an experiment in integrated multimedia conferencing that was intended to meet the last three definitions. Minimal effort was devoted to conference management functions—as defined, for example, by Sarin [21]—or the associated user interface issues; there was no attempt to produce a polished, production system. Instead, the intent was to demonstrate the *feasibility* of implementing conferencing facilities with no (or few) modifications to the existing software environment.

The remainder of the paper is organized as follows. Section 2 outlines the target environment. Section 3 presents the three basic architectural alternatives. Sections 4, 5, and 6 present the experiment in some detail. Section 7 concludes.

2 Target Environment

To provide a framework for the discussion that follows, it is useful to briefly discuss the system environment we have in mind as the target for our work.

2.1 Hardware

The basic hardware environment consists of relatively high-performance workstations interconnected by both local area and long-haul networks.

---

[3] Note, however, that programmers may *choose* to take conferencing issues into account.

The "base" workstation is a diskless, monochrome Sun-class workstation with a speech-processing peripheral.[4] We assume that all workstations are connected to an Ethernet (or equivalent LAN). This provides access to other workstations and servers within the same institution. Second, we assume that institutional LANs are interconnected by networks with delay and bandwidth characteristics *at least* as good as the ARPANET. However, we believe that adequate performance can be guaranteed only by using T1 (or equivalent) for long-haul interconnections. Fortunately, such long-haul interconnections are becoming increasingly common.

2.2 *Software*

The hardware environment just discussed implies a number of characteristics of the software environment. For example, we assume the availability of basic networking facilities, such as those provided by the Internet protocol suite [16]. We also assume an operating system/programming environment that supports the construction of software composed of multiple independent modules (typically processes). Of more interest, however, are the assumptions we make about the architecture of the user interface software, since it is into that software that the bulk of the multimedia conferencing facilities must be placed.

We assume an environment that distinguishes between the user interface to, and the algorithms implemented by an application. This *functional* decomposition, if reflected in the implementation, can lead to a core of interaction facilities that is common to all applications. It is in this core that we propose placing the conferencing facilities.

Perhaps the most common "cores" available today are the various standard graphics packages—including, of course, the proposed Core standard [8], which derived its name from this very concept. Unfortunately, these packages provide a fairly low level of commonality, corresponding to the lexemes of a natural language. What is needed is more uniformity with respect to dialogue management and workstation management. *Dialogue management* refers to the manner in which a user interacts with the system to specify commands and handle responses—to carry on a meaningful *dialogue* with the system. *Workstation management* refers to the manner in which a user controls multiple applications at the same time, including the positioning of "windows" on his display.

To date, the bulk of the work toward general facilities for dialogue and workstation management has been couched in terms of *user*

---

[4] However, no speech-processing peripherals were available in the course of this experiment.

interface management systems [18] and *window systems* [9], respectively. Our own current work is based on a decade of experience building virtual terminal/window systems, graphics packages, and command interpreters [11, 13, 14, 17]. This experience has culminated in a methodology for implementing user interfaces [12] that is based on a decomposition of user interface software into four basic components, namely:

1.   The *workstation agent*, responsible for providing the basic, device- and media-dependent I/O abstractions, such as graphics primitives.

2.   The *dialogue manager*, responsible for command specification and invocation, response handling, and intelligent information presentation. While application requirements are specified in a *media-independent* fashion, each user has his own style of interaction and each workstation places different constraints on the communications media that can be employed. Based on these preferences and constraints, the dialogue manager must decide what communications media to employ for different stages of the man-machine dialogue.

3.   The *workstation manager*, responsible for controlling multiple applications and multiple dialogue managers at a time.

4.   Application-specific *frontends*, which, for example, implement additional interaction primitives to the extent that they augment the above facilities.

The semantics of an application—its algorithms—are embedded in what we refer to as its *backend*. The dialogue manager and the application frontend invoke those algorithms as necessary. While the split of *frontend* from *backend* is inspired in part by our experience with distributed applications, it is equally applicable in a single-machine environment.

Referring to Figure 19.1, the basic flow of control through the components is as follows: When booted, the workstation manager creates a default dialogue manager. Later, the user may interact with the workstation manager to create other dialogue managers or to create new windows for existing applications.[5] Typically, however, one dialogue manager will suffice; it interacts with the user (via the workstation agent)

---

[5]   Note that the workstation manager is itself a form of dialogue manager; two different names are used to highlight the workstation manager's "root" position in the architecture. Also note that "workstation manager" is used instead of "window manager" primarily because the latter term does not suggest the reality that there are many devices other than displays (hence windows) that must be managed.

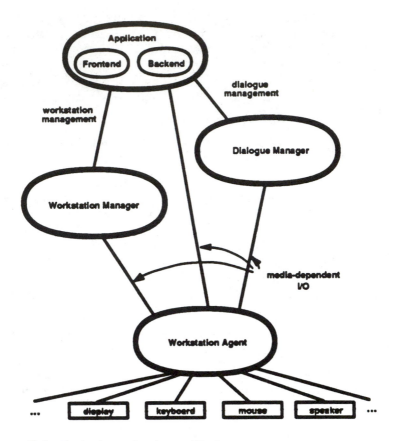

Figure 19.1 The basic user interface architecture.

to determine what applications (commands) should be run, to specify the parameters to those commands, and to invoke frontend and backend services as necessary. Naturally, any number of applications may be running at the same time; the user controls the input focus via the workstation manager.

This flow of control is typical of *external* control; the user guides the interaction. Unfortunately, the vast bulk of existing applications are written to use *internal* control; they drive the interaction. Such applications are dealt with in our architecture in two ways. First, all requests for "parameters" can be directed to the dialogue manager rather than to a specific workstation agent (or device driver). The dialogue manager can then determine the best interaction technique to use to specify that parameter—just as it determines the interaction technique(s) for specifying a complete command. Second, pre-existing "shells" or "executives" may be invoked as an application. The "real" applications may then be invoked from within the context of the shell.[6]

There are three principal motivations for this decomposition. First, it encapsulates common facilities in such a way that applications are encouraged to use those facilities, leading to greater consistency. Second, it facilitates experimentation with the user interface, since each component can be modified or replaced altogether (largely) independently of the others. Third, the decomposition facilitates porting of the user interface software across machines and operating systems, by encouraging better isolation of machine- or operating system-specific modules.

Of course, these things are true only if the implementation exhibits the modularity and well-defined interfaces of the architecture. That in turn is perhaps best achieved in a system that provides good support for the construction of software composed of multiple processes communicating via messages. While the experiment employed a system (the V-System [3]) that is nearly ideal in this regard, the same ideas could be applied, with some loss of performance, in the context of Berkeley UNIX.

3 Basic Architectural Alternatives

The basic goal of the experiment was to incorporate conferencing facilities into an existing system in such a way as to have minimal impact on existing applications and system software. The problems to be solved derive primarily from two characteristics of existing applications:

1. Most existing applications have been written under the assumption that they interact with only one user, whereas when the application is invoked from within the context of a conference it may have to interact (implicitly at least) with multiple users.

2. Most existing applications are sequential and nondistributed, while a conference is by its nature distributed and, in addition, could benefit from concurrency.

Fortunately, the modular software architecture advocated in the previous section provides the basis for a solution by enforcing a clean separation between applications and the system, and between the various components of the system. Extensions for multimedia conferencing require the addition of three principal components to the system (per conference):

---

[6] Note that a shell is yet another form of dialogue manager; again, a different name is used to highlight its status as a "lesser" entity in the hierarchy of dialogue managers.

1.   the *conference manager,* which provides floor control and other necessary synchronization functions;

2.   the *conference agent,* which mediates all I/O between shared applications and users (or, more precisely, their associated workstation agents); and

3.   the *conference frontend,* which provides user interface facilities specific to the conferencing environment, including those that support the invocation of shared applications.

The three principal architectures to be presented below assume the existence of exactly one conference manager and at least one conference agent. Further discussion of conference frontends is deferred until Section 4.

3.1 *A Centralized Architecture*

One approach is to emulate the manner in which timesharing systems provide "shared screen" support, that is, to interpose a single conference agent between the existing application and the conferees' workstation agents, as shown in Figure 19.2. The conference agent receives all user input and broadcasts all application output (destined for the user). To the application, the conference agent looks like a *virtual terminal* (or, more appropriately, a *virtual workstation*). To each workstation agent, the conference agent looks like an application. The data exchanged between conference agent and application is almost identical to that exchanged between conference agent and workstation agent; the conference agent only serves to multiplex low-level I/O.

This approach possesses the three significant advantages of minimal software development, minimal space requirements, and simple synchronization. Unfortunately, it also suffers from three equally significant disadvantages. First, it promises to provide poor response to all conferees except the one using the workstation on which the application (and presumably the conference agent) is running. This is particularly true when the second disadvantage manifests itself, namely, when there is so much user I/O that the conference agent becomes a bottleneck.

Finally, this simple centralized architecture imposes the heaviest network load since large amounts of low-level data must be passed between the conference agent and every other workstation. Note, however, there are many possible definitions of "low-level"—ranging from bitmaps to highly structured graphical data—depending on the interface provided by the workstation agent. If that interface is sufficiently high-level (as provided, for example, by the Virtual Graphics Terminal

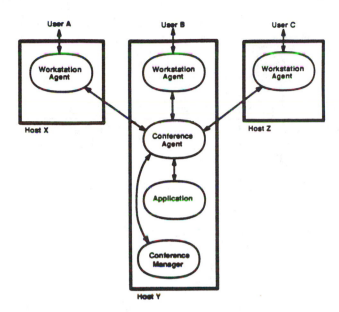

Figure 19.2   A centralized architecture.

Service [14, 15]), the network load will be nowhere near as severe as that suggested by Sarin and Greif [22].

3.2 A Fully Replicated Architecture

In the event that poor response or network saturation is seen as the major problem to be solved, we might choose to replicate both the application and a conference agent on every workstation, as seen in Figure 19.3. Each conference agent would be responsible for accepting media-dependent input from its associated workstation agent and relaying that input to all other conference agents. Upon receiving relayed input, a conference agent would pass the input to its co-resident application, which would then recompute and generate the necessary output. In general, it would not be necessary to direct that output through the conference agent, but rather, directly to the workstation agent.

Note that user input could be considerably "compressed" when being passed between conference agents. For example, our earlier work has demonstrated that the use of structured graphics (rather than the more common bitmaps or vector graphics) yields interactive applications that, when run on a host other than the workstation, are relatively insensitive to network bandwidth [14, 15, 17]. The use of multicast for "relaying" user input to all conference agents also serves to compress the data—by eliminating redundant point-to-point messages.

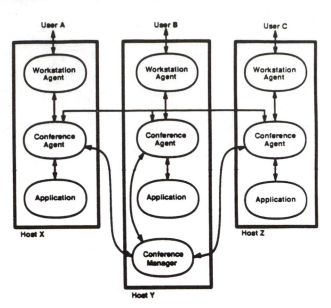

Figure 19.3   A fully replicated architecture.

We see, then, that the fully replicated architecture promises to sig-nificantly reduce network traffic. Moreover, because an instance of the application runs on every workstation, response, in general, should be improved. Unfortunately, depending on what language the application is written in, how much memory it consumes, and what devices it uses, it may prove impossible or impractical to run the application on every workstation.

This architecture also suffers from considerably more complex syn-chronization compared to the centralized architecture. In particular, if an application interacts with an I/O device not managed by the worksta-tion agent—for purposes of reading or writing a file, for example—each *instance* of the application may attempt to access the same device. The resulting synchronization problems could be disastrous.

3.3 *A Hybrid Architecture*

The two previous approaches approximate two ends of the spectrum for possible architectures. There are certainly other alternatives. Perhaps the most obvious one is a straightforward hybrid of the previous two, in which local clusters of users share a centralized architecture, and the collection of clusters together employ a replicated architecture. This approach is shown in Figure 19.4.

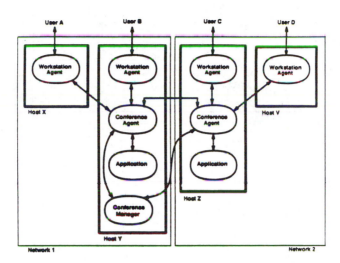

Figure 19.4   A hybrid architecture.

4 The Experiment

As an initial experiment with these ideas, the fully replicated architecture was applied in the context of the V-System. This choice was based on a desire to minimize network traffic and improve response, and was made possible by the homogeneity of the experimental environment. Note, again, that the intent of this experiment was not to produce a polished production system, but to demonstrate the feasibility of implementing conferencing facilities with no (or few) modifications to the existing software environment.

4.1 An Overview of the V-System

The V-System is a message-based distributed operating system designed primarily for high-performance workstations connected by local networks. It consists of a distributed kernel and a distributed set of server processes. The distributed kernel provides network-transparent interprocess communication based on synchronous message-passing—such that a sender blocks until a reply is received. Servers include device servers, storage servers, network servers, and, of course, dialogue managers and workstation agents.

The dialogue manager using this experiment is similar to the UNIX c-shell. It will be referred to below as the "executive." The workstation agent used, known simply as The Workstation Agent (TheWA), is a successor to the Virtual Graphics Terminal Service (VGTS) [14, 17]. Like the VGTS, TheWA provides multiple windows and a structured graphics system similar to PHIGS [4]. Unlike the VGTS, TheWA is composed of two distinct collections of processes, one for input (the WA-in) and one for output (the WA-out).

See [3] for a comprehensive overview of the V-System (Release 6.0) and pointers to the literature. An overview of TheWA is forthcoming.

4.2 The Conferencing Environment

The experimental conferencing environment reflects the following assumptions and constraints:

- Each conferee is using a Sun-class workstation connect to a local area network.

- A single file server serves all workstations.

- Each conferee is responsible for managing her own display; when conference-related windows are created, the user is responsible for positioning those windows in an appropriate place.

- Floor control is explicit and centralized within the conference manager.

- Shared windows maintain visual and functionality consistently across workstations.

- Each conferee's home directory acts as the working directory for each replicated version of the conference. Data files to be used by applications must be explicitly copied to each such directory before they are used in a conference.

4.3 Implementation Basics

Integration of conferencing facilities into the V-System required the addition of three new (types of) processes and minor modifications to TheWA. The three process types were discussed above, namely, conference frontend, conference agent, and conference manager. For each conference, there is one conference manager, while instances of the conference frontend and conference agent are replicated at every participating workstation.

In this implementation, the conference frontend provides only a rudimentary user interface for the conference manager. Indeed, the conference frontend and conference manager constitute the frontend and backend, respectively, of the conference management "application." The conference manager receives commands from the conference frontend, validates them, and if valid, broadcasts them to all conference agents.[7] The conference agents actual execute the commands with respect to their individual workstation environments.

In this implementation, the conference agent, rather than the conference frontend, is responsible for invocation of shared applications— applications that are to be run in the context of the conference. Of course, before invoking an application, it must first determine which application to invoke, and with what parameters; it must act as a dialogue manager. However, rather than reimplementing dialogue management functions within the conference agent, it was decided that the only application a conference agent could invoke would be an executive. Any other application can then be invoked from the executive.[8] Any executives invoked by the conference agents, and any applications invoked by those executives, are shared by all conferees.

4.3.1 *Mediating I/O*

Only one user may have the floor at any time. Therefore, all requests destined for the workstation's WA-in must be intercepted. What the conference agent does with these requests depends on whether or not its user has control of the floor. If not, the conference agent is said to be in *passive* mode; it simply buffers the input requests and waits for the input to arrive from the controlling conference agent. If the user has control of the floor, the conference agent is said to be in *control* mode; it responds to input requests by asking its co-resident WA-in for input.

When user input is received, the (controlling) conference agent broadcasts the input to all passive conference agents and passes it back to the requesting application. On receipt of the relayed input, each passive conference agent returns the input to its instance of the application, or buffers the input until a request for it is received.[9] Thus, regardless of source (WA-in or other conference agent), conference agents always pass user input on to their co-resident application. Each instance of the application proceeds to generate the same output—directly to the WA-out.

---

[7] Here and in the discussion to follow, "broadcast" is used as a placeholder for the sending of a message to a group of processes, whether by using *bona fide* broadcast or multicast facilities, or point-to-point messages.

[8] This is one example of a hierarchy of dialogue managers as discussed in Section 2.2.

[9] Since all instances of the application are not guaranteed to run in lock-step, it is possible for input to arrive from the controlling conference agent before a request for input is received by the passive conference agent.

5 Mediating I/O: Details

5.1 Opening Windows

There is one exception to the rule that output goes directly to the WA-out. To appreciate this exception, it is necessary to understand some details about the implementation of TheWA. Specifically, two streams are associated with each window—one for input (from the WA-in) and one for output (to the WA-out). When a window is opened, two separate open requests are generated, both of which are sent to the WA-out. Requests to open input streams are sent the WA-out so that it can initialize itself for echoing purposes; the WA-out then forwards the request to the WA-in. After opening the input stream, the WA-in records the output stream to be used for echoing and replies directly to the application, returning a unique identifier for the opened input stream. Given the semantics of message-passing in the V-System, this approach to opening input streams saves one message (yielding a total of three).

Unfortunately, if the conference agent did not intercept requests destined for the WA-out, it would miss the requests to open input streams and thus be unable to intercept subsequent requests destined for the WA-in. It is therefore necessary to intercept the messages containing these open requests, and it is desirable to intercept only those messages. The approach is to intercept requests to open *output* streams and then register the conference agent with the WA-in as an "intermediary" for input purposes.

Specifically, when applications make requests to open the output stream for a window, they determine the identity of the WA-out by resolving the name [defaultdisplay]. As shown in Figure 19.5 (where each arc represents a message), by binding the process identifier for the conference agent to [defaultdisplay], all such open requests are sent to the conference agent (message 1).

On receipt of such a request, the conference agent relays it to the WA-out (message 2), which replies with a unique identifier for the output stream and itself identified as the server for all subsequent interaction on that stream (message 3). The conference agent then proceeds to take advantage of the one change that had to be made to TheWA (specifically, the WA-in) to support conferencing: The conference agent registers itself with the WA-in to mediate all requests to open input streams associated with the just opened output stream (messages 4 and 5). Finally, the conference agent replies back to the requesting application with the information pertaining to the output stream (message 6)—which, remember, specifies the WA-out, not the conference agent, as the destination for all subsequent requests related to that stream. Subsequently, when the

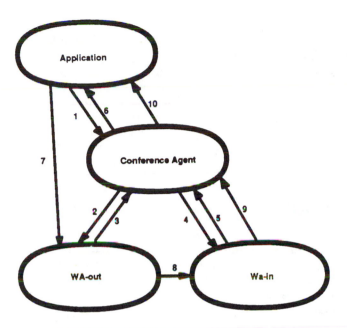

Figure 19.5 Opening a window.

application makes a request to open the input stream associated with the output stream, the request goes directly to the WA-out (message 7). As previously described, the WA-out eventually forwards this request to the WA-in (message 8). Now, however, after opening the input stream, the WA-in looks up the stream identifier for the output stream, notes that it is associated with an intermediary, and forwards the original request from the WA-out to the conference agent, along with the identifier for the newly opened input stream (message 9). The conference agent replaces the server identifier with its own so that all subsequent interaction on the input stream will be directed to the conference agent, and replies to the application (message 10).

5.2 *Stream Mapping*

Due to the replicated architecture, instances of the same (logical) I/O stream may have different stream identifiers on each workstation. In order for conference agents to agree on which stream(s) input is coming from, the workstation-specific identifiers must be bound to an identifier common to all conference agents. Fortunately, because only one person may have the floor (and thus invoke applications) at any time, stream open requests are guaranteed to arrive at every conference agent in the same order. Therefore, it suffices to use a monotonically increasing counter, initialized to the same value, to assign the common identifiers. This algorithm is completely decentralized.

Subsequently, whenever the controlling conference agent must broadcast input to the passive conference agents, it maps the workstation-specific identifier for the input stream to the common identifier and includes the latter in the broadcast message. Each passive conference agent then maps the common identifier into its workstation-specific identifier and includes the latter in its reply to the co-resident application.

5.3 *Change of Floor*

Another problem stems from the client/server model on which the V-System is based. Any application (client), when "at rest," is likely to have a read request outstanding on each of its input streams. Under normal circumstances, the server managing the stream responds only when input is available.

Conforming to this model, the controlling conference agent always has a read request outstanding to its co-resident WA-in for every conference-related window. Unfortunately, the associated user (who has the floor) may relinquish the floor at any time. Two major problems result if the outstanding read requests are not "withdrawn."

First, suppose the controlling user relinquishes the floor, but continues to generate input—either accidentally or forgetting he relinquished the floor. If the associated input stream is enabled for local echo, then any input will be echoed in the associated window. However, when the collected input is finally returned to the conference agent, it is thrown away, since that agent is no longer in control. This results in visual inconsistency across workstations. Worse, that inconsistency is reflected in the underlying data structures, such that subsequent output requests will generate different results on the various workstations.

Second, even if the former controlling user does not generate any additional input, conflicting read requests may result if the user regains the floor. Either the conference agent or the WA-in could treat a read request on a stream that already has a pending read as a duplicate, leaving the original request pending. Unfortunately, the second request may not be asking for the same type of input.

What is needed, then, is the ability to withdraw or abort outstanding read requests. Fortunately, this is possible in the V-System without further changes to system software. All servers are written to account for the death of clients. Read requests to the WA-in are generated only by helper processes within the conference agent—one per input stream.

Therefore, to abort an outstanding read, all that is required is to terminate the relevant helper processes. Of course, this also means that whenever a conference agent enters control mode, it must (re)create those processes.

6 Performance

At the time of this writing, no precise performance figures are available. A few observations can be made, however. First, the number of messages required to open a window has doubled—from 5 to 10, as documented in Section 5.1—and some additional processing is required. As a result, it appears to take twice as long to open a window. Fortunately, windows are created infrequently.

As for input and output requests: The number of messages required for the controlling application to get input has tripled, in the worst case (from 2 to 6). Add in some additional processing overhead, and it appears that the average input request also takes twice as long to process. On the other hand, the output from each instance of the application proceeds in parallel on each workstation, and goes directly to the WA-out, so output speed is not affected.

Finally, in situations where the participating workstations are equally loaded, we have observed negligible delay in the time it takes to generate output on all of them.

7 Conclusions

Overall, experience with the prototype has been promising. As described, no changes were made to existing applications and only one relatively minor change needed to be made to existing systems software. Moreover, while that change was inspired by the conferencing work, it can be employed by any application that needs to intercept input. Performance also does not appear to be a major problem. Since many other window systems, including X, are implemented in the server-based fashion of TheWA, the basic results should extend to them.

Of course, there are two significant features missing from our experimental environment: it does not support all the media (in particular, voice) typically associated with multimedia conferencing, and it does not include a long-haul network. As for additional media, we believe that they will introduce no new architectural problems—for the purposes of integration. Media-dependent I/O is handled, in our architecture, by the workstation agent, which is independent of the conferencing facilities;

any additional media will require modifications to the workstation agent regardless of how conferencing is implemented.

As for long-haul networks, we assume that our previous experience with distributed graphics applications [15] will apply in the conferencing environment. Specifically, delay and not bandwidth will be the major problem, and that problem is ameliorated by the fully replicated architecture. Moreover, both delay and bandwidth on long-haul interconnections will improve with the emergence of T1-equivalent networks. Nevertheless, we intend to pursue further experiments in this area.

A much more serious problem accrues to the fully replicated architecture, however. As previously discussed, if each instance of an application attempts to access the same device, the resulting synchronization problems could be disastrous. Most of these problems were avoided in the experimental environment by assuming that the only files accessed are named relative to the user's working directory, and that all such files are replicated in every user's working directory. Unfortunately, these assumptions are unreasonable in practice.

The techniques employed for workstation I/O could be extended to provide access to shared files, but only by changing significantly more systems software. There is also reason to believe that similar simplifying assumptions could be applied effectively to the hybrid architecture discussed in Section 3.3. However, further investigation is clearly required.

In addition to these problems, many extensions are possible. For example, as discussed thus far, each participant in a conference is assumed to be employing the same (logical) input and output devices. For the user who may wish to see different *views* of the shared data, this is undesirable. Fortunately, our user interface architecture permits conference agents to be extended to mediate all workstation input and output in the manner of a dialogue manager. Indeed, this is straightforward with the experimental conferencing architecture, since each conference agent already employs executives for command interpretation. Naturally, the conference agents would have to communicate amongst themselves using a standard representation for the input, and it would have to be possible to "snap back" to a common view—in order for participants to effectively discuss (using voice) the information being presented to them, for example.

Another major area of work will be determining the best implementation techniques to employ in different operating systems. The experimental implementation takes advantage of the multi-process structuring and interprocess communication facilities of the V-System. Unfortunately, these facilities are not so readily available in many other systems.

Acknowledgments

This research was supported in part by the National Aeronautics and Space Administration under contract NAGW-419. Judy Parkes, Amy Pearl, and Chris Lauwers were responsible for the prototype implementation; Judy and Amy also provided documentation that served as the basis for Sections 4 and 5. Joseph Pallas and Mike Slocum provided advice on the design. Robert Brown, Earl Craighill, Barry Leiner, and Raphael Rom provided commentary on Sections 1–3 when they were cast in the form of a proposal.

References

1. L. Aguilar, J. J. Garcia Luna Aceves, D. Moran, E. J. Craighill, and R. Brungardt. Architecture for a multimedia teleconferencing system. Proc. SIGCOMM '86 Symposium on Communications Architectures and Protocols, ACM, August 1986, pp. 126–136.

2. L. J. Bannon. Computer-mediated communication. In *User Centered System Design: New Perspectives on Human—Computer Interaction*, D. A. Norman and S. W. Draper, Eds. Lawrence Erlbaum Associates, 1986, pp. 433–456.

3. E. J. Berglund. "An introduction to the V-System." *IEEE Micro* (August 1986), 35–52.

4. M. Brown and M. Heck. *Understanding PHIGS: The Hierarchical Graphics Standard*. Megatek Corporation, San Diego, CA, 1985.

5. J. L. Edighoffer and K. A. Lantz. The impact of naming on computer bulletin boards. Submitted for publication.

6. H. C. Forsick. Explorations in real-time multimedia conferencing. Proc. 2nd International Symposium on Computer Message Systems, IFIP, September, 1985, pp. 299–315.

7. G. Foster. CoLab: Tools for computer-based cooperation. Tech. Rept. UCB/
CSD 84/215, Department of Electrical Engineering and Computer Science, University of California, Berkeley, 1984.

8. Graphics Standard Planning Committee. "Status report." *Computer Graphics 13*, 3 (August 1979), I.1-V.10.

9. F. R. A. Hopgood, D. A. Duce, E. V. C. Fielding, K. Robinson, and A. S. Williams. *Methodology of Window Management*. Springer-Verlag, 1986.

10. K. Kelleher and T. B. Cross. *Teleconferencing: Linking People Together Electronically*. Prentice-Hall, 1985.

11. K. A. Lantz. An architecture for configurable user interfaces. In *Foundation for Human—Computer Communication*, K. Hopper and I. A. Newman, Eds., North-Holland, 1986, pp. 257–275.

12. K. A. Lantz. On user interface reference models. To be published in *SIGCHI Bulletin.*

13. K. A. Lantz. *Uniform Interfaces for Distributed Systems.* Ph.D. Th., University of Rochester, 1980. TR63, Department of Computer Science.

14. K. A. Lantz and W. I. Nowicki. "Structured graphics for distributed systems." *ACM Transactions on Graphics 3*, 1 (January 1984), 23–51.

15. K. A. Lantz, W. I. Nowicki, and M. M. Theimer. "An empirical study of distributed application performance." *IEEE Transactions on Software Engineering SE-11*, 10 (October 1985), 1162–1174.

16. B. M. Leiner, R. Cole, J. Postel, and D. Mills. "The DARPA Internet protocol suite." *IEEE Communications Magazine 23*, 3 (March 1985), 29–34.

17. W. I. Nowicki. *Partitioning of Function in a Distributed Graphics System.* Ph.D. Th., Stanford University, 1985.

18. G. E. Pfaff (Ed.). *User Interface Management Systems.* Springer-Verlag, 1985.

19. W. Pferd, A. Peralta, and F. X. Prendergast. "Interactive graphics teleconferencing." *Computer 12*, 11 (November 1979), 62–72.

20. A. Poggio, J. J. Garcia Luna Aceves, E. J. Craighill, D. Moran, L. Aguilar, D. Worthington, and J. Hight. "CCWS: A computer-based multimedia information system." *Computer 18*, 10 (October 1985), 92–103.

21. S. K. Sarin. *Interactive On-line Conference.* Ph.D. Th., Massachusetts Institute of Technology, 1984. TR-330, Laboratory for Computer Science, Massachusetts Insitute of Technology.

22. S. K. Sarin and I. Greif. "Computer-based real-time conferencing systems." *Computer 18*, 10 (October 1985), 33–45.

III

CSCW DESIGN THEORIES

Recent Theoretical Approaches

The 1984 paper by Attewell and Rule (Reading 20, this volume) analyzes the then-current literature on the effects of computing in organizations and finds it to present inconsistent and inconclusive results. The other three papers (Readings 21–23)—all written since the Attewell review—are indicative of the progress we are making within the CSCW field. These papers present frameworks or theories that begin to bring order to our understanding of this subject.

The convergence of methodologies and models from organizational theory, computer systems, and linguistic theories of conversational discourse is the core of CSCW's identity. The impact on organizations may be the most important unknown to be explored in the field. Several researchers are trying to anticipate the effects and to formulate new design theories that can combine organizational and system design, so that people systems and computer systems can be jointly developed. These papers discuss the roles of underlying theories in system development and the implications of CSCW for organizations.

Malone's paper, *Electronic Markets and Electronic Hierarchies* (Reading 21), predicts a shift in organizational structure that can be directly attributed to coordination technologies. He analyses cost trade-offs—the costs of coordination as well as some more subtle costs—that have influenced past choices between markets and hierarchies. In some cases in which a hierarchy became a market, he can show the reasons to be a shift in these costs. He shows as well that electronic communication and shared databases will further tip the balance in ways that may bring the electronic "disintegration" of some vertically integrated production activities. There may also be a transition time during which we will see interesting variants of hierarchy that are made possible by technology. For example, an organization that grows to spread across large distances and time zones may preserve its hierarchical structure by using electronic media. Without the electronic support, the organization might have shifted sooner to a market structure owing to advantages that branches gain by dealing with local suppliers rather than with remote, centrally located ones. Trade-offs will still have to be made, but the costs change. Creative uses of the technology may also shift the balance to make new kinds of organizational structure feasible.

The Clement and Gotlieb paper (Reading 22) is a study that was influenced by Malone's work. It takes a look at work organization and computer system organization in the New Business Department at a large life insurance firm. The dynamics of the interaction between the two can be explained in terms of "the economic incentive to reduce the length of transaction processing chains and the more political goal of extending managerial control." He emphasizes the ways in which different perspectives and a concern for the human factors of organizations can influence system design. Political goals as well as economic ones might be achieved in part by changes in computer technology.

The Winograd paper (Reading 23) suggests yet another way to look at computer systems: the language/action perspective. This perspective is the basis for a commercial product, The Coordinator, developed by Action Technologies, Inc. In the paper, the language perspective is used in a case study that involves no computer systems. This perspective helps take into account the importance of the specialized language, or jargon, of a business. A system that does not support the jargon may not satisfy users. In the papers that emphasize the organizational perspective, we saw that the computer system can shape the organizational structure. In this paper, we see an analogous effect by which the computer system may end up changing the organization's language and conversation structures.

One of the most useful sections of the Winograd paper is its analysis of the "blindnesses" of the language/action perspective. These are highlighted by contrasting the perspective with several others, each of which has its strengths and weaknesses. The importance of this analysis is to highlight the complexity of designing systems for people in organizations: the full range of perspectives must be applied. This will be possible only with increased awareness of the failings of each perspective taken separately and with team design that brings together experts in the many perspectives. CSCW demands new design techniques; that is the primary message of this section.

Computing and Organizations: What We Know and What We Don't Know

Paul Attewell
James Rule

A few issues in the evolution of computing draw equal attention from specialists and from the public at large. Nearly everyone, for example, wants to know what kind of social world is emerging from the continuing permeation of organizational life by computing. The most urgent of these questions are socioeconomic—for instance, whether new technologies will reduce employment, enhance organizational efficiency, or strengthen managers' decision-making power. However, hardly of less interest are issues relating to the changing nature of social *experience* in the face of technological change: Is work becoming more or less fulfilling, thanks to the computer? Are computerized organizations more or less humane than their conventional counterparts?

We like to think of these questions as topical, yet they echo themes that have long played a part in the history of social and economic thought. They were by no means new, for example, when Marx entertained them. He and other nineteenth-century commentators devoted much attention to what we would now call automation and technologically induced unemployment. No less was Marx attentive to what he saw as degradation in the *content* of work through technologically induced deskilling. The widespread use of computing by government and private organizations is obviously a phenomenon of the last two or three decades. Yet the same questions we are now asking about computing, others have long asked about other technologies.

What puzzles us is that people remain so willing to speak and write as though the overall effects of computing technologies were a foregone conclusion, as though they could be determined a priori. People still make broad claims that computerized work is manifestly more fulfilling than conventional work or that computerization obviously and evidently robs work of its inherent rewards. Similar a priori claims are made on the effects of computing on employment or on its role in organizational decision making. Often buttressed by studies of small sets of cases, such works give people the impression that we understand more about the repercussions of computing in organizations than we really do and that research will only confirm what we already know.

We argue the opposite: that evidence on these subjects is actually fragmentary and very mixed, and that a priori arguments are particularly inappropriate in light of the range and variety of variables at work in these situations. In this article we examine the literature on the effects of computing on the numbers and quality of jobs, on management decision making, and on organizational dealings with clients and customers. We also consider various perspectives on the causes of organizational decisions to adopt computing in the first place. We pay much more attention to the first questions, where the existing literature is larger. However, our conclusions are similar for all of these areas: Virtually none of the studies mounted so far have been capable of yielding a persuasive and comprehensive view of computer-induced social change.

Quality of Work

The research literature on the impact of new information technologies on job content and job satisfaction provides a mass of contradictory findings. The wide range of informed opinion can best be defined by describing the two extreme positions: *deskilling* and *upgrading*.

The deskilling perspective suggests that automation is used to strip relatively skilled jobs of their conceptual content [13]. Those conceptual tasks previously integrated into work are either built into computer algorithms or transferred to a numerically smaller number of high-level specialists.

Deskilling manifests itself in two ways: *intra*occupational changes, where the skill content of a particular job decreases over time, and *inter*occupational changes, where the number of people in skilled jobs shrinks and the number in less skilled jobs increases. In the second of these cases, one empirical indicator of deskilling is a shift in the occupational distribution of the white-collar work force. Thus, the deskilling position implies that new information technologies produce a more polarized pyramidal distribution of skill: a mass of unskilled clerical workers at the bottom, and a small number of "conceptual workers" at the top, alongside management. James Driscoll of MIT [25] has put this rhetorically: "The office of the future would ... leave people in only two roles: bosses and garbage collectors."

In contrast, several researchers have argued that computerization and other new information technologies upgrade rather than deskill white-collar workers [8, 35, 81]. They maintain that automation primarily occurs in already-routinized work situations; the new technology takes the drudge work out of information processing by automating filing and information retrieval, preparing repetitious paperwork (e.g., form letters), doing simple computational tasks, moving messages, and so on. As automation absorbs many of the *manual aspects* of information processing, humans have more time to concentrate on conceptual and decision-making tasks.

The potential victims in this net upgrading of white-collar work are the lowest level clerical workers whose work consists almost entirely of manual manipulation of data (e.g., file clerks, correspondence typists, mailroom workers). These jobs can be largely replaced by the new technologies. However, proponents of the upgrading thesis argue that negative impacts need not occur even for this lowest stratum of workers. The process manifests itself in the relative growth of higher level white-collar jobs and the relative shrinkage of low-level jobs; the absolute number of low-level clerical workers need not decline in the short run. In addition, retraining schemes can modestly upgrade even lowest level clerical workers: File clerks become data-processing and entry clerks, bank tellers become officers or collections agents, typists retrain on text editors, and other workers join the computer operations staff (cf. [76, (p. 64)]).

With upgrading, then, the impact of computer technology is a net increase in skill and job satisfaction [35]. The occupational distribution of white-collar jobs shifts from a pyramid shape (few skilled, many semiskilled or unskilled) toward a diamond shape (few top managers, many professionals and middle managers, few low-skilled clericals) [124].

At the case-study level, many observers have described a loss of conceptual content, fragmentation, and deskilling of various clerical and professional white-collar jobs after computers were introduced [7, 20, 36–38, 46, 76, 116]. Groups representing clerical workers have also complained about computer-generated degradation of their work [41, 92].

On the other hand, several observers (sometimes the same observers!) give examples of the reversal of the division of labor with the introduction of new information technologies. Tasks are consolidated rather than further fragmented [20, 72, 76 (p. 62), 102].

The most plausible explanation for these opposed viewpoints is not that either group of observers is wrong but that both processes (deskilling and upgrading) are occurring within white-collar occupations. The riddle, then, is to determine which tendency predominates. For this purpose, single-case studies are not useful.

These difficulties are partially overcome in Attewell's [5] study of the insurance industry, utilizing Bureau of Labor Statistics (BLS) surveys on a large sample of insurance firms. Using detailed job descriptions, the BLS divides each occupation into several skill levels: file clerk A, file clerk B, file clerk C, etc. Since the surveys provide the numbers of persons in each skill category and since surveys have been carried out at five-year intervals during a period of rapid computer automation, one can analyze the data to determine intraoccupational skill changes over time. Consistent with the case studies above, Attewell reported a mixed picture. Four occupations showed modest but statistically significant downgrading over the last 15 years, six showed similarly significant upgrading, and three showed no trends. Thus both upgrading and deskilling are occurring within occupations as automation affects information-processing jobs. The unanswered question is, What is the overall effect of intraoccupational shifts in skills economywide? Are the findings for the insurance industry generalizable to other sectors?

Horowitz and Herrenstadt [47] examined intraoccupational skill changes in five industries between 1949 and 1965, using occupational skill data as determined by successive editions of the Department of Labor's *Dictionary of Occupational Titles (DOT)*, and found little overall change in skills. Spenner [107] examined change within 545 occupations using the 1965 and 1977 *DOT* skill measures and found "very little change—if any, a slight upgrading in the actual skill content of work over the last quarter century" [107 (p. 973)]. Rumberger [101] examined the *DOT* measure of educational requirements of jobs (as a proxy for skill) for the period 1960–1976. He found that intraoccupational change had led to a narrowing of skill differences: upgrading in lower occupations, downgrading in higher ones.

Although these *DOT* studies have a great advantage over the case studies in terms of correctly representing a large range of occupations and industries, they are unfortunately flawed. In an exhaustive study of the *DOT* skill-measurement system, carried out under the auspices of the National Academy of Science, Cain and Treiman [14] found that successive editions of the *DOT* do not accurately assess changes in skill content. They also echoed Howe's [48] criticism of the *DOT* as systematically biased because it undervalues the skill levels of many jobs predominantly held by women. Taken together, these objections vitiate the *DOT* as a tool for studying skill changes.

This leaves us with an unsatisfactory situation. We have a variety of case-study evidence indicating both upgrading and downgrading but no way to map this onto the economy as a whole or onto a representative sample of firms.

The evidence on interoccupational change (i.e., the relative growth of high-skill versus low-skill occupations) has similar difficulties. A series of early case studies reported that lower level clerical positions were eliminated by automation and that the proportion of higher level clerical jobs increased [18, 21, 43, 68, 94, 112, 120]. More recently, Menzies [76 (p. 63)] documented the retraining of displaced low-level clerical workers associated with "a radical upgrading of information work in Canadian industry, characterized by a diminishing demand for low-level clerical workers [and] increasing demand for technical and professional workers." Attewell [5], using BLS data on interoccupational shifts in the insurance industry from 1966 to 1980 (a period of intense automation), documents a marked growth in the proportion of insurance workers in higher level white-collar occupations (38 to 60 percent) and a corresponding decrease in the proportion of the work force in lower level jobs. These findings support the upgrading thesis.

Unfortunately, in attempting to generalize beyond these case-specific or industry-specific studies to the economy as a whole, we confront some of the problems encountered with the *DOT* data discussed above. Jaffe and Froomkin [51 (pp. 73–82)] suggested a modest aggregate upgrading of skills, most especially due to the changing industrial composition of the economy, rather than to an occupational mix within industries. Dubnoff [26] looked at the interoccupational distribution of jobs between 1900 and 1970, again using the *DOT* to measure skill levels. He found no aggregate deskilling in the nonfarm sector since 1900. Rumberger [101 (p. 578)] used *DOT* educational requirements as a proxy for skill and found that "between 1960 and 1976 changes in the distribution of employment have favored more-skilled jobs." But each of these studies stands or falls on the accuracy of *DOT* determinations of skill levels of jobs.

The third source of data for examining changes in the quality of worklife due to technological change comes from surveys of workers' own opinions. Muller [79] surveyed a representative sample of the U.S. work force (blue and white collar) about their experience of many kinds of technological change between 1962 and 1967. She found that reports of job enlargement and increased job satisfaction greatly exceeded reports of downgrading [79 (p. 14)]. More recently, Kling [59] surveyed 1200 managers, clerks, and data analysts in municipal government jobs about the impact of new information technologies on their work. He concluded that "computer use did not profoundly alter the character of their jobs." However, the new technology did have an effect on the quality of worklife. Kling found a modest upgrading of skill and job satisfaction across the occupational hierarchy from clerical to middle-level professionals to managers.

Kraemer and Danziger [62] also analyzed opinion survey data from a large sample of municipal government employees, examining several dimensions of job satisfaction and four levels of information workers (managers, staff professionals, bureaucrats who work with the public, and "desk-top bureaucrats"). Consonant with Kling's observations, they found that about half of the workers experienced an increased sense of accomplishment in computerized work, whereas only 4 percent reported a lowered sense. Most respondents did not experience computer-generated changes in supervision, nor did respondents report that computers diminished their control over others. Time pressure was experienced differentially: Forty-eight percent of the sample was unaffected, 29 percent reported decreased pressure, and 22 percent reported increased pressure. Overall, then, the effects of new technology were not dramatic, but where change was reported, computers were most often said to be enhancing job satisfaction.

Kraemer and Danziger's analysis did not support Kling's finding that the job-enhancing benefits of computerization increase as one climbs the organizational hierarchy. They found no significant differences between the occupational levels in terms of an increased sense of accomplishment. Surprisingly, they found that managers and bureaucrats directly serving the public reported higher increases in supervision than more routinized desk-top bureaucrats. Perceived changes in time pressure were also distributed across occupational strata in unexpected ways: Street-level bureaucrats experienced the highest incidence of decreased work pressure, followed by managers, desk-top bureaucrats, and professionals. The one finding that did support Kling's view of the hierarchical impact of the new technology concerned control over others. Computers allowed for an increased control over others toward the top of the occupational hierarchy.

Surveys of worker satisfaction in the private sector do not match in quality, detail, or representativeness the above research on the public sector [93, 114]. Shepard's [102] study remains the most ambitious. He compared various groups of blue- and white-collar workers on several dimensions of alienation. He found that automated workers were less alienated than both mechanized and nonmechanized groups. Unlike the surveys discussed earlier, Shepard's study did not ask workers within an occupation to compare their pre- and post-automation work, but instead contrasted quite different occupations cross-sectionally.

Since pay, promotion prospects, prestige, and other factors differentiated these occupations, in addition to level of technology, Shepard's observed difference in alienation/dissatisfaction between occupational groups may have little to do with technology.

To summarize: Surveys of workers' perceptions of the new technology generally contradict the deskilling/job degradation thesis. Most workers surveyed regard the new technologies in a positive light. There are, however, three caveats concerning these findings: First, existing opinion-survey data depend mainly on studies of public bureaucracies. The application of computer technology in the public sector may be more "humane" than in private-sector profit-oriented businesses that are pressured by competition—hence, the need to study a representative sample of businesses. Second, existing studies do not distinguish among levels of information technology. Thus we do not know whether the reports of job enhancement come from those individuals who work eight hours a day on state-of-the-art computer work stations or from individuals who only indirectly or intermittently use computer data. (Kraemer and Danziger [62] suggest this as a possible after-the-fact explanation for some of their findings.) The issue needs to be tested more rigorously. Finally, there is a possibility that increased satisfaction reflects a "novelty effect,"a temporary increase in interest that will fade as the technology becomes more familiar. Surveys therefore should take account of the length of time for which respondents have used the technology they are assessing.

Effects on Unemployment

Fears of automation-generated unemployment swept the United States and Europe in the 1950s and early 1960s, resulting in several volumes of research and commentary [1, 42, 50, 64, 82, 89, 109]. At that time, the main focus was on blue-collar unemployment and the automation of manual tasks, although computer impacts on white-collar workers were considered. These early concerns faded as the 1960s brought both increases in productivity and a rapid expansion of the American work force, thus apparently proving that automation need not generate unemployment.

However, by the early 1970s concerns over technologically generated unemployment surfaced again. By the late 1960s the manufacturing sector of the U.S. economy was exhibiting "jobless growth"—expansion in output with no corresponding increase in employment. In the industrialized nations of Europe and Japan there were absolute declines in manufacturing employment alongside increases in output [97 (pp. 3–4, 38–39)]. The rapid growth of the service sector (18.5 million new jobs in the United States between 1970 and 1981) seemed to offset stagnation and contraction in manufacturing employment during the 1970s, although some argued that this trend was heavily dependent on the expansion of government and would not continue into the 1980s, even in private-sector services (e.g., [34]).

A spate of studies then appeared, many sponsored by European governments, assessing the unemployment consequences of new microelectronic technology [2, 6, 15, 16, 29, 31, 53, 84–86, 104, 111]. These studies were generally pessimistic, predicting substantial levels of technologically induced unemployment (10 percent and greater). However, each national study concludes that the unemployment consequences for that nation of *not* adopting the new technology would be more severe than the consequences of adopting it, since nonadoption would result in loss of international competitive standing and hence loss of export markets. The pessimistic position is well expressed by the titles of books: *The Collapse of Work* [52] and *Automatic Unemployment* [45].

Pessimists point out that microelectronics technology is simultaneously affecting all parts of industry and commerce, from product and process design to welding, forging, molding, diecasting, and painting [55] to assembly [45 (pp. 21–24), 55] and office work [30, 35, 54]. Empirically, the pessimists' case rests on a series of daunting but quite unsystematic case studies, which show employment shrinkages of 50 percent in metalworking, 25 percent in telecommunications [97 (U.K. data)], 30 percent in banking [86 (French data)], 16–35 percent in female clerical work [76 (pp. 71–73, Canadian data)], and so on.

There are two major problems with the empirical bases of the pessimists' position. First, most of the national studies utilizing sophisticated input/output analyses (e.g., [69, 85]) are grounded in percentage estimates of the degree of increased productivity due to microelectronic technology for each industrial/commercial sector. These estimates are at best informed guesses and at worst complete speculation. There have been no systematic industrywide *measurements* of productivity increases resulting from the new technology because of the near impossibility of the task, from a methodological standpoint. Different firms take incompatible approaches to productivity measurement; many do not measure it at all. Attempts to compare productivity before and after automation in a few exemplary automated corporations are frustrated by the fact that such businesses often abandon or change their productivity measurement systems when production is reorganized around new technology, thus vitiating such comparisons. Separating the effects of the new technology from other factors affecting productivity (economic contractions, good or bad management, etc.) is also quite complex.

A second and easier approach has been to directly measure changes in employment in automating firms and to extrapolate these findings to the economy at large (e.g., [97]). This approach has similar pitfalls. If, as is often the case, one looks at firms in the avant-garde of computer automation, one risks choosing totally atypical businesses. Also, automating enterprises may be more competitive, stealing market shares from less advanced firms—the employment impact may be felt not in the automating firm itself but in backward noncompetitive firms in the same business.

Observed employment decreases may also be due to nationwide contraction rather than new technology, and so on.

A better way to assess employment changes due to the new technology would be to draw a systematic representative sample of businesses, study each firm's level of automation, and analyze changes in employment for each firm, controlling for (1) degree of automation and (2) changes in total constant dollar sales. Such a sample would have to include the full spectrum of automated and nonautomated businesses.

Optimists ague that studies of the apparent negative employment effects of the new technology are overstated, since they ignore several countertendencies. They maintain that by cutting the costs of goods and services, new technology stimulates increased demand. The work force need not shrink if increases in production balance increases in productivity. These "economic multiplier" effects might help to create a new technological "long wave" that could revive the international economy. Other such waves were triggered by the introduction of the railroads, electric power, etc. [17, 33] Optimists also point out that automation frequently occurs in industries experiencing a labor *shortage* and increased consumer demand. Automation in such industries only slows down the growth rate of labor; it does not shrink the labor force [30]. Again, these claims, although plausible, cannot be measured without a representative sampling of businesses and examination of their occupational and output growth rates.

Management Effects

Students of organizations have frequently observed that control of information is a source of power [19, 75, 91]. New technologies that alter the quality and availability of information are likely to shift balances of power between various groups of organizational actors—workers, supervisors, middle managers, executives, etc. [88]. The rerouting of information may also create new dependencies between parts of organizations and dissolve old ones, paving the way for structural changes.

One group of researchers finds evidence that such processes lead to increased centralization of power and decision making in computer-automated organizations [65]. Leavitt and Whisler [66] predicted in 1958 that the new information technologies would eliminate whole levels of middle management as improved information led to centralized decision making at the higher levels of the corporate hierarchy. Those middle-level managers who remained would have less discretion than before, since they would be supervising according to standardized procedures and decisions set from above, and since their clerical subordinates would face more routinized work [119]. Centralization would also lead to the merging of departments and a general simplification of organizational structure.

Early case-study research confirmed this prediction, especially as regards the decline of middle management [3, 49, 80, 81, 119].

Subsequent studies of computer mail systems have reinforced this view by showing the predominance of "top-down" communication [67, 70]. A further indication of centralization is the development of executive information systems that allow top executives to bypass line administrators and to monitor activity on the "factory floor" via computer tallies [12].

There is some evidence for an opposite view, however: The increase in communication resulting from new computer technologies may be *decentralizing* managerial decision making. Withington [122] reported case-study observations that management-information-system (MIS) data enhanced decision making by middle managers and strengthened their authority (cf. [58]). Pfeffer [90, 91] has argued that computerization allows for delegation of decision-making authority to lower level managers because such decisions can be easily monitored by higher level managers via MIS data. Blau et al. [10], in a comparative study of manufacturing companies, found that on-site computers do foster decentralized operational decisions, at least down to the level of plant manager. Also contra Whisler, Blau et al. and Blau and Schoenherr [11] found that, far from eliminating levels of middle management, computers are associated with an increase in the number of levels of line management and that differentiation into multiple departments increases with computerization. They contend computers lead to a more differentiated, more complex organizational structure.

Between the extremes of centralization and decentralization, we find a number of studies that suggest that power shifts resulting from computerization are complex and cannot be understood in terms of the single dimension of centralization/decentralization.

Kling [60 (p. 24)] has argued that even where new information technologies provide the potential for increased managerial surveillance, this potential has often not been used by managers.

He also cites instances where subordinates put false information into MIS systems in order to evade managerial control [60 (p. 84)].

Nor is it clear that upper management is always the group that benefits from improved access to information. Markus [74 (p. 55)] discusses a situation where junior officers in a U.S. military logistics group gained status vis-à-vis senior officers because of their access to on-line data. Bjorn-Anderson and Peterson [9] found that planners gained power at the expense of plant and production managers in several computerized Danish factories. Kraemer and Danziger [62] found in a sample of municipal governments that managers and staff did experience an increase in control over subordinates but that they themselves also experienced a relative increase in supervision. Meanwhile, a substantial proportion of their subordinates—"desk-top bureaucrats"—reported a lessening of supervision following computerization (see also [59 (p. 21)]). Such examples indicate that control is not a simple zero-sum relationship and that various groups may experience enhanced power and decision-making opportunities after computerization. Kling, Kraemer, and Dutton (summarized in [60 (p. 92)]) found that the pattern of power shifts following office automation in large municipalities differed from that found in smaller cities. Contextual variables thus play important mediating roles in influencing the outcome of the introduction of the new technology.

Robey [95, 96], in reviewing this literature and in presenting his own international case-study data, provided the following conclusion: "Computers do not *necessarily* affect the distribution of authority and control." In most cases either there is no change following the introduction of a MIS or an existing organizational structure is simply reinforced. Where changes are observed, centralization is a more common outcome than decentralization. Computerized information systems are clearly compatible with a wide variety of lateral and vertical power relationships in organizations [96].

Contradictory conclusions can be drawn from these case studies, if we assume that there must be a single accurate characterization of these effects. If we instead assume that a range of management effects is possible following the introduction of new information technology and that a variety of factors influences a particular outcome, our task becomes clear. We must identify those variables that can account for differential outcomes and examine them in a comparative study of a stratified sample of organizations. Variables include organizational size, industry type, degree of prior routinization or variability of work, degree of dependence upon a professional or high-skilled work force, and the patterns of information usage and information flow associated with the technologies in use.

Organizations and the Public

Social relationships within organizations are not the only ones to change in response to new bureaucratic uses of information. Relationships between organizations and their environments—particularly the general public—are also affected. It is easier to collect, disseminate, store, analyze, and use information with modern information technologies, and this is bound to make a difference in how organizations interact with the public.

This category of relationships has been the focus of much less theoretical attention and empirical investigation than those discussed earlier. To be sure, students of formal organization have long acknowledged that the flow of information between organizations and the public represents an important constraint on these relationships (see Deutsch [22] and Stinchcombe [108]). However, this recognition has not been attended by systematic attention to these issues in specific organizations. A few authors (e.g., Shils [103], Rule [98], and Rule et al. [99, 100]) have focused on the growing appetite of centralized organizations, especially governments, for information on the people with whom they deal. Other authors (e.g., Mowshowitz [77], Hiltz and Turoff [44], and Smith [106]) have speculated about new kinds of informational services that computerized organizations could provide and the concomitant changes that could be expected in modern ideas of what organizations are and do. However, none of these writings takes us close to a comprehensive assessment of how informational relations between organizations and the public are changing through the rise of computing.

Any perceptive casual observer could cite additional evidence that such relationships are indeed changing. All of us find ourselves interacting more with machines, and less with live human beings, as we deal with organizations. Bank accounts, bills, responses to complaints, correspondence, and other transactions are now routinely computerized. A few authors (e.g., Turkle [110] and Weizenbaum [117]) have begun to study the effects of these interactions, but we still know little about the prevailing forms and extent of computerized processes that organizations may substitute for direct dealings with people.

We suspect that profound economic forces will lead to further automation. It is widely acknowledged that human beings are becoming more and more expensive, relative to computer time. Hiring people to deal with the general public may thus become a luxury that organizations feel they cannot afford. A major New York bank recently tried to institute rules permitting only account holders with substantial deposits the privilege of doing business with a human teller. The effort was abandoned in the face of public protest and editorial reproach, but one can hardly doubt that similar moves will be attempted elsewhere.

Still, it would be wrong to conclude that the growing reliance on computing for mediation between organizations and the public must necessarily restrict and impoverish these relations. As with job content and worker satisfaction, a variety of tendencies and possibilities seems to be present. Computerization, after all, affords the capability of providing more information to more customers or account holders in less time. The only reliable grounds for judging which tendencies will prevail would be a study of a representative sample from a large and significant population of organizations.

The Impetus to Innovation

For most observers, the reasons for adopting computing in organizations are moot. It is taken as self-evident that organizations computerize in order to pursue long-standing goals of efficiency and cost-effectiveness. Rationalization, or the relentless effort to adopt the most efficient means to established ends, is seen as the hallmark of modern organizations. Computerization is considered the most eminently rational of present-day technological trends.

Against this view there is a long-standing alternative, originally and most persuasively articulated by Jacques Ellul [28]. In this view, new technologies do not arise simply as superior responses to preexisting problems. Rather, the "need" for innovation is the product of a mind-set that demands that every available technological possibility be developed as a matter of course. The evolution of technology is thus self-sustaining and autonomous—a catalyst for change in other sectors of society, rather than a response to interests generated elsewhere. Though planners may *believe* they are acting rationally in adopting new technologies, their decisions actually reflect a pervasive mystique that what can be developed, must be developed. This idea continues to have influence among modern critics of technology (e.g., Winner [121]).

In fact, this critical view is by no means unsupported in the empirical literature. True, the earliest writers on subjects like office automation considered the cost-benefit justifications of new technologies as too obvious to question [66]. However, other early studies that actually examined the effects of computer innovations in detail reported a more mixed picture [65, 118]. More recently, the URBIS study by the Irvine group has again shown how strong the tendency is, among managers in municipal governments, to perceive that the use of computers is the most rational choice (e.g., [27]). However, the participating authors themselves by no means take these perceptions at face value; indeed, they find savings through computing quite uneven among local governments and among departments within governments. They are confident that a savings is possible in the most favorable circumstances but unconvinced that any savings will necessarily be realized [57].

Downs [23] has pointed to some possible explanations. He shows, much as Laudon [65] has done, that changes in information organization may also be changes in power relations. Such findings suggest that efficiency claims for computing innovations may actually mask the political motives of the parties making the claims.

In the most penetrating empirically oriented study of these issues, King and Kraemer [57] examine why innovations in computing often seem to fail to yield expected benefits. They identify a number of hidden costs attached to new computing systems that are often ignored by planners—the interruption of established organizational routines brought about by computing use, for instance. Even more important, they offer what strikes us as a very telling observation: New computing systems are often applied not only to existing organizational problems but to qualitatively new organizational activities. Thus, a new computing system for an accounting and finance department may be used to undertake much more thorough and far-reaching audits of the activities of other departments than anyone had previously considered necessary. In such cases it may be more reasonable to conclude that the availability of the technology incited the organizational "needs" to which it was applied, rather than the other way around.

These and other findings by members of the Irvine group provide tentative and tantalizing support for some of Ellul's seemingly incredible ideas. To be sure, their observations at this stage must be considered straws in the wind. Dutton and Kraemer base their observation on their sample of 572 larger municipal and county governments, for example. Are profit-making organizations more rigorous in their cost-benefit rationality? Can managers in most organizations even cite evidence for the cost-effectiveness of their systems? Does adoption of such systems correspond to shifts in organizational agenda?

Conclusions

The sheer variety of disparate and seemingly conflicting conclusions that can be derived from the studies noted may seem to warrant despair. Why do all these works add up to so few conclusive results? Is there really so little to show, by way of direct answers to the questions with which this review began?

For our part, we are obviously skeptical but by no means discouraged. The literature reviewed offers important lessons for future inquiry, especially by way of cautionary conclusions on relations between theories and empirical investigation on these issues. In particular, we believe that a priori reasoning proceeding from assumptions about principles that logically *must* describe the social impacts of computing in organizations is unproductive. On the contrary, we suspect that the transformations in organizational life through computing are so multifarious as to encompass the most disparate cause-effect relations in different contexts. There is no reason why computing should not result in deskilling in some settings and the enhancement of job content elsewhere, or in greater responsiveness to public needs in some organizations and diminished responsiveness in others. Indeed, one might well expect quite different effects to ensue from what appear to be the "same" causes in similar or even identical organizations, according to contextual changes in such things as the environments in which organizations act. In short, we see no reason to believe that any simple set of theoretical relationships can account for all the data that one might expect empirical inquiry to bring to light on these subjects.

The problem for research, as we see it, is twofold. First, one must determine, as far as possible, what particular cause-effect relations prevail in specific contexts. Where, for example, is computerization an authentic response to needs that are demonstrably fulfilled by the new technologies; and where, by contrast, might computerization actually *create* the needs that it is supposed to be fulfilling? Second, one must locate such cases as closely as possible within larger ranges of cases in which similar cause-effect relations can be expected to prevail. Clearly these requirements point to an ambitious program of inquiry. They suggest that large samples and extensive replication will be necessary—not so much to *isolate* the effects of computing in organizations, but to characterize such effects in their full variety.

We do not expect any of the problems considered above to be "solved" definitively, no matter how widely they are investigated. This does not dismay us. We believe that the social impacts of computing are infinitely variable but that the sources of these variations are eminently accessible to study. As long as investigators continue to study new organizations in new settings, new effects can be expected to emerge. The essential thing is that we continue confronting our theories with new data and that we not be afraid to modify theories in light of such confrontations.

References

1. American Assembly. *Automation and Technological Change.* Prentice-Hall, Englewood Cliffs, N.J., 1962.

2. ANZAAS (Australian and New Zealand Association for the Advancement of Science). *Automation and Unemployment.* The Law Book Company, Sydney, Australia, 1979.

3. Argyris, C. Management information systems: The challenge to rationality and emotionality. *Manage. Sci. 17*, 6 (Feb. 1971), 275–292.

4. Attewell, P. The de-skilling controversy. Mimeo manuscr., Dept. of Sociology, State Univ. of New York, Stony Brook, 1982.

5. Attewell, P. Microelectronics and employment. Paper presented at the Conference on Microelectronics in Transition, Univ. of California, Santa Cruz, 1963.

6. Austrian Academy of Sciences. *Mikroelektronick: Anwendungen, Verbreitung und Auswirkungen: Am Beispiel Österreichisches.* Springer-Verlag, Berlin, West Germany, 1981.

7. Barker, J., and Downing, H. Word processing and the transformation of the patriarchial relations of control in the office. *Cap. Cl. 3* (1978), 64–99.

8. Bell, D. *The Coming of Post-Industrial Society.* Basic Books, New York, 1963.

9. Bjorn-Anderson, N., and Pederson, P. Computer facilitated changes in management power structures. *Account. Organ. Soc. 5*, 2 (1977), 203–216.

10. Blau, P. M., McHugh Falbe, C., McKinley, W., and Tracy, P. Technology and organizaton in manufacturing. *Adm. Sci. Q. 21*, 1 (Mar. 1976), 20–40.

11. Blau, P. M., and Schoenherr, R. *The Structure of Organizations.* Basic Books, New York, 1971.

12. Bralove, M. Direct data: Some chief executive bypass and irk staffs in getting information. *Wall St. J.* (Jan. 12, 1983), 1.

13. Braverman, H. *Labor and Monopoly Capital: The Degradation of Work in the Twentieth Century.* Monthly Review, New York, 1974.

14. Cain, P., and Treiman, D. The *D.O.T.* as a source of occupational data. *Am. Sociol. Rev. 46*, 3 (1981), 235–278.

15. Central Policy Review Staff. *Social and Employment Implications of Microelectronics.* H.M. Government, London, 1978.

16. Chern, A. B. Speculation on the social effects of new microelectronics technology. *Int. Labor Rev. 119,* 6 (Nov.–Dec. 1980), 705–721.

17. Cooper, C. M., and Clarke, J. A. *Employment, Economics and Technology: The Impact of Technological Change in the Labour Market.* St. Martin's Press, New York, 1982.

18. Craig, H. *Administering a Conversion to Electronic Accounting.* Division of Research, Graduate School of Business Administration, Harvard Univ., Boston, Mass., 1955.

19. Crozier, M. *The Bureaucratic Phenomenon.* Univ. of Chicago Press, Chicago, Ill., 1964.

20. DeKadt, M. Insurance: A clerical work factory. In *Case Studies in the Labor Process,* A. Zimbalist, Ed. Monthly Review, New York, 1979.

21. Delehanty, G. Office automation and occupation structure: A case study of five insurance companies. *Ind. Manage. Rev. 7* (Spring, 1966), 99–108.

22. Deutsch, K. *The Nerves of Government.* The Free Press, New York, 1966.

23. Downs, A. A realistic look at the final payoffs from urban data systems. *Public Adm. Rev. 27,* 3 (Sept. 1967), 204–209.

24. Driscoll, J. How to humanize office automation. *Off. Technol. People 1,* 2–3 (Sept. 1982), 167–176.

25. Driscoll, J. Office automation: The dynamics of a technological boondoggle. In *Emerging Office Systems,* R. M. Landau and J. H. Blair, Eds. Norwood, N.J., 1982.

26. Dubnoff, S. Inter-occupational shifts and changes in the quality of work in the American economy, 1900–1970. Paper presented at the annual meeting of the Society for the Study of Social Problems, San Francisco, Calif., 1978.

27. Dutton, W., and Kraemer, K. Determinants of support for computerized information systems: The attitude of local government chief executives. *Midwest Rev. Public Adm. 12,* 1 (Mar. 1978), 19–40.

28. Ellul, J. *The Technological Society.* Knopf, New York, 1964.

29. Equal Opportunities Commission. *New Technology and Women's Employment: Case Studies from West Yorkshire.* Equal Opportunities Commission, Manchester, England, 1962.

30. Ernst, M. The mechanization of commerce. *Scientific American 247,* 3 (Sept. 1982), 132–147.

31. ETUI (European Trade Union Institute). *The Impact of Microelectronics on Employment in Western Europe in the 1980s*. European Trade Union Institute, Brussels, Belgium, 1979.

32. Faunce, W. A. Automation and the division of labor. *Soc. Problems 13* (Fall 1965), 149–160.

33. Freeman, C., Clark, J., and Soete, L. *Unemployment and Technical Innovation: A Study of Long Waves and Economic Development*. Francis Pinter, London, 1982.

34. Gershuny, J. I. *After Industrial Society?* Humanities Press, Atlantic Highlands, N.J., 1978.

35. Giuliano, V. The mechanization of office work. *Scientific American 247*, 3 (Sept. 1982), 148–165.

36. Glenn, E., and Feldberg, R. Degraded and deskilled: The proletarianization of clerical work. *Soc. Probl. 25*, 1 (Oct. 1977), 52–64.

37. Glenn, E., and Feldberg, R. Proletarianization of clerical work: Technology and organizational control in the offeice. In *Case Studies on the Labor Process*, A. Zimbalist, Ed. Monthly Review, New York, 1979.

38. Glenn, E., and Feldberg, R. Technology and work degradation: Reexamining the impacts of office automation. Mimeo manuscr., Dept. of Sociology, Boston Univ., Boston, 1980.

39. Granovetter, M. Small is bountiful: Labor markets and establishment size. *Am. Sociol. Rev.* To be published.

40. Greenbaum, J. *In the Name of Efficiency: A Study of Change in Data Processing Work*. Temple Univ. Press, Philadelphia, Pa., 1979.

41. Gregory, J., and Nussbaum, K. Race against time: Automation in the office. *Off. Technol. People 1*, 2–3 (1982), 197–236.

42. Haber, W., Ferman, L., and Hudson, J. *The Impact of Technological Change: The American Experience*. W. E. Upjohn Institute for Employment Research, Kalamazoo, Mich., 1963.

43. Helfgott, R. B. EDP and the office workforce. *Ind. Labor Relat. Rev. 19* (July 1966), 503–517.

44. Hiltz, S. R., and Turoff, M. *The Network Nation*. Addison-Wesley, Reading, Mass., 1978.

45. Hines, C., and Searle, G. *Automatic Unemployment*. Earth Resources Research, London, 1979.

46. Hoos, I. *Automation in the Office*. Public Affairs Press, Washington, D.C., 1960.

47. Horrowitz, M., and Herrenstadt, I. Changes in skill requirements of occupations in selected industries. In *The Employment Impact of Technological Change*, vol. 2. National Commission on Technology, Automation, and Economic Progress, U.S. Government Printing Office, Washington, D.C., 1966.

48. Howe, L. *Pink Collar Workers*. G. P. Putnam, New York, 1977.

49. Huse, E. The impact of computers on managers and organizations: A case study in an integrated manufacturing company. In *The Impact of Computers on Management*, C. A. Myers, Ed. MIT Press, Cambridge, Mass., 1967.

50. International Conference on Automation, Full Employment, and a Balanced Economy. In *Proceedings*. American Foundation on Automation and Employment, 1967.

51. Jaffe, A. J., and Froomkin, J. *Technology and Jobs: Automation in Perspective*. Praeger, New York, 1966.

52. Jenkins, C., and Sherman, B. *The Collapse of Work*. Eyre Methuen, London, 1979.

53. JIPDEC (Japan Information Processing Development Center). The impact of microelectronics on employment. *JIPDEC Rep.* (Spring, 1980), 1–19.

54. JIPDEC (Japan Information Processing Development Center). The office of today and tomorrow. *JIPDEC Rep. 47* (1981).

55. JIPDEC (Japan Information Processing Center). The robots are coming. *JIPDEC Rep. 50* (1982).

56. Kahn, H. The future of the corporation. In *The Future of the Corporation*, H. Kahn, Ed. Mason and Lipscomb, New York, 1974.

57. King, J. L., and Kraemer, K. Cost as a social impact of telecommunications and other information technologies. Public Policy Research Organization, Irvine, Calif., 1980.

58. Klatzky, S. R. Automation, size, and locus of decision-making. *J. Bus. 43*, 2 (Apr. 1970), 141–151.

59. Kling, R. The impact of computing on the work of managers, data analysts and clerks. Mimeo manuscr., Dept. of Information and Computing Science, Univ. of California, Irvine, Calif., 1978.

60. Kling, R. Social analyses of computing: Theoretical perspectives in recent empirical research. *ACM Comput. Surv. 12*, 1 (Mar. 1980), 61–110.

61. Kling, R., and Scacchi, W. The web of computing: Computer technology as social organization. *Adv. Comput. 21* (1982), 1–90.

62. Kraemer, K., and Danziger, J. Computers and control in the work environment. Mimeo manuscr., Public Policy Research Organization, Irvine,

Calif., 1982.

63. Kraft, P. *Programmers and Managers: The Routinization of Computer Programming in the United States.* Springer-Verlag, New York, 1977.

64. Kreps, J. M. *Automation and Employment.* Holt, Rinehart and Winston, New York, 1964.

65. Lane, R. The decline of politics and ideology in a knowledgeable society. *Am. Sociol. Rev. 31,* 5 (Oct. 1966), 649–662.

66. Laudon, K. *Computers and Bureaucratic Reform.* Wiley, New York, 1964.

67. Leavitt, H., and Whisler, T. Management in the 1980s. *Harvard Bus. Rev. 36,* 6 (Nov.–Dec. 1985), 41–48.

68. Leduc, N. Communicating through computers. *Telecommun. Policy* (Sept. 1979), 235–244.

69. Lee, H. C. Electronic data processing and skill requirements. *Pers. Adm. 29* (May–June 1966), 50–53.

70. Leontief, W. The distribution of work and income. *Scientific American 247,* 3 (1982), 188–204.

71. Lippit, M., Miller, J. P., and Lalamaj, J. Patterns of use and correlates of adoption of an electronic mail system. *Proceedings of the American Institute of Decision Sciences,* Las Vegas, Nev., 1980.

72. Lowi, T. The information revolution, politics, and the prospects for an open society. In *Government Secrecy in Democracies,* I. Galnoor, Ed. Harper and Row, New York, 1977.

73. Mann, F., and Williams, L. Organizational impact of white collar automation. In *Annual Proceedings.* Industrial Relations Research Association, Madison, Wis., 1958, pp. 59–69.

74. Mann, F., and Williams, L. Some effects of the changing work environment in the office. *J. Soc. Issues 18* (1962), 90–11.

75. Markus, M. L. *Systems in Organizations.* Pitman Publishing, Marshfield, Mass., 1984.

76. Mechanic, D. Sources of power and lower participants in complex organizations. *Adm. Sci. Q. 7* (1962), 349–364.

77. Menzies, H. *Women and the Chip: Case Studies of the Effects of Informatics on Employment in Canada.* Institute for Public Policy, Montreal, Canada, 1981.

78. Mowshowitz, A. *The Conquest of Will: Information Processing in Human Affairs.* Addison-Wesley, Reading, Mass., 1976.

79. Moynihan, D. P. The professionalization of reform. *Public Interest 1,* 1 (Fall 1965), 6–16.

80. Mueller, E. *Technological Advance in an Expanding Economy: Its Impact on a Cross-Section of the Labor Force.* Institute for Social Research, Ann Arbor, Mich., 1969.

81. Mumford, E., and Banks, O. *The Computer and the Clerk.* Routledge, Kegan Paul, London, 1967.

82. Myers, C. *The Impact of Computers on Management.* MIT Press, Cambridge, Mass., 1967.

83. National Commission on Technology, Automation and Economic Progress. *Technology and the American Economy*, vol. 1. U.S. Government Printing Office, Washington, D.C., 1966.

84. National Commission on Technology, Automation and Economic Progress. The employment impact of technological change. In *Technology and the American Economy*, vol. 2. U.S. Government Printing Office, Washington, D.C., 1966.

85. Netherlands Government. *The Impact of Chip Technology on Employment and the Labor Market.* Ministerie Van Sociale Zaken, The Hague, The Netherlands, 1979.

86. Netherlands Government. *The Social Impact of Micro-Electronics.* Netherlands Government Publishing Office, The Hague, The Netherlands, 1980.

87. Nora, S., and Minc, A. *The Computerization of Society: A Report to the President of France.* MIT Press, Cambridge, Mass., 1980.

88. Olson, M. H. New information technology and organizational culture. *Manage. Inf. Syst. Q.* (1982).

89. Olson, M. H., and Lucas, H. C. The impact of office automation on the organization: Some implications for research and practice. *Commun. ACM 25*, 11 (Nov. 1982), 838–847.

90. Organization for Economic Cooperation and Development. *The Requirements of Automated Jobs.* OECD, Paris, France, 1965.

91. Pfeffer, J. *Organizational Design.* AHM Publishing, Arlington Heights, Ill., 1978.

92. Pfeffer, J. *Power in Organizations.* Pitman Publishing, Marshfield, Mass., 1981.

93. *Processed World 1*, 1 (Spring 1981).

94. Response Analysis Corporation. *Office Automation and the Workplace.* Honeywell, Minneapolis, Minn., 1983.

95. Rico, L. The staffing process and the computer. *Manage. Pers. Q. 1*, 4 (Autumn–Winter 1962), 32–38.

96. Robey, D. Computers and management structure: Some empirical findings re-examined. *Hum. Relat. 30*, 11 (1977), 963–976.

97. Robey, D. Computer information systems and organizational structure. *Commun. ACM 24*, 10 (Oct. 1961), 679–687.

98. Rothwell, R., and Zegveld, W. *Technical Change and Employment*. Frances Pinter, London, 1979.

99. Rule, J. *Private Lives and Public Surveillance*. Schocken, New York, 1974.

100. Rule, J., McAdam, D., Stearns, L., and Uglow, D. *The Politics of Privacy*. Elsevier, New York, 1980.

101. Rule, J., McAdam, D., Stearns, L., and Uglow, D. Documentary identity and bureaucratic surveillance in America. *So. Probl.* To be published.

102. Rumberger, R. The changing skill requirements of jobs in the U.S. economy. *Ind. Labor Relat. Rev. 34* (1981), 578–590.

103. Shepard, J. *Automation and Alienation: A Study of Office and Factory Workers*. MIT Press, Cambridge, Mass., 1971.

104. Shils, E. *Center and Periphery: Essays in Macrosociology*. Univ. of Chicago Press, Chicago, Ill., 1975.

105. Sleigh, J., Boatwright, B., Irwin, P., and Stanyan, R. *The Manpower Implications of Micro-Electronic Technology*. H.M. Stationery Office, London, 1979.

106. Smith, A. *The Geopolitics of Information*. Oxford Univ., New York, 1980.

107. Smith, A. *Goodbye Gutenberg*. Oxford Univ., New York, 1980.

108. Spenner, K. Temporal changes in work content. *Am. Sociol. Rev. 44* (1979), 965–975.

109. Stinchcombe, A. Institutions of privacy in the determination of police administrative practice. *Am. J. Sociol, 69*, 2 (Sept. 1983), 1–10.

110. Terborgh, G. *The Automation Hysteria*. W.W. Norton, New York, 1965.

111. Turkle, S. Study of human interactions with computers. *The Second Self*. Simon and Schuster, New York, 1984.

112. United Kingdom Government. *Technological Change: Threats and Opportunities for the United Kingdom*. H.M. Stationery Office, London, 1979.

113. U.S. Bureau of Labor Statistics. The introduction of an electronic computer in a large insurance company. In *Studies on Automation Technology* 2. U.S. Government Printing Office, Washington, D.C., 1955.

114. U.S. Dept. of Health, Education and Welfare. *Work in America*. MIT Press, Cambridge, Mass., 1973.

115. Verbatim Corporation. *The Verbatim Survey: Office Worker Views and Perceptions of New Technology in the Workplace.* The Verbatim Corporation, Sunnyvale, Calif., 1982.

116. Wallace, M., and Kalleberg, A. Industrial transformation and the decline of craft: The decomposition of skill in the printing industry, 1931–1978. *Am. Sociol. Rev. 47,* 3 (1982), 307–324.

117. Weber, C. E. Impact of electronic data processing on clerical skills. *Pers. Adm. 22–33,* 1 (Jan.–Feb. 1959), 20–26.

118. Weizenbaum, J. *Computer Power and Human Reason.* W.H. Freeman, San Francisco, Calif., 1976.

119. Westin, A., and Baker, M. *Databanks in a Free Society.* Quadrangle Times Books, New York, 1972.

120. Whisler, T. *The Impact of Computers on Organizations.* Praeger, New York, 1970.

121. Whisler, T., and Meyer, H. The impact of EDP on life company organization. Pers. Adm. Rep. 34, Life Office Management Association, 1967.

122. Winner, L. *Autonomous Technology.* MIT Press, Cambridge, Mass., 1977.

123. Withington, F. *The Real Computer: Its Influence, Uses and Effects.* Addison-Wesley, Reading, Mass., 1969.

124. Zimbalist, A., Ed. *Case Studies on the Labor Process.* Monthly Review, New York, 1979.

125. Zuboff, S. New worlds of computer-mediated work. *Harvard Bus. Rev.* (Sept.–Oct. 1982), 142–152.

21

Electronic Markets and Electronic Hierarchies[1]

Thomas W. Malone
Joanne Yates
Robert I. Benjamin

The innovations in information technologies of the past two decades have radically reduced the time and cost of processing and communicating information. These reductions have in turn brought many changes in the ways tasks are accomplished within firms. Data-processing systems have transformed the ways in which accounting data are gathered and processed, for example, and CAD/CAM has transformed the ways in which complex machinery is designed. Underlying (and often obscured by) these changes may be more fundamental changes in how firms and markets organize the flow of goods and services through their value-added chains (e.g., see [34]). In this paper we address the more basic issue of how advances in information technology are affecting firm and market structures and discuss the options these changes present for corporate strategies.

New information technologies are allowing closer integration of adjacent steps on the value-added chain through the development of electronic markets and electronic hierarchies. Although these mechanisms are making both markets and hierarchies more efficient, we argue that they will lead to an overall shift toward proportionately more market

---

[1]This research was supported in part by the Management in the 1990s Research Program and the Center for Information Systems Research at the Sloan School of Management, Massachusetts Institute of Technology.

coordination. Some firms will be able to benefit directly from this shift by becoming "market makers" for the new electronic markets. Others will be able to benefit from providing the interconnections to create electronic hierarchies. All firms will be able to benefit from the wider range of options provided by these markets and from the possibilities for closer coordination provided by electronic hierarchies.

The analytic framework on which our argument is based is useful in explaining several major historical changes in American market structures, as well as in predicting the consequences that changing information technologies should have for our current market structures. Since we are attempting to predict changes that have not yet occurred on a large scale, our forecasts are based on a simple conceptual analysis rather than on systematic empirical studies. A conclusive test of our model and our predictions will, therefore, require further empirical and analytical work. Nevertheless, in many cases, we are able to identify early examples of the predicted changes that have already occurred in some industries and to suggest implications of the predicted changes for corporate strategy.

In addition to the changes in information technology that we discuss here, there are, of course, other important forces—such as changes in stock prices, antitrust regulations, and interest rates—that might affect firm and market structures. The possible consequences of these other forces are outside the scope of this article. The examples we describe, however, illustrate the importance of changes in information technology, even in cases where other forces are involved as well.

Analytic Framework

Definitions of Markets and Hierarchies

Economies have two basic mechanisms for coordinating the flow of materials or services through adjacent steps in the value-added chain: markets and hierarchies (e.g., see [14] and [40]). *Markets* coordinate the flow through supply and demand forces and external transactions between different individuals and firms. Market forces determine the design, price, quantity, and target delivery schedule for a given product that will serve as an input into another process: The buyer of the good or service compares its many possible sources and makes a choice based on the best combination of these attributes.

Hierarchies, on the other hand, coordinate the flow of materials through adjacent steps by controlling and directing it at a higher level in the managerial hierarchy. Managerial decisions, not the interaction of market forces, determine design, price (if relevant), quantity, and delivery schedules at which products from one step on the value-added chain are procured for the next step. Thus buyers do not select a supplier from a group of potential suppliers; they simply work with a single predetermined one. In many cases the hierarchy is simply a firm, while in others it may span two legally separate firms in a close, perhaps electronically mediated, sole supplier relationship.

Variants of the two pure relationships exist, but can usually be categorized as primarily one or the other. When a single supplier serves one or more buyers as a sole source of some good, the relationship between the supplier and each buyer is primarily hierarchical, since the buyers are each procuring their supplies from a single, predetermined supplier, rather than choosing from a number of suppliers. On the other hand, the relationship between a single buyer and multiple suppliers serving only that buyer is governed by market forces, since the buyer is choosing between a number of possible suppliers. As the number of suppliers is reduced toward one, relationships that have characteristics of both types may exist.

Factors Favoring Markets or Hierarchies

A number of theorists (e.g., [14], [40], [41], [43], [44]) have analyzed the relative advantages of hierarchical and market methods of organizing economic activity in terms of various kinds of coordination or transaction costs. These coordination costs take into account the costs of gathering information, negotiating contracts, and protecting against the risks of "opportunistic" bargaining. Building on this and other work, Malone and Smith [27], [28] have summarized several of the fundamental trade-offs between markets and hierarchies in terms of costs for activities such as production and coordination. Table 1 summarizes the part of their analysis that is most relevant to our argument here.[2]

In the table the designations "Low" and "High" refer only to relative comparisons within columns, not to absolute values. Production costs include the physical or other primary processes necessary to create and distribute the goods or services being produced. Coordination costs include the transaction (or governance) costs of all the information processing necessary to coordinate the work of people and machines that perform the primary processes (e.g., see [23], [30], and [40]). For example, coordination costs include determining the design, price, quantity,

---

[2]In the terms used by Malone and Smith [27], [28], this table compares the performance that is achievable with separate divisions in a product hierarchy to the performance that is achievable with separate companies coordinated by a decentralized market (see [27, Table 2]). As noted by Malone [27, pp. 18–19], this comparison is equivalent to a comparison of coordination by separate hierarchical firms and coordination by a market.

Table 1   Relative Costs for Markets and Hierarchies

Organizational form	Production costs	Coordination costs
Markets	Low	High
Hierarchies	High	Low

delivery schedule, and other similar factors for products transferred between adjacent steps on a value-added chain. In markets, this involves selecting suppliers, negotiating contracts, paying bills, and so forth. In hierarchies, this involves managerial decision making, accounting, planning, and control processes. The classification of a specific task as a production or a coordination task can depend on the level and purpose of analysis, but at an intuitive level, the distinction is clear.

Table 1 is consistent with an analysis of both the simple costs involved in information search and load sharing [27] and the costs resulting from "opportunistic" behavior by trading partners with "bounded rationality" [40]. As Williamson [43, p. 558] summarizes, "tradeoffs between production cost economies (in which the market may be presumed to enjoy certain advantages) and governance cost economies (in which the advantages may shift to internal organization) need to be recognized."

In a pure market, with many buyers and sellers, the buyer can compare different possible suppliers and select the one that provides the best combination of characteristics (such as design and price), thus presumably minimizing production costs for the desired product. One of the obvious benefits of this arrangement is that it allows for pooling the demands of numerous buyers to take advantage of economies of scale and load leveling. The market coordination costs associated with this wide latitude of choice, however, are relatively high, because the buyer must gather and analyze information from a variety of possible suppliers. In some cases, these costs must also include additional negotiating or risk-covering costs that arise from dealing with "opportunistic" trading partners.

Since hierarchies, on the other hand, restrict the procurer's choice of suppliers to one predetermined supplier, production costs are, in general, higher than in the market arrangement. The hierarchical arrangement, however, reduces coordination costs over those incurred in a market by eliminating the buyer's need to gather and analyze a great deal of information about different suppliers.

Various factors affect the relative importance of production and coordination costs, and thus the relative desirability of markets and hierarchies (e.g., see [40], [41], [43], and [44]). We focus here, however, on those that are particularly susceptible to change by the new information technologies [13]. Clearly, at a very general level, one of these factors is coordination cost. Since the essence of coordination involves communicating and processing information, the use of information technology seems likely to decrease these costs (e.g., see [27]). Two other, more specific, factors that can be changed by information technology are also important in determining which coordination structures are desirable: *asset specificity* and *complexity of product description*. The importance of asset specificity has been amply demonstrated by previous analyses (e.g., [43], [44]), but the importance of the complexity of product descriptions has not, we believe, been satisfactorily analyzed.

Asset Specificity   An input used by a firm (or individual consumer) is highly asset specific, according to Williamson's definition [43], [44], if it cannot readily be used by other firms because of site specificity, physical asset specificity, or human asset specificity. A natural resource available at a certain location and movable only at great cost is site specific, for example. A specialized machine tool or complex computer system designed for a single purpose is physically specific. Highly specialized human skills—whether physical (e.g., a trade with very limited applicability) or mental (e.g., a consultant's knowledge of a company's processes)—that cannot readily be put to work for other purposes are humanly specific. We propose yet another type of asset specificity to add to Williamson's list: time specificity. An asset is time specific if its value is highly dependent on its reaching the user within a specified, relatively limited period of time. For example, a perishable product that will spoil unless it arrives at its destination and is used (or sold) within a short time after its production is time specific. Similarly, any input to a manufacturing process that must arrive at a specific time in relation to the manufacturing process to avoid great costs or losses is also time specific.

There are several reasons why a highly specific asset is more likely to be acquired through hierarchical coordination than through market coordination [41], [43], [44]. Transactions involving asset-specific products often involve a long process of development and adjustments for the supplier to meet the needs of the procurer, a process that favors the continuity of relationships found in a hierarchy. Moreover, since there are, by definition, few alternative procurers or suppliers of a product high in physical or human asset specificity, both parties in a given transaction are vulnerable. If either one goes out of business or changes its need for (or production of) the product, the other may suffer sizable losses. The greater control and closer coordination allowed by a hierarchical relationship are thus more desirable to both.

Complexity of Product Description   Complexity of product description refers to the amount of information needed to specify the attributes of a product in enough detail to allow potential buyers (whether producers acquiring production inputs or consumers acquiring goods) to make a selection. Stocks and commodities, for example, have simple, standardized descriptions, while those of business insurance policies or large and complicated computer systems are much more complex. This factor is frequently, but not always, related to asset specificity; that is, in many cases a highly specific asset, such as a specialized machine tool, will require a more complex product description than a less specific asset. The two factors are logically independent, however, despite this frequent correlation. Coal produced by a coal mine located adjacent to a manufacturing plant is highly site specific, though the product description is quite simple. Conversely, an automobile is low in asset specificity, since most cars can be used by many possible consumers, but the potential car buyer requires an extensive and complex description of the car's attributes in order to make a purchasing decision.

Other things being equal, products with complex descriptions are more likely to be obtained through hierarchical than through market coordination for reasons centering on the cost of communication about a product. We have already noted that coordination costs are higher for markets than for hierarchies, in part because market transactions require contacting more possible suppliers to gather information and negotiate contracts. Because highly complex product descriptions require more information exchange, they also increase the coordination cost advantage of hierarchies over markets. Thus buyers of products with complex descriptions are more likely to work with a single supplier in a close, hierarchical relationship (whether in-house or external), while buyers of simply described products (such as stocks or graded commodities) can more easily compare many alternative suppliers in a market.

As Figure 21.1 shows, then, items that are both highly asset specific and highly complex in product description are more likely to be obtained through a hierarchical relationship, while items that are not very asset specific and have simple product descriptions are more often acquired through a market relationship. The organizational form likely for items in the other two cells of the table will depend on which factor dominates.

Historical Changes in Market Structures

To illustrate the application of our analytic framework, we briefly examine the historical evolution of market structures in America, paying

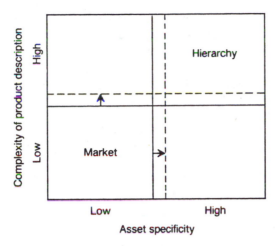

Figure 21.1   Product attributes affect forms of organization.

particular attention to the effects of a key nineteenth century information technology, the telegraph. (The analysis in this section draws on arguments by Chandler [12], Williamson [43], [44], Malone and Smith [28], Malone [27], and Duboff [16]. Yates [45] develops this application in more detail.)

Until the mid-nineteenth century, small-scale local and regional markets, not hierarchies, coordinated adjacent stages of American industrial activity. The three major functions of manufacturing—procurement, production, and distribution—were generally handled by different parties. By midcentury the dramatic improvements in communication and transportation provided by the telegraph and the railroads created a network for exchanging information and goods over great distances, thus effectively increasing the area over which markets or hierarchies might be established.

Our analytic framework helps explain how these developments encouraged larger and more efficient markets in some cases, and larger, multifunctional hierarchies in others. On the one hand, as Table 1 illustrates, markets are more communication intensive than hierarchies. Therefore, reducing the time and cost of communication favored—and thus encouraged—the growth of markets. On the other hand, the growth in market area increased the number of economic actors potentially involved in transactions as well as the total amount of communication necessary for efficient markets to operate, thus favoring hierarchies (see [27] and [28]). The net effect of the telegraph in different industries depended largely on the other factors from our framework.

Just as our framework would lead us to expect, nationwide markets mediated by telegraph developed for products such as stocks and commodities futures. These products were nonspecific assets with many potential buyers. In addition, they were easily describable and consequently susceptible to standardized designations that reduced telegraph costs further. The commodities futures market, for example, only emerged on a national scale after a uniform grading scheme that simplified product description was adopted [16].

The detailed evolutionary path of large integrated hierarchies was more complex than that of national markets and involved several factors other than the telegraph. Nevertheless, our framework again proves useful in the explanation of which conditions led to which forms. The growth of market areas, according to Chandler [12], encouraged manufacturers to increase their output, frequently by developing new techniques of mass production that offered economies of scale. Such firms, however, often found that existing procurement and distribution mechanisms did not support the high-volume throughput necessary to realize the economies, especially when specialized equipment or human expertise were required.

As Williamson [44] has pointed out, the companies that Chandler identifies as the first to vertically integrate procurement, production, and distribution within a hierarchy were those with asset-specific products, such as meat packers with perishable products requiring railroad refrigeration cars and rapid delivery, and manufacturers of complex machine tools with specialized sales and support needs. In the first case, high time specificity outweighed low complexity of product description. In the second case, the product description was complex, and the sales process was high in human specificity. For these firms, the telegraph provided a mechanism by which close hierarchical coordination could be wielded over great distances. Although the economies of scale were the major factor driving this integration, asset specificity and complexity of product description played a role in determining which firms were likely to integrate, using the telegraph as a mechanism of hierarchical coordination rather than of market communication.

Thus our analytic framework is useful in interpreting the impact of communication technology on past changes in organizational form, even when noncommunication factors also played a large role. In the next section, we apply the framework to contemporary developments.

Contemporary Changes in Market Structures

We can now give a fuller explanation of the nature of electronic hierarchies and markets, the conditions under which each is likely to emerge, and the reasoning behind our thesis that the balance is shifting toward electronic markets.

Emergence of Electronic Interconnection

Let us begin by looking briefly at the technological developments that make electronic interconnection of either type possible and desirable. New information technologies have greatly reduced both the time and cost of communicating information, just as the telegraph did when it was introduced. In particular, the use of computer and telecommunications technology for transferring information gives rise to what we term the *electronic communication effect.* This means that information technology may (1) allow more information to be communicated in the same amount of time (or the same amount in less time), and (2) decrease the costs of this communication dramatically. These effects may benefit both markets and hierarchies.

In addition to these well-known general advantages of electronic communication, electronic coordination can be used to take advantage of two other effects: the electronic brokerage effect and the electronic integration effect. The *electronic brokerage effect* is of benefit primarily in the case of computer-based markets. A broker is an agent who is in contact with many potential buyers and suppliers and who, by filtering these possibilities, helps match one party to the other. A broker substantially reduces the need for buyers and suppliers to contact a large number of alternative partners individually (see [1] and [27] for detailed formal analyses of the benefits of brokering). The electronic brokerage effect simply means that electronic markets, by electronically connecting many different buyers and suppliers through a central database, can fulfill this same function. The standards and protocols of the electronic market allow a buyer to screen out obviously inappropriate suppliers, and to compare the offerings of many different potential suppliers quickly, conveniently, and inexpensively. Thus the electronic brokerage effect can (1) increase the number of alternatives that can be considered, (2) increase the quality of the alternative eventually selected, and (3) decrease the cost of the entire product selection process.

When a supplier and a procurer use information technology to create joint, interpenetrating processes at the interface between value-added stages, they are taking advantage of the *electronic integration effect.* This effect occurs when information technology is used not just to speed communication, but to change—and lead to tighter coupling of—the processes that create and use the information. One simple benefit of this effect is the time saved and the errors avoided by the fact that data need only be entered once. Much more important benefits of close integration of processes are possible in specific situations. CAD/CAM technology, for example, often allows both design and manufacturing engineers to access and manipulate their respective data to test potential designs and to create a product more acceptable to both sides. As another example, systems linking the supplier's and procurer's inventory management processes, so that the supplier can ship the products "just in time" for use in the procurer's manufacturing process, enable the latter to eliminate inventory holding costs, thus reducing total inventory costs for the linked companies. The benefits of the electronic integration effect are usually captured most easily in electronic hierarchies, but they are sometimes apparent in electronic markets as well.

Electronic interconnections provide substantial benefits. The recipients of these benefits—either buyers or suppliers (or both)—should be willing to pay, either directly or indirectly, for them. The providers of electronic markets and electronic hierarchies should, in many cases, be able to realize significant revenues from providing these services.

The Shift from Hierarchies toward Markets

Our prediction that information technology will be more widely used for coordinating economic activities is not a surprising one, even though our analysis of the three effects involved (electronic communication, brokerage, and integration effects) is new. In this section we move to a more surprising and significant prediction: that the overall effect of this technology will be to increase the proportion of economic activity coordinated by markets.

Although the effects of information technology discussed above clearly make both markets and hierarchies more efficient, we see two arguments supporting an overall shift toward market coordination: The first is a general argument based on the analysis summarized in Table 1; the second is a more specific argument based on shifts in asset specificity and complexity of product descriptions.

General Argument Favoring Shift toward Markets
Our initial argument for the overall shift from hierarchies to markets is a simple one, based primarily on two components. The first is the assumption that the widespread use of information technology is likely to decrease the "unit costs" of coordination. As noted above, "coordination" refers to the information processing involved in tasks such as selecting suppliers, establishing contracts, scheduling activities, budgeting resources, and tracking financial flows. Since, by definition, these coordination processes involve communicating and processing information, it seems quite plausible to assume that information technology, when used appropriately, can reduce these costs. This is, of course, an empirically testable hypothesis,

and there are already some suggestive data that support it (e.g., [15], [23], [38]).

The second component of our argument is based on the trade-offs summarized in Table 1. As we noted above, and as Williamson [43] and numerous others have observed, markets have certain production cost advantages over hierarchies as a means of coordinating economic activity. The primary disadvantage of markets is the cost of conducting the market transactions themselves, which, for a number of reasons (including the "opportunistic" ones emphasized by Williamson and the purely "informational" ones emphasized by Malone [27]), are generally higher in markets than in hierarchies. An overall reduction in the "unit costs" of coordination would reduce the importance of the coordination cost dimension (on which markets are weak) and thus lead to markets becoming more desirable in some situations where hierarchies were previously favored. In other words, the result of reducing coordination costs without changing anything else should be an increase in the proportion of economic activity coordinated by markets. This simple argument does not depend on the specific values of any of the costs involved, on the current relative importance of production and coordination costs, or on the current proportion of hierarchical and market coordination.

We find the simplicity of this argument quite compelling, but its obviousness appears not to have been widely recognized. There is also another, less obvious, argument that leads to the same conclusion. This second argument is based on shifts in our key factors for determining coordination structures: asset specificity and complexity of product description.

Changes in Factors Favoring Electronic Markets versus Electronic Hierarchies As Figure 21.1 illustrates, some of the new, computer-based information technologies have affected both of our key dimensions so as to create an overall shift from hierarchies to markets. Databases and high-bandwidth electronic communication can handle and communicate complex, multidimensional product descriptions much more readily than can traditional modes of communication. Thus the horizontal line between high and low complexity in Figure 21.1 has, in effect, shifted upward so that some product descriptions previously classified as highly complex, such as those of airline reservations, may now be considered low in complexity relative to the capabilities of the technology to communicate and manipulate them. The line should continue to shift upward for some time as the capabilities of information technology continue to evolve.

The dimension of asset specificity has undergone a similar change. Flexible manufacturing technology allows rapid changeover of production lines from one product to another. Thus some physically asset-specific components that are similar to other, nonspecific components may begin to be produced by more companies. Companies that in the past would not have tooled up for such a small market now may produce small numbers of these components without significant switch-over costs. The vertical line in Figure 21.1 therefore moves slightly right because some asset-specific components have become, in essence, less specific.

Both these changes increase the region of the chart in which market modes of coordination are favored, lending more support to our argument that there will be an overall shift in this direction.

Examples of the Shift toward Electronic Markets   A dramatic example of the shift toward electronic markets has already occurred in the airline industry. When airline reservations are made by a customer calling the airline directly (and the commission is received by the airline's own sales department), the selling process is coordinated by the hierarchical relationship between the sales department and the rest of the firm. When airline reservations are made through a travel agent, the sale is made (and the commission is received) by the travel agent acting as an external selling agent for the airline. In this case, the selling process is coordinated by the market relationship between the travel agent and the airline. Due, presumably in large part, to the greater range of choices conveniently available through the electronic market, the proportion of total bookings made by travel agents (rather than by customers dealing with airline sales departments) has doubled from 35 to 70 percent since the introduction of the American Airlines reservations system [33, pp. 43–44].

Similarly, there are many recent examples of companies such as IBM, Xerox, and General Electric substantially increasing the proportion of components from other vendors contained in their products (e.g., see [10] and [35]). This kind of "vertical disintegration" of production activities into different firms has become more beneficial as computerized inventory control systems and other forms of electronic integration allow some of the advantages of the internal hierarchical relationship to be retained in market relationships with external suppliers.

The Evolution of Electronic Markets and Electronic Hierarchies

Motives for Establishing Electronic Markets: Possible Market Makers

An electronic market may develop either from a nonelectronic market or from an electronic hierarchy spanning firm boundaries. As Figure 21.2

indicates, any of several participants in an emerging electronic market may be its initiator or market maker, each with different motives. For a market to emerge at all, there must be both *producers* and *buyers* of some good or service. (Depending on the nature of the good or service and on the coordination mechanism used, *producers* may also be called *manufacturers* or *suppliers*, and we will continue to use these three terms as well as the terms *buyers*, *procurers*, and *consumers* interchangeably.) In addition to these primary participants, an existing market may also include two other kinds of participants: First, there may be various levels of "middlemen" who act as distributors, brokers, or agents in the transfer of the goods being sold (we will usually use the term *distributors* to refer to all these levels). Second, there may be various kinds of financial service firms such as banks and credit card issuers who store, transfer, and sometimes loan the funds involved in the transactions. Finally, we may regard as potential participants in any electronic marketplace the information technology vendors who can provide the networks, terminals, and other hardware and software necessary for a computer-based market. Each of these different market participants has different motivations and possibilities for helping to form electronic markets. Our framework suggests how these motivations and other forces such as the electronic brokering, electronic communication, and electronic integration effects may influence the evolution of electronic markets.

Producers   As the initial maker of a product, the producing firm is motivated to have buyers purchase its products rather than those of its competitors. This motivation has already led several producers to establish electronic interconnections with their buyers. In the airline industry, such electronic systems were originally established to encourage travelers to buy tickets from the airline providing the service; they were thus initially electronic hierarchies. Now, however, the travel agents' systems provide access to tickets from all airlines, thus creating electronic markets with an electronic brokering effect [9], [11], [33]. Another example of an electronic interconnection established by a producer is American Hospital Supply's (AHS's) ASAP system, by which several thousand hospitals are provided with on-site terminals that allow them to automatically enter orders for AHS's products [21], [33]. Since this system has only one supplier (AHS), we would classify it as an electronic hierarchy rather than an electronic market. As we will describe below, our framework suggests that, in spite of the original motivations of the producers, there are often strong forces that cause electronic hierarchies to evolve toward electronic markets that do not favor specific producers.

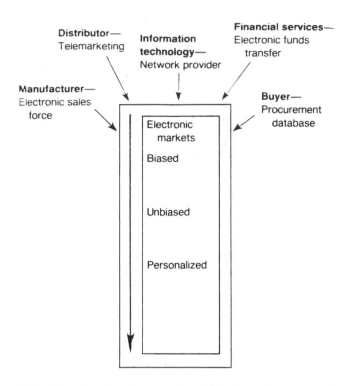

Figure 21.2 Evolution of electronic markets: Multiple starting points lead to a common evolutionary path.

Buyers In contrast to the producer, who wants to minimize the number of alternatives considered by buyers, the buyers themselves would like to maximize the number of alternatives considered and the ease of comparing them. One way of doing this is for buyers to begin using computer databases containing information about alternative products. In some cases, the buyers are powerful enough in a market that they can require suppliers to provide this information, thus creating an electronic market. For example, General Motors already requires its primary suppliers to conform to the computer hardware and communications standards established by the Automotive Industry Action Group [11]. These systems can then be used to speed order processing and implement innovations such as "just-in-time" inventory management [7]. Groups of buyers are currently developing similar electronic markets in the grocery, chemical, and aluminum industries as well [7]. Unlike systems provided by producers, which are motivated by the desire to establish an attractive distribution channel for certain products, these systems are established by buyers to make supplier selection, order processing, and inventory management more efficient.

Distributors   In some cases, the initiative for a computer-based market may come from distributors rather than directly from buyers or suppliers. In the pharmaceutical industry, for example, wholesale distributors such as McKesson have followed the lead of producers such as AHS in setting up electronic connections with their customers [8]. Like AHS, such distributors established the electronic links in an attempt to monopolize the business of their customers, and at this stage the systems are still electronic hierarchies rather than electronic markets. Just as with systems developed by producers, however, we expect that electronic links developed by distributors will often have an initial bias toward one or more producers, but that these biases will usually disappear under pressure from competitive and legal forces. Although the benefits to the distributor may initially have had their source in the bias, distributors may soon find that the greater efficiency offered by the electronic market allows adequate compensation for running an unbiased market.

Financial Services Providers   By transferring the funds and/or extending the credit required for transactions, banks and other financial institutions are already involved as participants in most markets. In some cases, this involvement can be the basis for providing a full-fledged electronic market. For example, some banks, such as Citicorp, offer their credit card holders a telephone shopping service for a wide variety of consumer goods [37]. The system keeps a log of the lowest retail prices available for all the products included. Cardholders can call for a price quotation, order the goods over the phone, and have them delivered to their door. In a similar spirit, Citicorp and McGraw-Hill have formed a joint venture to make information about alternative prices for crude oil and to match buyers and sellers [5]. Similarly, Louie [26] describes the evolution of the PRONTO home banking system at Chemical Bank in New York, from offering a single financial service (home banking) to becoming a full systems operator and providing home information services with stock prices and home retailing information. The initial motivation of the financial institution in these cases is presumably not to favor the sale of any particular supplier's products, but to increase the volume of transaction processing and credit-based income for the financial institution.

Information Technology Vendors   In all of the above examples, the hardware, networks, and often the software necessary to create computer-based markets are provided by information technology vendors.

Even though these examples illustrate how the line between these vendors and other kinds of firms is beginning to blur, there are still some cases where firms whose primary business is supplying information technology may be able to make computer-based markets themselves. For example, Western Union has a system for matching freight shippers with motor freight carriers and verifying that the latter have the necessary legal authorization and insurance coverage [20, p. 1199]. It is easy to imagine other examples of information technology vendors making markets. For example, a natural extension of telephone companies' classified directories would be "electronic yellow pages" which might include capabilities for actually placing orders as well as locating suppliers. (A directory-only service of this type is already offered by Automated Directory Services [25].)

Stages in the Evolution of Electronic Markets

The evolution of electronic markets from nonelectronic markets or from electronic or nonelectronic hierarchies frequently involves an intermediate stage—a biased market—but eventually proceeds to an unbiased market. In the future that evolution may continue to a personalized market.

From Biased to Unbiased Markets   Some of the initial providers of electronic markets have attempted to exploit the benefits of the electronic communication effect to capture customers in a system biased toward a particular supplier. We believe that, in the long run, the significant additional benefits to buyers possible from the electronic brokerage effect will drive almost all electronic markets toward being unbiased channels for products from many suppliers. For example, both American Airlines and United Airlines have introduced reservation systems that allow travel agents to find and book flights, print tickets, and so forth [9], [11], [33]. The United system was originally established as an electronic hierarchy that allowed travel agents to book only flights on United. To compete with this system, American established a system that included flights from all airlines (thus making it a true market), but with American flights for a given route listed first. This shift to a biased market was possible both because airline reservations are not asset specific and because they can be described in standardized forms and manipulated in standardized processes that may be quickly and easily handled by the new technology. United soon adopted the same strategy, and by 1983 travel agencies that used automated reservation systems used one of these two systems for 65 percent of the reservations they made [11, p. 139]. These systems' significant bias in favor of their suppliers' flights eventually led other airlines to protest, and recent rules from the Civil Aeronautics Board eliminated much of the bias in the systems. The systems now provide unbiased reservation service to other airlines for a significant fee.

A similar evolution may result in the case of the ASAP order entry system. AHS is apparently trying to prevent that outcome by making the shared processes themselves more asset specific. For instance, Jackson [21, p. 137] describes many features built into the ASAP system to customize the system to a particular hospital's needs, in effect creating a procedural asset specificity in the relationship between buyer and seller. These features include purchase history files, computation of economic order quantities, and basic order file templates. In each case, powerful one-to-one hierarchical relationships are established between buyer and seller. However, most of the medical products sold through the system meet the criteria listed above for electronic markets: They are not uniquely useful for specific customers, and their descriptions are relatively simple and standardized. Therefore, our model leads us to predict that this system (or its competitors) will move toward including products from many different suppliers. The same evolution is likely in the case of pharmaceutical distributors such as McKesson.

These examples illustrate what we suggest will be a very common case: Producers who start out by providing an electronic hierarchy or a biased electronic market will eventually be driven by competitive or legal forces to remove or significantly reduce the bias.

From Unbiased to Personalized Markets   One of the potential problems with unbiased electronic markets of the sort we have described is that buyers might be overwhelmed with more alternatives than they can possibly consider. This problem will be less important in commodity-like markets where the product descriptions are well-known standards and where the only dimension on which products are compared is price. The problem will be particularly acute, however, in markets for which the product descriptions involve a number of related attributes that are compared in different ways by different buyers. Retail sales of many consumer products, for example, would fall in this category.

In these cases, a final stage may be the development of electronic markets that provide personalized decision aids to help individual buyers select from the alternatives available, what we call "personalized markets." For example, at least one such system has been developed for airline reservations [6, p. 21]. Using this system, travel agencies and corporate travel departments can receive information about available flights with each flight automatically ranked on a scale from 1 to 100.

The rankings take into account "fares, departure times, and even the value of an executive's time."

It is easy to imagine even more sophisticated systems that use artificial intelligence (AI) techniques to screen advertising messages and product descriptions according to precisely the criteria that are important to a given buyer (e.g., see [29] for a similar system that filters electronic messages of all kinds). Air travelers, for instance, might specify rules with which their own "automated buyers' agents" could compare a wide range of possible flights and select the ones that best match that particular traveler's preferences. A fairly simple set of such rules could, in many cases, do a better job of matching travelers' preferences than all but the most conscientious and knowledgeable travel agents.

In addition to AI techniques for specifying complex qualitative reasoning processes, there are also a number of normative mathematical models [24] and descriptive behavioral models [22], [32], [36] that could help in designing such systems.

Clearly these techniques will be more useful for certain products (e.g., those that are easily described and nonspecific) and certain buyers (e.g., industrial buyers doing routine purchasing rather than consumers buying on impulse). Ultimately, however, such personalized decision aids may be widely useful in both industrial and consumer purchasing for screening large amounts of electronically stored product information on behalf of particular buyers.

Another intriguing possibility is that some of the preference rules specified by buyers might be made available to suppliers. There are obviously cases where protecting the privacy of buyers should preclude making this information available. In other cases, however, making buyer preferences automatically available (perhaps anonymously) to suppliers could dramatically improve the efficiency of certain kinds of market research as well as the responsiveness of suppliers. Instead of having to painstakingly infer consumer decision rules from surveys or experiments, suppliers might be able to simply observe the actual rules consumers had specified.

Motives for Establishing Electronic Hierarchies

There are still many cases of high asset specificity and complex product descriptions for which electronic hierarchies will be desirable. In particular, as Figure 21.3 suggests, electronic hierarchies will be established to improve product development or product distribution. In this section we discuss why and how companies may establish electronic hierarchies for each of these functions.

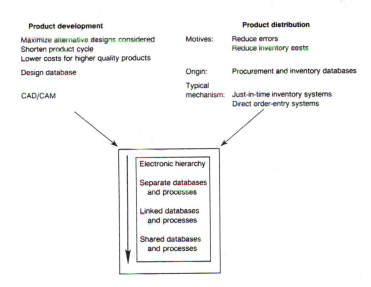

Figure 21.3 Evolution of electronic hierarchies: From separate to shared databases.

Product Development CAD/CAM, electronic mail, and other information technologies can be used in product development to enhance the hierarchical coordination between design and manufacturing groups. The electronic integration effect can be used, in this case, to (1) shorten the development cycle, (2) increase the number of alternative designs considered, (3) reduce development (i.e., coordination) costs, (4) reduce manufacturing costs (by involving manufacturing engineers in the design process), and (5) produce a higher quality product. The president of Xerox's newly integrated Engineering and Manufacturing Group, for example, says that such integration "is the key to faster and less costly development, to lower manufacturing costs, and to better products" [19, p. 12].

The key data that must be shared in the product development process are engineering drawings, parts descriptions, bills of materials, engineering change notices (ECNs), machine tool configurations, and so forth. For example, in many companies the ECN process is considered a people-intensive, time-consuming, and error-prone administrative activity. Because the shared database of an electronic hierarchy allows people directly involved in the change to work with the ECN process electronically, the large bureaucracy previously needed for administering this process coordination may be severely reduced (e.g., [30]).

Xerox's new electronic ECN process, for instance, involves three parties: the design engineer, who is also responsible for the manufacturability of the change and its entry in the spare parts ordering process; the manufacturing engineer, who designs the actual manufacturing process; and the manufacturing analyst, who updates the necessary manufacturing databases to accommodate the change. In the previous process, a number of other people were also involved: the advanced manufacturing engineer, who worked with the design engineer to determine general manufacturability; the administrator of the record center—where all data on the part were kept—who managed copying and distribution to necessary parties; the manufacturing configuration specialist, who provided information on the manufacturing bill of materials and maintained any changes required; and the spare-parts planner, who did the entering and ordering of spares for initializing the product in the distribution system. The electronic database permits significant reduction in administrative coordination costs and, more importantly, increases the quality and timeliness of the product development process as well.

Although the above example is of electronic integration within one organization, there have also been examples of linkages between design and manufacturing groups in different companies in both heavy manufacturing and the auto industry [11], [35]. In the design of semiconductor circuits, for instance, over 100 different processes and over 30–40 separate organizations have traditionally been involved [17], [38]. Use of the Mead Conway method for VLSI design and electronic integration between organizations has dramatically reduced these numbers. Designers in remote organizations use standardized languages in functionally rich workstations and then send their standardized design databases over a network to a supplier fabrication facility where they are linked to the supplier's manufacturing process databases. The end result is that the test circuits are delivered to the procurer more cheaply and quickly.

Thus electronic integration of product design and development, whether within or between firms, uses linked or shared databases to achieve more efficient and effective product development cycles. The electronic integration effect may also be realized in product distribution.

Product Distribution   The two primary participants in product distribution systems are the procurer and the supplier. The procurer's goal for establishing electronic hierarchies may be to have the inventory available to the factory production process "just in time," thus eliminating inventory carrying costs as well as all production control necessary to manage inventory [31]. That is, to lower inventory costs, procurers may raise the time specificity of the process. Firestone, for example, as part of the physical and electronic inventory system of two major car manufacturers, carries the tire inventories of both firms. The large battery manufacturer that supplies Firestone's retail stores is similarly tied into its distribution system and maintains the battery inventory for Firestone.

As we saw above, these electronic interconnections are allowing many manufacturers to rely increasingly on external suppliers of components rather than on manufacturing the components themselves (e.g., [35]). One somewhat paradoxical aspect of this shift is that, even though manufacturers are increasing the volume of components purchased externally, they are decreasing the number of suppliers from which these components are purchased [35, p. D5]. This paradox can be resolved, however, by noting that the reasons given for decreasing the number of suppliers (e.g., to become preferred customers and thus increase leverage with the suppliers) amount to ways of increasing the asset specificity of the products. In other words, these buyers are using information technology to "get the best of both worlds"—they are making increasing use of electronic markets, but their relationships with each of the suppliers in these markets are becoming increasingly like electronic hierarchies.

The supplier may be motivated to enter such a just-in-time arrangement for defensive reasons—doing so may be a condition of doing business with the procurer. Suppliers, however, may also perceive other advantages to an electronic arrangement. Jackson [21, p. 134] asserts that a buyer is unlikely to tamper with an established just-in-time relationship "because changing would require another substantial investment in learning to work with the new vendor." That is, the shared databases and physical and electronic processes may become physically, humanly, and time specific, increasing the likelihood of a hierarchical rather than market relationship. This is clearly a consideration in early systems such as that developed by AHS. As noted earlier, however, such electronic hierarchies frequently develop into biased, then unbiased electronic markets when the products themselves are not asset specific and are easily described in standardized terms.

In addition to these separate motives, both procurer and supplier may be motivated to reduce the time, cost, and errors produced by an extensive procurement system that requires repeated entries, transmissions, translations into different terms, and reentries of information between paper and computer systems of both parties. For the auto makers and component suppliers, for example, this costly process results in errors in approximately 5 percent of all procurer/supplier documents [7]. The Automotive Industry Action Group is now establishing standard forms and processes for the major auto companies and their many suppliers to use. Once these standards are established, the existing electronic hierarchies between buyers and sellers in this market are likely to evolve into electronic markets.

Relative Power of Participants

As these examples illustrate, one of the critical factors involved in the establishment of electronic interconnections is the relative power of the participants. The interconnections that emerge are determined, in part, by the preexisting power relationships of the participants, and these power relationships may, in turn, be changed by the new electronic arrangements. For example, suppliers may enter into a just-in-time inventory arrangement in order to continue doing business with a powerful buyer, and the knowledge this arrangement gives the buyer about the inventory positions of all its suppliers may enhance the buyer's power even more.

Sometimes, merely agreeing on the standards for electronic systems can be the battleground on which many of the power issues arise. In the insurance industry, for example, both the independent agents and the major commercial and property carriers are hotly contesting the control of standards [3]. The large carriers would like to tie independent agents to their own systems, and see their proprietary standards as a means to achieve this. However, the independent agents, through an industry association, are defining a set of standards for the primary insurance transactions that will give them the freedom to do business with multiple carriers. A number of large carriers have indicated that they will now live with the more general standards.

Stages in the Evolution of Electronic Hierarchies

Shared databases, made possible by advances in information technology, are at the core of electronic hierarchies. They provide the mechanism for integrating processes across organizational boundaries by allowing continuous sharing of information in easily accessible on-line form [4].

Our primary basis for predicting the evolutionary path of these mechanisms is the observation that both the benefits and the costs of electronic integration become greater as the coupling between adjacent steps on the value-added chain becomes tighter. Thus we would expect organizations to obtain limited benefits at low cost before moving to greater benefits at higher cost. Figure 21.3 indicates a plausible trajectory that this observation suggests: Stand-alone but mutually accessible databases should appear first, then be replaced by electronically linked databases and, eventually, by fully shared databases. We are not aware of good examples of all three stages of this trajectory occurring in a single system, but we can describe examples of systems at each of the three stages.

Stand-Alone Databases   In this stage one or both parties make their databases accessible to the other party in the electronic hierarchy. This often requires the other party to use a separate workstation. The early versions of the AHS order entry system, for example, required customers to use a separate workstation to access the AHS order entry programs and purchasing history databases [18]. Even though the database that is built up in this process is, in some sense, "shared" by the customers and AHS, it is not connected to the customer's accounting and other application systems, so we classify it as a stand-alone database.

Linked Databases   In this stage supplier and buyer databases are still separate, but a formal on-line mechanism passes information from one to the other. The most recent version of the AHS order entry system (see [18]) allows this kind of direct computer-to-computer communication. Orders are prepared by the customer's internal computer system and transmitted electronically to AHS, and order confirmations are returned to the customer's computer and used to update the hospital's files. Another example of this level of linking is provided by the Mead-Conway VLSI design methodology. Here, electronic networks are used to transfer product design specifications from the CAD system on the designer's workstation to a manufacturing system that is located at a remote site and owned by another organization.

Shared Databases   In this final stage, one database contains information of value for both parties in the electronic hierarchy. The ECN process we described above illustrates a simple example of this situation, and great effort is currently being expended by CAD/CAM vendors and manufacturing companies to implement and use the integrated engineering/manufacturing database environment successfully (e.g., [39]).

Conclusions and Strategic Implications

A casual reading of the business press confirms that electronic connections within and between organizations are becoming increasingly important (e.g., [2], [9], [11], [33]). The framework we have developed here helps illuminate many of these changes. We have shown how the increasing use of electronic interconnections can be seen as the result of three forces: the electronic communication effect, the electronic brokerage effect, and the electronic integration effect. We have analyzed how factors such as the ease of product description and the degree to which products are specific to particular customers affect whether these interconnections will take the form of electronic hierarchies or electronic markets. Finally, and perhaps most importantly, we have argued that, by reducing the costs of coordination, information technology will lead to an overall shift toward proportionately more use of markets rather than hierarchies to coordinate economic activity. By applying this framework, it is possible to see how many of the changes occurring today fit into a larger picture and to predict some of the specific evolutionary changes that are likely to occur as information technology becomes more widely used.

Our analysis has several implications for corporate strategy:

1.   All market participants should consider the potential advantages of providing an electronic market in their marketplace. For some participants, providing such a market may increase the sales of their current products or services. For all participants, it provides a potential source of new revenues from the market-making activity itself.

2.   All organizations should consider whether it would be advantageous for them to coordinate some of their own internal operations more closely or to establish tighter connections with their customers or suppliers using electronic hierarchies.

3.   Market forces make it likely that biased electronic sales channels (whether electronic hierarchies or biased electronic markets) for nonspecific, easily described products will eventually be replaced by unbiased markets. Therefore, the early developers of biased electronic sales channels for these kinds of products should not expect that the competitive advantages these systems provide will continue indefinitely. They should instead be planning how to manage the transition to unbiased markets in such a way that they can continue to derive revenues from the market-making activity itself.

4.   All firms should consider whether more of the activities they currently perform internally could be performed less expensively or more flexibly by outside suppliers whose selection and work could be coordinated by computer-based systems.

5.   Information systems groups in most firms should begin to plan the network infrastructure that will be necessary to support the kinds of internal and external interconnections we have described.

6.   Advanced developers of computer-based marketing technology should begin thinking about how to develop intelligent aids to help buyers select products from a large number of alternatives. Such intelligent aids may eventually be able to act, in part, as automated agents for the buyers. They may also, in some situations, be able

to provide detailed information to suppliers about their customers' preferences.

In short, if our predictions are correct, we should not expect the electronically interconnected world of tomorrow to be simply a faster and more efficient version of the world we know today. Instead, we should expect fundamental changes in how firms and markets organize the flow of goods and services in our economy. Clearly more systematic empirical study and more detailed formal analyses are needed to confirm these predictions, and we hope the conceptual framework presented here will help guide this research.

References

Note: References [39] and [42] are not cited in text.

1. Baligh, H. H., and Richartz, L. *Vertical Market Structures*. Allyn and Bacon, Boston, Mass., 1967.

2. Barrett, S., and Konsynski, B. Inter-organization information sharing systems. *Manage. Inf. Syst. Q.*, spec. ed. (Dec. 1982), 94.

3. Benjamin, R. What companies share is virtually a new game. *Inf. Syst. News* (Dec. 26, 1983), 11.

4. Benjamin, R., and Scott-Morton, M. S. Information technology, integration, and organizational change. *Interfaces*. [To be published.]

5. Bennett, R. A. Citibank, McGraw in a venture: Information service for oil. *New York Times* (Sept. 10, 1985), bus. sect., 1.

6. Brown, F. C., III. Automation brings travel service right to the traveler's doorstep. *Wall St. J.* (Aug. 7, 1986), 21.

7. *Business Week*. Detroit tries to level a mountain of paperwork. *Bus. Week* (Aug. 26, 1985), 94–96.

8. *Business Week*. For drug distributors, information is the Rx for survival. *Bus. Week* (Oct. 14, 1985), 116.

9. *Business Week*. Information power: How companies are using new technologies to gain a competitive edge. *Bus. Week* (Oct. 14, 1985), 108–116.

10. *Business Week*. The hollow corporation (a special report). *Bus. Week* (Mar. 3, 1986), 57–85.

11. Cash, J. I., and Konsynski, B. R. IS redraws competitive boundaries. *Harvard Bus. Rev. 64*, 2 (Mar.–Apr. 1985), 134–142.

12. Chandler, A. D. *Strategy and Structure*. Doubleday, New York, 1962.

13. Ciborra, C. U. Markets, bureaucracies, and groups in the information society. *Inf. Econ. Policy 1* (1983), 145–160.

14. Coase, R. H. The nature of the firm. *Econ. N.S. 4* (Nov. 1937), 386–405.

15. Crawford, A. B. Corporate electronic mail: A communication-intensive application of information technology. *Manage. Inf. Syst. Q. 6*, 3 (Sept. 1982), 1–13.

16. DuBoff, R. B. *The Telegraph and the Structure of Markets in the United States, 1845–1890.* Vol. 8, *Research in Economic History.* JAI Press, Greenwich, Conn., 1983, pp. 253–277.

17. Feigenbaum, E., and McCorduck, P. *The Fifth Generation: Artificial Intelligence and Japan's Challenge to the World.* Addison-Wesley, Reading, Mass., 1984.

18. Harvard Business School. American Hospital Supply Corp. (A) The ASAP system. HBS Case 0-186-005, Harvard Business School, Boston, Mass., 1985.

19. Hicks, W. A new approach to product development. *High Technol.* (Oct. 1984), 12.

20. Ives, B., and Learmonth, G. P. The information system as a competitive weapon. *Commun. ACM 27*, 12 (Dec. 1984), 1193–1201.

21. Jackson, B. *Winning and Keeping Industrial Customers.* Lexington Books, Lexington, Mass., 1985.

22. Johnson, E., and Payne, J. Effort, accuracy, and choice. *Manage. Sci. 31*, 4 (Apr. 1985), 395–414.

23. Jonscher, C. J. Information resources and productivity. *Inf. Econ. Policy 1*, 1 (1983), 13–35.

24. Keeney, R. L., and Raiffa, H. *Decision with Multiple Objectives: Preferences and Value Tradeoffs.* Wiley, New York, 1976.

25. Koenig, R. Call-in firms are taking on yellow pages. *Wall St. J.* (Mar. 1, 1983), 37.

26. Louie, B. Impact of information technology on the strategy-structure relationship. Master's thesis, Center for Information Systems Research, Sloan School of Management, Massachusetts Institute of Technology, Cambridge, Mass., 1985, pp. 58–59.

27. Malone, T. W. Organizational structure and information technology: Elements of a formal theory. *Manage Sci.* [To be published.] (Expanded version available: CISR WP 130, Sloan WP 1710-85, 90s WP 85-011, Center for Information Systems Research, Sloan School of Management, Massachusetts Institute of Technology, Cambridge, Mass., 1985.)

28. Malone, T. W., and Smith, S. A. Tradeoffs in designing organizations: Implications for new forms of human organizations and computer systems.

CISR WP 112, Sloan WP 1541-84, Center for Information Systems Research, Sloan School of Management, Massachusetts Institute of Technology, Cambridge, Mass., 1984.

29. Malone, T. W., Grant, K. R., Turbak, F. A., Brobst, S. A., and Cohen, M. D. Intelligent information-sharing systems. *Commun. ACM 30*, 5 (May 1987), 390–402.

30. Miller, J. G., and Vollmann, T. E. The hidden factory. *Harvard Bus. Rev. 63*, 5 (Sept.–Oct. 1985), 142–150.

31. Nakane, J., and Hall, R. Management specifications for stockless production. *Harvard Bus. Rev.* (May–June 1983), 84–91.

32. Payne, J. W., Braunstein, M. L., and Carroll, J. S. Exploring predecisional behavior: An alternative approach to decision research. *Organ. Behav. Hum. Performance 22*, 1 (Aug. 1978), 17–44.

33. Petre, P. How to keep customers happy captives. *Fortune 112*, 5 (Sept. 2, 1985), 42–46.

34. Porter, M. E., and Millar, V.E. How information gives you competitive advantage. *Harvard Bus. Rev. 63*, 4 (July–Aug. 1985), 149–160.

35. Prokesh, S. E. U.S. companies weed out many operations. *New York Times* (Sept. 22, 1985), A1, D5.

36. Russo, J., and Dosher, B. Strategies for multi-attribute binary choice. *J. Exp. Psychol. Learn. Mem. Cognition 9*, 4 (Oct. 1983), 676–696.

37. Stevenson, R. W. Credit card enhancements: Wider range of services. *New York Times* (Apr. 30, 1985), bus. sect., 1.

38. Strassman, P. *Information Payo–*. Free Press, New York, 1985.

39. Ware, M. A total integrated systems approach to CAD/CAM. *Computers* (Jan. 1982), 105–116.

40. Williamson, O. E. *Markets and Hierarchies*. Free Press, New York, 1975.

41. Williamson, O. E. Transaction cost economics: The governance of contractual relations. *J. Law Econ. 22*, 2 (Oct. 1979), 233–261.

42. Williamson, O. E. The organization of work: A comparative institutional assessment. *J. Econ. Behav. Organ. 1*, 1 (Mar. 1980), 6–38.

43. Williamson, O. E. The economics of organization: The transaction cost approach. *Am J. Sociol. 87*, 3 (Nov. 1981), 548–575.

44. Williamson, O. E. The modern corporation: Origins, evolution, attributes. *J. Econ. Lit. 19*, 4 (Dec. 1981), 1537–1568.

45. Yates, J. The telegraph's effect on nineteenth century markets and firms. In *Business and Economic History*. Series 2, vol. 15, 1986, pp. 149–163.

22

Evolution of an Organizational Interface: The New Business Department at a Large Insurance Firm

Andrew Clement
Department of Computer Science and Mathematics
Atkinson College, York University
North York, Canada

C. C. Gotlieb
Department of Computer Science
University of Toronto
Toronto, Canada

1 Introduction

Studies of computer-human interaction generally focus on the design of the interface between an individual user and a computer system while often ignoring the larger organizational and social contexts within which the interaction takes place. On the other hand, organizational studies tend to treat computer systems as a given and something from which social impacts flow deterministically. These models of computer-human interaction are being increasingly regarded as overly simplistic [5,15,18]. In particular, Malone [12] has recently suggested that this gap in research be addressed by paying more attention to organizational interfaces, rather than simply user interfaces, and by focussing on design issues rather than on explanatory or predictive theories.

There are several reasons why the concept of computer-human interaction should be extended to include consideration of organizations interacting with entire computer systems. Generally computer systems have been developed by organizations for use within organizations. It is through organizational processes that resources are invested in computer systems, the needs of various actors articulated and translated into systems specifications, working knowledge embedded in software, and so on.

The interaction process operates in the other direction as well. Once implemented, computer systems provide opportunities and constraints for organizational action. Even though there are no *necessary* impacts, numerous studies point to the influence of computer systems on the nature of organizational tasks, roles, relationships and behaviour [1,11].

Whereas the time period of interaction phenomena at the level of individual users and computers is typically on the order of seconds, the interactions between organizations and computer systems can be measured in months and years. Despite this difference in time scale, an understanding of the organizational context in which the individual user interaction takes place can be crucial in determining the success or failure of user interface designs—sometimes in unexpected ways [22].

The purpose of this paper is to describe one example of organization-computer interaction and draw from it some general principles that can explain the process. The implications for systems designers will then be discussed.

2 The Case of the New Business Department at Maple Leaf Life

The Maple Leaf Life Insurance Company (MLL)[1] is a major insurer and user of computers. The company has more than 90 branch offices in the U.S. and Canada and operates in 20 countries worldwide. Its assets exceed $16 billion, making it one of the 20 largest life insurance companies in North America. Generally it is quite profitable. MLL was one of the first companies to use computers in Canada, and by 1984 it operated an IBM 3081 connected on-line to more than 500 terminals spread through its offices. The principal user of computing services is the Individual Insurance Administration operation (IIA), which is located

---

[1]   Not its real name.

at the head office and in 1983 employed 230 people. One of the two main departments in IIA is New Business, which determines whether policy applications from the sales force are acceptable to the company and issues the policies in the case of successful applications.

The case study reported here is derived from Ph.D. dissertation research into the relationship between managerial control and on-line computer systems [4]. The research was conducted mainly in 1982 and 1983 through extensive, open-ended, on-site interviews (>60) with personnel at every corporate level and involved at every stage of the development and use of the major on-line computer systems in the IIA. Transaction processing work was observed directly and in addition numerous corporate documents (>70) were collected and analysed.[2]

As its name suggests, the New Business Department's function is to process new insurance policies as they are sold to individual customers. The key to understanding the interaction between this organization and its computer systems is the evolution in the way the department processes policy applications.

A transaction (i.e., application) processed by New Business passes through every major function in the department. Although there are variations in the types of policies handled, all applications generally follow the same route and are subjected to the same treatment. When an application arrives at Head Office, it is used to establish a temporary application file. Information on other policies the client has with the company is obtained by searching the Policy Holder Index (PHI). Results of previous attempts by the client to obtain insurance coverage from other companies is sought through the Medical Information Bureau (MIB). When the information from these sources has arrived, the "front-ending" stage is complete and the underwriter is in a position to assess whether the risk in providing the requested insurance is acceptable to the company. Additional information may be requested from the branch, such as extra medical tests in the case of particularly large policies or if there are indications of potential health problems.

If the underwriter deems the risk acceptable, as it is in the great majority of cases, then the "back-ending" is done. The premium payment and cash value table (page 3 of the policy) are calculated, printed and checked against the original application. Any special provisions, endorsements and subject-to forms are prepared and pre-printed policy clauses are pulled. All these pages are collated, checked, grommetted (i.e., fastened) together and then mailed to the branch for forwarding

---

[2] In the case of the New Business Department, the focus of this paper, the most relevant interviews were conducted with two Vice Presidents, the manager of New Business, two supervisors, two former supervisors, an underwriter and a systems specialist. These informants had between 10 and 30 years experience with New Business.

to the client. In addition, permanent company files such as the policy service masterfile, the policy holder index file, and agency file (for initiating commission payments) are updated with information from the new policy.

At the level of generality with which we have been discussing New Business, the processing pattern has remained approximately the same for at least the last twenty years. At a more detailed level, however, the processing has changed considerably over this period and so have the organizational structure and the control mechanisms.

Before the first use of on-line systems in New Business in 1973, computers played a minor role in the functionally organized department. Front-ending and back-ending were quite labor intensive. Each application was handled many (>23) times by a collection of people each fulfilling one of at least 12 specialized roles. Each of the major tasks (PHI, MIB, Underwriting, Stenography, Checking, "Pulling," "Subject-to") formed a separate work unit and many had their own supervisor. Only within Underwriting had a start been made to organize territorially. Teams of underwriters dealt with all applications from branches within each unit. There was no individual uniquely assigned responsibility for business originating in a particular branch. Furthermore, these territorial underwriting units were organized hierarchically by functional specialty. Particularly complicated or risky applications could pass through as many as four levels in Underwriting before a final decision was made —Control Clerk, First Reader (Junior Underwriter), Second Reader (Intermediate Underwriter), and Senior Underwriter. The Senior Underwriters also supervised each team and trained their subordinates.

Figure 22.1 shows a detailed picture of how applications were processed by the various sections of the New Business Department in the years immediately preceding the installation of the on-line system developed by Insurance Systems of America (ISA). At the top of the figure is represented a modified organization chart, while below it is a data flow diagram [7,8] showing the passage of an application and related information through the New Business Department. Generally information flows down the page with time and across the page when moving across organizational boundaries. In effect this diagram depicts in part the organization/computer system interface at one point in time.

Immediate, task-related control of the work process was exercised in a direct, personal fashion. Only basic overall volume counts were kept (e.g., number of applications processed, policies issued) and were not used to evaluate the performance of individual clerks or underwriters. Rather than depending on quantitative measures, supervisors maintained control over operations in the traditional manner—by directly observing work as it was carried out according to a highly fragmented and managerially specified division of labour.

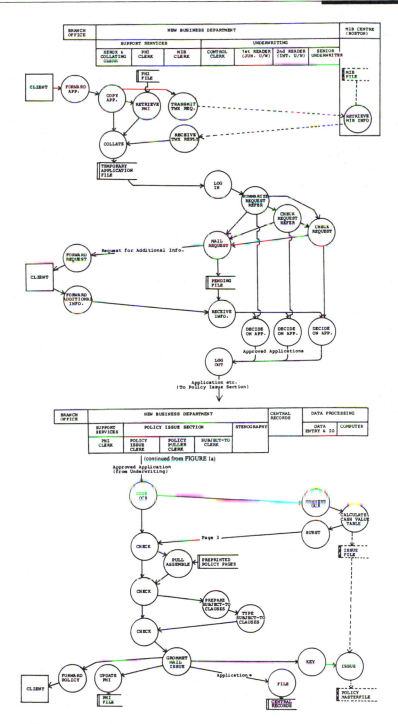

Figure 22.1

The picture that emerges of New Business in this period is that of a department which was difficult to manage on a day-to-day basis in anything other than this fairly personal way. An application was processed through many steps and crossed several organizational boundaries. No single Head Office person involved in the process was responsible for an application's safe passage through the system as a whole. Finding out where an application was at any particular time required manual searches through stacks of paper files. Trying to measure systematically the speed and accuracy of any individual employee based on their actual work performance would require considerably more effort. The difficulty in assessing the contribution of the individual to overall performance of the department was further compounded by the finely divided nature of the tasks and organization. These basic managerial problems would likely remain as long as the production process was serially fragmented and essential production information was relatively inaccessible by being tied to paper. This situation began to change noticeably in 1973, a year that marks a convenient dividing line in our historical discussion of the evolution of the New Business Department because this is when the ISA on-line computer system was installed.

The ISA system was first used to maintain a "pending" file for underwriters to keep track of the status of each application and determine whether outstanding requirements that have held up processing have been received. Once the basic infrastructure of on-line terminals and the routine updating of records throughout the application process has been put in place, it became much easier to incrementally enhance the functionality of the system by collecting more information and implementing new applications programs. In the decade since the ISA system was installed, the management in New Business has repeatedly extended and refined it to improve productivity and processing times, offer previously infeasible services to branches and gain greater control over New Business operations. PHI and MIB queries were automated and back-ending simplified and sped up by the printing of standardized insurance clauses and the numbers of pre-printed pages.

During the ten years of progressive enhancement to the computing systems in New Business, the department was also reorganized along much more territorial lines. New Business led the company in this direction and took territorialization far beyond the high level splitting into U.S. versus Canada/International. Each of these large areas was further subdivided into a number of smaller units, so that each underwriter dealt exclusively with a specified set of branches. The introduction of thorough territorialization meant that the craft-based hierarchy within the underwriting units was eliminated. As a long-time underwriter noted:

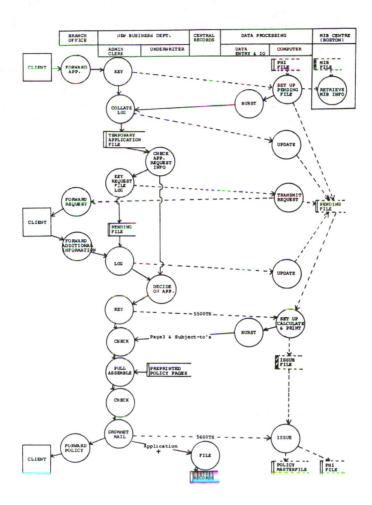

Figure 22.2

Now we [underwriters] are acting as units of one. I get absolutely piddly cases and I get million dollar cases. I act as my own first, second and third reader. [4, p. 8–36]

The differing grades of administrative staff were similarly collapsed into a single clerical level. The overall effect has been that the structure of both the organization and the non-computerized information processing task has been dramatically simplified in the ten years since the ISA system was introduced (see Figure 22.2).

Just as the structure has changed in concert with the computer system, so too has the way in which the employees in the department are managed. With detailed information about the status of each application automatically recorded by the computer system, managers have been able to obtain regular printouts showing volume counts, service times, application status lists, overdue lists, run logs and the like, broken down by territorial unit and in some cases by individual employee. Managers use the printouts not only for day-to-day operations, but also to evaluate the performance of individual workers. As such they play a role in decisions involving pay, promotion, demotion, transfer and dismissal. One of the underwriters noted that they were now "very much under scrutiny, basically because [of] the data from the computer system."

3 *Principles of Organization/Computer System Interaction*

Although the design of the organizational interface took place over a considerable period of time and in a largely ad hoc manner, we can discern definite principles that have informed the effort. The principles that can be seen to be followed are sufficiently common to the systems development process in large corporations that they are generally taken for granted and seldom made explicit.

3.1 *Collapsing the Processing Chain*

One pattern in the evolution of the organization/computer system interface that emerges strongly is the progressive collapse of the processing chain involved in the handling of policy applications. One can clearly see this phenomenon by comparing the information flow diagrams, Figures 22.1 and 22.2. The historic trend, at least until recently, in the industrialization of both factory and office work has been the fragmentation of tasks and the consequent increase in the number of processing steps. The New Business Department was a good example of this, but with the development of the on-line system the trend has been significantly reversed. This phenomenon, which has been observed in a number of other modern office settings [2,8,23], reaches its highest expression in on-line self-service systems such as direct distance dialing (DDD), automated teller machines (ATM), airline self-ticketing, and the like.

The collapse of transaction processing chains, which is likely to continue as part of the trend towards self-service operation, can be explained largely in economic terms. Most obviously, the lessening cost of computerizing routine information processing in relation to human labour makes it attractive for managers to automate away steps previously performed by their employees. In addition, the combining of steps allows faster, more accurate response to customer requests, thus increasing the apparent value of the service and offering competitive advantage. This change in production method, which reflects the systems analyst's imperative to "capture data at its source," also undermines the functional forms of organization which have traditionally prevailed.

3.2 *Extending Managerial Control*

Much as the principle of shortening processing chains, with its underlying economic rationale, helps explain the particular technical and organizational evolution that took place in the New Business Department, it does not in itself provide an adequate explanation. For instance, it does not explain the employee monitoring features of the software, nor does it account for why employees lost some of their control over the knowledge that was previously needed to perform the work. To find explanations for these changes, it is helpful to turn to longstanding principles of managerial control—scientific management and organizational decentralization.

Scientific management stresses the capture of knowledge of the work process by management and the related separation of conception from execution. The application of these principles has traditionally led to greater task fragmentation, but with new forms of computer-based automation, we can see that they are also compatible with task integration. The essential feature is that management takes the initiative in the capture and control of workplace knowledge [3,21]. Organizational decentralization compliments this approach by showing managers how to structure organizations and roles so that when they are unable to obtain detailed working knowledge they can still maintain overall control by delegating to subordinates operational decisions while retaining for themselves the more crucial policy decisions [5]. Together these two sets of principles have had a powerful influence on management thought and have provided a durable foundation for large modern corporations since the early decades of this century. In particular they are consistent with the collapse of processing chains and provide an additional political insight into the interaction of organizations and computing systems.

In the New Business Department these principles of managerial control are quite evident. At every stage of the development of the computer system, managers took the initiative and guided the effort. They oversaw the work of systems analysts as they interviewed the underwriters and clerks and incorporated their knowledge into company owned software. Once the on-line computer system was implemented, managers in New Business used it to obtain more detailed performance measures of their employees and to regulate (using IBM's ACF2 software) employee access to previously available information. Managerial control concerns were also a factor in the way tasks were integrated and the organization decentralized along territorial lines. The fact that increasing the accountability of individual employees was an incentive beyond simply the collapse of processing chains is revealed graphically in remarks by an Assistant Vice President responsible for Individual Insurance Administration:

> We brought underwriting and policy issue and all the underwriting support functions under one person. So, a couple of things: *you don't have the work bouncing back and forth*, between floors; and *you also have one person on the hook for the whole process*. (emphasis added) [4, p. 5–20]

This attempt to centralize effective control through computerization and decentralization of operational decision making supports observations Robey has made concerning computing systems and organization structure:

> By increasing the formalization of tasks and monitoring the lower level decision outcomes computer systems are a chief tool in the strategy of administrative control. *Thus, what appears to be greater decentralization may simply entail the delegation of more routine decisions whose outcomes are more closely controlled.* Power and control over the premises for decision making may actually be more concentrated than previously. (emphasis in original) [20, p. 681]

These comments fit the New Business case well. We can thus see that the collapse of processing chains and the extension of managerial control through the classic techniques of scientific management and organizational decentralization provide a good explanation of the evolution of both the computer system and the organization since 1973. Similar transformations have been observed in other large organizations which sell information intensive services [4,14]. Indeed, wherever profit-seeking, cost-reducing corporations process massive volumes of relatively routine, client initiated transactions we should expect to see similar patterns of evolution in the organization/computer system interface.

4 Implications for Interface Design

Attention to the organizational context of computer systems development and in particular understanding the principles which underlie the evolution of the organizational-computer system interface have important implications for systems designers. In the case of the New Business Department, we can draw two useful lessons.

We have noted earlier that as on-line systems are used to eliminate processing steps, tasks become increasingly integrated and the roles of individual workers are changed. This suggests designing the user interface to support the work role as it will be rather than as it was. Generally this will mean allowing users to access a broader range of processing functions than their jobs would have entailed before. Interfaces that offer a consistent, uniform pattern of interaction across a range of functions will be more likely to accommodate future evolution of the processing chain and not become obsolete as quickly as one that makes fine and rigid distinctions between its various users. For example, at MLL on-line screens were designed so that clerks can readily switch between different types of transactions, thus allowing them to fill more integrated job roles. However, the interface was not made sufficiently general in all cases to allow branch clerks to use them and this has slowed the transfer of on-line data entry from head office to branch locations.

The use of on-line systems to extend managerial control by technical means raises more fundamental issues for systems designers. The fact that computer systems are not developed purely out of a rational pursuit of generalized collective benefit but are also used by one group to gain advantage over another (in this case managers over workers) introduces a political dimension. That systems personnel tend to develop systems favoring management, whether deliberately or not, is hardly surprising. Managers, not workers, hire the programmers and, as some have noted, technical education in North America is geared to this scheme [12,17]. Only where unionization and support for industrial democracy is relatively strong, such as in Scandinavia, have there been significant attempts to develop computer systems from a worker rather than a management perspective [10,19]. The point remains, however, that it is technically and economically feasible to design systems that distribute power and influence differently than is now generally the case.

If designers aim to benefit users, then they might consider ways that provide them with greater control in the development and operation of systems. There is evidence that participative design can lead to greater satisfaction without necessarily sacrificing productivity [16]. The organizational context in which much development takes place imposes severe constraints on this approach but usually there is some flexibility. For example, in New Business it is possible that the systems could have been designed so that they provided more feedback to individual clerks and underwriters and less performance reporting to managers.

5 Conclusions

Organizational interfaces evolve over time under the influence of both economic and political factors. Designing such interfaces means not only specifying how a collection of people interact as individuals with a computer system, it also has to do with the relations between people. While computer systems have been developed in ways that reflect managerial control in the workplace and in turn help to reinforce that control, it is technically possible to create systems for which this is not the case. Paying attention to human factors at the organizational level could lead to computer system designs which better serve the people who interact with them.

References

1. Attewell, P., and Rule, J. Computing and organizations: What we know and what we don't know. *Commun. ACM 27*, 12 (Dec. 1984), 1184–1192.

2. Baran, B. Office automation and the technological transformation of the insurance industry. In M. Castells (Ed.), *High Technology*, Sage, Beverly Hills, 1985, pp. 142–171.

3. Braverman, H. *Labour and Monopoly Capital: The Degradation of Work in the Twentieth Century*. Monthly Review Press, New York, 1974.

4. Chandler, A. D. *Strategy and Structure: Chapters in the History of American Enterprise*. MIT Press, Cambridge, Mass., 1962.

5. Clement, A. *Managerial Control and On-line Processing at a Large Insurance Firm*. Ph.D. dissertation, Dept. of Computer Science, University of Toronto, 1986.

6. Cooley, M. *Architect or Bee: The Human/Technology Relationship*. Langley Technical Services, Slough, England, 1980.

7. De Marco, T. *Structured Analysis and Systems Specification*. Prentice-Hall, Englewood Cliffs, New Jersey, 1980.

8. Feldberg, R., and Glenn, E. N. New technology and its implications in U.S. clerical work. In D. Marschall and J. Gregory (Eds.), *Office Automation: Jekyll or Hyde?*, Working Women Education Fund, Cleveland, Ohio, 1983, pp. 89–95.

9. Gane, C., and Sarson, T. *Structured Systems Analysis*, Prentice-Hall, Englewood Cliffs, New Jersey, 1979.

10. Howard, R. UTOPIA: Where workers craft new technology. *Technology Review* (April 1985), 43–49.

11. Kling, R. Social analyses of computing: Theoretical perspectives in recent empirical research. *Computing Surveys 12*, 1 (March 1980), 61–110.

12. Kraft, P. *Programmers and Managers: The Routinization of Programming in the U.S.* Springer Verlag, New York, 1977.

13. Malone, T. Designing organizational interfaces. *Proceedings of the CHI'85 Conference on Human Factors in Computing Systems* (San Francisco, April 14–18, 1985), ACM, New York, 1985, pp. 66–71.

14. Matteis, R. J. The new back office focuses on customer service. *Harvard Business Review* (March–April, 1979), 146–159.

15. Mowshowitz, A. "Social change in the computer revolution." (mimeo), Science and Technology Studies Division, Rensselaer Polytechnic Institute, Troy, New York, 1983.

16. Mumford, E. Successful systems design. In H. Otway and M. Peltu (Eds.), *New Office Technology: Human and Organizational Aspects*, Ablex, Norwood, New Jersey, 1983.

17. Noble, D. *America by Design: Science, Technology and the Rise of Corporate Capitalism.* Oxford University Press, Oxford, 1977.

18. Noble, D. *Forces of Production: A Social History of Industrial Automation.* Alfred Knopf, New York, 1984.

19. Nygaard, K. Workers' participation in system development. In A. Mowshowitz (Ed.), *Human Choice and Computers*, North-Holland, Amsterdam, 1980, 71–75.

20. Robey, D. Computer information systems and organizational structure. *Commun. ACM 24*, 10 (1980), 679–687.

21. Taylor, F. *Principles of Scientific Management.* Norton, New York, 1967 (original published 1911).

22. Turner, J. Computer mediated work: The interplay between technology and structured jobs. *Commun. ACM 27*, 12 (1984), 1210–1217.

23. U.S. Congress, Office of Technology Assessment. *Automation of America's Offices.* OTA-CIT-287, U.S. Government Printing Office, Washington, D.C., December, 1985.

A Language/Action Perspective on the Design of Cooperative Work[1]

Terry Winograd
Standord University
Palo Alto, CA

1 Perspective and Design

Within the community concerned with the design of computer systems, there is a growing recognition of the importance of the designer's perspective—the concerns and interpretations that shape the design, whether they are articulated explicitly or are just part of the unexamined background of the work. A perspective does not determine answers to design questions, but guides design by generating the questions to be considered.

Many writers have identified useful perspectives on computer-based systems, and several classification schemes have been proposed (see, for example, Malone (1985), Kling (1980), and Nygaard & Sorgaard (1985)). As we will discuss in Section 7, no one perspective covers all of the relevant concerns. System design is a complex web. It can be picked up from any one point, and the others will follow along. If we start from implementation considerations (e.g., available hardware functions), we

[1] The work presented here was supported by the System Development Foundation under a grant to the Center for the Study of Language and Information at Stanford University.

will eventually have to define user interfaces. If we start by considering user interaction, we must eventually build concrete implementations that can run effectively on the hardware. But although the full range of perspectives must eventually be considered, the outcome will differ depending on where we start.

This paper presents a particular perspective: one that takes language as the primary dimension of human cooperative activity. It draws on work developed by Flores and his colleagues at Stanford University, Logonet, and Action Technologies (Flores, 1981; Flores and Ludlow, 1981; Winograd and Flores, 1986), and has been the basis for designing commercially successful computer systems. By starting with a language/action perspective, we have found it possible to create systems that can be effective in getting work done, whenever that work involves communication and coordinated action among a group of people.

We will illustrate the language/action perspective through an example: the nursing work in a hospital ward, as studied by Kaasbøll (1986, in press). This example was chosen for its careful description and analysis of the setting and the structure of work. No computer-based systems have been introduced into the work or designed in detail. The goal here is to illustrate the questions and concerns that would guide the design of such systems.

2 The Language/Action Perspective

One useful way to identify a perspective is by its declaration of what people do. From a language/action perspective we say that *People act through language*. As a contrast, consider the more predominant perspective that *People process information and make decisions*. Of course everyone in an organization can be described as doing both, but there is a difference of focus.

Consider a situation in which a hospital nurse calls the pharmacy, finds out what drugs are available, and orders one of them for a patient. From an information-processing perspective we could focus on the data base of information about the drugs and on the rules for deciding what drug to order. From a language/action perspective, we focus on the act of ordering and on the patterns of interaction in related conversations, such as the preliminary conversation about drug availability and the subsequent conversation that unfolds in the process of fulfilling the order. From other perspectives we might consider such things as the personal relationship between nurse and pharmacist, the cost-effectiveness of making the communication over a phone, or the legal status of orders placed by a nurse.

For a perspective to have analytical value, its focus on particular concerns must be combined with a systematic conceptual framework and methodology. For issues of cost effectiveness, we would turn to economic theory. For information processing we would look to theories of information and decision-making. The language/action perspective rests on theories of language, but not linguistics in the rather specialized sense that is often understood. We are not primarily concerned with the details of natural language utterances, but with the issues of form, meaning and use that are common to all human communication. We use the word 'language' rather than 'communication' to emphasize the relevance of symbols and interpretation, and also to avoid the connotations of 'communication theory' which has come to stand for a rather specialized mathematical approach.

As the following sections will demonstrate, there is a broad view of language activity, which includes a wide range of interactions with computers. The theories grow out of previous work in linguistics, but go beyond it and are still being developed. Our own work on design has been intermingled with research on linguistic theory (see Winograd & Flores, 1986).

As a broad framework for outlining a language/action perspective, we will adopt and extend the traditional subdivisions of linguistic theory: *syntax, semantics* and *pragmatics*.

Syntax is the structure of the visible (or audible) forms of language. The syntactic rules (or 'grammar') of a language determine the basic elements (letters, words, etc.) and the ways in which they can be combined. In an extended sense, one can talk about the syntax of an equation, a spreadsheet, or an invoice, or even of an event, such as buttoning a menu item on a screen. What distinguishes syntax from other levels of analysis is that it does not take into account interpretation or meaning.

Semantics is the systematic relation between structures in a language and a space of potential meanings. It includes the definitions of individual elements (e.g., words) and the meaning that is generated by combining them (e.g., the meaning of "Jill sees Bill" as different from "Bill sees Jill"). In extension, one can talk about the semantics of a blank on a form appearing on a workstation screen, or the semantics of an operating system command.

Pragmatics deals with issues of language use. A classical example is "It's cold in here" spoken by a master to a servant. Although the literal meaning is a statement about the temperature, the intent is to evoke an action by the servant. Our primary interest lies in this aspect of language—its role in evoking and interpreting actions.

Modern linguists have tended to adopt a 'cognitivist' approach (Haugeland, 1981), formalizing the structure of an individual language user's knowledge and mental processes. Our perspective leads us to deal with these three aspects of language in the reverse of the standard order—we take issues of meaning to be critically dependent on considerations of language action and context, and syntax to be of interest primarily in its ability to reflect meaningful distinctions in conversation.

3 *The Pragmatics of Language Action*

The language/action perspective emphasizes pragmatics—not the form of language, but what people do with it. The theory of speech acts is a starting point for developing the larger picture of the following sections.

3.1 *Speech Act Theory*

Austin (1962) noted that not all utterances are statements whose truth or falsity is at stake. Performatives, such as "I pronounce you husband and wife" are actions, which can be made appropriately ('felicitously') or not, but which are neither true nor false in a simple sense. Similarly, the language actions of commands, questions, and apologies are not descriptions of a non-linguistic world.

Searle (1975) identified five fundamental 'illocutionary points'— things you can *do* with an utterance:

> **Assertive:** Commit the speaker (in varying degrees) to something's being the case—to the truth of the expressed proposition.
>
> **Directive:** Attempt (in varying degrees) to get the hearer to do something. These include both questions (which can direct the hearer to make an assertive speech act in response) and commands (which direct the hearer to carry out some linguistic or non-linguistic act).
>
> **Commissive:** Commit the speaker (again in varying degrees) to some future course of action.
>
> **Declaration:** Bring about the correspondence between the propositional content of the speech act and reality (e.g., pronouncing a couple married).

Expressive: Express a psychological state about a state of affairs (e.g., apologizing and praising).

Three points deserve note:

1. The illocutionary point of an utterance is interpreted by speaker and hearer in a background. A commissive need not include the words "I promise" or "I will," but can be "I guess" or "a dollar" (in response to "Can you give me anything?") or just a facial gesture. The identification of a language act depends on the backgrounds of speaker and hearer, and is always open to differences of interpretation. "It's time for lunch" might be an assertive or a directive, depending on who says it to whom in what circumstances.

2. Directives and commissives (which will informally be called 'requests' and 'promises' here) always deal with a future action. They differ in whether the action is to be taken by the speaker or the hearer.

3. Speech acts take effect by virtue of public declaration—by mutual knowledge of hearer and speaker that the act has been made. This is especially obvious in the case of declarations and expressives (e.g., an apology muttered but not heard is not an apology), but is equally true of the others.

3.2 Conversations for Action

Speech acts are not unrelated events, but participate in larger conversation structures (Flores, 1981; Flores and Ludlow, 1981). An important example is the simple "conversation for action," in which one party (A) makes a request to another (B). The request is interpreted by each party as having certain conditions of satisfaction, which characterize a future course of actions by B. After the initial utterance (the request), B can accept (and thereby commit to satisfy the conditions); decline (and thereby end the conversation); or counter-offer with alternative conditions. Each of these in turn has its possible continuations (e.g., after a counter-offer, A can accept, cancel the request, or counter-offer back). The overall structure is diagrammed in Figure 23.1

This diagram is not a model of the mental state of a speaker or hearer, but shows the conversation as a 'dance,' in which the conversation steps proceed towards mutual recognition that the requested action has been done or that the conversation is complete without it having

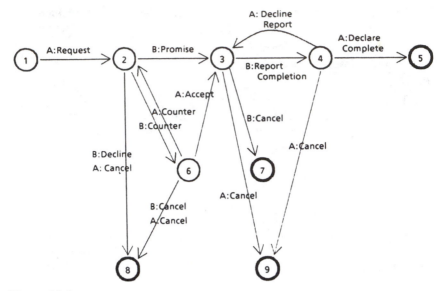

Figure 23.1   State transition network representing a conversation for action initiated by a request from speaker A to speaker B. The circles represent conversation states and the labelled lines represent speech acts. Heavy circles represent states of completion. (adapted from Winograd and Flores, 1986, p. 65.)

been done. The basic logic represented here deals with the central progression of acts. Other possibilities not shown in the diagram can emerge in related conversations, such as those in which the conversational acts themselves are taken as a topic. For example, a speaker might question intelligibility ("What, I didn't hear you") or legitimacy ("You can't order me to do that!").

If B commits to fulfill a request (moving to state 3), the natural continuation is that at some later point B reports to A that the conditions of satisfaction have been met (moving to state 4). If A declares that he or she is satisfied, the conversation reaches a successful completion (state 5). On the other hand, A may not interpret the situation in the same way and may decline the report, declaring that the conditions have not been met and thereby returning the conversation to state 3. In any state, either party may propose changes to the conditions of satisfaction or may back out on the deal, moving to a state of completion (7 and 9) that does not include satisfaction of the original request.

Several points about this conversation structure deserve note:

1.   We use 'conversation' in a very general sense to indicate a coordinated sequence of acts that can be interpreted as having linguistic meaning. It need not be a spoken conversation, or even involve the

use of ordinary language. A doctor who writes treatment requests on a patient form is engaged in a conversation with the nurse who will administer the treatments, even if they never speak face-to-face. Certain kinds of requests are made implicitly on the basis of a long-term declaration. A manager does not explicitly request each worker to come to work each morning, although the conversation proceeds (in those cases where there is a breakdown) as though he or she had. The recurrent request is listened to as an effect of the declaration "You're hired" within a shared understanding of common practices.

2. The conversation is initiated by a request (there is a similar network for conversations initiated by an offer), and therefore is rooted in the anticipation of some future action.

3. At each point in the conversation, there is a small set of possible action types, determined by the previous history. Each type has unlimited possibilities for detailed content. For example, a 'counter-offer' action specifies particular conditions of satisfaction.

4. All of the acts are linguistic—they represent utterances by parties to the conversation (or silences that are listened to as standing for an act). For example, the act that normally follows a promise is a report of completion (an assertive speech act) from the promisor to the requestor. It is followed by a declaration by the requestor that the action is satisfactory (or that it is not). The actual doing of whatever is needed to meet the conditions of satisfaction lies outside of the conversation structure.

5. Many acts are 'listened to' without being explicit. If the requestor can recognize satisfaction of the request directly, there may be no explicit report or completion. Other acts, such as declaring satisfaction, may be taken for granted if some amount of time goes by without a communication to the contrary. What is not said is listened to as much as what is said.

6. Conditions of satisfaction are not objective realities, independent of interpretations. They exist in the listening, and there is always the potential for difference among the parties. This can lead to breakdowns and to subsequent conversation about the understanding of the conditions.

7. There are states of completion (the heavy circles in the figure) in which it is mutually recognized that neither party is waiting for further action by the other. All other states represent an incomplete conversation. Completion does not guarantee satisfaction.

For example, if the promisor cancels after the promise is made, the conversation is completed without the original request being satisfied.

8.   The network does not say what people *should* do, or deal with consequences of their acts (such as backing out of a commitment). These are important human phenomena, but are not generated in the domain formalized in this network.

Conversations for actions are the central coordinating structure for human organizations. We work together by making commitments so that we can successfully anticipate the actions of others and coordinate them with our own. The emphasis here is on language as an activity, not as the transmission of information or as the expression of thought. Although people think when they use language, and they often describe their world in language, the relevant structures for analysis here are the language acts and the conversations into which they are woven. In applying this to computer system design, we are not concerned with duplicating the knowledge or thought patterns of people, but with the structure of their interactions and the embedding of those interactions in computer systems.

4 *Designing Conversations for Action*

We will illustrate the relevance of this analysis to computer systems, by describing The Coordinator,[2] a first-generation conversational system currently used for everyday communications in sales, finance, general management, operations, and planning functions in organizations of a variety of sizes and types. This system provides facilities for generating, transmitting, storing, retrieving and displaying messages that are records of moves in conversations. However, unlike electronic mail systems that take "messages" and "information" as their starting points, it is based on the conversation theory outlined above.

---

[2] The Coordinator is a workgroup productivity system created by Action Technologies, Inc., available for IBM PC-XT/AT™-compatible machines. The description here focusses on the conversation manager, which is one part of an integrated system that also includes word processing, formatting, calendar maintenance and communication over modems and LANs. "The Coordinator" is a registered trademark of Action Technologies. The interface design is copyrighted, and aspects of it are reproduced here by permission. A patent is pending on the system's conversation manager.

```
                        C O N V E R S E

OPEN CONVERSATION FOR ACTION           REVIEW / HANDLE
     Request                           Read new mail
     Offer                             Missing my response
                                       Missing other's response
OPEN CONVERSATION FOR POSSIBILITIES
     Declare an opening                My promises/offers
                                       My requests
ANSWER                                 Commitments due: 24-Sep-84

NOTES                                  Conversation records
```

Figure 23. 2   "Converse" menu from The Coordinator (reprinted by permission from Action Technologies, 1987).

4.1 Tools for Conversing

The use interface of The Coordinator is menu driven. The primary menu for conversing is shown in Figure 23.2. Some of the menu items indicate new actions the user may take. Others bring up displays of the records of conversations maintained by the system. Let us look first at ways of opening a conversation for action (answering is discussed below, and conversations for possibilities will be discussed in Section 5).

Rather than providing a uniform command to initiate a new message, The Coordinator system provides options for opening conversations that have different implicit structures of action. When "Request" is selected, templates appear prompting the user to specify an addressee, others who will receive copies, a "domain," which groups or categorizes related conversations, and an "action" description, corresponding to the subject header in traditional mail systems. The text of the message is prompted with the phrase "What is your request?," to which the user can enter any text whatsoever.

The system makes no attempt to interpret this text, relying on the users' understanding and cooperation that the message is properly identified as a request. This is a key design issue: Let people do the interpretation of natural language, and let the program deal with explicit declarations of structure (such as the user's declaration that this is a request). This leaves users free to communicate in ordinary language that depends on the background of the reader. A perfectly understandable request might contain the single word "Noon?" if the participants have a shared understanding (e.g., they often go to lunch together).

```
 ┌─────────────────────────────────────────────┐
 │ SPEAKING IN A CONVERSATION FOR ACTION         │
 │                                               │
 │ Acknowledge        Promise                    │
 │ Free-Form          Counter-offer              │
 │ Commit-to-commit   Decline                    │
 │ Interim-report     Report-completion          │
 └─────────────────────────────────────────────┘
```

Figure 23.3   Menu for responding to a request (reprinted by permission from Action Technologies, 1987).

When the user signals that the text is complete, the system prompts for three dates associated with the completion of the action: a "respond-by" date, a "complete-by" date, and an "alert" date. Date entries are optional, but experienced users almost always include one or more of them. Not only do they provide a structure for retrieval and for monitoring completion, but the use of specific dates plays a surprisingly large role in producing effective conversations. Although we will not emphasize this aspect in the present paper, the design of The Coordinator system grew out of Flores's work in training people in "communicative competence" (Flores & Graves; 1968a, 1968b). In that work, Flores has demonstrated that people's ability to communicate effectively (with or without support from computer systems) is improved when they develop facility in distinguishing the kinds of commitments people make in conversations for action, and the dimensions of time associated with the completion of those conversations.

When a user of the system receives a request (the details of message transmission and retrieval will not be discussed here), he or she has the option of responding by selecting "Answer" from a menu. This pops up a subsidiary menu as shown in Figure 23.3.

This menu is automatically generated by a conversational state interpreter from a network like that of Figure 23.1. The first three items in the right hand column ("Promise," "Counter-offer," and "Decline") represent the actions available to the responder (B) in state 2. The fourth choice ("Report-completion") is an action available in state 3, after B has promised. In some cases, it will turn out that B has already done what A requested, before having responded to initial request. In that case, the "Promise" act is implicit, and "Report-completion" is the next overt communication.

The left-hand column introduces conversation acts concerned with the conduct of the conversation itself, which do not advance its state.

```
┌──────────────────────────────────────────────┐
│ SPEAKING IN A CONVERSATION FOR ACTION          │
│                                                 │
│ Free-Form        Cancel/New-Promise             │
│ Interim-report   Cancel                         │
│                  Report-completion              │
└──────────────────────────────────────────────┘
```

Figure 23.4   Answer menu generated in continuing a promise (reprinted with permission from Action Technologies, 1987).

"Acknowledge" lets the requestor know that the request was received. "Free-form" allows any kind of communication relevant to the conversation that does not fit into the formal structure—most frequently, notes, comments, and questions. "Commit-to-commit" would be conveyed in natural language with sentences like "I'll let you know by Thursday if I can do it." That is, the speaker is committing to take the next conversational step (promising or declining) by a specific time.

When any answering action is selected, a new message is automatically generated with markers corresponding to the choice of act, and with a generic text. For example if the response is "Promise," the initial message is "I promise to do as you request." while for "Counter-offer" it is "No; I counteroffer:" The user can augment or replace this text using embedded word processing facilities. Experience has shown that a surprising number of messages need only the initial *pro forma* composition. The message initiating a request or offer needs to contain text that describes the action, such as "Can you send me that report we were talking about?", but often the subsequent steps can be made by simply selecting the appropriate menu item and hitting the button that sends a message.

Whenever "Answer" is selected, the menu displays only those actions that could sensibly be taken next by the current speaker. State 2 of Figure 23.1 shows a "Cancel" action by A, in which the request is withdrawn. This will appear on A's menu, but not on B's. Or, for example, after making a promise in a conversation, then the next time B selects "Answer" in that conversation (assuming no intervening action by A, the menu offered will be shown in Figure 23.4.

At this point, B no longer has the option to decline (having already promised), but can "Report-completion" (moving to state 4) or "Cancel" (moving to state 7) with or without initiating a new promise.

The Coordinator has no magic to coerce people to come through with what they promise, but it provides a straightforward structure in which they can review the status of their commitments, alter those commitments they are no longer in condition to fulfill, make new commitments to take care of breakdowns and opportunities appearing in their conversations, and generally be clear (with themselves and others) about the state of their work.

4.2 Retrieval and Monitoring

The structure and status of conversations is the primary basis for organizing retrieval and review in the system. To put it simply, the structure is organized to provide straightforward and relevant answers to the implicit question "What do I have to do now?".

In the main menu of Figure 23.2, under the heading "REVIEW/ HANDLE" we find items such as "Missing my response," "Missing other's response," "My promises/offer," and "My requests." When one of these is selected, the user is presented with a listing of conversations matching the selected item. Several things are of note:

1. The basic unit of work in the system is a conversation, not a message. In conventional electronic mail systems, messages in a conversation are often linked by conventions such as the use of "Re: ... " in headers. For The Coordinator, each message (including a "Free-form") belongs to a particular conversation. The retrieval structure is two-level, with the user first identifying a conversation, then selecting particular messages within it to be displayed.

2. The explicit use of conversation theory in the generation of messages makes it possible for retrieval to be based on status. There is a menu selection that selects and displays conversations in response to the question, "In which conversations is someone waiting for me to do something?" or "In which conversations have I promised to do things?" Note that these are different. For example, if you make an offer to me, then our conversation is in a state where the next move characteristically belongs to me, but I have made no promise to you.

3. The distinction between "open" and "closed" conversations is used to filter out those to be retrieved. Unless the user designates otherwise, The Coordinator will display only those conversations that are still open to further action (not in one of the final states as shown by heavy circles in Figure 23.1).

4. Explicit completion and alert dates are used for time-oriented retrieval. The item "Commitments due: ... " on the menu allows

retrieval of all conversations that need some action (either a response or a completion) on a date entered by the user. There is an additional menu that allows retrieval on precise combinations of dates, domains, and people involved in different conversational roles (e.g., the things Chauncey has promised to get done next week regarding programming). The calendar subsystem is integrated, so that all of these items can optionally appear at the appropriate places in a personal calendar, along with more conventional entries such as meetings and appointments.

The Coordinator is an example of basing a system on theories of language without attempting to program "understanding." All of the interpretations (e.g., that a particular message is a request, or that it should be done by a certain time) are made by the people who use the system, guided by appropriate menus and prompts. This is not experienced by users as an extra job of annotating, but in fact replaces typing parts of the contents with more direct and structured interactions, which are often more efficient. It is a generic tool in the sense that a word processor is—intended for a particular kind of communication, without regard to topic. A word processor is not equally well suited to generating all kinds of character sequences, but is specially designed for the words, sentences, paragraphs, and the like of ordinary written text. Similarly, The Coordinator system is not built for arbitrary sequences of messages, but for the requests, promises and completions that are at the heart of coordinated work.

5 Conversations in a Work Setting

Conversations for action (CfA) form the central fabric of cooperative work. However, many kinds of language acts do not participate directly in the completion of a CfA. Remarks such as "They're planning to remodel the West Wing next summer" need not relate directly to any specific future actions of speaker or hearer. From a cognitive perspective, one might choose to characterize these as "conveying information" without a particular motivation in action. From the perspective of language as action, the primary concern is with the role that all conversations (and all utterances within conversations) play with respect to action and potentials for action. We distinguish several additional kinds of conversation that go along with conversations for action: *conversation for clarification, conversation for possibilities*, and *conversation for orientation*. There is no sharp line between them, but they are accompanied by different moods.

In a **conversation for clarification**, the participants cope with or anticipate breakdowns concerning interpretations of the conditions of satisfaction for a CfA. The conditions are always interpreted with respect to an implicit shared background, but the sharing is partial and needs to be negotiated. As a simple example, the request "Give the patient some diazine" might evoke responses such as "Right now, or with the morning meds?" or "What dosage?". One can never guarantee that everything is totally precise. Precision is relative to each party's implicit anticipation that the other party will have a sufficiently shared background to carry out the action in a satisfactory way.

In a **conversation for possibilities**, the mood is one of speculation, anticipating the subsequent generation of conversations for action. Specific conditions of satisfaction will emerge in the course of the conversation, and associated conversations for action will be initiated. Many gatherings that are called 'meetings' are best conducted in this mood. The meeting is a failure if some action does not come out of the discussion. Some conversations for possibilities are highly routinized. For example, 'work rounds' on a hospital ward is a routine conversation for possibilities, during which the medical team visits each patient and specific requests and commitments are generated.

In a **conversation for orientation**, the mood is one of creating a shared background as a basis for future interpretation of conversations. This shared background includes specific knowledge, interpersonal relations, and general attitudes. The most obvious examples are meetings labelled "orientation," in which newcomers begin to develop the understanding that is required to function in the organization. Conversations for orientation are prominent in less formal settings ('shooting the bull'). Although the mood here is not directed towards action, it is important to recognize the importance of developing mutual orientation as the basis for future effective action and for appropriately shared interpretation of language acts.

Each of these types of conversation has its own regularities of structure, which in turn can be reflected in the design of the tools for conducting it. Just as the CfA structure of The Coordinator grew out of experience with conventional message systems, we can apply conversational analysis to the reinterpretation and redesign of other existing systems, such as help systems (which carry out a limited kind of conversation for clarification), group facilitation systems, such as Colab (Stefik et al., 1986) which are used in generating possibilities, and BBOARD and computer forum systems, which (among other things) facilitate conversations for orientation. We will not analyze these in detail, but will use the nursing example to show how conversations appear in the nursing setting, and to discuss some of the design considerations.

In the discussion we will comment on details of work on the hospital ward, as outlined in the Appendix. Although no computer applications were developed in that setting, one can imagine an integrated 'medication information system' through which many of the activities would be replaced by actions on terminals (or workstations) at various sites, including the ward, the examining rooms, and the pharmacy. Records needed in places where direct computer access was infeasible could be printed out and posted. The 'information flow' could be redesigned, eliminating redundancies and the need for manual copying or posting of information. It is far beyond the scope of this paper to develop a comprehensive design for such a system, but the setting can serve to illustrate our perspective.

5.1 Conversations for Action

In the hospital, there are many different conversations for action, with a variety of visible forms. Some are highly routinized, such as the primary CfA dealing with the administration of medications. Requests are made by doctors (either as standing cures or on the patient-carried paper scraps), to the treating nurse. Report of completion is represented on the curve sheet, and the declaration of completion is implicit in the doctor's review of the records on his or her next visit. As a precondition for satisfying these requests, the nurse must receive the medicine, and there are CfAs (with the pharmacy) to get the medications, using prescription forms to make requests. In general, conditions of satisfaction are determined in a rigid way by the codes and blanks, perhaps with extra notations in natural language. Acceptance of an offer or request is assumed whenever it is not explicitly rejected. Completion is reported on a standard form, which, like all of the other forms, is associated with standards for interpretation, which are learned as part of the relevant professional training. In addition to these routinized CfAs there are unscheduled verbal conversations. For example, a request may be made by a doctor to a nurse at the bedside, with immediate explicit accept, decline, or counter-offer. Completion may be reported later via a note in the patient's chart.

In a hospital, completion of conversations can be a life-or-death matter. There is a highly regularized structure of checks and crosschecks to ensure it, as illustrated in the Appendix. The regularization is both in the form of special activities (the various checklists) and the strict temporal routine. The fact that a particular action will be done at a particular time can be taken for granted on the basis of the daily schedule. The dependence on rigid forms and routines can be viewed as an attempt to assure that conversations proceed smoothly in cases where personal contact is not sufficient. This could potentially be reduced, adding work flexibility, through the use of a conversation-based system in which the monitoring of completion (and coaching towards completing conversations) is incorporated in a communication medium.

There is also the potential to replace routine CfAs with declarations of recurrent responses. For example, rather than responding to each drug request, a pharmacist might establish an automated 'prescription filling system,' which takes the data from the request and activates a mechanized dispensary. This is a common kind of computerization: computers take over those functions for which precise repetitive rules can be established. In designing these automated systems from a language/action perspective, we are led to consider the potential for secondary conversations. Who declares the distinctions that are embodied in the forms and rules? If the medication request does not match the standard form for designating medications, then who is involved in the conversation for clarification, and how? In conventional system design, there will always be *de facto* answers to such questions (especially after experience has pointed out the places for breakdown). Through a conversational analysis we can anticipate and design for them.

5.2 Conversations for Clarification

Conversations for clarification are much less regular (as we would expect) and are often verbal. The crosschecking of the various forms also triggers these conversations when the different forms are not directly contradictory, but are open to conflicting interpretations. In designing tools for conversations for clarification, it is important to recognize their relative lack of recurrence. Recurrent differences of interpretation will lead to the declaration of new distinctions or new forms for making requests and commitments that are clear. But there will always be irregular, unexpected cases, and computer-based systems that provide only rigid forms may make it difficult or impossible to deal with them.

5.3 Conversations for Possibilities

Much of what appears to be useless copying or verification of redundant information on the hospital ward is really a routine way of generating conversations for possibilities. For example, in the review of medications (see Appendix):

> Only a minor part of the 30 minutes was used for updating and comparing. The rest of the time was spent on small conversations, initiated by findings in the information they were handling. Some examples of what the nurses did: Reporting to each other about the patients' state and activities; deciding what were facts when inconsistencies were found; deciding changes in some medicines after small negotiations; reminding the treating nurse of a test that had been forgotten; investigating why a medicine was not delivered from the chemist's; finding out why a patient had to take a specific test.

If the medication review were replaced by an automated process, the opportunity for this kind of conversation could be lost. It could be reinstituted in other ways if it were recognized in the analysis. Similarly, if the curve sheet is replaced with a table of drugs, dosages and times, it is no longer possible for the nurses to use it as a vehicle of communication (in the notes) for the "small conversations" dealing with specific breakdowns and subsidiary CfAs. It might well be possible to replace it with a better vehicle for these conversations, once their importance is recognized.

5.4 Conversations for Orientation

When asked to comment on the systems analysis, the nurses felt that it did not capture the aspect of their activities that dealt with the "total picture" rather than with the specifics of particular medications and tests. The existing structure provides explicit routines to allow for open-ended conversation, such as the morning report, where "One nurse is informing the other staff of the status, changes and performed activities of each patient during the last day and night." Informal exchanges among the nurses include both explicit CfAs and more general orienting discussion about the "total picture." One form of orienting conversation is the telling of stories, whether in the direct line of work, or around the coffeepot. Orr (1986) describes the importance of relating "war stories" as part of technical training. One has only to spend a short time in the company of medical workers to realize how prevalent this activity is. Computer BBOARD systems sometimes play this role within the community of computer researchers. They often contain extended stories, commentaries and other forms of conversation that serve for mutual orientation. This would not be directly applicable to the hospital setting, where the workers do not spend long hours in front of a computer terminal, but it illustrates a potential for design.

5.5 *The Larger Web of Conversations*

Finally, the conversational analysis includes not only those immediately visible, but also the larger web of conversations in which they are situated (Kling & Scacchi, 1982). One obvious example in the hospital is the legal conversation about the quality of care. All written records are potential evidence in a malpractice suit, and the people who create and manipulate them are aware of this possibility. In addition to the legal conversation, there are ongoing conversations about the hiring, evaluation, and dismissal of employees. Kaasbøll notes (1986, p. 11): "If the nurses make mistakes, they may be sued by the patients, and they may be punished by the hospital administration. This gives an incentive for not recording mistakes in the Kardex."

Certain conversations will inevitably go on outside of any written (or electronically stored) system. Explicit records will never correspond to an objective reality, but are the result of declarations by individuals, with their own interpretations and purposes. No computer system can change these fundamental facts about how humans function in organizations, but an explicit understanding of the larger network of conversations can help to recognize the roles that language acts play in a variety of conversations, and to match expectations to those roles.

6 *Semantics*

The previous sections have introduced conversation types in a very general sense, without considering what the conversations are about. Of course there is also a high degree of recurrence in content, which is apparent in the amount of organizational communication conducted with forms of various kinds (including electronic forms). When a doctor requests medication for a patient, we can identify the generic action as a "Request" in terms of the CfA structure given above, and we could use a system like The Coordinator to monitor its completion. From a slightly different angle, we can see it as an instance of a "Medication Order" conversation, which is specified by filling in standard blanks, such as the patient's name, the identity and quantity of the drug, etc. The doctor could take a single action (e.g., a menu selection) to bring up a display with the relevant items indicated, and with some of them initially filled in (e.g., the date). Others might be filled automatically (for example, the standard dosage when the drug name is given), or with machine aid (e.g., providing generic drug names corresponding to brand names.)

None of this is new. Business programs along these lines can be found in every walk of life from the airline counter to the grocery store. We can think of these systems as embodying frozen conversation structures. In designing the forms and interactions, programmers embody their understanding of a specialized conversation structure and a set of procedures for completing the conversations. General facilities for specifying office information systems are described by Ellis and Nutt (1980), and in the more recent research exemplified by Malone et al. (in press). A flexible specification formalism for forms (or messages) and relationships among their parts makes it easier to design appropriate forms and blanks, and to support automation.

From a language/action perspective, two fundamental issues appear. First, there is the role of conversation structure. The "Medication Order" form encodes an action (a request) in a particular conversation. Another form, such as the "Nurse's patient report" may embody a further action in the conversation (e.g., reporting completion). These linkages can be the basis for retrieval and presentation, as well as providing structure for the overall system and the procedures that go with it.

Second, semantics is subordinate to language action. Traditionally, semantics has been described as a correspondence between the forms of a language and some kind of 'truth conditions' on the world of which it speaks. The analysis concentrates on deriving meaning from the systematic combination of elements. One takes for granted a collection of basic terms—the nouns, verbs, adjectives and the like—referring to identifiable objects, properties, relations, and events in the world. From the perspective of language as action, words cannot be defined in isolation from a particular conversational setting in which they are used. The distinctions that are reflected by the choices among words arise through recurrent patterns of conversation, in which breakdowns of action lead to new distinctions (Winograd, 1985; Winograd & Flores, 1986).

This is equally true in our extended linguistic perspective. A computer-based form has a syntax in which the individual fields and their fillers are the basic units. The interpretation of a field marked "Status" cannot be based on a general definition of what a "status" is. It will depend on the context and background of the people who enter, interpret, and use the records. The communication will be effective only to the extent that relevant background is shared. Texts on business data processing discuss the importance of 'data dictionaries,' which prescribe the meanings of the individual records and fields in a data base. Behind that activity there are questions as to where definitions come from, how they are represented, and how they are understood by the people who use them. These are analogous to problems in natural language.

6.1 *What Domains of Distinctions Are Taken as Background?*

Everyone in a normal work setting shares a natural language and a lifetime of cultural experience. The everyday use of language takes this for granted, using ordinary vocabulary along with common technical terminology, such as that of the clock and calendar. Other meanings will be specialized to a professional area such as medicine. The boundary between natural and specialized domains is not sharp—many words are used in both informal and semi-formalized, or stylized ways. "The patient is in stable condition" has a technical interpretation distinct from the natural one. In some cases, such distinctions may be set down by formal rules; in others, learned through practice.

A crucial part of professional training is learning a jargon—the distinctions and associated terms that provide a basis for inventing and taking relevant actions. 'Profession-oriented languages' (Kaasbøll, 1986) are an attempt to integrate this specialized language structure into the design of computer-based systems. Kaasbøll (in press) points out problems, such as locally-used distinctions that are not standard to the field and not immediately available to system designers. For example, the nurses in his study referred to a lung-function test apparatus as "the Ohio," which was its brand name, and they had no more general term. In some cases such matters are of critical importance to conditions of satisfaction. In the medical profession two different kinds of terms are used to describe medications: brand names ("Tylenol") and generic names ("Acetaminophen"). A request made for a brand name may or may not be satisfied by an equivalent generic, depending on a complex interaction of standard practices and local regulations.

Suchman (1987) describes the problems that arise from failing to account for differences in semantic interpretations when designing user interfaces. In a 'user-friendly' interface for a copier, language about the machine and the user's actions appeared in various forms on the screen, using distinctions and words that made perfect sense to the copier-designers, but that led to serious breakdowns for users without the same background. In one case, failure to distinguish the "document cover" from the "bound document aid" led to interpreting help instructions in a way completely different from what the designers intended.

The point here is that the system designer cannot assume that the semantics—the mapping from words to distinctions of interest—will either be 'natural' or follow some existing formal specification of the domain. This is especially relevant in a setting like the hospital, where conflicting languages are already in use (the language of doctors, nurses, ordinary language, etc.).

Along with the specific conversations and forms, the system designer participates in designing the professional language of the workplace. A new computer system will alter the language, both in interactions with the system, and in the work around it. Andersen and Madsen (1986) point out the change in usage of the word "document" when an indexing system was designed for a document collection, then extended to the whole library. All of the indexed items (including books, magazines, etc.) came to be called "documents," contrary to prior usage. There is both a danger of creating confusion and an opportunity to shape the conversations and the work itself.

6.2 *How Do New Distinctions Emerge?*

New distinctions are always emerging because of new breakdowns or anticipation of them. A frequent reason for the failure of computer systems is that they 'lock-in' a set of distinctions without provision for evolution. Gradually people find more and more need to 'work around' the system, leading to complexity and chaos.

For example, based on the manual forms used by the dieticians, a patient's diet might be recorded as one of a fixed set of choices, such as "no salt," "diabetic," etc. Imagine that a new kind of diet is added, such as limiting the cholesterol within the existing diets. The new distinction is not simply one more alternative but modifies each of the pre-existing choices. We might add a collection of new diets such as "no salt low cholesterol," "diabetic low cholesterol," etc. but this is a work-around. If a further qualification ("high potassium") is added, the system will begin to bog down. What is needed is an interpretation of diet as combining a set of separable dimensions, instead of as a simple choice. The original system designer could not anticipate this need. Gerson and Star (1986) describe the problems that arise and the need for what they call "due process" in maintaining shared understanding.

Kaasbøll (1986, p. 10) gives an example of a technical term whose meaning was subject to argument and the imposition of authority:

> During a doctor's visit, the doctor and two nurses started a conversation of what 'P1' means. P-values are measure of obstructions in the lungs.
>
> Doctor: It is the air in the lungs that counts, not the sounds.
>
> Nurse1: It is obvious that Peter (the chief physician) has a different opinion of P1 than you.
>
> Nurse2: One has to remember that there are individual discrepancies between the children, such that P1 does not mean the same for one child as for another.

> This discussion can be interpreted as a negotiation over the semantics of 'P1', and thus as a development of the language at the ward. It can also be seen as part of the power struggle between the two professions involved.

The larger pragmatic analysis of conversations and roles includes the conversations in which meaning is negotiated, and their reflection in a computer system.

6.3 *How Are Distinctions Indicated?*

Much of the traditional work on natural language semantics adopts the idealization of a relatively straightforward 'compositional' mapping from forms to meanings. Put simply, each basic term (word) has a meaning, and each phrase or sentence has a meaning made up from the meaning of its parts in a standard way. Some current research goes further, focussing on the effect of context on meaning. It is based on structured analyses of contexts (both the linguistic context and the situation of the speaker and hearer) and the relation between those structures and the meanings of utterances. There has been some interest in applying the resulting theoretical framework to non-natural languages, such as programming languages and human-computer interfaces (CSLI, 1984). It is beyond the scope of this paper to survey the relevant work. It has significant limitations, as discussed by Winograd (1985).

As an example, consider the meaning of filling in a "medicine card" listing a patient's medications. From a standard semantic view, each blank would be filled with a term that denoted a particular medication, and the card as a whole (analogous to a sentence) would enumerate all the medications to be given to the patient. This is typically the case, but according to Kaasbøll (in press, p. 4):

> The sheets were filled in properly during the 30 minutes, except for a couple of observed 'missing medicines' on the medicine cards. When asked about the 'mistakes' the treating nurse replied: 'Oh, but we know he (the patient) is going to have the medicines even if it is not written here. It is erased only because he has been under intensive care for some days.'

The issue here is not the exact form of the cards. It could just as well have been a computer system with database entries for medications. The situation-dependence of meaning is in the people who enter and access the data. Accuracy is not just a matter of having the computer keep its records straight. In designing and using a system, it is critical to understand the different potentials for interpretation and either cope with them or modify them through training.

The point of all this from the language/action perspective is to treat the generation and interpretation of semantic distinctions as an activity based on conversations that can be designed and facilitated through the computer. One general principle pointed out by Nygaard (1986) is the importance of having distinctions that are open to new interpretation by the workers. In practical terms, this may be as simple as having a "Notes" field in some data record, that allows the worker to enter (and retrieve) ordinary natural language text, as opposed to 'fixed fields,' in which the distinctions are fixed by system convention. It may also lead to new kinds of structured conversations within the work.

7 Blindnesses of the Language/Action Perspective

Technological impacts cannot be fully understood from any one perspective. Each perspective brings forth some concerns and is 'blind' to others. In designing a coherent system we are guided by a choice of perspective, but success comes from anticipating breakdowns that only become visible from other perspectives. A number of other perspectives will interact with a design generated from concerns of language action:

Implementation   From an implementation perspective we are concerned with issues of hardware, operating systems, languages, data formats, and the like. The vast bulk of the detailed literature on system design approaches problems from this perspective, as it must for practical reasons.

Web of Computing   As Kling and Scacchi (1982) point out, we cannot look at the computer system in isolation. The implementation design is part of a larger web of issues surrounding the computer system itself, such as the design, acquisition, installation, maintenance, and hiring and/or training of people to use a system. These include economic, political, and social considerations and each of these has its own domains of conversation, possibilities and breakdown. In a way, this perspective is at the opposite end from implementation—these are the concerns that ultimately must dominate practical choices, but they do not provide a structured basis for creating a design.

Information Processing   Traditional system perspectives have centered on the kinds of information being entered, stored and accessed, and on the logical rules relating them. As with implementation, this is obviously the perspective from which many details have to be approached. Our relative lack of attention to those issues here does not mean that they are unimportant. Our argument is that, like implementation, they should be looked at in a subordinate way, guided by considerations of the role they play in the structure of language actions by the people using the system.

Roles, Locations, and Materials Holt, Ramsey, and Grimes (1983) present a "role/activity theory" that focusses on people's roles (which specify sets of behaviors) and on the temporal and spatial structure of their potential interactions. Holt (1986) notes that "What first stands out in any work environment is its architecture—that is to say its spatial-functional organization. ... Functional proximity is what relates work places to each other. It is the relation which constrains and organizes the movement of people and materials. ... "

From a language/action perspective we can understand roles in terms of potentials for entering into particular recurrent conversations. But we do not have any tools for describing the distribution of materials or the physical potential for interaction. There may be a critical difference between putting a single terminal at the main nursing station, putting a terminal in each examining and activity room, and having one available by every bedside. In looking at the role of an individual, we need to recognize that his or her body can only be in one place at one time, and is limited in its ability to move from place to place. In a way this sounds mundane, but it is all too easy to design a system that would work wonderfully—if the nurse would walk over to the nursing station before giving each patient medication—but which doesn't succeed in practice.

Authority An important aspect of every human organization is the distribution of authority and the mechanisms by which it is maintained. The introduction of a new technology can perturb this structure in a variety of ways: facilitating detailed monitoring of performance; making it possible for subordinates to work in ways that are not understood by their superiors; and opening possibilities for communication that crosses lines of authority. An analysis of conversational roles can identify particular individuals as having the ability to initiate or respond in certain conversations, and this structure is the practical consequence of authority. But the mechanisms by which authority is established and maintained go beyond this. In contrasting the 'tool perspective' to a more traditional systems perspective, Ehn and Kyng (1984) focus on this issue, looking at ways to maintain the autonomy of workers in the face of computer-based changes that can potentially be used to expand centralized authority.

Group Interests   Work is not carried out by a homogeneous collection of individuals. Every work setting contains groups with collective interests, which can be affected by the introduction of computer systems. The redesign of work is a negotiation among the groups already doing and supervising the work, and the results will be shaped by the interests of these groups and the compromises among them. This kind of issue is often critical to system design, for example between journalists and typographers in newspaper-publishing systems (Howard, 1985) and between librarians and clerks in libraries (Andersen and Madsen, 1986). In the hospital, there are powerful constraints on the appropriate role behavior of doctors and nurses. The structure of interactions within the organization maintains this identity and changes can threaten it. In our example, one might imagine merging the various records and thus eliminating the Kardex. But, according to Kaasbøll (in press):

> Nurses are traditionally a paraprofession subordinate to the physicians and their medical knowledge.... In the nurses' struggle for acceptance of nursing as a profession, the theoretical concept 'nursing process' and its practical documentation in the Kardex is of central importance for developing nursing as a science on its own. In this struggle, the Kardex as a basis for nursing decisions may be seen as the nurses' answer to the physicians' medical records.

Conflict   Most of the organizational models applied to information system design are based on the assumption of shared goals among the participants. In real organizations there are always conflicts among competing goals held by different individuals and groups. In some cases this is institutionalized (as in contractual labor-management relations or internal market competition in a firm), but it is always present. A system that assumes idealized cooperation may easily fail as the result of behavior that the systems analysis might label as stupidity, sabotage, or just plain human stubbornness. An analysis that takes conflicting interests into account is not a vain attempt to dissolve them, but can channel them into explicit forms of mutually agreed-upon negotiation.

The language/action perspective establishes a structure for negotiation, based on a theory of cooperation that assumes the willingness to enter into serious conversation, without assuming shared goals or agreement. A conversation for clarification, for example, might involve each party's negotiating to get a 'favorable deal,' but it can nevertheless result in a mutual agreement. More work needs to be done in integrating a conflict perspective (Ciborra, 1985; Nygaard, 1986).

Interpersonal Relations One of the most obvious effects of computer systems is the replacement of face-to-face verbal interaction with computer-mediated exchange. Some of the potential problems can be characterized in conversational terms. A face-to-face interaction that is identified as playing a particular role in conversations for action (e.g., medication record entry) often has other components (conversations for possibilities) that are lost when it is replaced with computer interactions. Language acts, in general, can be less effective in the absence of personal relationships. In a study of the introduction of a production planning and control system into a factory, Schneider and Howard (1985, pp. 14-15) noted:

> In the contributing areas, Production Support personnel are constantly engaged in informal discussions, promises, and agreements.... Schedulers spend nearly half their time in meetings, competing with their colleagues over shop capacity and priority (one likens the process to 'butting heads'). Thus, a major part of the production planning and control process involves the extremely social acts of persuasion, negotiation, and, at times, argument. As one Production Control expeditor puts it, 'I'm just one leaf on the tree. I try to go in any and all directions in order to get a part out. It all depends on developing working relationships with people in other departments—purchasing, quality control, manufacturing engineering. It's a matter of trust built up over time. Personalities play a big role in it.'

In their study, they show the pitfalls of trying to redesign the work to eliminate these interactions. Although the language/action perspective focusses on the conversations among individuals it is structural, not psychological. It asks us to look at the potentials for interaction, but not the motivations and feelings that will lead to what people actually do. Questions of mood, motivation, and personal satisfaction go far beyond anything that has been dealt with here, and are essential to successful design.

8 Conclusion

We began with the declaration that a system designer benefits from having an explicit awareness of perspective. A perspective generates concerns and questions, and provides a structured analysis through which they can be addressed. Although every design must eventually confront issues from all perspectives, its overall direction is strongly affected by the ones taken as primary.

We have shown how cooperative work can be interpreted as the generation of language acts and conversations. Experience with The Coordinator has demonstrated the value of this perspective in designing workgroup communication tools. In its capacity as a general medium for conversations for action, it has improved work capacity and effectiveness in a variety of settings. The next step will be to apply the language/action perspective to the design of systems that deal with the recurrent content of conversations, with the other types of conversations, and with the relations linking one conversation to another.

There is little agreement as to what core issues will define the area of research in "office systems" and "computer-supported cooperative work." The fields cannot be defined by particular implementation techniques, or principles of information processing, since these apply to all computer systems. We believe that they are part of a new discipline that focuses on the interaction between the structure of systems and the structure of work, and we anticipate that the language/action perspective will play a major role in its development.

Acknowledgments

My conversations with Fernando Flores have been the basis for my understanding, in the most fundamental ways. Without his teaching, my perspectives would have been far different. I wish to thank the participants in the working meetings on system development at the Center for the Study of Language and Information at Stanford for their valuable contributions to the evolution of this work. Jens Kaasbøll and Kim Halskov Madsen were especially helpful in giving me access to and a better understanding of the work being done in the SYDPOL projects. Chauncey Bell, Bradley Hartfield, Francoise Herrmann, Mary Holstege, Judy Olson, and Liam Peyton gave insightful critiques of earlier drafts.

Appendix: Activities on a Hospital Ward [3]

In a case study described by Kaasbøll (1986), researchers in the Florence project of the Scandinavian research program on System Development and Profession Oriented Languages (SYDPOL) analyzed work on a ward of a Norwegian hospital, from what they call a "systems perspective." They focused on the tasks associated with giving medications in a ward for children with respiratory problems. The Appendix paraphrases Kaasbøll's verbal description of some of the activities that were analyzed.

---

[3] Adapted from [Kaasbøll, 1986, p. 3].

Each nurse has a special responsibility as the *team nurse* for a small group of patients.

On the day shift, one nurse (called the *treating nurse* has the task of giving medicines. Her working day may be characterized roughly by the sequence: attend the report meeting; give medicines; record the medicines given; take care of children in kindergarten or the dining hall.

The report meeting takes place from 7:45 to 8 am. One nurse informs the other staff of the status, changes and activities of each patient during the previous day and night. She has heard a vocal report from the night shift, and she reads the *Kardex* while reporting. The Kardex contains diagnosis, planning and evaluation for each patient, and a form with fixed main patient information. It is supposed to be up to date. Other staff take notes on their *program sheets*.

Medicines are prescribed by the doctors on *prescription forms* in cures lasting several days or in daily doses. Cures are recorded on the main patient information form and on the *medicine card*.

Medicines are given in a treatment room between 8 and 9:30 am. Patients enter after having been examined by a doctor,carrying with them a scrap of paper on which the doctor has written today's dose and possible changes in cures. Prescriptions for medicines during the intervals between the regular medicine hours are noted down on a *premedlist* hanging on the wall in the treatment room.

Some simple lung function tests are also performed in the treatment room to monitor the effects of the medicines. Tests to be taken are written on the prescription form and on a scrap taped to the medicine card or on the program sheet if there are changes. The test results are recorded on special forms.

After having given medicines, the treating nurse brings her papers to the ward office. Together with each of the team nurses, one at a time, she examines the papers. All medicines given are now registered on the *curve sheet*. Changes in cures are recorded in the Kardex, and on the medicine card and eventually on the premedlist. In addition, all sheets are compared for the sake of control.

The patients are processed one by one. The team nurse reads from her papers which medicines are to be given. The treating nurse answers by stating which are actually given, and the state of the patient. One day, when the load on the nurses was relatively low, this activity lasted from 9:30 am to 13:25 pm. During these 4 hours, at most 30 minutes were 'effective paper work.' The rest was delays, either because some of the papers were used by others, or because one of the nurses was engaged in handling interruptions. Only a minor part of the 30 minutes was used for updating and comparing. The rest of the time was spent on small conversations, initiated by findings in the information they were handling. These included:

- reporting to each other about the patients' state and activities

- deciding what were facts when inconsistencies were found

- deciding changes in some medicines after small negotiations

- reminding the treating nurse of a test that had been forgotten

- investigating why a medicine was not delivered from the chemist's

- finding out why a patient had to take a specific test.

References

Action Technologies, Inc. (1987). The Coordinator Workgroup Productivity System I. Version 1.5P. Emeryville, California.

Andersen, P. B., & Madsen, K. H. (1986). How to handle the intangible: Metaphors in design and use of computer system, Technical report, Aarhus University.

Austin, J. (1962). *How to Do Things with Words*. Cambridge, Massachusetts: Harvard University Press.

Ciborra, C. U. (1985). Reframing the role of computers in organizations, the transaction costs approach, *Sixth Annual International Conference on Information Systems*, Indianapolis.

Center for the Study of Language and Information (1984). Research Program on Situated Language, Report CSLI-1, Stanford University.

Ehn, P. & Kyng, M. (1984). A tool perspective on the design of interactive computer support for skilled workers. In M. Saaksjarvi (Ed.), *Report of the Seventh Scandinavian Research Seminar on Systemeering*, Helsinki.

Ellis, C. A. & Nutt, G. J. (1980). Office information systems and computer science. *Computing Surveys* 12, 27–60.

Flores, C. F. (1981). *Management and communication in the office of the future*. Unpublished doctoral dissertation, University of California at Berkeley.

Flores, C. F. & Graves, M. (1986a). Domains of permanent human concerns. Unpublished report, Logonet Inc., Berkeley.

Flores, C. F. & Graves, M. (1986b). Designing education. Unpublished report, Logonet Inc., Berkeley.

Flores, C. F. & Ludlow, J. (1981). Doing and speaking in the office. In G. Fick & R. Sprague (Eds.), *DSS: Issues and Challenges*. London: Pergamon Press, 1981.

Gerson, E. M. & Star, S. L. (1986). Analyzing due process in the workplace. *ACM Transactions on Office Information Systems* 4, 257–270.

Haugeland, J. (1981). The nature and plausibility of cognitivism. In J. Haugeland (Ed.), *Mind Design*. Cambridge, Massachusetts: Bradford/MIT Press, 1981.

Holt, A. (1986). Primitive man in the electronic work environment. *Conference on electronic work*, Milan.

Holt, A., Ramsey, H. R., & Grimes, J. D. (1983). Coordination system technology as the basis for a programming environment. *Electrical Communication* 57, 307–314.

Howard, R. (1985). UTOPIA: Where workers craft new technology. *Technology Review* 88, 43–49.

Kaasbøll, J. (1986). Intentional development of professional language through computerization: A case study and some theoretical considerations. *Proceedings of the IPIF Working Conference on System Design for Human Development and Productivity through Participation*. Amsterdam: North Holland.

Kaasbøll, J. (in press). Observation of people working with information: A case study. Submitted for publication.

Kling, R. (1980). Social analyses of computing: Theoretical perspectives in recent empirical research. *Computing Surveys* 12, 61–100.

Kling, R. & Scacchi, W. (1982). The web of computing: Computing technology as social organization. In M. Yovits (Ed.), *Advances in Computers*, Vol. 21, 1–90.

Malone, T. W. (1985). Designing organizational interfaces. *Proceedings of the CHI '85 Conference on Human Factors in Computer Systems*, 66–71. New York: ACM.

Malone, T. W., Grant, K. R., Turbak, F., Brobst, S. A., & Cohen, M. D. (in press). Intelligent information sharing systems, *Communications of the ACM*.

Malone, T. W., Grant, K. R., Lai, K. Y., Rao, R., & Rosenblitt, D. A. (in press). Semi-structured messages are surprisingly useful for computer-supported coordination, *ACM Transactions on Office Information Systems*.

Nygaard, K. (1986). Program development as a social activity. In H-J. Kugler (Ed.) *Information Processing 86*, 189–198. New York: Elsevier (North-Holland).

Nygaard, K. & Sorgaard, P. (1985). The perspective concept in informatics. *Precedings of the Aarhus 1985 Working Conference on Development and Use of Systems and Tools*. Aarhus University, 1985.

Orr, J. (1986). Narratives at work, story telling as cooperative diagnostic activity. *Proceedings of the Conference on Computer-Supported Cooperative Work*, 62–72. Austin, Texas: MCC.

Schneider, L. & Howard, R. (1985). Office automation in a manufacturing setting. Unpublished study prepared for the United States Office of Technology Assessment.

Searle, J. R. (1969). *Speech Acts*. Cambridge: Cambridge University Press.

Searle, J. R. (1975). A taxonomy of illocutionary acts. In K. Gunderson (Ed.), *Language, Mind and Knowledge*, 344–369. Minneapolis: University of Minnesota Press.

Stefik, M., Foster, G., Bobrow, D. G., Kahn, K., Lanning, S. & Suchman, L. (1987). Beyond the Chalkboard: Computer support for collaboration and problem solving in meetings. *Communications of the ACM*, 30, 32–47.

Suchman, L. (1987). *Plans and Situated Actions: The Problem of Human-machine Communication*. Cambridge: Cambridge University Press.

Winograd, T. (1985). Moving the semantic fulcrum. *Linguistics and Philosophy*, 8, 91–104.

Winograd, T. & Flores, F. (1986). *Understanding Computers and Cognition: A New Foundation for Design*. Norwood, New Jersey: Ablex.

Empirical Studies

These papers present several different methodologies for studying users of CSCW systems. The first two (Readings 24 and 25) analyze the applicability of social-psychology methods to the study of electronic communications and present the results of several studies. The three papers following (Readings 26–28), all presented originally at CSCW 1986, are groping for new methods and new models that seem to represent the core of what CSCW is about.

The Keisler, Siegel, and McGuire paper (Reading 24) looks at the application of the methods of the social psychologist to studying impacts of electronic media on group process and decision making. The paper emphasizes the fact that many of the issues raised by computing and technological change are researchable using such methods. It also raises the concern that very little literature in scientific journals reports experimental research studies of group behavior in modern computer-mediated communication. The authors describe suggestive studies based on older technologies such as the teletypewriter and then describe their own study of simultaneous computer-linked discourse and its effects on decision making.

The next paper (Reading 25), published a year later by Sproull and Kiesler, presents the results of empirical research on electronic mail to show the impact on the kinds of information exchanged. These results are applicable to systems design. For example, the effects of limited social context for interactions and the lack of conventions for usage can be emphasized as an advantage of a system, or compensated for when seen as a disadvantage. In particular, the lack of social context can make conversations less personal. For tasks where objective opinions are to be gathered with equal say from all involved, this can be an advantage. For tasks where sensitivity to personal feelings is important, system design should include features that compensate for the "coldness" of the medium and remind users that they are sending messages to people, not to computers.

Crowston, Malone, and Lin (Reading 26) are trying to develop new methodologies that combine concepts drawn from object-oriented programming and artificial intelligence to look at information processing in organizations. They characterize such processing in terms of the kinds of messages people exchange. The method is applied in a case analysis of the introduction of a computer conferencing system into an organization.

Relationships and Tasks in Scientific Research Collaborations (Reading 27) uses the results of studies of research collaborations among scientists to suggest design guidelines for computer technology aimed at supporting such collaboration. Their study, in the form of interviews with researchers in psychology, management science, and computer science, shows that a great deal of emphasis will have to be placed on how the researchers form and maintain personal relationships. The report is not focused on the technology, but rather on the collaborative work needs of a group of people, established by studying how they work with or without computer support. They propose a model of the stages of a research collaboration that can be used as a framework for design of computer-support tools for collaboration.

The paper by Blomberg (Reading 28) is an ethnographic study of the impact of computer technologies on work activities. The author, an anthropologist, argues that the impact of the technology must be understood in terms of the social environment into which it is introduced. She makes her point through a case study of the interplay between Trillium, a computer-based design environment employed in creating machine interface, and the users of this tool. The users are of two types: the designers of the interface to the target machine and the software engineers supporting Trillium. The use of Trillium has caused a restructuring of the social organization and of the design tasks.

Perhaps the most interesting aspect of Blomberg's work is that the software tool is *not* a group tool. Nevertheless, the tool has affected the teams of people that must collaborate on the interface design. Technology and people affect each other in ways that we are barely beginning to notice, let alone understand.

24

Social Psychological Aspects of Computer-Mediated Communication[1]

Sara Kiesler
Jane Siegel
Timothy W. McGuire
Carnegie-Mellon University
Pittsburgh, PA

Computer technologies are improving so swiftly these days that few of us comprehend even a small part of the change. Computers are transforming work and, in some cases, lives. Whether eager for this or resistant, many people believe the organizational, social, and personal effects of computers will be deeply felt (De Sola Poole, 1977, Hiltz & Turoff, 1978, Kling, 1980).

Today, no one can predict in any detail the nature of the transformations that computers will bring, but one aspect of life that will certainly be affected is communication. The use of electronic mail and messages, long-distance blackboards, computer bulletin boards, instantaneously transferable data banks, and simultaneous computer conferences is reportedly advancing "like an avalanche" (Stockton, 1981; also see Kraemer, 1981). The U.S. federal judiciary, for example, is using electronic mail to speed the circulation of appellate opinion drafts among panels of judges (Weis, 1983). Computer conferences are being used for such le-

[1] The research described in this article was supported by grants from the Robotics Institute, Carnegie-Mellon University, and from the National Science Foundation (Grant No. IST-8210701) to the first author. We are grateful to colleagues who commented on the manuscript: Vitaly Dubrovsky, Rob Kling, Allen Newell, Drury Sherrod, and Lee Sproull. Also, we thank Arlene Simon and Mary Jo Dowling for their help in preparing the text.

gal proceedings as admission of evidence, trial scheduling, giving parties access to documents, and expert interrogation (Bentz & Potrykus, 1976; "Party-Line Plea," 1981). Other government agencies, such as the Department of Defense, as well as private firms, such as Westinghouse Corporation and Xerox Corporation, and some universities, use computer-mediated communication extensively for both routine transfer of data and nonroutine interpersonal communication and project work (e.g., Licklider & Vezza, 1978; U.S. Department of Commerce, 1977; Wang Corporation, 1982).

Computer-mediated communication was once confined to technical users and was considered somewhat arcane. This no longer holds true. Computer-mediated communication is a key component of the emerging technology of computer networks. In networks, people can exchange, store, edit, broadcast, and copy any written document. They can send data and messages instantaneously, easily, at low cost, and over long distances. Two or more people can look at a document and revise it together, consult with each other on critical matters without meeting together or setting up a telephone conference, or ask for and give assistance interactively (Hiltz & Turoff, 1978; Williams, 1977).

Networks, and hence computer-mediated communications, are proliferating at a tremendous rate. In addition to the older long-distance networks that connect thousands of scientists, professionals, and managers (e.g., the Department of Defense's ARPANET, GTE's TELENET), there are more and more local-area networks that link up computers within a region, city, or organization (e.g., Nestar System's CLUSTER-BUS, Xerox's ETHERNET, Ford Aerospace's FLASHNET, and Wang Laboratories' WANGNET). Stimulating this growth are the decreasing costs and the advantages of networks over stand-alone systems, such as sharing high-speed printers and access to a common interface for otherwise incompatible equipment. The future of this technology cannot be foretold, but it is far from arcane.

The functions and impact of computer-mediated communication are still poorly understood. Critical information (such as who uses it for what purposes) is lacking, and the social psychological significance is controversial (see, e.g., Turoff, 1982). Computers could make communication easier, just as the canning of perishables and the development of can openers made food preparation easier, or they could have much more complex implications. For instance, access to electronic communication may change the flow of information within organizations, altering status relations and organizational hierarchy. When a manager can receive electronic mail from 10,000 employees, what happens to existing controls over participation and information? When people can publish and distribute their own electronic newspaper at no cost, does the distribution of power change too? When communication is rapid and purely textual, do working groups find it easier or harder to resolve conflict? These unanswered questions illustrate that, although the technology may be impressive, little systematic research exists on its psychological, social, and cultural significance. Given such conditions it seems sensible to try to understand the fundamental behavioral, social, and organizational processes that surround computer-mediated communication. We believe that ideas and approaches from social psychology and other areas of behavioral science can be applied to these questions.

This article is meant to describe some of the issues raised by electronic communication; to illustrate, from our own work, one empirical approach for investigating them; and to show why social psychological research might contribute to a deeper understanding of electronic communication specifically and of computers and technological change in society more generally. We begin by citing some existing research on computer-mediated communication. Most of this research addresses the technical capabilities of the electronic technologies. Next, we consider the possible social psychological impact, and we discuss some hypotheses and some possible implications for the outcomes of communication. Finally, we describe some of our own experiments on social psychological aspects of computer-mediated communication, using these to indicate potential lines of future research.

Existing Research

With a few pioneering exceptions (Hiltz, Johnson, Aronovitch, & Turoff, 1980; Hiltz, Johnson, & Turoff, 1982; Kling, 1982; Short, Williams, & Christie, 1976), research on and analyses of computer communication technologies evaluate the efficiency of these technologies based on their cost and technical capabilities (Bikson, Gutek, & Mankin, 1981). Representative of this orientation are discussions of how computer communications can work in organizations such as libraries and engineering firms (e.g., Lancaster, 1978; Tapscott, 1982); surveys of the introduction of computer networks in organizations (e.g., Rice & Case, 1982; Sinaiko, 1963); and also experimental studies comparing the effects of various communication channels (Chapanis, 1972; Geller, 1981; Kite & Vitz, 1966; Krueger, 1976; Morley & Stephenson, 1969; Weeks & Chapanis, 1976; Williams, 1973a, 1973b, 1975a, 1975b). In general, research on the technical capabilities of computers has addressed questions about how particular technical, economic, or ergonomic characteristics of the technology are related to organizational efficiency and effectiveness. The instantaneous information exchange provided by electronic mail, for example, might allow people to work without regard for their geographic dispersion, their schedules, time zones, access to secretaries, and energy costs (Kraemer, 1981). If computer mail discourages chatting and off-task interaction (Weeks & Chapanis, 1976) or if people read more effectively than they listen (Hiltz & Turoff, 1978), then managers might be more efficient.

The approach based on technical capability is a common and convenient means of analyzing new technologies. However, in real life, technological functions do not exist in isolation. Each technical component may be part of a larger context or may trigger certain social psychological processes (Pye & Williams, 1977; Williams, 1977). Thus, for instance, a broadly accessible communication network might not only increase total communication rates but also stimulate communication up and down the organization. If supervisors find it easy to keep tabs on subordinates and subordinates "copy up" to superiors, centralization of control might increase even while communication becomes more participative.

The prospect of enhanced or changed flows of information among people raises many other social psychological issues. For example, managers who use computer conferences to look at and discuss on-line computerized forecasts and analyses (Dutton & Kraemer, 1980) might persuade each other too readily. On the other hand, there are various computer-aided decision-making techniques, such as Delphi, that are designed to increase decision quality by removing status and other social cues (Martino, 1972; Price, 1975). It is conceivable that by providing groups with more "hard" information, computers would reduce the probability of "groupthink" (Janis, 1972) or "tunnel vision" (Hedberg, Nystrom, & Starbuck, 1976) in group decision making (Krueger, 1976; Vallee, Johansen, Lipinski, & Wilson, 1977).

As these speculations suggest, a focused effort on the psychological and social aspects of computing environments revealed by technical capability studies (but not pursued in these studies) is needed. In the new research efforts, social psychologists and other social scientists would use the wealth of theory and previous research in their fields to generate hypotheses about computing and to evaluate these hypotheses empirically. This would mean studying the implications of the social features of computing, not just its technical characteristics. We expand on this notion next.

Social Psychological Aspects of Computer-Mediated Communication

Computer-mediated communication differs in many ways, both technically and culturally, from more traditional communication technologies.

Technically, it has the speed (including simultaneity, if desired) and energy efficiency, but not the aural or visual feedback of telephoning and face-to-face communication. It has the adaptability of written text. Messages can be sent to groups of any size and can be programmed for such special functions as automatic copying to a prespecified distribution list. Culturally, computer-mediated communication is still undeveloped. Although computer professionals have used electronic communication for over two decades, and they make up a subculture whose norms influence computer users and electronic communication (Sproull, Kiesler, & Zubrow, in press), no strong etiquette as yet applies to how electronic communication should be used. A few user manuals devote a paragraph to appropriate uses of a computer network, but generally speaking, people do not receive either formal or informal instruction in an etiquette of electronic communication. These technical and cultural issues might be organized around the following questions.

Time and Information Processing Pressures

Does easy, rapid communication—messages exchanged literally at the touch of a key—change the quantity or the distribution or the timing of information exchanged? Availability of instantaneous electronic communication, for example, might lead people to expect immediate responses. (We have talked with a company president in Pittsburgh who sends computer mail at dinnertime asking his subordinates in Singapore for quarterly projections by breakfast.)

Absence of Regulating Feedback

Does communication through text alone reduce coordination of communication? In traditional forms of communication, head nods, smiles, eye contact, distance, tone of voice, and other nonverbal behavior give speakers and listeners information they can use to regulate, modify, and control exchanges. Electronic communication may be inefficient for resolving such coordination problems as telling another person you already have knowledge of something he or she is explaining (Kraut, Lewis, & Swezey, 1982).

Dramaturgical Weakness

Computer communication might weaken social influence by the absence of such nonverbal behavior as taking the head seat, speaking loudly, staring, touching, and gesturing (R. Kling, personal communication, May

1983). The opportunity to hear someone's voice or to look him or her in the eye changes how bargains are negotiated or whether any real bargaining occurs (e.g., Carnevale, Pruitt, & Seilheimer, 1981; Krauss, Apple, Morencz, Wenzel, & Winton, 1981). When using computers to communicate, how will people compensate for the dramaturgical weakness of electronic media? For example, Hiltz and Turoff reported that computer conferees have developed ways of sending computerized screams, hugs, and kisses (in Pollack, 1982, p. D2).

Few Status and Position Cues

Software for electronic communication is blind with respect to the vertical hierarchy in social relationships and organizations. Once people have electronic access, their status, power, and prestige are communicated neither contextually (the way secretaries and meeting rooms and clothes communicate) nor dynamically (the way gaze, touch, and facial and paralinguistic behavior communicate; Edinger & Patterson, 1983). Thus charismatic and high status people may have less influence, and group members may participate more equally in computer communication.

Social Anonymity

Is electronic communication depersonalizing? Because it uses printed text, without even the texture of paper to lend it individuality, electronic communication tends to seem impersonal. Communicators must imagine their audience, for at a terminal it almost seems as though the computer itself is the audience. Messages are depersonalized, inviting stronger or more uninhibited text and more assertiveness in return. It might be especially hard to communicate liking or intimacy, without writing unusually positive text. (At our university, a computer manual warns, "Sometimes ... users lose sight of the fact that they are really addressing other people, not the computer.")

Computing Norms and Immature Etiquette

Because electronic communication was developed and has been used by a distinctive subculture of computing professionals, its norms are infused with that culture's special language (i.e., people talk about "default" attitudes and "bogus" assertions) and its implicit rejection of organizational conventionality and 8-hour workdays. In our own university as well as other organizations (Sheil, personal communication, April 1982), people using electronic mail overstep conventional time boundaries dividing office and home; they mix work and personal communications; they use language appropriate for boardrooms and ballfields interchangeably; and they disregard normal conventions of privacy (for instance, by posting personal messages to general bulletin boards). This behavior is not counteracted by established conventions or etiquette for computer communication. There are few shared standards for salutations, for structuring formal versus informal messages, or for adapting content to achieve both impact and politeness. How do people develop a communication network social structure using a technology in cultural transition? Do they import norms from other technologies? Do they develop new norms?

From a social psychological perspective, this list of questions suggests that computer-mediated communication has at least two interesting characteristics: (a) a paucity of social context information and (b) few widely shared norms governing its use. These characteristics may affect communication via computer in at least three areas. First, the lack of social feedback and unpredictable style of messages might make it difficult to coordinate and comprehend messages (Kraut & Lewis, in press). Second, social influence among communicators might become more equal because so much hierarchical dominance and power information is hidden (Edinger & Patterson, 1983). Third, social standards will be less important and communication will be more impersonal and more free because the rapid exchange of text, the lack of social feedback, and the absence of norms governing the social interaction redirect attention away from others and toward the message itself. Indeed, computer-mediated communication seems to comprise some of the same conditions that are important for deindividuation—anonymity, reduced self-regulation, and reduced self-awareness (e.g., Diener, 1980; Festinger, Pepitone, & Newcomb, 1952; Forsyth, 1983, pp. 308–338).

This last point deserves some elaboration. Using traditional communication, norms, social standards, and inferences about individuals are made salient by observable social structural artifacts (such as prestige communicated through a person's dress or letterhead) and by communication itself, including nonverbal involvement (Edinger & Patterson, 1983; Patterson, 1982). However, terminals and electronic signals convey fewer historical, contextual, and non-verbal cues. Electronic media do not efficiently communicate nuances of meaning and frame of mind, organizational loyalties, symbolic procedural variations, and, especially, individuating details about people that might be embodied in their dress, location, demeanor, and expressiveness (e.g., Ekman, Friesen, O'Sullivan, & Scherer, 1980; Mehrabian, 1972). This situation, where personality and culture lack salience, might foster feelings of depersonalization. In addition, using the computer tends to be absorbing and conducive to quick response, which might reduce self-awareness and increase the feeling of being submerged in the machine. Thus, the overall weakening of self- or normative regulation might be similar to what happens when people become less self-aware and submerged in a group, that is, deindividuated (Dienes, Lusk, DeFour, & Flax, 1980; Scheier, 1976; Scheier & Carver, 1977; Scheier, Carver, & Gibbons, 1981).

Outcomes of Technology Use

Most existing discussions of computers focus on the advantages of computer-mediated communication for work: fast and precise information exchange, increased participation in problem solving and decision making, and reduction of "irrelevant" status and prestige differences (Lancaster, 1978; Linstone & Turoff, 1975; Martino, 1972). This orientation is illustrated by the following:

> The scientific literature will become unified ... Scientists everywhere will have equal access ... the advantage of being in a famous center of research will be substantially lessened. Scientists in obscure universities ... will be able to participate in scientific discourse more readily. (Folk, 1977, p. 80)

Existing social psychological studies do not entirely contradict the forecasts that communicating by computer will increase participation, objectivity, and efficiency of groups and organizations. For example, any communication technology that reduces the importance of status and dominance could increase the likelihood that opinions in groups are sampled more widely. If people who are high in status usually talk most and dominate decision making (Hoffman, 1978), then computer-mediated communication that deemphasizes the impact of status also might increase people's consideration of minority views. If minority opinions can enhance performance, then groups could be more effective when using computers to communicate.

On the other hand, equal participation, objectivity, and efficiency sometimes interfere with important group outcomes. To be effective, rather than encouraging equal participation, group members may need to organize themselves by discovering sources of information, deciding who can be depended on, distributing work to these people, and protecting their autonomy (e.g., Hackman & Morris, 1978). To be effective, rather than aiming at objectivity, groups may need affective bonds, a status distribution that helps sort out multiple objectives, and a hierarchy that determines influence, even if these behaviors interfere with "good" decisions (Kelley & Thibaut, 1978; March & Olsen, 1976; Salancik, 1977). For accomplishing these purposes, the social structure provided by roles, norms, and status and reinforced by trust and personal engagement with others is critical.

These ideas suggest that the use of computers for communication will be more complex than is typically envisioned in the computer technology literature. We have speculated that computer-mediated communication will influence group functions involving coordination of discussion, participation and influence of dominant individuals, and normative control. In technical problem solving, then, computer-mediated groups might be disorganized, democratic, unrestrained, and perhaps more creative than groups communicating more traditionally; they might have trouble reaching consensus if the "correct" answer is not obvious; they might not operate as cool, fast decision makers. What might be the outcome for real groups that have to deal with technical, political, and organizational tasks? Ultimately, it might depend on existing relationships. In computer-linked groups whose members are discontented and in conflict with one another, impersonal behavior might tend to polarize members, exacerbate aggressiveness, and cause negative attributions to others (e.g., Gibbons & Wright, 1981; Goldstein, Davis, & Herman, 1975; McArthur & Solomon, 1978; Prentice-Dunn & Rogers, 1980). However, in computer-linked groups that are on friendly, cooperative terms, impersonal behavior might actually encourage joint approaches to decision making or negotiating (see Druckman, 1977; Pruitt & Lewis, 1975), and it could reduce self-consciousness and promote intimacy. Some of our colleagues, for example, notice that their students are more often willing to approach a professor for assistance with assignments or a potential date through electronic mail than in face-to-face encounters (Larkin, personal communication, July 1982; Welsch, 1982).

These speculations must be evaluated empirically. There are no experimental research studies published in scientific journals that focus directly on group behavior in modern computer-mediated communication, such as electronic mail. However, earlier studies of the teletypewriter lend support to the analyses we have presented. Sinaiko's (1963) experiments at the Institute for Defense Analyses indicated that "teletype quite dramatically depersonalizes negotiations.... Differences in initial positions held by negotiators converge more in a face-to-face situation, next by telephone and least when the teletypewriter is the medium of communication" (p. 18). Morley and Stephenson (1969, 1970) found that tasks requiring dependence on interpersonal or interparty considerations interacted strongly with media. Three studies that focused on group processes showed that role differentiation was diminished and more unstable in the computer-mediated cases. Moreover, frequency of participation was most equal in the teletypewriting mode, less equal with audio only, and least equal when subjects were face to face (Krueger, 1976; Strickland, Guild, Barefoot, & Patterson, 1975; Williams, 1975a). Communication by teletype was both "egalitarian" and "disorganized" (Williams, 1977).

The findings from research on earlier technologies indicate that computer-mediated communication raises some old issues. Technologies that lacked a distinctive etiquette (teletype, for instance) and/or the opportunity to exchange a full range of paralinguistic cues (such as freeze-frame videoconferencing) caused special problems for groups. In earlier advances of communication technology, people had to learn how to organize new and disparate pieces of information, and they had to learn how to behave toward one another.

Electronic communication differs from any other communication in time, space, speed, ease of use, fun, audience, and opportunity for feedback. For example, in one firm where someone posted a new product idea on the computer network, the proposition was sent in one minute to 300 colleagues in branches across the country, and, within two days, sufficient replies were received to launch a new long-distance joint project. We do not present this anecdote as though we know its precise significance, but we do mean to argue that computers are different from previous technologies. Research must discover how groups respond to the difference; how, given time, groups work out new communication traditions and rules; and what the requirements of the new communication culture will be. The answers to these questions ultimately will determine the nature of the social revolution embodied in modern communication technologies.

The rest of this article describes one approach to studying the social psychological dimensions of computer-mediated communication. In the following section, we summarize experiments on the effects on groups of simultaneous terminal-to-terminal teleconferencing and of electronic mail. Also, we have begun to study underlying processes and to explore questions of external generalizability. The final section summarizes the direction of this work.

Studies of Participation, Choice, and Interaction in Computer-Mediated Groups

The purpose of our initial studies (Siegel, Dubrovsky, Kiesler, & McGuire, 1983) has been to explore, experimentally, the impact of computer-mediated communication, as used in our own local computer network, on group interaction and decisions. To our knowledge, these are among the first controlled experiments using modern, fast terminals and flexible computer conference and mail software (see also Hiltz, Johnson, & Turoff, 1982). We emphasized control over generalizability in the first three experiments, choosing a small group size of three. The subjects were students who had used the computer network previously. Also, we used a group task about which there is considerable knowledge, that is, the Stoner (1961) choice–dilemma problems (see, e.g., Dion, Baron, & Miller, 1978; Kogan & Wallach, 1964, 1967; Lamm & Kogan, 1970; Vinokur & Burnstein, 1974; Zajonc, 1969). This research was carried out in offices and rooms where terminals were already in use so as to duplicate the actual setting where communication typically takes place.

The first experiment is prototypical of the rest. The study compared three-person groups who were asked to reach consensus on a choice–dilemma problem in three different contexts: once face to face, once using the computer anonymously (i.e., not knowing by name who within their group was talking), and once using the computer nonanonymously. In the computer-mediated discussions, each person was separated physically from the others, and each used a computer terminal to communicate. Each group member typed his or her remarks into the computer using a program called "Converse," which divides the screen into three or more parts and allows messages from different people to appear simultaneously and scroll independently.

The main dependent variables in all of the experiments were (a) communication efficiency, (b) participation, (c) interpersonal behavior, and (d) group choice. We derived hypotheses for the experiments both from our observations of the technology and from the social psychological literature. We tried to examine whether computer communication is depersonalizing and lacking in social structure, and we tried to test our hunches about the implications. Hence, in the first experiment we predicted that participation would be more equal in the computer-mediated communication conditions. We thought that coming to consensus would be more difficult. In carrying out pilot work, we had seen many instances of what appeared to be uninhibited behavior—subjects swearing, individuals shouting at their terminals, and groups refusing to make a group decision until a group member gave in—and as a result we systematically evaluated interpersonal interactions as revealed in the transcripts of both face-to-face and computer-mediated groups. We predicted more uninhibited behavior in computer-mediated groups. Also, we added an anonymous computer-mediated communication condition in order to explore whether not knowing specifically who was talking would increase depersonalization (e.g., Williams, Harkins, & Latane, 1981).

We hypothesized that choice shift would be greater when people used the computer, generally because norms are weaker, and, hence, group members might be less likely to simply average initial opinions or obey the initial majority. According to social comparison theory (Brown, 1965; Goethals & Zanna, 1979; Sanders & Baron, 1977) and the persuasive arguments model (Vinokur & Burnstein, 1974, 1978), choice shift may occur in groups because people compare themselves to others with extreme or novel attitudes or because they are exposed to extreme arguments they would not otherwise hear (this assumes most people have moderate initial positions). If people in computer-mediated groups, as compared to face-to-face groups, are party to a broader distribution of opinions (because participation is spread more evenly across opinions) and extreme opinions are less likely to be withheld (because behavior is less inhibited), then we would predict more choice shift in computer-mediated groups.

Our data showed, in all three experiments, that computer-mediated communication had marked effects on communication efficiency, participation, interpersonal behavior, and decision making.

Communication Efficiency

Three measures bear on communication efficiency: time to decision, number of remarks exchanged, and percentage of discussion remarks about the group choice rather than about extraneous topics (e.g., school work). We found that in spite of the fact that messages arrived instantaneously, using a keyboard took time. Computer-mediated groups took longer to reach consensus than did face-to-face groups, and they exchanged fewer remarks in the time allowed them. We think groups in the computer-communication conditions took more time to reach consensus for reasons beyond technical difficulties. They might have had greater difficulties reaching agreement, judging by the vehemence of their arguments. Also, when we asked people to type out remarks that subjects had made face to face, we found typing time could not account for all the time taken by computer-mediated groups to reach consensus.

We found that computer-mediated groups were as task oriented as face-to-face groups. This tends to rule out the idea that groups using the computer were inefficient because they were not paying attention to the task. In Figure 24.1, we summarize effects on equality of participation, group choice shift, and uninhibited interpersonal behavior.

Participation, Group Choice, and Interpersonal Behavior

Based on analyses of who talked and how much they talked (i.e., the distribution of remarks among group members), group members using the computer participated more equally than they did when they talked

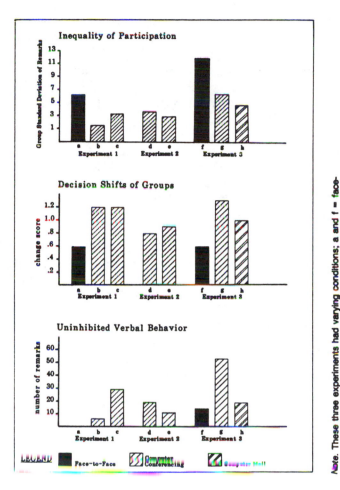

Figure 24.1   Inequality of Participation, Decision Shifts of Groups, and Uninhibited Verbal Behavior

face to face. Although one person tended to dominate in both face-to-face and computer-mediated interaction, this dominance was less strong in computer-mediated groups.

Computer-mediated groups showed significantly higher choice shift. We do not fully understand this finding. Analyses of the group process (e.g., extreme positions taken, use of decision rules such as majority rule or simple averaging, or repeated stating of positions) did not reveal differences in these processes between face-to-face and computer-mediated groups. People in computer-mediated groups used a higher proportion of numeric arguments, but this tendency was uncorrelated with choice shift. Perhaps if communication using the computer was depersonalized, people felt more able to abandon their previous positions or to ignore social pressure to reach consensus.

People in computer-mediated groups were more uninhibited than they were in face-to-face groups as measured by uninhibited verbal behavior, defined as frequency of remarks containing swearing, insults, name calling, and hostile comments.

In addition to what is shown in Figure 24.1, each experiment incorporated different computer communication design features and samples. By varying technical features of the communication programs and changing subject samples, we hoped to address some plausible alternative explanations of our results. Based on these variations we did reach certain conclusions. First, from using trained and practiced subjects in Experiment 2 (and adult managers in our fourth and fifth experiments), we concluded that our findings are generalizable to adults and nonstudents as well as to undergraduate students. Second, from comparing experienced and inexperienced computer network users, we concluded that our results apply not just to novices but also to people who use computers often and for whom electronic mail and message systems as well as simultaneous discussion systems are familiar. Third, we also have compared strangers and friends and obtained similar results.

Is computer-mediated communication simply disorderly, perhaps because there is no constraint on interruptions and distracting remarks? In Experiment 2, Vitaly Dubrovsky (Dubrovsky, Kiesler, & Siegel, 1983) devised a technical variation of the simultaneous computer conversation program to see whether imposing procedural order through technical features of the communication medium would increase its similarity to face-to-face communication. He designed a sequential computer conference program that forced group members to take turns speaking and to indicate to others when they wished to interrupt. Hence, the new software allowed only one person to talk at a time, and we compared how groups used this method with how they used the regular simultaneous computer conference program. The most important outcomes of this study were to establish that software developed to control the sequence of interaction is disliked and that it does not necessarily coordinate or control discussions. The effects of the computer-mediated communication programs were equal to those of computer communication in the first experiment.

Experiment 3 was intended primarily to extend the study to electronic mail, which is used extensively in most computer networks. Although electronic mail has some of the same cultural and technical characteristics as simultaneous computer conferences, it does not require communication in real time. There is time for reflection, for composing one's thoughts, and for side discussions with only part of a group. Hence, we thought it possible that electronic mail would be relatively conflict free and would produce about the same decisions as face-to-face communication. In spite of our expectations, the findings of Experiment 3 were similar to those of the other experiments. However, uninhibited behavior was somewhat higher in the computer conference condition than in the computer mail condition.

How might we explain the results as a whole? There are at least three alternatives, having to do with (a) difficulties of coordination from lack of informational feedback, (b) absence of social influence cues for controlling discussion, and (c) depersonalization from lack of nonverbal involvement and absence of norms. We will consider each briefly. First, we can explain the greater time people took to reach consensus and the evenness of participation rates by pointing to the absence of informational feedback between speakers and listeners in the computer-mediated communication condition. That is, the usual forms of discussion control through back-channel communications (Kraut et al., 1982) could not be exerted. People did not know exactly when their arguments were understood or agreed to, and consequently everyone believed they had to exert more effort to be understood. This explanation, however, does not account for the findings of greater choice shift and uninhibited behavior, except indirectly. Perhaps it was frustrating for people to be discussing a problem inefficiently; they might have become angry and, hence, more extreme in decision making and more uninhibited.

A second explanation of our findings is that in computer communication there is less influence and control of a dominant person, moderator, or leader. Lack of leadership could have caused difficulties in reaching a group decision efficiently. Without leadership, a group might ignore social norms, standards, and precedents, causing both choice shift and uninhibited behavior.

A final explanation for our results is that electronic communication involves a process of depersonalization or a redirection of attention away from one's audience. Suppose computer-mediated communication prevented personal feedback and individuating information and at the same time lacked a shared etiquette and, further, was influenced by norms from the computer subculture. This could have made group members more responsive to immediate textual cues, more impulsive and assertive, and less bound by precedents set by societal norms of how groups should come to consensus. This explanation fits our data. However, we emphasize that our own data do not provide any evidence to distinguish among these tentative and somewhat limited potential explanations.

Another issue with which we must deal is external validity, that is, to what degree our results can be generalized across people and technologies. Based on our own research and anecdotal evidence from reports of computer network behavior, we are relatively sure that our findings apply to a wide sample of both novice and experienced computer users. For example, observers of computer networks have noticed uninhibited behavior for years. In the computer subculture, the word *flaming* refers to the practice of expressing oneself more strongly on the computer than one would in other communication settings. The Defense Communications Agency, which manages the 12-year-old ARPANET, has had to police use of the network bulletin boards by manually screening messages every few days to weed out those deemed in bad taste. Nor is flaming confined to government-sponsored networks. When IBM installed the personal computer in offices and created an internal message system, VNET, to link them, a "GRIPENET" emerged—organized complaints against management practices and policies whose form and substance deviate considerably from standard IBM culture (Emmett, 1981). Of course, whether this behavior was caused specifically by a lack of shared etiquette, by computer culture norms, or by the impersonal and text-only form of communication is not clear.

We are not so sure how our findings would apply to more sophisticated technologies, say those that include video or audio channels in electronic mail. We suspect that combining telephone with electronic mail in the same facility would decrease the differences between electronic communication and face-to-face communication, if only because the amount of feedback is increased. Based on current trends, text-only electronic communication systems will become more popular. In that case, we should study both their transient effects (those likely to disappear when the technologies are mature) and their more permanent and secondary effects. Judging from our own observations of existing networks, both kinds of change are important. For example, absence of computer etiquette is a transient problem, but it is one that raises significant policy debates over rights of computer users to privacy and freedom of exploration. A more permanent effect might be the extension of participation in group or organizational communication. This is important because it implies more shared information, more equality of influence, and, perhaps, a breakdown of social and organizational barriers.

Implications for Future Research

The conceptual framework for studies of computer-mediated communication will develop mainly from studies of social process. These studies will provide either detailed descriptions of behavior or tests of alternative theoretical ideas. In our own laboratory, we have just collected additional data on the process of computer-mediated communication. In one new experiment, we asked business managers and university administrators to use simultaneous computer conferences to reach decisions involving multiattribute risky choices (Payne & Laughhunn, in press; Tversky & Kahneman, 1981). Preliminary analyses of the decisions and the content of discussions indicate that when the managers used the computer to consider the issues, they were less effective in considering all the issues and coordinating their discussion. The findings suggest that if computer-mediated communication is used by managers to make group decisions, those decisions may differ qualitatively from decisions reached face to face.

In another study (Kiesler, Zubrow, Moses, & Geller, 1983), we tested whether using a computer to communicate is physiologically arousing or has other affective consequences. In a 2 × 2 design, we manipulated anxiety (anticipation of evaluation) and computer-mediated versus face-to-face communication in a study of how two people get to know each other. In this study, we measured physiological arousal (pore size and pulse), emotionality, interpersonal attraction, responsiveness to others, self-disclosure, and other aspects of interpersonal communication. Our results suggest that computer-mediated communication is not physiologically arousing. Once again we discovered more uninhibited behavior when people communicated using the computer. We also found that although people felt more embarrassed meeting one another face to face, they ended up liking each other better. Because other research suggests that gaze, smiling, and other nonverbal feedback is important to establish attraction (Scherer, 1974), our data do support our hypothesis that the lack of nonverbal involvement is a critical dimension of electronic communication.

Much more work on affective and cognitive dimensions of computer-mediated communication is needed to understand the issues we raised earlier. For example, further studies of affective responses may establish whether absorption in computer messages is arousing (see Zajonc, 1965), why users are sometimes aggressive (see Goldstein et al., 1975), whether attention is submerged in messages (see McArthur & Solomon, 1978), and under what conditions people will be uninhibited (see Zillman, Bryant, Cantor, & Day, 1975). The research could build on recent studies of affect in social cognition (e.g., Isan, Shalker, Clark, & Karp, 1978) that show how mood and emotion are connected to information processing, memory, and overt behavior using computers.

In addition to identifying behavioral dimensions of computer-mediated communications, research could reveal more about fundamental group processes, both inside and outside of computer-mediated settings. For example, social norms play a critical role in models of group decision making developed by Davis and his colleagues (e.g., Davis, 1973). According to these models, changing the potential for normative influence, such as reducing face-to-face contact, changes the influence function (Stasser & Davis, 1981, p. 544). Because computers appear to alter the operation of normative influences, studies of computer-mediated decision making might contribute to our understanding of these and other models in social psychology that invoke group pressure, persuasion, and affectively relevant processes.

The potential for developing important organizational applications from social psychological studies of computer-mediated communication is also high. One avenue of development will be experimental research that suggests new ways to use computers in education (Lepper, 1982), public affairs, and mental health. It might be possible to turn computer networks into social support networks. Second, it might be possible, through experimental research, to establish the feasibility of using electronic communication for surveys, questionnaires, and interactive polling. A group at our university is carrying out what we believe are among the first controlled experiments on using the computer to collect survey data (Kiesler & Sproull, 1984).

Finally, quasi-experimental and field studies of networks will suggest applications for long-distance collaborative work and management. For example, geographically dispersed groups of scientists and their students are currently working to develop a common computer language (Common LISP) for artificial intelligence research. The groups have used electronic mail via ARPANET with everyone participating rather than forming committees and meeting face to face (Maddox, 1982). Reportedly, electronic mail was used during 1 year to discuss some 232 issues. About 150 of these issues were resolved before participants came to any face-to-face meeting. Most technical questions were resolved by someone in the group communicating a solution through the network. However, questions of style, for example, about programming conventions or systems architecture, evoked conflict and flaming on the computer. These matters had to be resolved by a mediator (appointed by the groups to organize the project) or in face-to-face meetings. Nonetheless, participants in the project report they have made more progress and acquired the active contribution of many more scientists by using the network. Their experience suggests that long-distance computer-mediated group problem solving could have many useful applications. Hiltz (1984) discussed many other instances of long-distance collaboration using the experimental Electronic Information Exchange System (EIES).

Although the social responses to computer-mediated communication described in this article occur in the situation in which the communication takes place, readers should not carry away the impression that all of the social implications are short term. Some effects, such as increased lateral communication in an organization or reduction in clerical staff, might develop over a long period through the actions and attitudes of many people (Hough & Panko, 1977). Others have examined organizational effects of computers generally (Boguslaw, 1981; Danziger, Dutton, Kling, & Kraemer, 1982; Whisler, 1970). Our aim has not been to delineate any particular social impact but to suggest, using our work as an example, the significance of understanding the broad range of social implications of computerization. Much of this work belongs in the field of social psychology, although the line between social psychology and other areas of psychology and social science is tenuous and arbitrary. Actually, studies of behavioral and social processes in computer-mediated communication (indeed of all computing) will be carried out best as an interdisciplinary effort.

References

Bentz, C. A., & Potrykus, T. M. (1976). *Visual communications in the Phoenix criminal justice system* (American Telephone and Telegraph Company Report No. 39-8-39-12). Morristown, NJ: American Telephone and Telegraph Company.

Bikson, T. K., Gutek, B. A., & Mankin, D. A. (1981). *Implementation of information technology in office settings: Review of relevant literature* (Report No. P-6691). Santa Monica, CA: Rand Corporation.

Boguslaw, R. (1981). *The new utopians: A study of system design and social change* (2nd ed.). New York: Irvington.

Brown, R. (1965). *Social psychology*. New York: Free Press.

Carnevale, P. J. E., Pruitt, D. G., & Seilheimer, S. D. (1981). Looking and competing: Accountability and visual access in integrative bargaining. *Journal of Personality and Social Psychology, 40*, 111–120.

Chapanis, A. (1972). Studies in interactive communication: The effects of four communication modes on the behavior of teams during cooperative problem-solving. *Human Factors, 14*, 487–509.

Danziger, J. N., Dutton, W. H., Kling, R., & Kraemer, K. L. (1982). *Computers and politics: High technology in American local governments*. New York: Columbia University Press.

Davis, J. H. (1973). Group decision and social interaction: A theory of social decision schemes. *Psychological Review, 80*, 97–125.

De Sola Poole, I. (1977). *The social impact of the telephone.* Cambridge MA: MIT Press.

Diener, E. (1980). Deindividuation: The absence of self-awareness and self-regulation in group members. In P. Paulus (Ed.), *The psychology of group influence* (pp. 209–242). Hillsdale, NJ: Erlbaum.

Diener, E., Lusk, R., DeFour, D., & Flax, R. (1980). Deindividuation: Effects of group size, density, number of observers, and group member similarity on self-consciousness and disinhibited behavior. *Journal of Personality and Social Psychology, 39,* 449–459.

Dion, K. L., Baron, R. S., & Miller, N. (1978). Why do groups make riskier decisions than individuals? In L. Berkowitz (Ed.), *Group processes* (pp. 227–299). New York: Academic Press.

Druckman, D. (1977). *Negotiations: Social-psychological perspectives.* London: Sage.

Dubrovsky, V., Kiesler, S., & Siegel, J. (1983, October). *Human factors in computer-mediated communication.* Paper presented at the meeting of the Human Factors Society, Baltimore, MD.

Dutton, W. H., & Kraemer, K. L. (1980). Automating bias. *Society, 17,* 36–41.

Edinger, J. A., & Patterson, M. L. (1983). Nonverbal involvement and social control. *Psychological Bulletin, 93,* 30–56.

Ekman, P., Friesen, W. V., O'Sullivan, M., & Scherer, K. (1980). Relative importance of face, body, and speech in judgments of personality and affect. *Journal of Personality and Social Psychology, 38,* 270–277.

Emmett, R. (1981, November). VNET or GRIPENET? *Datamation,* pp. 48–58.

Festinger, L., Pepitone, A., & Newcomb, T. (1952). Some consequences of deindividuation in a group. *Journal of Abnormal and Social Psychology, 47,* 382–389.

Folk, H. (1977). The impact of computers on book and journal publication. In J. L. Divilbiss (Ed.), *The economics of library automation: Proceedings of the 1976 clinic on library applications of data processing* (pp. 72–82). Urbana, IL: University of Illinois Graduate School of Science.

Forsyth, D. R. (1983). *An introduction to group dynamics.* Monterey, CA: Brooks/Cole.

Geller, V. J. (1981, September). *Mediation of social presence: Communication modality effects on arousal and task performance.* Murray Hill, NJ: Bell Laboratories.

Gibbons, F. X., & Wright, R. A. (1981). Motivational biases in causal attributions of arousal. *Journal of Personality and Social Psychology, 40,* 588–600.

Goethals, G. R., & Zanna, M. P. (1979). The role of social comparison in choice shifts. *Journal of Personality and Social Psychology, 37*, 1469–1476.

Goldstein, J. H., Davis, R. W., & Herman, D. (1975). Escalation of aggression: Experimental studies. *Journal of Personality and Social Psychology, 31*, 162–170.

Hackman, J. R., & Morris, C. G. (1978). Group tasks, group interaction process, and group performance effectiveness: A review and proposed integration. In L. Berkowitz (Ed.), *Group processes* (pp. 1–55). New York: Academic Press.

Hedberg, B. L. T., Nyston, P. C., & Starbuck, W. H. (1976). Camping on seesaws: Prescriptions for a self-designing organization. *Administrative Science Quarterly, 21*, 41–65.

Hiltz, S. R. (1984). *Online scientific communities: A case study of the office of the future.* Norwood, NJ: Ablex Press.

Hiltz, S. R., Johnson, K., Aronovitch, C., & Turoff, M. (1980, August). *Face-to-face vs. computerized conferences: A controlled experiment:Vol. 1. Findings* (Report No. 12). Newark, NJ: New Jersey Institute of Technology.

Hiltz, S. R., Johnson, K., & Turoff, M. (1982). *The effects of formal human leadership and computer-generated decision aids on problem solving via computer: A controlled experiment* (Report No. 18). Newark, NJ: New Jersey Institute of Technology.

Hiltz, S. R., & Turoff, M. (1978). *The network nation: Human communication via computer.* Reading, MA: Addison-Wesley.

Hoffman, L. R. (1978). The group problem-solving process. In L. Berkowitz (Ed.), *Group processes* (pp. 101–112). New York: Academic Press.

Hough, R. W., & Panko, R. R. (1977). *Teleconferencing systems: A state-of-the-art survey and preliminary analysis* (National Science Foundation Report No. RA 770103, PB268455). Washington, DC: National Science Foundation.

Isen, A. M., Shalker, T. E., Clark, M., & Karp, L. (1978). Affect, accessibility of material in memory, and behavior: A cognitive loop? *Journal of Personality and Social Psychology, 36*, 1–12.

Janis, I. L. (1972). *Victims of groupthink.* Boston: Houghton Mifflin.

Kelley, H. H., & Thibaut, J. W. (1978). *Interpersonal relations.* New York: Wiley.

Kiesler, S., & Sproull, L. (1984). *Response effects in the electronic survey.* Unpublished manuscript, Carnegie-Mellon University, Pittsburgh, PA.

Kiesler, S., Zubrow, D., Moses, A., & Geller, V. (1983). *Affect in computer-mediated communication.* Manuscript submitted for publication.

Kite, W. R., & Vitz, P. C. (1966). *Teleconferencing: Effects of communication medium, network, and distribution of resources.* Arlington, VA: Institute for Defense Analyses.

Kling, R. (1980). Social analyses of computing: Theoretical perspectives in recent empirical research. *Computing Surveys, 12*, 61–110.

Kling, R. (1982). *Visible opportunities and hidden constraints: Engagements with computing on a social terrain.* Unpublished manuscript, University of California at Irvine.

Kogan, N., & Wallach, M. A. (1964). *Risk taking: A study in copgnition and personality.* New York: Holt, Rinehart & Winston.

Kogan, N., & Wallach, M. A. (1967). Effects of physical separation of group decision-makers upon group risk taking. *Human Relations, 20*, 41–49.

Kraemer, K. L. (1981). *Telecommunications-transportation substitution and energy productivity: A re-examination.* Paris: Directorate of Science, Technology and Industry, Organization for Economic Cooperation and Development.

Krauss, R. M., Apple, W., Morencz, N., Wenzel, C., & Winton, W. (1981). Verbal, vocal, and visible factors in judgments of another's affect. *Journal of Personality and Social Psychology, 40*, 312–320.

Kraut, R. E., & Lewis, S. H. (in press). Some functions of feedback in conversation. In H. Applegate & J. Sypher (Eds.), *Understanding interpersonal communication: Social, cognitive, and strategic processes in children and adults.* Beverly Hills, CA: Sage.

Kraut, R. E., Lewis, S. H., & Swezey, L. W. (1982). Listener responsiveness and the coordination of conversation. *Journal of Personality and Social Psychology, 43*, 718–731.

Krueger, G. P. (1976). *Teleconferencing in the communication modes as a function of the number of conferees.* Unpublished doctoral dissertation, Johns Hopkins University, Baltimore, MD.

Lamm, H., & Kogan, N. (1970). Risk-taking in the context of intergroup negotiations. *Journal of Experimental Social Psychology, 6*, 351–363.

Lancaster, F. W. (1978). *Toward paperless information systems.* New York: Academic Press.

Lepper, M. R. (1982, August). *Microcomputers in education: Motivational and social issues.* Paper presented at the 90th annual convention of the American Psychological Association, Washington, DC.

Licklider, J. C. R., & Vezza, A. (1978). Applications of information networks. *Proceedings of the IEEE, 66*, 1330–1346.

Linstone, H. A., & Turoff, M. (Eds.). (1975). *The Delphi method: Techniques and applications.* Reading, MA: Addison-Wesley.

Maddox, W. (1982). *Computer communication in the Carnegie-Mellon University Spice Project*. Unpublished report, Carnegie-Mellon University, Pittsburgh, PA.

March, J. G., & Olsen, J. P. (1976). *Ambiguity and choice in organizations*. Bergen, Norway: Universitetsforiaget.

Martino, J. P. (1972). *Technological forecasting for decisionmaking*. New York: American Elsevier.

McArthur, L. Z., & Solomon, L. K. (1978). Perceptions of an aggressive encounter as a function of the victim's salience and the perceiver's arousal. *Journal of Personality and Social Psychology, 36*, 1278–1290.

Mehrabian, A. (1972). *Nonverbal communication*. Chicago: Aldine.

Morley, L. E., & Stephenson, G. M. (1969). Interpersonal and interparty exchange: A laboratory simulation of an industrial negotiation at the plant level. *British Journal of Psychology, 60*, 543–545.

Morley, L. E., & Stephenson, G. M. (1970). Formality in experimental negotiations: A validation study. *British Journal of Psychology, 61*, 383–384.

Party-line plea. (1981, January). *Time*, p. 49.

Patterson, M. L. (1982). A sequential functional model of nonverbal exchange. *Psychological Review, 89*, 231–249.

Payne, J. W., & Laughhunn, D. J. (in press). Multiattribute risky choice behavior: The editing of complex prospects. *Management Science*.

Pollack, A. (1982, May 27). Technology: Conference by computer. *New York Times*, p. D2.

Prentice-Dunn, S., & Rogers, R. W. (1980). Effects of deindividuating situational cues and aggressive models on subjective deindividuation and aggression. *Journal of Personality and Social Psychology, 39*, 104–113.

Price, C. R. (1975). Conferencing via computer: Cost effective communication for the era of forced choice. In H. A. Linstone & M. Turoff (Eds.), *The Delphi method: Techniques and applications* (pp. 497–516). Reading, MA: Addison-Wesley.

Pruitt, D. G., & Lewis, S. A. (1975). Development of integrative solutions in bilateral negotiations. *Journal of Personality and Social Psychology, 31*, 621–633.

Pye, R., & Williams, E. (1977). Teleconferencing: Is video valuable or is audio adequate? *Telecommunications Policy, 1*, 230–241.

Rice, R. E., & Case, D. (1982, May). Electronic messaging in the university organization. *Psychological Bulletin, 94*, 239–264.

Salancik, G. R. (1977). Commitment and the control of organizational behavior and belief. In B. M. Staw & G. R. Salacik (Eds.), *New directions in organizational behavior* (pp. 1–54). Chicago: St. Clair Press.

Sanders, G., & Baron, R. S. (1977). Is social comparison irrelevant for producing choice shifts? *Journal of Experimental Social Psychology, 13*, 303–314.

Scheier, M. F. (1976). Self-awareness, self-consciousness, and angry aggression. *Journal of Personality, 44*, 627–644.

Scheier, M. F., & Carver, C. S. (1977). Self-focused attention and the experience of emotion: Attraction, repulsion, elation, and depression. *Journal of Personality and Social Psychology, 35*, 625–636.

Scheier, M. F., Carver, C. S., & Gibbons, F. X. (1981). Self-focused attention and reactions to fear. *Journal of Research in Personality, 15*, 1–15.

Scherer, S. E. (1974). Influence of proximity and eye contact on impression formation. *Perceptual and Motor Skills, 38*, 538.

Short, J., Williams, E., & Christie, B. (1976). *The social psychology of telecommunications*. Longon: John Wiley & Sons.

Siegel, J., Dubrovsky, V., Kiesler, S., & McGuire, T. (1983). *Group processes in computer-mediated communications*. Manuscript submitted for publication.

Sinaiko, H. W. (1963). *Teleconferencing: Preliminary experiments*. (Research Paper P-108). Arlington, VA: Institute for Defense Analyses.

Sproull, L., Kiesler, S., & Zubrow, D. (in press). Encountering the alien culture. *Social Issues*.

Stasser, G., & Davis, J. H. (1981). Group decision making and social influence: A social interaction sequence model. *Psychological Review, 88*, 523–551.

Stockton, W. (1981, June 28). The technology race. *New York Times Magazine*, p. 14.

Stoner, J. (1961). *A comparison of individual and group decisions including risk*. Unpublished master's thesis. School of Industrial Management, Massachusetts Institute of Technology.

Strickland, L. H., Guild, P. D., Barefoot, J. R., & Patterson, S. A. (1975). *Teleconferencing and leadership emergence*. Unpublished manuscript, Carleton University, Ottawa, Canada.

Tapscott, D. (1982, March). Investigating the electronic office. *Datamation*, pp. 130–138.

Turoff, M. (1982). Interface design in computerized conferencing systems. In *NYU Symposium on User Interfaces*. New York: New York University, Graduate School of Business Administration, Computer Applications and Information Systems.

Tversky, A., & Kahneman, D. (1981). The framing of decisions and the psychology of choice. *Science, 211*, 453–458.

U.S. Department of Commerce. (1977). *Computers in the federal government: A compilation of statistics.* Washington, DC: U.S. Government Printing Office.

Vallee, J., Johansen, R., Lipinski, H., & Wilson, T. (1977). *Group communication through computers* (Vol. 4). Menlo Park, CA: Institute for the Future.

Vinokur, A., & Burnstein, E. (1974). The effects of partially shared persuasive arguments in group-induced shifts: A group problem-solving approach. *Journal of Personality and Social Psychology, 29*, 305–315.

Vinokur, A., & Burnstein, E. (1978). Novel argumentation and attitude change: The case of polarization following group discussion. *European Journal of Social Psychology, 8*, 335–348.

Wang Corporation. (1982). *Concepts.* Lowell, MA: Author.

Weeks, G. D., & Chapanis, A. (1976). Cooperative versus conflictive problem-solving in three telecommunication modes. *Perceptual and Motor Skills, 42*, 879–917.

Weis, J. F., Jr. (1983). Electronic mail. *Judges' Journal, 22*(3).

Welsch, L. A. (1982). Using electronic mail as a teaching tool. *Communications of the ACM, 23*, 105–108.

Whisler, T. L. (1970). *The impact of computers on organizations.* New York: Praeger.

Williams, E. (1973a). *Final report* (Reference No. P/73273/EL). (Available from Communications Studies Group, Wates House, 22 Gordon Street, London WC1H 0QB, England).

Williams, E. (1973b). *The scope of person-to-person telecommunications in government and business* (Reference No. P/73272/EL). (Available from Communications Studies Group, Wates House, 22 Gordon Street, London WC1H 0QB, England).

Williams, E. (1975a). *The effectiveness of person-to-person telecommunications systems research at the Communications Studies Group* (University College, Long Range Research Report 3, Reference No. LRRR 003/1TF). (Available from Communications Studies Group, Wates House, 22 Gordon Street, London WC1H 0QB, England).

Williams, E. (1975b). Medium or message: Communications medium as a determinant of interpersonal evaluation. *Sociometry, 38*, 963–976.

Williams, K., Harkins, S., & Latane, B. (1981). Identifiability as a deterrent to social loafing: Two cheering experiments. *Journal of Personality and Social Psychology, 40*, 310–311.

Zajonc, R. (1965). Social facilitation. *Science, 149*, 269–274.

Zajonc, R. (1969). Group risk-taking in a two-choice situation: Replication, extension, and a model. *Journal of Experimental Social Psychology, 5*, 127–140.

Zillman, D., Bryant, J., Cantor, J. R., & Day, K. D. (1975). Irrelevance of mitigating circumstances in retaliatory behavior at high levels of excitation. *Journal of Research in Personality, 9*, 282–293.

25

Reducing Social Context Cues: Electronic Mail in Organizational Communication

Lee Sproull
Sara Kiesler
College of Humanities and Social Sciences
Carnegie-Mellon University
Pittsburgh, PA

1 Introduction

The boss is always the last one to know. This aphorism summarizes both what is right and what is wrong about communication in organizations. The unequal distribution of information promotes organizational efficiency by shielding decision makers from unnecessary information (e.g., O'Reilly 1980). But it can also lead to organizational disaster by separating decision makers from information they need to know (Allison 1971; Shlaim 1976; Wohlstetter 1962). Who has what information is a perennially important organizational question.

The purpose of this paper is to investigate how a new communication technology—electronic mail—affects who has what information in organizations. Most analyses of electronic mail view it simply as an information accelerator, a tool that reduces the amount of time it takes for people to get information they otherwise would have received more slowly. For instance managers in Digital Equipment Corporation reported that electronic mail increased the speed of their decision making and saved them about seven hours a week (Crawford 1982, pp. 3–4). Managers at Manufacturers Hanover Trust reported that electronic mail saved them about three hours a week, mostly by eliminating unreturned phone calls and internal correspondence (Nyce and Groppa 1983, p. 65). Speeding up the flow of existing information may be sufficient justification for using electronic mail. But we believe that electronic mail may do more than speed up information exchange. It may also alter the distribution of information in organizations, that is, it may change who has what information. This paper investigates one way that electronic mail may change patterns of information distribution in organizations. It uses research on how social context cues regulate communication to predict how information exchange in electronic mail will differ from information exchange in other media.

§2 describes the basic features of electronic mail. §3 suggests how features of electronic mail are likely to diminish commonly available social context cues and predicts how reduced social context cues are likely to affect communication behavior. §§4 and 5 describe the methods and results of an empirical study of electronic mail communication in two divisions of a Fortune 500 company. §6 discusses some of the implications of our findings for organizational management.

2 What Is Electronic Mail?

In this section we describe the basic features of electronic mail and its characteristic implementations.

An electronic mail system (EMS) uses computer text-processing and communication tools to provide a high speed information exchange service. Anyone with a computer account can create and send information to anyone who has a mailbox on that computer or on any other computer to which it is connected through a computer network. The networked computers might be physically proximate and connected via a local area network, or they might be in different states, countries, or continents, and connected via long distance telecommunications.[1] Depending upon software sophistication, the mailed information can be

---

[1] Electronic mail services can be operated by an organization for its members or by a third party for extra-organizational traffic. Current commercially-available third party systems include The Source, Compuserve, and MCI Mail. The first large-scale computer communications network—the ARPANET—was begun in 1966 by the Department of Defense. It was designed to allow computer scientists at many locations to use special computing resources operating at only one location. Remote computers could log in to the special machine by using the communications network. It soon became evident that most

a message, a document, a computer program, statistical data, or even a collection of organized messages—a computer discussion—forwarded from some other mailbox. At the recipient's convenience, he can read the information, edit it, save it, delete it, move it to another computer file, forward it to other people, combine it with other computer mail, and/or reply to the sender.

The fundamental process of electronic mail, moving text from one computer mailbox to another, has three general characteristics. First, it is *asynchronous* or nonsimultaneous. That is, like memos or postal mail but unlike conversations, senders and receivers do not attend to the same communication simultaneously.[2] Second, it is *fast*. Unlike paper-based communication, electronic mail can be transmitted in seconds or minutes down a hall or across a continent. Replies can flow back just as rapidly. Third, it is *text-based*. Unlike facsimile or telephone, electronic mail has no picture or sound components. Messages can be conveyed only through text.

The general process of moving text from one mailbox to another can be implemented in a variety of ways. Currently the most common are mail, bulletin boards, and conferences. Some organizations use all three of these implementations, but the most common is mail. Mail systems transmit information to individually-addressed people, whereas bulletin boards and conferences transmit information to a named electronic location that is accessible to more than one person (e.g., "Science Fiction Lovers," "Macintosh Users"). Bulletin boards and conferences differ in that bulletin boards display messages chronologically as they are received; conferences group messages by topic and display grouped messages together (see Rice 1980, for a review of conferencing).

Within any general implementation, equipment, software, and organizational policy choices can create very different systems. The kind of i/o device is an important equipment choice. In some systems, people use hard copy terminals, like teletype terminals, for typing out sent and received information on paper. But most systems today are based on

---

of the traffic over the ARPANET was not machine to machine, but rather was researcher to researcher, using EMS (Licklider and Vezza 1978, p. 1331). Indeed the ARPANET helped form entire communities composed of researchers at various locations around the country who exchange papers, ideas, computer programs, gossip, restaurant reviews, and all forms of messages. Today the ARPANET has hundreds of thousands of users at over 1300 locations. Corporations have also begun using EMS for internal communications. The Manufacturers Hanover Trust network has over 3000 users (Nyce and Groppa 1983); the Digital Equipment Corporation network has over 6000 (Crawford 1982). Other corporations using EMS include AT&T, Bank of America, Hewlett-Packard, IBM, Westinghouse, Xerox, 3M, and Peat Marwick and Mitchell.

[2]   There are electronic communication programs for simultaneous communication. They are worthy of study in their own right but are not included in the domain of this paper which focuses on asynchronous communication.

video terminals, which display on a screen the information that people are typing or reading. An important software choice for mail implementations is presence or absence of a group mail facility. Some systems make it possible to send information only to individual recipients; others make it possible to send to groups of people via a distribution list mechanism. With this mechanism a sender sends one message to a group name, then the computer automatically sends a copy of the message to everyone belonging to the group. Most mail systems today have a group mail feature. Another important software choice is the extent to which people can edit and transmit "messages" of any length and style. Flexible message format makes it possible to exchange documents, computer programs, personal notes, and official announcements within the same medium. An important policy choice is how many people share a terminal. If many people share a single terminal, then the time-to-receipt of a sent message can become much longer than the real transmission time. At the extreme, if an entire building has only one terminal then people might have to make appointments to read their mail, or all mail might have to be printed and physically placed in people's office mailboxes once a day. Electronic mail systems are used most heavily by people who have a terminal on their desk. And, as the cost of computing continues to drop, the resulting trend is for more people to have good access to EMS.[3]

The organization we studied uses a sophisticated mail system, including video terminals, group distribution lists, and easy access. Henceforth our discussion assumes this type of system.

3 Social Context and Information Exchange

However sophisticated the communication system, information in organizations does not flow in a vacuum. Senders and receivers are situated within a social context that regulates or influences communication contact (who exchanges information with whom) and communication content (what information is communicated). Three kinds of variables contribute significantly to the social context: geographic, organizational, and situational variables. In this section we discuss variables in each category that influence communication.

---

[3] All is not rosy. There are potential serious problems with electronic mail including cost, privacy, security, and authentication of messages. These topics deserve attention in their own right; we cannot do them justice in this paper.

3.1 *What Social Context Variables Are Important?*

Geographic location, defined as a person's physical position in time and space, constrains the opportunity to communicate using some media, but not others. In order for people to communicate face to face, they must be in the same geographic location. Communication by telephone can occur across all geographic distances but large time zone differences constrain routine telephone contact. Hard copy communication (e.g., postal mail and interoffice memos) is constrained neither by geographic distance nor by time zones, but it is slow. Distance sometimes affects communication content as well as contact, independent of any other variables (Barnlund and Harland 1963; Baum and Valins 1977).

Organizational position is defined as a person's location in an organizational department, hierarchy, and job category. Like geographic distance, organizational distance also predicts communication contact and content independent of any other variables (O'Reilly and Roberts 1974; Tushman and Romanelli 1983). Information is more often exchanged within than across organizational units, chains of command, and job categories.

Situational variables describe features of the immediate communication situation, such as the relationships among senders and receivers, the topic of the communication, and the norms or social conventions appropriate to the situation. For instance, when senders and receivers have the same sex, race, and age, they contribute information more equally and their information is more equally valued than when they are dissimilar on these variables (Cohen and Roper 1972; Kanter 1977; Watson 1982).[4] The emotional compatibility and trust between senders and receivers also affects the content of what is communicated (O'Reilly and Roberts 1974). So does the topic of a communication. For example, people prefer not to communicate bad news (Rosen and Tesser 1970). Norms in the communication setting also influence what is communicated to whom. Some norms are relatively stable across organizations: for instance, be polite to your boss, don't reveal personal information to people you don't know well, lead the discussion if you are the highest status person in the room. Other norms vary across organizations, as recent case studies of organizational culture suggest (e.g., Kidder 1981; Wright 1979); for example, who should come to meetings, how candid should discussion be.

---

[4]   Most work investigating these variables has been conducted in face-to-face settings; some might wonder if they are irrelevant in hard copy communication. But some studies have demonstrated that the same written material is evaluated more highly when people think it is written by men than when they think it is written by women (Feldman-Summers and Kiesler 1974).

3.2 *How Does Social Context Affect Information Exchange?*

Social context influences information exchange through perception, cognitive interpretation, and communication behavior. (Figure 25.1 summarizes the process.) First, senders and receivers must perceive the social context of the communication. Social context barriers, such as status differences, will not constrain communication if senders and receivers are unaware of them. It is not sufficient for people simply to hold different positions; they must be aware of the fact that they do. Even the effects of geographic location are conditioned partially by perception because location covaries with situational variables, especially norms. Thus, although a person may have the technical capability to communicate with a business associate at any hour of the day or night via telephone, knowing that the associate is at home and it is evening or a weekend often deters communication. Communicators perceive the social context of a communication through both static and dynamic cues. Static cues emanate from peoples' appearance and artifacts such as a clock, a private office, a big desk, and a personal secretary. Dynamic cues emanate from peoples' nonverbal behavior which changes over the course of an interaction—for instance, nodding approval and frowning with displeasure.

Once people perceive social context cues, these cues can create or elicit cognitive interpretations and concomitant emotional states. People adjust the target, the tone and verbal content of their communications in response to their definition and interpretation of the situation. Typically, when social context cues are strong, behavior tends to be relatively other-focused, differentiated, and controlled. When social context cues are weak, people's feelings of anonymity tend to produce relatively self-centered and unregulated behavior. That is, people become relatively unconcerned with making a good appearance (Cottrell, Wack, Sekerak, and Rittle 1968). Their behavior becomes more extreme, more impulsive, and less socially differentiated (Diener, Fraser, Beamon, and Kelem 1976; Singer, Brush, and Lublin 1965).

All communications media attenuate to at least some degree the social context cues available in face-to-face conversation. The telephone reduces dynamic and static cues by eliminating visual information about communicators. Letters and memos reduce static cues by imposing standardized format conventions; they eliminate dynamic cues altogether. The relatively low level of social context cues in letters and memoranda can produce communication that is less well-regulated than face-to-face communication. In practice, we do not experience frequent unregulated paper communication because the social context cues attached to paper itself signal norms that paper communication not be used as a substi-

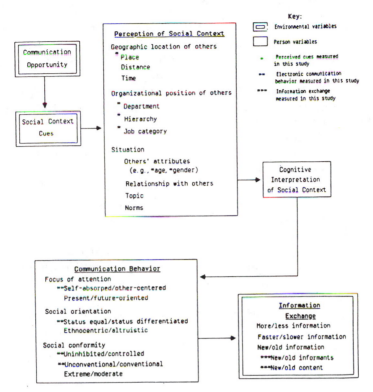

Figure 25.1 Theoretical framework for how social context information affects information exchange.

tute for conversation and discussion (Siegel 1985). But in experimental comparisons, paper questionnaires elicited more antisocial opinions and more personal revelations than face-to-face interviews did (Sudman and Bradburn 1974). Written notes elicited more swings of opinion in groups than face-to-face discussions did (Festinger 1950, p. 176).

3.3 *Electronic Mail and Social Context Cues*

Electronic mail is likely to greatly attenuate social context cues. Dynamic cues are eliminated; static cues are minimal. When information is sent via EMS, the only signs of organizational position and personal similarity for senders and receivers are names and addresses: missing are all indications of senders' and receivers' job title, level of the hierarchy, departmental affiliation, race, age, and appearance. Unless first names are used as well as last names, gender information is also missing. Furthermore, a situational definition is missing. When using EMS one does not expect or encounter reminders of the situation in which the communication is generated or received and interpreted, as one does using other communication technologies. Corporate memos, for example, are generated and read in some settings but not others, by some people and not others, and are about some topics but not others. The absence of situational cues is important in EMS because EMS can be used to exchange so many different kinds of information, from cafeteria menus to corporate strategy documents to love notes, all of which are conveyed within the same message format. People make announcements and suggestions using EMS, just as they do using paper memos, but people also carry on conversations, discussions, and exchanges of affection using EMS, just as they do in face-to-face and telephone conversations. Of course, people may possess knowledge of relevant social context information from other sources. But there are few cues in the EMS situation to evoke that knowledge.

There has been a small amount of experimental research on how electronic mail affects communication. In comparison with face-to-face groups, groups that communicated electronically had more antisocial behavior and made more extreme decisions (Siegel, Dubrovsky, Kiesler, and McGuire 1985). In comparison with paper and pencil responses, responses to an electronic mail questionnaire were more extreme, more revealing, and less socially desirable (Kiesler and Sproull 1986; Sproull 1986). But as far as we know, the processes described above and supported in experimental studies have not been investigated in ongoing formal organizations.[5]

3.4 Hypotheses

We propose five hypotheses about communication behavior in organizations when social context cues are weak or absent, which address the communication behavior described in Figure 25.1. Although these are not the only hypotheses about electronic mail to investigate, we believe they exemplify ways in which EMS can alter who has what information in organizations.

1.   Social context cues are relatively weak in electronic mail

    1a.   Messages from unknown senders will not reveal cues about their geographic location, organizational department, hierarchical position, job category, age, or sex.

---

[5]   Computer conferences have been the focus of research. But these studies have looked at extraorganizational conferences, whose participants have come from many different organizations (e.g., Rice 1982; Rice and Barnett 1986).

2. EMS behavior is relatively self-absorbed

2a. People focus more on themselves than on others in the social frame (salutation and closing) of EMS communications

2b. People overestimate their own contribution to EMS communications

2c. People underestimate the messages they receive as a consequence of group membership.

3. EMS behavior is relatively undifferentiated by status

3a. Messages from superiors look the same as messages from subordinates

3b. Messages to managers look the same as messages to nonmanagers

3c. People will more prefer to use EMS to send messages to superiors than they will to subordinates.

4. EMS behavior is relatively uninhibited and nonconforming

4a. People behave irresponsibly more often in EMS than they do in face-to-face conversations

4b. People violate the norm against sending bad news more with EMS than with other media

4c. People violate the norm against nonwork communication during the workday more with electronic mail than with other media

4d. People violate the norm against work communication at home more with electronic mail than with other media.

5. EMS provides new information, not just a faster way to receive old information

5a. EMS provides new information from new respondents

5b. EMS provides new information from old respondents.

4 Research Design

4.1 Overview

This research investigates EMS behavior in an ongoing formal organization. Ideally such research would be conducted in organizations that have used electronic mail for some time, so that any identified effects would not be attributable merely to initial reactions to a new technology. It would investigate use by people of different statuses, since status information is an important component of social context in communication situations. And it would compare communication behavior across media, since many of the hypothesized effects are relative to other media. The research reported here does examine behavior in an organization that has used electronic mail for a long time. It examines behavior for people of different statuses. It examines the contents of actual electronic messages, but relies on self-reports to compare electronic communication behavior with that using other media. Comparing actual communications from other media would be preferable but was not feasible.

In §3 we postulated a three-element process for how social context affects communication behavior: perception of social context cues, cognitive interpretation, and communication behaviors. We actually investigated the first and third of these elements, but not the second because cognitive states are extremely difficult to measure retrospectively. To investigate the first element, perception of social context cues, we measured respondents' knowledge of a set of social context cues about others: geographic location, organizational department, hierarchical position, job, age, and gender. (See Figure 25.1.) For a sample of messages, we asked senders if they were aware of this information about their receivers and we asked receivers if they were aware of this information about their senders. We investigated the third element by analyzing messages for self-absorbed behavior, status differentiation, and norm violations.

4.2 Sample

We collected data from EMS users in units of two divisions of a Fortune 500 office equipment firm employing over 100,000 people, with assets of over $7.5 billion, and 1982 sales of over $8 billion. The two divisions—R&D and Business Products—were the corporation's most extensive users of electronic mail. At the time of data collection in the late spring of 1983, the research unit employed 312 people organized into an administrative unit and 7 research laboratories. The product development unit employed 291 people.

The mail system used by this corporation supported over 3700 users and handled over 8000 messages each day, many of which were sent to multiple (sometimes hundreds of) people. The system provided good tools for editing mail, storing it, and forwarding it to others. It also provided good and extensively-used software for sending mail to groups of people via distribution lists. All the people in the units we studied used video terminals for input and output and most of them processed their own mail directly.

All EMS users ($n = 513$) were stratified on employment level (technical/clerical, professional, managerial) and gender, resulting in six strata. Each stratum containing at least 5% of the entire unit's population was sampled. Female managers, who represent less than 5% of each unit's population, were not sampled. A 10-person sample was drawn from each stratum in the research unit. In the product development unit 10-person samples were drawn when possible; census samples were drawn from strata with fewer than ten members. Out of the original 98-person sample, 11 were no longer employed by the company or were out of the country, 2 did not use EMS, and 4 declined to participate. Replacements were drawn for all nonparticipants, except in the case of census strata, resulting in a final sample of 96 people.

4.3 *Data Collection and Instruments*

Data were collected during an eight-week period in the spring of 1983 by interview, questionnaire, and content coding of actual mail. Every participant saved a hard copy of every message sent or received for the three days prior to a scheduled interview. During the interview the respondent was asked ten open-ended questions about each of 15 or fewer messages from the previous workday (henceforth, the focal messages). If the respondent had 15 or fewer messages, the questions were asked for each message. If the respondent had more than 15 messages, a random sample of 15 was used. Then the respondent filled out a separate 13-item partner characteristics sheet for each focal message partner while the interviewer recorded attributes of each focal message on a coding sheet. The respondent also filled out an 80-item fixed-response questionnaire about general EMS attitudes and behaviors. In summary, the data set contains self-reports about attributes of specific messages (from interview questions about the nature of each focal message and characteristics questions about each focal message partner), data on actual attributes of specific messages (recorded or coded directly from the focal messages themselves), and self-reports about general electronic mail behavior and attitudes (from the questionnaire).

4.4 *Measures and Analyses*

The general analysis strategy was to use actual message attributes to examine internal characteristics of electronic mail behavior and to use questionnaire date to examine perceived differences in behavior across different communications media. Respondent data were weighted by the appropriate stratum proportion; message data were weighted by the total number of messages per respondent, then by the appropriate stratum proportion (Cochran 1963; pp. 87–153). Questionnaire responses and message characteristics were compared using correlated t-tests or repeated measures analysis of variance.

4.4.1 *Message Attributes* Eight attributes characterized the messages: length, opening, closing, positive affect, negative affect, politeness, energy, and topic. Length was coded as the number of lines in the message text. Opening was coded as the number of words in the salutation; closing was the number of words in the closing. Positive affect was coded as the number of words or simple phrases expressing positive sentiment (such as "wonderful," "I love it"). Negative affect was coded as the number of words or simple phrases expressing negative sentiment (such as "terrible," "this is garbage"). Politeness was coded as the number of words or simple phrases expressing courtesy or etiquette (such as "please," "I would be grateful if...￼"). Energy was coded as the number of instances of typographic extremes, marked by exclamation points and words typed in all capital letters. The topic of each message was coded as either work or nonwork.[6]   Coding of these attributes was performed by two independent coders resulting in an overall agreement rate of 97%, ranging from a low of 83% for positive affect to a high of 100% for length. We constructed an index of message uninhibition (UMI) by adding together the number of instances of negative affect, energy, and overly long messages (ones at least two standard deviations greater than the mean length) and subtracting the number of positive affect and politeness instances. The UMI ranges from 0 to 29 with a mean of 8.1 (s.d. = 2.2).

4.4.2 *Partner Attributes* Seven attributes characterized the message partner for each focal message: geographic location, departmental location, hierarchical position, job category, age, gender, and how well the partner is known by the respondent (0 = not at all, 5 = very well). Each of these items was provided by the respondent for each message partner and was translated directly into numerical form for analysis. We constructed an index of perception of social context cues (SCI) for each message by adding together each of the first six attributes for which the

---

[6]   The topic is coded work if it has anything at all to do with the corporation, its employees, or their activities. This is an extremely liberal interpretation of "work." It includes, for example, messages announcing the week's menu in the company cafeteria and scores from the company softball games as well as laboratory reports, personnel announcements, and technical arguments. Examples of nonwork messages are movie reviews, requests for babysitters, and advice on where to find a second mortgage.

respondent had information. The SCI index ranges from 0 to 6, with a mean of 3.7 (s.d. = 2.1).

4.4.3 *Absorption Effects*

We used multiple measures to increase the reliability of measurement. This is particularly important in this case because our operationalizations are based on artifacts (messages) and self-report (questionnaires), hence are indirect measures of absorption. We used three indicators of absorption: the length of message salutations and closings, the difference between questionnaire estimates of total message volume and the actual message volume (computed from the average of the three days' worth of saved messages), and the difference between questionnaire estimates of group message volume and the actual group message volume. Because reminders of the presence of other people are relatively weak in EMS, people should focus relatively strongly on themselves and on what they want to say and less strongly on their audience. One indicator of this is that people dispense with direct acknowledgements of the other person, that is, salutations. Another indicator of this is that people are more likely to use a closing (i.e., the author's name) than a salutation (other's name). The total number of words in both salutations and closings is an indicator of the total attention paid by the sender to the social relationship. The number of words in the closing compared to the number in the salutation is an indicator of the relative focus on the self. The length of message openings and closings were compared using correlated *t*-tests. Another indicator of self-absorption is people's estimates of their behavior compared with their actual behavior; estimates larger than actual indicate relative self-absorption. Questionnaire estimates of message volume were compared with the actual volume using *t*-tests for the difference in proportions. Questionnaire estimates of group messages were compared with the actual number of group messages similarly. (In this case, estimates *lower* than actual indicate relative self-absorption.)

4.4.4 *Status Equalization Effects*

We compared message presentation for messages from partners subordinate to the respondent with those from partners superior to the respondent. In this analysis, we analyzed sent messages separately from received messages to preserve the directionality of hierarchy. (If we had looked at all messages together we would not have known if "partner's hierarchical status" characterized a sender or a receiver.) We also analyzed questionnaire responses to hypothetical tasks entailing communication up or down the hierarchy. People were asked to indicate what medium (face-to-face, EMS, telephone, or hardcopy mail) they would use to carry out four such tasks: asking your boss (secretary) to solve a problem, and negotiating with your boss (secretary) for more resources for a task you are working on. We assumed face-to-face is the norm for all four tasks. Responses were analyzed using repeated measures analysis of variance with medium and direction of communication as within-subjects variables.

4.4.5 Uninhibited Behavior   Because reminders of the presence of other people and of social norms are relatively weak in EMS, communication behavior should be relatively uninhibited. We used three indicators of uninhibited behavior from the questionnaire. People were asked how many times they saw flaming[7] in their electronic mail and in their conversations. Responses were compared using correlated t-tests. People were asked about six tasks related to communicating good or bad news: telling your secretary she had gotten a large (no) raise; providing an enthusiastic (half-hearted) recommendation for a colleague; providing compliments (criticisms) about a colleague's work. We assumed that face-to-face was the preferred medium and that communicating bad news was less normative than communicating good news. Responses were analyzed using repeated measures analysis of variance with medium and nature of news as within-subjects variables. A third indicator of uninhibited behavior compared questionnaire responses on the frequency of using EMS and telephone for nonwork messages at the office and for work messages at home. We assumed that nonwork messages at the office were less normative and work messages at home were less normative.

5 Findings

Table 1 describes the sample. The mean age of respondents is 36.5. On average, respondents have a college education, have worked for the PHC for 4.8 years, and have used EMS for 4.6 years. Twenty-five percent of them are in business or support positions. There are no differences between the two divisions on any of these characteristics. Men, in comparison with women, are better educated, have been in the organization longer, and are more likely to be in scientific and technical positions. Managers are older and have been in the organization longer; nonexempts have less education and are more likely to be in business and support positions.

---

[7]   "Flaming," a term coined by the hacker community, means to "speak rabidly or incessantly on an uninteresting topic or with a patently ridiculous attitude" (Steele et al. 1983).

Table 1 Sample Characteristics

Entire Sample ($n = 96$)	
	Mean Response
Characteristic	
Age	36.5
Education (2 = some college, 3 = college degree, 4 = graduate work, 5 = professional degree, 6 = Ph. D.)	3.5
Job Category (1 = scientific/technical, 2 = business/support)	1.25
Years in organization	4.8
Years using EMS	4.6
Sample Differences By Organization			
	Research ($n = 50$)	Prod. Dev. ($n = 46$)	*p*-value of *t*-statistic
Characteristic			
Age	37.3	35.7	n.s.
Education	3.6	3.4	n.s.
Job Category	1.2	1.3	n.s.
Years in organization	5.4	4.2	n.s.
Years using EMS	4.4	4.8	n.s.
Sample Differences By Gender			
	Male ($n = 58$)	Female ($n = 38$)	*p*-value of *t*-statistic
Characteristic			
Age	37.8	34.6	n.s.
Education	4.0	2.8	<0.01
Job Category	1.1	1.5	<0.01
Years in organization	5.6	3.6	<0.01
Years using EMS	4.9	4.1	n.s.
Sample Differences By Hierarchy			
	Mgrs. ($n = 21$)	Profs. ($n = 40$)	Non-exempt ($n = 35$)	*p*-value of *F*-ratio
Characteristic				
Age	43	34	35	<0.01
Education	5.0	4.1	1.9	<0.01
Job Category	1.2	1.1	1.4	<0.01
Years in organization	6.9	4.3	4.1	<0.01
Years using EMS	5.6	5.2	3.3	<0.01

5.1 *The Electronic Community*

Table 2 affirms that PHC does represent a well-established electronic community. On average PHC's policies and procedures made it very easy to use EMS; people found the program itself easy to use; they and their work colleagues had good access to EMS terminals; they used EMS quite extensively. People sent and received an average of 26 messages a day. Table 2 also displays differences in electronic community characteristics by group (division, sex, and hierarchy). There were no gender or hierarchy differences in EMS accessibility or volume of messages, suggesting that EMS had widely permeated the entire organization. The two organizations differed in EMS accessibility, although in both cases accessibility was relatively high. The biggest difference was that the product development organization had more message traffic than did the R&D organization—an average of 31 messages a day per person in the product development organization compared with 20 messages a day per person in the R&D organization.

Table 3 describes characteristics of message presentation and message partner attributes. Messages ranged in length from 0 lines to 1200 lines; in number of opening words from 0 to 9; in number of closing words from 0 to 5. They ranged in number of instances of positive affect from 0 to 15; in number of instances of negative affect from 0 to 12; in number of instances of politeness from 0 to 9; in number of instances of energy from 0 to 14. 60% of the messages were about work topics. The average age of message partners was 34.3; for message partners whose gender was known by the respondent, 71% of them were male. For received messages, 11% of the partners were subordinates, 17% were peers, 9% were superiors, and 63% were outside the chain of command. 52% of the received messages were from partners not known by the respondent. Eighty-six percent of the received messages were sent to more than one person, almost always via a distribution list.

5.2 *Reduced Social Context Information*

The SCI is our measure of social context information. When partners are known, awareness of social context information can come from many sources. When partners are unknown, the message itself is one of the very few available sources of such information. The mean SCI for messages whose partners were known was 5.2; the mean SCI for messages whose partners were unknown was 2.0 ($t = 40.11$, $p < 0.01$). The major mechanism for communicating with unknown partners is via group messages; 97% of all messages whose partner was unknown were group messages.

Table 2   Organizational Characteristics

Overall Characteristics ($n = 96$)			
			Mean Response
EMS Accessibility			
Organizational ease of use (1 = very easy, 5 = very hard)			1.2
Program ease of use (1 = very easy, 5 = very hard)			1.4
Office Access (% with terminal in own office)			85%
Colleague's access (% of work partners with terminal in own office)			87%
Messages			
Total daily			25.6
Sent			2.0
Received			23.6

Differences By Organization			
	Research ($n = 50$)	Prod. Dev. ($n = 46$)	p-value of t-statistic
EMS Accessibility			
Org. ease of use	1.4	1.0	<0.01
Program ease of use	1.6	1.2	<0.01
Office access	72%	99%	<0.01
Colleagues' access	77%	97%	<0.01
Messages			
Total Daily	19.8	31.4	<0.01
Sent	1.5	2.4	<0.01
Received	18.3	29.0	<0.01

Differences By Gender			
	Male ($n = 58$)	Female ($n = 38$)	p-value of t-statistic
EMS Accessibility			
Org. ease of use	1.2	1.2	n.s.
Program ease of use	1.4	1.2	n.s.
Office access	86%	82%	n.s.
Colleagues' access	89%	83%	n.s.
Messages			
Total Daily	26.6	22.5	n.s.
Sent	2.0	2.0	n.s.
Received	24.6	20.5	n.s.

Differences By Hierarchy			
	Mgrs. ($n = 21$)	Profs. ($n = 40$)	Non-exempt ($n = 35$)	p-value of F-ratio
EMS Accessibility				
Org. ease of use	1.0	1.2	1.3	n.s.
Program ease of use	1.4	1.4	1.3	n.s.
Office access	95%	82%	93%	n.s.
Colleagues' access	85%	87%	89%	n.s.
Messages				
Total Daily	23.0	27.2	19.6	n.s.
Sent	2.4	2.0	1.6	n.s.
Received	20.6	25.2	18.0	n.s.

Note: The data for each sampling stratum are weighted to reflect its proportion of the organization as a whole.

Table 3   Organizational Message Characteristics

All Messages ($n = 1248$)	
	Mean Characteristic
Message presentation	
Length (in lines)	12.6
Opening (number of words)	0.31
Closing (number of words)	0.94
Positive affect (number of instances)	0.52
Negative affect (number of instances)	0.15
Politeness (number of instances)	0.46
Energy (number of instances)	0.48
Topic (0 = nonwork; 1 = work)	0.60
Partner attributes	
Age	34.3
Job title (1 = scientific or technical;	
2 = business or support)	1.2
Sex (0 = male; 1 = female)	0.29
Hierarchy (1 = subordinate; 2 = peer;	
3 = superior; 4 = not in chain of command)	3.2
Know partner (1 = not at all to: 5 = very well)	2.1

Message Differences By Organization			
	Research ($n = 627$)	Prod. Dev. ($n = 621$)	p-value of t-statistic
Message presentation			
Length	12.5	12.7	n.s.
Opening	0.35	0.28	n.s.
Closing	0.85	1.01	<0.01
Positive affect	0.46	0.58	n.s.
Negative affect	0.14	0.15	n.s.
Politeness	0.50	0.42	n.s.
Energy	0.57	0.38	<0.01
Topic (% work)	54%	66%	<0.01
Partner Attributes			
Age	35.2	33.6	n.s.
Job title	1.3	1.2	n.s.
Sex	0.35	0.24	<0.01
Hierarchy	3.0	3.4	<0.01
Know partner	2.0	2.2	<0.01

Table 3   Organizational Message Characteristics (*continued*)

	Message Differences By Gender		
	Male ($n = 955$)	Female ($n = 293$)	*p*-value of *t*-statistic
Message presentation			
Length	13.1	10.3	<0.01
Opening	0.33	0.27	n.s.
Closing	0.91	1.02	n.s.
Positive affect	0.49	0.60	n.s.
Negative affect	0.15	0.14	n.s.
Politeness	0.45	0.48	n.s.
Energy	0.49	0.42	n.s.
Topic (% work)	60%	60%	n.s.
Partner attributes			
Age	34.0	35.7	n.s.
Job title	1.2	1.3	<0.01
Sex	0.29	0.28	n.s.
Hierarchy	3.2	3.4	<0.01
Know partner	2.2	2.1	n.s.

	Message Differences By Hierarchy			
	Mgrs. ($n = 114$)	Profs. ($n = 963$)	Non-exempt ($n = 171$)	*p*-value of *F*-ratio
Message presentation				
Length	18.5	11.9	12.4	<0.01
Opening	0.65	0.27	0.34	<0.01
Closing	0.89	0.95	0.88	n.s.
Positive affect	0.38	0.53	0.55	n.s.
Negative affect	0.32	0.11	0.22	<0.01
Politeness	0.42	0.45	0.54	n.s.
Energy	0.31	0.49	0.47	n.s.
Topic (% work)	84%	58%	55%	<0.01
Partner attributes				
Age	37.1	33.8	35.2	<0.01
Job title	1.29	1.17	1.49	<0.01
Sex	0.37	0.26	0.37	<0.01
Hierarchy	2.8	3.2	3.4	<0.01
Know partner	2.6	2.1	2.1	<0.01

Note: The data for each sampling stratum are weighted to reflect its proportion of the organization as a whole.

5.3 *Absorption*

The mean number of words in salutations was 0.31; the mean number of words in closings was 0.94 ($t = 13.9$, $p < 0.01$). People estimated that they send an average of 3.9 messages a day; they actually sent an average of 2.0 per day ($t = 20.4$, $p < 0.01$). They also overestimated the number they received (mean $= 27.6$) in comparison with the actual number they received (mean $= 25.6$) ($t = 6.83$, $p < 0.01$). But they *more* overestimated their sent messages than their received ones. The ratio of estimated messages sent to actual messages sent was 2:1; the ratio of estimated messages received to actual messages received was 1.1:1 ($t = 13.83$, $p < 0.01$). Another aspect of absorption is underestimating group membership. People underestimated the proportion of group messages (i.e., messages from distribution lists) they received in comparison with the actual proportion they received from distribution lists. People estimated that 79% of their received messages were group messages; 86% of their received messages were actually group messages ($t = 1.47$, n.s.).

Exhibit 1 displays one example of absorption effects. This message was sent in response to an earlier general information message on health effects of video display terminals. Note its chatty tone and how it reveals personal information about the sender (her physical ailments, how she broke her glasses). This message was sent to more than 3000 people.

5.4 *Status Equalization*

Messages from subordinates were no different from messages from superiors on the UMI or the other variables of message presentation. Messages from managers were more likely to be about work but there were no differences in the UMI or other variables of message presentation.

Table 4 reports the results of asking people how they would do a series of hypothetical tasks. We deliberately chose important tasks, ones in which a preference for face-to-face communication should dominate, in order to provide a strong test for any change in medium preference across tasks. People said they preferred EMS more when sending messages up the hierarchy than when sending them down, as shown by the last four tasks in Table 4. People more preferred EMS for communicating with their boss than with their secretary about project resources (the F-ratio for the interaction of medium and hierarchy was 3.71 (d.f. $= 3,285$), ($p < 0.05$). People more preferred EMS for communicating with their boss than with their secretary when solving an administrative problem, although the difference in preference was not significant (the F-ratio for the interaction of medium and hierarchy was 1.41 (d.f. $= 3,285$), ($p =$ n.s.). There are two plausible reasons why people might

Exhibit 1   Self-Absorbed Message

Date: 28 April 1983 2:38pm EDT (Thursday)
From:
Subject: Re: VDTs---A NEW SOCIAL DISEASE
In-reply-to: Menr's message of 17 April 1983
                               6:53 pm EDT (Wednesday)
To: ALLNYC ALLCHI ALLPGH
cc: ALLSEW ALLPHL ALLNEW
                               WOMEN.LA WOMEN.PGH
Reply-to:

As a user of glasses only for reading (you know, the
old age bit, where your
could see 500 miles away, but can't read 2 inches in
front of you, and your arms
aren't made of elastic, therefore won't stretch far
enough): I recently decided to
purchase bifocals (thinking they would be better than
my reading glasses) and I
definitely say they are only good for reading material
that you could position at
the level you want. I am not of the same opinion
as you in that it can be a
problem only if you make it a problem. Even if you
sit back and look through
top part of the lens, I find then that I'm better off
without my glasses. You have
to remember there are different degrees of distances
farsighted people can see.
My bifocals are not only entirely useless for the
screen AND keyboard, but in
trying to position my neck, face, head, shoulders, in
order to work at the
keyboard properly, I have worsened some very severe
problems in my neck.

I found that my very first reading glasses (with the
smallest prescription
possible) were the best for working with the screen.
The reason I say ''were''
is because I broke the frame the other day.

I sure hope someone comes up with a solution to all
this. Until all this started
coming over the electronic mail, I was silently
suffering to myself, thinking I
was the only one in such a dilemma.

Table 4   Preferred medium depending upon task and kind of information or hierarchical direction of communication. (Mean preference on a 10-point scale)

Task, Kind of Information, and Hierarchical Direction	Medium of Communication			
	FACE	EMS	PHONE	PAPER
Salary News				
Raise	9.4	0.3	0.2	0.1
No raise	8.6	0.9	0.3	0.2
Recommendation				
Enthusiastic	5.3	2.2	1.7	0.9
Half-hearted	4.4	2.8	1.9	0.9
Evaluate colleague				
Compliment	5.8	3.0	1.0	0.2
Criticize	7.1	2.1	0.7	0.1
Solve problem				
To Secy	6.0	2.8	1.0	0.05
To Boss	6.0	3.3	0.7	0.03
Negotiate				
To Secy	7.5	1.5	0.7	0.25
To Boss	7.3	2.3	0.3	0.06

prefer EMS for upward over downward communication. One is access equalization; that is, bosses may not be as accessible face-to-face as they are via EMS while secretaries are equally accessible in both media. The other is status equalization; that is, subordinates may prefer to have few reminders of status differences when talking with bosses but many when talking with secretaries. Our data do not allow us to distinguish between these explanations.

5.5 Uninhibited Behavior

People reported seeing flaming in their EMS messages a mean of 33 times a month; they reported seeing flaming in their face-to-face conversations a mean of 4 times a month ($t = 2.9$, $p < 0.01$). Exhibit 2 displays one example of an uninhibited message sent by a professional in the product development organization. Note the profanity, negative affect, and typographic energy (capitalizations and exclamation points). This message was sent to more than 100 people.

A second kind of uninhibited behavior is increased willingness to communicate bad news or negative information. People said they more preferred EMS to deliver bad salary news than good salary news (*F*-ratio for the interaction of medium and kind of information was 8.89 (d.f. $= 3,285$), $p < 0.01$). People said they more preferred EMS to deliver a

Exhibit 2 Uninhibited Message

Date: 26 Apr 83 19:53:38 EDT (Tuesday)
From:
Subject: That which is TRULY MONSTROUS
To: [Product] Interest.pa

It's great to worry about fine points, but I think we should concentrate on getting rid of those aspects of [product] which are
TRULY MONSTROUS to the native user (such as yours truly). I had
to ask about three people to figure out how to get the @#$%*ing
insertion point beyond a graphics frame. the answer, it appears,
is some incredibly arcane nonsense about show structure, select
after anchor, and repaginate. WHY CAN'T I JUST POINT THE BLOODY
MOUSE BELOW A GRAPHICS FRAME AND GET AN INSERTION POINT?

half-hearted recommendation than an enthusiastic one (*F*-ratio for the
interaction of medium and kind of information was 6.34 (d.f. = 3,285),
$p < 0.01$). But they said they preferred EMS less to criticize a colleague's
work than to compliment it (*F*-ratio for the interaction of medium and
kind of information was 15.75 (d.f. = 3,285), $P < 0.01$).

A third kind of uninhibited behavior is flouting social conventions.
One such convention marks the boundary between work and play, which
we expect would be attenuated by electronic mail. Forty percent of all
message traffic was totally unrelated to work, e.g., movie reviews, notices
about astronomy club meetings, recipes, advice about where to obtain
a second mortgage.[8]   People reported that they used EMS at the office
a mean of 31 times during the week for nonwork communication; they
used the telephone at the office a mean of 6 times during the week for
nonwork communication ($t = 5.74$, $p < 0.01$). Those with terminals at
home reported that they used EMS at home at least once a week to send
or receive messages about work matters. This was the same frequency
with which they used their home telephone for work ($t = 0.25$, $p =$
n.s.).

5.6 New Information

Sixty-two percent of the messages constituted "new" information; that
is, information respondents reported they would have gotten (or sent)

---

[8]   We do not know of good comparative data from other media for organizations generally, so it is difficult to know whether 40% is a small or large number. Some comparative
data are available for managers however. In one study of managerial time allocation,
managers spent about 6% of their time in nonwork activities (Sproull 1984, p. 19). In the
managers' subsample in this project, about 16% of their messages were unrelated to work.

Table 5 Relationship among nature of information, topic of message and knowledge of partner

| | Partner | | | |
| | Unknown | | Known | |
Topic of Message	Old Info	New Info	Old Info	New Info
Work	65	177	340	170
Nonwork	18	339	54	85

no other way if there were no electronic mail. Table 5 reveals that new information flowed in two ways. One was via access to unknown people. This was how the majority of new information arrived and much of it was nonwork related. The other way was via known people. Note that new work-related information was as likely to come from known partners (170 messages) as it was from unknown partners (177 messages). Examples of new information from the sample included an announcement of a house for sale (nonwork), a request for a baby sitter (nonwork), a report about a conference (work), a solicitation for ideas about a new product (work), and suggestions for new ways to use a particular piece of software (work).

6 Discussion

In a field study of organizational electronic mail, we found evidence that electronic mail reduced social context cues, provided information that was relatively self-absorbed, undifferentiated by status, uninhibited, and provided new information. Specifically, we found:

- Relatively weak social context cues in EMS
- People focused more on themselves than on others in message salutations and closings
- People overestimated their own contribution to EMS communications
- People underestimated their group messages
- Messages from superiors and managers looked no different from messages from subordinates and nonmanagers
- People more preferred to use EMS to send messages to superiors than to subordinates
- People behaved irresponsibly more often on EMS than they did in face-to-face conversations

- People preferred EMS for sending bad news
- People used EMS for nonwork communication during the workday
- 60% of the messages contained new information.

Three alternative explanations for these findings—technical unreliability, user inexperience, and lack of widespread access to the technology —can be considered. Some might argue that the technology is unreliable because it is new. Unreliability would lead to uncertainty and frustration, hence disinhibition and, perhaps, self-absorption. But the mail system in this research had been running continuously and reliably for ten years at the time of data collection. Some might argue that people have not yet learned how to use the technology "properly," even though it is reliable. Inexperience on the part of users would lead to uncertainty and inappropriate behavior. But respondents reported they had been using EMS extensively for as long as they had been in the organization. Some might argue that, although the technology is reliable and people are experienced, EMS communication is insignificant or trivial because only a very few people have access to it and none of those people are important. Insignificance would lead to uninhibited behavior and deviance. However, in this case the mail system was used by over 3700 people in the corporation. And in the divisions studied in this research, people at all hierarchical levels used EMS extensively. In sum, although we cannot rule these explanations out, it is unlikely that unreliable technology, inexperienced users, or lack of access produced the results of this study.

Further research should address two shortcomings in this study. The first is that the research was conducted within only one organization; therefore any claims to generalizability are problematic. The hypothesized processes have been observed in laboratory studies; however further field studies should be conducted in more than one organization. The second is that, because all mediated communication reduces social context information, further research should compare actual face-to-face conversations, telephone conversations, letters, and memoranda with electronic mail.

Each of the effects hypothesized and observed in this research can have important consequences for organizations. People's overestimating their personal contribution to and involvement in EMS communications is one of the self-absorption effects. Overestimation may have interesting implications for decision making. If people receive an EMS message announcing a decision or new policy, they may feel more committed to it than if it had come via a paper announcement. This might occur simply because people would feel a generalized sense of having contributed. On the other hand it may be more difficult for people to reach a decision using EMS than using face-to-face meetings or paper memoranda. If participants overestimate the value of their EMS contributions as much as they overestimate their frequency, people should be very reluctant to give up their initial positions conveyed via EMS to reach a consensus or compromise. But once consensus is reached, participants might value the decision more highly than one made using other media because they would overestimate the extent to which the decision reflected their own effort in reaching that decision.

A consequence of status equalization is that managers may have access to information that formerly would have been difficult if not impossible for them to get. During the period of research described in this paper, a product developer sent a message to distribution lists that reach thousands of people asking for suggestions about how to add a particular new product feature. Within two weeks, he had received over 150 messages in reply, cutting across geographical, departmental, divisional, and hierarchical boundaries, almost all from people the product developer did not know. Some of these messages even told the developer bluntly why it was a bad idea to add this feature. Status equalization may make people less unwilling to send bad news up the chain of command.

Uninhibited behavior may lead to more new ideas flowing through electronic mail, just as brainstorming techniques are supposed to release inhibitions so that ideas can flow in face-to-face groups. The extensive literature on communication and innovation (e.g., Allen and Cohen 1973; Ebadi and Utterback 1984) documents how structural and social variables can impede or channel technical information. Uninhibited behavior signals a decrease in the importance of these barriers to information flow. A topic for future research is how electronic mail networks affect the relative importance of structural and social variables in governing technical communication. For example, if everyone is easily accessible via electronic mail, what happens to the role of gatekeepers?

Another question is whether more information exchange is useful. Uninhibited behavior may lead to more "junk mail" as well as to more creative ideas. Proponents of new information technology often assert that it will remove "barriers" (geographic, temporal, departmental, and others) to communication. The assumption is that if these barriers are removed, large amounts of pent up task-relevant information will surge through the organization. In our study people did receive many work-related messages they said they would not have received other than through EMS. But they also received a great deal of new nonwork communication as well. The real value of this could be increased sociability and organizational attachment. People like to be sociable at work. A technology that makes it easy to be sociable—be it a water fountain, coffee pot, telephone, or EMS—will be used for sociability.[9] EMS has the potential to be a good technology for sociability. It reduces social reminders of norms against "goofing off." Furthermore, because it is asynchronous, it is a relatively efficient medium for sociability. Recipients are amused or enlightened on their own schedule, not that of the initiator. And recipients do not have to reciprocate; they can simply read their entertaining message and get back to work. Thus, even busy workers who otherwise would not take the time, or wallflowers who would not have the social skills, can participate in affable communication. One topic for future research is the relationship between EMS sociability and feeling of affiliation and commitment to the organization. Another is the relationship between sociability and work effectiveness.

All of these consequences bear on changing the distribution of information in organizations—who knows what. EMS can both add new recipients to information already being circulated within an organization and add genuinely new or previously uncirculated information. These are managerial issues, not technical ones. The technology of electronic mail simply moves text from one computer mailbox to another. Organizational policy will determine who has access to those mailboxes, how easy the access is, who can create distribution lists, who can join them, who can send mail to whom, and how closely, if at all, messages are monitored. In the case of the organization studies in this research, access was easy and widespread, anyone could create distribution lists, and the management was not heavy-handed in policing the system. The costs were in computer resources necessary to support a very heavily-used mail system and in people's sometimes receiving inappropriate messages. The benefits were in expanding and changing the distribution of information within the organization. The results of our research suggest that much of the power of EMS may stem from changing the nature of information and informants, not just the quantity and speed of information.[10]

References

Allen, Thomas J. and Stephen I. Cohen, "Information Flow in Research and Development Laboratories," *Admin. Sci. Quart.*, 18 (1973), 12–19.

[9] Two of the most frequently-run computer programs at Carnegie-Mellon University are JOKE and COOKIE. The first prints a joke on the user's screen; the second prints a fortune-cookie fortune. JOKE is run an average of 150 times a day; COOKIE is run an average of 2300 times a day (Blackwell 1986).

[10] We are grateful for financial assistance from the Stanford/NIMH Organization Research Training Program and the System Development Foundation. Jonathan Cender, Martha Feldman, Tom Finholt, James March and Allen Newell were helpful friends and critics.

Allison, Graham, *Essence of Decision*. Little, Brown, Boston, 1971.

Barnlund, Dean C., and Carroll Harland, "Propinquity and Prestige as Determinants of Communication Networks." *Sociometry*, 26 (1963), 466–479.

Baum, Andrew, and Stuart Valins, *Architecture and Social Behavior*. Erlbaum, Hillsdale, N.J., 1977.

Blackwell, Mike, "Electronic Observations of Computer User Behavior," in Sara Kiesler, Lee Sproull, and Associates, *From Chalkboards to BBoards: Computing and Organizational Change on Campus*, Carnegie-Mellon University, CSSRC unpublished monograph, 1986.

Cochran, William, *Sampling Techniques*. 2nd ed., John Wiley and Sons, New York, 1963.

Cohen, Elizabeth, and Susan Roper, "Modification of Interracial Interaction Disability," *Amer. Sociological Rev.*, 37 (1972), 643–665.

Cottrell, Nicholas, Dunstan Wack, Gary Sekerak, and Robert Rittle, "Social Facilitation of Dominant Responses by the Presence of an Audience and the Mere Presence of Others," *J. Personality and Social Psychology*, 9 (1968), 245–250.

Crawford, Albert B., "Corporate Electronic Mail—A Communication-Intensive Application of Information Technology," *MIS Quart.*, 6 (1982), 1–14.

Diener, Ed, Scott Fraser, A. L. Beaman, and R. T. Kelem, "Effects of Deindividuating Variables on Stealing by Halloween Trick-or-Treaters," *J. Personality and Social Psychology*, 33 (1976), 178–183.

Ebadi, Yar M., and James M. Utterback, "The Effects of Communication on Technological Innovation," *Management Sci.*, 30 (1984), 572–585.

Festinger, Leon, "Informal Social Communication," *Psychological Rev.*, 57 (1950), 271–282.

Kanter, Rosabeth, "Some Effects of Proportions in Group Life: Skewed Sex Ratios and Responses to Token Women," *Amer. J. Sociology*, 82 (1977), 965–990.

Kiesler, Sara, and Lee Sproull, "Response Effects in the Electronic Survey," *Public Opinion Quart.*, 50 (1986), 243–254.

Kidder, Tracy, *The Soul of a New Machine*. Avon, New York, 1981.

Licklider, J. C. R., and Albert Vezza, "Applications of Information Networks," *IEEE Proc.*, 66 (1978), 1330–1346.

Nyce, H. Edward, and Richard Groppa, "Electronic Mail at MHT," *Management Technology* (May 1983), 65–72.

O'Reilly, Charles, "Individuals and Information Overload in Organizations: Is More Necessarily Better?" *Acad. Management J.*, 23 (1980), 684–696.

_____ and Karlene Roberts, "Information Filtration in Organizations: Three Experiments," *Organizational Behavior and Human Performance*, 11 (1974), 253–265.

Rice, Ronald, "Computer Conferencing," in Brenda Dervin and Melvin Voight (Eds.), *Progress in Communication Sciences*, II, Ablex, Norwood, N.J., 215–240, 1980.

_____, "Communication Networking in Computer-Conferencing Systems: A Longitudinal Study of Group Roles and System Structure," in Michael Burgoon (Ed.), *Communication Yearbook.* 6, Sage, Beverly Hills, 925–944, 1982.

_____ and George Barnett, "Goups Communication Networking in an Information Environment: Applying Metric Multidimensional Scaling," in Margaret McLaughlin (Ed.), *Communication Yearbook.* 9, Sage, Beverly Hills, 315–338, 1986.

Rosen, Sidney, and Abraham Tesser, "On Reluctance to Communicate Undesirable Information: The MUM Effect," *Sociometry*, 33 (1970), 253–263.

Shlaim, Avi, "Failures in National Intelligence Estimates: The Case of the Yom Kippur War," *World Politics* 28 (1976), 348–380.

Siegel, Jane, "Managers' Communication and Telecommunications Technology Use," Carnegie-Mellon University. Unpublished doctoral dissertation, 1986.

_____, Vitaly Dubrovsky, Sara Kiesler and Timothy W. McGuire, "Group Processes in Computer-Mediated Communication," *Organization Behavior and Human Decision Processes* 37 (1986), 157–187.

Singer, Jerome, Claudia Brush and Shirley Lublin, "Some aspects of deindividuation: Identification and conformity," *J. Experimental Social Psychology* 1 (1965), 365–568.

Sproull, Lee, "The Nature of Managerial Attention," in Lee Sproull and Patrick Larkey (Eds.), *Advances in Information Processing in Organizations*, 1, JAI Press, Greenwich, Conn, 1984.

_____, "Using Electronic Mail for Data Collection in Organizational Research," *Acad. Management J.*, 29 (1986), 159–169.

Steele, Guy, Donald Woods, Raphael Finkel, Mark Crispin, Richard Stallman, and Geoffrey Goodfellow, *The Hackers Dictionary*. Harper and Row, New York, 1983.

Sudman, Seymour, and Norman M. Bradburn, *Response E–ects in Surveys*, Aldine, Chicago, 1974.

Tushman, Michael L., and Elaine Romanelli, "Uncertainty, Social Location and Influence in Decision Making: A Sociometric Analysis." *Management Sci.*, 29 (1983), 12–23.

Watson, Kathleen, "An Analysis of Communication Patterns: A Method for Discriminating Leader and Subordinate Roles," *Acad. Management J.*, 25 (1982), 107–120.

Wohlstetter, Roberta, *Pearl Harbor*, Stanford University Press, Stanford, 1962.

Wright, J. Patrick, *On a Clear Day You Can See General Motors*, Avon, New York, 1979.

Cognitive Science and Organizational Design: A Case Study of Computer Conferencing

Kevin Crowston
Thomas W. Malone
Felix Lin
Sloan School of Management
Massachusetts Institute of Technology
Cambridge, MA

Introduction

Since soon after the invention of computers, researchers have attempted to investigate the relationship between information technology (IT) and organizational structure. For instance, as long ago as in 1958, Leavitt and Whisler predicted that IT would lead to a dramatic reduction in numbers of middle managers. Recently there has been a flood of articles in the popular business press describing individual organizations where the introduction of IT seems to be associated with large organizational changes (Business Week, 1984, 1985). We are thus apparently beginning to see the effects of IT, but as yet we understand them only vaguely.

Our research involves a new perspective to investigate this link. The technique analyzes information processing in organizations in a much more detailed way than most previous work. Using concepts of object-oriented programming from artificial intelligence, we characterize the information processing that occurs in organizations in terms of the kinds of messages people exchange and the ways they process those messages. The models that can be developed using these object-oriented concepts have more of the precision and flavour of cognitive science theories than most previous models based on the information processing view of organizations.

We begin with a review of the literature on the impact of IT on organizations, from which we develop a new information processing approach to the problem. The utility of this technique is demonstrated through the analysis of a case, one in which a reduction in levels of management is coupled with the introduction of a computer conferencing system. The model developed in this case agrees with data about the changes in the organizational structure, qualitative comments about changes in job roles and detailed analyses of message contents. We conclude by sketching possible future directions for research using our perspective.

Literature Review

Studies of IT and Organizational Structure

Many researchers have investigated the link between information technology and organizational structure. There seems to be a general expectation that IT can eliminate levels of management (Whisler, 1970), as originally predicted by Leavitt and Whisler (1958). The popular press is filled with anecdotes about firms that have reduced the number of their middle managers using IT (Business Week, 1984), but the empirical evidence is contradictory (Attewell and Rule, 1984). The results for the related question of centralization versus decentralization are similarly mixed, although centralization is seen somewhat more often (Robey, 1981; Rowe, 1984; Attewell and Rule, 1984; Carter, 1984; Pfeffer and Leblebici, 1977). Carter (1984) points out that studies conducted prior to 1970 favour centralization, and those after, decentralization, suggesting an increased familiarity with or improved computing technology. Pfeffer and Leblebici (1977) note that smaller firms are usually more centralized, and that IT may indirectly cause centralization by reducing the number of workers. Predictions of IT-induced unemployment, usually of clerical or production workers, have been pessimistic (Attewell and Rule, 1984), but these studies have a number of methodological problems that make firm conclusions difficult. The evidence regarding deskilling versus job enhancement is mixed, although "most workers surveyed regard the new technologies in a positive light" (Attewell and Rule, 1984: 1187). A number of studies have shown that IT can change work roles (Zuboff, 1983a; Foster and Flynn, 1984; Mohrman, 1982; Pfeffer, 1978; Pfeffer and Leblebici, 1977). Foster and Flynn (1984), for example, showed a change from hierarchically-based to competency-based roles in their study of the impact of a teleconferencing system. IT generally seems to increase the level of communication in organizations (Freeman, 1984; Sanders, Courtney and Loy, 1984; Foster and Flynn, 1984), although Robey (1981) found mixed results concerning the effect on lateral communications.

Limitations

Limited view of causality: These ambiguous conclusions seem to indicate that there are many contingent factors that have not been included in past analyses and demonstrate the weakness of current theories for analyzing such effects. One limitation of past approaches was pointed out by Robey (1983) and further discussed by Markus and Robey (1986). These authors note that organizations are designed to achieve certain goals and that these designs include the information systems as well as the formal organizational structure. Neither directly causes the other; rather, both are intended as solutions to perceived problems. Studies that view IT as a cause of change rather than one of many factors that enable change may therefore find inconsistent results. For example, Robey (1983) notes instances where a system was introduced after a reorganization. In these cases, IT clearly cannot be the cause of the change; however, there may still be a link between the two, which a less causal and more "interactionist" analysis might illuminate.

Scattered results: A second problem with the existing literature is that results are scattered. Although IT is likely to have multiple effects, many studies have focused on only a single aspect of organizational structure. With no theory predicting multiple effects and few comprehensive studies, it is difficult to gauge the total effect of IT on an organization.

Blunt measures: A final problem is the use of very blunt measures. IT (or information, uncertainty, or communication) is often viewed as a binary variable. At best, the total dollar investment in IT is measured, as if every dollar spent or every application had identical effects. Information and interaction are also grossly measured. As Freeman (1984: 205) notes, "structural studies of social networks typically ignore the content of the relations under examination; we act as if we expect to find some universal structural laws that can be applied equally well to friendship and to corporate interlocks." Walker (1985), in a study of the communication patterns of a software firm, showed that there were different networks for technical and administrative information, again demonstrating that different kinds of information are treated differently.

The Information Processing Perspective

The solution to some of these problems is to examine more closely the link between IT and organizational structure. To do this, however, we need a perspective in which the effects of IT are more easily interpretable. For this purpose, the information processing (IP) view of organizations (Galbraith, 1974, 1977; Tushman and Nadler, 1978) seems likely to be fruitful. Tushman and Nadler (1978: 292) outline three basic assumptions of the IP perspective: organizations must deal with work-related uncertainty; organizations can fruitfully be seen as information processing systems; and organizations can be viewed as composed of sets of groups or departments (which they refer to as subunits, and which we will call agents). In this view, organizational structure is the pattern and content of the information flowing between the agents and the way they process this information. The IP view has a major, although as yet mostly unexploited advantage, for investigating possible effects of IT, since it directly includes what IT can do: process information.

The IP perspective of organizations grew from the "Carnegie school" of decision making (March and Simon, 1958; Cyert and March, 1963), whose authors attempted to model how organizations make decisions. They noted such key factors as the limited rationality of human beings, which led them to consider explicitly the way people and organizations gather and process information. Their analysis, however, emphasized factors such as the steps involved in decision making, and did not focus much at all on the amount and kinds of communication between different agents. Galbraith (1974, 1977) expanded on their work, explicitly considering an organization's need to process information and reduce environmental uncertainty, and strategies by which it could achieve this goal. Tushman and Nadler (1978) hypothesized that different organizations face different levels of uncertainty and that an organization's effectiveness would depend on the fit between its information processing capacity and its environment. They discussed ways to improve this fit and noted that, "the information processing model holds promise as a tool for the problem of designing organizations" (Tushman and Nadler, 1978:300).

Limitations   The limitations of these theories are similar to those of previously discussed. The major problem is that the concepts discussed in these studies are still very aggregate. Galbraith and Tushman and Nadler treat information almost like a fluid, and uncertainty, its lack. An organization's structure then is like plumbing that directs the flow of information to where it is needed to reduce uncertainty. Such general factors are, as Galbraith notes, very difficult to measure, as it is unclear, for example, exactly what is and what is not information. Such simplifications are useful for general studies, but permit only very general conclusions. A more detailed analysis would attempt to characterize the content of the messages that comprise the flow of information and examine the processing that these messages require. The need for greater detail was anticipated by Galbraith, who noted, "to determine uncertainty, the required task information must be defined" (Galbraith, 1977: 37).

Toward More Precise Information Processing Models

Our perspective attempts to make such a finer analysis. One of the methods other information-processing-based disciplines use to gain insight into complex behaviours is to imagine how a computer could be programmed to reproduce them. In cognitive psychology, for example, computer models of learning or memory have been used to make theories about human information processing concrete and to generate further empirically testable hypotheses. The organizational models developed using our perspective are similar in flavour and purpose.

Like many earlier IP theories, we treat the organization as a collection of intercommunicating agents. In addition to looking for the presence of information or uncertainty, however, we attempt to identify the content and purpose of the messages being exchanged and the actions that these messages trigger in the agents. Models developed using our technique are thus similar to a programme written in an object-oriented language (Goldberg and Robson, 1983; Stefik and Bobrow, 1986), since they specify the different classes of agents, the messages they understand, and the processing they do for each message. We can simplify the description of the agents and highlight their similarities using the concept of inheritance. Some types of agents can be considered specializations of other, more basic types, inheriting some behaviours while adding or modifying others. By modelling these features of an organization's information processing capability, we make concrete our assumptions about the organization, and can more quickly examine the effects of changes in its structure or in the technology used.

It is important to realize that our primary goal here is to emphasize a perspective towards organizations rather than any detailed theory. This "pretheoretical" perspective disposes us to build models or theories that emphasize certain aspects of organizational behaviour, specifically, agent and message types and the patterns of communications and information processing. In particular, these detailed models of communications and computation may be especially useful for analyzing directly the changes that information technology may allow in the costs and capabilities for organizational information processing.

One criticism of this perspective is that it is rather mechanistic. We model the organization simply, focusing on the pattern of communication and the types of messages sent. While these simplifications allow us to model computer systems quite accurately, they clearly do not address all aspects of human organizations. To include all features of organizations, however, would make our analysis hopelessly complicated. Furthermore, our simple theories do not have any particular advantage for analyzing issues such as power, opportunism or satisfaction. Although we do not consider such features unimportant, omitting them and concentrating on those features which seem easier to model makes it possible for us to derive unambiguous conclusions, which may still explain substantial parts of the behaviour of the organizations we study.

Example: The Task Assignment Problem

To illustrate our perspective, we will present a specific model, the model of the task assignment problem developed by Malone and Smith (1984) and further expanded by Malone (1986). The model describes an organization in which tasks arise that must be assigned to "processors" (persons, machines or combinations) to be performed. The tasks may in turn be composed of subtasks, and different tasks or subtasks may require processing by specific classes of agent. For example, a manufacturing organization may receive orders for a product, the subparts of which must be manufactured by one division, assembled by another, and shipped by a third. An organization to process tasks can have a number of possible structures; four simple ones are shown in Figure 26.1. These four organizations are simple forms of what in human organizations would be called, respectively, a functional hierarchy, a product hierarchy, a decentralized market and a centralized market with brokers.

These structures are clearly much simpler than those of any real organizations. However, they serve as analytic building blocks with which larger and more complex organizations can be described. As in many other sciences, study of such extremely simple forms may produce results that are more easily interpretable than those for realistic mixed forms, and which still offer insight into many real world situations.

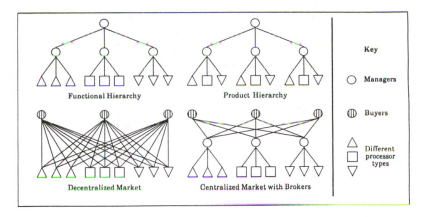

Figure 26.1

Agents and Messages   The agents in these organizations communicate by sending each other messages. Again, for ease of analysis we reduce complex behaviours to the minimum set of messages necessary to perform the function. Messages observed in real organizations, however, can often by interpreted in this framework. The simplest protocol is followed in the two hierarchical organizations: a manager with a task to be done chooses a subordinate who is able to do it, and assigns the task by sending it a *DoTask* message. When the subordinate finishes the task, it notifies the manager who assigned the task by sending a *FinishedTask* message. Note that the agent to whom the task was assigned may in turn decompose or delegate it using the same protocol; for example, the middle managers in some organizations are assigned tasks, which they in turn assign to their own subordinates.

The difference between the two hierarchies is the level at which the task is decomposed. In the functional hierarchy, the general manager at the top of the hierarchy decomposes incoming tasks and assigns each subtask to the appropriate functional manager, who in turn assigns it to a subordinate. Each functional division is specialized to perform a single type of task. In the product hierarchy, the divisions are split along geographical or product lines rather than by function, and each division is therefore self-contained. Tasks arrive at the appropriate division and the manager of that division decomposes the task and assigns the subtask to the appropriate functional specialists in the division.

Markets add another set of messages to control a manager's choice of subordinate. A manager with a task to be done (a buyer) requests bids by broadcasting a *RequestForBids(RFB)* message; an agent who is interested in doing the task (a seller) then responds with a *Bid* message. The manager chooses (by some criteria) the best bid from those received, and assigns the task to that agent, using the protocol presented above. In a decentralized market, the manager will solicit bids from all of the agents in the market capable of doing the task. In a centralized market, the manager may simply contact a smaller number of brokers with "subordinates" capable of performing the task.

A summary of the different agent types, the messages they understand and the actions they take on receiving these messages is given in Table 1. Note that a *Manager* agent can be viewed as a special kind of *Processor*. It should also be noted that some of these descriptions are incomplete. For example, *Seller* agents are described as understanding only *RFB* messages. These roles do not stand by themselves, but are rather used to supplement others. For example, combining the description of a *Seller* with that of a *Processor* gives an appropriate description for a *Processor* in a decentralized market; combining a *Seller* and a *Functional Manager*, the description for a *Broker* in a centralized market (see Table 2).

Comparing Organizational Forms Each of these different organizational forms is capable of performing the tasks. They differ, however, in other properties, such as cost (the number of messages that must be exchanged to assign the task and the amount of processing that must be done) and flexibility (the response of the organization to the possible failure of some agent). For example, assigning a task in a functional hierarchy is simple: the manager simply sends the task to the division responsible for that type of task. In a market, the manager must do more work to handle the many messages necessary to solicit and receive bids, process the bids and assign the task. If one of the managers in the functional hierarchy fails, however, the entire organization will be disrupted, because no work can be done without that division. If a seller in a market fails, it will simply not bid on tasks, and none will be assigned to it. The additional cost of the market is balanced by its increased flexibility. Different organizations will make different tradeoffs between these costs, depending on their environment and their needs.

A queuing-theory analysis of the different simple organizations is presented by Malone and Smith (1984) and Malone (1986). The total costs of the different organizational forms depend on a number of parameters, such as the cost of sending a message or of searching for a supplier. These parameters may be set to appropriate values to simulate existing organizations, or modified to identify the effects of the introduction of IT. For example, an electronic mail system may reduce the cost of internal communications; an electronic market, the cost of searching

Table 1   Agents and Messages for the Task Assignment Problem

Agent Type	Message	Action
Processor	*DoTask*	Perform the given task: when done, notify the assigning manager by sending a *FinishedTask* message.
General Manager	*DoTask*	Decompose the task into subtasks and assign each task to an appropriate subordinate by sending a *DoTask* message.
	FinishedTask	Note that a subordinate has finished its subtask. If all the subtasks of a task have been finished, notify the assigning manager by sending a *FinishedTask* message.
Functional Manager	*DoTask*	Assign the task to an appropriate subordinate by sending a *DoTask* message.
	FinishedTask	Note that a subordinate has finished a task and notify the assigning manager by sending a *FinishedTask* message.
Seller	*RequestForBids*	If the task is one that this agent can do, send the buyer a *Bid* message; otherwise, do nothing.
Buyer	*Bid*	Add this bid to the set of bids received. If it was the final bid expected or if enough time has passed since the initial *RFB*, then evaluate and choose the best bid and assign the task using the given protocol.

for a supplier (Malone, Benjamin and Yates, 1986). Either change might shift the tradeoff, making market-like organizations more desirable. As Malone (1986) shows, this model is consistent with two kinds of empirical observations, generalizations from previous work on organizational design and major changes in the structures of American businesses over the last century, such as are discussed by Chandler (1962).

Table 2   "Combination" Agents

Base Agent Type	Supplement	Result
Processor	Seller	Processor in a decentralized market.
General Manager	Seller	Broker in a centralized market, although of a different kind than that shown. This type of agent would bid on and perform complete tasks, much like a firm in a competitive market.
	Buyer	Buyer in a decentralized or centralized market of the type shown.
	Seller and Buyer	Buyer in a centralized market, although again of a different kind than that shown. This type of agent would bid on complete tasks, and then subcontract the subtasks, much like a prime contractor might.
Functional Manager	Seller	Broker in a centralized market of the type shown.
	Buyer	Buyer in a decentralized or centralized market. This type of manager would work in a hierarchical firm, but would contract out all tasks assigned.
	Seller and Buyer	Broker in a centralized market, although again of a different kind than that shown. This type of agent would bid on subtasks, which it would then subcontract. A temp-agency works in this way, centralizing a supply of free-lancers.

Advantages

An integrative approach: Our perspective has several advantages for study in the areas it addresses. First, it offers an integrated framework for studying organizational structure. In previous studies, different aspects of organizational structure had unrelated definitions, drawn from many different reference disciplines, and it was unclear how the different effects fit together. Our perspective provides coherent definitions for many of these aspects, based on the flow of messages. The different sets of messages exchanged implement different *organizational processes*. The *structure* is the pattern of messages exchanged, that is, which agents are communicating and which messages they send. The set of messages to which a given agent responds, and the processing it therefore does, can be seen as that agent's *role*. With these definitions, we can begin to assess the link between IT and the whole structure of an organization.

Measurement: Since organizational structure is defined in terms of messages sent and received, it is also easier to measure these different aspects. The IP view provides a framework to guide the collection and interpretation of the necessary data. The view suggests the examination of the sources and uses of data, the types of messages sent and received, and the actions agents take when they receive certain messages. Existing techniques, such as network analysis, may be used to reveal the pattern of communications. A protocol analysis of tasks can be done by examining the contents of a person's "in box" and watching as they read and act on the messages in it (*e.g.,* Malone *et al.,* 1986). Sometimes messages sent using a computer system can be unobtrusively collected for later analysis. McKenney, Doherty and Sviokla (1986) performed such an analysis in a software firm, tracing the flow of messages and drawing flowcharts to describe the processing involved in certain tasks.

Organizational simulations: Finally, the IP view suggests and facilitates the use of organizational simulations. Simulations have at least two advantages for research that make them desirable in this area. First, simulations require that assumptions be made explicit, making them easier to see and the results of changing them easier to test. Second, simulations make it possible to analyze systems that are too complex for analytic solution.

An Example Case

To test and further develop this perspective, we attempted to apply it to the analysis of a real organization. We examined an organizational change that took place in one part of a large electronics manufacturing firm, which we will refer to as the Electronic Manufacturing Firm (EMF).[1]   This case was selected because it appeared to be one in which

---

[1]   The names of the corporation and divisions have been changed to avoid revealing the identity of the organization studied.

an important organizational structure change was associated with the introduction of IT—in this case, a computer conferencing system.

Method

We developed a model of the organization in an iterative fashion, switching between data collection and model development. Our perspective led us to attempt to identify the basic task of the organization, the different kinds of agents in it, and the sorts of messages those agents exchanged. From this analysis, we constructed two initial models, which differed in their treatment of the computer conferencing system. The construction of each tentative model revealed areas where our understanding of the situation was weak, thus focusing further investigations. We also attempted to test each model by looking for data that would disconfirm key assumptions or predictions. Based on our findings in subsequent rounds of data collection, we chose one model over the other and refined it by adding new processes and message types.

The data for the model came from a variety of sources. Some data were collected in face-to-face and telephone interviews conducted with knowledgeable individuals in the organization ("key informants") between April 1985 and September 1986. This key informant method is limited, in that it relies heavily on retrospection. For instance, individuals may remember details incorrectly or give answers biased by new information or a desire to make a good impression. To reduce these effects, we interviewed a number of people in different parts of the organization and attempted to resolve any conflicting reports we received in follow up interviews.

We also collected more objective data to support our model. First, we observed our interviewees using the conferencing system. We also examined and classified 331 messages stored in the system. Two of the interviewees reviewed drafts of this paper for accuracy and provided detailed information about the organizational structure before and after the change, including the approximate number and job grades of persons at each level of the organization.

History

The Organization   The organization discussed in this paper is the Compensation and Benefits (C&B) organization of EMF. The C&B organization is a part of the Personnel Department that manages the compensation and benefits policy (*e.g.*, pay programmes) for the corporation. Because EMF is a decentralized company, the C&B organization is geographically and administratively dispersed.

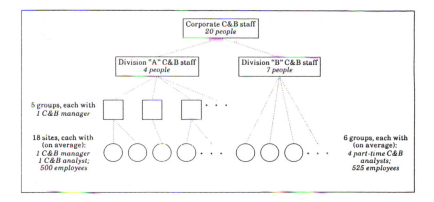

Figure 26.2

In the part of EMF we studied, there were originally two divisions (see Figure 26.2). The first, division "A", was composed of five groups, each with an average of four sites of 500 employees each (there were 18 sites in total). At each level of the hierarchy—corporate, division, group and site—there were C&B managers who reported to the local personnel manager, and had a dotted-line relationship with other C&B personnel at different levels. In large sites, there might have been one or two C&B analysts who reported directly to the site C&B manager. The site managers were all at about the same job grade, while the group managers were at a higher level.

The second division, "B", had a more centralized structure. Each group had a few C&B analysts, but only one had a group C&B manager. In terms of job grade, however, most of the central staff members were about equal to the division "A" site managers.

The Change In the fall of 1982, these two divisions of EMF were merged. The C&B manager for the new division felt that there was "too much buffering" between the policy makers at the corporate level and the policy implementors at the sites and that as a result the organization was not "generating enough new ideas". Furthermore, he felt that it was too expensive to maintain both the division C&B managers and the group C&B managers, and that IT could be used to eliminate the middle level of management.

The new C&B manager therefore initiated a number of changes (see Figure 26.3). First, the old division staffs were merged and a new group formed to handle C&B for the new division. At this time, C&B managers were appointed for each of the groups in division "B". (Generally these were C&B analysts already in the group who had been informally performing this role.) It should be noted, however, that a "B" group is

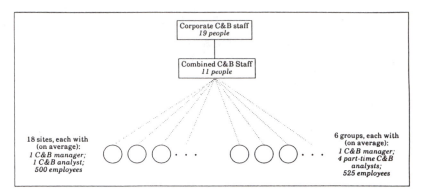

Figure 26.3

comparable in size to a single "A" site, and that the new "B" group managers were at the same job level as the "A" site managers. Second, with the agreement of the group personnel managers, the group level of C&B managers in division "A" was eliminated and the managers placed elsewhere in the company. Given the similarity between "A" sites and "B" groups, this left the entire organization with a fairly uniform structure. The transition to this new structure took place during the summer of 1983 and was completed by September, 1983.

The Use of Computer Conferencing In the original organization, the group managers coordinated the 18 division "A" sites, and helped formulate and distribute new policies and answer questions about existing ones. In the fall of 1983, after the elimination of the group managers the head of the combined C&B division arranged for the introduction of a computer conferencing system to serve some of these functions. It was intended that some communication between the different parts of the organization would take place via this system.

The manager responsible for the introduction of the system felt it had several advantages. First, since the information in the system was available to everyone in the organization, the corporate level staff did not have to answer the same questions repeatedly, as had been the case before. Second, the system sped up some communications and facilitated new interactions, both lateral and vertical. He also credited the system with increasing feedback from the site managers on new policies proposed by the corporate staff. A final hope was that sharing information would lead to better agreement on what the policies were.

An Explanatory Model

It is clear that no model can capture all of the events associated with this change or explain every detail of what happened. Our goal is therefore

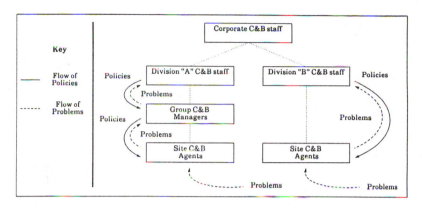

Figure 26.4

more modest. We will simply use our modelling technique to show why the elimination of the group managers and the introduction of computer conferencing made sense in light of the problems described, and why this change was better than the other options considered. Note too that this case is one in which the organizational change happened before the introduction of IT, and both were designed to address a perceived problem with the existing organization. An advantage of our technique is that it can be used to explain the fit between the two, rather than the impact of one on the other.

Model Development   A key step in the model building process is characterizing the function the organization performs. The function of the C&B organization was assumed to be solving any problems that arose by applying the policies created at the corporate level. This process might be called the policy development and application process (*e.g.*, see Barber, 1985). Different policies were assumed to be useful for solving different problems.

The model developed for the original organization is shown in Figure 26.4. The important paths that messages follow are the hierarchical dotted-line relationships. In this model, there are two kinds of information: problems and policies. Problems flow in at the bottom of the hierarchy, where the site C&B analysts see and attempt to solve them. Policies flow from the top, where they are created by the corporate and division C&B staffs. Each policy tells the C&B people how to deal with some of the problems. Problems also flow from the site analysts up and correspond to requests for clarification of a policy or for help in solving the problem.

Agents and Messages Based on job descriptions obtained in the interviews and presented above, a very simplified and somewhat abstract message protocol was developed to model the way members of the organization handle problems. The process starts with the receipt of a *Problem* message by a site agent. This agent is either a site analyst or manager. Normally, when a site agent gets a problem s/he looks for the policy that covers the situation. If s/he finds the policy, then s/he simply handles the problem. Otherwise, s/he resends the *Problem* message to the manager above him or her, asking for help. If a site or group manager is sent a *Problem* message that s/he knows how to solve, then s/he replies immediately by sending back an appropriate *Policy* message to the site manager, who then applies the policy; otherwise the process is repeated. The corporate C&B managers can always respond with a *Policy* message, since they know all the current policies and can create new ones when faced with new problems.

Part of the process of policy development involves consultations with agents in other parts of the organization. To model this process two additional messages, *RequestForComments* (RFC) and *Comment*, are used. The corporate C&B staff can send *RFC* messages, to which site managers can reply with *Comment* messages. Site managers may also treat *Policy* messages as implicit *RFC*s and sent *Comments*. Note that we do not attempt to mimic the entire consultation process, but rather simply model the minimum communication that must take place. A summary of the agent types, the messages they understand, and the processing they do when receiving a message is given in Table 3. (To simplify the terminology, we use site analyst to refer to any site agent with no subordinates.)

Modelling Computer Conferencing Our approach to modelling the use of the computer conferencing system is to simply change the pattern of linkages as shown in Figure 26.5. Computer conferencing can be used either to store information for later retrieval or to quickly disseminate it to individuals in the organization. We have chosen to emphasize the latter function. In this model, everyone has an opportunity to see and respond to all messages. Note, however, that the basic function of the organization and the capabilities of the individual agents are unaltered—only the communication paths have been changed.

Support for the Model

Content Analysis of Messages One form of support for our model comes from a detailed analysis of a sample of messages from the conferencing system. From one of our interviewees, we obtained copies of 331

Table 3 Agents and Messages for the EMF Case Model

Agent Type	Message	Action
Site C&B Analyst or Manager	*Problem*	Look up the appropriate policy for the problem. If it is found, use it to solve the problem. Otherwise, refer the problem to the next level by sending a *Problem* message.
	Policy	Note the new policy. If it can be used to solve a currently outstanding problem, then use it.
	RFC	Possibly return a *Comment* message.
Site or Group C&B Manager	*Problem*	Look up the appropriate policy for the problem. If it is found, then send the referring agent a *Policy* message. Otherwise, refer the problem to the next level by sending a *Problem* message.
	Policy	Note the new policy. If it can be used to solve a currently outstanding problem, then send the referring agent a *Policy* message.
	RFC	Possibly return a *Comment* message.
Corporate C&B Manager	*Problem*	Look up the appropriate policy for the problem. If it is found, then send the referring agent a *Policy* message. Otherwise, create a new policy to solve the problem, possibly asking for comments by sending an *RFC* message.
	Comment	Note the comment.

messages in four conferences, three complete ones containing a total of 202 messages about the development and implementation of new computer tools for salary management, and the most recent 129 messages (out of a total of about 450) in the general "catch-all" group. In order to protect the sensitive information discussed in some of the conferences,

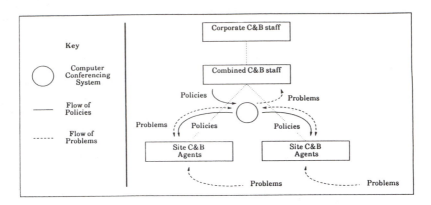

Figure 26.5

the three specialized conferences we analyzed contained few messages that related directly to the C&B "business" of the organization. They can, however, be interpreted as discussions of the implementation of a new policy, namely the new salary management system.

Based on the model and a preliminary analysis of the messages, we prepared descriptions (included in the appendix) of the four expected classes of messages, namely *Policy*, *Problem*, *Request For Comments* and *Comment*, as well as a category for other messages that used the broadcast capabilities of the system (such as announcements of meetings, job openings, Christmas greetings, and so forth).

The messages were then read and classified by five graduate students in management, none of whom were aware of our hypotheses. Since coding messages was somewhat time-consuming, one coder read and classified every message; the others classified some of the messages as a check on the first. Each message was read by at least two coders and many were read by three. At least two coders agreed on the classification of 79% (261) of the messages, and only these messages are analyzed further.

The results of the classification, presented in Table 4, tend to support our model. Most of the messages fell into one of the four message types we expected. Of the remainder, most took advantage of the capability to broadcast to the entire organization.

We then used the messages in the four expected classes to test one hypothesis from the model about the direction of flow of different kinds of messages, namely:

Most *Policy* and *RFC* messages will be sent by division C&B staff members.

Most *Problem* and *Comment* messages will be sent by site C&B managers.

The number of each class of message, broken down by organizational location of sender, is shown in Table 5. The distribution is significantly different from that expected by chance ($x^2 = 61.43$, $df = 3$, $p << 0.005$) and examination of the table shows the deviations to be in the direction predicted by the hypothesis, with the exception of the non-significant difference for *RFC* messages.

Structural Changes   Another support for this model comes from its ability to explain the observed structural changes by showing how the implemented changes address the perceived problems with the organization. We examine three such changes here.

Elimination of middle managers: As mentioned above, the manager largely responsible for the final organizational change had two complaints about the presence of group C&B managers in the organization: (1) maintaining the middle level of management in Division "A" was too expensive; (2) the group C&B managers "buffered" the division and corporate C&B staff from the problems being experienced by the site agents. It is clear that eliminating the group C&B managers will help the first problem by directly reducing the payroll costs for the organization. The second problem can be interpreted in the framework of the model by noting that in the original organization the division managers

Table 4   Number of messages in each category

Policy	Problem	Request For Comment	Comment	Broadcast	Other
87	47	16	41	66	4
33%	18%	6%	16%	25%	2%

Table 5   Message categories, broken down by organizational location of sender. Expected values are in parentheses.

Organizational Location of Sender	Policy	Problem	Request For Comment	Comment	Total
Site	16	41	8	24	89
	(40.5)	(21.9)	(7.5)	(19.1)	
Corporate	71	6	8	17	102
	(46.5)	(25.1)	(8.5)	(21.9)	
Total	87	47	16	41	191

communicate only with the group managers and never directly with the site managers. This has two effects. First, the division managers never receive *Problem* messages directly from the site managers, but only indirectly through the group managers. Second, the division managers can exchange *RFC* and *Comment* messages only with the group managers and not the sites, thus reducing the variety (and perhaps immediacy) of the comments received. Clearly, removing the group managers will make both of these types of communication possible and thus should reduce the sense of buffering.

Use of computer conferencing: After the divisions were merged and the division "A" group managers eliminated, however, some new mechanism was necessary to coordinate the 24 site level managers. In an interview, the new C&B manager listed four alternatives he considered to solve this problem of a large "span of control":

- local peer communication (where one of the site managers would be responsible for coordinating the other sites in his or her group);

- dividing the division staff geographically (with each division staff member responsible for a different group of sites);

- large face-to-face meetings (where all site managers could hear the answers to each other's questions simultaneously); and

- use of computer conferencing (where again all site managers could see the answers to all questions).

In terms of structure, these changes reduce to a choice between some variant on the previous hierarchical structure and a market-like meeting structure, where everyone is connected to everyone else in the organization. It seems clear from our analysis that maintaining a hierarchical structure will maintain the problem of lack of feedback to the corporate level, without affecting the ability of the corporate level to poll the site managers. This suggests that a meeting-like structure is preferable, eliminating the first two alternatives considered. Computer conferencing was chosen as a technology to drive the organizational change because it seems to have a lower cost for day-to-day operations, although the interviews revealed that face-to-face meetings are also still held (biweekly between the managers in adjacent levels; quarterly for others).

Increase in staff specialists: One surprising finding of the case was that the total number of managers appears not to have gone down when the system was installed (see Table 6). One common prediction is that

Table 6 Number of staff members at each organizational level, before and after the reorganization

	Before		After	
Organizational Level	Job Grade 1	Job Grade 2	Job Grade 1	Job Grade 2
Site	18		24	
Group		5		
Division	4	3	2	5
Total	22	8	26	5

increased use of IT will lead to reduction in middle management. Such a reduction seems to have been a motive here, but, in fact, the total number of people did not go down. Instead, it seems that people were removed from group manager positions in division "A" and others of the same grade were added as staff specialists to the division staff, while the opposite happened in division "B". In total effect, there was a centralization, with more staff and decisions made higher up in the hierarchy. Accompanying this centralization was a specialization, since the staff added at the corporate level were responsible for specific programmes, unlike the generalist group managers they replaced. Lawrence and Lorsch (1967) note that such increased differentiation requires higher communication; similarly, Malone and Smith (1985) predicted that cheaper communication could lead to the use of functional rather than product or geographic hierarchies, as discussed above. The centralization and specialization seem to have been made possible by the reduction in communications cost and the broadcast capability offered by the system.

This finding suggests that technology-induced elimination of middle managers is actually a result of two causes: the introduction of some technology to make the elimination of the managers possible, and a resource constraint making such reductions important. In the absence of resource constraints, management resources that are no longer needed for mediating communication may be applied to other tasks such as formulating better policies. For instance, one manager we interviewed commented that, "the complexity of the work being accomplished has deepened and the quality has increased ... I don't really know if some of those things would have been tackled a few years ago; I don't think they were."

Characteristics of System Usage Our model also exhibits a number of features that agree well with our observations and with comments made by our interviewees.

Job enlargement for site managers: Our model predicts a change in the role of site managers. Before the introduction of the computer conferencing system, site managers never saw *Problem* messages from their peers. Also because of the hierarchy, they would not see *RFC*s from the corporate or divisional C&B managers, and so would not participate in policy development. After the introduction of the conferencing system, however, site managers could receive both kinds of messages and could send *Policy* or *Comment* messages in reply, thus taking a more active role in the organization. Interviews with some of the division level managers indicated that such an upgrade in the status of site managers was in fact one of the goals of the organizational change, and one that they felt had been achieved.

System used for broadcasting messages, not information retrieval: The fact that the system was used primarily as a broadcast medium rather than as a data base was confirmed by a number of behavioural observations. First, most people in the organization subscribe to every conference they can, instead of only the ones in which they are currently interested, a fact brought up by the managers we interviewed and partially confirmed by examining the membership list for several conferences. Second, a division C&B manager reported that he checks who has read the messages in each conference and calls to remind those who are not caught up. We found some evidence that messages are reread from the system only in special cases. For example, when new employees joined the organization, they would be told to read the old messages in order to catch up. Also, at one point instructions for the use of a new system were made available on the system, but in a separate file, not as a conference message. Finally, there seemed to be few provisions for searching the messages, and managers interviewed indicated that they rarely did that. These observations support our claim that the system was used primarily as a broadcast medium.

Conclusions

Using our technique we have been able to develop a model that incorporates observations at two levels. At the macro level, it offers an explanation for the structural changes that took place. At the micro level, it incorporates observed individual use of the conferencing system, reflected in the messages sent as well as the participants' impressions. We believe that this twofold support highlights the more inclusive nature of our perspective.

Our perspective seems likely to be further applicable in two distinct ways. First, it is useful, as demonstrated by the case above, for explaining and perhaps predicting the kinds of changes associated with the introduction of IT. As our review of the literature has shown, studies using only gross operationalizations of IT have only led to uninterpretable results. Studies based on a much more detailed understanding of the use of IT may lead to more generalizable results. This suggests performing a number of case studies of the sort presented here, and looking for common features.

A second use of this methodology was suggested by Tushman and Nadler (1978): design of organizations. A prior analysis of this type might be used to identify the organizational processes that can be effectively supported and the information systems and organizational structures that will be useful. A computer simulation of an organization, based on a model such as that developed above could be used by a designer to quickly and easily experiment with new organizational forms, predict the effects of different kinds of IT. A general design tool such as this could also be used to examine the properties or organizations that are not yet feasible, and thus explore the potential of future technologies.

Acknowledgments

This research was supported by the Center for Information Systems Research and the Management in the 1990s Project at the Sloan School of Management, Massachusetts Institute of Technology.

The authors would especially like to thank the managers at "EMF" for their generous contributions of time and data.

Appendix: Instructions for Coding Message Categories

The code for each type of message is given in *italics* after the description. Note that some messages may have more than one type (*e.g.*, a message giving a policy and asking about another policy). If so, please note all message types. Be CAREFUL to analyze the **content** of the message rather than its form. For example, "Would you send me documentation to help me with System X..." is a *PROB* and not a *RFC*.

Policy (Pol)

A message *outlining* some policy or *answering a procedural question*, including *capabilities or use* of a system. *NOT* a message giving a comment or opinion about some policy or describing a problem with it. For example:

"To login to System-X, type 'LOGON <user>'..."

"Plan B will not update the database records..."

"Don't use the system on Fridays because..."

"To answer Fred's question, yes, we do enter that data..."

Comment (Com)

A message giving a *comment on or opinion* about a policy. Note that comment may be in reply to **Policies** as well as **RFCs**. *NOT* a message outlining a policy or answering a procedural question. For example:

"We have reviewed the planning policy and suggest the following revisions..."

"I should clarify my view... The system should verify..."

"To answer Jane's question, I agree, we should use a review board for..."

RFC (RFC)

A message *asking for comments* on a policy or system. *NOT* a message asking for help implementing a policy. For example:

"Please send a note with the following information..."

"Would someone tell me how you think we should handle..."

"Who's using review boards..."

Problem (Prob)

A message from a site person *asking the staff for help* with or for *clarification* of a policy. *NOT* a message asking for comments on a policy or system. For example:

"What is the contingency plan...?"

"What will happen to us under those rules?"

"Since when have we treated CPR teams that way?"

Other, Classified (Other)

A message of one of the following types:

Personnel (*e.g.*, "Please welcome Mary to the group" or "Goodbye");

Conference system related (*e.g.*, branching a group or drawing attention to a new group or message);

Announcements of job openings;

Personal (*e.g.*, "Merry Christmas");

Thank you's for some answer;

Meeting or meeting attendance announcements and questions (*e.g.*, "Can we not meet on Sunday?"; "No, we have to meet then.").

Other, Unclassified

A message that can't otherwise be classified.

References

P. Attewell and J. Rule, "Computing and Organizations: What We Know and What We Don't Know", *Communications of the ACM*, Volume 27, Number 12, December 1984.

O. R. Barber, "An Office Study: Its Implications on the Understanding of Organizations", Unpublished Paper, Massachusetts Institute of Technology, 1985.

U. Briefs, "Re-Thinking Industrial Work: Computer Effects on Technical White-Collar Workers", *Computers in Industry*, Volume 2, pp. 76–81, 1981.

S. A. Brobst, T. W. Malone, K. R. Grant and M. D. Cohen, "Toward intelligent message routing systems", *Computer message systems—85: Proceedings of the Second International Symposium on Computer Message Systems*, R. Uhlig (ed), Amsterdam: North-Holland, 1986.

Business Week, "A New Era for Management", *Business Week*, pp. 50–86, 25 April 1983.

Business Week, "Office Automation Restructures Business", *Business Week*, pp. 118–142, 8 October 1985.

N. Carter, "Computerization as a Predominate Technology: Its Influence on the Structure of Newspaper Organizations", *Academy of Management Journal*, Volume 27, Number 2, pp. 247–270, June 1984.

A. D. Chandler, Jr., *Strategy and structure: Chapters in the history of the American industrial enterprise*, Cambridge, MA: MIT Press, 1962.

M. D. Cohen, *Artificial Intelligence and the Dynamic Performance of Organizational Designs*, Discussion Paper Number 204, Institute of Public Policy Studies, University of Michigan, June 1984.

T. D. Cook and D. T. Campbell, *Quasi-Experimentation: Design and Analysis Issues for Field Settings*, Boston: Houghton Mifflin, 1979.

A. B. Crawford, Jr., "Corporate Electronic Mail—A Communication-Intensive Application of Information Technology", *MIS Quarterly*, pp. 1–13, September 1982.

R. M. Cyert and J. G. March, *A Behavioural Theory of the Firm*, Englewood Cliffs, NJ: Prentice-Hall, 1963.

J. J. Elam, J. C. Henderson and J. B. Thomas, *Diagnostic Approach for Analyzing the Impact of the Information Systems Function*, Unpublished Working Paper, University of Texas at Austin, 1984.

L. W. Foster and D. M. Flynn, "Management Information Technology: Its Effects on Organizational Form and Function", *MIS Quarterly*, pp. 229–235, December 1984.

L. C. Freeman, "The Impact of Computer Based Communication on the Social Structure of an Emerging Scientific Specialty", *Social Networks*, Volume 6, pp. 201–221, 1984.

J. R. Galbraith, "Organization Design: An Information Processing View", *Interfaces*, Volume 4, Number 5, pp. 28–36, May 1974.

J. R. Galbraith, *Organization Design*, Reading, MA: Addison-Wesley, 1977.

A. Goldberg and D. Robson, *Smalltalk-80: The Language and Its Implementation*, Reading, MA: Addison-Wesley, 1983.

S. R. Hiltz and M. Turoff, "The Evolution of User Behavior in a Computerized Conferencing System", *Communications of the ACM*, Volume 24, Number 11, pp. 739–751, November 1981.

R. Kling, "Social Analyses of Computing: Theoretical Perspectives in Recent Empirical Research", *ACM Computing Surveys*, Volume 12, Number 1, pp. 61–110, March 1980.

H. J. Leavitt and T. L. Whisler, "Management in the 1980's", *Harvard Business Review*, Volume 36, Number 6, pp. 41–48, November/December 1958.

P. Lawrence and J. Lorsch, *Organization and Environment*, Boston: Division of Research, Harvard Business School, 1967.

F. Lin, *The Organizational Impact of Electronic Conferencing*, Unpublished Bachelors Thesis, Department of Electrical Engineering and Computer Science, Massachusetts Institute of Technology, May 1985.

T. W. Malone, *Organizational Structure and Information Technology: Elements of a Formal Theory*, Working Paper Number 130, Center for Information Systems Research, MIT Sloan School of Management, August 1985a.

T. W. Malone, *Computer Support for Organizations: Towards an Organizational Science*, Working Paper Number 85-012, Management in the 1990s, MIT Sloan School of Management, September 1985b.

T. W. Malone, R. I. Benjamin and J. Yates, *Electronic Markets and Electronic Hierarchies: Effects of Information Technology on Market Structure and Corporate Strategies*, to appear in *Proceedings of the Seventh International Conference on Information Systems*, December 1986.

T. W. Malone and S. A. Smith, *Tradeoffs in Designing Organizations: Implications for New Forms of Human Organizations and Computer Systems*, Working Paper Number 112, Center for Information Systems Research, MIT Sloan School of Management, March 1984.

J. G. March and H. A. Simon, *Organizations*, New York: John Wiley and Sons, 1958.

M. L. Markus and D. Robey, *Information Technology and Organizational Change: Conception of Causality in Theory and Research*, Unpublished Paper, University of California, Los Angeles, June 1986.

D. McArthur, P. Klahr and S. Narain, *ROSS: An Object-Oriented Language for Constructing Simulations*, Project AIR FORCE Report Number R-3160-AF, The Rand Corporation, December 1984.

J. L. McKenney, V. S. Doherty and J. J. Sviokla, *The Impact of Electronic Networks on Management Communication: An Information Processing Study*, Working Paper 1-786-041, Harvard Business School, June, 1986.

A. M. Mohrman, Jr., "The Impact of Information Processing Technology on Office Roles", Paper Presented at the Annual Meeting of the World Futures Society, Washington, D. C., 21 July 1982.

A. Newell and H. A. Simon, "Computer Science as Empirical Inquiry: Symbols and Search", *Communications of the ACM*, Volume 19, pp. 113–126, 1976.

M. H. Olson, "New Information Technology and Organizational Culture", *MIS Quarterly*, Special Issue, pp. 71–92, 1982.

C. Perrow, "A Framework for the Comparative Analysis of Organizations", *American Sociological Review*, Volume 32, pp. 194–208, 1967.

C. Perrow, *Complex Organizations: A Critical Essay*, 2nd ed., New York: Random House, 1979.

J. Pfeffer, *Organizational Design*, Arlington Heights, Illinois: Harlan Davidson, Inc., 1978.

J. Pfeffer and H. Leblebici, "Information Technology and Organizational Structure", *Pacific Sociological Review*, Volume 20, Number 2, pp. 241–261,

April 1977.

D. F. Robey, "Computer Information Systems and Organization Structure", *Communications of the ACM*, Volume 24, Number 10, pp. 679–687, October 1981.

D. F. Robey, "Information Systems and Organizational Change: A Comparative Case Study", *Systems, Objectives, Solutions*, Volume 3, pp. 143–154, 1983.

C. Rowe, "The Impact of Computers on the Work Organisation: Centralisation or Decentralisation?" *Industrial Management and Data Systems*, pp. 13–15, November/December 1984.

G. L. Sanders, J. F. Courtney and S. L. Loy, "The Impact of DSS on Organizational Communication", *Information and Management*, Volume 7, pp. 141–148, 1984.

H. Simon, "Rationality as a Process and the Product of Thought", *American Economic Review*, Volume 68, pp. 1–16, 1986.

M. Stefik and D. G. Bobrow, "Object-Oriented Programming: Themes and Variations", *The AI Magazine*, pp. 40–62, 1986.

M. Tushman and D. Nadler, "Information Processing as an Integrating Concept in Organization Design", *Academy of Management Review*, Volume 3, pp. 613–624, 1978.

G. Walker, "Network Position and Cognition in a Computer Software Firm", *Administrative Science Quarterly*, Volume 30, March 1985.

R. E. Walton, "Social Choice in the Development of Advanced Information Technology", *Technology in Society*, Volume 4, pp. 41–49, 1982.

T. L. Whisler, *Information Technology and Organizational Change*, Belmont, CA: Wadsworth, 1970.

O. E. Williamson, *Markets and Hierarchies: Analysis and Antitrust Implications*, New York: The Free Press, 1975.

S. Zuboff, *Some Implications of Information Systems Power for the Role of the Middle Manager*, Working Paper Number 84-29, Harvard Business School, May 1983a.

S. Zuboff, "New Worlds of Computer-Mediated Work", *Harvard Business Review*, pp. 142–152, September–October 1983b.

Relationships and Tasks in Scientific Research Collaborations

Robert Kraut
Bell Communications Research

Jolene Galegher
University of Arizona

Carmen Egido
Bell Communications Research

Most computer-based aids for researchers and other workers have had individuals, rather than groups or teams, as their beneficiaries. This is unfortunate, since much work in business and academia is performed by groups of people (Bair, 1985). It is especially unfortunate for researchers in the sciences and social sciences. Examinations of patterns of authorship reveal that collaborative research is increasing in many disciplines. In psychology, for example, the mean number of authors per published article rose from 1.5 in 1949 to 2.2 in 1979 (Over, 1982), and, in 1981, over 65% of articles in a sample of six social psychology journals were jointly authored (Mendenhall, Oddou & Franck, 1984). A variety of factors including increases in the professionalization of science and in research funding can partially explain these trends, but, so far, improvements in technology do not seem to have caused or even facilitated this increase (Beaver & Rosen, 1978, 1979; Heffner, 1981; Over, 1982). With the important exception of improvements in the quality and cost of telecommunications transmission, information technology has not evolved to meet the needs of collaborating research scientists. The trends noted above, however, suggest that opportunities to test and implement technologies that support collaborative research are proliferating and seem likely to grow in the years ahead. The premise of this report is that understanding the nature of collaborative work relationships can help to make those efforts a success.

In this paper we propose a framework for describing research collaboration that we hope will provide guidance to those developing technology to aid collaborative work. Our general approach has been to specify the hurdles or dilemmas that researchers must overcome in order to collaborate successfully. These are real problems, although most research scientists do not see them as major or particularly difficult to handle. Institutional arrangements resolve many before they occur, and others are solved naturally in the course of doing research. They are resolved through the behaviors and techniques for doing work that are built into the structure of the scientific community, learned through observation of the experiences of others, absorbed from the organizational culture, or worked out in explicit discussions between research partners. In dealing with these potential dilemmas, researchers illustrate the current technologies for collaborative work. We use the term "technologies" here in its broadest sense, to include not only hardware and software, but also institutional arrangements and work techniques that the institution of science itself, the organizations that employ researchers, and individual researchers have adopted to get the work of science done. As such these technologies provide a baseline that computer scientists and engineers must understand in order to not disrupt on-going adaptations and to offer better solutions to partially solved problems.

Our framework was derived from semi-structured interviews with one member from each of 50 pairs of researchers in social psychology, management science, and computer science, as well as on our experience with long-distance collaboration in producing this and other research products. We selected our interviewees from among those who had published a jointly-authored paper in a small number of prestigious refereed journals in 1986. One-hour telephone interviews were conducted with one member of each collaborative pair. In 36 of the interviews we asked collaborators to describe the production of the published article, while in 14 we asked them to describe projects they defined as problematic. During the interview, respondents provided a narrative history of their collaboration, from first meeting to the time of the interview. Through

Figure 27.1 Model of research collaboration

follow-up questions and probes, respondents were encouraged to discuss the following topics: the decision to work together; the evolution of the project; the division of labor between the collaborators; the apportioning of recognition and reward for the project; coordination of the work in progress; problems that arose during the collaboration; and the advantages and disadvantages of collaborative work.

1 Overview

Figure 27.1 shows the path that collaborative research relationships typically follow. We propose that research collaborations progress through three stages—initiation, execution and public presentation—and that at each stage activity takes place on two levels—a relationship level and a task level. Remarkably different problems confront the collaborators at each of these stages. In the initiation stage potential collaborators establish a personal relationship, commit themselves to working together, and plan a project. Their primary goal is to establish an interpersonal relationship based on shared interests. To do so they must identify commonalities or, at least, compatibilities in research interests, in professional goals, and in individual work styles. In addition, they must come to an agreement about the broad outline of their research objectives and the approach they will take to reach them. These goals in the initiation stage were very general across disciplines.

The central goal of the execution stage of the collaboration is to move from the specification of a research objective through the many and varied tasks that must be carried out to complete the project. In this stage, plans become more detailed and specific; they are often revised and occasionally abandoned without the research collaboration disintegrating. Ultimately, for successful collaborations, the work itself is executed. The nature of activities during the execution stage, of course, depends on the research being carried out. But regardless of these topic-specific activities, most collaborators are confronted with the complexities of developing an equitable division of labor, of subtly supervising a peer, of sharing private and ill-formed information, and of coordinating activity that is continually evolving.

In the public presentation stage, researchers document and disseminate their research. This activity is, again, similar across disciplinary lines. The physical task of writing most often involves a division of labor, but, in the course of developing a final product, the collaborators must come to a common understanding of what they want to say and how to say it. In addition, they must make decisions about order of authorship and responsibility for public talks. The necessity to allocate credit and the opportunity to be in the spotlight force collaborators to evaluate each other's contribution to the joint project explicitly.

It typically takes 18 months to 2 years for a pair of researchers to move through these stages (Garvey, Lin, & Nelson, 1970). At a minimum, this time span suggests that technologies focusing on collaborative tasks, with time spans ranging from minutes (e.g., making plans and arrangements, exchanging information via conference calls), to days (e.g., writing and editing using word processing) or even to months (e.g., idea generation and evaluation via computer conferences), will only nibble at the large problem of supporting research collaborations. In this paper we will describe individual and social factors that facilitate or hinder accomplishment of the goals we described above and discuss technological needs and difficulties that arise at each stage.

2 Initiation Stage

Researchers become involved in collaborative relationships for a variety of reasons. As one might expect, combining resources to accomplish a project was a major reason why researchers collaborated. These resources included material ones (e.g., grant money, research assistants, labor, computer time) and intellectual ones (e.g., substantive knowledge and methodological skills). Second, people collaborated because collaboration changed the process of research for them in desirable ways. In particular, for many of our respondents, working with another person was simply more fun than working alone. Similarly, they also believed that working with another improved the quality of the research product, because of the synthesis of ideas it allowed, the feedback they received from each other, and the new skills they learned. Third, a number of our respondents collaborated primarily to maintain a pre-established personal relationship, especially one that was threatened by physical separation. The collaboration provided a raison d'etre for contact. Fourth, researchers collaborated for self-presentational or political reasons, because they believed that working with a particular person or being in a collaborative relationship per se was valuable for their careers. As Crane (1965) has demonstrated, multiple publications in an area are crucial to becoming a recognized leader in a field and having multiple authors does not hinder this process (Innes, 1980). Of course, these motives are not mutually exclusive, and in most cases respondents cited a combination of them to explain why they collaborated with their partners. These motivations represent a mix of task and relationship factors, and the development of a satisfactory and productive collaborative relationship requires activity on both of these levels.

To start a research collaboration, potential collaborators must become acquainted with each other, identify their common interests and the mutual benefit that might come from working together, become committed to working together, and establish a preliminary agenda and division of labor. Below we discuss each of these aspects of the development of a collaborative relationship.

2.1 *Relationship Level*

The essential relationship-level activity during the initiation stage is determining whether potential collaborators are suitable work partners. This means determining whether they are smart enough to help think through problems and responsible enough to do their share of the work, as well as whether they are sympathetic enough with one's research perspective and compatible enough in work style and personality to make working together pleasant. Ideally, one would like to make these judgments *before* one is committed to the execution of a long and difficult project with a less than compatible partner. We will see below that the organizational arrangements of their work places enable most researchers to make these assessments unobtrusively, perhaps without even being aware of the process.

2.1.1 *Getting Connected* The most fundamental requirement for the development of a collaborative relationship is that potential collaborators have the opportunity to make contact with each other. Then, in order for the relationship to grow beyond acquaintance, the individuals must come to see each other as intellectually and interpersonally suitable collaborators. The opportunity to make contact can be provided by geographical proximity or institutional norms or can be created by special events such as a professional conference or the collaborators' own actions. Each of these mechanisms has different implications for how potential collaborators manage the problem of establishing suitability.

Proximity effects: The frequent, low-cost contact that is made possible by physical proximity creates many opportunities for potential collaborators to become acquainted, to identify common interests and to assess interpersonal compatibility. People with interests in common are often geographically clustered. But even if potential collaborators were evenly distributed across the social environment, pairs of them are more likely to get acquainted and identify shared interests and world views the more opportunities they have to communicate and the easier these opportunities are. As we found in our interviews, the identification of shared interests was likely to occur with a potential collaborator who sat across the lunch table, who was down the corridor, or who was in the same academic department. The effects of simple proximity and frequency of interaction seem to be as powerful in facilitating research collaborations as they are in social relations more generally (e.g., Festinger, Schachter, & Back, 1950; Kerchhoff, 1974).

One reason for the powerful effect of proximity is that it enables people to solve the primary relationship-level concern of this stage—establishing compatibility—easily and at low personal cost. They can exchange ideas, comments, news of their own activities and interests casually over lunch or a cup of coffee. If both individuals find the conversations and each other stimulating and enjoyable, they may discuss the possibilities for joint research more seriously and directly. But the casual conversation implies no commitment, and if a research collaboration does not develop, neither participant has lost face.

Well-documented tendencies in human judgment may help to explain why proximity plays such a dominant role in determining who collaborates with whom. Years of research on person perception processes have shown that individuals overestimate their ability to make complex judgments about other people. They feel that they can make better judgments about another when presented with the complex array of data that face-to-face interaction makes available than when presented with only a few relevant facts about the stimulus person or than when they interact with a partner over a limited channel like the telephone, even though the extra information rarely improves their judgments (Dawes, 1971, 1979; Sawyer, 1966; Zuckerman, DePaulo, & Rosenthal, 1981). In the development of collaborations, therefore, people are more likely to feel confident about making commitments to work together when each has had the opportunity to size up the other face-to-face than if they learn about each other in an indirect way such as by reading each other's prior publications. These tendencies to prefer face-to-face contact and to attribute to ourselves complex powers of judgment combine to make proximity a frequent solution to the relationship-level problem of establishing compatibility with a potential collaborator.

Thus we see that proximity not only enables potential collaborators to make contact with each other, but also makes it possible for them to make unobtrusive and psychologically satisfying assessments of the likelihood that they would be able to work together productively and amicably. Reaching agreement to work with another individual on a specific project requires both interpersonal compatibility and mutual substantive interests. That both of these elements seem to be present in collaborations that are described by the participants as successful may establish boundary conditions on technologies supporting cooperative work. Such technologies are geared toward allowing individuals to learn about each other's ideas and interests or to accomplish tasks, but do not provide a sustained opportunity to learn about each other as people. Technologies such as computer conferencing or readily available video links between organizational locations (Goodman & Abel, 1986) combine the opportunity for chance meetings and low cost contacts with the opportunity to seek out a particular other on the basis of mutual interests. They could be used more extensively to promote the initiation of research collaborations at a distance. We wonder, however, whether potential collaborators will be able to or willing to use them to discover personal compatibilities.

Institutional norms: In addition to proximity, institutional norms create opportunities to make contact with potential collaborators and strongly influence who collaborates with whom. Many respondents mentioned the existence of an environment that encourages or, at least, does not actively discourage collaboration as a factor shaping their research activities. The most typical of collaborations—between professor and student or between principal investigator and paid research assistant—are defined almost totally by reference to social norms. Depending on the local supply and demand, faculty will work with almost any student who walks in the door and students with any faculty who will take them. Only in the context of these role obligations, do individual tastes in research topic or personal style come into play. In these situations, then, the relationship-level problem of making contact is obviated by a social system that requires particular people to make contact with particular others.

Extra-Institutional contact mechanisms: Collaborations between investigators within the same institution (or who were within the same institution when the collaboration started) were, by far, the most common in our research. But we did find instances of collaborative relationships that were initiated outside an institutional framework. In a number of cases, including our own, people began to work together after an initial conversation at a professional meeting.

We observed two different patterns in the development of relationships after an initial meeting at a conference. In some cases, individuals with only remotely overlapping research interests met and liked each other at a conference and then later found a way to work together. In one of these instances, a now very close and productive collaborative relationship turned into a work relationship only after meetings at three successive annual meetings. In other cases, one party sought out the other because a conference presentation or published work was of particular interest. In these situations, the issue of intellectual compatibility was already resolved—at least at a superficial level—and, in our interviews, people seemed to assume that interpersonal compatibility would follow. It's worth noting, however, that even in these cases where seeming strangers came together, contact at meetings was preceded by contact with the potential collaborator's reputation. Research communities are small and provide many opportunities for individuals to know about each other without ever having met. The existence of a research community is a surrogate for physical proximity, and professional meetings provide the intellectual and social benefits of proximity to colleagues, if only on a short-term basis. Thus, even when researchers do not share an institutional home, social structures—in this case, professional organizations—play an important role in bringing them together.

2.1.2 *Moving toward Commitment*   The initial contact between potential collaborators sets the stage for a series of conversations or long-distance interactions that leads to a commitment to work together on a specific project. We identified two dominant routes through which potential collaborators moved from mere acquaintance to commitment. In some collaborations, informal contact evolved into commitment, similarly to the way in which informal contact often evolves into friendship. Here collaborators could not identify a precise time when informal discussion turned into collaboration. For other collaborators, however, the process was more analogous to courtship and marriage, in which one partner proposed collaboration to the other. The proposal was accepted or rejected on the basis of explicit evaluations of mutual interests and feasibility. In addition, we found a few cases of arranged marriages, where a high status person ordained that two people he or she was responsible for should work together.

As might be expected, the nature of the commitment process varies with distance. The gradual, informal contact-to-commitment evolution was by far the more frequent and occurred in situations where individuals had the opportunity for frequent interaction, and the more explicit, formal proposal-acceptance process occurred in situations where both proposing and executing the collaborative work required structured, intentional communication.

2.2 *Task-Level*

In the initiation stage, as elsewhere, relationships and tasks often blend, but the distinction between the two is useful to illuminate the complexity of the process through which researchers come together and begin to formulate a research project or program. The major goal at this point is to merge differing perspectives and interests into a framework that will provide the basis for a joint project.

2.2.1 *Idea Generation*   The initial task-level activity in a collaborative relationship usually consists of multiple face-to-face discussions, occurring over the course of days, or, more typically, weeks or even months. These discussions are the most intensely interactive aspect of a collaborative project. The investigators we interviewed reported that they are also the most intellectually exciting and rewarding aspect of collaborative work. It is here that ideas are really joined. In these talks, the collaborators moved from the general ideas that brought them together to a specific research question and the outline of a plan for executing the project.

The mechanics of these meetings are simple: they take place in faculty offices or conference rooms and, typically, the only technologies involved are paper, pencils, and blackboard. The participants, except for graduate students, do not prepare for these meetings in any formal sense. There is little reliance on pre-written documents or diagrams as a basis for the discussion; instead, collaborators seem to value the opportunity for spontaneous, informal, and unstructured exchange of ideas. The participants talk, argue, interrupt, write equations, draw sketches, and modify both their own and their partners' work. Participants may take notes in order to have a record of important observations or issues that arise in the conversation or to remind themselves of things to do—articles to read, people to contact, purchases to make—but there is usually no explicit effort to make a formal record of the proceedings. Among peer collaborators, only one pair in our sample wrote a formal proposal or memorandum of understanding to each other to document and clarify the work they intended to do together. Such formal documents were more typical of graduate student research proposals to faculty. In listening to reports of these conversations, one has the sense of high energy levels and a high level of concentration on the serious, substantive intellectual questions involved.

Our analysis of these discussions revealed two styles of project development and planning. In the first, the research question and project plan grew directly out of the joint conversations. In these cases, individuals did not seem to be able to identify idea ownership. In the other, one partner presented his or her ideas for a project and the other partner served as a sounding board, presenting critiques, alternative approaches, and refinements, until they had come to agreement about the questions they wanted to pursue and outlined an approach for their empirical work. This second pattern was more common for both peer and faculty-student collaborations. However, despite the fact that collaborators could frequently identify ownership of the initial idea, they also acknowledged that initial ideas usually underwent major transformations before work was done. Indeed, many interviewees seemed to feel the opportunity to do this kind of intellectual work with another person was the primary benefit of collaboration.

By this point, then, the collaborators have developed a specific research plan and some general ideas as to how to carry it out. All of this has been accomplished with little reliance on sophisticated technology of any sort, including the telephone. In order to preserve the value that researchers currently find in these intense face-to-face interactions, technology builders must concentrate on supporting the highly interactive, real-time, spoken, non-text-oriented, multi-media work style we have described above. Although visual nonverbal behavior (e.g., quizzical expressions, nodding to indicate agreement) no doubt plays a role in helping researchers understand each other at this point, these behaviors are probably not crucial and are redundant with parallel auditory nonverbal behavior (Krauss, Garlock, Bricker, & McMahon, 1977). Technology that allows researchers to talk and to pass and modify brief handwritten documents quickly would be more useful. Especially if individuals are already acquainted, it is less important to be able to see each other than to be able to work with and have records of sketches, equations and other notes.

Although our research indicates that the initiation and planning of research occurs most frequently when individuals are physically close, we found a few cases in which collaborators maintained research activity after one member moved and face-to-face meetings became rare. In these instances, individuals had developed both a shared world view and a shorthand way of communicating that diminished the impact of distance on their ability to do the awkward, ill-defined idea generation and specification work that seems to be particularly difficult to do at a distance.

However, we should not conclude that a well-developed research relationship can be easily maintained at a distance. Indeed, one of our colleagues, a veteran of many collaborative projects, commented that after his research partner moved to a new institution they hadn't initiated any new projects despite their intentions to do so—intentions that were reaffirmed over drinks when they saw each other at annual conferences. His explanation for the gap between their intentions and their behavior was that, "We never got to have the second conversation." Thus, despite a long history of successful collaboration and intentions to continue to work together, these individuals seemed to be hampered by distance in their ability to formulate new plans and projects.

3 Execution Stage

Assuming that a pair of individuals has arrived at an agreement to work together and a general plan about work topic and agenda, they must then plan in detail and execute the actual tasks required to carry out and document their research. Some problems confronting collaborators are universal—achieving an equitable division of labor, dealing with intellectual and other disagreements, coordinating work, monitoring progress, and overcoming the derailing effects of personal problems, conflicting commitments, and procrastination—while other problems in collaborations were more domain specific. Social psychologists rarely had to solve the algorithm problems that plagued computer scientists. Computer scientists didn't have to negotiate access to organizations as management scientists do. We will not discuss these domain-specific problems below. Rather, we will attempt to portray the issues involved in the execution of collaborative work at a more general level.

In carrying out their research plan, collaborators have two primary missions. First, they must accomplish the work they have set for themselves, overcoming both practical barriers and sloth as they proceed. Second, they must maintain an interpersonal relationship that is at least minimally cordial, often in the face of stressful circumstances. These goals are potentially in conflict, but collaborators are helped in trying to achieve them by the commitments developed earlier in the relationship. Our respondents reported that although their initial research plan might have foundered or required substantial reshaping, the idea of working together remained intact; the commitment to work on a particular project with a particular other made it possible for their collaboration to withstand disruptions, conflicts, and hurdles that would have been fatal at the earlier stage.

3.1 *Task Level*

Here we reverse the order of the discussion of relationship and task level issues. This is a reflection of a switch in what might be called the motive force for execution stage activity. In the initiation stage, tasks typically flowed from a personal relationship; in the execution stage relationship-level issues seemed to arise from the task-level concerns that govern this production-oriented phase.

3.1.1 *Coordinating Activity and Sharing Information*   Whenever two or more people work together, they must share information and coordinate activities in ways that solo researchers need not do (cf., Galbraith, 1973). For collaborators, information-sharing means that some information that would have remained implicit throughout a solo research project must become explicit so that it can be communicated to a research partner. The requirement to make implicit knowledge explicit surfaces throughout the collaboration process. For example, collaborators must explicitly delineate their research direction and methodological approach, translate idiosyncratic shorthands, and summarize meetings with external contacts. This can be particularly difficult when people are involved in complex technical tasks such as programming and data analysis where knowledge of what has been done, what has been learned, and what remains to be done exists at a pre-verbal level in the mind of one member of the collaborative pair.

In addition to sharing information, people who work together need to coordinate their activities. In general this means they must mesh their work so that all of it gets done, that it isn't done redundantly, and that components of the work are handed off in a timely manner without impeding another's progress on a different part of the project.

We had hypothesized that both information sharing and activity coordination would be among the major unresolved problems of collaborative research, but collaborators didn't experience them as such. They identified some difficulties in cramming meetings and research activities into overloaded schedules, but in general they did not experience problems in the mechanics of sharing information or meshing activities. By drawing conclusions from a sample of small and relatively successful collaborations, however, we have underestimated the importance of this set of problems.

Reducing the needs for information sharing: The reason for this difference between our expectations and our findings was that collaborators developed work strategies that reduced the need for information sharing and activity coordination. We identified three mechanisms that collaborators use to minimize coordination problems: division of labor, encapsulation, and sequential processing.

By dividing tasks among themselves, collaborators turned many potentially joint tasks into individual ones. For example, in the modal collaboration in our sample—an empirical, social science research project—data collection, data analysis, and writing the first draft were each typically the responsibility of one member of the collaboration. In other collaborations, the division was at finer levels, for example developing questionnaires, drawing figures, or handling contacts with human subjects committees. Whatever the level of granularity, the division of labor had the consequence of allowing a single individual to handle all of the details of one phase in the research process so that information sharing and activity coordination needs were reduced. While division of labor has many functions, simplification of the communication task among collaborators was an important one in our sample.

Collaborators used encapsulation in conjunction with division of labor to reduce needs for activity coordination and information sharing. Encapsulation means that the researcher who had primary responsibility for a piece of a project often presented his or her partner with a completed subunit, but generally did not communicate in detail the processes by which these subunits were produced. By keeping intervening processes private, collaborators reduced the need to turn inchoate material into a form that was comprehensible to another. For example, after planning an experiment, the collaborators generally did not meet to discuss it in detail until the responsible partner had collected some pretest data and then not again until all of the data had been collected and made ready for analysis. Encapsulation was a technique practiced more among peer collaborators than among unequal collaborators: faculty often didn't trust the competence of their student collaborators and demanded more active supervision.

Finally, during the execution and especially during the writing stages of research, collaborators used sequential processing to minimize the need for coordinating activity and sharing information. Sequential processing means that a passive partner becomes activated only when he or she received a completed subunit from the then active partner. For example, one partner started data entry after the active partner handed off a set of completed questionnaires and another started writing the first draft of a manuscript after the active partner handed off the results of the data analysis.

As a result of these three techniques—division of labor, encapsulation, and sequential processing—many collaborations can be characterized as threaded collections of jointly planned but individually executed products. The highly interactive and integrative aspects of the collaboration come primarily in the planning stages for both the project as a whole and for the documentation; the execution of these plans, however, tends to be done as the exclusive responsibility of one party or another.

Annotation: One way in which collaborators did share information was to annotate the products they passed to their collaborators, thus making explicit some information that they would have kept implicit if they had been working by themselves. In data analysis, for example, they would pencil in label definitions to annotate the brief variable labels common in some statistical software. But this static annotation was the exception rather than the rule. Instead collaborators typically handed off products, passed information, and briefed their partners in person. Providing such information during face-to-face meetings takes much less thought and effort than providing clear asynchronous textual annotations. In addition, feedback from the partner being briefed allowed the briefer to tailor the communication to the partner's concerns and confusions (Kraut, Lewis, & Swezey, 1982). In speech, communicators indicate mutual understanding through the use of back channel responses—nods, eye movements and "uh-hums." These are one mechanism that allows research collaborators to develop rich and meaningful, partner-specific abbreviations and short-hands, which would be incomprehensible to an outsider (Krauss & Weinheimer, 1966). These back channel responses are peppered throughout ordinary speech many times a minute, but they seem to have no analog in current asynchronous electronic communication systems. Kiesler, Siegal, & McGuire (1984) report that the absence of such feedback has a detrimental effect on electronically transmitted messages.

Joint supervision of the project: In peer collaborations one member occasionally adopted the role of project manager. More frequently, though, this leadership and project monitoring role was shared, if only to minimize status differentiations between the supposed peers. Their need to jointly supervise the progress of their research demonstrates an interesting conjunction of information sharing and activity coordination that deserves special attention.

Collaborators typically monitored the progress of a project by passing brief messages about project status during meetings with other primary purposes. These meetings were of two sorts. First were scheduled meetings in which decisions were made and substantive work on the project was done. These meetings could either be event driven (e.g., when the first test results of a computer program came in or when stimulus materials for an experiment had to be selected) or they could be periodically scheduled (e.g., weekly group meetings). The second type of meeting was brief hallway, mailroom, or lunchroom encounters. Both types of meeting provided collaborators an opportunity to alert their partners to deviations from normal progress about which the partner should be aware. The ritual dialogue

"How's it going"

"Fine"

which seems to carry little information is a sign from one partner to another that the agreed upon division of labor is working satisfactorily and doesn't require active intervention on the part of the passive partner. The failure to provide status information in the face of easy opportunities to do so is often taken as evidence that all is copacetic.

More generally, low cost communication and the opportunity for quick and easy access to a partner are crucial for collaborators' joint supervision of the project and each other's work. As a result proximity plays an important role in project management. Many of the sticking points in conducting research are minor. They consist of questions like: Should I change the wording of a question in a questionnaire? At what points should we break the program into modules? While working alone, one would simply make a decision. When working with a collaborator, researchers often want to share the decision, if only to preserve the balance of control they and their partner share in the project. Distance raises the personal costs of communication, so that short messages become uneconomical. As a result, distance cuts down on nags and feedback, both so crucial to accomplishing collaborative activities. One collaborator told us that her relationship with her partner deteriorated in part because personal commitments prevented them from having lunch together; as a result they had difficulty solving the minor problems of their on-going research, minor problems unworthy of a meeting or even a telephone call.

Computer mail can certainly supplement the face-to-face message passing now used by collaborators, although it runs the danger of appearing to be unwarranted nagging if it is frequently used for the sole purpose of requesting status reports. In computers with shared workspaces for the collaboration, each collaborator should be able to directly view the other's files to check on progress; how this procedure will affect issues of privacy and trust remains to be seen.

Rarely did collaborators use even shades of formal project management techniques. Only one respondent reported estimating how long tasks should take and then intervening when the actual time to accomplish the work took substantially longer than the scheduled time. This reluctance suggests that collaborators are unlikely to use formal project management techniques, including software, even though avoidable or unexplainable delays were a major problem in a minority of collaborative projects and researchers frequently complained that collaborative research took longer than solo research. Furthermore, in peer collaborations, the use of such techniques runs the risk of generating unequal leadership roles and a sense of distrust among partners that may damage the collaborative relationship.

3.1.2 *Sustaining progress* In executing their work, collaborators are confronted with many of the same problems that confront solo researchers. Both collaborators and solo researchers have similar impediments to progress from competing commitments, recalcitrant research topics, and logistical difficulties and use many of the same mechanisms for solving these problems. However, collaborators have additional mechanisms for sustaining progress that are unavailable to solo researchers.

For example, like solo researchers, collaborators motivate themselves by setting deadlines with external consequences, e.g., by promising to give talks at conferences before the work is actually completed. But in addition, collaborators set internal deadlines as well, in the form of promises to their partners or of preparations for regularly scheduled meetings. This is one of the many ways that collaborators act as external consciences for each other: the guilt and embarrassment from disappointing a partner's expectations drives the work. Frequent hallway meetings between collaborators give the conscience its sting.

In addition to being an external conscience, collaborators also served the roles of cheerleader and social support agent. Collaborators reported that when things were not going well, they used each other as "shoulders to cry on" and, in general, helped convince each other that the project was worthwhile and would turn out well. A supportive partner that believed in the value of the project was especially important in the face of rejections from journal reviewers and other peers (c.f., Festinger, Schachter, & Reicken, 1956, and Sherif, 1935, for more general demonstrations of the power of social support in sustaining a view of reality in the face of social opposition).

3.2 Relationship Level

3.2.1 *Equitable Division of Labor* The major potential strain on a collaborative relationship during the execution of the work was an imbalance between collaborators in both the amount of work they were doing and the credit they claimed. We discuss the credit imbalance in detail in the following section, since it is the major relationship issue during the public presentation stage of a research product, while work imbalance is more central to the execution stage. Among peers, at least, collaborators go to great lengths to insure that they and their partners do comparable amounts of work. In one collaboration, for example, when one partner supervised data collection, the second felt compelled to supervise the data entry, merely to even the score. Sometimes, recognition of the need to divide labor (and credit) leads the collaborators to initiate more than one project simultaneously, in order to insure that both bear an equal share of the burden of routine work and both will have an equal opportunity to be recognized as project leader. Since many collaborations extend over multiple projects, the time span for achieving equity in contributions can be similarly extended. Peer research collaborations, however, disintegrate, if over the long term one member feels that another is not doing his or her part or is getting more than his or her share of the rewards. One of our interviewees told us he now takes pains to avoid having his former collaborator find out about his current activities because, in the past, the collaborator frequently "weaseled" his way into a research project, made only minor contributions and then insisted on sharing authorship.

Achieving an equitable division of labor generally does not appear to be a goal for faculty-student collaborations. When faculty members collaborate with their students, both individuals typically assume that the student will be responsible for carrying out the work of the project under the supervision of the faculty member. However, students are often resentful of the credit faculty members receive for their minimal contributions.

Individuals use a variety of principles to divide responsibility for carrying out specific tasks. For instance, relative status, the possession of a necessary skill or available time, access to resources such as research facilities or participants, and simple preferences for particular tasks were all used as criteria for deciding who would do what. Division of labor between faculty and students was strongly governed by institutional norms. Students were invariably responsible for data collection and analysis and writing code. In collaborations involving advanced graduate students, faculty often acted as advisors; with less experienced graduate students they were more actively involved in planning and writing.

In addition to variations in the principles used to divide work, our respondents also varied in the extent to which they held explicit discussions of dividing their labor. In established relationships and those that evolved out of an extended series of informal contacts, the division of labor seemed to just happen, perhaps because of some implicit, shared knowledge about preferences or talents. With new and with the relatively formal collaborations that were initiated at a distance, the collaborators are careful to discuss both who will do what and the rationale for particular task assignments.

3.2.2 *Establishing Trust*   Throughout a collaboration, partners act individually in ways that have the potential to influence the outcome of their joint work and each other's good name. Consequently, they must rely on the good sense and noble motives of their partners. This reliance requires affirmative answers to questions such as: Will my partner give this project as much attention as I have? Should I trust the data analysis or the writing of a difficult section to my partner? Will he or she acknowledge my contribution when talking about our work? Our sense is that being able to trust a collaborator in these and other ways is a crucial determinant of both the productivity and longevity of the relationship, but we have very little specific information as to how collaborators assess or monitor trustworthiness.

We suspect that, like so many aspects of a collaborative relationship, research partners are helped in this respect by proximity and that proximity is especially important early in the relationship. Being close at hand provides the opportunity to observe how one's partner spends time and whether he or she does, in fact, acknowledge one's contributions in informal discussions. As in any relationship, trust between collaborators grows out of experience. Over time, collaborators who observe that their partners carry out their work promptly and accurately and do not trample on each other's interests or reputation will come to trust each other and the need for continued monitoring will decline.

4 Public Presentation

As we have seen, collaboration has the potential for improving both the quality of a research product and the process by which it is made. In addition, collaboration on average increases the extrinsic rewards of research. In the most straightforward way, joint projects increase the visibility of the collaborators, associating each of them with more projects than they could accomplish independently and often increasing audiences for each project. Increases in audience are particularly likely if the collaborators are affiliated with different institutions or if they identify themselves with different fields and professional communities.

Successful research collaboration culminates in the documentation and publication of the work effort, but publication is only one of many avenues for public presentation of work. Throughout the entire course of a research project many occasions arise for both formal and informal public discussion of the work. The occasional hallway encounter with one's department head, the casual lunchtime conversation with colleagues, and the semi-formal presentations at seminars and progress review meetings all provide opportunities to publicize one's professional activities.

Much of what goes on during this phase recapitulates the earlier stages of the collaborative process. Collaborators must plan their work, divide the labor, and do the work. Even though the problems are similar, some solutions are different during this stage and we concentrate on these differences. In addition, because the written record leaves little room for the ambiguity that can help gloss over differences during working discussions, during the public presentation stage final disagreements must be resolved and individual ideas and perceptions must converge to a common perspective. Finally, the public presentation stage is the time when researchers must allocate rewards and credit for their joint product to individual researchers.

4.1 *Relationship Level*

When a research project goes public, collaborators must decide how to divide credit for the work between themselves, and they must also figure out how to control outsiders' perceptions of each collaborator's relative contributions. These dilemmas are starkly highlighted in the collaborators' decision about the ordering of authorship, but also show up in decisions about who should give formal and informal presentations of the work, and how casual discussion about the work should be handled. Outsiders' views about each collaborator's contributions to a project are shaped by the nature of these public presentations. First authorship or public presentation of jointly executed work often leads the audience to view the highlighted member as the principal contributor. Thus, the desire to publicize work as widely as possible in one's own professional circles must be carefully balanced with the distribution of credit to one's collaborator. Particularly where there is significant overlap between collaborators' professional communities, managing this balance is an important requirement for sustaining a long-term collaborative research relationship.

In computer science, professional norms make authorship strictly alphabetical. In psychology and management science, professional norms make ordering of authorship reflect ordering of contributions. Within this general framework, collaborators that we interviewed used a variety of rules to determine order of authorship. Ownership of the original ideas seemed to be the strongest determinant, as long as the initial ideas had not been modified too extensively by the second member of the team. No other kind of work is valued as highly as the intellectual work involved in the initial formulation of the research plan. The ability to formulate interesting research questions and translate them into research plans is the *sine qua non* of being a scientist and those who contribute to the execution of a project in this way are generally seen as project leaders, the most important members of the team, despite the fact that they may be almost totally reliant on others to carry out the plan. Thus, even in cases where the second member had played a major role in actually carrying out the research plan, the generator of the original ideas became the first author. One important exception to this rule is in cases of faculty-student collaborations surrounding dissertation topics, where institutional norms dictated that the student should get first authorship.

Many of our interviewees stated that first authorship belonged to the writer of the first draft, but in cases where ownership of the seed ideas was clear this writing task was taken on by the original owner. Thus, idea ownership often determined who would write the first draft and, in turn, who would be first author.

In cases where initial ownership is less clear, credit is allotted according to the perceived amount of work done by each member of the collaboration. Interestingly, however, the relative amounts of work are not measured using a straightforward metric such as time spent executing it. Almost invariably intellectual work was judged as more valuable than work the collaborators thought was menial (e.g., running subjects), clerical (e.g., keypunching data), or routine (e.g., coding software), regardless of the time and effort needed to do these tasks. Need occasionally played a role in authorship decisions. A collaborator on the job-market or up for tenure was more likely to get first authorship. Very senior faculty were sometimes magnanimous in assigning authorship.

In formal and informal oral presentation, it was common for collaborators to use an alternation rule in deciding who should give the presentations. Less commonly, collaborators divided presentations by topic or section, although this made the logistics of the presentation difficult.

Although a shared view of who principally owns or leads the project must at least begin to be achieved in the handling of formal and informal oral presentations, many collaborators do not explicitly discuss order of authorship for the written document until they are ready to begin the actual task of writing. In many cases both collaborators have independently arrived at the same conclusion about deserved order, but they often still feel a need to discuss the issue openly at some point. In one case where explicit discussion had never taken place, one of our respondents felt insulted to see her name appear second on the first draft written by her colleague, even though in fact she had always assumed second authorship for herself.

Although authorship and credit issues are highlighted at the stage of public presentation, they are latent issues throughout the collaborative process and inform decisions all of the way through, from the initial decision of whom to collaborate with to decisions about how to divide the labor. For example, some junior faculty members noted that, although some of their research is collaborative, they felt pressure to produce papers on their own in order to demonstrate their competence as independent researchers to tenure committees. For much the same kind of public relations reason, they also expressed reluctance to become involved with senior faculty unless they could clearly demonstrate their independent contribution and leadership role in the project.

4.2 Task-Level

4.2.1 Planning Like the collaboration process as a whole, writing is typically planned over highly interactive, face-to-face meetings during which the collaborative pair makes extensive use of multiple media such as blackboards, data printouts, graphs and sketches to supplement their discussion. Document planning meetings accomplish at least two goals. First, the collaborators begin to achieve a common understanding of what should be said and how. A few of our interviewees in fact reported having to resolve divergences of views that had developed during the low-communication project execution stage. Second, they come to an agreement as to how the writing tasks are to be divided between the two of them. As in the early meetings, the outcome is a jointly developed plan for work tasks that will be executed individually.

This jointly developed plan is frequently made explicit in the form of a written outline for the document, which, unlike other written records produced during earlier meetings, can constitute a binding agreement between the two members of the collaborative team. Surprisingly, though, given their importance, these outlines were very sketchy, rarely longer than a handwritten page.

4.2.2 *Writing* The division of the writing tasks minimized the need to share and coordinate information, much the same way that division of work tasks did in earlier stages. Thus, subdividing the writing task by document section was not common in our sample, particularly among collaborators of equal status. Working together in the same place to produce a paper was extremely rare. In the modal case, one member of the collaboration assumed responsibility for writing a first draft, and the second collaborator took on the role of editor and reviewer.

As we noted above, physical proximity between collaborators plays important though distinct roles in the initiation and execution stages. In contrast, proximity is not as important a factor during the document writing period. Distance can add considerable delay in exchanging document drafts. However, distance is, by this time, much less of an impediment at the relationship level because the need for direct, frequent communication during the documentation stage is limited. Documentation tasks are, for the most part, very compartmentalized, with each collaborator having very specific individual responsibilities. Thus, while researchers find it difficult to initiate and execute collaborative projects at a distance, they usually succeed in writing a paper at a distance. Only in cases where geographic separation had occurred prior to planning the document did collaborators fail to produce a final document.

Before conducting our interviews we hypothesized that the difficulty of accepting criticism from collaborators would emerge most strongly in the documentation stage, where changes to one's work are unambiguous. To our surprise, few of our respondents considered this a problem. In general, collaborators felt free to make changes to each other's work without needing to justify or explain them, and, in turn, they accepted most changes to their work without question. In fact, more than one research pair adopted a "Don't tell me about it; change it" rule. Similarly, in cases where equipment incompatibilities made it difficult for collaborators to rework the writing themselves, they often fell naturally into editor-clerk roles, where the "editor" rewrote and the "clerk" simply entered the changes into the word processor.

For many researchers a major attraction of working with another is that the collaborator will be involved enough to read the work carefully and help to improve the writing. Although one can sometimes get feedback from a colleague prior to submitting a manuscript, the critical scrutiny and effort necessary to point out subtle flaws in arguments or clearer ways of stating an argument is not likely to come from a casual reader. We encountered agreement among our interviewees about this point in many different ways. One researcher to whom we spoke thought highly enough about this function that he routinely granted second authorship on his papers to anyone who offered him significant comments, regardless of whether they had any other connection with the research. In another case, a collaboration is thriving between two scientists whose primary language is not English largely because they carefully corrected each other's grammar and style.

4.2.3 *Technology for Multi-Author Documents* Almost all of the papers produced by the collaborators in our sample were written using computers or word processors. They make revision easy and encourage collaborators to pass work back and forth and to make changes or additions. The combination of interlocation computer networks, electronic mail and word processing could make the process of long-distance editing and revising much more efficient and less expensive than shipping paper manuscripts back and forth, and for some could even be an improvement over face-to-face meetings. However, in 1984 and 1985, when many of the manuscripts in this sample were written, collaborators rarely passed manuscripts back and forth in electronic form; instead they passed paper copies. This reliance on paper occurred in part because collaborators rarely had compatible hardware or software. But even when transferring electronic files was technologically feasible, i.e., compatible hardware and software or interlocation networks, researchers still often passed paper. The use of paper copies minimized the need for collaborators to keep track of multiple versions of a manuscript and made it very easy to detect changes, since they were usually in the margins or the backs of the pages. Few word processing systems provide mechanisms to track or compare versions or to allow annotations analogous to penciling in the margins of a paper. Some collaborators overcame this limitation by writing notes to each other within the manuscript they were working on. They expressed uncertainties about what they had written, asked for evaluations of particular points, and explained changes that they had made from previous versions. These comments and questions are a useful means of drawing attention to problematic parts of the paper or of discussing the rationale for specific decisions, but they often created discontinuities in the flow of the text. Furthermore, they interfered with some of the housekeeping aspects of document writing, such as monitoring length or previewing the final appearance of the manuscript.

5 Conclusions

The dominant conclusion that emerges from our research is that the establishment and maintenance of a personal relationship is the glue that holds together the pieces of a collaborative research effort. Often, it is at least as important as the content of the work itself. When collaborators describe collaborations as problematic, they inevitably point to problems in the personal relationships: untrustworthy or irresponsible colleagues who don't do their part, who assume too much control, or who seize too much credit for the work they have done. They sometimes point to difficulties in the intellectual tasks: e.g., improving on an algorithm or describing a theoretical approach in a way that satisfies reviewers. But rarely do they point to difficulties in the process by which the collaborative work gets done. Instead they generally have institutional arrangements and work techniques—technologies in the broadest sense—that solve potential problems in the work process before they arise.

The challenge we see for information technology developers is to create tools that not only facilitate task completion but also support productive personal relationships. By contrast, the main technologies that have been developed so far to support group work focus primarily on task completion, and we believe, have been largely unsuccessful precisely because of this.

To take but one example, consider the use of teleconferencing to support group work. Marketing strategies for teleconferencing systems and services typically have focused on the electronic replacement of face-to-face meetings to reduce travel time and cost. But this replacement is sold without regard to the consequences of reducing opportunities for personal contact. For research collaboration in particular, where frequent personal contact is a major facilitator of the process, care must be taken to prevent the damage to personal relationships that may result from reducing opportunities for communication and spontaneity. A wiser approach may be to provide communications technologies that will supplement or enhance, rather than replace, existing communication modes.

A second major conclusion of our research is that no single technology for supporting collaboration will adequately satisfy researchers' needs throughout the collaborative process. Although we started our research with the aim of investigating how particular intellectual products—i.e., publications in scholarly journals—were created, we were immediately pushed into investigating the collaborative relationship, which often had a life of multiple products and many years. The extended time course of research collaboration and the diversity of goals and tasks that characterize each phase of the process call for a rich palette of collaborative work tools to choose from. For example, the techniques and technologies one might use to introduce potential collaborators to each other are certainly not what would be useful to coordinate the writing and revision by collaborators who have worked with each other in previous projects.

A related point is that a single technique currently used during various stages of the collaborative process may serve different functions at each stage. As a result, these techniques may have multiple technological translations. Consider, for example, the role that proximity plays in research collaborations and the ways one might devise technological solutions to allow collaborations to occur at a distance. During the initiation stage proximity provides low cost communication that allows potential collaborators to form impressions of each other and feel each other out before committing to work together. Computer conferencing with facilities for private side conversations might be a possible technological substitute. So, too, might be a continuous video link between the lunchrooms of two compatible research institutions. But during the planning stages of execution and documentation, proximity supports intense, unstructured, multi-media meetings for completing highly interactive intellectual work. The slow speed of computer conferences and electronic mail and the relative formality of writing would not serve these ends. Instead audio conferences that allowed participants to pass documents and scribbled notes and figures back and forth, to modify these materials interactively, and to retain paper copies of their work would be a useful tool. Next, during the rest of the execution stage, proximity is used to supervise and sustain progress by providing the low cost communications to catalog what has been done, to alert partners to minor problems, and to enforce guilt. Some of this work could be done automatically by the electronic monitoring of shared files and other parts can be done using a regimen of computer-assisted project management techniques. But more generally and throughout the collaborative process, proximity supports the maintenance of a warm personal friendship among the collaborators that aids them through the travails of working together, and it is possible that no electronic aids will substitute for its role in this domain.

When considering technologies that could support collaborations, one must consider at least three classes of tools: a) those that collaborators use to accomplish the many individually performed activities in the collaboration, b) technologies and protocols that would allow them to integrate these individually accomplished products, and c) communication technologies that allow them to be in touch and work jointly as easily as if their offices were next door to each other.

We can illustrate this point by describing ways to improve the documentation phase of a research collaboration. As we have reported, most researchers use computers or word processors for their writing. Many of the irritating problems with these programs remain, in part, because word processing systems are designed to produce polished final copy, but not to support the process of writing itself, much less collaborative writing. For instance, few word processing systems provide mechanisms to track or compare versions or to allow side annotations analogous to penciling in the margins of a paper. Word processors with built in version control and annotation would aid many writers, among them collaborative writers for whom the difficulties of annotating and comparing versions are great. While most collaborators found word processors easier than typewriters for making revisions and incorporating another's comments, many of them had difficulties with the incompatibilities among programs and computing environments. Along with the reasons of control discussed above, this incompatibility was one reason why a single partner in the collaboration typically controlled the manuscript and incorporated the other's handwritten annotations and changes into an electronic version of the text. Common protocols for word processing programs or translation programs that would convert text between them without losing structure and formatting information would be a highly valuable addition to the tools for collaborative work. Finally, we have discussed the need for an array of communications facilities that would allow collaborators to intensively discuss material during the planning section, to view, talk about and modify sections of a manuscript, and to monitor and help sustain each other's progress on a manuscript.

The conclusions we have presented here, while based on careful examination of a moderate number of research collaborations, should be considered tentative and possibly of restricted generality for a number of reasons. First, they are based on a sample of voluntary two-person scholarly research collaborations, with all of the limitations that this implies. These collaborations were typical of traditional science as described by Hagstrom (1964). The scientists had relative freedom to choose their research partners and topics, had long and flexible deadlines for their work, and were rewarded intangibly through reputation and esteem. Whether our conclusions about the dominance of relationship issues would hold for collaborations with shorter deadlines among people assigned to their topics and partners is an open question. In addition, we suspect that the task of coordinating activity would become substantially more difficult if more than two parties were involved. Second, our sample is biased toward successful collaborations and collaborators. The primary sample discussed published research articles, although a supplementary sample was asked to describe problematic collaborations. Third, we examined the relationships between the principal research scientists in these collaborations. We did not, however, extend our focus to the numerous supporting roles, ranging from secretaries and research assistants to department heads and grant officers, whose work contributes to the successful completion of a research project. Finally, the methodology we used—retrospective interviewing—is not the optimal way to learn about how people perform tasks that seem to them routine. Interviewees often cannot describe how they made decisions, how they assigned responsibilities, how they knew what a partner was doing, or how often they met, because these issues were forgotten, out of their awareness, or uninteresting to them. Systematic observation or experimental methodology may be a more appropriate methodology for capturing this type of detail, although these techniques place different constraints on the unit of work that can be analyzed.

Despite these caveats, our research has sketched a framework for describing research collaborations that can provide some guidance to those developing technology to support collaborative work. We have stressed the importance of the communication and the social psychological component of research collaboration and have suggested some shortcomings of current technology designed to support collaborations. Our most important advice to those who develop technology for collaborative work is that the technology needs to support people and their relationships as well as the tasks that they perform.

Acknowledgments

This research was supported by funding from Bell Communications Research. Please send correspondence concerning this article to Robert Kraut, Room 2E-232, Bell Communications Research, 435 South Street, Morristown, New Jersey, 07960 or to Jolene Galegher, Department of Management and Policy, University of Arizona, Tucson, AZ 85721.

We would like to thank the many researchers who took time from their busy schedules to talk to us about their processes of doing work. Without them and their insightful comments on their own work, our research would have been impossible.

References

Aucella, A. F. & Ehrlich, S. F. (1986). Voice Messaging: Enhancing the User Interface Based on Field Performance *Human Factors in Computing Systems. Proceedings of the ACM SIGCHI '86 Conference.* Boston, Mass. April, 1986. pp. 156–161.

Bair, J. H. (1985). The Need for Collaboration Tools in Offices. *Proceedings of the 1985 Office Automation Conference (AFIPS).* Atlanta, Georgia. February, 1985. pp. 59–68.

Beaver, D. deB. & Rosen, R. (1978). Studies in scientific collaboration, Part I: The professional origins of scientific co-authorship. Scientometrics, 1, 65–84.

Beaver, D. deB. & Rosen, R. (1979). Studies in scientific collaboration, Part II: Scientific co-authorship, research productivity and visibility in the French scientific elite, 1799–1830. Scientometrics, 1, 133–149.

Crane, Diana (1965). Scientists at major and minor universities: A study of productivity and recognition. *American Sociological Review, 30*, 699–714.

Dawes, R. M. (1971). A case study of graduate admissions: Applications of three principles of human decision making. *American Psychologist, 26*, 180–188.

Dawes, R. M. (1979). The robust beauty of improper linear models in decision making. *American Psychologist, 34*, 571–582.

Festinger, L., Schachter, S., & Back, K. (1950). *Social pressure in informal groups: A study of human factors in housing.* New York: Harper & Row.

Festinger, L., Schachter, S., & Reicken, H. (1956). *When prophecy fails.* Minneapolis: University of Minnesota Press.

Galbraith, J. (1973). *Designing complex organizations.* New York: Addison-Wesley.

Garvey, W., Lin, N., & Nelson, C. E. (1979). Communications in the physical and the social sciences. *Science, 170*, 1166–1173.

Goodman, George O., & Abel, Mark J. (1986, Dec. 3–5). Collaboration research in SCL. *Proceedings of the Conference on Computer-Supported Cooperative Work.* pp. 246–251. Austin, TX.

Hagstrom, W. O. (1964). Traditional and modern forms of scientific teamwork. *Administrative Science Quarterly, 9*, 241–263.

Heffner, A. G. (1981). Funded research, multiple authorship, and subauthorship collaboration in four disciplines. Scientometrics, 3(1), 5–12.

Innes, J. M. (1980). Psychology of the scientist: XLV. Collaboration and productivity in social psychology. *Psychological Reports, 47*, 1331–1334.

Kerckhoff, (1974). The social context of interpersonal attraction. In T. Huston (ed). *Foundations of interpersonal attraction.* NY; Appleton-Century-Crofts.

Kiesler, S., Siegel, J., & McGuire, T. (1984). Social psychological aspects of computer-mediated communication. *American Psychologist, 39*, 1123–1134.

Krauss, R., Garlock, C., Bricker, P., & McMahon, L. (1977). The role of audible and visible back-channel responses in interpersonal communication. *Journal of Personality and Social Psychology, 35*, 523–529.

Krauss, R. & Weinheimer, S. (1966). Concurrent feedback, confirmation, and the encoding of referents in verbal interaction. *Journal of Personality and Social Psychology*, 4, 342–346.

Kraut, R., Lewis, S., & Swezey, L. (1982). Listener responsiveness and the co-ordination of conversation. *Journal of Personality and Social Psychology*, *43*, 718–731.

Malone, T. W., Grant, K. R., & Turbak, F. A. (1986). The Information Lens: An Intelligent System for Information Sharing. *Human Factors in Computing Systems. Proceedings of the ACM SIGCIII '86 Conference*. Boston, Mass. April, 1986. pp. 1–8. in Organizations.

Mendenhall, M., Oddou, G. & Franck, L. (1984). The trend toward research collaboration in social psychological research. *Journal of Social Psychology*, *122*, 101–103.

Over, R. (1982). Collaborative research and publication in psychology. *American Psychologist, 37*, 996–1001.

Sawyer, J. (1966). Measurement *and* prediction, clinical *and* statistical. *Psychological Bulletin*, 66, 178–200.

Sherif, M. (1935). A study of some social factors in perception. *Archives of Psychology, 27*. Whole no. 187.

Zuckerman, M., DePaulo, B. & Rosenthal, R. (1981). Verbal and nonverbal communication of deception. In L. Berkowitz (Ed.). *Advances in experimental social psychology, Vol. 14*. New York: Academic Press.

28

The Variable Impact of Computer Technologies on the Organization of Work Activities

Jeanette L. Blomberg
Intelligent Systems Laboratory
Xerox Palo Alto Research Center
Palo Alto, CA

Introduction

As Malone (1985) has pointed out, much of the research on the effect of new computer technologies on the social organization of work makes the implicit assumption that the impact of a technology is uniform across adopting groups.[1] By contrast, the position taken in this paper is that the interplay between a technology and the characteristics of the adopting group will affect the nature and extent of the changes that result. This is not to argue that technology is neutral with respect to social change, but that its impact must be understood in terms of the social environment into which it is introduced. Furthermore, contrary to the prevailing unidirectional emphasis on how technology shapes the social environment of use, this paper explores the reciprocal relationship that obtains between a technology and the social organization

[1] There is a considerable body of research (cf. Bikson et al., 1983, 1985; Kimberly and Evanisko, 1981; Lucas, 1978) suggesting that the way a technology is introduced into an organization will affect the success or failure of the technology. However, this work typically does not consider how the technology changes the social organization of work.

of work (Blomberg, 1986). Not only does a technology exert pressures for change on the social environment of its use, but that environment, in turn, exerts selective pressure on a technology, thereby shaping its meaning and influencing its evolution. Finally, this paper suggests that because computer technologies have been designed primarily with an implicit model of isolated users performing specific tasks, these tools have failed to support the inherently cooperative nature of most work activities. It is hoped that recent interest in computer tools that support notably collaborative tasks (e.g., co-authorship, group meetings, etc.) will not draw attention away from the cooperative aspect of most human activities and the need for computer technologies that support them.

The Trillium Example

To illustrate the reciprocal nature of the relationship between a technology and the people who use it and the variable impact a technology can have on the social organization of work, examples from an ethnographic study of the introduction of a computer-based design environment called Trillium into the machine interface design community of a large American corporation will be presented. Trillium is used in the creation of the layout and logic of interaction for Control/Display interfaces on a wide variety of machines such as copiers, duplicators, and printers. In other words, Trillium supports the design of both the appearance and the behavior of user interfaces. Designers use Trillium to develop the look and placement of objects on an interface and to specify the sequencing of events necessary for use of the machine. Trillium adopts a construction set notion of design, where a set of pieces are available which the designer puts together to create interfaces. These pieces are both physical objects (such as a back lit number pad) and specifications for how objects interact (such as the presentation of a particular message when some action is taken by the user). Trillium also allows new pieces to be added to the original set as new design concepts are developed (for a more complete description of Trillium see Henderson, 1986).

Trillium was developed to enable designers who had little or no computer programming background to create prototype designs for the user interfaces of machines under development. Designers who generally had backgrounds in either industrial design or human factors psychology were to develop new design abstractions and modify existing ones directly on the computer without the assistance of a computer programmer. While it was recognized that some radically different design concepts might require that a support programmer implement them initially, it was hoped that the involvement of support programmers in the basic design process would be limited and that the tool would shorten the iterative process from design concept to implementation by taking the computer programmer out of the loop. In practice, however, Trillium has proven difficult for designers lacking a computer background, and in some cases the involvement of either support programmers or "expert" Trillium users has been greater than anticipated.

Prior to the introduction of Trillium, designers used paper and pencil to specify the look of the interface and flow charts, diagrams or some other way of specifying the behavior of the interface. Sometimes the behavior of the interface was not completely or clearly specified prior to implementation on the target machine. In such cases, the software engineers responsible for implementing the design might make design decisions themselves rather than take the time to request clarification from the UI designers. Generally, the paper and pencil drawings, along with some representation of the behavior of the interface, would be given to the software engineers, who would use the design to program the target machine to look and behave as specified. A frequent problem with this procedure, however, was that something was lost in the translation between the designer's original conception of the interface and the software engineer's implementation. When the implementation was completed it often didn't look or behave as the designer intended. Even though modifications often were needed to make the software implementation congruent with the designer's original concept, these changes sometimes were not made because they would be costly in terms of the software engineer's time. Furthermore, since software implementation came so late in the product development process, additional time constraints were imposed on modifying the user interface. Designers had to struggle to get interface changes made, and those that were made often were band-aids concealing a design problem, not significant adjustments to the basic design concepts employed. Needless to say, there was a problem in communication between what was in the designer's head and how the pencil and paper specifications of the design were understood and translated by the software engineers. Trillium was developed, in part, to allow designers to do their own implementations in the hope that this would enable them to specify more precisely the look and behavior of their designs. At the same time, Trillium was to provide software engineers with a more accurate representation of the design, thereby minimizing or eliminating problems with translation. Furthermore, the iterative loop from design concept to implementation was to be made shorter and less time consuming since changes could be made using Trillium before they were implemented on the target machine.

The development of user interfaces for major new products typically has involved the cooperative efforts of several designers, each taking responsibility for particular aspects of the interface design. Coordinating their activities always has been a part of the design process. Although Trillium was intended for use by individual designers, its use has not eliminated the need for cooperation among designers. However, because Trillium was not designed to support the cooperative aspect of the design process, difficulties have arisen over the sharing of design pieces, updating Trillium files, and coordinating the release of new versions of the Trillium implemented design.

Impact on the Design Process

Although Trillium was developed, in part, to facilitate the communication between designers and software engineers, its introduction has resulted in a reallocation and redefinition of the work tasks undertaken in the design process. To illustrate these changes and to demonstrate the variable impact a technology can have on the environment of its use, I will describe Trillium's impact on the definition of the design process and on the allocation of tasks in two of the design groups using Trillium. The first group was composed primarily of designers hired prior to the introduction of Trillium. These designers were asked to use Trillium to design the user interface for a major new product. The second group consisted primarily of designers hired after Trillium had been introduced into the design community and after it had been selected as the design tool to be employed in the development of another new product. The two groups were similar in that their task was to design the user interfaces for major future products.

Design Group Hired Prior to Trillium's Introduction

Although Trillium was intended for use by designers with no computer background, it has been difficult for them to use. For example, there were some designers in this group who had taken at least one training course, who had experimented with the system over a period of several months, who had been assigned tasks where Trillium was to be used, but who nonetheless were unable to become accomplished enough with Trillium to employ it in the completion of their design tasks. These individuals, mostly trained in industrial design or human factors psychology, did not necessarily have the incentive to sit for hours at a time in front of a computer terminal trying to figure out how to get particular design effects. From their perspective, using Trillium required that they spend too much time massaging the computer tool and not enough time designing. Many didn't see using Trillium as part of the design process itself, but instead a necessary evil to be tolerated if they were to implement their design concepts prior to the involvement of software engineers. Consequently, in the design group hired in pre-Trillium days, many of the designers chose not to use Trillium themselves, but instead to rely on someone else to implement their designs using Trillium. These so-called "Trillium implementors" either were designers with a special aptitude for computer technologies or people hired after Trillium was introduced specifically to implement interface designs using Trillium. It is unclear whether the designers in this group chose not to use Trillium because it was so difficult to master or because they would rather spend their time in more traditional design activities, such as discussing design concepts with other designers and developing paper and pencil representations of those concepts. In any event, it appears they would rather leave the actual implementation to someone else.

In this design group a new role has emerged, that of the Trillium implementor. The implementor's activities fell somewhere between those of a traditional designer and those of a computer programmer. Trillium implementors were more intimately involved in the design of the user interface, but their expertise was sought primarily for their knowledge of Trillium. Despite this, because the Trillium implementors were not software engineers, they still required the assistance of support programmers to develop new design pieces that reflected new design abstractions.

Superficially, it may seem that Trillium only has served to add an additional step in the design process and that it has not significantly enhanced the ability of designers in this group to develop prototype designs. However, Trillium has made it easier for the designer to experiment with design concepts, because it has shortened the iterative loop between design concept and the representation of that concept. The effort involved in implementing interface designs using Trillium was much less than that required to implement them on the target product. If problems were encountered with the Trillium-implemented design, they could be corrected before the software engineer became involved in the process. As such, even those designers who did not use Trillium directly benefited from the ability to see their design concepts implemented. In addition, Trillium implementors were more likely to be familiar with the design task than were the software engineers, so communication between the two was less burdened than it was between designer and software engineer.

Although Trillium's introduction did not create the problem of coordinating the activities of the various designers involved in the design of the user interface, it added some new contingencies. Designers still met frequently to discuss the progress and direction of their designs, but they now had to coordinate their activities with those of the Trillium implementor. In turn, the Trillium implementor's job required integrating the work of several designers. The Trillium implementor often was under pressure to complete an implementation either because the designer wanted to see his/her design embodied in a functioning interface or because of a deadline set by the program committee for review of the interface. Furthermore, in those situations where the Trillium implementor required the assistance of a support programmer in order to create a design piece capable of producing some new effect specified by a designer, meeting this deadline was dependent on the cooperation of the support programmers, who frequently were burdened with competing work demands.

In the past, once an interface design was completed, the paper and pencil representation was given to software engineers to encode in the target machine using a computer language that is understood by the processor that runs the final product. Certain aspects of the Trillium implemented design are being machine translated into the computer language that runs the target machine, taking the code generated using Trillium and translating it into the required computer language. This will reduce some of the differences between the designer's conception of the user interface and the software engineer's understanding of that design as it is embodied in the Trillium implementation. However, for those aspects of the interface design that are not being machine translated, the problem of correspondence between the designer's intentions and the final look and behavior of the user interface remain. Those aspects of the design that are not being machine translated are being specified using the old method of flow charts and other diagrammatic ways of specifying the design.

Design Group Hired After Trillium's Introduction

By contrasting the design team hired in pre-Trillium days with the design team composed primarily of designers hired after the introduction of Trillium, the variable impact of a technology on the social organization of work can be illustrated. When the second design team was assembled, it was clear that Trillium would be used in the design process, and this fact clearly influenced the skills sought in the new recruits. A requirement for the job of designer was some computer experience and a willingness to spend much of the day in front of a computer terminal. Job applicants were screened for these characteristics. In addition, some background in cognitive science or human factors psychology was desired, although not all those hired met this standard. The belief seemed to be that it would be easier to teach new recruits how to design user interfaces than it would be to teach designers with no background or facility in computers how to use Trillium. In this second group, user interface design and Trillium implementation were both done by the same set of individuals. The actual process involved going back and forth from paper and pencil drawings to the computer with some of the actual design work done using Trillium. In the process of implementing the design using Trillium, unforeseen problems could be taken into consideration and sometimes overcome by the designer.

Although the design and Trillium implementation were done by the same individuals, a design task that previously had been distributed throughout an entire design team was concentrated in the hands of the few experienced, senior designers who evaluated the designs created by other members of the team. Since the new designers had limited experience designing user interfaces, it became necessary to have senior designers or "evaluators" critique their work. The principal evaluator for this design team had been involved in the design of numerous user interfaces prior to the introduction of Trillium and, while she did not use Trillium, she provided experience and expertise not present in the new recruits.

Because of the way Trillium was being used by this design team there were greater requirements on these designers to coordinate their activities. Since each designer implemented his/her own design that later had to be assembled into a single user interface, it was necessary that the design team agree on the design pieces they would employ, on naming conventions for these design pieces and on a system for filing both design pieces and the individual interface implementations. Otherwise it would be very difficult and time consuming to produce the interface composed of the work of all the designers. In addition, elaborate social conventions were created to orchestrate access to the evolving interface. For example, write access to the directories containing the compiled interface was denied all designers except a designated "integrator" and his/her manager.

In this second group, all aspects of the user interface design implemented using Trillium were machine translated into the computer language that was to run the target product, reducing the communication problem between designers and software engineers. Even so, there remained some incongruity between the Trillium-implemented design and the resulting user interface on the target machine. Some adjustments still will be required and there is early indication these will involve negotiations between the designers and the software implementors.

Redistribution of Power

The introduction of Trillium has not only redefined the design process, but also has redistributed power within each of the design groups. Prior to the introduction of Trillium, the software engineers had a great deal to say about the final interface design. In pre-Trillium days, they essentially used the designers' paper and pencil drawings as guidelines for their implementation. Since communication between designers and software engineers was limited and problematic, the designers had little input during the period of time after they completed their designs and before the implementation had been accomplished. By the time the software engineers had finished the implementation, designers had little power to make significant changes to the design. The power was in the hands of the software engineers who in response to objections from designers that a particular effect was not what they had intended could claim the designers had not been precise enough in the representation of their designs. However, after Trillium was introduced, the balance of power shifted to the side of the designers, since they now were able to produce a functioning interface as a representation of their designs. Software engineers could no longer claim that the designers had not been precise enough in the representation of their designs.

On the other hand, designers are now dependent on software engineers to help them build demonstratively different design pieces and in some cases on Trillium implementors to embody their designs in a functioning interface. In some cases designers have made the decision to modify their designs instead of waiting for the software engineers to build a new design piece. While the impact on the designer's work is more indirect, it still has an effect on the final user interface design.

In the second design group (those hired after the introduction of Trillium) the software engineers have re-established some control over the interface design in another way. Since the Trillium implementation is being automatically translated into the computer language that will run the target product, software engineers have restricted the design options available to the designers to help assure that the automatic translation runs smoothly. The argument they made was that if the designers were free to develop new design pieces at will, the computer program might fail to correctly translate them. In this instance, designers were in the position of having to justify their use of design pieces that had not been formally approved. While this did not prevent them from experimenting with new design concepts, it required that they obtain approval if they planned to use these design concepts in the user interface design for the product under development. Within this group, the software engineers had re-established their influence on the way the final user interface would look and function, which limited the power of the designers.

Trillium has had another impact on the power of UI designers in that it allows a functioning interface to be produced much earlier in the product development process. Program planners were now able to see a functioning interface prior to its implementation on the target product, which put the designers in a better position to argue for the re-direction and increased allocation of resources to the user interface. The planners were better able to see what they would be getting for their investment and, consequently, were better equipped to evaluate the benefits of a user interface with the particular capabilities represented in the design. Members of one of the design teams cited with a sense of accomplishment an occasion when they presented a Trillium-implemented design to a Program team, and as a result of this presentation, expectations concerning the quality and capability of the final product were modified to incorporate ideas observed in the demo interface. The implication was that the design concepts reflected in the Trillium-implemented design had more power to change the thinking of the Program team than paper and pencil drawings or some other design representation.

The Evolution and Meaning of Trillium

I began this paper by suggesting that the relationship between technology and the social environment should not be viewed as unidirectional, but reciprocal. In the case examples I've reviewed, Trillium not only has affected the social organization of the design process, but, in turn, the evolution and meaning of Trillium has been shaped by the re-allocation of design tasks within each of the design groups. In the first group, initially there was a great deal of pressure on Trillium to become easier to use. The belief was that designers were resisting this new technology simply because it was too difficult to use, and that if Trillium could be made easier, designers would begin to use it in the creation of their designs. However, either because Trillium was inherently difficult to use or because modifications to Trillium's user interface were too slow in coming, the design group adjusted to the situation by re-defining the design tasks. Once the design process had been re-partitioned to include the Trillium implementor, the pressure to change Trillium moved in the direction of increased functionality and speed of use. Because Trillium implementors were not as handicapped by the opaqueness of the Trillium user interface, they were more interested in increasing Trillium's power and speed than improving its ease of use. From their point of view these other changes would make their work implementing user interfaces easier and less time consuming. This is not to say that ease of use did not remain an important concern within the design community, but since designers lacking computer experience were not expected to use the tool, the issue diminished in importance.

For each of the groups using Trillium the meaning of the technology has been influenced and shaped by the way in which Trillium has been embedded in the design process. From the perspective of the first group, Trillium was not so much a tool for designers as it was a rapid and flexible vehicle through which their design concepts could be embodied in a functioning interface. However, for the design team assembled since Trillium's introduction, Trillium came to mean something quite different. In this group Trillium was seen as a tool for designers even though these designers must possess a different set of skills than those traditionally required. The ability to master a complex computer tool became requisite to being an accomplished designer. For both groups the tool enhanced the power of the designers in relation to software engineers and program planners, although the control of designers over the interface design was weakened by the design restrictions resulting from the use of machine translation programs.

Summary

A new technology does not exert a singular force on the people who adopt it, nor is its meaning shared equally by all. It is important to consider the interplay between the technology and the social organization of use, exploring the ways in which pre-existing social patterns alter responses to the use of such technologies. A technology can only be described and its significance appreciated in the context of its uses and its users. Trillium, like any technology, can best be understood as it is embedded in a particular social structure; removing it from its environment changes the meaning, character, and practice of the technology.

Most human activities require some degree of coordination with others and the recognition of this fact can contribute to the design of computer technologies that support the cooperative aspect of human endeavors. The Trillium technology would have benefited from a greater appreciation of the fact that Trillium would be used by multiple users and that part of its functionality would depend on the ability of these users to interact and share information with one another. To say this is not to minimize the obstacles to be overcome in providing the electronic and human infrastructure that would support such interactions. The emergence of a Trillium community, where users have access to the social resources of other users, and the development of elaborate social conventions for using Trillium are testimony to this fact.

References

Bikson, T. K., B. Gutek, and D. Mankin (1983). "Factors in Successful Implementation of Office Information Systems." In *Academy of Management Review*.

Bikson, T. K., C. Stasz, and D. A. Mankin (1985). *Computer-Mediated Work: Individual and Organizational Impact in One Corporate Headquarters*. Rand Corporation, Santa Monica, CA.

Blomberg, J. L. (1986). "Social Interaction and Office Communication: Effects on User Evaluations of New Technologies." In R. Kraut (ed.), *Transformation of White Collar Work*, Erlbaum, New Jersey.

Henderson, D. Austin (1986). "The Trillium User Interface Design Environment," in M. Mantei and P. Orbeton (eds.), *Human Factors in Computing Systems*, SIGCHI '86 Proceedings, April 13–17, 221–227.

Lucas, H. (1978). "Unsuccessful Implementation: The Case of a Computer-based Order Entry System." In *Decision Sciences*, 9, 68–79.

Malone, Thomas (1985). "Designing Organizational Interfaces," in L. Borman and B. Curtis (eds.), *Human Factors in Computing Systems*, SIGCHI '85 Proceedings, April 14–18, 66–71.

Index

Note: Index references are to introductory sections only; from these sections, the reader will be referred to the articles that discuss indexed concepts in detail.

783

Physical Therapy for Children With Cerebral Palsy

An Evidence-Based Approach

Physical Therapy for Children With Cerebral Palsy

An Evidence-Based Approach

MARY RAHLIN, PT, DHS, PCS
Associate Professor
Department of Physical Therapy
Rosalind Franklin University of Medicine and Science
North Chicago, Illinois

SETON HALL UNIVERSITY
UNIVERSITY LIBRARIES
SOUTH ORANGE, NJ 07079

SLACK
INCORPORATED

www.Healio.com/books

ISBN: 978-1-61711-065-8

Physical Therapy for Children With Cerebral Palsy: An Evidence-Based Approach includes ancillary materials specifically available for faculty use. Included are PowerPoint Slides. Please visit http://www.efacultylounge.com to obtain access.

The procedures and practices described in this publication should be implemented in a manner consistent with the professional standards set for the circumstances that apply in each specific situation. Every effort has been made to confirm the accuracy of the information presented and to correctly relate generally accepted practices. The authors, editors, and publisher cannot accept responsibility for errors or exclusions or for the outcome of the material presented herein. There is no expressed or implied warranty of this book or information imparted by it. Care has been taken to ensure that drug selection and dosages are in accordance with currently accepted/recommended practice. Off-label uses of drugs may be discussed. Due to continuing research, changes in government policy and regulations, and various effects of drug reactions and interactions, it is recommended that the reader carefully review all materials and literature provided for each drug, especially those that are new or not frequently used. Some drugs or devices in this publication have clearance for use in a restricted research setting by the Food and Drug and Administration or FDA. Each professional should determine the FDA status of any drug or device prior to use in their practice.

Any review or mention of specific companies or products is not intended as an endorsement by the author or publisher.

SLACK Incorporated uses a review process to evaluate submitted material. Prior to publication, educators or clinicians provide important feedback on the content that we publish. We welcome feedback on this work.

Published by: SLACK Incorporated
                  6900 Grove Road
                  Thorofare, NJ 08086 USA
                  Telephone: 856-848-1000
                  Fax: 856-848-6091
                  www.Healio.com/books

Contact SLACK Incorporated for more information about other books in this field or about the availability of our books from distributors outside the United States.

Library of Congress Cataloging-in-Publication Data

Names: Rahlin, Mary, - author.
Title: Physical therapy for children with cerebral palsy : an evidence-based
  approach / Mary Rahlin.
Description: Thorofare, NJ : SLACK Incorporated, [2016] | Includes
  bibliographical references and index.
Identifiers: LCCN 2016015539 (print) | LCCN 2016016592 (ebook) | ISBN
  9781617110658 (hardcover : alk. paper) | ISBN 9781630913892 (epub) | ISBN
  9781630913908 (web)
Subjects: | MESH: Cerebral Palsy--therapy | Physical Therapy Modalities |
  Evidence-Based Practice | Child
Classification: LCC RJ496.C4 (print) | LCC RJ496.C4 (ebook) | NLM WS 342 |
  DDC 618.92/836--dc23
LC record available at https://lccn.loc.gov/2016015539

Printed in the United States of America.

Last digit is print number: 10 9 8 7 6 5 4 3 2 1

DEDICATION

This book is dedicated to children with cerebral palsy and their families who inspire clinicians to never stop thinking, contemplating, hypothesizing, testing, creating, analyzing, learning, and, most importantly, caring.

CONTENTS

ACKNOWLEDGMENTS

I would like to thank Dr. Donna Frownfelter, an accomplished author and my colleague and friend, for her enthusiasm in encouraging me to take on this project, for her support throughout the writing process, and for contributing to this book. My sincere gratitude goes to all of the contributors for their dedication to this project and for putting endless hours and their hearts into developing their chapters. I am honored by having the Foreword to this book written by Dr. Toby Long, my teacher and mentor, who has been my role model during my entire professional career and for whom I have great respect and admiration. I would also like to thank Brien Cummings, Tony Schiavo, April Billick, and Dani Malady at SLACK Incorporated for their guidance, expertise, support, and patience during the manuscript preparation and book production.

I am very grateful to my dear friends and colleagues Barbara Womack, Joyce Barnett, Reggie Harbourne, and Bernadette Sarmiento for taking time to read and comment on drafts of several chapters, and to my daughter Sasha for her gift of time and effort in preparing one of the figures. A special thank you goes to all children and adults, with and without cerebral palsy, whose photos and videos are featured in this book and its supplemental materials, and to their parents for their unwavering support of this endeavor.

Finally, I would like to thank my husband, Val, for being there for me, day and night, to provide his computer expertise, edit and format the figures, remove the burden of everyday responsibilities, offer advice and words of encouragement at difficult times, and celebrate together at the times of joy. Without you, my love, this book would not have been written!

About the Author

Mary Rahlin, PT, DHS, PCS received her Bachelor of Arts degree in Physical Education and a Physical Therapist ("Therapeutic Physical Culture Instructor") Certificate from the State Central Institute of Physical Culture in Moscow, Russia. Subsequently, she received her Bachelor of Science and advanced Master of Science degrees in physical therapy from Finch University of Health Sciences/The Chicago Medical School in North Chicago, Illinois, and her Doctor of Health Science degree from the University of Indianapolis in Indiana. Dr. Rahlin is a Board Certified Clinical Specialist in Pediatric Physical Therapy. She is a member of the American Physical Therapy Association, Section on Pediatrics and Education Section, and a member of the American Academy for Cerebral Palsy and Developmental Medicine. Dr. Rahlin is Associate Professor in the Department of Physical Therapy, College of Health Professions, at Rosalind Franklin University of Medicine and Science in North Chicago, IL. Besides teaching pediatric physical therapy and related curricular content, she provides continuing education courses for practicing clinicians. Her research interests are in the areas of assessment and management of therapy-related behavior and physical therapy intervention for children with cerebral palsy and congenital muscular torticollis. Dr. Rahlin has developed and validated the Therapy Behavior Scale that was published in 2012. She is the first author of a number of peer-reviewed publications in *Pediatric Physical Therapy, Physiotherapy Theory and Practice*, and *Infant Behavior and Development*. In addition, she has authored two book chapters, spoken and presented numerous posters at APTA meetings, and serves as a reviewer for *Pediatric Physical Therapy*. Dr. Rahlin has practiced pediatric physical therapy in a variety of settings and has over 20 years of clinical experience. Currently, she maintains a small private practice, primarily in Early Intervention.

Contributing Authors

Donna Frownfelter, PT, DPT, MA, CCS, RRT, FCCP (Chapter 24)
Assistant Professor
Program Director, tDPT Program
Department of Physical Therapy
Rosalind Franklin University of Medicine and Science
North Chicago, Illinois

Regina T. Harbourne, PhD, PT, PCS (Chapter 14)
Assistant Professor
Duquesne University
John G. Rangos School of Health Sciences
Pittsburgh, Pennsylvania

Roberta Henderson, PT, PhD (Chapter 10)
Associate Professor and Chair
Department of Physical Therapy
Rosalind Franklin University of Medicine and Science
North Chicago, Illinois

Donald McGovern, CPO, FAAOP (Chapter 20)
Certified Prosthetist Orthotist
Prosthetics Orthotics Clinical Center
Rehabilitation Institute of Chicago
Chicago, Illinois

Elaine Owen, MSc, SRP, MCSP, Clinical Specialist Physiotherapist (Chapters 19, 21)
Child Development Centre
Bangor, United Kingdom

Wendy Rheault, PT, PhD, FASAHP, FNAP (Chapter 6)
Provost
Professor of Physical Therapy
Rosalind Franklin University of Medicine and Science
North Chicago, Illinois

FOREWORD

Pediatric physical therapists serve children with a wide variety of disabilities. With an incidence of approximately 2 to 3 per 1000 live births, cerebral palsy is the most common physical disability in childhood[1]; thus, most if not all pediatric physical therapists will serve children with cerebral palsy and their families at some point during their career. For many pediatric physical therapists, cerebral palsy is the condition that piqued our interest in serving children with disabilities.

Cerebral palsy is one of the most challenging conditions that pediatric therapists encounter given the complexity of the condition. *Physical Therapy for Children With Cerebral Palsy: An Evidence-Based Approach* is long overdue and is the most comprehensive text on cerebral palsy published in recent memory. Previous texts have described the condition, its impairments, limitations, and co-occurring conditions[2-4] or presented strategies that clinicians have developed to help promote developmental skill acquisition in children with cerebral palsy.[5] Based on a neuromaturational perspective on development, these texts often focused on body structure or function restrictions and limitations. For physical therapists and other service providers, the explanations, suggestions, and treatment options proposed by the traditional perspective of cerebral palsy are less than helpful and often do not support contemporary research on child development, treatment efficacy, and the evolving view of disability within society.

Dr. Rahlin presents an extensive analysis of research related to the diagnosis and management of children with cerebral palsy based on the International Classification of Functioning, Disability, and Health (ICF).[6] The ICF, a biopsychosocial model of disability, integrates individual personal characteristics and external societal characteristics as contributing to a person's health.[6] Helping a child with a disability to become an integrated member of society becomes the goal of services rather than remediating an individual's impairments in hopes of promoting "normal" behavior. Practicing therapists as well as students will benefit greatly from this text. The practicing therapists will elevate their intervention incorporating contemporary practices by using this text. For the student physical therapists, *Physical Therapy for Children With Cerebral Palsy: An Evidence-Based Approach* illustrates how contemporary neuroscience is incorporated into practice. This is especially relevant before students or early career therapists are influenced by traditional cerebral palsy intervention paradigms.

The 24 chapters of *Physical Therapy for Children With Cerebral Palsy: An Evidence-Based Approach* provide the necessary information needed to implement intervention that will operationalize the ICF and contemporary research. All information relates to integrating contemporary research into practice. Traditionally, professionals who serve children with cerebral palsy have focused on the impairments of body structure and function within treatment programs. A variety of surgical, pharmacological, and physical handling strategies have been used to counteract these impairments with limited long-term functional results. Dr. Rahlin presents a comprehensive examination of these impairments and limitations, illustrating the significant complexity and interaction among them (Chapter 4). The analysis of this information underscores the importance of using contemporary practice paradigms that are outcome-driven and life span–oriented.

In Chapter 14, Therapeutic Approaches, Dr. Rahlin and her colleague Dr. Reggie Harbourne compare and contrast a variety of common intervention strategies based on theories underpinning the strategy and its major concepts and principles. Research evidence and a critical evaluation of each approach are presented. The approaches presented include traditional approaches such as neurodevelopmental treatment (NDT) as well as more contemporary approaches such as the participation-based approach. The information discussed allows the reader to judge the evidence and determine the usability of the various approaches within his or her own individual intervention plans. The explanations help us individualize our intervention strategies based on the unique characteristics of the child and family and outcomes desired.

Of particular interest to therapists who serve infants and toddlers or newly trained therapists with little professional experiences is Chapter 5, Evidence for Prognosis for Ambulation, Employment, and Independent Living. In this chapter, Dr. Rahlin provides research evidence that helps therapists to collaborate with families in decision making and developing a comprehensive program plan. Information not only explains short-term ambulation prognosis, but also maintenance of ambulation through adulthood. A thorough description of the personal and environmental factors that influence ambulation is provided.

These are only a few examples of the breadth and depth of information presented in *Physical Therapy for Children With Cerebral Palsy: An Evidence-Based Approach*. Therapists will find each chapter crucial in creating comprehensive management programs for children with cerebral palsy. Those therapists who take the time to read this text and integrate its principles, philosophy, and concrete suggestions will create program plans with families that are practical, functional, and meaningful, providing the anticipatory guidance necessary to help children with cerebral palsy participate in the activities they want to or are expected to throughout their life time.

I have had the pleasure of knowing Mary Rahlin for close to 20 years. I am proud to have been her teacher, her dissertation adviser, her co-author, and her friend. I am humbled to have been invited to write this foreword. Finally, I am awestruck by this text and the information Dr. Rahlin has integrated and presented in such a readable and practical manner. I am confident that *Physical Therapy for Children With Cerebral Palsy: An Evidence-Based Approach* will be the gold standard of texts about cerebral palsy for many years.

Toby M. Long, PhD, PT, FAPTA
Professor, Georgetown University
Director, Georgetown University, Certificate in Early Intervention
Associate Director for Training, Georgetown University Center for Child and Human Development
Washington, DC

References

1. Arneson CL, Durkin MS, Benedict RE, et al. Prevalence of cerebral palsy: autism and developmental disabilities monitoring network, three sites, United States, 2004. *Disabil Health J.* 2009;2(1):45-48.
2. Miller F. *Physical Therapy of Cerebral Palsy.* New York, NY: Springer; 2007.
3. Miller F, Bachrach S. *Cerebral Palsy: A Complete Guide for Caregiving.* Baltimore, MD: Johns Hopkins Press Health; 2006.
4. Miller F. *Cerebral Palsy.* New York, NY: Springer; 2005.
5. Martin S. *Teaching Motor Skills to Children with Cerebral Palsy and Similar Movement Disorders: A Guide for Parents and Professionals.* Rockville, MD: Woodbine House; 2006.
6. World Health Organization. *International Classification of Functioning, Disability and Health.* Geneva, Switzerland: World Health Organization; 2001.

INTRODUCTION

This book examines cerebral palsy (CP) as a life span condition and focuses on physical therapy management of children with this most common physical disability encountered in pediatric practice.[1] It is a comprehensive, evidence-based text that analyzes and synthesizes a vast volume of research literature while using the framework of the International Classification of Functioning, Disability and Health (ICF).[2] The ICF model emphasizes the person's health and functional level regardless of presence or absence of disability, and recognizes the interaction of environmental and personal contextual factors with the individual's health condition.[2,3] The ICF classifies body functions, activities, and participation that comprise the term *functioning* and describes *disability* based on alterations in body structures and functions, limitations in activity, and restrictions in participation.[2,3]

The new edition of the *Guide to Physical Therapist Practice (Guide 3.0)*[4] lists the biopsychosocial ICF[2] model as a major foundational construct that informs the physical therapist's decision-making process. Evidence-based practice (EBP) is another such construct. EBP integrates best available evidence with clinical expertise and the patient/client circumstances and values.[4,5] So, what is best available evidence? According to the latest version of the levels of evidence published by the Oxford Centre for Evidence-Based Medicine in 2011, random sample-based surveys and systematic reviews are considered the highest level of evidence (level 1).[6] These are followed by individual randomized controlled clinical trials (RCTs), inception cohort studies, and systematic reviews of surveys (level 2); nonrandomized controlled cohort studies and case series (levels 3 and 4, respectively); and mechanism-based reasoning that links interventions with clinical outcomes and occupies the lowest level in this hierarchy.[6]

Guide 3.0[4] suggests that, before making a decision in regard to the application of research evidence to management of a specific patient, physical therapists must access that evidence and critically assess its quality. According to *Guide 3.0*,[4] best evidence is provided by clinical practice guidelines, followed by systematic reviews, clinical prediction rules, and single research articles, such as RCTs. However, recent literature suggests that practical clinical trials (PCTs) may be of greater value than RCTs, for example, for research related to intervention dosing parameters for children with CP.[7] PCTs require large and diverse samples that are recruited from heterogeneous settings and, therefore, may be expensive to conduct.[8] However, PCTs may also be cost-effective because they compare interventions of choice across a large number of health outcomes and allow for documentation of a wide variety of intervention attributes and contextual factors.[7,8] Another recent recommendation is to use repeated measures rather than pretest–post-test designs.[7,9] Within-subject repeated measures design studies may be a powerful alternative to RCTs, and their quality can be assessed using 5 levels of evidence and 14 rigor criteria for single-subject research published by Logan et al.[10]

After examining several available methods for critical appraisal of research literature, a logical question to be asked in this context is: What place do textbooks occupy in the hierarchy of evidence? One way to answer this question is by burning all traditional textbooks as suggested by Sackett et al.[11] This sounds like an extreme measure; however, the argument for this solution is that, because of the rapid advancement of science we are experiencing, many textbooks become outdated even before they are published. According to Sackett et al,[11] a textbook can be spared such fate if it is revised every year, is heavily referenced, and the references are selected based on "explicit principles of evidence."[11(p 31)] These are extremely rigorous criteria that are very difficult and, perhaps, even impossible to meet, but they are worth striving for.

It is important to note that a review of literature that took place at the inception of the idea for this book revealed that just in *Pediatric Physical Therapy*, the journal of the American Physical Therapy Association (APTA) Section on Pediatrics, roughly 50% of all research articles published from the mid-1990s to date were devoted to topics related to children with CP. This discovery highlights the major place these children occupy in pediatric physical therapy practice and suggests that the overall body of general knowledge and research related to this complex condition is enormous. At the same time, while this body of research certainly contains high-level evidence, there are many publications that cannot be classified as such; some areas of practice are better researched than others; and on some subjects, evidence is completely missing.

Although many pediatric therapists strive to embrace EBP, the lack of time and incentives for EBP-related activities have been identified as barriers to its implementation, and the development of user-friendly clinical practice guidelines and continued professional education have been suggested as practical solutions.[12] The complexity of CP as a life span condition that affects the structures and functions of multiple body systems, activity and participation, and the heterogeneity of clinical presentation in this patient population complicate the design and implementation of research studies, the development of evidence-based clinical practice guidelines, and the every-day clinical decision making. At the same time, it is difficult to imagine that a single clinician, student, educator, or researcher may be capable of keeping up with the entire body of literature that covers all areas of practice related to the management of children and adults with CP. Therefore, it appears that an evidence-based text that summarizes the available research may be able to fill this void, serve as a source of foundational knowledge, and stimulate critical thinking by bringing up issues deliberated in recent literature. While it is not realistic to expect this text to be revised every year and while the best available evidence it cites may, at times, fall short of the rigor that one would desire, every attempt has been made here to bring the contemporary view of pediatric physical therapy practice to the reader.

This book is intended for Doctor of Physical Therapy students, physical therapy educators, new graduates and expert clinicians, pediatric physical therapists and other members of the interdisciplinary team, pediatric physical therapy residents, therapists studying for a pediatric physical therapy specialty certification examination, and researchers working with children with CP. It examines the current approach to the diagnosis and classification of CP and explores the research evidence related to prognosis; medical management; and physical therapy examination, evaluation, and intervention for children with this condition.

Although it focuses on only one developmental disorder, this book contains many features of a comprehensive pediatric text that can serve as a foundation for the discussion of physical therapy management of children with other movement disorders and disabilities. These include such topics as typical and atypical development of movement and postural control; physical therapy examination, evaluation, and intervention approaches, strategies, and techniques; concepts of motor learning and issues related to family education and family-centered care; assessment and management of pain and therapy-related behavior; therapy settings and delivery models; assistive technology; and transition to adulthood. In discussions of specific conditions other than CP, research articles and additional classroom materials can be used to supplement this text.

Online access to video clips that accompany the text is available for the readers. The videos can be used for individual or classroom observation, laboratory sessions, written projects, and class discussions, with suggestions for such activities provided for each video and linked to specific chapters. In addition, complementary PowerPoint slides for each chapter are included for use by physical therapy educators.

This book was written with the intent to encourage the readers to think critically and form their own opinions regarding important issues and controversies existing in current literature. The Questions to Ponder at the end of each of its 6 sections are offered to create opportunities for classroom discussions among entry-level physical therapy students and for a healthy professional debate among experienced clinicians on such topics as functional outcomes of spasticity management, intervention dosing, theoretical foundation and efficacy of therapeutic approaches, the role of manual guidance in pediatric physical therapy intervention, and others. Finally, questions for future research are proposed to challenge the reader to look ahead and plan new studies in search for evidence that would move the pediatric practice forward.

Mary Rahlin, PT, DHS, PCS

References

1. Reddihough DS, Collins KJ. The epidemiology and causes of cerebral palsy. *Aust J Physiother.* 2003;49:7-12.
2. World Health Organization. *International Classification of Functioning, Disability and Health.* Geneva, Switzerland: World Health Organization; 2001.
3. World Health Organization. Towards a common language for functioning, disability and health: ICF, the International Classification of Functioning, Disability and Health. *World Health Organization.* http://www.who.int/classifications/icf/training/icfbeginnersguide.pdf?ua=1. Published 2002. Accessed March 8, 2015.
4. American Physical Therapy Association. *Guide to Physical Therapist Practice 3.0.* http://guidetoptpractice.apta.org/. Published August 2014. Accessed March 8, 2015.
5. Sackett DL, Rosenberg WM, Muir Gray JA, et al. Evidence-based medicine: what it is and what it isn't. *BMJ.* 1996;312:71-72.
6. OCEBM Levels of Evidence Working Group. The Oxford 2011 Levels of Evidence. *Oxford Centre for Evidence-Based Medicine.* http://www.cebm.net/. Accessed March 8, 2015.
7. Gannotti ME, Christy JB, Heathcock JC, Kolobe TH. A path model for evaluating dosing parameters for children with cerebral palsy. *Phys Ther.* 2014;94(3):411-421.
8. Tunis SR, Stryer DB, Clancy CM. Practical clinical trials: increasing the value of clinical research for decision making in clinical and health policy. *JAMA.* 2003;290(12):1624-1632.
9. Kolobe TH, Christy JB, Gannotti ME, et al and Research Summit III Participants. Research summit III proceedings on dosing in children with an injured brain or cerebral palsy: executive summary. *Phys Ther.* 2014;94(7):907-920.
10. Logan LR, Hickman RR, Harris SR, Heriza CB. Single-subject research design: recommendations for levels of evidence and quality rating. *Dev Med Child Neurol.* 2008;50(2):99-103.
11. Sackett DL, Straus SE, Richardson WS, Rosenberg W, Haynes RB. *Evidence-Based Medicine: How to Practice and Teach EBM.* 2nd ed. Ediburgh, Scotland: Churchill Livingstone; 2000.
12. Schreiber J, Stern P, Marchetti G, Provident I. Strategies to promote evidence-based practice in pediatric physical therapy: a formative evaluation pilot project. *Phys Ther.* 2009;89(9):918-933.

TYPICAL AND ATYPICAL DEVELOPMENT OF MOVEMENT AND POSTURAL CONTROL

Theoretical Perspectives on Motor Development

...a theory is not a theory unless it can be disproved.

John R. Platt, *Strong Inference: Certain Systematic Methods of*
Scientific Thinking May Produce Much More Rapid Progress Than Others

Theories are developed out of necessity to classify, categorize, and explain a set of facts or observed phenomena.[1,2] Based on theories, hypotheses are generated, tested, and then supported or refuted through observation, research, and practice, thus giving rise to new ideas.[1,2] As this cycle continues, theories are refined and reformulated in attempts to provide a more precise explanation for observable facts.[1] All of this is true when applied to the field of human development where, over the years, researchers proposed several theories that explained the development of movement and postural control in infancy and childhood and offered their views of these phenomena.

Motor development refers to changes in motor behavior exhibited by the individuals over their life span.[3] In clinical practice, therapists encounter children who develop typically and atypically. The term *typical* is synonymous with "normal," "healthy," or "usual."[4] Thus, the term *atypical* can be defined as "abnormal," "unhealthy," or "unusual." Knowledge of typical motor development is crucial for understanding atypical development[5] as it provides the foundation for intervention. As clinicians assimilate new theoretical knowledge and apply it to their practice, new therapeutic approaches emerge.[2] Each approach relies on a specific theory or a set of theories to explain the typically occurring developmental changes and the characteristics of atypical development. This chapter highlights the neuromaturational, dynamic systems, perception-action, and neuronal group selection theories, and examines and analyzes their views of typical motor development.

NEUROMATURATIONAL THEORY

The neuromaturational theory related the changes in motor behavior exhibited during infancy and childhood to the maturation of the central nervous system (CNS) as their primary catalyst.[3,6] The maturation processes, such as the appearance and integration of primitive reflexes, the development of righting and equilibrium reactions (Table 1-1), and the progression of myelination were used to explain the sequential emergence of new motor skills in infants, from functioning in recumbent positions, to quadruped, and then to upright mobility.[2,3,7,8] The hierarchic maturation of the CNS toward the dominance of cerebral cortex over the lower levels of the brain was thought to be primarily responsible for guiding motor development.[2,6] Gesell[9,10] and McGraw[11] were prominent researchers who held maturationist views. They are widely credited for their work in defining developmental stages and providing detailed descriptions of a sequential progression of movement skills acquisition in infants.[2,12,13]

Rahlin M. *Physical Therapy for Children With Cerebral Palsy:*
An Evidence-Based Approach (pp 3-23).
© 2016 SLACK Incorporated.

TABLE 1-1

PRIMITIVE REFLEXES AND RIGHTING AND EQUILIBRIUM REACTIONS

PRIMITIVE REFLEXES

Reflex	Stimulus[8]	Response[8]	Onset[3,7]	Integration[3,7]
Rooting	Stroking of the corner of the mouth	Turning face and tongue to the side of the stimulus; sucking activation	28 weeks gestation	3 months
Crossed extension	Noxious stimulus to the sole of the foot	LE flexion on stimulus side and extension and adduction of the other LE	28 weeks gestation	1 to 2 months
Moro	Sudden head drop in posterior direction after the infant is positioned in reclined sitting	(B) shoulder abduction, elbow extension, and hand opening, followed by shoulder adduction and elbow flexion; (B) LE flexion	28 weeks gestation	4 to 6 months
Plantar grasp	Pressure to the sole of the foot in the area of metatarsal heads	Strong toe flexion (stronger with ankle dorsiflexion)	28 weeks gestation	9 to 12 months
Primary standing (positive support)	Contact of the feet with supporting surface when the infant is supported in vertical suspension	Weight-bearing through (B) LE, without full extension of the trunk, (B) hip, and knee	35 weeks gestation	1 to 2 months
Primary walking (automatic stepping)	Placing infant in supported standing with his or her trunk tipped forward	Taking steps forward	38 weeks gestation	1.5 to 2 months
Palmar grasp	Pressure to the palm of the hand	Strong finger flexion	Birth	9 months
Asymmetrical tonic neck reflex (ATNR)	Rotation of the head to the side to 90 degrees	UE and LE extension on the face side and UE and LE flexion on the skull side of the head; response is stronger in UEs	Birth	4 to 6 months
Symmetrical tonic neck reflex (STNR)	Head flexion or head extension	UE flexion, LE or UE extension, LE flexion	4 to 6 months	8 to 12 months

RIGHTING REACTIONS

Reflex	Stimulus[8]	Response[8]	Onset[3,7]	Integration[3,7]
Derotative neck	Neck rotation in supine	Immature: "log rolling" in the same direction	34 weeks gestation	4 to 6 months
		Mature: segmental rolling from shoulder to pelvis in the same direction	4 to 6 months	5 years
Lateral (labyrinthine)	Lateral displacement of weight	Restoration of the upright position of the head while using flexors and extensors of the neck simultaneously	Birth to 2 months	Persists
Optical	Visual input	Head elevation against gravity	Birth to 2 months	Persists

(continued)

TABLE 1-1 (CONTINUED)

PRIMITIVE REFLEXES AND RIGHTING AND EQUILIBRIUM REACTIONS

RIGHTING REACTIONS (CONTINUED)

Reflex	Stimulus[8]	Response[8]	Onset[3,7]	Integration[3,7]
Body on body	Rotation of a part of the body	Immature: "log rolling"	34 weeks gestation	4 to 6 months
		Mature: segmental rolling	4 to 6 months	5 years
Landau	Positioning in prone suspension. May gently raise/lower the infant	Head, trunk, and LE extension against gravity	3 to 4 months	1 to 2 years
Downward parachute	Quick displacement in downward direction in vertical suspension	(B) hip flexion, abduction, external rotation, and knee flexion followed with hip and knee extension of (B) LE as they bear weight	4 months	Persists
Forward protective	Quick displacement of the infant toward a flat surface, head first	(B) shoulder flexion, elbow extension, wrist extension, hand opening, finger extension, and abduction	6 to 7 months	Persists
Lateral protective	Quick displacement of weight in lateral direction	Shoulder abduction and elbow, wrist, and finger extension on the side of displacement	7 to 8 months	Persists
Backward protective	Quick displacement of weight in posterior direction	Backward extension of (B) UE to protect against a fall	9 months	Persists
Staggering (LE stepping)	Quick displacement of weight in anterior, posterior, or lateral direction in standing	Taking several steps in the direction of displacement to regain balance	15 to 17 months	Persists

EQUILIBRIUM REACTIONS

Reflex	Stimulus[8]	Response[8]	Onset[3,7]	Integration[3,7]
Prone	Lateral tilt of the supporting surface	Lateral flexion of the trunk and extension and abduction of UE and LE on the upward (non–weight-bearing) side, with trunk elongation on the weight-bearing side	6 months	Persists
Supine			7 to 8 months	Persists
Sitting			7 to 8 months	Persists
Quadruped			9 to 12 months	Persists
Standing			12 to 24 months	Persists

Abbreviations: (B), bilateral; LE, lower extremity; UE, upper extremity.

Onset and integration data from Cech and Martin.[3] Stimulus and response description adapted from *Normal Infant Reflexes and Development* [video]. Tuscon, AZ: Therapy Skill Builders; 1988.

Gesell pioneered developmental testing,[12,13] and a significant part of his research was dedicated to establishing norms in various areas of development.[14] Many of the items contained in current developmental tests were derived from his work.[12,13]

The sequential nature of motor development was subsequently highlighted by multiple authors,[2,3,5,15-17] and for years to come, the developmental sequence, along with postural reactions, became the foundation of therapeutic intervention for infants and children who developed atypically.[13,16,17] A typical sequence of gross motor skill development in the first year of life, with the emphasis on these components,[15] is summarized in Table 1-2 and illustrated by Figures 1-1 through 1-21.

	TABLE 1-2			

TYPICAL SEQUENCE OF MOVEMENT SKILL ACQUISITION IN THE FIRST YEAR OF LIFE

AGE (MONTHS)	POSITION			
	Prone	*Supine*	*Sitting*	*Standing*
Newborn (Figure 1-1)	• Physiological flexion • Weight shifted anteriorly • Able to clear airway by turning head to side • AG head elevation is minimal but present • Full forward flexion posture in horizontal suspension	• Physiological flexion • Random movement of UE and LE • Able to briefly bring head to midline • No active antigravity flexion • Pull to sit: some initial activation of neck flexors, then full head lag	• Full forward flexion posture in supported sitting • May elevate head only momentarily	• Primary standing • Automatic stepping
1 (Figure 1-2)	• Less physiological flexion • Decreased hip flexion, less anterior weight shift • Increased activation of neck extensors, including horizontal suspension	• Less physiological flexion • Pull to sit: full head lag	• Head still falls forward in supported sitting • Attempts to elevate head against gravity	• Continues WB through LE • Automatic stepping still may be present
2 (Figures 1-3 and 1-4)	• Decreased physiological flexion • Decreased hip flexion • Increased head elevation, with wide position of the hands, with elbows behind shoulders • Asymmetrical posture • Increased head/neck and upper trunk extension in horizontal suspension	• Decreased physiological flexion • Increased extension of extremities due to gravity • Asymmetrical posture • ATNR • Uncontrolled swiping at toys at one side • Increased lateral vision • Pull to sit: briefly assists with head lifting, then head lag	• Head bobbing in supported sitting • Lack of trunk control	• Astasia-abasia (inability to take weight through (B) LE) • Absent automatic stepping
3 (Figures 1-5 and 1-6)	• Developing midline skills, more symmetry • (B) LE abduction and external rotation • Rubbing feet together (with knees flexed) • Forearm WB, elbows directly under the shoulders, elevation of upper chest, with head elevated to 90 degrees • Neck and trunk extensors and upper chest and neck flexors working together (stability)	• Developing midline skills, more symmetry • Decreased ATNR • Midline head position • Chin tuck • Hands and feet may come together at midline • Increased midline vision • More antigravity flexor control with pull to sit, but not maintaining midline head yet	• Rounded back, but some neck elongation is seen in supported sitting • Head elevation with neck hyperextension and elevation of scapulae • May open mouth	• Takes weight through (B) LE • Variable LE movement • Absent automatic stepping

(continued)

TABLE 1-2 (CONTINUED)				
TYPICAL SEQUENCE OF MOVEMENT SKILL ACQUISITION IN THE FIRST YEAR OF LIFE				
AGE (MONTHS)	**POSITION**			
	Prone	*Supine*	*Sitting*	*Standing*
4 (Figures 1-7 and 1-8)	• Symmetrical posture, midline skills are formed • Increased anterior pelvic tilt, legs are closer together, scapular adduction • Alternates between anterior and posterior pelvic tilt positions • Head elevation to 90 degrees, chest elevation, forearm WB, elbows in front of shoulders • Rolling from prone to side as an accident • Full Landau response	• Symmetrical posture, midline skills are formed • Hands to knees, posterior pelvic tilt • Active rolling to the side following rotation of the head led by vision • Initiates lateral head righting in side-lying • Pull to sit: midline head; activates neck flexors, abdominals, elbow and hip/knee flexors, with head in line with body; shoulder elevation for stability	• More upper spinal extension in supported sitting, kyphotic posture below T-level	• Takes weight through (B) LE • Increased trunk and hip control
5 (Figure 1-9)	• Prone on extended arms, more stability • Weight shifting on forearms, reaching with one upper extremity • Emerging lateral righting and prone equilibrium reactions • Emerging mature weight shift (trunk elongation on WB side, trunk lateral flexion on non-WB side, and LE dissociation, with hip adduction, extension and medial rotation on WB side and hip abduction, flexion and lateral rotation on non-WB side) • Accidental rolling into supine, but no controlled rolling	• Hand to foot, foot to mouth • AG pelvic elevation and posterior tilt • Active rolling to side-lying with lateral head righting and LE dissociation; may attempt rolling to prone • Pull to sit: chin tuck, (B) UE and (B)LE flexion and abdominal activation	• Tripod sitting (leans forward and props on extended arms) • L-spine still rounded • May balance in this position but cannot be left alone	• Takes full weight through (B) LE
6 (Figures 1-10 and 1-11)	• Good AG head control • Balanced neck, trunk, hip flexor and extensor, and abdominal muscle activity • Increased shoulder girdle and pelvic stability • Weight shift on extended arms; reaching with one UE	• Good AG head control • Plays with feet • Active rolling into prone with lateral trunk flexion and LE dissociation • Pull to sit: pulls him- or herself up holding on to an adult's fingers	• Good AG head control • Increased hip extensor control • Attempts independent sitting with a chin tuck present	• Good AG head control • Able to hold on to support to stand and bounce • Wide BOS

(continued)

TABLE 1-2 (CONTINUED)				
TYPICAL SEQUENCE OF MOVEMENT SKILL ACQUISITION IN THE FIRST YEAR OF LIFE				
AGE (MONTHS)	POSITION			
	Prone	*Supine*	*Sitting*	*Standing*
7 (Figures 1-12 and 1-13)	• Preferred position • Pivoting prone • Reciprocal belly crawling • Controlled rolling from prone to side-lying • Plays in side-lying propped on one elbow • Assumes an immature quadruped position • May rock back and forth and diagonally • Transitions from quadruped to sitting with trunk rotation	• Is rarely in this position	• Hands free in unsupported sitting • Trunk rotation and mature weight shifting	• Starting to pull up to stand at support from quadruped using UE, without LE dissociation • Requires (B) UE support for standing, continues bouncing
8 (Figures 1-14 and 1-15)	• Immature reciprocal creeping	• Is rarely in this position	• Increased trunk control in sitting • Long sitting and half-long sitting positions are used • Transitions in and out of sitting from/ to quadruped with trunk rotation	• Transitions to standing through half-kneeling but still uses (B) UE more than (B) LE • Cruising sideways along furniture • Unable to transition from standing in a controlled manner
9 (Figures 1-16 and 1-17)	• Develops a more mature creeping pattern • Creeping is the predominant method of locomotion • Climbing with UE and LE dissociation	• Is rarely in this position	• Sitting in a variety of ways • Independently transitions in and out of sitting	• Pulls to stand through half-kneeling • Still lacks full LE dissociation • Cruising with partial rotation in direction of movement
10 (Figures 1-18 and 1-19)	• Continues creeping and climbing with more pelvic-hip control	• Is rarely in this position	• Continues using a variety of sitting positions	• Half-kneeling is the predominant way of pulling up to stand • Can lower self from standing in a controlled manner • Increased trunk rotation with cruising • Walks forward with two hands held with improved control

(continued)

AGE (MONTHS)	POSITION			
	Prone	*Supine*	*Sitting*	*Standing*
11 (Figure 1-20)	• Continues creeping and climbing		• Well-developed postural reactions • Smooth transitions between sitting, quadruped, and creeping	• Uses LE muscles more than UE muscles when pulling up to stand through half-kneeling • Minimal use of (B) UE for support • Transitions in and out of standing through half-kneeling • Attempts to stand alone with high guard position of (B) UE • Wide BOS • Walks with one hand held
12 (Figure 1-21)	• Equilibrium reactions are present • Full trunk control	• Equilibrium reactions are present	• Equilibrium reactions are present • Full trunk control	• Transitions to standing without use of furniture for support • Initiates steps with high guard position of (B) UE

TABLE 1-2 (CONTINUED)

TYPICAL SEQUENCE OF MOVEMENT SKILL ACQUISITION IN THE FIRST YEAR OF LIFE

Abbreviations: AG, antigravity; (B), bilateral; BOS, base of support; LE, lower extremity; UE, upper extremity; WB, weight-bearing.
Compiled from Bly.[15]

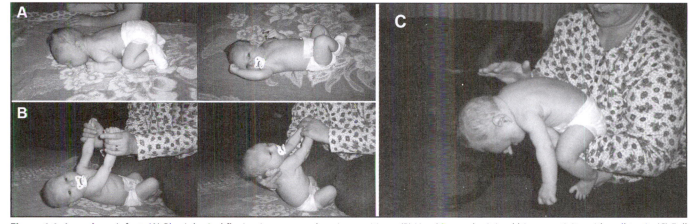

Figure 1-1. A newborn infant. (A) Physiological flexion in prone and supine positions. (B) Head lag and minimal biceps activity with pull to sit. (C) Full forward flexion posture in horizontal suspension.

Besides his research related to developmental stages and developmental testing, Gesell formulated several major concepts or principles of development, including directionality, reciprocal interweaving, functional asymmetry, and self-regulation.[14,18,19] He suggested that motor behavior progressed 1) in a cephalocaudal direction, with head control developing before trunk control, and upper extremity control emerging before infants are able to control their lower extremities; and 2) in the direction from proximal to distal, with the midline neck and trunk control established before shoulder and

pelvic girdle control, followed by control of upper extremities, hands, and feet.[3,14,19]

Gesell[18] created the term *reciprocal interweaving* to describe development as a spiral process, with alternating periods of relative equilibrium and disequilibrium that are characterized by stable and unstable behaviors, respectively. In this process, less mature behaviors seem to disappear only to re-emerge later in a more mature form, which Gesell attributed to reciprocal excitation and inhibition occurring at subcortical level of the CNS.[18] This concept was applied not

Figure 1-2. A 1-month-old infant. (A) Decreased physiological flexion as compared to a newborn. (B) Still minimal head control in a supported sitting position. (C) Weight-bearing through lower extremities.

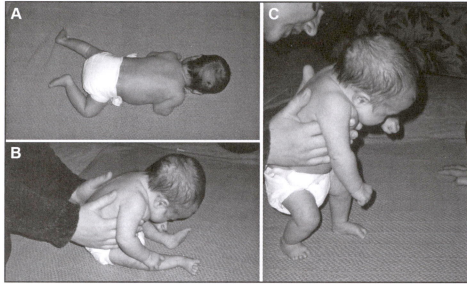

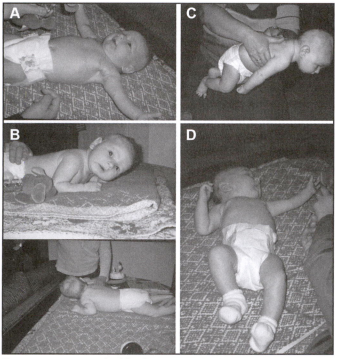

Figure 1-3. A 2-month-old infant. (A) Markedly decreased physiological flexion in supine as compared to younger infants. (B) Asymmetrical posture and decreased hip flexion in prone, with head elevation to 30 degrees, and elbows positioned behind shoulders. (C) Increased head/neck and upper trunk extension in horizontal suspension as compared to younger infants. (D) Asymmetrical tonic neck reflex.

Figure 1-4. A 2-month-old infant: astasia abasia.

only to motor, but also to personal-social, language and other areas of development.[3,14,18,19] In addition, Gesell recognized the importance of asymmetry in human development, from the asymmetrical structure of organ systems to the development of functional hand dominance,[14,18,19] and formulated his principle of self-regulation that proposed that the human organism imposes inherent protective limits on the bursts and pauses or retreats that occur in its developmental process.[14,19]

Although Gesell insisted on genetics and maturation playing a major role in guiding development,[9,12-14,19] he acknowledged the role of environment, especially in cognitive development, and the existence of individual differences among developing children.[12-14] He recognized the role of vision in motor development,[14,20] viewed the human organism as a whole, and appreciated the importance of all developmental domains.[14] As Thelen and Adolph[14] pointed out, these ideas and Gesell's developmental concepts, such as reciprocal interweaving and self-regulation, could be considered precursors to the current views of dynamic systems and perception-action theories, which are discussed further in this chapter.

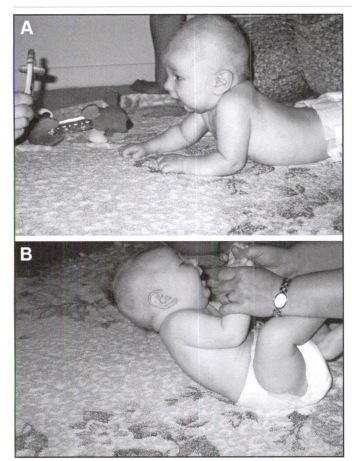

Figure 1-5. A 3-month-old infant. (A) Forearm weight-bearing in a prone position, with head elevation to 90 degrees and elbows directly under the shoulders. (B) More antigravity flexor control with a pull-to-sit maneuver as compared to younger infants.

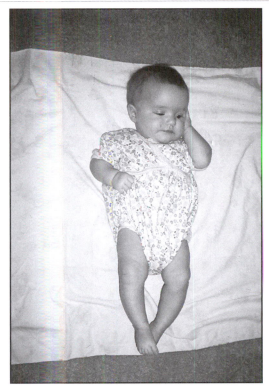

Figure 1-6. A 3-month-old infant: developing midline skills.

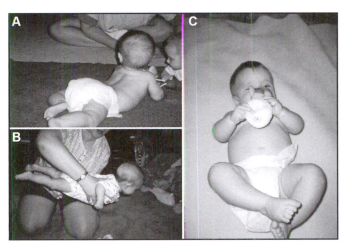

Figure 1-7. A 4-month-old infant. (A) Increased anterior pelvic tilt and scapular adduction in a prone position, with forearm weight-bearing and head elevation to 90 degrees; elbows in front of shoulders. (B) Full Landau response in horizontal suspension. (C) Symmetrical posture and formed midline skills in a supine position.

Figure 1-8. A 4-month-old infant: posterior pelvic tilt, hands to knees in a supine position.

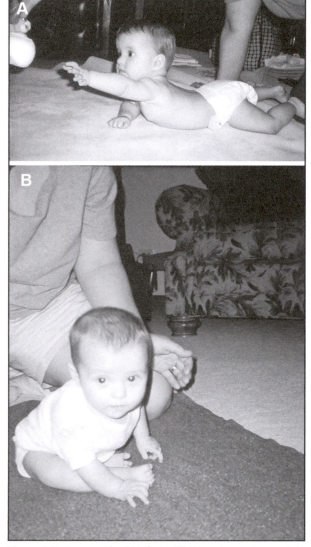

Figure 1-9. Five-month-old infants. (A) Emerging mature weight shift onto one elbow and reaching for a toy against gravity with the other upper extremity in a prone position. (B) Tripod sitting.

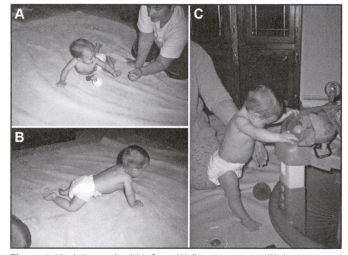

Figure 1-12. A 7-month-old infant. (A) Pivoting prone. (B) An immature quadruped position, with insufficient hip flexion and hip abduction and external rotation. (C) Standing with bilateral upper extremity support, hip flexion, and knees locked in extension.

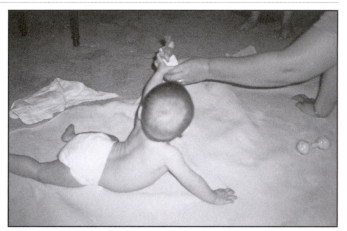

Figure 1-10. A 6-month-old infant: mature weight shifting on extended arms in a prone position and reaching for a toy with one upper extremity in an upward direction.

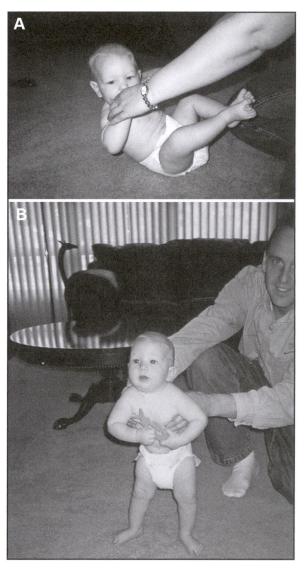

Figure 1-11. A 6-month-old infant. (A) Pulling himself up to sitting holding on to an adult's fingers. (B) Good antigravity head control in a supported standing position.

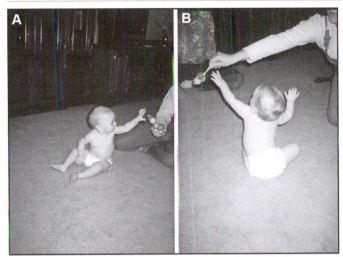

Figure 1-13. A 7-month-old infant: trunk rotation and mature weight shifting in a ring sitting position, hands free.

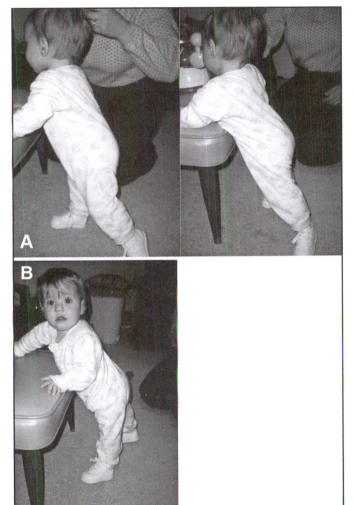

Figure 1-15. An 8-month-old infant. (A) Still using upper extremities and upper body strength greater than lower extremities to pull up to standing and leaning into support during play in a standing position. (B) Cruising sideways along furniture.

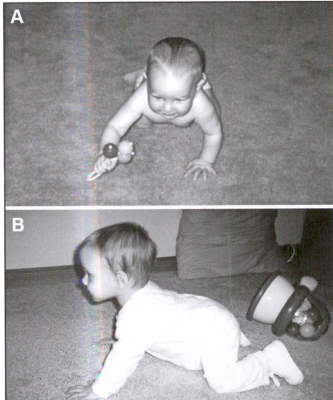

Figure 1-14. Two 8-month-old infants: an immature reciprocal creeping pattern, with a wide base of support, lumbar lordosis and hip flexion, abduction, and external rotation.

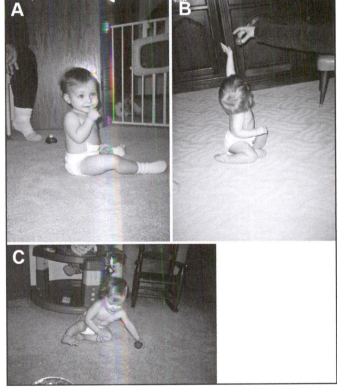

Figure 1-16. A 9-month-old infant. (A) Long sitting with hips abducted. (B) Side-sitting. (C) Half-long sitting.

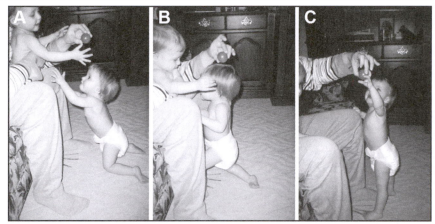

Figure 1-18. A 10-month-old infant: pulling up to stand through a half-kneeling position.

Figure 1-17. A 9-month-old infant: cruising along a coffee table with partial rotation in the direction of movement.

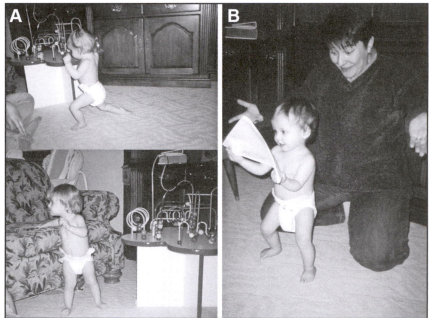

Figure 1-20. Two 11-month-old infants. (A) Predominant use of lower extremities when pulling up to stand and minimal use of upper extremities for support during cruising. (B) A successful attempt to stand alone.

Figure 1-19. A 10-month-old infant: ability to lower self from standing in a controlled manner.

Figure 1-21. A 12-month-old infant. (A) Transition to standing without using furniture for support. (B) Taking independent steps walking.

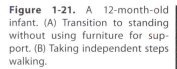

Dynamic Systems Theory

Systems View of Movement

The application of quantitative methods used in advancing movement science to developmental research led to findings that challenged the maturationist view of development.[21,22] These methods, such as electromyography and kinematic analysis, provided researchers with opportunities to study muscle activity and spatio-temporal characteristics of human movement, including that of a developing child.[21] Bernstein,[23] who pioneered such approach to movement analysis, formulated his famous "degrees of freedom" problem by asking, "How is the human organism able to create a single motor act that matches the task at hand when it possesses an endless number of options inherent in its redundant anatomical structure, with multiple possible combinations of body segments' positions and movements that may be achieved by many different muscles?" In the process of answering this question, he defined *motor coordination* as "overcoming excessive degrees of freedom of our movement organs, that is, turning the movement organs into controllable systems."[23(p 41)] Bernstein[23] suggested that the human body solved the motor control problem by forming functional synergies from actions of different muscle groups, and that other factors besides the CNS, such as external forces (eg, gravity) and internal forces (eg, inertia), as well as the input from the proprioceptive, kinesthetic, tactile, visual, auditory, and other systems, were also responsible for movement organization. He proposed that human movement was fundamentally complex and had to be flexible in order to match the demands of a specific task in a constantly changing environment. Therefore, movement was the result of a flexible interaction between 3 major components: the person, the task at hand, and the environment in which the task was being performed. This meant that instead of following a central command originating in the human brain, the responsibility for the production of movement was distributed among these 3 elements, and that even in a series of repetitive movements, the trajectory of each of them would be unique and at least slightly different from the previous one and the one to follow.[23]

Principles of Dynamic Systems Theory

Bernstein's ideas were taken further by other scientists who developed the dynamic systems theory or DST.[2,3,21,22,24,25] This theory has been used to explain many natural phenomena, from changes in the state of matter and patterns of cloud formation to motor development.[25] The major premises of the DST as applied to motor development include self-organization; nonlinearity; and the role of control parameters, attractors, and rhythmical stereotypies or oscillations in driving the developmental process.[21,22,24,25]

Self-organization is the fundamental principle of the DST.[2,3,21,22,24-27] It implies that nervous, musculoskeletal, cardiovascular and pulmonary, vestibular, and somatosensory systems work together as equal contributors to the task-related behavior exhibited by an individual in his or her physical, psychological, and social environments. Thus, the emergent movement results from the interaction of all, equally important, subsystems that self-organize to accomplish a specific task under specific conditions determined by all external and internal forces acting on the human body.[2,3,21,22,24-27]

In DST, the human organism is viewed as a complex and multidimensional system that has a nonlinear pattern of development.[2,3,21,22,24-27] According to this view, not all systems comprising the human body mature at the same time.[27] Periods of accelerated development of one or several body systems may coincide with slow periods or pauses in the development of other systems.[27] The nonlinearity of the developmental process means that the human organism is sensitive to control parameters.[2,3,21,22,24-27] A control parameter is a variable that is capable of producing a qualitative change in the behavior of the entire system.[28] A system behaves in a nonlinear fashion when its output is not proportional to the input it receives.[28-30] To illustrate this notion, Kamm et al[21] provided an example of the "last straw" that broke a camel's back. When the weight added to the camel's back reached a critical value, the camel collapsed as it was no longer able to remain standing.[21] Other examples of the effects of control parameters observed in nature include the transformation of water from liquid to gaseous state as it reaches its boiling temperature (a control parameter) or a locomotor pattern of walking changing into running with its distinct flight phase when its speed increases to a critical value (another control parameter).[31]

Studies of Infant Kicking and Stepping Behaviors

Thelen and Smith[22] described a series of elegant experiments that were conducted using electromyography, kinematics, and observation to study stepping and kicking behaviors in infants and to investigate the seeming disappearance of the newborn stepping movements by 2 months of age. When Thelen and Fisher[32,33] compared spontaneous newborn kicking in supine with infant early stepping behavior, they found that these 2 cyclical patterns were very similar in their kinematics (motion of the body segments) and in the sequence of muscle activation for flexion and extension movements of the legs. As shown in other studies, both types of movement intensified with increased arousal.[34-37] While the newborn stepping declined between 2 and 6 weeks of life and "disappeared" around 2 months of age, supine kicking persisted.[22] Thelen et al[37,38] discovered that newborn stepping disappeared at a faster rate in those infants who displayed the highest rate of weight gain. When small weights were added to the legs of 4-week-old infants, they displayed a significant decrease in their stepping behavior as compared to the testing condition without weights.[38] In addition, when 3-month-old infants were supported in the upright position in trunk-deep water, they performed frequent steps, although they did not demonstrate any stepping when held in an upright standing

Figure 1-22. A child with cerebral palsy in a W-sitting position.

position on land.[38] The results of these experiments demonstrated that the disappearance of newborn stepping could rather be explained by the weight gain in an infant with an immature musculoskeletal apparatus than the maturation of the nervous system.[21,22,24,25]

Continuing with her examination of infant stepping behavior in a series of treadmill studies, Thelen[39] found that 7-month-old infants who did not demonstrate any stepping on a stationary surface were able to generate steps while held upright on a moving treadmill. These infants produced very well-coordinated, alternating steps, and as the treadmill speed increased, they were able to increase the rate of stepping by decreasing the single stance time as is typical for locomotion in adults.[39] Further research showed that when held upright with one leg on a slower moving and the other one on a faster moving treadmill belt, 7-month-old infants were still able to produce remarkably coordinated alternating steps.[40] The examination of infant treadmill stepping at ages 1 to 10 months demonstrated that their stepping pattern changed as their muscle strength increased.[41] In addition, during treadmill experiments, some of the infants displayed a distinct heel strike at the initial contact phase of gait.[42] Movement patterns elicited in these studies are commonly seen after the emergence and during further development of independent walking.[22,24,25] As they were "uncovered" by the treadmill, Thelen and Ulrich[41] called them the *hidden skills*. In these experiments, the treadmill speed served as a control parameter that allowed the system to self-organize for a stepping behavior that was not normally seen on a stationary surface, and changes in muscle strength led to a nonlinear increase in alternating stepping behavior, usually at 3 months of age.[25]

To summarize, Thelen's research of stepping and kicking behaviors led to the discovery that leg movements in infants depended on such factors as the baby's state of arousal, his or her position in space, the environment (submerged in water vs supported on a treadmill vs standing on a stationary supporting surface), and the desire to deliberately use leg movements for environmental exploration.[22] Therefore, the development of walking could not be explained by a single cause, such as brain maturation. Instead, it was found to be multidimensional in nature, including such equally important dimensions as the organic structures (the musculoskeletal, nervous, and other body systems), the task at hand, and the environment or context.[22]

Developmental Change

According to the DST, the human body is a complex, self-organizing, dynamic system that is sensitive to control parameters, which cause dramatic changes in its behavior.[2,3,21,22,24-27] The adjustments of this system to the demands of the task and its context bring about movement variability, which is an inherent characteristic of typical development.[2,3,30] Optimal amount of movement variability allows the child to adapt to the requirements of a task and its environmental constraints.[2,3,30] Little variability signifies stable movement patterns or attractor states, while an increase in variability indicates the disorganization of the system when a movement pattern becomes unstable.[2,3,43] A period of instability leads to a phase shift when a significant change in behavior is achieved by reaching a new stable behavior or a new "attractor state."[43] An attractor can be defined as a preferred movement pattern or posture used to perform a common activity.[21] This pattern or posture is not obligatory or mandatory for completion of the task, but its resistance to perturbation maintains its stability.[21] Thelen[24] described the developmental change as "a series of states of stability, instability, and phase shifts in the attractor landscape."[(p 84)] The degree to which it is possible to change the preferred movement pattern has been described as the depth of an attractor well.[21] When explaining the concept of attractor wells, Shumway-Cook and Woollacott[2] provided an analogy with riverbeds. When the riverbed is deep, it is not very likely that the water will flow outside its banks. However, when it is shallow, the likelihood of such an occurrence is much higher.[2] For example, children developing typically may temporarily play in a W-sitting position but would have many other sitting positions available to them, which would make their W-sitting attractor well very shallow. However, it is not uncommon for children with cerebral palsy to develop a very deep W-sitting attractor well as this may be the only floor sitting position that would allow them to use both hands to manipulate a toy (Figure 1-22).

Thelen[34-36] suggested that rhythmical behaviors or oscillations played a special role in the formation of new attractor states. She looked at such behaviors as kicking, waving, quadruped rocking, and bouncing in supported standing as the precursors of a significant change in motor behavior or a phase shift, from uncoordinated to complex, well-coordinated, purposeful movement.[34-36] Her research showed that kicking increased significantly just prior to the emergence of independent locomotion, quadruped rocking intensified before the onset of creeping, and more frequent oscillations in sitting and standing positions were followed by significant gains in sitting and standing postural control.[35,36]

Thelen's Dynamic Systems Theory Concepts and Links to Other Theories

Spencer et al[25] listed 4 major DST concepts developed by Esther Thelen through her research. These concepts were as follows:

1. The importance of time: A single behavior occurs "in the moment," but multiple behavioral decisions the child makes have a cumulative effect on developmental change that occurs over a long period of time, and each change serves as a precursor for the changes to follow.

2. The multifaceted nature and flexibility of behavior: Multiple factors interact to produce a motor behavior, but their "soft assembly" and nonlinear relationship provide an opportunity for the child to adjust his or her actions to the task and its environmental constraints.

3. "Embodiment": The inseparable nature of perception, action, and cognition, with cognition existing only in connection with perception and movement

4. The significance of individuality: The child perceives a specific motor problem in his or her own, unique way, and selects a unique solution through the process of active exploration.[24,25]

The first 2 of these concepts build upon the DST ideas related to the role of attractors and control parameters in developmental change. However, the third and the fourth concepts may be looked at as the links to the perception-action theory described by Gibson[44] and the theory of neuronal group selection (TNGS) pioneered by Edelman.[45,46] These 2 theories are presented further in this chapter.

PERCEPTION-ACTION THEORY

The "Scribble" Experiment

In 1955, James and Eleanor Gibson described an experiment that involved having the subjects look at a spiral drawing or a "scribble" and then identify from a set of "scribbles" those that were identical to the initial drawing.[47] Children aged 6 to 11 years and adults were shown the "scribbles" one after another and were not given any feedback regarding their success in completing the identification task. They were also asked to verbally describe each item. The experiment consisted of several consecutive trials that were continued until the participants correctly recognized only one drawing as being identical to the first one they had seen. The results showed that although the subjects' performance was directly related to their age, all participants demonstrated decreased errors

and improved ability to differentiate the items based on their distinct characteristics as the trials progressed.[47]

The clever structure of this experiment allowed the authors to demonstrate that the observed improvement in subjects' performance did not signify a response to stimulation and could not be related to the knowledge of results of their actions as they had not been provided with any extrinsic feedback.[47,48] Instead, their performance improved because their perception had been enhanced by having a repeated opportunity to inspect and analyze the drawings. Through practice, the subjects learned the qualities that distinguished the items from each other. Thus, the learning process could be looked at in 2 different ways: 1) as "learning to perceive," or achieving enhanced perception through practice or experience; and 2) as "perceiving to learn," or improving performance by achieving a higher level of perception.[47,48]

Central Concepts of Perception-Action Theory

In their subsequent work, James and Eleanor Gibson continued their discussion of the mechanism, role, and importance of perceptual learning.[44,48-50] The nature of human perception, the interaction between perception and action, the role of cognition in that interaction, the relationship between the organism and the environment, and the role of active exploration in developmental process are the central concepts of their perception-action or ecological theory. The Gibsons argue that improvement in perception results from learning to differentiate a greater and greater number of distinct qualities and aspects of visual, auditory, tactile, olfactory, and gustatory information about the environment that the human organism acquires through its sensory channels. The organism always exists in some kind of environment, and that environment has specific characteristics. The organism is not passive in receiving and responding to stimuli. It actively seeks and obtains external information through its perceptual systems, and then matches what the environment has to offer with its own internal capabilities.[44,48-50]

Gibson[44] introduced the concept of affordance that can be described as a quality or a characteristic of the environment or of an object in that environment that provides the individual with a possibility to act. The action will depend on how this individual perceives the affordance in a specific situation.[44,48-50] For example, a dining room chair affords a woman an opportunity to sit down, but her toddler son may perceive the same chair as an object under which he can crawl while "driving" a toy car.

Perception leads to action, but each action also serves as a source of information, which further enhances perception.[44,48-50] To illustrate, let us consider the woman from the previous example who decides to sit down in the dining room chair. Once she does so, she finds that, although it initially looked very comfortable, the chair is actually too firm for her liking. As her perception of the opportunity provided to her by the chair changes, she chooses to move to the couch in the living room instead. In the meantime,

		TABLE 1-3	

THREE PHASES OF EXPLORATORY DEVELOPMENT IN INFANCY

PHASE NUMBER	APPROXIMATE TIMING[a]	EXPLORATION MODES
1	Birth to ~4 months of age	• Attention to surroundings in immediate visual field available for tracking • Minimal visual attention to specific objects • Tracking movement (visual exploration) • Mouthing objects (tactile exploration) • Attention to sounds associated with events (auditory exploration)
2	Starts in the fifth month of age	• Attention to objects • Reaching for and grasping objects • Visual exploration using depth perception
3	Starts at 8 to 9 months of age	• Attention to the world expands with onset of locomotion • Exploration through movement (attention to surroundings beyond visible space [eg, behind objects and people, including the child; around the corners; enclosed hiding places])

[a] These are overlapping phases.

Compiled from Gibson.[50]

her son who was crawling under the chair discovers that it may be fun to "drive" his toy car up the chair's leg, and in the process, he kneels and then stands up next to it. This example demonstrates that there is a continuous interaction between perception and action, which, as Gibson[50] pointed out, are linked by affordances. Cognition plays a major role in this interaction as it allows the individual to process and interpret the information acquired from the environment and from his or her own organism.[44,50] The latter refers to vestibular, tactile, proprioceptive, and kinesthetic information that is used to analyze the possibility for action as it relates to physical capabilities of the human body in a specific situation.[44,50] The chair afforded the little boy an opportunity to enhance his play, and he acted on it as his physical abilities allowed him to act in this situation.

Gibson[44] made a distinction between sensation and perception. He emphasized that to perceive did not mean to have sensations, but that it meant to detect information.[44,50] The process of sensation is passive while perception is an active one. For example, the visual system has both motor and sensory components. The motor components serve to adjust the position of the head and the eyes and to focus on an object while seeking, obtaining, and processing visual information. Using touch to actively explore the environment is another example of perception as an active process.[44,50]

The environment has both constant and changing properties.[44] The human organism receives varied sensations that reflect environmental changes in lighting, smell, texture, and sound; however, it also perceives constant, or invariant, properties of the environment in spite of changes in sensation.[44]

The woman in the previous example would perceive a chair as being a chair in spite of the differences of seeing the chair in the morning sun light or in the light of a floor lamp at night. If her son called for her, she would be able to detect where the sound originated from, no matter how loud or quiet her son's voice might be.

The interaction between the human organism and its environment is reciprocal and dynamic.[44] Perception links the individual and the environment. When the individual perceives the environmental changes, his or her actions change, and the individual's actions also change the environment.[44] To illustrate, let us imagine that, as the toddler mentioned earlier continues "driving" his toy car on the floor, he encounters a tower made of wooden blocks and knocks it over. Now the blocks are all around him. The environment has changed and it is offering the little boy new affordances for action. He may choose to "drive" his car around the blocks; push the blocks out of his way; sit down and rebuild the tower; or stand up, pick up the blocks and put them in a container.

As stated previously, active exploration of the environment is one of the central concepts of the perception-action theory.[44,48-50] Perception is an active process.[44] As Eleanor Gibson stated, "We don't simply see, we look."[50(p 5)] Active exploration drives perceptual development and learning, and thus, both perception and action are inseparable from cognition.[44,48-50] Gibson[50] identified 3 overlapping phases of exploratory development in infancy that signified the cooperation between perception and action in developmental process (Table 1-3).

While exploring the possibilities for action, children select specific information that is important for the task at hand.[44,48-50] They use this information to adapt their actions in order to satisfy the demands of the task and the environment in which they are functioning. For example, for an infant considering crawling up the stairs, the information relevant to the task would include the following:

- Specific characteristics of the environment, such as the length of the staircase; the height, width, and surface texture of the steps; and what or who is waiting for them at the top
- The relationship between the child's body and the environment, specifically, his or her height and leg length as compared to the size of the steps
- The crawler's own physical capabilities, such as the range of motion in various joints, muscle strength, and the preferred method of locomotion.

If the analysis of this information leads to the infant perceiving this situation as an affordance for action, crawling up the stairs will be attempted.

Studies of Relationship Between Perception and Action

The perception-action theory inspired a large body of research that investigated the relationship between perception and action in motor development,[24] looking at perception as the guide for action[50-54] and at action as the means to enhance perception.[54,55] Only a few of these studies will be mentioned here to give the reader a glimpse into the investigation of these fascinating topics abundant with research possibilities. These studies showed that motor skills and postural control developed as infants moved and extracted perceptual information simultaneously, in an organized, coordinated way.[24]

In one of their experiments, Gibson and Walker[51] investigated tactile exploratory behaviors in infants and demonstrated that 1 month olds could visually differentiate rigid and elastic objects after a 60-second period of mouthing a hard or a soft toy. In another series of studies, Gibson et al[52] showed that infants and toddlers who preferred different patterns of locomotion (walking vs crawling) demonstrated different behaviors when faced with the task of moving across a hard or a flexible supporting surface. The two surfaces were a plywood walkway and a waterbed, both covered with the same textured material. The surface of the waterbed was moved by an experimenter concealed from the baby. The plywood walkway appeared to be hard when examined visually and felt hard to touch, and the waterbed surface looked and felt flexible. The majority of 16 crawling infants easily crossed both surfaces to their parent. Fourteen of 16 infants and toddlers who could walk crossed the plywood walkway, 9 by crawling and only 5 by walking. The walkers stopped to explore the flexible waterbed, both visually and by touching its surface, and then 12 of 16 babies crawled across and none of them walked. These results highlighted the role of affordances and

the close relationship among exploration, perception, and action in developmental process. Active exploration allowed the infants and toddlers to detect the affordances for action, which led to the selection of a specific method of locomotion that matched their physical capabilities.[52]

Other researchers investigated the human ability to perceive affordances for action when negotiating stairs[53] and slopes[54,56] and reaching for objects.[57] Warren[53] conducted several experiments with adult participants that examined the role of visual perception in the human action of stair climbing. The results showed that, regardless of the participants' leg length, the stairs were perceived as "climbable" until the step height/leg length ratio reached a critical value of .88, and the step height was both perceived and estimated to be optimal when this ratio was equal to .25. Thus, Warren[53] demonstrated that visual perception played a major role in extracting crucial information from the environment to be applied in a given situation. This information was then matched with the individual's physical capabilities, which resulted in finding the optimal movement solution for a task at hand.[53]

Adolph[56] studied infants' ability to detect affordances for the task of negotiating slopes as they progressed from crawling to walking. She found that learning to move over the slopes was specific to the infant's preferred locomotor pattern and resulted from spontaneous exploration of the environment on even surfaces rather than from direct practice of crawling and walking over the slopes.[54,56] In another series of experiments. Adolph[57] studied 9-month-old infants' perception of affordances for reaching across an adjustable gap in the supporting surface in sitting and quadruped positions. The accuracy of the infants' perception that led to their decision to reach or avoid reaching was found to be related to the amount of overall sitting and crawling experience rather than to the fear or experience of falling.[57] The specificity of learning discovered in these studies will be discussed in greater detail in Chapter 2.

As Thelen[24] pointed out, movement experience is critical for exploration, learning, and adaptation to the environment. As the baby learns new skills, motor activity enhances perception. Bushnell and Boudreau[55] illustrated this notion by highlighting the connection between motor development and the development of depth perception and tactile discrimination, including the objects' hardness or stiffness, shape, size, temperature, texture, and weight. Their analysis of research literature showed that infants' perception of properties of objects develops as allowed by the level of their manual manipulation skills. They also found that the development of depth perception is closely related to mastering head control, oculomotor control, and the ability to hold and manipulate an object in one hand.[55]

Proposed Agreement With Other Theories

In agreement with Gibson,[44] Thelen[24,58,59] emphasized the link between perception and action and their strong connection to cognition, but she also suggested that action is a form of perception that allows a human being to learn about the surrounding world and then act on that knowledge, thus perpetuating a continuous flow of multimodal and multisensory information. Furthermore, she proposed that developmental change is grounded in the fundamental dynamic processes of exploration and selection that can be explained by the TNGS.[24,58,59] According to Thelen,[24] this theory "is consistent with both, dynamic/Gibsonian behavioral perspectives and with current findings on brain function and plasticity."(p 90)

THEORY OF NEURONAL GROUP SELECTION

Mechanisms of Developmental and Experiential Selection

The TNGS formulated by Gerald Edelman rejected a popular hypothesis that the human brain functions in a way similar to a computer by processing information it receives from the environment and then generating responses to stimuli.[45,60] Instead, this theory proposed that adaptive behavior develops via a combination of spontaneous exploration and selection.[45,60] According to the TNGS, the brain of a newborn baby contains a population of diverse neuronal groups (clusters of hundreds and thousands of brain cells connected together in different ways as predetermined by evolution).[45,60,61] These structurally variable groups located in cortical and subcortical areas of the brain constitute basic functional units, or units of selection, which are genetically programmed to control specific motor behaviors.[45,60,61] These units form what Edelman[45,60] called the *primary neuronal repertoire*. The primary repertoires are not precisely identical in all newborn infants because of the dynamic variation in the regulatory processes of cell production, adhesion, and death, and because of varied early activity of the infant's movement apparatus that forms or selects many groups of active synaptic connections and retracts those connections that are not being used.[45,60] Edelman[60] identified this process of formation of the primary repertoire as the first selection mechanism and called it *developmental selection*.

The TNGS proposed that human brain uses a method similar to the Darwinian selection to choose those functional units that match the production of the most efficient movement for a particular task, which would allow the individual to adapt to each specific situation.[45,60,61] When an infant attempts to solve a motor problem, many neuronal groups respond in a competition for finding a motor solution that would fit the task's demands. Some of the groups are structured better to produce the most efficient response in order to allow the infant to adapt to that particular situation. Spontaneous exploration of the environment plays a major role in the discovery of possible solutions to this problem. In the process of trial and error, the infant attempts a variety of strategies before achieving the desired movement

outcome.[45,60,61] In addition, during spontaneous exploration, the infant learns what the results of these attempts mean to him or her, representing what Sporns and Edelman[61] called an *adaptive value*, which guides the selection process. Synapses in the neuronal groups that are ultimately selected for the successful execution of the task are strengthened and are likely to be used in the future, and the synaptic networks of other neuronal groups are weakened.[45,60,61] Once the selection is completed, the variation in motor behavior briefly decreases, but the newly found stability is quickly followed by an increase in variation because of the changes continuously occurring in the environment, in the task demands, and in the biomechanical characteristics of the growing and developing infant's body. This second selection mechanism that Edelman[60] called *experiential selection* forms the secondary neuronal repertoire.[45,60,61]

To illustrate, let us consider a 9-month-old baby girl who is trying to obtain her favorite toy placed on the couch by her mother. The baby crawls up to the couch and gets up on her knees while holding on to it with both hands. She tries to touch the toy but it is still outside her reach. She grabs on to the couch upholstery and uses all of her arm strength to pull herself up. She does not yet possess sufficient lower body strength to accomplish this task and her legs extend simultaneously in an attempt to assist with pulling up to stand. Unfortunately, she is not successful this time as she loses balance and lands on her buttocks, but the baby's mother pushes a button on the toy, it starts playing a tune and once again attracts the little girl's attention. This time, she tries to pull up directly from a sitting position, but this appears to be even more difficult, so she transitions into a tall kneeling position and tries again. Finally, after several attempts of spontaneous exploration when she tries a variety of movement transition strategies, the little girl succeeds in standing up at the couch by using mostly her arms and assisting with both legs, and then happily grabs the toy.

Once the baby is again sitting on the floor and her mother places the toy on the couch for her to reach, she is likely to select the same strategy more frequently as at the moment, it has the highest *adaptive value*[61] and, therefore, the synaptic connections responsible for this movement solution will be strengthened. However, in a few days, while playing with toys on the couch, she may remain in a tall kneeling position for a while and may discover that she can shift her weight from side to side as she reaches for toys located further away from her center of gravity. Through spontaneous exploration, she may also discover that she can place one of her feet flat on the floor, which would lead to standing on one knee. With time, this would, in turn, lead to the development of a new strategy for pulling up to stand through a half-kneeling position. The baby may use both of the discussed transition patterns for some time, which would signify an increase in variation in her motor behavior. As she eventually discovers that the half-kneeling position yields a more efficient way of accomplishing the task of pulling up to stand, she will select this strategy more and more frequently, leading to strengthening corresponding synaptic connections in her brain. At the same time, she will gradually abandon the other transition pattern, which would lead to weakening its respective synapses. This way, once again, a new stable adaptive motor behavior will be found and used for a while.

Reentrant Signaling as a Higher-Level Selection Mechanism

According to the TNGS, the brain is organized into constantly changing "maps" that reflect the new solutions found by the child's changing movement system in order to adapt to a given situation, which is modified by changing environmental constraints.[45,60,61] The greater the environmental and task constraints, the more specific is the solution that emerges from the selection process.[60-62] This theory proposes that the mapped regions of the brain are connected with each other, which allows them to exchange and coordinate information obtained by separate neuronal groups at the same time, in a parallel fashion.[45,60] This ongoing process that Edelman[45,60] called *reentrant signaling* is accomplished through dynamic reciprocal connections that exist within specific maps, between different maps (for example, the corticothalamic and thalamocortical connections), and among remote areas of the brain, such as the cerebellum, cerebral cortex, and basal ganglia. The neuronal groups in different areas of the brain are activated simultaneously and communicate with each other in the process of finding the best solution to the task at hand. After repeated activation of these connections in the same situation, the synapses that accomplish the reentrant signaling between these neuronal groups would strengthen or weaken, depending on the achieved results.[60] This higher-level selection mechanism integrates and synchronizes multimodal sensory and motor information across different areas of the brain and coordinates a multimodal response in real time, which leads to constant remapping of existing neuronal connections.[24,60] Computer simulation experiments conducted to test several models of a nervous system that functioned based on the selection mechanisms proposed by the TNGS showed that such methodology could be successfully used to model and analyze the development of adaptive behavior.[63,64]

Intermodal Connections, Developmental Change, and Relationship Between Action and Perception

When a baby is born, objects and experiences in her environment are unknown, unfamiliar to her. Edelman[45,60] proposed that reentrant signaling plays a major role in recognition and labeling of all entities in the outside world (its "perceptual categorization"), leading to successful learning and development of adaptive behavior. He emphasized that perceptual categorization involves multiple interconnected sensory and motor maps.[60] Perception and action are interdependent. When the humans move, the neuronal group selection in visual, auditory, and tactile maps of their brains occurs continuously with the selection process in their proprioceptive and kinesthetic maps, organized in dynamic

reentrant signaling loops. This means that movement itself plays a major role in the process of perception; in other words, action is a part of perception.[60]

Thelen[24] gave an example of an infant kicking an overhead mobile to explain developmental change using the TNGS. In her experiment, she used a string to attach the left ankles of 3-month-old infants to an overhead mobile.[65] Some of the babies had their legs loosely bound with an elastic cord that allowed different kicking patterns to occur, but they could elicit the most movement and sound from the mobile when they kicked both legs simultaneously as compared to using a single-limb or an alternating movement pattern. Only those babies whose lower extremities were bound together showed an increasingly stronger preference for kicking both legs simultaneously.[65] Thelen[24] suggested that this example illustrated the dynamic and self-organizing nature of learning related to the recognition and categorization of multimodal signals by diverse neural structures in the process of reentrant signaling. As the infant kicked her leg in an act of a spontaneous, exploratory movement, that movement activated the mobile, and the baby looked at the moving mobile and listened to the sound it was making.[24,65] With repeated kicking, the infant made a connection between the movements of her legs and the movement and the sound of the activated mobile. The reciprocal synaptic connections among the neuronal groups that were simultaneously receiving proprioceptive, visual, and auditory information from kicking of the baby's legs and movement of the mobile became stronger over time. Furthermore, when the infant's legs were loosely bound with an elastic cord, she tried different kicking patterns and discovered through spontaneous exploration that simultaneous kicking with both legs had the greatest effect on the mobile. This led her to select and use this pattern more frequently.[24,65]

Other authors reported on research that supported the notions that neuronal groups responsible for different perceptual modalities are interconnected and that the human brain is built to integrate this information in the process of spontaneous exploration occurring in real time.[24,51,58,66] For example, a series of experiments conducted by Bahrick and Watson[66] highlighted the ability of young infants to integrate information from different modalities. The researchers presented 5-month-old babies with a live recording of their own leg movements occurring in real time, side by side with a recording of movements of another baby. The infants were able to match proprioceptive information obtained from their own moving bodies with visual information provided by the recordings and spent a significantly longer time watching the recordings of other babies as compared to the recordings of their own movement. Such preference was observed even when the infants' view of their own legs was occluded. This indicated that they were able to visually identify the real time recording of their own movement and thus directed their attention to movement of another baby that was more interesting for them. Furthermore, when the infants were presented with a video of their own movement recorded earlier and thus not synchronized with their current motor activity, they showed visual preference for that recording as compared to the one that was displaying their own movement in the real time. These results suggest that the ability to make a connection between proprioceptive and visual information may play a crucial role in the development of self-perception.[66]

The Theory of Neuronal Group Selection and Bernstein's Problem: Proposed Unity With Other Theories

Sporns and Edelman[61] addressed the Bernstein's degrees of freedom problem by applying the TNGS to human development. As discussed previously in this chapter, according to Bernstein,[23] in spite of its enormous inherent anatomical redundancy, the human organism is able to accomplish coordinated movement by organizing muscle activity into functional synergies. Sporns and Edelman[61] proposed that the formation of synergies occurs as the result of neuronal group selection processes, via strengthening of synaptic connections responsible for movements that successfully accomplish a specific task in a given context. They emphasized that possible solutions to motor problems are discovered and selected as entire movement patterns and not as their separate parts. With changes in biomechanics of the developing organism and in environmental and task constraints, the child's movement repertoire continues to evolve and modify to adapt to these changes.[61]

Thelen[24] suggested that the TNGS idea of "development as selection" provided a very appealing explanation for the variability in individual movement repertoires and their adaptability to ongoing changes in environmental constraints, task demands, growth, and proportions of the child's body, and his or her level of activity. Furthermore, she saw the DST, TNGS, and perception-action theory as complementing each other in their depiction of developmental change as a dynamic unity and interdependence of perception and action, which is driven by processes of spontaneous exploration and selection.[24,46,58] All 3 of these theories emphasized the role cognition plays in developmental change through its link with perception and action.[24,25,44,50,59-61] The perception-action theory was the first to acknowledge the importance of this connection[44,50]; the DST took it further through the concept of embodiment[24,59]; and the TNGS explained it using the term *adaptive value*.[61] In addition, these theories explained the organization of movement at 3 different but complementary levels: the perception-action theory emphasized the role of multiple perceptual systems[44,50]; the DST stressed the self-organization process[21,22,24,25]; and the TNGS explained the mechanism of self-organization using the concepts of selection and reentrant signaling.[45,60,61] This integrated theoretical view is important for further understanding of the concepts of variability, complexity, and adaptability discussed in Chapter 2.

The current chapter provides merely a glimpse into the complex world of motor development, with its fascinating questions and an enormous body of past, ongoing, and future research. Theoretical explanations of the developmental process will continue to evolve and will be supported or refuted by careful observation, well-designed research and successful clinical practice, leading to further progress in developmental science.

Complete video-based activities for Chapter 1 (see Activity Set 1 on the book website).

REFERENCES

1. Portney LG, Watkins MP. The role of theory in clinical research. In: Portney LG, Watkins MP, eds. *Foundations of Clinical Research: Applications to Practice.* 3rd ed. Upper Saddle River, NJ: Pearson Education, Inc.; 2009:33-46.
2. Shumway-Cook A, Woollacott MH. Motor control: issues and theories. In: Shumway-Cook A, Woollacott MH, eds. *Motor Control: Translating Research Into Clinical Practice.* 4th ed. Philadelphia, PA: Lippincott Williams and Wilkins; 2012:3-20.
3. Cech D, Martin S. Motor development. In: Cech D, Martin S, eds. *Functional Movement Development Across the Life Span.* 3rd ed. St, Louis, MO: Saunders; 2012:45-67.
4. Hensyl WR, ed. *Stedman's Pocket Medical Dictionary.* Baltimore, MD: Williams and Wilkins; 1987.
5. Bly L. *Components of Typical and Atypical Motor Development.* Laguna Beach, CA: Neuro-Developmental Treatment Association, Inc.; 2011.
6. Cech D, Martin S. Theories affecting development. In: Cech D, Martin S, eds. *Functional Movement Development Across the Life Span.* 3rd ed. St, Lois, MO: Saunders; 2012:14-44.
7. Cech D, Martin S. Posture and balance. In: Cech D, Martin S, eds. *Functional Movement Development Across the Life Span.* 3rd ed. St, Louis, MO: Saunders; 2012:263-287.
8. *Normal Infant Reflexes and Development* [video]. Tuscon, AZ: Therapy Skill Builders; 1988.
9. Gesell A. Behavior patterns of fetal-infant and child; with evidence of innate growth factors. *Res Publ Assoc Res Nerv Ment Dis.* 1954;33:114-126.
10. Gesell A, Amatruda C. *Developmental Diagnosis: Normal and Abnormal Child Development.* New York, NY: Paul Hoeber; 1947.
11. McGraw MB. *The Neuromuscular Maturation of the Human Infant.* New York, NY: Columbia University Press; 1943.
12. Dalton TC. Arnold Gesell and the maturation controversy. *Integr Physiol Behav Sci.* 2005;40(4):182-204.
13. Campbell SK. The child's development of functional movement. In: Campbell SK, Palisano RJ, Orlin MN, eds. *Physical Therapy for Children.* 4th ed. St. Louis, MO: Saunders; 2012:37-86.
14. Thelen E, Adolph KE. Arnold L. Gesell: The paradox of nature and nurture. *Dev Psychol.* 1992;28(3):368-380.
15. Bly L. *Motor Skills Acquisition in the First Year.* San Antonio, TX: Therapy Skill Builders; 1994.
16. Bobath K, Bobath B. The neuro-developmental treatment. In: Scrutton D, ed. *Management of the Motor Disorders of Children With Cerebral Palsy.* Philadelphia, PA: Lippincott; 1984:6-18.
17. Butler C, Darrah J. AACPDM evidence report: effects of neurodevelopmental treatment (NDT) for cerebral palsy. *Dev Med Child Neurol.* 2001;43(11):778-790.
18. Gesell A. Reciprocal interweaving in neuromotor development. *J Comp Neurol.* 1939;70(2):161-180.
19. Gesell A. *Infant Development: The Embryology of Early Human Behavior.* New York, NY: Harper; 1952.
20. Gesell A, Ilg FL, Bullis G. *Vision: Its Development in Infant and Child.* New York, NY: Paul B. Hoeber; 1949.
21. Kamm K, Thelen E, Jensen JL. A dynamical systems approach to motor development. *Phys Ther.* 1990;70:763-775.

22. Thelen E, Smith LB. Lessons from learning to walk. In: Thelen E, Smith LB, eds. *A Dynamic Systems Approach to the Development of Cognition and Action.* Cambridge, MA: MIT Press; 1994:3-20.

23. Bernstein NA. On dexterity and its development. In: Latash ML, Turvey MT, eds. *Dexterity and Its Development.* Mahwah, NJ: Lawrence Erlbaum Associates, Publishers; 1996:3-244.

24. Thelen E. Motor development. A new synthesis. *Am Psychol.* 1995;50(2):79-95.

25. Spencer JP, Clearfield M, Corbetta D, Ulrich B, Buchanan P, Schöner G. Moving toward a grand theory of development: in memory of Esther Thelen. *Child Dev.* 2006;77(6):1521-1538.

26. Kelso JAS. *Dynamic Patterns: The Self-Organization of Brain and Behavior.* Cambridge, MA: The MIT Press; 1995.

27. Thelen E, Kelso JAS, Fogel A. Self-organizing systems and infant motor development. *Dev Review.* 1987;7(1):39-65.

28. Latash ML. The Bernstein problem: how does the central nervous system make its choices? In: Latash ML, Turvey MT, eds. *Dexterity and Its Development.* Mahwah, NJ: Lawrence Erlbaum Associates, Publishers; 1996:277-303.

29. Liebovich LS. *Fractals and Chaos Simplified for the Life Sciences.* New York, NY: Oxford University Press; 1998:225-235.

30. Harbourne RT, Stergiou N. Movement variability and the use of nonlinear tools: principles to guide physical therapist practice. *Phys Ther.* 2009;89(3):267-282.

31. Rahlin M. TAMO therapy as a major component of physical therapy intervention for an infant with congenital muscular torticollis: a case report. *Pediatr Phys Ther.* 2005;17:209-218.

32. Thelen E, Fisher DM. Newborn stepping: an explanation for a "disappearing" reflex. *Dev Psychol.* 1982;18(5):760-775.

33. Thelen E, Fisher DM. The organization of spontaneous leg movements in newborn infants. *J Mot Behav.* 1983;15(4):353-377.

34. Thelen E. Rhythmical stereotypies in normal human infants. *Anim Behav.* 1979;27:699-715.

35. Thelen E. Kicking, rocking and waving: contextual analysis of rhythmic stereotypies in normal human infants. *Anim Behav.* 1981;29(1):3-11.

36. Thelen E. Rhythmical behavior in infancy: an ethological perspective. *Dev Psychol.* 1981;17(3):237-257.

37. Thelen E, Fisher DM, Ridley-Johnson R, Griffin NJ. Effects of body build and arousal on newborn infant stepping. *Dev Psychobiol.* 1982;15(5):447-453.

38. Thelen E, Fisher DM, Ridley-Johnson R, Griffin NJ. The relationship between physical growth and a newborn reflex. *Infant Behav Dev.* 1984;7(4):479-493.

39. Thelen E. Treadmill-elicited stepping in seven-month-old infants. *Child Dev.* 1986;57:1498-1506.

40. Thelen E, Ulrich BD, Niles D. Bilateral coordination in human infants: stepping on a split-belt treadmill. *J Exp Psychol Hum Percept Perform.* 1987;13(3):405-410.

41. Thelen E, Ulrich BD. Hidden skills: a dynamic systems analysis of treadmill stepping during the first year. *Monogr Soc Res Child Dev.* 1991;56(1):1-98.

42. Thelen E, Bril G, Breniere Y. The emergence of heel strike in newly walking infants: a dynamic interpretation. In: Woollacott M, Horak F, eds. *Posture and Gait Control Mechanisms.* Eugene, OR: University of Oregon Books; 1992:334-337.

43. Thelen E, Smith LB. Dynamic systems: exploring paradigms of change. In: Thelen E, Smith LB, eds. *A Dynamic Systems Approach to the Development of Cognition and Action.* Cambridge, MA: MIT Press; 1994:45-69.

44. Gibson JJ. *The Senses Considered as Perceptual Systems.* Boston, MA: Houghton Mifflin; 1966.

45. Edelman GM. *Neural Darwinism.* New York, NY: Basic Books; 1987.

46. Thelen E, Smith LB. Dynamics of neural organization and development. In: Thelen E, Smith LB, eds. *A Dynamic Systems Approach to the Development of Cognition and Action.* Cambridge, MA: MIT Press; 1994:129-160.

47. Gibson JJ, Gibson EJ. Perceptual learning: differentiation or enrichment? *Psychol Rev.* 1955;62(1):32-41.

48. Pick H. Eleanor Gibson: learning to perceive and perceiving to learn. *Dev Psychol.* 1992;28(5):787-794.

49. Gibson EJ. What does infant perception tell us about theories of perception? *J Exp Psychol Hum Percept Perform.* 1987;13(4):515-523.

50. Gibson EJ. Exploratory behavior in the development of perceiving, acting, and the acquiring of knowledge. *Annu Rev Psychol.* 1988;39:1-41.

51. Gibson EJ, Walker AS. Development of knowledge of visual-tactual affordances of substance. *Child Dev.* 1984;55(2):453-460.

52. Gibson EJ, Riccio G, Schmuckler MA, Stoffregen TA, Rosenberg D, Taormina J. Detection of the traversability of surfaces by crawling and walking infants. *J Exp Psychol Hum Percept Perform.* 1987;13(4):533-544.

53. Warren WH. Perceiving affordances: visual guidance of stair climbing. *J Exp Psychol Hum Percept Perform.* 1984;10(5):683-703.

54. Adolph KE, Berger SE. Motor development. In: Damon W, Lerner R, Kuhn D, Siegler RS, eds. *Handbook of Child Psychology, Vol. 2: Cognition, Perception, and Language.* New York, NY: Wiley; 2006:161-213.

55. Bushnell EW, Boudreau JP. Motor development and the mind: the potential role of motor abilities as a determinant of aspects of perceptual development. *Child Dev.* 1993;64(4):1005-1021.

56. Adolph KE. Learning in the development of infant locomotion. *Monogr Soc Res Child Dev.* 1997;251-62(3):v,1-162.

57. Adolph KE. Specificity of learning: why infants fall over a veritable cliff. *Psychol Sci.* 2000;11:290-295.

58. Thelen E, Smith LB. The dynamics of selection in human infants. In: Thelen E, Smith LB, eds. *A Dynamic Systems Approach to the Development of Cognition and Action.* Cambridge, MA: MIT Press; 1994:187-211.

59. Thelen E. Grounded in the world: developmental origins of the embodied mind. *Infancy.* 2000;1(1):3-28.

60. Edelman GM. Neural Darwinism: selection and reentrant signaling in higher brain function. *Neuron.* 1993;10(2):115-125.

61. Sporns O, Edelman G. Solving Bernstein's problem: a proposal for the development of coordinated movement by selection. *Child Dev.* 1993;64(4):960-981.

62. Hadders-Algra M. Early brain damage and the development of motor behavior in children: clues for therapeutic intervention? *Neural Plast.* 2001;8:31-49.

63. Sporns O, Gally JA, Reeke GN, Edelman GM. Reentrant signaling among simulated neuronal groups leads to coherency in their oscillatory activity. *Neurobiol.* 1989;86:7265-7269.

64. Edelman GM, Reeke GN, Gall WE, Tononi G, Williams D, Sporns O. Synthetic neural modeling applied to a real-world artifact. *Neurobiol.* 1992;89:7267-7271.

65. Thelen E. Three-month-old infants can learn task-specific patterns of interlimb coordination. *Psychol Sci.* 1994;5(5):280-285.

66. Bahrick LE, Watson JS. Detection of intermodal proprioceptive-visual contingency as a potential basis of self-perception in infancy. *Dev Psychol.* 1985;21(6):963-973.

2

Variability, Complexity, and Adaptability in Typical and Atypical Motor Development

Humans are designed not only <u>with</u> variability but <u>for</u> variability.

Linda Fetters[1]

VARIABILITY: DEFINITIONS, TYPES, AND ROLE IN DEVELOPMENTAL PROCESS

Theories discussed in Chapter 1 highlighted the role of variability in the developmental process. Although in the past, variability was mostly looked at as a statistical characteristic that reflected errors of performance or errors of measurement, a more current view of variability suggests that it is an inherent trait of the human organism observed at multiple levels, such as in the structure and function of body systems, growth patterns, behavior, coordination, and motor performance, to name a few.[1,2] Variability in neuronal connections of the developing brain,[3-5] abundance of possible configurations in the alignment of body segments,[6] variability in movement and posture related to changing body proportions of a growing child,[7,8] and variability in motor solutions to a given task[1,6] all illustrate this notion.

Current literature contains several definitions of movement variability.[9-11] It may be defined as "variations… in motor performance across multiple repetitions of a task"[9(p 120)] or referred to as the ability to select a specific movement strategy appropriate for a specific situation.[10] Dusing and Harbourne[11] described several types of movement variability, including the following:

- Variability within a single movement, such as seen in a spontaneous arm or leg movement of a newborn infant, which is irregular in its velocity and amplitude
- Variability in strategies used to complete a task within a single attempt, for example, when a baby uses a sequence of reciprocal belly crawling and scooting forward without reciprocation to propel her body forward across the room
- Variability in biomechanical characteristics of skills emerging over time, such as seen during gait development[11]

Hadders-Algra[12,13] distinguished between primary and secondary variability observed during typical motor development. She explained these phenomena from the perspective of the theory of neuronal group selection (TNGS) by linking them to the primary and secondary neuronal repertoires described by Edelman[3,4] (see Chapter 1). Primary variability is seen during the fetal period and in early infancy.[12,13] It is characterized by high variation in postural adjustments and in spontaneous movements of extremities, including their quantity and spatial and temporal characteristics. Newborn infants actively explore all movement possibilities available to them from their primary neuronal repertoires. Two types of movements are observed at this time: general movements and the initial attempts at goal-directed movements. General

Rahlin M. *Physical Therapy for Children With Cerebral Palsy: An Evidence-Based Approach* (pp 25-46).
© 2016 SLACK Incorporated.

movements can be defined as movements of all body parts that are not arranged in a specific sequence and are varied in amplitude and speed. These movements generate afferent information that is used to modify synaptic connections in the infant's brain, but they do not serve to adapt his or her motor behavior to the environment.[12,13]

As goal-directed movement gradually replaces general movements starting at the age of approximately 4 months, high variation in reaching and grasping patterns is observed in the process of spontaneous exploration.[12,13] This is followed by variable postural control exhibited in stationary positions and during locomotion. The exploratory behavior and processing of the afferent information it generates eventually allow the infant to select the movement pattern that would best match a specific task. This selection process gives rise to the secondary (adaptive) variability, which develops starting from mid-infancy, becomes evident at 2 to 3 years of age, and matures during adolescence. Development of secondary variability corresponds to the formation of secondary neuronal repertoires. It allows the individual to find multiple solutions to a given motor task and to adapt his or her movements precisely to its specific conditions.[12,13]

Variability plays an important role in the development of human action.[1] It supports spontaneous exploration, and exploration leads to the development of new skills through the process of trial and error. As the infants explore their environment and consequences of their own actions, they learn which actions succeed and which do not.[1] When they first start walking, they exhibit high variability in step length, single leg stance time, and other gait parameters, which decreases over time with walking practice.[14,15] As shown by research, the amount of walking activity varies within each day and from day to day, but on average, infants cover a distance greater than the length of 29 football fields and take approximately 9,000 steps per day.[14] This massive amount of practice occurs under varied environmental constraints, such as different walking surfaces, indoor and outdoor locations, and contextual situations, and is accompanied by frequent loss of balance followed by safe falls that occur 15 times per hour on average.[14,15] Through this experience that involves a continuous interaction between perception and action, infants learn about their bodies, their proportions, postural alignment and stability, and the amount of effort required to control dynamic balance in a variety of situations.[16] They develop an understanding of consequences of their movements and use that knowledge when they face a new task in a new situation.[16] This process illustrates the concept of embodiment described by Thelen[17]—the dynamic unity and interrelationship of perception, action and cognition.

RELATIONSHIP BETWEEN VARIABILITY AND COMPLEXITY

Motor development is complex.[2] This complexity is related to inter- and intra-individual variability. Inter-individual variability refers to variability of movement solutions for the same task observed across different children.[2] This can be illustrated by looking at 3 healthy infants functioning at the same motor skill level when they are positioned supine and encouraged to obtain a toy placed outside of their reach. One infant may sit up, another one may roll over and transition into a quadruped position, the third infant may move onto her side and scoot forward by using one arm and one leg, but all 3 will complete the task successfully.

Intra-individual variability can be described as variability of movement trajectories exhibited by the same child performing the same movement several times,[2] such as when a toddler takes blocks out of a container one by one, with each movement following a slightly different path. Another way to describe intra-individual variability is by looking at different movement solutions for the same task exhibited by the same child,[2] such as when an infant uses several different strategies to pull up to stand within seconds of each other.

Dusing and Harbourne[11] defined *complexity* as "a measure of the structure of variability"(p 1840) and suggested that predictable, regular variability lacks complexity. This notion can be illustrated through an examination of postural adjustments in infants by recording the displacement of their center of pressure (COP) over time. Shumway-Cook and Woollacott[18] referred to the COP as "the center of the distribution of the total force applied to the supporting surface."(p 162) The analysis of the COP trajectory in a child who rhythmically rocks in the anterior-posterior direction in a ring sitting position would show that the COP movement is highly variable statistically as it would be characterized by a large standard deviation.[11] However, this COP trajectory would lack complexity as there will be little change noted in the direction of the rocking motion. On the other hand, for a child who makes very small postural adjustments in various directions while maintaining his or her upright sitting balance, the assessment of the COP trajectory will yield low statistical variability signified by a small standard deviation, but at the same time, this trajectory will be very complex. The presence of these small but complex postural adjustments is crucial for the development of healthy postural control that would allow the infant to pick up necessary information from the changing environment and plan a subsequent action, thus adapting his or her posture to a specific situation.[11]

A significant body of research on variability, complexity, and adaptability in motor development has emerged in the recent years. For example, the relationship between variability and complexity in the development of postural control was investigated in several studies.[11,19,20] The COP trajectories were recorded and analyzed in infants positioned supine[19] and in sitting[20] on a force platform. Dusing et al[19] studied postural control in healthy infants born full term and in infants born prematurely who were assessed at the age of 1 to 3 weeks post-term. As they were moving spontaneously in a supine position, the neonates born full term maintained an antigravity flexion alignment of their trunk and demonstrated caudal-cephalic displacements of their COP characterized by smaller amplitude and, thus, lower variability compared to infants born prematurely. However, the structure of variability of the COP movement exhibited by the full-term infants was more irregular and less predictable and, thus, it was more complex.[19] Dusing and Harbourne[11] suggested that this early complexity in the presence of minimal postural sway was necessary for the development of the infants' abilities to orient to stimuli, manipulate objects, and address other functional needs while exploring a variety of movement possibilities.[11]

An investigation of sitting postural control in 4- to 8-month-old infants developing typically yielded similar results.[20] Harbourne and Stergiou[20] examined the infants' motor behavior at 3 stages of sitting: stage 1 was characterized by the baby's ability to maintain head elevation against gravity with trunk support provided by an adult; at stage 2, the infant was able to maintain a stable prop-sitting position or to sit unsupported, hands free, for a few seconds; and at stage 3, safe and stable independent sitting was observed. As they were learning to sit, younger infants displayed many complex strategies of postural control, which supported the exploration of movement possibilities and selection of successful strategies for future use.[11,19] Other findings highlighted a significant decrease in degrees of freedom between stages 1 and 2 of sitting, which was consistent with the Bernstein's view of the process of acquisition of new motor skills (see Chapter 1).[20,21] This was followed by a subsequent release of degrees of freedom at stage 3, which signified an increase in adaptability of postural control as the infants learned to sit independently.[20]

ADAPTABILITY AND ITS RELATIONSHIP TO VARIABILITY AND COMPLEXITY

Adaptability is the ability to modify action or movement strategy as the result of perceiving and processing information received from the environment or from a previous action.[11] Karen Adolph proposed another term for adaptability.[22] She described it as *flexibility*, or the ability to select an adaptive movement solution to a new problem, adapt movement occurring in real time to "changes in local conditions,"(p 399) and discover new ways to attain desired results. Flexibility is crucial for achieving the functional goals of everyday actions because constant changes occurring in the child's environment require movement modifications that would match the task demands in the constraints of a specific situation.[22] Adaptability or flexibility is possible because variability observed in a human organism at multiple levels provides it with many options for action and allows it to select the best strategy for the task at hand.[23]

In the first 2 years of life, infants show an incredible developmental change; their body dimensions and proportions change rapidly as they acquire new motor skills, and the environment they can explore expands with their increase in mobility.[24,25] As the infants develop postural control in sitting, quadruped, and standing positions, they have to learn to maintain balance in 3 different situations. Adolph[24] pointed out that the skills of sitting, creeping (crawling on hands and knees), and walking involve different rotation points for maintaining balance during postural sway and different muscle groups for performing movement and generating compensatory strategies to respond to balance perturbations. In addition, they provide different points for viewing the supporting surface and different flows of visual, vestibular, and kinesthetic information. By exploring movement possibilities in each posture, infants learn to control and fine-tune its perception-action system.[24,25]

Several studies showed that the difference between the parameters of these 3 systems translates into a specificity of learning.[24,25] When looking at how infants learn to maintain postural control while negotiating slopes and judge depth and distance as they reach across gaps in a supporting surface, Adolph[24] found that learning was specific to each of the 3 developmental milestones (sitting, creeping, and walking). In other words, the perception-action systems using depth information for motor planning were specific to the system of postural control involved in the task. For example, in order to crawl to and reach across a gap in a supporting surface in a safe manner, the infants relied on the depth and distance information obtained while functioning in a quadruped position, but not while sitting or standing. Infants who had extensive sitting experience and less extensive crawling experience were found to overestimate their ability to reach across dangerous gaps while on hands and knees, although they could safely avoid such unsafe reaching in a sitting position. Therefore, learning within a sitting posture did not carry over to the quadruped position. Similarly, there was no carryover between the quadruped and standing postures. After first starting to walk, the same infants who had avoided the risky slopes while crawling attempted to walk down these slopes. Thus, they had to relearn the same task while relying on a standing-specific as compared to a quadruped-specific perception-action system. It is interesting to note that learning within each posture did not depend on the infants' experience of loss of balance and falling from heights and down the slopes. Instead, it depended on massive daily experience of exploring the environment on safe, firm surfaces.[24] These findings suggest that varying the environmental set-up that provides the infant with many opportunities for spontaneous exploration within each posture may lead to increased movement variability, thus building a foundation for increased flexibility or adaptability of movement and postural control.

Besides a specific postural control system involved in finding a solution for a given task, other factors play an important role in the developmental process. The acquisition of functional skills may be dependent on how complex the postural control variability is in the first year of life.[11] Complexity allows infants to develop the ability to adapt to changing environments, task requirements, and their own limitations, thus leading to the development of adaptability.[11] In this context, the infants' limitations may be related to their anthropometric characteristics (large head, long trunk, short extremities) that determine the position of their center of gravity. In addition, an increase in the percentage of body fat and an insufficient amount of muscle mass in the second month after birth have been shown to be responsible for the temporary loss of the automatic stepping reflex.[7] Alternatively, the infant's limitations may be related to the alterations of structures and functions of different body systems that are associated with atypical development. These may affect the variability of movement and posture, the complexity of postural control, and, thus, the development of adaptability.[9,11,23]

OPTIMAL VARIABILITY

To introduce their model of variability of human movement, Stergiou et al[9] used an analogy with chaotic variation exhibited by the human body, including its heart rhythms, blood cell counts, blood pressure measures, and other signals related to a state of health. These authors suggested that movement of healthy individuals, similar to their physiological characteristics, is characterized by optimal variability that has a chaotic (complex) structure.[9] Decreased variability would limit adaptability and the ability to develop new skills,[2] and make the system more rigid.[9] Excessive variability would lead to decreased consistency of motor performance, decreased adaptability to changing demands of the task, and decreased carryover of the task mastered in one environment or context to other situations.[1] In addition, increased variability would make the system unstable.[9] Such motor behavior may be observed in children with dyskinetic (athetoid and dystonic) cerebral palsy (CP).[26] Both situations, of decreased and excessive variability, would negatively affect the child's ability to adapt his or her movement and posture to a specific situation.[9] Therefore, one of the goals of physical therapy intervention should be to help promote the optimal level of movement variability,[9] and clinicians should focus their attention on movement variability, complexity, and adaptability when conducting patient evaluations and developing intervention plans.[9,19,27] As discussed next, this would require a paradigm shift.

TRADITIONAL APPROACH TO DEVELOPMENTAL TESTING

Pediatric physical therapists have traditionally used standardized assessment instruments to assess motor development in infants and children.[28-30] Developmental testing is an important part of the patient evaluation process and is employed in a variety of pediatric settings, from neonatal intensive care units to outpatient pediatrics.[28-32] Percentile ranks based on the normal distribution of test scores allow therapists to compare the child's performance to that of his or her peers and to determine the amount of developmental delay, if present.[29]

Many standardized developmental tools are available to pediatric physical therapists.[28-32] Selection of a specific instrument depends on the child's age; the purpose of assessment and the setting in which it will be performed; the areas of development being evaluated; and the test's validity, reliability, and other psychometric properties.[28-30,33] Table 2-1 summarizes relevant information on selected norm-referenced instruments used to assess motor development in infants and children.[34-47]

CHALLENGING THE TRADITIONAL APPROACH

Standardized instruments used to evaluate motor development are based on typical developmental sequence and motor milestones.[28-30,48] Intervention for infants and children with developmental delays and movement disorders is often recommended based on the standardized testing results.[28-30,48] Many developmental tools have been normed on a large number of children.[34,37,38,40,44] The normative sample may be stratified by age, gender, ethnicity, geographical area, parental education, and other factors[34,37,38,40,44] that are representative of the population from which the potential patients will be later identified.[49] Although such sampling efforts help prevent testing bias,[49] they do not account for wide variation in the timing of onset, sequence of emergence, and prevalence of specific types of postures and movements among infants and children who are brought up in different cultures around the world.[48] Cross-cultural research has revealed that parenting practices prevalent in different cultural environments can greatly affect motor development. For example, crawling facilitation activities performed by some Ugandan mothers reportedly lead to accelerated development of this skill, with the average age of its onset being 5.5 months.[48] On the other hand, the insufficient amount of time spent in a prone position because of restrictions imposed by the "Back to Sleep" campaign in the United States has been shown to result in delayed onset not only for crawling, but also for other prone milestones and for some supine and sitting skills.[50]

Another important factor to consider in regard to the traditional approach to developmental testing is that, in clinical practice, standardized assessment is commonly performed at single points in time and, specifically, during the initial evaluation and when tracking the child's progress. Re-evaluations usually occur in 3- to 6-month intervals, depending on the therapy setting, third-party payer requirements, and other factors. The single-point assessments performed at such long intervals fail to account for intra-individual variability that infants exhibit in their daily motor performance, which may lead to errors in interpreting test results.[51] For example, Adolph et al[15] showed that, when learning to walk, infants demonstrate highly variable behavior, with bursts and pauses in activity observed from day to day. After taking their first steps, they may revert to crawling and return to attempts in upright mobility only several days or even weeks later.

	TABLE 2-1			
	GENERAL CHARACTERISTICS AND PSYCHOMETRIC PROPERTIES OF SELECTED NORM-REFERENCED STANDARDIZED INSTRUMENTS USED TO ASSESS MOTOR DEVELOPMENT IN INFANTS AND CHILDREN			
TEST NAME	**AGE RANGE**	**SUBSCALES**	**USES BY PHYSICAL THERAPISTS FOR CHILDREN WITH OR AT RISK FOR CP**	**PSYCHOMETRIC PROPERTIES**

Alberta Infant Motor Scale (AIMS)[34-36]	Birth to 18 months	• One scale only	• Identify infants exhibiting atypical movement patterns and developmental delay
			• Not for monitoring progress over time in presence of atypical movement and posture
				• Interrater reliability: Pearson r=0.96-1.00
				• Test-retest reliability: Pearson r=0.86-0.99
				• Predictive validity: Suggested cut-off points for atypical/suspicious vs typical development
				  ○ 10% at 4 months of age (sensitivity=58.3%; specificity=82.8%)[a]
				  ○ 5% at 8 months of age (sensitivity=63.9%; specificity=95.3%)[a]

Bayley Scales of Infant and Toddler Development III (Bayley III)[37]	1 to 42 months	• Cognition • Language • Motor • Social-emotional • Adaptive behavior • Behavior rating (optional)	• Identify children with developmental delay	• Concurrent validity: with PDMS-2 (Total Motor) Pearson r=0.55 • Internal consistency: Chronbach's α=0.77-0.96 • Test-retest reliability: Pearson r=0.67-0.86

Peabody Developmental Motor Scales 2 (PDMS-2)[38,39]	Birth to 72 months	• Gross motor
		• Fine motor
			• Identify level of development
			• Detect changes in motor development in children with CP, ages 2 to 5 years
				• Interrater reliability: Pearson r=0.97-0.99
				• Test-retest reliability: Pearson r=0.82-0.94
				• Content validity: Pearson r=0.35-0.69
				• In children with CP, ages 2 to 5 years:
				  ○ Sensitivity to change coefficient: 1.6-2.1
				  ○ Responsiveness coefficient: 1.7-2.

Test of Infant Motor Performance (TIMP)[40-43]	<u>Preterm:</u> 34 weeks PCA to 4 months post-term
	<u>Full-term:</u> Birth to 4 months
		• Observed items
		• Elicited items
			• Assess development of postural control and selective control of upper and lower extremities
			• Identify infants with motor delays and atypical development
			• Predict developmental outcome
				• Test-retest reliability: Pearson r=0.89
				• Content validity: established by 21 experts
				• Discriminant validity: discriminates between infants with different levels of risk for a poor outcome in motor performance
				• Concurrent validity
				  ○ With the AIMS raw scores: Pearson r=0.64, p<0.0001
				  ○ With the AIMS percentile ranks: Pearson r=0.60, p<0.0001

(continued)

TABLE 2-1 (CONTINUED)				
GENERAL CHARACTERISTICS AND PSYCHOMETRIC PROPERTIES OF SELECTED NORM-REFERENCED STANDARDIZED INSTRUMENTS USED TO ASSESS MOTOR DEVELOPMENT IN INFANTS AND CHILDREN				
TEST NAME	AGE RANGE	SUBSCALES	USES BY PHYSICAL THERAPISTS FOR CHILDREN WITH OR AT RISK FOR CP	PSYCHOMETRIC PROPERTIES

Test of Infant Motor Performance (TIMP)[40-43] (continued)				• Predictive validity with the AIMS
				  ◦ Scores on the TIMP at 90 days after term age predict the infant's performance on the AIMS at 12 months: Pearson r=0.67, p=0.0001
				 • Predictive validity with the PDMS-2
				  ◦ The TIMP cut-off score of 0.5 SD below the mean at ages 30, 60, and 90 days after term predicts performance at 2 SD below the mean on the PDMS-2 at 57+4.8 months of age
				  ◦ The TIMP score at 90 days post-term is the strongest predictor of the later performance on the PDMS-2: Pearson r=0.69, p=0.001

Toddler and Infant Motor Evaluation (TIME)[44-47]	Birth to 42 months	• Mobility subtest
		 • Stability subtest
		 • Motor Organization subtest
		 • Functional Performance subtest
		 • Social-Emotional Abilities subtest
			• Identify children with motor delays and atypical movement patterns
			 • Measure change over time (interpret results with caution in children with atypical movement patterns)
				• Reliability
				  ◦ Test-retest: Pearson r=0.99-1.00
				  ◦ Interrater: Pearson r=0.90-1.00
				  ◦ Intrarater: Spearman Rho=0.98-1.00; Pearson r=0.995; ICC(3,1)=0.997
				 • Internal consistency
				  ◦ Cronbach's α=0.72-0.96
				 • Construct validity: age trends for mobility, stability, and motor organization subtests demonstrated in 14 normative age groups
				 • Discriminant validity of mobility subtest:
				  ◦ Specificity: 85.9% to 92.6%
				  ◦ Sensitivity: 88.2% to 93.8%
				 • Discriminant validity of stability subtest:
				  ◦ Specificity: 90.0% to 96.9%
				  ◦ Sensitivity: 80.6% to 97.2%
				 • Responsiveness: may be affected by scoring and structural issues revealed by research

Abbreviations: PTs, physical therapists; CP, cerebral palsy; PCA, postconceptional age; SD, standard deviation

[a] Sensitivity—percent of infants identified as developing atypically or suspicious for atypical development at 18 months of age and correctly categorized by the cut-off at an earlier age.[36] Specificity—percent of infants identified as developing typically at 18 months of age and correctly categorized by the cut-off at an earlier age.[36]

Furthermore, their motor behavior within the same day may vary as well, with bouts of increased locomotion alternating with periods of quiet play.[15] This means that, if the child is tested on a "less active" day or during their "quiet" time, the results may be quite different from those obtained when he or she is more active. In addition, longitudinal research has shown that more frequent assessments would reveal a different pattern of developmental change compared to that obtained when testing at longer intervals.[51-54] Therefore, single assessment results may not accurately reflect the true level of the child's development at that point in time. Based on their research findings, several authors recommended that serial standardized assessments be performed for both screening and diagnostic purposes.[52,53] This would help account for high intra-individual variability in test scores over time so that the infants at risk for and with motor delays can be identified more accurately.[52,53]

Eldred and Darrah[54] performed cluster analysis of gross motor percentile scores obtained from 66 typically developing infants and children in 2 longitudinal studies. Infants were tested on the Peabody Developmental Motor Scales (PDMS)[55] at ages of 9, 11, 13, 16, and 21 months,[53] and children were tested on the Peabody Developmental Motor Scales, Second Edition (PDMS-2),[38] at ages of 4, 4.5, 5, and 5.5 years.[56] Information on participants' demographics and medical history, family socioeconomic status, and parental level of education was also obtained.[54] Analysis of testing results yielded 4 different clusters of percentile scores, with each possessing a unique pattern of score variability (see Table 2-2 for cluster-specific characteristics and clinical implications). The clusters did not differ based on the additional data collected in these studies, except for the significant difference found in the total number of illnesses between clusters 3 and 4, with the greatest number reported for cluster 3 and the lowest for cluster 4. This was surprising, considering that children in cluster 4 demonstrated consistently low developmental scores. The authors acknowledged that further longitudinal studies conducted with children at a higher risk for developmental problems would be needed to validate the clinical use of the 4 clusters. However, these results still had several important implications for pediatric practice, including the following:

- Typical development is characterized by variability in the emergence of motor skills.
- Results of a single-point standardized assessment cannot be the only factor taken into consideration when making clinical decisions.
- Serial standardized testing should be used instead.
- Several patterns of typical development characterized by different scoring profile clusters exist that can be used to interpret the child's assessment results over time.
- Other important factors, including parental concerns, medical and developmental history, and results of skilled observation of quality of movement need to be carefully considered when assessing motor development.[54]

ASSESSMENT OF QUALITY OF MOVEMENT

Differences in the quality of movement exhibited by infants and children developing typically and atypically are widely documented.[1,9-11,19,20,57-61] Quality of movement can be evaluated in several ways, including the identification of specific movement components through traditional clinical observation[57,58] (see Table 1-2 and Figures 1-1 through 1-21) and the use of standardized developmental assessment tools.[34,40,44]

Observation of general movements present in early infancy,[59-63] standardized testing based on the TNGS,[64,65] and the use of nonlinear tools[9,11,19,20,23,66-68] are other methods of evaluation of quality of movement. These methods take into consideration movement variability and complexity as the inherent characteristics of typical motor development.[9,11,19,20,23,59-68] Clinical and research findings that can be obtained using these assessment methods in children with typical and atypical development are discussed next.

Traditional Clinical Observation

Observation or visual movement analysis is an invaluable tool used by clinicians to recognize the signs of atypical motor development. Because the same child may demonstrate both typical and atypical components of movement and posture, training and experience in clinical observation are required to make that distinction.[58]

According to Bly,[58] many movement components seen in the process of typical development may be missing from the repertoire of infants developing atypically. This would lead to the development and prolonged use of atypical compensatory strategies or secondary impairments, which may result in joint deformities that frequently require surgical intervention later in life. In many of these babies, antigravity flexion fails to develop or its development is insufficient. Therefore, the antigravity trunk extension that typically precedes the emergence of antigravity flexion remains unbalanced and results in overactivity of extensor musculature.[58] To compensate, these infants develop "fixing" patterns by "freezing" the degrees of freedom[21] they need to control in order to maintain a posture or to achieve a functional movement.[58] In babies who develop atypically, flexor and extensor muscle imbalance persists and prevents the acquisition of stability that would normally allow the infant to move one part of the body on another, stabilized part. Therefore, the release of degrees of freedom[21] that typically occurs when stability is achieved does not take place or is insufficient, and these fixing patterns again, persist.[58]

Bly[58] described 4 main fixing patterns or "blocks" to typical development that significantly affect the quality of movement in infants and children who develop atypically (Table 2-3 and Figures 2-1 through 2-6). These "blocks" disrupt control of the following areas of the body: head and neck, shoulder girdle and upper extremities, and pelvis and

Table 2-2

Characteristics of Four Clusters of Percentile Scores Obtained From PDMS and PDMS-2 Standardized Testing Performed With 66 Infants and Children Who Were Developing Typically

Cluster Number	Intra-Individual Variability Scoring Pattern From Infancy to Preschool Age	Percentile Score Range	Number of Children Included	Number of Children With at Least One Score at or Below 16th Percentile[a]	Number of Children With Developmental Delays and/or Another Diagnosis at 8 Years of Age	Clinical Implications
1	"Robust scores"	13-91	22	4	0	Serial assessments would reveal no developmental concerns.
2	"Decreasing scores"	4-82	14	13	0	Therapists may not be aware of this scoring pattern as the developmental delay would not be identified until preschool age. Parents can be advised that developmental concerns related to serial assessment scores may not be justified.
3	"Increasing scores"	1-88	11	10	1	No intervention was provided in infancy to these children. Therapists should be aware that children in this cluster may show spontaneous improvement in their percentile scores.
4	"Low scores"	1-71	19	18	5	Consistently low percentile scores may be indicative of future motor difficulties, but not in all children.

[a] Gross motor development of children who score at or below the 16th percentile on the PDMS and PDMS-2 is identified as suspicious.

Data from Eldred and Darrah.[54]

TABLE 2-3

BLOCKS TO TYPICAL MOTOR DEVELOPMENT, THEIR COMPONENTS, AND CONSEQUENCES

BLOCK	COMPONENTS	POSTURAL CONSEQUENCES	MOVEMENT CONSEQUENCES
Head and Neck Block – Neck Hyperextension (Figure 2-1)	• Flexion of the head and neck is not developed. • Imbalance between anti-gravity extension and flexion	• Head and neck hyperextension • Head is stabilized via bilateral shoulder elevation • Mouth opening • Jaw protrusion	• Active chin tuck does not develop • Disrupted development of righting reactions • Decreased active cervical spine and scapulae movement • Difficulty with upper extremity reaching
Head and Neck Block – Head and Neck Asymmetry (Figure 2-2)	• Asymmetrical activation of head and neck flexor and extensor musculature • Strong ATNR	• Asymmetrical head position • Rotation and flexion of the spine in the same direction leading to the development of scoliosis • Strong rotation of the head and spine in one direction causing anterior pelvic rotation on the skull side followed by medial rotation of the femur, with predisposition for hip subluxation or dislocation • "Wind-swept" deformity	• Inability to bring head to midline • Difficulty bringing hands to midline • Difficulty bringing hand to mouth • Compensatory functional use of the ATNR • Unilateral upper extremity use leading to poor ocular control and decreased visual perception
Shoulder Block (Figure 2-3)	• Decreased or absent scapular stability • Blocked external rotation, flexion and adduction of the humerus • Disrupted scapulohumeral rhythm • Lack of shoulder girdle control	• Scapular winging • Scapulohumeral muscle tightness • Difficulty with forearm weight-bearing • Compensatory patterns: primitive trunk extension with scapula adduction or humeral adduction reinforcing elevation of the trunk	• Poor upper extremity coordination for reaching, grasping, and fine motor skills • Poor upper extremity weight-bearing for movement transitions, crawling, and creeping

(continued)

lower extremities.[58] It is important to mention that Bly's description of the anterior and posterior pelvic tilt blocks does not seem to cover a combination of low postural tone and hypertonicity or spasticity in extremities. For example, the child depicted in Figures 2-4 and 2-1D displays a standing posture described as an anterior pelvic tilt block and a sitting posture described as a posterior pelvic tilt block, respectively, and yet she presents with hypotonic trunk musculature combined with spasticity in hip flexors, adductors, and medial rotators, as well as hamstring and gastrocnemius muscles bilaterally. Also, in standing and during walking, the same child may display the features of a posterior pelvic tilt block and "scissoring gait" with a narrow base of support but transition to an anterior pelvic tilt block alignment when the base of support is increased (Figure 2-7). Nevertheless, using the descriptions of the fixing patterns provided by Bly (see Table 2-3),[58] physical therapists can analyze posture and movement exhibited by their patients and identify specific atypical or missing components.

TABLE 2-3 (CONTINUED)			
BLOCKS TO TYPICAL MOTOR DEVELOPMENT, THEIR COMPONENTS, AND CONSEQUENCES			
BLOCK	**COMPONENTS**	**POSTURAL CONSEQUENCES**	**MOVEMENT CONSEQUENCES**
Hypotonia – Anterior Pelvic Tilt Block (Figure 2-4)	• Hypotonia • Insufficient abdominal muscle control • Imbalance of trunk, pelvic, and hip musculature	• Hip flexion, abduction, and external rotation (a "frog-legged" position) in supine, prone, and ring sitting • Rib cage elevation and lower rib flaring • Excessive extension in T12-L1 spinal segment observed in quadruped and tall kneeling • Trunk flexion in ring sitting with widely abducted hips • Anterior pelvic tilt, wide BOS, and hip flexion in supported standing • Achieving stability in standing by lowering COG through bilateral hip adduction and knee flexion leading to increased foot pronation and eversion, with toe clawing	• Use of hip flexion, abduction, and external rotation for stability in prone and ring sitting positions • Decreased active hip extension, adduction and medial rotation • Limited weight shifting in supine, prone, and sitting positions • Disrupted development of righting and equilibrium reactions • Mature weight shift does not develop • Difficulty with lateral weight shift from quadruped leading to a posterior transition into W-sitting • Lack of lower extremity dissociation leads to a "bunny hopping" creeping pattern • Immature weight shift during gait
Hypertonicity – Posterior Pelvic Tilt Block (Figures 2-5 and 2-6)	• Hypertonicity and tightness of extensor musculature • Inactivity of abdominal muscles • Imbalance of flexor and extensor musculature • Lack of flexion, abduction, and lateral rotation of the hip	• Very strong lumbar extension with hip extension and adduction in supine and prone positions • Hip extensor tightness leading to posterior pelvic tilt, increased knee flexion, lumbar and thoracic spine rounding, and sacral weightbearing in sitting • Narrow BOS due to hip adduction in fully supported standing	• Impaired function in all positions • Use of total extension pattern for rolling from supine to prone • Lack of function in flexed sitting leading to use of W-sitting • Belly crawling without reciprocation in prone (if achieved) • "Bunny hopping" in quadruped (if achieved)

Abbreviations: ATNR, asymmetrical tonic neck reflex; BOS, base of support; COG, center of gravity.

Compiled from Bly.[58]

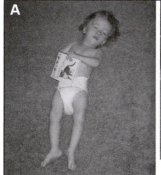  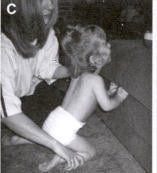 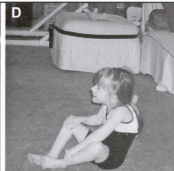

Figure 2-1. Head and neck block—neck hyperextension, observed in (A) supine, (B) prone, (C) tall kneeling, and (D) sitting positions.

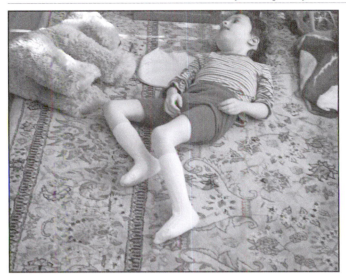

Figure 2-2. Head and neck block—head and neck asymmetry. Persistent head rotation to the right may lead to an asymmetrical position of lower extremities and a predisposition to hip subluxation on the left.

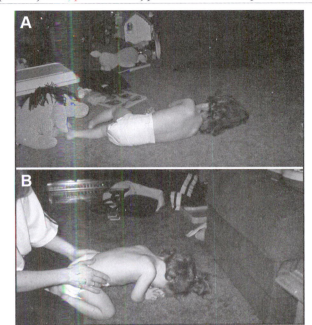

Figure 2-3. Shoulder block. (A) Scapula winging in a side-lying position. (B) Difficulty bearing weight through upper extremities in a quadruped position.

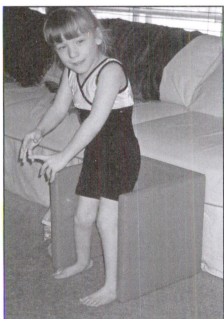

Figure 2-4. Anterior pelvic tilt block observed in a standing position.

Figure 2-5. Hypertonicity—posterior pelvic tilt block observed in a prone position.

Figure 2-6. Posterior pelvic tilt block observed in a sitting position.

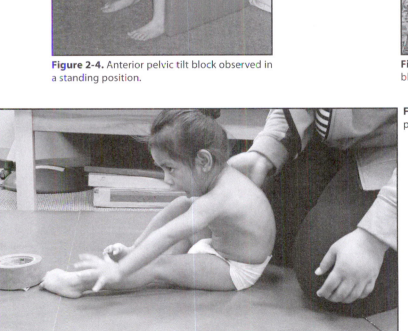

Figure 2-7. Features of 2 different pelvic blocks displayed during gait and supported standing by the same child. (A) Posterior pelvic tilt block and a narrow base of support. (B) Anterior pelvic tilt block and a wide base of support.

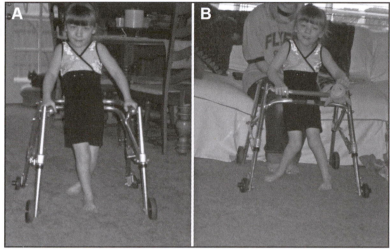

Standardized Developmental Testing With Emphasis on Movement Components

Standardized developmental testing is another way to evaluate quality of movement (see Table 2-1). Specifically, the Alberta Infant Motor Scale (the AIMS)[34] and the Toddler and Infant Motor Evaluation (the TIME)[44] allow therapists to identify infants and toddlers who exhibit atypical movement patterns. However, tracking developmental progress while using the AIMS in these infants will not be valid because the test scores received by these infants will be affected by their quality of movement and will not reflect improvements in their functional performance achieved over time.[34]

Similar to the AIMS, the Mobility subtest of the TIME[44] takes into account the child's quality of movement.[44,46] However, research has identified several problems that may be affecting the responsiveness of the TIME when evaluating progress in motor development.[46] For example, scores assigned to some of the items on the Mobility subtest incorrectly reflect the item difficulty, and, similar to the AIMS, the Mobility score would not reflect functional improvements demonstrated by a child who exhibits atypical movement patterns. Clinicians need to be aware of these limitations when interpreting the TIME testing results in this patient population.[46]

Unlike the AIMS and the TIME, the Test of Infant Motor Performance (the TIMP)[40] looks specifically at selective control of upper and lower extremities and documents the presence or absence of several types of general movements. This feature of the TIMP allows clinicians to identify those infants who are developing atypically up to the age of 4 months postterm and recommend early intervention when appropriate.[40]

Assessment of General Movements

Observation of quality of general movements is an examination technique that sharply varies from the regular neurological examination and from the standardized testing based on the developmental sequence of motor milestones.[59-63] Table 2-4 contains information on the types, description, and timing of general movements observed in typical development as described by Prechtl.[59]

The standardized procedure for the Prechtl's method of assessment of general movements is summarized in Table 2-5.[60] According to Einspieler and Prechtl,[60] accurate application of this assessment method requires training. After the completion of a standardized basic training course, the results of 9000 assessments performed by 800 observers showed 83% to 89% accuracy.[60,61] Based on their analysis of multiple research studies, Einspieler and Prechtl[60] reported good interobserver agreement of this assessment method (89% to 93%; average kappa of 0.88) and good test-retest reliability (85% to 100%).

The types of general movements observed during early infant development include gross movements that involve the entire body, as well as writhing and fidgety movements (see Table 2-4).[59] Using a standardized procedure for the Prechtl's method of assessment (see Table 2-5), clinicians are able to identify typical and atypical quality of general movements.[60,61] This observational method was shown to be valid not only for use with video recordings of infants at preterm and post-term age, but also with recordings of fetal movement obtained by means of ultrasonography.[59] Based on the analysis of findings in several studies,[69-74] Prechtl's assessment of general movements was reported to predict the developmental outcomes at the age of 2 years with high sensitivity (94%), varied specificity when used at preterm age and until 8 weeks post-term (46% to 93%), and increased specificity in the third month of age (82% to 100%).[60] This method was repeatedly found to be more effective than the neurological examination in predicting developmental outcomes.[71-74] It was also reported to be a more accurate predictor of CP than the ultrasonography of the brain.[69]

Table 2-6 provides a description of several types of general movements that can be observed in infants developing atypically.[59,60] Consistently present cramped-synchronized movements and absent fidgety movements were shown to be the strongest predictors of CP.[59-61,69,70,74] Based on previously reported research findings,[69,70,74-77] Einspieler and Prechtl[60] identified other specific characteristics of general movements

TABLE 2-4		
TYPES, DESCRIPTION, AND TIMING OF GENERAL MOVEMENTS OBSERVED IN TYPICAL DEVELOPMENT		
TYPE OF GENERAL MOVEMENTS	**DESCRIPTION**	**TIMING**
Gross movements involving entire body	• Have a gradual beginning and end and last a few seconds to several minutes or longer • Movements of the neck, trunk, arms, and legs variable in sequence, speed, force, and intensity • Mostly complex sequences of arm and leg flexion-extension movements, with superimposed rotations and frequent subtle changes in the direction of movement • Elegant and fluent quality, complex, and variable to the observer	Prenatal and preterm age
Writhing movements	• Small to moderate amplitude • Slow to moderate speed • Elliptical in form, which creates the writhing impression of movement quality • At times, may be accompanied with large and fast extension movements, especially in the arms	Term age to 8 weeks post-term
Fidgety movements	• Have a gradual onset, followed by an increase, and then a gradual decrease in frequency • Circular movements characterized by small amplitude, moderate speed, and variable acceleration of all body parts in all directions • Continuously observed in awake infants, except when fussing, crying, or focusing attention • May be accompanied by kicking, wiggling-oscillating, and swiping movements of the arms	6 to 20 weeks (most commonly 9 to 15 weeks) post-term

Adapted with permission from Prechtl HFR. General movement assessment as a method of developmental neurology: new paradigms and their consequences. The 1999 Ronnie Mac Keith Lecture. *Dev Med Child Neurol.* 2001;43:836-842. Copyright © 2001 John Wiley & Sons, Inc. All Rights Reserved.

that predict unfavorable outcomes of spastic and dyskinetic CP, and those that predict the anatomical distribution of involvement of extremities and trunk in children with spastic CP (see Chapter 3 for classification of CP). This information is summarized in Tables 2-7 and 2-8.[60]

The assessment of general movements focuses on their quality, and specifically, on their variation, complexity, and fluency.[63] Complex general movements are characterized by frequently changing spatial parameters (joint abduction-adduction, flexion-extension, and medial-lateral rotation).[63] Therefore, complexity reflects the spatial structure of movement variability.[11,63] The continuous change in movement patterns over time represents the temporal aspect of variability.[63] As for the fluency component of movement, it can be defined as the absence of stiffness, tremors, or jerky appearance.[63]

The overall quality of general movements has been classified in 4 groups (Table 2-9).[78] This classification emphasizes the importance of variation and complexity of movement but not necessarily its fluency as a significant number of infants developing typically may lack this movement characteristic.[63,78] Approximately 10% to 20% of infants developing typically demonstrate optimal typical general movements, while the majority of them display suboptimal typical movements.[63] In comparison, mildly atypical and definitely atypical general movements are observed in infants who develop atypically.[63,78] According to Hadders-Algra,[63] the finding of definitely atypical general movements observed at a "fidgety" age indicates a very high risk for the development of CP and, thus, warrants a referral for physical therapy intervention.

Standardized Testing Based on the Theory of Neuronal Group Selection

The Infant Motor Profile (IMP)[64,65] is a standardized, video-based assessment instrument that is used to

	TABLE 2-5

SUMMARY OF THE STANDARDIZED PROCEDURE FOR THE PRECHTL'S METHOD FOR ASSESSMENT OF QUALITY OF GENERAL MOVEMENTS

STEP	PROCEDURE	COMMENTS
1	Position the infant supine.	Dress the infant comfortably, with arms and legs unclothed. The infant can be asleep or awake but not fussing or crying.
2	Create a video recording of the infant.	The recording duration depends on the infant's age: • 30 to 60 minutes at preterm age • 5 to 10 minutes at term and post-term age
3	Review the recording and identify 3 sequences of general movements for further analysis.	It is recommended to store the sequential video recordings of the same infant taken at different ages in the same file to document the developmental trajectory.
4	Assess the quality of general movements through observation and pattern recognition.	Watch the recording without the sound, avoid attention to detail, and ignore other people and objects present in the recording.
5	Use the infant's developmental trajectory to report consistent or inconsistent typical or atypical findings and to predict his or her neurological development.	The developmental trajectory should consist of 2 or 3 recordings at preterm age (if applicable), one recording at term age and/or early after term, and one or more recordings at 9 to 15 weeks post-term.

Compiled from Einspieler and Prechtl.[60]

	TABLE 2-6

TYPES, DESCRIPTION, AND TIMING OF GENERAL MOVEMENTS OBSERVED IN INFANTS DEVELOPING ATYPICALLY

TYPE OF ATYPICAL GENERAL MOVEMENTS	DESCRIPTION	TIMING	PREDICTIVE VALUE
Poor repertoire of general movements	• Decreased complexity of movements of body parts • A monotonous sequence of successive movement components is observed	Prenatal and preterm age	Low
Cramped-synchronized movements	• Rigid appearance • Lack smoothness and fluency • Almost simultaneous contraction and subsequent relaxation of all extremity and trunk muscles	Preterm, term, and post-term age	High for spastic cerebral palsy
Chaotic movements	• Abrupt movements of large amplitude • Chaotic order of movements • Absent smoothness and fluency	Preterm, term, and early post-term age	High for development of cramped-synchronized movements
Absent fidgety movements	• Fidgety movements are not observed • Other movements can be observed	6 to 20 weeks post-term	High
Atypical fidgety movements	• Moderately or greatly exaggerated speed, amplitude, and jerkiness of fidgety movements	6 to 20 weeks post-term	Low

Adapted with permission from Prechtl HFR. General movement assessment as a method of developmental neurology: new paradigms and their consequences. The 1999 Ronnie Mac Keith Lecture. *Dev Med Child Neurol.* 2001;43:836-842. Copyright © 2001 John Wiley & Sons, Inc. All Rights Reserved. Additional data from Einspieler and Prechtl.[60]

TABLE 2-7

CHARACTERISTICS OF ATYPICAL GENERAL MOVEMENTS PREDICTING THE TYPE OF CEREBRAL PALSY

PREDICTED TYPE OF CEREBRAL PALSY	TYPE OF OBSERVED ATYPICAL GENERAL MOVEMENTS	COMMENTS
Spastic	Consistent cramped-synchronized movements	• Earlier onset of cramped-synchronized general movements correlates with greater severity of impairment
	Absent fidgety movements	• May be preceded by poor repertoire or cramped-synchronized general movements
	Transient cramped-synchronized movements followed by absent fidgety movements	• Neurological outcome is normal if transient cramped-synchronized movements are followed by typical fidgety movements
Dyskinetic (dystonia or athetosis)[12]	Poor repertoire of general movements; atypical circular UE movements; and finger splaying	• All 3 types are seen together until the second post-term month. • Circular UE movements are slow forward rotations of the shoulder. They are monotonous in their amplitude and speed. • Circular movements and finger splaying persist until at least the fifth post-term month.
	Lack of midline skills (foot to foot, hand to hand contact and hand to mouth movement)	• Seen at 3 months of age and later
	Absence of fidgety movements	• Seen between 3 and 5 months of age

Abbreviation: UE, upper extremity.

Compiled from Einspieler and Prechtl.[60]

evaluate spontaneous and elicited movement in infants of 3 to 18 months of age and in older children with moderate to severe motor disorders. The evaluation is conducted in 4 positions (supine, prone, sitting, and standing) and during walking. This test contains 80 items arranged in 5 subscales, including Variability—size of repertoire, Variability—ability to select, Symmetry, Fluency, and Performance.[64] While the assessment of general movements allows clinicians to evaluate the quality of movement in early infancy (the phase of primary variability), the IMP serves the same purpose during the development of secondary variability.[12,13,64] Because the variability subscales of the IMP[64] assess the size of the child's movement repertoire and his or her ability to select the best movement strategy in the process of spontaneous exploration, with a goal to match the task at hand, this test's conceptual framework is consistent with the TNGS.[12,13]

The IMP was standardized on 40 low-risk, full-term and 40 high-risk, preterm infants.[64] It was shown to have good intra- and interobserver reliability (Spearman rho = 0.9 for the total IMP score).[64,79] For the individual subscales, intraobserver reliability varied from poor to good, with Spearman rho ranging from 0.4 to 1.0. The reported

concurrent validity of the IMP with the AIMS[34] was also good (Spearman rho = 0.8, p < 0.005).[64,79] Construct validity of this instrument was established with 30 full-term and 59 prematurely born infants.[65] Significant associations were found between the IMP scores and pertinent risk factors for neuromotor developmental problems.[65]

In a pilot study, Heineman et al[64] showed that infants born preterm scored lower on the IMP than those who were born full term, and infants with significant brain pathology identified by ultrasound scans demonstrated significantly lower total and subscale IMP scores than those with minor brain lesions or negative scan results. Subsequent research confirmed these findings.[65]

In a study with 30 full-term and 59 prematurely born infants, the IMP was administered at the ages of 4, 6, 10, 12, and 18 months.[65] Results revealed significant associations between the IMP scores and pertinent risk factors for neuromotor developmental problems, including gestational age at birth, 5-minute Apgar scores, and parental socioeconomic status. Infants born prematurely exhibited greater variation in their IMP scores obtained over time compared to infants born full term. This finding pointed to the need for serial

TABLE 2-8

CHARACTERISTICS OF ATYPICAL GENERAL MOVEMENTS PREDICTING THE ANATOMICAL DISTRIBUTION OF INVOLVEMENT OF EXTREMITIES AND TRUNK

PREDICTED ANATOMICAL DISTRIBUTION OF INVOLVEMENT[12]	CHARACTERISTICS OF OBSERVED ATYPICAL GENERAL MOVEMENTS	COMMENTS
Movement and posture of all 4 extremities and trunk are impaired (diplegia or quad-riplegia—bilateral CP).[a]	Consistent cramped synchronized movements	• If this movement type has a later onset and is present for a shorter period of time, UEs are more likely to be less involved than LEs, resulting in diplegic and not quadriplegic CP. • Concurrent presence of isolated movements of hands and fingers that occur separately or a part of general movements predicts diplegic CP. • In the absence of isolated movements, UEs and LEs are more likely to be equally involved, resulting in quadriplegic CP.
Movement and posture of trunk as well as UE and LE on one side of the body are primarily impaired (hemiplegia—unilateral CP).[a]	Poor repertoire of general movements or cramped syn-chronized movements followed by absent fidgety movements, with decreased or absent iso-lated movements of hands, fin-gers, feet and toes on the side contralateral to the brain lesion.	• Asymmetry in presentation of isolated movements is seen in infants born prematurely starting from the third post-term month of age. • In full-term infants with neonatal cerebral infarction, this asymmetry can be present in the second month of life.

Abbreviations: CP, cerebral palsy; UEs, upper extremities; LEs, lower extremities; UE, upper extremity; LE, lower extremity.

[a] Current classification of CP requires that all affected body parts be listed and their involvement be described in detail. It calls for discontinuation of terms diplegia, quadriplegia, and hemiplegia because of their lack of precision in the identification of specific impairments.[26] These terms are used here for consistency with the original source of information presented in this table.

Compiled from Einspieler and Prechtl.[60]

TABLE 2-9

CLASSIFICATION OF QUALITY OF GENERAL MOVEMENTS

CLASS OF GENERAL MOVEMENTS	COMPLEXITY	VARIATION	FLUENCY
Optimal typical	Abundantly present (+++)	Abundantly present (+++)	Present (+)
Suboptimal typical	Sufficiently present (++)	Sufficiently present (++)	Absent (–)
Mildly atypical	Present, but insufficiently (++)	Present, but insufficiently (++)	Absent (–)
Definitely atypical	Virtually absent or absent (–)	Virtually absent or absent (–)	Absent (–)

Adapted from Hadders-Algra M, Mavinkurve-Groothuis AMC, Groen SE, Stremmelaar EF, Martijn A, Butcher PR. Quality of general movements and the development of minor neurological dysfunction at toddler and school age. *Clin Rehabil.* 2004;18:287-299, copyright ©2004 by Arnold Publishers. Adapted by permission of SAGE.

assessments of neuromotor function in infants with high risk for poor developmental outcomes. In addition, in the group of infants born prematurely, those whose neonatal ultrasound scans revealed major brain pathology scored significantly lower on the IMP at 4 of 5 assessment points.[65] Neonatal ultrasound scans positive for significant brain lesions have

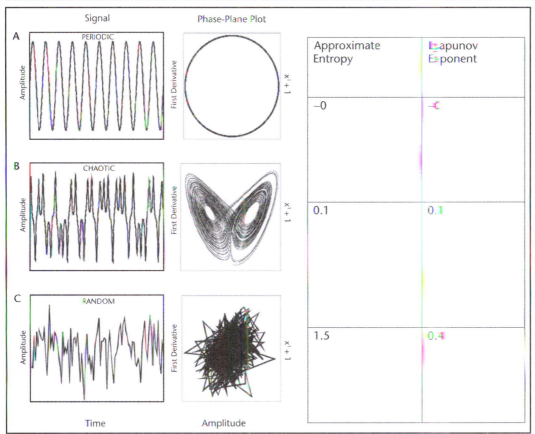

Figure 2-8. Time series and corresponding phase-plane plot: (A) periodic function; (B) time series from a chaotic system, the Lorenz attractor; (C) random time series. (Reprinted from Harbourne RT, Stergiou N. Movement variability and the use of nonlinear tools: principles to guide physical therapist practice. *Phys Ther.* 2009;89:267-282, with permission of the American Physical Therapy Association. This material is copyrighted, and any further reproduction or distribution requires written permission from APTA.)

been shown to predict unfavorable developmental outcomes at 3.6 years of age.[80] Because the IMP scores in the study conducted by Heineman et al[64] correlated with the ultrasound findings, the results clearly supported the construct validity of the IMP as an instrument that can be used to assess neuromotor function in high-risk infants, with the emphasis on evaluation of variability.[65]

Nonlinear Tools

Nonlinear measures have been repeatedly shown to be very useful in the evaluation of complexity of postural control in typical development.[11,20,23,66-68] Harbourne et al[66] analyzed data in a COP time series when studying independent sitting in infants. While the amount of postural sway in anterior-posterior and mediolateral directions could be quantified using linear measures of displacement of the COP, such as its length, frequency, and time, they could not be used to analyze the complexity of postural adjustments. The researchers delineated 2 important features of complexity of postural control that can be examined by using nonlinear tools: its regularity and dynamic stability.[66]

Regularity of postural control can be assessed using a statistic called *Approximate Entropy* or ApEn.[19,20,23,66,68,81,82] ApEn is a nonlinear estimate of the complexity of the system, which is based on the calculation of frequency with which different length patterns, such as the lengths of the COP displacement path, are repeated within the same time series. This quantifies the predictability or regularity of the system's

behavior.[19,20,23,66,81] The ApEn values vary from 0 to 2, with higher values indicating greater complexity or irregularity and lower predictability (Figure 2-8).[20,23,66,81,82]

The second feature of complexity—dynamic stability—can be assessed using a nonlinear tool called the *Lyapunov Exponent*, or LyE, which "measures the divergence of the data trajectories in phase space."[66(p 127)] A postural sway example illustrates the meaning of this measure.[20,66] Consider a situation when the LyE is used to assess data obtained from a hypothetical time series when a sine wave depicting rhythmical and periodic (back and forth) postural sway of a standing person follows multiple trajectories that overlap with each other completely, without any divergence. In this situation, the structure of variability will not change over time, the corresponding phase-plane plot will be a perfect circle, and the LyE will be equal to zero (see Figure 2-8). If, on the other hand, the data in the time series change over time, the data trajectories will vary and will show maximal divergence when the data are completely random.[20,66] The LyE value measuring dynamic stability in this case will increase above 0.4.[23] If the postural adjustments occur to adapt to changes in the environment, the LyE value will be between 0 and 0.4, which would reflect a chaotic organization of variability of postural control in the standing person (see Figure 2-8). This will indicate the presence of normal dynamic stability and complexity of postural control.[20,23,66]

Harbourne and Stergiou[20] illustrated the usefulness of linear and nonlinear measures for the evaluation of postural control by comparing data obtained from the recordings of

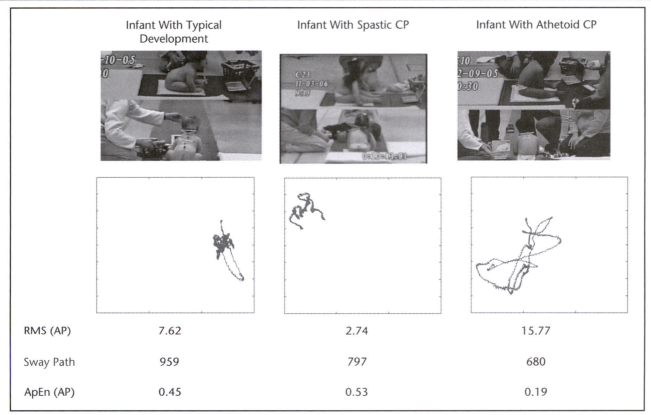

	Infant With Typical Development	Infant With Spastic CP	Infant With Athetoid CP
RMS (AP)	7.62	2.74	15.77
Sway Path	959	797	680
ApEn (AP)	0.45	0.53	0.19

Figure 2-9. Three children at sitting stage 1 and respective center-of-pressure (COP) tracings in the first row. The first picture shows an infant with typical development, the second picture shows an infant with spastic quadriplegic cerebral palsy (CP), and the third picture shows an infant with athetoid CP. Beneath the COP tracings are examples of the linear and nonlinear measures. RMS (AP)=linear measure of overall postural variability, the standard deviation of the length samples in the anterior-posterior direction; sway path=linear measure of the velocity of the COP; ApEn (AP)=approximate entropy, a measure quantifying the regularity or predictability of the COP in the anterior-posterior direction. (Reprinted from Harbourne RT, Willett S, Kyvelidou A, Deffeyes J, Stergiou N. A comparison of interventions for children with cerebral palsy to improve sitting postural control: a clinical trial. *Phys Ther.* 2010;90:1881-1898, with permission of the American Physical Therapy Association. This material is copyrighted, and any further reproduction or distribution requires written permission from APTA.)

a COP time series in infants developing typically and atypically who were placed in a prop-sitting position on a force platform (Figure 2-9). While the infant developing typically was observed to continuously perform frequent small movements in different parts of her body that were indicative of relative dynamic stability and some ability to adapt to the sitting task, the infant with spastic CP displayed a static posture and was unable to make any adjustments. This was reflected in decreased values of the root mean square (RMS), a linear measure of variability that signified a decreased COP excursion in the anterior-posterior direction.[20]

The infant with athetoid CP demonstrated postural adjustments but had difficulty adapting to the sitting task, most likely because of excessive postural sway.[20] This observation was confirmed by increased RMS values that indicated a greater anterior-posterior displacement of the COP and, thus, greater variability as compared to the infant developing typically. At the same time, a low ApEn value for the infant with athetoid CP signified a less complex structure of variability of postural control and, therefore, a more predictable and regular pattern of the COP displacement. In comparison, an increased ApEn value obtained for the infant with spastic CP suggested a less predictable and more irregular pattern than

displayed by the infant with athetoid CP, but it was combined with an overall decrease in movement. This example shows that a combination of linear and nonlinear measures allows for a comprehensive, qualitative assessment of postural control.[20]

In another study that examined postural control in a supine position in 1- to 3-week-old infants, Dusing et al[19] obtained RMS and ApEn values indicative of decreased postural stability and increased regularity of COP movement in infants born prematurely compared to those born full term. The authors emphasized the importance of complexity of postural control and recommended that, besides focusing on movement speed and magnitude, clinicians who observe developing infants should also pay close attention to the variety of motor control strategies available to them.[19]

The last statement can be supported by an example provided by Dusing and Harbourne,[11] who assessed the COP movement of 2 infants in a supine position at term age. One infant was born full term, and the other one was born prematurely. The full-term neonate used a wide variety of movement strategies. He elevated his lower extremities against gravity and kicked them reciprocally, brought his hands to mouth, and moved his head without difficulty. The displacement of his

	TABLE 2-10	

EXAMPLES OF INTERVENTIONS FOR VARIABILITY AND COMPLEXITY DEFICITS IDENTIFIED THROUGH CLINICAL OBSERVATIONS

VARIABILITY/ COMPLEXITY DEFICIT	CLINICAL OBSERVATION	SUGGESTED INTERVENTION
Overall reduced range of movement	• Poverty of movement strategies • Very little active movement	• Provide manual guidance • Increase sensory information to help guide and learn movement possibilities
Increased regularity	• Static posture • Stiffness, rigidity, or hypotonia • Making the same errors repeatedly	• Adapt the environment to encourage slight active movement out of preferred posture
Decreased regularity	• Constant pushing or pulling into extreme ranges (eg, extensor thrusting) • Varied errors that generally follow the same theme	• Provide flexible constraints to suggest a reduced range • Provide a reward within the reduced range

Adapted from Dusing SC, Harbourne RT. Variability in postural control during infancy: implications for development, assessment, and intervention. *Phys Ther*. 2010;90:1838-1849, with permission of the American Physical Therapy Association. This material is copyrighted, and any further reproduction or distribution requires written permission from APTA.

COP was small, but its trajectory was complex. In comparison, the infant born prematurely displayed a limited number of movement strategies, which were simple and repetitive in nature. He was repeatedly unsuccessful in his attempts to lift his lower extremities off of the supporting surface and keep them elevated against gravity. As a result, he rolled to his side every time. In addition, he had difficulty rotating his head from side to side and lifting one lower extremity without lifting the other. This infant's COP movement was characterized by greater excursion and lower complexity compared to the infant born full term. This example demonstrates that 1) nonlinear measures are very useful in detecting complexity as an important characteristic of postural control that reflects the structure of its variability, and 2) clinical observation focused on detecting the variability of movement strategies available to the infant may point to the signs of decreased complexity even in the absence of special equipment that would allow a trained observer to assess complexity more objectively.[11]

Harbourne and Stergiou[23] noted that nonlinear measures are currently used primarily in research that involves the analysis of time series data while employing mathematics and specially designed software. They hypothesized that, with the development of technology, these tools may become available in the clinic in the form of an electronic device that will be used to assess variability. In the meantime, to bridge this gap between research and clinical practice, physical therapists need to be trained in understanding variability and complexity and in using that understanding when performing patient examination and evaluation, and while developing intervention programs.[23]

OPTIMAL VARIABILITY AS A GOAL OF THERAPEUTIC INTERVENTION

As discussed earlier in this chapter, Stergiou et al[9] proposed that a healthy state of a biological system is characterized by optimal variability that allows the system to adapt to a variety of environmental and internal conditions. A child who is developing typically may be an example of such a biological system. Conversely, children with atypical motor development demonstrate stereotypical, repetitive, and predictable movement or highly variable, irregular, and unpredictable movement leading to a loss of adaptability. In other words, decreased complexity associated with both suboptimal and excessive variability[9] indicates that the child's ability to adapt to external and internal changes is also decreased and, therefore, he or she may be at risk for developmental delays and disabilities.[11,20] Early identification of such deficits should lead to an early referral for therapeutic intervention,[11] which must promote optimal variability and, thus, complexity and adaptability of movement and postural control.[9]

Dusing and Harbourne[11] suggested interventions that can be used to promote the complexity of postural control, including environmental adaptation, exposure to varied tasks, and manual guidance in the form of light touch that encourages varied and spontaneous exploration of the environment (Table 2-10). Spontaneous exploration will allow for varied and meaningful errors made while finding the best solution to a motor task. These errors are different from those made by a child who demonstrates repetitive and predictable or random and unpredictable postural control (see Table 2-10).[11]

Appropriately designed intervention should encourage more divergent and better graded movement, with the ultimate goal of reaching the optimal level of variability.[9,11]

Fetters[1] emphasized skillful environmental design as a strategy to promote spontaneous exploration. She stressed the necessity to allow the infant to experience success as the reward for multiple attempts at finding a solution to a motor task. This would require the therapist to be proficient in setting up the environment that encourages "discovery learning," which would eventually lead to a successful resolution of a motor problem.[1]

SUMMARY AND IMPLICATIONS FOR CLINICAL PRACTICE

Movement variability and complexity are inherent characteristics of typical motor development that lead to the development of adaptability, which allows the human being to select the best possible solution for a motor task.[23] Infants and children with atypical development frequently display stereotypical movement and posture[10,13,58] that lack optimal variability[9] and are less complex than seen in children developing typically.[27,66-68] Current evidence[1,2,9,11,23] points to the need for a paradigm shift from relying heavily on the timing of acquisition of developmental milestones to focusing on variability, complexity, and adaptability in physical therapy examination, evaluation, and intervention, with a goal of achieving optimal movement variability. Physical therapists should employ a variety of appropriate methods to evaluate quality of movement in developing infants and children. In addition, the evaluation of motor development should take into consideration the parental practices used in different cultural environments, which affect the timing and sequence of acquisition of motor milestones.[48] The recommendations for early therapeutic intervention need to be made based on the assessment of quality of movement[40,57-65] and on a series of standardized developmental testing results as compared to a single-point assessment.[51-54] Evidence for intervention developed through research using nonlinear measurement tools[11,19,20,23,66-68] should be incorporated into clinical practice. Therapists should promote variability and complexity of movement and postural control in infants and children by using interventions that encourage spontaneous exploration, which would help increase the number of strategies available to them for active problem solving.[11]

Complete video-based activities for Chapter 2 (see Activity Sets 1 and 2 on the book website).

REFERENCES

1. Fetters L. Perspective on variability in the development of human action. *Phys Ther.* 2010;90:1860-1867.
2. Vereijken B. The complexity of childhood development: variability in perspective. *Phys Ther.* 2010;90:1850-1859.
3. Edelman GM. *Neural Darwinism.* New York, NY: Basic Books; 1987.
4. Edelman GM. Neural Darwinism: selection and reentrant signaling in higher brain function. *Neuron.* 1993;10(2):115-125.
5. Sporns O, Edelman G. Solving Bernstein's problem. *Child Dev.* 1993;64(4):960-981.
6. Bernstein N. *The Co-ordination and Regulation of Movements.* Oxford: Pergamon Press; 1967.
7. Thelen E, Smith LB. Lessons from learning to walk. In: Thelen E, Smith LB, eds. *A Dynamic Systems Approach to the Development of Cognition and Action.* Cambridge, MA: MIT Press; 1994:3-20.
8. Thelen E, Fisher DM, Ridley-Johnson R, Griffin NJ. The relationship between physical growth and a newborn reflex. *Infant Behav Dev.* 1984;7(4):479-493.
9. Stergiou N, Harbourne RT, Cavanough JT. Optimal movement variability: a new theoretical perspective for neurologic physical therapy. *J Neurol Phys Ther.* 2006;30(3):120-129.
10. Hadders-Algra, M. Variation and variability: key words in human motor development. *Phys Ther.* 2010;90:1823-1837.
11. Dusing SC, Harbourne RT. Variability in postural control during infancy: implications for development, assessment, and intervention. *Phys Ther.* 2010;90:1838-1849.
12. Hadders-Algra M. The neuronal group selection theory: a framework to explain variation in normal motor development. *Dev Med Child Neurol.* 2000;42(8):566-572.
13. Hadders-Algra M. Reduced variability in motor behaviour: an indicator of impaired cerebral connectivity? *Early Hum Dev.* 2008;84(12):787-789.
14. Adolph KE, Berger SE. Motor development. In: Damon W, Lerner R, Kuhn D, Siegler RS, eds. *Handbook of Child Psychology, Vol. 2: Cognition, Perception, and Language.* New York, NY: Wiley; 2006:161-213.
15. Adolph KE, Vereijken B, Shrout PE. What changes in infant walking and why. *Child Dev.* 2003;74:475-497.
16. Thelen E, Smith LB. Hard problems: toward a dynamic cognition. In: Thelen E, Smith LB, eds. *A Dynamic Systems Approach to the Development of Cognition and Action.* Cambridge, MA: MIT Press; 1994:311-339.
17. Thelen E. Grounded in the world: developmental origins of the embodied mind. *Infancy.* 2000;1(1):3-28.
18. Shumway-Cook A, Woollacott MH. Normal postural control. In: Shumway-Cook A, Woollacott MH, eds. *Motor Control: Translating Research into Clinical Practice.* 4th ed. Philadelphia, PA: Lippincott Williams and Wilkins; 2012:161-194.
19. Dusing SC, Kyvelidou A, Merecer VS, Stergiou N. Infants born preterm exhibit different patterns of center-of-pressure movement than infants born at full term. *Phys Ther.* 2009;89:1354-1362.
20. Harbourne RT, Stergiou N. Nonlinear analysis of the development of sitting postural control. *Dev Psychobiol.* 2003;42:368-377.
21. Bernstein NA. On dexterity and its development. In: Latash ML, Turvey MT, eds. *Dexterity and Its Development.* Mahwah, NJ: Lawrence Erlbaum Associates, Publishers; 1996:3-244.
22. Adolph KE. Joh AS, Franchak JM, Ishak S, Gill-Alvarez SV. Flexibility in the development of action. In: Bargh J, Gollwitzer P, Morsella E, eds. *The Psychology of Action.* Vol. 2. New York, NY: Oxford University Press; 2008: 399-426.
23. Harbourne RT, Stergiou N. Movement variability and the use of nonlinear tools: principles to guide physical therapist practice. *Phys Ther.* 2009;89(3):267-282.
24. Adolph KE. Specificity of learning: why infants fall over a veritable cliff. *Psychol Sci.* 2000;11:290-295.
25. Adolph KE, Joh AS. Multiple learning mechanisms in the development of action. In: Woodward A, Needham A, eds. *Learning and the Infant Mind.* New York, NY: Oxford University Press; 2009:172-207.
26. Rosenbaum P, Paneth N, Leviton A, et al. A report: the definition and classification of cerebral palsy April 2006. *Dev Med Child Neurol.* 2007;49(suppl 109):8-14.

27. Harbourne RT, Willett S, Kyvelidou A, Deffeyes J, Stergiou N. A comparison of interventions for children with cerebral palsy to improve sitting postural control: a clinical trial. *Phys Ther.* 2010;90:1881-1898.

28. Campbell SK. The child's development of functional movement. In: Campbell SK, Palisano RJ, Orlin MN, eds. *Physical Therapy for Children.* 4th ed. St. Louis, MO: Saunders; 2012:37-86.

29. Long TM, Toscano K. Measurement. In: *Handbook of Pediatric Physical Therapy.* 2nd ed. Philadelphia, PA: Lippincott Williams and Wilkins; 2002:85-178.

30. Effgen SK, Howman J. Child appraisal: examination and evaluation. In: Effgen SK, ed. *Meeting the Physical Therapy Needs of Children.* 2nd ed. Philadelphia, PA: F. A. Davis Company; 2013:107-152.

31. Kahn-D'Angelo L, Blanchard Y, McManus B. The special care nursery. In: Campbell SK, Palisano RJ, Orlin MN, eds. *Physical Therapy for Children.* 4th ed. St. Louis, MO: Saunders; 2012:903-943.

32. Rahlin M. Impaired ventilation, respiration/gas exchange and aerobic capacity/endurance associated with respiratory failure in the neonate. In: Moffat M, Frownfelter D, eds. *Cardiopulmonary Essentials: Preferred Physical Therapist Practice Patterns.* Thorofare, NJ: SLACK Incorporated; 2007:237-264.

33. Effgen SK, Howman J. Serving the needs of children and their families. In: Effgen SK, ed. *Meeting the Physical Therapy Needs of Children.* 2nd ed. Philadelphia, PA: F. A. Davis Company; 2013:3-40.

34. Piper MC, Darrah J. *Motor Assessment of the Developing Infant.* Philadelphia, PA: W.B. Saunders Company; 1994.

35. Blanchard Y, Neilan E, Busanich J, Garavuso L, Klimas D. Interrater reliability of early Intervention providers scoring the Alberta Infant Motor Scale. *Pediatr Phys Ther.* 2004;16:13-13.

36. Darrah J, Piper M, Watt MJ. Assessment of gross motor skills of at-risk infants: predictive validity of the Alberta Infant Motor Scale. *Dev Med Child Neurol.* 1998;40:485-491.

37. Bayley, N. *Bayley Scales of Infant and Toddler Development (Bayley-III®).* 3rd ed. San Antonio, TX: Harcourt Assessment; 2005.

38. Folio MR, Fewell RR. *Peabody Developmental Motor Scales.* 2nd ed. Austin, TX: Pro-Ed, Inc.; 2000.

39. Wang HH, Liao HF, Hsieh CL. Reliability, sensitivity to change, and responsiveness of the Peabody Developmental Motor Scales – second edition for children with cerebral palsy. *Phys Ther.* 2006;86:1351-1359.

40. Campbell SK. *The Test of Infant Motor Performance. Test User's Manual Version 2.0.* Chicago, IL: Infant Motor Performance Scales, LLC; 2005.

41. Campbell SK. Test-retest reliability of the Test of Infant Motor Performance. *Pediatr Phys Ther.* 1999;11:60-66.

42. Campbell SK, Kolobe TH, Wright BD, Linacre JM. Validity of the Test of Infant Motor Performance for prediction of 6-, 9- and 12-month scores on the Alberta Infant Motor Scale. *Dev Med Child Neurol.* 2002;44:263-272.

43. Kolobe TH, Bulanda M, Susman L. Predicting motor outcomes at preschool age for infants tested at 7, 30, 60, and 90 days after term using the Test of Infant Motor Performance. *Phys Ther.* 2004;84:1144-1156.

44. Miller LJ, Roid GH. *The T.I.M.E.™ Toddler and Infant Motor Evaluation, a Standardized Assessment.* San Antonio, TX: Therapy Skill Builders™; 1994.

45. Rahlin M, Stoecker J, Cech D, Henderson R, Rheault W. Intrarater reliability of the Toddler and Infant Motor Evaluation (pilot studies 1 and 2) (abstract). *Phys Ther.* 2000;80:S28.

46. Rahlin M, Rheault W, Cech D. Evaluation of the primary subtests of Toddler and Infant Motor Evaluation: implications for clinical practice in pediatric physical therapy. *Pediatr Phys Ther.* 2003;15:176-183.

47. Tieman BL, Palisano RJ, Sutlive AC. Assessment of motor development and function in preschool children. *Ment Retard Dev Disabil Res Rev.* 2005;11:189-196.

48. Adolph KE, Karasik LB, Tamis-Lemonda CS. Motor skill. In: Bornstein MH, ed. *Handbook of Cultural Developmental Science.* New York, NY: Taylor & Francis Group, LLC; 2010:61-88.

49. Portney LG, Watkins MP. Sampling. In: Portney LG, Watkins MP, eds. *Foundations of Clinical Research: Applications to Practice.* 3rd ed. Upper Saddle River, NJ: Pearson Education, Inc.; 2009:143-159.

50. Dudek-Shriber L, Zelazny S. The effects of prone positioning on the quality and acquisition of developmental milestones in four-month-old infants. *Pediatr Phys Ther.* 2007;19:48-55.

51. Adolph KE, Robinson SR, Young JW, Gill-Alvarez, F. What is the shape of developmental change? *Psychol Rev.* 2008;115:527-543.

52. Darrah J, Redfern L, Maguire TO, Beaulne AP, Watt J. Intra-individual stability of rate of gross motor development in full-term infants. *Early Hum Dev.* 1998;52(2):169-179.

53. Darrah J, Hodge M, Magill-Evans J, Kembhavi G. Stability of serial assessments of motor and communication abilities in typically developing infants – implications for screening. *Early Hum Dev.* 2003;72(2):97-110.

54. Eldred E, Darrah J. Using cluster analysis to interpret the variability of gross motor scores of children with typical development. *Phys Ther.* 2010;90:1510-1518.

55. Folio MR, Fewell RP. Peabody *Developmental Motor Scales and Activity Card Manual.* Allen, TX: DLM Teaching Resources; 1983.

56. Darrah J, Magill-Evans J, Volden J, Hodge M, Kembhavi G. Scores of typically developing children on the Peabody Developmental Motor Scales: infancy to preschool. *Phys Occup Ther Pediatr.* 2007;27(3):5-19.

57. Bly L. *Motor Skills Acquisition in the First Year.* San Antonio, TX: Therapy Skill Builders; 1994.

58. Bly L. *Components of Typical and Atypical Motor Development.* Laguna Beach, CA: Neuro-Developmental Treatment Association, Inc.; 2011.

59. Prechtl HFR. General movement assessment as a method of developmental neurology: new paradigms and their consequences. The 1999 Ronnie Mac Keith Lecture. *Dev Med Child Neurol.* 2001;43:836-842.

60. Einspieler C, Prechtl HFR. Prechtl's Assessment of General Movements: a diagnostic tool for the functional assessment of the young nervous system. *Ment Retard Dev Disabil Res Rev.* 2005;11:61-67.

61. Einspieler C, Prechtl HFR, Bos AF, Ferrari F, Cioni G. *Prechtl's Method on the Qualitative Assessment of General Movements in Preterm, Term and Young Infants.* London, UK: MacKeith Press; 2004.

62. Einspieler C, Prechtl HF, Ferrari F, Cioni G, Bos AF. The qualitative assessment of general movements in preterm, term and young infants – review of the methodology. *Early Hum Dev.* 1997;50(1):47-60.

63. Hadders-Algra M. General movements: a window for early identification of children at high risk for developmental disorders. *J Pediatr.* 2004;145:S12-S18.

64. Heineman KR, Bos AF, Hadders-Algra M. The Infant Motor Profile: a standardized and qualitative method to assess motor behavior in infancy. *Dev Med Child Neurol.* 2008;50:275-282.

65. Heineman KL, La Bastide-Van Gemert S, Fidler V, Middelburg KJ, Bos AF, Hadders-Algra M. Construct validity of the Infant Motor Profile: relation with prenatal, perinatal, and neonatal risk factors. *Dev Med Child Neurol.* 2010;52:e209-e215.

66. Harbourne RT, Deffeyes JE, Kyvelidou A, Stergiou N. Complexity of postural control in infants: linear and nonlinear features revealed by principal component analysis. *Nonlinear Dynamics Psychol Life Sci.* 2009;13(1):123-144.

67. Smith BA, Stergiou N, Ulrich BD. Lyapunov exponent and surrogation analysis of patterns of variability: profiles in new walkers with and without Down syndrome. *Motor Control.* 2010;14:126-142.

68. Deffeyes JE, Harbourne RT, Kyvelidou A, Stuberg WA, Stergiou N. Nonlinear analysis of sitting postural sway indicates developmental delay in infants. *Clin Biomech (Bristol, Avon).* 2009;24:564-570.

69. Prechtl HF, Einspieler C, Cioni G, Bos AF, Ferrari F, Sontheimer D. An early marker for neurological deficits after perinatal brain lesions. *Lancet*. 1997;349(9062):1361-1363.

70. Ferrari F, Cioni G, Prechtl HF. Qualitative changes of general movements in preterm infants with brain lesions. *Early Hum Dev*. 1990;23(3):193-231.

71. Prechtl HF, Ferrari F, Cioni G. Predictive value of general movements in asphyxiated fullterm infants. *Early Hum Dev*. 1993;35(2):91-120.

72. Cioni G, Ferrari F, Einspieler C, Paolicelli PB, Barbani MT, Prechtl HF. Comparison between observation of spontaneous movements and neurological examination in preterm infants. *J Pediatr*. 1997;130(5):704-711.

73. Cioni G, Prechtl HF, Ferrari F, Paolicelli PB, Einspieler C, Roversi MF. Which better predicts later outcome in full-term infants: quality of general movements or neurological examination? *Early Hum Dev*. 1997;50(1):71-85.

74. Ferrari F, Cioni G, Ferrari F, et al. Cramped synchronized general movements in preterm infants as an early marker for cerebral palsy. *Arch Pediatr Adolesc Med*. 2002;156:460-467.

75. Cioni G, Bos AF, Einspieler C, et al. Early neurological signs in preterm infants with unilateral intraparenchymal echodensity. *Neuropediatrics*. 2000;31(5):240-251.

76. Guzzetta A, Mercuri E, Rapisardi G, et al. General movements detect early signs of hemiplegia in term infants with neonatal cerebral infarction. *Neuropediatrics*. 2003;34(2):61-66.

77. Einspieler C, Cioni G, Paolicelli PB, et al. The early markers for later dyskinetic CP are different from those for spastic CP. *Neuropediatrics*. 2002;33(2):73-78.

78. Hadders-Algra M, Mavinkurve-Groothuis AMC, Groen SE, Stremmelaar EF, Martijn A, Butcher PR. Quality of general movements and the development of minor neurological dysfunction at toddler and school age. *Clin Rehabil*. 2004;18:287-299.

79. Portney LG, Watkins MP. Reliability of measurements. In: Portney LG, Watkins MP, eds. *Foundations of Clinical Research: Applications to Practice*. 3rd ed. Upper Saddle River, NJ: Pearson Education, Inc.; 2009:77-96.

80. Weisglas-Kuperus N, Baerts W, Fetter WP, Sauer PJ. Neonatal cerebral ultrasound, neonatal neurology and perinatal conditions as predictors of neurodevelopmental outcome in very low birthweight infants. *Early Hum Dev*. 1992;31(2):131-148.

81. Pincus SM. Approximate entropy as a measure of system complexity. *Proc Natl Acad Sci USA*. 1991;88:2297-2301.

82. Pincus SM, Gladstone IM, Ehrenkranz RA. A regularity statistic for medical data analysis. *J Clin Monit*. 1991;7(4):335-345.

Please see videos on the accompanying website at

www.healio.com/books/videosrahlin

Section I

QUESTIONS TO PONDER

1. Is there enough research evidence to support the theoretical premises of each of the theories discussed in Chapter 1? Please justify your answer.

2. Is there enough research evidence to support the unity of the perception-action theory, the DST, and the TNGS? Please explain your answer.

3. How do theoretical assumptions translate into clinical practice?

4. Considering the impact of variability in skill acquisition, is there still a place for the developmental sequence to be used in clinical practice as a guide for planning intervention?

5. Should the standardized developmental assessment instruments based on the developmental sequence of acquisition of motor milestones be discarded? Please explain your answer.

6. What may be the barriers to implementation of serial assessment practices?

7. Can an intervention approach be effective if it is based on a theory that is no longer valid? Please explain your answer.

8. How can the research evidence related to variability, complexity, and adaptability of movement and postural control be translated into clinical practice, and what barriers need to be overcome to accomplish this goal?

9. How would pediatric physical therapy change if the entire body of research evidence on variability, complexity, and adaptability of movement and postural control were translated into clinical practice?

SUGGESTED QUESTIONS FOR FUTURE RESEARCH

1. Is there a relationship between the timing of acquisition of motor milestones and variability of movement and postural strategies available to typically developing infants observed in similar cultural environments and brought up using similar parenting practices?

2. What are the effects of the "Back to Sleep" program on variability and complexity of movement and postural control in developing infants?

3. Is there a way to objectively assess the complexity of movement and postural control without the need to use sophisticated and expensive equipment?

4. What are the effects of serial assessment practices on the cost of Early Intervention services?

5. What are the effects of serial assessment practices on the decision-making process in pediatric physical therapy?

6. Which interventions used by physical therapists are most effective in helping infants and children who develop atypically make the greatest gains toward achieving optimal movement variability?

7. Considering the massive amounts of practice required for typically developing infants to achieve meaningful gains in their motor development, what is the optimal amount of movement practice needed for infants and children with atypical development?

CEREBRAL PALSY AS A DEVELOPMENTAL DISORDER

3

Definition, Incidence, Etiology, Classification, and Diagnosis of Cerebral Palsy

...definitions stand and fall by what they include and what they exclude.

Lewis Rosenbloom[1]

In 1843, Dr. William Little, an orthopedic surgeon, first described *spastic rigidity* seen in infants and young children and linked it to *cerebral disease* related to premature birth and perinatal asphyxia.[2-5] For many years, this condition was called *Little's disease*.[3,5,6] In 1889, Sir William Osler used the term *cerebral palsies* in his description of 151 patients that varied in their anatomical distribution of paralysis.[5-7] He classified all cases into 3 groups, including *infantile hemiplegia, bilateral spastic hemiplegia,* and *spastic paraplegia*.[5-7] Sigmund Freud also contributed to the study of this condition and published his work on *infantile cerebral paralysis* in 1897.[5,6,8] By the 20th century, the diagnostic term evolved into *cerebral palsy* (CP).[5,6] For over 100 years, CP has been the topic of multiple publications, and many authors have worked on and refined its definition and classification.[5,8,9]

DEFINITION OF CEREBRAL PALSY

The current definition of CP provided next was developed by the participants of an International Workshop on Definition and Classification of Cerebral Palsy held in Bethesda, Maryland, on July 11-13, 2004.[9] Rosenbaum et al[9] cited a number of factors that contributed to the need to reconsider and update the definition and classification of CP, including advances in diagnostic imaging technology, changing standards of care for children with disabilities, the existing relationship between motor impairments of a developing child and other disabilities, and new insights related to the etiology of and risk factors for CP.

Cerebral palsy (CP) describes a group of permanent disorders of the development of movement and posture, causing activity limitation, that are attributed to non-progressive disturbances that occurred in the developing fetal or infant brain. The motor disorders of cerebral palsy are often accompanied by disturbances of sensation, perception, cognition, communication, and behaviour, by epilepsy, and by secondary musculoskeletal problems.[9(p 9)]

According to this definition, a person is not considered to have CP if he or she has the following:

- A neurodevelopmental disability that does not "primarily affect movement and posture"[9(p 10)]
- Motor deficits caused by a diagnosed progressive disorder of the brain
- A severe cognitive impairment without any present motor signs, except for some hypotonia[9]

Rahlin M. *Physical Therapy for Children With Cerebral Palsy: An Evidence-Based Approach* (pp 51–62).

CLASSIFICATION OF CEREBRAL PALSY

Historically, CP was classified based on the type of movement abnormality related to muscle tone,[10-12] the anatomical distribution of the involved areas of the body, the severity of motor involvement, and functional abilities.[13-15] Spastic, dyskinetic, ataxic, and mixed types of CP were identified based on the examination of muscle tone abnormalities.[15] The types described relative to the anatomical distribution of involvement included monoplegia, in which only one extremity was affected; hemiplegia, in which upper and lower extremity and the trunk on one side of the body were involved; diplegia, in which all extremities and trunk were affected, with the upper extremities less involved than lower extremities; and quadriplegia, which was characterized by relatively equal involvement of all extremities and trunk.[15-17] The lack of standardization in defining these terms showed to be detrimental to the reliability and validity of this topographic approach.[13,15] A network of 14 centers in 8 European countries, Surveillance of Cerebral Palsy in Europe (SCPE) proposed that CP should be identified as spastic, ataxic, and dyskinetic, with spastic CP differentiated into unilateral or bilateral, and dyskinetic CP further classified into dystonic or choreoathetotic.[18] This effectively implied that the traditional topographic approach to the classification of CP should be abandoned[18]; however, it continues to be widely used in current literature. The degree of involvement described as mild, moderate, or severe proved to be even more subjective,[13] and is now rarely utilized to classify CP.

In 1997, Palisano et al[14] published their Gross Motor Function Classification System (GMFCS) for children with CP that, since that time, has been widely used in research and clinical practice throughout the world.[19] The Delphi Survey methodology was applied to validate the original GMFCS that classified CP into 5 functional levels in the area of gross motor skills for 4 age groups of children (younger than 2 years, 2 to 4 years, 4 to 6 years, and 6 to 12 years).[14] In 2007, the GMFCS was expanded and revised into the GMFCS—E&R to include youth ages 12 to 18 years,[20] and its content validity was established in 2008.[21] This classification system focuses on such meaningful, self-initiated activities of daily living as mobility, sitting, and transfers.[14,20] Children classified in level I demonstrate the most and children in level V the least functional independence (Figure 3-1).[14,20]

The GMFCS is consistent with the International Classification of Functioning, Disability and Health (ICF) that was published by the World Health Organization in 2001.[20-23] Figure 3-2 represents the ICF model that emphasizes the person's health and functional level regardless of whether they have a disability.[23] The ICF classifies the individual's body functions, activities, and participation that comprise the term *functioning*, while *disability* is described in terms of the changes observed in body structures and functions, as well as the limitations in activity and restrictions in participation.[22,23] The ICF model recognizes the interaction of contextual (environmental and personal) factors with the individual's health conditions.[22,23] A children and youth version of the ICF (ICF-CY) was published in 2007.[24] Similar to the ICF-CY, the GMFCS—E&R focuses on the current abilities and limitations exhibited by children and youth in a variety of settings, but specifically, in their gross motor function, while taking into consideration the environmental and personal factors that may affect their functional performance.[20] The reader is referred to Chapter 4 for further discussion of the ICF[22] and ICF-CY.[24]

Research of the psychometric properties of the original GMFCS demonstrated moderate to good interrater reliability[25] and stability of the GMFCS levels over time.[14,26-28] The kappa statistic used as an estimate of interrater reliability in 2 studies was 0.55 to 0.65 for children with CP assessed before their second birthday, and 0.74 to 0.75 for older children.[14,26] A retrospective study that involved a review of 85 charts of children with CP by a developmental pediatrician and a physical therapist yielded a generalizability coefficient of 0.93 as an interrater reliability estimate of the GMFCS.[27]

Research evidence suggests that a child with CP would remain in the same GMFCS level from the age of 1 or 2 years to the age of 12 years.[26-28] This stability of the GMFCS levels over time allowed Wood and Rosenbaum[27] to show that this classification system can be used to predict ambulation in younger children with CP at a later point in time (see Chapter 5). Besides predicting outcomes, other uses of this functional classification system in clinical practice include planning intervention and counseling families of children with CP.[19,27] In addition, according to Gray et al,[19] the GMFCS is widely and increasingly used in research, including both experimental and observational studies. It is important to emphasize that the application of this classification system to different patient populations, such as children with conditions other than CP, as well as individuals older than 18 years, is not appropriate. Finally, because of the GMFCS level stability over time, the use of this system as an outcome measure will not be valid.[19]

Current Classification

As its current definition, the most recent classification of CP was proposed by the participants of the 2004 International Workshop on Definition and Classification of Cerebral Palsy.[9] This classification describes the origin of the problem and the level of involvement exhibited by a person with CP; contains predictive information that can be used by providers of services to ascertain the patient's health care needs; compares the clinical presentation of the individual with CP to that observed in other cases; and allows for tracking the patient's progress over time.[9] Table 3-1 summarizes the components of the current classification system that are discussed next. These components described by Rosenbaum et al[9] include *motor abnormalities, accompanying impairments, anatomical and neuroimaging findings,* and *causation and timing.*[9]

A GMFCS E & R Descriptors and Illustrations for Children between their 6th and 12th birthday

GMFCS Level I

Children walk at home, school, outdoors and in the community. They can climb stairs without the use of a railing. Children perform gross motor skills such as running and jumping, but speed, balance and coordination are limited

GMFCS Level II

Children walk in most settings and climb stairs holding onto a railing. They may experience difficulty walking long distances and balancing on uneven terrain, inclines, in crowded areas or confined spaces. Children may walk with physical assistance, a hand-held mobility device or used wheeled mobility over long distances. Children have only minimal ability to perform gross motor skills such as running and jumping

GMFCS Level III

Children walk using a hand-held mobility device in most indoor settings. They may climb stairs holding onto a railing with supervision or assistance. Children use wheeled mobility when traveling long distances and may self-propel for shorter distances.

GMFCS Level IV

Children use methods of mobility that require physical assistance or powered mobility in most settings. They may walk for short distances at home with physical assistance or use powered mobility or a body support walker when positioned. At school, outdoors and in the community children are transported in a manual wheelchair or use powered mobility.

GMFCS Level V

Children are transported in a manual wheelchair in all settings. Children are limited in their ability to maintain antigravity head and trunk postures and control leg and arm movements.

GMFCS descriptors copyright © Palisano et al. (1997) Dev Med Child Neurol 39:214-23
CanChild: www.canchild.ca

Illustrations copyright © Kerr Graham, Bill Reid and Adrienne Harvey,
The Royal Children's Hospital, Melbourne

Figure 3-1. The Gross Motor Function Classification System (GMFCS) – Expanded and revised for children (A) from 6 to 12 years and (B) from 12 to 18 years of age. (Reproduced with permission from CanChild: www.canchild.ca. GMFCS Descriptors Copyright © Palisano RJ, Rosenbaum PL, Walter SD, Russell DJ, Wood EP, Galuppi BE. Development and reliability of a system to classify gross motor function in children with cerebral palsy. *Dev Med Child Neurol.* 1997;39(4):214-223; and Palisano R, Rosenbaum P, Bartlett D, Livingston M. Content validity of the expanded and revised Gross Motor Function Classification System. *Dev Med Child Neurol.* 2008;50(10):744-750. Illustrations Copyright © Kerr Graham, Bill Reid and Adrienne Harvey, The Royal Children's Hospital, Melbourne, Australia.) *(continued)*

Motor Abnormalities

Motor abnormalities can be classified relative to the abnormal muscle tone and associated atypical movement patterns exhibited by the individual (see Table 3-1).[9] The associated types of CP include spastic, dyskinetic (dystonic or athetoid), and ataxic. Because many children display signs of several tonal abnormalities, Rosenbaum et al[9] recommended that, rather than identifying their presentation as "mixed" as was commonly practiced previously, each case should be classified based on the dominant type of abnormal muscle tone the child exhibits, with other types of tone and involuntary movements described as secondary, if present.[9]

Children with spastic CP demonstrate atypical postures and movement.[15] Spasticity is caused by pyramidal lesions that affect corticobulbar and corticospinal tracts.[10] It can be defined as velocity-dependent hypertonicity characterized by resistance to passive stretch that increases with the increasing speed of movement in the joint and varies depending on the direction of movement (eg, flexion vs extension). A "catch" is usually felt when a quick stretch is applied to a spastic muscle, which results from achieving a threshold joint angle or a threshold speed of passive movement. Spasticity implies the presence of positive and negative neurological signs. The positive signs include hyperreflexia, presence of overflow reflexes, and positive Babinski reflex; the negative signs are muscle weakness, low muscle endurance, and decreased dexterity. Spasticity varies with changes in posture, activity, level of alertness, pain, other sensory input, or emotional state of the child.[10]

Dyskinetic CP is thought to result from lesions to the basal ganglia.[10-12,15] Children with dyskinetic CP may exhibit dystonia or athetosis.[9,15] These two terms describe specific types of movement abnormalities observed in these children.[12]

Figure 3-1 (continued). The Gross Motor Function Classification System (GMFCS) – Expanded and revised for children (A) from 6 to 12 years and (B) from 12 to 18 years of age. (Reproduced with permission from CanChild: www.canchild.ca. GMFCS Descriptors Copyright © Palisano RJ, Rosenbaum PL, Walter SD, Russell DJ, Wood EP, Galuppi BE. Development and reliability of a system to classify gross motor function in children with cerebral palsy. *Dev Med Child Neurol.* 1997;39(4):214-223; and Palisano R, Rosenbaum P, Bartlett D, Livingston M. Content validity of the expanded and revised Gross Motor Function Classification System. *Dev Med Child Neurol.* 2008;50(10):744-750. Illustrations Copyright © Kerr Graham, Bill Reid and Adrienne Harvey, The Royal Children's Hospital, Melbourne, Australia.)

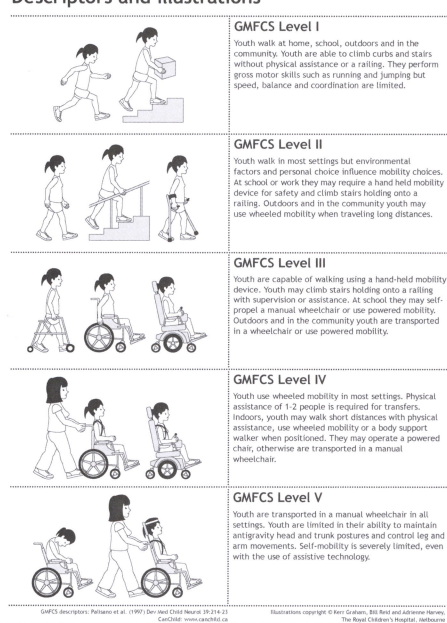

Figure 3-2. The interactive components of the ICF model. (Reproduced with permission from World Health Organization. Towards a common language for functioning, disability and health: ICF, the International Classification of Functioning, Disability and Health. Geneva, Switzerland: World Health Organization; 2002. http://www.who.int/classifications/icf/training/icfbeginnersguide.pdf. Copyright © World Health Organization. All rights reserved.)

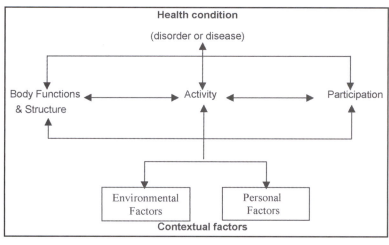

Table 3-1

Components of Cerebral Palsy Classification

DIMENSIONS	COMPONENTS	DESCRIPTION
Motor abnormalities	Nature and typology of the motor disorder	The observed tonal abnormalities assessed on examination (eg, hypertonia, hypotonia) as well as the diagnosed movement disorders present, such as spasticity, ataxia, dystonia, athetosis
	Functional motor abilities	The extent to which the individual is limited in his or her motor function, including oromotor and speech function
Accompanying impairments	Later-developing musculoskeletal problems	Presence or absence
	Non-motor neuro-developmental or sensory problems	The presence or absence of seizures; hearing or vision impairments; or attentional, behavioral, communicative, and/or cognitive deficits, and the extent to which impairments interact in individuals with CP
Anatomical and neuro-imaging findings	Anatomic distribution	The parts of the body (limbs, trunk, bulbar region, etc) affected by motor impairments or limitations
	Neuro-imaging findings	The neuroanatomic findings on CT or MRI imaging, such as ventricular enlargement, white matter loss, or brain anomaly
Causation and timing	Causation	Whether there is a clearly identified cause, as is usually the case with post-natal CP (eg, meningitis, head injury) or when brain malformations are present
	Timing	The presumed time frame during which the injury occurred, if known

Abbreviations: CP, cerebral palsy; CT, computerized tomography; MRI, magnetic resonance imaging.

Adapted with permission from Rosenbaum P, Paneth N, Leviton A, et al. A report: the definition and classification of cerebral palsy April 2006. *Dev Med Child Neurol.* 2007;49(s109):8-14. Copyright © 2007 John Wiley & Sons, Inc. All Rights Reserved.

Dystonia is characterized by involuntary muscle contractions that can be sustained or intermittent, which are usually elicited or exaggerated by attempted active movement.[10-12] Similar to variation in spasticity discussed previously, atypical postures and repetitive movements seen in children with dystonia vary in their quality and severity depending on the child's level of alertness or emotional state, as well as on the specific task at hand and the position of the child's body.[10,12] Athetosis can be described as uncontrolled, continuous, and slow writhing movements that result in the inability to maintain postural stability.[12,15] Athetosis affects hands and feet greater than proximal parts of extremities, but can be also observed in the trunk, neck, and face.[12] Unlike dystonia, it can be seen at rest, but, similar to dystonia, it may also increase during active movement and attempts to maintain a stable posture.[12]

Ataxic CP results from cerebellar lesions.[15,29] Sanger et al[29] defined ataxia as "an inability to generate a normal or expected voluntary movement trajectory that cannot be attributed to weakness or involuntary muscle activity about the affected joints."(p 2159) Ataxia is characterized by dysmetria (under- or overshooting when reaching for a target), dyssynergia (inability to coordinate movements that involve multiple joints at the same time), and dysdiadochokinesia (inability to perform rapidly alternating, rhythmic movements). Children with ataxic CP may demonstrate intention tremor and excessive movement variability. Many parts of the body may be affected, which results in inaccurate movements of extremities, decreased trunk control, and atypical gait.[29]

Another way to classify *motor abnormalities* in children with CP, besides the muscle tone assessment, is through the examination of their motor function, including gross motor, manual, oral motor, and speech-related skills (see Table 3-1).[9] As discussed earlier, the GMFCS is used to classify CP into five functional levels based on the child's gross motor skills (see Figure 3-1).[14,20] The development of classification systems for the arm and hand function,[30] as well as for communication,[31] followed the development of the GMFCS. Similar to the GMFCS, the Manual Ability Classification System (MACS)[30] and the Communication Function Classification System (CFCS)[31] were designed to classify function in individuals with CP into 5 distinct levels, with level I designated as the highest, and level V as the lowest functional level (Table 3-2). The MACS and the CFCS are also consistent with the ICF model as they look at the manual ability and communication function, respectively, look at their activity and participation level, and acknowledge the contribution of personal and environmental factors to functional performance in children with CP.[30-32]

		TABLE 3-2	

THE FIVE LEVELS OF GROSS MOTOR FUNCTION (GMFCS), MANUAL ABILITY (MACS), AND COMMUNICATION FUNCTION (CFCS) CLASSIFICATION SYSTEMS

	CLASSIFICATION SYSTEMS		
Levels	*GMFCS*	*MACS*	*CFCS*
I	Walks without limitations	Handles objects easily and successfully	Sends and receives with familiar and unfamiliar partners effectively and efficiently
II	Walks with limitations	Handles most objects but with somewhat reduced quality and/or speed of achievement	Sends and receives with familiar and unfamiliar partners but may need extra time
III	Walks using a hand-held mobility device	Handles objects with difficulty; needs help to prepare and/or modify activities	Sends and receives with familiar partners effectively, but not with unfamiliar partners
IV	Self-mobility with limitations; may use powered mobility	Handles a limited selection of easily managed objects in adapted situations	Inconsistently sends and/or receives even with familiar partners
V	Transported in a manual wheelchair	Does not handle objects and has severely limited ability to perform even simple actions	Seldom effectively sends and receives, even with familiar partners

The MACS focuses on the manual ability in children with CP, including the use of hands and handling objects in their everyday life.[30] It does not report on the level of function of each hand but rather looks at the bilateral hand use during age-appropriate activities, such as playing, eating, dressing, writing, and other tasks, that are performed within the child's base of support. The functional levels differ depending on the quality and quantity of upper extremity movement and required adaptations or assistance provided to complete the everyday activities. Research conducted by the MACS authors supported its construct validity. The interrater reliability was shown to be good[25] for therapists and also for pairs of therapists and parents of children with CP, with the ICC values of 0.97 and 0.96 reported, respectively.[30]

The focus of the CFCS is on the effectiveness of communication with a partner.[31] Communication is looked at as the result of an interaction of relevant ICF components of body structure and function, activity, and participation with the contextual factors. The ICF components relevant to communication are speech production, use of language, and the child's hearing skills. Some examples of contextual factors include a specific setting where communication takes place, methods of augmentative and alternative communication used, and family culture. Content validity of the CFCS was established using the Delphi Survey methodology applied with health care practitioners, educators, adults with CP, and caregivers of children with CP. The interrater reliability of

the CFCS was shown to be moderate,[25] with weighted kappa statistic of 0.49 and 0.66 reported for the parent-professional pairs and professionals only, respectively. Weighted kappa increased to 0.77 for professionals who used this classification system with children older than 4 years of age.[31] The test-retest reliability of the CFCS was good,[25] with the reported weighted kappa statistic of 0.82.[31]

Cooley Hidecker et al[32] used a case series of 222 children with CP, age range 2 to 17 years, to examine the relationships among the GMFCS, MACS, and CFCS levels. The results showed moderate correlation[33] of the GMFCS and MACS, as well as MACS and CFCS levels, with Spearman rs equal to 0.69 and 0.54, respectively. Fair correlation[33] between the GMFCS and CFCS levels was found (Spearman rs equal to 0.47).[32] Only 16% of the study participants were assigned the same level of classification in all 3 systems. This indicated that using 1 of 3 classification system would have a low predictive value for classifying the child's function in the other 2 areas. Cooley Hidecker at el[32] suggested that using a functional profile that consists of the child's CFCS, GMFCS, and MACS levels may be helpful for interprofessional and professional-family communication, as well as for planning appropriate intervention that would address the individual's mobility, object manipulation, and communication activity needs and their relationship to participation in meaningful situations of daily life.

Another area of motor function besides gross motor, manual ability and communication that requires special attention is the oral motor function.[9] In spite of the fact that 21% of children with CP have difficulties chewing and swallowing,[34] a classification system that addressed this functional area was not published until 2014.[35] Sellers et al[35] developed and validated the Eating and Drinking Ability Classification System (EDACS) for use with individuals with CP older than 3 years of age. Similar to the classification systems discussed earlier, the EDACS categorizes this area of functioning into 5 levels, with level I being the highest ("Eats and drinks safely and efficiently"), and level V being the lowest ("Unable to eat and drink safely; tube feeding may be considered to provide nutrition"). In addition, the EDACS specifies 3 levels of assistance the person would need in order to eat and drink efficiently and safely: *independent, requires assistance,* and *totally dependent.* This classification system was shown to have good reliability[25] for speech-language pathologists (SLPs) and also for pairs of SLPs and parents of children and young adults with CP, with the ICC values of 0.93 and 0.86 reported, respectively. It is important to note that Sellers et al[35] suggested that, because the association between the EDACS and the GMFCS levels in their study was found to be only moderate, the eating and drinking abilities of a person with CP would need to be considered separately from his or her level of gross motor function.

Accompanying Impairments

Other impairments, besides motor, negatively affect function and limit activity in children and adults with CP.[9] These *accompanying impairments* are numerous and include alterations of structure and function of many body systems that will be discussed in greater detail in Chapter 5. The current classification of CP calls for careful documentation of presence or absence of seizures; cognitive, behavioral, attentional, or emotional problems; vision and hearing deficits; as well as secondary musculoskeletal impairments (see Table 3-1). Specifically, epilepsy should be acknowledged as present when the individual has been observed to have "two or more afebrile, non-neonatal seizures."[9(p 13)] The degree of visual impairment needs to be recorded separately for each eye, if present, and the decibel loss assessed and documented separately for each ear, if applicable. Finally, the IQ score should be obtained to identify the presence or absence and the extent of intellectual disability, if any.[9]

Anatomical and Neuroimaging Findings

According to the current classification of CP, the *anatomic distribution* of motor involvement needs to be described as specific impairments of posture and movement in the person's trunk, each upper and lower extremity, and oropharynx.[9] Rosenbaum et al[9] recommended that the use of the terms *diplegia* and *quadriplegia* be avoided unless their precise definitions are provided. These authors suggested that the terms *unilateral* and *bilateral* may be better suited to classify CP based on the anatomical findings. However, they also acknowledged that children with unilateral CP may exhibit motor deficits on the "uninvolved" side of the body,

and children with bilateral CP may demonstrate asymmetrical involvement of their upper and lower extremities and trunk.[9] Furthermore, Dobson et al[36] showed that children with unilateral CP display a wide spectrum of variation in clinical presentation, including muscle tone, strength and isolated movement of the "involved" extremities, and gait patterns. Their levels of gross motor and upper extremity function also vary. Therefore, separate systems to classify the upper and lower extremity function in these children need to be used to supplement the information provided by the GMFCS and MACS.[36]

In the past, the relationship between the extent of disability and the amount of brain damage in children with CP was found to be weak.[9] However, the ongoing advances in diagnostic imaging technology and the development of objective functional assessment instruments are making this relationship stronger.[9] Therefore, the American Academy of Neurology recommends that *neuroimaging findings* be obtained for every child with CP.[37] Ashwal et al[37] reviewed relevant diagnostic imaging studies published between 1966 and 2002 and found that 62% to 93% of children with CP (77% on average) were reported to have abnormal computed tomography (CT) scans, and 68% to 100% (89% on average) had abnormal magnetic resonance imaging (MRI) results. This indicated that an MRI study would be the preferred imaging method for this patient population. In addition, in many cases, a combination of medical history and neuroimaging findings was found to be helpful in determining the etiology of CP and the timing of brain insult.[37]

Causation and Timing

Causes of CP are rarely clear-cut.[9,15,37] A combination of risk factors and prenatal, perinatal, or postnatal adverse events makes the identification of the exact cause in each specific case difficult.[9,15,37] If the child's medical history and physical examination are suggestive of the diagnosis of CP, an MRI study should be ordered. If the MRI results are abnormal, an attempt should be made to establish the etiology of CP. When the neuroimaging findings show a malformation of the brain, the child may need to be referred for genetic testing. If, on the other hand, the MRI study suggests a stroke in a child with unilateral involvement, further diagnostic testing for blood coagulation problems is indicated.[37] It is important to note that Rosenbaum et al[9] cautioned clinicians against running to conclusions regarding the *timing* of the neurological insult, unless there was a clear indication that a specific contributing event had occurred "in a specific time-window."[(p 13)]

Implications of the Shift to Current Definition and Classification of Cerebral Palsy

As stated earlier in this chapter, despite a significant shift in the definition and classification of CP[9,13] that has gained momentum since its publication, many authors continue using the language of traditional topographic classification.[37-40] Furthermore, Bax et al,[39] in departure from the definition and classification proposed by the 2004 International Workshop,[9] advocated for abandoning the diagnostic term *CP* in favor of another term, a *neurodevelopmental disorder of childhood*, that would place less emphasis on motor problems and, besides the motor concerns, encompass all other deficits while stressing those related to vision, hearing, cognition, behavior, epilepsy, and autism. This indicates that the shift to the new definition and classification, although widely spread, is far from being completed, and one should expect a continued discussion on the topic in current literature, which is likely to lead to further change. In the meantime, being aware of differences in opinion is important for the reader so that any confusion associated with this process may be avoided.

It is also important to mention that, although the terms *hemiplegia*, *diplegia*, and *quadriplegia* are still frequently found in published literature, the use of these terms in this book will be avoided whenever possible for consistency with the new CP classification. Instead, the terms *unilateral* and *bilateral* will be utilized to classify spastic CP. If the authors of a cited study do not specify the GMFCS and MACS levels of the participants with bilateral spastic CP and report on them as having *diplegia* or *quadriplegia*, an effort will be made to describe motor abnormalities related to the amount of their upper and lower extremity involvement as equal (quadriplegia) or greater involvement of lower than upper extremities (diplegia). This approach will bridge the gap between the new and traditional topographic classifications of CP only partially, but at the same time, it will preserve the meaning of diagnostic terms used by the authors of published research.

Some of the implications of the shift to current definition and classification of CP are related to medicolegal practices.[41] Mantovani[41] highlighted the importance of the *neuroimaging* and *causation and timing* aspects of the new CP classification for handling litigation related to a common perception that the diagnosis of CP is linked to a perinatal brain injury. The emphasis on the need for a diagnostic MRI study would allow one to rule out the injury to the brain as the cause of CP in cases when a congenital brain malformation is present, or when a metabolic or a genetic disorder is the primary cause of the motor problems exhibited by the infant.[41] In addition, the new classification acknowledges that, in many cases, a multitude of factors identified in the infant's prenatal, perinatal, and postnatal history may interact and create a complex situation, in which it may not be possible to determine the specific cause of CP and/or the specific timing of the brain insult.[9,41] This acknowledgment would play an important role in the testimony on the subject provided by legal experts.[41]

INCIDENCE AND ETIOLOGY OF CEREBRAL PALSY

The incidence of CP is reported to be 2 to 3 per 1000 live births,[5,15,38,42] with increased rates identified in infants born prematurely (11% to 20%).[43,44] Because of the increased survival of infants born preterm, the overall rates of CP have remained relatively unchanged in spite of significant advances in medical technology and neonatal care.[15,42]

By definition, CP results from "non-progressive disturbances" that occur in the brain of a developing infant or a fetus.[9(p 9)] The results of MRI scans performed in a European study of a population sample of 351 children with CP demonstrated that 42.5% of these children had periventricular leukomalacia, 12.8% had lesions in basal ganglia, 9.4% had cortical and subcortical lesions, and 7.4% had focal infarcts.[38] Brain malformations were found in 9.1% of the study participants; 7.1% had miscellaneous lesions, while the results of 11.7% of MRI scans were normal.[38]

The etiology of the brain insult leading to CP is complex and its causes can be classified into prenatal, perinatal, or postnatal.[15,42] In addition, risk factors that create a chain of events leading to CP have been identified. These risk factors are multiple and may exist before and during pregnancy, during labor and delivery, and early after birth.[15,42] Reddihough and Collins[42] emphasized the importance of making a distinction between the risk factors for CP and its causes because medical histories of many individuals with this disorder may not point to a specific identifiable single cause, but may rather paint a sequential picture of events associated with the subsequent diagnosis of CP. Information on the known causes of CP and its risk factors is summarized in Tables 3-3 and 3-4, respectively.[42,45]

Contrary to a previously common belief, only a small percentage of cases of CP result from perinatal causes (see Table 3-3).[41,42] In the absence of clear-cut evidence pointing to a perinatal or a postnatal brain insult, a prenatal cause is considered to be more likely.[42] Furthermore, even if specific perinatal problems are identified as possible causative factors for hypoxia leading to CP, specific essential criteria need to be present before a determination confirming a cause-and-effect relationship can be made.[42,46] These criteria include the presence of metabolic acidosis in samples of fetal intrapartum, umbilical arterial, or early neonatal blood; moderate or severe neonatal encephalopathy of early onset in infants born at or after 34 weeks gestation; and presentation consistent with dyskinetic or spastic quadriplegic CP.[46] In the majority of cases, neural injury leading to CP occurs in the prenatal period.[42] Besides those listed by Reddihough and Collins[42] based on their review of literature (see Table 3-3), other prenatal causes of brain insult include placental lesions affecting maternal-fetal circulation,[47-49] and congenital heart disease (CHD).[50] According to Limperopoulos,[50] CHD may compromise fetal blood flow and, specifically, cerebral perfusion, leading to a neurological insult, with structural brain damage identified via cranial ultrasound in 40% to 60% of infants with CHD born full term.

DIAGNOSIS OF CEREBRAL PALSY

Obtaining a definitive diagnosis of CP is not a simple task.[1,5,9,15,37] The current definition and classification of CP

	TABLE 3-3	
PRENATAL, PERINATAL, AND POSTNATAL CAUSES OF CEREBRAL PALSY		
TIMING OF BRAIN INSULT (% OF CASES OF CP)	**CAUSES OF BRAIN INSULT**	**COMMENTS**
Prenatal (75%)	Congenital brain malformations	Are often associated with abnormalities of other body systems besides CNS. Some cortical malformations have genetic origin.
	Vascular events	Example: occlusion of middle cerebral artery
	Maternal infections in the first and second trimesters	Examples: rubella, cytomegalovirus, toxoplasmosis
	Rare genetic syndromes, maternal ingestion of toxins, metabolic disorders	Less common causes
Perinatal (6-8%)	Problems during labor and delivery associated with perinatal asphyxia	Hypoxia may be caused by umbilical cord prolapse, obstructed labor, or antepartum hemorrhage.
	Neonatal problems	Examples: untreated jaundice, hypoglycemia, severe infection
Postnatal (10-18%)	Infections	Examples: meningitis, septicemia, malaria
	Injuries	Examples: MVA, near-drowning, non-accidental injuries
	Life-threatening events	Examples: CVA, sequelae of surgical intervention for congenital malformations

Abbreviations: CP, cerebral palsy; MVA, motor-vehicle accident; CVA, cerebrovascular accident.

Compiled from Reddihough and Collins.[42]

call for giving a careful consideration to all aspects of the child's presentation before making such a diagnosis.[1,9,15,37] Physical therapists are important members of the interdisciplinary team who are able to accurately identify the signs of atypical motor development, including the abnormalities of muscle tone, movement, and postural control; the anatomical distribution of involvement; and activity limitations and participation restrictions, all of which may point to a possible diagnosis of CP.[15] When this is the case, the physical therapist communicates the evaluation findings to the child's pediatrician, pediatric neurologist, and other medical professionals working with the child's family. The interprofessional collaboration is crucial for the success in ruling out other conditions and making an accurate diagnosis of CP whenever possible.[1,15] The roles and responsibilities of the members of the interdisciplinary team in this process and in the overall management of children and adults with CP, and the interprofessional approach to patient care will be discussed in Chapter 6.

When *motor abnormalities* are present and *accompanying impairments* are observed, a diagnostic imaging study may greatly contribute to obtaining more definitive information about the child's condition.[1,9,15,37] Therefore, the physical therapy evaluation may lead to a referral to a pediatric neurologist who would consider ordering an MRI of the brain. Based on the *neuroimaging findings*, further testing may be required to identify the possible causes and timing of the brain insult, if present.[9,37] A common problem that arises when a diagnostic MRI study is ordered is the need for anesthesia or sedation of an infant or a young child to prevent motion artifacts from interfering with the MRI examination quality.[51-55] Children require more frequent and "deeper" sedation and are at a higher risk for related adverse events than adults.[51] Hypoxia has been reported as the most common adverse event associated with sedation or anesthesia in infants and children undergoing nonsurgical procedures, including diagnostic imaging.[51,52] Other adverse events may include vomiting, excessive secretions, unexpected apnea, stridor, and laryngospasm.[51-53]

As frequently seen in clinical practice, parents are often concerned about the side effects of general anesthesia or sedation and may not be inclined to agree to a diagnostic imaging test unless they see it as being absolutely necessary. Physicians frequently have the same concerns and may not order or may postpone an MRI especially when its results are not expected to alter the services the child is already receiving. Studies that used an infant immobilizer device instead of anesthesia or sedation during diagnostic imaging procedures showed

	TABLE 3-4	

RISK FACTORS FOR CEREBRAL PALSY

TIMING WHEN PRESENT	RISK FACTORS	COMMENTS
Before pregnancy	Maternal factors	Delayed menstruation onset, irregular periods, too short or too long intervals between pregnancies; maternal seizures, intellectual disability, or thyroid disease; age over 35 years
	Advanced paternal age	Associated with dyskinetic CP
	Sibling factors	Previous fetal death, sibling with motor deficits
	Parental race	Increased risk of prematurity and CP in Black infants
During pregnancy	Pre-eclampsia	Increases risk for CP in infants born full-term
	Maternal hormone therapy	Estrogen or thyroid hormone
	Antepartum hemorrhage	Increases risk of CP in infants born prematurely
	Vascular events associated with genetic mutations	Placental thrombosis or neonatal stroke
	Multiple pregnancy, including twins	Associated with premature birth, IUGR, complications during delivery and birth defects
	Antenatal death of a twin	Associated with a 20% risk of brain damage in the live-born twin
	Severe IUGR	Strongly associated with white matter lesions
During labor	Events leading to perinatal asphyxia	Massive hemorrhage, maternal shock, prolapsed umbilical cord, abnormal presentation, cephalopelvic disproportion, shoulder dystocia in a large infant, prolonged labor, emergency C-section, premature separation of placenta
	Chorioamnionitis	Associated with CP in infants born full term and with PVL in full-term and preterm infants
	Meconium stained amniotic fluid	Associated with meconium aspiration syndrome, which may lead to CP
During delivery	Low birth weight	Depends on intrauterine growth and gestational age at birth
	Low Apgar scores	Scores of 0 to 3 at 5 minutes are highly associated with CP
In neona-tal period	Neonatal seizures	Strong association with CP
	Parenchymal brain damage with ventricular dilation	Identified via cerebral ultrasound in infants born preterm
	Cardiovascular and pulmonary problems	Respiratory disease in full-term and preterm infants; PDA, blood transfusion, hypotension, pneumothorax, prolonged ventilation in infants born preterm
	Sepsis, hyponatremia, total parenteral nutrition	In infants born preterm

Abbreviations: C-section, cesarean section; CP, cerebral palsy; IUGR, intrauterine growth restriction; PDA, patent ductus arteriosus; PVL, periventricular leukomalacia.

Compiled from Reddihough and Collins[42] and Wu et al.[45]

promising results that may help in the decision-making process in such cases.[54,55] The use of a device that consisted of a bean bag and a vacuum pump during imaging studies for 6-month-old and younger infants yielded motion artifact-free MRI and CT scans in 92.8% to 100% of cases.[54,55]

Rosenbloom[1] emphasized that, when attempting to answer the question of whether a child has CP, all pieces of the puzzle need to be examined in depth. The child's family should be given a comprehensive and accurate description of all components that comprise the diagnosis, and their meaning, including the information on prognosis, needs to be explained in reasonable detail whenever possible.[1] When the diagnosis of CP is obtained and discussed with the family, appropriate services that address the alterations in the child's body structures and functions, activity limitations and participation issues can be initiated. Once the physical therapist establishes a rapport with the family, the child's parents can be provided with important evidence-based information related to the prognosis for ambulation, employment, and independent living, when appropriate.

REFERENCES

1. Rosenbloom L. Definition and classification of cerebral palsy. Definition, classification, and the clinician. *Dev Med Child Neurol.* 2007;49(suppl 109):43.

2. Little WJ. Hospital for the cure of deformities: course of lectures on the deformity of the human frame. *Lancet.* 1843;41:350-354.

3. Brand RA. Biographical sketch: William John Little, FRCS (1810-1894). *Clin Orthop Relat Res.* 2012;470(5):1249-1251.

4. Little WJ. Hospital for the cure of deformities: course of lectures on the deformity of the human frame. *Lancet.* 1843;41:318-322.

5. Morris C. Definition and classification of cerebral palsy: a historical perspective. *Dev Med Child Neurol.* 2007;49(suppl 109):3-7.

6. Kavcic A, Vodušek DB. A historical perspective on cerebral palsy as a concept and a diagnosis. *Eur J Neurol.* 2005;12:582-587.

7. Osler W. *The Cerebral Palsies of Children.* Philadelphia, PA: P. Blakiston, Son & Co; 1889.

8. Freud S. *Infantile Cerebral Paralysis.* Coral Gables, FL: University of Miami Press; 1968.

9. Rosenbaum P, Paneth N, Leviton A, et al. A report: the definition and classification of cerebral palsy April 2006. *Dev Med Child Neurol.* 2007;49(suppl 109):8-14. Erratum in: *Dev Med Child Neurol.* 2007;49(6):480.

10. Sanger TD, Delgado MR, Gaebler-Spira D, Hallet M, Mink JW, Task Force on Childhood Motor Disorders. Classification and definition of disorders causing hypertonia in childhood. *Pediatrics.* 2003;111(1):e89-e97.

11. Sanger TD. Toward a definition of childhood dystonia. *Curr Opin Pediatr.* 2004;16(6):623-627.

12. Sanger TD, Chen D, Fehlings DL, et al. Definition and classification of hyperkinetic movements in childhood. *Mov Disord.* 2010;25(11):1538-1549.

13. Gorter JW, Rosenbaum PL, Hanna SE, et al. Limb distribution, motor impairment, and functional classification of cerebral palsy. *Dev Med Child Neurol.* 2004;46:461-467.

14. Palisano RJ, Rosenbaum PL, Walter SD, Russell DJ, Wood EP, Galuppi BE. Development and reliability of a system to classify gross motor function in children with cerebral palsy. *Dev Med Child Neurol.* 1997;39(4):214-223.

15. Wright M, Wallman L. Cerebral palsy. In: Campbell SK, Palisano RJ, Orlin MN, eds. *Physical Therapy for Children.* 4th ed. St. Louis, MO: Saunders; 2012:577-627.

16. Balf CL, Ingram TTS. Problems in classification of cerebral palsy in childhood. *Br Med J.* 1955;2:163-166.

17. Minear WL. A classification of cerebral palsy. *Pediatrics.* 1956;18:841-852.

18. Surveillance of cerebral palsy in Europe (SCPE). Surveillance of cerebral palsy in Europe: a collaboration of cerebral palsy surveys and registries. *Dev Med Child Neurol.* 2000;42:816-824.

19. Gray L, Ng H, Bartlett D. The Gross Motor Function Classification System: an update on impact and clinical utility. *Pediatr Phys Ther.* 2010;22:315-320.

20. Palisano R, Rosenbaum P, Bartlett D, Livingston M. *GMFCS – E & R, Gross Motor Function System, Expanded and Revised.* http://cpnet.canchild.ca/en/resources/42-gross-motor-function-classification-system-expanded-revised-gmfcs-e-r. Accessed January 23, 2016.

21. Palisano R, Rosenbaum P, Bartlett D, Livingston M. Content validity of the expanded and revised Gross Motor Function Classification System. *Dev Med Child Neurol.* 2008;50(10):744-750.

22. World Health Organization. *International Classification of Functioning, Disability and Health.* Geneva, Switzerland: World Health Organization; 2001.

23. World Health Organization. Towards a common language for functioning, disability and health: ICF, the International Classification of Functioning, Disability and Health. Geneva, Switzerland: World Health Organization. http://www.who.int/classifications/icf/training/icfbeginnersguide.pdf?ua=1. Published 2002. Accessed March 8, 2015.

24. World Health Organization. *International Classification of Functioning, Disability and Health: Children and Youth Version.* Geneva, Switzerland: World Health Organization; 2007.

25. Portney LG, Watkins MP. Reliability of measurements. In: Portney LG, Watkins MP, eds. *Foundations of Clinical Research: Applications to Practice.* 3rd ed. Upper Saddle River, NJ: Pearson Education, Inc.; 2009:77-96.

26. Liu UM, Thawinchain N, Palisano RJ, Valvano J. The interrater reliability and stability of the Gross Motor Function Classification System. *Pediatr Phys Ther.* 1998;10:174-175.

27. Wood E, Rosenbaum P. The Gross Motor Function Classification System for cerebral palsy: a study of reliability and stability over time. *Dev Med Child Neurol.* 2000;42:292-296.

28. Bodkin AW, Robinson C, Perales F. Reliability and validity of the Gross Motor Function Classification System for cerebral palsy. *Pediatr Phys Ther.* 2003;15:247-252.

29. Sanger TD, Chen D, Delgado MR, Gaebler-Spira D, Hallet M, Mink JW, Task Force on Childhood Motor Disorders. Definition and classification of negative motor signs in childhood. *Pediatrics.* 2006;118:2159-2167.

30. Eliasson AC, Krumlinde-Sundholm L, Rösblad B, et al. The Manual Ability Classification System (MACS) for children with cerebral palsy: scale development and evidence of validity and reliability. *Dev Med Child Neurol.* 2006;48(7):549-554.

31. Cooley Hidecker MJ, Paneth N, Rosenbaum P, et al. Developing and validating the Communication Function Classification System for individuals with cerebral palsy. *Dev Med Child Neurol.* 2011;53:704-710.

32. Cooley Hidecker MJ, Ho NT, Dodge N, et al. Inter-relationships of functional status in cerebral palsy: analyzing gross motor function, manual ability, and communication function classification systems in children. *Dev Med Child Neurol.* 2012;54:737-742.

33. Portney LG, Watkins MP. Correlation. In: Portney LG, Watkins MP, eds. *Foundations of Clinical Research: Applications to Practice.* 3rd ed. Upper Saddle River, NJ: Pearson Education, Inc.; 2009:523-538.

34. Parkes J, Hill N, Platt MJ, Donnelly C. Oromotor dysfunction and communication impairments in children with cerebral palsy: a register study. *Dev Med Child Neurol.* 2010;52(12):1113-1119.

35. Sellers D, Mandy A, Pennington L, Hankins M, Morris C. Development and reliability of a system to classify the eating and drinking ability of people with cerebral palsy. *Dev Med Child Neurol.* 2014;56(3):245-252.

36. Dobson F, Morris ME, Baker R, Graham HK. Unilateral cerebral palsy: a population-based study of gait and motor function. *Dev Med Child Neurol.* 2011;53(5):429-435.

37. Ashwal S, Russman BS, Blasco PA, et al. Practice parameter: diagnostic assessment of the child with cerebral palsy: report of the Quality Standards Subcommittee of the American Academy of Neurology and the Practice Committee of the Child Neurology Society. *Neurology.* 2004;62(6):851-63.

38. Bax M, Tydeman C, Flodmark O. Clinical and MRI correlates of cerebral palsy: the European cerebral palsy study. *JAMA.* 2006;296(13):1602-1608.

39. Bax M, Flodmark O, Tydeman C. From syndrome toward disease. *Dev Med Child Neurol.* 2007;49(suppl 109):39-41.

40. Majnemer A, Shevell M, Hall N, Poulin C, Law M. Developmental and functional abilities in children with cerebral palsy as related to pattern and level of motor function. *J Chil Neurol.* 2010;25:1236-1241.

41. Mantovani JF. Definition and classification of CP: medical-legal and service implications. *Dev Med Child Neurol.* 2007;49(suppl 109):42.

42. Reddihough DS, Collins KJ. The epidemiology and causes of cerebral palsy. *Aust J Physiother.* 2003;49:7-12.

43. Msall ME. Complexity of the cerebral palsy syndromes: toward a developmental neuroscience approach. *JAMA.* 2006;296(13):1650-1652.

44. Vohr BR, Wright LL, Poole WK, McDonald SA. Neurodevelopmental outcomes of extremely low birth weight infants <32 weeks' gestation between 1993 and 1998. *Pediatrics.* 2005;116:635-643.

45. Wu YW, Croen LA, Shah SJ, Newman TB, Najjar DV. Cerebral palsy in a term population: risk factors and neuroimaging findings. *Pediatrics.* 2006;118(2):690-697.

46. MacLennan A. A template for defining a casual relation between acute intrapartum events and cerebral palsy: international consensus statement. *BMJ.* 1999;319:1054-1059.

47. Redline RW. Disorders of placental circulation and the fetal brain. *Clin Perinatol.* 2009;36(3):549-559.

48. Scher MS, Belfar H, Martin J, Painter MJ. Destructive brain lesions of presumed fetal onset: antepartum causes of cerebral palsy. *Pediatrics.* 1991;88(5):898-906.

49. Redline RW. Infections and other inflammatory conditions. *Semin Diagn Pathol.* 2007;24(1):5-13.

50. Limperopoulos C. Disorders of the fetal circulation and the fetal brain. *Clin Perinatol.* 2009;36(3):561-577.

51. Cravero JP, Blike GT, Beach M, et al. Incidence and nature of adverse events during pediatric sedation/anesthesia for procedures outside the operating room: report from the Pediatric Sedation Research Consortium. *Pediatrics.* 2006;118(3):1087-1096.

52. Kannikeswaran N, Chen X, Sethuraman U. Utility of endtidal carbon dioxide monitoring in detection of hypoxia during sedation for brain magnetic resonance imaging in children with developmental disabilities. *Pediatr Anesth.* 2011;21(12):1241-1246.

53. Lee YJ, Kim do K, Kwak YH, Kim HB, Park JH, Jung JH. Analysis of the appropriate age and weight for pediatric patient sedation for magnetic resonance imaging. *Am J Emerg Med.* 2012;30(7):1189-1195.

54. Golan A, Marco R, Raz H, Shany E. Imaging in the newborn: infant immobilizer obviates the need for anesthesia. *Isr Med Assoc J.* 2011;13(11):663-665.

55. Neubauer V, Griesmaier E, Baumgartner K, Mallouhi A, Keller M, Kiechl-Kohlendorfer U. Feasibility of cerebral MRI in non-sedated preterm-born infants at term-equivalent age: report of a single centre. *Acta Paediatr.* 2011;100(12):1544-1547.

Alterations in Body Structures and Functions, Activity Limitations, and Participation Issues in Children With Cerebral Palsy

...a detailed analysis of the domains that make up health and disability shows that these two basic constructs are in fact different manifestations of the same domains of functioning...

Nenad Kostanjsek[1]

The International Classification of Functioning, Disability and Health (ICF) places health and disability on a single but multidimensional "ruler" that measures human functioning.[1-3] Since the time of its publication in 2001, the ICF has been widely adopted throughout the world, including the United States.[1,4-6] This classification is applicable not only to persons with disabilities, but to all people throughout their life span as they proceed along a continuous change in their state of health.[1-3] At every given point in time, each person exhibits a specific level of functional abilities in multiple areas that can be viewed at different levels, including body structures and functions, individual activities, and participation in the society. In addition, one's functioning and disability are observed in a unique context of a variety of environmental and personal factors. As discussed in Chapter 3, all components of the ICF Model interact with each other (see Figure 3-2), and this complex relationship determines the individual's current state of health, functioning, and disability.[1-3]

The ICF components can be described using both positive and negative terms.[2] The classification of *body structures and functions* is related to body systems, with structures representing each system's anatomical parts and functions associated with its physiology. A problem or alteration in the structure or function of a body system constitutes its *impairment*.

The term *activity* refers to the performance of a specific task; thus, difficulties encountered during the task completion are seen as *activity limitations*. Being involved in a specific life situation constitutes *participation*, which may be negatively affected by obstacles or problems that would represent *participation restrictions*. The environmental and personal factors comprise the context in which each individual lives and functions. The *environmental factors* include physical, psychological, and social living and working environments, as well as such societal entities as social services, government agencies, the legal system and its norms, and others. These factors may affect the person's body structures and functions, activities, or participation in a positive or a negative way. As for the *personal factors*, these constitute a set of specific traits of each individual, including his or her gender, age, lifestyle, education, past experiences, patterns of behavior, temperament, and other characteristic features and, as such, they are not included into the ICF classification system. However, these factors may play a positive or a negative role in rehabilitation and affect the results of health-related interventions or contribute to the person's disability.[2]

According to WHO,[2] the ICF does the following:

- Serves as a scientific foundation for studying the determinants of health and the outcomes of health-related states

Rahlin M. *Physical Therapy for Children With Cerebral Palsy: An Evidence-Based Approach* (pp 63-85).
© 2016 SLACK Incorporated.

- Provides a universal language for multiple users, from health care professionals, to policymakers, to general public
- Allows practitioners and researchers throughout the world to collect, record, and compare data
- Establishes a standardized health information coding system

Therefore, the ICF can be used as a multipurpose tool in many areas, from research and survey data collection and analysis to planning assessment, intervention, and evaluation of outcomes, and to education and making changes to social policy.[2]

A children and youth version of the ICF (ICF-CY) published in 2007 acknowledges and categorizes the rapid changes related to physical growth and development observed during infancy, childhood and adolescence.[7] It includes the category of developmental delay, which assists teachers, parents, and clinicians in assessing the child's needs related to education and health. In addition, this classification recognizes the effects of the child's social and physical environments on his or her growth, learning, and development; helps identify the areas where changes in education, health care, and social services are necessary; and provides a unified framework for related coding. The ICF-CY includes modified and new classification codes for body structures and functions, activity, and participation, as well as for the environmental contextual factors that play a significant supporting or restricting role in the daily activities of children and youth.[7]

ALTERATIONS IN BODY STRUCTURES AND FUNCTIONS IN CHILDREN WITH CEREBRAL PALSY

This chapter focuses on the ICF[2] components of body structures and functions, activities, and participation in children with cerebral palsy (CP) while building upon the classification of this condition discussed in Chapter 3.[8] As shown in Table 4-1, brain lesions and alterations in structures and functions of the neuromuscular system[9-23] are related to the dimensions of Motor Abnormalities and Anatomical and Neuroimaging Findings of the current CP classification.[8] Seizures and non-motor neurodevelopmental problems, as well as the alterations in structures and functions of the musculoskeletal and sensory systems, are viewed under the dimension of Accompanying Impairments.[8] In addition, although not included in the classification of CP, impairments of cardiovascular and pulmonary, digestive, and urogenital systems, as well as pain that may have multiple origins need to be discussed (see Table 4-1).

Neurological System

Brain lesions identified via diagnostic imaging that lead to motor abnormalities in children with CP were discussed in

Chapter 3. The accompanying impairments of the neurological system are described next.

Seizures

Epilepsy is an accompanying impairment present in 22% to 62% of children and adults with CP.[24-26] Several reports point to a relationship between the presence of seizures and intellectual disability, with higher frequency of epilepsy observed in children with CP who have decreased cognitive abilities.[24-27] The age of onset and prevalence of epilepsy vary with the etiology and type of CP, and with the anatomic distribution of involvement.[24-26] The youngest age of onset (6 months) has been reported in children with bilateral spastic CP and significant involvement of all 4 extremities (quadriplegia).[25] In a study of 100 children with CP, the average age of onset was 12 months, with the first seizure recorded before the first birthday in 74.2% of participants.[26] Reports on the highest prevalence of epilepsy by the anatomic distribution of involvement compete between unilateral CP (28-35% to 70.6%)[24-27] and bilateral CP with equal impairment of upper and lower extremities (19-36% to 100%).[24-28] Most likely, this inconsistency results from dissimilarities among study samples of children with CP examined by different researchers.[24-28] The lowest prevalence (16% to 27%) has been found in children with bilateral spastic CP characterized by greater involvement of lower than upper extremities (diplegia).[15,27] Children with spastic CP who are born full term are diagnosed with epilepsy more frequently than those born prematurely, with a higher risk reported in cases of central nervous system (CNS) infection, CNS malformation, and gray matter damage as compared to those with seizures of unknown etiology.[25] The presence of neonatal seizures that occur in the first 4 postnatal weeks and a family history of epilepsy have been implicated as significant risk factors for the development of epilepsy in this patient population.[25,26]

Seizures are characterized by abnormal electrical activity in the brain that can be recorded via electroencephalography (EEG).[29-31] Children with CP may have different types of seizures, but generalized and partial types are most common.[24-27] Generalized seizures involve both hemispheres, and partial or focal seizures occur in a localized area of the brain.[29,30] Secondary generalization of partial seizures may also occur when abnormal electrical activity spreads from a limited area to the entire brain.[29,30] Partial seizures are most common in children with unilateral CP, and generalized seizures are most frequently observed in those with bilateral CP.[25,27]

Other types of seizures reported in this patient population include infantile spasms, status epilepticus, and indeterminate or unclassified seizures.[25,26] Infantile spasms, or *West syndrome*, is a seizure disorder diagnosed between 4 and 8 months of age.[32] It is characterized by regression in development and usually subsides by the age of 5 years. The EEG of this type of seizure activity would show chaotic brain waves or hypsarrhythmia. Children who have infantile spasms frequently develop other types of seizures later in life.[32] Status epilepticus is a prolonged single epileptic seizure or a series of

TABLE 4-1

IMPAIRMENTS OF BODY SYSTEMS VIEWED FROM A COMBINED PERSPECTIVE OF ICF[2] AND CEREBRAL PALSY CLASSIFICATION

Involved Body Systems	Alterations in Body Structures and Functions	DIMENSIONS OF CEREBRAL PALSY CLASSIFICATION[8]		Anatomical and Neuroimaging Findings	
		Motor Abnormalities	Accompanying Impairments	Anatomic Distribution	Neuroimaging Findings
Neurological	• Brain lesions[9-15]	X			X
	• Seizures[8,15,24-34]	X	X		
	• Neurodevelopmental deficits (non-motor)[8,24,27,28,35-43]	X	X		
Neuromuscular	• Muscle tone abnormalities[9-12]	X		X	
	• Atypical posture and movement patterns, including gait[16-19,64,65,74,76,78-90]	X		X	
	• Postural control and balance deficits[20-23,46-57,59-63]	X		X	
	• Oral-motor problems (motor speech, drooling, feeding difficulties)[27,36,43,93-105]	X		X	
Musculoskeletal	• Low BMD[24,106,108,109]		X		
	• Muscle weakness[12,73,110-120]		X		
	• ROM limitations, joint contractures, musculoskeletal deformities[12,75,106-108,121-137]		X		
Sensory (visual, auditory, somatosensory) and neurological	• Visual, visual-perceptual, visual-spatial, visual memory deficits[12,24,28,37,139-141]	X	X		
	• Hearing problems[12,24,37]		X		
	• Tactile, proprioceptive and kinesthetic deficits[12,138,142-144]		X		
Cardiovascular and pulmonary	• Atypical development of the chest wall[135,149,152,153]	N/A	N/A	N/A	N/A
	• Increased work of breathing[149,152,153]				
	• Insufficient breath support for speech[149,153]				
	• Decreased lung function[149,154]				
	• Decreased cardiopulmonary fitness[154-157]				
	• Increased energy expenditure[83-87,158]				
	• Inefficient cough[103,135,146,149,159]				

(continued)

Table 4-1 (continued)

Impairments of Body Systems Viewed from a Combined Perspective of ICF[2] and Cerebral Palsy Classification

| Involved Body Systems | Alterations in Body Structures and Functions | DIMENSIONS OF CEREBRAL PALSY CLASSIFICATION[8] | | | |
| | | Motor Abnormalities | Accompanying Impairments | Anatomical and Neuroimaging Findings | |
				Anatomic Distribution	Neuroimaging Findings
Digestive	• Gastroesophageal reflux[27,93,103,104]	N/A	N/A	N/A	N/A
	• Colorectal problems[24,27,93,104,160,161]				
	• Nutritional issues[24,27,98,105,162-165]				
Urogenital	• Primary urinary incontinence[24,166,167]	N/A	N/A	N/A	N/A
	• Other lower urinary tract problems[167-169]				
	• Neurogenic bladder[167,170,171]				
Multiple	• Pain[12,91,92]	N/A	N/A	N/A	N/A

Abbreviations: BMD, bone mineral density; ICF, International Classification of Functioning, Disability and Health; N/A, not applicable; ROM, range of motion.

TABLE 4-2

TYPES AND SYMPTOMS OF SEIZURES REPORTED IN CHILDREN WITH CEREBRAL PALSY

TYPES OF SEIZURES		SYMPTOMS
Generalized	Absence	Motionless staring spells lasting less than 15 seconds with instantaneous return to activity after the seizure subsides. May occur multiple times in 1 day
	Atonic	Also known as *drop attacks*. A sudden decrease in muscle tone leads to a fall that may cause injury.
	Clonic	Muscle spasms and jerks, with initially rapid alternating flexion and relaxation of the neck, upper and lower extremities, and subsequent decrease in frequency. After the seizure subsides, a deep sigh is usually heard followed by normal breathing.
	Myoclonic	A sudden increase in muscle tone with physical manifestation resembling an electric shock
	Tonic	Stiffening of muscles of extremities and trunk with loss of consciousness and back arching. Eyes roll back, breathing becomes difficult, and gargling noises may be heard.
	Tonic-clonic	A combination of tonic and clonic seizures preceded by an aura (sensory changes, dizziness, or hallucinations). Consist of a tonic phase followed by a clonic phase that usually lasts no longer than a few minutes. Unconsciousness continues for a few minutes or longer in the post-seizure (postictal) period, with muscle aching, fatigue, or confusion frequently reported upon waking up.
Partial	Simple	Localized to one side of the brain but may spread further. Occurs without loss of consciousness. Symptoms can be motor, such as jerking movements of a part of the body; sensory (eg, hallucinations or abnormal sensations [numbness, tingling, etc]); autonomic, such as changes in heart rate, blood pressure, nausea, or sweating; or psychological (eg, feelings of anxiety or déjà vu).
	Complex	Is preceded by an aura (a simple partial seizure) and affects awareness and memory of events as the seizure activity spreads. May manifest as staring spells or automatisms (repetitive movements), such as lip smacking, eye turning, muscle contraction and relaxation on one side of the body, etc.
	Secondary generalized	Partial seizure that spreads to the other side of the brain. Presents as muscle spasms or a decrease in or loss of muscle tone.
Infantile spasms		A series of myoclonic seizures. Each seizure consists of a sudden jerk followed by muscle stiffening, with abducted upper extremities, flexed hips and knees, and forward flexion of the trunk. Commonly occur upon waking up and rarely when asleep
Status epilepticus		Prolonged single or repetitive seizures that last longer than 30 minutes. Classified into simple partial, complex partial, absence, myoclonic, and nonconvulsive types
Indeterminate		Unclassified as any other type of seizures

Compiled from Carlsson et al,[25] Bruck et al,[26] Jasmin,[29,30] Ramachandrannair,[33] and Johns Hopkins Medicine Website.[34]

2 or more seizures that is characterized by a failure to regain consciousness between seizures.[25] This is a neurological emergency in which seizure activity lasts longer than 30 minutes.[25,33] Table 4-2 summarizes the types and symptoms of seizures observed in children with CP.[25,26,29,30,33,34]

Non-Motor Neurodevelopmental Deficits

Non-motor accompanying impairments in the areas of cognition, attention, and communication, as well as behavioral problems and learning disabilities have been documented in people with CP.[24,27,28,35-43] According to Odding

et al,[24] 23% to 44% of children and adults with this condition have cognitive deficits, with prevalence of intellectual disability increasing to 59% to 77% in those who also have epilepsy. The prevalence of cognitive impairments varies depending on the anatomic distribution of involvement and the level of motor function.[24,35] Children with unilateral CP, Gross Motor Functions Classification System (GMFCS)[44] level I, tend to demonstrate the highest, and children with bilateral CP, GMFCS levels IV and V, the lowest intelligence quotients (IQ).[24,35] In a study of 40 individuals with bilateral spastic and/or dyskinetic CP, Pueyo et al[37] reported high prevalence of intellectual disability as well as language, abstract reasoning, and memory deficits, with short-term memory being greater affected in those born with low birth weight or small for gestational age.[37]

It is important to note that 40% of children with unilateral CP have normal IQ,[24] and not every person with bilateral CP and significant involvement of all 4 extremities (quadriplegia) has an intellectual disability.[27] In a study of 95 participants, Majnemer et al[35] showed that IQ test results may be skewed by intellectual and language difficulties that children with CP with the lowest levels of physical functioning may encounter during standardized testing. The IQ scores for this group of children were overestimated as only those with higher cognitive abilities were able to take the test.[35] Additionally, the IQ scores may be skewed in the opposite direction when visual, auditory, motor, and speech deficits in children with CP interfere with their test performance.[27] Such problems need to be taken into consideration when interpreting the IQ test results in this patient population.[27]

Besides cognitive deficits, children with CP frequently exhibit problems with attention, behavior, and socialization.[24,35,38-40] Attention deficit disorder (ADD) and attention deficit hyperactivity disorder (ADHD) are not uncommon findings in this patient population.[24,38] In one study conducted in Norway with 67 children with CP, 42% of participants met the criteria for the diagnosis of ADD.[38] Results of another study showed an association between symptoms of hyperactivity and limitations in functional skills in adolescents with CP.[39] Bottcher et al[40] reported deficits in sustained and divided attention in all 33 children with this condition who were assessed on the Test of Everyday Attention for Children (TEA-Ch).[45] Finally, in 2 consecutive population-based studies conducted in Sweden and published in 2006 and 2011, a significant proportion of participants with CP had learning disability, and its prevalence increased from 40% to 45% over the course of 5 years.[28,41] According to the results of the later study, fewer children with unilateral spastic CP had a learning disability (16%) compared to children with bilateral spastic and dyskinetic types (56% and 77%, respectively).[41]

According to Odding et al,[24] children with CP are 5 times more likely than their typically developing peers to demonstrate such behavioral problems as hyperactivity, stubbornness, and dependency. Other reports suggest that emotional symptoms, peer problems, and poor socialization skills are also prevalent in children and adolescents with this condition, which may negatively affect their psychosocial well-being.[35,39,42] In a study of 160 adolescents with CP, mean age 15.4 years, 59 participants were found to have behavioral difficulties.[39] These included peer problems (61.9%), emotional symptoms (34.4%), conduct problems (21.3%), hyperactivity (20%), and borderline or abnormal prosocial behaviors (15.6%).[39] As recommended by several authors, problems with attention and behavior need to be assessed and monitored in all children with CP, and addressed when necessary.[35,38]

Many people with CP have communication difficulties related to their cognitive development.[36,41-43] Parkes et al[36] reported impairments of communication (excluding motor speech problems) in 42% of 1268 children with CP. Forty-five percent of children with speech and language difficulties were completely unable to communicate. Moderate to profound impairments of communication were found in only 7% of children classified in GMFCS levels I through III, but in 77% of those in GMFCS levels IV and V. These results pointed to a relationship between the gross motor function and the communication ability in this patient population.[36]

Two smaller studies conducted with 186 and 243 children with CP, respectively, yielded similar results, but it is important to note that in both studies, the researchers did not discriminate between motor and cognitive aspects of speech impairments.[41,43] Himmelmann and Uvebrant[41] reported that, in their research, 49% of participants had verbal communication impairments and 64% of those were unable to speak. In the study by Shevell et al,[43] absence of verbal communication was found in 20%, 35%, and 82% of children with GMFCS levels III, IV, and V, respectively. In addition, 45% of children with bilateral spastic CP and significant involvement of all extremities (quadriplegia) and 50% of children with dyskinetic CP did not have any verbal skills. For comparison, only 3% of children with unilateral CP and 4% of those with bilateral CP affecting lower extremities greater than upper extremities (diplegia) had the same problem.[43]

Neuromuscular System

The reader is referred to Chapters 2 and 3 for the description of such alterations in structures and functions of the neuromuscular system in children with CP as muscle tone abnormalities, atypical posture and movement patterns, and postural control deficits in infants with atypical development. Additional impairments of this system listed in Table 4-1 that are related to the Motor Abnormalities and Anatomical and Neuroimaging Findings dimensions of CP classification[8] will be discussed next.

Postural Control and Balance Deficits

Postural control includes the abilities to organize the orientation of the body in space and to maintain its equilibrium, with both processes resulting from the interaction of multiple systems.[46,47] The first component of postural control refers to the body alignment in the system of coordinates defined by gravity and the supporting surface, relative to the person's visually observable environment and based on the tactile, proprioceptive, and kinesthetic information derived from his or her own body. This requires the individual to simultaneously process and interpret information received from visual, vestibular, and somatosensory perceptual systems. The second equilibrium component of postural control involves the ability to stabilize the center of mass (COM) of the body within its base of support (BOS) when postural stability is disturbed.[46]

Researchers have studied both components of postural control in children with CP by looking at their ability to maintain static postures[48-50] and by assessing their postural responses to destabilizing forces.[51-56] A destabilization by an external force, such as a tilt of a supporting surface, induces compensatory postural adjustments (CPAs), while a destabilization related to self-initiated movements is typically preceded by anticipatory postural adjustments (APAs) that occur before a person performs the actual purposeful movement.[51-56]

Research conducted by Saavedra and Woollacott[57] showed that typically developing infants assessed between 3 and 9 months of age develop sitting trunk control sequentially, from the top down, and demonstrate decreased agonist/antagonist and bilateral extensor muscle co-activation when greater stability is achieved. In addition, they display an increase in co-activation of bilateral internal oblique muscles, which is essential for stabilization of the lumbar spine.[57] As postural control develops and infants learn to sit independently, a gradual release of degrees of freedom[58] is observed, and the infants learn to adapt their posture to the task at hand (see Chapter 2).[57,59,60] In contrast, researchers who studied postural control in children with CP found that these children demonstrate persistent compensatory strategies in the form of cephalocaudal ("top-down") recruitment of muscles used for postural control and excessive co-activation of agonist and antagonist musculature, which impedes postural adaptation to the demands of a specific task.[48,51-53,61]

Saavedra et al[48] observed that, compared to typically developing children and adults, children with spastic, ataxic, and dystonic CP, age range 6 to 16 years, demonstrated insufficient head stability during static sitting. Specifically, they showed significantly greater velocity and amplitude of head movement when maintaining quiet bench sitting, unsupported or with pelvic support. When they closed their eyes, children with dyskinetic CP demonstrated an improvement in head stability, which may be explained by the presence of dyskinetic eye movements that would destabilize the head in these children when their vision is not occluded. Children with spastic CP showed an increase in amplitude of their head movement with eyes closed across all trunk support conditions, which may be attributed to vestibular deficits. This hypothesis requires further investigation because increased postural sway while maintaining static balance without reliance on vision may be used as a strategy to self-assess one's limits of postural stability.[48]

Postural control in children with CP in quiet standing was investigated in several studies.[49,50] Results showed the following:

- Visual feedback played similar roles in standing balance control for children with and without CP[49]

- Vestibular and musculoskeletal deficits, such as lower extremity muscle weakness and insufficient passive range of motion (ROM), may have impact on stance stability in children with CP[49,50]

- Because of musculoskeletal problems, these children may have difficulty using the ankle and hip strategies

for maintaining standing balance that are normally available to their typically developing peers[50]

Balance perturbations can be induced by external forces or active movements of one's own body.[51-56] When a person stands on a movable supporting surface, its forward displacement causes a posterior body sway, which leads to a direction-specific activation of ventral musculature of the body.[61] A backward displacement of the supporting surface would induce an anterior sway response, with the activation of dorsal musculature. These direction-specific responses have been registered using electromyography (EMG) technology in both sitting and standing positions.[61]

Studies of sitting postural adjustments in children with CP showed that, similar to children developing typically, most of them were capable of generating direction-specific responses to perturbations.[52,61,62] However, in general, the organization of postural adjustments varied depending on the child's level of disability.[52,61] Children with bilateral spastic CP who were able to sit unsupported assumed an upright trunk posture but recruited antagonistic (neck extensor) muscles to stabilize their head in space.[61] Those who were unable to sit unsupported exhibited deficits in basic direction-specific muscle activation, demonstrated longer response latencies for the onset of muscle recruitment, initiated postural adjustments with the recruitment of their neck musculature, and were unable to modulate their muscle activity relative to the demands of a specific task.[52,61]

Nashner et al[51] were first to assess and describe standing postural adjustments in 10 children with different types of CP during perturbations induced by a movable platform, movable visual environment, and active movement. Their findings revealed deficits in the organization of postural responses to sensory stimuli and in the timing and patterns of muscle activation in children with CP compared to children and adults without disabilities. This study became a foundation for future research in this area,[51] including the investigations of standing CPAs and APAs.[54-56,63]

In a small study of standing CPAs during backward displacement of a movable platform, children with bilateral spastic CP demonstrated excessive recruitment of antagonist muscles and decreased activation of trunk musculature compared to the control group.[63] These findings were attributed to crouched stancing and to the nervous system impairments observed in participants with spastic CP.[63]

While the CPAs occur in response to a perturbation, the APAs constitute active movements that occur approximately 100 ms prior to the anticipated disturbance of equilibrium.[54] Thus, the CPAs use sensory feedback received from a disturbance of balance while the APAs signify the feed-forward, proactive control of postural stability.[54] A number of studies conducted with children with CP examined their APAs associated with reaching arm movements in comparison to children developing typically.[54-56] Data were collected using the recordings of COP displacement with the participants standing on a force platform,[54,56] and the EMG recordings of trunk and lower extremity muscle activity.[55,56] The results showed that, similar to children developing typically, children with CP demonstrated direction-specific changes in COP and EMG activity prior to bilateral upper extremity reaching into shoulder flexion[54-56] and extension.[56] However, Liu et al[54] found that children with spastic CP, GMFCS level II, displayed greater variability in their COP excursion, and Tomita et al[55] reported smaller anticipatory activity changes in dorsal postural musculature, less frequent anticipatory activation of gastrocnemius muscles, and later onset times for gastrocnemius activity, when present, in children and young adults with bilateral spastic CP compared to that in participants without disability. Finally, Girolami et al[56] showed the following:

- Children with unilateral CP demonstrated greater anticipatory muscle activity and COP excursion than those with bilateral CP.

- Children with bilateral CP displayed greater baseline activity in their lower extremity and trunk musculature.

- Children with bilateral CP showed a COP displacement in posterior direction prior to performing upper extremity extension movements, instead of the anterior displacement demonstrated by children with unilateral CP and the control group.

The researchers hypothesized that differences in postural alignment among the three groups of study participants might have played a role in the observed differences in their APAs.[56]

Gait Dysfunction

Gait dysfunction in people with CP is a complex issue that can be approached in many different ways. Typically, clinicians "dissect" the walking patterns exhibited by children and adults with this condition from the perspective of specific gait deviations and differences in gait parameters in comparison with people without disabilities. Several gait classification systems for children with unilateral and bilateral spastic CP have been developed.[64,65] However, a larger question brought up by Latash and Anson[66] in 1996 also needs to be considered. This question was, "What are 'normal' movements' in atypical populations?" In other words, should the deviations from typical movement patterns observed in people with disabilities be viewed as impairments that need to be addressed by intervention, or are such deviations "normal" for the patient population in question?[66]

Latash and Anson[66] suggested that the CNS chooses specific motor control patterns based on the priorities related to the current state of the human organism (a biological system). If this biological system is healthy, "normal" movement patterns are selected, and in presence of atypical conditions, the CNS priorities are reconsidered. Factors that would cause such a change in priorities may include structural or biochemical CNS abnormalities, structural changes in the musculoskeletal system, disorders of perception, or cognitive difficulties that affect decision-making processes. A change in selection priorities leads to the development of new movement patterns that may be considered adaptive or even

optimal for the current state of the biological system.[66] This answer to the stated question implies that changing the movement patterns selected by the CNS should not be a priority for therapeutic intervention as such approach may be not only unsuccessful but also detrimental to intervention outcomes. To analyze this suggestion, it may be helpful to examine gait dysfunction in people with CP from the ICF[2] perspective by looking at walking as an activity that is interrelated with body structures and functions. A discussion of essential requirements or factors important for the achievement of skilled upright locomotion[67,68] may assist with this task.

Five requirements for successful and safe walking described by Patla[67] and applied to human development by Hanke and Cech[68] include *progression*, *stability*, *adaptability*, *long-term viability*, and *long-distance navigation*. Weight support and active propulsion are the components of *progression*, or "the ability to walk from point A to point B,"[68] which are regulated by the brain and spinal cord.[67]

Dynamic equilibrium, or *stability* of the moving body, is vital for the ability to ambulate[67,69] and is achieved through the use of the visual, kinesthetic, and vestibular systems in order to coordinate the position of one's COM during walking.[67,68] In addition, during gait, dynamic equilibrium in the frontal plane results from a specific interaction between moments produced by active muscle groups, passive joints, and gravity.[70] The reactive control of dynamic equilibrium involves the ability to detect unexpected perturbations by multiple sensory systems and make necessary adjustments.[67] The proactive control is achieved in 2 ways: 1) by predicting disturbances generated by ambulation itself, which include the necessary movements of extremities and trunk; and 2) by recognizing a potential threat to stability that comes from the obstacles encountered along the way. In both instances, the appropriate strategies to preserve the dynamic equilibrium are selected and implemented.[67]

Adaptability allows humans to accomplish the task of walking in various functional contexts.[68] They adapt to their behavioral goals and external constraints of this task[69] by selecting different strategies to negotiate various environments and to walk on even and uneven surfaces of different configurations, or of different compliance and friction qualities, such as stairs and ramps, ice, linoleum floor, grass, or sand.[67,68] During a transition from one supporting surface to another, walking patterns are first modulated by the visual system, followed by the kinesthetic system that comes into play once the foot is placed onto the new supporting surface.[67]

While *progression*, *stability*, and *adaptability* are the requirements related to the ability to execute the action of walking, the abilities to maintain the structural integrity of the musculoskeletal system and to minimize energy expenditure during gait preserve the *long-term viability* of the human body.[67,68] This is accomplished by achieving the optimal posture and joint alignment and by selecting the optimal movement trajectory and walking speed during locomotion.[67]

Purposeful long-distance travel, or *long-distance navigation*, requires the person to have adequate cognitive abilities, including perception, memory, and judgment,[68] as well as the ability to develop cognitive spatial maps.[67,68] These maps are stored in the brain and retrieved when necessary to allow the human being to navigate to a point not visible from the point of origin.[67]

In the process of normal development, infants, toddlers, and young children typically acquire the skills necessary to meet the requirements for safe upright locomotion described previously.[68] On average, they usually start walking independently at approximately 12 months of age (range 8.2 to 16.8 months) and demonstrate rapid changes in gait pattern and parameters during the first 9 months of walking.[71-74] The use of muscle co-activation allows a new walker to achieve stability during gait by decreasing the number of degrees of freedom[58] that need to be controlled.[75] As the child practices independent ambulation, the degrees of freedom are gradually released,[58,75] and reciprocal muscle activation begins after 6 months of walking.[68,75] The refinement of gait continues until approximately 7 years of age when its characteristics approximate that of an adult.[68,74-77]

When discussing gait development in children with CP, the multidimensionality of this process needs to be taken into consideration. The primary impairments of the nervous and neuromuscular systems discussed previously, and secondary musculoskeletal impairments that will be described later in this chapter contribute to changing the CNS priorities for the selection of movement patterns that would allow these children to develop upright locomotion.[66,74,76] Several authors compared gait development in children developing typically and children with CP.[74,78-81] Research suggested that children with CP failed to transition to a mature walking pattern from the one commonly seen during supported stepping in typically developing infants.[74,78,79] Berger[78,79] reported that children with bilateral spastic CP, age range 7 to 16 years, who achieved independent ambulation, demonstrated muscle activation patterns resembling those of 7- to 10-month-old infants learning to walk, specifically, the antagonist muscle co-activation in the stance phase and enhanced short latency stretch reflexes.[78,79]

Further research revealed additional differences in walking parameters displayed by children with CP compared to children developing typically.[80,81] These included the following:

- Children with CP walked at a slower self-selected speed and displayed increased activation and co-activation of trunk and hip musculature.[80]
- They displayed lower mean step length, single support time, walking velocity, and cadence.
- Stride-to-stride variability in cadence and single support time was higher in children with CP.[81]

Prosser et al[80,81] suggested that excessive activity in the trunk and hip musculature exhibited by children with CP might serve as a strategy they used in order to maintain antigravity postural control, so that they could accomplish walking in spite of the numerous neurological and neuromuscular system impairments they were facing. On one hand, this hypothesis echoes the previously discussed answer to the question posed by Latash and Anson.[66] However, on the other hand, the strategy of excessive muscle activation and co-activation may limit the postural adjustments available to people with CP who can walk.[80] This would negatively affect their ability to fully meet the *stability* and *adaptability* requirements for successful and safe locomotion.[68,80]

Not all children with CP are able to achieve independent upright mobility with or without assistive devices.[45,82] The *progression* requirement is not satisfied by children functioning at GMFCS level V and is only partially met in those classified in level IV.[45,68,82] In addition, in people with CP who meet this requirement and at least partially satisfy the requirements of *stability* and *adaptability*,[68] the *long-term viability* of body systems is frequently compromised by the development of abnormal joint alignment leading to deformities[12,74,76] and by high-energy expenditure during gait.[83-86] For instance, the energy cost of walking was shown to be 1.3 times higher in children with unilateral spastic CP than in children without disabilities.[83] In children with bilateral spastic CP, the mechanical cost of walking was 1.5 times greater than in children developing typically, with the lower extremity work increased by 37% and the upper body work increased by up to 222%.[84] Excessive movements of the trunk, head, and upper extremities were used by these children as compensatory strategies.[84,87]

Significant relationships between several other kinematic variables and energy cost of walking were also observed in children with bilateral spastic CP, with the highest correlations found for the amount of pelvic tilt and the speed of walking (Pearson r equal to 0.73 and 0.64, respectively).[85] In another study, the physiological cost indices (PCI) obtained for children with CP who walked with and without assistive devices were over 2.5 times higher than those calculated for children without disabilities.[86] The PCI was calculated as the difference between the walking and resting heart rates (HRs) divided by the walking speed.[86]

Several authors reported on age-related deterioration of gait in this patient population assessed using kinematic and temporospatial parameters, such as the ROM at lower extremity joints, single limb and double stance support time, walking velocity, cadence, and the timing of toe off.[88-90] An increase in the net oxygen cost of walking was also documented.[90] All of these findings point to a *long-term viability* requirement compromise in this patient population.[67,68] Additionally, pain that may originate from multiple sources may lead to gait deterioration and limit walking activity in children and adults with CP.[12,91,92] An in-depth discussion of pain assessment and management will be provided in Chapter 10.

Finally, the presence of cognitive, attentional, and behavioral problems discussed earlier in this chapter[24,37,39,40] may potentially have a negative effect on perception, memory, and judgment, as well as on the ability to develop cognitive spatial maps in children and adults with CP. Because these attributes are required for independent purposeful travel, this kind of deficiency may prevent them from meeting the *long distance navigation* requirement for successful and safe walking.[67,68]

The current discussion of walking requirements applied to people with CP suggests that on one hand, atypical gait patterns observed in this patient population seem to result from the changing CNS priorities as suggested by Latash and Anson.[66] On the other hand, the limitations in the ability of these individuals to meet the requirements for successful and safe ambulation[67,68] point to the need for intervention that would target specific deficits related to each requirement. Therefore, the question, "What are 'normal movements' in atypical populations?" posed by Latash and Anson,[66] remains open for discussion and will be revisited later in this book. In addition, in light of the complexity of this issue, making an accurate prognosis for independent ambulation for children with CP may be a difficult task that will be examined separately in Chapter 5.

Oral-Motor Problems

Oral-motor deficits listed in Table 4-1 are additional impairments of the neuromuscular system related to the Motor Abnormalities and Anatomical and Neuroimaging Findings dimensions of CP classification.[8] Muscles of the mouth, pharynx, and esophagus responsible for oral-motor function are controlled by cranial nerves V, VII, and IX through XII, as well as by the brainstem and cerebral cortex.[27,93] The disruption of coordination of this musculature by the CNS leads to alterations in oral-motor function in children with CP, including motor speech deficits, feeding difficulties related to problems with chewing and swallowing, and excessive drooling (see Table 4-1).[93] In one population-based study, 18% of participants with different types of CP had all of these impairments.[36] Generally, such deficits are most prevalent in children with bilateral CP and the greatest motor involvement (GMFCS levels IV and V).[27,93,94] Frequently, these problems are interrelated (eg, swallowing difficulties may lead to excessive drooling, which, in turn, may contribute to dysarthria).[36,95]

Dysarthria is a motor speech problem that manifests itself in articulation difficulties, while *anarthria* refers to the inability to pronounce remembered words, with both disorders caused by a brain lesion.[96,97] Children with CP who have dysarthria or anarthria may use alternative or augmentative methods of communication, such as sign language, pictures, or electronic devices.[36,98] Parkes et al[36] reported motor speech impairments in 37% of 1006 individuals with CP, with prevalence varying from 23% of cases classified in GMFCS levels I through III to 73% of those in GMFCS levels IV and V.[36] Children with dyskinetic CP were shown to lack verbal communication most frequently,[44,98] followed by children with bilateral spastic CP with significant involvement of all 4 extremities (quadriplegia).[44] In a study of 48 children with dyskinetic CP conducted by Himmelman et al,[98] 38 (79%) had anarthria and the rest had dysarthria.

Excessive drooling, or *sialorrhea*, is another impairment documented in children with CP and, primarily, with its bilateral spastic type with severe motor involvement (GMFCS levels IV and V).[27,36,99] Senner et al[95] showed that the severity of drooling was associated with the severity of dysarthria, with a Spearman rho correlation coefficient of 0.82, $p < 0.0001$. The overall prevalence of drooling problems in individuals with CP was reported to be between 40% and 58%, with severe sialorrhea found in 15% to 33%.[99-101] Significantly higher rates of drooling were observed in children with poor head control, feeding difficulties, and impaired lip closure.[99] Erasmus et al[102] showed that sialorrhea in children with CP was not caused by hypersalivation. Instead, abnormal posturing, such as maintaining a habitual open-mouth position; dental malocclusion; and oral-motor dysfunction, including low tone in oral musculature and impaired tongue movements and swallowing, were thought to contribute to the etiology of excessive drooling in this patient population.[27,100,102] It was also suggested that, in children with dyskinetic CP, increased salivation may result from hyperkinetic movements of the mouth.[102]

Excessive drooling may have a variety of negative consequences, including hygiene, integumentary and dental problems, dehydration, unpleasant odor, and communication and socialization difficulties that may lead to low self-esteem and social isolation.[27,95,99,100] Additionally, together with swallowing impairments, it may contribute to aspiration.[93,100] Oropharyngeal aspiration (inhalation) of saliva, fluids or food that results from poor planning, and coordination of swallowing and breathing is common in children with neurologic disorders and may lead to respiratory infections, chronic airway disease, or aspiration pneumonia.[27,103,104] Overt aspiration is characterized by attempts to expel the foreign material via reflexive cough produced by the stimulation of the receptors of the larynx and hypopharynx.[103] Silent aspiration is much more difficult to detect than overt aspiration because it occurs in the absence of a reflexive cough. This type of aspiration is very common in children with neurologic disorders and feeding problems, including those with CP. Therefore, Weir et al[103] advocated for videofluoroscopic swallow studies to be performed in children with CP who have feeding difficulties to determine whether silent aspiration may be present.

Difficulty swallowing, or *dysphagia*, is prevalent in children with CP.[27,36,94] In a large epidemiological study, the overall rate of chewing and swallowing problems was 21%.[36] These problems were present in 57% of individuals classified in GMFCS levels IV and V and in only 7% of those functioning at GMFCS levels I through III. Additionally, a higher risk for chewing and swallowing deficits was significantly associated with the level of intellectual disability.[36]

Dysphagia in individuals with CP involves impairments of the voluntary muscular control and of the reflexive pharyngeal swallowing phase.[104] Field et al[94] documented food refusal in 30%, oral-motor delays in 68%, and dysphagia in 32% of 44 toddlers and preschoolers with CP as the most prevalent feeding difficulties compared to food selectivity by type or texture (14% and 16%, respectively). The oral-motor delays included tongue movement, chewing, and lip closure deficits.[94] Dysphagia may lead to pulmonary aspiration, very long feeding times, and inadequate caloric intake causing malnutrition and growth problems.[27,93,103]

A gastrostomy feeding tube insertion is an intervention that may be recommended for children whose swallowing in unsafe, or for whom oral feedings are difficult and ineffective in maintaining sufficient caloric intake necessary for adequate growth.[27,93] The prevalence of gastrostomy tube (G-tube) feeding varies depending on a variety of factors.[105] A large study conducted in 6 European countries that included 1295 children with CP showed an overall prevalence of G-tube feeding of 11%.[105] The highest rates were found in children with bilateral and dyskinetic CP (15% and 33%, respectively), as well as in those classified in GMFCS levels IV and V (32%). It is interesting to note that the prevalence of the G-tube placement varied across countries, from 22% in Western Sweden to 6% in England and Portugal, and 3% in Iceland. The authors hypothesized that this variation may be attributed to differences in clinical practice, availability of access to care, and parental views on oral and tube feeding.[105]

Musculoskeletal System

Although impairments of the neurological and neuromuscular systems are primary in people with CP,[8,12] muscle imbalances related to abnormal muscle tone lead to atypical posturing, which negatively affects the musculoskeletal system development and, over time, results in abnormal joint formation, alignment, and deformities.[12,106,107] In the process of atypical development, the structure and function of both bone and muscle components of this body system are altered.[106-110] These and other accompanying musculoskeletal impairments listed in Table 4-1 will be discussed next.

Low Bone Mineral Density

Delayed and insufficient weight-bearing, as well as abnormal muscle pull, contribute to joint malformations and decreased bone mineral density (BMD) in children and adults with CP.[24,106,108] Low BMD is a common problem that strongly correlates with the inability to stand, thus affecting the individuals in the GMFCS levels IV and V greater than those in levels I through III.[24] Decreased BMD is associated with the development of osteoporosis and a higher incidence of fractures.[106,109] Based on their review of multiple sources, Fehlings et al[109] listed decreased weight-bearing, as well as poor nutrition, decreased sunlight exposure, and the use of anticonvulsant drugs as the risk factors for osteoporosis in children with CP.

Muscle Weakness

Muscle weakness or deficit of strength is a significant impairment in people with CP.[12,110-112] It is defined as "the inability to generate normal voluntary force in a muscle or normal voluntary torque about a joint."[113(p 2159)] Sanger et al and the Task Force on Motor Disorders[113] clarified the meaning of the term *normal* as related to individuals without disabilities, and the term *voluntary* as produced upon command or following a demonstration. Strength, therefore, can be defined as the ability to produce maximal voluntary force or torque of a normal value.[110,113]

Mockford and Caulton[110] conducted an extensive review of published literature and found that muscle strength deficits in children and adults with CP had both neurologic and muscle tissue origins.[110] The following neurologic components of muscle weakness pathophysiology were identified:

- Damage to pyramidal tracts leading to the insufficient motor drive of the agonist musculature[110,112]
- Inefficient recruitment of motor units in a spastic muscle leading to early fatigue, difficulty generating torque, and impaired selective motor control,[110,114] or the inability "to isolate the activation of muscles in selected pattern in response to demands of a voluntary posture or movement"[113]
- The repetitive use of neural circuits[74,110] under the conditions of inadequate myelination, decreased apoptosis ("programmed cell death"[115]) and insufficient feedback related to neural damage[74]
- Prolonged activity of spastic antagonist musculature leading to inadequate force generation by the agonists[110,112,116]
- Continuous shortening of spastic muscles negatively affecting the timing of peak torque generation by chronically lengthened opposing musculature.[110,117]

To add to this list, it is important to mention the work of Tedroff et al[118,119] that showed that, when a muscle was engaged in a maximum contraction, the EMG activity was also present in more distal musculature in children with and without CP.[118] However, in children with CP, activation of adjacent and distal muscles occurred earlier and in an atypical sequence, so that contraction of a different muscle preceded the activation of the intended agonist.[118] In addition, although muscle co-activation was found to be a normal response during a maximal isometric contraction, children with CP displayed significantly higher muscle co-activation than children without disabilities, which possibly contributed to decreased selective motor control and agonist muscle weakness in these children.[119] Tedroff et al[119] proposed that, when engaged in strengthening exercises, children with spastic CP may end up working on other muscles rather than those they intend to strengthen. This hypothesis, if supported by further research, would have implications for the development of strength training programs for this patient population.[119]

Current evidence suggests that, besides its neurologic origins, pathophysiology of muscle weakness in children with CP also includes components directly related to the structure and properties of muscle tissue.[110] These include the following:

- Selective atrophy of type 2 (fast-twitch) muscle fibers
- Changes in myosin expression
- Abnormally long sarcomeres with varied fiber size
- Reduced muscle cross-sectional area
- Increased stiffness of individual muscle fibers and decreased elasticity of muscle tissue
- Altered length-tension relationship[110]

Overall, muscle weakness has been shown to negatively affect motor function and limit daily activity in children and adolescents with CP.[12,110,111,114,120]

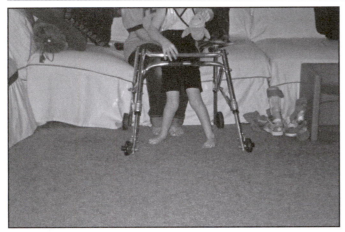

Figure 4-1. Crouch knee and genu valgum induced by ankle and foot malalignment in a child with bilateral spastic cerebral palsy.

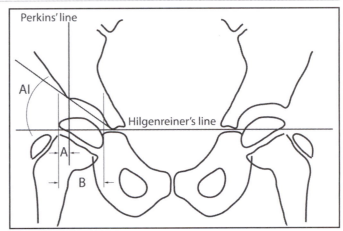

Figure 4-2. A representation of the acetabular index (AI) and migration percentage measurements of right hip dysplasia. The migration percentage is equal to the distance A divided by the distance B and multiplied by 100%.

Range of Motion Limitations, Joint Contractures, and Musculoskeletal Deformities

The overactivity of spastic musculature, muscle weakness, and muscle imbalance around the joints in children and adults with CP often lead to ROM limitations and bone and joint deformities.[12,106,107] These include hip and knee flexion contractures; torsional deformities of the femur and tibia; hip dysplasia, subluxation, and dislocation; ankle equinus and foot deformities; and abnormal spinal curvatures.[75,106-108] Upper extremity joint contractures are also common in people with CP.[108] Shoulder adduction and medial rotation contractures cause hygiene and dressing problems and may also lead to spiral humeral fractures. Elbow flexion, forearm pronation, and wrist and finger flexion contractures, when present, severely limit the hand function.[108]

McDowell et al[121] documented a significantly reduced hip flexor and adductor, knee flexor, and plantarflexor length in a population-based sample of 178 children with spastic CP, GMFCS levels I through IV, age range 4 to 17 years, compared to their peers without disabilities. Knee joint contractures were present in many children with CP, with the degree of passive ROM (PROM) limitation associated with a lower functional level.[121]

Crouching is considered to be the most common knee deformity in people with spastic CP,[107] with hip and knee flexor spasticity and contractures, and weakness of knee extensor muscles being contributing factors.[107,122,123] With increased knee flexion, quadriceps muscle fibers and patella tendon overstretch, leading to patella alta prevalence of 58% to 72% in this patient population.[107] A genu recurvatum deformity of the knee that results from rectus femoris muscle tightness may also cause patella alta.[122] Consequences of patella alta may include disturbances of ossification, stress fractures, chondromalacia, and subluxation or dislocation of the patella.[107,123] Genu valgum and varum deformities may also occur, mostly because of excessive femoral anteversion and malalignment of the foot and ankle (Figure 4-1).[107]

Hip development in children with CP is impeded by delayed weight-bearing, followed by abnormal alignment during standing, which is related to muscle imbalances and abnormal muscle pull that result in torsional deformities, including excessive femoral anteversion.[106,107] Gudjonsdottir and Stemmons Mercer[106] reported femoral anteversion values in 3- to 11-year-old children with CP that were approximately 15 degrees higher than in their peers without disabilities. Adults with spastic CP demonstrate 55 to 57 degrees of femoral anteversion on average, while its normal values range from 8 to 15 degrees.[107] Excessive femoral anteversion contributes to increased medial rotation of the hip.[76] The development of compensatory lateral tibial torsion helps to align the foot with the line of progression.[76] A combination of femoral torsion, hip adductor and flexor spasticity, and hip abductor and extensor muscle weakness leads to progressive subluxation of the hip joint.[106,107,124] If untreated, it may progress to acetabular dysplasia and deformation of the femoral head as it continues to migrate laterally, and would ultimately result in hip dislocation, most commonly, in posterior direction.[106,107,124]

Hip subluxation or dislocation is the second most common musculoskeletal deformity in people with CP, with those with bilateral spastic type and low level of gross motor function affected most frequently.[107,124,125] Results of 2 studies showed that walking 10 steps unsupported and unassisted by 30 months of age highly correlated with the preservation of hip joint stability in children with bilateral CP.[126,127] The degree of hip joint integrity is assessed using the acetabular index and the migration percentage that measure the amount of hip dysplasia and femoral head coverage by the acetabulum, respectively (Figure 4-2).[106,126] The acetabular index is measured as the angle between the Hilgenreiner's line connecting the triradiate cartilage of the acetabula located at the junction of the ischium, ilium, and pubis on each side of the pelvis and the line connecting the triradiate cartilage and the ossified lateral margin of the acetabulum on the same side.[106,126] Normal acetabular index values for newborns are

TABLE 4-3	
MIGRATION PERCENTAGE VALUES AND PROGRESSION RISK FOR NORMAL, SUBLUXED, AND DISLOCATED HIPS IN CHILDREN AND ADULTS WITH CEREBRAL PALSY	
MIGRATION (%)	**LEVEL OF HIP STABILITY AND RISK OF PROGRESSION**
< 30	Normal, stable hip, very low risk of progression
30-60	Mild to moderate subluxation, 25% risk of progression
61-90	Severe subluxation, high risk of dislocation
> 90	Dislocated hip
Data from Miller and Bagg.[128]	

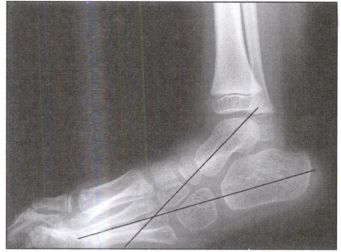

Figure 4-3. Equinovarus: lateral radiograph shows hindfoot equinus and hindfoot varus, which is characterized by increased parallelism of the talus and calcaneus (ie, decreased talocalcaneal angle). (Reprinted with permission from Morrell DS, Pearson MJ, Sauser DD. Progressive bone and joint abnormalities of the spine and lower extremities in cerebral palsy. *Radiographics.* 2002;22(2):257-268. Copyright © 2002 by RSNA.)

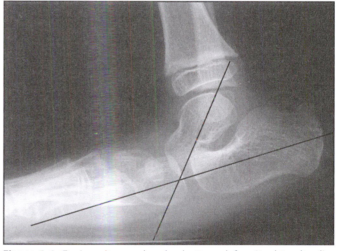

Figure 4-4. Equinovalgus and rocker-bottom deformity: lateral radiograph shows equinus deformity (plantarflexed calcaneus) and hindfoot valgus (increased talocalcaneal angle), which result in rocker-bottom deformity. (Reprinted with permission from Morrell DS, Pearson MJ, Sauser DD. Progressive bone and joint abnormalities of the spine and lower extremities in cerebral palsy. *Radiographics.* 2002;22(2):257-268. Copyright © 2002 by RSNA.)

between 27 and 42 degrees and decrease to 11 degrees by the age of 11 years, which frequently does not occur in children with CP.[106] As shown in Figure 4-2, the migration percentage is estimated as the percentage of the width of the femoral head that has migrated laterally beyond the Perkins' line, which is a vertical line drawn through the lateral acetabular margin.[106,126] Migration percentage values for normal, subluxed, and dislocated hips are given in Table 4-3.[128]

A windswept deformity that manifests itself as an abduction contracture of one hip and an adduction contracture of the other occurs in 12% to 52% of children and adults with bilateral spastic CP.[107,125] It results from muscle tone asymmetry and is associated with a persistent asymmetrical tonic neck reflex, scoliosis, pelvic obliquity, and hip subluxation or dislocation.[125,129] Young et al[125] reported a fixed hip adduction deformity or hip dislocation most often occurring on the side of the body with the strongest hip adductor tone and the least hip abduction and lateral rotation ROM. The windswept deformity may severely compromise the child's functional abilities, including sitting and walking.[107,125]

Ankle equinus or plantarflexion contracture is the most common musculoskeletal deformity in people with spastic CP.[107] It results from the overactivity, tightness, and spasticity of the gastrocnemius-soleus muscle group.[107,130,131] Associated deformities of the foot are also frequently present in this patient population.[107,108] In one longitudinal study, higher muscle tone was shown to be associated with lower ankle dorsiflexion PROM in children with all types of CP functioning at all GMFCS levels, with an average PROM decline of 19 degrees reported during the first 18 years of life.[130]

A child with CP may have an equinus deformity combined with a hindfoot valgus or varus.[107,131] The equinovarus deformity is less common and is characterized by a decreased

talocalcaneal angle (Figure 4-3), which is frequently accompanied with forefoot adduction and hindfoot inversion.[107] Spasticity in the gastrocnemius, soleus, and peroneus brevis muscles and overactivity of the peroneus longus muscle during gait may lead to the equinovalgus deformity.[107,131] A posterolateral displacement and eversion of the calcaneus associated with muscle shortening that leads to equinovalgus results in a more vertical position of the talus and a rocker-bottom deformity of the foot (Figure 4-4).[107]

Further progression of the equinovalgus deformity may cause chondromalacia of other foot joints and pes planovalgus.[107,131] The planovalgus deformity consists of talonavicular

Table 4-4

Prevalence of Sensory and Perceptual Impairments in Children With Cerebral Palsy

IMPAIRMENT TYPE	PREVALENCE (%)
Visual (low acuity, strabismus, retinopathy, cortical visual impairment)[24]	62-71
Hearing[24]	25
Tactile (stereognosis and 2-point discrimination)[37]	44-51
Proprioception (position sense)[138]	22-32
Visual-perceptual[37]	60
Visual-spatial[37]	90
Visual memory[37]	21-29
Auditory comprehension[37]	48

Visual and hearing impairment data from Odding et al.[24] Tactile, visual-perceptual, visual-spatial, visual memory, and auditory comprehension data from Pueyo et al.[37] Proprioception data from McLaughlin et al.[138]

subluxation, hindfoot valgus, and forefoot abduction and leads to collapse of the longitudinal arch of the foot.[132,133] In individuals with bilateral CP, it is often caused by muscle imbalance, including spasticity in peroneal muscles and tibialis posterior muscle weakness. The foot collapse is further exacerbated by decreased shock absorption during gait.[133] The resultant gait pattern alterations and skin breakdown over the prominent talar head and navicular tuberosity may lead to pain upon weight-bearing, which further complicates walking.[132,134]

Besides the development of bone and joint deformities in extremities, abnormal muscle tone, muscle imbalance, and atypical posturing also lead to the development of pelvic obliquity, scoliosis, and deformities of the thorax in children with CP.[106,107] Pelvic obliquity may occur as the result of hip abductor weakness, hip adductor or iliotibial band contractures, and medial hamstring muscle tightness.[106] It is frequently accompanied with variable amounts of pelvic tilt and pelvic rotation that contribute to postural malalignment.[106]

The prevalence of neuromuscular scoliosis in this patient population is 25% on average,[135] ranging from 7% to 61%, with higher numbers reported in older and nonambulatory individuals with bilateral spastic CP.[106,107] Scoliosis progression occurs more rapidly during growth spurts, and larger curves may continue progressing even after the skeletal maturity is achieved.[107] Thoracolumbar scoliotic curves are most common and most severe,[106,107] followed by lumbar curves.[106] Thoracic hyperkyphosis and lumbar hyperlordosis deformities are observed less frequently than scoliosis.[107,136] Hyperlordosis may result in spondylolysis and spondylolisthesis leading to low back pain.[107,123] Spondylolysis is a stress fracture of the pars interarticularis,[123] and spondylolisthesis involves the slippage of a lumbar vertebra in anterior direction on the vertebra below.[137] Postural deficits in children and adults with CP negatively affect their sitting, standing, and walking abilities[135] and often lead to cardiovascular and pulmonary complications that will be discussed later in this chapter.[135]

Sensory Systems

Children who suffered early brain injury, including those with CP, frequently demonstrate difficulty processing visual, auditory, tactile, and proprioceptive information (see Table 4-1).[12,24,28,37,138-145] Data on prevalence of sensory and perceptual impairments in this patient population obtained from published literature are summarized in Table 4-4.[24,37,138] Research evidence related to these deficits is discussed next.

Vision Deficits

Although vision in children with CP may be affected by eye abnormalities, such as retinopathy or cataracts, their visual and visual-perceptual deficits are more commonly related to cerebral lesions, and specifically, damage to the retrochiasmic visual pathway.[139,140] In a study of 353 children with CP, 19% had severe visual impairment.[28] Its prevalence varied depending on muscle tone abnormalities and the anatomical distribution of involvement, and was the greatest (87%) in those with bilateral CP. Among children born prematurely, prevalence of severe visual impairment was the highest in those who were born before 31 weeks gestation (27% to 30%). It was 18% in children born full term who sustained a neonatal stroke, cerebral infection, or hypoxic-ischemic encephalopathy.[28]

Children born prematurely may suffer from periventricular leukomalacia (PVL), an ischemic lesion of the brain caused by the reduction of blood flow to the periventricular white matter.[145] Among other brain structures, PVL may affect optic radiations, which would lead to cerebral visual impairment, including visual perceptual disorders.[141,145] Children with PVL are frequently diagnosed with a bilateral CP characterized by spasticity in all four limbs, with lower extremities involved greater than upper extremities (spastic diplegia).[8,12,141,145] Fazzi et al[141] identified visual-perceptual and visual-motor integration deficits in 65% to 85% of their study participants with PVL and bilateral CP. Because all 20 children who participated in this study had normal or mildly reduced visual acuity and 75% of them had parietal white matter damage confirmed by an MRI, the authors hypothesized that the visual-perceptual deficits were likely to be related to the dysfunction in the occipital-parietal pathway of visual integration.[141]

Tactile and Proprioceptive Deficits

As shown in Table 4-4, children with CP have significant tactile and proprioceptive deficits.[37,138] Cooper et al[142] and Klumlinde-Sundholm and Eliasson[143] reported on 2 independent studies that compared tactile sensitivity and proprioception in the hands of children with unilateral CP (hemiplegia) and children developing typically. In both studies, the researchers assessed the participants' sensitivity to pressure, stereognosis of familiar objects and shapes, and 2-point discrimination.[142,143] In addition, Cooper et al[142] used a proprioception test, and Klumlinde-Sundholm and Eliasson[143] used a pick-up test performed with and without visual feedback. It is interesting to note that, while Cooper et al[142] found significant sensory deficits in both hands of study participants, specifically in stereognosis and proprioception, Klumlinde-Sundholm and Eliasson[143] observed deficient performance only on the involved side, except for the stereognosis of shapes, in which the deficits were present bilaterally. In addition, a significant relationship between sensory deficits and dexterity in these children was reported in the latter study.[143] These findings warrant a recommendation for conducting a thorough bilateral sensory assessment in children with unilateral CP.

Besides purely sensory tactile and proprioceptive problems, children with CP have been shown to have difficulties with sensorimotor integration.[144] Gordon et al[144] investigated the origins of deficient anticipatory control during grasping in the involved hand of children with unilateral CP. Typically, when manipulating a small object, one needs to grade the fingertip forces depending on the object's weight and surface friction. When a person lifts such an object with one hand, the weight and friction information is obtained through experience and then can be successfully used to grade the fingertip forces while manipulating the same object with the other hand. Gordon et al[144] showed that children with hemiplegia had difficulty with anticipatory control for grasping with their involved hand. However, they could transfer the information regarding the object's weight and surface friction between the hands, even when first handling it with their involved hand. This suggested that the deficit in the anticipatory control of the involved hand may be related to impaired sensorimotor integration as opposed to decreased or altered sensation.[144]

Cardiovascular and Pulmonary System Impairments

Although the impairments of cardiovascular and pulmonary systems are not included in the classification of CP,[8] they may have significant impact on the quality of life of children and adults with this condition (see Table 4-1).[135,146] Premature birth plays a significant role in the etiology of many cases of CP.[147,148] Prevalence of chronic lung disease related to bronchopulmonary dysplasia (BPD) is the highest in infants born at 32 weeks gestation or earlier, and BPD is associated with a high incidence of neurodevelopmental

problems, including CP.[149-151] Therefore, history of prematurity contributes to the respiratory dysfunction in this patient population.[149,150] In infants born full term, meconium aspiration syndrome may also lead to chronic lung disease and neurologic sequelae, such as CP and seizure disorders.[149,150]

Children with CP demonstrate atypical development of the rib cage, with a high, flattened chest wall and lower rib flaring caused by abnormal tone-related weakness in their abdominal musculature.[149] Decreased chest expansion, increased work of breathing, shallow respiration, and impaired breath support for speech production are common in this patient population.[149,152,153] When present, spinal deformities further alter the physiological function that can be expressed in such measures as HR, respiratory rate (RR), oxygen saturation (SaO_2), and excursion of the chest wall (CWE).[135] Progressive neuromuscular scoliosis adds to morbidity and mortality in children and adults with CP.[135]

Impaired lung function is manifested in hypoventilation and decreased aerobic capacity,[149,154] contributing to low walking endurance and impaired cardiopulmonary fitness.[155-157] Verchuren and Takken[154] examined the aerobic capacity measured as peak oxygen uptake (VO_{2peak}) in children and adolescents with CP, GMFCS levels I and II, and found that it was significantly lower than in their typically developing peers and decreased with age, especially in girls.[154]

Children with CP demonstrate increased energy expenditure during ambulation[158] that complicates meeting the long-term viability requirement for safe and successful locomotion.[83-87] Furthermore, in one study, participants with CP did not only demonstrate significantly higher energy expenditure and oxygen consumption during physical activity, but also had a higher VO_2 at rest compared to the control group.[158]

Additional respiratory problems observed in this patient population include ineffective cough and airway clearance deficits.[146,149] Children with CP may display an insufficient coughing response to aspiration[103,146] and have difficulty coughing up secretions during respiratory infections.[146,149] Respiratory compromise is frequently reported as the most common cause of death in people with CP.[135,159] However, in a very large population-based mortality study, Strauss et al[159] found that cardiovascular problems, including heart disease and cerebrovascular disease, were the most common cause of death among its 45,292 participants.

Digestive System Impairments

Digestive system problems are common in children with CP, and associated growth and nutritional issues may significantly affect quality of life of these children and their caregivers.[27,93] Gastroesophageal reflux, a pathological process leading to the gastroesophageal reflux disease (GERD), is observed in 15% to 75%.[27,93,104] It is thought to be caused by the CNS dysfunction that impedes the motility of the esophagus and stomach and disrupts the work of the lower esophageal sphincter.[93,104] This neuromuscular incoordination leads to the reflux of stomach contents back into the esophagus and toward the larynx, which, in turn, may result in pulmonary aspiration.[93,103,104] Additional factors that contribute to the etiology of GERD in children with CP may include prolonged supine positioning, hiatal hernia, scoliosis, seizures, and spasticity-related increased intra-abdominal pressure.[27,93]

Prevalence of colorectal problems among children with CP is also very high, with constipation affecting 26% to 90%, and fecal incontinence present in 47%.[24,27,93,104,160,161] Chronic constipation refers to the occurrence of bowel movements with the frequency lower than 3 times per week, or the persistent need for the use of laxatives.[93] Its etiology in this patient population is related to bowel dysmotility caused by CNS lesions, combined with decreased physical activity, musculoskeletal deformities, and generalized hypotonia or increased extensor muscle tone. The use of medications with a side effect of constipation may contribute to this problem. Such medications include aluminum antacid, anticonvulsant, antihistamine, antispasmodic, and opioid drugs.[93] Because children with CP have multiple health issues, constipation may be overlooked, which may lead to permanent dysmotility of the gut and even to bowel perforation.[27] Chronic constipation may be associated with other gastrointestinal symptoms, such as chronic nausea, recurrent vomiting, abdominal pain, and decreased appetite, which may lead to feeding problems.[27,93] Chronic constipation may also contribute to urogenital system impairments.[93]

Greater than 50% of children with CP have weight problems, with many being underweight and others overweight, and almost 25% are small for their age.[24,162] Stallings et al[162] reported significant difference in linear growth between children with and without CP, with 30% of 154 study participants with unilateral and bilateral CP being undernourished. Improved growth and nutritional status were shown to correlate with improvements in gross motor function.[27,163] Results of several studies pointed to a relationship between the G-tube placement and nutritional status and growth in children classified in GMFCS levels IV and V.[98,105,164] Specifically, Dahlseng et al[105] reported on a strong association between restricted growth and low prevalence of G-tube placement; Himmelmann et al[98] showed that children who were fed using G-tubes had significantly higher weight and BMI than those who were not; and Day et al[164] obtained similar results related to height and weight. These findings suggested that the use of G-tube feedings, when available, may, indeed, improve growth in children with the lowest levels of motor function.[105]

It is important to mention that energy expenditure variability among individuals with CP functioning at different GMFCS levels while performing different physical tasks makes the development of specific caloric intake guidelines difficult.[27] In addition, standard growth charts may not be appropriate for use with this patient population.[27] Joint contractures may make the height measurement process difficult and less reliable, and the body mass index (BMI) may not be

an accurate nutritional status measure because of the lower BMD and lower muscle mass findings in children and adults with CP compared to people without disabilities. Therefore, it appears to be more appropriate to use patient population-specific growth charts.[27,164,165] Based on the data obtained in a very large study of 24,920 children and adolescents with CP, age range 2 to 20 years, Day et al[164] developed height and weight growth charts that can be used specifically for this patient population at all functional levels. In a smaller study of 273 children with CP, Stevenson et al[165] created gender-specific growth curves for 6 different anthropometric measures, including weight, upper arm length, knee height, triceps and subscapular skinfolds, and muscle area of the mid-upper arm.

Urogenital System Impairments

Primary urinary incontinence affects a significant number of children with CP.[24,166,167] This term refers to involuntary loss of urine one time per week or more frequently, to the extent that necessitates the use of diapers or having to change the person's clothing as it becomes wet.[166] Incontinence that occurs after complete bladder control has been achieved and practiced for a period of time is referred to as *secondary urinary incontinence.* Roijen et al[166] reported on a study conducted with 601 children and adolescents with unilateral and bilateral spastic, dyskinetic, and ataxic CP, age range 4 to 18 years. Prevalence of primary urinary incontinence in this sample was 23.5%, while in a subset of 4- to 10-year-old participants, it was 33.6%. Results indicated delayed development of bladder control in children with CP. Only 54% of participants with bilateral spastic CP and lower functional level, and 38% of those with significant intellectual disability achieved urinary continence spontaneously, compared to 80% of participants with unilateral and bilateral spastic CP who had higher levels of motor and cognitive functions.[166]

Other types of lower urinary tract dysfunction observed in children with CP include urinary tract infections (UTIs), increased voiding frequency, urinary hesitancy, and urgency.[167] *Urinary hesitancy* is defined as difficulty starting the flow of urine,[168] and urgency refers to a sudden onset of a strong need to urinate.[169] Abnormal urodynamic findings, such as decreased bladder capacity, incomplete bladder emptying, detrusor overactivity and detrusor sphincter dyssynergia were also reported.[167,170,171] In a study of 214 individuals with CP, urodynamic findings consistent with the diagnosis of neurogenic bladder were present in 16.4% of participants, ages 5 to 57 years, who functioned at variable educational and GMFCS levels.[170] Eighty percent of them had spastic hyperreflexic bladders.[170] It is important to keep in mind that lower urinary tract dysfunction may be indicative of the upper urinary tract problems in individuals with CP.[171] Specifically, Gündoğdu et al[171] identified such symptoms as febrile UTIs and detrusor sphincter dyssynergia as important factors that may point to the presence of upper urinary tract deterioration.

ACTIVITY LIMITATIONS AND PARTICIPATION RESTRICTIONS IN CHILDREN WITH CERERBRAL PALSY

In the past, physical therapy research focused mainly on the outcomes related to body structures and functions but not necessarily to daily activity and participation across different settings.[5] Therefore, therapists emphasized addressing impairments and functional limitations in habilitation and rehabilitation processes as compared to focusing on increasing their patients' activity and enhancing their participation in life situations. The adoption of ICF[2] provided pediatric physical therapists and other health care practitioners with a new perspective that supports their professional role as health enablement specialists. The orientation toward enhancing activity and participation gives pediatric clinicians an opportunity to make a difference in the lives of children with CP and their families by helping them achieve desired, meaningful goals within the context of their daily lives.[5]

CP is a chronic health condition that is associated with limitations in physical activity and restrictions in participation in family, school, and community situations.[172] The results of a large population-based study of 15,300 third graders showed that 3210 of them (21%) had chronic health conditions, including physical disabilities. A higher BMI in these children was associated with decreased physical activity compared to their peers without chronic health conditions. Additional factors that contributed to being at risk for or being overweight included living in an urban area, spending more time watching television, being cared for by individuals other than their parents, having fewer siblings, Hispanic ethnicity, low socioeconomic status, the diagnosis of asthma, and having parents with poor mental or physical health.[172]

Another study examined physical activity in 81 ambulatory children with CP, age range 10 to 13 years and GMFCS levels I through III.[173] The participants with CP walked significantly less and were overall less physically active than children without disabilities. However, when examined by the GMFCS level, the amount of activity in children with CP who functioned at level I was similar to children developing typically, while children who functioned at GMFCS level III displayed the greatest activity limitations.[173] In that study, the participants' quality of life and physical, behavioral, and emotional aspects of health were also assessed.[174] The amount of self-reported daily activity affected the physical, behavioral, and emotional health reports by the participants, but not their reports of quality of life. Other interesting findings in this study were that those children who functioned at GMFCS levels I and II rated their physical health lower than children without disabilities, and children in GMFCS level I also reported lower ratings of their emotional health. To explain these results, the authors suggested that perhaps children with CP who had the highest levels of physical functioning were more acutely aware of the differences in performance between them and children with typical development.

Although these differences may appear insignificant to other people, the heightened awareness negatively affected self-assessment ratings in these children.[174] Research results obtained by Majnemer et al[175] can be used to support this explanation. In their study, children with CP who had higher levels of motor function were found to have an emotional response to failure more frequently, which negatively affected their motivation to persist in their attempts to complete difficult tasks.[175]

The lack of relationship between self-reported physical activity and quality of life in the study by Bjornson et al[174] was explained using the Theory of Subjective Well-Being Homeostasis.[176] According to this theory, people feel satisfied with their lives because of a homeostatic mechanism that is grounded in such cognitive concepts as perception of being in control, self-esteem, and optimism. Self-perception based on these concepts is influenced by one's personality and allows the individual to interpret life situations in a positive way.[174,176] This theory may help explain how people with physical disabilities can have a positive outlook on life despite of everyday challenges they face.[174] Highly variable findings of a quality of life study conducted by Majnemer et al[43] with 95 school-aged children with CP support this theory. The quality of life of approximately 50% of the study participants was reportedly similar to that of those developing typically, and activity limitations were not found to affect their psychosocial well-being. Instead, social-emotional adaptation in these children was related to such factors as the level of parental stress, behavioral problems, and motivation.[43] In a later study by the same authors, high levels of motivation were also found to be associated with a reduced number of activity limitations, fewer behavioral problems, and decreased burden on the family.[175]

Participation is a multidimensional construct that encompasses being involved in a variety of life situations in different settings, and it is related to activity or the ability to perform specific tasks.[2,177] Carey and Long[177] brought up an important issue that had to do with the difficulty separating participation from activity as a construct and measuring its outcomes. These authors emphasized that eliminating a limitation in a specific activity may not necessarily lead to enhanced participation. A child with CP may learn to use a reverse wheeled walker to achieve independent ambulation and, thus, an increased activity level. However, the same child still may have difficulty playing with peers developing typically if that involves negotiating stairs or if he or she has communication deficits. Based on their review of current literature, Carey and Long[177] identified positive and negative personal and environmental factors that affect participation in children with disabilities (Table 4-5).

Amount of participation in different life situations encountered across different settings varies among children with disabilities, but overall, their participation levels are lower than in children with typical development.[177-180] Factors that reportedly enhance or impede participation in educational settings are similar to those identified in Table 4-5.[177] Additional barriers encountered in a school setting may

TABLE 4-5

PERSONAL AND ENVIRONMENTAL FACTORS AFFECTING PARTICIPATION IN CHILDREN WITH DISABILITIES

FACTORS	POSITIVE	NEGATIVE
Child-related	• Enjoyment of activities • Ability to experience enjoyment • Ability to select preferred activities • Ability to identify preferences	• Greater limitations in motor function and mobility corresponding to GMFCS and MACS levels • Intellectual disability • Deficits in adaptive skills • Communication deficits
Family-related	• Cohesive and stable families • Participation in recreational and social life as a family • Positive views of participation by the caregiver • Ability to identify priorities for activities • Ability to advocate for the child's participation needs	• Lower household income • Lower level of parental education • Decrease in caregiver's physical function • Higher level of parental stress • Perceived community participation barriers • Difficulties with the child's transportation
Environment-related	• Availability of equipment and structural environmental adaptations • Access to private transportation options • Availability of transportation services or assistance • Availability of financial assistance through social services	• Prohibitive cost of equipment and structural adaptations • Difficulty accessing public transportation • Negative attitudes of others • Poor social support • Inadequate institutional and government policies • Insufficient knowledge of disability-related laws

Abbreviations: GMFCS, Gross Motor Function Classification System; MACS, Manual Ability Classification System.

Compiled from Carey and Long.[177]

include difficulty making friends, bullying by peer students, and social isolation.[177] Thomas and Rosenberg[178] described other barriers to participation that exist in the areas of leisure and recreation, such as insufficient knowledge of available resources by health professionals involved in the child's care, prohibitive cost of community participation, and misunderstanding or misinformation.[178] Majnemer et al[179] found that children with CP enjoyed participation in a wide variety of leisure activities, which was enhanced by such factors as motivation in mastering difficult tasks and receiving rehabilitation services. However, these children were involved in a lower number of physical activities and those related to specific skills, such as playing musical instruments or taking art lessons.[179] Data obtained from a large European study that examined participation in children with CP demonstrated considerable geographic and inter-individual variability, but certain consistently present barriers were identified.[180] Besides limitations in fine motor skills, walking, intellectual abilities, and communication, presence of pain was another significant factor that was found to impede participation across most areas of daily life.[180]

Participation in exercise and fitness programs is of special interest to pediatric physical therapists as it is seen as the means to prevent the development of accompanying impairments in children with CP.[181,182] Brunton and Bartlett[181] conducted a 4-year Adolescent Study of Quality of Life, Mobility and Exercise (ASQME). They described exercise participation, weekly duration of fitness activities, and change in participation over time in 130 adolescents with CP, mean age 14.7 years. The participants' activity levels were compared to Canadian national health guidelines that, at the time of the study, recommended 60 minutes of moderate or 30 minutes of vigorous daily physical activity.[181] Currently, Public Health Agency of Canada recommends 60 minutes of moderate to vigorous daily exercise for the 12 to 17 years age group.[183]

The results showed low overall participation rates, with greater moderate and vigorous exercise participation recorded in adolescents with CP who had higher levels of motor function.[181] The exercise guidelines were met by 9.4% to 11.4% of the study sample. The participants functioning at GMFCS levels I through III preferred walking to other exercise activities, and swimming was the preferred type of exercise among those who functioned at GMFCS levels IV and V. There was an inverse relationship found between the amount of stretching performed and the GMFCS level, and female participants reported performing more stretching than male.[181]

Other findings included a 50% rate of participation in strengthening exercise; low levels of participation in cardiovascular fitness activities, especially by youth functioning at GMFCS levels IV and V; and declining exercise participation rates over time.[181] These results are concerning because a sedentary life style continuing into adulthood may greatly contribute to further development of accompanying musculoskeletal impairments and secondary health conditions. Moreover, these results underscore the urgent need for pediatric physical therapists to engage in promotion of exercise participation among adolescents with CP, with the emphasis on the importance of continuing an active life style into adulthood.[181]

REFERENCES

1. Kostanjsek N. Use of the International Classification of Functioning, Disability and Health (ICF) as a conceptual framework and common language for disability statistics and health information systems. *BMC Public Health.* 2011;11(suppl 4):53.

2. World Health Organization. *International Classification of Functioning, Disability and Health.* Geneva, Switzerland: World Health Organization; 2001.

3. World Health Organization. Towards a common language for functioning, disability and health: ICF, the International Classification of Functioning, Disability and Health. Geneva, Switzerland: World Health Organization. http://www.who.int/classifications/icf/training/icfbeginnersguide.pdf?ua=1. Published 2002. Accessed March 8, 2015.

4. Jette AM. Toward a common language for function, disability, and health. *Phys Ther.* 2006;86:726-734.

5. Goldstein DN, Cohn E, Coster W. Enhancing participation for children with disabilities: application of the ICF enablement framework to pediatric physical therapist practice. *Pediatr Phys Ther.* 2004;16:114-120.

6. Palisano RJ, Campbell SK, Harris SR. Evidence-based decision-making in pediatric physical therapy. In: Campbell SK, Palisano RJ, Orlin MN, eds. *Physical Therapy for Children.* 4th ed. St. Louis, MO: Saunders; 2012:1-36.

7. World Health Organization. *International Classification of Functioning, Disability and Health: Children and Youth Version.* Geneva, Switzerland: World Health Organization; 2007.

8. Rosenbaum P, Paneth N, Leviton A, et al. A report: the definition and classification of cerebral palsy April 2006. *Dev Med Child Neurol.* 2007;49(suppl 109):8-14. Erratum in: *Dev Med Child Neurol.* 2007;49(6):480.

9. Sanger TD, Delgado MR, Gaebler-Spira D, Hallet M, Mink JW, Task Force on Childhood Motor Disorders. Classification and definition of disorders causing hypertonia in childhood. *Pediatrics.* 2003;111(1):e89-e97.

10. Sanger TD. Toward a definition of childhood dystonia. *Curr Opin Pediatr.* 2004;16(6):623-627.

11. Sanger TD, Chen D, Fehlings DL, et al. Definition and classification of hyperkinetic movements in childhood. *Mov Disord.* 2010;25(11):1538-1549.

12. Wright M, Wallman L. Cerebral palsy. In: Campbell SK, Palisano RJ, Orlin MN, eds. *Physical Therapy for Children.* 4th ed. St. Louis, MO: Saunders; 2012:577-627.

13. Sanger TD, Chen D, Delgado MR, Gaebler-Spira D, Hallet M, Mink JW, Task Force on Childhood Motor Disorders. Definition and classification of negative motor signs in childhood. *Pediatrics.* 2006;118:2159-2167.

14. Ashwal S, Russman BS, Blasco PA, et al. Practice parameter: diagnostic assessment of the child with cerebral palsy: report of the Quality Standards Subcommittee of the American Academy of Neurology and the Practice Committee of the Child Neurology Society. *Neurology.* 2004;62(6):851-863.

15. Bax M, Tydeman C, Flodmark O. Clinical and MRI correlates of cerebral palsy: the European cerebral palsy study. *JAMA.* 2006;296(13):1602-1608.

16. Hadders-Algra, M. Variation and variability: key words in human motor development. *Phys Ther.* 2010;90:1823-1837.

17. Bly L. *Components of Typical and Atypical Motor Development.* Laguna Beach, CA: Neuro-Developmental Treatment Association, Inc.; 2011.

18. Einspieler C, Prechtl HFR. Prechtl's Assessment of General Movements: a diagnostic tool for the functional assessment of the young nervous system. *Ment Retard Dev Disabil Res Rev.* 2005;11:61-67.

19. Dobson F, Morris ME, Baker R, Graham HK. Unilateral cerebral palsy: a population-based study of gait and motor function. *Dev Med Child Neurol.* 2011;53(5):429-435.

20. Deffeyes JE, Harbourne RT, Kyvelidou A, Stuberg WA, Stregiou N. Nonlinear analysis of sitting postural sway indicates developmental delay in infants. *Clin Biomech (Bristol, Avon).* 2009;24:564-570.

21. Harbourne RT, Willett S, Kyvelidou A, Deffeyes J, Stergiou N. A comparison of interventions for children with cerebral palsy to improve sitting postural control: a clinical trial. *Phys Ther.* 2010;90:1881-1898.

22. Stergiou N, Harbourne RT, Cavanough JT. Optimal movement variability: a new theoretical perspective for neurologic physical therapy. *J Neurol Phys Ther.* 2006;30(3):120-129.

23. Dusing SC, Harbourne RT. Variability in postural control during infancy: implications for development, assessment, and intervention. *Phys Ther.* 2010;90:1838-1849.

24. Odding E, Roebroeck ME, Stam HJ. The epidemiology of cerebral palsy: incidence, impairments and risk factors. *Disabil Rehabil.* 2006;28(4):183-191.

25. Carlsson M, Hagberg G, Olsson I. Clinical and aetiological aspects of epilepsy in children with cerebral palsy. *Dev Med Child Neurol.* 2003;45(6):371-376.

26. Bruck I, Antoniuk SA, Spessatto A, Schmitt de Bem R, Hausberger R, Pacheco CG. Epilepsy in children with cerebral palsy. *Arq Neuropsiquiatr.* 2001;59(1):35-39.

27. Pruitt DW, Tsai T. Common medical comorbidities associated with cerebral palsy. *Phy Med Rehabil Clin N Am.* 2009;20(3):453-467.

28. Himmelmann K, Beckung E, Hagberg G, Uvebrant P. Gross and fine motor function and accompanying impairments in cerebral palsy. *Dev Med Child Neurol.* 2006;48(6):417-423.

29. Luc Jasmin, David Zieve; MedlinePlus Medical Encyclopedia. Partial (focal) seizure. http://nlm.nih.gov/medlineplus/ency/article/000697.htm. Updated August 3, 2015. Accessed September 7, 2015.

30. Luc Jasmin; MedlinePlus Medical Encyclopedia. Generalized tonic-clonic seizure. http://nlm.nih.gov/medlineplus/ency/article/000695.htm. Updated August 3, 2015. Accessed September 7, 2015.

31. Panayiotopoulos CP. Clinical aspects of the diagnosis of epileptic seizures and epileptic syndromes. In: Panayiotopoulos CP, ed. *The Epilepsies: Seizures, Syndromes and Management.* Oxfordshire, UK: Bladon Medical Publishing; 2005. http://www.ncbi.nlm.nih.gov/books/NBK2609/. Accessed September 7, 2015.

32. National Institute of Neurological Disorders and Stroke. NINDS infantile spasms information page. http://www.ninds.nih.gov/disorders/infantilespasms/infantilespasms.htm. Updated July 17, 2015. Accessed September 7, 2015.

33. Ramachandrannair R. Pediatric status epilepticus. *Medscape*. http://emedicine.medscape.com/article/908394-overview. Updated October 4, 2014. Accessed September 7, 2015.

34. Types of seizures. Johns Hopkins *Medicine*. http://www.hopkins-medicine.org/neurology_neurosurgery/specialty_areas/epilepsy/seizures/types/. Accessed on September 7, 2015.

35. Majnemer A, Shevell M, Hall N, Poulin C, Law M. Developmental and functional abilities in children with cerebral palsy as related to pattern and level of motor function. *J Child Neurol.* 2010;25(10):1236-1241.

36. Parkes J, Hill N, Platt MJ, Donnelly C. Oromotor dysfunction and communication impairments in children with cerebral palsy: a register study. *Dev Med Child Neurol.* 2010;52(12):1113-1119.

37. Pueyo R, Junqué C, Vendrell P, Narberhaus A, Segarra D. Neuropsychologic impairment in bilateral cerebral palsy. *Pediatr Neurol.* 2009;40(1):19-26.

38. Bjorgaas HM, Hysing M, Elgen I. Psychiatric disorders among children with cerebral palsy at school starting age. *Res Dev Disabil.* 2012;33(4):1287-1293.

39. Brossard-Racine M, Waknin J, Shikako-Thomas K, et al. Behavioral difficulties in adolescents with cerebral palsy. *J Chil Neurol.* 2013;28(1):27-33.

40. Bottcher L, Meulengracht Flachs E, Uldall P. Attentional and executive impairments in children with spastic cerebral palsy. *Dev Med Child Neurol.* 2010;52(2):e42-e47.

41. Himmelmann K, Uvebrant, P. Function and neuroimaging in cerebral palsy: a population-based study. *Dev Med Child Neurol.* 2011;53(6):516-521.

42. Majnemer A, Shevell M, Rosenbaum P, Law P, Poulin C. Determinants of life quality in school-age children with cerebral palsy. *J Pediatr.* 2007;151(5):470-475.

43. Shevell MI, Dagenais L, Hall N; REPACQ Consortium. Comorbidities in cerebral palsy and their relationship to neurologic subtype and GMFCS level. *Neurology.* 2009;72(24):2090-2096.

44. Palisano RJ, Rosenbaum PL, Walter SD, Russell DJ, Wood EP, Galuppi BE. Development and reliability of a system to classify gross motor function in children with cerebral palsy. *Dev Med Child Neurol.* 1997;39(4):214-223.

45. Manly T, Robertson IH, Anderson V, Nimm-Smith I. *The Test of Everyday Attention for Children: Manual.* Bury St. Edmunds, UK: Thames Valley Test Company; 1999.

46. Horak FB. Postural orientation and equilibrium: what do we need to know about neural control of balance to prevent falls? *Age Ageing.* 2006;35(suppl 2):ii7-iii1.

47. Shumway-Cook A, Woollacott MH. Normal postural control. In: Shumway-Cook A, Woollacott MH, eds. *Motor Control: Translating Research into Clinical Practice.* 4th ed. Philadelphia, PA: Lippincott Williams and Wilkins; 2012:161-194.

48. Saavedra S, Woollacott M, van Donkelaar P. Head stability during quiet sitting in children with cerebral palsy: effect of vision and trunk support. *Exp Brain Res.* 2010;201:13-23.

49. Rose J, Wolff DR, Jones VK, Bloch DA, Oehlert JW, Gamble JG. Postural balance in children with cerebral palsy. *Dev Med Child Neurol.* 2002;44(1):58-63.

50. Pax Lowes L, Westcott SL, Palisano RJ, Effgen SK, Orlin MN. Muscle force and range of motion as predictors of standing balance in children with cerebral palsy. *Phys Occup Ther Pediatr.* 2004;24(1/2):57-77.

51. Nashner LM, Shumway-Cook A, Marin O. Stance posture control in select groups of children with cerebral palsy: deficits in sensory organization and muscular coordination. *Exp Brain Res.* 1983;49(3):393-409.

52. Brogren Carlberg E, Hadders-Algra M. Postural dysfunction in children with cerebral palsy: some implications for therapeutic guidance. *Neural Plast.* 2005;12(2):221-228.

53. Bigongiari A, de Andrade e Souza F, Fraciulli PM, Neto Sel R, Araujo RC, Mochizuki L. Anticipatory and compensatory postural adjustments in sitting in children with cerebral palsy. *Hum Mov Sci.* 2011;30(3):648-657.

54. Liu W-Y, Zaino CA, Westcott McCoy S. Anticipatory postural adjustments in children with cerebral palsy and children with typical development. *Pediatr Phys Ther.* 2007;19:188-195.

55. Tomita H, Fukaya Y, Ueda T, et al. Deficits in task-specific modulation of anticipatory postural adjustments in individuals with spastic diplegic cerebral palsy. *J Neurophysiol.* 2011;105(5):2157-2168.

56. Girolami GL, Shiratori T, Aruin AS. Anticipatory postural adjustments in children with hemiplegia and diplegia. *J Electromyogr Kinesiol.* 2011;21(6):988-997.

57. Saavedra S, van Donkelaar P, Woollacott M. Learning about gravity: segmental assessment of upright control as infants develop independent sitting. *J Neurophysiol.* 2012;108(8):2215-2229.

58. Bernstein NA. On dexterity and its development. In: Latash ML, Turvey MT, eds. *Dexterity and Its Development.* Mahwah, NJ: Lawrence Erlbaum Associates, Publishers; 1996:3-244.

59. Harbourne RT, Stergiou N. Nonlinear analysis of the development of sitting postural control. *Dev Psychobiol.* 2003;42:368-377.

60. Harbourne RT, Stergiou N. Movement variability and the use of nonlinear tools: principles to guide physical therapist practice. *Phys Ther.* 2009;89(3):267-282.

61. Brogren E. Influence of two different sitting positions on postural adjustments in children with spastic diplegia. *Dev Med Child Neurol.* 2001;43(8):534-546.

62. Hadders-Algra M, van der Fits IBM, Stremmelaar EF, Touwen BCL. Development of postural adjustments during reaching in infants with CP. *Dev Med Child Neurol.* 1999;41:766-776.

63. Burtner PA, Qualls C, Woollacott MH. Muscle activation characteristics of stance balance control in children with spastic cerebral palsy. *Gait Posture.* 1998;8(3):163-174.

64. Winters TF, Gage JR, Hicks R. Gait patterns in spastic hemiplegia in children and young adults. *J Bone Joint Surg Am.* 1987;69(3):437-441.

65. Rodda JM, Graham HK, Carson L, Galea MP, Wolfe R. Sagittal gait patterns in spastic diplegia. *J Bone Joint Surg (Br).* 2004;86-B(2):251-258.

66. Latash ML, Anson JG. What are "normal movements" in atypical populations? *Behav Brain Sci.* 1996;19:55-106.

67. Patla AE. The neural control of locomotion. In: Spivack BS, ed. *Evaluation and Management of Gait Disorders.* New York, NY: Marcel Dekker, Inc.; 1995:53-78.

68. Hanke, T, Cech DJ. Locomotion. In: Cech DJ, Martin S. *Functional Movement Development across the Life Span.* 3rd ed. St. Louis, MO: Saunders; 2012:288-308.

69. Barbeau H, Ladouceur M, Norman KE, Pepin A, Leroux A. Walking after spinal cord injury: evaluation, treatment, and functional recovery. *Arch Phys Med Rehabil.* 1999;80:225-235.

70. MacKinnon CD, Winter DA. Control of whole body balance in the frontal plane during human walking. *J Biomechanics.* 1993;26:633-644.

71. Effgen SK. Child development. In: Effgen SK, ed. *Meeting the Physical Therapy Needs of Children.* 2nd ed. Philadelphia, PA: F. A. Davis Company; 2013:41-105.

72. Campbell SK. The child's development of functional movement. In: Campbell SK, Palisano RJ, Orlin MN, eds. *Physical Therapy for Children.* 4th ed. St. Louis, MO: Saunders; 2012:37-86.

73. Berger SE, Theuring C, Adolph KE. How and when infants learn to climb stairs. *Infant Behav Dev.* 2007;30(1):36-49.

74. Farmer SE. Key factors in the development of lower limb co-ordination: implications for the acquisition of walking in children with cerebral palsy. *Disabil Rehabil.* 2003;25:807-816.

75. Shumway-Cook A, Woollacott MH. A life span perspective on mobility. In: Shumway-Cook A, Woollacott MH, eds. *Motor Control: Translating Research into Clinical Practice.* 4th ed. Philadelphia, PA: Lippincott Williams and Wilkins; 2012:348-380.

76. Stout JL. Gait: development and analysis. In: Campbell SK, ed. *Physical Therapy for Children*. 3rd ed. Philadelphia, PA: W.B. Saunders Company; 2006:161-190.

77. Sutherland DH, Olshen R, Cooper L, Woo SL. The development of mature gait. *J Bone Joint Surg Am*. 1980;62(3):336-353.

78. Berger W. Characteristics of locomotor control in children with cerebral palsy. *Neurosci Biobehav Rev*. 1998;22:579-582.

79. Berger W. Normal and impaired development of gait. *Adv Neurol*. 2001;87:65-70.

80. Prosser LA, Lee SCK, VanSant AF, Barbe MF, Lauer RT. Trunk and hip muscle activation patterns are different during walking in young children with and without cerebral palsy. *Phys Ther*. 2010;90(7):986-997.

81. Prosser LA, Lauer RT, VanSant AF, Barbe MF, Lee SCK. Variability and symmetry of gait in early walkers with and without bilateral cerebral palsy. *Gait Posture*. 2010; 31(4):522-526.

82. Palisano R, Rosenbaum P, Bartlett D, Livingston M. *GMFCS – E & R, Gross Motor Function System, Expanded and Revised*. http://cpnet.canchild.ca/en/resources/42-gross-motor-function-classification-system-expanded-revised-gmfcs-e-r. Accessed January 23, 2016.

83. van den Hecke A, Malghem C, Renders A, Detrembleur C, Palumbo S, Lejeune TM. Mechanical work, energetic cost, and gait efficiency in children with cerebral palsy. *J Pediatr Orthop*. 2007;27(6):643-647.

84. Van de Walle P, Hallemans A, Truijen S, et al. Increased mechanical cost of walking in children with diplegia: the role of the passenger unit cannot be neglected. *Res Dev Disabil*. 2012;33(6):1996-2003.

85. Rosen S, Tucker CA, Lee SCK. Gait energy efficiency in children with cerebral palsy. *Conf Proc IEEE Eng Med Biol Soc*. 2006;1:1220-1223.

86. Bratteby Tollerz LU, Olsson RM, Forslund AH, Norrlin SE. Reliability of energy cost calculations in children with cerebral palsy, cystic fibrosis an healthy controls. *Acta Paediatr*. 2011;100(12):1616-1620.

87. Romkes J, Peeters W, Oosterom AM, Molenaar S, Bakels I, Brunner R. Evaluating upper body movements during gait in healthy children and children with diplegic cerebral palsy. *J Pediatr Orthop*. 2007;16(3):175-180.

88. Johnson DC, Damiano DL, Abel MF. The evolution of gait in childhood and adolescent cerebral palsy. *J Pediatr Orthop*. 1997;17:392-396.

89. Bell KJ, Ounpuu S, DeLuca PA, Romness MJ. Natural progression of gait in children with cerebral palsy. *J Pediatr Orhop*. 2002;22(5):677-682.

90. Kerr C, McDowell BC, Parkes J, Stevenson M, Cosgrove AP. Age-related changes in energy efficiency of gait, activity, and participation in children with cerebral palsy. *Dev Med Child Neurol*. 2011;53(1):61-67.

91. McKearnan KA, Kieckhefer GM, Engel JM, Jensen MP, Labyak S. Pain in children with cerebral palsy: a review. *J Neurosci Nurs*. 2004;36(5):252-259.

92. Tervo RC, Symons F, Stout J, Novacheck T. Parental report of pain and associated limitations in ambulatory children with cerebral palsy. *Arch Phys Med Rehabil*. 2006;87(7):928-934.

93. Sullivan PB. Gastrointestinal disorders in children with neurodevelopmental disabilities. *Dev Disabil Res Rev*. 2008;14(2):128-136.

94. Field D, Garland M, Williams K. Correlates of specific childhood feeding problems. *J Paediatr Child Health*. 2003;39(4):299-304.

95. Senner JE, Logemann J, Zecker S, Gaebler-Spira D. Drooling, saliva production, and swallowing in cerebral palsy. *Dev Med Child Neurol*. 2004;46(12):801-806.

96. Dysarthria – definition and more from the Free Merriam-Webster Dictionary. *Merriam-Webster Online*. http://www.merriam-webster.com/dictionary/dysarthria. Accessed September 7, 2015.

97. Anarthria – medical definition and more from the Free Merriam-Webster Dictionary. *Merriam-Webster Online*. http://www.merriam-webster.com/medical/anarthria. Accessed September 7, 2015.

98. Himmelmann K, Hagberg G, Wiklund LM, Eek MN, Uvebrant P. Dyskinetic cerebral palsy: a population-based study of children born between 1991 and 1998. *Dev Med Child Neurol*. 2007;49(4):246-251.

99. Reid SM, McCutcheon J, Reddihough DS, Johnson H. Prevalence and predictors of drooling in 7- to 14-year-old children with cerebral palsy: a population study. *Dev Med Child Neurol*. 2012;54(11):1032-1036.

100. Reddihough D, Erasmus CE, Johnson H, McKellar GMW, Jongerius PH. Botulinum toxin assessment, intervention and aftercare for paediatric and adult drooling: international consensus statement. *Eur J Neurol*. 2010;17(suppl 2):109-121.

101. Tahmassebi JF, Curzon MEJ. Prevalence of drooling in children with cerebral palsy attending special schools. *Dev Med Child Neurol*. 2003;45(9):613-617.

102. Erasmus CE, van Hulst K, Rotteveel LJC, et al. Drooling in cerebral palsy: hypersalivation or dysfunctional oral motor control? *Dev Med Child Neurol*. 2009;51(6):454-459.

103. Weir KA, McMahon S, Taylor S, Chang AB. Oropharyngeal aspiration and silent aspiration in children. *Chest*. 2011;140(3):589-597.

104. Erasmus CE, van Hulst K, Rotteveel LJC, Willemsen MA, Jongerius PH. Swallowing problems in cerebral palsy. *Eur J Pediatr*. 2012;171(3):409-414.

105. Dahlseng MO, Andersen GL, Da Graca Andrada M, et al; Surveillance of Cerebral Palsy in Europe Network. Gastrostomy tube feeding of children with cerebral palsy: variation across six European countries. *Dev Med Child Neurol*. 2012;54(10):938-944.

106. Gudjonsdottir B, Stemmons Mercer V. Hip and spine in children with cerebral palsy: musculoskeletal development and clinical implications. *Pediatr Phys Ther*. 1997;9(4):179-185.

107. Morrell DS, Pearson M, Sauser DD. Progressive bone and joint abnormalities of the spine and lower extremities in cerebral palsy. *Radiographics*. 2002;22(2):257-268.

108. Horstmann HM, Hosalkar H, Keenan MA. Orthopaedic issues in the musculoskeletal care of adults with cerebral palsy. *Dev Med Child Neurol*. 2009;51(suppl 4):99-105.

109. Fehlings D, Switzer L, Agarwal P, et al. Informing evidence-based clinical practice guidelines for children with cerebral palsy at risk of osteoporosis: a systematic review. *Dev Med Child Neurol*. 2012;54(2):106-116.

110. Mockford M, Caulton JM. The pathophysiological basis of weakness in children with cerebral palsy. *Pediatr Phys Ther*. 2010;22(2):222-233.

111. Goh H-T, Thompson M, Huang W-B, Schafer S. Relationships among measures of knee musculoskeletal impairments, gross motor function and walking efficiency in children with cerebral palsy. *Pediatr Phys Ther*. 2006;18(4):253-261.

112. Damiano DL, Dodd K, Taylor NF. Should we be testing and training muscle strength in cerebral palsy? *Dev Med Child Neurol*. 2002;44(1):68-72.

113. Sanger TD, Chen D, Delgado MR, Gaebler-Spira D, Hallet M, Mink JW, Task Force on Childhood Motor Disorders. Definition and classification of negative motor signs in childhood. *Pediatrics*. 2006;118:2159-2167.

114. Damiano DL, Quinlivan J, Owen BF, Shaffrey M, Abel MF. Spasticity versus strength in cerebral palsy: relationships among involuntary resistance, voluntary torque, and motor function. *Eur J Neurol*. 2001;8(suppl 5):40-49.

115. Apoptosis – medical definition and more from the Free Merriam-Webster Dictionary. *Merriam-Webster Online*. http://www.merriam-webster.com/medical/apoptosis. Accessed September 7, 2015.

116. Myklebust BM, Gottlieb GL, Penn RD, Agarwal GC. Reciprocal excitation of antagonistic muscles as a differentiating feature in spasticity. *Ann Neurol*. 1982;12(4):367-374.

117. Engsberg JR, Hollander KW. Hip spasticity and strength in children with spastic diplegic cerebral palsy. *J Appl Biomech*. 2000;16:221-233.

118. Tedroff K, Knutson LM, Soderberg G. Synergistic muscle activation during maximum voluntary contraction in children with and without spastic cerebral palsy. *Dev Med Child Neurol.* 2006;48:789-796.

119. Tedroff K, Knutson LM, Soderberg G. Co-activity during maximum voluntary contraction: a study of four lower-extremity muscles in children with and without cerebral palsy. *Dev Med Child Neurol.* 2008;50:377-381.

120. Ohata K, Tsuboyama T, Haruta T, Ichibashi N, Kato T, Nakamura T. Relation between muscle thickness, spasticity, and activity limitations in children and adolescents with cerebral palsy. *Dev Med Child Neurol.* 2008;50(2):152-156.

121. McDowell BC, Salazar-Torres JJ, Kerr C, Cosgrove AP. Passive range of motion in a population-based sample of children with spastic cerebral palsy who walk. *Phys Occup Ther Pediatr.* 2012;32(2):139-150.

122. Joseph B, Reddy K, Varghese RA, Shah H, Doddabasappa SN. Management of severe crouch gait in children and adolescents with cerebral palsy. *J Pediatr Orthop.* 2010;30(8):832-839.

123. Murphy KP. Cerebral palsy lifetime care – four musculoskeletal conditions. *Dev Med Child Neurol.* 2009;51(suppl 4):30-37.

124. Picciolini O, Albisetti W, Cozzaglio M, Spreafico F, Mosca F, Gasparroni V. "Postural management" to prevent hip dislocation in children with cerebral palsy. *Hip Int.* 2009;19(suppl 6):S56-S62.

125. Young NL, Wright JG, Lam TP, Rajaratnam K, Stephens D, Wedge JH. Windswept hip deformity in spastic quadriplegic cerebral palsy. *Pediatr Phys Ther.* 1998;10:94-100.

126. Scrutton D, Baird G. Surveillance measures of the hips of children with bilateral cerebral palsy. *Arch Dis Child.* 1997;76(4):381-384.

127. Scrutton D, Baird G, Smeeton N. Hip dysplasia in bilateral cerebral palsy: incidence and natural history in children aged 18 months to 5 years. *Dev Med Child Neurol.* 2001;43(9):586-600.

128. Miller F, Bagg MR. Age and migration percentage as risk factors for progression in spastic hip disease. *Dev Med Child Neurol.* 1995;37(5):449-455.

129. Bly L. *Components of Typical and Atypical Motor Development.* Laguna Beach, CA: Neuro-Developmental Treatment Association, Inc.; 2011.

130. Hägglund G, Wagner P. Spasticity of the gastrocnemius muscle is related to the development of reduced passive dorsiflexion of the ankle in children with cerebral palsy: a registry analysis of 2,796 examinations in 355 children. *Acta Orthop.* 2011;82(6):744-748.

131. Boulay C, Pomero V, Viehweger E. Dynamic equinus with hindfoot valgus in children with hemiplegia. *Gait Posture.* 2012;36(1):108-112.

132. Sung KH, Chung CY, Lee KM, Lee SY, Park MS. Calcaneal lengthening for planovalgus foot deformity in patients with cerebral palsy [published online ahead of print November 21, 2012]. *Clin Orthop Relat Res.* doi:10.1007/s11999-012-2709-5

133. De Moraes Barros Fucs PM, de Assumpção RMC, Yamada HH, Simis SD. Surgical technique: medial column arthrodesis in rigid spastic planovalgus feet. *Clin Orthop Relat Res.* 2012;470(5):1334-1343.

134. Kadhim M, Holmes Jr., L, Miller F. Correlation of radiographic and pedobarograph measurements in planovalgus foot deformity. *Gait Posture.* 2012;36(2):177-181.

135. 135. Littleton SR, Heriza CB, Mullens PA, Moerchen VA, Bjorson K. Effects of positioning on respiratory measures in individuals with cerebral palsy and severe scoliosis. *Pediatr Phys Ther.* 2011;23:159-169.

136. Kotwicki T, Jozwiak M. Conservative management of neuromuscular scoliosis: personal experience and review of literature. *Disabil Rehabil.* 2008;30(10):792-798.

137. Spensylolisthesis – medical definition and more from the Free Merriam-Webster Dictionary. *Merriam-Webster Online.* http://www.merriam-webster.com/medical/spondylolisthesis. Accessed September 7, 2015.

138. McLaughlin JF, Felix SD, Nowbar S, Ferrel A, Bjorson K, Hays RM. Lower extremity sensory function in children with cerebral palsy. *Pediatr Rehabil.* 2005;8(1):45-52.

139. Guzzetta A, Cioni G, Cowan F, Mercuri E. Visual disorders in children with brain lesions: 1. Maturation of visual function in infants with neonatal brain lesions: correlation with neuroimaging. *Eur J Paediatr Neurol.* 2001;5(3):107-114.

140. Guzzetta A, Mercuri E, Cioni G. Visual disorders in children with brain lesions: 2. Visual impairment associated with cerebral palsy. *Eur J Paediatr Neurol.* 2001;5(3):115-119.

141. Fazzi E, Bova SM, Uggetti C, et al. Visual-perceptual impairment in children with periventricular leukomalacia. *Brain Dev.* 2004;26:506-512.

142. Cooper J, Majnemer A, Rosenblatt B, Birnbaum R. The determination of sensory deficits in children with hemiplegic cerebral palsy. *J Child Neurol.* 1995;10:300-309.

143. Klumlinde-Sundholm L, Eliasson AC. Comparing tests of tactile sensibility: aspects relevant to testing children with spastic hemiplegia. *Dev Med Child Neurol.* 2002;44:604-612.

144. Gordon AM, Charles J, Steenbergen B. Fingertip force planning during grasp is disrupted by impaired sensorimotor integration in children with hemiplegic cerebral palsy. *Pediatr Res.* 2006;60(5):587-591.

145. Kahn-D'Angelo L, Blanchard Y, McManus B. The special care nursery. In: Campbell SK, Palisano RJ, Orlin MN, eds. *Physical Therapy for Children.* 4th ed. St. Louis, MO: Saunders; 2012:903-943.

146. Seddon PC, Khan Y. Respiratory problems in children with neurological impairment. *Arch Dis Child.* 2003;88(1):75-78.

147. Msall ME. Complexity of the cerebral palsy syndromes: toward a developmental neuroscience approach. *JAMA.* 2006;296(13):1650-1652.

148. Vohr BR, Wright LL, Poole WK, McDonald SA. Neurodevelopmental outcomes of extremely low birth weight infants <32 weeks' gestation between 1993 and 1998. *Pediatrics.* 2005;116:635-643.

149. Rahlin M, Moerchen VA. Infants and children with cardiovascular and pulmonary dysfunction. In: Frownfelter D, Dean E, eds. *Cardiovascular and Pulmonary Physical Therapy: Evidence to Practice.* 5th ed. St, Louis, MO: Mosby, Inc.; 2012:600-624.

150. Rahlin M. Impaired ventilation, respiration/gas exchange and aerobic capacity/endurance associated with respiratory failure in the neonate. In: Frownfelter D, ed. *Cardiopulmonary Essentials: Preferred Physical Therapist Practice Patterns.* Thorofare, NJ: SLACK Incorporated; 2007:237-264.

151. Jobe AH, Bancalari E. Bronchopulmonary dysplasia. *Am J Respir Crit Care Med.* 2001;163:1723-1729.

152. Ersöz M, Selçuk B, Gündüz R, Kurtaran A, Akyüz M. Decreased chest mobility in children with spastic cerebral palsy. *Turk J Pediatr.* 2006;48(4):344-350.

153. Alexander R. Respiratory and oral-motor functioning. In: Connolly BH, Montgomery PC, eds. *Therapeutic Exercise in Developmental Disabilities.* 3rd ed. Thorofare, NJ: SLACK Incorporated; 2005:285-306.

154. Verchuren O, Takken T. Aerobic capacity in children and adolescents with cerebral palsy. *Res Dev Disabil.* 2010;31(6):1352-1357.

155. Mattern-Baxter K, Bellamy S, Mansoor JK. Effects of intensive locomotor treadmill training on young children with cerebral palsy. *Pediatr Phys Ther.* 2009;21:308-319.

156. van Brussel M, van der Net J, Hulzebos E, Helders PJM, Takken T. The Utrecht approach to exercise in chronic childhood conditions: the decade in review. *Pediatr Phys Ther.* 2011;23:2-14.

157. Wind WM, Schwend RM, Larson J. Sports for the physically challenged child. *J Am Acad Orthop Surg.* 2004;12(2):126-137.

158. Norman JF, Bossman S, Gardner P, Moen C. Comparison of the energy expenditure index and oxygen consumption index during self-paced walking in children with spastic diplegic cerebral palsy and children without physical disabilities. *Pediatr Phys Ther.* 2004;16:206-211.

159. Strauss D, Cable W, Shavelle R. Causes of excess mortality in cerebral palsy. *Dev Med Child Neurol.* 1999;41(9):580-585.

160. Krogh K, Christensen P, Lauberg S. Colorectal symptoms in patients with neurological diseases. *Acta Neurol Scand.* 2001;103(6):335-343.

161. Agnarsson U, Warde C, McCarthy G, Clayden GS, Evans N. Anorectal function in children with neurological problems. II: cerebral palsy. *Dev Med Child Neurol.* 1993;35(10):903-908.

162. Stallings VA, Charney EB, Davies JC, Cronk CE. Nutritional status and growth of children with diplegic or hemiplegic cerebral palsy. *Dev Med Child Neurol.* 1993;35(11):997-1006.

163. Campanozzi A, Capano G, Miele E. Impact of malnutrition on gastrointestinal disorders and gross motor abilities in children with cerebral palsy. *Brain Dev.* 2007;29(1):25-29.

164. Day SM, Strauss DJ, Vachon PJ, Rosenbloom L, Shavelle RM, Wu YW. Growth patterns in a population of children and adolescents with cerebral palsy. *Dev Med Child Neurol.* 2007;49(3):167-171.

165. Stevenson RD, Conaway M, Chumlea WC, et al. Growth and health in children with moderate-to-severe cerebral palsy. *Pediatrics.* 2006;118(3):1010-1018.

166. Roijen LE, Postema K, Limbeek VJ, Kuppevelt VH. Development of bladder control in children and adolescents with cerebral palsy. *Dev Med Child Neurol.* 2001;43(2):103-107.

167. Silva JA, Alvares RA, Barboza AL, Monteiro RT. Lower urinary tract dysfunction in children with cerebral palsy. *Neurourol Urodyn.* 2009;28(8):959-963.

168. David C. Dugdale, III, Scott Miller, David Zieve; MedlinePlus Medical Encyclopedia. Urination – difficulty with flow. http://www.nlm.nih.gov/medlineplus/ency/article/003143.htm. Updated August 3, 2015. Accessed September 7, 2015.

169. Linda J. Vorvick, Scott Miller, David Zieve; Medline Plus Medical Encyclopedia. Frequent or urgent urination. http://www.nlm.nih.gov/medlineplus/ency/article/003140.htm. Updated August 3, 2015. Accessed September 7, 2015.

170. Murphy KP, Boutin SA, Ide KR. Cerebral palsy, neurogenic bladder, and outcomes of lifetime care. *Dev Med Child Neurol.* 2012;54(10):945-950.

171. Gündogdu G, Kömür M, Avlan D, et al. Relationship of bladder dysfunction with upper urinary tract deterioration in cerebral palsy. *J Pediatr Urol.* 2013;9(5):659-64. doi: 10.1016/j.jpurol.2012.07.020. Epub 2012 Aug 21.

172. Gannotti M, Veneri D, Roberts D. Weight status and physical activity in third graders with chronic health conditions. *Pediatr Phys Ther.* 2007;19(4):301-308.

173. Bjornson KF, Belza B, Kartin D, Logsdon R, McLaughlin JF. Ambulatory physical activity performance in youth with cerebral palsy and youth who are developing typically. *Phys Ther.* 2007;87(2):248-257.

174. Bjornson KF, Belza B, Kartin D, Logsdon R, McLaughlin JF, Thompson EA. The relationship of physical activity to health status and quality of life in cerebral palsy. *Pediatr Phys Ther.* 2008;20(3):247-253.

175. Majnemer A, Shevell M, Law M, Poulin C, Rosenbaum P. Level of motivation in mastering challenging tasks in children with cerebral palsy. *Dev Med Child Neurol.* 2010;52(12):1120-1126.

176. Cummins RA, Nistico H. Maintaining life satisfaction: the role of positive cognitive bias. *J Happiness Stud.* 2002;3(1):37-69.

177. Carey H, Long T. The pediatric physical therapist's role in promoting and measuring participation in children with disabilities. *Pediatr Phys Ther.* 2012;24(2):163-170.

178. Thomas AD, Rosenberg A. Promoting community recreation and leisure. *Pediatr Phys Ther.* 2003;15:232-246.

179. Majnemer A, Shevell M, Law M, et al. Participation and enjoyment of leisure activities in school-aged children with cerebral palsy. *Dev Med Child Neurol.* 2008;50(10):751-758.

180. Fauconnier J, Dickinson HO, Beckung E, et al. Participation in life situations of 8-12 year old children with cerebral palsy: cross sectional European study. *BMJ.* 2009;338:b1458.

181. Brunton LK, Bartlett DJ. Description of exercise participation of adolescents with cerebral palsy across a 4-year period. *Pediatr Phys Ther.* 2010;22(2):180-188.

182. Fowler EG, Kolobe TH, Damiano DL, et al; Section on Pediatrics Research Summit Participants; Section on Pediatrics Research Committee Task Force. Promotion of physical fitness and prevention of secondary conditions for children with cerebral palsy: section on pediatrics research summit proceedings. *Phys Ther.* 2007;87(11):1495-1510.

183. Public Health Agency of Canada. Physical activity tips for youth (12-17 years). http://www.phac-aspc.gc.ca/hp-ps/hl-mvs/pa-ap/06paap-eng.php. Modified April 25, 2012. Accessed September 7, 2015.

Evidence for Prognosis for Ambulation, Employment, and Independent Living

Families are encouraged to assume an active role in making decisions
concerning their child's education, rehabilitation, living arrangements and employment.

Johanna Darrah, Joyce Magill-Evans, and Robin Adkins[1]

Parents of children with cerebral palsy (CP) are faced with many questions and concerns throughout their lives.[1-4] One of the first questions they usually ask is whether their child will be able to walk,[3,4] possibly because they view walking as a measure of independence and associate it with social acceptance.[4] Questions emerging later are those related to what to expect and prepare for in the future.[2,5] Will their children be able to live on their own and support themselves financially? If yes, what would be their living arrangements and working opportunities? If not, what happens then, and who will take care of them when the parents are no longer able to do that?[2,5] Adolescents with CP share their concerns with their parents in regard to many issues related to their future as adults.[5] They have similar aspirations for their future as youth without disabilities, such as being able to go to college, lead an independent life, work, have a family, and engage in leisure and recreational activities in their communities.[6,7]

In the family-centered rehabilitation model, therapists and other pediatric clinicians have a unique opportunity to provide the families of children, adolescents, and adults with CP with crucial information that would help them make many important decisions.[1] Instead of prescribing the course of action, health care providers should collaborate with the families and support them in their problem-solving and decision-making processes.[1] This chapter focuses on prognostic information related to such important aspects of life as walking, independent living, and employment. Other life span issues and planning the child's transition to adulthood will be covered in Chapters 23 and 24.

PROGNOSIS FOR AMBULATION

Children with CP do not necessarily view their functional abilities, including walking, as the determinants of their satisfaction with life.[8] Results of several studies showed that the functional level of participants with CP did not correlate with their psychosocial health[9] or psychosocial well-being as a component of quality of life.[10,11] Nevertheless, walking is viewed as a major motor milestone in many cultures and usually is of great importance to parents of children with CP.[3,4,12] As observed in clinical practice and reflected in the Gross Motor Function Classification System (GMFCS),[13,14] not all children with CP attain independent ambulation with or without assistive devices. Prognosis for ambulation has been the subject of multiple investigations.[3,12,15-23] Research evidence can be used for family education while setting realistic functional goals, planning intervention, and discussing the child's future needs.[12]

Rahlin M. *Physical Therapy for Children With Cerebral Palsy:*
An Evidence-Based Approach (pp 87-98).
© 2016 SLACK Incorporated.

Bartlett and Palisano[15] studied perceptions of 60 pediatric physical therapists with an average of 13.7 years of experience to ascertain specific factors that affect the attainment of motor milestones in children with CP. This group identified the distribution of involvement, muscle tone, and movement patterns, as well as balance and sensory problems as the most important primary impairments that would determine motor outcomes in these children. The secondary impairments perceived as being the most important were deficits in range of motion (ROM) and joint alignment, muscle strength and force production, overall health, and endurance. Personal and environmental factors that the participating physical therapists thought were important included the child's level of motivation, support the child receives from the family, family expectations, and support provided to the family.[15]

In their study, Bartlett and Palisano[15] used focus groups and surveys to obtain data based on the clinical experience of pediatric physical therapists. Other investigators conducted longitudinal, retrospective, and prospective studies with children, adolescents, and adults with CP to identify the objective criteria for their prognosis for ambulation.[3,17-23] Evidence yielded by these and other research studies is summarized next.[3,17-23]

Type of Cerebral Palsy, Primitive Reflexes, and Precursor Motor Skills as Predictors of the Walking Ability

According to published literature, children with CP have different outcomes in achieving the ability to ambulate depending on their anatomical distribution of motor involvement.[3,12,15-18] All or almost all children with unilateral CP learn to walk independently.[3,16,17] Children with bilateral spastic CP and greater involvement of lower than upper extremities (diplegia) have a more favorable prognosis for ambulation than those with significant involvement of all extremities (quadriplegia).[3,12,16,18] Specifically, the proportions of ambulatory children with spastic diplegia and quadriplegia reported in earlier studies were 86% to 91%[16] and 0% to 72%, respectively.[3,12,16,18] Such extensive variability in the walking ability observed in the latter group may be related to the disparities in definitions used by different authors to classify CP as spastic diplegia or quadriplegia.[16]

A more recent study examined ambulation in 9012 children with CP who were included in the Surveillance of Cerebral palsy in Europe (SCPE) database.[17] Results showed a significant relationship between the probability of being able to walk at 5 years of age and the type of CP. Ninety-six percent of children with unilateral spastic CP and 90% of those with the ataxic type walked with or without assistive devices, while children with bilateral spastic CP and dyskinetic CP were the least likely to walk, with only 57% and 41% of them achieving this skill, respectively. In addition, the presence of severe intellectual impairment highly reduced the probability of walking in children with all types of CP. The intelligence quotient (IQ) of < 50 combined with the inability to walk was defined as *severe CP* in this research. Among

1607 participants classified in that category, 40% had dyskinetic CP and 30% had bilateral spastic CP, while only 4% and 3% had ataxic and unilateral spastic CP, respectively. Other factors that showed significant inverse relationships with the ability to walk were presence of active epilepsy and severe visual or hearing impairment.[17]

Several authors implicated persistent presence of primitive reflexes at 2 years of age and, specifically, obligatory asymmetrical and symmetrical tonic neck reflexes and Moro, and tonic labyrinthine reflexes as negative predictors of ambulation.[3,12,16] Additionally, specific motor milestones attained by a certain age were identified as positive predictors of walking ability in children with CP.[3,12,16,18] In a retrospective, 22-year study of 272 children with spastic CP, Campos da Paz et al[18] showed that favorable prognosis for ambulation with or without assistive devices was associated with the ability to achieve antigravity head control in a prone position by 9 months, independent sitting (when placed) by 24 months, and crawling on hands and knees by 30 months of age. The same milestones were found to be negative predictors of walking in children with CP if they were attained after 20, 36, and 61 months, respectively.[18]

The ability to sit independently by 2 years of age was reported to be the most consistent positive predictor of ambulation at a later time.[3,12,16,18,19] In 1989, Watt et al,[3] who coined the statement "sitting by two years, walking by eight,"(p 768) reported on a longitudinal study conducted with 74 children with CP who had been born prematurely. Independent sitting at 2 years of age was identified as the strongest predictor of becoming a community ambulator by the age of 8 years. In that study, independent sitting was defined as the ability to maintain hands-free sitting, when placed, for an indefinite amount of time. Being a community ambulator was defined as being able to walk a 15-meter distance on even surfaces, independently, with or without an assistive device or ankle-foot orthoses.[3] More recently, in a very large retrospective study of 5366 children with CP who were not walking at ages 2 to 3.5 years, Wu et al[19] confirmed that independent sitting at 2 years of age was a strong positive predictor of the future walking ability. However, it was also found that not being able to pull up to stand in addition to sitting at the age of 2 reduced the probability of walking at the age of 6 years to 50%, compared to 76% for those children who had attained both skills.[19]

Use of the Gross Motor Function Classification System, Motor Development Curves, and Reference Curves

Several prognostic methods for children with CP[13,20-23] were developed based on standardized assessments conducted with the Gross Motor Function Measure (GMFM).[24] The GMFM is a standardized assessment instrument designed to measure change in gross motor functional skills in children with CP. It includes 5 dimensions: Lying and Rolling; Sitting; Crawling and Kneeling; Standing; and Walking, Running, and Jumping. The original version, the GMFM-88, consisted of 88 items. It was modified into the 66-item GMFM-66 using Rasch analysis.[24-26] A more detailed discussion of the GMFM will follow in Chapter 11.

The GMFCS published in 1997 was developed based, in part, on the results of GMFM-88 assessments performed with 215 children with CP and 60 children with typical development[13] (see Chapter 3 for a detailed discussion of the GMFCS). Research demonstrated that GMFCS levels were stable over time, meaning that the classification of a child with CP as functioning at a specific GMFCS level was unlikely to change as he or she became older.[27-29] Wood and Rosenbaum[28] used this stability of the GMFCS levels to predict future ambulation. They compared the GMFCS levels of children with CP in which they were classified at the age of 1 to 2 years with their GMFCS levels identified at later times to calculate predictive values for their ability to walk. For children functioning at GMFCS levels I, II, or III at 1 to 2 years of age, the positive predictive value of the ability to walk at 6 to 12 years of age, at least indoors, was 0.74. This meant that these children would have a 74% chance to achieve this level of functioning. The negative predictive value for children classified in levels III, IV, and V was 0.90. This indicated that they would have a 90% chance of being in need of wheeled mobility, at least in the community, by the age of 6 to 12 years.[28]

Palisano et al[20] constructed 5 distinct cross-sectional curves that reflected the nonlinear relationship between gross motor function and age and predicted maximum GMFM scores that could be obtained at each GMFCS level. The probabilities of attaining specific functional skills were estimated based on the total GMFM scores. For example, a child with a total GMFM score of 70 was estimated to have a 50% chance to achieve the ability to take 10 steps walking unsupported, while a total GMFM score of 87 would increase the probability of achieving this GMFM item to 95%. The correlation between the GMFM scores and GMFCS levels obtained in that study was high (-0.91).[20,30] The negative correlation coefficient indicated that higher GMFM scores corresponded to the lower-numbered GMFCS levels, such as levels I and II, which reflected more advanced gross motor function.[20] This study effectively validated the use of the GMFCS to predict gross motor function, including the ability to walk, in children with CP.[20]

Subsequently, the same group of researchers constructed motor development curves for children with CP based on results of a Canadian longitudinal study conducted with 657 children, GMFCS levels I through V, ages 1 to 13 years.[21] Patterns of gross motor development were described based on 2632 GMFM-66[24] assessments. The researchers created 5 curves that varied significantly in the limits and rates of gross motor skill development in children functioning at different GMFCS levels. Based on these curves, the estimated limits in gross motor development were lower for children with a higher severity of impairment, and children with a lower motor development potential tended to reach their limit more quickly. Rosenbaum et al[21] used the term *Age-90* to identify the age at which children with CP would attain 90% of their potential highest GMFM-66 score. The

estimated Age-90 for children in GMFCS level I was 4.8 years, and for those in GMFCS level V, it was 2.7 years.[21]

Although this research evidence provided more accurate prognostic information, it also led to an important question: should therapy be discontinued soon after the child reaches his or her developmental limit as suggested by the motor development curve?[21] To address this question, Rosenbaum et al[21] provided the following comments:

- In this study, the participants were tested on the GMFM-66 without the use of orthoses or assistive devices and, therefore, the curves outlined the lower limits of what these children could have accomplished if these aids had been used.
- The curves did not assess changes in the quality of movement and the carryover of the functional skills to the child's everyday life because the GMFM-66 does not measure these attributes.
- The study sample did not include children who were undergoing muscle tone reduction procedures such as selective dorsal rhizotomy, intrathecal baclofen treatment, or botulinum toxin injections, which might have an effect on their gross motor function.

This discussion led to the recommendation that clinicians should not discontinue therapy when the curves seem to level off, especially because of the development of new therapies that may benefit children with CP and help improve their function. Instead, intervention should focus on addressing accompanying impairments, activity and participation.[21]

Data collected in the study by Rosenbaum et al[21] described previously were used for further research.[22] Hanna et al[22] created cross-sectional reference percentile curves that can be used to assess the child's standing relative to a normative sample of other children with CP who function at the same GMFCS level, and to track progress over time. Children who function at different GMFCS levels may receive the same GMFM-66 score, which can be interpreted differently. For example, a GMFM-66 score of 52 can be interpreted as average for a 6-year-old girl who functions at GMFCS level III as it is located close to the 50th percentile on the reference curve. However, because the same score corresponds to the 95th reference percentile for a child of the same age classified in GMFCS level IV, it can be interpreted as an indicator of very high functioning.[22]

To evaluate change in the child's relative standing within a GMFCS level, his or her GMFM-66 change score can be compared to the mean changes in percentiles obtained by Hanna et al[22] (Table 5-1). It is important to remember that large changes in percentiles are common for children with CP. For example, for children functioning at GMFCS level I, there is an 80% chance that their GMFM-66 score obtained 1 year after the first assessment would increase or decrease by up to 20 points (see Table 5-1). In this situation, a change score greater than 20 points would be interpreted as an indicator of greater progress than expected, while a lower change score may mean that the child "is falling behind" other children within his or her GMFCS level.[22] The tabulated

TABLE 5-1

MEAN CHANGES IN PERCENTILES OVER 2 ASSESSMENTS, WITH PROBABILITY INTERVALS

PARAMETER	GMFCS[a]				
	I	II	III	IV	V
No. of children	147	78	107	121	117
Mean change	3.0	−0.8	3.3	2.5	3.6
SD for change	15.6	15.5	12.4	11.8	13.2
PROBABILITY[b]	INTERVAL OF CHANGE IN PERCENTILES BETWEEN ASSESSMENTS				
20%	±4.0	±3.9	±3.1	±3.0	±3.3
50%	±10.5	±10.5	±8.4	±8.0	±8.9
80%	+20.0	+19.9	+15.9	+15.1	+16.9

Abbreviations: GMFCS, Gross Motor Function Classification System; SD, standard deviation.

[a]The median time between assessments was 1 year.

[b]Probability that observed change falls within the corresponding interval.

Reprinted from Hanna SE, Bartlett DJ, Rivard LM, Russell DJ. Reference curves for the Gross Motor Function Measure: percentiles for clinical description and tracking over time among children with cerebral palsy. *Phys Ther.* 2008;88(5):596-607, with permission of the American Physical Therapy Association. Copyright © 2008 American Physical Therapy Association.

reference percentiles can be accessed online and should be utilized together with the GMFM-66 manual.[24,31] Clinicians and researchers should refer to the original publication of the reference curves to ensure their appropriate use.[22]

It is important to remember that the gross motor development curves and reference percentiles should not be used in isolation.[21,22] Other pertinent information, such as the meaning of the child's raw GMFM-66 score in the context of his or her medical history, current clinical situation, use of orthoses and assistive devices, and possible effects of medical interventions the child may be undergoing at the time of evaluation must be also taken into consideration.[21,22] In addition, because of a wide variability of percentile scores observed in children with CP over time, change scores need to be interpreted with caution.[22,31]

Variability in Mobility of Children With Cerebral Palsy Within the Same GMFCS Level

As proposed by the International Classification of Functioning, Disability and Health (ICF), function and disability of every individual should be viewed in a unique context of a variety of environmental and personal factors.[32] These contextual factors may have a positive or negative effect on functional mobility, overall activity, and participation in children with CP.[32,33] This is one of the reasons why children who are classified within the same GMFCS level may vary in their mobility modes and independence in different environmental settings.[33]

Tieman et al[33] investigated the variability in this area of function among 183 children with CP, age range 6 to 12 years, GMFCS levels II through IV. Results showed that, at home, children across all examined GMFCS levels usually used mobility methods that required greater motor control and independence than at school, and the least physically demanding, least independent mobility methods were used outdoors and in the community. Additionally, children classified in each GMFCS level differed in the mobility methods and the amount of independence they had moving around within each setting. For example, at home, the majority of children who functioned at level III used floor mobility (rolling, crawling, or creeping) or walked with an assistive device. However, others walked holding on to the walls or to an adult's hand, or used a manual wheelchair, and one participant was carried by an adult.[33]

Tieman et al[33] proposed that, while children with CP have similar limitations in what they are able to do at their specific GMFCS level, their actual performance depends on a variety of environmental and personal factors. Features of the environment specific to each setting may restrict or enhance the child's mobility. For example, home environments are usually less demanding than school or community settings in terms of the distance the children have to cover, the speed with which they have to move, the predictability of encountered obstacles, and the expectations for their performance.[33]

Personal factors that may affect mobility include the level of cognition; personality traits, such as the tendency for risk-taking or excessive apprehension; health conditions; and personal preference.[33] For example, in spite of her slow walking speed, a child functioning at GMFCS level III may prefer using her walker to move to the kitchen from the living room to have dinner with her family, while another child may prefer to propel her manual wheelchair because she would rather get to the kitchen quickly. The modes of mobility the child uses in different settings and related environmental and personal factors need to be examined and addressed when designing intervention as they have a considerable potential to influence therapy outcomes.[33] Although not directly related to making a prognosis for ambulation for children with CP, the study by Tieman et al[33] highlighted the complexity of this task as it requires taking into consideration multiple variables, some of which are more subjective than others.

Palisano et al[23] addressed this complex problem in their longitudinal study conducted with 642 children and adolescents with CP, GMFCS levels I through V, age range 16 to 21 years. The researchers modeled the changes in probability of using specific methods of mobility in different environmental settings with increasing age. The methods of mobility that were investigated were as follows:

- Independent walking with or without an assistive device or while holding on to furniture
- Independent wheeled mobility, either manual or power
- Assisted mobility, such as taking steps with adult assistance, moving on the floor independently, and being carried or pushed in a wheelchair by an adult[23]

The variability of mobility methods used by children within GMFCS levels I and V in this study was very low.[23] The majority of participants classified in level I were able to walk in all settings by 3 years of age, and the majority of those in level V used assisted mobility and were primarily carried or pushed in a wheelchair by an adult. The probability of walking for participants classified in levels II and III varied considerably by setting and age. For instance, for children and adolescents in level II, the probability of walking at 4, 9, and 18 years of age was the highest in a school setting (76%, 93%, and 93%, respectively) and the lowest at home (50%, 86%, and 78%, respectively). This finding differed from that obtained by Tieman et al,[33] as in their research, the majority of the children who functioned at level II walked in the home setting. In the study by Palisano et al,[23] the highest probability of walking for children classified in level III was estimated to be at school at the age of 9 years (68%). By the age of 18 years, it was approximately 50% for all settings. Children in level IV had a zero or near zero probability of walking in all settings. However, they had a 50% chance of using either wheeled or assisted mobility at 7 and 12 years of age, and a 57%, 45%, and 37% chance of using wheeled mobility outdoors, at school, and at home, respectively, by the age of 18 years.[23]

The results confirmed that personal and environmental factors had an effect on the selected mobility methods, which varied by the GMFCS level.[23] An important conclusion that can be made based on the research findings discussed previously is that what children with CP can do when assessed on a standardized test varies from their *actual performance* in daily life, which supports the ICF emphasis on contextual factors as playing a major role in the person's function, disability, and health.[23,32,33]

Probability of Maintaining Ambulatory Function Into Adulthood

Functional and ambulatory prognosis after childhood is very important for the families of children with CP, clinicians involved in their care, and researchers.[34] Many authors documented evidence of a decline in motor function and age-related changes in ambulatory ability in adolescence and into adulthood in persons with CP.[34-40] In a longitudinal study, Hanna et al[34] found no functional deterioration in most adolescents with CP classified in GMFCS levels I and II. However, in those in levels III through V, gross motor function assessed with GMFM-66[24] peaked at approximately 7 or 8 years of age before an observed decline through adolescence.[34] Gait deterioration marked by changes in kinematic and spatiotemporal parameters and related to the loss of ROM and increased energy cost over time was reported in this patient population.[35-37] Bottos et al[38] described loss of independent and supported ambulation in many adults with CP and decreased ability to walk longer distances in others.

Jahnsen et al[39] conducted a survey study of 406 individuals with CP, age range 18 to 72 years. While 44% of respondents reported the deterioration of walking observed prior to age 35 years, there was no change over time in 28%, and 27% noted an improvement in ambulation before the age of 25 years. The deterioration of upright locomotion was associated with a later vs earlier onset of walking skills, older age, and the diagnosis of bilateral spastic CP with significant involvement of all extremities (quadriplegia). The authors cited fatigue, pain, and insufficient opportunities for adapted exercise as the causes of the locomotor decline characterized by decreased walking distance and speed, increased use of support during ambulation, and increased community use of a wheelchair.[39]

As evident from the discussed research, multiple factors may affect function and the ability to walk in people with CP in adolescence and young adulthood.[34-39] In a very large retrospective study, Day et al[40] estimated the probabilities of change in the ambulatory status in youth and young adults with CP over a 15-year period starting at the age of 10 years (7550 participants) and the age of 25 years (5721 participants). Four possible types of initial ambulatory status were considered:

1. Unsupported independent walking at least 6 meters with good balance and negotiating stairs without a handrail
2. Unsupported independent walking at least 6 meters with good balance and negotiating stairs with a handrail only
3. Walking with difficulty at least 3 meters or walking with an assistive device combined with using a wheelchair (3a) or not using a wheelchair (3b)
4. Being unable to walk[40]

Results showed that, overall, the participants in both starting age groups had a high probability of maintaining their ambulatory status in the next 15 years.[40] As anticipated, those who had the highest initial level of functional

TABLE 5-2

POSITIVE AND NEGATIVE PREDICTORS OF AMBULATION IN CHILDREN WITH CEREBRAL PALSY

PREDICTORS	POSITIVE	NEGATIVE
Type of CP: Muscle tone-related motor abnormalities and anatomical distribution of involvement[17]	• Unilateral spastic CP • Ataxic CP	• Bilateral spastic CP • Dyskinetic CP
Accompanying non-motor impairments[17]	• IQ > 85 • Absence of active epilepsy • Absence of severe visual or hearing impairment	• Severe intellectual disability (IQ < 50) • Active epilepsy • Severe visual impairment • Severe hearing impairment
Primitive reflexes[3,12,16]		• Persistent presence of ATNR, STNR, Moro reflex, and TLR
Age of acquisition of motor milestones[3,12,16,18,19]	• Independent sitting, when placed, by 24 months of age • Head control in prone by 9 months • Crawling on hands and knees by 30 months • Pulling up to stand by 24 months	• Inability to sit independently until after 36 months of age • Prone head control not attained until after 20 months • Crawling on hands and knees not present until after 61 months • Inability to pull up to stand at 24 months
GMFCS level[20-23,28,31,40]	• I and II • III, not using a wheelchair at 10 years of age	• IV and V • III, using a wheelchair at 10 years of age
Environmental factors[23,33]	• Setting (size, layout, predictability of obstacles) • Social norms, expectations of others	
Personal factors[23,33]	• Child's age • Personality traits • Personal preference	

Abbreviations: ATNR, asymmetrical tonic neck reflex; CP, cerebral palsy; IQ, intelligence quotient; STNR, symmetrical tonic neck reflex; TLR, tonic labyrinthine reflex.

ambulation at ages 10 and 25 years (status 1) had the best prognosis for being able to maintain it in the future (a 63% and 75% chance, respectively). Participants with the ambulatory status 2 at 10 years of age had a 54% chance for no change in ambulation and roughly equal probabilities of improvement or decline (approximately 20%). A surprising finding of this research was a significant probability of improvement (33%) for children who had the initial status 3b at the age of 10 years. This was unexpected because Rosenbaum et al[21] had demonstrated that the motor development curves constructed for children with CP plateaued around 7 years of age, and, thus, further increase in function would be unlikely. The participants with the initial status of 3a at 10 years of age had a 34% chance of losing their ability to ambulate.[40] Results for adults with the initial status 2 and 3 were similar to those obtained for the youth group, but with a greater probability of functional decline. Day et al[40] demonstrated that adolescents and adults with CP were likely to maintain and sometimes improve their ambulation over time. Their findings confirmed the need to use other pertinent factors, besides the information provided by the motor development curves, to determine prognosis for ambulation in persons with CP.[21,40]

Table 5-2 compiled from published research lists positive and negative predictors of ambulation in this patient population.[3,12,16-23,28,31,40] Clinicians should consider all available evidence to communicate the prognostic information to their patients' families and exercise caution in their interpretation of the evaluation findings. Besides probability estimates and motor development and reference percentile curves,[21,22,31,40] other variables, such as medical and developmental history, use of technology, and environmental and personal factors need to be considered.[3,12,16,18,21-23,33,40]

PROGNOSIS FOR EMPLOYMENT

Being able to work constitutes a major part of being an adult.[7] *Competitive employment* can be defined as "working on equal terms"[p 644] with people without disabilities.[41] When considering employment opportunities, adults with CP are faced with many concerns, which may include the need for accommodations to perform their job duties; being able to access transportation in order to reach their work destination; the need for appropriate assistive technology that would allow them to move around in their work place; what a paid job may mean for their disability benefits; and how they will be perceived by their co-workers.[42] Rutkowski and Riehle[42] listed several challenges young adults with CP may encounter on their way to competitive employment, including the following:

- Low expectations for their employment-related performance from teachers, family members, and the society as a whole
- Inadequate preparation for the desired work, such as insufficient social and technical skills, resulting from the lack of emphasis on work-related education
- Lack of community resources
- Inadequate planning of the transition to adult life and employment

Between years 2000 and 2013, researchers from different countries reported varied employment statistics for adults with CP, but overall, the proportion of those who were competitively employed was very low (Table 5-3).[41,43-48] Nevertheless, literature shows that people with this condition may be capable of performing a wide variety of jobs.[43,47] The employed participants of a Danish CP registry-based study worked in the following fields: nursing and early childhood education (19%); commerce (17%), real estate, and information technology (13%); manufacturing (11%); and office positions in a variety of sectors (11%).[43] Authors of a smaller study conducted in Taiwan also listed many different occupations held by individuals with CP that varied from a car washer to a web designer.[47]

Table 5-4 summarizes the positive and negative predictors of employment in people with CP.[43,45-50] Although the type of CP and the level of motor function were strong predictors of employment,[43,45-48,50] the severity of motor involvement in ambulatory individuals was not.[43] Murphy et al[48] implicated education beyond the level of high school as the most significant positive factor leading to competitive employment for people with severe motor involvement. Other authors indicated that mainstream schooling assisted adults with CP in obtaining a job.[45,47,48,50] However, in the study by Michelsen et al,[43] only 47% of participants educated in a regular classroom were able to find competitive employment. To explain this phenomenon, the authors referred to such possible reasons as the presence of cognitive and perceptual deficits; environmental factors, including building accessibility, societal attitudes, and employment policies; and the lack

of social skills. Huang et al[47] showed that social interaction was important in assisting adults with CP in their job search as they used personal networking and communication with public employment agencies when looking for a job. In addition, social skills were needed to obtain rides to work from family members and friends.[47] Magill-Evans et al[49] also cited transportation difficulties as a major barrier to employment for people with CP.

Overall, the employment rates in this population remain low.[41,43-48] However, they may be rising with progress in rehabilitation and assistive and computer technology that leads to increased opportunities for social participation and adaptation.[41,48]

PROGNOSIS FOR INDEPENDENT LIVING

Besides being able to work, living independently and having one's own family are also major parts of being an adult.[7] In spite of progress in rehabilitation and technology,[48] many adults with CP continue living with their parents, and others require placement in specialized facilities or other institutions (Table 5-5).[41,44,46,48] While 68% of participants with CP aged 21 to 35 years in the study by Mechelsen et al[41] lived independently, this number was 92% for the comparison group derived from general population of the same age. In Denmark, adults with disabilities who require assistance with their care may live in "accommodation facilities" available through their county where they receive care and services but also have control over their pension. Mechelsen et al[41] documented the housing arrangements for the study participants who lived in accommodation facilities, which included specialized homes for people with significant cognitive or physical impairments (45%), nursing homes for older adults (22%), and an unknown type (34%).

It is interesting to note that in 3 of 4 studies included in Table 5-5, 67% to 89% of participants lived independently,[41,46,48] while in the study by Mesterman et al,[44] 78% lived with their parents. It is possible that this difference may be explained by a somewhat younger age range of the participants of the latter research. Whether this discrepancy may be also explained by other characteristics of the study sample is difficult to discern because, unfortunately, Mesterman et al[44] reported on the distribution of gender and the types of CP only for their entire sample of 163 individuals, including children (not shown in the table), but not for the 95 participants who were older than 18 years (see Table 5-5). In the study by Murphy et al,[48] approximately 33% of the sample lived with their parents, with the majority of participants in this group being diagnosed with bilateral spastic CP characterized by weakness of all extremities (quadriparesis or quadriplegia). However, 54% of all participants with this type of CP lived independently, with 80% of them receiving assistance from an attendant. For comparison, 17% of participants with unilateral spastic CP and 42% of those with dyskinetic CP who lived independently required attendant services.[48] Although

TABLE 5-3

EMPLOYMENT STATISTICS FOR PEOPLE WITH CEREBRAL PALSY REPORTED BASED ON RESULTS OF RESEARCH CONDUCTED AROUND THE WORLD

COUNTRY	STUDY	N (MALE/FEMALE)	AGE RANGE (YEARS)	TYPE(S) OF CP	EMPLOYED (%)	
					Competitively	Noncompetitively
Denmark	Michelsen et al, 2005[43]	819 (471/348)	21-35	Unilateral spastic (31%)	46	6
				Bilateral (LE > UE) (43%)	26	7
				Bilateral (LE = UE) (18%)	12	1
				Other (8%)	10	4
				All types (100%)	29	5
Israel	Mesterman et al, 2010[44]	95 (gender not specified)	18-30	Unilateral spastic	Employment % not broken down by type of CP	
				Bilateral spastic		
				Dyskinetic		
				Ataxic		
				All types	23	15
Japan	Tobimatsu and Nakamura, 2000[45]	99 (54/45)	18-33	Spastic (57%)	36	9
				Dyskinetic (43%)	27	5
Netherlands	Van der Slot et al, 2010[46]	56 (35/21)	25-45	Bilateral spastic	54	14
				• GMFCS levels I-II (73%)		
				• GMFCS Levels III-V (27%)		
Taiwan	Huang et al, 2013[47]	279 (170/109)	18-54	Spastic (52.1%)	Employment % not broken down by type of CP	
				Dyskinetic (28.6%)		
				Ataxic (19.4%)		
				Not sure (28.6%)		
				All types (100%)	18.6	4.3
United States	Murphy et al, 2000[48]	101 (53/48)	27-74	Unilateral spastic (10%)	78	20
				Bilateral (LE > UE) (11%)	64	9
				Bilateral (LE = UE) (28%)	43	21
				Dyskinetic (51%)	52	17
				All types (100%)	53	18

Abbreviations: CP, cerebral palsy; LE > UE, lower extremities involved greater than upper extremities (diplegia); LE = UE, all extremities equally involved (quadriplegia) ; N, number of subjects.

TABLE 5-4

POSITIVE AND NEGATIVE PREDICTORS OF EMPLOYMENT IN ADULTS WITH CEREBRAL PALSY

PREDICTORS	POSITIVE	NEGATIVE
Type of CP: Muscle tone-related motor abnormalities and anatomical distribution of involvement	• Unilateral spastic CP[43,48] • Ataxic CP[47]	• Bilateral spastic CP[43] • Dyskinetic CP[43,47]
Accompanying non-motor impairments	• Higher IQ[49] • Good expressive language skills[50]	• Severe cognitive or learning impairment (DQ < 85)[43] • Active epilepsy[43] • Limited receptive language[50]
Level of motor function	• Ability to walk[43,45] • Higher level of motor function[46] • Higher level of community mobility[47] • Greater independence in ADLs[47] • Using a wheelchair[50]	• Higher GMFCS level indicating lower level of motor function[49]
Environmental factors	• Assistive technology[48] • Computer technology[48] • Community resources[48]	• Transportation dependence[49]
Personal factors	• Relatively older age[46,47] • Mainstream schooling[45] • Higher educational level[47,48] • Receipt of high school diploma or certificate[50]	• Female gender[49] • Nonwhite race[50] • No high school diploma or certificate[50]

Abbreviations: ADLs, activities of daily living; CP, cerebral palsy; DQ, developmental quotient; IQ, intelligence quotient.

these numbers suggest that the type of CP and the severity of motor involvement play a role in the level of independence the person may be able to attain, Murphy et al[48] documented a positive trend in a greater number of adults with CP achieving independent living, possibly because of advances in assistive technology and rehabilitation and improvements in home support services. It is important to note that many participants of their study were in contact with the Center for Independent Living located in Berkeley, California, which may have made a difference in their success in this area.[48]

In a later study, Michelsen et al[41] demonstrated that the inability to walk documented at 6 years of age in children with CP was a statistically significant predictor of being unable to live independently in adulthood. Other negative prognostic factors for independent living identified with statistical significance (p = 0.05) included severe cognitive impairment, with the developmental quotient (DQ) lower than 50, and the presence of epilepsy. Such factors as the parental area of residence, income, educational level, and cohabitation (living as a family) were not found to be significant predictors of living arrangements for their adult children with CP.[41]

PROGNOSTIC INFORMATION AND SOCIAL INTEGRATION OF ADULTS WITH CEREBRAL PALSY

The information on predictors of independent living and data presented in Tables 5-2 and 5-4 suggest that the level of motor function, presence or absence of epilepsy, and the level of cognition may serve as common determinants of prognosis for ambulation, employment, and independent living for people with CP. In addition, as discussed previously, the ability to walk was shown to be a positive predictor of employment,[43,45] while the inability to walk was found to be a negative predictor of independent living.[41] Although children with CP do not always view walking as the determinant of their satisfaction with life[8] and their functional level does not necessarily correlate with such components of quality of life as psychosocial health[9] or psychosocial well-being,[10,11] research evidence[41,43,45] suggests that walking during childhood may have an important value for future social participation and integration in adulthood.

TABLE 5-5

LIVING ARRANGEMENTS' STATISTICS FOR PEOPLE WITH CEREBRAL PALSY REPORTED BASED ON RESULTS OF RESEARCH CONDUCTED IN SEVERAL WORLD COUNTRIES

COUNTRY	STUDY	N (MALE/FEMALE)	AGE RANGE (YEARS)	TYPE(S) OF CP	LIVING ARRANGEMENTS (%)		
					Independent	With Parents	In a Facility[b] or an Institution
Denmark	Michelsen et al, 2006[41]	416 (243/173)	29-35	Unilateral spastic, bilateral spastic and other[a]	68	13	16
Israel	Mesterman et al, 2010[44]	95 (gender not specified)	18-30	Unilateral spastic, bilateral spastic, dyskinetic, and ataxic[a]	12	78	10
Netherlands	van der Slot et al, 2010[46]	56 (35/21)	25-45	Bilateral spastic	89	7	4
United States	Murphy et al, 2000[48]	101 (53/48)	27-74	Unilateral spastic (10%)	60	40	Not identified
				Bilateral (LE>UE) (11%)	73	27	
				Bilateral (LE=UE) (28%)	54	46	
				Dyskinetic (51%)	69	31	
				All types (100%)	~67	~33	

Abbreviations: CP, cerebral palsy; LE>UE, lower extremities involved greater than upper extremities (diplegia); LE=UE, all extremities equally involved (quadriplegia); N, number of subjects.

[a] Living arrangement statistics were not broken down by the type of CP.

[b] Facility = an "accommodation facility" in Denmark where an adult with disability receives care and services but also has control over his or her pension,[41] which may be different from specialized institution, nursing homes, or sheltered housing in other countries.

Michelsen at al[41] described complete social integration as a combination of independent family living, having children, and being competitively employed. In their study, 55% of the sample (age range 29 to 35 years) did not succeed in any of these areas. Although 28% of the participants had their own family and 15% lived with a partner and their biological and nonbiological children, only 11% were able to obtain all 3 components of social integration, including competitive employment. The authors explained this phenomenon by citing published literature that pointed to premature aging in people with disabilities and documented significant levels of physical fatigue reported by adults with CP, which impacted their life satisfaction.[41,51,52] Addressing physical symptoms and cognitive deficits through early intervention and subsequent continuation of services into adulthood may lead to improvement in social integration of people with CP.[41] Further research is needed to obtain evidence that would substantiate this hypothesis.

REFERENCES

1. Darrah J, Magill-Evans J, Adkins R. How well are we doing? Families of adolescents or young adults with cerebral palsy share their perceptions of service delivery. *Disabil Rehabil.* 2002;24(19):542-549.

2. Wright M, Wallman L. Cerebral palsy. In: Campbell SK, Palisano RJ, Orlin MN, eds. *Physical Therapy for Children.* 4th ed. St. Louis, MO: Saunders; 2012:577-627.

3. Watt JM, Robertson CMT, Grace MGA. Early prognosis for ambulation of neonatal intensive care survivors with cerebral palsy. *Dev Med Child Neurol.* 1989;31(6):766-773.

4. Stout JL. Gait: development and analysis. In: Campbell SK, ed. *Physical Therapy for Children.* 3rd ed. Philadelphia, PA: W.B. Saunders Company; 2006:161-190.

5. Davis E, Shelly A, Waters E, et al. Quality of life of adolescents with cerebral palsy: perspectives of adolescents and parents. *Dev Med Child Neurol.* 2009;51(3):193-199.

6. Cussen A, Howie L, Imms C. Looking to the future: adolescents with cerebral palsy talk about their aspirations – a narrative study. *Disabil Rehabil.* 2012;34(24):2103-2110.

7. Liptak GS. Health and well being of adults with cerebral palsy. *Curr Opin Neurol.* 2008;21(2):136-142.

8. Chong J, Mackey AH, Broadbent E, Stott NS. Children's perceptions of their cerebral palsy and their impact on life satisfaction. *Disabil Rehabil.* 2012;34(24):2053-2060.

9. Wake M, Salmon L, Reddihough D. Health status of Australian children with mild to severe cerebral palsy: cross-sectional survey using the Child Health Questionnaire. *Dev Med Child Neurol.* 2003;45(3):194-199.

10. Shelly A, Davis E, Waters E, et al. The relationship between quality of life and functioning for children with cerebral palsy. *Dev Med Child Neurol.* 2008;50(3):199-203.

11. Pirpiris M, Gates PE, McCarthy JJ, et al. Function and well-being in ambulatory children with cerebral palsy. *J Pediatr Orthop.* 2006;26(1):119-124.

12. Montgomery PC. Predicting potential for ambulation in children with cerebral palsy. *Pediatr Phys Ther.* 1998;10(4):148-155.

13. Palisano RJ, Rosenbaum PL, Walter SD, Russell DJ, Wood EP, Galuppi BE. Development and reliability of a system to classify gross motor function in children with cerebral palsy. *Dev Med Child Neurol.* 1997;39(4):214-223.

14. Palisano R, Rosenbaum P, Bartlett D, Livingston M. *GMFCS – E & R, Gross Motor Function System, Expanded and Revised.* https://canchild.ca/en/resources/42-gross-motor-function-classification-system-expanded-revised-gmfcs-e-r. Accessed October 22, 2015.

15. Bartlett DJ, Palisano RJ. Physical therapists' perceptions of factors influencing the acquisition of motor abilities of children with cerebral palsy: implications for clinical reasoning. *Phys Ther.* 2002;82:237-248.

16. Sala DA, Grant AD. Prognosis for ambulation in cerebral palsy. *Dev Med Child Neurol.* 1995;37(11):1020-1026.

17. Beckung E, Hagberg G, Uldall P, Cans C. Probability of walking in children with cerebral palsy in Europe. *Pediatrics.* 2008;121(1):e187-e192.

18. Campos da Paz A Jr, Burnett SM, Braga LW. Walking prognosis in cerebral palsy: a 22-year retrospective analysis. *Dev Med Child Neurol.* 1994;36(2):130-134.

19. Wu YW, Day SM, Strauss DJ, Shavelle RM. Prognosis for ambulation in cerebral palsy: a population-based study. *Pediatrics.* 2004;114(5):1264-1271.

20. Palisano RJ, Hanna SE, Rosenbaum PL, et al. Validation of a model of gross motor function for children with cerebral palsy. *Phys Ther.* 2000;80(10):974-985.

21. Rosenbaum PL, Walter SD, Hanna SE, et al. Prognosis for gross motor function in cerebral palsy. *JAMA.* 2002;288(11):1357-1363.

22. Hanna SE, Bartlett DJ, Rivard LM, Russell DJ. Reference curves for the Gross Motor Function Measure: percentiles for clinical description and tracking over time among children with cerebral palsy. *Phys Ther.* 2008;88(5):596-607.

23. Palisano RJ, Hanna SE, Rosenbaum PL, Tieman B. Probability of walking, wheeled mobility, and assisted mobility in children and adolescents with cerebral palsy. *Dev Med Child Neurol.* 2010;52(1):66-71.

24. Russell DJ, Rosenbaum PL, Avery LM, Lane M. *Gross Motor Function Measure (GMFM-66 & GMFM-88) User's Manual.* Lavenham, Suffolk: Mac Keith Press; 2002.

25. Linacre JM. Rasch analysis of rank-ordered data. *J Appl Meas.* 2006;7(1):129-139.

26. Portney LG, Watkins MP. Surveys and Questionnaires. In: Portney LG, Watkins MP, eds. *Foundations of Clinical Research: Applications to Practice.* 3rd ed. Upper Saddle River, NJ: Pearson Education, Inc. 2009:325-355.

27. Liu UM, Thawinchain N, Palisano RJ, Valvano J. The interrater reliability and stability of the Gross Motor Function Classification System. *Pediatr Phys Ther.* 1998;10:174-175.

28. Wood E, Rosenbaum P. The Gross Motor Function Classification System for cerebral palsy: a study of reliability and stability over time. *Dev Med Child Neurol.* 2000;42(5):292-296.

29. Bodkin AW, Robinson C, Perales F. Reliability and validity of the Gross Motor Function Classification System for cerebral palsy. *Pediatr Phys Ther.* 2003;15(4):247-252.

30. Portney LG, Watkins MP. Correlation. In: Portney LG, Watkins MP, eds. *Foundations of Clinical Research: Applications to Practice.* 3rd ed. Upper Saddle River, NJ: Pearson Education, Inc.; 2009:523-538.

31. Hanna SE, Bartlett DJ, Rivard LM, Russell DJ. Tabulated reference percentiles for the 66-item Gross Motor Function Measure for use with children having cerebral palsy. http://canchild.ocean.factore.ca/en/resources/237-motor-growth-curves. Accessed October 18, 2015.

32. World Health Organization. *International Classification of Functioning, Disability and Health.* Geneva, Switzerland: World Health Organization; 2001.

33. Tieman B, Palisano RJ, Gracely EJ, Rosenbaum PL. Variability in mobility of children with cerebral palsy. *Pediatr Phys Ther.* 2007;19(3):180-187.

34. Hanna SE, Rosenbaum PL, Bartlett DJ, et al. Stability and decline in gross motor function among children and youth with cerebral palsy aged 2 to 2 years. *Dev Med Child Neurol.* 2009;51(4):295-302.

35. Johnson DC, Damiano DL, Abel MF. The evolution of gait in childhood and adolescent cerebral palsy. *J Pediatr Orthop.* 1997;17:392-396.

36. Bell KJ, Ounpuu S, DeLuca PA, Romness MJ. Natural progression of gait in children with cerebral palsy. *J Pediatr Orhop.* 2002;22(5):677-682.

37. Kerr C, McDowell BC, Parkes J, Stevenson M, Cosgrove AP. Age-related changes in energy efficiency of gait, activity, and participation in children with cerebral palsy. *Dev Med Child Neurol.* 2011;53(1):61-67.

38. Bottos M, Feliciangeli A, Sciuto L, Gericke C, Vianello A. Functional status of adults with cerebral palsy and implications for treatment of children. *Dev Med Child Neurol.* 2001;43(8):516-528.

39. Jahnsen R, Villien L, Egeland T, Stanghelle JK, Holm I. Locomotion in adults with cerebral palsy. *Clin Rehabil.* 2004;18(3):309-316.

40. Day SM, Wu YW, Strauss DJ, Shavelle RM, Reynolds RJ. Change in ambulatory ability of adolescents and young adults with cerebral palsy. *Dev Med Child Neurol.* 2007;49(9):647-653.

41. Michelsen SI, Uldall P, Hansen T, Madsen M. Social integration of adults with cerebral palsy. *Dev Med Child Neurol.* 2006;48(8):643-649.

42. Rutkowski S, Riehle E. Access to employment and economic independence in cerebral palsy. *Phys Med Rehabil Clin N Am.* 2009;20(3):535-547.

43. Michelsen SI, Uldall P, Kejs AMT, Madsen M. Education and employment prospects in cerebral palsy. *Dev Med Child Neurol.* 2005;47(8):511-517.

44. Mesterman R, Leitner Y, Yifat R, et al. Cerebral palsy – long-term medical, functional, educational, and psychosocial outcomes. *J Child Neurol.* 2010;25(1):36-42.

45. Tobimatsu Y, Nakamura R. Retrospective study of factors affecting employability of individuals with cerebral palsy in Japan. *Tohoku J Exp Med.* 2000;192(4):291-299.

46. Van der Slot WMA, Nieuwenhuijsen C, van der Berg-Emons RJG, Wensink-Boonstra AE, Stam HJ, Roebroeck ME; Transition Research Group South West Netherlands. Participation and health-related quality of life in adults with spastic bilateral cerebral palsy and the role of self-efficacy. *J Rehabil Med.* 2010;42:528-535.

47. Huang I-C, Wang Y-T, Chan F. Employment outcomes of adults with cerebral palsy in Taiwan. *Disabil Rehabil.* 2013;35(3):228-235.

48. Murphy KP, Molnar GE, Lankasky K. Employment and social issues in adults with cerebral palsy. *Arch Phys Med Rehabil.* 2000;81(6):807-811.

49. Magill-Evans J, Galambos N, Darrah J, Nickerson C. Predictors of employment for young adults with developmental motor disabilities. *Work.* 2008;31(4):433-442.

50. Bjornson K, Kobayashi A, Zhou C, Walker W. Relationship of therapy to postsecondary education and employment in young adults with physical disabilities. *Pediatr Thys Ther.* 2011;23(2):179-186.

51. Kemp BJ. What the rehabilitation professional and the consumer need to know. *Phys Med Rehabil Clin N Am.* 2005;16(1):1-18,vii.

52. Jahnsen R, Villien L, Stanghelle JK, Holm I. Fatigue in adults with cerebral palsy in Norway compared with general population. *Dev Med Child Neurol.* 2003;45(5):2960303.

Section II

QUESTIONS TO PONDER

1. What is the clinical significance of obtaining an accurate diagnosis of CP?

2. Is there enough evidence to justify the need for a shift to the new definition and classification of CP published by Rosenbaum et al[1] in 2007? Please explain your answer.

3. Should deviations from typical movement patterns observed in people with CP be viewed as impairments that need to be addressed by intervention, or should these deviations be considered "normal" for their "current state of the system" as Latash and Anson[2] suggested?

4. Is walking an important ability for children with CP considering that many of them do not view it as a determinant of their satisfaction with life and may end up giving it up in adulthood? Please explain your answer.

5. What would provide a clinician with more meaningful information regarding the true functional abilities of a child with CP, the GMFM[3] score or the information on his or her performance related to specific personal and environmental factors?

6. How should clinicians approach counseling families of children with CP using the research evidence related to the prognosis for ambulation, employment and independent living?

7. How should pediatric physical therapists address the long-term goal of complete social integration of people with CP while working with them in their childhood years?

SUGGESTED QUESTIONS FOR FUTURE RESEARCH

1. Is there a difference in interrater reliability estimates for the traditional topographic classification of spastic CP into monoplegia, hemiplegia, diplegia, quadriplegia, and the new CP classification that includes unilateral and bilateral spastic CP, combined with the GMFCS and MACS?

2. Do interventions targeting neuromuscular and musculoskeletal impairments in children with CP lead to the achievement of the requirements for safe and successful ambulation?

3. Does the presence of cognitive, attentional, or behavioral problems in children and adults with CP prevent them from meeting the *long distance navigation* requirement for successful and safe locomotion? If yes, then to what extent?

4. Do interventions targeting neuromuscular and musculoskeletal impairments translate into increased participation in individuals with CP?

5. What is the relationship between exercise participation and general health in adolescents and young adults with CP?

6. What is the relationship between exercise participation and development of secondary impairments in individuals with CP?

7. Is there a way to quantify the prognosis for ambulation for people with CP across the life span while taking into account both objective functional measures and contextual factors?

8. Is early intervention at a young age effective in improving social integration of adults with CP?

9. Is continuation of rehabilitation services into adulthood effective in improving social integration of adults with CP?

References

1. Rosenbaum P, Paneth N, Leviton A, et al. A report: the definition and classification of cerebral palsy April 2006. *Dev Med Child Neurol.* 2007;49(suppl 109):8-14. Erratum in: *Dev Med Child Neurol.* 2007;49(6):480.
2. Latash ML, Anson JG. What are "normal movements" in atypical populations? *Behav Brain Sci.* 1996;19:55-106.
3. Russell DJ, Rosenbaum PL, Avery LM, Lane M. *Gross Motor Function Measure (GMFM-66 & GMFM-88) User's Manual.* Lavenham, Suffolk: Mac Keith Press; 2002.

MEDICAL MANAGEMENT

The Interdisciplinary Team and Effective Interprofessional Collaboration in Health Care

Mary Rahlin, PT, DHS, PCS and Wendy Rheault, PT, PhD, FASAHP, FNAP

A team is a small number of people with complementary skills who are committed to a common purpose, set of performance goals, and approach for which they hold themselves mutually accountable.

Jon R. Katzenbach and Douglas K. Smith, *The Discipline of Teams*

Care for children with developmental disabilities, including cerebral palsy (CP), requires teamwork.[1] Patel et al[1] reported on the following benefits of teamwork in caring for children with disabilities:

- Development of new approaches to problem-solving when faced with complex cases and when both medical and psychological issues need to be addressed
- Enhanced efficiency of service delivery and convenience for the patient and his or her family, which lead to increased satisfaction with health care
- Reduction in duplication of services and errors
- Increased collaboration among multiple providers while individual professional development is enhanced

How effective the team is depends on whether multiple professionals work well together in order to fully address their patient's needs[1] and, thus, for a health care team, interprofessional (IP) collaboration is a must.[2,3]

INTERPROFESSIONAL COLLABORATION, TYPES OF TEAMS, AND TEAM MEMBERS' AREAS OF EXPERTISE IN CARING FOR CHILDREN WITH CEREBRAL PALSY

According to D'Amour et al,[3] IP collaboration needs to be viewed as an interactive dynamic process that encompasses such concepts as *sharing, partnership, interdependency,* and *power*. These collaboration-related concepts are described in Table 6-1. IP collaboration is exercised by members of *multidisciplinary, interdisciplinary,* and *transdisciplinary* teams, but to a different extent.[3] Professionals working on a *multidisciplinary* team have the least interaction among them and work toward the same goal independently or in parallel with each other. However, mutual respect and recognition of each member's contribution and expertise, as well as coordination of their efforts, are still important components of the multidisciplinary teamwork.[3,4]

Rahlin M. *Physical Therapy for Children With Cerebral Palsy: An Evidence-Based Approach* (pp 103-110).
© 2016 SLACK Incorporated.

TABLE 6-1

INTERPROFESSIONAL COLLABORATION-RELATED CONCEPTS

CONCEPT	DESCRIPTION
Sharing	Collaboration includes shared health care philosophy, values, responsibilities, decision making, planning, intervention, and sharing varied professional perspectives among the members of the team.
Partnership	Collaboration involves the presence of a constructive and genuine collegial relationship, which is characterized by open communication, honesty, mutual respect, and trust, with collaborating partners having a good understanding of each other's contributions to the pursuit and achievement of specific common goals.
Interdependency	Individual contributions of different professionals to meeting the needs of their patient are maximized when they become aware of their mutual dependence as opposed to functioning autonomously. This interdependence allows them to truly work together to solve complex problems.
Power	Professionals that comprise a health care team share power and acknowledge each other's knowledge and expertise as opposed to the held position or title.

Compiled from D'Amour et al.[3]

A greater degree of collaboration is observed in an *interdisciplinary* team whose members work closely together throughout patient evaluation, goal setting, and intervention planning processes.[3,4] They exhibit greater flexibility than a multidisciplinary team in carrying out intervention by sharing their professional responsibility across the boundaries of their disciplines. This flexibility may translate into scheduling co-treatment therapy sessions, such as conducted by a physical therapist and a speech-language pathologist or an occupational therapist; or into having a health care provider of one discipline incorporate into their sessions specific strategies or activities developed by a provider of another discipline, so that several important goals could be worked on at the same time. This requires frequent, well-coordinated interactions among the team members to ensure effective problem solving, decision making, and continuity of care.[3,4]

Finally, a *transdisciplinary* team is characterized by role release due to open and often almost nonexistent boundaries among professional disciplines, when various members educate representatives of other disciplines in specific interventions they may carry out instead of them, or even select one primary member who delivers care to the patient.[3,4] Such model requires the greatest amount of IP collaboration and close communication and involves a planned transfer of knowledge and skills among members in a well-coordinated fashion.[3,4]

Traditionally, the interdisciplinary team is the one most frequently observed in current clinical practice at different points on the continuum of care for children with CP and their families. However, the transdisciplinary teams are becoming more and more common, especially in an Early Intervention setting. Therapy settings and service delivery models will be discussed further in Chapter 12. Table 6-2 lists the professionals who comprise the team caring for children with CP, their areas of expertise, and responsibilities.[4-33] It is obvious from this table that regardless of the type of the team, its members cannot work in isolation and require effective communication and close collaboration when making clinical decisions and addressing the same patient-related goals. Chapter 3 highlighted the role of the physical therapist as a member of the interdisciplinary team in the diagnostic process leading to the definitive diagnosis of CP when other conditions are being ruled out. Once the diagnosis is established, the physical therapist continues to be a valuable team member who actively participates in the overall decision-making process, including goal setting, planning, implementing and modifying intervention, and assessing its outcomes.

The roles of clinicians of different disciplines may overlap as, for example, in a situation when a recommendation for a seating mobility device is being made for a child with CP. The child's physical or occupational therapist would frequently be the one to initiate this process and consult with the child and his or her family, other therapists, and an assistive technology supplier. The child's pediatrician, orthopedic surgeon, neurologist, or physiatrist would write a prescription for the device; the therapist would compose a letter of medical necessity; the social worker would look into the funding options; and the case manager (if applicable) would coordinate the entire process. Once the seating mobility device is received, the child, his or her family, the supplier, and the therapist would participate in its fitting.

TABLE 6-2

TEAM MEMBERS, THEIR AREAS OF EXPERTISE, AND RESPONSIBILITIES IN CARING FOR CHILDREN WITH CEREBRAL PALSY[4-33]

TEAM MEMBER	AREA OF EXPERTISE/RESPONSIBILITIES
Assistive technology or rehabilitation technology supplier or vendor[5]	Supplies positioning, seating, mobility, and other types of adaptive equipment to the child; may lend equipment to the child/family on a trial basis; provides information on available options and costs of the required device. Participates in assistive technology evaluations, delivers and adjusts equipment when necessary.
Audiologist[6]	Performs hearing evaluation; suggests and provides appropriate intervention when hearing loss is confirmed to support the child's ability to comprehend spoken language and to communicate with other people.
Augmentative and alternative communication (AAC) specialist[7,8]	A speech-language pathologist who provides AAC assessment, consultation, and intervention options to the child and family, when appropriate, from low tech symbol charts to high tech speech synthesizers. This promotes the development of communication and supports the acquisition of language and literacy skills by the child.
Case manager or service coordinator[4,9]	Coordinates services for the child and family; ensures ongoing communication and exchange of information among the team members; holds team meetings.
Developmental optometrist[10,11]	Performs an examination of visual function and provides appropriate intervention, when necessary, including bifocal or multifocal lenses and/or vision therapy, such as eye patching and vision exercises.
Education specialist or special educator[5,12]	Ensures and supports the child's active participation in school education. Identifies specific classroom-related and educationally relevant demands that the child has difficulty meeting and appropriate teaching methods to address the identified deficits.
Gastroenterologist[13,14]	Evaluates the child's gastrointestinal function; orders diagnostic tests; suggests and provides appropriate medical intervention, from nutritional recommendations and medication prescription to gastrostomy tube placement and other surgical procedures; and addresses such problems as gastroesophageal reflux disease, constipation, fecal incontinence, feeding difficulties, swallowing problems, and other issues.
Neurologist[14-16]	Evaluates the child's neurological function; orders diagnostic tests; establishes medical diagnosis of cerebral palsy; suggests and provides appropriate medical interventions for identified neurological and neuromuscular problems and deficits, such as seizures and muscle tone abnormalities; generates referrals to rehabilitation professionals to address neuromotor deficits and developmental problems.
Neurosurgeon[17,18]	Evaluates the child's need for invasive management of muscle tone abnormalities; orders diagnostic tests; suggests and provides available options (eg, the insertion of an intrathecal Baclofen pump, deep brain stimulation, or selective dorsal rhizotomy).
Nutritionist[12,14]	Assesses the child's growth and nutritional status; suggests and implements appropriate intervention (eg, dietary and caloric intake recommendations to address growth and weight management).
Occupational therapist[12,16,19]	Evaluates the child's upper extremity function, ability to participate in activities of daily living (bathing, dressing, feeding, toileting, etc), and the need for adaptive equipment. Suggests and implements appropriate interventions, such as functional training, sensory-motor training, oromotor and feeding therapy, splinting, use of adaptive equipment, and child/family education and counseling.
Ophthalmologist[11,12]	Evaluates the child's vision; suggests and implements interventions appropriate for identified deficits, such as prescription of glasses, vision therapy, or surgery.

(continued)

TABLE 6-2 (CONTINUED)	
TEAM MEMBERS, THEIR AREAS OF EXPERTISE, AND RESPONSIBILITIES IN CARING FOR CHILDREN WITH CEREBRAL PALSY[4-33]	
TEAM MEMBER	**AREA OF EXPERTISE/RESPONSIBILITIES**
Orthopedic surgeon[12,20]	Performs an examination of the child's bone and joint integrity and alignment; orders diagnostic tests; identifies, monitors, and addresses musculoskeletal deformities of the lower extremity, upper extremity, and spine; and suggests and implements intervention to address prevention and management of joint contractures and dislocations, bone and joint deformities, and abnormal spinal curvatures. Available intervention options vary from observation and monitoring by means of diagnostic imaging to orthotic prescription, to surgeries.
Orthotist[21]	Evaluates the child's functional and cosmetic needs; designs, fabricates, and fits appropriate lower extremity, upper extremity or spinal orthoses; and educates the child and family in their use.
Parents and family[4,9,22,23]	Provide history information to health care providers. In a family-centered environment, actively participate in all aspects of care, including examination and evaluation, goal setting, planning and implementing intervention, and coordination of therapy schedules. Carry out home programs to address the child's deficits in multiple areas.
Pediatrician[17,24]	Performs physical examination to evaluate the child's general health; performs a neurological examination; orders diagnostic tests; establishes medical diagnosis of cerebral palsy. Generates referrals to medical specialists to address the child's diagnostic and medical management needs. Generates referrals to rehabilitation professionals to address neuromotor and developmental problems.
Pediatric nurse[16,25]	Evaluates and addresses the child's general health needs; may implement case coordination and/or participate in coordination of communication between the child's family, primary care physician, and other health care providers.
Physiatrist[18,26]	Performs an evaluation of the child's physical function and identifies his or her rehabilitation needs, including management of muscle tone; coordinates therapy services and communication between the rehabilitation specialists and the child's family.
Physical therapist[12,16,27]	Evaluates the child's gross motor development and gross motor function, including posture, movement transitions, and mobility; assesses cardiovascular and pulmonary function in relation to movement and position change; identifies the need for assistive devices, orthoses and positioning and mobility equipment; suggests and implements intervention to address the child's gross motor function, postural alignment, mobility, fitness, overall activity and participation, and prevention of secondary impairments.
Psychologist[28-31]	Evaluates the child's psychological functioning and psychosocial well-being and provides psychological counseling to address behavioral and psychosocial adjustment problems, when necessary. Provides psychological support to the child's family to address parental stress.
Social worker[16,32,33]	Evaluates psychosocial needs of the child and family. Assists the child's family in finding and enrolling in educational and community assistance programs, and with planning and implementing transitions within the continuum of care.
Speech-language pathologist[6-8,12,16]	Evaluates the child's communication, speech and language skills, oral-motor function, and feeding. Identifies the need for video-swallow studies and augmentative and alternative communication. Suggest and implements appropriate interventions to address feeding, receptive and expressive language, articulation, and overall communication deficits. Trains communication partners.

Interprofessional Approach to Patient Care in the Changing Health Care Environment

In the changing landscape of health care environment in the United States, new entities, such as accountable care organizations (ACO) and patient-centered medical homes, are taking charge of addressing and improving health of the country's population.[34,35] IP collaboration as the determinant of health care quality is critical in this process.[2,35] Berry and Beckham[34] suggested that the success of an ACO lies in its adherence to two important values: team-based medicine and putting the patient's needs first. The teamwork needs to be integrated both culturally and structurally. Cultural integration comes from sharing values among the team members, and structural integration supports the team through the development of information technology, payment plans, organizational charts, and financial and non-financial incentives. Only when IP collaboration is viewed as critical to the delivery of high-quality, patient-centered care can a health care organization that otherwise consists of distinct, independent teams become truly integrated.[34]

Besides the integration of care as opposed to its fragmentation, benefits of IP collaboration include improved health of the population and improved quality, increased efficiency and effectiveness, and reduced costs of health care.[34,36] The IP approach to clinical practice is challenged by the following:

- The resistance generated by previously established patterns of behavior observed in health care
- Concerns related to a perceived threat to the professional identity and the lack of acknowledgment of one's professional contributions to the team
- Greater reliance on structure, such as incentives, than on value-based team culture
- Organizational difficulties in unifying professionals and different administrative entities in their approach to health care and teamwork
- Budget cuts[34,36]

One way to address the required paradigm shift is through IP education (IPE) that would bring together health care practitioners and educators working on a common goal of preparing future clinicians for a successful transition to the new health care environment.[35]

Interprofessional Education as a Stepping Stone for the Interprofessional Clinical Practice

According to the World Health Organization (WHO),[37] IPE is the key to strengthening health systems by moving them away from fragmentation and toward collaborative practice. IPE "occurs when students from two or more professions learn about, from and with each other to enable effective collaboration and improve health outcomes."[37(p 7)] Once armed with the knowledge and understanding of IP practice, these students will be ready to enter the workforce as members of collaborative health care teams.[37]

A framework for action provided by the WHO[37] includes educator and curricular mechanisms for the development and delivery of IPE that would translate into collaborative clinical practice. The educator mechanisms include the following:

- Institutional policies and management that support IPE
- Ongoing communication among all involved parties
- Enthusiasm for and shared vision of the IP curriculum and its benefits
- Designation of a "champion," a leader who coordinates educational processes and identifies barriers to IPE-related progress

The proposed key curricular mechanisms that can help overcome organizational difficulties in implementing the IPE are mandatory attendance and flexible scheduling that offers a number of learning options available at varied times and locations. Other effective curricular mechanisms include using adult learning principles and providing "real life" and interactive practical experiences to students.[37]

Several authors reported on best practice IPE models developed in university settings in the United States.[38,39] For example, at Rosalind Franklin University of Medicine and Science (RFUMS) in North Chicago, Illinois, collaborative student experiences include two Foundations for Interprofessional Practice courses as required curricular offerings for the first-year students in all university programs.[38,39] Medical, podiatric medicine, nurse anesthesia, pathologists' assistant, physician assistant, physical therapy, and clinical psychology students are grouped in 16-member IP teams with a faculty mentor who guides them through the didactic, service learning and clinical course components.[38,39]

The University of Florida offers the Interdisciplinary Family Health course to all first-year students educated in its medical, dental, pharmacy, nursing, physical therapy, psychology, and nutrition programs. This course includes small group meetings and home visits performed by a 3-member IP student team supervised by 2 faculty members who represent different professions. Course assignments build upon previously learned didactic curricular components. The Center for Health Sciences Interprofessional Education at the University of Washington offers more than 50 collaborative IP courses and experiential training and service learning activities for health sciences students. The developing IP team simulation program is an example of an experiential training activity that allows the students to practice their communication, leadership, mutual support, and situation monitoring team-based skills.[38]

Western University in Pomona, California, which educates health professions students in dental medicine, graduate nursing, osteopathic medicine, pharmacy, physical therapy,

Figure 6-1. Inter-professional education for family-centered collaborative care practice.

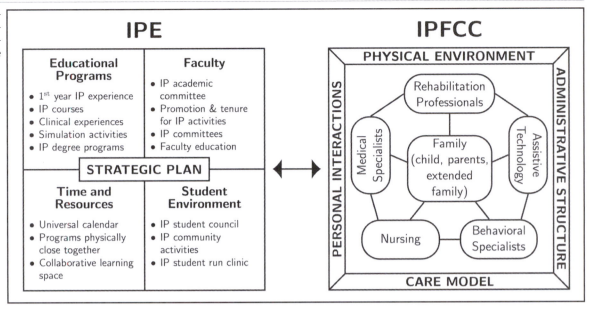

physician assistant, podiatric medicine, and other areas, is yet another example of a best practice IPE model.[39] It includes a 3-phase IPE curriculum, with phase I composed of 2 case-based courses that emphasize such competencies as communication, professional roles, team building, and others. In phase II, which offers experiential teamwork, the students enroll in a one-credit hour IP course each semester. Phase III is designated for the clinical care part of the IPE curriculum, with an IP student and clinical faculty team providing collaborative, patient-centered care.[39]

Bridges et al[38] identified developing the students' understanding of their own profession in conjunction with their appreciation of the professional roles of other team members as the common theme among several described IPE models. Other elements that determined the students' success in IPE included having opportunities to witness and reflect upon the results of collaborative IP effort, participation in graded experiences, faculty mentor training, and effective communication of the importance of IPE to the faculty.[38]

Aston et al[39] recommended that, to ensure success, IPE programs should receive strong administrative support and funding; develop specific IP courses and activities; and carefully plan the logistics of the academic structure, designated physical space, and required faculty and support staff. Figure 6-1 illustrates the relationship between IPE and IP family-centered care (IPFCC) commonly practiced in pediatrics that incorporates some of these recommendations. Important components of planning for and implementation of successful IPE are depicted on the left side of the figure, and an IPFCC model is provided on the right. The connecting lines in this part of the figure represent the ongoing communication and collaboration among the team members functioning within a clinical environment characterized by specific administrative and physical structure and quality of personal interactions typical of family-centered care. The IPE program quality, IP involvement of the program faculty, invested time and resources, and the cultivated IP student

environment are expected to promote successful participation of students and program graduates in the IPFCC collaborative practice. At the same time, the practice set-up and the ongoing collaboration among multiple professionals within the family-centered practice should facilitate improvements in IPE based on the patient care-related feedback.

The resultant outcomes of the IPE-IPFCC relationships and interactions can be assessed at several levels by focusing on patient, professional, and organizational outcomes.[40] At the patient and family level, these would include specific clinical outcomes, patient and family satisfaction, and quality of care. At the professional level, health care providers' satisfaction with their workplace and their perception of their accomplishments can be assessed. Finally, at the organizational level, the efficiency and cost effectiveness of care are the outcomes that need to be evaluated.[40]

The complexity of the IPE-IPFCC relationships and interactions offers new possibilities for research. Angelini[41] examined benefits of and barriers to IPE in the context of health care environment changing toward collaborative IP practice. Some of the benefits of IPE are changing attitudes, improving communication, increasing cultural sensitivity, and enhancing professional confidence while improving mutual understanding and respect among professions. Some of the barriers to successful implementation of IPE may include lack of administrative support and funding, geographical separation of professional student groups, lack of perceived value and mutual respect, insufficient faculty training, resistance to curricular changes, biases related to culture and gender, and perceived need to protect professional and organizational boundaries.[41]

The effectiveness of IPE was evaluated in multiple studies of varied rigor and quality.[37,42,43] One systematic review examined 6 studies, 4 randomized controlled trials (RCTs), and 2 controlled before and after (CBA) design.[42] Results showed that the studies varied in the timing of data collection, evaluated outcomes, and overall quality. The heterogeneity of described IPE interventions and methodology-related limitations made the assessment of IPE effects on professional practice and health care outcomes difficult, especially because all examined studies compared the IPE to control groups that did not receive any educational intervention, and none of them compared the IPE to professional education in isolation.[42]

Another systematic review that examined the effects of IPE on professional practice and health care outcomes contained 15 studies that also lacked control groups that would receive uniprofessional education.[43] Seven of the examined studies reported positive outcomes of IPE for clinical practice in emergency departments; operating rooms; and the areas of mental health, diabetes care, and care related to domestic violence. Mixed outcomes were obtained in 4 studies and, the other 4 had no effect on clinical practice. The authors of this systematic review proposed the following steps to address the quality of research in this area:

- Conducting studies that would compare IPE to profession-specific educational interventions
- Conducting qualitative research to evaluate IPE-related processes and their effects on changes in clinical practice
- Performing IPE-related cost-benefit analyses[43]

This chapter provided the reader with information on structure and characteristics of different types of health care teams, with the emphasis on the interdisciplinary team and the roles of its members; described the current trends in the development of IP collaboration among clinicians of different disciplines in the changing health care environment; and highlighted the role of IPE in this process. The next several chapters will address medical and surgical management of alterations in structures and functions of several major body systems in children with CP. In collaboration with other members of the interdisciplinary team, pediatric therapists make meaningful contributions to habilitation and rehabilitation of these children.

REFERENCES

1. Patel DR, Pratt HD, Patel ND. Team processes and team care for children with developmental disabilities. *Pediatr Clin North Am.* 2008;55(6):1375-1390.
2. Zwarenstein M, Goldman J, Reeves S. Interprofessional collaboration: effects of practice-based interventions on professional practice and healthcare outcomes. *Cochrane Database Syst Rev.* 2009;(3):CD000072.
3. D'Amour D, Ferrada-Videla M, San Martin Rodriguez L, Beaulieu M-D. The conceptual basis for interprofessional collaboration: core concepts and theoretical frameworks. *J Interprof Care.* 2005;19(suppl 1):116-131.
4. Atkinson H. Rehabilitation settings. In: Effgen SK, ed. *Meeting the Physical Therapy Needs of Children.* 2nd ed. Philadelphia, PA: F. A. Davis Company; 2013:583-597.
5. Angelo J. A guide for assistive technology therapists. In: Angelo J, Lane S, eds. *Assistive Technology for Rehabilitation Therapists.* Philadelphia, PA: F. A. Davis Company;1997;1-14.
6. McLaughlin MR. Speech and language delay in children. *Am Fam Physician.* 2011;83(10):1183-1188.
7. Pennington L, Goldbart J, Marshall J. Speech and language therapy to improve the communication skills of children with cerebral palsy. *Cochrane Database Syst Rev.* 2004;(2):CD003466.
8. Light J, McNaughton D. Supporting the communication, language, and literacy development of children with complex communication needs: state of the science and future research priorities. *Assist Technol.* 2011;24(1):34-44.
9. O'Regan Kleinert J, Effgen SK. Early intervention. In: Effgen SK, ed. *Meeting the Physical Therapy Needs of Children.* 2nd ed. Philadelphia, PA: F. A. Davis Company; 2013:475-493.
10. Bodack MI. Eye and vision assessment of children with special needs in an interdisciplinary school setting. *Optom Ves Dev.* 2011;42(3):220-226.
11. Jackson J, Castleberry C, Galli M, Arnoldi KA. Cerebral palsy for the pediatric eye care team Part II: diagnosis and treatment of ocular motor deficits. *Am Orthopt J.* 2006;56:86-96.
12. Dodge NN. Cerebral palsy: medical aspects. *Pediatr Clin N Am.* 2008;55(5):1189-1207.
13. Sullivan PE. Gastrointestinal disorders in children with neurodevelopmental disabilities. *Dev Disabil Res Rev.* 2008;14(2):128-136.
14. Pruitt DW, Tsai T. Common medical comorbidities associated with cerebral palsy. *Phy Med Rehabil Clin N Am.* 2009;20(3):453-467.
15. Ashwal S, Russman BS, Blasco PA, et al. Practice parameter: diagnostic assessment of the child with cerebral palsy: report of the Quality Standards Subcommittee of the American Academy of Neurology and the Practice Committee of the Child Neurology Society. *Neurology.* 2004;62(6):851-863.
16. Aisen ML, Kerkovich D, Mast J, et al. Cerebral palsy: clinical care and neurological rehabilitation. *Lancet Neurol.* 2011;10(9):844-852.
17. Fairhurst C. Cerebral palsy: the whys and hows. *Arch Dis Child Educ Pract Ed.* 2012;97(4):122-131.
18. Deon LL, Gaebler-Spira D. Assessment and treatment of movement disorders in children with cerebral palsy. *Orthop Clin N Am.* 2010;41(4):507-517.
19. Steultjens EM, Dekker J, Bouter LM, van de Nes JC, Lambregts BL, van den Ende CH. Occupational therapy for children with cerebral palsy: a systematic review. *Clin Rehabil.* 2004;18(1):1-14.
20. Morrell DS, Pearson M, Sauser DD. Progressive bone and joint abnormalities of the spine and lower extremities in cerebral palsy. *Radiographics.* 2002;22(2):257-268.
21. Nielsen CC. Orthotics and prosthetics in rehabilitation: the multidisciplinary approach. In: Lusardi MM, Nielsen CC, eds. *Orthotics and Prosthetics in Rehabilitation.* 2nd ed. St. Louis, MO: Elsevier Inc.; 2007:3-14.
22. Bamm EL, Rosenbaum P. Family-centered theory: origins, development, barriers, and supports to implementation in rehabilitation medicine. *Arch Phys Med Rehabil.* 2008;89:1618-1624.
23. Jeglinsky I, Autti-Rämö I, Brogren Carlberg E. Two sides of the mirror: parents' and service providers' view on the family-centredness of care for children with cerebral palsy. *Child Care Health Dev.* 2012;38(1):79-86.
24. Aneja S. Evaluation of a child with cerebral palsy. *Indian J Pediatr.* 2004;71(7):627-634.
25. Hayes C. Cerebral palsy: classification, diagnosis and challenges of care. *Br J Nurs.* 2010;19(6):368-373.
26. Gaebler-Spira D, Revivo G. The use of botulinum toxin in pediatric disorders. *Phys Med Rehabil Clin N Am.* 2003;14(4):703-725.
27. Wright M, Wallman L. Cerebral palsy. In: Campbell SK, Palisano RJ, Orlin MN, eds. *Physical Therapy for Children.* 4th ed. St. Louis, MO: Saunders; 2012:577-627.
28. Odding E, Roebroeck ME, Stam HJ. The epidemiology of cerebral palsy: incidence, impairments and risk factors. *Disabil Rehabil.* 2006;28(4):183-191.
29. Majnemer A, Shevell M, Rosenbaum P, Law P, Poulin C. Determinants of life quality in school-age children with cerebral palsy. *J Pediatr.* 2007;151(5):470-475.

30. Brossard-Racine M, Waknin J, Shikako-Thomas K, et al. Behavioral difficulties in adolescents with cerebral palsy. *J Child Neurol.* 2013;28(1):27-33.

31. Park MS, Chung CY, Lee KM, Sung KH, Choi IH, Kim TW. Parenting stress in parents of children with cerebral palsy and its association with physical function. *J Pediatr Orthop B.* 2012;21(5):452-456.

32. Cerebral Palsy: Hope Through Research. *National Institute of Neurological Disorders and Stroke.* http://www.ninds.nih.gov/disorders/cerebral_palsy/detail_cerebral_palsy.htm. Accessed May 27, 2013.

33. Shanske S, Arnold J, Carvalho M, Rein J. Social workers as transition brokers: facilitating the transition from pediatric to adult medical care. *Soc Work Health Care.* 2012;51(4):279-295.

34. Berry LL. Beckham D. Team-based care at Mayo Clinic: a model for ACOs. *J Healthc Manag.* 2014;59(1):9-13.

35. Garr DR, Margalit R, Jameton A, Cerra FB. Commentary: educating the present and future health care workforce to provide care to populations. *Acad Med.* 2012;87(9):1159-1160.

36. Jones R, Bhanbhro SM, Grant R, Hood R. The definition and deployment of different core professional competencies in multiprofessional health and social teams. *Health Soc Care Community.* 2013;21(1):47-58.

37. World Health Organization. Framework for action on interprofessional education & collaborative practice. http://whqlibdoc.who.int/hq/2010/WHO_HRH_HPN_10.3_eng.pdf. Published 2010. Accessed May 25, 2014.

38. Bridges DR, Davidson RA, Odegard PS, Maki IV, Tomkowiak J. Interprofessional collaboration: three best practice models of interprofessional education. *Med Educ Online.* 2011;16: doi:10.3402/meo.v16i0.6035.

39. Aston SJ, Rheault W, Arenson C, et al. Interprofessional education: a review and analysis of programs from three academic health centers. *Acad Med.* 2012;87(7):949-955.

40. D'Amour D, Oandasan I. Interprofessionality as the field of interprofessional practice and interprofessional education: an emerging concept. *J Interprof Care.* 2005;19(suppl 1):8-20.

41. Angelini DJ. Interdisciplinary and interprofessional education: what are the key issues and considerations for the future? *J Perinat Neonatal Nurs.* 2011;25(2):175-179.

42. Reeves S, Zwarenstein M, Goldman J, et al. The effectiveness of interprofessional education: key findings from a new systematic review. *J Interprof Care.* 2010;24(3):230-241.

43. Reeves S, Perrier L, Goldman J, Freeth D, Zwarenstein M. Interprofessional education: effects on professional practice and healthcare outcomes (update). *Cochrane Database Syst Rev.* 2013;3:CD002213.

7

Neurological and Neuromuscular Systems
Medical and Surgical Management of Alterations in Body Structures and Functions

…it is important that all child health workers have an understanding of the basic mechanisms of neurological, biomechanical and pharmacological management of children with CP and how that may have an effect on their general or specialist areas of intervention.

Charlie Fairhurst[1]

Teamwork is essential in order to provide effective care for children with cerebral palsy (CP), and interprofessional communication and collaboration among the team members is crucial for addressing the needs of the whole child (see Chapter 6).[1-3] In order to be effective members of the interdisciplinary team, physical therapists need to have sufficient knowledge of medical and surgical management of alterations of structures and functions exhibited by these children and understand the rationale for these interventions. This chapter focuses on the neurological and neuromuscular systems and, specifically, on medical and surgical management of brain lesions, seizures, muscle tone abnormalities, and oral-motor problems, which were discussed in detail in Chapter 4 and summarized in Table 4-1.

NEUROLOGICAL SYSTEM

Stem Cell Therapies

While other medical interventions focus on secondary neurological and neuromuscular problems affecting children with CP, the emerging stem cell therapies have a potential to directly address the primary impairment, namely, the brain lesions.[1,4-6] Intervening early, when the infant's brain has the highest potential for plasticity, would be best.[1,4] If successful, stem cells may, hypothetically, repair or regenerate brain tissue and, thus, prevent secondary impairments.[1,4] However, despite the excitement caused by this idea in both the scientific community and lay public, much still needs to be done in order to determine the best route for cell transplantation, as well as its dose, timing, efficacy, and most importantly, safety.[1,4-6]

Ruff et al[4] described stem cells as "multipotential cells that exist in both adult and developing tissue."(p 689) In the process of development, the ability of stem cells to form different tissues, proliferate, and self-renew decreases as their differentiation increases. Not all types of stem cells are appropriate for transplantation for therapeutic purposes. For example, the earlier lineage cells have a high proliferative and self-renewal capability, but they have been linked to a high risk of formation of teratomas.[4] Congenital teratoma is a type of a tumor that is usually benign but may also be malignant.[7] Table 7-1 contains information on different types of stem cells, their level of differentiation, and potential clinical use.[4] There are 3 possible mechanisms of neural repair that have been investigated in animal studies using mesenchymal stem cells (MSCs), neural precursor cells (NPCs), and more mature progenitor cells (Schwann cells and olfactory ensheathing glia, or OEG). These mechanisms include the repair of damaged brain tissue by providing it with structural support;

Rahlin M. *Physical Therapy for Children With Cerebral Palsy: An Evidence-Based Approach* (pp 111-124).

TABLE 7-1		
STEM CELL TYPES AND THEIR DIFFERENTIATION LEVEL, SOURCE, AND POTENTIAL CLINICAL USE FOR NEURAL REPAIR		
TYPE OF STEM CELLS	LEVEL OF DIFFERENTIATION AND SOURCE	POTENTIAL CLINICAL USE FOR NEURAL REPAIR
Totipotent stem cells	Cells found at the earliest stage of division, capable of producing all cell types	Usually are not used for transplantation as they are not specialized and have been linked to high risk for formation of teratomas
Pluripotent stem cells		
Embryonic stem cells (ESCs)	Cells obtained from the inner cell mass formed after approximately 4 days of a blastocyst cell division	Are not appropriate for clinical use because of high level of plasticity. In order to be used for transplantation, these cells need to be further differentiated into multipotent stem cells or fate-restricted progenitor cells
Induced pluripotent stem cells (iPSCs)	Cells derived from human blood or skin tissue to create patient-specific cells	
Multipotent stem cells	Cells formed from pluripotent cells later in the developmental process	Most promising for clinical use as the teratoma formation risk is low
Mesenchymal stem cells (MBCs)	Cells isolated from placenta, umbilical cord, bone marrow, and fat	Are used for transplantation aimed at neural repair with variable and at times, contradictory results. Currently used in several human trials
Neural precursor cells (NPCs)	Exist in adult brain, spinal cord, and neural parenchyma. Can be differentiated from pluripotent cells or derived from fetal tissue	Potentially, most useful for neural repair, but cell harvesting is difficult and ethically challenging. Safety for use in humans has not been fully established
Fate-restricted progenitor cells	Are not stem cells but rather more mature precursor cells	Used in preclinical and clinical trials with experimental neurological injuries for trophic and structural support and remyelination, but with variable results
Schwann cells	Peripheral glial cells	
Olfactory ensheathing glia (OEG)	Glial cells derived from the olfactory bulb or olfactory mucosa	

Compiled from Ruff et al.[4]

remyelination of affected axons; and expression of neuro-trophic growth factors.[4]

As emphasized by several authors, safety of stem cell transplantation still needs to be investigated and confirmed in human studies.[1,4-6] However, in spite of the lack of evidence on the subject, expensive stem cell therapies are currently offered at multiple clinical sites in Asia, Central America, Europe, and Middle East[1,4,5] leading to what has been termed *medical* or *stem cell tourism*.[4,5] Patients who use these clinics may be exposed to unregulated and scientifically unsupported interventions that put their health at risk for complications and even death, and that may also render them ineligible for participation in future, appropriately designed stem cell clinical trials.[4,5] It is important for clinicians, including those working with children with CP, to be aware of this issue so that they can advise their patients' parents accordingly.[5]

Clinical trials conducted with children with CP around the world, including the United States, use stem cells derived from bone marrow and umbilical cord blood (UCB) and deliver them intravenously or intrathecally.[4,8-10] Min et al[10] completed a double-blind, randomized, placebo-controlled clinical trial with 105 children with CP, ages 10 months to 10 years, to investigate the efficacy and safety of intravenously administered allogeneic UCB potentiated with human erythropoietin (rhEPO).[8] Participants were randomly assigned to 1 of 3 groups. Group 1 received UCB potentiated with rhEPO, group 2 received placebo UCB and rhEPO, and group 3 (control group) received placebo UCB and placebo rhEPO. All groups underwent intensive inpatient rehabilitation for 1 month and continued with therapies 3 times per week until the final assessment conducted 6 months after treatment.[10]

Significantly greater improvement in motor and cognitive functioning and superior brain imaging results that indicated both structural and metabolic changes were obtained for group 1.[10] Serious adverse events that necessitated hospitalization were reported in 9 participants and included pneumonia, seizure, influenza, and urinary tract infection. The incidence of adverse events was similar among the study groups. One death determined to be unrelated to the study was also reported. This study was an important step in establishing efficacy and safety of this medical intervention for children with CP.[10]

Management of Seizures

The prevalence of epilepsy among children with CP and the types and symptoms of seizures were discussed in Chapter 4 and Table 4-2. There are several treatment options available for this patient population, including antiepileptic drugs, dietary therapies, vagal nerve stimulation, and surgical intervention.[11-13]

Antiepileptic Drugs

Antiepileptic drugs (AEDs) are usually used for the initial treatment of seizures in children with developmental disabilities.[11] The AED selection is guided by the child's history of seizures, presence or absence of intellectual disability and behavioral problems, other comorbidities, drug interaction precautions, and side effects.[11,12] The medication benefits need to be compared against the risks of adverse effects that may potentially negatively affect the child's quality of life.[11,12] Several authors emphasized the importance of an individualized approach to the AED prescription while taking into account the child's psychological and educational needs and priorities in order to ensure compliance with the medication regimen and safety of its administration.[11,12,14] Epilepsy may be accompanied by behavioral and cognitive dysfunction, which, in turn, may be accentuated by the use of anti-seizure medications.[11] Table 7-2 lists selected AEDs used to treat different types of seizures and their reported side effects. Another problem in children with CP is the development of osteoporosis associated with prolonged administration of AEDs combined with decreased weight-bearing and exposure to sunlight, and insufficient intake of calcium and vitamin D.[11,15] The discontinuation of AEDs in patients who are seizure free for 2 years was shown to improve complex cognitive functioning and increase the speed of cognitive processing. However, it was also found to be associated with the recurrence of seizures in 14% to 62% of children with CP.[11]

Besides other types of seizures, children with CP may suffer from electrical status epilepticus in sleep (ESES).[16] ESES can be defined as "epilepsy with continuous spike-waves during slow-wave sleep."[16,17(p 799)] Kramer et al[16] described successful use of steroids, levetiracetam, and intravenous immunoglobulin for treatment of ESES in children with unilateral CP after a failure of multiple drug interventions while none of the agents used for a child with bilateral spastic CP worked. The terms *refractory* and *intractable* can be used to describe epilepsy resistant to multiple AEDs.[12] In one study,

clinical predictors of a poor response to AEDs in children with CP included the diagnosis of bilateral spastic CP with equal involvement of upper and lower extremities (quadriplegia), intellectual disability, and the presence of myoclonic seizures.[18]

Dietary Therapies

Refractory childhood epilepsy can be treated using dietary therapies, including the ketogenic diet (KD), the medium chain triglyceride (MCT) diet, the low glycemic index treatment (LGIT), and the modified Atkins diet (MAD).[11-13,19,20] The KD includes high fat and adequate protein intake, but is low on carbohydrates.[11-13] It mimics the fasting effects by creating an overabundance of ketones[11-13] and is used over 2 years or longer if it is successful, or over a 3- to 6-month period if it is not.[13] This intervention was shown to be effective in alleviating seizures completely in 15.6% of children with refractory epilepsy and in reducing seizure frequency by greater than 50% in at least one-third of the patients who used it for 6 months.[21] In a study conducted with 38 children with catastrophic epileptic encephalopathies (74% of them had CP), 28.9% of participants who used the KD for 12 months demonstrated a greater than 50% decrease in seizure frequency, and in 23.7%, the seizures stopped completely.[20]

Other dietary therapies have been used as alternatives to the KD because they are less restrictive and may be better tolerated.[12,13] The MCT diet is similar to the KD but uses more ketogenic oil and greater levels of carbohydrates.[13,22] The LGIT includes berries, green vegetables, and whole grain to supply carbohydrates with glycemic indices below 50 to keep the patient's blood glucose level stable.[13,23] The *glycemic index (GI)* reflects the effect of specific types of food on blood glucose.[24] In comparison to the LGIT, the MAD restricts carbohydrates to 10 grams per day and is very high on fat, but does not limit calories, protein, or fluids.[13,25] Evidence shows that these diets are at least as effective as the KD in reducing seizures in children with refractory epilepsy.[12,13,25-28] Most frequently reported side effects of dietary therapies include vomiting, hyperlipidemia, acidosis, constipation, weight loss, and kidney stones.[13,20,21]

More Invasive Interventions: Vagus Nerve Stimulation, Deep Brain Stimulation, and Surgery

In 1997, Federal Drug Administration (FDA) approved vagus nerve stimulation for the treatment of refractory epilepsy.[12,29] It can be used as adjunctive therapy for children older than 12 years of age who suffer from complex partial seizures[12,30,31] (see Table 4-2) but was also shown to be effective in younger children.[30] Vagus nerve stimulation is accomplished by using a contact wrapped around the trunk of the nerve on the left side of the neck to deliver intermittent electrical stimulation.[12,29] It was reported to decrease the seizure frequency by greater than 50% in 35% to 45% of patients on average; completely alleviate seizures in 2% to 10%[11,12,29,31,32]; decrease the number of hospitalizations and emergency room visits; and lower the health care costs.[30]

TABLE 7-2

SELECTED ANTIEPILEPTIC DRUGS AND THEIR SIDE EFFECTS IN TREATMENT OF DIFFERENT TYPES OF SEIZURES

AEDa	SEIZURE TYPES	SIDE EFFECTS				
		Behavioral/Psych	GI	Metabolic	Neuro	Skin
Carbamazepine	Generalized tonic-clonic; partial	Affective disorder		Water retention, anemia	Dizziness, ataxia, blurred vision	
Clonazepam	Most types of generalized and partial seizures	Aggression, attention problems, hyperactivity, irritability			Ataxia, sedation	
Ethosuximide	Generalized absence seizures	Psychosis	Nausea, vomiting		Dizziness, fatigue, headache, lethargy	Rash and itching
Felbamate	Generalized absence; partial	Agitation and irritability	Anorexia, nausea, vomiting	Aplastic anemia, liver failure	Dizziness, headache, insomnia	
Gabapentin	Partial seizures	Aggressive and oppositional behaviors, agitation, hyperactivity			Ataxia, dizziness, fatigue, sedation	
Lamotrigine	Most types of generalized and partial seizures	Anxiety, aggressive behavior, irritability, hypomania			Ataxia, dizziness, headaches, vision issues	Rash
Levetiracetam	Generalized atonic, tonic, tonic-clonic; partial	Agitation, aggression, irritability			Sedation	
Phenobarbital	Generalized atonic, tonic, tonic-clonic; partial	Depression, hyperactivity, irritability		Deficiency of folate and vitamin K	Ataxia, nystagmus, paradoxical increase in seizures, sedation	Skin problems
Phenytoin	Generalized tonic and tonic-clinic	Aggressive behavior, anxiety, confusion, slow movement, depression	Gastric irritation		Ataxia and other cerebellar signs, dizziness, headache, sedation	Hirsutism and skin problems

(continued)

TABLE 7-2 (CONTINUED)

SELECTED ANTIEPILEPTIC DRUGS AND THEIR SIDE EFFECTS IN TREATMENT OF DIFFERENT TYPES OF SEIZURES

AED[a]	SEIZURE TYPES	SIDE EFFECTS				
		Behavioral/Psych	GI	Metabolic	Neuro	Skin
Tiagabine	Partial seizures	Anxiety, depression, irritability, drowsiness			Dizziness and weakness	
Topiramate	Most types of generalized and partial seizures	Acute psychosis, depression, paranoia			Ataxia, dizziness, fatigue, sedation	
Valproic acid	Most types of generalized and partial seizures	Depression	GI distress	Impaired platelet function, weight gain/loss	Encephalopathy	Temporary hair loss
Vigabatrin[b]	Infantile spasms				Permanent loss of peripheral vision; MRI changes of unknown significance[c]	

Abbreviations: AED, antiepileptic drug; GI, gastrointestinal; Neuro, neurological; Psych, psychiatric; SHARE, Support, Help, And Resources for Epilepsy.

[a] Only generic drug names are listed.

[b] Available only through a SHARE program.

[c] Per http://www.sabril.net/. Accessed June 30, 2013.

Compiled from Depositario-Cabacar and Zelleke[11] and Ciccone.[14]

TABLE 7-3

EFFECTS OF MEDICAL AND SURGICAL ANTISPASTICITY INTERVENTIONS

EFFECTS	REVERSIBLE	NONREVERSIBLE
Focal	Intramuscular injections/neurolytic blocks • Botulinum toxin A • Phenol • Alcohol	Orthopedic surgery
Regional	Intrathecal baclofen	Orthopedic surgery Selective dorsal rhizotomy
Systemic	Oral medications Cerebellar stimulation	

Compiled from Graham et al,[48] Gormley et al,[46] and Harat et al.[49]

Observed side effects may include hoarse voice, coughing, throat pain, dyspnea, nausea, and infection at the implantation site.[12,29,31]

Another, emerging intervention for intractable epilepsy is deep brain stimulation (DBS).[12,29] So far, electrical stimulation of the anterior nuclei of the thalamus and the hippocampus has been researched mostly in adult patients.[12,29,32,33]

Finally, surgery is a treatment of choice for children with refractory partial seizures.[11,12,34] Depending on the etiology, hemispherectomy; frontal, central, or temporal resection; callosotomy; and other surgical procedures may be performed.[34,35] During childhood, seizures may be detrimental to the neurodevelopmental process, and this problem serves as one of the evaluative criteria for surgical intervention.[34,35] However, while the reported seizure-related surgical outcomes are generally good in approximately 80% of patients,[12,35-37] the results in the area of motor function may vary from motor deterioration to functional improvement.[35-37]

NEUROMUSCULAR SYSTEM

Management of Spasticity: Theoretical Foundation and Research Evidence

The term *spasticity* refers to velocity-dependent hypertonicity characterized by resistance to passive stretch that increases with the increasing speed of movement in the joint, and varies depending on the direction of movement.[38] *Reduced selective motor control* or difficulty activating specific muscles during voluntary movement is one of the negative

signs present in individuals with spasticity related to the upper motor neuron syndrome.[38,39] During a maximum muscle contraction, children with CP demonstrate abnormal timing and sequencing of muscle recruitment, and a higher level of muscle coactivation than observed in children developing typically.[40,41] Tedroff et al[40] suggested that the altered patterns of muscle activation may contribute to the limited functional effects of medical interventions used to decrease spasticity in this patient population, and that the removal of spasticity may lead to an increased use of co-contraction of weak musculature to achieve adequate postural stability.

While atypical movement patterns result from a combination of spasticity, muscle weakness, and low muscle endurance,[38,39,41] it is unclear how much each of these components contributes to movement abnormalities and impedes function in people with CP.[41] To add to this controversy, it is important to revisit the question asked by Latash and Anson,[42] "What are 'normal movements' in atypical populations?" The reader is referred back to Chapter 4 for the initial discussion of the proposed notion that new movement patterns exhibited by a person with a neurological disorder develop based on changed central nervous system (CNS) priorities and can be viewed as adaptive and, perhaps, even optimal for the current state of the biological system.[42] This would mean that altering these new movement patterns by alleviating abnormal muscle tone may result in suboptimal functioning of the individual. To test this hypothesis, one must examine the available research evidence on the subject.

The idea that the inhibition of abnormal muscle tone would help to normalize movement in affected individuals served as one of the foundational premises of the Neurodevelopmental Treatment Approach (see Chapter 14).[43,44] The same idea, in combination with the goal of minimizing contractures, led to the development of multiple medical interventions, such as oral drugs, intrathecal baclofen (ITB), intramuscular injections and neurolytic blocks, selective dorsal rhizotomy (SDR), cerebellar stimulation, and orthopedic surgeries.[45-47] Depending on whether they affect specific muscles, a particular region of the body, or have a generalized effect, these interventions can be classified as focal, regional, or systemic, and their effects can be reversible or permanent (Table 7-3).[46,48,49] Published evidence of the outcomes and side effects of these treatment methods is discussed next, with the exception of orthopedic surgeries that will be reviewed in Chapter 8.

Oral Antispasticity Medications

Oral medications have a systemic effect on muscle tone (see Table 7-3). They may act at different levels, from multiple CNS sites to the skeletal muscle itself.[45,47] Most of these drugs increase the release of inhibitory or inhibit the release of excitatory neurotransmitters.[45,46] Dantrolene is the only antispasticity medication that acts at the skeletal muscle level.[45,47] According to Damiano et al,[45] it is typical for the clinician to see varied responses to the same drug and variations in efficacy and side effects in different patients. Furthermore, while only 30% of patients with spasticity have a favorable response to oral medications,[45] only partial decrease in spasticity is usually

TABLE 7-4

COMMON ORAL ANTISPASTICITY MEDICATIONS AND THEIR MECHANISMS OF ACTION, REPORTED BENEFITS, AND SIDE EFFECTS

MEDICATION	MECHANISM OF ACTION	REPORTED ANTISPASTICITY BENEFITS AND RELATED EFFECTS	SIDE EFFECTS
Benzodiazepines (eg, diazepam, nitrazepam, and clonazepam)	GABA mediated inhibition at the supraspinal and spinal cord levels via increased transmission at $GABA_A$ receptors	Decrease in generalized spasticity, muscle spasms, and hyperreflexia Decrease in anxiety and improvement of sleep	Sedation, drowsiness, ataxia, memory and attention problems, hyperactive behavior, weakness, constipation, urinary retention, hypersalivation, and increase bronchial secretion Physical dependence with prolonged use Withdrawal symptoms when discontinued abruptly: agitation, hyperpyrexia, insomnia, irritability, nausea, seizures, and tremor
Baclofen	Presynaptic inhibition of monosynaptic and polysynaptic spinal reflexes by binding to the $GABA_B$ receptors	Inconsistent reports on antispasticity effects Decrease in clonus, spasms, and resistance to passive stretch; increase in passive range of motion reported	Sedation, hypotonia; cognitive impairments, including attention and memory problems and confusion; ataxia, dizziness, orthostatic hypotension, and weakness Withdrawal symptoms when discontinued abruptly: increased spasticity with spasms, confusion, hallucinations, hyperthermia, and seizures
Dantrolene sodium	Impedes the release of calcium from the sarcoplasmic reticulum at the skeletal muscle level	Inconsistent reports on antispasticity effects Decrease in clonus and muscle spasms	Mild sedation, malaise, nausea, vomiting, diarrhea, dizziness, and paresthesias In rare cases, hepatotoxicity and fatal hepatitis
Alpha 2 adrenergic agonists (clonidine and tizanidine)	Hyperpolarization of motoneurons at the brain and spinal cord levels	Decrease in spasticity; insufficient evidence for use in children with CP	Hypotension, sedation, depression, dizziness, dry mouth, nausea, hepatotoxicity, and reversible elevations of liver enzymes

Abbreviations: GABA, γ-aminobutyric acid; $GABA_A$, γ-aminobutyric acid type A; $GABA_B$, γ-aminobutyric acid type B.

Compiled from Deon and Gaebler-Spira,[47] Quality Standards Subcommittee of the American Academy of Neurology and the Practice Committee of the Child Neurology Society et al,[50] and Verotti et al.[51]

achieved,[45,46] and there is still insufficient evidence to recommend one drug over another or to support the use of any of these drugs to address motor function in children with CP.[45,50]

Table 7-4 lists the mechanisms of action, benefits, and side effects of the most common oral antispasticity medications used with this patient population.[47,50,51] It is important to mention that oral baclofen was found to induce new or increased seizure activity in children with CP,[52,53] with new-onset seizures documented in 14% of 54 participants in one study 1 to 2.5 months after starting on this drug or increasing its dose.[53]

Intrathecal Baclofen

The administration of ITB is an invasive method of delivery of the drug to achieve a regional effect on spasticity (see Table 7-3).[45-48,50,51] Pump implantation is a neurosurgical procedure that requires general anesthesia.[47] The pump is implanted in the lower abdomen, and a catheter attached to the pump is inserted intrathecally for continuous delivery of baclofen into the subarachnoid space.[46,47,51] The dose can be adjusted throughout the day using an external remote control, and the refills are performed by injecting the drug

	TABLE 7-5

SIDE EFFECTS AND COMPLICATIONS OF MEDICAL AND SURGICAL ANTISPASTICITY INTERVENTIONS[a]

INTERVENTION	SIDE EFFECTS AND COMPLICATIONS	
ITB[46,47,50,51,54,57,60]	Catheter kinking or malfunction	Meningitis
	CSF leaks	Respiratory depression from an overdose
	Decreased bladder control	Seromas
	Decreased trunk control	Spinal headaches
	Drooling	Superficial skin, pump pocket, and wound infections
	Hypotonia	Urinary retention
	Increased constipation	Withdrawal symptoms when ITB level is low
	Increased depression symptoms	
BTX-A[45,47,50,61,62]	Decreased balance	Risk of development of neutralizing antibodies
	Fatigue	Systemic effects with excessive dose administration
	Focal muscle weakness	• Dysphagia, dysphonia, dyspnea, respiratory distress, severe generalized weakness
	Localized pain	Urinary incontinence
Phenol and ethyl alcohol[46,61,62]	Dysesthesias	Prolonged localized pain
	Muscle necrosis	Significant procedural pain that requires sedation
	Muscle weakness	Transient anaesthesia
	Paresthesias	Vascular complications
Cerebellar stimulation[49]	CSF accumulation	Wound infection
SDR[46,47,61,75,77,78]	Back pain	Muscle weakness
	Decrease in functional skills in older children	Spinal abnormalities
	Exacerbation of dystonia	• Back pain, black discs, disc protrusion, increased lumbar lordosis, kyphosis, scoliosis, spinal stenosis, spondylolysis, spondylolisthesis
	Hip subluxation	

Abbreviations: BTX-A, botulinum toxin type A; CSF, cerebrospinal fluid; ITB, intrathecal baclofen; SDR, selective dorsal rhizotomy.

[a] Excludes oral medications and orthopedic surgeries.

solution into the pump port every 2 to 6 months.[47,54] The catheter insertion sites vary depending on the desired effects and, besides the most common thoracic level, a lumbar, sacral, or cervical site may be used.[55] While the catheter insertion at the cervical level may be beneficial for management of upper extremity spasticity, an associated decrease in postural tone may compromise head and upper trunk control and, thus, the child's sitting function.[46,54] However, in a prospective cohort study of 108 children with spastic CP, the catheter insertion site had no significant effects on the ITB antispasticity benefits or complication rate.[55]

While the intrathecal administration of baclofen circumvents the unfavorable systemic effects of the oral drug,[54-56] including the potentiation of seizure activity,[56] this intervention is expensive and has a number of side effects and complications that may outweigh its benefits[50] (Table 7-5). Additionally, failure to refill a pump in a timely manner may result in withdrawal symptoms that vary from bothersome

to dangerous, including dyskinesias, dysphoria, dystonia, hallucinations, hypertonia, hypotension or unstable blood pressure, itching, mental status changes, paresthesias, psychosis, rebound spasticity, seizures, and even death.[47,54,57,58] Nevertheless, research has shown that this intervention has not been associated with increased mortality in children and adults with CP.[57]

Published literature indicates that the ITB therapy is effective in achieving significant reduction in spasticity in children and adults with severe CP.[46,50,51,54-57,59] However, its efficacy in improving function has not been clearly established.[50,59] In fact, two systematic reviews concluded that the published studies of the clinical use of continuous ITB treatment lacked rigor, and that the evidence of positive effects of ITB on functional skills was insufficient,[50,60] especially in ambulatory people with CP.[60] Considering the methodological difficulties and ethical dilemmas that involve the withholding of treatment in conducting randomized controlled trials (RCTs) with this patient population, Krach[59] recommended that single subject research design be used instead or, alternatively, functional outcomes of the ITB therapy be compared to those observed in patients who refuse this intervention.

Intramuscular Injections and Neurolytic Blocks

Intramuscular injections of botulinum toxin type A (BTX-A) and phenol or alcohol blocks are focal antispasticity interventions (see Table 7-3) that target specific muscles to address clearly defined functional goals.[44-47] BTX is a product of *Clostridium botulinum*, which causes tetanus.[47] BTX-A acts presynaptically at the neuromuscular junction by blocking the release of acetylcholine.[46,47,61] This causes chemodenervation of the muscle resulting in weakness and decreased tone that become apparent in 5 to 7 days, peak at approximately 4 weeks, and last up to 3 to 6 months.[46,47,61] Palpation, electromyography (EMG), electrical stimulation, and ultrasound can be used to ensure accurate administration of BTX-A within the target musculature.[45] This intervention is very expensive, and in a child with generalized spasticity, only a limited number of muscles can be selected for BTX-A injections as there are limits on the safe medication doses that the patients can receive.[46,47] These limits are calculated per kilogram of body weight.[46,47] Using a combination of BTX-A and phenol or ethyl alcohol may allow the physician to circumvent the dose restrictions and target additional musculature in a single treatment.[45,46,61]

Phenol and ethyl alcohol have been used much longer than BTX-A to address focal spasticity.[47,61] These agents are injected in immediate proximity of a motor nerve, causing the denaturation of the protein and thus inducing chemical lysis, which results in muscle denervation through degeneration of axons.[46,47,61] The injection procedure guided by electrical stimulation to localize the nerve is lengthy and painful, and patient sedation is usually required.[46,47] The effects of a neurolytic block are evident immediately after the injection and last from 3 to 12 months.[47] This intervention is very cheap but is certainly less well tolerated than BTX-A.[46,47] Injection of phenol next to a nerve that contains a large number of sensory fibers may lead to painful sensory dysesthesias that may last for several months.[46] Therefore, Gormley et al[46] recommended avoiding the use of phenol injections on such nerves.

Table 7-5 contains information on side effects and complications associated with the intramuscular injections of BTX-A, phenol, and alcohol. Generally, the BTX-A therapy is better tolerated than phenol and alcohol injections, which are associated with more bothersome and frequent side effects.[46,61,62] In a retrospective cohort study of 336 children with CP who received a total of 764 multilevel BTX or BTX and phenol injections, adverse effects were observed more frequently in patients who received injections with both agents, with the reported complication rate of 2.5% and 7.6%, respectively.[62] Another group of researchers reported adverse effects in 3.3% of 1382 BTX-A injections and 8.7% of 356 participants with CP.[63] Interesting results were obtained by Williams et al[64] who demonstrated a combined effect of a 4.47% gastrocnemius muscle atrophy, a 3.96% soleus muscle hypertrophy, and no change in the total volume of the plantarflexor muscle group in 15 children with CP immediately after the BTX-A injections of spastic gastrocnemius muscles. The authors explained the soleus muscle hypertrophy as a possible compensatory response to the gastrocnemius muscle atrophy induced by BTX-A.[64]

BTX-A, phenol, and ethyl alcohol injections have been used in children and adults with CP with a primary goal to reduce spasticity.[45-48,50,51,61-64] Other reported therapeutic goals were to increase or preserve range of motion (ROM); prevent contractures; improve active movement, gait, and other functional skills; and delay orthopedic surgeries.[45,48,50,51] In addition, BTX-A injections have been used in combination with serial casting, splinting, and bracing to address ROM issues and hip joint development.[45,47,65] In a systematic review of literature that examined pharmacologic antispasticity interventions, none of the phenol or alcohol injection studies met the inclusion criteria.[50] As for the BTX-A, results of 3 systematic reviews showed that it was effective in decreasing focal spasticity in children with CP, but evidence of its functional effects was found to be inconclusive.[50,66,67] Another systematic review found limited or inconclusive evidence of BTX-A effectiveness in managing postoperative pain, achieving functional goals, and addressing hip integrity and general pain reduction in children classified in Gross Motor Function Classification System (GMFCS)[68] levels IV and V.[69]

Cerebellar Stimulation

Cerebellar stimulation was introduced in the 1970s with the idea that chronic stimulation of the superior-medial cerebellar cortex would have an inhibitory effect on spasticity.[70,71] Davis[71] reported on the results of a number of small studies that used this intervention with patients with CP with such benefits as decreased generalized spasticity, athetosis, and seizures in over 50% of participants. However, these studies lacked rigor and appropriate outcome measures, and some of them documented limited or no response to cerebellar stimulation. This led to a controversy regarding the use of this intervention in clinical practice, which was further fueled by the insufficient reliability of calibration of radiofrequency-linked stimulators, and by the use of different implantation sites and stimulation parameters.[71]

In a more recent study of 13 nonambulatory adolescents and young adults with CP, Harat et al[49] used deep stimulation of the superior cerebellar peduncle and reported decreased spasticity in 11 participants within the first 6 months, which was maintained at 1 and 2 years post-implantation. Other reported benefits included improvements in visual-motor coordination, cognitive function, self-care, and social function. Unfortunately, no validity and reliability information was provided for the questionnaire used to assess functional skills. Complications included wound infection that required stimulator explantation and accumulation of the cerebrospinal fluid superior to the stimulator in 3 and 2 participants, respectively. Because of the small sample size and the use of an inadequately described functional outcome measure, this study provided insufficient evidence for making a connection between the reduction of spasticity and reported functional improvement.[49]

Selective Dorsal Rhizotomy

SDR is a neurosurgical procedure that involves lamino-plasty followed by the separation and stimulation of dorsal nerve rootlets at the T_{12}-S_1 levels.[47,61] The electromyographic response to stimulation is recorded. If specific rootlets, when stimulated, produce excessive response in the corresponding muscles, they are selectively cut in order to decrease the abnormal afferent input and, ultimately, decrease spasticity. During surgery, approximately 25% to 60% of examined nerve rootlets are severed.[47,61] Patient selection plays an important role in the rate of success of this intervention.[45,47,61,72] Children with bilateral spastic CP who are 3 to 8 years old, are able to walk, show a hip adductor spasticity score lower than 3 on the Modified Ashworth Scale,[73] and receive preoperative Gross Motor Function Measure (GMFM-88)[74] scores greater than 60% are best candidates for this procedure.[45,47,61,72]

In a longitudinal retrospective study of ambulatory children with bilateral spastic CP, MacWilliams et al[75] showed that SDR performed in patients older than 10 years of age may lead to significant deterioration of higher-level gross motor functional skills that involve single leg stance. This finding suggests that SDR is not appropriate for ambulatory older children and adolescents.[75,76] In addition to age, functional skills, and the presence of spasticity, the presence of dystonia and muscle weakness also need to be considered.[46,47,70] SDR is not recommended for children with dystonia because it may make this type of muscle tone abnormality more pronounced.[46,47] Strength assessment prior to surgery is necessary as SDR frequently results in muscle weakness, and it may take the child longer than 6 months of physical therapy to return to the preoperative level of strength.[47,61] Reported long-term complications following SDR include spinal problems, back pain, and hip subluxation (see Table 7-5).[61,77,78]

According to published literature, SDR results in short-term gains at the level of body structures and functions and at the activity level of the International Classification of Functioning, Disability and Health (ICF)[79] manifested in decreased spasticity and improvements in ROM, gait parameters, and gross motor function.[61,77] Long-term, follow-up data point to continued improvements in lower extremity muscle tone, activities of daily living (ADLs), and gross motor function in children who meet the best candidate selection criteria discussed previously.[72] However, many children still require orthopedic surgeries performed prior to or after SDR to address the development of contractures and to maintain their ability to ambulate.[45,72,80,81]

Tedroff et al[80] reported on a prospective study of children with bilateral spastic CP who demonstrated a decrease in ROM and gross motor function at the 10-year follow-up, with 16 of 19 participants requiring orthopedic surgeries, all despite a long-term significant decrease in spasticity induced

by SDR. This pointed to the possibility of other causes of contracture development besides spasticity in this patient population.[80] Bolster et al[78] obtained different results that showed no long-term deterioration of gross motor function in children with bilateral spastic CP at the 10-year follow-up after an SDR surgery based on the GMFM-66 reference curves[82] used to track their progress. Nevertheless, 16 of 29 participants still underwent subsequent orthopedic surgeries 2 to 9 years following SDR.[78]

A systematic review of literature published in 2011 found limited evidence of long-term effects of SDR on activity and no studies that would provide level III or higher evidence of participation-related long-term outcomes.[77] In the same year, Langerak et al[83] reported on an observational 17- to 26-year follow-up study of 31 individuals with bilateral spastic CP, GMFCS levels I through III, who had undergone an SDR surgery between 1981 and 1991. The outcome measures included the Functional Mobility Scale (FMS)[84] and the Life-Habit Questionnaire (LIFE-H).[85] The FMS evaluates functional mobility in children with CP over 5, 50, and 500 meters in 3 different settings (home, school, and community).[84] The LIFE-H is a measure of activity and social participation that consists of 77 life habit items divided into 6 ADL and 6 Social Roles categories.[85,86] Results showed high functional mobility levels of the majority of participants when assessed with the FMS, but 48% reported difficulty and 6% dissatisfaction with their mobility on the LIFE-H.[83] Other LIFE-H results included 81% and 79% of participants reporting independence with ADLs and 5 of 6 Social Roles items, respectively. The level of satisfaction with the life habits was generally high as well. Overall, these results reflected good long-term activity and participation outcomes of SDR but need to be interpreted with caution because of the small sample size and the absence of a control group in this study.[83]

In summary, the use of interventions discussed in this section is generally supported by research of varied quality and quantity as effective in managing spasticity. However, evidence of an existing relationship between the reduction of spasticity and functional improvement, activity, or participation is absent or insufficient. Therefore, rigorous research is necessary to establish a clear connection between these variables, and other interventions that affect function, activity, and participation in this patient population need to be investigated.

Management of Dystonia

Dystonia is caused by lesions to basal ganglia and is characterized by involuntary muscle contractions that are usually elicited or exaggerated by attempted active movement.[38,87] Dystonia can be managed with oral medications, BTX-A injections, ITB therapy, or DBS, with more invasive therapies selected when the less invasive ones are not effective.[47]

Because basal ganglia lesions affect the synthesis of dopamine, carbidopa/levodopa is an oral drug of choice for children with dystonia.[47,88] Its dose-limiting side effects include confusion, hallucinations, and memory problems.[47]

Anticholinergics, such as trihexyphenidyl, have also been used.[47,88,89] Their side effects are similar but may also include blurred vision, changes in behavior, constipation and other gastrointestinal problems, dry mouth, nightmares, skin rash, and urinary retention.[47,88] Other drugs used for management of dystonia are oral baclofen and benzodiazepines such as clonazepam.[47,88] Their side effects are listed in Table 7-4.

When oral medications are not effective, BTX-A injections can address focal dystonia or target selected muscles in children with generalized dystonia.[45,47,88] If less invasive options fail, the ITB pump placement can be considered, although it is less effective in the treatment of dystonia than spasticity,[47] and a recent systematic review found no evidence of its use in ambulatory children with dyskinetic CP.[59]

DBS is a neurosurgical intervention that has been used in children with CP with variable results.[47,70,88,90,91] It targets the globus pallidus internus and, in some cases, other thalamic and subthalamic nuclei may be also stimulated.[90] The DBS surgery involves an MRI-guided targeted placement of electrodes performed under general anaesthesia, followed by computed tomography that confirms the lead placement.[92] Results of a meta-analysis indicated that DBS may be effective in addressing dystonia in children with dyskinetic CP.[90] Additionally, in a retrospective cohort study, Lumsden et al[92] showed that DBS was more effective in children treated within the 5 years of its onset compared to later in life, and that it was more effective in patients with primary dystonia compared to those with secondary dystonia, such as children with dyskinetic CP. Further collaborative research, preferably in the form of prospective clinical trials, should examine the efficacy of this intervention in addressing dystonia, function, and quality of life in these children.[92,93]

Management of Oral-Motor Problems

Oral-motor problems related to the disrupted CNS coordination of muscles of the mouth, pharynx, and esophagus include motor speech deficits, feeding difficulties, and sialorrhea.[94] The reader is referred to Chapter 4 for a detailed discussion of these issues and for the description of gastrostomy tube placement in medical management of dysphagia and its sequelae.

Medical management of sialorrhea includes oral anticholinergic drugs,[95-97] focal injections of BTX-A into submandibular and parotid glands,[95-99] and surgical interventions.[95,99,100] Anticholinergic medications, including glycopyrrolate, benztropine, and scopolamine, affect drooling by blocking parasympathetic innervation to salivary glands.[95-97] Their use is frequently discontinued because of their side effects, which may include blurred vision, heat insensitivity, irritability, sedation, and urinary retention.[95,96]

BTX-A injections for sialorrhea are performed under ultrasound guidance and lead to a temporary reduction in saliva secretion.[99] The reported side effects include pain, hematoma, bleeding, swelling, and infection at the injection site, as well as dry mouth, saliva thickening, and problems with chewing and swallowing related to the BTX-A diffusion into the oral musculature.[99] According to Erasmus et al,[101] the thickening of saliva may also cause chewing and swallowing difficulties. This issue needs to be considered when making clinical decisions regarding the use of BTX-A for a specific patient.[101] Surgeries, such as salivary duct ligation or rerouting and salivary gland excision, are considered to be the most definitive type of treatment for sialorrhea.[96] Their side effects may include discomfort at incision site, potential for tooth decay, and a risk of formation of salivary retention cysts.[95,96]

A Cochrane review of interventions for sialorrhea used in children with CP found insufficient evidence in support of one treatment option over another, and there were no studies that investigated the effects of these interventions on the participants' psychological well-being or quality of life.[97] Therefore, this topic needs to be examined further through well-designed RCTs. Additionally, the efficacy of conservative treatment options, such as behavioral, occupational, speech, and physical therapies aimed at improved lip closure and active swallowing to control saliva, and the use of mouth appliances and acupuncture for the same purposes should be investigated through rigorous research.[97]

REFERENCES

1. Fairhurst C. Cerebral palsy: the whys and hows. *Arch Dis Child Educ Pract Ed.* 2012;97(4):122-131.
2. Patel DR, Pratt HD, Patel ND. Team processes and team care for children with developmental disabilities. *Pediatr Clin North Am.* 2008;55(6):1375-1390.
3. Aisen ML, Kerkovich D, Mast J, et al. Cerebral palsy: clinical care and neurological rehabilitation. *Lancet Neurol.* 2011;10(9):844-852.
4. Ruff CA, Faulkner SD, Fehlings MG. The potential for stem cell therapies to have an impact on cerebral palsy: opportunities and limitations. *Dev Med Child Neurol.* 2013;55(8):689-697.
5. Regenberg AC, Hutchinson LA, Schanker B, Matthews DJ. Medicine on the fringe: stem cell-based interventions in advance of evidence. *Stem Cells.* 2009;27(9):2312-2319.
6. Pabon MM, Borlongan CV. Advances in the cell-based treatment of neonatal hypoxic-ischemic brain injury. *Future Neurol.* 2013;8(2):193-203.
7. Boston Children's Hospital. Teratoma in children at CHB. http://www.childrenshospital.org/az/Site1691/mainpageS1691P0.html. Accessed June 22, 2013.
8. James E. Carroll Georgia Health Sciences University. Safety and effectiveness of cord blood stem cell infusion for the treatment of cerebral palsy in children. *ClinicalTrials.gov.* http://www.clinicaltrials.gov/ct2/show/NCT01072370?term=NCT01072370&rank=1. Updated October 4, 102. Accessed June 23, 2013.
9. James E. Baumgartner; Memorial Hermann Healthcare System. Umbilical cord blood in the treatment of stroke in children (Pedi Stroke). *ClinicalTrials.gov.* http://www.clinicaltrials.gov/ct2/show/NCT01700166?term=NCT01700166&rank=1. Published October 2, 2012. Accessed June 23, 2013.
10. Min K, Song J, Kang JY, et al. Umbilical cord blood therapy potentiated with erythropoietin for children with cerebral palsy: a double-blind, randomized, placebo-controlled trial. *Stem Cells.* 2013;31(3):581-591.
11. Depositario-Cabacar DF, Zelleke T-G. Treatment of epilepsy in children with developmental disabilities. *Dev Disabil Res Rev.* 2010;16(3):239-247.

12. Cross JH, Kluger G, Lagae L. Advancing the management of childhood epilepsies. *Eur J Paediatr Neurol.* 2013;17(4):334-347.

13. Kossoff EH, Wang HS. Dietary therapies for epilepsy. *Biomed J.* 2013;36(1):2-8.

14. Ciccone CD. Antiepileptic drugs. In: Ciccone CD, ed. *Pharmacology in Rehabilitation.* 3rd ed. Philadelphia, PA: F.A. Davis Company; 2002:110-122.

15. Smith MC. Optimizing therapy of seizures in children and adolescents with developmental disabilities. *Neurology.* 2006;67(12 suppl 4):S52-S55.

16. Kramer U, Sagi L, Goldberg-Stern H, Zelnik N, Nissenkorn A, Ben-Zeev B. Clinical spectrum and medical treatment of children with electrical status epilepticus in sleep (ESES). *Epilepsia.* 2009;50(6):1517-1524.

17. Engel J Jr.; International League Against Epilepsy (ILAE). A proposed diagnostic scheme for people with epileptic seizures and with epilepsy: report of the ILAE Task Force on Classification and Terminology. *Epilepsia.* 2001;42(6):796-803.

18. Aneja S, Aneja B, Taluja V, Bhatia VK. Epilepsy in children with cerebral palsy. *Indian J Pediatr.* 2001;68(2):111-115.

19. Cervenka MC, Kossoff EH. Dietary treatment of intractable epilepsy. *Continuum (Minneap Minn).* 2013;19(3 Epilepsy):756-766.

20. Coppola G, Verrotti A, Ammendola E, et al. Ketogenic diet for the treatment of catastrophic epileptic encephalopathies in childhood. *Eur J Paediatr Neurol.* 2010;14(3):229-234.

21. Keene DL. A systematic review of the use of the ketogenic diet in childhood epilepsy. *Pediatr Neurol.* 2006;35(1):1-5.

22. Schwartz RH, Eaton J, Bower BD, Aynsley-Green A. Ketogenic diets in the treatment of epilepsy: short-term clinical effects. *Dev Med Child Neurol.* 1989;31(2):145-151.

23. Pfeifer HH, Thiele EA. Low-glycemic-index treatment: a liberalized ketogenic diet for treatment of intractable epilepsy. *Neurology.* 2005;65(11):1810-1812.

24. Jenkins DJ, Wolever TM, Taylor RH, et al. Glycemic index of foods: a physiological basis for carbohydrate exchange. *Am J Clin Nutr.* 1981;34(3):362-366.

25. Kossoff EH, Krauss GL, McGrogan JR, Freeman JM. Efficacy of the Atkins diet as therapy for intractable childhood epilepsy. *Neurology.* 2003;61(12):1789-1791.

26. Kossof EH, McGrogan JR, Bluml RM, Pillas DJ, Rubenstein JE, Vining EP. A modified Atkins diet is effective for the treatment of intractable pediatric epilepsy. *Epilepsia.* 2006;47(2):421-424.

27. Kang HC, Lee HS, You SJ, Kang du C, Ko TS, Kim HD. Use of a modified Atkins diet in intractable childhood epilepsy. *Epilepsia.* 2007;48(1):182-6.

28. Muzykewicz DA, Lyczkowski DA, Memon N, Conant KD, Pfeifer HH, Thiele EA. Efficacy, safety, and tolerability of the low glycemic index treatment in pediatric epilepsy. *Epilepsia.* 2009;50(5):1118-1126.

29. Stacey WC, Litt B. Technology insight: neuroengineering and epilepsy-designing devices for seizure control. *Nat Clin Pract Neurol.* 2008;4(4):190-201.

30. Helmers SL, Duh MS, Guérin A, et al. Clinical outcomes, quality of life, and costs associated with implantation of vagus nerve stimulation therapy in pediatric patients with drug-resistant epilepsy. *Eur J Paediatr Neurol.* 2012;16(5):449-458.

31. Mapstone TB. Vagus nerve stimulation: current concepts. *Neurosurg Focus.* 2008;25(3):E9.

32. Fisher RS, Krauss GL, Ramsay E, Laxer K, Gates J. Assessment of vagus nerve stimulation for epilepsy: report of the Therapeutics and Technology Assessment Subcommittee of the American Academy of Neurology. *Neurology.* 1997;49(1):293-297.

33. Velasco AL, Velasco F, Velasco M, Trejo D, Castro G, Carrillo-Ruiz JD. Electrical stimulation of the hippocampal epileptic foci for seizure control: a double-blind, long-term follow-up study. *Epilepsia.* 2007:48(10):1895-1903.

34. Cross JH, Jayakar P, Nordli D, et al; International League against Epilepsy, Subcommission for Paediatric Epilepsy Surgery; Commissions of Neurosurgery and Paediatrics. Proposed criteria for referral and evaluation of children for epilepsy surgery: recommendations of the Subcommission for Pediatric Epilepsy Surgery. *Epilepsia.* 2006;47(6):952-959.

35. van Empelen R, Jennekens-Schinkel A, Gorter JW, et al; Dutch Collaborative Epilepsy Surgery Programme. Epilepsy surgery does not harm motor performance of children and adolescents. *Brain.* 2005;128(Pt 7):1536-1545.

36. Daniel RT, Thomas SG, Thomas M. Role of surgery in pediatric epilepsy. *Indian Pediatr.* 2007;44(4):263-273.

37. Hemb M, Velasco TR, Parnes MS, et al. Improved outcomes in pediatric epilepsy surgery: the UCLA experience, 1986-2008. *Neurology.* 2010;74(22):1768-1775.

38. Sanger TD, Delgado MR, Gaebler-Spira D, Hallet M, Mink JW, Task Force on Childhood Motor Disorders. Classification and definition of disorders causing hypertonia in childhood. *Pediatrics.* 2003;111(1):e89-e97.

39. Sanger TD, Chen D, Delgado MR, Gaebler-Spira D, Hallet M, Mink JW, Task Force on Childhood Motor Disorders. Definition and classification of negative motor signs in childhood. *Pediatrics.* 2006;118:2159-2167.

40. Tedroff K, Knutson LM, Soderberg G. Synergistic muscle activation during maximum voluntary contraction in children with and without spastic cerebral palsy. *Dev Med Child Neurol.* 2006;48(10):789-796.

41. Tedroff K, Knutson LM, Soderberg G. Co-activity during maximum voluntary contraction: a study of four lower-extremity muscles in children with and without cerebral palsy. *Dev Med Child Neurol.* 2008;50(5):377-381.

42. Latash ML, Anson JG. What are "normal movements" in atypical populations? *Behav Brain Sci.* 1996;19:55-106.

43. Bobath B, Bobath K. *Motor Development in the Different Types of Cerebral Palsy.* London, UK: William Heinemann Medical Books Limited; 1975.

44. Semans S. The Bobath concept in treatment of neurological disorders; a neuro-developmental treatment. *Am J Phys Med.* 1967;46(1):732-788.

45. Damiano DL, Alter KE, Chambers H. New clinical and research trends in lower extremity management for ambulatory children with cerebral palsy. *Phys Med Rehabil Clin N Am.* 2009;20(3):469-491.

46. Gormley ME Jr, Krach LE, Piccini L. Spasticity management in the child with spastic quadriparesis. *Eur J Neurol.* 2001;8(suppl 5):127-135.

47. Deon LL, Gaeblar-Spira D. Assessment and treatment of movement disorders in children with cerebral palsy. *Orthop Clin N Am.* 2010;41(4):507-517.

48. Graham HK, Aoki KR, Autti-Rämö I, et al. Recommendations for the use of botulinum toxin type A in the management of cerebral palsy. *Gait Posture.* 2000;11(1):67-79.

49. Harat M, Radziszewski K, Rudas M, Okon M, Galanda M. Clinical evaluation of deep cerebellar stimulation for spasticity in patients with cerebral palsy. *Neurol Neurochir Pol.* 2009;43(1):36-44.

50. Quality Standards Subcommittee of the American Academy of Neurology and the Practice Committee of the Child Neurology Society, Delgado MR, Hirtz D, et al. Practice parameter: pharmacologic treatment of spasticity in children and adolescents with cerebral palsy (an evidence-based review): report of the Quality Standards Subcommittee of the American Academy of Neurology and the Practice Committee of the Child Neurology Society. *Neurology.* 2010;74(4):336-343.

51. Verotti A, Greco R, Spalice A, Chiarelly F, Iannetti P. Pharmacotherapy of spasticity in children with cerebral palsy. *Pediatr Neurol.* 2006;34(1):1-6.

52. De Rinaldis M, Losito L, Gennaro L, Trabacca A. Long-term oral baclofen treatment in a child with cerebral palsy: electroencephalographic changes and clinical adverse effects. *J Child Neurol.* 2010;25(10):1272-1274.

53. Hansel DE, Hansel CR, Shindle MK, et al. Oral baclofen in cerebral palsy: possible seizure potentiation? *Pediatr Neurol.* 2003;29(3):203-206.

54. Zdolsek H, Olesch C, Antolovich G, Reddihough D. Intrathecal baclofen therapy: benefits and complications. *J Intellect Dev Disabil.* 2011;36(3):207-213.

55. Sivakumar G, Yap Y, Tsegaye M, Vloeberghs M. Intrathecal baclofen therapy for spasticity of cerebral origin—does the position of the intrathecal catheter matter? *Childs Nerv Syst.* 2010;26(8):1097-1102.

56. Buonaguro V, Scelsa B, Curci D, Monforte S, Iuorno T, Motta F. Epilepsy and intrathecal baclofen therapy in children with cerebral palsy. *Pediatr Neurol.* 2005;33(2):110-113.

57. Krach L, Kriel RL, Day SM, Strauss DJ. Survival of individuals with cerebral palsy receiving continuous intrathecal baclofen treatment: a matched-cohort study. *Dev Med Child Neurol.* 2010;52(7):672-676.

58. Specchio N, Carotenuto A, Trivisano M, Cappelletti S, Vigevano F, Fusco L. Prolonged episode of dystonia and dyskinesia resembling status epilepticus following acute intrathecal baclofen withdrawal. *Epilepsy Behav.* 2011;21(3):321-323.

59. Krach L. Intrathecal baclofen and motor function in cerebral palsy. *Dev Med Child Neurol.* 2011;53(5):391.

60. Pin TW, McCartney L, Lewis J, Waugh M-C. Use of intrathecal baclofen therapy in ambulant children and adolescents with spasticity and dystonia of cerebral origin: a systematic review. *Dev Med Child Neurol.* 2011;53(10):885-895.

61. Tilton AH. Therapeutic interventions for tone abnormalities in cerebral palsy. *NeuroRx.* 2006;3(2):217-224.

62. Kolaski K, Ajizian SJ, Passmore L, Pasutharnchat N, Koman LA, Smith BP. Safety profile of multilevel chemical denervation procedures using phenol or botulinum toxin or both in a pediatric population. *Am J Phys Med Rehabil.* 2008;87(7):556-566.

63. Papavasiliou AS, Nikaina I, Foska K, Bouros P, Mitsou G, Filiopoulos C. Safety of botulinum toxin A in children and adolescents with cerebral palsy in a pragmatic setting. *Toxins.* 2013;5:524-536.

64. Williams SA, Reid S, Elliott C, Shipman P, Valentine J. Muscle volume alterations in spastic muscles immediately following botulinum toxin type A treatment in children with cerebral palsy. *Dev Med Child Neurol.* 2013;55(9):813-820.

65. Willoughby K, Ang SG, Thomason P, Graham HK. The impact of botulinum toxin A and abduction bracing on long-term hip development in children with cerebral palsy. *Dev Med Child Neurol.* 2012;54(8):743-747.

66. Koog YH, Min B-I. Effects of botulinum toxin A on calf muscles in children with cerebral palsy: a systematic review. *Clin Rehabil.* 2010;24(8):685-700.

67. Ryll U, Bastiaenen C, De Bie R, Staal B. Effects of leg muscle botulinum toxin A injections on walking in children with spasticity-related cerebral palsy: a systematic review. *Dev Med Child Neurol.* 2011;53(3):210-216.

68. Palisano RJ, Rosenbaum PL, Walter SD, Russell DJ, Wood EP, Galuppi BE. Development and reliability of a system to classify gross motor function in children with cerebral palsy. *Dev Med Child Neurol.* 1997;39(4):214-223.

69. Pin TW, Elmasry J, Lewis J. Efficacy of botulinum toxin A in children with cerebral palsy in Gross Motor Function Classification System levels IV and V: a systematic review. *Dev Med Child Neurol.* 2013;55(4):304-313.

70. Lynn AK, Turner M, Chambers HG. Surgical management of spasticity in persons with cerebral palsy. *PM R.* 2009;1(9):834-838.

71. Davis R. Cerebellar stimulation for cerebral palsy spasticity, function, and seizures. *Arch Med Res.* 2000;31(3):290-299.

72. Dudley RW, Parolin M, Gagnon B, et al. Long-term functional benefits of selective dorsal rhizotomy for spastic cerebral palsy. *J Neurosurg Pediatr.* 2013;12(2):142-150.

73. Bohannon RW, Smith MB. Interrater reliability of a Modified Ashworth Scale of muscle spasticity. *Phys Ther.* 1987;67(2):206-207.

74. Russell DJ, Rosenbaum PL, Avery LM, Lane M. *Gross Motor Function Measure (GMFM-66 & GMFM-88) User's Manual.* Lavenham Suffolk: Mac Keith Press; 2002.

75. MacWilliams BA, Johnson BA, Shuckra AL, D'Astous JL. Functional decline in children undergoing selective dorsal rhizotomy after age 10. *Dev Med Child Neurol.* 2011;53(8):717-723.

76. Baker R, Graham K. Functional decline in children undergoing selective dorsal rhizotomy after age 10. *Dev Med Child Neurol.* 2011;53(8):577.

77. Grunt S, Becher JG, Vermeulen RJ. Long-term outcome and adverse effects of selective dorsal rhizotomy in children with cerebral palsy: a systematic review. *Dev Med Child Neurol.* 2011;53(6):490-498.

78. Bolster EA, van Schie PE, Becher JG, van Ouwerkerk WJ, Strijers RL, Vermeulen RJ. Long-term effect of selective dorsal rhizotomy on gross motor function in ambulant children with spastic bilateral cerebral palsy, compared with reference centiles. *Dev Med Child Neurol.* 2013;55(7):610-616.

79. World Health Organization. *International Classification of Functioning, Disability and Health.* Geneva, Switzerland: World Health Organization; 2001.

80. Tedroff K, Löwing K, Jacobson DN, Åström E. Does loss of spasticity matter? A 10-year follow-up after selective dorsal rhizotomy in cerebral palsy. *Dev Med Child Neurol.* 2011;53(8):724-729.

81. Langerak NG, Tam N, Vaughan CL, Fieggen AG, Schwartz MH. Gait status 17-26 years after selective dorsal rhizotomy. *Gait Posture.* 2012;35(2):244-249.

82. Hanna SE, Bartlett DJ, Rivard LM, Russell DJ. Reference curves for the Gross Motor Function Measure: percentiles for clinical description and tracking over time among children with cerebral palsy. *Phys Ther.* 2008;88(5):596-607.

83. Langerak NG, Hillier SL, Verkoeijen PP, Peter JC, Fieggen AG, Vaughan CL. Level of activity and participation in adults with spastic diplegia 17-26 years after selective dorsal rhizotomy. *J Rehabil Med.* 2011;43(4):330-337.

84. Graham HK, Harvey A, Rodda J, Nattrass GR, Pirpiris M. The Functional Mobility Scale. *J Pediatr Orthop.* 2004;24(5):514-520.

85. Fougeyrollas P, Noreau L, Bergeron H, Cloutier R, Dion SA, St-Michel G. Social consequences of long term impairments and disabilities: conceptual approach and assessment of handicap. *Int J Rehabil Res.* 1998;21(2):127-141.

86. Resnik L, Plow MA. Measuring participation as defined by the International Classification of Functioning, Disability and Health: an evaluation of existing measures. *Arch Phys Med Rehabil.* 2009;90(5):856-866.

87. Sanger TD. Toward a definition of childhood dystonia. *Curr Opin Pediatr.* 2004;16(6):623-627.

88. Langlois M, Richer F, Chouinard S. New perspectives on dystonia. *Can J Neurol Sci.* 2003;30(suppl 1):S34-S44.

89. Carranza-del Rio J, Clegg NJ, Moore A, Delgado MR. Use of trihexyphenidyl in children with cerebral palsy. *Pediatr Neurol.* 2011;44(3):202-206.

90. Koy A, Hellmich M, Pauls AM, et al. Effects of deep brain stimulation in dyskinetic cerebral palsy: a meta-analysis. *Mov Disord.* 2012;28(5):647-654.

91. Tierny TS, Lozano AM. Surgical treatment for secondary dystonia. *Mov Disord.* 2012;27(13):1598-1605.

92. Lumsden DE, Kaminska M, Gimeno H, et al. Proportion of life lived with dystonia inversely correlates with response to pallidal deep brain stimulation in both primary and secondary childhood dystonia. *Dev Med Child Neurol.* 2013;55(6):567-574.

93. Rosenbaum P. Deep brain stimulation in cerebral palsy: an opportunity for collaborative research. *Dev Med Child Neurol.* 2013;55(7):584-585.

94. Sullivan PB. Gastrointestinal disorders in children with neurodevelopmental disabilities. *Dev Disabil Res Rev.* 2008;14(2):128-136.

95. Pruitt DW, Tsai T. Common medical comorbidities associated with cerebral palsy. *Phy Med Rehabil Clin N Am.* 2009;20(3):453-467.

96. Hockstein NG, Samadi DS, Gendron K, Handler SD. Sialorrhea: a management challenge. *Am Fam Physician.* 2004;69(11):2628-2634.

97. Walshe M, Smith M, Pennington L. Interventions for drooling in children with cerebral palsy (review). *Cochrane Database Syst Rev.* 2012;11:CD008624.

98. Reid SM, Johnstone BR, Westbury C, Rawicki B, Reddihough DS. Randomized trial of botulinum toxin injections into the salivary glands to reduce drooling in children with neurological disorders. *Dev Med Child Neurol.* 2008;50(2):123-128.

99. Reddihough D, Erasmus CE, Johnson H, McKellar GMW, Jongerius PH. Botulinum toxin assessment, intervention and aftercare for paediatric and adult drooling: international consensus statement. *Eur J Neurol.* 2010;17(suppl 2):109-121.

100. Scheffer AR, Bosch KJ, van Hulst K, van den Hoogen FJ. Salivary duct ligation for anterior and posterior drooling: our experience in twenty one children. *Clin Otolaryngol.* 2013;38(5):425-429. doi: 10.1111/coa.12146.

101. Erasmus CE, Van Hulst K, Van Den Hoogen FJ, et al. Thickened saliva after effective management of drooling with botulinum toxin A. *Dev Med Child Neurol.* 2010;52(6):e114-e118.

8

Musculoskeletal System
Medical and Surgical Management of
Alterations in Body Structures and Functions

Early recognition of progressive deformity in patients with cerebral palsy allows
timely treatment and prevention of irreversible change.

David S. Morrell, J. Michael Pearson, and Donald D. Sauser[1]

Bone and joint deformities in extremities and spine as well as osteoporosis are frequently observed in children with cerebral palsy (CP) and may lead to chronic pain[1-3] (see Chapter 4). Knowledge and understanding of timely medical and surgical management of the musculoskeletal system impairments affecting these children are very important for physical therapists who are involved in their pre- and post-surgical care.[3,4] This chapter will focus on medical management of osteopenia and osteoporosis and on the types and outcomes of orthopedic surgeries that aim to address bone and joint deformities, associated pain, as well as spasticity as one of the causes of muscle contractures and limitations in range of motion (ROM) in this patient population. Pain assessment and management will be discussed in Chapter 10, and Chapter 15 will cover interventions for muscle weakness as another alteration of body structures and functions related to the musculoskeletal system.

MEDICAL MANAGEMENT OF OSTEOPENIA AND OSTEOPOROSIS

While *osteopenia* is defined as the "reduction in bone volume to below normal levels especially due to inadequate replacement of bone lost to normal lysis,"[5] *osteoporosis* is a condition characterized by bone weakness and fragility leading to fractures.[6] Both conditions are related to decreased bone mineral density (BMD), but in osteoporosis, it is more severe.[5,6] Children with CP frequently demonstrate decreased bone mass that puts them at risk for painful fractures.[7-11] Several methods can be used to assess bone health.[7] Blood tests, such as complete blood cell count (CBC), serum creatinine, albumin, calcium, phosphorus, serum 25-hydroxyvitamin D, and alkaline phosphatase, would provide relevant laboratory values for the examination of a patient with or at risk for osteoporosis. Structural bone changes and fractures related to osteoporosis can be identified with plain film radiographs. However, only dual-energy x-ray absorptiometry or DEXA would offer the most objective quantitative assessment of BMD. It is recommended that, in children and adolescents, BMD be expressed as a z score for gender and age to account for developmental variations related to these variables. If a child's BMD is identified as low, meaning that his or her corresponding z score is below -2.0,[7] possible interventions may include weight-bearing activities, proper nutrition, supplemental calcium and vitamin D, the use of bisphosphonates, and possible reduction or discontinuation of medications that negatively affect bone health, such as antiepileptic drugs.[7-14]

Rahlin M. *Physical Therapy for Children With Cerebral Palsy:*
An Evidence-Based Approach (pp 125-141).
© 2016 SLACK Incorporated.

Weight-bearing activities, including standing programs and mechanical loading of low magnitude[11,15-17] will be discussed in Chapter 22. Because normal development and mineralization of bone depends on adequate intake of calcium and vitamin D,[10] nutritional recommendations for children and youth include foods that contain vitamin D, such as egg yolks and fortified cereals and milk, as well as calcium and vitamin D supplementation.[7] Efficacy of medical interventions used to address osteopenia and osteoporosis in children with CP was examined in a number of studies.[8-13] Kilpinen-Loisa et al[10] documented a significant increase in vitamin D levels in 40 children and adolescents with CP after a 10-week regimen of high intake of vitamin D_3, but the results failed to show any effects on bone turnover in the study participants.[10] Other authors reported a significant increase in BMD in response to calcium and vitamin D supplementation in non-ambulatory children with bilateral CP and epilepsy,[12-14] and polytherapy with vitamin D (alfacalcidol) and oral bisphosphonate (risedronate) was shown to be even more effective in increasing the BMD of lumbar spine.[13,14] Bisphosphonates inhibit the resorption of bone in the presence of continued bone formation.[7] Other bisphosphonate interventions besides risedronate, such as oral alendronate and intravenously administered pamidronate, were also reported to be successful and safe in the treatment of osteopenia and osteoporosis in children with CP.[8,9,11]

In order to determine the strength of evidence that supports specific interventions and to develop evidence-based clinical guidelines, studies need to be evaluated for their size, design, and rigor.[11] A systematic review of interventions used to address osteoporosis in this patient population showed that bisphosphonates were probably effective in increasing BMD and possibly effective in preventing fractures related to bone weakness. The same review demonstrated that evidence in regard to calcium and vitamin D supplementation was not as strong and only pointed to a possible resultant increase in BMD, with insufficient information available to support the use of these interventions for fracture prevention.[11]

MEDICAL AND SURGICAL MANAGEMENT OF RANGE OF MOTION LIMITATIONS, JOINT CONTRACTURES, AND MUSCULOSKELETAL DEFORMITIES

Multiple antispasticity interventions shown to improve ROM were discussed in Chapter 7. Orthopedic surgery is another intervention that addresses spasticity in a short term, with its longer lasting effects observed in muscle length, bone and joint alignment, pain, function, and ease of hygiene.[18] Orthotic management that is often indicated to maintain the surgical correction will be examined in Chapters 20 and 21. Musculotendinous or tendon lengthening, tendon transfer, rotational osteotomy, and arthrodesis or joint fusion are the most common types of orthopedic surgeries children with CP may undergo.[18,19] Table 8-1 contains brief descriptions and goals of these surgeries.[18,19] Specific surgical procedures performed on the upper and lower extremities and spine will be described later in this chapter.

Some of the most common side effects of orthopedic surgeries are muscle weakness and pain related to muscle spasms.[20,21] Botulinum toxin A (BTX-A) may be used preoperatively to assist the interdisciplinary team in the decision-making process and to address postoperative muscle spasms.[20,21] Rutz et al[20] showed that specific muscles that would or would not benefit from tendon lengthening surgeries could be identified based on the amount of muscle weakness and its effects on gait documented post-BTX injections in children with CP, Gross Motor Function Classification System (GMFCS)[22] levels I through III. Results of an earlier randomized clinical trial (RCT) demonstrated other benefits of preoperative application of BTX-A, such as significant reduction in postoperative pain scores, decreased requirements for analgesia, and shorter lengths of hospital stay in children with bilateral spastic CP, GMFCS[22] levels IV and V.[21] Iatrogenic tendon overlengthening is another complication of orthopedic surgeries that needs to be avoided.[18,19,23,24] A common example of such problem is crouching during standing and walking activities as the result of an isolated Achilles tendon lengthening procedure.[23,24] In the past, single-level orthopedic surgeries were frequently performed to address specific contractures and deformities.[18,25,26] However, more recently, single-event multilevel surgeries (SEMLS) became more common,[18,25,26] especially for the lower extremity, with improved outcomes reported in multiple studies.[18,23,25]

Management of the Lower Extremity

Making a decision regarding the best course of action in the orthopedic management of lower extremity impairments in children with CP involves multiple factors, including the child's and family goals and expectations, the child's age, ambulatory status, gait pattern (if applicable), and specific problems with the lower extremity alignment and ROM that negatively affect physical activity.[27-30] Interprofessional collaboration among multiple members of the interdisciplinary team is crucial for determining the best course of action.[18,19,27] Current evidence-based consensus is that, whenever possible, orthopedic surgeries need to be delayed until the elementary school age because growth spurts in early childhood would prevent long-lasting improvements in the lower extremity alignment, and the recurrence of contractures would necessitate additional surgeries.[18,19,27,28] Because of the resultant postsurgical muscle weakness, avoiding repeated soft tissue procedures may be beneficial for children with CP.[20,28] In many cases, conservative interventions, including BTX-A injections, physical therapy techniques, and orthotic management, may help delay orthopedic surgeries in this patient population.[28]

Computerized gait analysis is an effective assessment tool that enhances the decision-making process in regard to

TABLE 8-1

TYPES, BRIEF DESCRIPTION, AND GOALS OF COMMON ORTHOPEDIC SURGERIES PERFORMED IN CHILDREN WITH CEREBRAL PALSY

TYPE OF SURGERY	DESCRIPTION	GOALS
Musculotendinous or tendon lengthening	Lengthens musculotendinous unit via tenotomy, Z-type incision, or isolated recession through the fascia at the musculotendinous junction	• Temporarily decrease spasticity • Increase range of motion
Tendon transfer	Repositions a spastic muscle or its part so that it serves a different function	• Correct deformity • Improve joint alignment • Increase active range of motion • Improve function
Osteotomy	Corrects bony malrotation and disrupted joint mechanics by performing a cut in the affected bone	• Realign the joint for improved function • Reduce joint subluxation or dislocation • Increase movement efficiency • Decrease energy expenditure during functional movement
Arthrodesis	Fuses the joint	• Correct deformity of a distal extremity joint when recurrence is likely • Correct progressive neuromuscular scoliosis • Achieve optimal alignment of extremity or spine

Compiled from Damiano et al[18] and Lynn et al.[19]

the best surgical or nonsurgical intervention for a specific child.[27,29,30] It was shown to improve surgical outcomes in several studies.[29-31] In addition, Wren et al[32] demonstrated that children who had undergone preoperative clinical gait analysis required fewer additional surgeries than those who had not. It is important to note that gait immaturity and inconsistency in children with CP younger than 7 or 8 years of age would typically preclude obtaining meaningful results from preoperative gait analysis, which is another reason to delay a surgery, if possible.[18,19,27,33] However, because of the heterogeneity of presentation in children with CP, the discussion of the best timing of orthopedic surgeries still persists in published literature.[33,34] There is a general agreement that hip subluxation or dislocation is a major exception to delaying surgical intervention as it needs to be addressed early in the developmental process in order to assure a good outcome.[18,19,35-37]

Management of the Hip Joint

Chapter 4 contains detailed information on anatomy, pathophysiology, and clinical presentation of hip dysplasia in children with CP, and the methods of assessment of hip joint integrity (see also Table 4-3 for information on the migration percentage values and progression risk).[38-40] Currently, structural hip problems in this patient population are addressed by initiating a systematic radiological surveillance program for each child.[37,41-43] This approach was shown to be crucial for preventing hip dislocations in children with CP.[37,41-43] Its benefits include early identification of the risk for hip subluxation leading to a timely preventive surgical intervention, and the resultant significant decrease in the need for complex reconstructive surgeries.[41-43] It is recommended that such programs be initiated between the ages of 12 and 24 months.[37,41,44] Wynter at el[44] published a consensus statement with specific recommendations for a hip surveillance schedule for children with CP classified in GMFCS[22] levels I through V (Table 8-2).

Physical therapy is usually indicated as a conservative intervention to maintain flexibility of musculature around the hip joint and attempt to prevent hip subluxation in young children with CP through positioning, weight-bearing programs, and ROM interventions.[35,45] In the presence of hip displacement, conservative and minimally invasive measures used to address its progression and prevent hip dislocation, such as abduction bracing and BTX-A injections, were not found to be effective.[35,37,46] In children who underwent invasive antispasticity interventions, joint displacement continued to progress in 25% to 33% of the hips.[47,48] Orthopedic surgeries are usually recommended to address spastic hip dysplasia.[35,37,41,42] Preventive tendon lengthening is the first line of defense against hip subluxation, followed by bony osteotomies with or without acetabular reconstruction in

TABLE 8-2

HIP SURVEILLANCE SCHEDULE FOR CHILDREN WITH CEREBRAL PALSY BY GMFCS LEVEL

HIP SURVEILLANCE FREQUENCY AND POINTS	GMFCS LEVEL[22]				
	I	*II*	*III*	*IV*	*V*
Initial clinical assessment and AP pelvic radiograph	12-24 months of age or at the time of received diagnosis of CP if later than at the age of 24 months				
Repeat clinical assessment	3 and 5 years of age	• Every 12 months if MP is unstable or abnormal, until MP stability is achieved • 4-5 and 8-10 years of age if MP is stable	• Every 6 months if MP is unstable or abnormal, until MP stability is achieved • Every 12 months if MP is stable • Discontinue at 7 years of age if MP is stable • Resume with 12-month intervals prior to puberty	• Same as for GMFCS level III • Every 6 months in presence of scoliosis or pelvic obliquity at 7 years of age	• Every 6 months until 7 years of age • Every 12 months after 7 years of age if MP is stable • Every 6 months in presence of scoliosis or pelvic obliquity
Repeat AP pelvic radiograph	N/A				
Discharge from surveillance	5 years of age if hips are clinically stable	8-10 years of age if MP is stable	Skeletal maturity		

Abbreviations: AP, anteroposterior; CP, cerebral palsy; GMFCS, Gross Motor function Classification System; MP, migration percentage; N/A, not applicable.

Compiled from Wynter et al.[44]

children with significant hip displacement. Salvage or palliative surgeries are indicated for patients with painful dislocated hips (Table 8-3).[35,37,41,42]

Clinical decision making in the hip joint management includes taking into consideration possible postsurgical complications.[35,37] According to Dobson et al,[41] approximately 25% of children with CP who undergo preventive surgical procedures may still require reconstructive surgeries in the future. Injury to the medial circumflex artery during psoas muscle tenotomy may result in avascular necrosis of the femoral head, and mild to moderate heterotopic ossification is a relatively common complication seen in hip adductor lengthening.[35,37,49] In addition, the neurectomy of the anterior branch of the obturator nerve sometimes performed as a part of a soft tissue lengthening surgery may lead to a hip abduction contracture and needs to be avoided in children who are able to walk.[35,37]

Hip reconstruction surgeries are usually more successful, with follow-up procedures but not salvage surgeries required in some cases.[41] Complications may include

infection, avascular necrosis of the femoral head, prolonged hip pain, femoral fractures, and cast-related superficial pressure ulcers.[35,37,41,50] Early postsurgical mobilization and decreased use of casting have been advocated to reduce the complication rates.[35] As for the salvage procedures, besides complications similar to those seen after hip reconstructions surgeries, other problems may include pneumonia, loosening of prosthetic components, femoral head migration, and joint stiffness.[37,51] Raphael et al[52] reported permanent pain relief and functional improvement in the majority of patients with CP who underwent total hip arthroplasty, with a 15% revision rate documented within 6 months to 17 years postsurgically.

Management of the Knee Joint

Table 8-4 contains information on the surgical procedures used to address several common knee problems that negatively affect standing and gait in ambulatory children with CP. Besides spasticity, contractures, and muscle tightness, abnormal knee alignment and atypical gait patterns in this patient population may result from iatrogenic causes, such as

TABLE 8-3

SURGERIES PERFORMED TO ADDRESS HIP SUBLUXATION AND DISLOCATION IN CHILDREN WITH CEREBRAL PALSY

TYPE OF SURGERY[35,37,41]	INDICATIONS[35,41]	SPECIFIC PROCEDURES[35,37,41,42]
Soft tissue lengthening	• Migration percentage[a] of >40% • Migration increase >10% in a period of 1 year • Acetabular index[b] of >27	• Hip adductor longus tenotomy • Adductor brevis and gracilis myotomies • Iliopsoas lengthening
Joint reconstruction	• Soft tissue surgery and appropriate positioning and bracing ineffective in stopping progressive hip displacement • Migration percentage of >50% and progressing	• Varus derotation osteotomy of the proximal femur • Pelvic osteotomy • Femoral osteotomy with acetabular reconstruction
Salvage surgeries	• Painful hip dislocation • Advanced arthritic changes in the spastic hip joint • Difficulty sitting and skin breakdown related to postural alignment • Poor perineal hygiene	• Valgus redirectional osteotomy • Femoral head resection • Interposition arthroplasty[c] • Total hip arthroplasty • Hip arthrodesis

[a] Migration percentage measures the amount of hip dysplasia.[38]

[b] Acetabular index measures the femoral head coverage by the acetabulum.[38]

[c] Involves placing surrounding tissues or a prosthetic device between the joint surfaces.[35,37]

TABLE 8-4

SURGERIES PERFORMED TO ADDRESS ATYPICAL KNEE ALIGNMENT IN STANDING AND GAIT IN INDIVIDUALS WITH CEREBRAL PALSY

ATYPICAL KNEE ALIGNMENT	SURGERIES
Crouching	Hamstring lengthening[53,54] Anterior stapling of distal femur[55] Guided growth using 2 anterior tension band plates[57] DFEO[58,59] PTA[58,59] DFEO/PTA combined procedure[58,59]
Genu valgum or varum	Hemiepiphysiodesis or guided growth with a single extraperiosteal plate and 2 screws[56]
Genu recurvatum	Calf muscle lengthening as a part of SEMLS[62]
Stiff knee	Distal rectus femoris tendon transfer to gracilis, sartorius, or semitendinosus tendon or to iliotibial band[53,65,66]

Abbreviations: DFEO, distal femoral extension osteotomy; PTA, patellar tendon advancement; SEMLS, single-event multilevel surgery.

crouch gait seen in patients who underwent isolated Achilles tendon lengthening surgeries.[18,19,23,24,53] When hamstring tightness or spasticity is the main cause of crouch gait, tendon lengthening surgeries help improve knee alignment in children with CP.[53,54] However, over time, hamstring contractures and crouch gait pattern may recur. A retrospective study of 39 patients with CP showed that repeat hamstring lengthening surgeries failed to produce a long-term improvement of crouch gait.[54] The authors suggested that quadriceps muscle weakness and other causes might be contributing to the recurrent crouching and that alternative surgical procedures should be used to address this problem.[54]

Anterior stapling of the distal femur and hemiepiphysiodesis or guided growth can help attain angular correction of the knee joint alignment in sagittal and frontal planes.[55-57] The hemiepiphysiodesis guided growth procedure addresses the genu valgum or varum deformity via insertion of an extraperiosteal plate secured with 2 screws to the femoral and/or tibial physis.[56] To correct knee flexion contractures through guided growth, 2 anterior tension band plates are used on the distal femur.[57] These procedures performed in patients who had not yet achieved skeletal maturity were described as less invasive and less expensive than corrective osteotomies.[55-57] Stevens[56] reported a more rapid correction rate and fewer complications with the guided growth procedure as compared to stapling, which may result in staple breakage, migration, and extrusion in some cases.[55,56] Unlike osteotomies, both of these methods did not require immobilization or hospitalization and allowed the operated children to resume physical therapy and bracing immediately after the surgery.[55-57]

Distal femoral extension osteotomy (DFEO) involves the removal of a wedge of the distal femur, realignment of the ends of the bone to achieve knee extension, and fixation using hardware.[58,59] Patellar tendon advancement (PTA) is a surgical technique that repositions patella alta distally by aligning its inferior pole with the knee joint line in order to restore the length-tension relationship of the quadriceps muscle and allow for full knee extension in the stance phase of gait. In a retrospective, nonrandomized, repeated-measures design study of 73 adolescents and young adults with CP, a combination of DFEO with PTA showed the best surgical results compared to each of these 2 procedures performed in isolation, while the osteotomy alone achieved only partial correction of crouch gait.[58,59] In addition, in a retrospective study of 51 limbs in 32 patients with CP, Healy et al[60] demonstrated that, although a concomitant hamstring lengthening procedure was not performed to complement a combined DFEO/PTA surgery, hamstring length and contraction velocity improved in 94% and 80% of the operated limbs, respectively.

Similar to crouching, genu recurvatum alignment is another example of surgical overcorrection, which in this case, occurs because of excessive hamstring lengthening.[53,61,62] Plantarflexor muscle spasticity leading to equinus ankle alignment at initial contact is another common reason for this type of abnormality in the stance phase of gait.[53,61,63]

This problem may be addressed via aponeurotic calf muscle lengthening (see Table 8-4) performed as a part of SEMLS.[62]

Stiff knee pattern commonly results from the overactivity of a spastic rectus femoris muscle that is manifested in reduced dynamic knee ROM in the swing phase of gait, usually with insufficient knee flexion and foot clearance.[53,64-67] Another manifestation of the stiff knee gait pattern is walking with severely flexed knees that negatively affects dynamic ROM of the knee joint in the entire cycle.[53] Currently, the problem of decreased peak swing knee flexion is frequently addressed through a distal rectus femoris tendon transfer to one of several possible sites (see Table 8-4).[53,65,66] Several authors reported that the transfer site did not seem to affect the surgical outcomes that targeted improved knee motion, timing of the peak knee flexion in the swing phase, and knee extension at the initial contact.[65,66] The improvement in knee flexion commonly observed after such procedures may be attributed to the resultant decrease in the rectus femoris muscle knee extension moment.[67]

Outcome predictors for this type of surgery were examined in 2 studies that reviewed pre- and postoperative gait analysis data.[68,69] A positive preoperative result of the Duncan-Ely test that indicated the presence of spasticity in the rectus femoris muscle was shown to be a positive predictor of a good surgical outcome,[68] while being classified in GMFCS[22] level IV was found to be a negative predictor.[69] The latter study results showed that children functioning at level IV may not be appropriate candidates for the distal rectus femoris tendon transfer surgery because of the increase in crouch they displayed postoperatively.[69] Good outcomes in children with decreased swing knee motion were reported by multiple authors.[53,65,66,70] However, based on the results of an RCT, Dreher et al[70] cautioned against using this surgery as a "prophylactic" procedure with patients who demonstrate severe flexed-knee gait with decreased dynamic knee ROM but normal or increased peak knee flexion in the swing phase as it would not lead to gait improvement in these children.

Management of the Ankle and Foot

Ankle equinus, equinovarus, equinovalgus, and planovalgus deformities are common in children and adults with CP.[23,24,27,71-73] The equinovarus ankle alignment is more frequently observed in individuals with unilateral involvement while equinovalgus and planovalgus are more prevalent in those with bilateral CP.[23,24,27,73] When conservative intervention methods are not effective in the management of these deformities, a surgical approach is usually indicated.[71] Surgeries aim to address ankle and foot stability for standing and walking and to prevent or alleviate skin breakdown and pain that may result from abnormal alignment of these structures during weight-bearing activities.[23,24,27,71-73] Indications for common surgical procedures and reported postoperative complications[23,24,27,71-75] are summarized in Table 8-5, and brief descriptions of selected soft tissue and bony surgeries[23,24,27,71,76-86] are provided in Table 8-6.

TABLE 8-5

INDICATIONS FOR AND COMPLICATIONS OF SURGICAL PROCEDURES PERFORMED TO ADDRESS COMMON ANKLE AND FOOT DEFORMITIES IN CHILDREN AND ADULTS WITH CEREBRAL PALSY

DEFORMITY	INDICATIONS FOR SURGERY	SURGICAL PROCEDURES	COMPLICATIONS
Equinus[23,24,27,71,74]	Increased gastrocnemius-scleus muscle spasticity during gait Plantarflexion contracture Toe walking	Achilles tendon lengthening Gastrocnemius aponeurotic recession	Overcorrection Calcaneus gait and calcaneus deformity Recurrent equinus deformity
Equinovarus[27,71]	Flexible hindfoot deformity difficult to control with orthoses	Split posterior tibialis tendon transfer Posterior tibialis tendon lengthening Anterior tibialis tendon transfer to the middle or lateral cuneiform Split anterior tibialis tendon transfer (SPLATT) Posterior tibialis muscle lengthening combined with Achilles tendon lengthening and SPLATT	Incomplete correction Overcorrection leading to valgus alignment
	Rigid hindfoot deformity	Calcaneal osteotomy Triple arthrodesis	
Equinovalgus and planovalgus[27,72,73,75]	Orthotic interventions are ineffective in correcting the deformity and addressing pain and callus formation Moderate to severe rigid deformity	Calcaneal lengthening Calcaneal osteotomy Arthrodesis	Recurrent deformity Incomplete correction Degenerative changes Calcaneocuboid subluxation Overcorrection Pseudarthrosis Pain

In conjunction with the ankle and foot deformities, the alignment of the toes, and especially the big toe, needs to be addressed. For example, the extensor hallucis longus (EHL) muscle hyperactivity in the presence of the equinovarus deformity may be observed in some children with CP.[27] This problem can be managed by the EHL transfer to the peroneus brevis and the interphalangeal joint arthrodesis.[27] Another common problem is the hallux valgus deformity.[87,88] It is thought to result from an abnormal muscle pull in the spastic foot and from disrupted forefoot mechanics in the stance phase of gait, which is associated with the planovalgus deformity. The big toe malalignment may cause it to overlap or underlap the second toe, which frequently leads to pain, atypical gait, and hygiene and footwear problems. Although surgical management of hallux valgus may include soft tissue procedures and osteotomies, metatarsophalangeal arthrodesis in combination with other surgeries designed to improve the foot alignment and gait have been described as the best treatment of choice.[87,88]

As evident from Tables 8-5 and 8-6, a variety of surgical procedures are available to address foot and ankle deformities. Currently, single-level orthopedic surgeries are rarely performed as multilevel surgeries have been reported to provide a more balanced approach to correcting the lower extremity alignment.[18,23,25,26] For example, the gastrocnemius-soleus intramuscular aponeurotic recession included in the SEMLS was shown to be effective in correcting mild to moderate equinus deformities in 44 children with bilateral spastic CP, and its risk of overcorrection was significantly lower than in the Achilles tendon lengthening surgery.[23,24]

Outcomes of Lower Extremity Multilevel Surgeries

The SEMLS is a combination of multiple soft tissue and/or bony surgical procedures that aims to address gait deviations by correcting all related musculoskeletal deformities at once.[89] Efficacy of SEMLS for children with CP was

TABLE 8-6

BRIEF DESCRIPTIONS OF SELECTED SURGICAL PROCEDURES PERFORMED TO ADDRESS ANKLE AND FOOT DEFORMITIES IN CHILDREN AND ADULTS WITH CEREBRAL PALSY

DEFORMITY	SURGICAL PROCEDURE	BRIEF DESCRIPTION
Equinus	Achilles tendon lengthening[24,27]	Percutaneous or open "Z" lengthening is performed using 2 or 3 partial horizontal tenotomies with the foot in a plantigrade position.
	Gastrocnemius aponeurotic recession[23,24,27]	Release of the overlying fascia of the gastrocnemius muscle is performed with muscle fibers left intact and correction achieved via the incision separation during ankle dorsiflexion.
Equinovarus	Split posterior tibialis tendon transfer[27,71,76-78]	Distal detachment of the posterior half of the tibialis posterior tendon is performed, with its subsequent posterior routing around the tibia, and lateral attachment under tension into the peroneus brevis tendon to serve as a foot evertor. Alternatively, the detached tendon half is routed through the interosseous membrane, with subsequent attachment to the middle cuneiform bone or to the distal peroneus brevis tendon.
	Split anterior tibialis tendon transfer (SPLATT) to the cuboid[27,71,79]	This procedure involves detaching the lateral half of the tibialis anterior tendon from the first metatarsal bone, splitting it longitudinally, routing it laterally under the extensor retinaculum, and inserting it into a tunnel drilled in the cuboid. The intended result is active ankle dorsiflexion without supination.
	Combined procedure[27,80]	Tibialis posterior muscle lengthening is combined with SPLATT, with or without Achilles tendon lengthening.
	Triple arthrodesis[27,81,82]	Surgical fusion of the talocalcaneal, calcaneocuboid, and talonavicular joints is performed to establish a plantigrade foot alignment.
Equinovalgus and planovalgus	Calcaneal osteotomy[27,83,84]	An oblique calcaneal osteotomy is performed through a lateral incision, and the distal fragment is shifted medially, often in combination with Achilles and peroneal tendon lengthening to achieve a plantigrade foot alignment. Sliding calcaneal osteotomy may also be combined with cuboid and cuneiform osteotomies.
	Calcaneal lengthening[27,72,85]	Calcaneal osteotomy is performed 1 to 1.5 cm proximal to the calcaneocuboid joint, distracted to achieve realignment of the talonavicular joint and lateral column, and supported with a bone graft. A concomitant Achilles and peroneal tendon lengthening may also be required.
	Arthrodesis procedures[27,73,75,81,82,86]	Possible options include extra-articular subtalar arthrodesis using a fibular graft; medial column arthrodesis (fusion of the talus, navicular, medial cuneiform, and first metatarsal bones); talonavicular arthrodesis; and triple arthrodesis.

examined in multiple studies that varied in their design and quality,[25] from retrospective studies and a case series,[89-91] to prospective single-subject,[92] cohort[93] and RCT[94] research. A systematic review of literature on the topic revealed that most of the examined studies used outcome measures pertinent to the body structures and functions domain of the International Classification of Functioning, Disability and Health (ICF)[95]; only few used measures of activity and participation, and only 2 investigated the effects of SEMLS on health-related quality of life (HRQoL).[25] More recent investigations were found to be of better quality compared to earlier research, but the lack of RCTs published on the subject was also highlighted. Nevertheless, the results of this systematic review suggested that SEMLS was effective in improving passive ROM, several kinematic and kinetic gait parameters, and the overall quality of gait in children with CP.[25]

In a prospective study, Gorton et al[93] compared function and gait in 2 cohorts of 75 children with spastic CP

TABLE 8-7

PROBABILITY OF CHANGE IN MOBILITY MODE AFTER SEMLS IN CHILDREN WITH CEREBRAL PALSY CLASSIFIED IN GMFCS[22] LEVEL III

PRIOR TO SEMLS		% CHANCE AT FIVE YEARS POST-SEMLS				
Device	Setting	Independent Walking or Crutches	Crutches	Crutches or Walker	Walker or Wheelchair	Wheelchair
Crutches	Home	75				
	School		54		40	
Walker	Home	70				
	School	50				23
Wheelchair	Community			32		68

Abbreviation: SEMLS, single-event multilevel surgery.

Compiled from Harvey et al.[89]

matched based on their gender, type of CP, and GMFCS[22] level. Participants in the surgical cohort underwent single- or multilevel orthopedic surgeries, and the nonsurgical cohort served as a control group. Gait assessment using Gillette Gait Index (GGI)[96] revealed significant improvement in the surgical group and minimal change in the nonsurgical group over a 12-month period.[93] The GGI is a measure of gait deviation based on assessment of 16 gait parameters, with a higher score indicating greater gait deviations.[96] In a pilot RCT, Thomason et al[94] provided additional strong evidence of significant gait improvement in children with CP assessed using the Gait Profile Score (GPS)[97] and the GGI[96] 12 months post-SEMLS, with a 34% and 57% increase in outcome scores, respectively, and a "highly significant" difference in change scores between the surgical and control groups reported on both measures. Children who underwent the multilevel surgery demonstrated a significant improvement in their gross motor function on the Gross Motor Function Measure (GMFM-66).[94,98] Finally, a subsequent prospective cohort study with 18 participants of the RCT showed the stability of their gains in gross motor function and gait up to 5 years after SEMLS.[99]

Because SEMLS is now the standard of care for this patient population,[89] it is important to examine its effects on functional mobility and on the amount of assistance needed for ambulation. Harvey et al[89,90] conducted 2 studies with children and adolescents with CP, GMFCS[22] levels I through III, that used Functional Mobility Scale (FMS)[100] as an outcome measure. The FMS assesses functional mobility in children with CP over 5, 50, and 500 meters in 3 different settings (home, school, and community).[100] In the first study, participants' mobility deteriorated significantly at 3 and 6 months after SEMLS, improved to the baseline level at 12-month follow-up, and demonstrated further improvement at 24 months.[90] Children classified in level III of GMFCS[22] remained in the same level, while 86% of those classified in levels I and II were reclassified into level III at 3 months postsurgically, which indicated a short-term decrease in mobility. However, by 1-year follow-up, only 19% of these children remained classified in level III, while the rest were again reclassified in levels I and II.[90]

The second study examined a longitudinal change in mobility and the use of assistive devices at 2 and 5 years after SEMLS in 156 children with CP.[89] For the majority of participants, mobility remained stable or improved long term, with those functioning in GMFCS level III showing the greatest improvement. The probability of change in the mode of mobility after SEMLS for this group of children is shown in Table 8-7.[89] The most important finding of this research was that the multilevel surgery may be able to stabilize mobility in children whose ambulation is otherwise likely to deteriorate with age.[89] Earlier, Gannotti et al[91] reported similar results in their case study series conducted with young adults with CP whose walking capability remained the same as prior to surgery or improved 11 to 15 years after SEMLS.

In their systematic review, McGinley et al[25] pointed out such weaknesses of the SEMLS research as the lack of control; insufficient reporting of adverse events; limited description of surgical, postoperative, and rehabilitation management; and inadequate outcome measures used in some studies.[25] In their subsequent RCT, Thomason et al[94] reported several adverse events, including mild problems related to malfunction of epidural pain management after surgery, and constipation and emesis in response to excessive use of codeine. Moderate adverse events were also pain-related, with the removal of femoral osteotomy plates required in one case and post-calcaneal lengthening pain that lasted for 6 months in another.[94] Other adverse effects described in literature were persistent crouching after Achilles tendon lengthening performed as a part of SEMLS[101] and muscle weakness evident at 6 and 12 months postoperatively. Results of 2 RCTs suggested some benefits of strength training programs in addressing muscle weakness and gait parameters after SEMLS in children with bilateral spastic CP.[102,103]

The same systematic review revealed mixed activity and participation results, and most outcome measures that assessed quality of life did not show change after SEMLS.[25] In their single-subject design study, Åkerstedt et al[92] used the Child Health Questionnaire (CHQ)[104] to assess HRQoL in 11 children and adolescents with CP at baseline and repeatedly after SEMLS. The CHQ is a self-report questionnaire for children and youth that evaluates HRQoL from physical and psychological perspectives.[104] Eight participants showed improvement in CHQ physical summary scores at 1 year after SEMLS, and 6 of them maintained this improvement at 2 years. Only 3 of 11 participants received increased CHQ[104] psychosocial summary scores at 1 year after SEMLS.[92] Thomason et al[94] also used the CHQ to assess HRQoL in participants of their RCT. A significant decrease in the social/emotional domain scores at the 12-month follow-up time was reported in the SEMLS group, while the control group showed improvement, and the physical function domain scores increased significantly in the surgical group at 24-month follow-up.[94]

In an earlier multicenter prospective trial, Cuomo et al[105] used the Pediatric Outcomes Data Collection Instrument (PODCI),[106] Pediatric Quality of Life Inventory (PedsQL),[107] and Gillette Functional Assessment Questionnaire (FAQ) Walking Score[108] to assess HRQoL in 57 ambulatory children with CP before and after a multilevel soft tissue surgery. Results showed significant improvement in the FAQ Walking Score[108]; the Transfers/Mobility, Sports/Physical Function, and Global outcome scores on the PODCI[106]; and the PedsQL[107] scores that reflected parent perception of their child's functional well-being. However, the PODCI[106] results also indicated that the SEMLS had no effect on the parent-reported perception of happiness or pain in their children. Based on these findings, the authors recommended that families of children with CP be informed that postsurgical improvements in functional well-being would not necessarily lead to improvements in psychosocial well-being. Further rigorous research is warranted to examine the relationship between physical and psychological well-being in children with CP who undergo multilevel surgeries and to identify factors that affect different aspects of their HRQoL.[105]

Surgical Management of the Upper Extremity

In spite of functional activity limitations frequently observed in the upper extremities of children with CP, less than 20% of them undergo surgical procedures that address this problem.[109] Horstmann et al[110] reported that 114 adult patients with CP referred to their facility had 369 lower extremity procedures and only 16 upper extremity (UE) surgeries as children. Conservative interventions aimed at preserving the UE ROM, preventing contractures and deformities, and improving function may include physical and occupational therapy, casting, splinting, electrical stimulation, antispasticity medications, and BTX-A injections.[109] When these measures fail, UE surgery for spastic and fixed joint contractures may be indicated.[109,111] Interprofessional

collaboration among members of the interdisciplinary team, careful preoperative evaluation, and well-planned postoperative rehabilitation are crucial for the success of surgical intervention.[109]

Besides the patient's medical history, physical examination, and reports from multiple professionals working with the child, the preoperative evaluation should include a thorough assessment of the UE function.[109] The House scale[112] is frequently used to evaluate the results of UE surgeries.[109,113,114] It rates the UE function at 9 levels, from the score of 0 ("does not use") to the score of 8 ("spontaneous use, complete")."[111,112] The amount of functional improvement is quantified by calculating the difference between the pre- and postoperative House scores. The Manual Ability Classification System (MACS)[115] is different from the House scale[111,112] as it does not reflect the level of function of each hand, but rather looks at the child's bilateral hand use for completion of everyday tasks (see Chapter 3). Children with CP classified into different MACS[115] levels may display varied amount of improvement after UE surgery.[114]

Other measures, besides the House scale,[112] that are used to assess surgical outcomes may include such standardized assessment instruments as the Melbourne Assessment of Unilateral Upper Limb Function,[116] the Upper Extremity Rating Scale (UERS),[109,117] and the Jebsen-Taylor Hand Function Test.[118] The Melbourne Assessment[116] is a clinical test of unilateral UE function that contains 12 items that include grasp, release, reach, and manipulation tasks. The UERS[117] is used to evaluate passive and active ROM in UE joints and the child's grasp and release skills in each hand. The Jebsen-Taylor test[118] is a norm-referenced instrument that consists of 7 subtests that assess such functional skills as writing, turning pages, picking up objects, using a spoon, and stacking checkers. Each subtest is administered in a standardized manner and timed for each hand.[118] The patient's hand use in self-care skills can be assessed using the Functional Independence Measure for Children (WeeFIM).[109,119,120] Finally, the preoperative evaluation should also include clinical observation of the child during activities of daily living, a video recordings of hand use, UE sensory testing, diagnostic imaging studies of joint alignment, and the electromyographic (EMG) testing of UE muscles for possible transfer surgery.[109]

The overall goals of surgical intervention are to improve function, reduce pain, facilitate care, and improve the child's self-esteem.[109] Although these goals can be met to some extent, in most cases, it would be unrealistic to expect that the surgery would yield normalized hand function. Therefore, it is the responsibility of the interdisciplinary team to convey this information to the child and his or her family.[109] UE surgeries indicated for children and adults with CP may include soft tissue releases, tendon lengthenings, tendon transfers, joint fusions or arthrodeses,[109-111] and single-event multilevel surgeries.[14,26] Surgical procedures specific to each UE joint or segment with their goals and possible risks or complications are summarized in Table 8-8.[26,109-111,113,114,121-131]

TABLE 8-8

SURGERIES FOR COMMON UPPER EXTREMITY DEFORMITIES IN CHILDREN AND ADULTS WITH CEREBRAL PALSY, THEIR GOALS, AND RISKS

JOINT/SEGMENT	COMMON PROBLEMS/ DEFORMITIES	SURGICAL GOALS	SURGICAL PROCEDURES	POSSIBLE RISKS/ REPORTED COMPLICATIONS
Shoulder[109,110,121]	Adduction and medial rotation contractures/deformity Glenohumeral joint subluxation or dislocation Arthritis	Increase ROM Stabilize glenohumeral joint Decrease pain	Pectoralis major and subscapularis muscle lengthening Joint capsule release Transfer of latissimus dorsi and teres major to posterolateral humerus Latissimus dorsi and teres major muscle release Humeral derotation osteotomies Shoulder arthrodesis Shoulder arthroplasty	Spasticity-related failure of soft tissue procedures Limited ROM Medial rotator and abductor muscle weakness Anterior subluxation of prosthesis after arthroplasty Persistent pain
Elbow[26,109-111,122-124]	Flexion contracture Flexion deformity (contracture with/without radial head subluxation/dislocation)	Improve active elbow extension, UE function, and cosmesis Decrease pain	Brachioradialis, biceps tendon and brachialis muscle lengthening, with/without flexor-pronator origin release and anterior elbow capsulotomy Elbow arthrodesis	Increased pronation deformity after biceps lengthening Mild to moderate loss of active elbow flexion ROM
Forearm[26,109-111,114,122,123,125]	Pronation contracture or deformity Impaired selective control of forearm supination	Improve active forearm supination and associated hand function	Flexor-pronator release Pronator teres lengthening or rerouting Pronator quadratus release Brachioradialis rerouting Flexor carpi ulnaris transfer Rotational osteotomies Radioulnar arthrodesis	Insufficient forearm supination Supination deformity Loss of active pronation

(continued)

TABLE 8-8 (CONTINUED)

SURGERIES FOR COMMON UPPER EXTREMITY DEFORMITIES IN CHILDREN AND ADULTS WITH CEREBRAL PALSY, THEIR GOALS, AND RISKS

JOINT/SEGMENT	COMMON PROBLEMS/ DEFORMITIES	SURGICAL GOALS	SURGICAL PROCEDURES	POSSIBLE RISKS/REPORTED COMPLICATIONS
Wrist[26,109,110,113,114,122,123,126]	Flexion contracture Flexion and ulnar deviation deformity Impaired grasp and release Skin lesions due to hygiene problems	Improve wrist alignment Increase active wrist extension ROM Support active grasp and release Decrease pain Improve hygiene and cosmesis	FCU transfer to ECRB, ECRL, or EDC tendon Flexor tendon releases Flexor muscle lengthening ECU transfer to ECRB Pronator teres or brachioradialis tendon transfer to ECRB tendon Wrist arthrodesis with or without proximal row carpectomy	Decreased grip strength Decreased fine motor control Dynamic wrist extension deformity Prominent hardware, pain, extensor tendon adhesions, development of finger swan-neck deformities, and distal radioulnar joint instability after arthrodesis
Thumb[26,109,110,114,123,126-129]	Thumb-in-palm deformity Flexion deformity First MCP joint hyperextension instability	Increase thumb abduction and extension ROM Improve grasp and release function Improve thumb alignment	Adductor pollicis and/or first dorsal interosseous muscle release Adductor pollicis lengthening First web space Z-plasty Brachioradialis transfer to APL or EPB FDS, FCR, ECRL, or palmaris longus transfer to APL, EPL, or EPB EPL rerouting FPL lengthening FCU transfer to EPL MCP joint sesamoid capsulodesis CMC, MCP, or IP arthrodesis	Failure of soft tissue procedures MCP joint instability after soft tissue procedures performed without MCP arthrodesis Epiphyseal plate damage with arthrodesis Delayed union of MCP arthrodesis
Fingers[26,109,110,114,126,130,131]	Finger flexion deformity Swan-neck deformity (flexion deformity of distal interphalangeal joint with hyperextension of proximal interphalangeal joint)	Increase finger extension ROM Improve grasp and release function Improve finger alignment	FDS and/or FDP lengthening FCU or FDS tendon transfers to EDC tendon FDS transfer to FDP Flexor-pronator origin release For swan-neck deformity: Central slip tenotomy Lateral band rerouting PIP tenodesis	Flexor-pronator overlengthening Swan-neck deformity after finger flexor lengthening Persistent swan-neck deformity, Boutonnière deformity in PIP joints and lack of active extension in PIP joints after swan-neck deformity surgery

Abbreviations: APL, abductor pollicis longus; CMC, carpometacarpal joint; ECRB, extensor carpi radialis brevis; ECRL, extensor carpi radialis longus; ECU, extensor carpi ulnaris; EDC, extensor digitorum communis; EPB, extensor pollicis brevis; EPL, extensor pollicis longus; FCR, flexor carpi radialis; FCU, flexor carpi ulnaris; FDP, flexor digitorum profundus; FDS, flexor digitorum superficialis; FPL, flexor pollicis longus; IP, interphalangeal joint; MCP, metacarpophalangeal joint; PIP, proximal interphalangeal joint; ROM, range of motion; UE, upper extremity.

Compared to single-level surgical procedures, the SEMLS addresses all UE deformities and impairments at the same time while targeting both functional and cosmetic goals, and is designed to eliminate the need for repeated or serial procedures.[26]

Specific single-level UE surgical techniques were described in multiple publications, with many authors reporting on positive surgical outcomes related to body structures and functions, but not to the activity and participation domains of the ICF[95] or quality of life.[109,110,112,121,122,124,125,127-131] The same was true in regard to SEMLS, with only few exceptions.[26,111,114,126] In a retrospective, control-series study, Smitherman et al[26] reported on statistically significant but not clinically important improvement in the spontaneous use of UE in children with unilateral spastic CP who underwent SEMLS. Gong et al[114] showed that children with CP classified in MACS[115] levels I and II demonstrated greater postsurgical functional improvement and greater satisfaction with outcomes of multilevel surgeries than children classified in levels III through V, but children in lower functional abilities achieved greater improvement in their hygiene status. The authors suggested that the MACS[115] level could be used as a predictor of surgical outcome in children with CP. In that study, activity and participation were not directly assessed.[114]

Finally, Wesdock et al[126] published 3 case exemplars of adolescents with unilateral spastic CP who were assessed before and after UE SEMLS. The authors used the Pediatric Evaluation of Disability Inventory (PEDI)[132] and the modified Jebsen-Taylor Test of Hand Function[118] as measures of activities of daily living, and Goal Attainment Scaling (GAS)[133] as a measure of participation. The PEDI[132] is a standardized questionnaire that evaluates the child's functional skills in self-care, mobility, and social function domains and the required amount of caregiver assistance. The GAS[133] rates the attainment of child-specific goals on a 5-point ordinal scale. Children described in the case reports demonstrated varied impairment-level postsurgical improvements and uneven changes in activity and participation.[126] Specifically, all participants showed minimal to moderate improvement on the Jebsen-Taylor test,[118] 2 of 3 attained increased scores on the PEDI,[132] and only 1 achieved all but one individual goal. The low goal attainment correlated with low satisfaction with surgical outcomes reported in all 3 cases.[114] Future research should be designed to assess participation as a surgical outcome, and quality of life changes need to be examined when determining the value of specific orthopedic surgeries to children and their families.

Surgical Management of the Spine

Spinal deformities observed in children and adults with CP were described in Chapter 4.[1,38,134,135] When conservative interventions used to address these deformities fail and the scoliotic curve progresses beyond 40 degrees and negatively affects the child's sitting balance, comfort, and respiratory function, surgery is usually indicated.[136] Because of a high complication rate, such surgeries warrant an extensive preoperative evaluation that includes pulmonary, gastrointestinal, nutritional, neurological, and musculoskeletal systems and urinary tract assessment. Subsequent decision making includes considerations related to specific patient presentation.[136]

Several types of instrumentation and bone grafts can be used for surgical fixation of the spine and pelvis in neuromuscular scoliosis.[136] Harrington rods[137] have been largely replaced by segmental fixation with unit rods and sublaminar wires[138] and, more recently, by hybrid instrumentation that uses laminar hooks and pedicle screws in addition to sublaminar wires,[139,140] or pedicle screw fixation alone.[141] It is recommended to extend the spinal fusion to pelvis in non-ambulatory patients with severe pelvic obliquity.[136] This procedure may also be beneficial for some patients who present with pelvic obliquity but are able to walk, if they do not use the lumbar flexion and extension strategy for ambulation.[136] The anterior release surgical approach is used for children and adults with severe kyphosis, large stiff thoracolumbar curves with significant pelvic obliquity, and children who have not reached skeletal maturity and may benefit from the growth plate disruption to arrest growth of their anterior column.[136,142,143] Auerbach et al[142] showed that posterior spinal fusion alone was effective in correcting relatively flexible smaller curves, while a combination of anterior release and posterior fusion was needed for larger and more rigid deformities.

High complication rates in spinal surgeries performed in individuals with CP, together with limited resultant functional improvements, have contributed to the controversy related to the surgical benefits.[136,144] Watanabe et al[144] classified complications of spinal surgeries into intraoperative and early and late postoperative. Early postoperative or acute complications reported by multiple authors may have serious effects on the cardiovascular, pulmonary, digestive, integumentary, neurologic, and other major body systems.[136,141,142,144,145] Wound infection and implant failure issues may complicate the late postoperative period.[136,141,144,145] The intraoperative blood loss is a major concern and may lead to serious consequences, including death.[136,144] This problem needs to be addressed by careful positioning of the patient for surgery to avoid an increase in venous pressure and by thorough considerations given to the selection of instrumentation and the overall surgical approach.[136] A combined anterior release/posterior spinal fusion is associated with increased duration of the surgery and, therefore, potentially with more prolonged bleeding.[136] However, Watanabe et al[144] reported the same rate of complications in patients who underwent posterior fusion only and those who had combined surgeries.

Although spinal surgeries result in significant improvement of postural alignment in children and adults with CP, this benefit does not necessarily translate into a functional improvement.[136,145] In one study, limited improvements in walking, UE use, eating, and dressing were documented; however, the majority of participants reported improvement in their posture and sitting balance and were satisfied with the surgical outcomes.[144] A later study showed similar results, with the surgical outcome satisfaction rate of 91.7% among 50 patients with CP, age range 8.8 to 33.2 years.[145] The authors reported a 64.3% spinal curvature correction and a 57.7% pelvic tilt correction on average, and average improvements in apical vertebral rotation and translation of 53% and 67.2%, respectively. A major finding of that study was a significant (71%) improvement in participants' HRQoL. It is interesting to note that changes in postsurgical HRQoL reported by the caregivers did not correlate with the objective changes in spinal alignment. Bohtz et al[145] interpreted this finding as an indication that the amount of achieved surgical correction was sufficient to improve the HRQoL of their patients.

REFERENCES

1. Morrell DS, Pearson M, Sauser DD. Progressive bone and joint abnormalities of the spine and lower extremities in cerebral palsy. *Radiographics*. 2002;22(2):257-268.

2. Fowler EC, Kolobe TH, Damiano DL, et al; Section of Pediatrics Research Summit Participants, Section of Pediatrics Research Committee Task Force. Promotion of physical fitness and prevention of secondary conditions in children with cerebral palsy: Section of Pediatrics Research Summit proceedings. *Phys Ther*. 2007;87(11):1495-1510.

3. Harryman SE. Lower-extremity surgery for children with cerebral palsy: physical therapy management. *Phys Ther*. 1992;72:16-24.

4. McLellan A, Cipparone C, Giancola D, Armstrong D, Bartlett D. Medical and surgical procedures experienced by young children with cerebral palsy. *Pediatr Phys Ther*. 2012;24(3):268-277.

5. Osteopenia – medical definition and more from the Free Merriam-Webster Dictionary. *Merriam-Webster Online*. http://www.merri-am-webster.com/medical/osteopenia. Accessed October 13, 2013.

6. Osteoporosis – definition and more from the Free Merriam-Webster Dictionary. *Merriam-Webster Online*. http://www.mer-riam-webster.com/dictionary/osteoporosis. Accessed October 13, 2013.

7. Aronson E, Stevenson SB. Bone health in children with cerebral palsy and epilepsy. *J Pediatr Health Care*. 2012;26(3):193-199.

8. Paksu MS, Vurucu S, Karaoglu A, et al. Osteopenia in children with cerebral palsy can be treated with oral aledronate. *Childs Nerv Syst*. 2012;28(2):283-286.

9. Allington N, Vevegnis D, Gerard P. Cyclic administration of pamidronate to treat osteoporosis in children with cerebral palsy or a neuromuscular disorder: a clinical study. *Acta Orthop Belg*. 2005;71(1):91-97.

10. Kilpinen-Loisa P, Nenonen H, Pihko H, Mäkitie O. High-dose vitamin D supplementation in children with cerebral palsy or neuromuscular disorder. *Neuropediatrics*. 2007;38(4):167-172.

11. Fehlings D, Switzwer L, Agarwal P, et al. Informing evidence-based clinical practice guidelines for children with cerebral palsy at risk for osteoporosis: a systematic review. *Dev Med Child Neurol*. 2012;54(2):106-116.

12. Jekovec-Vrhovsek M, Kocijancic A, Preželj J. Effect of vitamin D and calcium on bone mineral density in children with CP and epilepsy in full-time care. *Dev Med Child Neurol*. 2000;42(6):403-405.

13. Iwasaki T, Takei K, Nakamura S, Hosoda N, Yokota Y, Ishii M. Secondary osteoporosis in long-term bedridden patients with cerebral palsy. *Pediatr Int*. 2008;50(3):269-275.

14. Iwasaki T, Nonoda Y, Ishii M. Long-term outcomes of children and adolescents who has cerebral palsy with secondary osteoporosis. *Curr Med Res Opin*. 2012;28(5):737-747.

15. Pin TW. Effectiveness of static weight-bearing exercises in children with cerebral palsy. *Pediatr Phys Ther*. 2007;19(1):62-73.

16. Paleg GS, Smith BA, Glickman LB. Systematic review and evidence-based clinical recommendations for dosing of pediatric supported standing programs. *Pediatr Phys Ther*. 2013;25(3):232-247.

17. Ward K, Alsop C, Caulton J, Rubin C, Adams J, Mughal Z. Low magnitude mechanical loading is osteogenic in children with disabling conditions. *J Bone Miner Res*. 2004;19(3):360-369.

18. Damiano DL, Alter KE, Chambers H. New clinical and research trends in lower extremity management for ambulatory children with cerebral palsy. *Phys Med Rehabil Clin N Am*. 2009;20(3):469-491.

19. Lynn AK, Turner M, Chambers HG. Surgical management of spasticity in persons with cerebral palsy. *PM R*. 2009;1(9):834-838.

20. Rutz E, Hofmann E, Brunner R. Preoperative botulinum toxin test injections before muscle lengthening in cerebral palsy. *J Orthop Sci*. 2010;15(5):647-653.

21. Barwood S, Baillieu C, Boyd R, et al. Analgesic effects of botulinum toxin A: a randomized, placebo-controlled clinical trial. *Dev Med Child Neurol*. 2000;42(2):116-121.

22. Palisano RJ, Rosenbaum PL, Walter SD, Russell DJ, Wood EP, Galuppi BE. Development and reliability of a system to classify gross motor function in children with cerebral palsy. *Dev Med Child Neurol*. 1997;39(4):214-223.

23. Dreher T, Buccoliero T, Wolf SI, et al. Long-term results after gastrocnemius-soleus intramuscular aponeurotic recession as a part of multilevel surgery in spastic diplegic cerebral palsy. *J Bone Joint Surg Am*. 2012;94(7):627-637.

24. Borton DC, Walker K, Pirpiris M, Nattrass GR, Graham HK. Isolated calf lengthening in cerebral palsy. Outcome analysis of risk factors. *J Bone Joint Surg Br*. 2001;83(3):364-370.

25. McGinley JL, Dobson F, Ganeshalingam R, Shore BJ, Rutz E, Graham HK. Single-event multilevel surgery for children with cerebral palsy: a systematic review. *Dev Med Child Neurol*. 2012;54(2):117-128.

26. Smitherman JA, Davids JR, Tanner S, et al. Functional outcomes following single-event multilevel surgery of upper extremity for children with hemiplegic cerebral palsy. *J Bone Joint Surg Am*. 2011;93(7):655-661.

27. Karol LA. Surgical management of the lower extremity in ambulatory children with cerebral palsy. *J Am Acad Orthop Surg*. 2004;12(3):196-203.

28. Molenaers G, Campenhout AV, Fagard K, De Cat J, Desloovere K. The use of botulinum toxin A in children with cerebral palsy, with a focus on the lower limb. *J Chid Orthop*. 2010;4(3):183-195.

29. Chang FM, Seidl AJ, Muthusamy K, Meininger AK, Carollo JJ. Effectiveness of instrumented gait analysis in children with cerebral palsy—comparison of outcomes. *J Pediatr Orthop*. 2006;26(5):612-616.

30. Wren TA, Otsuka NY, Bowen RE, et al. Influence of gait analysis on decision-making for lower extremity orthopaedic surgery: baseline data from a randomized controlled trial. *Gait Posture*. 2011;34(3):364-369.

31. Wren TA, Otsuka NY, Bowen RE, et al. Outcomes of lower extremity orthopaedic surgery in ambulatory children with cerebral palsy with and without gait analysis: results of a randomized controlled trial. *Gait Posture*. 2013;38(2):236-241.

32. Wren TA, Kalisvaart MM, Ghatan CE, et al. Effects of preoperative gait analysis on cost and amount of surgery. *J Pediatr Orthop*. 2009;29(6):558-563.

33. Švehlík M, Steinwender G, Kraus T, et al. The influence of age at single-event multilevel surgery on outcome in children with cerebral palsy who walk with flexed knee gait. *Dev Med Child Neurol*. 2011;53(8):730-735.

34. Hoffinger S. The influence of age on timing of single-event multilevel surgery: are adolescents with cerebral palsy comparable to a younger cohort? *Dev Med Child Neurol*. 2011;53(8):675-683.

35. Flynn JM, Miller F. Management of hip disorders in patients with cerebral palsy. *J Am Acad Orthop Surg*. 2002;10(3):198-209.

36. Khot A, Sloan S, Desai S, Harvey A, Wolfe R, Graham HK. Adductor release and chemodenervation in children with cerebral palsy: a pilot study in 16 children. *J Pediatr Orthop.* 2008;2(4):293-299.

37. Valencia FG. Management of hip deformities in cerebral palsy. *Orhop Clin N Am.* 2010;41(4):549-559.

38. Gudjonsdottir B, Stemmons Mercer V. Hip and spine in children with cerebral palsy: musculoskeletal development and clinical implications. *Pediatr Phys Ther.* 1997;9(4):179-185.

39. Scrutton D, Baird G. Surveillance measures of the hips of children with bilateral cerebral palsy. *Arch Dis Child.* 1997;76(4):381-384.

40. Miller F, Bagg MR. Age and migration percentage as risk factors for progression in spastic hip disease. *Dev Med Child Neurol.* 1995;37(5):449-455.

41. Dobson F, Boyd RN, Parrott J, Nattrass GR, Graham HK. Hip surveillance in children with cerebral palsy: impact of the surgical management of spastic hip disease. *J Bone Joint Surg Br.* 2002;84(5):720-726.

42. Hägglund G, Andersson S, Düppe H, Lauge-Pedersen H, Nordmark E, Westbom L. Prevention of dislocation of the hip in children with cerebral palsy. The first ten years of a population based prevention programme. *J Bone Joint Surg Br.* 2005;87(1):95-101.

43. Gordon GS, Simkiss DE. A systematic review of the evidence for surveillance in children with cerebral palsy. *J Bone Joint Surg Br.* 2006;88(11):1492-1496.

44. Wynter M, Gibson N, Kentish M, Love S, Thomason P, Graham JK. The Consensus Statement on Hip Surveillance for Children with Cerebral Palsy: Australian Standards of Care. *J Pediatr Rehabil Med.* 2011;4(3):183-195.

45. Pountney TE, Mandy A, Green E, Gard PR. Hip subluxation and dislocation in cerebral palsy – a prospective study on the effectiveness of postural management programs. *Physiother Res Int.* 2009;14(2):116-127.

46. Graham HK, Boyd R, Carlin JB, et al. Does botulinum toxin A combined with bracing prevent hip displacement in children with cerebral palsy and "hips at risk"? A randomized, controlled trial. *J Bone Joint Surg Am.* 2008;90(1):23-33.

47. Krach LE, Kriel RL, Gilmartin RC, et al. Hip status in cerebral palsy after one year of continuous intrathecal baclofen infusion. *Pediatr Neurol.* 2004;30(3):163-168.

48. Silva S, Nowicki P, Caird MS, et al. A comparison of hip dislocation rates and hip containment procedures after selective dorsal rhizotomy versus intrathecal baclofen pump insertion in nonambulatory cerebral palsy patients. *J Pediatr Orthop.* 2012;32(8):853-856.

49. Krum SD, Miller F. Heterotopic ossification after hip and spine surgery in children with cerebral palsy. *J Pediatr Orthop.* 1993;13(6):739-743.

50. Huh K, Rethlefsen SA, Wren TA, Kay RM. Surgical management of hip subluxation and dislocation in children with cerebral palsy: isolated VDRO or combined surgery? *J Pediatr Orthop.* 2011;31(8):858-863.

51. Muthusamy K, Chu HY, Friesen RM, Chou PC, Eilert RE, Chang FM. Femoral head resection as a salvage procedure for severely dysplastic hip in nonambulatory children with cerebral palsy. *J Pediatr Orthop.* 2008;28(8):884-889.

52. Raphael BS, Dines JS, Akerman M, Root L. Long-term followup of total hip arthroplasty in patients with cerebral palsy. *Clin Orthop Relat Res.* 2010;468(7):1845-1854.

53. Chambers HG. Treatment of functional limitations at the knee in ambulatory children with cerebral palsy. *Europ J Neurol.* 2001;8(suppl 5):59-74.

54. Rethlefsen SA, Yasmeh S, Wren TA, Kay RM. Repeat hamstring lengthening for crouch gait in children with cerebral palsy. *J Pediatr Orthop.* 2013;33(5):501-504.

55. Kramer A, Stevens PM. Anterior femoral stapling. *J Pediatr Orthop.* 2001;21(6):804-807.

56. Stevens PM. Guided growth for angular correction: a preliminary series using a tension band plate. *J Pediatr Orthop.* 2007;27(3):253-259.

57. Klatt J, Stevens PM. Guided growth for fixed knee flexion deformity. *J Pediatr Orthop.* 2008;28(6):626-631.

58. Stout JL, Gage JR, Schwartz MH, Novacheck TF. Distal femoral extension osteotomy and patellar tendon advancement to treat persistent crouch gait in cerebral palsy. *J Bone Joint Surg Am.* 2008;90(11):2470-2484.

59. Novacheck TF, Stout JL, Gage JR, Schwartz MH. Distal femoral extension osteotomy and patellar tendon advancement to treat persistent crouch gait in cerebral palsy. *J Bone Joint Surg Am.* 2009;91(suppl 2):271-286.

60. Healy MT, Schwartz MH, Stout JL, Gage JR, Novacheck TF. Is simultaneous hamstring lengthening necessary when performing distal femoral extension osteotomy and patellar tendon advancement? *Gait Posture.* 2011;33(1):1-5.

61. Zwick EB, Svehlík M, Steinwender G, Saraph V, Linhart WE. Genu recurvatum in cerebral palsy – part B: hamstrings are abnormally long in children with cerebral palsy showing knee recurvatum. *J Pediatr Orthop B.* 2010;19(4):373-378.

62. Dreher T, Vegvari D, Wolf SI, et al. Development of knee function after hamstring lengthening as a part of multilevel surgery in children with spastic diplegia: a long-term outcome study. *J Bone Joint Surg Am.* 2012;94(2):121-130.

63. Klotz MC, Wolf SI, Heitzmann D, Krautwurst B, Braatz F, Dreher T. Reduction in primary genu recurvatum gait after aponeurotic calf muscle lengthening during multilevel surgery. *Res Dev Disabil.* 2013;34(11):3773-3780.

64. Sutherland DH, Davids JR. Common gait abnormalities of the knee in cerebral palsy. *Clin Orthop Relat Res.* 1993;288:139-147.

65. Scully WF, McMulkin ML, Baird GO, Gordon AB, Tompkins BJ, Caskey PM. Outcomes of rectus femoris transfers in children with cerebral palsy: effect of transfer site. *J Pediatr Orthop.* 2013;33(3):303-308.

66. Õunpuu S, Muik E, Davis RB, Gage JR, DeLuca PA. Rectus femoris surgery in children with cerebral palsy. Part I: the effect of rectus femoris transfer location on knee motion. *J Pediatr Orthop.* 1993;13(3):325-330.

67. Fox MD, Reinbolt JA, Õunpuu S, Delp SL. Mechanisms of improved knee flexion after rectus femoris transfer surgery. *J Biomech.* 2009;42(5):614-619.

68. Kay RM, Rethlefsen SA, Kelly JP, Wren TA. Predictive value of the Duncan-Ely test in distal rectus femoris transfer. *J Pediatr Orthop.* 2004;24(1):59-62.

69. Rethlefsen SA, Kam G, Wren TA, Kay RM. Predictors of outcome of distal rectus femoris transfer surgery in ambulatory children with cerebral palsy. *J Pediatr Orthop.* 2009;18(2):58-62.

70. Dreher T, Götze M, Wold SI, et al. Distal rectus femoris transfer as part of multilevel surgery in children with spastic diplegia—a randomized clinical trial. *Gait Posture.* 2012;36(2):212-218.

71. Greene WB. Cerebral palsy. Evaluation and management of equinus and equinovarus deformities. *Foot Ankle Clin.* 2000;5(2):265-280.

72. Yoo WJ, Chung CY, Choi IH, Cho TJ, Kim DH. Calcaneal lengthening for the planovalgus foot deformity in children with cerebral palsy. *J Pediatr Orthop.* 2005;25(6):781-785.

73. De Moraes Barros Fucs PM, de Assumpção RMC, Yamada HH, Simis SD. Surgical technique: medial column arthrodesis in rigid spastic planovalgus feet. *Clin Orthop Relat Res.* 2012;470(5):1334-1343.

74. Chen L, Greisberg J. Achilles lengthening procedures. *Foot Ankle Clin N Am.* 2009;14(4):627-637.

75. De Coulon G, Turcot K, Canavese F, Dayer R, Kaelin A, Ceroni D. Talonavicular arthrodesis for the treatment of neurological flat foot deformity in pediatric patients: clinical and radiographic evaluation of 29 feet. *J Pediatr Orthop.* 2011;31(5):557-63.

76. Kling TF, Kaufer H, Hensinger RN. Split posterior tibial-tendon transfers in children with cerebral spastic paralysis and equinovarus deformity. *J Bone Joint Surg Am.* 1985;67(2):186-194.

77. Moran MF, Sanders JO, Sharkey NA, Piazza SJ. Effect of attachment site and routing variations in split tendon transfer of tibialis posterior. *J Pediatr Orthop.* 2004;24(3):298-303.

78. Mulier T, Moens P, Molenaers G, Spaepen D, Dereymaeker G, Fabry G. Split posterior tibial tendon transfer through the interosseus membrane in spastic equinovarus deformity. *Foot Ankle Int.* 1995;16(12):754-759.

79. Hoffer MM, Reiswig JA, Garrett AM, Perry J. The split anterior tibial tendon transfer in the treatment of spastic varus hindfoot in childhood. *Orthop Clin North Am.* 1974;5(1):31-38.

80. Barnes MJ, Herring JA. Combined split anterior tibial-tendon transfer and intramuscular lengthening of the posterior tibial tendon. Results in patients who have a varus deformity of the foot due to spastic cerebral palsy. *J Bone Joint Surg Am.* 1991;73(5):734-738.

81. Saltzman CL, Fehrle MJ, Cooper RR, Spencer EC, Ponseti IV. Triple arthrodesis: twenty-five and forty-four-year average follow-up of the same patients. *J Bone Joint Surg Am.* 1999;81(10):1391-1402.

82. Tenuta J, Shelton YA, Miller F. Long-term follow-up of triple arthrodesis in patients with cerebral palsy. *J Pediatr Orthop.* 1993;13(6):713-716.

83. Koman LA, Mooney JF 3rd, Goodman A. Management of valgus hindfoot deformity in pediatric cerebral palsy patients by medial displacement osteotomy. *J Pediatr Orthop.* 1993;13(2):180-183.

84. Rathjen KE, Mubarak SJ. Calcaneal-cuboid-cuneiform osteotomy for the correction of valgus foot deformities in children. *J Pediatr Orthop.* 1998;18(6):775-782.

85. DeYoe BE, Wood J. The Evans calcaneal osteotomy. *Clin Podiatr Med Surg.* 2005;22(2):265-276.

86. Mazis GA, Sakellariou VI, Kanellopoulos AD, Papagelopoulos PJ, Lyras DN, Soucacos PN. Results of extra-articular subtalar arthrodesis in children with cerebral palsy. *Foot Ankle Int.* 2012;33(6):469-474.

87. Davids JR, Mason TA, Danko A, Banks D, Blackhurst D. Surgical management of hallux valgus deformity in children with cerebral palsy. *J Pediatr Orthop.* 2001;21(1):89-94.

88. Bishay SN, El-Sherbini MH, Lotfy AA, Abdel-Rahman HM, Iskandar HN, El-Sayed MM. Great toe metatarsophalangeal arthrodesis for hallux valgus deformity in ambulatory adolescents with spastic cerebral palsy. *J Child Orthop.* 2009;3(1):47-52.

89. Harvey A, Rosenbaum P, Hanna S, Yousefi-Nooraie R, Graham HK. Longitudinal changes in mobility following single-event multilevel surgery in ambulatory children with cerebral palsy. *J Rehabil Med.* 2012;44(2):137-144.

90. Harvey A, Graham HK, Morris ME, Baker R, Wolfe R. The Functional Mobility Scale: ability to detect change following single event multilevel surgery. *Dev Med Child Neurol.* 2007;49(8):603-607.

91. Gannotti ME, Gorton GE 3rd, Nahorniak MT, Masso PD. Walking abilities of young adults with cerebral palsy: changes after multilevel surgery and adolescence. *Gait Posture.* 2010;32:46-52.

92. Åkerstedt A, Risto O, Ödman P, Öberg B. Evaluation of single event multilevel surgery and rehabilitation in children and youth with cerebral palsy – a 2-year follow-up study. *Disabil Rehabil.* 2010;32(7):530-539.

93. Gorton GE 3rd, Abel MF, Oeffinger DJ, et al. A prospective cohort study of the effects of lower extremity orthopaedic surgery on outcome measures in ambulatory children with cerebral palsy. *J Pediatr Orthop.* 2009;29(8):903-909.

94. Thomason P, Baker R, Dodd K, et al. Single-event multilevel surgery in children with spastic diplegia: a pilot randomized controlled trial. *J Bone Joint Surg Am.* 2011;93(5):451-460.

95. World Health Organization. *International Classification of Functioning, Disability and Health.* Geneva, Switzerland: World Health Organization; 2001.

96. Schutte LM, Narayanan U, Stout JL, Selber P, Gage JR, Schwartz MH. An index for quantifying deviations from normal gait. *Gait Posture.* 2000;11(1):25-31.

97. Baker R, McGinley JL, Schwartz MH, et al. The gait profile score and movement analysis profile. *Gait Posture.* 2009;30(3):265-269.

98. Russell DJ, Rosenbaum PL, Avery LM, Lane M. *Gross Motor Function Measure (GMFM-66 & GMFM-88) User's Manual.* Lavenham, Suffolk: Mac Keith Press; 2002.

99. Thomason P, Selber P, Graham HK. Single event multilevel surgery in children with bilateral spastic cerebral palsy: a 5 year prospective cohort study. *Gait Posture.* 2013;37(1):23-28.

100. Graham HK, Harvey A, Rodda J, Nattrass GR, Pirpiris M. The Functional Mobility Scale. *J Pediatr Orthop.* 2004;24(5):514-520.

101. Bernthal NM, Gamradat SC, Kay RM, et al. Static and dynamic gait parameters before and after multilevel soft tissue surgery in ambulating children with cerebral palsy. *J Pediatr Orthop.* 2010;30(2):174-179.

102. Seniorou M, Thompson N, Harrington M, Theologis T. Recovery of muscle strength following multi-level orthopaedic surgery in diplegic cerebral palsy. *Gait Posture.* 2007; 26(4):475-481.

103. Patikas D, Wolf SI, Mund K, Armbust P, Schuster W, Döderlein L. Effects of a postoperative strength-training program on the walking ability of children with cerebral palsy: a randomized controlled trial. *Arch Phys Med Rehabil.* 2006;87(5):619-626.

104. Landgraf JM, Abetz L, Ware JE. *Child Health Questionnaire (CHQ): A User's Manual.* Boston, MA: HealthAct; 1999.

105. Cuomo AV, Gamradt SC, Kim CO, et al. Health-related quality of life outcomes improve after multilevel surgery in ambulatory children with cerebral palsy. *J Pediatr Orthop.* 2007;27(6):653-657.

106. Daltroy LH, Liang MH, Fossel AH, Goldberg MJ. The POSNA pediatric musculoskeletal functional health questionnaire: report on reliability, validity, and sensitivity to change. Pediatric Orthopaedic Society of North America. *J Pediatr Orthop.* 1998;18(5):561-571.

107. Varni JW, Seid M, Kurtin PS. The Peds QLTM 4.0: reliability and validity of the Pediatric Quality of Life InventoryTM version 4 generic core scales in healthy and patient populations. *Med Care.* 2001;39(8):800-812.

108. Novacheck TF, Stout JL, Tervo R. Reliability and validity of the Gillette Functional Assessment Questionnaire as an outcome measure in children with walking disabilities. *J Pediatr Orthop.* 2000;20(1):75-81.

109. Koman LA, Sarlikiotis T, Smith BP. Surgery of the upper extremity in cerebral palsy. *Orthop Clin North Am.* 2010;41(4):519-529.

110. Horstmann HM, Hosalkar H, Keenan MA. Orthopaedic issues in the musculoskeletal care of adults with cerebral palsy. *Dev Med Child Neurol.* 2009;51(suppl 4):99-105.

111. Van Heest AE, House JH, Cariello C. Upper extremity surgical treatment of cerebral palsy. *J Hand Surg Am.* 1999;24(2):323-330.

112. House JH, Gwathmey FW, Fidler MO. A dynamic approach to the thumb-in palm deformity in cerebral palsy. *J Bone Joint Surg Am.* 1981;63(2):216-225.

113. Alexander RD, Davids JR, Peace LC, Gidewall MA. Wrist arthrodesis in children with cerebral palsy. *J Pediatr Orthop.* 2000;20(4):490-495.

114. Gong HS, Chung CY, Park MS, Shin HI, Chung MS, Baek GH. Functional outcomes after upper extremity surgery for cerebral palsy: comparison of high and low manual ability classification system levels. *J Hand Surg Am.* 2010;35(2):277-283.

115. Eliasson AC, Krumlinde-Sundholm L, Rösblad B, et al. The Manual Ability Classification System (MACS) for children with cerebral palsy: scale development and evidence of validity and reliability. *Dev Med Child Neurol.* 2006;48(7):549-554.

116. Johnson LM, Randall MJ, Reddihough DS, Oke LE, Byrt TA, Bach TM. Development of a clinical assessment of quality of movement for unilateral upper-limb function. *Dev Med Child Neurol.* 1994;36(11):965-973.

117. Koman LA, Williams RM, Evans PJ, et al. Quantification of upper extremity function and range of motion in children with cerebral palsy. *Dev Med Child Neurol.* 2008;50(12):910-917.

118. Jebsen RH, Taylor N, Trieschmann RB, Trotter MJ, Howard LA. An objective and standardized test of hand function. *Arch Phys Med Rehabil.* 1969;50(6):311-319.

119. *Guide for Uniform Data Set for Medical Rehabilitation for Children (WeeFIM) Version 4.0 – Community Outpatient.* Buffalo, NY: Uniform Data System for Medical Rehabilitation; 1994.

120. Msall ME, DiGaudio K, Duffy LC, LaForest S, Braun S, Granger CV. WeeFIM. Normative sample of an instrument for tracking functional independence in children. *Clin Pediatr (Phila).* 1994;33(7):431-418.

121. Hattrup SJ, Cofield RH, Evidente VH, Sperling JW. Total shoulder arthroplasty for patients with cerebral palsy. *J Shoulder Elbow Surg.* 2007;16(5):e5-e9.

122. Özkan T, Tunçer S. Tendon transfers for the upper extremity in cerebral palsy. *Acta Orthop Traumatol Turc.* 2009;43(2):135-148.

123. Van Heest AE, Ramachandran V, Stout J, Wervey R, Garcia L. Quantitative and qualitative functional evaluation of upper extremity tendon transfers in spastic hemiplegia caused by cerebral palsy. *J Pediatr Orthop.* 2008;28(6):679-683.

124. Carlson MG, Hearns KA, Inkellis E, Leach ME. Early results of surgical intervention for elbow deformity in cerebral palsy based on degree of contracture. *J Hand Surg Am.* 2012;37(8):1665-1671.

125. Gschwind CR. Surgical management of forearm pronation. *Hand Clin.* 2003;19(4):649-655.

126. Wesdock KA, Kott K, Sharps C. Pre- and postsurgical evaluation of hand function in hemiplegic cerebral palsy: exemplar cases. *J Hand Ther.* 2008;21(4):386-397.

127. Tonkin M, Freitas A, Koman A. Leclercq C, Van Heest A. The surgical management of thumb deformity in cerebral palsy. *J Hand Surg Eur.* 2008;33(1):77-80.

128. Davids JR, Sabesan VJ, Ortmann F, et al. Surgical management of thumb deformity in children with hemiplegic-type cerebral palsy. *J Pediatr Orthop.* 2009;29(5):504-510.

129. Van Heest AE. Surgical technique for thumb-in-palm deformity in cerebral palsy. *J Hand Surg Am.* 2011;36(9):1526-1531.

130. Tonkin MA, Hughes J, Smith KL. Lateral band translocation for swan-neck deformity. *J Hand Surg Am.* 1992;17(2):260-267.

131. Carlson MG, Athwal GS, Bueno RA. Treatment of the wrist and hand in cerebral palsy. *J Hand Surg Am.* 2006;31(3):483-490.

132. Haley et al. *Pediatric Evaluation of Disability Inventory (PEDI).* Boston, MA: Trustees of Boston University; 1998.

133. King GA, McDougall J, Palisano RJ, Gritzan J, Tucker MA. Goal attainment scaling: its use in evaluating pediatric therapy programs. *Phys Occup Ther Pediatr.* 1999;15:31-52.

134. Kotwicki T, Jozwiak M. Conservative management of neuromuscular scoliosis: personal experience and review of literature. *Disabil Rehabil.* 2008;30(10):792-798.

135. Murphy KP. Cerebral palsy lifetime care – four musculoskeletal conditions. *Dev Med Child Neurol.* 2009;51(suppl 4):30-37.

136. Jones-Quaidoo SM, Yang S, Arlet V. Surgical management of spinal deformities in cerebral palsy. A review. *J Neurosurg Spine.* 2010;13(6):672-685.

137. Harrington PR. Treatment of scoliosis: correction and internal fixation by spinal instrumentation. *J Bone Joint Surg Am.* 1962;44-A(4):591-610.

138. Luque ER. Segmental spinal instrumentation for correction of scoliosis. *Clin Orthop Relat Res.* 1982;(163):192-198.

139. Teli MG, Cinnella P, Vincitorio F, Lovi A, Grava G, Brayda-Bruno M. Spinal fusion with Cotrel-Dubousset instrumentation for neuropathic scoliosis in patients with cerebral palsy. *Spine.* 2006;3(14):E441-E447.

140. Cheng I, Kim Y, Gupta MC, et al. Apical sublaminar wires versus pedicle screws - which provides better results for surgical correction of adolescent idiopathic scoliosis? *Spine.* 2005;30(18):2104-2112.

141. Modi HN, Hong J-Y, Mehta SS, et al. Surgical correction and fusion using posterior-only pedicle screw construct for neuropathic scoliosis in patients with cerebral palsy. *Spine.* 2009;34(11):1167-1175.

142. Auerbach JD, Spiegel DA, Zgonis MH, et al. The correction of pelvic obliquity in patients with cerebral palsy and neuromuscular scoliosis. *Spine.* 2009;34(21):E766-E774.

143. Dohin B, Dubousset JF. Prevention of the crankshaft phenomenon with anterior spinal epiphysiodesis in surgical treatment of severe scoliosis of the younger patient. *Eur Spine J.* 1994;3(3):165-168.

144. Watanabe K, Lenke LG, Daubs MD, et al. Is spine deformity surgery in patients with spastic cerebral palsy truly beneficial? *Spine.* 2009;34(20):2222-2232.

145. Bohtz C, Meyer-Heim A, Min K. Changes in health-related quality of life after spinal fusion and scoliosis correction in patients with cerebral palsy. *J Pediatr Orthop.* 2011;31(6):668-673.

Cardiovascular and Pulmonary, Digestive, Integumentary, Urogenital, and Sensory Systems

Medical and Surgical Management of Alterations in Body Structures and Functions

Management of the associated medical conditions that accompany CP can have a significant impact on the health, function, and quality of life of the child and family.

David W. Pruitt and Tobias Tsai[1]

Management of multiple medical problems observed in children with cerebral palsy (CP) requires the attention of many members of the interdisciplinary team.[1] The current chapter describes medical and surgical management of common co-morbidities affecting the pulmonary, digestive, integumentary, and urogenital systems in these children and examines a number of treatment options for vision and hearing deficits. Although these problems are primarily addressed by pediatricians, family practitioners, and medical specialists,[1,2] general knowledge related to all areas of complex care provided to children with CP and their families is very important for rehabilitation professionals, including physical therapists. Such knowledge is necessary for planning, implementing, and modifying safe and effective therapeutic intervention; providing education and support to the family; and making decisions about appropriate referrals to medical specialists. Finally, the team members' understanding of co-morbidities and their management is crucial for smooth coordination of complex interdisciplinary care and for prevention or timely treatment of possible complications.[1,2]

CARDIOVASCULAR AND PULMONARY SYSTEMS

According to Jones et al,[2] every child with CP should undergo a complete cardiovascular evaluation. This includes obtaining a history of possible signs of cardiac dysfunction, such as cyanosis, pallor, or excessive fatigue,[2] and screening for possible congenital cardiac anomalies.[3,4] Results of a large study that used a population-based register of children with CP showed that these children were 5 times more likely to be born with a heart defect than children in the general population.[3] If present, cardiac anomalies will be addressed by appropriate medical or surgical means. Additionally, children with unilateral CP should be screened for coagulopathy that contributes to the etiology of neonatal stroke because an increased prevalence of prothrombotic risk factors has been reported in this diagnostic group.[4] Although circulatory problems are not discussed in relation to the diagnosis of CP as frequently as other impairments, cardiovascular disease has been implicated as the leading cause of death in adults with this condition.[5] This finding supports the importance of

Rahlin M. *Physical Therapy for Children With Cerebral Palsy: An Evidence-Based Approach (pp 143-156).*

a thorough cardiovascular evaluation by a primary care physician,[2] followed by a referral to a cardiologist, if necessary.

Pulmonary system co-morbidities in children with CP may arise from such factors as history of premature birth and respiratory distress, need for mechanical ventilation and oxygen supplementation leading to bronchopulmonary dysplasia (BPD),[6-10] or, if born full-term, history of meconium aspiration.[8,9] Other factors may include aspiration related to gastroesophageal reflux, swallowing dysfunction, or excessive drooling1,[2,6,11,12]; atypical development of the rib cage, chest wall spasticity, and weakness of respiratory musculature leading to ineffective cough[1,2,6,8]; and spinal deformities.[6,13] A thorough pulmonary examination needs to be conducted for every child with CP to establish the presence or absence of such respiratory problems as recurrent upper or lower respiratory tract infections, breathing and airway clearance difficulties, sleep apnea, and swallowing dysfunction that may lead to aspiration.[1,2,6,14] The child's nutritional status also needs to be assessed as malnutrition may lead to increased susceptibility to infection and, conversely, improved nutritional status has been linked to decreased incidence of lower respiratory tract infections.[14,15]

Medical Management of Respiratory Infections and Lung Disease

Besides adequate nutrition, other measures used to prevent respiratory infections include routine immunizations with influenza and pneumococcal vaccines,[2] and the administration of palivizumab as a prophylaxis for the respiratory syncytial virus infection that may be very dangerous for a young child with CP who has BPD.[16] Prophylactic antibiotics, such as nebulized tobramycin and oral azithromycin, can be used to prevent or decrease the frequency of episodes of pneumonia and related hospitalizations.[17,18] A timely referral for a videofluoroscopic swallow study may also be viewed as a preventive measure.[19] Its results may suggest the need for feeding modifications necessary to prevent chronic aspiration, aspiration pneumonia, and bronchiectasis.[14,19] Such modifications may include a variety of measures, from changing the feeding strategies and food or formula consistency, to nasogastric or gastrostomy tube feedings.[2,14]

Unfortunately, in spite of preventive measures, lung disease remains prevalent in children and adolescents with CP, with recurrent and persistent pneumonia being a common occurrence, and respiratory symptoms of asthma, such as coughing, wheezing, and segmental atelectasis, also frequently documented.[6,20] Published literature suggests that some asthmatic symptoms in individuals with CP may result from pulmonary aspiration, bronchiectasis, and insufficient airway clearance that contribute to the overall development of lung disease and, thus, asthma medications may be overused in this patient population. Several authors recommend a trial of nebulized bronchodilators (eg, albuterol) and a short course of systemic corticosteroids when the acute symptoms, such as wheezing and segmental atelectasis, are present. If ineffective, these medications should not be continued.[6,20]

In the meantime, an effort must be made to run laboratory tests to determine whether a specific infection is present.[6] Bronchoscopy that allows for the analysis of airway secretions may be helpful in the diagnostic process, and plain film radiographs must be obtained. However, if the child has a history of BPD, a comparison to the previously taken chest images needs to be made to ensure that chronic lung disease is not mistaken for an acute episode.[6] Antibiotic treatment of respiratory infections needs to be instituted early and should be based on the obtained sputum cultures.[20] A prolonged course of antibiotics that lasts 3 or 4 weeks is commonly necessary.[20]

Management of Airway Clearance Problems

Ineffective cough, respiratory muscle weakness, aspiration, and recurrent infections impede airway clearance in individuals with CP.[6,20-22] Chest physical therapy, including postural drainage, percussion, and vibration, is usually recommended to improve airway clearance in patients with respiratory problems.[6,8,20,21] Unfortunately, evidence of efficacy of these techniques in children with CP is limited.[6,20] There are several devices that can be used to enhance airway clearance in these children (Table 9-1).[6,8,21-29] It is important to keep in mind the following:

- The efficacy of most of these interventions, except for the high-frequency chest wall oscillation (HFCWO),[22,25] has been researched in children with cystic fibrosis and neuromuscular disease, but not in children with CP.[6,21]
- The positive expiratory pressure (PEP) oscillation devices may be ineffective in children with CP with significant muscle weakness.[21]
- Patient motivation and skilled respiratory coaching are required for the success of mechanical insufflation-exsufflation (MI-E) therapy.[6]

Although the HFCWO has gained some attention from researchers working with this patient population, evidence in its support is still sparse.[6,22,25,30] Plioplys et al[25] reported on a longitudinal study of 7 patients with bilateral CP, with data collected for 12 months prior to initiating the oscillating vest intervention and for 12 months of HFCWO therapy. Manual chest physical therapy techniques were used throughout the study. Results showed a significant decrease in the incidence of pneumonia and the number of pneumonia-related hospitalizations, and an increase in the frequency of effective suctioning in response to the HFCWO therapy.[25]

While Plioplys et al[25] did not report any adverse events, Willis and Warren[30] described a case of acute respiratory failure that occurred after a 2-month period of HFCWO administration in an 11-year-old child with bilateral CP, severe scoliosis, and ineffective cough fed via a gastrostomy tube (G-tube). Chest radiographs taken upon hospital admission showed bilateral infiltrates. The authors raised a concern regarding the use of the oscillating vest to mobilize secretions in children who are unable to produce an effective cough as the accumulation of secretions may lead to aspiration.

	TABLE 9-1		
	AIRWAY CLEARANCE INTERVENTION OPTIONS FOR CHILDREN WITH CEREBRAL PALSY		
METHOD	**MECHANISM OF ACTION**	**DEVICE (MANUFACTURER)**	**BRIEF DESCRIPTION**
PEP oscillatory devices[6,8,21]	The PEP devices use a one-way breathing valve and adjustable expiratory resistance, which helps maintain an open airway during exhalation, resulting in improved gas exchange, ventilation, and airway clearance.	Acapella (DHD Healthcare)	The mouthpiece (or an optional mask) is attached to the body of the device that contains a vibratory mechanism and a dial that is used to modify the expiratory resistance.
		Flutter VRP1 (VarioRaw)	This is a pipe-shaped device with a steel ball contained inside a plastic cone. During exhalation, the ball rolls up and down the cone, producing vibration. Pressure and frequency of vibration can be adjusted by moving the device in an upward or downward direction.
IPV[6,8,21,24]	The device delivers air and aerosol to the lungs via high-flow-rate mini-bursts during inspiration and maintains positive expiratory pressure during exhalation. The intra-airway percussion helps mobilize secretions.	The IPV Impulsator (Percussionnaire)	This is a pneumatic device that delivers breaths via a mouthpiece at 200 to 300 cycles per minute and peak pressure of 20 to 40 cm H_2O, with intervals of 5 to 15 seconds.
HFCWO[6,8,21,22,25-27]	Oscillation provided by the device is thought to assist in mobilizing secretions by inducing a change in mucus consistency and by creating a nonsymmetrical airflow, with expiration occurring faster than inspiration.	The Vest (Hill-Rom, Inc)	An inflatable vest is attached to a pulse generator via flexible hoses and provides external thoracic oscillation via its rapid inflation/deflation with adjustable pressure and at the frequency that can vary from 5 to 25 Hz.
MI-E[6,21,28,29]	Positive pressure is gradually applied to the airway, followed by a quick shift to negative pressure, to simulate a cough by producing high expiratory flow.	CoughAssist Mechanical In-Exsufflator (Philips Respironics)	The device consists of a centrifugal blower with preset pressure, duration, and inspiratory rate parameters, and a flexible hose connected to a mask or a tracheostomy tube. Treatment includes 3 to 5 in-exsufflation cycles and a 30-second rest period, repeated several times.

Abbreviations: HFCWO, high-frequency chest wall oscillation; IPV, intrapulmonary percussive ventilation; MI-E, mechanical insufflation-exsufflation; PEP, positive expiratory pressure.

They proposed that additional interventions, besides the HFCWO, should be used to assist with the removal of secretions in such situations.[30]

In their exploratory prospective randomized controlled trial (RCT), Yuan et al[22] compared the effects of standard chest physical therapy and the HFCWO on the number of hospitalizations, use of antibiotics, chest radiographs, and sleep parameters in 23 patients—9 with CP and 14 with neuromuscular disease. No significant differences between the groups were reported on most outcome measures, except for a significant increase in maximum oxygen saturation, a trend for fewer respiratory infection-related hospitalizations, and significantly higher compliance with intervention regimen observed in the HFCWO group. There were no reported adverse events, and the authors concluded that the HFCWO therapy was safe and well-tolerated by the participants. However, these results still need to be confirmed with future, larger clinical trials.[22]

Medical Management of Disturbances of Sleep and Obstructive Sleep Apnea

Breathing problems during sleep are common in children with CP and may include central and obstructive apnea, obstructive hypopnea, and paradoxical movement of the chest wall with oxygen desaturation.[20,31] Altered sleep cycles, fragmented sleep, and insomnia have been also documented.[20,32] Frequent awakenings may disrupt sleep of the entire family, lead to the child's daytime sleepiness, and have a tremendous negative effect on cognitive and social skills, and on the overall quality of life.[20,33] In a study of 41 children with CP and 91 children developing typically, excessive daytime sleepiness predicted lower Pediatric Quality of Life Inventory (PedsQL)[34] Physical Summary Scores, and the presence of insomnia negatively affected the Psychosocial Summary Scores received by participants with CP.[33] These results emphasized the importance of sleep assessment in the comprehensive evaluation of children with CP.[33]

Fitzgerald et al[20] asserted that sleep disturbances in this patient population were most likely underreported and given insufficient attention by medical professionals. The issue of possible obstructive sleep apnea is usually raised when consistent snoring is reported. Upper airway obstruction may be caused by pharyngeal collapse, enlargement of tonsils and adenoids, or glossoptosis.[20] Alterations in sleep cycles and insomnia may be caused by brainstem dysfunction, discomfort related to musculoskeletal deformities, pain from hypertonia-related muscle spasms, difficulty changing body positions, epilepsy, night-time cough, and pulmonary aspiration.[20,31,32] Recommendations for a sleep assessment include a thorough history; a physical examination; a lateral radiograph of the airway; as well as blood gas screening tests, oximetry during sleep, and polysomnography, which would help identify the presence of and the reasons for the nighttime breathing problems.[6,20] Table 9-2 lists interventions for sleep disturbances and obstructive sleep apnea that may be used in children with CP.[6,20,31,32,35-37]

A systematic review conducted by Galland et al[32] revealed no studies that would specifically target sleep improvement in children with CP. In published research, sleep outcomes were usually reported as secondary, and the quality of methodology was variable. Overall, there was insufficient evidence in support of specific interventions aimed at improving sleep in this patient population, except for melatonin, which was widely researched and shown to produce consistently positive sleep outcomes. However, it was reported to increase the frequency of seizures in children with neurologic disorders.[38] This side effect needs to be taken into consideration before suggesting melatonin as an intervention for sleep

disturbances in patients with epilepsy.[32] Multicenter studies focusing on specific sleep interventions for children with CP are necessary to establish their efficacy.[32]

DIGESTIVE SYSTEM

Digestive system impairments and nutrition and growth issues in children with CP that are often challenging to manage may have a significant effect on the quality of life of these children and their caregivers.[1,2,11] Medical and surgical interventions for gastroesophageal reflux disease (GERD) and colorectal problems, and general nutritional considerations will be discussed next.

Medical and Surgical Management of Gastroesophageal Reflux Disease

Children with CP who are diagnosed with GERD usually exhibit such chronic symptoms as peptic esophagitis with burning epigastric pain, recurrent vomiting, and tooth erosion.[1,11] In addition, in many cases, chronic dysphagia, irritability, and feeding-related behavior problems are observed. GERD may also contribute to pulmonary aspiration and other respiratory complications, especially in the presence of dysphagia.[1,2,11] Table 9-3 lists medical and surgical intervention options for GERD used in children with CP.[1,2,11,14,39-47] Usually, the most conservative measures are employed first, followed by the use of medications and, if not effective, surgical procedures.[1,11,14]

According to Sullivan,[11] who reported on data from multiple sources, decision making in regard to medical management of GERD in children with neurologic dysfunction is difficult because they are frequently excluded from drug efficacy studies. Proton pump inhibitors (PPI) were shown to be more effective in the management of GERD in children than histamine-2 receptor antagonists.[11,40] The use of PPI is associated with decreased feeding-related acid secretion, healing of esophagitis, and decreased need for antireflux surgeries; however, vomiting may still persist.[11,40] There is insufficient evidence to provide firm support for the use of prokinetic agents, although domperidone is frequently prescribed.[11,41] Baclofen that is used as an antispasticity medication in children with CP was shown to inhibit transient relaxation of the lower esophageal sphincter and accelerate gastric emptying in typically developing children with GERD,[42] and decrease the frequency of episodes of acid reflux and emesis in children with neurologic impairment.[43]

Unfortunately, medical antireflux interventions frequently fail in children with CP and, therefore, surgery may be indicated.[1,11] Such surgeries are associated with a high rate of complications, and repeat procedures may be required.[11,40] Brief descriptions of several surgical options and their complications are provided in Table 9-4.[11,44,45,48-51] A recent systematic review of complete and partial fundoplication surgeries conducted in children revealed that evidence-based decision making related to the selection of the most

TABLE 9-2

INTERVENTION OPTIONS FOR SLEEP DISTURBANCES AND OBSTRUCTIVE SLEEP APNEA IN CHILDREN WITH CEREBRAL PALSY DESCRIBED IN LITERATURE

SLEEP PROBLEM	INTERVENTIONS
Alteration of sleep cycles and insomnia[20,32,35]	Acupuncture[a] Baclofen for reduction of spasticity[a] Massage[a] Osteopathic intervention[a] Sleep setting routines • Bathing routine at bedtime • Cognitive behavioral therapies • Decreased stimulation close to bedtime • Maintaining a sleep diary to help modify bedtime routines Over-the-counter medications (from most to least frequently recommended)[32] • Antihistamines • Melatonin[a] • Herbal preparations • Pain reliever combinations Prescription medications (from most to least frequently prescribed)[32] • Sedating antidepressants • Alpha agonists • Trazodone • Atypical antipsychotics • Selective serotonin reuptake inhibitors • Anticonvulsants • Tricyclics • Benzodiazepines • Short-acting hypnotics
Obstructive sleep apnea and disordered breathing during sleep[6,20,31,36,37]	Adenoidectomy and tonsillectomy BiPAP[b] CPAP[b] Mandibular advancement surgery Mandibular distraction osteogenesis procedure Multilevel upper airway reconstruction surgery[c] Tongue base suspension surgery[d] Tongue-hyoid advancement surgery Tonsillectomy Tracheostomy Uvulopalatoplasty UPPP[a]

Abbreviations: BiPAP, bilevel positive airway pressure; CPAP, continuous positive airway pressure; UPPP, uvulopalatopharyngoplasty.

[a] Sleep disturbance reduction reported in published studies.[32]

[b] For noninvasive respiratory support.[20]

[c] Performed to avoid tracheostomy.[36]

[d] Performed to augment other surgeries for obstructive sleep apnea.[37]

TABLE 9-3
MEDICAL AND SURGICAL INTERVENTION OPTIONS FOR THE TREATMENT OF GASTROESOPHAGEAL REFLUX DISEASE IN CHILDREN WITH CEREBRAL PALSY

TYPE OF INTERVENTION	INTERVENTION OPTIONS
Conservative measures[1,2,14,39,40]	Positioning
	Diet changes
	Thickening of formula and food
Medications[1,11,40-43]	PPI
	• Omeprazole
	• Lansoprazole
	H2RA
	• Ranitidine
	• Famotidine
	Prokinetic agents
	• Domperidone
	• Metoclopramide
	Baclofen
Surgical procedures[1,11,44-47]	Nissen fundoplication
	Thal fundoplication
	Laparoscopic fundoplication
	Vertical gastric plication
	Gastrojejunal tube insertion
	Laparoscopic assisted jejunostomy
	Total esophagogastric disconnection

Abbreviations: H2RA, histamine-2 receptor antagonists; PPI, proton pump inhibitors.

appropriate procedure for a specific patient may be complicated by the lack of well-designed clinical trials.[49] As evident from Table 9-4, numerous and serious complications reported by multiple authors[11,44,45,48-51] make this process even more complex.

G-Tube Feeding

G-tube placement in children with dysphagia and pulmonary aspiration, ineffective oral feeding and inadequate nutritional status,[1,11] and its prevalence and effects on growth and body mass index in children with CP[52-54] were discussed in Chapter 4. GERD is frequently associated with respiratory complications in these children, and aspiration is one of the reasons for the G-tube placement.[11] However, gastrostomy feedings may worsen the symptoms of gastroesophageal reflux, with a subsequent fundoplication surgery required after the G-tube placement in some cases.[11,55-57] Early complications and associated risks of the percutaneous endoscopic gastrostomy procedure may include esophageal laceration, peritonitis, pneumoperitoneum, colonic perforation, a risk of

colo-gastric fistula formation, and general anesthesia risk.[11] Later and less significant complications may include cellulitis, granulation tissue formation around the insertion site, and stoma leakage.[11]

Medical and Surgical Management of Constipation

Because of the high prevalence of colorectal problems in children with CP, it is important to ask related questions when taking the child's history.[1,11] Clinicians should inquire about bowel problems, such as chronic constipation or fecal incontinence, as well as nausea, vomiting, and abdominal pain.[1,11] Additional information can be obtained through a colonic motility examination accomplished by taking serial plain film radiographs or via anorectal and colonic manometry.[11] When a colorectal problem is identified, depending on its severity and present complications, it is addressed through dietary modifications, the use of over-the-counter and prescription medications, or, when necessary, by surgical means.[1,2,11,58] Using a bowel habit diary may assist with

TABLE 9-4

BRIEF DESCRIPTIONS OF SELECTED SURGICAL OPTIONS AND THEIR COMPLICATIONS IN THE TREATMENT OF GASTROESOPHAGEAL REFLUX DISEASE IN CHILDREN WITH NEUROLOGIC DYSFUNCTION, INCLUDING CEREBRAL PALSY

SURGICAL PROCEDURE	BRIEF DESCRIPTION	REPORTED COMPLICATIONS
Nissen fundoplica-tion[11,44,48,49]	Gastric fundus is completely wrapped around the abdominal esophagus to reinforce the lower esophageal sphincter.	• Bowel perforation • Gas bloat syndrome • Death • Death of unrelated causes • Intraoperative bleeding • Laceration of hepatic vein • Need for repeat surgery • Paraesophageal hernia • Postoperative dysphagia • Recurrent gastroesophageal reflux • Recurrent hiatal hernia • Small bowel obstruction • Tension pneumothorax • Valve migration
Thal fundoplication[45,49]	Partial fundoplication is performed, with anterior wrapping of the fundus around the esophagus.	• Bowel perforation • Death • Ineffective wrap • Intraoperative bleeding • Need for repeat surgery • Postoperative feeding difficulties • Recurrent hiatal hernia • Recurrent gastroesophageal reflux
Vertical gastric plication[44,50]	Lengthening of the abdominal esophagus and stapling of anterior and posterior gastric walls are performed to create a vertical partition parallel to the stomach's lesser curvature.	• Death of unrelated causes • Paraesophageal hernia • Pneumonia • Urinary tract infection
Total esophagogastric disconnection[11,51]	Disconnection of the esophagus from the stomach and closure of the gastroesophageal junction are performed; a jejunal limb is prepared and attached to the esophagus via an esophagojejunal anastomosis; bowel continuity is restored via a jejunojejunal anastomosis; a gastrostomy tube is inserted to allow bolus feedings.	• Death • Death of unrelated causes • Dislodged gastrostomy tube • Enterocolitis with enterocutaneous fistula • Esophageal stenosis • Leak at esophagojejunal anastomosis • Pancreatitis • Paraesophageal hernia • Pneumonia • Slow gastric emptying • Small bowel obstruction • Urinary tract infection • Wound dehiscence and infection

TABLE 9-5

INTERVENTIONS FOR COLORECTAL PROBLEMS, THEIR INDICATIONS, AND ADVERSE EFFECTS IN CHILDREN WITH NEUROLOGIC DISORDERS

INDICATIONS	INTERVENTIONS	ADVERSE EFFECTS
Mild constipation without complications[1,2,11]	• Customized daily bowel program • Dietary modifications, including fluid and fiber intake • Stool softener (eg, lactulose) • Mineral oil • Mild stimulant medications (eg, senna)	• Gas, abdominal distension, pain from lactulose • Colicky abdominal pain from stimulant medications • Aspiration of mineral oil
Megarectum and rectal impaction[1,11]	• Sodium acid phosphate or sodium citrate enema, followed by the use of stool softener (docusate sodium or psyllium husk) and stimulants	• Distress from enema • Electrolyte imbalance • Ineffective enema treatment
Anal fissure[11,59]	• Stool softener • Topical lidocaine • Topical glyceryl trinitrate • Transcutaneous needle-free botulinum toxin injection into external anal sphincter	• Headache from topical glyceryl nitrate • Recurrent constipation and stool withholding 4 to 6 months after botulinum toxin administration
Failed medical interventions for constipation and fecal incontinence[11,58,60]	• Colostomy • The Malone antegrade continence enema procedure[a] • Laparoscopic-assisted endoscopic cecostomy (LAPEC)[b]	• Abdominal discomfort • Appendicostomy leak • Risk of appendix perforation with catheter • Post-LAPEC procedure low-grade fever, cecostomy tube dislodgement with subsequent repeat surgery, minor skin erosion and skin breakdown leading to tube removal

[a] A surgical procedure for constipation or fecal incontinence when appendix is moved to the skin and a small appendicostomy is created, through which a catheter is inserted into the cecum to administer the antegrade enema with a saline, polyethylene glycol, or phosphate solution to facilitate a bowel washout through the anus.

[b] A minimally invasive surgical technique for the antegrade continence enema procedure.

monitoring the child's treatment response.[11] Interventions for chronic constipation and fecal incontinence in children with neurologic disorders are presented in Table 9-5.[1,2,11,58-60] It is important to note that the use of some of these treatment methods have not been adequately researched in children with CP.

Nutritional Considerations

To perform an objective assessment of nutritional status for a child who demonstrates inadequate growth, his or her caloric intake should be compared to the established daily energy needs.[2] Because of the heterogeneity of presentation in children with CP, it may be difficult to estimate their projected energy expenditure and, thus, the development of general nutritional guidelines for this group of patients may be challenging.[1] For example, the caloric intake requirements

in children with spastic CP are usually lower than in those developing typically but would vary depending on whether the child is able to ambulate, and in children with dyskinetic CP, energy needs may be twice as high as typically expected.[61] Krick et al[62] developed a formula for calculating the energy needs for children with CP based on their basal metabolic rate, muscle tone, ambulatory status, and expected growth. Using growth charts specific to this patient population is also recommended.[53,63]

In a study conducted with 45 children with bilateral spastic CP who received a nutritional support intervention, a significantly greater number of children were classified into the group below the 10th percentile for growth by national standards developed for children without disabilities compared to the diagnosis-specific growth charts. In response to nutritional support, the study participants demonstrated significant improvements on a number of anthropometric measures, and the overall nutritional status improved in 4 children whose pre-intervention weight-for-height values had been below the 10th percentile. In addition, a significant decrease in the number of lower respiratory tract infections and in the constipation rate was observed.[15]

An important issue to consider when evaluating the nutritional status of a child with CP is whether the caloric intake received by mouth is adequate or whether a G-tube placement may be required.[2] This may be difficult for a number of reasons, including the emotional implications of this procedure for the child's parents and the lack of definitive recommendations on the subject in published literature.[1,64] After an extensive search of multiple databases, a recent Cochrane review found no RCTs that would compare the effects of G-tube or jejunostomy tube feedings and oral feedings in children with CP. This problem poses a significant barrier to evidence-based decision making in this area and needs to be resolved by timely and well-designed research.[64]

Although many children with CP are underweight, the problem of obesity should not be overlooked as it is not uncommon in children who are overfed via a G-tube.[2,65] If the child is ambulatory, being overweight will be detrimental to the ability to maintain functional walking over time. If the child is unable to walk, excessive weight would make it more difficult for the caregiver to manage transfers and position changes and to lift the child, if required.[2] Caregiver education on the appropriate caloric intake and adequate amount of fluid, vitamins, minerals, and protein for the child is imperative so that obesity or excessive weight gain can be prevented or addressed.[2]

Research demonstrates that energy intake of less than 75% of the estimated requirement may be sufficient for a child with CP, Gross Motor Function Classification System (GMFCS)[65] level IV or V, who is fed via a G-tube. In a prospective feasibility study, Vernon-Roberts et al[66] demonstrated that a low-energy, high-fiber diet with a complete set of required micronutrients provided to G-tube fed children with bilateral spastic CP, median age 2 years, could effectively support their growth without a detriment to their body composition. However, the results of this research need to be taken with caution because of its small sample size, the young age of the participants, and the normal content of body fat they demonstrated at the baseline.[66,67] Many older children with CP classified in GMFCS[65] level V and fed via a G-tube present with decreased body fat even when aggressive nutritional intervention is instituted.[67,68] Therefore, the nutritional regimen used in the study by Vernon-Roberts et al[66] may not be effective in these children.[67,68] This argument illustrates the challenge the development of uniform nutritional guidelines for children with CP may present.

INTEGUMENTARY SYSTEM

Although children with CP are at risk for skin breakdown for a variety of reasons,[2] there is not much information in published literature that would directly address medical management of the integumentary system problems in this patient population. Clinicians need to be aware of the potential development of calluses and skin thickening on the hands and upper and lower extremity bony prominences in those individuals who use floor mobility past the infant or toddler age.[2] Pressure ulcers related to musculoskeletal deformities[69] and to splint and orthotic wear may also form, and the caregivers need to be instructed in performing daily skin inspections as a preventive measure.[2] In addition, although prevalence of obesity among adolescents with CP is lower than in other groups of youth with disabilities, those of them who are overweight are more likely to develop pressure ulcers than their peers who are not.[70]

Integumentary complications related to the insertion of intrathecal baclofen pumps[71,72] and to orthopedic surgeries and procedures[73-78] raise another concern. Children with CP are at a greater risk of developing a postoperative infection if they present with respiratory co-morbidities, poor nutritional status, poor skin condition, and preoperative infections.[74] In such cases, a thorough preoperative evaluation and an intraoperative administration of prophylactic antibiotics may be necessary.[74] Additionally, new techniques are being developed to address postsurgical deep wound infections.[78] For example, Vacuum-Assisted Closure (KCI, Inc) has been successfully applied in treatment of deep spinal infections in children and adolescents with disabilities, including CP, who underwent spinal fusion surgeries.[78] This method involves using a negative pressure device to increase the blood flow and the rate of granulation tissue formation, and to decrease edema and bacterial counts.[78-80]

UROGENITAL SYSTEM

Delayed development of bladder control, urinary incontinence, urinary tract infections (UTIs) and neurogenic bladder problems affect many children and adults with CP.[2,81,82] As well-stated by Murphy et al,[82] urinary continence is "part of basic human dignity,"(p 949) and "it should not be denied to anyone within the context of patient-centered, professional, medical, and surgical care."(p 949) Parents, health care providers, and school personnel may be involved in helping the child achieve urinary continence by instituting a toilet training program.[2] Such programs are often included into the Individualized Education Plan in a school setting (see Chapter 12). Physical, occupational, and nursing assessments are indicated for individuals with neurogenic bladder problems.[82] An evaluation for adaptive toileting equipment may also be necessary. Hygiene issues related to UTIs and urinary incontinence need to be addressed through caregiver education and discussed with the child, when appropriate. Another related problem is the proper management of menstrual periods in girls with CP and intellectual disability or communication difficulties who may not be able to express the associated discomfort or handle the hygiene issues without

	TABLE 9-6	
INDICATIONS FOR INTERVENTIONS USED IN MANAGEMENT OF LOWER URINARY TRACT DYSFUNCTION AND NEUROGENIC BLADDER IN PERSONS WITH CEREBRAL PALSY		
INDICATIONS		**INTERVENTIONS**
UTI or UTI prophylaxis[81,85]		Antibiotics
Neurogenic bladder[81,82,85,86]	Detrusor overactivity and detrusor sphincter dyssynergia	Anticholinergic medications (oxybutynin, hyoscyamine sulfate, propantheline)
		Clean intermittent catheterization
	Detrusor underactivity	Alpha-blockers
		Monitoring for upper urinary tract dysfunction
		Clean intermittent catheterization
		Foley catheter
	Detrusor areflexia	Clean intermittent catheterization
Neurogenic overactivity of pelvic floor[82]		Adapted toileting equipment or seating positioning modifications
		Biofeedback
		Pelvic floor spasticity management
Abbreviation: UTI, urinary tract infection.		

external assistance.[2] These issues create unique challenges for parents and health care providers.

The overall intervention goals for children with CP and urinary tract dysfunction are to prevent kidney damage, achieve urinary continence, and improve the child's quality of life.[83,84] Besides toilet training programs,[2] other measures may be required. Urodynamic studies, such as filling and voiding cystometry, assessment of flow rate and residual urine volume, and external urethral sphincter electromyography, are helpful in the evaluation of lower urinary tract dysfunction.[81,85] When upper urinary tract pathology is suspected, a renal ultrasound and a voiding cystourethrogram (VCUG) study can be performed.[82] Table 9-6 contains indications for specific interventions used in the management of lower urinary tract dysfunction and neurogenic bladder in this patient population.[81,82,85,86] A patient-specific toileting schedule and environmental modifications may also be helpful in addressing incontinence.[82] Finally, surgical intervention may be required for children with upper urinary tract dysfunction or those with persistent urinary incontinence that fails to respond to conservative management.[84,87]

The efficacy of anticholinergic drugs in the treatment of neurogenic bladder was established in multiple studies.[83] A number of interventions that address urinary incontinence in children and adults with CP were described,[81-87] with positive results reported by several authors.[82,87] However, studies comparing the efficacy of different interventions are still necessary to provide much needed guidance to clinical practice in this area.

SENSORY SYSTEMS

Auditory System

Although hearing loss in children with CP is not as prevalent as visual impairments (see Table 4-4),[88,89] this problem should not be overlooked.[2] It is particularly necessary to keep this issue in mind when the child with CP has a history of extremely low birth weight (ELBW) with hospitalization in a Neonatal Intensive Care Unit (NICU) because sensory-neural hearing loss that requires hearing aides has been documented in up to 7% of the ELBW NICU survivors.[90] Another point important for every child with CP is that, when the newborn screening does not show a hearing deficit, some degree of impairment still may be present, and an audiology evaluation may be required at a later time, especially if this child demonstrates a speech delay.[2]

For children with CP and hearing loss who do not receive sufficient assistance from the hearing aides, and for those who are born with profound hearing impairment, cochlear implants may be used to improve their auditory function and assist with speech development.[91-94] Cochlear implants are surgically installed electronic devices that provide direct stimulation to the auditory nerve.[93,94] Improvements in sound perception, production of speech, and the use of verbal language are expected following the device implantation.[91-94] However, this procedure is expensive,[93] and its adverse effects may include cholesteatoma formation, cutaneous infections, device failure, electrode placement errors, facial palsy, magnet

TABLE 9-7

INTERVENTION OPTIONS AND THEIR REPORTED ADVERSE EFFECTS IN MANAGEMENT OF OCULAR MOTOR AND VISUAL DISORDERS IN CHILDREN WITH CEREBRAL PALSY

DISORDERS		INTERVENTIONS	REPORTED ADVERSE EFFECTS
Ocular motor[100,104-107]	Strabismus	Eye glasses	Surgical overcorrection
		Vision therapy	Surgical undercorrection
		Surgical recession of medial or lateral rectus muscle(s)	Need for repeat surgeries
		Botulinum toxin A injections for esotropia	Need for repeat botulinum toxin injections
	Eye movement abnormalities	Vision therapy	Persistent dysfunction
Visual[101,104]	Refractive errors	Eye glasses	No improvement in vision
	Amblyopia	Eye patching	
		Atropine eye drops	

displacement, pain leading to implant removal, persistent ear infections, and vertigo,[91,93-95] with a complications-related reimplantation rate of 7% to 30.2%.[91,95]

Approximately 33% of children who receive cochlear implants have additional disabilities besides hearing loss.[91] Significant differences in outcomes of cochlear implantation were reported in children with and without additional disabilities[91] and in children with CP who functioned at different GMFCS[65] levels.[92] Specifically, having an additional disability and greater physical, cognitive, and social interaction deficits were shown to be associated with significantly less favorable auditory and speech outcomes.[91,92]

Visual System

Accompanying visual system impairments that are most commonly related to brain lesions in children with CP[89,96-98] were discussed in Chapter 4. Because of the high prevalence of visual abnormalities (see Table 4-4),[89,96] every child with or at risk for CP needs to have a thorough visual assessment early in life, followed by annual eye examinations.[2,98] Visual impairment in this patient population may manifest itself as a combination of ocular motor, visual, and sensory deficits.[99-101] Assessment of visual acuity and ocular motor function in children with CP is often difficult because their primary motor impairment may prevent them from producing an adequate response during testing, leading to incorrect diagnosis.[101] Ocular motor problems may include strabismus, nystagmus, inaccurate saccades (fast eye movements), unstable fixation, smooth pursuit deficits, and paroxysmal eye deviations.[99,100] Esotropia or medial deviation of the eye is more frequently observed in children with CP than exotropia or lateral eye deviation.[100,102] Visual disorders commonly

documented in this patient population include optic nerve abnormalities; refractive errors, such as hyperopia (upward vertical deviation of one eye), myopia and astigmatism; and amblyopia or decreased visual acuity, which, in children with CP, is most often related to strabismus and refractive errors.[101-103]

Table 9-7 contains information on management options for oculomotor and visual disorders.[100,101,104-107] Persistent visual and ocular motor dysfunction in children with CP is not uncommon and is most likely the result of underlying pathology of the central nervous system.[100,101] There is insufficient evidence related to the efficacy of vision therapy for eye movement abnormalities in this patient population, and described surgical outcomes are variable, with high overcorrection rates reported after strabismus surgeries.[100,105] A higher surgical success rate (71%) was documented in children with mild to moderate CP compared to 56% in those with severe motor involvement. However, the use of eye glasses for refractive errors and conservative interventions for amblyopia may have comparable effects in children with CP and their peers without disabilities.[101]

REFERENCES

1. Pruitt DW, Tsai T. Common medical comorbidities associated with cerebral palsy. *Phy Med Rehabil Clin N Am.* 2009;20(3):453-467.
2. Jones MW, Morgan E, Shelton JE. Primary care of the child with cerebral palsy: a review of systems (part II). *J Pediatr Health Care.* 2007;21(4):226-237.
3. Pharoah PC. Prevalence and pathogenesis of congenital anomalies in cerebral palsy. *Arch Dis Child Fetal Neonatal Ed.* 2007;92(6):F489-F493.

4. Senbil N, Yüksel D, Yilmaz D, Gürer YK. Prothrombotic risk factors in children with hemiplegic cerebral palsy. *Pediatr Int.* 2007;49(5):600-602.

5. Strauss D, Cable W, Shavelle R. Causes of excess mortality in cerebral palsy. *Dev Med Child Neurol.* 1999;41(9):580-585.

6. Toder DS. Respiratory problems in the adolescent with developmental delay. *Adolesc Med.* 2000;11(3):617-631.

7. Vohr BR, Wright LL, Poole WK, McDonald SA. Neurodevelopmental outcomes of extremely low birth weight infants <32 weeks' gestation between 1993 and 1998. *Pediatrics.* 2005;116:635-643.

8. Rahlin M, Moerchen VA. Infants and children with cardiovascular and pulmonary dysfunction. In: Frownfelter D, Dean E, eds. *Cardiovascular and Pulmonary Physical Therapy: Evidence to Practice.* 5th ed. St, Louis, MO: Mosby, Inc; 2012:600-624.

9. Rahlin M. Impaired ventilation, respiration/gas exchange and aerobic capacity/endurance associated with respiratory failure in the neonate. In: Frownfelter D, ed. *Cardiopulmonary Essentials: Preferred Physical Therapist Practice Patterns.* Thorofare, NJ: SLACK Incorporated; 2007:237-264.

10. Jobe AH, Bancalari E. Bronchopulmonary dysplasia. *Am J Respir Crit Care Med.* 2001;163:1723-1729.

11. 11. Sullivan PB. Gastrointestinal disorders in children with neurodevelopmental disabilities. *Dev Disabil Res Rev.* 2008;14(2):128-136.

12. Reddihough D, Erasmus CE, Johnson H, McKellar GMW, Jongerius PH. Botulinum toxin assessment, intervention and aftercare for paediatric and adult drooling: international consensus statement. *Eur J Neurol.* 2010;17(suppl 2):109-121.

13. Littleton SR, Heriza CB, Mullens PA, Moerchen VA, Bjornson K. Effects of positioning on respiratory measures in individuals with cerebral palsy and severe scoliosis. *Pediatr Phys Ther.* 2011;23:159-169.

14. Seddon PC, Khan Y. Respiratory problems in children with neurological impairment. *Arch Dis Child.* 2003;88(1):75-78.

15. Soylu OB, Unalp A, Uran N, et al. Effect of nutritional support on children with spastic quadriplegia. *Pediatr Neurol.* 2008;39(5):330-334.

16. Jamroz E, Kordys-Darmolinska B, Głuszkiewicz E, Wos H. The diagnostic and therapeutic difficulties of the recurrent lower respiratory tract infections in children with neurological disorders. *Pediatr Pol.* 2011;86(5):474-480.

17. Plioplys AV, Kasnicka I. Nebulized tobramycin: prevention of pneumonias in patients with severe cerebral palsy. *J Pediatr Rehabil Med.* 2011;4(2):155-158.

18. Kirk CB. Is the frequency of recurrent chest infections, in children with chronic neurological problems, reduced by prophylactic azithromycin? *Arch Dis Child.* 2008;93(5):422-444.

19. Kim JS, Han ZA, Song DH, Oh HM, Chung ME. Characteristics of dysphagia in children with cerebral palsy, related to gross motor function. *Am J Phys Med Rehabil.* 2013;92(10):912-919.

20. Fitzgerald DA, Follett J, Van Asperen PP. Assessing and managing lung disease and sleep disordered breathing in children with cerebral palsy. *Paediatr Respir Rev.* 2009;10(1):18-24.

21. Finder JD. Airway clearance modalities in neuromuscular disease. *Paediatr Respir Rev.* 2010;11(1):31-34.

22. Yuan N, Kane P, Shelton K, Matel J, Becker BC, Moss RB. Safety, tolerability, and efficacy of high-frequency chest wall oscillation in pediatric patients with cerebral palsy and neuromuscular disease: an exploratory randomized controlled trial. *J Child Neurol.* 2010;25(7):815-821.

23. Mejia-Downs A. Airway clearance techniques. In: Frownfelter D, Dean E, eds. *Cardiovascular and Pulmonary Physical Therapy: Evidence to Practice.* 5th ed. St, Louis, MO: Mosby, Inc; 2012:309-336.

24. Reardon CC, Christianson D, Barnett ED, Cabral HJ. Intrapulmonary percussive ventilation vs incentive spirometry for children with neuromuscular disease. *Arch Pediatr Adolesc Med.* 2005;159(6):526-531.

25. Plioplys AV, Lewis S, Kasnicka I. Pulmonary vest therapy in pediatric long-term care. *J Am Med Dir Assoc.* 2002;3(5):318-321.

26. Tomkiewicz R, Bivij A, King M. Effects of oscillating air flow on the rheological properties and clearability of mucous gel simulants. *Biorheology.* 1994;31(5):511-520.

27. Chang HK, Weber ME, King M. Mucus transport by high-frequency nonsymmetrical oscillatory airflow. *J Appl Physiol.* 1988;65(3):1203-1209.

28. Miske LJ, Hickey EM, Kolb SM, Weiner DJ, Panitch HB. Use of the mechanical in-exsufflator in pediatric patients with neuromuscular disease and impaired cough. *Chest.* 2004;125(4):1406-1412.

29. Homnick DN. Mechanical insufflation-exsufflation for airway mucus clearance. *Respir Care.* 2007;52(10):1296-1305.

30. Willis LD, Warren RH. Acute hypoxemia in a child with neurologic impairment associated with high-frequency chest-wall compression. *Respir Care.* 2007;52(8):1027-1029.

31. Kotagal G, Gibbons VP, Stith JA. Sleep abnormalities in patients with severe cerebral palsy. *Dev Med Child Neurol.* 1944;36(4):304-311.

32. Galland BC, Elder DE, Taylor BJ. Interventions with a sleep outcome for children with cerebral palsy or post-traumatic brain injury: a systematic review. *Sleep Med Rev.* 2012;16(6):561-573.

33. Sandella DE, O'Brien LM, Shank LK, Warschausky SA. Sleep and quality of life in children with cerebral palsy. *Sleep Med.* 2011;12(3):252-256.

34. Varni JW, Seid M, Kurtin PS. The PedsQLTM 4.0: reliability and validity of the Pediatric Quality of Life InventoryTM version 4 generic core scales in healthy and patient populations. *Med Care.* 2001;39(8):800-812.

35. Owens JA, Rosen CL, Mindell JA, Kirchner HL. Use of pharmacotherapy for insomnia in child psychiatry practice: a national survey. *Sleep Med.* 2010;11(7):692-700.

36. Cohen SR, Lefaivre JF, Burstein FD, et al. Surgical treatment of obstructive sleep apnea in neurologically compromised patients. *Plast Reconstr Surg.* 1997;99(3):638-646.

37. Hartzell LD, Guillory RM, Munson PD, Dunham AK, Bower CM, Richter GT. Tongue base suspension in children with cerebral palsy and obstructive sleep apnea. *Int J Pediatr Otorhinolaryngol.* 2013;77(4):534-537.

38. Sheldon SH. Pro-convulsant effects of oral melatonin in neurologically disabled children. *Lancet.* 1998;351(9111):1254.

39. Miyazawa R, Tomomasa T, Kaneko H, Arakawa H, Shimizu N, Morikawa A. Effects of pectin liquid on gastroesophageal reflux disease in children with cerebral palsy. *BMC Gastroenterol.* 2008;8:11.

40. Hassall E. Decisions in diagnosing and managing chronic gastroesophageal reflux disease in children. *J Pediatr.* 2005;146(suppl 3):S3-S12.

41. Tighe MP, Afzal NA, Bevan A, Beattie RM. Current pharmacological management of gastro-esophageal reflux in children: an evidence-based systematic review. *Paediatr Drugs.* 2009;11(3):185-202.

42. Kawai M, Kawahara H, Hirayama S, Yoshimura N, Ida S. Effect of baclofen on emesis and 24-hour esophageal pH in neurologically impaired children with gastroesophageal reflux disease. *J Paediatr Gastroenterol Nutr.* 2004;38(3):317-323.

43. Omari TI, Benninga MA, Sansom L, Butler RN, Dent J, Davidson GP. Effect of baclofen on esophagogastric motility and gastroesophageal reflux in children with gastroesophageal reflux disease: a randomized controlled trial. *J Pediatr.* 2006;149(4):468-474.

44. Durante AP, Schettini ST, Fagundes DJ. Vertical gastric plication versus Nissen fundoplication in the treatment of gastroesophageal reflux in children with cerebral palsy. *Sao Paolo Med J.* 2007;125(1):15-21.

45. Ramachandran V, Ashcraft KW, Sharp RJ, et al. Thal fundoplication in neurologically impaired children. *J Pediatr Surg.* 1996;31(6):819-822.

46. Esposito C, van der Zee DC, Settimi A, Doldo P, Staiano A, Bax NM. Risks and benefits of surgical management of gastroesophageal reflux in neurologically impaired children. *Surg Endosc.* 2003;17(5):708-710.

47. Esposito C, Settimi A, Centonze A, Capano G, Ascione G. Laparoscopic-assisted jejunostomy. *Surg Endosc.* 2005;19(4):501-504.

48. GERD Surgery – Mayo Clinic Medical Information and Tools for Healthy Living. *Mayo Clinic.* http://www.mayoclinic.com/health/medical/IM03999. Accessed December 26, 2013.

49. Mauritz FA, Blomberg BA, Stellato RK, van der Zee DC, Siersema PD, van Herwaarden-Lindeboom MY. Complete versus partial fundoplication in children with gastroesophageal reflux disease: results of a systematic review and meta-analysis. *J Gastrointest Surg.* 2013;17(10):1883-1892.

50. Taylor TV, Knox RA, Pullan BR. Vertical gastric plication: and operation for gastro-oesophageal reflux. *Ann R Coll Surg Engl.* 1989;71(1):31-36.

51. Danielson PD, Emmens RW. Esophagogastric Disconnection for gastroesophageal reflux in children with severe neurological impairment. *J Pediatr Surg.* 1999;34(1):84-87.

52. Himmelmann K, Hagberg G, Wiklund LM, Eek MN, Uvebrant P. Dyskinetic cerebral palsy: a population-based study of children born between 1991 and 1998. *Dev Med Child Neurol.* 2007;49(4):246-251.

53. Day SM, Strauss DJ, Vachon PJ, Rosenbloom L, Shavelle RM, Wu YW. Growth patterns in a population of children and adolescents with cerebral palsy. *Dev Med Child Neurol.* 2007;49(3):167-171.

54. Dahlseng MO, Andersen GL, Da Graca Andrada M, et al; Surveillance of Cerebral Palsy in Europe Network. Gastrostomy tube feeding of children with cerebral palsy: variation across six European countries. *Dev Med Child Neurol.* 2012;54(10):938-944.

55. Sulaeman E, Udall JN, Brown RF, et al. Gastroesophageal reflux and Nissen fundoplication following percutaneous endoscopic gastrostomy in children. *J Pediatr Gastroenterol Nutr.* 1998;26(3):269-273.

56. Ponsky TA, Gasior AC, Parry J, et al. Need for subsequent fundoplication after gastrostomy based on patient characteristics. *J Surg Res.* 2013;179(1):1-4.

57. Samuel M, Holmes K. Quantitative and qualitative analysis of gastroesophageal reflux after percutaneous endoscopic gastrostomy. *J Pediatr Surg.* 2002;37(2):256-261.

58. Krogh K, Christensen P, Lauberg S. Colorectal symptoms in patients with neurological diseases. *Acta Neurol Scand.* 2001;103(6):335-343.

59. Keshtgar AS, Ward HC, Clayden GS. Transcutaneous needle-free injection of botulinum toxin: a novel treatment of childhood constipation and anal fissure. *J Pediatr Surg.* 2009;44(9):1791-1798.

60. Rodriguez L, Flores A, Gilchrist BF, Goldstein AM. Laparoscopic-assisted percutaneous endoscopic cecostomy in children with defecation disorders (with video). *Gastrointest Endosc.* 2011;73(1):98-102.

61. Herman R, Btaiche I, Teitelbaum DH. Nutrition support in the pediatric surgical patient. *Surg Clin North Am.* 2011;91(3):511-541.

62. Krick J, Murphy PE, Markham JF, Shapiro BK. A proposed formula for calculating energy needs of children with cerebral palsy. *Dev Med Child Neurol.* 1992;34(6):481-487.

63. Stevenson RD, Conaway M, Chumlea WC, et al. Growth and health in children with moderate-to-severe cerebral palsy. *Pediatrics.* 2006;118(3):1010-1018.

64. Gantasala S, Sullivan PB, Thomas AG. Gastrostomy feeding versus oral feeding alone for children with cerebral palsy. *Cochrane Database Syst Rev.* 2013;7:CD003943.

65. Palisano RJ, Rosenbaum PL, Walter SD, Russell DJ, Wood EP, Galuppi BE. Development and reliability of a system to classify gross motor function in children with cerebral palsy. *Dev Med Child Neurol.* 1997;39(4):214-223.

66. Vernon-Roberts A, Wells J, Grant H, et al. Gastrostomy feeding in cerebral palsy: enough and no more. *Dev Med Child Neurol.* 2010;52(12):1099-1105.

67. Somerville H, O'Loughlin E. Gastrostomy feeding in cerebral palsy: enough and no more. *Dev Med Child Neurol.* 2010;52(12):1076.

68. Arrowsmith F, Allen J, Gaskin K, Somerville H, Clarke S, O'Loughlin E. The effect of gastrostomy tube feeding on body protein and bone mineralization in children with quadriplegic cerebral palsy. *Dev Med Child Neurol.* 2010;52(11):1043-1047.

69. Noonan KJ, Jones J, Pierson J, Honkamp NJ, Leverson G. Hip function in adults with severe cerebral palsy. *J Bone Joint Surg Am.* 2004;86(12):2607-2613.

70. Rimmer JH, Yamaki K, Lowry BM, Wang E, Vogel LC. Obesity and obesity-related secondary conditions in adolescents with intellectual/developmental disabilities. *J Intellect Disabil Res.* 2010;54(9):787-794.

71. Quality Standards Subcommittee of the American Academy of Neurology and the Practice Committee of the Child Neurology Society, Delgado MR, Hirtz D, et al. Practice parameter: pharmacologic treatment of spasticity in children and adolescents with cerebral palsy (an evidence-based review): report of the Quality Standards Subcommittee of the American Academy of Neurology and the Practice Committee of the Child Neurology Society. *Neurology.* 2010;74(4):336-343.

72. Pin TW, McCartney L, Lewis J, Waugh M-C. Use of intrathecal baclofen therapy in ambulant children and adolescents with spasticity and dystonia of cerebral origin: a systematic review. *Dev Med Child Neurol.* 2011;53(10):885-895.

73. Auerbach JD, Spiegel DA, Zgonis MH, et al. The correction of pelvic obliquity in patients with cerebral palsy and neuromuscular scoliosis. *Spine.* 2009;34(21):E766-E774.

74. Jones-Quaidoo SM, Yang S, Arlet V. Surgical management of spinal deformities in cerebral palsy. A review. *J Neurosurg Spine.* 2010;13(6):672-685.

75. Watanabe E, Lenke LG, Daubs MD, et al. Is spine deformity surgery in patients with spastic cerebral palsy truly beneficial? *Spine.* 2009;34(20):2222-2232.

76. Bohtz C, Meyer-Heim A, Min K. Changes in health-related quality of life after spinal fusion and scoliosis correction in patients with cerebral palsy. *J Pediatr Orthop.* 2011;31(6):668-673.

77. Stasikelis PJ, Lee DD, Sullivan CM. Complications of osteotomies in severe cerebral palsy. *J Pediatr Orthop.* 1999;19(2):207-210.

78. Canavese F, Krajbich JI. Use of vacuum assisted closure in instrumented spinal deformities for children with postoperative deep infections. *Indian J Orthop.* 2010;44(2):177-183.

79. Contractor D, Amling J, Brandoli C, Tosi LL. Negative pressure wound therapy with reticulated open cell foam in children: an overview. *J Orthop Trauma.* 2008;22(suppl 10):S167-S176.

80. Morykwas MJ, Argenta LC, Shelton-Brown EI, McGuirt W. Vacuum-assisted closure: a new method for wound control and treatment: animal studies and basic foundation. *Ann Plast Surg.* 1997;38(6):553-562.

81. Silva JA, Alvares RA, Barboza AL, Monteiro RT. Lower urinary tract dysfunction in children with cerebral palsy. *Neurourol Urodyn.* 2009;28(8):959-963.

82. Murphy KP, Boutin SA, Ide KR. Cerebral palsy, neurogenic bladder, and outcomes of lifetime care. *Dev Med Child Neurol.* 2012;54(10):945-950.

83. Chancellor MB, Anderson RU, Boone TB. Pharmacotherapy for neurogenic detrusor overactivity. *Am J Phys Med Rehabil.* 2006;85(6):536-545.

84. Ellsworth P, Cone EB. Neurogenic detrusor overactivity: an update on management options. *R I Med J.* 2013;96(4):38-40.

85. Karaman MI, Kaya C, Caskurlu T, Guney S, Ergenekon E. Urodynamic findings in children with cerebral palsy. *Int J Urol.* 2005;12(8):717-720.

86. Wang MH, Harvey J, Baskin L. Management of neurogenic bladder in patients with cerebral palsy. *J Pediatr Rehabil Med.* 2008;1(2):123-125.

87. Reid CJ, Borzyskowski M. Lower urinary tract dysfunction in cerebral palsy. *Arch Dis Child.* 1993;68(6):739-742.

88. Evans P, Elliott M, Alberman E, Evans S. Prevalence and disabilities in 4 to 8 year olds with cerebral palsy. *Arch Dis Child.* 1985;60(10):940-945.

89. Odding E, Roebroeck ME, Stam HJ. The epidemiology of cerebral palsy: incidence, impairments and risk factors. *Disabil Rehabil.* 2006;28(4):183-191.

90. Msall ME. Neurodevelopmental surveillance in the first 2 years after extremely preterm birth: evidence, challenges, and guidelines. *Early Hum Dev.* 2006;82(3):157-166.

91. Birman CS, Elliott EJ, Gibson WP. Pediatric cochlear implants: additional disabilities prevalence, risk factors, and effect on language outcomes. *Otol Neurotol.* 2012;33(8):1347-1352.

92. Byun H, Moon IJ, Kim EY, et al. Performance after timely cochlear implantation in prelingually deaf children with cerebral palsy. *Int J Pediatr Otolaryngol.* 2013;77(6):1013-1018.

93. Özdemir S, Tuncer Ü, Tarkan Ö, Kiroglu M, Çetik F, Akar F. Factors contributing to limited or non-use in the cochlear implant systems in children: 11 years experience. *Int J Pediatr Otolaryngol.* 2013;77(3):407-409.

94. O'Donoghue GM. Cochlear implants in children: principles, practice and predictions. *J R Soc Med.* 1996;89(6):345P-347P.

95. Loundon N, Blanchard M, Roger G, Denoyelle F, Garabedian EN. Medical and surgical complications in pediatric cochlear implantation. *Arch Otolaryngol Head Neck Surg.* 2010;136(1):12-15.

96. Pueyo R, Junqué C, Vendrell P, Narberhaus A, Segarra D. Neuropsychologic impairment in bilateral cerebral palsy. *Pediatr Neurol.* 2009;40(1):19-26.

97. Guzzetta A, Cioni G, Cowan F, Mercuri E. Visual disorders in children with brain lesions: 1. Maturation of visual function in infants with neonatal brain lesions: correlation with neuroimaging. *Eur J Paediatr Neurol.* 2001;5(3):107-114.

98. Guzzetta A, Mercuri E, Cioni G. Visual disorders in children with brain lesions: 2. Visual impairment associated with cerebral palsy. *Eur J Paediatr Neurol.* 2001;5(3):115-119.

99. Dutton GN, Jacobson LK. Cerebral visual impairment in children. *Semin Neonatol.* 2001;6(6):477-485.

100. Jackson J, Castleberry C, Galli M, Arnoldi KA. Cerebral palsy for the pediatric eye care team – part II: diagnosis and treatment of ocular motor deficits. *Am Orthopt J.* 2006;56:86-96.

101. Arnoldi KA, Pendarvis L, Jackson J, Batra NN. Cerebral palsy for the pediatric eye care team – part III: diagnosis and management of associated visual and sensory disorders. *Am Orthopt J.* 2006;56:97-107.

102. Scheiman M. Three component model of vision, part two: visual efficiency skills. In: Scheiman M, ed. *Understanding and Managing Vision Deficits: A Guide for Occupational Therapists.* 3rd ed. Thorofare, NJ: SLACK Incorporated; 2011:57-78.

103. Appel SD, Ciner EB. Oculo-visual disorders associated with developmental and sensory disabilities. In: Scheiman M, ed. *Understanding and Managing Vision Deficits: A Guide for Occupational Therapists.* 3rd ed. Thorofare, NJ: SLACK Incorporated ; 2011:233-251.

104. Ciner EB, Appel SD, Graboyes M. Management of vision problems for children with special needs. In: Scheiman M, ed. *Understanding and Managing Vision Deficits: A Guide for Occupational Therapists.* 3rd ed. Thorofare, NJ: SLACK Incorporated; 2011:253-275.

105. Ma DJ, Yang HK, Hwang JM. Surgical outcomes of medial rectus recession in esotropia with cerebral palsy. *Ophthalmology.* 2013;120(4):663-667.

106. Petrushkin H, Oyewole K, Jain S. Botulinum toxin for the treatment of early-onset esotropia in children with cerebral palsy. *J Pediatr Ophthalmol Strabismus.* 2012;49(2):125.

107. Malgorzata M, Wojciech K, Alina BŁ, Artur B. Botulinum toxin injection as primary treatment for esotropia in patients with cerebral palsy. *Klin Oczna.* 2013;115(1):13-14.

Pain Assessment and Management

Roberta Henderson, PT, PhD and Mary Rahlin, PT, DHS, PCS

Pain assessment and management should be part of the educational curriculum of all health professionals who care for children.

American Pain Society Pediatric Chronic Pain Task Force[1]

Pain may bring about significant physical and psychological sequelae for children and their families, and yet, the pain experience of children is poorly understood and often difficult to assess due to the subjective nature of pain and the child's lack of verbal skill required for its self-report.[1-3] Pain assessment by physical therapists has implications for intervention planning and selection, establishing the diagnosis and prognosis, and evaluating intervention efficacy and outcomes.[4] Pain itself can be a limiting factor in physical therapy sessions, performance of home exercise and activity programs, and in the quality of a child's life.[2,5] Thus, it is imperative for physical therapists to include assessment and management of pain in pediatric clinical practice.[2]

The physical sensation of pain is a universal experience of the human condition, including that of infants and children.[1-3,6] Pain is now regarded as the fifth vital sign.[3,7] There has been an implicit common assumption that pain in adults differs from pain in infants and children.[6,8,9] Much more attention has been historically devoted to pain in adults.[10] Far less is known about pain in infants and children, although it can undeniably affect all aspects of their lives.[10]

The International Association for the Study of Pain (IASP)[11] defines pain as "an unpleasant sensory and emotional experience associated with actual or potential tissue damage, or described in terms of such damage." Pain is a subjective construct, and "each individual learns the application of the word through experiences related to injury in early life." This definition links pain *early in life* to that of the adult, suggests an evolution of the pain experience, and, as such, declares that pain in infants and children differs from adult pain.[11] This generates important questions. How do past experiences of pain and environment influence an infant's or child's pain and his or her experience of pain as an adult? How do infants and children perceive and express pain, and what factors influence these processes? What effect does the child's pain have on the caregiver and the family? How can pain be meaningfully assessed and effectively managed in pediatric clinical practice?

Historically, assessment of pain in infants and children was not a priority of the clinician.[2,3,6,10] Perhaps this is because of a presumption that a child's pain is somehow less than that of an adult, acceptance of the inevitable presence of pain in children resulting from falls and play, inability of infants and some children to verbalize the pain experience, increasing demands on the clinician in the clinical setting, or insufficient knowledge of valid and reliable pain assessment methods. Lacking formal pain assessment, pain was underestimated and undertreated in infants and children of all ages.[2,3,6,10]

Rahlin M. *Physical Therapy for Children With Cerebral Palsy: An Evidence-Based Approach* (pp 157-169).

More recently, pain assessment and management in pediatric populations were recognized as important problems. In the past 2 decades, numerous national and international clinical practice guidelines and policy statements pertaining specifically to pain in infants and children were developed.[1,2,12,13] Examples range from an international consensus statement for prevention and management of pain in the newborn,[12] to a position statement by the American Pain Society detailing assessment and management of chronic pain in children,[1] to clinical practice recommendations for pain assessment in the nonverbal patient.[13] In a recent survey study of physical therapists in pediatric practice, most stated that it was important to assess and manage pain in infants and children, yet reported using a limited number of pain assessment scales.[14] Furthermore, most of the pain scales that they used did not universally meet their patients' pain assessment needs nor did all the respondents routinely apply the results of pain assessment in their practice.[14]

PAIN IN INFANTS AND CHILDREN

The IASP definition of pain[11] suggests that, in addition to the immediate effects of pain on the child, there are future, less obvious implications. Research has demonstrated that pain early in life is related to future differences in pain perception and behavior.[15-19] A child's pain perception and behavior are influenced by a multitude of personal and environmental factors, including age, gender, level of development, verbal and cognitive ability, context, cultural and social influences, as well as prior experiences and duration of pain.[1,20]

Acute Pain in Infants and Its Sequelae

For a long time, it was thought that newborns experienced less pain than older children and adults due to the immaturity of their nervous system.[2,16,21] We now know from animal and developmental studies that, although the ascending pain transmission pathways are developed by 20 weeks gestational age, the development of descending inhibitory pathways lags behind.[16,21] This suggests that preterm neonates may actually have more pain than older infants and children.[16,21] Furthermore, in response to recurrent painful stimuli and experiences, it appears that newborns are particularly vulnerable because of increased excitability in the nociceptive neurons of the dorsal horn resulting in hyperalgesia that persists and alters pain perception in childhood and, perhaps, as an adult.[21-25] Acute pain exposure in the Neonatal Intensive Care Unit (NICU) was shown to heighten motor responses of preterm neonates to clustered care[15] and change stress responses to novelty stimuli later in infancy.[17] In addition, the available evidence points to potential alterations in long-term social-emotional and neurodevelopmental functioning related to prolonged and repeated episodes of physical pain experienced in early infancy.[18,23]

Chronic Pain in Infants and Children

Chronic pain in infants is difficult to define.[26] According to a 2012 position statement from the American Pain Society, chronic pain is "persistent and recurring pain" that continues "beyond the expected healing time" of 3 to 6 months.[1] However, this definition cannot be applied to neonates and young infants hospitalized in the NICU who experience persistent pain because they may not have lived as long as 3 or 6 months and because their "expected healing time" may not be the same as in a child or in an adult.[26] Pillai Riddell et al[26] researched the parameters for the definition and assessment of chronic pain in infants. These authors interviewed 45 expert clinicians of different disciplines working in several NICUs and Pediatric Intensive Care Units (PICUs). The following categories of symptoms potentially indicative of chronic pain in infants were identified:

- Inability to settle or restlessness
- Body tension
- Constant grimacing
- Hypo- and hyper-reactivity to painful stimuli manifested as absent or heightened responses, respectively
- Disrupted feeding and sleeping patterns
- Social withdrawal

These findings can serve as the foundation for the development of the definition of chronic pain in future studies.[26]

The definition of chronic pain provided earlier implies that chronic pain differs appreciably from acute self-limited pain following a direct bodily injury in that it persists or recurs beyond an expected time for healing.[1] As such, the perception and behavioral manifestations of chronic pain are the result of operant biological processes and psychological, cultural, and social factors. In chronic pain, central sensitization occurs, characterized by generalized increased responsiveness to stimuli. Thus, manifestation of chronic pain can include fatigue as well as sleep, mood, and cognitive dysfunctions.[1] Chronic pain in children negatively affects their quality of life regardless of etiology.[1,5,27] Pain may have an impact on school attendance and social participation,[28] and there appears to be a relationship between the intensity of pain and depression.[29,30] Research substantiates that children with cerebral palsy (CP) who have pain also have a significantly lower quality of life.[31]

Children with CP regularly experience pain and, for some, it is a daily occurrence.[5,32-36] Pain in children and adults with this condition may originate in multiple body systems (see Chapter 4 and Table 4-1).[33,37-39] Pain etiology can be classified into 6 categories: gastrointestinal, orthopedic, neuromuscular, procedural, rehabilitative, and surgical.[36] Gastrointestinal problems that may cause pain in individuals with CP include gastroesophageal reflux, gastrostomy tube infection, constipation, and other colorectal and gastrointestinal disturbances.[5,36,40,41] Orthopedic causative agents include biomechanical abnormalities and musculoskeletal deformities.[36-38] Spasticity is the primary neuromuscular causative agent,[5] with radiculopathy, myelopathy, and nerve entrapment also playing a role.[36,42] The rehabilitative etiology of pain is related to therapeutic procedures that are designed to improve the child's functioning and, paradoxically, reduce pain.[36] In a survey study by Hadden and von Baeyer,[43] stretching was identified as a painful intervention by 93% of parents of children with CP. Other rehabilitative causative agents included donning splints and performing functional activities, such as assisted sitting, independent standing, and assisted walking.[43] Physical therapists working with this patient population need to be aware of the impact the interventions they provide may have on the child's motivation to participate in therapy and on future health and fitness behaviors, if these interventions are associated with pain.[5,36]

In a recent Canadian study of 230 adolescents with CP, 64% of girls and 50% of boys reported experiencing pain within the past month, most frequently in the feet, ankles, knees, or lower back.[44] Overall, pain intensity was surprisingly high, and a strong negative correlation with performance of daily activities was found (Spearman rho = 0.75, p < 0.01, for girls and Spearman rho = 0.82, p < 0.01, for boys).[44] Similar findings came from a large parallel European study, in which the prevalence of self-reported pain within the past week was 60% while prevalence of parent-reported pain was 73%. In addition, the parent-reported but not self-reported frequency and severity of pain correlated with the severity of the child's impairment.[45]

Russo et al[31] demonstrated the lack of correlation between the level of physical involvement and presence and severity of pain in children with unilateral CP who are typically classified in the Gross Motor Function Classification System (GMFCS)[46] level I. Of 107 study participants, 48% reported having pain that was mostly mild in severity, described as aching, and was present most frequently on the involved side of the body. However, 35% of children who had pain described it as moderate to severe; in 29%, pain was present bilaterally or on the uninvolved side; and 43% of participants reported tingling, sharp, numb, or burning sensations. Pain affected movement and activity and was aggravated by movement, immobility, and fatigue. In addition, children who reported chronic pain, compared to those without pain, achieved significantly lower scores on the Pediatric Quality of Life Inventory[47] and the Self-Perception Profile for Children,[48] which indicated negative effects of pain on quality of life and self-concept.[31]

Another important finding in the study by Russo et al[31] was that only 16% of children who experienced pain were treated with medication, while the most common methods of pain relief were massage, sleep, and rest, or a combination of these nonpharmacological methods. Furthermore, in 14% of the participants who reported pain, it was not addressed. The authors explained these findings by the families' and clinicians' perception of pain as being an inevitable part of the child's medical condition resulting in families not seeking and clinicians not offering pharmacological interventions.[31]

These findings underscore the importance of pain assessment and management in children with CP regardless of their GMFCS[46] level.[31] Other related research showed that chronic pain can negatively impact activities of daily living (ADLs), life-style, mobility, self-care, productivity, and leisure, and that prevalence of pain may increase with age as evidenced by studies of adolescents and adults with CP.[32,38,44,49] Health professionals should be prepared to address this problem in their daily practice and educate their patients and their families about pain being common and treatable.[31]

Effects of the Child's Pain on the Caregiver

Pain experienced by their child is worrisome for parents. Published research highlighted the negative impact the child's pain may have on the caregivers, including dissatisfaction with pain management; loss of income that may result from taking time off of work to care for a child with chronic pain; and negative changes in marital well-being, mood, parenting, stress, and overall functioning.[50-53] Complex manifestations and effects of chronic pain need to be addressed early through careful assessment and appropriate intervention designed to improve function, participation, and quality of life for the children and their families.[1]

ASSESSMENT OF PAIN IN INFANTS, CHILDREN, AND ADOLESCENTS

The importance of pain assessment and management was emphasized by the publication and enforcement of related standards by the Joint Commission on Accreditation of Healthcare Organizations in 2000.[54] These standards stipulated that patients had the right to have their pain appropriately assessed and managed and outlined the related responsibilities of accredited health care organizations that were to be addressed from the patient's admission to discharge.[54] Consequently, interest in all aspects of pain assessment and management increased, and so did efforts to implement them.[55]

Instruments to assess pain in infants and children are classified as physiological (biological), observational (behavioral), and self-report.[55] Physiological measures include heart rate, oxygen saturation, sweating, and stress hormone levels. Observational instruments are used to assess such pain behaviors as body movements, facial expressions, and vocalizations. The use of self-report instruments involves obtaining information about the pain experience from the child, which may include the use of pain adjective lists; direct questioning; visual analog scales (VAS); category rating and numerical rating scales; and nonverbal assessment methods, such as pain drawings.[55] Both observational and self-report measures are problematic because they elicit subjective assessment of a subjective phenomenon. In adults, such scales are often underused and misinterpreted by clinicians.[56-59] The additional challenge in pediatric populations is to assess pain in an infant or a child who cannot understand the construct of pain and cannot verbalize to offer self-report.[55]

Selection of a specific pain scale depends on multiple factors, including the child's age, level of development, ability to communicate and cognitive ability, and assessment context.[55] Behavioral scales are specifically indicated for infants and children younger than age 6 years, as well as for children with intellectual disability that would limit the use of a self-report scale. Self-report "faces" scales can generally be used by children older than age 6 years. At 8 years of age, children are typically able to use self-report visual analog and numerical rating scales to assess their pain.[55]

Pain Assessment Scales for Neonates and Infants

Numerous pain scales and their revisions are available for use with infants and children, yet few are universally known and used in the pediatric physical therapy practice.[14] Several scales with established psychometric properties are available for the assessment of acute procedural or postoperative pain in preterm and full-term neonates.[60-66] Examples include the Neonatal Infant Pain Scale (NIPS),[60-62] Premature Infant Pain Profile (PIPP),[63,64] and Crying, Requires increased oxygen administration, Increased vital signs, Expression, Sleeplessness (CRIES).[65,66] A revised version of the PIPP (PIPP-R) was also recently developed.[67,68] The NIPS uses 6 behavioral indicators, including cry, facial expression, breathing pattern, motor activity in upper and lower extremities, and state of arousal.[60,61] The PIPP is composed of 3 observational facial expression indicators, 2 physiological indicators, such as oxygen saturation and heart rate, and 2 contextual indicators, including the infant's behavioral state and gestational age.[63,64] The CRIES instrument also uses a combination of observational and physiological indicators that were found to be reflective of neonatal pain.[65] The observational variables include crying, expression, and sleeplessness, and physiological variables include vital signs and oxygen administration requirement.[65]

Conversely to acute pain, chronic pain in neonates and young infants is much more difficult to define and assess, although important ground work for the development of the definition of chronic pain in this population has begun.[26] Scales developed for assessment of persistent or prolonged pain in neonates and preterm infants use varied indicators and observation timing, which, again, points to the need to define pain that persists beyond acute.[26] The EDIN (Échelle Douleur Inconfort Nouveau-Né) scale developed in France is an example of an observational instrument validated for use with preterm neonates.[69] It has 5 behavioral indicators of prolonged pain: facial activity, body movements, quality of sleep, quality of contact with nurses, and consolability. Each is scored on a 4-point scale from 0 to 3, with a concise description provided for each score. The internal consistency of the EDIN scale was established with Cronbach's alpha of 0.86-0.94.[69] Its interrater reliability was found to be moderate,[70] with weighted Kappa varying from 0.59 to 0.74.[69]

Other examples of such scales include the Neonatal Pain, Agitation and Sedation Scale (N-PASS)[71] and the COMFORT scale.[72,73] The N-PASS is a measure of prolonged acute pain and sedation in preterm infants assessed postoperatively and during mechanical ventilation.[71] It has good psychometric properties, including construct validity, internal consistency, and interrater reliability. Its convergent validity with the PIPP was shown by obtaining a Spearman rho of 0.61 to 0.83 for low and high pain scores, respectively.[71]

The COMFORT scale was originally developed to assess distress in infants, children, and adolescents hospitalized in the PICU[72] and was subsequently validated for the NICU use with ventilated infants born prematurely.[73] It is a reliable and valid instrument that rates 8 behaviors, including alertness, calmness/agitation, respiratory response, physical movement, mean arterial blood pressure, heart rate, muscle tone, and facial tension, on a scale from 1 to 5, with a total score varying from 8 to 40.[72] Ambuel et al[72] reported moderate to good[70] interrater reliability for each of the scale dimensions and the total score, with Pearson r equal to 0.51-0.75 and 0.84, respectively. Strong evidence of internal consistency of the scale was also demonstrated, with correlations between the individual items and the total score varying from 0.60 to 0.90, except for the Muscle Tone dimension with r=0.30. Finally, construct validity of the COMFORT scale was established by obtaining a correlation of 0.75 between its total scores and VAS ratings assigned by experienced nurses.[72]

Pain Assessment Scales for Children and Adolescents With and Without Disabilities

Multiple pain measures have been developed for toddlers, children, and adolescents, with many of them used to assess postoperative or procedural pain in children without developmental or intellectual disabilities. Scale examples include such self-report measures as the Poker Chip Tool, which is also known as the Pieces of Hurt,[74-76] the Wong-Baker FACES scale,[75-77] the Faces Pain Scale-Revised,[78-81] the Oucher,[82-86] and the VAS.[80,84,87-89] In their systematic review of self-report pain scales, Stinson et al[89] found these instruments to have sound psychometric properties. In addition, this review revealed that all of these scales can be used in assessment of acute and disease-related or chronic pain in children, except for the Poker Chip Tool/Pieces of Hurt,[74] which is not appropriate for the evaluation of chronic or recurrent pain.[89]

The Poker Chip Tool/Pieces of Hurt is administered by asking the child to select the number of red poker chips that represents his or her amount of pain, with 1 chip representing "a little hurt" and 4 chips corresponding to "the most hurt you could ever have," with pain intensity scored from 0 to 4.[74,89] To administer the Wong-Baker FACES Pain Rating Scale, the child is asked to point to 1 of the 6 face drawings that are arranged from smiling ("no hurt") to crying ("hurts worst") to identify how much pain he or she has, which is scored from 0 to 10.[75] The Faces Pain Scale-Revised also uses 6 faces but yields a score from 0 to 5 or 0 to 10, with the score of 0 being "no pain," and the score of 5 or 10 indicating the "most pain possible," reflected in corresponding facial expressions.[78] The Oucher tool combines a photographic face scale scored from 0 to 5 with a vertical numerical rating scale that has a score range from 0 to 100.[82,89] Finally, the VAS is a premeasured horizontal or vertical line, on which the child marks a spot to report pain intensity.[89]

Based on their systematic review of literature, Stinson et al[89] provided age-related recommendations for the use of these self-report pain scales with children and adolescents in clinical trials. The Poker Chip Tool/Pieces of Hurt[74] was suggested as the best instrument for preschool children; the Faces Pain Scale-Revised[78] for children of school age; and the VAS[87] for older school-aged children and adolescents. The Faces Pain Scale-Revised,[78] the Wong-Baker FACES Pain Rating Scale,[75] and the Oucher scales would also be quite appropriate for the older age group.[89] In addition, a Coloured Analogue Scale (CAS) was suggested as an easier to administer alternative to the VAS for clinical application with younger children.[89,90]

The administration of self-report instruments may not be feasible with children who are unable to report pain verbally or understand its construct.[55] This may be the case when the child is too young or has an intellectual disability. It may be difficult to distinguish the signs and symptoms of pain in children with intellectual and developmental disabilities from the signs of stress or general arousal and, in some cases, children demonstrate atypical expressions of pain.[91] Historically, the majority of pain research excluded children with developmental disabilities, which resulted in a limited number of available assessment options. At the same time, it is important to remember that, while pain behaviors in children with disabilities may be more difficult to understand, this does not mean that these children do not have pain or have less pain than children developing typically. Therefore, it is imperative that clinicians take into the account the child's cognitive level when selecting the most appropriate pain scale for clinical use. As suggested by current evidence, self-report measures may not be the best choice for children with developmental and intellectual disabilities, which makes observational instruments most useful.[91] Table 10-1 contains information on some of the more commonly used and researched observational pain scales that can be administered with this patient population.[55,88,92-103]

Besides pain scales, other instruments can be used in pediatric practice to assess pain and its impact on function and quality of life in children and adolescents with CP. Examples of such instruments include the CP Module of the Pediatric Quality of Life Inventory (PedsQL)[104] that contains a Pain and Hurt scale and can be administered by child self-report or parent proxy-report; the Cerebral Palsy Quality of Life Instrument for children with CP (CP QOL-Child)[105] that has a Pain and Impact of Disability subscale; and the Caregiver Priorities and Child Health Index of Life with Disabilities (CPCHILD),[106] a parent-report measure that includes a Comfort and Emotions section with 7 questions inquiring about frequency and intensity of pain or discomfort the child experienced in the past 2 weeks (see Chapter 11 and Table 11-17).

PAIN MANAGEMENT IN INFANTS, CHILDREN, AND ADOLESCENTS

In light of the future consequences of experiencing pain early in life, it is important to minimize pain in infants and children to the extent possible.[1,107] Barriers to pain management in children include the lack of knowledge of the pathophysiological mechanisms of pain, reluctance to address pain with pharmacologic agents, beliefs and values of health care professionals, and the lack of awareness of appropriate pain assessment instruments.[6]

Recognizing that an infant or a child is in pain is an important first step in its management.[107] Besides the administration of pain scales, behavioral cues are most often used for this purpose. The child's irritability, facial expressions, vocalizations, and crying were found to be the behavioral cues most commonly used by physical therapists.[20] The next most common cues were muscle tone changes, reluctance to participate in activities, withdrawal, and requests for rest.[20] Once pain presence is identified, it needs to be addressed by selecting the most appropriate strategy. Pain management includes pharmacological and nonpharmacological methods. Although physical therapists do not routinely administer pain medications, they need to be aware of pharmacological approaches to pain management in infants and children.

Pharmacological Methods of Pain Management

Pharmacological methods of pain management are used with reservation related to the potential for side-effects and challenges of dosage, particularly in the neonate, because of the physiologic and metabolic immaturity.[107] To be effective, near-toxic doses of analgesics may have to be used. *Balanced analgesia*, the use of more than one approach to pain management simultaneously, can be employed to address this issue, with a lower dose of each medication necessary to achieve a cumulative analgesic effect. Infants born prematurely who require prolonged mechanical ventilation frequently experience such painful procedures as venipuncture, placement of an intravenous catheter, or lumbar puncture. According to a Policy Statement of the American Academy of Pediatrics and the Canadian Paediatric Society, continuous infusions of sedatives and pain medications such as morphine, midazolam, or fentanyl are no longer recommended in ventilated neonates born preterm.[107] Adverse effects of such drugs in this patient population include a significantly longer need for administration of mechanical ventilation,[108-110] increased ventilator setting requirements,[109] and unchanged or increased risk of poor neurologic outcomes.[107,110,111]

Topical local anesthetics are helpful for reduction of pain from minor needle procedures in infants born prematurely and full-term, except for the heel-stick blood draws, for which nonpharmacological pain management is recommended.[107] Topical medications are also used in children for similar procedures that may cause anxiety and pain.[112,113]

	TABLE 10-1	
	BRIEF DESCRIPTION AND PSYCHOMETRIC PROPERTIES OF SELECTED OBSERVATIONAL PAIN SCALES THAT CAN BE USED FOR CHILDREN AND ADOLESCENTS WITH DEVELOPMENTAL AND INTELLECTUAL DISABILITIES	
PAIN SCALE	**BRIEF DESCRIPTION**	**PSYCHOMETRIC PROPERTIES**[a]
Children's Hospital of Eastern Ontario Pain Scales (CHEOPS)[55,88,92-95]	Used for assessment of postoperative and procedural pain in children aged 1 to 12 years, including children with intellectual disabilities Scores 6 behaviors, including cry (1-3), facial (0-2), child verbal (0-2), torso (1-2), touch (1-2) and legs (1-2) Total score range: 4-13	*Intrarater reliability:* ICC = 0.87-0.99[94] *Inter-rater reliability:* r = 0.90-0.99[92] ICC = 0.92[94] ICC = 0.54-0.72[95] Cohen's Kappa = 0.50-0.61[95] *Concurrent validity with the VAS, Faces Scale, FLACC, other scales:* Pearson r = 0.74-0.92[88] Spearman rho = 0.62-0.82[94]
Face, Leg, Activity, Cry, Consolability (FLACC) scale[93,96-98]	Used for assessment of post-operative pain in children aged 2 months to 19 years, including those with cognitive impairment Scores from 0 to 2 are obtained in each of 5 categories included in the scale title A revised and individualized version with specific descriptors and unique behaviors identified by parents is available[98] Total score range: 0-10	*Inter-rater reliability:* Weighted kappa = 0.85[97] Simple kappa = 0.73-0.91[97] ICC = 0.76-0.90[98] *Concurrent validity with the CAS:* Spearman rho = 0.50-0.59[97] *Criterion validity:* Spearman rho = 0.65-0.87[98]
Non-Communicating Children's Pain Checklist-Revised (NCCPC-R)[99] and Non-Communicating Children's Pain Checklist – Postoperative Version (NCCPC-PV)[100]	Used for assessment of pain related to a chronic condition, illness, injury, medical procedure or an unknown cause in children with intellectual disabilities aged 3-18 years[99] Scores items on each of 7 subscales (vocal, eating/sleeping, social, facial, activity, body/limb, and physiological signs) from 0 to 3 based on observation frequency within 2 hours The postoperative version does not include the Eating/Sleeping subscale and uses a 10-minute observation[100] Total score range: 0-90	*Internal consistency:* Cronbach's alpha = 0.91-0.93[99,100] Established discriminant validity[99] *Cut-off score:* A total score of 7 or > indicates presence of pain with 84% sensitivity, 77% specificity[99] *Inter-rater reliability:* Pearson r = 0.72[100]
		(continued)

However, limiting the repeated use of topical anesthetics is recommended because of their link to methemoglobinemia.[107,114,115] Alternatives to anesthetic creams and gels that can be used in children in some instances include lidocaine iontophoresis and vapocoolant sprays.[113]

Aspirin use is not recommended for children due to its link to Reye's syndrome (hepatic encephalopathy); however, it is still helpful in the management of pain associated with rheumatologic conditions and in inhibition of platelet aggregation.[112,116] *Acetaminophen*, which replaced aspirin, is widely used in children for fever control and mild analgesia.[112] *Nonsteroidal anti-inflammatory drugs (NSAIDs)* are effective in decreasing mild to moderate pain, inflammation, and fever, and can be also used in combination with opioids for

TABLE 10-1 (CONTINUED)		
BRIEF DESCRIPTION AND PSYCHOMETRIC PROPERTIES OF SELECTED OBSERVATIONAL PAIN SCALES THAT CAN BE USED FOR CHILDREN AND ADOLESCENTS WITH DEVELOPMENTAL AND INTELLECTUAL DISABILITIES		
PAIN SCALE	**BRIEF DESCRIPTION**	**PSYCHOMETRIC PROPERTIES[a]**
Pediatric Pain Profile (PPP)[91,101-103]	Used for assessment and monitoring of pain over time in children "with severe to profound" neurologic impairment aged 1 to 18 years	*Internal consistency:* Cronbach's alpha = 0.75-0.89[101]
	A semi-individualized parent-held record of the child's pain (parents retrospectively rate the child's behavior "on a good day" and on a day when they had "most troublesome pain" that provides a baseline for future assessments)	*Intrarater reliability:* ICC = 0.90[102] *Inter-rater reliability:* ICC = 0.70-0.87[101] ICC = 0.62[102]
	Can be used across a variety of settings	*Concurrent validity with a NRS:* Pearson r = 0.76-0.90[102]
	May be difficult to use in inpatient settings[103]	*Cut-off scores:*
	Scores 20 items from 0 ("not at all") to 3 ("a great deal") based on the amount of time a behavior was observed during a specific time period, with an "unable to assess" option available	A total raw score of 14.4 (24%) or > indicates moderate or worse pain with 100% sensitivity, 95% specificity[102]
	Total score range: 0-60	A total raw score of 7.5 (12.5%) or > indicates mild or worse pain with 100% sensitivity, 88% specificity[102]

Abbreviations: CAS, Coloured Analogue Scale; ICC, intraclass correlation coefficient; NRS, Numerical Rating Scale.

[a] Not all inclusive.

severe pain and perioperatively.[112,113,117] However, NSAIDs' side effects may include gastritis, gastric or duodenal ulceration, and bleeding.[113,117] Selective cyclooxygenase-2 (COX-2) inhibitors is a class of NSAIDs designed to decrease the occurrence of such side effects.[112,113] *Tramadol* is another analgesic intended for mild to moderate acute or chronic pain.[113] Although it is thought to have a low potential for addiction, physical dependence may still occur, and withdrawal symptoms may be present if it is discontinued abruptly.[113]

Opioids (morphine or fentanyl) are widely used postoperatively in infants, children, and adolescents.[112,113] Oral *long-acting opioids*, such as oxycodone and morphine, can be prescribed for chronic pain but not for acute pain management; however, their use has decreased due to the associated fear of drug abuse.[113] Other side effects of opioids include constipation, dysphoria, pruritus, sedation, and respiratory depression. *Gabapentin* (typically prescribed for partial seizures) as well as other antiepileptic drugs can be helpful in treating chronic neuropathic pain; and *alpha-2 agonists*, such as clonidine, typically prescribed for hypertension, can be effective in the management of intraoperative, postoperative, and chronic pain, and in reduction of withdrawal symptoms in patients being weaned off opioids.[113]

Management of pain in children with neurologic disorders, including CP, requires special attention because, for a long time, it was handled inadequately as reflected in recent literature.[5,20,91,113,118] Besides the pharmacological methods of pain management examined previously, knowledge of medical interventions specifically aimed at reducing pain with neuromuscular and musculoskeletal etiology in this patient population is important for physical therapists. Children with CP frequently undergo surgical procedures and suffer from pain-inducing alterations of body structures, such as spasticity, contractures, and musculoskeletal deformities.[118] Intrathecal baclofen (ITB) therapy and botulinum toxin A (BTX-A) injections that are used to manage spasticity in children and adults with CP were reported to be effective in decreasing spasticity-related pain in this patient population.[119-123] In addition, there is evidence derived from a double-blind randomized placebo-controlled trial that BTX-A can be effective in reducing postoperative pain, analgesia requirement, and hospital stay in children with CP classified in GMFCS[46] levels IV and V.[123,124] Perioperative methods of pain management have been also explored, and epidural analgesia has been suggested as a superior alternative to the systemic pain management method for selective dorsal rhizotomy and, potentially, some other surgeries.[125]

Nonpharmacological Methods of Pain Management

Nonpharmacological methods of pain management are preferred for infants and children, when possible,[107,113] with the recommendation to use a child-centered approach in a child-friendly environment.[6,126] To the extent possible, the child should be involved in making decisions about pain management, and the caregiver and family involved in a positive way as active assistants, not merely to provide passive restraint. This approach promotes autonomy and control on the part of the participants, as well as effective therapeutic relationships with a focus on the child. When appropriate, a combination of pharmacological and nonpharmacological methods of pain control should be used.[6,126]

Nonpharmacological interventions are often described as psychological or psychosocial methods of pain management that can be categorized into cognitive and behavioral teachniques.[5,6,127] Some examples of cognitive interventions are imagery, providing the child with information about pain and painful procedures, and instruction in positive coping strategies.[6] Breathing exercises, positive reinforcement with rewards for desired behaviors, and desensitization by gradually introducing a painful procedure are some examples of behavioral interventions.[6] Distraction is a commonly used nonpharmacological intervention in which a child's attention is diverted toward an activity and away from the pain experience.[5,6,127] Distraction can be passive, with the child's attention drawn away from pain by actions of another (eg, someone talking, singing, or reading a book to the child) or by having the child listen to music.[6,128,129] In active distraction, the child actually participates in an activity during a painful procedure.[6,128,129]

The nonpharmacological interventions should be age appropriate. Table 10-2 compiled from multiple sources contains suggestions for the selection of such interventions for procedural and needle-related pain in infants, children, and adolescents.[6,107,126,127,129-142]

Literature related to the effectiveness of nonpharmacological methods of pain management in children and adolescents with developmental disabilities and, specifically, those with CP, is sparse at best.[5,20] Furthermore, there is a paucity of available information in regard to physical therapy interventions as causative agents of pain and as methods of pain management in this patient population.

Physical Therapy Interventions for Pain Management in Children and Adults With Cerebral Palsy

Results of a survey conducted with pediatric physical therapists showed that, among 107 respondents, the most frequently used interventions to manage therapy-related pain were distraction, talking during a painful procedure, and praise.[20] Other commonly used interventions included allowing rest periods, relaxation, and calming techniques.

Massage, rewards, and reassurance were used less frequently, and the least common interventions for rehabilitative pain included the use of thermal agents and transcutaneous electrical nerve stimulation.[20] Another important finding was that some of the therapists thought that, contrary to published literature,[36,43] pain was not present during physical therapy sessions.[20] Furthermore, while the use of appropriate methods of pain management, such as caregiver-generated distraction and self-coping strategies, were reported by some of the respondents, others used strategies that the researchers found to be "potentially harmful," such as pain-contingent rest and apologizing for inflicting pain.[20]

Chronic pain management in adults with CP was studied by several authors.[120,143-146] Physical therapy interventions and coping strategies that were found to be helpful were biofeedback-assisted relaxation,[120,143] exercise,[120,144] and task persistence,[145] while resting, catastrophizing, and seeking social support were associated with depression and pain-related disability.[145,146] Biofeedback-assisted autogenic relaxation was shown to reduce pain intensity in 2 of 3 adults with CP who used this intervention in a multiple baseline design study.[143] In the follow-up period, pain remained at a lower level of intensity or continued to decrease.[143] As for the exercise intervention, Vogtle et al[144] reported significant decrease in pain and fatigue experienced by ambulatory adults with CP who participated in a nonstandardized community-based exercise program 3 times per week for 1 hour over a period of 3 months. Chair exercises; sit to stand transitions; leg exercises; arm ergometer or stationary bicycle; and flexibility, resistive strengthening, and endurance activities were included. Unfortunately, the nonambulatory adults with CP who participated in this study reported a significant increase in lower extremity pain. Hypothetically, this negative result might be avoided if the participants were transferred out of their chairs for the duration of the class sessions, and if different, more appropriate activities were included in their exercise programs. These hypotheses will need to be explored in future research.[144]

IMPLICATIONS FOR FUTURE RESEARCH AND PEDIATRIC PHYSICAL THERAPY PRACTICE

The assessment and management of pain in infants and children of all ages are receiving increasing attention from pediatric physical therapists. In a recent survey study of this professional group, all respondents stated that pain in infants and children should be assessed.[14] Most participants reported that they thought that pain medication was appropriate for infants and very young children, that the lack of pain expression did not indicate the lack of pain, and that children were the most accurate judges of their pain.[14] However, only a little more than half of the respondents asserted that parents could give an accurate estimate of their child's pain.[14] This is bothersome, considering that many established pain

TABLE 10-2

SUGGESTED NONPHARMACOLOGICAL PAIN MANAGEMENT INTERVENTIONS IN INFANTS, CHILDREN, AND ADOLESCENTS[a]

NEONATES AND INFANTS	CHILDREN AND ADOLESCENTS
Developmentally supportive care in a family-centered environment using the Newborn Individualized Developmental Care and Assessment Program (NIDCAP)[130-133] • Observation-based individualized care • Clustered and paced caregiving • Soothing environment with reduced noise and lighting • Individualized positioning and feeding Avoiding recurrent painful stimuli[12] Breastfeeding[107,134] Use of oral sucrose[107,134] Use of a pacifier and other non-nutritive sucking interventions[6,107,135] Swaddling[107,136] Flexed positioning (facilitated tucking)[107,137] Skin-to-skin contact with the parent (Kangaroo care)[107,138] Passive distraction techniques • Visual, such as pictures, mirrors, or videos[6,139,140] • Auditory, such as singing or playing music to the baby[6,129,141]	Cognitive techniques[6,126] • Answering the child's questions • Introduction of coping statements and strategies • Mental rehearsal • Modelling • Providing the child with explanation of the procedure in an age-appropriate manner • Providing the child with information and opportunity to make a choice • Role-playing Hypnosis[125,127,142] Active distraction techniques[6,126,127,142] • Reading books • Blowing bubbles • Counting objects • Deep breathing • Engaging in a conversation • Playing with toys and electronic devices • Progressive relaxation techniques • Using squeeze balls Passive distraction techniques[6,126,127,142] • Listening to music • Reading, story-telling, singing to the child • Videos

[a] Not all inclusive.

scales and assessment instruments that contain pain items or subscales, especially those used for children who cannot report pain, rely on parental report.[98,99,101,104-106]

Because of the significant lack of available evidence on pain assessment and management in children with developmental disabilities as opposed to children developing typically, there is an urgent need of research in this important area of practice.[5,91] What is known is that pain is a critical factor to consider and address in this patient population and, specifically, in infants and children with CP. Future studies should compare self-reported and parental perceptions of pain experienced by children with CP and examine pain assessment instruments, their psychometric properties, and interventions used by physical therapists to manage pain.[5]

Frequent and prolonged contact that pediatric physical therapists have with children with CP and their families allows them to address pain in these children.[5] In order to do that, physical therapists must recognize and acknowledge pain as an existing problem, expand their knowledge of pain assessment and management, encourage the use of parent-report standardized measures, widely apply psychosocial interventions during physical therapy sessions and in home programs, abandon distress-generating approaches to therapy-related pain, and instead encourage the child's use of physical activity and appropriate coping strategies.[5] Finally, Doctor of Physical Therapy curricula must contain pertinent evidence-based information related to pain assessment and management in children, including those with CP and other developmental disabilities.[1]

Complete a video-based activity for Chapter 10 (see Activity Set 2 [activity 1] on the book website).

REFERENCES

1. Palermo T, Eccleston C, Goldschneider K, et al; Pediatric Chronic Pain Task Force. Assessment and management of children with chronic pain. A position statement from the American Pain Society. *American Pain Society.* http://americanpainsociety.org/about-us/position-statements/overview. Approved January 4, 2012. Accessed March 12, 2015.

2. O'Rourke D. The measurement of pain in infants, children, and adolescents: from policy to practice. *Phys Ther.* 2004;84(6):560-570.

3. Mathews L. Pain in children: neglected, unaddressed and mismanaged. *Indian J Palliat Care.* 2011;17(suppl):S70-S73.

4. American Physical Therapy Association. *Guide to Physical Therapist Practice 3.0.* http://guidetoptpractice.apta.org/. Published August 2014. Accessed March 12, 2015.

5. Swiggum M, Hamilton ML, Gleeson P, Roddey T. Pain in children with cerebral palsy: implications for pediatric physical therapy. *Pediatr Phys Ther.* 2010;22(1):86-92.

6. Srouji R, Ratnapalan S, Schneeweiss S. Pain in children: assessment and nonpharmacological management. *Int J Pediatr.* 2010;2010. pii:474838.doi:10.1155/2010/474838.

7. Lynch M. Pain as the fifth vital sign. *J Intraven Nurs.* 2001;24(2):85-94.

8. McLaughlin CR, Hull JG, Edwards WH, Cramer CP, Dewey WL. Neonatal pain: a comprehensive survey of attitudes and practices. *J Pain Symptom Manage.* 1993;8(1):7-16.

9. Salanterä G. Finnish nurses' attitudes to pain in children. *J Adv Nurs.* 1999;29(3):727-736.

10. Baker CM, Wong DL. Q.U.E.S.T.: a process of pain assessment in children (continuing education credit). *Orthop Nurs.* 1987;6(1):11-21.

11. International Association for the Study of Pain. IASP taxonomy: pain. *IASP.* http://www.iasp-pain.org/Taxonomy. Updated May 22, 2012. Accessed March 12, 2015.

12. Anand KJ; International Evidence-Based Group for Neonatal Pain. Consensus statement for the prevention and management of pain in the newborn. *Arch Pediatr Adolesc Med.* 2001;155(2):173-180.

13. Herr K, Coyne PJ, Key T, et al; American Society for Pain Management Nursing. Pain assessment in the nonverbal patient: position statement with clinical practice recommendations. *Pain Manag Nurs.* 2006;7(2):44-52.

14. Henderson R, Mentz M, Rourke N, Kim M, Kloker K, Swanson M. Selection and use of pain assessment instruments by physical therapist in pediatric practice, and attitudes of pediatric physical therapists towards pain in children. Poster presented at: American Physical Therapy Association Combined Sections Meeting; February 4-7, 2015; Indianapolis, IN.

15. Holsti L, Grunau RE, Oberlander TF, Whitfield MF. Prior pain induces heightened motor responses during clustered care in preterm infants in the NICU. *Early Hum Dev.* 2005;81(3):293-302.

16. Johnston C. Experience in a neonatal intensive care unit affects pain response. *Pediatrics.* 1996;98(5):925-930.

17. Grunau RE, Weinberg J, Whitfield MF. Neonatal procedural pain and preterm infant cortisol response to novelty at 8 months. *Pediatrics.* 2004;114(1):e77-e84.

18. Whitfield MF, Grunau RE. Behavior, pain perception, and the extremely low-birth weight survivor. *Clin Perinatol.* 2000;27(2):363-729.

19. Sternberg WF, Scorr L, Smith LD, Ridgway CG, Stout M. Long-term effects of neonatal surgery on adulthood pain behavior. *Pain.* 2005;113(3):347-353.

20. Swiggum M, Hamilton ML, Gleeson P, Roddey T, Mitchell K. Pain assessment and management in children with neurologic impairment: a survey of pediatric physical therapists. *Pediatr Phys Ther.* 2010;22(3):330-335.

21. Fitzgerald M. Development of pain mechanisms. *Br Med Bull.* 1991;47(3):667-675.

22. Fitzgerald M. Hyperalgesia in premature infants. *Lancet.* 1988;1(8580):292.

23. Grunau R. Early pain in preterm infants. A model of long-term effects. *Clin Perinatol.* 2002;29:373-394.

24. Hermann C, Hohmeister J, Demirakça S, Zohsel K, Flor K. Long-term alteration of pain sensitivity in school-aged children with early pain experiences. *Pain.* 2006;125(3):278-285.

25. Grunau RE, Holsti L, Peters JW. Long-term consequences of pain in human neonates. *Semin Fetal Neonatal Med.* 2006;11(4):268-275.

26. Pillai Riddell RR, Stevens BJ, McKeever P, et al. Chronic pain in hospitalized infants: health professionals' perspective. *J Pain.* 2009;10(12):1217-1225.

27. Schanberg LE, Sandstrom MJ. Causes of pain in children with arthritis. *Rheum Dis Clin North Am.* 1999;25(1):31-53.

28. Eccleston C, Clinch J. Adolescent chronic pain and disability: a review of the current evidence in assessment and treatment. *Paediatr Child Health.* 2007;12(2):117-120.

29. Gauntlett-Gilbert J, Eccleston C. Disability in adolescents with chronic pain: patterns and predictors across different domains of functioning. *Pain.* 2007;131(1-2):132-141.

30. Oddson BE, Clancy CA, McGrath PJ. The role of pain in reduced quality of life and depressive symptomology in children with spina bifida. *Clin J Pain.* 2006;22(9):784-789.

31. Russo RN, Miller MD, Haan E, Cameron ID, Crotty M. Pain characteristics and their association with quality of life and self-concept in children with hemiplegic cerebral palsy identified from a population register. *Clin J Pain.* 2008;24(4):335-342.

32. Castle K, Imms C, Howie L. Being in pain: a phenomenological study of young people with cerebral palsy. *Dev Med Child Neurol.* 2007;49(6):445-449.

33. Tervo RC, Symons F, Stout J, Novacheck T. Parental report of pain and associated limitations in ambulatory children with cerebral palsy. *Arch Phys Med Rehabil.* 2006;87(7):928-934.

34. Houlihan CM, O'Donnell M, Conaway M, Stevenson RD. Bodily pain and health-related quality of life in children with cerebral palsy. *Dev Med Child Neurol.* 2004;46(5):305-310.

35. Engel JM, Petrina TJ, Dudgeon BJ, McKearnan KA. Cerebral palsy and chronic pain: a descriptive study of children and adolescents. *Phys Occup Ther Pediatr.* 2005;25(4):73-84.

36. McKearnan KA, Kieckhefer GM, Engel JM, Jensen MP, Labyak S. Pain in children with cerebral palsy: a review. *J Neurosci Nurs.* 2004;36(5):252-259.

37. Gajdosick CG, Cicirello N. Secondary conditions of the musculoskeletal system in adolescents and adults with cerebral palsy. *Phys Occup Ther Pediatr.* 2001;21(4):49-68.

38. Jensen MP, Engel JM, Hoffman AJ, Schwartz L. Natural history of chronic pain and pain treatment in adults with cerebral palsy. *Am J Phys Med Rehabil.* 2004;83(6):439-445.

39. Wright M, Wallman L. Cerebral palsy. In: Campbell SK, Palisano RJ, Orlin MN, eds. *Physical Therapy for Children.* 4th ed. St. Louis, MO: Saunders; 2012:577-627.

40. Pruitt DW, Tsai T. Common medical comorbidities associated with cerebral palsy. *Phy Med Rehabil Clin N Am.* 2009;20(3):453-467.

41. Sullivan PB. Gastrointestinal disorders in children with neurodevelopmental disabilities. *Dev Disabil Res Rev.* 2008;14(2):128-136.

42. Roscigno CI. Addressing spasticity related pain in children with spastic cerebral palsy. *J Neurosci Nurs.* 2003;34(3):123-133.

43. Hadden KL, von Baeyer CL. Pain in children with cerebral palsy: common triggers and expressive behaviors. *Pain.* 2002;99(1-2):281-288.

44. Doralp S, Bartlett DJ. The prevalence, distribution, and effect of pain among adolescents with cerebral palsy. *Pediatr Phys Ther.* 2010;22(1):26-33.

45. Parkinson KN, Gibson L, Dickinson HO, Colver AF. Pain in children with cerebral palsy: a cross-sectional multicenter European study. *Acta Paediatr.* 2010;99(3):446-451.

46. Palisano RJ, Rosenbaum PL, Walter SD, Russell DJ, Wood EP, Galuppi BE. Development and reliability of a system to classify gross motor function in children with cerebral palsy. *Dev Med Child Neurol.* 1997;39(4):214-223.

47. Varni JW, Seid M, Kurtin PS. Peds QL 4.0: reliability and validity of the Pediatric Quality of Life Inventory version 4.0 generic core scales in healthy and patient populations. *Med Care.* 2001;39(8):800-812.

48. Harter S. *Manual for the Self-Perception Profile for Children.* Denver, CO: University of Denver; 1985.

49. Sobus KM, Karkos JB. Rehabilitation care and management for the individual with cerebral palsy, ages 13 through early adulthood. *Crit Rev Phys Rehabil Med.* 2009;21(2):117-165.

50. Gill M, Drendel AL, Weisman SJ. Parent satisfaction with acute pediatric pain treatment at home. *Clin J Pain.* 2013;29(1):64-69.

51. Lewandowski J, Lukaszewska K. Characteristics of back pain in Polish youth depending on place of residence. *Ann Agric Environ Med.* 2014;21(3):644-648.

52. Walker SM. Pain in children: recent advances and ongoing changes. *Br J Anaesth.* 2008;101(1):101-110.

53. Jordan A, Eccleston C, McCracken LM, Connell H, Clinch J. The Bath Adolescent Pain-Parental Impact Questionnaire (BAP-PIQ): development and preliminary psychometric evaluation of an instrument to assess the impact of parenting an adolescent with chronic pain. *Pain.* 2008;137(3):478-487.

54. Joint Commission on Accreditation of Healthcare Organizations. *Pain Assessment and Management: An Organizational Approach.* Oak-Brook Terrace, IL: Author; 2000.

55. McGrath PJ, Unruh AM. Measurement and assessment of pediatric pain. In: McMahon SB, Koltzenburg M, Tracey I, Turk DC, eds. *Wall and Melzack's Textbook of Pain.* 6th ed. Philadelphia, PA: Saunders; 2013:320-327.

56. Henderson RJ, Primack M. Interrater and interdevice reliability of physical therapist and client rating of low back pain with a visual analogue scale and a picture scale. Poster presented at: The 2nd Joint Scientific Meeting of the American Pain Society and the Canadian Pain Society; May 6-9, 2004; Vancouver, Canada.

57. Henderson RJ, Primack M, Jennings E, Levine J, Fertig-Tabao J. Congruence between physical therapist and client picture scale ratings of low back pain. Poster presented at: Physical Therapy 2004: The Annual Conference and Exposition of the American Physical Therapy Association; June 30-July 3, 2004; Chicago, IL.

58. Suarez-Almazor ME, Conner-Spady B, Kendall CJ, Russell AS, Skeith K. Lack of congruence in the ratings of patients' health status by patients and their physicians. *Med Decis Making.* 2001;21(2):113-121.

59. Harrison A. Comparing nurses' and patients' pain evaluations: a study of hospitalized patients in Kuwait. *Soc Sci Med.* 1993;36(5):683-692.

60. Lawrence J, Alcock D, McGrath P, Kay J, MacMurray SB, Dulberg C. The development of a tool to assess neonatal pain. *Neonatal Netw.* 1993;12(6):59-66.

61. Bellieni CV, Cordelli DM, Caliani C, et al. Inter-observer reliability of two pain scales for newborns. *Early Hum Dev.* 2007;83(8):549-552.

62. Suraseranivongse S, Kaosaard R, Intakong P, et al. A comparison of postoperative pain scales in neonates. *Br J Anaesth.* 2006;97(4):540-544.

63. Stevens B, Johnston C, Petryshen P, Taddio A. Premature Infant Pain Profile: development and initial validation. *Clin J Pain.* 1996;12(1):13-22.

64. Stevens B, Johnston C, Taddio A, Gibbins S, Yamada J. The Premature Infant Pain Profile: evaluation 13 years after development. *Clin J Pain.* 2010;26(9):813-830.

65. Krechel SW, Bildner J. CRIES: a new neonatal postoperative pain measurement score. Initial testing of validity and reliability. *Paediatr Anaesth.* 1995;5(1):53-61.

66. Pasero C. Pain assessment in infants and young children: neonates. *Am J Nurs.* 2002;102(8):61-64.

67. Stevens BJ, Gibbins S, Yamada J, et al. The premature infant pain profile-revised (PIPP-R): initial validation and feasibility. *Clin J Pian.* 2014;30(3):238-243.

68. Gibbins S, Stevens BJ, Yamada J, et al. Validation of the Premature Infant Pain Profile-Revised (PIPP-R). *Early Hum Dev.* 2014;90(4):189-193.

69. Debillon T, Zupan V, Ravault N, Magny JF, Dehan M. Development and initial validation of the EDIN scale, a new tool for assessing prolonged pain in preterm infants. *Arch Dis Child Fetal Neonatal Ed.* 2001;85(1):F36-F41.

70. Portney LG, Watkins MP. Reliability of measurements. In: Portney LG, Watkins MP, eds. *Foundations of Clinical Research: Applications to Practice.* 3rd ed. Upper Saddle River, NJ: Pearson Education, Inc.; 2009:77-96.

71. Hummel P, Puchalski M, Creech SD, Weiss MG. Clinical reliability and validity of the N-PASS: neonatal pain, agitation and sedation scale with prolonged pain. *J Perinatol.* 2008;28(1):55-60.

72. Ambuel B, Hamlett KW, Marx CM, Blumer JL. Assessing distress in pediatric intensive care environments: the COMFORT scale. *J Pediatr Psychol.* 1992;17(1):95-109.

73. Wielenga JM, De Vos R, de Leeuw R, De Haan RJ. COMFORT scale: a reliable and valid method to measure the amount of stress of ventilated preterm infants. *Neonatal Netw.* 2004;23(2):39-44.

74. Hester NK. The preoperational child's reaction to immunization. *Nurs Res.* 1979;28(4):250-255.

75. Wong-Baker FACES® Pain Rating Scale. *Wong-Baker FACES Foundation.* http://wongbakerfaces.org/. Accessed October 15, 2015.

76. Gharaibeh M, Abu-Saad H. Cultural validation of pediatric pain assessment tools: Jordanian perspective. *J Transcul Nurs.* 2002;13(1):12-18.

77. Keck JF, Gerkensmeyer J, Joyce B, Schade J. Reliability and validity of the Faces and Word Descriptor Scales to measure procedural pain. *J Pediatr Nurs.* 1996;11(6):368-374.

78. Hicks CL, von Baeyer CL, Spafford PA, van Korlaar I, Goodenough B. The Faces Pain Scale-Revised: toward a common metric in pediatric pain measurement. *Pain.* 2001;93(2):173-183.

79. Miró J, Huguet A. Evaluation of reliability, validity, and preference for a pediatric pain intensity scale: the Catalan version of the faces pain scale – revised. *Pain.* 2004;111(1-2):59-64.

80. Migdal M, Chudzynska-Pomianowska E, Vause E, Henry E, Lazar J. Rapid, needle-free delivery of lidocaine for reducing the pain of venipuncture among pediatric subjects. *Pediatrics.* 2005;115(4):e393-e398.

81. Taddio A, Soin HK, Schuh S, Koren G, Scolnik D. Liposomal lidocaine to improve procedural success rates and reduce procedural pain among children: a randomized controlled trial. *CMAJ.* 2005;172(13):1691-1695.

82. Beyer J. *The Oucher: A User Manual and Technical Report.* Evanston, IL: Judson; 1984.

83. Beyer JE, Aradine CR. Content validity of an instrument to measure young children's perceptions of the intensity of their pain. *J Pediatr Nurs.* 1986;1(6):386-395.

84. Beyer JE, Aradine CR. Convergent and discriminant validity of a self-report measure of pain intensity for children. *Child Health Care.* 1988;16(4):274-281.

85. Beyer JE, Denyes MJ, Villarruel AM. The creation, validation, and continuing development of the Oucher: a measure of pain intensity in children. *J Pediatr Nurs.* 1992;7(5):335-346.

86. Luffy R, Grove SK. Examining the validity, reliability, and preference of three pediatric pain measurement tools in African-American children. *Pediatr Nurs.* 2003;29(1):54-59.

87. Scott J, Huskisson EC. Vertical or horizontal visual analogue scales. *Ann Rheum Dis.* 1979;38:560.

88. Tyler DC, Tu A, Douthit J, Chapman CR. Toward validation of pain measurement tools for children: a pilot study. *Pain.* 1993;52(3):301-309.

89. Stinson JN, Kavanagh T, Yamada J, Gill N, Stevens B. Systematic review of the psychometric properties, interpretability and feasibility of self-report pain intensity measures for use in clinical trials in children and adolescents. *Pain.* 2006;125(1-2):143-157.

90. McGrath PA, Seifert CE, Speechley KN, Booth JC, Stitt L, Gibson MC. A new analogue scale for assessing children's pain: an initial validation study. *Pain.* 1996;64(3):435-443.

91. Oberlander TF, Burkitt CC, Symons FJ, Johnston C. Sensory functions: pain (b280-b289). In: Majnemer A. *Measures for Children with Developmental Disabilities: An ICF-CY Approach.* London, UK: Mac Keith Press, Clinics in Developmental Medicine No. 194-195; 2012:170-180.

92. McGrath PJ, Johnson G, Goodman JT, et al. CHEOPS: a behavioral scale for rating postoperative pain in children, In: Fields HL, Dubner R, Cervero F, eds. *Advances in Pain Research and Therapy.* New York, NY: Raven Press; 1985:395-402.

93. Crellin D, Sullivan TP, Babl FE, O'Sullivan R, Hutchinson A. Analysis of the validation of existing behavioral pain and distress scales for use in the procedural setting. *Paediatr Anaesth.* 2007;17(8):720-733.

94. Suraseranivongse S, Santawat U, Kraiprasit K, Petcharatana S, Prakkamodom S, Muntraporn N. Cross-validation of a composite pain scale for preschool children within 24 hours of surgery. *Br J Anaesth.* 2001;87(3):400-405.

95. Massaro M, Ronfani L, Ferrara G, et al. A comparison of three scales for measuring pain in children with cognitive impairment. *Acta Paediatr.* 2014;103:e495-e500.

96. Merkel SI, Voepel-Lewis T, Shayevitz JR, Malviya S. The FLACC: a behavioral scale for scoring postoperative pain in young children. *Pediatr Nurs.* 1997;23(3):293-297.

97. Nilsson S, Finnström B, Kokinsky E. The FLACC behavioral scale for procedural pain assessment in children aged 5-16 years. *Paediatr Anaesth.* 2008;18(8):767-774.

98. Malviya S, Voepel-Lewis T, Burke C, Merkel S, Tait AR. The revised FLACC observational pain tool: improved reliability and validity for pain assessment in children with cognitive impairment. *Paediatr Anaesth.* 2006;16(3):258-265.

99. Breau LM, McGrath PJ, Camfield CS, Finley GA. Psychometric properties of the non-communicating children's pain checklist-revised. *Pain.* 2002;99(1-2):349-357.

100. Breau LM, Finley GA, McGrath PJ, Camfield CS. Validation of the Non-Communicating Children's Pain Checklist-Postoperative Version. *Anesthesiology.* 2002;96(3):528-535.

101. Hunt A, Goldman A, Seers K, et al. Clinical validation of the Paediatric Pain Profile. *Dev Med Child Neurol.* 2004;46(1):9-18.

102. Hunt A, Wisbeach A, Seers K, et al. Development of the paediatric pain profile: role of video analysis and saliva cortisol in validating a tool to assess pain in children with severe neurological disability. *J Pain Symptom Manage.* 2007;33(3):276-289.

103. Hunt KA, Franck LS. Special needs require special attention: a pilot project implementing the paediatric pain profile for children with profound neurological impairment in an in-patient setting following surgery. *J Child Health Care.* 2011;15(3):210-220.

104. Varni JW, Burwinkle TM, Berrin SJ, et al. The PedsQL in pediatric cerebral palsy: reliability, validity, and sensitivity of the Generic Core Scales and Cerebral Palsy Module. *Dev Med Child Neurol.* 2006;48(6):442-449.

105. Waters E, Davis E, Mackinnon A, et al. Psychometric properties of the quality of life questionnaire for children with CP. *Dev Med Child Neurol.* 2007;49(1):49-55.

106. Narayanan UG, Fehlings D, Weir S, Knights S, Kiran S, Campbell K. Initial development and validation of the Caregiver Priorities and Child Health Index of Life with Disabilities (CPCHILD). *Dev Med Child Neurol.* 2006;48(10):804-812.

107. American Academy of Pediatrics Committee on Fetus and Newborn; American Academy of Pediatrics Section on Surgery; Canadian Paediatric Society Fetus and Newborn Committee, Batton DG, Barrington KJ, Wallman C. Prevention and management of pain in the neonate: an update. *Pediatrics.* 2006;118(5):2231-2241.

108. Bhandari V, Bergqvist LL, Kronsberg SS, Barton BA, Anand KJ; NEOPAIN Trial Investigators Group. Morphine administration and short-term pulmonary outcomes among ventilated infants. *Pediatrics.* 2005;116(2):352-359.

109. Aranda JV, Carlo W, Hummel P, Thomas R, Lehr VT, Anand KJ. Analgesia and sedation during mechanical ventilation in neonates. *Clin Ther.* 2005;27(6):877-899.

110. Ng E, Taddio A, Ohlsson A. Intravenous midazolam infusion for sedation of infants in the neonatal intensive care unit. *Cochrane Database Syst Rev.* 2012;6:CD002052.

111. Anand KJ, Hall RW, Desai N, et al; NEOPAIN Trial Investigators Group. Effects of morphine analgesia in ventilated preterm neonates: primary outcomes from the NEOPAIN randomised trial. *Lancet.* 2004;363(9422):1673-1682.

112. Berde CB, Sethna NF. Analgesics for the treatment of pain in children. *N Engl J Med.* 2002;347(14):1094-1103. Erratum in: *N Engl J Med.* 2011;364(18):1782.

113. Zempsky WT, Schechter NL. What's new in the management of pain in children. *Pediatr Rev.* 2003;24(10):337-348.

114. Larson A, Stidham T, Banerji S, Kaufman J. Seizures and methemoglobinemia in an infant after excessive EMLA application. *Pediatr Emerg Care.* 2013;29(3):377-379.

115. So TY, Farrington E. Topical benzocaine-induced methemoglobinemia in the pediatric population. *J Pediatr Health Care.* 2008;22(6):335-339.

116. Belay ED, Bresee JS, Holman RC, Khan AS, Shahriari A, Schonberger LB. Reye's syndrome in the United States from 1981 through 1997. *N Engl J Med.* 1999;340(18):377-382.

117. Romsing J, Walther-Larsen S. Peri-operative use of nonsteroidal anti-inflammatory drugs in children: analgesic efficacy and bleeding. *Anesthesia.* 1997;52(7):673-683.

118. Hadden KL, von Baeyer CL. Global and specific behavioral measures of pain in children with cerebral palsy. *Clin J Pain.* 2005;21(2):140-146.

119. Gooch JL, Oberg WA, Grams B, Ward LA, Walker ML. Care provider assessment of intrathecal baclofen in children. *Dev Med Child Neurol.* 2004;46(8):548-552.

120. Vogtle LK. Pain in adults with cerebral palsy: impact and solutions. *Dev Med Child Neurol.* 2009;51(suppl 4):113-121.

121. Lundy CT, Doherty GM, Fairhurst CB. Botulinum toxin type A injections can be an effective treatment for pain in children with hip spasms and cerebral palsy. *Dev Med Child Neurol.* 2009;51(9):705-710.

122. Chaléat-Valayer E, Parratte B, Colin C, et al. A French observational study of botulinum toxin use in the management of children with cerebral palsy: BOTULOSCOPE. *Eur J Paediatr Neurol.* 2011;15(5):439-448.

123. Pin TW, Elmasry J, Lewis J. Efficacy of botulinum toxin A in children with cerebral palsy in Gross Motor Function Classification System levels IV and V: a systematic review. *Dev Med Child Neurol.* 2013;55(4):304-313.

124. Barwood S, Bailloeu C, Boyd R, et al. Analgesic effects of botulinum toxin A: a randomized, placebo-controlled clinical trial. *Dev Med Child Neurol.* 2000;42(2):116-121.

125. Moore RP, Wester T, Sunder R, Schrock C, Park TS. Peri-operative pain management in children with cerebral palsy: comparative efficacy of epidural vs systemic analgesia protocols. *Paediatr Anaesth.* 2013;23(8):720-725.

126. The Royal Australasian College of Physicians, Paediatrics and Child Health Division. Guideline statement: management of procedure related pain in children and adolescents. *J Paediatr Child Health.* 2006;42(suppl 1):S1-S29.

127. Uman LS, Birnie KA, Noel , et al. Psychological interventions for needle-related procedural pain and distress in children and adolescents. *Cochrane Database Syst Rev.* 2013;10:CD005179.

128. Murphy G. Distraction techniques for venipuncture: a review. *Paediatr Nurs.* 2009;21(3):18-20.

129. Klassen JA, Liang Y, Tjosvold L, Klassen TP, Hartling L. Music for pain and anxiety in children undergoing medical procedures: a systematic review of randomized controlled trials. *Ambul Pediatr.* 2008;8(2):117-128.

130. Sizun J, Ansquer H, Browne J, Tordjman S, Morin JF. Developmental care decreases physiologic and behavioral pain expression in preterm neonates. *J Pain*. 2002;3(6):446-450.

131. Als H, Gibes R. *Newborn Individualized Developmental Care and Assessment Program (NIDCAP)*. Boston, MA: Children's Hospital; 1986.

132. Als H, Gilkerson L. The role of relationship-based developmentally supportive newborn intensive care in strengthening outcome of preterm infants. *Semin Perinatol*. 1997;21:178-189.

133. Westrup B, Sizun J, Lagercrantz H. Family-centered developmental supportive care: a holistic and humane approach to reduce stress and pain in neonates. *J Perinatol*. 2007;27(suppl 1):S12-S18.

134. Shah PS, Herbozo C, Aliwalas LL, Shah V. Breastfeeding or breast milk for procedural pain in neonates. *Cochrane Database Syst Rev*. 2012;12:CD004950.

135. Bo LK, Callahan P. Soothing pain-elicited distress in Chinese infants. *Pediatrics*. 2000;105(4):E49.

136. Huang CM, Tung WS, Kuo LL, Ying-Ju C. Comparison of pain responses of premature infants to the heelstick between containment and swaddling. *J Nurs Res*. 2004;12(1):31-40.

137. Ward-Larson C, Horn RA, Gosnell F. The efficacy of facilitated tucking for relieving procedural pain of endotracheal suctioning in very low birthweight infants. *MCN Am J Matern Child Nurs*. 2004;29(3):151-156.

138. Johnston CC, Stevens B, Pinelli J, et al. Kangaroo care is effective in diminishing pain response in preterm neonates. *Arch Pediatr Adolsec Med*. 2003;157(11):1084-1088.

139. Cohen LL. Reducing infant immunization distress through distraction. *Health Psychol*. 2002;21(2):207-211.

140. Cohen LL, MacLaren JE, Fortson BL, et al. Randomized clinical trial of distraction for infant immunization pain. *Pain*. 2006;125(1-2):165-171.

141. Hartling L, Shaik MS, Tjosvold L, Leicht R, Liang Y, Kumar M. Music for medical indications in the neonatal period: a systematic review of randomised controlled trials. *Arch Dis Child Fetal Neonatal Ed*. 2009;94(5):F349-F354.

142. Birnie KA, Noel M, Parker JA, et al. Systematic review and meta-analysis of distraction and hypnosis for needle-related pain and distress in children and adolescents. *J Pediatr Psychol*. 2014;39(8):783-808.

143. Engel JM, Jensen MP, Schwartz L. Outcome of biofeedback-assisted relaxation for pain in adults with cerebral palsy: preliminary findings. *Appl Psychophysiol Biofeedback*. 2004;29(2):135-140.

144. Vogtle LK, Malone LA, Azuero A. Outcomes of an exercise program for pain and fatigue management in adults with cerebral palsy. *Diabil Rehabil*. 2014;36(10):818-825.

145. Jensen MP, Engel JM, Schwartz L. Coping with cerebral palsy pain: a preliminary longitudinal study. *Pain Med*. 2006;7(1):30-37.

146. Engel JM, Jensen MP, Schwartz L. Coping with chronic pain associated with cerebral palsy. *Occup Ther Int*. 2006;13(4):224-233.

Please see videos on the accompanying website at

www.healio.com/books/videosrahlin

Section III

QUESTIONS TO PONDER

1. When the students are trained in an interprofessional education (IPE) environment, would this translate into good clinical outcomes if the clinical practice setting where they work does not use a collaborative care approach?

2. Do medical interventions that target the alterations of structures and functions in children with CP improve their quality of life? Please explain your answer.

3. What is the best approach to counseling patient families in regard to the benefits of spasticity management?

4. Do the benefits of invasive methods used to address spasticity in children with CP, such as intrathecal baclofen, neurolytic block interventions, selective dorsal rhizotomy, and orthopedic surgeries, outweigh their risks? Please justify your answers.

5. What is the clinical significance of the knowledge of cardiovascular and pulmonary co-morbidities and their medical management for physical therapists working with children and adults with CP?

6. Based on the current literature, what is the relationship between G-tube feedings and nutritional status in children with CP?

7. What is the potential impact, if any, that auditory and visual system impairments and their medical management may have on physical therapy intervention provided to children with CP?

8. Should pharmacological methods be widely used to manage chronic pain in children with developmental disabilities, including CP? Please explain your answer.

9. How can physical therapists minimize PT intervention-related pain in their patients with CP?

SUGGESTED QUESTIONS FOR FUTURE RESEARCH

1. At what point in professional programs should the IPE be initiated to be most effective in its translation to clinical practice?

2. What are the effects of specific medical antispasticity interventions on gross motor function, activity, participation, and quality of life in children with CP?

3. Which of the available interventions for sialorrhea has the most impact on the psychological well-being, social participation, and quality of life in individuals with CP?

4. What is the best timing for orthopedic surgeries to address growth-related contracture development in children with CP?

5. What is the relationship between physical and psychological well-being in children with CP who undergo single-event multilevel surgeries?

6. What are the effects of single-event multilevel surgeries, upper extremity surgeries, and spinal surgeries on activity, participation, and different aspects of health-related quality of life in children with CP?

7. What are the effects of chest PT and airway clearance interventions on the incidence of pneumonia, hospitalization rate, and health-related quality of life in children and adults with CP?

8. What are the effects of interventions aimed at improving sleep in individuals with CP on their physical and psychological well-being and quality of life?

9. Which medical interventions are most effective in addressing urinary incontinence in children and adults with CP?

10. Is vision therapy effective in managing visual and ocular motor dysfunction in children with CP, and how does it affect their activity and participation?

11. Which pain scale(s) is/are most accurate in assessing pain in children and adults with CP?

12. Which non-pharmacological method(s) of chronic pain management is/are most effective in individuals with CP of different ages?

SECTION IV

PHYSICAL THERAPY MANAGEMENT
THEORETICAL FOUNDATION,
RESEARCH EVIDENCE, AND PRACTICE

11

Physical Therapy
Examination and Evaluation
Tests and Measures, Anticipated Goals,
Expected Outcomes, and Tracking Progress

Within the enablement perspective, how children with disabilities participate in
daily routines that promote their health and well-being is a central concern in the evaluation process.

Diana Nathan Goldstein, Ellen Cohn, and Wendy Coster[1]

A world-wide acceptance of the framework provided by the International Classification of Functioning, Disability and Health (ICF)[2] led to a paradigm shift in patient/client management by health care professionals, from focusing on disease, impairments, and disability to emphasizing health, activity, and participation.[1,3] The reader is referred to Chapter 4 for a discussion of the ICF Model,[2] its components, and uses. In contemporary clinical practice, pediatric physical therapists are in a unique position to enhance activity and participation in children with cerebral palsy (CP) and, thus, make a meaningful difference in the lives of these children and their families,[1] with the ultimate goal of improving their quality of life.[4] This idea should transcend all aspects of patient/client management[1,3] identified in the *Guide to Physical Therapist Practice 3.05 (Guide 3.0)*: designing patient examination and evaluation; determining appropriate diagnosis, prognosis, and plan of care; planning and implementing intervention; and assessing outcomes.

According to *Guide 3.0*,[5] the initial *physical therapy examination* is a process that consists of the patient history, systems review, and selected tests and measures. The *evaluation* of information obtained during the initial examination allows the therapist to interpret the clinical findings and determine the patient's *diagnosis* that identifies the primary impact of his or her condition on function at a body system or a whole person level. In addition, the evaluation process

may result in the need for a consultation with or a patient *referral* to another health care professional. The arrival at a physical therapy *diagnosis* is followed by the development of *prognosis* that contains the anticipated amount of and the time frame for improvement that would result from physical therapy *intervention*. The *plan of care* is determined based on the patient's examination, diagnosis, and prognosis. It contains specific patient goals, interventions to be used, suggested therapy frequency and duration required to achieve these goals, and the level of improvement anticipated as the result of provided intervention.[5] The current chapter will encompass a discussion of all elements of patient/client management related to children with CP, except for intervention, which will be covered later in this book.

The initial evaluation can be structured using a bottom-up or a top-down approach described in rehabilitation literature and shown in Figure 11-1.[6-8] The therapist who uses the bottom-up approach would perform the physical therapy examination and evaluation to identify the child's strengths and problems, and to develop his or her physical therapy goals. The therapist would then design the plan of care and implement intervention, followed by the assessment of outcomes.[6,7] The bottom-up approach was traditionally used in medical settings, but it is now more and more frequently replaced with the top-down approach, the first step in which is for the therapist is to inquire about the child's and caregiver's concerns

Rahlin M. *Physical Therapy for Children With Cerebral Palsy:*
An Evidence-Based Approach (pp 173-206).
© 2016 SLACK Incorporated.

Evaluation Approaches

Top Down	Bottom Up
• Parental/patient concerns and desired outcomes	• Develop and implement plan of care
• PT examination	• Set PT goals
• PT evaluation: identify strengths and obstacles	• Identify strengths and problems
• Develop and implement plan of care	• PT examination and evaluation

Figure 11-1. Top-down and bottom-up approaches to physical therapy evaluation.

and about the desired outcomes or intervention goals (see Figure 11-1).[6-8] The extent to which children can participate in this process depends on their ability to communicate and comprehend the discussion. The information obtained from the child and his or her family helps the therapist to structure the physical therapy examination and select measures appropriate for the set goals. In the process of the subsequent physical therapy evaluation, the child's strengths that would assist in meeting the goals, as well as obstacles to goal achievement are identified. This is followed by the development and implementation of the plan of care, with the ongoing re-evaluation of the child's progress toward intervention outcomes.[6-8] The top-down approach is predominantly used in early intervention that employs family-centered care[7] (see Chapter 12). However, the current trend observed in other clinical settings is to include the child and the family in the decision-making process whenever possible, which indicates a continued shift from prescriptive to collaborative care and away from the bottom-up approach. The process of physical therapy examination and evaluation will be discussed next from the top-down approach perspective.

PHYSICAL THERAPY EXAMINATION OF A CHILD WITH CEREBRAL PALSY

Components of physical therapy examination and general categories and subcategories of related examination procedures are shown in Table 11-1, with concerns expressed by the child and his or her family and their desired intervention outcomes added to the examination components listed in *Guide 3.0*.[5] Tests and measures are organized by the ICF Model[2] components, and methods used to assess quality of life are also included. The examination procedures related to body structures and functions are listed by body system. In addition, the table contains the assessment of pain that may originate from an alteration of structure or function of one or several body systems. A detailed discussion of pain assessment in children with CP was provided in Chapter 10

and will not be covered here. Finally, as shown in Table 11-1, the examination of environmental and personal factors that comprise the context in which the child lives and functions[2] can be performed through taking the patient's history (when appropriate), by observation, or by using specific tests and measures. These contextual factors may have an effect on the child's body structures and functions, activity, and participation, and contribute to or impede the success of physical therapy intervention[2,3] (see Chapter 4 and Table 4-5).

In the process of physical therapy examination, physical therapists select appropriate tests and measures based on the subjective information obtained from the interview conducted with the child and his or her caregiver, and from the child's history and systems review[5,7] (see Table 11-1). A variety of tests and measures can be used to conduct the initial physical therapy examination and evaluation and to develop the diagnosis, prognosis, and plan of care.[5,7] However, as observed in clinical practice, it may be beneficial, when possible, to select such examination procedures and instruments that would not only help the therapist to identify the pertinent variables expected to have an effect on the desired intervention outcomes, but also assist with the processes of ongoing re-evaluation, tracking progress toward the set goals, and goal modification, when necessary. Another important criterion for the selection of specific tests and measures is the need to discern the possible causes of alterations of the child's body structures and functions, activity limitations, and restrictions in participation that may negatively affect his or her quality of life.[4,5,7]

In order to serve their purposes to the benefit of the patient, tests and measures the physical therapist selects need to have good psychometric properties, such as *reliability* and *validity*.[5,9] This means that they need to be reliable when used repeatedly by the same therapist or used by different therapists with the same child.[10] This also means that they need to be valid for the assessment of specific constructs, content, or characteristics in specific patient populations and age groups,[11] and, sometimes, in specific settings, as may be the case with some of the standardized tools.[12]

Based on their purpose, standardized assessment instruments can be classified as *discriminative*, *evaluative*, and *predictive*, and some of them possess the required properties of 2 or all 3 types.[13] Pediatric physical therapists use discriminative tools to accurately identify presence or absence of developmental delay, atypical development, or disability.[9,13] Therefore, these instruments need to possess high *sensitivity* and *specificity* values.[14] Evaluative tools are used to measure change over time, which means that for these instruments, *responsiveness*, or the ability to detect small increments of change, is important.[9,11-13] Finally, the purpose of predictive measures is to determine if the child will have a developmental delay or disability in the future or to predict their outcomes and, therefore, these tools should possess good *predictive validity*.[9,11,13] To summarize, in order to select the most appropriate standardized assessment instrument, the physical therapist needs to take into consideration the child's age, the purpose of assessment, the setting where it will be used, and its psychometric properties.

TABLE 11-1

COMPONENTS OF PHYSICAL THERAPY EXAMINATION OF A CHILD AND RELEVANT CATEGORIES OF EXAMINATION PROCEDURES

EXAMINATION COMPONENTS	GENERAL CATEGORIES AND SUBCATEGORIES OF PHYSICAL THERAPY EXAMINATION METHODS AND PROCEDURES[a]		
Concerns expressed by the child, parent, or guardian	Interview with the child/parent/guardian		
Intervention outcomes desired by the child/family	May be related to general health, development, body structures or functions, activities, participation, or overall quality of life		
History	Written reports and an interview with the child/parent/guardian, to include the following: • Demographic and general health information • Developmental, educational, family, medical, and social history • Reported levels of activity and participation • Environmental factors, such as physical, psychological, and social living and educational environments; available services and their utilization • Personal factors, such as patterns of behavior, temperament, interests, play preferences, and other characteristic features		
Systems review	Screening of major body systems and general affect, cognition, communication, and use of language		
Tests and measures	Assessment of body structures and functions (by system)	Neuromuscular	• Muscle tone • Deep tendon reflexes, primitive reflexes, and postural reactions • Motor development tests • Movement patterns (with or without use of orthoses/other adaptive equipment) • Sensory integrity
		Musculoskeletal	• Range of motion • Muscle performance • Joint integrity • Static and dynamic postural alignment (with or without use of orthoses/other adaptive equipment)
		Cardiovascular and pulmonary	• Cardiovascular and pulmonary vital signs • Aerobic capacity, energy expenditure, cardiorespiratory endurance • Respiration/gas exchange and ventilation
		Integumentary	• Skin characteristics and integrity • Present or potential effects of positioning or equipment on skin integrity

(continued)

	TABLE 11-1 (CONTINUED)	
COMPONENTS OF PHYSICAL THERAPY EXAMINATION OF A CHILD AND RELEVANT CATEGORIES OF EXAMINATION PROCEDURES		
EXAMINATION COMPONENTS	**GENERAL CATEGORIES AND SUBCATEGORIES OF PHYSICAL THERAPY EXAMINATION METHODS AND PROCEDURES**a	
Tests and measures *(continued)*	Assessment of pain related to one or several body systems	• Pain drawings, pictures, and other graphic representation • Observational, numeric, visual analog, and other pain scales • Pain indices and questionnaires
	Assessment of activity	• Motor capacity and functional mobility, including movement transitions, transfers, locomotion, and gait (with or without use of orthoses/other adaptive equipment) • Physical fitness • Play activities • Functional performance of daily activities • Task-related static and dynamic balance and safety (with or without use of orthoses/other adaptive equipment) • Standardized functional scales and questionnaires • Surveys
	Assessment of participation	• Involvement in specific life situations with peers and family in a variety of settings and environments (with or without use of orthoses/other adaptive equipment) • Involvement in life situations based on personal preferences and priorities • Checklists, surveys, and standardized questionnaires
	Assessment of quality of life and health-related quality of life	• Physical, economic, and psychological well-being • Self-determination • Social integration • Health status questionnaires • Child-related and caregiver-related measures • Self-report and parent-/caregiver-report instruments • Surveys
	Identification of relevant personal factors	• Expressed levels of enjoyment, motivation, interest, and persistence in activities and participation • Observation of ability to communicate, patterns of behavior, temperament, general interests, play preferences, and other characteristic features • Scales, questionnaires, and surveys
a Not all inclusive.		

Selected Tests and Measures

Neuromuscular System

The presence of abnormal muscle tone contributes to the classification of motor abnormalities observed in individuals with CP.[15] This makes the assessment of muscle tone an important component of physical therapy examination. Muscle tone can be defined as the degree of partial contraction of a muscle at rest that creates its resistance to passive elongation or stretch.[16-18] Children with CP may demonstrate several types of increased muscle tone (hypertonia or hypertonicity), including spasticity, dystonia, rigidity, or

	TABLE 11-2

MODIFIED ASHWORTH SCALE FOR GRADING SPASTICITY

GRADE	DESCRIPTION
0	No increase in muscle tone
1	Slight increase in muscle tone, manifested by a catch and release or by minimal resistance at the end of the range of motion when the affected part(s) is moved in flexion or extension
1+	Slight increase in muscle tone, manifested by a catch, followed by minimal resistance throughout the remainder (less than a half) of the ROM
2	More marked increase in muscle tone through most of the ROM, but affected part(s) easily moved
3	Considerable increase in muscle tone, passive movement difficult
4	Affected part(s) rigid in flexion or extension

their combinations.[18] A complete discussion of definitions of spasticity, dystonia, athetosis, and ataxia, with the description of associated atypical movement patterns, was provided in Chapter 3.[18-21] Spasticity is usually accompanied by positive neurological signs, including hyperreflexia,[18] which can be assessed using a reflex hammer to elicit deep tendon reflexes.[5] Hypotonia is another type of abnormal tone that is frequently observed in children with CP, especially in the trunk musculature.[22] It is defined as low resistance to passive movement and is subjectively classified as mild, moderate, or severe,[22] which obviously presents a measurement reliability problem as definitions of these categories may differ among clinicians.

Muscle Tone Assessment

Assessment of increased muscle tone can be performed using several different methods described in the literature, with the modified Ashworth scale (MAS)[23] and the modified Tardieu scale (MTS)[24,25] being the most common and most researched. The MAS is used to grade spasticity, hypertonicity, or resistance to passive stretch.[23] The joint is moved through its available range of motion (ROM) at a standard speed (within approximately 1 second), and the resistance of stretched muscle(s) is assessed on a 6-point scale (Table 11-2).[23]

To assess spasticity on the MTS, the examiner uses goniometry to measure 2 joint angles at different velocities.[24-26] Three stretching velocities used by the Tardieu scale[27] are V1 (as slow as possible); V2 (the speed at which the limb would fall when acted upon by gravity); and V3 (as fast as possible). Joint angle R1 is obtained when the muscle is stretched at a fast velocity to the point when a "catch" is felt, which signifies presence of a spasticity-related overactive stretch reflex and determines the dynamic length of the tested muscle.[24-26] Velocity V2 or V3 is used for this measurement, depending on the specific muscle tested. Joint angle R2 is obtained by

stretching the muscle at a slow velocity (V1). This measure reflects the joint ROM or the resting length of the tested muscle. The difference between the R2 and R1 angles is then calculated. A small R2-R1 value signifies the presence of a fixed muscle contracture. When this value is large, it indicates that the muscle contracture is for the most part dynamic (related to spasticity), and that it may be possible to address the limitation in dynamic ROM by applying an antispasticity intervention[24-26] (see Chapter 7).

Research of the MAS and MTS psychometric properties yielded variable results. Pandyan et al[28] reported poor criterion validity of the MAS investigated in 63 adult patients with stroke. Although resistance to passive movement was significantly higher in the participants' involved arm compared to their uninvolved side, no significant difference was found in resistance to passive movement among the MAS grades of 1, 1+, and 2.[28] As for the MTS, Boyd et al[24] found it to be valid for quantifying and documenting change in spasticity in 16 children with CP.[24] Table 11-3 contains information on reliability of the MAS and the MTS. As suggested by general guidelines, poor, moderate, and good reliability are indicated by reliability coefficients below 0.50, between 0.50 and 0.75, and above 0.75, respectively.[10] As evident from the table, in 2 of 3 studies that investigated both scales, the reliability of the MAS was poor to moderate, while for the MTS, it was mostly moderate to good.[30,31] There was significant variability in the ICC values for test-retest reliability of both scales in the study by Fosang et al,[30] while Numanoğlu and Günel[31] reported on interrater reliability that was significantly higher for the MTS than for the MAS. Because of the variable results, several authors suggested that clinicians exercise caution when using these scales to assess spasticity in children with CP and interpreting their assessment findings.[29,30,32]

Another method of muscle tone assessment involves using the Myotonometer (Neurogenic Technologies, Inc), a patented electronic and computerized tissue compliance device,[35]

TABLE 11-3				
RELIABILITY OF THE MODIFIED ASHWORTH SCALE AND THE MODIFIED TARDIEU SCALE IN ASSESSMENT OF SPASTICITY IN CHILDREN WITH CEREBRAL PALSY				
STUDY	PARTICIPANTS (NUMBER AND DIAGNOSIS)	RELIABILITY	MAS	MTS
Yam and Leung[29]	17 children with spastic CP	Interrater	ICC = 0.41-0.73	ICC = 0.22-0.71
Fosang et al[30]	18 children with spastic CP	Interrater	ICC = 0.27-0.56	ICC = 0.58-0.74
		Test-retest	ICC = -0.07-0.85	ICC = 0.38-0.93
Numanoğlu and Günel[31]	37 children with spastic CP	*Intrarater (overall)*	ICC = 0.26-0.66	ICC = 0.54-0.95
		LE muscles	ICC = 0.26-0.64	ICC = 0.54-0.95
		Wrist and elbow flexors	ICC = 0.57 & 0.66	ICC = 0.63-0.93
			MAS ONLY	
Clopton et al[32]	17 children with CP, DD, and TBI	*Interrater (overall)*	ICC(2,1) = 0.33-0.79	
		Hamstrings and elbow flexors	ICC(2,1) = 0.79	
		LE muscles besides hamstrings	ICC(2,1) = 0.33-0.45	
		Intrarater (overall)	ICC(3,1) = 0.54-0.80	
		Hamstrings	ICC(3,1) = 0.80	
		Other LE muscles and elbow flexors	ICC(3,1) = 0.54-0.67	
Mutlu et al[33]	38 children with bilateral spastic CP	Interrater	ICC = 0.61-0.87	
		Intrarater	ICC = 0.36-0.83	
Klingels et al[34]	30 children with unilateral CP	Interrater (UE muscles)	ICC = 0.52-0.88	
		Test-retest (UE muscles)	ICC = 0.57-0.90	

Abbreviations: CP, cerebral palsy; DD, developmental delay; ICC, intraclass correlation coefficient; LE, lower extremity; TBI, traumatic brain injury; UE, upper extremity.

which has a potential for clinical use when it becomes commercially available. This instrument measures resting muscle tone by quantifying the amount of displacement of muscle tissue per unit force applied by placing the Myotonometer probe onto the skin and pushing it into the underlying muscle.[36] When applied during maximal isometric muscle contraction, the Myotonometer measures muscle torque production. The severity of spasticity can be quantified based on the percentage difference between the applied force and muscle tissue displacement when the muscle is relaxed and when it is contracted. As measurements are taken every 0.25 kg of force and up to 2.0 kg, the Myotonometer software produces force/displacement curves for the 2 muscle conditions. The smaller the difference between the "resting" and "contracted" measurements, the greater the amount of muscle spasticity.[36]

Leonard et al[36] reported on the validity of this device for the assessment of spasticity and identification and quantification of muscle paresis in persons with upper motoneuron involvement. Significant differences between the Myotonometer measurements of muscle tone in the participants of the experimental and control groups, as well as in the involved and uninvolved extremities of patients with CP and stroke, were documented. In addition, moderate to good correlation was demonstrated between the MAS grades and the Myotonometer percentage differences obtained from measurements performed under relaxed and contracted muscle conditions.[36] These findings supported the construct validity of the Myotonometer.[11,36]

The reliability of tone assessment in biceps brachii and medial gastrocnemius muscles when using the Myotonometer was examined in 10 children with unilateral and bilateral spastic CP, age range 5 to 12 years.[37] Results showed moderate to good intrarater and interrater reliability,[10] with the ICC values ranging from 0.54 to 0.99,[37] except for the interrater reliability in the tone assessment of the uninvolved medial gastrocnemius muscle, for which the ICC values ranged from 0.05 to 0.99.[37]

In another study, Lidström et al[38] obtained similar results when assessing the rectus femoris muscle tone in 15 children with CP, with the ICC values ranging from 0.67 to 0.95 and from 0.57 to 0.89 for the intrarater and interrater reliability, respectively. Based on their research data, the authors suggested that the most reliable measurements can be performed when the Myotonometer probe is applied to the muscle at the 0.75- to 1.50-kg force level. However, they questioned the validity of the Myotonometer and argued that because this device is used at rest and during an isometric muscle contraction, its measurements do not fully reflect spasticity as a velocity-dependent type of abnormal muscle tone. Therefore, the researchers proposed that the use of the Myotonometer should be complemented with the assessment of spasticity under dynamic conditions on one of the available ordinal scales.[38] This brought back the issue of subjective assessment of muscle tone using the MAS and the MTS, and the variable reliability of these scales.[22-26,28-34] To address this problem, a Haptic Elbow Spasticity Simulator or HESS, was developed.[39] This device was programmed to recreate conditions that simulated the MAS grades of 1, 1+, 2, and 3. The HESS was successfully used by 7 clinicians in its accuracy and reliability study. Potentially, this device may become a helpful training tool in making clinical assessment of spasticity more reliable.[39]

Other Measures of the Neuromuscular System Structures and Functions

Other physical therapy examination procedures used for the assessment of body structures and functions pertaining to the neuromuscular system were discussed previously. The reader is referred to Chapter 1 and Table 1-1 for the description of primitive reflexes and postural reactions and for the discussion of their role in the CNS maturation. Because of the advances in movement science and the associated changes in the theoretical foundation for current understanding of motor development, primitive reflexes are no longer viewed as the central part of developmental assessment.[22] Postural reactions are frequently tested by placing children on moveable surfaces to elicit righting and equilibrium responses and to determine whether they demonstrate adequate compensatory postural adjustment strategies; however, this examination procedure is not very reliable.[22] Researchers can examine the compensatory and anticipatory postural adjustments (CPAs and APAs) using electromyography (EMG) and center of pressure (COP) data obtained from force platforms (see Chapter 4),[40,41] but usually, this equipment is not readily available in a clinical setting.

Skilled clinical observation employed in a traditional movement analysis and its significance for the identification of the signs of atypical development were emphasized in Chapter 2. While the reliability of this examination procedure has not been established, several standardized developmental assessment instruments can be used to evaluate the quality of movement in infants and toddlers with a high degree of reliability (see Table 2-1).[42-44] In addition, assessment methods that take into account movement variability and complexity have been shown to be reliable and valid for the evaluation of quality of movement and prediction of developmental outcomes in young infants (see Chapter 2).[45-47]

Finally, sensory integrity needs to be evaluated in children with CP. Although sensory problems may contribute to decreased hand function, they may be overlooked because of the high prevalence of motor deficits observed in these children.[48] Specific examination procedures used to assess sensory integrity may include pressure sensitivity, proprioception, 2-point discrimination, and stereognosis.[48,49] Published literature contains very limited information on psychometric properties of sensory assessment in this patient population, but Klingels et al[34] showed good interrater and test-retest reliability[10] of these tests in 30 children with unilateral CP.

Musculoskeletal System

While quality of movement is included in the examination of the neuromuscular system, postural alignment is a part of the musculoskeletal assessment,[5] which is especially important in children with CP who frequently present with such accompanying impairments[15] as muscle weakness, ROM limitations, joint contractures, and musculoskeletal deformities (see Table 4-1).[50,51] One of the major reasons for the use of orthoses, assistive devices, and other adaptive equipment is to improve the child's postural alignment (see Chapters 20 through 22), which, therefore, needs to be assessed with and without the use of assistive technology, when applicable.

Joint Range of Motion Assessment

Assessment of joint ROM is a standard physical therapy examination procedure that is used with a wide variety of patients.[52] In children with CP, when ROM limitations and joint contractures are present, ROM measurements help determine the appropriate timing of conservative and surgical interventions that address these problems and their outcomes.[52-54] Goniometry is used most commonly,[52-56] but sometimes, therapists may rely on visual estimation.[53,55,56] Visual estimation may be useful when a very quick assessment of ROM is needed, for example, when a child is seen in a diagnostic clinic by multiple professionals, with a limited time available for the physical therapy examination. When using visual estimation, the physical therapist can move and stabilize the child's body parts with both hands, without the need to position the goniometer for measurement.[53] This may be helpful because abnormal posturing and joint alignment may make it difficult for the therapist to perform goniometry in a proper way, which would potentially compromise both the validity and reliability of measurement.[53]

Several studies examined the psychometric properties of goniometry and visual estimation methods used for the assessment of passive ankle,[53,55] popliteal angle,[55,56] and hip abduction and extension[55] ROM in children with CP. The results showed no significant difference in reliability between the 2 methods.[53,55,56] Additionally, Glanzman et al[55] established the validity of visual estimation for the assessment of lower extremity passive ROM by examining a correlation between visual estimation measurements and goniometry, with Pearson r ranging from 0.89 to 0.96.

TABLE 11-4

RELIABILITY OF GONIOMETRY AND VISUAL ESTIMATION IN ASSESSMENT OF LOWER EXTREMITY PASSIVE RANGE OF MOTION IN CHILDREN WITH CEREBRAL PALSY

STUDY	PARTICIPANTS' NUMBER AND TYPE OF CEREBRAL PALSY	JOINT MOTION(S)	RELIABILITY/ NUMBER OF LOWER EXTREMITIES (NUMBER OF CLINICIANS PERFORMING EACH MEASUREMENT[a])	GONIOMETRY	VISUAL ESTIMATION
Allington et al[53]	24 children with spastic CP	Ankle dorsiflexion, ankle plantarflexion, subtalar inversion and eversion	Intrarater/46 LEs (2-person)	Pearson $r=0.78-0.95$ $P>0.05$	Pearson $r=0.75-0.94$ $P>0.05$
			Interrater/46 LEs (2-person)	Pearson $r=0.80-0.95$ $P>0.05$	Pearson $r=0.81-0.94$ $P>0.05$
Ten Berge et al[56]	15 children with unilateral and bilateral CP	Popliteal angle	Intrarater/15 LEs (1-person)	$ICC=0.77$	$ICC=0.82$
			Interrater/15 LEs (1-person)	$ICC=0.68$	$ICC=0.72$
			GONIOMETRY ONLY		
McWhirk and Glanzman[52]	25 children with spastic CP	Hip extension, hip abduction, popliteal angle, knee extension, ankle dorsiflexion	Interrater/46 LEs (2-person)	$ICC=0.58-0.93$	
Multu et al[54]	38 children with bilateral spastic CP	Hip extension, hip abduction, hip external rotation, hip flexion with knee extended, ankle dorsiflexion	Interrater/76 LEs (2-person)	$ICC=0.61-0.95$	
			Test-retest/60 LEs (2-person)	$ICC=0.48-0.99$	
Glanzman et al[55]	25 children with spastic CP	Ankle dorsiflexion, hip abduction, popliteal angle, hip extension	Intrarater/50 LEs (1-person and 2-person)	$ICC(3,1)=0.96-0.98$	

Abbreviations: CP, cerebral palsy; ICC, intraclass correlation coefficient; LEs, lower extremities.

[a] When a 2-person measurement is performed, one clinician assists in positioning and stabilizing the child's LEs, and the other clinician measures the angle.

Table 11-4 contains information on reliability of the 2 methods of ROM measurement derived from research conducted in children with CP.[52-56] Results of the studies included in the table demonstrated moderate to good intrarater and interrater reliability[10] of lower extremity ROM measurements.[52-56] Mutlu et al[54] reported poor to good test-retest reliability[10] of goniometry, with a low ICC value (0.48) obtained for the hip abduction measurement by 1 of 3 testers. The rest of the ICC values were in the moderate to good[10] reliability range.[54] In the study by Glanzman et al,[55] hip extension measurements yielded good intrarater reliability[10] for both the Staheli[57] and Thomas tests used to assess the amount of hip flexion contracture[58] ($ICC(3,1)=0.98$).[55] The interrater and test-retest reliability of the Thomas test reported by other authors was moderate to good,[10] with the ICC values ranging from 0.58 to 0.95 and from 0.73 to

TABLE 11-5			
SELECTED RANGE OF MOTION MEASUREMENT PROCEDURES PERFORMED USING ONE-PERSON GONIOMETRY[a]			
GONIOMETRY PROCEDURE	**PURPOSE**	**CHILD'S POSITION**	**MEASUREMENT PROCEDURE**
Staheli test[55,57,58]	Assess the amount of hip flexion contracture by measuring hip extension ROM	• Prone, with the head, trunk, and abdomen supported on a table • Left hip flexed to 90 degrees over the edge of the table toward the floor, right LE supported by the examiner	• Place the goniometer axis at the right greater trochanter, the stationary (proximal) arm along the side of the pelvis, parallel to the supporting surface, and the moveable (distal) arm pointing to the right lateral femoral epicondyle. • While manually stabilizing the child's pelvis and keeping the goniometer in place at the same time, move the right LE into hip extension until movement toward anterior pelvic tilt is first felt. • Measure the angle between the supporting surface and the femur.
Thomas test[52,55,58]		• Supine, with the left hip flexed to achieve a neutral pelvic alignment[b] • Right LE positioned on the table, with the lower leg "hanging" over its edge	• Place the goniometer axis at the right greater trochanter, the stationary arm along the side of the pelvis, parallel to the supporting surface, and the moveable arm pointing at the right lateral femoral epicondyle. • While maintaining the flexion alignment of the left hip and keeping the goniometer in place, measure the angle between the supporting surface and the femur.
Popliteal angle[52,55,56,58]	Assess hamstring muscle length	• Supine, with the left LE stabilized against the supporting surface in a neutral alignment to prevent hip flexion[c] • Right hip and knee flexed to 90 degrees	• Place the goniometer axis at the right femoral epicondyle, the stationary arm aligned along the long axis of the femur and pointing at the greater trochanter, and the moveable arm pointing at the right lateral malleolus. • While stabilizing the child's left LE and maintaining the goniometer in place, slowly extend the child's right knee toward the vertical position. • Measure the angle between the thigh and the lower leg • Calculate the popliteal angle as the amount of ROM lacking from complete knee extension by subtracting the measured angle from 180 degrees.

Abbreviations: LE, lower extremity; PSIS, posterior superior iliac spine; ROM, range of motion.

[a] Described for the right LE.

[b] Determined by the perpendicular position of the imaginary line drawn through the ASIS and PSIS to the supporting surface.[52]

[c] The therapist can use his or her LEs to stabilize the child's left leg while handling the right LE for measurement.

0.99, respectively.[52,54] The descriptions of the Staheli[57] and Thomas tests are provided in Table 11-5.

As shown in Table 11-4, many reliability studies were conducted with the researchers using a 2-person measurement method, with one therapist positioning and stabilizing the child's lower extremities, and the other one performing the ROM measurement.[52-55] This brings about the question of applicability of this procedure to clinical practice, as in real life, therapists do not necessarily have help available each time they examine a patient. However, Glanzman et al[55] showed good reliability[10] of goniometry in several lower extremity joints while using both 1- and 2-person assessment methods. In another study, moderate to good reliability[10] of goniometry and visual estimation was obtained with one person performing the popliteal angle measurements.[55]

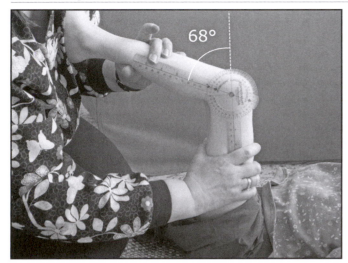

Figure 11-2. Popliteal angle measurement in a child with spastic cerebral palsy.

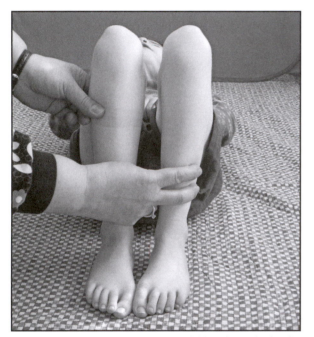

Figure 11-3. The Galeazzi sign in a child with cerebral palsy yields a negative result.

TABLE 11-6
NORMAL VALUES OF THE POPLITEAL ANGLE RANGE OF MOTION IN TYPICALLY DEVELOPING CHILDREN

AGE	POPLITEAL ANGLE RANGE OF MOTION (DEGREES)
Newborn	20-40
1 month	20-30
2 months	15-35
3 months	15-30
4 months	10-25
5 months	10-20
6 months	5-15
7 months	0-15
8-9 months	0-10
10 months	0-5
11-12 months	0
12-24 months	0-15
2-5 years	10-15
6-12 years	25-30
13-19 years	25-40
Data from Reade et al,[59] Katz et al,[60] and Stout.[61]	

Assessment of the popliteal angle ROM is widely used in pediatric physical therapy practice (see Table 11-5 and Figure 11-2 for the description and illustration of the measurement procedure).[56] It provides clinicians with valuable information about the hamstring muscle length, which is especially important when working with children with CP who frequently demonstrate hamstring contractures affecting their sitting and standing posture and gait.[56,58] This measure is critical in the decision-making process related to medical and surgical interventions aimed at alleviating these problems and in the assessment of outcomes of these interventions.[56] Normal values of the popliteal angle ROM in typically developing children, from infancy through adolescence, are listed in Table 11-6.[59-61]

Measures of Joint Integrity and Skeletal Alignment

Because of the high prevalence of hip joint pathology and torsional bone deformities,[51,62] assessment of the hip joint integrity and femoral and tibial torsion in children with CP is important for the development of the plan of care and for making appropriate referrals to other members of the interdisciplinary team, when necessary. Additionally, leg length discrepancy (LLD) is not uncommon in children with unilateral and bilateral CP and may negatively affect their gait, leading to the need for orthotic intervention or surgery.[63-65] Table 11-7 describes several examination procedures used by physical therapists to assess these skeletal deformities and contains information on their psychometric properties.[58,66-74]

The Galeazzi sign is frequently used in clinical practice to assess hip integrity in children with CP (see Table 11-7, Figure 11-3).[58,66] A positive finding may be indicative of a posterior subluxation or dislocation of the hip.[58,66] However, a false negative result may be obtained when both hips are dislocated.[66] Therefore, the assessment of hip abduction ROM should complement the Galeazzi sign procedure, with the hip abduction measurement performed with the hip and knee flexed expected to be greater than 60 degrees to rule out

TABLE 11-7

MEASURES OF SKELETAL ALIGNMENT USED IN CHILDREN WITH CEREBRAL PALSY AND THEIR PSYCHOMETRIC PROPERTIES

EXAMINATION PROCEDURE	PURPOSE	MEASUREMENT PROCEDURE	VALIDITY	RELIABILITY
Galeazzi sign[58,66]	Assess hip joint integrity	• Position the child supine with hips adducted, and feet placed flat on the supporting surface. • Document a positive sign if the knees are of unequal height. • Document a negative sign if the knee height is equal. • Bilateral hip dislocation will also yield a negative finding.	Not established	Not established
Trochanteric prominence angle test (TPAT)[58,67-71]	Assess femoral anteversion	• Position the child prone and passively flex one knee to 90 degrees. • Move the hip between medial and lateral rotation positions with one hand while palpating the greater trochanter with the other hand. • When the greater trochanter is in the most lateral ("prominent") position, use the goniometer to measure the angle between the long axis of the lower leg and an imaginary vertical line. • If the resultant angle is measured with the hip in a medial rotation position, record its value as femoral anteversion; if measured in lateral rotation, record the angle as femoral retroversion.	• TPAT found to underestimate femoral anteversion values obtained by CT scans (mean difference of 9.2 to 18 degrees)[67,69] • Good concurrent validity with intraoperative measurements[70] • Concurrent validity with CT scan measurements: Pearson r = 0.86, p < 0.001[71]	Statistical difference of 3 degrees between raters reported and explained by the inexperience of 1 of 3 raters[67] Interrater reliability: ICC = 0.81[71]
Thigh-foot angle[58,72]	Assess tibial torsion	• Position the child prone, flex one knee to 90 degrees. • With the ankle in a neutral alignment and the foot sole positioned parallel to the table, use the goniometer to measure the angle between the long axis of the foot drawn through the second metatarsal bone and the long axis of the thigh.	Concurrent validity with CT scan measurements: r = 0.52, p = 0.001[72]	Interrater reliability: ICC = 0.74[72]
Transmalleolar angle test[58,72]	Assess tibial torsion	• Position the child prone, flex one knee to 90 degrees. • With the ankle in a neutral alignment and the foot sole positioned parallel to the table, draw a line ("axis") connecting the malleoli and the second line perpendicular to the transmalleolar axis. • Use the goniometer to measure the angle between the second line and the long axis of the thigh.	Concurrent validity with CT scan measurements: r = 0.62, p < 0.001[72]	Interrater reliability: ICC = 0.91[72]
Tape measure method[58,73,74]	Assess leg length and LLD	• Position the child supine, with hips in a neutral alignment and knees extended. • Use the tape measure to determine the distance between the most prominent points of the ASIS and the medial malleolus.	Concurrent validity with CT scan measurements: ICC = 0.98-0.99[73] ICC = 0.81-0.85[74]	Intrarater reliability: ICC = 0.99[73] Interrater reliability: ICC = 0.99[73] ICC = 0.92[74]

Abbreviations: ASIS, anterior superior iliac spine; CP, cerebral palsy; CT, computed tomography; LLD, leg length discrepancy.

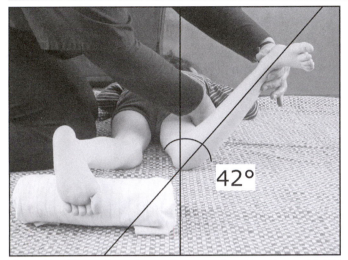

Figure 11-4. The trochanteric prominence angle test in a 7-year-old child with cerebral palsy shows presence of significant femoral anteversion.

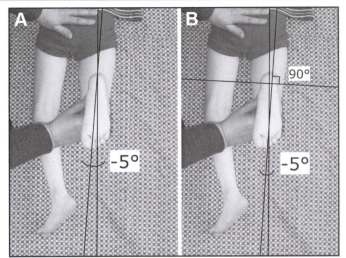

Figure 11-5. (A) The thigh-foot angle and (B) the transmalleolar angle tests in a child with cerebral palsy indicate presence of medial tibial torsion.

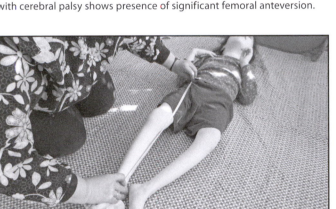

Figure 11-6. Leg length assessment in a child with cerebral palsy using a tape measure. Because of knee flexion contractures, segmental measurements are indicated.

a dislocation.[66] Additionally, as observed in clinical practice, a false positive Galeazzi sign may be obtained because of muscle imbalance or an asymmetrical position of the child's trunk and pelvis during testing. Because the psychometric properties of this examination procedure have not been established, its results should be interpreted with caution.

The trochanteric prominence angle test (TPAT) has been described and researched more widely.[67-71] It can be performed with the child positioned in a sitting or a prone position and yields a clinical measure of femoral anteversion, which needs to be compared to the normal values documented in children developing typically.[68] Table 11-7 describes and Figure 11-4 illustrates the prone positioning TPAT method. At birth, the amount of femoral anteversion is between 25 and 30 degrees and decreases gradually to 8 to 16 degrees by the time of skeletal maturity,[75] while children and adults with CP demonstrate much higher values (see Chapter 4).[51,76] As evident from Table 11-7, studies that compared the results of this test with measures of femoral anteversion received from computed tomography (CT) scans produced variable results.[67-70] Several authors suggested the

presence of a systematic error, with the CT yielding femoral anteversion values 10 to 20 degrees greater than the physical examination.[58,67-69] Therefore, a recommendation was made that 20 degrees be added to the goniometric measurements obtained from the TPAT.[58,68] However, 2 other studies demonstrated a good agreement between the TPAT and the amount of femoral anteversion measured during orthopedic surgeries,[70] and between the TPAT and the CT scan results.[71] Further research is required to resolve this controversy.

Tibial torsion can be assessed using the thigh-foot angle and the transmalleolar angle tests (see Table 11-7 and Figure 11-5).[58,72] For both tests, the measured angle is assigned a negative value that designates medial tibial torsion (the foot turned in) or a positive value that designates lateral tibial torsion (the foot turned out). A typically developing newborn infant demonstrates between 0 and 5 degrees of medial tibial torsion, which changes to 23 to 25 degrees of lateral torsion by the time of skeletal maturity.[75] Many children with CP demonstrate excessive lateral tibial torsion for their age, and some of them display excessive medial or insufficient lateral tibial torsion.[62,72] The presence of foot deformities (eg, metatarsus adductus) may compromise the validity and reliability of the thigh-foot angle measurements because the long axis of the foot should be drawn through the second metatarsal bone[58,72] (see Table 11-7). This problem is eliminated when the transmalleolar angle test is used instead.[58] Another advantage of this measure is that it was shown to possess superior psychometric properties examined when both of these tests were applied in children with CP.[72]

The tape measure method used for the assessment of leg length[58,73,74] is described in Table 11-7 and depicted in Figure 11-6. The psychometric properties of this examination procedure were not assessed in children with CP. However, its validity and reliability studies in the assessment of leg length in adults[73] and LLD in children and adults with hip dislocation and hip abduction or adduction contractures[74] yielded good results (see Table 11-7).[73,74] In a child with CP, LLD may be present because of the hip and knee flexion and ankle plantarflexion contractures,[58] which would warrant performing thorough measurements of the femoral and tibial segment lengths, as well as the lower extremity joint ROM to determine the true cause of LLD.

Spinal deformities are also frequently documented in children with CP, which necessitates regular screening.[51,77,78] Persson-Bunke et al[78] described a scoliosis monitoring program that was organized for children included in a Swedish CP registry. In this program, children with CP, ages 2 to 6 years, undergo standardized biannual spinal examination conducted by physical therapists, followed by annual examinations after the age of 6 years. The physical therapist performs a standing or sitting screening of the spinal alignment, depending on the child's ability to stand. The spine is assessed in extension, followed by a forward bending test, and the scoliotic curve is rated as mild, moderate, or severe as outlined in Table 11-8. Plain film radiography of the spine and, subsequently, the Cobb angle[79] measurements are performed for further evaluation in children younger than 8 years of age who have structural scoliotic curves and in older children who present with moderate to severe scoliosis. The frequency of radiographic examinations depends on the child's age and on the progression of scoliosis. It is important to note that, although the spinal examination the therapist performs is subjective, it plays a vital role in the scoliosis screening and monitoring program.[78]

While a scoliometer is often used to assess the degree of axial trunk rotation upon forward bending in a standing position in patients with idiopathic scoliosis,[80-82] its psychometric properties have not been examined in children with CP. Furthermore, the validity and reliability of scoliometer in this patient population may be potentially compromised because scoliosis is most prevalent in children and adults with CP classified in the Gross Motor Function Classification System (GMFCS)[83] levels IV and V[78] who are unable to maintain a stable standing position and will need to be examined in supported sitting.

Assessment of Muscle Performance

Muscle strength, power, and endurance are the indicators of muscle performance that can be examined through observation of movement or functional activities, and by using manual muscle tests, hand-held dynamometry, or other assessment methods.[5,58] The application of many of these examination procedures in infants and young children is limited by their age-related ability to understand instructions, follow directions, or stay on task for the sufficient amount of time.[58] The same concerns apply to older children with intellectual disability. Additionally, the reliability of testing may vary with the time of the day, the child's willingness to participate, the environment in which the physical therapy examination is performed, and the therapist's rapport with the child.[84] It is important to standardize the strength testing procedures so that the most accurate results can be obtained. However, besides the factors listed previously, the validity and reliability of measurement may be negatively affected by the presence of abnormal muscle tone and the degree to which the child may be able to produce consistent force.[84]

TABLE 11-8
RATING OF SCOLIOSIS BASED ON A CLINICAL EXAMINATION

SCOLIOSIS RATING	DESCRIPTION
Mild	A distinct curve is seen upon a thorough clinical exam.
Moderate	The scoliotic curve is obvious upon observation in a spinal extension position and during the forward bending test.
Severe	A marked scoliotic curve requires external support to achieve an upright position of the trunk.

Compiled from Persson-Bunke et al.[78]

As the result, the physical therapist is commonly faced with the task of selecting the most appropriate method of strength testing in each specific patient. Several examination procedures utilized in clinical practice are described next.

Manual muscle testing (MMT) is a common measure used by clinicians to assess strength.[5] Because the application of a standard MMT[85] with infants, young children, and many children with intellectual disabilities is not possible, physical therapists frequently rely on the observation/movement activation/palpation method of muscle testing.[86,87] This method was described for infants with spina bifida[86] and brachial plexus injury[87] but is also clinically applicable in infants and children with CP.

The therapist first observes the child's posture and active movement in a variety of positions.[86,87] When the lack of movement in a joint is observed, tactile input such as light touch, stroking, or tapping is provided to the muscle in question in an attempt to elicit movement. If the effect of gravity is questioned as the factor impeding movement, the child can be placed in a "gravity assisted," "reduced gravity," or "gravity eliminated" position.[86,87] In addition, facilitation of movement in other parts of the body may elicit activity in the muscle being tested. For example, if an infant is placed in a side-lying position and rolling toward prone and back to side-lying is facilitated, muscle activity in quadriceps, hamstring, and/or ankle muscles may be observed. Stabilization or gentle resistance provided to the proximal part of the upper or lower extremity may also promote increased activity in the distal musculature that is being tested.[86] When facilitation, stabilization, or resistance are applied, palpation is very helpful in determining whether a muscle contraction is, indeed, taking place.[86] While using this MMT method, the therapist assigns muscle grades based on the combined observed, elicited, and palpated response. Clinically, several scales have been used (Table 11-9),[86,87] but their psychometric properties have not been examined.

TABLE 11-9
OBSERVATION/MOVEMENT ACTIVATION/PALPATION MANUAL MUSCLE TESTING SCALES USED IN CLINICAL PRACTICE

SCALE	GRADES			
Observed clinically	Muscle contraction present X	Muscle contraction present but weak X-	Muscle contraction questionable ?	Muscle contraction absent 0
Described by Tappit-Emas[86]	Strong movement present X	Trace contraction T	Reflex response R	Absent response 0
Described by Shepherd[87]	Muscle contraction present through full ROM 2	Muscle contraction present through partial ROM 1	Muscle contraction absent 0	
Abbreviation: ROM, range of motion.				

TABLE 11-10
CLINICALLY USED MODIFIED MANUAL MUSCLE TESTING SCALE

GRADE	CORTICAL CONTROL	IN PATTERN	MOVEMENT DESCRIPTION
5/5	X		Complete AROM AG, ability to resist maximal pressure
4/5	X		Complete AROM AG, ability to resist moderate pressure
3+/5	X		Complete AROM AG, able to resist minimal pressure
3/5	X		Complete AROM AG, unable to resist pressure
3-/5	X		Partial AROM AG
3-/5		X	Complete AROM AG, with substitutions/synergies present
2+/5	X		Initiates movement AG, unable to move through available range
2/5		X	Initiates movement AG with substitutions/synergies present, unable to move through available range
2/5	X		Complete AROM in GE position
2-/5	X		Initiates movement in GE position, unable to move through available range
2-/5		X	Complete AROM in GE position, with substitutions/synergies present
1+/5		X	Initiates movement in GE position with substitutions/synergies present, unable to move through available range
1/5	X		Trace muscle contraction, observed or palpated, no joint motion
0/5	X		No muscle contraction palpated
Abbreviation: ROM, range of motion.			

A modified MMT scale that has been utilized in some clinical settings is another method of strength testing that does not have established validity or reliability (Table 11-10). The rationale for the selection of this scale compared to a standard MMT[85] is that it can capture muscle substitutions, abnormal muscle synergies, or compensations observed in children who exhibit atypical movement patterns due to the presence of spasticity. This MMT method can be used with 3 to 4 year olds and older children who exhibit atypical movement patterns but are able to understand instructions, follow directions, and stay on task for a sufficient amount of time for testing to be completed. Besides the child's ability to move a joint through the available ROM against gravity or under "gravity eliminated" conditions, the quality of movement is also assessed, with the grade assigned to movement that is performed *with cortical control* as opposed to movement *in pattern*. Movement *with cortical control* implies the ability to perform isolated movements, and movement *in pattern* refers to impaired selective motor control when abnormal muscle synergies, substitutions, or compensations are present as is frequently observed in children with CP. When the modified MMT scale is used, resistance to active movement is applied only when the child is able to perform an isolated movement.

Two other tests can be used to assess selective control of lower extremity musculature in children with CP.[25,88] The first selective motor control (SMC) test quantifies the child's ability to isolate ankle dorsiflexion movement using a 5-point scale from 0 to 4, with attention given to the recruitment of specific musculature.[25] The second instrument, the modified Trost SMC test,[88] can be used to assess the child's ability to perform isolated hip flexion, hip abduction, knee extension, and ankle dorsiflexion movements with the amount of selective control rated on a 3-point scale from 0 to 2: 0 = total synergy, 1 = partial synergy, and 2 = no synergy. An additional score, "unable," is assigned if the child is not capable of performing a voluntary movement in the designated joint because of muscle weakness or difficulty understanding the task.[88] Higher interrater reliability was reported for the modified Trost SMC test (Cohen's Kappa = 0.57-0.71) compared to the Boyd and Graham[25] SMC test for ankle dorsiflexion (Cohen's Kappa = 0.55).[88]

Hand-held dynamometry (HHD) is a method of isometric muscle force measurement that has been widely researched in children developing typically and atypically, including children with CP.[88-96] The application of this method of strength testing in children developing typically yielded reference values for 11 muscle groups in 4 to 16 year olds[89] and for lower extremity musculature in 6 to 8 year olds.[90] In addition, Gajdosik[91] demonstrated that typically developing children as young as 2 to 4 years of age were able to produce consistent isometric muscle contractions that could be reliably measured with HHD.

Macfarlane et al[90] described the testing procedure using a Microfet II HHD (Hoggan Health Industries) that had the sensitivity of 0.1 lbs and range of 0.8 to 150 lbs. The positions of the child and his or her examiner, methods of stabilization of the participant's body parts, the HHD placement, and its distance from the axis of joint rotation were clearly defined for 6 tested lower extremity muscle groups. For example, to test the muscle force of hip abductors, the patient was positioned supine with both lower extremities in a neutral alignment, knees extended. The examiner was positioned on the side of the extremity that was being tested and stabilized the child's pelvis at the iliac crest. The examiner placed the HHD against the lateral femoral condyle, maintained it in place, instructed the child to "push as hard as he or she could"

for a "make test," and then recorded the value of the force the child generated. The distance from the hip joint axis at greater trochanter to the center of the HHD was measured and used to calculate the muscle torque (Torque = Force x Perpendicular Distance between the axis of rotation and the force application point). The torque values reflect muscle strength of a growing child and allow clinicians to compare strength in children of different heights. The reference and cut-off values for force and torque generated by this research are useful for detecting muscle weakness in 6- to 8-year-old patients of the same height and weight as the Macfarlane et al[90] study participants.

The psychometric properties of the HHD method of muscle strength assessment in children and adolescents with CP who functioned in GMFCS[83] levels I through IV were examined in several studies that focused on lower extremity musculature.[92-96] In most of these studies, a "make test" was used (see previous) as opposed to a "break test," for which the child is instructed to hold the limb in place while resisting the force applied to it by the examiner.[92-95] Two groups of researchers reported good within-session intrarater reliability of HHD[10] for most lower extremity muscle groups,[92,93] while between-session reliability was variable (ICC = 0.0.71-0.97 in the study by Berry et al[92] and ICC = 0.26-0.91 in the study by Crompton et al[93]). In an interrater reliability study, the "make" and "break" tests were compared, and the "make" test was found to be slightly more reliable, but overall, the interrater reliability was poor to good[10] (ICC = 0.42-0.82).[96] Two other groups of researchers obtained moderate to good test-retest reliability[10] of HHD, with the ICC values ranging from 0.78 to 0.99 in one study[94] and from 0.70 to 0.97 in the other.[95] Because a large standard error of measurement (SEM) was reported by several authors,[92-95] it was recommended that calculating the average of 2 trials over 2 or 3 test occasions scheduled 2 to 5 days apart might help decrease the SEM and improve the HHD responsiveness to small increments of change in muscle strength.[94,95]

In ambulatory children with CP, muscle performance can be assessed using functional strength tests.[94,96] Similar to observation/movement activation/palpation method, it is a dynamic method of strength testing, but it uses either the repetition maximum[96-98] or the repetition rate[99,100] to quantify muscle strength during a functional activity. Table 11-11 contains information on several functional strength tests and their reliability.[94,96-100]

Finally, results of several studies showed the feasibility of using an objective measure of rectus femoris and vastus lateralis muscle thickness obtained through ultrasound imaging to estimate the force-generating capacity of these muscles.[101,102] This method of "surrogate" strength assessment may be helpful for the evaluation of the effects of a variety of medical, surgical, and physical therapy interventions in children with CP who have trouble understanding instructions and following directions or have visual, hearing, or motor control deficits that invalidate the use of other objective strength measures.[101,102]

TABLE 11-11

FUNCTIONAL TESTS AND THEIR RELIABILITY IN ASSESSMENT OF LOWER EXTREMITY STRENGTH IN AMBULATORY CHILDREN WITH CEREBRAL PALSY

FUNCTIONAL STRENGTH TEST	DESCRIPTION	RELIABILITY
One-leg standing heel rise[94,97]	Standing on one foot and touching the examiner with one finger to maintain balance, the child performs heel rises to a set ROM, as many repetitions as he or she can. The test is stopped if the child does the following: • Leans or pushes down onto the examiner • Flexes his or her knees • Gives up • Asks to stop the test	Test-retest reliability: $ICC = 0.86$-0.99[94]
The lateral step-up test[96,99]	The child stands with the tested LE on the step, with feet shoulder width apart and parallel to each other. The lateral step-up repetition is counted as appropriately performed if the child's stance knee joint attains a position within 15 degrees of full extension during testing. The repetition ends when the other foot touches the floor after the step-up is completed.	Interrater reliability: $ICC = 0.94$[96]
Sit-to-stand test[96,98]	From sitting on a bench, with knees flexed to 90 degrees and feet flat on the ground, the child stands up without UE support. The repetition is completed when the hip and knee joints attain a position within 15 degrees of full extension.	Interrater reliability: $ICC = 0.91$[96]
Five-repetition sit-to-stand test[100]	The child is positioned sitting in a chair without arm rests, with hip flexed to 90 degrees, knees flexed to 105 degrees, bare feet placed on a firm mat, and arms folded across the chest. A rope stretched at the child's body height is used as a marker of a fully extended standing position. The examiner instructs the child to stand up, touch the rope with his or her head, and sit back down 5 times as quickly as he or she can. The time needed to complete 5 sit-to-stand-to-sit cycles is recorded, and the mean of 3 trials is calculated.	Intra-session reliability: $ICC = 0.95$ Test-retest reliability: $ICC = 0.97$-0.99
Half-kneel to stand without UE support[96]	From standing on one knee with the opposite foot in a plantigrade position and with buttocks not touching the lower legs or the floor, the child transitions to standing without UE support. The repetition is completed when both of his or her hip and knee joints attain a position within 15 degrees of full extension.	Interrater reliability: $ICC = 0.93$-0.96

Abbreviations: LE, lower extremity; ROM, range of motion; UE, upper extremity.

Cardiovascular and Pulmonary Systems

Because children with CP frequently demonstrate atypical development of the rib cage, decreased chest expansion, shallow respiration, and increased work of breathing,[103,104] the cardiovascular and pulmonary system assessment plays an important role in their physical therapy examination.[105] Heart rate (HR), respiratory rate (RR), oxygen saturation (SaO$_2$), and chest wall excursion (CWE) measurements taken at rest, in different positions, and during physical activity provide the therapist with information regarding the child's physiological function.[106-108] The HR variability can be used as an indicator of the efficiency of the cardiac autonomic mechanism and its adaptability to exercise in children with CP.[107] In addition, energy cost indices, such as the physiological cost index (PCI) and the total cost index (TCI), are based on the HR values obtained at rest and during ambulation (PCI) or during ambulation only (TCI) and can serve as measures of energy expenditure and walking efficiency used to evaluate the effects of intervention.[108-110] Formulas for the PCI and TCI calculations[108] are as follows:

$$PCI \text{ (beats/m)} = \frac{\text{Work Heart Rate - Resting Heart Rate (beats/min)}}{\text{Walking Velocity (m/min)}}$$

$$TCI \text{ (beats/m)} = \frac{\text{Mean of Work Heart Rate Recordings (beats/min)}}{\text{Walking Velocity (m/min)}}$$

The TCI formula includes the mean of all heart rate recordings obtained during walking or the mean of steady-state heart rate recordings.[108] Bratteby Tollerz et al[108] defined the steady-state work heart rate as the mean of walking heart rate recordings registered at 5-second intervals within 5 beats of each other. These authors examined the PCI and the TCI in a reliability study and showed that both indices were useful for the assessment of energy cost in children with CP and could be calculated with good test-retest reliability[10] (ICC = 0.99 for the PCI and ICC = 0.96-0.97 for the TCI).[108]

In a child with CP and chronic lung disease or respiratory illness, the HR, RR, and SaO_2 values, combined with a subjective observation of the rib cage structure and the chest wall movement, provide the therapist with crucial information.[105,106] It helps to plan and implement intervention, monitor the child's responses to position change or exercise, and determine when a break between activities may be needed.[105,106] A portable pulse oximeter serves as a valuable tool that allows for timely spot checks of the SaO_2 levels.[106] The RR values can be obtained through observation and palpation of the chest wall and upper abdominal movements during respiration, with their frequency recorded over a 1-minute time period.[106] The CWE assessment using a tape measure to capture the tidal volume and the maximal voluntary effort chest expansion at the level of the xiphoid process, as well as the upper abdominal excursion measurement performed at the waist level provide additional information.[106,111] Finally, pulmonary function tests, such as forced vital capacity (FVC) and forced expiratory volume in 1 second (FEV_1), can be performed using a spirometer.[111] In a study that examined position-related changes in respiration in adolescents and adults with CP and severe scoliosis, Littleton et al[106] demonstrated good intrarater and interrater reliability[10] of HR, RR, SaO_2, and CWE measures. The intrarater and interrater percent agreement varied from 80% to 100% and from 94% to 100%, respectively.[106]

Many children with CP present with insufficient breath support for vocalization that negatively affects their speech production,[103,105] which can be assessed by examining phonation expressed as the number of syllables pronounced per breath and the timed ability to phonate a vowel sound during a controlled exhalation.[105] The results can then be compared to normal values of 8 to 10 syllables per breath and 10 to 12 seconds, respectively.[105] Additional information related to the child's respiratory function, including cough effectiveness, sleeping and feeding patterns, as well as breathing patterns during movement, can be obtained through the patient and parent interview and by observation. This information helps the therapist to draw conclusions in regard to the impact of the pulmonary impairments on the child's activity, participation, and quality of life.[105]

Ambulatory children and adolescents with CP demonstrate diminished aerobic capacity compared to their peers without disabilities.[112] In these children, aerobic capacity and cardiorespiratory endurance can be assessed in laboratory conditions using treadmill or cycle ergometer tests, which are performed using a heart rate monitor and a gas analysis system.[113,114] Alternatively, shuttle run tests can be used in the clinic to estimate the child's aerobic capacity from the continuous heart rate data obtained from a portable monitor.[113,115,116] Table 11-12 contains information on 3 shuttle run tests, SRT-I, SRT-II, and SRT-III, developed by Verschuren et al[113,116] for children and adolescents with CP classified in GMFCS[83] levels I, II, and III, respectively.

The validity of SRT-I and SRT-II was established by using gas analysis to compare peak oxygen consumption values (VO_{2peak}) obtained during shuttle run tests and treadmill tests performed with the same participants (Pearson r = 0.96).[113] Height-related shuttle run reference values for young people with CP functioning in GMFCS[83] levels I and II were also developed.[115] The centile curves based on these reference values can be used to predict aerobic fitness in individuals with CP from childhood to young adulthood.[115] In addition, a 10-meter shuttle ride test (SRiT) was developed to evaluate exercise capacity and cardiorespiratory fitness in children and adolescents with CP who use a self-propelled manual wheelchair for mobility. Validity of this test was established by assessing the association between the VO_{2peak} values obtained for the SRiT and a graded arm exercise test (Pearson r = 0.84, p < 0.01). The description of the SRiT and its reliability data are shown in Table 11-12.[117]

Integumentary System

Skin integrity is a concern in children and adults with CP[118-120] and should be assessed as a part of physical therapy examination.[5] Skin should be inspected for redness, blisters, calluses, thickening, and pressure ulcers that may develop because of joint contractures leading to difficulties with hygiene, and musculoskeletal deformities that make the appropriate fit of supportive and positioning devices challenging.[118-120] The initial signs of skin breakdown may indicate that the child is in need of a new splint, orthosis, or positioning device to accommodate for growth, which requires a timely action to prevent further development of skin problems.[118]

Assessment of the risk for pressure ulcer development is an important preventive measure in addressing skin integrity.[121] Several pediatric pressure ulcer risk assessment scales can be used for these puproses.[121-126] Examples include the Braden Q Scale,[121] the Garvin Scale,[122] and the Glamorgan Scale[123] that were developed for hospitalized children. The risk factors assessed using these instruments are listed in Table 11-13.[121-125] Because hospitalizations related to orthopedic surgeries and respiratory infections are not uncommon in children with CP,[51,126] the use of such scales may be helpful for prevention of pressure ulcers in this patient population. However, a systematic review showed that, although

	TABLE 11-12	
	SHUTTLE RUN AND SHUTTLE RIDE TESTS FOR ASSESSMENT OF EXERCISE CAPACITY AND CARDIORESPIRATORY FITNESS IN CHILDREN AND YOUTH WITH CEREBRAL PALSY: DESCRIPTION AND RELIABILITY	
TEST	**DESCRIPTION**	**TEST-RETEST RELIABILITY**
SRT-I[113]	• Population: children, adolescents, and young adults[115] with CP classified in GMFCS[83] level I • Distance between markers: 10 meters • Procedure: walking or running between 2 markers and making 180-degree turns at each marker with the starting speed of 5 km/h; speed is increased by 0.25 km/hour every minute following a signal provided by an audio recording • Outcome measure: exercise capacity expressed as total exercise time or the number of attained shuttle run levels	HR_{peak}: ICC = 0.87 Ex. Time: ICC = 0.97
SRT-II[113]	• Population: children, adolescents, and young adults[115] with CP classified in GMFCS[83] level II • Distance between markers: 10 meters • Procedure: walking or running between 2 markers and making 180-degree turns at each marker with the starting speed of 2 km/h; speed is increased by 0.25 km/hour every minute following a signal provided by an audio recording • Outcome measure: exercise capacity expressed as total exercise time or the number of attained shuttle run levels	HR_{peak}: ICC = 0.94 Ex. Time: ICC = 0.99
SRT-III[116]	• Population: children and adolescents with CP classified in GMFCS[83] level III • Distance between markers: 7.5 meters • Procedure: walking or running in squares between 4 markers while making 90-degree turns at each marker with the starting speed of 1.5 km/h; speed is increased by 0.19 km/hour every minute following a signal provided by an audio recording • Outcome measure: exercise capacity expressed in total exercise time or the number of attained shuttle run levels	Ex. Time: ICC = 0.99
SRiT[117]	• Population: children and adolescents with CP who use a self-propelled manual wheelchair for mobility • Distance between markers: 10 meters • Procedure: propelling the wheelchair between 2 markers and making 180-degree turns at each marker with the starting speed of 2 km/h; speed is increased by 0.25 km/hour every minute following a signal provided by an audio recording • Outcome measure: exercise capacity expressed in total exercise time	HR_{peak}: ICC = 0.99 Ex. Time: ICC = 0.99

Abbreviations: CP, cerebral palsy; Ex., exercise; GMFCS, Gross Motor Function Classification System; HR_{peak}, peak heart rate; ICC, intraclass correlation coefficient; SRiT, shuttle ride test; SRT, shuttle run test.

some of these scales have sound psychometric properties, the impact of their use on incidence of pressure ulcers has not been investigated.[127] The authors of this review suggested that, in absence of such evidence, clinical judgment might be more effective as a risk assessment measure.[127]

Activity

The term *activity* as a component of the ICF Model[2] refers to the performance of a specific task. Activity-related physical therapy examination methods are listed in Table 11-1, and selected specific examination procedures, such as standardized functional tests, gait assessment scales, functional mobility, balance, physical fitness, and other activity measures will be discussed next.

Selected Standardized Functional Tests

The Gross Motor Function Measure (GMFM)[128] and the Pediatric Evaluation of Disability Inventory (PEDI)[129] are 2 standardized functional assessment instruments that have been most commonly used in children with CP. The GMFM is a criterion-referenced test that was specifically designed for children with CP to assess change in gross motor functional skills related to 5 dimensions, A through E:

A. Lying and Rolling
B. Sitting
C. Crawling and Kneeling
D. Standing
E. Walking, Running and Jumping[128]

There are 2 different versions of this test, GMFM-88 that consists of 88 items and GMFM-66 that was developed from GMFM-88 using the Rasch analysis.[128,130] Rasch analysis determined the hierarchical order of the scale items, converted the ordinal scale of measurement into a unidimensional interval scale, eliminated those items that did not fit the dimension of gross motor function, and provided an opportunity to estimate a total GMFM score when some of the data were missing.[131] For both GMFM versions, the therapist administers the test and scores the child's performance on a 4-point ordinal scale from 0 to 3.[128] The GMFM-88 yields a percent score for each of its 5 dimensions, while for the GMFM-66, a Gross Motor Ability Estimator (GMAE) computer program is used to convert raw ordinal scores for each item into a total score on an interval scale.[128] Brunton and Bartlett[132] tested 2 abbreviated versions of the GMFM-66 and found them to be highly reliable and valid.

The PEDI[129] is a norm-referenced functional questionnaire that was developed for children with disabilities. It has been used to identify the child's functional abilities; assess and monitor progress in performance of functional skills using specially designed scaled scores; and evaluate program outcomes. The test is administered through a structured interview, by parental report, or via observation of the child's functional behavior. It examines 3 major domains: Self-Care, Mobility, and Social Function. The Functional Skills items scored on a dichotomous scale across the 3 domains are used to evaluate the child's overall functional capability. The Modifications and the Caregiver Assistance scales provide additional information in regard to the child's use of supportive or adaptive equipment and to the amount of required caregiver assistance.[129] As the GMFM-66,[128] the PEDI[129] was also designed using the Rasch analysis.[130]

More recently, a computer adaptive test (CAT) version of the PEDI, the PEDI-CAT[133] was developed. It was standardized on a normative sample of children developing typically and 703 children with disabilities aged birth to 21 years, which significantly expanded the age range of the original PEDI.[129] The CAT methodology serves to individualize the test administration to each child by preselecting the items based on previous responses. This minimizes the number of items that need to be administered, thus effectively decreasing the test administration time.[133]

TABLE 11-13

FACTORS EVALUATED USING PEDIATRIC PRESSURE ULCER RISK ASSESSMENT SCALES

SCALE	EVALUATED FACTORS
The Braden Q Scale[121,124]	*Pressure Intensity and Duration*
	Mobility
	Activity
	Sensory perception
	Soft Tissue Tolerance
	Moisture
	Friction-shear
	Nutrition
	Tissue perfusion and oxygenation
The Garvin Scale[122,125]	Mobility
	Sensory perception
	Nutrition
	Moisture
The Glamorgan Scale[123,125]	Mobility
	Equipment pressing or rubbing on skin
	Anemia
	Pyrexia
	Peripheral perfusion
	Nutrition
	Serum albumin
	Weight
	Continence

Both the GMFM[128] and the PEDI[129] have been extensively researched and found to be reliable, valid, and responsive to change[128,129,131-137] In addition, these instruments were shown to complement each other in the assessment of different areas of motor function, which helps the examiner to obtain the most comprehensive testing results.[137] Debuse and Brace[138] conducted a systematic review of activity assessment tools available for children with CP, including the GMFM,[128] the original PEDI,[129] the Paediatric Outcomes Data Collection Instrument (PODCI),[139] the Functional Independence Measure for Children (WeeFIM),[140] and the Gilette Functional Assessment Questionnaire (FAQ).[141] Results of this review revealed that further research was needed to establish the psychometric properties of most of the examined functional measures for use with this diagnostic group, except for the GMFM and the PEDI.[139] A brief summary of general characteristics and selected psychometric properties of these standardized instruments are provided in Table 11-14.[128,129,134,142]

TABLE 11-14

GENERAL CHARACTERISTICS AND PSYCHOMETRIC PROPERTIES OF THE GMFM-88, GMFM-66,[128] PEDI,[129] AND THE PEDI-CAT[133]

TEST TITLE	INTENDED POPULATION	AGE RANGE	SUBSCALES AND SCORING	PSYCHOMETRIC PROPERTIES
GMFM-88[128]	Children and adolescents with CP	5 months to 16 years	*Dimensions* A: Lying and Rolling B: Sitting C: Crawling and Kneeling D: Standing E: Walking, Running and Jumping *Scoring* Percent score for each dimension and the total score are calculated	*Reliability* Intrarater: ICC = 0.92-0.99 Interrater: ICC = 0.87-0.99 *Face and Content Validity* Established through evaluation of test items and their format by a group of experts. *Responsiveness to Change* Correlations between GMFM-88 change scores and judgments of change by therapists (r = 0.65), parents (r = 0.54), and video analysis of item performance (r = 0.82)
GMFM-66[128]	Children and adolescents with CP	5 months to 16 years	*Dimensions* Same as above *Scoring* Only the total score is obtained	*Reliability* • Test-retest: ICC = 0.99[134] • Reliability of Item Difficulties Over Time: ICC = 0.97, p < 0.001[128] • Reliability of child ability scores with different items used for testing: ICC = 0.98, p < 0.001[128] *Face Validity* Established through evaluation of item difficulty and distribution of test scores by GMFCS[83] level and type of CP[134] *Responsiveness to Change* • Significant interaction of time, age and GMFCS[83] level[134] • Greater change over time in children younger than 5 years • Greater change observed in children functioning at GMFCS levels I and II compared to other GMFCS levels[134]

(continued)

TABLE 11-14 (CONTINUED)

GENERAL CHARACTERISTICS AND PSYCHOMETRIC PROPERTIES OF THE GMFM-88, GMFM-66,[128] PEDI,[129] AND THE PEDI-CAT[133]

TEST TITLE	INTENDED POPULATION	AGE RANGE	SUBSCALES AND SCORING	PSYCHOMETRIC PROPERTIES
PEDI[129]	Children with disabilities	6 months to 7.5 yrs or older children functioning below the age level of 7.5 years	*Domains* • Self-Care • Mobility • Social Function *Scales* • Functional Skills • Caregiver Assistance • Modifications *Scoring* • Normative and scaled scores are available	*Interrater Reliability* ICC = 0.84-1.00 *Construct Validity* • PEDI scores demonstrated age trends expected of developing functional skills • Functional Skills and Caregiver Assistance scales were shown to be separate functional constructs *Discriminant Validity* Correctly classified children as having or not having a disability (47-75% and 59-100%, respectively) *Responsiveness to Change* Selective responsiveness to change demonstrated in varied clinical samples, with children with mild to moderate injuries showing statistically significant change over time, and children with multiple disabilities demonstrating significant change in scores in the Mobility Domain but not in other domains.
PEDI-CAT[133]	Children and youth with behavioral, cognitive and physical disorders	Birth through 20 years (3-20 years for Responsibility Domain)	*Domains* • Daily Activities • Mobility • Social-Cognitive • Responsibility *Scoring* • Normative and scaled scores are available	*Test-Retest Reliability* ICC(3,1) = 0.96-1.00 *Discriminant Validity* Significantly lower scores obtained for children with disabilities compared to children without disabilities for all domains *Concurrent Validity of PEDI-CAT and PEDI Scaled Mobility Scores* Pearson r = 0.82, P < 0.001[142]

Abbreviations: GMFM, Gross Motor Function Measure; PEDI, Pediatric Evaluation of Disability Inventory; PEDI-CAT, Pediatric Evaluation of Disability Inventory Computer Adaptive Test.

		TABLE 11-15	

SELECTED ACTIVITY MEASURES FOR USE IN CHILDREN WITH CEREBRAL PALSY: MOTOR CAPACITY, FUNCTIONAL MOBILITY, AND BALANCE

INSTRUMENT	POPULATION	DESCRIPTION	PSYCHOMETRIC PROPERTIES[a]
SWOC[143,144]	Children with developmental disabilities who can walk without assistance and without an assistive device and follow directions	This is a test of ambulatory capacity. The child walks on a path of designated length, width, and directional turn parameters and is required to step over and around obstacles, walk on several different surfaces, and perform sit to stand and stand to sit transitions using a chair with and without armrests. The course can be completed by walking under 3 different conditions: with arms down, while carrying a set lunch tray, and while wearing shaded glasses. The time and the number of steps required for the course completion, as well as the number of step stumbles off the designated path are recorded.	*Concurrent Validity with the TUG* Pearson r=0.63-0.92, p<0.05 *Intrarater Reliability* ICC(3,2)=0.90-0.97 *Interrater Reliability* ICC(2,2)=0.99 Sensitivity: 67.6-72.3% Specificity: 68.8-79.7%
TUG[143,145,146]	Children with developmental disabilities; children with CP, GMFCS[83] levels I through III	This is a test of functional mobility and dynamic balance. The child is required to stand up from an armchair, walk 3 meters forward, turn around, walk back, and sit down. Test completion time and the number of walked steps are recorded.	*Concurrent Validity with the SWOC* Pearson r=0.63-0.92, p<0.05[143] *Concurrent Validity with the GMFM Dimensions D[145] and E[146]* Spearman rho=-.052[145] and -0.89[146] *Discriminant Validity* Significant differences demonstrated in the TUG scores among children in GMFCS levels I, II, and III[145,146] but not between levels I and II[146] *Test-Retest Reliability* ICC=0.98-0.99[145,146]
6MWT[147-149]	Children and adolescents with CP, GMFCS[83] levels I through III	This is a self-paced test of functional walking capacity. The child is asked to walk (not run) as many 30-meter laps as he or she can within 6-minute time, with a standardized verbal cue given every 30 seconds by an accompanying assessor. Distance walked is recorded.	*Convergent Validity* Association of 6MWT results with parental reports of the child's ambulatory abilities Spearman rho=0.70, p<0.01[149] *Test-Retest Reliability* ICC=0.91-0.98[147,148]

(continued)

Selected Measures of Motor Capacity, Functional Mobility, and Balance

As shown in Table 11-1, besides standardized functional assessment scales, activity measures may include those that evaluate such aspects of the child's motor capacity and functional mobility as movement transitions, transfers, locomotion, and gait, as well as task-related balance and safety. Selected tools from this category are listed in Table 11-15.[143-153] A systematic review of instruments used for balance assessment in children and adults with CP revealed that most of these tools, including, among others, the Pediatric Balance Scale (PBS),[151] the Timed Up and Go test (TUG),[145,146] and the Timed Up and Down Stairs test (TUDS),[150] were lacking evidence on responsiveness with the

TABLE 11-15 (CONTINUED)

SELECTED ACTIVITY MEASURES FOR USE IN CHILDREN WITH CEREBRAL PALSY: MOTOR CAPACITY, FUNCTIONAL MOBILITY, AND BALANCE

INSTRUMENT	POPULATION	DESCRIPTION	PSYCHOMETRIC PROPERTIES[a]
TUDS[150]	Children with CP, GMFCS[83] levels I and II	This is a test of functional mobility and balance. The child is asked to ascend a 14-step flight of stairs with a railing "quickly but safely," turn around and descend the same flight of stairs using any walking or running method of stair climbing. Time required to complete the task is recorded.	*Construct Validity* Significant difference found between the TUDS scores in 3 groups of children: developing typically, GMFCS level I, and GMFCS level II, $p < 0.001$ *Concurrent Validity with the TUG* Spearman rho $= 0.68$, $p < 0.02$ *Intrarater and Interrater Reliability* ICC $= 0.99$ *Test-Retest Reliability* ICC $= 0.94$
PBS[151-153]	Children with mild to moderate motor impairments; children with CP, GMFCS[83] levels I through III	This is a test of functional balance that includes 14 items that examine static and dynamic sitting and standing balance, and balance during transfers and transitions between sitting and standing positions. The items are scored on a 4-point ordinal scale, and the examiner may opt to record the item completion time.	*Concurrent Validity* • With the GMFM-88[128] total score: rs $= 0.93$, $p < 0.001$[152] • With the GMFM-66[128] total score: rs $= 0.90$, $p < 0.001$[152]; Pearson r $= 0.89$-0.95, $p < 0.01$[153] • With the PEDI[129] scaled Mobility Domain score: rs $= 0.64$-0.71, $p < 0.001$ *Discriminant Validity* Significant differences in PBS scores were shown among the GMFCS levels I through III[152] *Predictive Validity* Correlation with GMFM-66 scores at follow-up r $= 0.90$-0.92, $p < 0.01$[153] Responsiveness: moderate (SRM $= 0.75$)[153] *Test-Retest Reliability* For individual items: k $= 0.87$-1.0[151] Spearman rho $= 0.89$-1.0[151] For total score: ICC(3,1) $= 1.00$ *Interrater Reliability* ICC $= 1.00$[151]

Abbreviations: 6MWT, six-minute walk test; CP, cerebral palsy; GMFCS, Gross Motor Function Classification System; GMFM, Gross Motor Function Measure; ICC, intraclass correlation coefficient; PBS, Pediatric Balance Scale; PEDI, Pediatric Evaluation of Disability Inventory; SWOC, Standardized Walking Obstacle Course; TUDS, Timed Up and Down Stairs test; TUG, Timed Up and Go test.

[a] Not all inclusive.

emphasis on clinically meaningful change, and that larger reliability studies were needed.[154] However, Chen et al[153] did investigate the responsiveness, minimal detectable change (MDC), and minimal clinically important change (MCIC) of the PBS[151] in children with CP. The researchers found this test to be moderately responsive to change (see Table 11-15) and identified its MDC and MCID values.[153]

Gait assessment measures that examine its quality based on a series of temporal spatial and/or kinematic gait parameters, such as the Gillette Gait Index (GGI),[155] the Gait Deviation Index (GDI),[156] and the Gait Profile Score (GPS),[157] are not included in Table 11-15 because they quantify gait-related alterations of body structures and functions, which differs from the activity component of the ICF.[2] Instead, the table contains information on tests of functional walking capacity, such as the Standardized Walking Obstacle Course (SWOC),[143,144] the Six-Minute Walk Test (6MWT),[147-149] and 2 instruments that combine the examination of functional mobility and dynamic balance (the TUG[145,146] and the TUDS[150]).

It is important to understand that walking activity has two aspects: capacity and performance, with the former reflecting what the child *can* do and the latter assessing what the child *actually does* every day.[158] Actual physical activity can be quantified using a pedometer or an accelerometer by recording the total step count, the percentage of active time, and the levels of activity, from low to high, throughout the day. Bjornson et al[158] used this method to examine ambulatory activity in children with CP, GMFCS[83] levels I through III, and in children developing typically, and reported it to be a "valid and feasible" measure of mobility intervention outcomes in this patient population.

Selected Physical Fitness Tests

Children with CP frequently demonstrate poor physical fitness, especially in the areas of flexibility, muscle strength, aerobic capacity, agility, and anaerobic muscle power.[159,160] Methods of assessment of joint ROM, muscle performance, and aerobic capacity were described earlier in this chapter. These procedures can be used to obtain information about the child's muscle strength and aerobic capacity as components of physical fitness. Verschuren et al[159] investigated the link between physical fitness and gross motor capacity in 68 children with spastic CP and found no relationship between the aerobic capacity and scores on the GMFM-88[128] dimensions D and E. However, moderate correlations were obtained between the D and E dimension scores and functional muscle strength, short-term muscle power, and agility. Earlier, Bar-Or[161] proposed that maximal aerobic power was not the main factor that limited daily activity in children with neurologic dysfunction. Findings reported by Verschuren et al[159] suggest that aerobic capacity might be a less valuable measure of gross motor capacity than short-term muscle power.

Two running-based tests are available to assess agility and anaerobic muscle power in children with CP, the 10 X 5-Meter Sprint Test[162,163] and the Muscle Power Sprint Test (MPST).[163] The 10 X 5-Meter Sprint Test[162,163] involves running 10 times between 2 lines separated by a 5-meter distance, at a maximal speed and without stopping while making 180-degree turns at the lines, and with the time of the test completion recorded by an observer. For the MPST,[163] the child is required to run 15 meters 6 times at a maximal speed, with timed 10-second rest periods in between runs. Verschuren et al[163,164] applied both tests in children with CP and established the construct validity and reliability of these measures. Construct validity was supported by significantly different test findings obtained for children classified in GMFCS[83] levels I and II.[164] Inter-observer and test-retest reliability values were good[10] (ICC = 1.00 and 0.97 for the 10 X 5-Meter Sprint Test, and ICC = 0.97-0.99 and 0.98-0.99 for the

MPST, respectively).[164] A later study established the concurrent validity of the MPST with the Wingate Anaerobic Cycling Test[165] (Pearson r = 0.73-0.90, P < 0.01), which supported the use of the MPST as an anaerobic capacity test in children with CP.[166]

Surveys and Questionnaires

Several subjective measures of physical activity are available to examine the child's activity performance,[167] such as the Activities Scale for Kids – performance version (ASKp),[168] the Children's Assessment of Participation and Enjoyment/Preferences for Activity of Children (CAPE/PAC),[169] the Canada Fitness Survey,[170] and the Physical Activity Questionnaire – Adolescents (PAQ-A).[171] Capio et al[167] conducted a systematic review of measures of physical activity that can be used for children with CP and determined that only the ASKp[168] and the CAPE/PAC[169] had been found to be reliable and valid when used in children with physical disabilities, including CP.

The CAPE/PAC[169] is an instrument that primarily measures participation. However, it incorporates the assessment of physical activity and the child's preferences for specific tasks, including physical activities.[167] The ASK[168] has 2 parts: the ASK capability (ASKc) and the ASK performance (ASKp). The ASKp consists of 30 items that cover personal care, dressing, transfers, standing, locomotion, play, and other skills, which are scored on a 5-point ordinal scale. The questionnaire is completed by the child in his or her home based on the recollection of activities performed in the previous week.[168,172] Evidence of its content, discriminant, and concurrent validity was obtained by several authors, and good[10] test-retest, intrarater, and interrater reliabilities were also reported, including the corresponding ICC values of 0.97, 0.94-0.97, and 0.96.[168,173,174]

Participation

As a component of the ICF Model,[2] the term *participation* is defined as being involved in a variety of life situations. Because participation is closely related to activity or being able to perform specific tasks, it may be difficult to measure these 2 constructs separately from each other.[3] This relationship is complicated by the fact that eliminating a limitation in activity may not necessarily lead to increased participation. As discussed previously in regard to activity, the child's capacity may not necessarily translate into his or her actual performance.[3,158] Furthermore, enhanced performance, in turn, does not necessarily translate into increased participation.[3] Thus, when measuring participation outcomes, therapists should assess the impact of both the capacity and performance variables, on the child's involvement in life situations.[3]

A published review of participation assessment instruments available to pediatric physical therapists identified their strengths and limitations that are summarized in Table 11-16.[3,169,175-177] Carey and Long[3] selected only 3 instruments for this review because of their design as participation measures and their availability for clinical use.[3] They argued that if an outcome measure does not have a

TABLE 11-16

Participation Assessment Instruments Available to Physical Therapists Working With Children With Disabilities

INSTRUMENT	INSTRUMENT TYPE, PURPOSE, AND AGE RANGE	ICF²-BASED PARTICIPATION ITEMS (%)	ICF² CHAPTERS COVERED BY PARTICIPATION ITEMS	STRENGTHS	LIMITATIONS
CAPE[169]	A questionnaire used to directly assess participation in daily activities in home and community settings (6-21 years)	96.4	• Community, Social, and Civic Life (majority of items) • Domestic Life • Major Life Areas	• Adequate reported test-retest, interrater reliability, and internal consistency[169] • Established construct validity[177]	• No research reports on responsiveness to change • Not designed for children younger than 6 years of age and those with severe intellectual and physical disabilities
SFA[175]	A questionnaire used in an educational setting to assess participation in a variety of situations; and also, task supports and activity performance (grades K through 6)	42.9	• Self-Care • Major Life Areas	• Established construct validity and responsiveness to change • Good[10] test-retest reliability and internal consistency values	• Limited age range • Participation assessment limited to educational settings and situations • May take a long time to administer and requires collaboration of at least 2 professionals
M-FUN[176]	A developmental assessment of effects of motor abilities on engagement in activities and social participation in home and school settings (2 years, 6 months to 7 years, 11 months)	25.0	• Self-Care • Domestic Life • Interpersonal Interactions and Relationships • Major Life Areas	• Established reliability and validity of test components that assess performance • Participation Assessment checklists allow to obtain a complete picture of the child's function	• No evidence of validity and reliability of Participation Assessment checklists • Not designed for children older than 7 years • Thorough observation of participation in life situations is needed

Abbreviations: CAPE, the Children's Assessment of Participation and Enjoyment; ICF, International Classification of Functioning, Disability and Health; K, Kindergarten; M-FUN, the Miller Function & Participation Scales; SFA, the School Function Assessment.

Compiled from Carey and Long.[3]

sufficient number of items that directly assess participation, or if it does not cover the entire spectrum of this construct, the testing results may not accurately reflect the involvement in life situations desired by or expected from the child. Table 11-16 contains information on the percentage of participation-related items identified in each of the reviewed instruments and lists the ICF[2] participation chapters these items cover.[3] As evident from the table, the CAPE[169] has the highest percentage of its items that assess participation, but mostly related to community, social, and civic life. At the same time, although the M-FUN[176] contains only 25% participation-related items, they cover 4 of 5 ICF[2] chapters that address its participation component. It is important to keep in mind the limitations of the existing participation assessment tools when using them in clinical practice, and, as recommended by Carey and Long,[3] new instruments that may be developed in the future should cover the full spectrum of the person's involvement in life situations.

Chiarello et al,[178] who examined family priorities in the areas of activity and participation for children and adolescents with CP, emphasized the importance of interviewing the child's family in order to determine activity and participation outcomes that would be meaningful for everyone involved. Besides the participation-specific outcome measures or their relevant parts discussed previously, physical therapists can also use individualized instruments to assess participation as suggested by Palisano et al.[179] The Goal Attainment Scaling (GAS)[180] and the Canadian Occupational Performance Measure (COPM)[181] are 2 examples of such instruments.

The GAS[180] is a highly individualized measure of change that is based on set criteria specific to the area in which the goal is established. It can be used to set meaningful goals for the child and his or her family.[180] These goals can be established at the level of any of the ICF[2] components, from the alterations in body structures and functions to participation.[182] In order to set a participation goal, the therapist needs to first interview the child and the family to identify their participation priorities.[179]

According to the GAS procedure, once a meaningful goal is identified, a range of its possible outcomes is determined on a 5-point ordinal scale from -2 to +2.[180] The lowest score on the scale (-2) would represent the child's level of participation prior to intervention. The score of 0 would represent being on target for the attainment of the set goal. The scores of -1, +1, and +2 would correspond to different levels of goal attainment, from a measurable but insufficient improvement (-1) to outcomes that exceed expectations set by the goal but may still be realistic in a better (+1) or the best (+2) case scenario.[180] This method of assessing intervention outcomes was shown to be responsive to change and has evidence of adequate content validity.[182] Its interrater reliability was examined in a study conducted with 23 children with CP whose GAS scales were rated by several pairs of physical, occupational, and speech therapists.[183] The scales constructed by the therapists who knew the children well were found to have good[10] interrater reliability (Cohen's kappa = 0.82), while moderate[10]

interrater reliability was obtained for the scales constructed by independent therapists (Cohen's kappa = 0.64).[183]

The COPM[181] is another individualized instrument that can be used to assess activity and participation outcomes, set goals, and track changes in self-perception for people of all ages and with a variety of disabilities in regard to their occupational performance and satisfaction.[184,185] When it is applied with very young children, parental report[184] and an adapted version of this measure[186] can be used with adequate reliability. The COPM is administered as a semi-structured interview to identify, rate the importance of, and prioritize problems related to 3 areas of occupational performance: self-care, including personal care, functional mobility, and community management; productivity in play, school, or work activities; and leisure, including socialization and quiet and active recreation.[181,184,185] For the top 5 problems, the child's performance and satisfaction are rated on a scale from 1 to 10, with better performance and higher satisfaction rated higher. This assessment process leads to writing meaningful intervention goals for the child.[181,184,185] Cusick et al[186] obtained evidence of acceptable construct and content validity, internal consistency, and responsiveness to change of the adapted version of the COPM when it was used in 41 children with unilateral spastic CP. In addition, Sakzewski et al,[185] who conducted a systematic review of participation assessment instruments that can be used in children with CP, reported that only the COPM[181] and the GAS[180] demonstrated adequate responsiveness, and were able to detect change that was clinically significant.

Quality of Life

As discussed previously, besides participation, quality of life (QoL) should be considered the most important outcome of intervention, and, thus, it needs to be assessed.[187] The World Health Organization (WHO)[187] defined QoL as "the individual's perception of their position in life in the context of the culture and value systems in which they live, and in relation to their goals, expectations, standards and concerns."(p. 1403) Many other definitions of QoL exist as it is a subjective multidimensional construct that encompasses the person's view of the place they have in the society, including his or her emotional, social, material, and physical well-being, as well as self-esteem and self-determination.[188,189]

Health-related quality of life, or HRQL, is a part of QoL that is in direct relationship with one's health.[188,190] This concept can be interpreted as the person's perception of his or her health and different components of QoL that are related to and affected by a specific medical condition; the consequences of this condition; and the characteristics of QoL the health professionals working with this person may be able to change.[188] Parents, clinicians, and the child may have different perspectives on the child's QoL.[190] Self-reported HRQL is probably the most valid, but for children who are very young or unable to communicate, parents or caregivers would be the best reporters.[190]

	TABLE 11-17	
	CEREBRAL PALSY-SPECIFIC MEASURES OF HEALTH-RELATED QUALITY OF LIFE, THEIR DESCRIPTION, AND PSYCHOMETRIC PROPERTIES	
INSTRUMENT	**DESCRIPTION**	**PSYCHOMETRIC PROPERTIES**
PedsQL 3.0 CP Module[199]	This is a questionnaire for children and adolescents with CP, ages 2 to 18 years, that consists of 35 items distributed in 7 scales: Daily Activities, School Activities, Movement and Balance, Pain and Hurt, Fatigue, Eating Activities, and Speech and Communication. A modified parent-report form that contains fewer scales and items is available for toddlers. Items are scored on a 5-point ordinal scale. Item scores are transferred onto a scale from 0 to 100, and higher scores correspond to better HRQL.	*Internal Consistency* Self-report: Cronbach's alpha = 0.63-0.93 Parent proxy-report: Cronbach's alpha = 0.88-0.96 *Sensitivity* Test scores were higher for children in GMFCS[83] level I and lower in level V. *Construct Validity* Intercorrelations between CP Module and generic PedsQL total score: Pearson r = 0.31-0.65 (self-report) Pearson r = 0.38-0.54 (parent proxy-report)
		(continued)

HRQL measures available for use in children with disabilities can be classified as generic and condition-specific.[188] The Child Health Questionnaire (CHQ)[191] and the KIDSCREEN-52[192] are examples of generic HRQL instruments. The CHQ[191] was developed to assess functional health in such domains as mobility, behavior, social, school and family functioning, pain, general and mental health, and parental impact in the areas of emotional and physical functioning. Bjornson and McLaughlin[190] suggested that, because the CHQ[191] was not designed to measure change over time, it was not appropriate for application in intervention efficacy studies. In addition, a European study of psychometric properties of the CHQ[191] parent report form (PF-50) conducted with 818 parents of children with CP showed "limited applicability" of this generic instrument with this diagnostic group.[193]

The KIDSCREEN-52[192] is another generic questionnaire for children and adolescents that consists of 52 items, with the self-report and parent-report versions available. It is a cross-cultural instrument developed in Europe that covers 10 dimensions of HRQL, including Physical Well-Being, Psychological Well-Being, Moods and Emotions, Self-Perception, Autonomy, Relations with Parents and Home Life, Social Support and Peers, School Environment, Social Acceptance (Bullying), and Financial Resources.[192,194] The items are scored on a 5-point ordinal scale, and subsequently, a Rasch[130] score is calculated for each dimension.[194] In a very large study conducted in 13 European countries, this questionnaire was found to have acceptable psychometric properties, including internal consistency (Cronbach's alpha = 0.77-0.89), test-retest reliability (ICC = 0.56-0.77), and convergent validity with other generic instruments that assessed similar constructs (Pearson r = 0.44-0.61). In addition, statistically different KIDSCREEN scores were obtained for children with and without mental and physical health issues,[194] and, unlike the CHQ,[191,193] both the self-report and parent-report versions of the KIDSCREEN-52 were found to be valid for use in 8 to 12 year olds with CP and their parents.[195]

The Pediatric Quality of Life Inventory (PedsQL) version 4.0 contains 4 generic core scales (Emotional, Physical, School, and Social).[196] It is a reliable and valid measure of HRQL in healthy children and adolescents, ages 2 to 18 years, and those with acute and chronic health conditions.[196] It was used in studies with children with CP[197,198] and was found to discriminate well between these children and children without disabilities.[199] A CP-specific module of the PedsQL is also available.[199] This and several other condition-specific HRQL instruments designed for children and adolescents with CP, including the Cerebral Palsy Quality of Life Questionnaire (CP QOL) – Child and Teen versions,[200,201] and the Caregiver Priorities and Child Health Index of Life with Disabilities (CPCHILD),[202] with their psychometric properties, are briefly described in Table 11-17.[199-202] Condition-specific instruments capture the QoL domains that are important to that particular diagnostic group and that are not covered by generic questionnaires.[201] Results of a systematic review of 5 instruments designed to assess QoL in school-aged children with CP suggested that the CP QOL-Child[200] and CPCHILD[201] were superior to the PedsQL 3.0 CP Module[199] in their psychometric properties and clinical utility, such as cost, completion time, and the ease of access.[203]

TABLE 11-17 (CONTINUED)

CEREBRAL PALSY-SPECIFIC MEASURES OF HEALTH-RELATED QUALITY OF LIFE, THEIR DESCRIPTION, AND PSYCHOMETRIC PROPERTIES

INSTRUMENT	DESCRIPTION	PSYCHOMETRIC PROPERTIES
CP QOL-Child[200]	This is an ICF[2] Model-based questionnaire administered by caregiver-proxy report in 4- to 12-year-old children and by self-report in 9- to 12-year-old children with CP. It consists of 7 subscales: Social Well-Being and Acceptance, Functioning, Participation and Physical Health, Emotional Well-Being, Access to Services, Pain and Impact of Disability, and Family Health. Its 52 items are scored on a 9-point ordinal scale. Domain scores are obtained by calculating the sum of and averaging their item scores.	*Internal Consistency* Self-report: Cronbach's alpha=0.80-0.90 Primary caregiver proxy-report: Cronbach's alpha=0.74-0.92 *Test-Retest Reliability* Primary caregiver proxy-report: ICC=0.76-0.89 *Concordance between Proxy-Report and Self-Report Scores* r=0.52-0.77 *Concurrent Validity* Supported by correlation patterns with other HRQL tool scores
CP QOL-Teen[201]	This is an extension of the CP QOL-Child[200] developed for adolescents with CP, ages 13 to 18 years. The adolescent questionnaire consists of 70 and the primary caregiver version of 87 items scored similarly to the CP QOL-Child.[200] Its 7 subscales include Wellbeing and Participation, Communication and Physical Health, School Wellbeing, Social Wellbeing, Access to Services, Family Health and Wellbeing, and Feelings about Functioning.	*Internal Consistency* Adolescent: Cronbach's alpha=0.78-0.96 Primary caregiver: Cronbach's alpha=0.81-0.96 *Test-Retest Reliability* Adolescent: ICC=0.57-0.88 Primary caregiver: ICC=0.29-0.83 *Concordance Between 2 Versions:* ICC=0.40-0.61 *Concurrent Validity:* Similar to CP QOL-Child[200]
CPCHILD[202]	This is a caregiver-report questionnaire for children with severe CP, ages 5 to 18 years, which contains 36 items distributed in 6 domains: Personal Care; Positioning, Transferring and Mobility; Communication and Social Interaction; Comfort, Emotions, and Behavior; Health; and Overall Quality of Life. The items are scored on a 6-point ordinal scale, with discomfort and behavioral problems also rated on a 3-point Intensity scale.	*Test-Retest Reliability* Domain Scores: ICC=0.88-0.99 Total: ICC=0.97 *Face Validity* Established by caregiver examination of item importance for the child's QoL. *Construct Validity* Supported by children with CP, GMFCS levels IV and V, obtaining higher scores than those classified in levels I through III, which indicated lower HRQL in nonambulatory children.

Abbreviations: CP, cerebral palsy; CPCHILD, Caregiver Priorities and Child Health Index of Life with Disabilities; CP QOL, Cerebral Palsy Quality of Life instrument; GMFCS, Gross Motor Function Classification System; ICC, Intraclass Correlation Coefficient; PedsQL, Pediatric Quality of Life Inventory; QoL, quality of life.

PHYSICAL THERAPY EVALUATION, DIAGNOSIS, PROGNOSIS, AND DECISION MAKING

As described in *Guide 3.0,*[5] the evaluation process may be more or less complex, depending on a variety of variables. These variables include the physical therapy examination findings related to the child's primary condition of CP and to the existing comorbidities that affect his or her body structures and functions, activity, participation, and quality of life. In addition, the child's personal factors, living environment, and family situation and social supports need to be considered.[2,5,204] All of these components contribute to the clinical reasoning that leads to the development of the lists of strengths and problems or challenges that would support or impede the achievement of goals identified at the beginning of the top-down structured initial physical therapy evaluation.[6-8]

The physical therapy evaluation report should include the therapist's hypotheses in regard to the sources of the child's movement disorder, leading to the appropriate physical therapy diagnosis that would describe the child's motor problems, such as decreased functional mobility for the patient's age[205] (activity) or the inability to participate in age-appropriate play situations with peers (participation).[2] In addition, based on the analysis of the identified strengths and challenges, the physical therapist must be able to discern to what extent the physical therapy intervention may help alleviate the discovered problems (prognosis), and whether the child's referral to another health care professional may be needed[205] to address specific alterations in structures and functions of various body systems and possible presence of chronic pain (see Chapters 6 through 10). The reader is referred to Chapter 5 for a detailed discussion of factors affecting the prognosis for ambulation, employment, and independent living in children and adults with CP.

Following the top-down approach to the evaluation process, the plan of care should be developed in collaboration with the child (when appropriate) and his or her family.[6-8] The anticipated goals and expected outcomes should be based on the outcome priorities identified during the initial family interview. These may be refined and modified through the discussion of pertinent examination findings.[206] This process would ensure that the set goals are meaningful to the child and the family and may lead to improvements in their quality of life[4] as such goals will address specific functional activities and participation needs of the child as opposed to the remediation of alterations in body structures and functions.[8] Finally, the therapist should decide what frequency, duration, and intensity of services provided in a given therapy setting and which interventions would result in the best possible outcomes.[205] Dosing of intervention is a complex issue that will be discussed in detail in Chapter 18, preceded by several other chapters that will describe therapy settings, delivery models, and intervention approaches, strategies, and techniques used by physical therapists working with children with CP.

Complete video-based activities for Chapter 11 (see Activity Set 2 [activities 2 and 3] and Activity Set 3 on the book website).

REFERENCES

1. Goldstein DN, Cohn E, Coster W. Enhancing participation for children with disabilities: application of the ICF enablement framework to pediatric physical therapist practice. *Pediatr Phys Ther.* 2004;16(2):114-120.
2. World Health Organization. *International Classification of Functioning, Disability and Health.* Geneva, Switzerland: World Health Organization; 2001.
3. Carey H, Long T. The pediatric physical therapist's role in promoting and measuring participation in children with disabilities. *Pediatr Phys Ther.* 2012;24(2):163-170.
4. Bjornson KF, Belza B, Kartin D, Logsdon R, McLaughlin JF, Thompson EA. The relationship of physical activity to health status and quality of life in cerebral palsy. *Pediatr Phys Ther.* 2008;20(3):247-253.
5. American Physical Therapy Association. *Guide to Physical Therapist Practice 3.0.* http://guidetoptpractice.apta.org/. Published August 2014. Accessed August 30, 2014.
6. Campbell PH. Evaluation and assessment in early intervention for infants and toddlers. *J Early Interv.* 1991;15(1):36-45.
7. Effgen SK. Serving the needs of children and their families. In: Effgen SK, ed. *Meeting the Physical Therapy Needs of Children.* 2nd ed. Philadelphia, PA: F. A. Davis Company; 2013:3-40.
8. McEwen IR, Meiser MJ, Hansen LH. Children with motor and intellectual disabilities. In: Campbell SK, Palisano RJ, Orlin MN, eds. *Physical Therapy for Children.* 4th ed. St. Louis, MO: Saunders; 2012:539-576.
9. Long TM, Toscano K. Measurement. In: Long TM, Toscano K, eds. *Handbook of Pediatric Physical Therapy.* 2nd ed. Philadelphia, PA: Lippincott Williams and Wilkins; 2001:85-178.
10. Portney LG, Watkins MP. Reliability of measurements. In: Portney LG, Watkins MP, eds. *Foundations of Clinical Research: Applications to Practice.* 3rd ed. Upper Saddle River, NJ: Pearson Education, Inc.; 2009:77-96.
11. Portney LG, Watkins MP. Validity of measurements. In: Portney LG, Watkins MP, eds. *Foundations of Clinical Research: Applications to Practice.* 3rd ed. Upper Saddle River, NJ: Pearson Education, Inc.; 2009:97-118.
12. Tieman BL, Palisano RJ, Sutlive AC. Assessment of motor development and function in preschool children. *Ment Retard Dev Disabil Res Rev.* 2005;11(3):189-196.
13. Kirshner B, Guyatt G. A methodological framework for assessing health indices. *J Chronic Dis.* 1985;38(1):27-36.
14. Portney LG, Watkins MP. Statistical measures of validity. In: Portney LG, Watkins MP, eds. *Foundations of Clinical Research: Applications to Practice.* 3rd ed. Upper Saddle River, NJ: Pearson Education, Inc.; 2009:619-658.
15. Rosenbaum P, Paneth N, Leviton A, et al. A report: the definition and classification of cerebral palsy April 2006. *Dev Med Child Neurol.* 2007;49(suppl 109):8-14. Erratum in: *Dev Med Child Neurol.* 2007;49(6):480.
16. Tonus – medical definition and more from the Free Merriam-Webster Dictionary. *Merriam-Webster Online.* http://www.merriam-webster.com/medical/tonus. Accessed January 12, 2014.
17. *Inductel Illustrated Medical Dictionary* [computer program]. Version M7. Monte Sereno, CA: Inductel, Inc.; 2003.
18. Sanger TD, Delgado MR, Gaebler-Spira D, Hallet M, Mink JW, Task Force on Childhood Motor Disorders. Classification and definition of disorders causing hypertonia in childhood. *Pediatrics.* 2003;111(1):e89-e97.
19. Sanger TD. Toward a definition of childhood dystonia. *Curr Opin Pediatr.* 2004;16(6):623-627.

20. Sanger TD, Chen D, Fehlings DL, et al. Definition and classification of hyperkinetic movements in childhood. *Mov Disord.* 2010;25(11):1538-1549.

21. Sanger TD, Chen D, Delgado MR, Gaebler-Spira D, Hallet M, Mink JW; Task Force on Childhood Motor Disorders. Definition and classification of negative motor signs in childhood. *Pediatrics.* 2006;118:2159-2167.

22. Goulet C, Furze J. Neuromuscular system: examination. evaluation and diagnosis. In: Effgen SK, ed. *Meeting the Physical Therapy Needs of Children.* 2nd ed. Philadelphia, PA: F. A. Davis Company; 2013:269-346.

23. Bohannon RW, Smith MB. Interrater reliability of a Modified Ashworth Scale of muscle spasticity. *Phys Ther.* 1987;67(2):206-207.

24. Boyd R, Barwood SA, Baillieu CE, Graham HK. Validity of a clinical measure of spasticity in children with cerebral palsy in a double-blind randomized controlled clinical trial [AACPDM Annual Meeting abstract B:2]. *Dev Med Child Neurol.* 1998;40(suppl 78):7.

25. Boyd RN, Graham KH. Objective measurement of clinical findings in the use of botulinum toxin type A for the management of children with cerebral palsy. *Eur J Neurol.* 1999;6(suppl 4):S23-S35.

26. Mackey AH, Walt SE, Lobb G, Stott NS. Intraobserver reliability of the modified Tardieu scale in the upper limb of children with hemiplegia. *Dev Med Child Neurol.* 2004;46(4):267-272.

27. Tardieu G, Shentoub S, Delarue R. Research on a technic for measurement of spasticity [in French]. *Rev Neurol.* 1954;91(2):143-144.

28. Pandyan AD, Price CI, Barnes MP, Johnson GR. A biomechanical investigation into the validity of the modified Ashworth Scale as a measure of elbow spasticity. *Clin Rehabil.* 2003;17(3):290-293.

29. Yam WK, Leung MS. Interrater reliability of Modified Ashworth Scale and Modified Tardieu Scale in children with spastic cerebral palsy. *J Child Neurol.* 2006;21(12):1031-1035.

30. Fosang AL, Galea MP, McCoy AT, Reddihough DS, Story I. Measures of muscle and joint performance in the lower limb of children with cerebral palsy. *Dev Med Child Neurol.* 2003;45(10):664-670.

31. Numanoglu A, Günel MK. Intraobserver reliability of modified Ashworth scale and modified Tardieu scale in the assessment of spasticity in children with cerebral palsy. *Acta Orthop Traumatol Turc.* 2012;46(3):196-200.

32. Clopton N, Dutton J, Featherston T, Grigsby A, Mobley J, Melvin J. Interrater and intrarater reliability of the Modified Ashworth Scale in children with hypertonia. *Pediatr Phys Ther.* 2005;17(4):268-274.

33. Mutlu A, Livanelioglu A, Gunel MK. Reliability of Ashworth and modified Ashworth scales in children with spastic cerebral palsy. *MBC Musculoskel Disord.* 2008;9:44.

34. Klingels K, De Cock P, Molenaers G, et al. Upper limb motor and sensory impairments in children with hemiplegic cerebral palsy. Can they be measured reliably? *Disabil Rehabil.* 2010;32(5):409-416.

35. Leonard CT, Mikhailenok EL, inventors. Apparatus for measuring muscle tone. US patent 6,063,044. May 16, 2000.

36. Leonard CT, Stephens JU, Stroppel SL. Assessing the spastic condition of individuals with upper motoneuron involvement: validity of the Myotonometer. *Arch Phys Med Rehabil.* 2001;82(10):1416-1420.

37. Aarrestad DD, Williams MD, Fehrer SC, Mikhailenok W, Leonard CT. Intra- and interrater reliability of the Myotonometer when assessing the spastic condition of children with cerebral palsy. *J Child Neurol.* 2004;19(11):894-901.

38. Lidström A, Ahlsten G, Hirchfeld H, Norrlin S. Intrarater and interrater reliability of Myotonometer measurements of muscle tone in children. *J Child Neurol.* 2009;24(3):267-274.

39. Kim J, Park H-S, Damiano DL. Accuracy and reliability of haptic spasticity assessment using HESS (Haptic Elbow Spasticity Simulator). *Conf Proc IEEE Eng Med Biol Soc.* 2011;2011:8527-8530.

40. Brogren E. Influence of two different sitting positions on postural adjustments in children with spastic diplegia. *Dev Med Child Neurol.* 2001;43(8):534-546.

41. Liu W-Y, Zaino CA, Westcott McCoy S. Anticipatory postural adjustments in children with cerebral palsy and children with typical development. *Pediatr Phys Ther.* 2007;19:188-195.

42. Piper MC, Darrah J. *Motor Assessment of the Developing Infant.* Philadelphia, PA: W.B. Saunders Company; 1994.

43. Miller LJ, Roid GH. *The T.I.M.E.™ Toddler and Infant Motor Evaluation, a Standardized Assessment.* San Antonio, TX: Therapy Skill Builders™; 1994.

44. Campbell SK. *The Test of Infant Motor Performance. Test User's Manual Version 2.0.* Chicago, IL: Infant Motor Performance Scales, LLC; 2005.

45. Einspieler C, Prechtl HFR, Bos AF, Ferrari F, Cioni G. *Prechtl's Method on the Qualitative Assessment of General Movements in Preterm, Term and Young Infants.* London, UK: MacKeith Press; 2004.

46. Heineman KR, Bos AF, Hadders-Algra M. The Infant Motor Profile: a standardized and qualitative method to assess motor behavior in infancy. *Dev Med Child Neurol.* 2008;50:275-282.

47. Heineman KR, La Bastide-Van Gemert S, Fidler V, Middelburg KJ, Bos AF, Hadders-Algra M. Construct validity of the Infant Motor Profile: relation with prenatal, perinatal, and neonatal risk factors. *Dev Med Child Neurol.* 2010;52:e209-e215.

48. Cooper J, Majnemer A, Rosenblatt B, Birnbaum R. The determination of sensory deficits in children with hemiplegic cerebral palsy. *J Child Neurol.* 1995;10:300-309.

49. Klumlinde-Sundholm L, Eliasson AC. Comparing tests of tactile sensibility: aspects relevant to testing children with spastic hemiplegia. *Dev Med Child Neurol.* 2002;44:604-612.

50. Mockford M, Caulton JM. The pathophysiological basis of weakness in children with cerebral palsy. *Pediatr Phys Ther.* 2010;22(2):222-233.

51. Morrell DS, Pearson M, Sauser DD. Progressive bone and joint abnormalities of the spine and lower extremities in cerebral palsy. *Radiographics.* 2002;22(2):257-268.

52. McWhirk LB, Glanzman AM. Within-session inter-rater reliability of goniometric measures in patients with spastic cerebral palsy. *Pediatr Phys Ther.* 2006;18(4):262-265.

53. Allington NJ, Leroy N, Doneux C. Ankle joint range of motion measurements in spastic cerebral palsy children: intraobserver and interobserver reliability and reproducibility of goniometry and visual estimation. *J Pediatr Orthop B.* 2002;11(3):236-239.

54. Mutlu A, Livanelioglu A, Gunel MK. Reliability of goniometric measurements in children with spastic cerebral palsy. *Med Sci Monit.* 2007;13(7):CR323-CR329.

55. Glanzman AM, Swenson AE, Kim H. Intrarater range of motion reliability in cerebral palsy: a comparison of assessment methods. *Pediatr Phys Ther.* 2008;20(4):369-372.

56. Ten Berge SR, Halbertsma JP, Maathuis PG, Verheij NP, Dijkstra PU, Maathuis KG. Reliability of popliteal angle measurement: a study in cerebral palsy patients and healthy controls. *J Pediatr Orthop.* 2007;27(6):648-652.

57. Staheli LT. The prone hip extension test: a method for measuring hip flexion deformity. *Clin Orthop Relat Res.* 1977;(123):12-15.

58. Orlin MN, Pax Lowes L. Musculoskeletal system: structure, function, and evaluation. In: Effgen SK, ed. *Meeting the Physical Therapy Needs of Children.* 2nd ed. Philadelphia, PA: F. A. Davis Company; 2013:183-218.

59. Reade E, Hom L, Hallum A, Lopopolo R. Changes in popliteal angle measurement in infants up to one year of age. *Dev Med Child Neurol.* 1984;26(6):774-780.

60. Katz K, Rosenthal A, Yosipovitch Z. Normal ranges of popliteal angle in children. *J Pediatr Orthop.* 1992;12(2):229-231.

61. Stout JL. Physical fitness during childhood and adolescence. In: Campbell SK, Palisano RJ, Orlin MN, eds. *Physical Therapy for Children.* 4th ed. St. Louis, MO: Saunders; 2012:205-238.

62. Lee KM, Chung CY, Sung KH, Kim TW, Lee SY, Park MS. Femoral anteversion and tibial torsion only explain 25% of variance in regression analysis of foot progression angle in children with diplegic cerebral palsy. *J Neuroeng Rehabil.* 2013;10:56.

63. Riad J, Finnbogason T, Broström E. Leg length discrepancy in spastic hemiplegic cerebral palsy: a magnetic resonance imaging study. *J Pediatr Orthop.* 2010;30(8):846-850.

64. Saraph V, Zwick EB, Steinwender G, Auner C, Schneider F, Linhart W. Leg lengthening as part of gait improvement surgery in cerebral palsy: an evaluation using gait analysis. *Gait Posture.* 2006;23(1):83-90.

65. Owen E. Optimisation and normalisation of segment lengths (2) equalising leg lengths in AFOFCs. In: *Advanced Paediatric Gait Analysis and Orthotic Management with AFO Footwear Combinations: A Segmental Kinematic Approach to Rehabilitation* [course manual]. Presented at: Rehabilitation Institute of Chicago, May 10-11, 2012; Chicago, IL.

66. Noordin S, Umer M, Hafeez K, Nawaz H. Developmental dysplasia of the hip. *Orthop Rev.* 2010;2(2):e19.

67. Stuberg WA, Koehler A, Wichita M, Temme J, Kaplan P. Comparison of femoral torsion assessment using goniometry and computerized tomography. *Pediatr Phys Ther.* 1989;1(3):115-118.

68. Cusick B, Stuberg WA. Assessment of lower-extremity alignment in the transverse plane: implications for management of children with neuromotor dysfunction. *Phys Ther.* 1992;72:3-15.

69. Davids JR, Benfanti P, Blackhurst DW, Allen BL. Assessment of femoral anteversion in children with cerebral palsy: accuracy of the trochanteric prominence angle test. *J Pediatr Orthop.* 2002;22(2):173-178.

70. Ruwe PA, Gage JR, Ozonoff MB, DeLuca PA. Clinical determination of femoral anteversion. A comparison with established techniques. *J Bone Joint Surg Am.* 1992;74(6):820-830.

71. Chung CY, Lee KM, Park MS, Lee SH, Choi IH, Cho T-J. Validity and reliability of measuring femoral anteversion and neck-shaft angle in patients with cerebral palsy. *J Bone Joint Surg Am.* 2010;92(5):1195-1205.

72. Lee SH, Chung CY, Park MS, Choi IH, Cho T-J. Tibial torsion in cerebral palsy: validity and reliability of measurement. *Clin Orthop Relat Res.* 2009;467(8):2098-2104.

73. Neelly K, Wallmann HW, Backus CJ. Validity of measuring leg length with a tape measure compared to a computed tomography scan. *Physiother Theory Pract.* 2013;29(6):487-492.

74. Jamaluddin S, Sulaiman AR, Imran MK, Juhara H, Ezane MA, Nordin S. Reliability and accuracy of the tape measurement method with a nearest reading of 5 mm in the assessment of leg length discrepancy. *Singapore Med J.* 2011;52(9):681-684.

75. Bernhardt DB. Prenatal and postnatal growth and development of the foot and ankle. *Phys Ther.* 1988;68(12):1831-1839.

76. Gudjonsdottir B, Stemmons Mercer V. Hip and spine in children with cerebral palsy: musculoskeletal development and clinical implications. *Pediatr Phys Ther.* 1997;9(4):179-185.

77. Frere HA, Green SM, Patrick CR. Spinal conditions. In: Campbell SK, Palisano RJ, Orlin MN, eds. *Physical therapy for Children.* 4th ed. St. Louis, MO: Saunders; 2012:271-291.

78. Persson-Bunke M, Hägglund G, Lauge-Pedersen H, Wagner P, Westbom L. Scoliosis in a total population of children with cerebral palsy. *Spine.* 2012;37(12):E708-E713.

79. Cobb JR. Outline of the study of scoliosis. In: *The American Academy of Orthopedic Surgeons Instructional Course Lectures.* Ann Arbor, MI: Edwards; 1948;5:261-275.

80. Amendt LE, Ause-Ellias KL, Eybers JL, Wadsworth CT, Nielsen DH, Weinstein SL. Validity and reliability testing of the Scoliometer. *Phys Ther.* 1990;70(2):108-117.

81. Côté P, Kreitz BG, Cassidy JD, Dzus AK, Martel J. A study of the diagnostic accuracy and reliability of the Scoliometer and Adam's forward bend test. *Spine.* 1998;23(7):796-802.

82. Coelho DM, Bonagamba GH, Oliveira AS. Scoliometer measurements of patients with idiopathic scoliosis. *Braz J Phys Ther.* 2013;17(2):179-184.

83. Palisano RJ, Rosenbaum PL, Walter SD, Russell DJ, Wood EP, Galuppi BE. Development and reliability of a system to classify gross motor function in children with cerebral palsy. *Dev Med Child Neurol.* 1997;39(4):214-223.

84. Pax Lowes L, Sveda M, Gajdosik CG, Gajdosik RL. Musculoskeletal development and adaptation. In: Campbell SK, Palisano RJ, Orlin MN, eds. *Physical Therapy for Children.* 4th ed. St.Louis, MO: Saunders; 2012:175-204.

85. Kendall FP, Kendall McCreary E. Fundamental principles in manual muscle testing. In: Kendall FP, Kendall McCreary E, eds. *Muscles, Testing and Function.* 3rd ed. Baltimore, MD: Williams & Wilkins; 1983:1-15.

86. Tappit-Emas E. Spina bifida. In: Tecklin JS. *Pediatric Physical Therapy.* 3rd ed. Philadelphia, PA: Lippincott Williams & Wilkins; 1999:163-222.

87. Shepherd RB. Brachial plexus injury. In: Campbell SK. *Decision Making in Pediatric Neurologic Physical Therapy.* Philadelphia, PA: Churchill Livingstone; 1999:235-259.

88. Smits D-W, van Groenestijn AC, Ketelaar M, Scholtes VA, Becher JG, Gorter JW. Selective motor control of the lower extremities in children with cerebral palsy: inter-rater reliability of two tests. *Dev Neurorehabil.* 2010;13(4):258-265.

89. Beenakker EA, van der Hoeven JH, Fock JM, Maurits NM. Reference values of maximum isometric muscle force obtained in 270 children aged 4-16 years by hand-held dynamometry. *Neuromuscul Disord.* 2001;11(5):441-446.

90. Macfarlane T, Larson CA, Stiller C. Lower extremity muscle strength in 6- to 8-year-old children using hand-held dynamometry. *Pediatr Phys Ther.* 2008;20(2):128-136.

91. Gajdosik CG. Ability of very young children to produce reliable isometric force measurements. *Pediatr Phys Ther.* 2005;17(4):251-257.

92. Berry ET, Giuliani CA, Damiano DL. Intrasession and intersession reliability of handheld dynamometry in children with cerebral palsy. *Pediatr Phys Ther.* 2004;16(4):191-198.

93. Crompton J, Galea MP, Phillips B. Hand-held dynamometry for muscle strength measurement in children with cerebral palsy. *Dev Med Child Neurol.* 2007;49(2):106-111.

94. Van Vulpen LF, De Groot S, Becher JG, De Wolf GS, Dallmeijer AJ. Feasibility and test-retest reliability of measuring lower-limb strength in young children with cerebral palsy. *Eur J Phys Rehabil Med.* 2013;49:1-11.

95. Willemse L, Brehm MA, Scholtes VA, Jansen L, Woudenberg-Vos H, Dallmeijer AJ. Reliability of isometric lower-extremity muscle strength measurements in children with cerebral palsy: implications for measurement design. *Phys Ther.* 2013;93(7):935-941.

96. Verschuren O, Ketelaar M, Takken T, Van Brussel M, Helders PJ, Gorter JW. Reliability of hand-held dynamometry and functional strength tests for the lower extremity in children with cerebral palsy. *Disabil Rehabil.* 2008;30(18):1358-1366.

97. Lunsford BR, Perry J. The standing heel-rise test for ankle plantar flexion: criterion for normal. *Phys Ther.* 1995;75(8):694-698.

98. Bohannon RW. Sit-to-stand test for measuring performance of lower extremity muscles. *Percept Mot Skills.* 1995;80(1):163-166.

99. Ross M. Test-retest reliability of the lateral step-up test in young adult healthy subjects. *JOSPT.* 1997;25(2):128-132.

100. Wang T-H, Liao H-F, Peng Y-C. Reliability and validity of the five-repetition sit-to-stand test for children with cerebral palsy. *Clin Rehabil.* 2011;26(7):664-671.

101. Moreau NG, Simpson KN, Teefey SA, Damiano DL. Muscle architecture predicts maximum strength and is related to activity levels in cerebral palsy. *Phys Ther.* 2010;90(11):1619-1630.

102. Dew AP, Moreau NG. A comparison of 2 techniques for measuring rectus femoris muscle thickness in cerebral palsy. *Pediatr Phys Ther.* 2012;24(3):218-222.

103. Rahlin M, Moerchen VA. Infants and children with cardiovascular and pulmonary dysfunction. In: Frownfelter D, Dean E, eds. *Cardiovascular and Pulmonary Physical Therapy: Evidence to Practice.* 5th ed. St. Louis, MO: Mosby, Inc.; 2012:600-624.

104. Ersöz M, Selçuk E, Gündüz R, Kurtaran A, Akyüz M. Decreased chest mobility in children with spastic cerebral palsy. *Turk J Pediatr.* 2006;48(4):344-350.

105. Massery M. Multisystem clinical implications of impaired breathing mechanics and postural control. In: Frownfelter D, Dean E, eds. *Cardiovascular and Pulmonary Physical Therapy: Evidence to Practice.* 5th ed. St, Louis, MO: Mosby, Inc.; 2012:633-653.

106. Littleton SR, Heriza CB, Mullens PA, Moerchen VA, Bjorson K. Effects of positioning on respiratory measures in individuals with cerebral palsy and severe scoliosis. *Pediatr Phys Ther.* 2011;23:159-169.

107. Kholod H, Jamil A, Katz-Leurer M. The associations between motor ability, walking activity and heart rate and heart rate variability parameters among children with cerebral palsy and typically developed controls. *NeuroRehabilitation.* 2013;33(1):113-119.

108. Bratteby Tollerz LU, Olsson RM, Forslund AH, Norrlin SE. Reliability of energy cost calculations in children with cerebral palsy, cystic fibrosis and healthy controls. *Acta Paediatr.* 2011;100(12):1616-1620.

109. Raja K, Joseph B, Benjamin S, Minocha V, Rana B. Physiological cost index in cerebral palsy: its role in evaluating the efficiency of ambulation. *J Pediatr Orthop.* 2007;27(2):130-136.

110. Norman JF, Bossman S, Gardner P, Moen C. Comparison of the energy expenditure index and oxygen consumption index during self-paced walking in children with spastic diplegic cerebral palsy and children without physical disabilities. *Pediatr Phys Ther.* 2004;16(4):206-211.

111. Kwon YH, Lee HY. Differences of the truncal expansion and respiratory function between children with spastic diplegic and hemiplegic cerebral palsy. *J Phys Ther Sci.* 2013;25(12):1633-1635.

112. Verchuren O, Takken T. Aerobic capacity in children and adolescents with cerebral palsy. *Res Dev Disabil.* 2010;31(6):1352-1357.

113. Verschuren O, Takken T, Ketelaar M, Gorter JW, Helders PJ. Reliability and validity of data for 2 newly developed shuttle run tests in children with cerebral palsy. *Phys Ther.* 2006;86(8):1107-1117.

114. Brehm M-A, Balemans AC, Becher JG, Dallmeijet AJ. Reliability of a progressive maximal cycle ergometer test to assess peak oxygen uptake in children with mild to moderate cerebral palsy. *Phys Ther.* 2014;94(1):121-128.

115. Verschuren O, Bloemen M, Kruitwagen C, Takken T. Reference values for aerobic fitness in children, adolescents, and young adults who have cerebral palsy and are ambulatory. *Phys Ther.* 2010;90(8):1148-1156.

116. Verschuren O, Bosma L, Takken T. Reliability of a shuttle run test for children with cerebral palsy who are classified at Gross Motor Function Classification System level III. *Dev Med Child Neurol.* 2011;53(5):470-472.

117. Verschuren O, Zwinkels M, Ketelaar M, Reijnders-van Son F, Takken T. Reproducibility and validity of the 10-meter shuttle ride test in wheelchair-using children and adolescents with cerebral palsy. *Phys Ther.* 2013;93(7):967-974.

118. Jones MW, Morgan E, Shelton JE. Primary care of the child with cerebral palsy: a review of systems (part II). *J Pediatr Health Care.* 2007;21(4):226-237.

119. Noonan KJ, Jones J, Pierson J, Honkamp NJ, Leverson G. Hip function in adults with severe cerebral palsy. *J Bone Joint Surg Am.* 2004;86(12):2607-2613.

120. Horstmann HM, Hosalkar H, Keenan MA. Orthopaedic issues in the musculoskeletal care of adults with cerebral palsy. *Dev Med Child Neurol.* 2009;51(suppl 4):99-105.

121. Quigley SM, Curley MA. Skin integrity in the pediatric population: preventing and managing pressure ulcers. *J Soc Pediatr Nurs.* 1996;1(1):7-18.

122. Garvin G. Wound and skin care for the PICU. *Crit Care Nurs Q.* 1997;20(1):62-71.

123. Willock J, Baharestani MM, Anthony D. The development of the Glamorgan paediatric pressure ulcer risk assessment scale. *J Wound Care.* 2009;18(1):17-21.

124. Noonan C, Quigley S, Curley MA. Using the Braden Q scale to predict pressure ulcer risk in pediatric patients. *J Pediatr Nurs.* 2011;26(6):566-575.

125. Anthony D, Willock J, Baharestani M. A comparison of Braden Q, Garvin and Glamorgan risk assessment scales in paediatrics. *J Tissue Viability.* 2010;19(3):98-105.

126. Plioplys AV, Kasnicka I. Nebulized tobramycin: prevention of pneumonias in patients with severe cerebral palsy. *J Pediatr Rehabil Med.* 2011;4(2):155-158.

127. Kottner J, Hauss A, Schlüer AB, Dassen T. Validation and clinical impact of pediatric pressure ulcer risk assessment scales: a systematic review. *Int J Nurs Stud.* 2013;50(6):807-818.

128. Russell DJ, Rosenbaum PL, Wright M, Avery LM. *Gross Motor Function Measure (GMFM-66 & GMFM-88) User's Manual.* 2nd ed. Plymouth, Devon: Mac Keith Press;2013.

129. Haley SM, Coster WJ, Ludlow LH, Haltiwanger JT, Andrellos PJ. *Pediatric Evaluation of Disability Inventory (PEDI).* Boston, MA: Trustees of Boston University; 1998.

130. Linacre JM. Rasch analysis of rank-ordered data. *J Appl Meas.* 2006;7(1):129-139.

131. Avery LM, Russell DJ, Raina PS, Walter SD, Rosenbaum PL. Rasch analysis of the Gross Motor Function Measure: validating the assumptions of the Rasch model to create an interval-level measure. *Arch Phys Med Rehabil.* 2003;84:697-705.

132. Brunton LK, Bartlett DJ. Validity and reliability of two abbreviated versions of the Gross Motor Function Measure. *Phys Ther.* 2011;91(4):577-588.

133. Haley SM, Coster WJ, Dumas HM, Fragala-Pinkham MA, Moed R. *PEDI-CAT Version 1.3.6: Development, Standardization and Administration Manual.* Boston, MA: Trustees of Boston University; 2011.

134. Russell DJ, Avery LM, Rosenbaum PL, Raina PS, Walter SD, Palisano RJ. Improved scaling of the Gross Motor Function Measure for children with cerebral palsy: evidence of reliability and validity. *Phys Ther.* 2000;80:873-885.

135. Bjornson KF, Graubert CS, Buford VL, McLaughlin J. Validity of the Gross Motor Function Measure. *Pediatr Phys Ther.* 1998;10(2):43-47.

136. Ko J, Kim M. Reliability and responsiveness of the Gross Motor Function Measure-88 in children with cerebral palsy. *Phys Ther.* 2013;93(3):393-400.

137. Nordmark E, Jarnlo G-B, Hägglund G. Comparison of the Gross Motor Function Measure and Paediatric Evaluation of Disability Inventory in assessing motor function in children undergoing selective dorsal rhizotomy. *Dev Med Child Neurol.* 2000;42(4):245-252.

138. Debuse D, Brace H. Outcome measures of activity for children with cerebral palsy: a systematic review. *Pediatr Phys Ther.* 2011;23(3):221-231.

139. Daltroy LH, Liang MH, Fossel AH, Goldberg MJ. The POSNA pediatric musculoskeletal functional health questionnaire: report on reliability, validity, and sensitivity to change. Pediatric Orthopaedic Society of North America. *J Pediatr Orthop.* 1998;18(5):561-571.

140. McCabe M, Granger C. Content validity of a pediatric functional independence measure. *Appl Nurs Res.* 1990;3(3):120-122.

141. Novacheck TF, Stout JL, Tervo R. Reliability and validity of the Gillette Functional Assessment Questionnaire as an outcome measure in children with walking disabilities. *J Pediatr Orthop.* 2000;20(1):75-81.

142. Dumas HM, Fragala-Pinkham MA. Concurrent validity and reliability of the pediatric evaluation of disability inventory-computer adaptive test mobility domain. *Pediatr Phys Ther.* 2012;24(2):171-176.

143. Held SL, Kott KM, Young BL. Standardized Walking Obstacle Course (SWOC): reliability and validity of a new functional measurement tool for children. *Pediatr Phys Ther.* 2006;18(1):23-30.

144. Kott KM, Held SL, Giles EF, Franjoine MR. Predictors of Standardized Walking Obstacle Course outcome measures in children with and without developmental disabilities. *Pediatr Phys Ther.* 2011;23(4):365-373.

145. Williams EN, Carroll SG, Reddihough DS, Phillips BA, Galea MP. Investigation of the timed 'Up & Go' test in children. *Dev Med Child Neurol.* 2005;47(8):518-524.

146. Gan S-M, Tung L-C, Tang Y-H, Wang C-H. Psychometric properties of functional balance assessment in children with cerebral palsy. *Neurorehabil Neural Repair.* 2008;22(6):745-753.

147. Maher CA, Williams MT, Olds TS. The six-minute walk test for children with cerebral palsy. *Int J Rehabil Res.* 2008;31(2):185-188.

148. Thompson P, Beath T, Bell J, et al. Test-retest reliability of the 10-metre fast walk test and 6-minute walk test in ambulatory children with cerebral palsy. *Dev Med Child Neurol.* 2008;50(5):370-376.

149. Chong J, Mackey AH, Broadbent E, Stott NS. Relationship between walk tests and parental reports of walking abilities in children with cerebral palsy. *Arch Phys Med Rehabil.* 2011;92(2):265-270.

150. Zaino CA, Marchese VG, Westcott SL. Timed Up and Down Stairs test: preliminary reliability and validity of a new measure of functional mobility. *Pediatr Phys Ther.* 2004;16(2):90-98.

151. Franjoine MR, Gunther JS, Taylor MJ. Pediatric Balance Scale: a modified version of the Berg Balance Scale for the school-age child with mild to moderate motor impairment. *Pediatr Phys Ther.* 2003;15(2):114-128.

152. Yi SH, Hwang JH, Kim SJ, Kwon JY. Validity of pediatric balance scales in children with spastic cerebral palsy. *Neuropediatrics.* 2012;43(6):307-313.

153. Chen CL, Shen IH, Chen CY, Wu CY, Liu WY, Chung CY. Validity, responsiveness, minimal detectable change, and minimal clinically important change of Pediatric Balance Scale in children with cerebral palsy. *Res Dev Disabil.* 2013;34(3):916-922.

154. Saether R, Helbostad JL, Riphagen II, Vik T. Clinical tools to assess balance in children and adults with cerebral palsy: a systematic review. *Dev Med Child Neurol.* 2013;55(11):988-999.

155. Schutte LM, Narayanan U, Stout JL, Selber P, Gage JR, Schwartz MH. An index for quantifying deviations from normal gait. *Gait Posture.* 2000;11(1):25-31.

156. Schwartz MH, Rozumalski A. The gait deviation index: a new comprehensive index of gait pathology. *Gait Posture.* 2008;28(3):351-357.

157. Baker R, McGinley JL, Schwartz MH, et al. The gait profile score and movement analysis profile. *Gait Posture.* 2009;30(3):265-269.

158. Bjornson KF, Belza B, Kartin D, Logston R, McLaughlin JF. Ambulatory physical activity performance in youth with cerebral palsy and youth who are developing typically. *Phys Ther.* 2007;87(3):248-257.

159. Verschuren O, Ketelaar M, Gorter JW, Helders PJ, Takken T. Relation between physical fitness and gross motor capacity in children and adolescents with cerebral palsy. *Dev Med Child Neurol.* 2009;51(11):866-871.

160. Jeng SC, Yeh KK, Liu WY, et al. A physical fitness follow-up in children with cerebral palsy receiving 12-week individualized exercise training. *Res Dev Disabil.* 2013;34(11):4017-4024.

161. Bar-Or O. Role of exercise in the assessment and management of neuromuscular disease in children. *Med Sci Sports Exerc.* 1996;28(4):421-427.

162. Tsimeas PD, Tsiokanos AL, Koutedakis Y, Tsigilis N, Kellis S. Does living in urban or rural settings affect aspects of physical fitness in children? An allometric approach. *Br J Sports Med.* 2005;39(9):671-674.

163. Verschuren O, Ketelaar M, Takken T, Helders PJ, Gorter JW. Development of two running-based anaerobic field exercise tests for children and adolescents with cerebral palsy. *Dev Med Child Neurol.* 2005;47(suppl 103):60.

164. Verschuren O, Takken T, Ketelaar M, Gorter JW, Helders PJ. Reliability for running tests for measuring agility and anaerobic muscle power in children and adolescents with cerebral palsy. *Pediatr Phys Ther.* 2007;19(2):108-115.

165. Bar-Or O. The Wingate anaerobic test: an update on methodology, reliability and validity. *Sports Med.* 1987;4(6):381-394.

166. Verschuren O, Bongers BC, Obeid J, Ruyten T, Takken T. Validity of the Muscle Power Sprint Test in ambulatory youth with cerebral palsy. *Pediatr Phys Ther.* 2013;25(1):25-28.

167. Capio CM, Sit CH, Abernethy B, Rotor ER. Physical activity measurement instruments for children with cerebral palsy: a systematic review. *Dev Med Child Neurol.* 2010;52(10):908-916.

168. Young NL. *The Activities Scale for Kids (ASK).* Ontario: Laurentian University; 2007.

169. King G, Law M, King S, et al. *Children's Assessment of Participation and Enjoyment (CAPE) and Preferences for Activities of Children (PAC).* San Antonio, TX: Harcourt Assessment; 2004.

170. Canadian Fitness and Lifestyle *Research Institute (CFLRI). Canada Fitness Survey.* Ottawa, ON:CFLRI; 1981.

171. Kowalski KC, Crocker PRE, Kowalski NP. Convergent validity of the physical activity questionnaire for adolescents. *Pediatr Exerc Sci.* 1997;9:342-352.

172. Klepper SE. Measures of pediatric function. *Arthritis Care Res.* 2011;63(suppl 11):S371-S382.

173. Young NL, Yoshida KK, Williams JI, Bombardier C, Wright JG. The role of children in reporting their physical disability. *Arch Phys Med Rehabil.* 1995;76(10):913-918.

174. Young NL, Williams JI, Yoshida KK, Wright JG. Measurement properties of the activities scale for kids. *J Clin Epidemiol.* 2000;53(2):125-137.

175. Coster W, Deeney T, Haltingwanger J, Haley S. *School Function Assessment User's Manual.* San Antonio, TX: The Psychological Corporation; 1998.

176. Miller LJ. *Miller Function & Participation Scales.* San Antonio, TX: Harcourt Assessment; 2006.

177. King GA, Law M, King S, et al. Measuring children's participation in recreation and leisure activities: construct validation of the CAPE and PAC. *Child Care Health Dev.* 2007;33(1):28-39.

178. Chiarello LA, Palisano RJ, Maggs J, et al. Family priorities for activity and participation of children and youth with cerebral palsy. *Phys Ther.* 2010;90(9):1254-1264.

179. Palisano RJ, Chiarello LA, King GA, Novak I, Stoner T, Fiss A. Participation-based therapy for children with physical disabilities. *Disabil Rehabil.* 2012;34(12):1041-1052.

180. King GA, McDougall J, Palisano RJ, Gritzan J, Tucker MA. Goal attainment scaling: its use in evaluating pediatric therapy programs. *Phys Occup Ther Pediatr.* 1999;19(2):31-52.

181. Law M, Baptiste S, Carswell A, McColl M, Polatajko H, Pollock N. *Canadian Occupational Performance Measure (COPM) Manual.* 4th ed. Toronto, Ontario: CAOT; 2005.

182. Steenbeek D, Ketelaar M, Galama K, Gorter JW. Goal attainment scaling in paediatric rehabilitation: a critical review of the literature. *Dev Med Child Neurol.* 2007;49(7):550-556.

183. Steenbeek D, Ketelaar M, Lindeman E, Galama K, Gorter JW. Interrater reliability of goal attainment scaling in rehabilitation of children with cerebral palsy. *Arch Phys Med Rehabil.* 2010;91(3):429-435.

184. Verkerk GJ, Wolf MJ, Louwers AM, Meester-Delver A, Nollet F. The reproducibility and validity of the Canadian Occupational Performance Measure in parents of children with disabilities. *Clin Rehabil.* 2006;20(11):980-988.

185. Sakzewski L, Boyd R, Ziviani J. Clinimetric properties of participation measures for 5- to 13-year-old children with cerebral palsy: a systematic review. *Dev Med Child Neurol.* 2007;49(3):232-240.

186. Cusick A, Lannin NA, Lowe K. Adapting the Canadian Occupational Performance Measure for use in a paediatric clinical trial. *Disabil Rehabil.* 2007;29(10):761-766.

187. The World Health Organization Quality of Life assessment (WHOQOL): position paper from the World Health Organization. *Soc Sci Med.* 1995;41(10):1403-1409.

188. Colver A. Quality of life and participation. *Dev Med Child Neurol.* 2009;51(8):656-659.

189. Zecovic B, Renwick R. Quality of life for children and adolescents with developmental disabilities: review of conceptual and methodological issues relevant to public policy. *Disabil Soc.* 2003;18:19-34.

190. Bjornson KF, McLaughlin JF. The measurement of health-related quality of life (HRQL) in children with cerebral palsy. *Eur J Neurol.* 2001;8(suppl 5):183-193.

191. Landrgaf J, Abetz L, Ware JE. *The CHQ User's Manual.* Boston, MA: The Health Institute, New England Medical Center; 1996.

192. Ravens-Sieberer U, Gosch A, Rajmil L, et al. KIDSCEEN-52 quality-of life measure for children and adolescents. *Expert Rev Pharmacoecon Outcomes Res.* 2005;5(3):353-364.

193. McCullough N, Parkes J, White-Koning M, Beckung E, Colver A. Reliability and validity of the Child Health Questionnaire PF-50 for European children with cerebral palsy. *J Pediatr Psychol.* 2009;34(1):41-50.

194. Ravens-Sieberer U, Gosch A, Rajmil L, et al. The KIDSCREEN-52 quality-of life measure for children and adolescents: psychometric results from a cross-cultural survey in 13 European countries. *Value Health.* 2008;11(4):645-658.

195. Erhart M, Ravens-Sieberer U, Dickinson HO, Cover A, the European SPARCLE and KIDSCREEN Groups. Rasch measurement properties of the KIDSCREEN Quality of life instrument in children with cerebral palsy and differential item functioning between children with and without cerebral palsy. *Value Health.* 2009;12(5):782-792.

196. Varni JW, Seid M, Kurtin PS. Peds QL 4.0: reliability and validity of the Pediatric Quality of Life Inventory version 4.0 generic core scales in healthy and patient populations. *Med Care.* 2001;39(8):800-812.

197. Shikako-Thomas K, Dahan-Oliel D, Shevell M, et al. Play and be happy? Leisure participation and quality of life in school-aged children with cerebral palsy. *Int J Pediatr.* 2012;2012:387280. doi:10.1155/2012/387280.

198. Engsberg JR, Ross SA, Collins DR. Increasing ankle strength to improve gait and function in children with cerebral palsy: a pilot study. *Pediatr Phys Ther.* 2006;18(4):266-275.

199. Varni JW, Burwinkle TM, Berrin SJ, et al. The PedsQL in pediatric cerebral palsy: reliability, validity, and sensitivity of the Generic Core Scales and Cerebral Palsy Module. *Dev Med Child Neurol.* 2006;48(6):442-449.

200. Waters E, Davis E, Mackinnon A, et al. Psychometric properties of the quality of life questionnaire for children with CP. *Dev Med Child Neurol.* 2007;49(1):49-55.

201. Davis E, Mackinnon A, Davern M, et al. Description and psychometric properties of the CP QOL-Teen: a quality of life questionnaire for adolescents with cerebral palsy. *Res Dev Disabil.* 2013;34(1):344-352.

202. Narayanan UG, Fehlings D, Weir S, Knights S, Kiran S, Campbell K. Initial development and validation of the Caregiver Priorities and Child Health Index of Life with Disabilities (CPCHILD). *Dev Med Child Neurol.* 2006;48(10):804-812.

203. Carlon S, Shields N, Yong K, Gilmore R, Sakzewski L, Boyd R. A systematic review of the psychometric properties of Quality of Life measures for school aged children with cerebral palsy. *BMC Pediatr.* 2010;10:81.

204. Johnson CC, Long T. Use of diagnosis and prognosis by pediatric physical therapists. *Pediatr Phys Ther.* 2010;22(4):392-398.

205. O'Neil ME, Fragala-Pinkham MA, Westcott SL, et al. Physical therapy clinical management recommendations for children with cerebral palsy – spastic diplegia: achieving functional mobility outcomes. *Pediatr Phys Ther.* 2006;18(1):49-72.

206. Darrah J, Wiart L, Magill-Evans J. Do therapists' goals and interventions for children with cerebral palsy reflect principles in contemporary literature? *Pediatr Phys Ther.* 2008;20:334-339.

Please see videos on the accompanying website at

www.healio.com/books/videosrahlin

12

Therapy Settings and Service Delivery Models

In rehabilitation, the philosophy of service delivery for children with disabilities has moved from primarily a medical model, with service providers perceived as the experts and decision makers, to a family-centered model.

Johanna Darrah, Joyce Magill-Evans, and Robin Adkins[1]

Over the last 20 to 25 years, parents of children and adolescents with cerebral palsy (CP) have become dramatically more involved in making decisions on their behalf compared to a more passive role they played in the past.[1] This transformation was brought about by changes in both the societal views on the place of people with disabilities in the community and the rehabilitation service delivery.[1] The concept of disability is complex and widely debated,[2] but the world-wide adoption of the International Classification of Functioning, Disability and Health (ICF)[3] provided a new perspective for this debate.

The ICF Model uses a *biopsychosocial* model of disability that integrates its *medical* and *social* models.[2,3] In the *medical* model view, disability is a personal problem or characteristic directly caused by a health condition that needs the attention of medical professionals. The goal of medical management of disability is to cure the condition or help the person with disability adjust to it. Therefore, the main issue highlighted by the *medical* model is medical care, and health care policy is the main factor in solving the problem. For comparison, in the *social* model view, disability is not a problem of a person but rather a social problem of full integration of the person into the society. It is determined by a complex set of factors, many of which arise from the social environment itself. In this context, the goal of disability management is to provide sufficient environmental modifications that would allow the

person's full participation in the life of society. Therefore, the main issues highlighted by the *social* model are attitude, ideology, and human rights and, thus, social change is the main factor in solving the problem. By integrating the *medical* and *social* models of disability, the ICF provides a combined biological, individual, and social view of a person's health.[2,3] This integrated view leads to the responsibility for disability management to be shared between the individual and the society, which, in turn, supports the paradigm shift from a medical model of rehabilitation service delivery to a family-centered model[1] that is now believed to be a best practice in a variety of pediatric settings.[4-6]

The *CanChild* Centre for Childhood Disability Research in Ontario, Canada developed the following definition of family-centered service:

> Family-centered service is made up of a set of values, attitudes, and approaches to services for children with special needs and their families. Family-centered service recognizes that **each family is unique**, that the family is the **constant in the child's life**, and that they are the **experts on the child's abilities and needs**. The family works together with service providers to make informed decisions about the services and supports the child and family receive. In family-centered service, the strengths and needs of all family members are considered.[7(p 2)]

Rahlin M. *Physical Therapy for Children With Cerebral Palsy: An Evidence-Based Approach (pp 207-221).*
© 2016 SLACK Incorporated.

This definition encompasses the main premises of family-centered care that include the acknowledgment of parental expertise and uniqueness of each family, as well as the fact that the child functions best when supported by the family, which, in turn, is a part of a community.[7] The family-centered service provision is guided by the following principles:

- Parental participation in the decision-making process
- Partnership and mutual respect between parents and health care providers
- The supportive role of service providers who seek and respect the family opinions and accept decisions the families make
- The providers' focus on the strengths of the child and the family while taking into consideration the family priorities, concerns, needs, and resources[7]

This philosophy is different from the professional-centered medical model in which expert health care professionals make decisions and inform the family of what is to be done.[1] Family-centered care involves two important processes—*empowering* and *enabling*—that support the family expertise and autonomy in decision making.[8] The term *empowering* refers to providing parents with information that they can use to make informed decisions in regard to the child's plan of care and give informed consent for its implementation, while the term *enabling* means acknowledging the expertise and competence of the family, thus creating an environment for success.[8,9]

Rehabilitation services for children with disabilities, including those with and at risk for CP, need to be individualized to fit their and their families' needs in order to enhance the child's participation across his or her immediate and expanded environments, such as home, day care, school, and community.[4] As stated previously, in many therapy settings, services are provided while following the family-centered care philosophy. Such settings may include the neonatal intensive care unit (NICU) where the neonates at risk for CP may be hospitalized after birth,[10] the early intervention setting for infants and toddlers from birth to 3 years of age,[11] and the outpatient rehabilitation and home-based therapy settings.[12]

Therapeutic intervention provided in educational settings in the United States follows a different philosophy of child-centered, educationally relevant service delivery.[13] Provision of services at school is governed by a different set of laws, rules, and regulations compared to family-centered settings, which is reflected in the differences in eligibility criteria, goal writing, decision making, and service delivery.[12,13] When the child moves along the continuum of care transitioning from one setting to another or receives therapies concurrently in several different settings, knowledge of their similarities and differences allows clinicians to provide the child's parents with important information that would help them learn their rights, understand their responsibilities, and confidently navigate the maze of rules and regulations. These and other issues will be discussed next.

THE NEONATAL INTENSIVE CARE UNIT

Chapter 3 highlighted the link between the increased survival of infants born preterm and the incidence of CP, with the risk of unfavorable developmental outcome among the neonatal intensive care survivors increasing with lower gestational age at birth.[14-16] The complex etiology and timing of brain insult and risk factors for CP were also discussed in that chapter (see Tables 3-3 and 3-4).[14,17]

Neonatal practice is an advanced, specialized area of pediatric physical therapy that places extensive training demands on the health care professionals working with this fragile, vulnerable, physiologically unstable patient population.[18,19] As clearly stated in the clinical practice guidelines (Guidelines) for provision of physical therapy services in the NICU published by the American Physical Therapy Association (APTA) Section of Pediatrics, the intensive care nursery setting is not appropriate for physical therapists who lack specialized knowledge and experience in this area of practice, as well as for physical therapist assistants and students.[18] To prepare for neonatal practice, physical therapists would require 2 to 6 months of training that may be conducted as a precepted practicum, an APTA-accredited neonatology fellowship, or as a part of a pediatric physical therapy residency. The therapists' previous exposure to hospital-based pediatrics and early intervention practice would be very helpful in their preparation for meeting the NICU clinical competencies. Sweeney et al[18] provided an extensive list of the physical therapist's roles, clinical proficiencies, and corresponding knowledge in specific areas of neonatal practice, including screening, examination and evaluation, planning and implementing intervention, consultation, scientific inquiry, clinical education, self-learning and professional development, and administration.

The NICU Practice Guidelines[18] are based on the ICF Model,[3] premises of family-centered care, the dynamic systems and neuronal group selection theories (see Chapter 1), and the Synactive Theory of Development described by Als.[20,21] The Synactive Theory of Development is a dynamic systems model of the neonatal process of behavioral organization that is based on physiologic stability as the foundation for the completion of the infant's goals or tasks.[22] The Newborn Individualized Developmental Care and Assessment Program (NIDCAP) developed by Als[22] is grounded in this theory and follows 3 major principles:

1. Observation serves as the basis for actions that lead to minimizing the infant's stress and optimizing development.
2. Caregiver education and support are critical for the implementation of recommendations derived from observing the infant's behavior.
3. These efforts lead to improved functioning of the infant and increased confidence and competence of his or her parents.

A clinical decision-making algorithm described in the Guidelines[18] delineates evidence-based pathways for physical

Figure 12-1. Examples of strengths and challenges lists that illustrate the analysis and synthesis of data obtained at different points of physical therapy examination conducted with a hypothetical infant hospitalized in the Neonatal Intensive Care Unit.

PFSCL
Strengths:
1. Family-expressed desire to participate in the infant's care
2. Parent-reported infant's brief ability to visually focus on caregiver's face

Challenges:
1. Extremely low birth weight
2. Need for assisted ventilation
3. Need for NG feeding
4. Nurse-reported bradycardia during routine handling
5. Difficulty bonding

ISCL
Strengths:
1. Absence of abnormal reflexes or posturing observed during caregiving procedures
2. Observed infant's ability to briefly focus on the caregiver's face

Challenges:
1. Transient bradycardia during routine nursing procedures
2. Lethargy
3. Excessive extension of all extremities in a supine position

TSCL
Strengths:
1. Handling-related bradycardic episode resolved spontaneously
2. Appropriate responses to auditory stimuli
3. Parents present and interested in results of PT examination

Challenges:
1. Excessive hypotonia for PCA
2. Excessive drowsiness for PCA during handling
3. Poor head control for PCA
4. Weak non-nutritive suck

Merged Lists (PFSCL, ISCL and TSCL)

Strengths: Infant's ability to briefly focus on caregiver's face; appropriate responses to auditory stimuli; minimal negative effects of handling on heart rate; parental interest and active involvement in infant's care.

Challenges: Infant's need for assisted ventilation; need for NG feeding and weak non-nutritive suck; parental difficulty bonding; excessive hypotonia, extension of extremities and drowsiness for PCA; poor head control for PCA.

Abbreviations: PFSCL, primary care team and family identified strength and challenges list; NG, nasogastric; ISCL, infant strengths and challenges list; TSCL, therapist identified strengths and challenges list; PCA, post-conceptional age.

therapy examination, evaluation, intervention, and re-examination. The ability of a high-risk infant to adapt to the extra-uterine environment is systematically observed at rest and during and after caregiving procedures in order to develop an individualized examination, intervention, and parent education plan that emphasizes developmentally supportive care.[22] The physical therapy examination process starts with collecting history information, which includes data related to the infant's birth and current status, family history, feeding history, current environment, as well as the medical chart review and information provided by the primary care team. Based on the analysis of history data, the therapist generates a list of primary care team and family identified strengths and challenges (PFSCL).[18] Examples of such strengths and challenges are provided in Figure 12-1.[23] The next step in the examination process is to observe the infant's behavioral organization, self-regulation, and physiological responses demonstrated during routine caregiving procedures, as well as the extent of developmental support provided to the infant by the family members and clinicians.[18] Based on these observations, the infant's strengths and challenges list (ISCL) is generated (see Figure 12-1).[18,23] This process is followed by the infant's examination conducted at all levels of the ICF[3] and supplemented by the identification of contextual (personal and environmental) factors. The analysis of data obtained during the physical therapy examination yields a therapist generated strengths and challenges list (TSCL). When all 3 lists of strengths and challenges (PFSCL, ISCL, and TSCL) are merged as shown in Figure 12-1,[23] reasonable, family-centered, measurable goals are written for each identified challenge, followed by the development and implementation of an intervention plan.[18]

Physical therapy intervention is designed to address the infant's needs related to his or her cardiovascular and pulmonary, musculoskeletal, neuromuscular and integumentary systems; behavioral organization and responsivity to external stimuli; as well as the family needs for support, education, and training.[18,23] Family education, environmental modification, and direct intervention are provided to target the infant's alterations in body structures and functions, activity limitations, and restrictions in participation, which is followed by a physical therapy re-examination to reassess the infant's status, determine his or her progress toward achieving the set goals, and modify the plan of care accordingly.[18,23]

The models of delivery of neonatal therapy services include developmentally supportive care and direct intervention.[19] Developmental care can be implemented as general behavioral, environmental, and neonatal care modifications aimed at the modulation of behavioral and physiological responses of all infants. In comparison, the individualized developmental care following the NIDCAP approach[22] includes designing and implementing an infant-specific plan, followed by ongoing infant observation, plan re-evaluation, and modification. This differs from direct therapy services when a neonatal therapist provides direct intervention to an infant who exhibits alterations of body structures and functions and activity limitations that can be addressed by specific interventions.[19] The NICU Practice Guidelines[19] provide evidence-based recommendations for the selection of neonatal interventions, including infant positioning; joint range of motion (ROM) exercise; therapeutic handling; multimodal sensory stimulation; feeding support; and adjunct interventions, such as neonatal massage, swaddling, kangaroo care, and neonatal hydrotherapy. It is important to note that regardless of the service delivery model, parent education is considered to be of the utmost importance for infant and parent outcomes and, therefore, constitutes the therapist's primary role in the NICU.[19]

At the time of their discharge from the NICU, infants who are considered to be at risk for an unfavorable developmental outcome are referred to the NICU Follow-up Clinic, Early Intervention services, or both.[23] The NICU Clinic is usually staffed by an interdisciplinary team of health care professionals who re-evaluate the child's developmental status at regular intervals and consider or recommend intervention or further referrals, including the referral for Early Intervention services when appropriate.[23]

EARLY INTERVENTION

The provision of Early Intervention (EI) services to infants and toddlers with disabilities who are younger than 3 years of age is governed by federal and state laws.[24] An infant or a toddler is deemed eligible for EI services if he or she exhibits a documented delay in one or more areas of development, has a specific diagnosis that typically results in developmental delays, or will be at risk for developmental delays and disabilities in the absence of EI services.[24,25] The history of Federal legislation that regulates and provides funding for these services is summarized in Table 12-1.[24-28] The following is the definition of EI services provided by Public Law (PL) 108-446, Individuals with Disabilities Education Improvement Act (IDEIA) of 2004[24]:

developmental services that –

(A) are provided under public supervision;

(B) are provided at no cost except where Federal or State law provides for a system of payments by families, including a schedule of sliding fees;

(C) are designed to meet the developmental needs of an infant or a toddler with disability, as identified by the individualized family service plan team, in any 1 or more of the following areas:

(i) physical development;

(ii) cognitive development;

(iii) communication development;

(iv) social or emotional development; or

(v) adaptive development[(118 STAT.2744-2745)]

The amount of impairment or developmental delay that would make the child eligible for EI services is determined by each state.[24,25] The child referred to the EI system must undergo a timely multidisciplinary evaluation, with the identification of the child's and his or her family needs directed by the family. The provided services must meet the standards of the specific state in which they are taking place and, whenever possible, offered in *natural environments* (home and community settings) where children without disabilities typically participate.[24,25] In addition, the EI principles dictate that the services must be family-centered, strengths- and evidence-based, developmentally supportive, comprehensive, and individualized.[29] These services include family counseling; training; home visits; service coordination; occupational, physical, and speech therapies; medical diagnostic services and other medical services that enable the child's participation in other EI services; and early identification, screening, assessment, special instruction, social work, vision services, assistive technology, transportation and other services.[24,25] The EI services are provided by qualified professionals according to an individualized family service plan (IFSP). The IFSP is developed by the EI multidisciplinary team that includes the infant's or toddler's parents, as well as special educators, physical therapists, occupational therapists, speech therapists and audiologists, psychologists, nurses, social workers, pediatricians and other physicians, registered dietitians, and vision and other specialists.[24,25]

Referral, Initial Evaluation, and Ongoing Assessment

If an infant was hospitalized in the NICU, a referral to the EI system may be made by his or her neonatologist at the time of discharge or by a member of the interdisciplinary NICU Follow-up Clinic team when the need for an EI evaluation is determined. Other referral sources include pediatricians, other physicians, therapists, nurses, and other clinicians familiar with the child and the family or involved in child find activities, such as developmental screenings, and parental self-referrals are also common.[29] After the initial intake process, the child and the family are assigned a service coordinator who arranges for a timely multidisciplinary evaluation and guides all subsequent EI processes, including the development of the IFSP, finding and assigning providers of recommended interventions, ongoing communication among the team members, and the transition to preschool services upon the child's third birthday.[11,24]

The initial EI *Evaluation* is conducted by 2 or more clinicians to determine the child's level of development in several areas and to establish the eligibility for services.[6,29,30] The evaluation includes the following:

- A parent interview that allows the EI providers to identify parental concerns, priorities, and resources, as well as family activities, daily routines, and available supports

- A review of the child's medical history that is obtained from the interview and from available diagnostic and medical reports

- The administration of a standardized test to determine the amount of developmental delay the child exhibits

- An observation of the child's movement and posture, play, behavioral organization, and interactions with family members and therapists

TABLE 12-1

HISTORY OF FEDERAL LEGISLATION GOVERNING THE PROVISION OF EARLY INTERVENTION SERVICES IN THE UNITED STATES

YEAR	PUBLIC LAW	CONTENT/SIGNIFICANCE
1975	PL 94-142, Education for All Handicapped Children Act[26]	All children with disabilities, ages 6 to 21 years, should receive "free and appropriate public education."
1986	PL 99-457, Education of the Handicapped Amendments Act[27]	Provided federal funds to the states for EI services for children ages birth to 36 months who have or are at risk for having a disability
1991	PL 102-119, Individuals with Disabilities Education Act (IDEA) Amendments[28]	Reauthorized and amended PL 94-142 and PL 99-457.
1997	PL 105-17, IDEA Amendments[25]	Part C, Infants and Toddlers with Disabilities, outlined the federal policy for the following: • Developing and implementing a statewide early intervention system • Facilitating the coordination of payment for EI services • Enhancing the states' capacity to provide EI services • Encouraging the states to expand the opportunities for infants and toddlers at risk for a substantial developmental delay
2004	PL 108-446, Individuals with Disabilities Education Improvement Act (IDEIA)[24]	Expanded requirements for the IFSP to include the following: • A statement of specific EI services based on peer-reviewed research • A statement of measurable results or outcomes as appropriate for the child's developmental level • A description of transition services appropriate for the child A new option for Early Childhood Transition (section 633) is as follows: • The term *infant* or *toddler with disability* may include children who previously received services under Part C of IDEA, until they enter or are eligible to enter kindergarten or elementary school • May be implemented at a state's discretion • Program is to include an educational component • Parents must be notified in writing about their rights and responsibilities in making a decision regarding continuation of services for their child under Part C or participation in preschool programs under Section 619 New Child Find criteria for infants and toddlers to cover those who are in foster care, homeless, the wards of the state, "involved in a substantiated case of child abuse or neglect," affected by substance abuse or withdrawal symptoms due to prenatal drug exposure, or exposed to family violence

Abbreviations: EI, early intervention; IFSP, individualized family service plan.

The physical therapist selects and performs other tests and measures, as appropriate, and their findings contribute to the team's evaluation of the child's performance and lead to forming judgments in regard to the child's and family strengths and challenges, as well as the areas of development that require intervention.[29,30]

The EI evaluation results are discussed at an IFSP meeting, with all members of the team participating in a collaborative process of developing the IFSP outcomes and an intervention plan while taking into consideration the family wishes, culture, priorities, and resources.[29,30] The IFSP outcomes address the child's need for participation in family routines and community activities and are written in family terms. At that point, the child's needs for specific services and their location, frequency, and duration, as well as specific strategies that will be used to achieve the outcomes of intervention are

TABLE 12-2	
TYPES OF TEAMS OBSERVED IN EARLY INTERVENTION	
TYPE OF TEAM	**CHARACTERISTICS**
Multidisciplinary	• Does not meet the Part C requirements for EI services • Team members individually evaluate the child and provide reports • The least interaction among team members
Interdisciplinary	• A better teaming model more common in EI • More interaction among team members • Formal communication channels are set up • All information is shared among the team members who may submit combined assessment reports signed by all providers
Transdisciplinary	• Frequently used in EI • Team members share all information, skills, programming, goals, and strategies • Extensive communication among team members • Characterized by integrated programming, co-treatment, and role release
Abbreviation: EI, early intervention. Compiled from Kleinert and Effgen.[11]	

determined and included into the IFSP that is reviewed every 6 months.[29,30] The annual IFSP review requires a formal meeting, but the team may also meet at any point in time if a modification to the plan is necessary.[30] The ongoing re-evaluation of the family strengths and needs, and of the child's progress toward the IFSP outcomes, developmental performance, health status, and needs for services, with a generated a written report, is known as the EI *Assessment*.[11,31]

Teaming and Service Delivery Models

The EI services can be provided by a *multidisciplinary*, *interdisciplinary*, or *transdisciplinary* team. The characteristics of each of these team types are highlighted in Table 12-2.[11] As evident from the table, the transdisciplinary team is considered to be the most appropriate for team collaboration in EI.[30] It designates a primary service provider who directly works with the family on the IFSP implementation while consulting with other team members and crossing the boundaries between disciplines. It is important to note that in order for the child and the family to receive adequate support and services, the transdisciplinary framework should include the possibility of direct services provided by other members of the team, if necessary.[30] Coaching, a specific type of interaction common for transdisciplinary teams, consists of the following components:

- The therapist performs observations and leads collaborative discussions with the family in regard to imbedding specific intervention strategies into their daily routines.
- The therapist models and has the caregiver practice these interventions.

- At a follow-up appointment, the therapist evaluates the effects of interventions implemented by the family.
- The therapist and the family work together to identify changes that may be needed to achieve the intervention goals and ways to progress intervention if the goals have been met.[30]

Family-centered intervention includes routine-, activity-, context-, and participation-based approaches, all of which are collaborative consultative models of service delivery as compared to the traditional service delivery model in which a therapist provides a direct service to the child.[29] However, the direct service can be also structured using family-centered intervention principles, with the relationship and collaboration between the provider and the family being its central component. As observed clinically, many EI therapists successfully practice a combination of the "hands-on" and "hands-off" approaches by providing both the consultation and collaborative education to the family, as well as the skillful handling to the child. Results of a study of physical therapists' attitudes toward decision making in regard to EI services showed that the therapists supported the family-centered care approach but also valued direct intervention focused on functional activities as compared to intervention aimed at alleviating impairments.[32]

Depending on the delivery model predominantly utilized in a specific state, frequency and intensity of EI services may vary.[11,30] Typically, therapy frequency may range from 2 times per month to 1 time per month when the coaching model is used, with the parents expected to incorporate the learned skills into the infant's daily routine, to 1 time per week when the direct service model or a combination of coaching and direct models is used. Additionally, based on the clinical experience of the author of this chapter, when the infant reaches the age of 1 year and continues to demonstrate considerable developmental delays as is common in children with CP, depending on the state where the child lives, it may be possible to increase the therapy frequency to 2 times per week.

Variable results related to the efficacy of coaching and direct physical therapy services were reported in literature. For example, Hielkema et al[33] found no difference in motor outcomes achieved in infants who underwent coaching and traditional physical therapy interventions, while Harbourne et al[34] reported greater progress in overall motor development for the children who received direct physical therapy services. Lobo et al[35] offered a thought-provoking perspective on the efficacy of EI based on the concept of grounded cognition. The authors argued that, because cognition is formed through or is grounded in perceptual-motor experiences within different social and cultural contexts, limited exploratory abilities put infants and toddlers with special needs at risk for global developmental delays and disabilities. Therefore, EI must focus on perceptual-motor activities that would not be merely aimed at improving the child's motor skills in his or her immediate future, but would promote global development in the long term. Such an approach would address the primary EI goal that is to help these young children achieve a higher level of cognitive readiness for learning in a school setting.

Lobo at al[35] proposed that physical therapists should design interventions that provide opportunities for children to actively explore their environment while interacting with people and objects in different situations when challenged in dynamic sitting positions and during locomotion. Some of such interventions listed by these authors as effective in enhancing global development were reaching and prolonged object exploration, sitting postural control, and mobility activities that required active problem solving on the part of the child.[35] Specific examples included using movement training (general, midline, and specific movements performed in a supine position) to enhance interaction with objects in infants born preterm[36]; a perceptual-motor intervention that used environmental set-up and manual guidance techniques to advance the child's sitting postural control[34] (see Perception-Action Approach in Chapter 14); and the use of power mobility for very young children who were unable to walk to promote their cognitive, language, and social development (see Power Mobility in Chapter 22).[35,37,38]

Transition to Preschool

Unless the new option for the Early Childhood Transition outlined in the IDEIA of 2004[24] is exercised (see Table 12-1), the eligibility for EI services will no longer apply upon the child's third birthday.[29] Transition planning is a vital part of the IFSP, and the transition process usually starts at the age of approximately 2 years, 6 months.[29] It includes but is not limited to the following:

- Parental education on the Part B Preschool Services[24]
- The initial Individualized Education Program (IEP) meeting
- Collaboration between the EI and preschool teams in regards to the child's safety and learning needs in the educational environment
- Assisting the child in the development of play, self-care, communication, and adaptive skills in preparation for functioning in a preschool setting
- Encouraging the family to play an active role in this important process[29,30]

These steps serve to decrease parental stress and ensure the timeliness, effectiveness, and smoothness of the preschool transition.[29,30] Myers et al[39] identified collaboration, open communication, and positive relationships between the EI and preschool programs as supportive of the physical therapists' participation in the transition process. The therapists' perception of being valued by staff in both settings predicted their collaboration during the planning process.[39] As observed clinically, parents of children who are moving from EI to preschool may not always know what to expect or what questions to ask during the transition process and the initial IEP meeting. Therefore, the EI therapists' participation and support they provide to the child's parents are crucial for the success of the preschool transition.

SCHOOL SETTING

The provision of therapy services to children and adolescents with disabilities is governed by Part B of IDEA legislation,[25] titled Assistance for Education of All Children with Disabilities, which upheld and amended the initial provisions of PL 94-142, Education for All Handicapped Children Act of 1975 (Table 12-3).[26] The IDEA Amendments of 1997[25] established the right to a "free appropriate public education"[(111 STAT.42)] in public schools for all children with disabilities, ages 3 to 21 years, and emphasized the provision of special education and related services to meet "the unique needs"[(111 STAT.42)] of each child and to prepare the child "for employment and independent living."[(111 STAT.42)] The IDEIA of 2004[24] took this further by designating the improvement of education for children with disability as "an essential element of our national policy of ensuring equality of opportunity, full participation, independent living, and economic self-sufficiency for individuals with disability."[(118 STAT.2648-2649)]

According to another public law, the No Child Left Behind Act of 2001,[40] all children, including children with disabilities, should receive a quality education and must be tested annually to assess their progress. After the implementation of this law, many concerns in regard to its provisions, including its failure to ensure adequate testing of children with disabilities, were voiced by national organizations.[41] This led to the adoption of new federal provisions, which gave greater flexibility in meeting the law requirements to local school systems and transferred the responsibility for determining

TABLE 12-3

MAJOR PROVISIONS OF PL 94-142, EDUCATION FOR ALL HANDICAPPED CHILDREN ACT[26] OF 1975 UPHELD BY SUBSEQUENT LEGISLATION[24,25,28]

PROVISION	DESCRIPTION
Zero reject	All children, including those with severe physical and intellectual disabilities, must receive school education.
Least restrictive environment	Whenever possible, children with disabilities are to be educated with children without disabilities. Participation in special education classes and removal from a regular classroom may occur <u>only</u> if the child cannot be provided with satisfactory education in a regular classroom with the use of additional aids and services.
Right to due process	Includes parental rights to the following: • An impartial hearing • Be represented by counsel • Receive a transcript of meetings • Have an interpreter at the meetings • Reimbursement for legal fees if the parents prevail in a court case
Parent participation	Parents are encouraged to actively participate in the development of the IEP for their child. They give permission for their child's evaluation, can restrict the release of information, have access to the child's records, and can request a hearing to follow the due process.
Nondiscriminatory evaluation	The child's evaluation to determine appropriate placement and educational program must be conducted without racial or cultural discrimination, including testing in the child's "native language or mode of communication"[26] whenever possible, with no test results used as a single criterion in the decision-making process. Under the IDEIA 2004,[24] re-evaluations must be performed at least every 3 years but no more frequently than every year.
Development of an IEP	A comprehensive program must be developed for the child annually, including the following: • A statement of the child's present levels of academic and functional performance[24] • Special education, related services and supports needed • Measurable goals A comprehensive multi-year IEP can be developed for the child to allow for long-term planning, including planning transition to post-school activities and participation in the community.
Related services	Include educationally relevant physical, occupational, speech-language therapy services; as well as transportation, audiology, psychological, social work and counseling, recreation, orientation and mobility services, and medical diagnostic and evaluation services.

Abbreviation: IEP, individualized education program.

academic content and achievement standards, including those for children with disabilities, to individual states.[41-43]

Under the IDEA legislation,[24-26] children are considered eligible for special education and related services, including physical therapy, if they are identified as having one or more disabilities listed in Table 12-4.[44] As evident from the table, CP is not designated as a specific disability category; however, children with CP may qualify for services under several other categories. In addition, when a student does not qualify for special education and related services under IDEA,[24-26] it may be possible for that student to access these services under Section 504 of the Rehabilitation Act of 1973,[45] which prohibits discrimination against individuals with disabilities in programs that receive federal funding. According to Title 34, Section 104.3 of the Code of Federal Regulations,[46] a person is considered to have a disability if he or she:

(i) "Has a physical or mental impairment which substantially limits one or more major life activities

(ii) Has a record of such an impairment, or

(iii) Is regarded as having such an impairment"

Furthermore, the Code[46] defines *major life activities* as "…functions such as caring for one's self, performing manual tasks, walking, seeing, hearing, speaking, breathing, learning, and working."

It is important to note that across the United States, there is considerable variation in the interpretation of Section 504, which leads to discrepancies in provision of services not only among different states, but also among different school districts.[41]

Physical Therapy as a Related Service

Therapy services provided in a school setting are child-centered and, as indicated in Table 12-3, must be educationally relevant.[24-26,28] Physical therapy is a related service that addresses the child's academic needs in the context of functioning in the school environment, with the ultimate goal to enhance the student's ability to become an independent and economically self-sufficient member of the society after graduation.[13] The Competencies for Physical Therapists Working in Schools[13] document that is consistent with the *Guide to Physical Therapist Practice, 2nd Edition*[47] and uses the ICF[2] language outlines knowledge and skills necessary for the provision of physical therapy services in educational settings. These competencies encompass 9 main content areas: context of therapy practice, prevention and wellness, team collaboration, physical therapy examination and evaluation, planning, intervention, documentation, administration, and research.[13]

As a part of a team of professionals, the physical therapist conducts a school-based physical therapy examination and evaluation to identify the student's strengths; to determine whether he or she has a disability and specific educational needs; and to assess whether these needs are adequately met or impeded by alterations of body structures or functions, activity limitations, or participation restrictions.[13,24] The evaluation findings are used to determine the child's eligibility for special education and related services. Subsequently, as a member of the team, the physical therapist participates in the development of the Individualized Education Program (IEP) for the child (see Table 12-3 for its components).[13,24]

The IEP team consists of the child's parents; a regular education teacher if the child is to be included in a regular classroom; a special education teacher; a local education agency (LEA) representative who has knowledge of special education and general curricular instruction, as well the knowledge of available resources; a person who is able to interpret the results of the child's evaluation in relation to classroom instruction, which may be any of the members of the team; "at the discretion of the parent or the agency, other individuals,"[24(118 STAT.2710)] such as related service providers, who have specific knowledge about the child and can offer valuable expert information to the IEP team; and finally, the child, when appropriate.[24,30,48] The participation of related services professionals in IEP meetings is not required.[24] However, whenever possible, related services personnel, including physical therapists, should make every effort to take part in these meetings to be able to weigh in on decisions in regard to the services the child will be receiving.[30,48]

The IEP should include both academic and functional goals that must be individualized, context-specific, and measurable, and are agreed upon at the IEP meeting.[24,49] Annual goals or long-term objectives are set at the activity

TABLE 12-4	
FEDERALLY DEFINED DISABILITY CATEGORIES CONSIDERED WHEN DETERMINING ELIGIBILITY FOR SPECIAL EDUCATION AND RELATED SERVICES	
DISABILITY CATEGORY	**COMMONLY USED FOR CHILDREN WITH CEREBRAL PALSY**
Autism	
Deaf-blindness	
Deafness	
Developmental delay[a]	X
Emotional disturbance	
Hearing impairment	
Mental retardation	
Multiple disabilities	X
Orthopedic impairment	X
Other health impairment	
Specific learning disability	
Speech and language impairment	
Traumatic brain injury	
Visual impairment including blindness	

[a] A disability category used for children ages 3 through 9 years, with developmental delay defined by the State. The child shows delays in physical, cognitive, communication, social or emotional, or adaptive development and requires special education and related services. This category is often used for children who do not fit any other category.

and participation levels of the ICF.[2,30] Short-term objectives or benchmarks are not required by the law, but are considered best practice and may be written at the body structures and functions, activity, or participation levels.[2,30] An example of a long-term objective and related benchmarks is provided in Table 12-5. McConlogue and Quinn[49] analyzed 249 physical therapy goals written by physical therapists in IEPs of 32 students. Results revealed that 84% of examined goals were measurable, while only 28% were context-specific, with 21% addressing the students' life skills, 6% related to academic tasks, and 1% directed toward training personnel. The authors emphasized that, in a school setting, educational goals must be written that include the following areas:

- Address activities meaningful to the child
- Are important for his or her academic learning and functioning in a school environment
- Acknowledge the need for training of the support personnel[49]

	TABLE 12-5	
	AN EXAMPLE OF A LONG-TERM OBJECTIVE WITH RELATED BENCHMARKS INCLUDED INTO A CHILD'S INDIVIDUALIZED EDUCATION PROGRAM	
LONG-TERM OBJECTIVE	**SHORT-TERM OBJECTIVES (BENCHMARKS)**	
By the end of the school year, Betsy will stand up from her desk chair, cruise to her walker, and walk to the classroom door in preparation to walking to lunch room with other children, all with adult supervision, 5 days per week.[a]	By the end of the first marking period, Betsy will stand up from her desk chair with verbal cues, cruise to her walker with contact guard assistance, and walk to the classroom door with contact guard assistance, at least 3 days per week.[a]	
	By the end of the second marking period, Betsy will stand up from her desk chair with adult supervision, cruise to her walker with contact guard assistance, and walk to the classroom door with verbal cues, at least 4 days per week.[a]	
	By the end of the third marking period, Betsy will stand up from her desk chair with adult supervision, cruise to her walker with verbal cues, and walk to the classroom door with verbal cues, at least 4 days per week.[a]	
	By the end of the fourth marking period and school year, Betsy will stand up from her desk chair, cruise to her walker, and walk to the classroom door, all with adult supervision, 5 days per week.[a]	

[a] Adult supervision, verbal cues, and contact guard assistance will be provided by a classroom aide, teacher or special education teacher trained by the physical therapist.

It is important to note that, because impairment-related benchmarks may not be relevant to the child's education, they are not included into the IEP but may still be important from the perspective of timely documentation of the child's progress toward intervention outcomes as required by the Physical Therapy Practice Acts in each state.[30] Under IDEIA 2004,[24] the IEP is reviewed at least annually, with re-evaluations performed at least every 3 years but no more frequently than every year, to assess the child's progress toward the IEP goals. According to the law, the IEP can be changed without calling an IEP meeting if agreed upon by the parent and the LEA. In this case, a written document to amend the child's IEP is written.[24] Effgen and Kaminker[41] suggested that, potentially, such approach may create problems for the child and for providers of related services if a specific service is added, modified, or removed without consulting the child's therapist.

Therapy Frequency and Service Delivery Models

The IEP document must contain information on the frequency, duration, and location of physical therapy services the child will be receiving and modifications he or she may require, all of which are determined at the IEP meeting, in collaboration with other team members.[24,41] As there are no nation-wide guidelines available, the unique needs of each child and the therapist's professional judgment guide the decision-making process in this area of practice.[41] In addition, individual states have developed documents to assist school-based therapy providers in determining the frequency and duration of services they provide.[50,51]

According to one such document, the Considerations for Educationally Relevant Therapy for Occupational Therapy and Physical Therapy (CERT)[51] developed in the state of Florida, the therapist should fill out the Student Profile Tool prior to the IEP meeting. The Student Profile consists of the following sections: Personal Care, Mobility, Gross Motor, Fine Motor/Visual Motor, and Sensory Processing. At the IEP meeting, the team will fill out the Therapy Profile that includes information on the number of years the student has been receiving educationally relevant therapy services, his or her potential response to such therapy, as well as the learning environment and therapy and support services to be provided. If the child's scores show that the services are indicated, the available options may vary from periodic to intensive services (Table 12-6).[51]

Unfortunately, besides the existing guidelines and the needs of a specific child, another variable that determines how much therapy the child will receive and what service delivery model will be used is the limited availability of pediatric physical therapists and other related service providers working in a school setting.[41] Effgen and Kaminker[41] listed such reasons for a shortage of school physical therapists as insufficient compensation, difficulty working with children, relative professional isolation experienced by therapists in an educational setting, and benefits of working in other therapy settings. Table 12-7 contains information on service delivery models used in schools.[41,52] In addition to individual intervention models, group sessions are also common in educational settings.[13]

The collaborative model of service delivery can be viewed as the most advantageous for children with disabilities as it supports inclusion of these children in regular classrooms.[53]

	TABLE 12-6	
GUIDELINES FOR INTERPRETATION OF THE STUDENT PROFILE SCORING GRID		
DECISION	**DESCRIPTION**	**EXAMPLES OF THERAPY FREQUENCY AND DURATION**
Services are not indicated	Student is able to function independently in the school environment OR Classroom curriculum or other current services address the student's needs	N/A
Periodic services	Environmental/equipment modifications Training/consultation with parents/school staff	2 times/month 2 times/grading period 1 time/semester
Regular services	Specific therapeutic strategies Multiple environmental/equipment modifications Parental/school staff training	2 times/month 1 time/week 30-45 minutes/week
Intensive services	Intensive therapeutic strategies Multiple environmental/equipment modifications Parental/school staff training	1-2 times/week 45-60 minutes/week

Compiled from The Bureau of Exceptional Education and Student Services, Florida Department of Education *Considerations for Educationally Relevant Therapy (CERT) Form Training Tool: SCRIPT.* Tallahassee, FL: State of Florida Department of State; 2006.

Nochajski[53] explored views of 51 school professionals on collaboration. Results indicated that regular and special educators and related services personnel differed in their definitions of collaboration, with the majority attributing this term to activities associated with collaboration, such as communication and coordination, but not to a process of problem solving. The top 3 most frequently practiced types of collaborative activities, as well as the top 3 advantages of and barriers to collaboration, are listed in Table 12-8. Suggestions for improvement included educational activities provided to staff, improvement in communication between special and regular educators, increased administrative support and staffing, and provision of therapy services in the classroom.[53]

Kaminker et al[54,55] examined pediatric physical therapists' decision making related to physical therapy service delivery in an educational setting via a nationwide, case-based survey. The majority of respondents selected direct individual services over indirect and group services for children described in the hypothetical case scenarios, and significant variability was found in the respondents' decisions in regard to therapy frequency.[54] For example, recommendations for frequency of intervention for a 6-year-old child with CP and a 4-year-old child with developmental delays varied from 0 to 20 times per month.[54] When data were examined further, the authors found an association between the recommended service delivery models and frequency of therapy, and the geographic location of the physical therapy practice.[55] Specifically, fewer respondents from the Northeastern region of the United States recommended service provision in natural settings, while their recommendations for therapy

frequency were at least one session per month greater than suggested by respondents practicing in Midwest, South, and West regions of the country.[55]

These findings highlight the need for further research to improve our understanding of the reasons for regional differences in decision making regarding service provision in a school setting.[55] It would be especially important to investigate the relationship between different service delivery models, therapy frequency, and outcomes of intervention.[55] Furthermore, the dissemination of results of such research and its translation into clinical practice would be a significant step toward the use of evidence by pediatric physical therapists working in educational settings. In a small school-based study, pediatric physical therapists demonstrated insufficient confidence in their ability to implement evidence-based practice and demonstrated varied knowledge of the subject.[56] They were more likely to consult with colleagues or their supervisor and rely on their clinical experience than to use evidence when making practice-related decisions.[56]

Transition Services

The Early Childhood Transition from EI to Preschool was discussed previously. Transitions from preschool to elementary school, from elementary to middle school, and from middle school to high school are not outlined in the IDEA legislation.[25] Regardless, they may be stressful for the child, his or her family, and school personnel.[48] The new school environment may be demanding for all children as they enter an unfamiliar building, meet new teachers, and interact

TABLE 12-7		
SERVICE DELIVERY MODELS IN AN EDUCATIONAL SETTING		
SERVICE DELIVERY MODEL	**DESCRIPTION**	**SERVICE LOCATION**
Direct	• Traditional service delivery model • Therapist is the primary provider • Includes direct interaction with the student, as well as teacher and parent instruction	Classroom or special room
Integrated	• Therapist interacts with the student, teacher, paraprofessional(s), and parents • Frequently includes direct and consultative services • Therapist collaborates with other team members in development of goals and objectives • Therapist instructs all service providers in ways to implement the student's therapy program	Learning environment (classroom, school hallway, cafeteria, etc) or special room
Consultative	• Therapist consults the members of the educational team, including the parent and the child • Appropriate team members implement the activities suggested by the therapist and are responsible for outcomes • No direct intervention provided	Learning environment (classroom, school hallway, cafeteria, etc)
Monitoring	• Therapist shares information with/instructs the team members • Therapist reassesses the student's status on a regular basis and is responsible for outcomes • No direct intervention provided	Learning environment (classroom, school hallway, cafeteria, etc) or special room
Collaborative	• A combination of an integrated service delivery model and transdisciplinary team interaction • Services are provided by all team members with the role release and crossing disciplinary boundaries, which are greater than in an integrated model	Learning environment (classroom, school hallway, cafeteria, etc)

Compiled from Effgen and Kaminker[41] and Effgen and Howman.[52]

TABLE 12-8		
SCHOOL PROFESSIONALS' VIEWS ON COLLABORATION		
TOP THREE REPORTED		
Most Frequently Practiced Types of Collaborative Activities *(% participants)*	*Advantages of Collaboration* *(% participants)*	*Barriers to Collaboration* *(% participants)*
Informal daily discussions (100%)	Positive effects on students' progress and goal achievement (86%)	Lack of support from school administration (88%)
Monthly team meetings (61%)	Team members' learning from each other (80%)	Insufficient on-site presence of therapists (82%)
Monthly planning meetings (38%)	Therapists and teachers being able to work together (63%)	Lack of time (76%)

Data from Nochajski.[53]

with peers they may not have met before. For children with disabilities, successful adjustment to such changes would depend on their ability to navigate the new physical layout of the school; access to mobility, computer, and activities of daily living (ADL) equipment similar to what they used in a previous school setting; or the success of their training in the use of new, unfamiliar equipment. Therefore, timely transition planning is imperative and must begin in advance of the anticipated change.[48]

Physical therapists actively participate in transition services, including the following:

- Assessing the new environment and its demands
- Determining the needs for and assisting with obtaining and learning to use the adaptive equipment necessary for the student's function in the new environment
- Communicating with the transition team, including the child's family, regarding the physical expectations and requirements of the new environment, preparation for mobility and other functional activities in that environment, and the accessibility of the transportation system
- Consulting with and educating the student, family, and staff in regard to the strategies for the student's physical functioning in the new environment[41]

Transition from high school to adult community is covered by federal law.[24,25] Under IDEIA 2004,[24] a Transition IEP should be developed at age 16 years, with the emphasis on goals related to daily living, personal/social, and vocational skills, as well as on services needed to reach these goals. According to the law, transition services are designed based on the needs, strengths, and interests of the individual child to promote a smooth transition to post-secondary education, vocational training, employment, continuing education, therapy services for adults, as well as independent living and community participation.[24] Issues related to the transition to adulthood will be discussed in Chapter 24.

OUTPATIENT PEDIATRIC MEDICAL SETTING AND HOME-BASED PRIVATE THERAPY

Families of children with disabilities often access pediatric outpatient clinics and outpatient departments of hospitals regardless of whether they receive EI or school-based therapy services.[57] The demand for services increases with the severity of disability as it is associated with increased risk of the child's rehabilitation needs being unmet.[57,58] Among children with CP, those classified in Gross Motor Function Classification System (GMFCS)[59] levels IV and V were reported to have the highest need for developmental, educational, medical, and other community services.[57,60] In addition, parents of children who used wheeled mobility had the highest financial needs and needs for information and supports.[60]

While many families opt to utilize outpatient therapy services, others prefer having their children seen at home by private providers. The home-based setting offers the child and the family an opportunity for evaluation and modification of their home environment to address the child's functional needs related to maximizing his or her independence when participating in family routines, with the ultimate goal to improve the quality of life.[12,61] Regardless of the setting, the use of family-centered philosophy and parental involvement in the development and implementation of intervention goals have been shown to be effective in improving outcomes, increasing parent satisfaction with the services received by their child, supporting parental competency, and strengthening family partnerships with health care providers.[62,63]

New family-centered pediatric rehabilitation service delivery models developed in Canada for children with disabilities and their families were described in literature.[64,65] Although the American and Canadian health care systems are quite different, experience related to these service delivery models shared by the authors may be helpful to health care organizations in the United States, especially in the currently changing health care climate. The first model, the Life Needs Model of Pediatric Service Delivery, aims to meet long-term participation and quality of life goals of children and youth with disabilities.[64] This model addresses personal, interpersonal, and external needs of the child and the family from the child's birth to adulthood. The short-term goals identified at each point in time focus on the child's physical, social-emotional, communication, and behavioral functioning in the personal sphere of life, and his or her functional competence related to the interpersonal sphere, including the home, school, and community settings. Additionally, the short-term goals target such factors as the family competency and relationships in the interpersonal sphere, and the attitudes, restrictions, program availability, and adoption of policies and supportive legislation in the community, which are associated with the external sphere of life.[64]

In the Life Needs Model, a transdisciplinary team delivers both direct therapy and community participation-oriented services.[64] A similar Canadian model, the Apollo model of pediatric rehabilitation service delivery, addresses the need to shorten the waiting times for the families and includes individual, group, and community interventions.[65] Community interventions target the development of an inclusive community and facilitation of social participation for all children with disabilities in that community. The implementation of community interventions may be associated with an apparent decrease in productivity because they are not targeting a specific child, and this may negatively affect billing and reimbursement for such services. Individual interventions are personalized to each child while group interventions are used to motivate children through peer modeling and help them develop social skills. Group interventions are more cost-effective and cover a greater number of children. However, limiting individual interventions may be challenging because of the differences in opinion among clinicians in regard to the value of group interventions.[65]

Størvold and Jahnsen[66] showed that a combination of individual and group sessions may be effective in achieving family-centered intervention goals when intensive therapy is used for children with CP who vary in their age and GMFCS[59] levels. However, overall, frequency and intensity of intervention provided to children with CP in outpatient and private home-based settings may vary significantly as these variables may be affected by many factors, and the consensus on dosing parameters of therapy services for this patient population has not been reached.[58,67] These issues will be explored in detail in Chapter 18.

REFERENCES

1. Darrah J, Magill-Evans J, Adkins R. How well are we doing? Families of adolescents or young adults with share their perceptions of service delivery. *Disabil Rehabil.* 2002;24(19):542-549.
2. World Health Organization. *Towards a Common Language for Functioning, Disability and Health: ICF, the International Classification of Functioning, Disability and Health.* Geneva, Switzerland: World Health Organization. http://www.who.int/classifications/icf/training/icfbeginnersguide.pdf. Published 2002. Accessed March 9, 2014.
3. World Health Organization. *International Classification of Functioning, Disability and Health.* Geneva, Switzerland: World Health Organization; 2001.
4. Jeglinsky I, Salminen A-L, Carlberg EB, Autti-Rämö I. Rehabilitation planning for children and adolescents with cerebral palsy. *J Pediatr Rehabil Med.* 2012;5(3):203-215.
5. King S, Teplicky R, King G, Rosenbaum P. Family-centered service for children with cerebral palsy and their families: a review of literature. *Semin Pediatr Neurol.* 2004;11(1):78-86.
6. Bamm EL, Rosenbaum P. Family-centered theory: origins, development, barriers, and supports to implementation in rehabilitation medicine. *Arch Phys Med Rehabil.* 2008;89(8):1618-1624.
7. Law M, Rosenbaum P, King G, et al. *What is Family-Centered Service? FCS Sheet # 1.* Hamilton, ON, Canada: McMaster University, CanChild Centre for Childhood Disability Research. https://canchild.ca/system/tenon/assets/attachments/000/001/266/original/FCS1.pdf Accessed February 9, 2016.
8. Chiarello LA. Family-centered care. In: Effgen SK. *Meeting the Physical Therapy Needs of Children.* 2nd ed. Philadelphia, PA: F. A. Davis Company; 2012:153-180.
9. Dunst CJ, Trivette CN, Davis M, Cornwell J. Enabling and empowering families of children with health impairments. *Children's Health Care.* 1988;17(2):71-81.
10. Maitre NL, Slaughter JC, Aschner JL. Early prediction of cerebral palsy after neonatal intensive care using motor development trajectories in infancy. *Early Hum Dev.* 2013;89(10):781-786.
11. Kleinert JO, Effgen SK. Early intervention. In: Effgen SK. *Meeting the Physical Therapy Needs of Children.* 2nd ed. Philadelphia, PA: F. A. Davis Company; 2012:475-493.
12. Atkinson H. Rehabilitation settings. In: Effgen SK. *Meeting the Physical Therapy Needs of Children.* 2nd ed. Philadelphia, PA: F. A. Davis Company; 2012:583-597.
13. Effgen SK, Chiarello L, Milbourne SA. Updated competencies for physical therapists working in schools. *Pediatr Phys Ther.* 2007;19(4):266-274.
14. Reddihough DS, Collins KJ. The epidemiology and causes of cerebral palsy. *Aust J Physiother.* 2003;49:7-12.
15. Msall ME. Complexity of the cerebral palsy syndromes: toward a developmental neuroscience approach. *JAMA.* 2006;296(13):1650-1652.
16. Vohr BR, Wright LL, Poole WK, McDonald SA. Neurodevelopmental outcomes of extremely low birth weight infants <32 weeks' gestation between 1993 and 1998. *Pediatrics.* 2005;116:635-643.
17. Wu YW, Croen LA, Shah SJ, Newman TB, Najjar DV. Cerebral palsy in a term population: risk factors and neuroimaging findings. *Pediatrics.* 2006;118(2):690-697.
18. Sweeney JK, Heriza CB, Blanchard Y. Neonatal physical therapy. Part I: clinical competencies and Neonatal Intensive Care Unit clinical training models. *Pediatr Phys Ther.* 2009;21:296-307.
19. Sweeney JK, Heriza CB, Blanchard Y, Dusing SC. Neonatal physical therapy. Part II: practice frameworks and evidence-based practice guidelines. *Pediatr Phys Ther.* 2010;22:2-16.
20. Als H. Toward a synactive theory of development: promise for the assessment and support of infant individuality. *Infant Mental Health J.* 1982;3(4):229-243.
21. Als H. A synactive model of neonatal behavioral organization: framework for the assessment of neurobehavioral development in the premature infant and for support of infants and parents in the neonatal intensive care environment. *Phys Occup Ther Pediatr.* 1986;6:3-53.
22. Als H. Newborn Individualized Developmental Care and Assessment Program (NIDCAP): new frontier for neonatal and perinatal medicine. *J Neonatal Perinatal Med.* 2009;2:138-147.
23. Rahlin M. Impaired ventilation, respiration/gas exchange and aerobic capacity/endurance associated with respiratory failure in the neonate. In: Moffat M, Frownfelter D, eds. *Cardiopulmonary Essentials: Preferred Physical Therapist Practice Patterns.* Thorofare, NJ: SLACK Incorporated; 2007:237-264.
24. Pub L No 108-446, Individuals with Disabilities Education Improvement Act of 2004, 118 Stat 2647-2808.
25. Pub L No 105-17, Individuals with Disabilities Education Act Amendments of 1997, 111 Stat 37-157.
26. Pub L No 94-142, Education for All Handicapped Children Act of 1975, 89 Stat. 773-796.
27. Pub L No 99-457, Education of the Handicapped Amendments Act of 1986, 100 Stat 1145-1177.
28. Pub L No 102-119, Individuals with Disabilities Education Act Amendments of 1991, 105 Stat 587-608.
29. Long T. Early intervention. In: Batshaw ML, Roizen NJ, Lotrecchiano GR. *Children with Disabilities.* 7th ed. Baltimore, MD: Paul H. Brookes Publishing Co; 2013:547-557.
30. Chiarello, LA. Serving infants, toddlers, and their families: early intervention services under IDEA. In: Campbell SK, Palisano RJ, Orlin MN, eds. *Physical Therapy for Children.* 4th ed. St. Louis, MO: Saunders; 2012:944-967.
31. Campbell PH. Evaluation and assessment in early intervention for infants and toddlers. *J Early Interv.* 1991;15(1):36-45.
32. O'Neil ME, Palisano RJ. Attitudes toward family-centered care and clinical decision making in early intervention among physical therapists. *Pediatr Phys Ther.* 2000;12(4):173-182.
33. Hielkema T, Blauw-Hospers CH, Dirks T, Drijver-Messelink M, Bos AF, Hadders-Algra M. Does physiotherapeutic intervention affect motor outcome in high-risk infants? An approach combining a randomized controlled trial and process evaluation. *Dev Med Child Neurol.* 2011;53(3):e8-e15.
34. Harbourne RT, Willett S, Kyvelidou A, Deffeyes J, Stergiou N. A comparison of interventions for children with cerebral palsy to improve sitting postural control: a clinical trial. *Phys Ther.* 2010;90:1881-1898.
35. Lobo MA, Harbourne RT, Dusing SC, McCoy SW. Grounding early intervention: physical therapy cannot just be about motor skills anymore. *Phys Ther.* 2013;93(1):94-103.
36. Healthcock JC, Lobo MA, Galloway JC. Movement training advances the emergence of reaching in infants born at less than 33 weeks of gestational age: a randomized controlled clinical trial. *Phys Ther.* 2008;88(3):310-322.
37. Lynch A, Ryu J, Agrawal S, Galloway JC. Power mobility training for a 7-month-old infant with spina bifida. *Pediatr Phys Ther.* 2009;21(4):362-368.

38. Ragonesi CB, Chen X, Agrawal S, Galloway JC. Power mobility and socialization in preschool: a case study of a child with cerebral palsy. *Pediatr Phys Ther.* 2010;22(3):322-329.

39. Myers CT, Effgen SK, Blanchard E, Southall A, Wells S, Miller E. Factors influencing physical therapists' involvement in preschool transitions. *Phys Ther.* 2011;91(5):656-664.

40. Pub L 107-110, No Child Left Behind Act of 2001, 115 Stat 1425-2094.

41. Effgen SK, Kaminker MK. The educational environment. In: Campbell SK, Palisano RJ, Orlin MN, eds. *Physical Therapy for Children.* 4th ed. St. Louis, MO: Saunders; 2012:968-1007.

42. Department of Education. *Improving the Academic Achievement of the Disadvantaged, Final Rule.* 34 CFR Part 200, Title I. Federal Register. 68(236):68697-68708 (2003).

43. Department of Education. *Improving the Academic Achievement of the Disadvantaged, Individuals with Disabilities Education Act (IDEA), Final Rule.* 34 CFR Parts 200 and 300, Title I. Federal Register. 72(67):17748-17781 (2007).

44. National Dissemination Center for Children with Disabilities. Categories of disability under IDEA. http://nichcy.org/disability/categories. Published March 2012. Accessed April 6, 2014.

45. Pub L No 93-112, Rehabilitation Act of 1973. http://www.usbr.gov/cro/pdfsplus/rehabact.pdf. Accessed April 6, 2014.

46. Title 34: Education, Part 104 – Nondiscrimination on the basis of handicap in programs or activities receiving federal financial assistance. *Electronic Code of Federal Regulations.* http://www.ecfr.gov/cgi-bin/text-idx?SID=f89938887ed08292e46fc597f23c6639&node=34:1.2.1.1.3.1.134.3&rgn=div8. Updated April 3, 2014. Accessed April 6, 2014.

47. American Physical Therapy Association. *Guide to Physical Therapist Practice.* Rev 2nd ed. Alexandria, VA: APTA; 2003.

48. Effgen SK. Schools. In: Effgen SK. *Meeting the Physical Therapy Needs of Children.* 2nd ed. Philadelphia, PA: F. A. Davis Company; 2012:495-514.

49. McConlogue A, Quinn L. Analysis of physical therapy goals in a school-based setting: a pilot study. *Phys Occup Ther Pediatr.* 2009;29(2):154-169.

50. Iowa Department of Education. *Iowa Guidelines for Educationally Relevant Physical Therapy Services.* Des Moines, IA: Iowa Department of Education, 2001.

51. The Bureau of Exceptional Education and Student Services, Florida Department of Education. *Considerations for Educationally Relevant Therapy (CERT) Form Training Tool: SCRIPT.* Tallahassee, FL: State of Florida Department of State; 2006.

52. Effgen SK, Howman J. Serving the needs of children and their families. In: Effgen SK. *Meeting the Physical Therapy Needs of Children.* 2nd ed. Philadelphia, PA: F. A. Davis Company; 2012:3-40.

53. Nochajski SM. Collaboration between team members in inclusive educational settings. *Occup Ther Health Care.* 2002;15(3-4):101-112.

54. Kaminker MK, Chiarello LA, O'Neil ME, Dichter CG. Decision making for physical therapy service delivery in schools: a nationwide survey of pediatric physical therapists. *Phys Ther.* 2004;84(10):919-933.

55. Kaminker MK, Chiarello LA, Chiarini Smith JA. Decision making for physical therapy service delivery in schools: a nationwide analysis by geographic region. *Pediatr Phys Ther.* 2006;18(3):204-213.

56. Schreiber J, Steen P, Marchetti G, Provident I, Turocy PS. School-based pediatric physical therapists' perspectives on evidence-based practice. *Pediatr Phys Ther.* 2008;20(4):292-302.

57. Nageswaran S, Silver EJ, Stein RE. Association of functional limitation with healthcare needs and experiences of children with special health care needs. *Pediatrics.* 2008;121(5):994-1001.

58. Bailes AF, Succop P. Factors associated with physical therapy services received for individuals with cerebral palsy in an outpatient pediatric medical setting. *Phys Ther.* 2012;92(11):1411-1418.

59. Palisano RJ, Rosenbaum PL, Walter SD, Russell DJ, Wood EP, Galuppi BE. Development and reliability of a system to classify gross motor function in children with cerebral palsy. *Dev Med Child Neurol.* 1997;39(4):214-223.

60. Palisano RJ, Almarsi N, Chiarello LA, Orlin MN, Bagley A, Maggs J. Family needs of parents of children and youth with cerebral palsy. *Child Care Health Dev.* 2010;36(1):85-92.

61. Kolobe TH, Arevalo A, Catalino TA. The environment for intervention. In: Campbell SK, Palisano RJ, Orlin MN, eds. *Physical Therapy for Children.* 4th ed. St. Louis, MO: Saunders; 2012:879-902.

62. Baker T, Haines S, Yost J, DiClaudio S, Braun C, Holt S. The role of family-centered therapy when used with physical or occupational therapy in children with congenital or acquired disorders. *Phy Ther Rev.* 2012;17(1):29-36.

63. Øien I, Fallang B, Østensjø S. Goal-setting in paediatric rehabilitation: perceptions of parents and professional. *Child Care Health Dev.* 2010;36(4):558-565.

64. King GA, Tucker MA, Baldwin PJ, LaPorta JA. Bringing the Life Needs Model to life: implementing a service delivery model for pediatric rehabilitation. *Phys Occup Ther Pediatr.* 2006;26(1/2):43-70.

65. Camden C, Swaine B, Tétreault S, Bergeron S, Lambert C. development, implementation, and evaluation of the Apollo model of pediatric rehabilitation service delivery. *Phys Occup Ther Pediatr.* 2013;33(2):213-229.

66. Størvold GV, Jahnsen R. Intensive motor skills training program combining group and individual sessions for children with cerebral palsy. *Pediatr Phys Ther.* 2010;22:150-160.

67. Gannotti ME, Christy JB, Heathcock JC, Kolobe TH. A path model for evaluating dosing parameters for children with cerebral palsy. *Phys Ther.* 2014;94(3):411-421.

Assessment and Management of Therapy-Related Behavior

Respect the children by carefully monitoring their facial expressions, their body language, their emotional state, and their attention to your therapy activities. These overt behaviors speak volumes regarding approval or displeasure with therapy.

David G. Embrey, Linda Yates, Brett Nirider, Nancy Hylton, and Lauren S. Adams[1]

Clinical decision making for children with cerebral palsy (CP) is a complex process.[1,2] Components of physical therapy examination discussed in Chapter 11 include, among others, the identification of relevant personal factors,[3] such as the levels of enjoyment, motivation, interest, and persistence in accomplishing tasks exhibited by the child (see Table 11-1). These factors may affect participation in a variety of life situations, including therapy sessions, and may be positive, such as the child's ability to select a preferred activity, or negative, such as communication deficits (see Table 4-5 in Chapter 4).[4] It is important to note that some confusion exists in regard to the definition of personal factors provided by the International Classification of Functioning, Disability and Health (ICF).[3,5] This definition incorporates the following statement:

> These factors may include gender, race, age, other health conditions, fitness, life-style, habits, upbringing, coping styles, social background, education, profession, past and current experience (past life events and concurrent events), overall behavior pattern and character style, individual psychological assets and other characteristics, all or any of which may play a role in disability at any level.[3(p 17)]

This statement may be perceived as too broad, which may lead to an overlap between the construct of personal factors and the ICF[3] components of body structures and functions, activity, and participation.[5] For example, communication difficulties mentioned earlier may be related to an alteration in structure or function of a specific body system or classified as an activity limitation. Simeonsson et al[5] cautioned against documenting personal factors and their effects on function of the individual while using the ICF.[3] However, based on clinical experience and available research evidence, one may argue that personal factors may play an important role in intervention success or failure. As discussed next, motivation is one such factor.

While motivation to move was shown to lead to earlier acquisition of motor milestones in typically developing infants in one longitudinal study,[6] other research highlighted the relationship between motivation and effectiveness of intervention.[7-12] In their investigation of physical therapists' perceptions of characteristics that affected motor skills acquisition in children with CP, Bartlett and Palisano[7] found that motivation was the most important personal factor for the therapists to consider when setting and working toward the child's intervention goals. Other research showed that higher

Rahlin M. *Physical Therapy for Children With Cerebral Palsy: An Evidence-Based Approach (pp 223-230).*
© 2016 SLACK Incorporated.

motivation in learning difficult tasks observed in children and adolescents with CP correlated positively with higher activity levels, interest in skill-based activities, and fewer behavioral problems; and lower motivation might have a negative effect on participation in therapy and other challenging activities.[8-11] Furthermore, Morris et al[12] demonstrated that physical abilities of children with CP did not fully explain their engagement in activities and life situations. The available research evidence highlights the importance of documenting patients' behavioral characteristics in clinical practice, as this information, when used appropriately, may enhance clinical reasoning and assist in decision making, which, in turn, may lead to improved intervention outcomes.[1,2,7]

THERAPY-RELATED BEHAVIORS

Behaviors a child exhibits during physical or occupational therapy sessions may have a positive or a negative effect on participation in therapeutic activities and on the immediate success of intervention.[13] These behaviors may not necessarily be related to the child's developmental or functional level. For example, a toddler with a mild developmental delay may consistently refuse to participate and throw temper tantrums in response to a slight change in activity, while another toddler of the same age may be fully engaged throughout every session in presence of significant physical disability.[13] Besides crying and temper tantrums, some of the behaviors that would typically interfere with therapy sessions may include noncompliance, resistance, or aggression toward the therapist; avoidance and delay tactics; inattention, passive behavior, and general lack of interest in people, toys, and environment; low tolerance to physical handling; and irritability related to unmet physiological needs, such as being hungry, thirsty, sleepy, or tired.[13-17]

Research suggests that therapy-related behavior is a multidimensional construct.[13,15,16] Crying is probably the most common negative behavior younger children exhibit during physical therapy sessions, and yet, it may have a variety of different causes, so the same intervention aimed at calming a crying child may produce variable results in different children and situations.[13,14,16] Brazelton[18] listed discomfort, pain, boredom, overstimulation, attention seeking, and limit testing as some of the reasons for crying in infants and toddlers. Rahlin and Stefani[16] found that other behavioral characteristics besides general irritability may be responsible for crying behaviors exhibited during therapy. As mentioned previously, motivation is another personal factor that requires attention from clinicians.[7-11] Assessment of therapy-related behavior may provide pediatric therapists with valuable information that would help them modify their approach to intervention and meet the unique needs of a specific child.[13] It would also provide parents with recommendations for the most appropriate set-up of their child's home exercise program activities, as these recommendations will be based on objective data.[13]

ASSESSMENT OF THERAPY-RELATED BEHAVIOR

Therapy Behavior Scale

As shown in Table 13-1, the Therapy Behavior Scale (TBS) is a standardized assessment instrument that is used to assess infant and toddler behavior during physical, occupational, and developmental therapy sessions.[13,19] It consists of 11 items scored from 1 to 4 on an ordinal scale and takes on average 5 minutes to administer. The TBS allows clinicians to assess infant and toddler therapy-related behavior through direct observation. It is applicable in home-based and outpatient therapy settings, and is appropriate for use with children from birth to 3 years of age, regardless of their level of development or disability.[13,19]

This instrument was developed with the intent to use objective behavioral data derived from the TBS testing to assist pediatric therapists in their efforts to individualize and structure intervention.[13] Another consideration was that the scores children receive on specific TBS items may be used for educating the caregivers on the ways they may interact with the children to promote their participation in daily activities, routines, and home exercise programs.[13]

The psychometric properties of the TBS are displayed in Table 13-1.[13,19] Six pediatric physical, occupational, and developmental therapists participated in the development and content evaluation of the TBS original version, which led to its modification into the TBS Version 1.0. Subsequently, several additional scale revisions were performed through the TBS pilot testing, small reliability studies, and content validation,[13,19] which ultimately resulted in its current Version 2.2 [unpublished data]. Research into the use of the TBS by novice raters (NRs) indicated that, to obtain valid testing results, only those raters who have sufficient training in development and therapeutic intervention, such as physical, occupational, and developmental therapists, but not student therapists, should use this assessment instrument in the clinic and in future research [unpublished data]. Further reliability studies of the TBS Version 2.2 are currently being planned.

The Dimensions of Mastery Questionnaire

The Dimensions of Mastery Questionnaire (DMQ)[20] is used to evaluate the perceptions of the child's parent or teacher and, when appropriate, the child's own perceptions in regard to his or her mastery-related behaviors, from infancy to adolescence (see Table 13-1). Mastery motivation is the central concept that is assessed using the DMQ.[20] Morgan et al[21] defined mastery motivation as "a psychological force that stimulates an individual to attempt independently, in a focused and persistent manner, to solve a problem or master a skill or task which is at least moderately challenging for him or her."(p 319) The DMQ assesses 2 major aspects of mastery motivation: instrumental and expressive.[20] The instrumental aspect motivates the individual to persist in attempting a difficult task, while the

TABLE 13-1
BRIEF DESCRIPTION AND PSYCHOMETRIC PROPERTIES OF TWO INSTRUMENTS USED FOR ASSESSMENT OF THERAPY-RELATED BEHAVIOR

INSTRUMENT	POPULATION	DESCRIPTION	PSYCHOMETRIC PROPERTIES
Therapy Behavior Scale (TBS)[13,19]	Infants and toddlers, ages birth to 3 years, regardless of their level of development or disability	The scale is designed to assess behavior during physical, occupational, and developmental therapy sessions, with its 11 items reflecting specific therapy-related behaviors: 1. Physiological Needs 2. Willingness to Engage in Play 3. Self-Calming and Calming Ability 4. Interest in Toys and Environment 5. Ability to Cope With Change 6. Attention Level 7. Ability to Respond Socially to Therapist 8. Tolerance to Physical Handling 9. Level of Physical Activity 10. Ability to Communicate Wants and Needs 11. Ability to Cooperate With Limits Set by Therapist Items are scored on an ordinal scale from 1 to 4, and a total score is obtained by adding the item scores.	*Novice Rater Interrater Reliability* Version 1.1: ICC (2,1) = 0.75[19] Version 2.0: ICC(2,1) = 0.83[a] *Novice and Expert Rater Interrater Reliability* Version 1.1: ICC(2,1) = 0.68-0.86[19] Version 2.0: ICC(2,1) = 0.24-0.36[a] *Content Validity* Established via scale evaluation by a group of experts.[13] Version 2.1 validated and modified into Version 2.2.[a]
Dimensions of Mastery Questionnaire (DMQ)[20]	Several versions are available for different age groups (Infant [6-18 months], Preschool [1.5-5 years], Child [6-12 years] and Teen [13-19 years])	The questionnaire is designed to assess the parent's or teacher's perceptions and self-perceptions of the child's mastery-related behaviors across 7 scales/ 45 items rated on a 5-point ordinal scale: • Instrumental aspects of mastery motivation (object-oriented persistence, and for older children, persistence at cognitive tasks; gross motor persistence; and social persistence with children and adults) • Expressive aspects (mastery pleasure and negative reactions to failure) • General competence (the child's ability to master tasks vs being motivated to do so) Scale, summary, and total scores can be calculated.	*Internal Consistency* Cronbach's alpha = 0.60-0.90 *Test-Retest Reliability* r = 0.68-0.89 *Discriminant Validity and Responsiveness to Change* Established
[a] Unpublished data.			

expressive aspect reflects the feelings this individual has while working on or having completed a task. General competence is another mastery-related concept that the DMQ measures, which reflects the actual abilities of the individual rather than his or her motivation to master a skill.[20]

Over the years of research, the original instrument was expanded to include additional scales and items.[20] The scales that comprise the instrumental, expressive, and general competence domains of the current version of the DMQ, and a summary of its psychometric properties are shown in Table 13-1. Multiple reliability and validity studies of different versions of the test were conducted with over 9000 children aged 6 months to 18 years of both genders and different ethnicities, including children who were developing typically and those who had developmental delays and disabilities. The authors of the DMQ recommended using this instrument as a part of a comprehensive clinical evaluation performed in a variety of settings with different patient populations.[20]

MANAGEMENT OF
THERAPY-RELATED BEHAVIOR

When children with movement disorders demonstrate such behavioral problems as stubbornness, dependency, aggression, hyperactivity, or anxiety at home and during therapy sessions, a consultation with behavioral specialists may be indicated.[22] McDermott et al[22] reported statistically significant improvements in adaptive behaviors displayed by children with CP, developmental delays, and other conditions after monthly consultative meetings held between behavioral specialists and rehabilitation professionals working with these children. The consultations and training were provided by a team that consisted of a developmental pediatrician, a pediatric psychiatrist, psychologists, and a preventive medicine specialist. Improvements in parental attitudes toward their children and an increase in the therapists' knowledge of behavioral problems and related intervention strategies were additional significant positive findings in this research. The therapists reported that their newly acquired ability to use behavioral guidance had enhanced their rapport with the families. The behavioral guidance included providing the child's parents with advice and support, when appropriate, or with a referral to a specialist, when necessary. These results highlighted the importance of ongoing behavioral assessment as a part of rehabilitation services for children with disabilities.[22]

Systematic observation of play behaviors displayed during therapy sessions can help increase the number of available options and improve the selection of activities the therapist can use for a specific child.[1] Additionally, a formal assessment of therapy-related behaviors may provide therapists with valuable information they can use to modify physical, psychological, and social environments in which the child functions during therapy.[13,23,24] Along with the child's personal factors, these environmental modifications may play a major role in the success of intervention. For instance, when using the TBS with infants and toddlers to evaluate their responses to a variety of interventions, the therapist may be able to do the following:

- Determine possible reasons for uncooperative behavior and crying
- Form an opinion on the immediate success of a specific intervention strategy and its environmental set-up
- Make necessary changes to the surface on which the child is playing, toys introduced to the child, or people present
- Change the therapy timing or setting[13]

Psychological and social environments deserve special attention as it was suggested that providing the child with reasonable freedom of choice, allowing creativity, and encouraging social interactions could enhance playfulness.[23] Playfulness is an important aspect of behavior that many pediatric clinicians use to engage children in therapeutic activities. The definition of playfulness proposed by Bundy[25] includes 4 factors:

1. Intrinsic motivation (a characteristic of a specific activity that serves as a stimulus for the child to participate)[26,27]
2. Internal control (being "in charge" of one's actions and to some extent, of the play outcome)
3. Freedom to suspend reality (ability to decide how close to objective reality the play process will be)
4. Framing (giving, receiving, and interpreting social cues during play)[25-27]

Chang et al[23] found playfulness to be a major indicator of self-determined behavior in children with CP who had limited self-mobility. Self-determination is a personal characteristic that develops across the life span and can be described as taking charge of problem solving and decision making in regard to one's life, its goals, and quality.[23,28,29] When their playfulness is supported, children with mobility limitations may be more likely to discover new problem-solving and decision-making strategies, thus demonstrating self-determination.[22] Activity accommodations; environmental modifications; as well as opportunities for peer interactions, making a choice, and trying new things support the child's participation in therapy sessions and other life situations.[23]

Besides promoting self-determination in children with disabilities,[23] rehabilitation professionals need to educate their patients' parents in regard to the parenting styles that may reinforce or impede their child's persistence in performing challenging tasks.[24] Miller et al[24] demonstrated that consistent discipline, structured environment, and clarity in outlining directions and consequences, as opposed to inconsistency, laxity in discipline, and verbosity in parenting, were associated with significantly greater mastery motivation in children with unilateral CP. These findings may serve as a guide for therapists who can model appropriate interaction practices for the caregivers with a goal of carrying them over to their home environments. Examples of such practices may include providing the child with optimally challenging tasks and properly structured feedback, and using supportive strategies appropriate for the child's age, communication skills, and functional level. Consistent application of these practices may have a positive effect on mastery motivation and, ultimately, on the outcomes of therapeutic intervention.[24] Several motivational strategies will be discussed next.

Motivational Strategies

When developing therapy programs for children with movement disorders, clinicians should select tasks that would be optimally challenging for their patients.[24] This is because children tend to demonstrate less interest in performing tasks that are too easy and less persistence in learning those that they perceive as too difficult.[30] Wang et al[30] reported that toddlers with motor delays diagnosed with CP, genetic disorders, and other developmental conditions displayed the same levels of pleasure and persistence as children who were developing typically when faced with moderately challenging structured tasks.

Another important point clinicians should keep in mind is that the individual preferences of children and adolescents with movement disorders need to be supported when developing programs targeting their activity and participation.[24,31] Shikako-Thomas et al[31] examined participation and enjoyment in leisure activities in 175 adolescents with CP and found that they highly valued opportunities to interact with their friends and their autonomy in selecting the activities in which they would like to participate. While the greatest levels of participation and enjoyment were reported for social activities, participation in skill-based and self-improvement activities was lower, which may be related to the lack of appropriate environmental modifications and specialized programs available to this patient population. This finding suggests that to promote healthy development in adolescents with disabilities and increase their engagement in physical activities, not only their personal preferences but also the environmental factors[3] must be considered.[31]

Research related to the outcomes of motivational rehabilitation interventions is sparse, and many studies in this area are limited in their internal validity.[32] A recent systematic review of literature showed that virtual reality technology was the method most frequently used as a motivational intervention.[32] Virtual reality is a computer-generated interactive system that simulates realistic sensory environments for the user.[33,34] Some of the available options include video game consoles, head-mounted displays, and robotic devices that create opportunities for interaction with virtual events and objects that may look, sound, and feel as if they are encountered in the real world.[32-34] In the past decade, virtual reality systems were increasingly applied in rehabilitation and rehabilitation research.[32-36] Although some studies showed that virtual reality can be successfully used as a motivational strategy with a potential to enhance intervention outcomes and increase exercise effectiveness and compliance in some cases,[32,35,36] the evidence in its support is still insufficient to draw meaningful conclusions.[32] Because motivation is a multidimensional construct[32] and mastery motivation reflects only several of its dimensions,[20,21] other reliable and valid assessment instruments (besides the DMQ[20]) need to be developed in order to evaluate the effects of motivational strategies, including virtual reality, on outcomes of rehabilitation interventions.[32]

Motivational Difficulties

Pediatric therapists are trained to consider such personal factors as age and cognitive and functional levels when attempting to engage the child in therapeutic activities.[37] In many instances, children may not be able to understand verbal instructions or follow directions the therapist provides. The clinician's creativity in setting up therapeutic play and, more importantly, the ability to engage in play with the child as an equal may greatly affect the success of intervention. However, sometimes, even very creative therapists may encounter situations when all of their efforts to motivate the child fail.[37] As observed in clinical practice, motivational difficulties may

stem from a variety of personal and environmental factors. Examples of such personal factors include profoundly passive behavior in a child with an intellectual disability who is not interested in toys, people, or surroundings in general, or similar behavior in a child with a physical disability who is clinically depressed. Another example is perfectionism that leads to the reluctance to participate out of the fear for less-than-perfect performance. As for the environmental factors, having too many toys or people present in the treatment room may lead to overstimulation, and excessive sound or light may be overwhelming for some children. While in some of the described situations, a referral to a behavioral specialist may be necessary,[22] in others, the therapist can successfully use the behavior management techniques described next.

Common Behavior Management Techniques

Pediatric therapists use behavior management techniques to structure the therapeutic environment that would promote their patients' participation in activities aimed at acquiring targeted skills.[38] These techniques may be very simple, such as distracting a crying infant with a toy or a sound, by looking in a mirror, or by moving to another room. The older the infant, the less effective distraction will become.[39] Infants and toddlers may need to be redirected by physically removing them from a dangerous situation, such as from the edge of the bed to which they crawled or from an unprotected electrical outlet.[40] A good strategy in such situations would be to suggest an alternative, safe activity. Although therapy rooms and infants' homes ideally must be made childproof, in real life, it is not always the case. When removing a potentially dangerous object, such as a sharp pencil or a pen from the hand of an infant or a toddler, it may be helpful to substitute it with a safe toy. In other, less critical situations, verbal redirection may be used by letting the child know that a certain behavior (eg, biting) is not acceptable.[40] This needs to be done in a firm, consistent, and nonthreatening way.

During therapy sessions, children may cry for a variety of reasons.[16] Soothing instrumental classical music can be used for calming purposes, and nursery rhyme songs can be played to motivate the child to participate.[15,16] Rahlin et al[15,16] showed that playing music during physical therapy sessions was effective in reducing the amount of crying in infants and toddlers with or at risk for developmental disabilities. In another study, the use of music helped reduce the frequency and duration of inconsolable crying and improve vital signs in infants who were born prematurely and hospitalized in a Neonatal Intensive Care Unit.[41]

Temper tantrums is another behavior that needs to be addressed. It is important to remember that attempts to distract, redirect, or reason with a toddler who is having a temper tantrum, or asking why he or she is crying, may only prolong the duration of the tantrum.[40] A much more effective solution is to make sure that the child is safe and then walk out of the room or ignore the tantrum altogether until it subsides.[40] In a therapy situation, using a one-way mirror to observe the child may be helpful to ensure safety. One-way mirrors available in some clinical settings allow the observer to view the session while staying outside of the treatment room. Being in agreement with the parent in regard to the use of this strategy is imperative for maintaining trust and respect in the parent-therapist relationship.

When it is difficult to engage a child in therapeutic activities, the therapist should consider applying behavioral programming that involves the following:

- Systematic manipulation of the environment in which therapy is provided
- The use of positive reinforcement to encourage wanted behaviors
- Ignoring undesirable behaviors (when appropriate)[37,38]

Physical environment can be manipulated by changing the size and physical layout of the treatment room; and changing the amount of light and sound, as well as the number of toys to which the child is exposed during the therapy session. The selection of toys, tasks, and therapeutic activities should match the child's age, cognitive and functional levels, and personal interests.[24,31,42] The manipulation of social environment may involve engaging the child's siblings and caregivers in therapeutic activities to encourage the child's participation,[42] or having the parent observe from a distance or through a one-way mirror when the child is reluctant to interact with the therapist in the parent's presence.

Different reward systems are used for positive reinforcement of wanted behaviors.[37,42] The reward is offered to the child upon the completion of a task, a series of tasks, or the entire therapy session. It is important to remember that over time, the frequency and type of reinforcement should "fade" so that the child learns to engage in the desired behavior spontaneously, without an obvious reward. Examples of rewards include sticker charts; toys; the child's favorite activity or game; or simple praise, a smile, a hug, or a "high five."[37] It is not uncommon for a parent to suggest food as a reward to give to their child during a physical therapy session. Most of the time, this may not be the best choice as it may disrupt the feeding schedule, support unhealthy eating practices, or lead to the loss of therapy time as it would be unsafe for the child to chew and swallow while actively moving to complete a physical task.

Negative reinforcement is a behavioral technique that may result in encouraging an undesirable behavior.[37] Negative reinforcement occurs when a stimulus aversive to the child is removed if he or she acts as asked. Effgen and Howman[37] described a situation when the therapist stopped the child's therapy session if the child agreed to perform a disliked task. This is an example of an inappropriate use of behavior management because in the future, this child will be likely to refuse participation and expect the session to end as the result.

Providing negative consequences is a technique that is different from negative reinforcement. Negative consequences may include removing a privilege or issuing a time-out when the child exhibits an unacceptable behavior (eg, aggression toward the therapist, a parent, or a sibling).[43,44] An example

of the removal of a privilege may be the therapist's or parent's refusal to play the child's favorite game at the end of the session as a consequence to "bad" behavior. Consistency in using negative consequences and remaining calm on the part of the adults involved in such situations are very important for reducing the unwanted behaviors.[43,44]

Using time-outs within a therapy session may not be feasible because of ethical considerations related to billing for therapy time. However, it is not uncommon for parents to ask for the therapist's advice regarding the use of discipline with their child. Brazelton[40] suggested that if a time-out is used as a consequence, it needs to be short, and Phelan[43] recommended using 5-minute time-outs. For children younger than 5 years of age, the amount of time spent in a time-out may be assigned based on their age. For example, a 2-minute time-out may be used for a 2-year-old toddler, while a 5-year-old child will spend 5 minutes in a time-out. Phelan[43,44] developed a "1-2-3 Magic" system, which has been successfully implemented by many parents, teachers, and child care workers. It combines rewards for good behavior with an effective way to address disruptive behaviors. Counting to 3 is used as a warning to stop an undesired behavior. If not successful, a time-out follows or a privilege is removed. This behavior management system emphasizes the importance of consistency in following the rules and controlling emotions on the part of the parents.[43,44] This program was effective in improving parenting practices by increasing positive behaviors and decreasing anxiety in parents, and in reducing problem behaviors in children.[45,46]

Learning of motor skills during therapy sessions can be enhanced by using chaining and shaping behavioral techniques.[37,38] Chaining involves breaking up a task and teaching its parts to the child in a sequence. In forward chaining, the parts of a task are taught from the beginning to the end, with the next step completed after the previous one. At the end, the task is performed as a whole. In backward chaining, the order of the practiced parts is reversed, with the last part of the task completed first.[37,38] An example of forward chaining is teaching a little girl how to remove her shoes by having her open the Velcro strap first, followed by assisting her with the rest of the task. On the second attempt, the child will undo the strap and open the shoe, and the therapist will finish by removing the shoe, and so on, until the child is able to complete the entire task by herself. Sometimes, backward chaining may be more effective than forward chaining because the ability to successfully complete the last step of the task without assistance may be more motivating for the child than being able to complete the first step and watching the caregiver to do the rest.[38] For example, when putting on a brace, the last step would be closing a Velcro strap, which would provide the child with a feeling of accomplishment, even if this is the only part of the task that could be completed without assistance at that time.

Shaping is different from chaining in that shaping involves providing positive reinforcement for behaviors that approximate the desired behavior, with the child's attempts to perform a skill being rewarded, even if they are unsuccessful.[37,47]

However, with each attempt or each set of attempts, the expectations for the child's performance increase, and the reward is given for a closer approximation of the desired behavior than previously.[47]

This chapter examined therapy-related behavior and emphasized the importance of its ongoing assessment and management. Relevant standardized assessment instruments were discussed and the state of the evidence linking therapy-related behaviors to therapy outcomes was explored. Finally, motivational strategies and common behavior management techniques were presented. The ability of pediatric clinicians to assess and manage therapy-related behavior while planning and implementing intervention will enhance their interactions with children and their families and may improve intervention outcomes.

REFERENCES

1. Embrey DG, Yates L, Nirider B, Hylton N, Adams LS. Recommendations for pediatric physical therapists: making clinical decisions for children with cerebral palsy. *Pediatr Phys Ther.* 1996;8(4):165-170.

2. Campbell SK. Models for decision making in pediatric neurologic physical therapy. In: Campbell, SK. *Decision Making in Pediatric Neurological Physical Therapy.* Philadelphia, PA: Churchill Livingstone; 1999:1-22.

3. World Health Organization. *International Classification of Functioning, Disability and Health.* Geneva, Switzerland: World Health Organization; 2001.

4. Carey H, Long T. The pediatric physical therapist's role in promoting and measuring participation in children with disabilities. *Pediatr Phys Ther.* 2012;24(2):163-170.

5. Simeonsson RJ, Lee A, Ellingsen KM. Personal factors. In: Majnemer A. *Measures for Children with Developmental Disabilities: An ICF-CY Approach.* London, UK: Mac Keith Press, Clinics in Developmental Medicine No. 194-195; 2012:435-439.

6. Atun-Einy O, Berger SE, Scher A. Assessing motivation to move and its relationship to motor development in infancy. *Infant Behav Dev.* 2013;36(3):457-469.

7. Bartlett DJ, Palisano RJ. Physical therapists' perceptions of factors influencing the acquisition of motor abilities of children with cerebral palsy: implications for clinical reasoning. *Phys Ther.* 2002;82(3):237-248.

8. Majnemer A, Shevell M, Law M, Poulin C, Rosenbaum P. Level of motivation in mastering challenging tasks in children with cerebral palsy. *Dev Med Child Neurol.* 2010;52(12):1120-1126.

9. Majnemer A, Shikako-Thomas K, Chokron N, et al. Leisure activity preferences for 6- to 12-year-old children with cerebral palsy. *Dev Med Child Neurol.* 2010;52(2):167-173.

10. Majnemer A, Shikako-Thomas K, Lach L, Shevell M, Law M, Schmitz N; QUALA group. Mastery motivation in adolescents with cerebral palsy. *Res Dev Disabil.* 2013;34(10):3384-3392.

11. Shikako-Thomas K, Majnemer A, Law M, Lach L. Determinants of participation in leisure activities in children and youth with cerebral palsy: systematic review. *Phys Occup Ther Pediatr.* 2008;28(2):155-169.

12. Morris C, Kurinczuk JJ, Fitzpatrick R, Rosenbaum PL. Do the abilities of children with cerebral palsy explain their activities and participation? *Dev Med Child Neurol.* 2006;48(12):954-961.

13. Rahlin M, McCloy C, Henderson R, Long T, Rheault W. Development and content validity of the Therapy Behavior Scale. *Infant Behav Dev.* 2012;35(3):452-465.

14. Hoffman SJ. *Enhancing Productive Physical Therapy in Children Using Strategic Interaction Training* [dissertation]. Gainesville: University of Florida; 1999.

15. Rahlin M, Cech D, Rheault W, Stoecker J. Use of music during physical therapy intervention for an infant with Erb's palsy: a single subject design. *Physiother Theory Pract.* 2007;23(2):105-117.

16. Rahlin M, Stefani J. Effects of music on crying behavior of infants and toddlers during physical therapy intervention. *Pediatr Phys Ther.* 2009;21(4):325-335. Erratum in: *Pediatr Phys Ther.* 2010;22(1):85.

17. Rahlin M. Case report: an individualized intermittent intensive physical therapy schedule for a child with spastic quadriparesis. *Physiother Theory Pract.* 2011;27(7):512-520.

18. Brazelton TB. Crying. In: Brazelton TB. *Touchpoints: Your Child's Emotional and Behavioral Development.* Reading, MA: Perseus Books; 1992:231-238.

19. Rahlin M, Easshauer L, Linden J, Morris K, O'Donnell K. Interrater reliability of the Therapy Behavior Scale used by novice raters with infants and toddlers: a pilot study. In: Abstracts of Poster and Platform Presentations at the 2012 Combined Sections Meeting. *Pediatr Phys Ther.* 2012;24(1):121. Abstract.

20. Morgan GA. Busch-Rossnagel NA, Barrett KC, Wang J. *The Dimensions of Mastery Questionnaire (DMQ): A Manual about Its Development, Psychometrics, and Use.* Fort Collins, CO: Colorado State University; 2009.

21. Morgan GA, Harmon RJ, Maslin-Cole CA. Mastery motivation: definition and measurement. *Early Educ Dev.* 1990;1:318-339.

22. McDermott S, Nagle R, Wright HH, Swann S, Leonhardt T, Wuori D. Consultation in paediatric rehabilitation for behaviour problems in young children with cerebral palsy and/or developmental delay. *Pediatr Rehabil.* 2002;5(2):99-106.

23. Chang HJ, Chiarello LA, Palisano RJ, Orlin MN, Bundy A, Gracely EJ. The determinants of self-determined behaviors of young children with cerebral palsy. *Res Dev Disabil.* 2014;35(1):99-109.

24. Miller L, Ziviani J, Ware RS, Boyd RN. Mastery motivation in children with congenital hemiplegia: individual and environmental associations. *Dev Med Child Neurol.* 2014;56(3):267-274.

25. Bundy AC. Play and playfulness: what to look for. In: Parham LD, Fazio LS, eds. *Play in Occupational Therapy for Children.* St. Louis, MO: Mosby, 1997;52-66.

26. Bundy AC, Nelson L, Metzger M, Bingaman K. Validity and reliability of a Test of Playfulness. *Occup Ther J Research.* 2001;21:276-292.

27. Reid D. The influence of virtual reality on playfulness in children with cerebral palsy: a pilot study. *Occup Ther Int.* 2004;11:131-144.

28. Wehmeyer ML. Self-determination as an educational outcome: Why it is important to children, youth, and adults with disabilities. In: Sends DJ, Wehmeyer ML. *Self-Determination across the Life Span: Independence and Choice for People with Disabilities.* Baltimore, MD: Paul H. Brooks; 1996;15-34.

29. Brotherson MJ, Cook CC, Erwin EJ, Weigel CJ. Understanding self-determination and families of young children with disabilities in home environments. *J Early Interv.* 2008;31(1):22-43.

30. Wang P-J, Morgan GA, Hwang A-W, Liao H-F. Individualized behavioral assessments and maternal ratings of mastery motivation in mental age-matched toddlers with and without motor delay. *Phys Ther.* 2013;93(1):79-87.

31. Shikako-Thomas K, Shevell M, Lach L, et al; QUALA group. Picture me playing – a portrait of participation and enjoyment of leisure activities in adolescents with cerebral palsy. *Res Dev Disabil.* 2013;34(3):1001-1010.

32. Tatla SK, Sauve K, Virji-Babul N, Holsti L, Butler C, Van Der Loos HF. Evidence for outcomes of motivational rehabilitation interventions for children and adolescents with cerebral palsy: an American Academy for Cerebral Palsy and Developmental Medicine systematic review. *Dev Med Child Neurol.* 2013;55(7):593-601.

33. Laufer Y, Weiss PL. Virtual reality in the assessment and treatment of children with motor impairment: a systematic review. *J Phys Ther Educ.* 2011;25(1):59-71.

34. Levac DE, Galvin J. When is virtual reality "therapy"? *Arch Phys Med Rehabil*. 2013;94(4):795-798.

35. Harris K, Reid D. The influence of virtual reality play on children's motivation. *Can J Occup Ther*. 2005;72(1):21-29.

36. Bryanton C, Bossé J, Brien M, McLean J, McCormick A, Sveistrup H. Feasibility, motivation, and selective motor control: virtual reality compared to conventional home exercise in children with cerebral palsy. *Cyberpsychol Behav*. 2006;9(2):123-128.

37. Effgen SK, Howman J. Serving the needs of children and their families. In: *Meeting the Physical Therapy Needs of Children*. 2nd ed. Philadelphia, PA: F. A. Davis Company; 2013:3-40.

38. McEwen IR, Meiser MJ, Hansen LH. Children with motor and intellectual disabilities. In: Campbell SK, Palisano RJ, Orlin MN, eds. *Physical Therapy for Children*. 4th ed. St. Louis, MO: Saunders; 2012:539-576.

39. Brazelton TB. Nine months. In: Brazelton TB. *Touchpoints: Your Child's Emotional and Behavioral Development*. Reading, MA: Perseus Books; 1992:119-131.

40. Brazelton TB. Discipline. In: Brazelton TB. *Touchpoints: Your Child's Emotional and Behavioral Development*. Reading, MA: Perseus Books; 1992:252-260.

41. Keith DR, Russell K, Weaver BS. The effects of music listening on inconsolable crying in premature infants. *J Music Ther*. 2009;46(3):191-203.

42. Ratliffe KT. The typically developing child. In: Ratliffe KT. *Clinical Pediatric Physical Therapy*. St. Louis, MO: Mosby, Inc.; 1998:23-68.

43. Phelan T. *1-2-3 Magic: Training Your Children to Do What You Want*. Glen Ellyn, IL: Child Management, Inc.; 1990.

44. Phelan TW. *1-2-3 Magic: Effective Discipline for Children*. 4th ed. Glen Ellyn, IL: ParentMagic; 2010.

45. Bradley SJ, Jadaa DA, Brody J, et al. Brief psychoeducational parenting program: an evaluation and 1-year follow-up. *J Am Acad Child Adolesc Psychiatry*. 2003;42(10):1171-1178.

46. Porzig-Drummond R, Stevenson RJ, Stevenson C. The 1-2-3 Magic parenting program and its effects on child problem behaviors and dysfunctional parenting: a randomized controlled trial. *Behav Res Ther*. 2014;58C:52-64.

47. Thorwarth Bruey C. Treatment. In: *Demystifying Autism Spectrum Disorders. A Guide to Diagnosis for Parents and Professionals*. Bethesda, MD: Woodbine House; 2004:181-212.

14

Therapeutic Approaches

Regina T. Harbourne, PhD, PT, PCS and Mary Rahlin, PT, DHS, PCS

As professionals, we must be ready to give up older ideas in favor of newer concepts with firm grounding in research.

Anne F. VanSant, *Are We Anchored to NDT?*

Every practical approach to habilitation or rehabilitation of children with neuromotor disorders such as cerebral palsy (CP) theorizes about the mechanism underlying the approach, or an overall construct from which the principles emerge. Often, the original basis of the approach includes theory that eventually proves faulty or limited, which may not ultimately translate to the users of the approach. Thus, the resulting approach to rehabilitation may be an amalgam of techniques that were originally linked to theory, but have "taken on a life of their own." These clinical tools are utilized because therapists take ownership of a collection of techniques, but may not recognize that the original logic of the approach is no longer valid according to current scientific evidence. However, theory helps us to understand why an approach is selected for a particular constellation of problems in a child with a movement disorder. Theory also allows the development of research questions to assist in determining the success of the approach. In this exposition of approaches, we attempt to separate the original theory from a current rendition of the theory (if applicable), which may have changed over time. We also provide a sample of principles and try to link theory, concepts, and principles where possible. We follow these explanations of each approach with research evidence and a critical evaluation of the current rendition of the approach.

NEURODEVELOPMENTAL TREATMENT APPROACH

The origin of this approach, as of many intervention approaches for individuals with motor deficits, is rooted in clinical experience. Berta Bobath developed ideas about how to handle and habilitate the movement problems of children and adults with a brain injury.[1] Her ideas and experiences in the clinic were then supported by her physician husband, Karel Bobath, who used current neurophysiologic science evidence of their time.[2,3] The significant revelation in the Bobath approach, compared to previous approaches to neurologic motor deficits, was the focus on changing the neurologic signs and symptoms and movement patterns, rather than supporting orthopedically or adapting to the peripheral effects of altered neurologic status.[1,4]

Original Theoretical Foundation

The overarching theory behind the Bobath approach was, and is, neuroplasticity, although the Bobaths did not use that term, except in a very general sense when writing about the advantage of very early treatment.[5] Nevertheless, they did expand the role of rehabilitation to include the idea that the

Rahlin M. *Physical Therapy for Children With Cerebral Palsy: An Evidence-Based Approach (pp 231-248).*

nervous system changes as a result of sensorimotor activity. This was novel and exciting, and even at the end of their lives, the Bobaths maintained that their idea that "spasticity can change" was the centerpiece of their theory.[6] However, embedded in the original theory was a model of the nervous system that is no longer viable. The original theory stipulated a reflex model[7] and also a hierarchical model of the nervous system, which supports the neuromaturational theory of development (Chapter 1) and which differs greatly from the current model of the nervous system as a distributed and redundant system.[8]

The model, at the time of the origination of the theory, assumed that higher parts of the nervous system (cortical centers), when activated, could inhibit primitive reflexes and movements that were "released" from the lower levels of the nervous system due to injury.[5] Certain movement patterns or strategies were assigned to these different levels, and given priority accordingly (see Chapter 1, Table 1-1). Because the hierarchical nature of the nervous system was assumed, the approach focused on inhibiting reflexes that came from lower centers and facilitating reactions from higher centers, based on a model of integration of reflexes within the human nervous system.[8] Another related assumption was that the elimination or inhibition of abnormal muscle tone or spasticity would reveal normal movement, or allow normal patterns of movement to emerge.[1]

When the Neurodevelopmental Treatment (NDT) approach originated, the theory, principles, and practices (techniques) fit together well. However, since that time, revolutions in science, including brain imaging, have revealed that the motor system is not organized in a hierarchical manner exclusively.[9] Recent research shows that the nervous system operates in a more distributed manner, and is far more plastic than depicted in early studies.[10] Thus, the original theory underlying the NDT approach is no longer viable. As an example, a procedure for inhibiting an abnormal motor pattern (which originated in a lower part of the nervous system), and facilitating a normal pattern (which originated in the cortical centers) would not be supported by current neuroscience theory of distributed control systems.[11]

Current Theoretical Assumptions

Current users of the NDT approach postulate that some newer principles should be utilized when evaluating and treating patients with a neurologic disorder,[12] but the connections between the original theory and current practice are tenuous. Howle[12] lists many assumptions related to motor learning, motor control, and neuroscience theories as accepted by the NDT approach. These theoretical assumptions include task-specific practice (motor learning),[13] multiple systems affect movement (systems theory),[14] and practice of a "good" pattern leads to functional use of that pattern (theory of neuronal group selection).[15,16] One might say that the practice of NDT currently utilizes a set of techniques and concepts but is still in search of one good, overarching theory.

Primary Concepts

Focus on Patterns of Movement

From a clinical experience perspective, one of the positive aspects of the NDT approach is the emphasis on observation of movement to provide an in-depth analysis of the individual movement strategies. Importantly, theory contributes to how information is gleaned from observation and interpreted to create an intervention plan or select techniques. Imagine that, as a therapist observes a child's movements, she classifies them into typical and atypical. At the end of the observation, the therapist has a list of 2 typical and 10 atypical strategies or movement patterns. What comes next in the problem-solving process? Using the NDT approach, one goal choice would be to try to eliminate the atypical movement choices and increase the more typical movements toward a functional end. Although the goal may have a functional endpoint, within the NDT approach, the movement pattern selected for that function is deemed to be important and also a feature of the overall goal of therapy. For example, the functional goal may be to roll over to acquire a distant toy, but the movement pattern elicited during that function would be selected by the therapist to be less atypical.[17] Thus, instead of allowing the child to roll over by arching his or her back (a pattern considered atypical), the therapist would use physical guidance to facilitate lateral trunk flexion and a combination of balanced trunk flexion and extension (considered a more typical pattern).[18] This would also require the early stages of weight-shift, an important component of the NDT approach.[18]

Consequently, the original theory of lower level, atypical movements revealing less maturity (neuromaturational or hierarchical theory) than higher-level movement patterns has already led to the therapist's direction within her intervention. This leads to the next concept, which is that synergies (movement patterns) are built over time through practice and reinforcement.[1,12,18] A therapist practicing the NDT approach might plan an intervention to reduce atypical movement because if it is repeated or practiced, it will be reinforced. By extension, this atypical movement may not be useful for accomplishing a functional task; conversely, a more typical or normal movement may lead to greater success.[12]

Synergies Can Be Good or Bad and Are Built Over Time Through Practice and Reinforcement

The Bobaths did not use the term *synergies* in a way that would describe typical movement.[5] They utilized the term *synergy* to describe atypical movement (ie, a spastic synergy of the upper or lower extremity).[19] Techniques directed at reducing or normalizing muscle tone, and thus helping a patient move out of the synergistic pattern, are included in this intervention approach.[19]

Abnormal Muscle Tone and Patterns of Movement Are Inhibited or Blocked, and Typical Movement Patterns Are Facilitated

Abnormal muscle tone is a central concept in the NDT approach.[1] However, it is vaguely defined. The Bobaths considered muscle tone to be not only the passive elasticity of the muscle, but also a "state of readiness to move" and a reflection of the nervous system overall.[7] Therefore, muscle tone is something that is felt as well as determined from overall observations of behavior. The Bobaths used the concept of the "postural reflex mechanism," which was thought to contribute to normalizing muscle tone,[5] to the maintenance of postural control against gravitational forces,[1,7] and to the integration of reflexes of the lower levels of the nervous system with balance and righting reactions generated by its higher levels.[20]

Movement Patterns Can Change With Practice

Both in the original version of the NDT approach, and the current rendition, practice to improve a motor pattern is an essential component.[12] Activities to facilitate or promote more normal movement patterns are encouraged in the therapeutic, home, and community settings to provide greater opportunities for practice. In addition, blocking or inhibiting a movement pattern is suggested to reduce the practice of abnormal movement strategies.[12]

The International Classification of Functioning, Disability and Health Can Be Applied Within the Neurodevelopmental Treatment Approach

According to the current interpretation of the NDT approach, practicing/learning a more typical movement pattern (body structure level of International Classification of Functioning, Disability and Health [ICF])[21] will lead to more efficient function (activity level), which will result in greater involvement in life situations (participation).[12] However, this assumes a linear relationship among the ICF model components while, in fact, that relationship is nonlinear and complex.[21] The origination of the NDT approach preceded the development of the ICF framework, which was published in 2001.[21] Thus, the application of the ICF within the NDT approach is post hoc. The original approach was focused on engaging the child in therapeutic activities that were not necessarily part of daily function.[1] The assumption was that the practiced movements would then be incorporated into the functions of the individual within their daily lives. However, as the NDT approach spread in popularity, equipment and positioning techniques were added to facilitate carryover into the daily functional activities.[22] As currently practiced, NDT principles and techniques are applied most often in the clinic, with efforts to set functional goals.[12] However, NDT intervention has not been explicitly presented in the context of the participation level of the ICF. Because its focus is on building more normal motor patterns that may not be naturally selected by the individual, function with a more typical pattern of movement is generally a goal and endpoint rather than aiming toward the participation level of the ICF.

Fundamental Principles of Manual Guidance

The NDT system of therapeutic intervention was developed at a point in time when hands-on approaches dominated the field of physical therapy. Thus, one of the strengths of NDT lies in developing the therapists' ability to use their hands and interact with the child with a neuromotor disorder. A focus on key points of control, facilitation, and inhibition of motor patterns influenced by special handling techniques adapted in real time is perceived as a characteristic of a skilled NDT therapist.[23,24] The blending of techniques to meet the goals of an individual child is an integral part of this approach.[12]

One of the fundamental principles of NDT manual guidance is that the therapist works to normalize muscle tone as a way to teach the child's nervous system more typical and efficient patterns of movement.[25] In the presence of spasticity, therapeutic handling will generally be slow and rhythmical, and the child's movements will be guided into patterns to "break up," inhibit, or discourage spastic movement patterns. In the presence of hypotonia, handling will be quicker, and faster tactile or proprioceptive stimuli will be used to try and increase the muscle tone. If a child has fluctuating muscle tone, such as athetosis, general steady and mid-range movement will be encouraged. Overall, efforts are made to normalize muscle tone prior to encouraging movement for a functional goal, and the use of key points of control is suggested.[23,24] A key point of control is any place on the child's body that is used to impart control so that the muscle tone can be influenced or movement patterns can be guided. Therefore, there may be multiple key points of control for any one child, and the key point may change depending on the current activity.[23] Key points of control are also used to guide bringing the child's center of mass (COM) within the base of support (BOS), and to provide controlled weight shift that helps initiate movement.[23,24]

Another NDT principle is that active movement initiated by the patient is the goal of therapy.[12] Note that this is the goal of therapeutic intervention, not a guiding principle during the intervention. Thus, guidance of movement is a strong part of this approach, and the guidance should be gradually reduced to allow the child to take over movement as he or she is able. Progress in therapy is noted by the reduction of assistance or guidance required by the therapist, as well as by the change toward functional goals.[12,26]

In this approach, therapists use the environmental setup, guidance of movement, and positioning to reduce the effects of abnormal reflexes and muscle tone, and reinforce normal movement patterns by rewarding feedback to the child.[25] The environmental setup is often accomplished by the use of specialized equipment to facilitate more typical and functional movement patterns, both during active intervention (as an extra pair of hands for the therapist), and to carry over intervention goals to functional, everyday activities. The concept of keeping the COM over the BOS and promoting optimal alignment of the body segments carries over into the way that equipment is used. Some equipment that is typically used within the NDT approach includes balls or moveable surfaces, walking assistive devices that encourage positioning out of spastic patterns, or stabilizing devices for one or more joints that reduce the effects of spasticity or abnormal movement patterns, and maintain optimal alignment of body segments within the BOS.

Summary of Research Evidence

The efficacy of the NDT approach has not been well supported by randomized controlled clinical trials (RCTs) when compared to other approaches in preschool population, school-age children, or across age groups of those older than 3 years.[27] Criticism of the efficacy research touches multiple issues, including the use of varying clinical outcome measures so that studies are difficult to compare; varying intensities or frequencies of intervention between studies; and, probably most importantly, the lack of standardization of the approach, so the intervention may differ from study to study or even from therapist to therapist.[27] Another very important problem observed in children with CP who receive NDT intervention is that the effects of the therapy, when positive, seem to be short lived.[28] This may be reflective of a focus on movement patterns, which may indicate short-term responsiveness to therapeutic handling.[28] However, when improvements in function or participation are observed, they do not necessarily appear to be a direct consequence of a change in motor patterns. Thus, movement that is generated within a therapeutic setting may not directly impact movement that is self-generated within activities of daily life.[28] In spite of the lack of efficacy generally found in research conducted with children with CP older than 3 years of age,[27] efficacy has been demonstrated in studies with younger children, specifically in infancy, by improved postural control in preterm infants,[29] and improved trunk control in infants with CP.[17] However, the positive effects of NDT in infants are also not consistent across studies, with a lack of efficacy noted in an RCT with high-risk preterm infants.[30]

Other research has moved to different questions, such as the issues of dosage, brain imaging to determine what changes in the nervous system with activity intervention, and life-course issues related to participation. Research of the NDT approach as a unique intervention is unlikely to be a priority of clinical scientists. Rather, efficacy studies must be described with clarity in regard to motor learning principles, manual guidance techniques, and measurement methods, which may be difficult because of the variety of clinical procedures used under the umbrella of "NDT." In fact, the intensity of intervention and individualized goal setting appear to be more important predictors of functional change than the treatment method or intervention approach used.[31-33]

Because the NDT approach is widespread and was originally formulated in the 1950s and 60s, research conducted over time has provided us with evidence that, overall, the efficacy of this intervention is questionable.[27,34] However, many studies can be criticized as poorly designed or faulty, leading to suggestions for continuing investigation. Major problems that should be addressed in future research of NDT include the need to standardize the approach by changing the focus to function/participation outcome measures, defining selected age groups (infancy, pre-school, etc) within the studies to identify if and when the approach should be used, and determining the interaction of dosage with technique. Research designs that contrast the specific procedures used in the NDT approach with another treatment option are necessary to sort out its efficacy and any interaction effects of the intensity of therapy. However, with current studies of the effects of physical activity on the nervous system, and new tools to measure change in both brain and behavior, research efforts are likely to de-emphasize the investigation of a particular therapeutic approach and focus on principles of motor learning, practice, and a set of axioms to guide intervention built on current scientific findings.[34]

PERCEPTION-ACTION APPROACH

Theoretical Foundation

This approach was also originally built upon the clinical experiences and observations of a master clinician, just as the NDT approach was built upon the experience of Berta Bobath. In fact, Ingrid Tscharnuter, the originator of this approach, began as an NDT instructor. However, through her clinical experience, self-evaluation, and extensive reading of the literature on motor control and perceptual development, her ideas about intervention began to change. Ingrid Tscharnuter abandoned NDT and built a new approach based on the direct perception ideas of Gibson.[35] As she changed in her point of view, she had a conversation with Berta Bobath, who specifically noted that the new approach was not a component or inclusive of NDT (I. Tscharnuter, oral communication, October, 1994). This therapeutic approach was initially known as Tscharnuter Akademie for Movement Organization or TAMO therapy.[36] Subsequent advances in understanding the perception-action contributions to the emergence of movement suggested a renaming of the therapy perspective as the Perception-Action (P-A) approach. Also embedded in Tscharnuter's ideas of the theoretical foundation of the P-A approach were the writings of Bernstein,[37] Gibson,[35] and Thelen.[38] Although the current teachers of the NDT approach also refer to the work of these researchers, the connection between the theory and clinical reasoning is not closely drawn, as it is in the P-A approach.[36,39] While Bernstein,[37] Gibson,[35] and Thelen[38] did not develop or support any therapeutic approach, they had in common that they looked at movement as a system that is interactive, complex,

TABLE 14-1

COMPARISON OF NEURODEVELOPMENTAL TREATMENT AND PERCEPTION-ACTION APPROACHES

THERAPEUTIC FOCUS	NEURODEVELOPMENTAL TREATMENT[5,7]	PERCEPTION-ACTION[36,39]
Perspective	Feeling an abnormal or a normal movement perpetuates that movement	Picking up information about the environment under different conditions affects action
	Linear connection between sensory input and motor patterns (specific therapy handling gives correct motor output)	Nonlinear connection between control parameter reaching a critical value and self-organization of the system
General evaluation	Evaluates postural control, muscle tone, movement patterns, function	Evaluates perception of environment and how information is picked up
Guidance	Therapist inhibits and facilitates movement that is considered by therapist to be normal and efficient	Therapist uses hands to provide information to suggest exploration of strategies, and to inform the therapist of child's intentions and perceptions of action
Inefficient movement	Therapist guides with hands or verbally to reduce errors	Errors are allowed as they are useful in learning
Progression	Developmental motor milestones used as guideline	Developmental consideration, but in purest form, only child initiated movement utilized
	Child may be placed in positions and supported to move within them	Movement variability encouraged rather than developmental positions

and embedded in the environment rather than hierarchical or reflexive. Unlike NDT, the P-A approach, described and taught by Ingrid Tscharnuter, does not focus fundamentally on the motor system.[36,39] The approach is based on a dynamic systems model of the human-environment interaction, and thus starts with environmental forces and the child's perception within that system. Another primary construct in the approach is the idea of self-organization, which holds that the system will re-organize in a way that is highly sensitive to initial conditions.[36,39] Thus, the theory accepts the model of the nervous system as a distributed system that works dynamically to support the interest of the child.[10] As discussed in Chapter 1, Edelman's theory of neuronal group selection[15] explains the mechanism of the self-organization process, which complements the contributions of the dynamic systems[38] and P-A[35] theories to an integrated theoretical view of developmental change.[40,41] This view is embraced by the current users of the P-A approach as its foundation.

Because the theoretical model for this approach relates to the self-organization of complex systems,[38,39] Dr. Tscharnuter focused on the interaction of perception and action as complex systems.[39] Within a complex, dynamic system, the outcome or endpoint of the system's path is highly dependent on initial conditions. In other words, a very small change in the path of the system at the start of a process of change can make a large change further down the path. This point is important

theoretically and practically because the P-A approach does not attempt to forcefully control movement by inhibition or facilitation. Rather, small changes in perceiving a movement and setting up the action via environmental forces and constraints are expected to suggest new motor strategies for the child. Part of this "setup" of movement is capitalizing on the genesis of a motor strategy; that is, creating initial conditions for a movement that is just forming, within a specific context. These motor strategies cannot be fully predicted by the therapist, but will have an emergent quality. They may differ from child to child, or within one child, and are not categorized into typical or atypical forms.[36,39]

Primary Concepts

Dr. Tscharnuter launched the P-A approach, which has been built upon while still leaving her original thoughts as a basis. Let us examine several concepts originated by Dr. Tscharnuter that distinguish this intervention from the NDT approach (Table 14-1). Within the P-A approach, there is no focus on a "normal typical movement pattern."[39] Rather, the therapist focuses on the child's exploration of forces within the environment to build strategies for further interaction with that environment. This may lead to the child using movement strategies that are immature or inefficient, which would not be resisted or inhibited by the therapist.[39]

Although the therapist does not resist inefficient or immature movement, a lack of variability would be noted and addressed in treatment.[39] The P-A approach promotes early variability of movement as a means of exploration and perceiving the affordances of actions.[42] This view is in contrast to the NDT approach because movement patterns are not classified as typical or atypical; rather, the focus is on variability. In this vein, no movement is discouraged or considered an error because all movements are thought to be necessary in learning how to create ongoing, adaptive action strategies.[43]

Because the NDT approach is built on an original theory of a reflexive model of the motor system,[5,7] there is no real place for perception or cognition within the approach, although therapists certainly consider cognition as an overall factor in a child's development. However, in the P-A approach, perception and cognition are at the core of the therapeutic intervention.[39] Although the NDT approach includes attention to sensory systems,[12] perception and sensation are not the same[35] (see the discussion of P-A theory in Chapter 1). In the P-A approach, the concept of whether a child perceives the affordances of his or her body or the environment is a major focus.[43] Perception and action are intimately linked so that a change in perception can be causal in the emergence of a new motor strategy.[39] In addition, the linkage to building cognitive concepts is integral to this approach, so play that builds cognitive concepts through action and perception is part of the therapeutic strategy.[44]

Action, or movement, organizes around the environment in the P-A approach, and this central construct is illustrated by 4 principles.[39] These 4 principles guide both assessment and intervention in this approach because they are considered key factors in organizing motor strategies.

Principle 1: Movement Organization Within the Environment as a System of Coordinates

The first principle is related to the organization of movement in a system of coordinates defined by gravity and supporting surface.[39] Gravity is always present in the world as a constant, and we must learn to use it to our best advantage.[35] Thus, the pressure against the ground due to gravity, also known as support surface contact, can be utilized as an organizer of movement.[39] A child who can adapt his or her body or body parts and utilize the support surface contact to provide leverage for movement can be successful in producing actions. In addition, the support surface can provide information to orient and inform the perception of body location in space. Thus, the force of gravity and the support surface define a perceptual space in which the other principles of the approach fit.[39] The following principles build on this as a basic tenet. Thus, the first aspect generally examined in the child is the support surface contact in various positions, and how the child utilizes that contact in an active, explorative way to work with gravitational forces.

Principle 2: Relationship of the Center of Mass to the Base of Support

This principle is closely linked to the first because it is necessary for engaging in ongoing movement and exploration to develop the perceptual capability to adapt and balance the body within the BOS.[39] There are countless ways that this can be accomplished, with perception being built and constantly updated over many instances of interaction with the environment, and driven by action initiated by the child.[39] Although the NDT approach also includes a discussion of the COM over the BOS,[18] the NDT intervention uses this concept in a biomechanical way. Guidance from the therapist, or equipment, is used to align the child's body within the BOS in NDT, in attempts to give the child the feedback about proper alignment. In the P-A approach, the emphasis is on perception, such that the therapist evaluates where the child perceives the position of the COM, and how the pressure at the BOS is altering the COM.[39] In addition, active movement at the BOS is a focus because the action at the base forms the perception of orientation within the ongoing dynamic exchange with the environment.[39]

Principle 3: Orientation of the Body Segments in Relation to the Force of Gravity

Gravity is a constant within the world.[35] The child must learn in both a perceptual and cognitive sense how to adapt each body segment to gravitational forces. For example, one must prospectively predict how much force is needed, when to apply that force, and in what direction to apply it to initiate and control any movement. Orienting a body segment prepares for the application of forces in a controlled and functional way. Integral to action then are the perception of the orientation of a body segment to the force of gravity and the interaction with the support surface (principle 1), which can provide for further action.[35,39] For example, a child can make a crawling motion with the legs, but unless the thigh and leg are oriented appropriately to the support surface and to vertical, the child will not advance forward. When the orientation of the body segment is explored with a successful action, the perception of the legs as "movers" is achieved.

Principle 4: Distribution of Stability and Mobility, or Dynamic Stability

In order for movement to be functional and adaptive, body segments are utilized in multiple ways for different tasks.[39] This is very apparent during self-mobility such as crawling or walking. At one moment, the leg or arm is mobile in order to be placed on the ground, and then that same limb must act in a stable way to allow the other side to move. During each activity, the distribution of mobility and stability changes dynamically from moment to moment. Hence, there is no assignment of stability to proximal parts of the body, but rather a continuous change depending on the function being performed and the forces needing to be controlled. This is also a perceptual capability that is built over time and experience, and one which can be manipulated by the environmental setup.[39]

Fundamental Principles of Manual Guidance

One of the most fundamental and defining principles of the P-A approach, compared to NDT, is the minimal control over the child's movement that is provided by the therapist (see Table 14-1).[36,39] The therapist's hands are extremely light on the child, partly because the therapist cannot perceive the child's movement intentions if too much force is used.[39] Within this approach, the therapist should never resist or force a movement. Movements are suggested, not facilitated. This suggestion is made by allowing the child to accommodate to the light touch of the therapist prior to any information being provided by hand pressure. Before any hands-on intervention, the therapist would change the environment to allow for exploration of movement first.[39]

Once the child has accommodated to the therapist's hands, light touch provides a vector of force directed gently into the support surface that is the child's center of pressure (COP).[39] The therapist may then adjust that vector of force in very slight increments to suggest the perception of new possibilities of movement, such as actively changing the contact with the support surface. Therapeutic manual guidance is meant to be informational, rather than guiding a movement into a particular pattern. Therefore, the child may select a movement strategy that is surprising to the therapist and initiate the movement without any assistance from the therapist. The performance of a self-initiated strategy is a goal of intervention because if the child initiates a movement based on a perception that he or she has formed, it is likely that such action will be repeated in a similar situation.[39]

Manual guidance in the P-A approach is kept to a minimum to allow the child to perceive the natural forces within the environment without the interference of the therapist.[39] Gentle manual loading is gradually and softly added by the therapist to emphasize an existing force acting on the child's body (such as gravity causing pressure on the support surface), and then exploration outside the "comfort zone" is suggested. Often, the therapist's hands are removed to allow the child to explore a new strategy independently. This enhances the child's perceptual experience, as well as allows the therapist to take stock of progress that has been made and determine the next steps of progression needed.[39]

"Errors" that cause the failure of movement intent are not blocked.[43] They are imagined as a learning device to help the child map a configuration of a space and his or her body parameters within that space. For example, if a child vigorously extends the trunk in the sitting position, the therapist would allow a safe backward "fall," but then use the child's new body orientation by emphasizing the new support surface and affordances in the supine position. The therapist would not push the child further into the sitting flexion position (as might be done in the NDT approach to overcome extensor muscle tone) because that would reinforce an erroneous perception in the child that pushing backward would make him or her move forward. Thus, in this example, the therapist using the NDT approach would use manual guidance in a way that would be the direct opposite of the type of guidance provided in the P-A approach.

Variability and complexity are central to the P-A approach.[43] Variable movement, or actions, allow the child to have adaptive strategies for many different situations encountered in the environment. Variable perceptions are also important because the environment can be perceived in different ways depending on the orientation of one's body and the way one interacts with the world.[42]

Concepts of movement organization can be perceived and learned by the child, just as cognitive concepts are learned. Thus, handling or manual guidance may not be the focus at all, but rather lessons that can be learned about the nature of the physical functioning within the world, such as learning about the effects of gravity by manipulating objects.

Summary of Research Evidence

The P-A approach is relatively new, so it is less well studied. One study showed early success in the treatment of a child with torticollis in changing the way he perceived and adapted to gravitational forces.[45] However, this was a case report, and it needs to be extended to more children.[45] Two more recent studies conducted with children with and at risk for CP are promising.[43,44] An RCT comparing the P-A approach to home-based caregiver coaching showed improvements in utilization of the support surface for the enhancement of sitting postural control, and greater progress in overall motor development for the children in the P-A group.[43] Specifically, the group receiving the P-A intervention improved in postural stability measures in the sitting position, over and above the postural scores of the infants in the group receiving weekly home visits. Furthermore, after the P-A approach intervention, sitting postural adjustment patterns in infants with CP resembled those of infants developing typically, which was reflected in their COP variables (see Chapter 2 for a discussion of nonlinear measures of variability). In addition, 40% of the P-A approach group participants crawled by the end of the study, compared to 20% in the home program group. Because this study compared 2 groups that were randomized and the number of participants was relatively high (30 infants), the evidence suggests support of the P-A approach.[43] Another recent study utilizing the P-A approach showed improvements in sitting postural control with concurrent changes in cognitive and play skills for children ages 1 to 6 years with moderate and severe CP.[44]

Other related research in perception that may support the theory underlying this approach relates to the importance of variability and complexity in early motor development.[42] In addition, this research supports the importance of the linkage between motor skills, perception, and cognition as the building blocks of future functional skills.[46,47]

PARTICIPATION-BASED APPROACH

Theoretical Foundation

This therapeutic approach is fundamentally different from 2 other approaches discussed previously in this chapter as it does not specifically focus on the motor system and movement patterns[5,7,12] or address the development of movement strategies through the interaction of perception and action.[36,39] Instead, this approach[48] is grounded in the concept of *participation* as an important component of the ICF Model,[21,49] which results from the interaction between the individual, a specific life situation, and the environment in which this situation takes place. The ICF Model,[21,49] as well as the activity and participation issues in the lives of children with CP, were discussed in detail in Chapter 4. Pediatric therapists have an opportunity to enhance participation of these children in activities meaningful to them and their families and, thus, make a real difference in their daily lives by helping them achieve their desired goals.[50]

Primary Concepts

The participation-based approach is founded on the conceptual framework of *optimal participation*.[48] According to Palisano et al,[48] optimal participation is a subjective construct, the meaning of which is determined by each person relatively to his or her own engagement in life situations. Optimal participation of children with physical disabilities can be defined as the result of a dynamic relationship between the *determinants* and *dimensions* of participation. The intensity of participation is affected by specific attributes (determinants) of the child, his or her family, and the environment in which they interact with each other. Physical, social, and "self" dimensions of participation reflect the child's actual engagement in a specific activity, activity-related interactions with other people, and developing understanding of one's self, respectively. The latter encompasses such constructs as the sense of enjoyment of and learning from the activity, and acquiring a self-concept in the process.[48]

Research conducted with children with CP identified such determinants of participation as the child's motivation in mastering difficult tasks; receiving rehabilitation services; age; behavior; cognitive, functional, and communication levels; family stress and activity levels; and the availability of community leisure and recreation programs.[51-54] Chiarello et al[55] demonstrated that taking into consideration the family's priorities for the child's activity and participation was critical for clinicians involved in the development of intervention plans. In a study conducted with 585 families of children and youth with CP, the researchers found that parental priorities were related to their child's Gross Motor Function Classification System (GMFCS)[56] level and age, with daily activities, including self-care, mobility, and communication, identified as the priority most frequently. These findings highlighted the importance of conducting family interviews that would allow therapists to establish the most meaningful rehabilitation outcomes for the child in collaboration with his or her parents.[55]

Fundamental Principles

According to the 6 fundamental principles of participation-based therapy listed by Palisano et al,[48] this intervention must be collaborative, ecological, goal-oriented, family-centered, self-determined, and strength-based. The therapist is expected to collaborate with the child, his or her family, as well as community providers and agencies while working with them in the child's natural environments to implement home and community participation goals, which are identified by the child and the family and need to be realistic and attainable within 4 months. The emphasis is placed on "real-life" experiences that build on the child's and family's strengths and community resources, and are fulfilling for the child. The therapist provides information and guides the child and the family in a manner that enables them in their problem solving and decision making, ultimately leading to enhanced participation.[48]

Palisano et al[48] developed a 5-step process for the implementation of participation-based therapy, which includes the following:

1. Development of a collaborative relationship
2. Forming an agreement on home and community participation goals
3. Assessment of child-, family-, and environment-related strengths and needs
4. Development and implementation of the intervention plan
5. Evaluation of the child- and family-related outcomes

A major premise of this approach is that rehabilitation services should focus on optimal participation as an essential outcome of intervention. Such focus during childhood would address the fundamental need for integration of people with physical disabilities into the society by helping them to develop abilities critical for forming friendships and other social relationships, as well as for employment and independent living.[48] The reader is referred to Chapter 5 for a detailed discussion of these important issues.

Another area of focus of this approach is empowering families with necessary skills and knowledge that build the child's capacity for home and community participation and enhance the parents' ability to advocate for their child's inclusion into the society as its valuable member.[48] The therapist's role is of a consultant who does the following:

- Collaborates with the child, his or her family, and community entities
- Guides the child and the family to set specific, realistic, and attainable participation goals
- Initiates a short-term, strength-based, family-centered intervention provided in the child's natural environment
- Encourages the child and the family to actively seek solutions to participation problems

It is important to note that the participation-based approach is complementary in nature and is not used in place of other interventions designed to address health, fitness, and impairment prevention needs of children with disabilities.[48]

The authors of this approach advocate for the use of individualized assessment instruments, such as Goal Attainment Scaling[57] and the Canadian Occupational Performance Measure,[58] to evaluate participation outcomes.[48] Additionally, they recommend that self-report instruments be used to assess the level of self-determination achieved by the child and the level of empowerment achieved by the parents.[48] Such instruments may include the American Institute of Research Self-Determination Scale[59] and the Psychological Empowerment Scale.[60]

It is important to note that significant barriers may exist in the implementation of this approach in a health care environment. On the one hand, because this approach calls for short-term interventions, which ultimately lead to independent participation and problem solving,[48] it has a potential to be quite cost-effective. However, on the other hand, while working with a child and his or her family, the therapist would spend a significant amount of time communicating not only with them, but also with appropriate community organizations and people to enable problem solving and facilitate the implementation of the intervention plan. Attending community events and making relevant observations would also take a significant amount of time. Although such activities are essential to the success of this intervention,[48] related billing and reimbursement issues may arise as possible barriers to a wide implementation of this approach in clinical practice. Therefore, it appears critical that a mechanism for addressing these issues be developed.

Summary of Research Evidence

Because the participation-based therapy is a very new approach to management of children with disabilities, it is in a great need of clinical trials that would evaluate its effectiveness.[48] However, research evidence from such fields as models of service delivery and pediatric quality of life may provide support for its principles.[48] A number of studies have shown that the practice of meaningful activities that occurs in natural environments and is directed at collaboratively set goals leads to the success of intervention programs.[61-63] Published literature indicates that building collaborative family-provider relationships is crucial for this success,[64,65] and the family-centered service delivery model is effective in empowering families, supporting their psychosocial well-being, and increasing their satisfaction with community-based services.[66,67]

King et al[68] described changes observed in therapists working in rehabilitation as they develop expertise in clinical practice. Specifically, the results of a qualitative study conducted with 11 therapists functioning at novice, intermediate, and expert levels demonstrated that expert clinicians educate, support, and empower the child and his or her family by providing them with necessary information and emotional support that instills in them the sense of control over the situation. In addition, they use a strength-based, individualized approach to support the family's hope and a positive vision of the child's future. Finally, expert therapists facilitate problem solving to encourage the child and the family to find possible participation solutions, and to become self-efficient in this area of their lives.[58]

Palisano et al[48] proposed that a change toward self-determination occurs when the family develops a belief in the benefits of a specific intervention. This leads to increased involvement not only in the therapeutic activities, but also in the decision-making processes related to setting meaningful goals and developing strategies for their attainment.[48,68] Self-determination becomes possible when a person's inherent human needs are fulfilled, leading to improved self-motivation and sense of well-being.[69] Such needs include the feeling of competence while performing an activity, autonomy or self-determined behavior, and relatedness or secure relationships with other people.[69] The participation-based approach builds on this premise, and its self-determination principle is supported by studies that examined outcomes of interventions used to enhance self-determination and enable participation in children and adults with disabilities.[70,71]

CONTEXT THERAPY APPROACH

Theoretical Foundation and Primary Concepts

Context therapy[72,73] is another new intervention approach. It is based on the dynamic systems theory application to development[40,41] that was discussed in detail in Chapter 1, and on the family-centered theory[74] that was described in Chapter 12. This intervention is built on the premise of the systems theory that a motor solution to a functional task evolves from an interaction of the person, the task at hand, and the environment in which it is to be performed.[75] Although the P-A[36,39] and participation-based[48] approaches also use this premise, the emphasis of context therapy is different from these approaches as it focuses on changing the demands of the task and the environmental constraints,[72,73] but not the child's or family attributes. The dynamic systems theory emphasizes the role of "phase shifts" in the developmental process, when new behaviors emerge as the result of a disorganization of the system that brings about variable behaviors.[40,41] In the context therapy approach, the caregivers' perception of their child's readiness for a transition to a new behavior is used in order to develop appropriate intervention goals.[72,73] Goal setting, assessment, and intervention are accomplished through a collaboration between clinicians and the family, with the primary therapist directly interacting with the child and the family in their natural environments, and other health care providers playing a consultative role.[72,73]

Fundamental Principles

Similar to the participation-based approach,[48] context therapy calls for active involvement of the family at all stages of its implementation.[72] Parents are interviewed using the Canadian Occupational Performance Measure.[58] They identify and prioritize their child's functional needs and are encouraged to concentrate on those activities that appear to be "in transition," meaning that the child has motivation to perform them but has not been successful in doing so.[72] This leads to setting meaningful goals, which is accomplished in collaboration with the therapist. The child's performance of the activities related to the intervention goals is videotaped, and the therapist and the family discuss the characteristics of the task and the environment that appear to assist the child's efforts and those that impede his or her performance. Next, the intervention strategies aimed at modifying the task and the environment are considered and agreed upon, without any consideration given to the child's alterations of body structures or functions, and without any movement solution discarded because of being immature or atypical. In the context therapy approach, the best solution to the problem is the one that is the quickest in allowing the child to achieve the functional goal, with the lack of success within 2 weeks indicating to the therapist that the intervention strategy needs to be reassessed. The therapist's involvement in intervention is episodic and is more intensive until the best working strategy is discovered through a trial and error process, followed by independent practice by the child and his or her family. For example, as described by Darrah et al,[72] a successful solution may entail requesting a school bus that has steps that are less steep for the child to be able to climb them, or changing his position by the toilet from standing in front of it to approaching it from the side, so that he can use the sink for support and become independent with using the bathroom. Because all parts of this approach are applied in the child's natural environments, such as his or her home, school, or community, there is no concern about the carryover of the acquired skill from the clinic to a "real life" situation.[72]

Summary of Research Evidence

Although this approach is very new, its efficacy has been examined through a very carefully designed and implemented RCT. Context therapy was compared to a traditional child-centered intervention aimed at addressing impairments and functional limitations, and both were provided weekly over a period of 6 months.[73] This study was conducted with 128 children with CP, GMFCS[56] levels I through V, age range 12 months to 5 years, 11 months. Ninety-one occupational and physical therapists were randomly assigned to a child-focused or a context therapy group, and recruited participants followed their therapists to the same group. Results demonstrated no significant differences between the groups, with both approaches found to be effective in improving the participants' self-care and mobility skills, increasing their participation, and empowering their families. Thus, the context therapy approach was shown to be as successful as traditional therapy applied with the same patient population at the same frequency of intervention. The authors indicated that further research would be required in order to establish the optimal dose-response relationship between the maximal functional change and frequency of context therapy.[73]

THERAPEUTIC APPROACHES BASED ON MOTOR LEARNING THEORY, CONCEPTS, AND PRINCIPLES

Theoretical Foundation and Primary Concepts

Shumway-Cook and Woollacott[76] defined motor learning as "the study of the acquisition and/or modification of movement."(p 21) Newell,[77] who examined motor learning from the perspective of the systems and P-A theories, proposed that it arises from the interaction between the individual, the task at hand, and the environment in which the search for the motor solution to the task occurs. Therefore, motor learning was also defined as "the coordination of the perceptual environment with the action environment in a way consistent with the task constraints."[77](p 225) Gibson[78] and, later, Thelen[79] emphasized the link between perception and action and their strong connection to cognition, and argued that cognition is embodied or grounded in perceptual-motor experiences (see Chapter 1). Because a significant body of research supports the view of grounded cognition, Lobo et al[80] proposed the need for a shift from focusing on the concepts of motor learning in isolation to considering learning as a global phenomenon that spans multiple domains. This shift has to occur in teaching physical therapy students and clinicians about learning processes, as well as in the ways intervention is designed and its outcomes are assessed in the clinic.[80] General concepts of motor learning are summarized in Table 14-2.[37,76,81-85]

Fundamental Principles

Table 14-3 contains principles of practice organization that originated from motor learning studies conducted with healthy adults.[76,81,85] Although a number of these principles are applicable in children, it is important to emphasize that learning in infants and children should be considered from a developmental perspective of motor and cognitive abilities emerging over time.[81] In addition to development, the child's growth, changes in body proportions, and maturation of body systems also lead to differences in learning processes exhibited by children compared to adults.[81]

It is obvious that motor learning principles, especially those related to feedback, cannot be applied to infants because of the limitations in the amount and quality of information that infants can process.[81] However, in children, some of these principles were examined in studies that

TABLE 14-2
GENERAL CONCEPTS OF MOTOR LEARNING

CONCEPT	DESCRIPTION
Implicit (nondeclarative) learning[76,81]	Nonassociative: occurs with repeated exposure to the same stimulus • Habituation: responsiveness decreases when a nonpainful stimulus is presented repeatedly • Sensitization: responsiveness increases when a noxious stimulus is presented repeatedly Associative • Classical conditioning: learning to associate one stimulus with another • Operant conditioning: learning to associate a behavior with a consequence Procedural: learning to perform a task automatically, without thinking about or paying attention to it
Explicit (declarative) learning[76,81]	Occurs when • Specific knowledge can be retrieved through the processes of attention, awareness, and reflection • It involves factual knowledge • It can be expressed verbally
Gentile's taxonomy of motor tasks[82]	Environmental conditions or context • Stationary • In motion Intertrial variability • Absent: no change in environmental conditions from trial to trial • Present: environment changes from trial to trial Tasks • Closed: performed under stationary environmental conditions with absent intertrial variability • Variable motionless: performed under stationary environmental conditions but with changes in stationary features • Consistent motion: performed under "in motion" environmental conditions with absent intertrial variability • Open: performed under "in motion" environmental conditions with present intertrial variability Body orientation • Stable positions • Body transport (movement from point A to point B) is required Object manipulation • Absent • Present

(continued)

investigated the application of different feedback frequencies and the relationship between the task difficulty and feedback frequency.[86,87]

Results of one study indicated that children differ from young adults in their use of feedback during motor learning, which may be related to cognitive processing differences that affect the challenge points for these 2 age groups[86] (see Table 14-2 for the explanation of the challenge point framework).[85] Specifically, children obtain greater benefits from a 100% feedback than a faded feedback schedule in

	TABLE 14-2 (CONTINUED)
	GENERAL CONCEPTS OF MOTOR LEARNING
CONCEPT	**DESCRIPTION**
Stages of motor learning[76,82-84]	Fitts and Posner[83] • Cognitive stage: gathering information about the skill and creating a plan for performance • Associative stage: practice and refinement of the skill • Autonomous stage: efficient, "automatic" performance of the skill without conscious attention Gentile[82] • Initial phase: active exploration and problem solving • Later phases: task-dependent adaptation of movement Vereijken et al,[84] derived from the work of Bernstein[37] • Novice stage: simplification of movement by "freezing" the degrees of freedom • Advanced stage: gradual release of degrees of freedom to involve a greater number of joints in performing the skill • Expert stage: all degrees of freedom are released and optimal movement efficiency is achieved
Instruction[81]	Demonstration: modeling a skill or activity for the learner Verbal instructions • Appropriate amount, clear, and concise • Focus attention on movement characteristics or on its outcome
Types of practice[76,81]	Massed: practice time in each trial is greater than rest time between trials Distributed: rest time between trials is the same or greater than the practice time in a trial Blocked: each skill or variation in activity is performed separately in sets of trials or for a specific amount of time Random: all skills or variations in activity are practiced in a random order Part: breaking down a skill into components and practicing each component separately, followed by putting the skills together Whole: practicing a skill as a whole Mental: performing a skill in one's mind without engaging in actual movement
Transfer of skill[76,81]	Generalization of the learned skill to a different task or environment
Types of feedback[76,81]	Intrinsic: Based on self-perception of one's movement and performance Extrinsic or augmented: Information provided to the learner
Types of extrinsic feedback[76,81]	Concurrent: given during the performance of a skill or activity Terminal: given after the skill or activity is completed Knowledge of results (KR): a type of terminal feedback that provides information about the movement or activity outcome Knowledge of performance (KP): feedback regarding the characteristics or pattern of performed movement or activity
	(continued)

TABLE 14-2 (CONTINUED)	
GENERAL CONCEPTS OF MOTOR LEARNING	
CONCEPT	**DESCRIPTION**
Challenge point framework[85]	Task-related information available for processing and interpretation challenges the performer to learn • Presence of information is necessary for learning • Too little or too much information impedes learning • Effective learning requires optimal amount of information (a challenge point). Challenge points vary depending on the difficulty of the task at hand and the learner's level of the skill. Task difficulty • Nominal: constant perceptual-motor characteristics of the task that are independent of its environmental context and of the learner's skill level • Functional: varied characteristics of the task related to the learner's skill level and the environmental context of the task or practice conditions Fundamental assumptions • Learning requires problem solving • Learning requires an action plan and intrinsic and extrinsic (augmented) feedback

the acquisition phase of learning and may require longer practice time.[86] In addition, if a faded feedback schedule is used with children, a slower reduction in feedback than with adults is advised.[86] Findings of another study conducted with typically developing 10- and 11-year-old children revealed that a 33% feedback frequency was a more optimal learning condition for a task with a lower nominal difficulty, while a 100% feedback frequency was more beneficial for learning a higher nominal difficulty task.[87] This research supported the optimal challenge point prediction in regard to the frequency of feedback (see Table 14-3), and provided evidence for clinical application of this prediction with children developing typically.[85,87]

There is limited and conflicting evidence to suggest specific practice schedules that would benefit learning in children.[81] As proposed by the challenge point framework (see Tables 14-2 and 14-3), the advantage of blocked or random practice may depend on the child's age and skill level, as well as on the complexity of the task.[81,85] Perhaps, carefully designed studies of varied types of practice and graded task difficulties applied in children of different age and skill level may help answer the question of when blocked or random practice may be most beneficial for the child's motor learning.

Motor Learning in Children With Cerebral Palsy: Summary of Research Evidence

Application of Motor Learning Strategies in Function-Based Therapeutic Interventions

The primary focus of physical therapy intervention for children with movement disorders is learning skills that would support their participation in daily life situations.[88,89] Thus, intervention must promote the transfer of skills acquired in the clinic to real life environments.[88] Functional activities in a therapy session can be structured using a number of motor learning strategies that include providing verbal instructions, varying the schedule and amount of practice, and selecting a specific type and frequency of feedback.[88] Levac et al[89] examined the application of such strategies in several function-based therapeutic approaches, 2 of which (family-centered functional therapy [FCFT][90,91] and activity-focused motor interventions [AFMI])[88] had been used for children with CP. Literature related to these approaches was found to contain good, replicable descriptions of motor learning strategies, which emphasized transfer of learned skills to different tasks and their generalization from clinical to other environments.[88-91]

The FCFT approach[90] that more recently was termed *context therapy*[72,91] has been already described in this chapter. The AMFI approach is another function-based intervention that involves the following:

- The analysis of the child's learning-related strengths and problems
- A collaboration with the child and the family in developing activity-related goals that target participation and quality of life
- An intervention plan that is activity-focused and includes motor learning strategies geared toward the child's individual strengths and needs
- The use of a combination of impairment- and activity-focused interventions when the development of secondary impairments needs to be addressed[88,92]

TABLE 14-3
PRINCIPLES OF PRACTICE ORGANIZATION FOR HEALTHY ADULTS[76,81,85]

PRACTICE ORGANIZATION COMPONENT	PRINCIPLES
Selecting the type of practice	Distributed practice is more effective than massed practice for continuous skills (eg, walking, running, swimming, cycling, etc). Massed practice creates less fatigue for discrete skills (eg, reaching and grasping) compared to continuous skills.
	In general, blocked practice is more effective during the acquisition stage of learning, but random practice is more effective for transfer of skill.
	Transfer of skill is supported by organizing practice in such a way that the skill components and practice environment closely resemble the real life situations to which the skill needs to be generalized.
	If the task can be broken down into natural units that comprise the skill, parts can be practiced separately before combining them into the whole skill. Practice of parts must occur in the context of the whole skill (eg, parts of a closed chain skill need to be practiced in a closed chain position).
	Mental practice is effective in enhancing learning, especially when combined with physical practice.
	Predictions regarding optimal challenge points are as follows:
	• Random (compared to blocked) practice will be most beneficial for tasks with lowest nominal difficulty and least beneficial for tasks with highest nominal difficulty.
	• Low contextual interference will be more beneficial for beginners, and high contextual interference will be more beneficial for highly skilled learners.
Selecting the knowledge of results feedback schedule	Feedback given with less than 100% frequency is more beneficial for learning than feedback given after every trial.
	Immediate feedback impedes learning.
	Fading feedback frequency is beneficial for retention of skill.
	Predictions regarding optimal challenge points are as follows:
	• The largest learning effects will be achieved with more immediate and frequent knowledge of results provided for tasks with high nominal difficulty, and the opposite will be true for tasks with low nominal difficulty.
	• Random presentation of augmented feedback will be more beneficial for learning tasks with low nominal difficulty, and blocked augmented feedback presentation will be more beneficial for learning tasks with high nominal difficulty.

In addition to the FCFT and AMFI approaches, motor learning coaching also serves as an example of application of motor learning concepts in pediatric clinical practice.[93] This approach uses the Gentile's taxonomy of tasks[82] and Fitts and Posner's learning stages[83] (see Table 14-2) to structure activity-focused therapy sessions. The emphasis is placed on random practice in varied environments and on the use of augmented feedback appropriate for the specific stage of motor learning.[82,83,93] Bar-Haim et al[93] compared the use of this approach to NDT5,[94] in 78 children with spastic CP, aged 6 to 12 years, who functioned at GMFCS[56] levels II and III. Children classified in level II and enrolled in the motor learning coaching group demonstrated a significantly better 6-month retention of functional skills and generalization of gains in mobility to outdoor and community environments than children in the NDT group who functioned at the same GMFCS level. However, these differences were not observed in children classified in level III, which suggested that motor learning coaching may not be as beneficial for children with greater physical involvement.[93]

Implicit and Explicit Learning, and Practice Schedules

To provide effective intervention to the population of children and adults with CP, it is necessary to determine how they learn best. Based on their review of available evidence,

Steenbergen et al[95] argued that individuals with CP have working memory deficits that may impede explicit learning (see Table 14-2) and suggested that implicit learning may be more beneficial for this patient population. These authors cited a study conducted with highly skilled soccer players with unilateral CP, results of which indicated that its participants with right hemiparesis used implicit and not explicit learning to master a dribbling task.[95,96] Gofer-Levi et al[97] investigated this issue further by having children and adolescents with bilateral spastic CP and their peers developing typically perform a serial reaction time task. Results suggested that individuals with CP may not be able to identify the hidden patterns or regularities in common sequential daily activities, which is related to implicit learning, and suggested that explicit learning of necessary steps by following instructions may lead to a greater success in acquiring such motor skills.[97]

Mixed results obtained in the discussed 2 studies highlight the need for further investigation of implicit and explicit learning in this patient population.[95-97] Differences in learning related to variations in cognitive functioning and to motor involvement in children with unilateral and bilateral CP also need to be examined. Furthermore, there is a great need for research comparing different practice schedules and their effects on motor learning in these children. Results of one study that compared blocked and random practice schedules in children with unilateral CP who performed an upper extremity task demonstrated greater benefits of blocked practice in the acquisition phase of learning, while there was no difference in the effects of the 2 schedules on skill retention.[98]

Feedback Type and Frequency

Selection of the most appropriate type and frequency of feedback may enhance motor learning. In children with CP, as in children developing typically, there is very limited research on the use of augmented feedback, especially in the form of knowledge of performance (KP).[99] One multiple baseline single subject study was conducted with children with CP classified in GMFCS[56] level III who worked on learning to move a therapeutic exercise apparatus, Pedalo, in a backward direction.[99] Practice without feedback, practice with KP feedback, and practice with KP feedback supplemented by the use of a cognitive strategy were compared. The cognitive strategy involved mental rehearsal of practice based on verbal instructions and previously viewed pictures. Results indicated that 62% of study participants benefited from practice by learning a novel task, and while some of them learned from practice without augmented feedback, supplementing KP with a cognitive strategy was beneficial for others.[99]

In a study by Burtner et al,[100] effects of combined knowledge of results (KR) and KP feedback provided on every trial were compared to combined feedback faded from 100% to 25% of trials in children with unilateral CP and their peers developing typically. Although children with CP demonstrated improvement in their performance of a discrete arm movement as the result of practice with augmented feedback, their movements were significantly less consistent and accurate than in children with typical development. In addition,

results indicated that children with CP may require a greater number of augmented feedback trials in order to learn new skills. However, all participants used feedback in a similar way, with greater retention demonstrated when feedback was provided to them more frequently.[100]

These results were similar to a previous study conducted with typically developing children and young adults[86] but differed from those obtained by another group of researchers who compared practice without feedback to 50% and 100% KR feedback practice of throwing darts.[101] In the latter study, children with unilateral CP demonstrated best retention of the learned skill with reduced (50%) feedback frequency.[101] As Burtner et al[100] suggested, this discrepancy in research findings between studies may be explained by the difference in complexity between a simpler task of dart throwing and a more complex discrete arm movement with predetermined spatiotemporal parameters examined in their study.

Self-controlled KR feedback is another type of feedback that received some attention in research. Hemayattalab et al[102] reported on a study that compared a throwing skill acquisition in children with unilateral CP who received self-controlled or yoked feedback. Participants assigned to the self-controlled feedback group were able to request feedback when needed while the yoked group participants were required to receive feedback with the same frequency as the participants of the self-controlled feedback group with whom they were paired. Although there was no difference between the groups demonstrated in the acquisition phase of learning, children with the self-controlled feedback group performed better on retention and transfer of skill.[102]

Evidence-Based Clinical Implications

Based on the reviewed literature, function-based intervention approaches that incorporate motor learning principles have been increasingly used in clinical practice and have shown promising results in children with CP.[72,73,88-93] However, there is an insufficient amount of evidence to conclude which of these approaches would benefit these children the most. It is also still unknown whether implicit or explicit learning is of greater benefit to this patient population,[95-97] and different practice schedules require further investigation.[98] Children with CP differ in their responses to KP feedback, and in some of them, supplementing KP with the use of cognitive strategies may improve learning.[99] In general, children with CP may require a greater number of practice trials with augmented feedback to learn a new skill, but they use feedback the same way as children developing typically.[100] In addition, consistent with the challenge point framework,[85] more frequent feedback may be beneficial for learning a complex task, while less frequent feedback would enhance simple task learning.[100,101] Finally, self-controlled feedback has been shown to be beneficial for skill retention and transfer in this patient population.[102] It is important to note that most of the studies discussed in this section were conducted with children with unilateral CP.[96,98,100-102] This observation highlights the need for expanding research in the area of motor learning to children with bilateral involvement.

Eclectic Approach

According to the Free Merriam-Webster Dictionary,[103] the word *eclectic* means "selecting what appears to be best in various doctrines, methods, or styles", or "composed of elements drawn from various sources." Many pediatric therapists consider themselves practicing an eclectic approach, which involves combining a variety of strategies employed in different therapeutic approaches and using techniques that appear to be effective and/or are supported by research.[34] The information on several intervention approaches presented in this chapter points to the fact that some of these treatment methods, such as the NDT[5,7] and P-A[36,39] approaches, cannot and should not be used together as their theoretical foundations and principles contradict each other. The context therapy approach is also fundamentally different in its philosophy from the sensory-motor NDT intervention,[5,7] as context therapy aims to change the characteristics of the task and the environment in which it is performed and not the characteristics of the child.[72] At the same time, context therapy is similar to the participation-based approach in its pursuit of activity and participation goals and the use of the child and family enabling strategies.[48,72] As for the participation-based approach, according to its authors, it is not intended to be used instead of other types of intervention but is rather complementary in nature.[48] This makes it compatible with any other approach that addresses goals related to the development of functional skills, including interventions grounded in the motor learning theory.[37,76,81-85]

The clinician who considers evidence to be a guide to the selection of interventions and is well-versed in the theoretical underpinnings of each approach is in the best position for making a decision regarding their use in his or her clinical practice, either alone or in combination with one another. As described in the next chapter of this book, techniques that address alterations of structures and functions in children with CP are supported by varied levels of research evidence. Many of these interventions can be used in combination with each other and with the approaches described previously. At the same time, it is important to mention that research has shown that cognition and its development are grounded in perceptual-motor experiences[38,78-80]; therefore, as Lobo et al[80] pointed out, "physical therapy cannot just be about motor skills anymore."[(p 94)] Clinicians should strive to address activity, participation, and global development of their patients, which means looking beyond their motor skills alone.[80] Thus, practicing a truly eclectic approach would mean selecting interventions that are supported by current theories of development and motor control, such as the dynamic systems,[38,40,79] P-A,[35,78] and neuronal group selection[15,104] theories (see Chapter 1) and moving away from those that are founded in the concepts of neuromaturation, hierarchic structure, and reflex integration.[8,34,80]

Complete video-based activities for Chapter 14 (see Activity Set 2 [activities 1, 2, and 4] and Activity Set 3 [activities 1, 2, and 4] on the book website).

References

1. Bobath B, Bobath K. *Motor Development in the Different Types of Cerebral Palsy.* London, UK: William Heinemann Medical Books Limited; 1975.
2. Twitchell TE. On the motor deficit in congenital bilateral athetosis. *J Nerv Ment Dis.* 1959;129(2):105-132.
3. Illingworth RS. *The Development of the Infant and the Young Child, Normal and Abnormal.* Edinburgh and London, UK: E. & S. Livingstone; 1960.
4. Phelps WM. The management of the cerebral palsies. *JAMA.* 1941;117:1621-1625.
5. Bobath K. *A Neurophysiological Basis for Treatment of Cerebral Palsy.* Lavenham, UK: Mac Keith Press; 1980.
6. Bobath B, Bobath K. *Interview for Neurodevelopmental Treatment Association.* Baltimore, MD; 1981.
7. Bobath B. *Abnormal Postural Reflex Activity Caused by Brain Lesions.* London, UK: William Heinemann Medical Books Limited; 1971.
8. Burke RE. Sir Charles Sherrington's the integrative action of the nervous system: a centenary appreciation. *Brain.* 2007;130(4):887-894.
9. Debaere F, Swinnen SP, Beatse F, Sunaert S, Van Hecke P, Duysens J. Brain areas involved in interlimb coordination: a distributed network. *Neuroimage.* 2001;14(5):947-958.
10. Johnson MH. Developmental neuroscience, psychophysiology, and genetics. In: Bornstein MH, Lamb ME, eds. *Developmental Science: An Advanced Textbook.* 6th ed. New York, NY: Psychology Press; 2011:201-239.
11. Horak F. Assumptions underlying motor control for neurologic rehabilitation. In: *Contemporary Management of Motor Control Problems. Proceedings of the II Step Conference.* Alexandria, VA: American Physical Therapy Association; 1991:11-27.
12. Howle J. *Neuro-Developmental Treatment Approach: Theoretical Foundations and Principles of Clinical Practice.* Laguna Beach, CA: NDTA; 2002.
13. Schmidt RA, Lee TD. *Motor Control and Learning: A Behavioral Emphasis.* 4th ed. Champaign, IL: Human Kinetics Publishers; 2005.
14. Shumway-Cook A, Woollacott MH. Motor control: issues and theories. In: Shumway-Cook A, Woollacott MH, eds. *Motor Control: Translating Research into Clinical Practice.* 4th ed. Philadelphia, PA: Lippincott Williams and Wilkins; 2012:3-20.
15. Edelman GM. *Neural Darwinism.* New York, NY: Basic Books; 1987.
16. Edelman GM. *Bright Air, Brilliant Fire: On the Matter of the Mind.* New York, NY: Basic Books; 1992.
17. Arndt SW, Chandler LS, Sweeney JK, Sharkey MA, Johnson McElroy J. Effects of a neurodevelopmental treatment-based trunk protocol for infants with posture and movement dysfunction. *Pediatr Phys Ther.* 2008;20(1):11-22.
18. Bly, L. *The Components of Normal Movement during the First Year of Life and Abnormal Motor Development, Monograph.* Laguna Beach, CA: Neurodevelopmental Treatment Association, Inc.; 1983.
19. Bouman HD. An exploratory and analytical survey of therapeutic exercise. Sixth question and discussion period. Proceedings, Northwestern University Special Therapeutic Exercise Project, NUSTEP, July 25, 1966 to August 19, 1966, Northwestern University Medical School, Chicago, Illinois. Am J Phys Med. 1967;46(1):667-680.
20. Fulton JF. *Physiology of the Nervous System.* New York, NY: Oxford University Press; 1951.
21. World Health Organization. *International Classification of Functioning, Disability and Health.* Geneva, Switzerland: World Health Organization; 2001.
22. Finnie NR. *Handling the Young Child with Cerebral Palsy at Home.* Boston, MA: Butterworth-Heinemann; 1997.

23. Bly L. *Baby Treatment Based on NDT Principles*. Austin, TX: Therapy Skill Builders; 1999.

24. Bly L, Whiteside A. *Facilitation Techniques Based on NDT Principles*. Austin, TX: Therapy Skill Builders; 1997.

25. Boehme R. *Improving Upper Body Control: An Approach to Assessment and Treatment of Tonal Dysfunction*. Tucson, AZ: Therapy Skill Builders; 1988.

26. Wright M, Wallman L. Cerebral palsy. In: Campbell SK, Palisano RJ, Orlin MN, eds. *Physical Therapy for Children*. 4th ed. St. Louis, MO: Saunders; 2012:577-627.

27. Butler C, Darrah J. AACPDM evidence report: effects of neuro-developmental treatment (NDT) for cerebral palsy; 2001-2002. Available at: www.aacpdm.org. Accessed: March 31, 2013.

28. Kluzik J, Fetters L, Coryell J. Quantification of control: a preliminary study of effects of neurodevelopmental treatment on reaching in children with spastic cerebral palsy. *Phys Ther*. 1990;70(2):65-76; discussion 76-78.

29. Girolami G, Campbell SK. Efficacy of a neuro-developmental treatment program to improve motor control in infants born prematurely. *Pediatr Phys Ther*. 1994;6(4):175-184.

30. Piper MC, Kunos I, Willis DM, Mazer BL, Ramsay M, Silver KM. Early physical therapy effects on the high-risk infant: a randomized controlled trial. *Pediatrics*. 1986;78(2):216-224.

31. Fetters L, Kluzik J. Neurodevelopmental treatment versus practice for the treatment of children with spastic cerebral palsy. *Phys Ther*. 1996;76(4):346-358.

32. Bower E, McLellan M, Arney J, Campbell MJ. A randomized controlled trial of different intensities of physiotherapy and different goal-setting procedures in 44 children with cerebral palsy. *Dev Med Child Neurol*. 1996;38(3):226-237.

33. Bar-Haim S, Harries N, Belokopytov M, et al. Comparison of efficacy of Adeli suit and neurodevelopmental treatments in children with cerebral palsy. *Dev Med Child Neurol*. 2006;48(5):325-330.

34. Damiano D. Pass the torch, please! *Dev Med Child Neurol*. 2007;49(10):723.

35. Gibson JJ. *The Senses Considered as Perceptual Systems*. Boston, MA: Houghton Mifflin; 1966.

36. Tscharnuter I. A new therapy approach to movement organization. *Phys Occup Ther Pediatr*. 1993;13:19-40.

37. Bernstein NA. *The Co-ordination and Regulation of Movements*. Oxford: Pergamon Press; 1967.

38. Thelen E, Smith LB, eds. *A Dynamic Systems Approach to the Development of Cognition and Action*. Cambridge, MA: MIT Press; 1994.

39. Tscharnuter I. Clinical application of dynamic theory concepts according to Tscharnuter Akademie for Movement Organization (TAMO) therapy. *Pediatr Phys Ther*. 2002;14:29-37.

40. Thelen E. Motor development. A new synthesis. *Am Psychol*. 1995;50(2):79-95.

41. Spencer JP, Clearfield M, Corbetta D, Ulrich B, Buchanan P, Schöner G. Moving toward a grand theory of development: in memory of Esther Thelen. *Child Dev*. 2006;77(6):1521-1538.

42. Dusing SC, Harbourne RT. Variability in postural control during infancy: implications for development, assessment, and intervention. *Phys Ther*. 2010;90(12):1838-1845.

43. Harbourne RT, Willett S, Kyvelidou A, Deffeyes J, Stergiou N. A comparison of interventions for children with cerebral palsy to improve sitting postural control: a clinical trial. *Phys Ther*. 2010;90:1881-1898.

44. Harbourne R, Willett SL, Ryalls B, Stergiou N. The use of stochastic noise during intervention to improve sitting postural control in children with cerebral palsy. In: Abstracts of Poster Presentations at the 2013 Combined Sections Meeting. *Pediatr Phys Ther*. 2013;25(1):105-106. Abstract.

45. Rahlin M. TAMO therapy as a major component of physical therapy intervention for an infant with congenital muscular torticollis: a case report. *Pediatr Phys Ther*. 2005;17(3):209-218.

46. Adolph KE, Berger SE. Physical and motor development. In: Bornstein MH, Lamb ME, eds. *Developmental Science: An Advanced Textbook*. 5th ed. New York, NY: Psychology Press; 2011:241-302.

47. Soska KC, Adolph KE, Johnson SP. Systems in development: motor skill acquisition facilitates three-dimensional object completion. *Dev Psychol*. 2010;46(1):129-138.

48. Palisano RJ, Chiarello LA, King GA, Novak I, Stoner T, Fiss A. Participation-based therapy for children with physical disabilities. *Disabil Rehabil*. 2012;34(12):1041-1052.

49. World Health Organization. *International Classification of Functioning, Disability and Health: Children and Youth Version*. Geneva, Switzerland: World Health Organization; 2007.

50. Goldstein DN, Cohn E, Coster W. Enhancing participation for children with disabilities: application of the ICF enablement framework to pediatric physical therapist practice. *Pediatr Phys Ther*. 2004;16:114-120.

51. Majnemer A, Shevell M, Law M, et al. Participation and enjoyment of leisure activities in school-aged children with cerebral palsy. *Dev Med Child Neurol*. 2008;50(10):751-758.

52. Palisano RJ, Chiarello LA, Orlin M, et al; Children's Activity and Participation Group. Determinants of intensity of participation in leisure and recreational activities by children with cerebral palsy. *Dev Med Child Neurol*. 2011;53(2):142-149.

53. Palisano RJ, Kang L-J, Chiarello LA, Orlin M, Oeffinger D, Maggs J. Social and community participation of children and youth with cerebral palsy is associated with age and gross motor function classification. *Phys Ther*. 2009;89(12):1304-1314.

54. Kang L-J, Palisano RJ, Orlin M, Chiarello LA, King GA, Polansky M. Determinants of social participation – with friends and others who are not family members – for youths with cerebral palsy. *Phys Ther*. 2010;90(12):1743-1757.

55. Chiarello LA, Palisano RJ, Maggs J, et al. Family priorities for activity and participation of children and youth with cerebral palsy. *Phys Ther*. 2010;90(9):1254-1264.

56. Palisano RJ, Rosenbaum PL, Walter SD, Russell DJ, Wood EP, Galuppi BE. Development and reliability of a system to classify gross motor function in children with cerebral palsy. *Dev Med Child Neurol*. 1997;39(4):214-223.

57. King GA, McDougall J, Palisano RJ, Gritzan J, Tucker MA. Goal attainment scaling: its use in evaluating pediatric therapy programs. *Phys Occup Ther Pediatr*. 1999;19(2):31-52.

58. Law M, Baptiste S, Carswell A, McColl M, Polatajko H, Pollock N. *Canadian Occupational Performance Measure (COPM) Manual*. 4th ed. Toronto, Ontario: CAOT; 2005.

59. Wolman J, Campeau P, Dubois P, Mithaug D, Stolarski V. *AIR Self-Determination Scale and User Guide*. Palo Alto, CA: American Institute for Research; 1994.

60. Akey TM, Marquis JG, Ross ME. Validation of scores on the psychological empowerment scale: a measure of empowerment for parents of children with a disability. *Educ Psychol Meas*. 2000;60(3):419-438.

61. Novak I, Cusick A, Lannin N. Occupational therapy home programs for cerebral palsy: double-blind, randomized, controlled trial. *Pediatrics*. 2009;124(4):e606-e614.

62. Van den Broeck C, De Cat J, Molenaers G, et al. The effect of individually defined physiotherapy in children with cerebral palsy. *Eur J Paediatr Neurol*. 2010;14(6):519-525.

63. Mastos M, Miller K, Eliasson AC, Imms C. Goal-directed training: linking theories of treatment to clinical practice for improved functional activities in daily life. *Clin Rehabil*. 2007;21(1):47-55.

64. Peterander F. The best quality cooperation between parents and experts in early intervention. *Infant Young Child*. 2000;12(3):32-45.

65. King G. A relational goal-oriented model of optimal service delivery to children and families. *Phys Occup Ther Pediatr*. 2009;29(4):384-408.

66. Dunst CJ, Trivette CM. Empowerment, effective help giving practices and family-centered care. *Pediatr Nurs*. 1996;22(4):334-337.

67. King S, Teplicky R, King G, Rosenbaum P. Family-centered service for children with cerebral palsy and their families: a review of literature. *Semin Pediatr Neurol.* 2004;11(1):78-86.

68. King G, Currie M, Bartlett DJ, et al. The development of expertise in pediatric rehabilitation therapists: changes in approach, self-knowledge, and use of enabling and customizing strategies. *Dev Neurorehabil.* 2007;10(3):223-240.

69. Ryan RM, Deci EL. Self-determination theory and the facilitation of intrinsic motivation, social development, and well-being. *Am Psychol.* 2000;55(1):68-78.

70. Algozzine B, Browder D, Karvonen M, Test DW, Wood WM. Effects of interventions to promote self-determination for individuals with disabilities. *Rev Educ Res.* 2001;71(2):219-277.

71. Graham F, Rodger S, Ziviani J. Coaching parents to enable children's participation: an approach for working with parents and their children. *Aust Occup Ther J.* 2009;56(1):16-23.

72. Darrah J, Law MC, Pollock N, et al. Context therapy: a new intervention approach for children with cerebral palsy. *Dev Med Child Neurol.* 2011;53(7):615-620.

73. Law MC, Darrah J, Pollock N, et al. Focus on function: a cluster, randomized controlled trial comparing child- versus context-focused intervention for young children with cerebral palsy. *Dev Med Child Neurol.* 2011;53(7):621-629.

74. Bamm EL, Rosenbaum P. Family-centered theory: origins, development, barriers, and supports to implementation in rehabilitation medicine. *Arch Phys Med Rehabil.* 2008;89:1618-1624.

75. Bernstein NA. On dexterity and its development. In: Latash ML, Turvey MT, eds. *Dexterity and Its Development.* Mahwah, NJ: Lawrence Erlbaum Associates, Publishers; 1996:3-244.

76. Shumway-Cook A, Woollacott MH. Motor learning and recovery of function. In: Shumway-Cook A, Woollacott MH, eds. *Motor Control: Translating Research into Clinical Practice.* 4th ed. Philadelphia, PA: Lippincott Williams and Wilkins; 2012:21-44.

77. Newell KM. Motor skill acquisition. *Annu Rev Psychol.* 1991;42:213-237.

78. Gibson EJ. Exploratory behavior in the development of perceiving, acting, and the acquiring of knowledge. *Annu Rev Psychol.* 1988;39:1-41.

79. Thelen E. Grounded in the world: developmental origins of the embodied mind. *Infancy.* 2000;1(1):3-28.

80. Lobo MA, Harbourne RT, Dusing SC, Westcott McCoy S. Grounding early intervention: physical therapy cannot just be about motor skills anymore. *Phys Ther.* 2013;93(1):94-103.

81. Gordon AM, Magill RA. Motor learning: application of principles to pediatric rehabilitation. In: Campbell SK, Palisano RJ, Orlin MN, eds. *Physical Therapy for Children.* 4th ed. St. Louis, MO: Saunders; 2012:151-174.

82. Gentile AM. Skill acquisition: action, movement, and neuromotor processes. In: Carr JH, Shepherd RB, eds. *Movement Science: Foundations for Physical Therapy and Rehabilitation.* 2nd ed. Rockville, MD: Aspen; 2000:111-187.

83. Fitts PM, Posner MI. *Human Performance.* Belmont, CA: Brooks/Cole; 1967.

84. Vereijken B, van Emmerik RE, Whiting HT, Newell KM. Freezing degrees of freedom in skill acquisition. *J Motor Behav.* 1992;24:133-142.

85. Guadagnoli MA, Lee TD. Challenge point: a framework for conceptualizing the effects of various practice conditions in motor learning. *J Mot Behav.* 2004;36:212-224.

86. Sullivan KJ, Kantak SS, Burtner PA. Motor learning in children: feedback effects on skill acquisition. *Phys Ther.* 2008;88(6):720-732.

87. Sidaway B, Bates J, Occhiogrosso B, Schlagenhaufer J, Wilkes D. Interaction of feedback frequency and task difficulty in children's motor skill learning. *Phys Ther.* 2012;92(7):948-957.

88. Valvano J. Activity-focused motor interventions for children with neurological conditions. *Phys Occup Ther Pediatr.* 2004;24(1-2):79-107.

89. Levac D, Wishart L, Missiuna C, Wright V. The application of motor learning strategies within functionally based interventions for children with neuromotor conditions. *Pediatr Phys Ther.* 2009;21:345-355.

90. Darrah J, Law M, Pollock N. Innovations in practice. Family-centered functional therapy – a choice for children with motor dysfunction. *Infants Young Child.* 2001;13(4):79-87.

91. Law M, Darrah J, Pollock N, et al. Focus on function – a randomized controlled trial comparing 2 rehabilitation interventions for young children with cerebral palsy (study protocol). *BMC Pediatr.* 2007;7:31.

92. Valvano J, Rapport MJ. Activity-focused motor interventions for infants and young children with neurological conditions. *Infants Young Child.* 2006;19(4):292-307.

93. Bar-Haim S, Harries N, Nammourah I, et al. Effectiveness of motor learning coaching in children with cerebral palsy: a randomized controlled trial. *Clin Rehabil.* 2010;24(11):1009-1020.

94. Bobath K, Bobath B. The facilitation of normal postural reactions and movements in the treatment of cerebral palsy. *Physiotherapy.* 1964;50:246-262.

95. Steenbergen B, van der Kamp J, Verneau M, Jongbloed-Pereboom M, Masters SW. Implicit and explicit learning: applications from basic research to sports for individuals with impaired movement dynamics. *Disabil Rehabil.* 2010;32(18):1509-1516.

96. Steenbergen B, van der Kamp J. Attentional processes of high-skilled soccer players with congenital hemiparesis: differences related to the side of the hemiparetic lesion. *Motor Control.* 2008;12(1):55-68.

97. Gofer-Levi M, Silberg T, Brezner A, Vakil E. Deficit in implicit motor sequence learning among children and adolescents with spastic cerebral palsy. *Res Dev Disabil.* 2013;34(11):3672-3678.

98. Duff SV, Gordon AM. Learning of grasp control in children with hemiplegic cerebral palsy. *Dev Med Child Neurol.* 2003;45(11):746-757.

99. Thorpe DE, Valvano J. The effects of knowledge of performance and cognitive strategies on motor skill learning in children with cerebral palsy. *Pediatr Phys Ther.* 2002;14(1):2-15.

100. Burtner PA, Leinwand R, Sullivan KJ, Goh H-T, Kantak SS. Motor learning in children with hemiplegic cerebral palsy: feedback effects on skill acquisition. *Dev Med Child Neurol.* 2014;56(3):259-266.

101. Hemayattalab R, Rostami LR. Effects of frequency of feedback on the learning of motor skill in individuals with cerebral palsy. *Res Dev Disabil.* 2010;31(1):212-217.

102. Hemayattalab R, Arabameri E, Pourazar M, Ardakani MD, Kashefi M. Effects of self-controlled feedback on learning of a throwing task in children with spastic hemiplegic cerebral palsy. *Res Dev Disabil.* 2013;34(9):2884-2889.

103. Eclectic – Definition and More from the Free Merriam-Webster Dictionary. *Merriam-Webster Online.* http://www.merriam-webster.com/medical/eclectic. Accessed April 28, 2013.

104. Edelman GM. Neural Darwinism: selection and reentrant signaling in higher brain function. *Neuron.* 1993;10(2):115-125.

Please see videos on the accompanying website at

www.healio.com/books/videosrahlin

Common Intervention Strategies and Techniques

Therapists have a professional and an ethical responsibility to use intervention strategies that are supported by research or at a minimum are supported by sound physiologic theories.

Meg Stanger and Susan Oresic[1]

Clinical decision making in regard to the selection of interventions for children with cerebral palsy (CP) is a complex process.[1] It is guided by the conceptual framework of the International Classification of Functioning, Disability and Health (ICF)[2] used to structure a thorough assessment and by the research evidence that supports, questions, or opposes the use of specific interventions to address the assessment findings.[1,3] The application of evidence to clinical practice requires a careful interpretation of study results, and therapists are often challenged to combine a variety of intervention strategies and techniques to achieve meaningful outcomes for the child and his or her family.[3]

The term *intervention strategy* has a wider meaning than the term *intervention technique*. In this context, a *strategy* is a term that describes the general approach to intervention, which may encompass a variety of specific *techniques*. For example, the cardiovascular and pulmonary intervention strategy includes airway clearance, respiratory training, aerobic exercise, and other intervention techniques, which are selected based on the patient's needs. This chapter provides a brief description and a summary of evidence in support of a number of common physical therapy intervention strategies and techniques that are used in children with CP.

Aquatic Intervention

Aquatic interventions include aquatic therapy and aquatic exercise, which use water properties, such as buoyancy, viscous drag, and hydrostatic pressure to decrease the effects of gravity and joint loading while providing postural support and resistance to active movement.[4,5] *Aquatic therapy* includes activities that generally do not lead to improved fitness, whereas *aquatic exercise* is expected to produce positive fitness effects, such as increased strength, flexibility, and cardiorespiratory endurance.[4] Aquatic therapy may include activities targeting the child's abilities to float, move extremities, kick, relax, submerge face, and blow bubbles in the water, with the progression to learning breath control and transitional mobility, and swimming skills.[6,7] Balance activities performed at varied water depths and a variety of standing play activities may also be used during aquatic therapy sessions.[5,7]

Aquatic exercise includes aerobic, strengthening, and stretching activities.[4,5] In-the-water kicking, stride jumps, jumping in place, step-ups, walking and running on the pool floor or on an underwater treadmill, shuttle running, and length swimming are some examples of aquatic aerobic

Rahlin M. *Physical Therapy for Children With Cerebral Palsy: An Evidence-Based Approach* (pp 249-261).
© 2016 SLACK Incorporated.

exercise.[4,5] Progressive resistive exercise using the velocity of movement in the water and its viscous drag property, and various paddles, kick boards, and other devices that allow to vary the amount of resistance can be utilized for strengthening. Passive and active stretching activities can be performed to improve flexibility.[4,5]

There are several important considerations for planning and implementing aquatic exercise programs for children with CP.[4] First, the treatment pool environment needs to be safe and appropriate for this patient population.[4] The water should be shallow enough so that the children can touch the bottom of the pool with their feet; floatation devices should be used when necessary; and water should be warmer than in a community pool to support relaxation and prevent the undesired temporary increase in muscle tone that may occur if the water temperature is lower than 95°F.[4-7]

Second, to achieve a desired fitness effect, aquatic exercise should be of appropriate frequency, duration, and intensity.[4] Literature reports on aerobic exercise parameters used in children with CP vary from 20 to 60 minutes for duration, from 50% to 80% of maximal heart rate for intensity, and from 2 to most days of the week for frequency of exercise,[4,5,7-9] which reflect significant heterogeneity in functional presentation within this patient population. The child's heart rate can be monitored during aquatic aerobic activities by using a water-proof telemetry strap or a heart rate monitor.[4,10] To increase muscle strength, progressive resistive exercise in the water can be performed 2 times per week, 8 to 12 repetitions for each muscle group,[4] and clinically significant improvements in lower extremity range of motion (ROM) can be observed after passive and active stretching performed in the pool.[5]

The third important consideration is whether the child would benefit from participation in a group aquatic exercise program.[4] Group environments provide unique opportunities for children with CP as they help engage them through races, games, and participation in a variety of activities that promote interaction with their peers. Peer modeling and healthy competition may make the exercise environment more exciting and stimulating, thus motivating the child to succeed.[4] In addition, participation in a community-based aquatic program together with children without disabilities may lead to greater acceptance of children with disabilities by their typically developing peers.[11]

In most studies that evaluated the effectiveness of aquatic interventions, they were used in combination with or as an adjunct to land-based therapy.[5,7-10] The reported benefits of aquatic therapy for children with movement disorders included clinically significant improvements in ROM, muscle strength, pain reduction, walking speed, and functional mobility.[5,7] As for aquatic exercise, favorable statistically significant outcomes were documented at all ICF[2] levels in a well-designed single-subject study.[8] These were increased walking efficiency and endurance (body function), gross motor function (activity), and increased community mobility performance (participation) in a 5-year-old girl with bilateral spastic CP.[2,8] Additionally, significant gains in cardiorespiratory endurance were demonstrated in an A-B multiple single

subject design with 16 participants with disabilities, but that study had weaker methodological quality.[9] Finally, in a pretest–post-test experimental design study with 12 adolescents with CP, significant improvement in gait efficiency was observed as the outcome of group aquatic training, which the authors attributed to "systemic cardiorespiratory adaptations"(p 1616) that resulted from this intervention.[10] Overall, further, more rigorous research is needed to establish sound clinical guidelines for implementation of aquatic programs.

CARDIOVASCULAR AND PULMONARY INTERVENTIONS

Airway Clearance and Respiratory Training Techniques

Because of decreased pulmonary function and chest mobility reported in children with CP, physical therapists must include respiratory training activities in their exercise programs.[12,13] Many individuals with CP present with ineffective cough, combined with respiratory muscle weakness, aspiration, and recurrent infections, which impede their airway clearance.[14-17] Usually, chest physical therapy, including postural drainage, percussion, and vibration, is recommended as the "gold standard" intervention to improve airway clearance in patients with respiratory problems.[14-16,18] However, there is insufficient evidence to suggest the effectiveness of these techniques in children with CP.[14,15] Head down postural drainage positions were shown to exacerbate symptoms of gastroesophageal reflux in infants with cystic fibrosis.[19,20] Because infants and children with CP are frequently affected by gastroesophageal reflux disease (GERD),[21] these head down positions may not be indicated for their respiratory management.[14,15,18] Therefore, modified postural drainage positions suggested by Button et al[19] for infants with cystic fibrosis are currently used for children with CP.[18]

Respiratory muscle training is necessary to improve ventilation, breathing control and efficiency, and the ability to cough in children with CP.[18] Younger children enjoy blowing bubbles, whistles, and simple horns, as well as singing nursery rhyme songs. If the infant or a toddler is unable to cough spontaneously or demonstrates a weak cough, nasopharyngeal suctioning may be needed to clear secretions. Older children who can follow directions may be able to learn formal breathing exercises. Ineffective cough in these children may be addressed by manual assistance provided by the therapist, but care must be taken to avoid scheduling airway clearance activities soon after a meal as this may lead to gagging or vomiting.[18] In a study with 30 children with CP, Wang et al[22] reported a fair to moderate positive correlation[23] between the participants' respiratory muscle strength and the Self-Care and Social Function scores on the Pediatric Evaluation of Disability Inventory (PEDI).[24] Lee et al[25] showed that strength of respiratory musculature in 6 to 12 year olds with

TABLE 15-1

TYPES OF CONSTRAINT-INDUCED MOVEMENT THERAPY MODELS

MODEL TYPE	COMPONENTS	BRIEF DESCRIPTION
Signature CIMT	Restraint of the uninvolved UE for at least 2 weeks during ≤0% of awake time Intensive training of the involved UE for 3 hours per day or more	Original model developed initially for adults with stroke
Modified CIMT	Restraint and intensive training components similar to signature model Components vary by the restraint type, type and daily duration of structured training, program duration, location and context, and provider training	Modification of the signature model
Hybrid CIMT	Restraint and intensive training Bimanual training component added	Significant alteration of the original single limb use model

Abbreviations: CIMT, constraint-induced movement therapy; UE, upper extremity.

Compiled from Eliasson et al.[35]

CP can be increased by respiratory training performed with an auditory and visual feedback breathing device, with significant improvement in pulmonary function demonstrated by study participants.

Aerobic Exercise

Compared to their typically developing peers, individuals with CP demonstrate decreased aerobic capacity that tends to decrease further with age.[26] Current rehabilitation programs for children with disabilities more and more frequently incorporate aerobic exercise components, which target cardiorespiratory endurance, aerobic capacity, weight management, and gross motor function.[3,27,28] Aerobic exercise can be used separately or in combination with strengthening and stretching activities, thus addressing the overall health-related physical fitness.[28,29] Examples of aerobic exercise interventions investigated in research literature include walking, interval training, step-ups, running, cycling, wheelchair driving, swimming, and other activities.[3,27-33]

Several systematic reviews of literature examined the effects of cardiorespiratory endurance training in children with CP.[27-29] Varied exercise activities and parameters were reported, and a variety of outcome measures, most of which focused on body structures and functions and activity levels of the ICF,[2] were used in published research.[27-29] The exercise program duration ranged from 6 weeks to 16 months, with reported aerobic exercise frequency of 1 to 4 times per week, 20 to 45 minutes in duration, at 60% to 75% of maximal heart rate. The participants' ages varied from 7 to 25 years, and they represented the Gross Motor Function Classification System (GMFCS)[34] levels I through IV. The overall methodological quality of examined research was rated as mostly low.[27-29] Although all 3 systematic reviews agreed in their finding that aerobic fitness in children with CP may increase as the result of cardiorespiratory endurance training,[27-29] Butler et al[28] also suggested that such an increase in fitness does not seem to carry over into activity, and Verschuren et al[29] recommended that future research should focus on effects of training on daily activity, participation, self-competence, and quality of life of children with CP.

CONSTRAINT-INDUCED MOVEMENT THERAPY

Constraint-induced movement therapy (CIMT) is an intervention strategy that involves restraining the uninvolved or better functioning upper extremity, with structured, intensive training provided for the involved arm to improve its functional use.[1,35] The CIMT is based on research conducted with monkeys, which showed that following a single upper limb deafferentation and the subsequent restraint of the unaffected limb, the monkey was able to purposefully use the deafferented limb.[36,37] The uninvolved limb can be restrained using a bivalved cast,[38] a sling,[39] a glove with a built-in plastic splint,[40] or a soft mitt.[41] There are several CIMT models (Table 15-1), all of which were demonstrated to be effective in improving functional use of the involved upper extremity in children with unilateral CP, regardless of the device used to restrain the uninvolved limb.[35] It is important to note that a similar intervention, termed forced use, is not included in Table 15-1 because this strategy does not include any specific training of the affected extremity while the unaffected arm is restrained.[35]

Results of a systematic review of literature demonstrated that the most rigorous of published research studies supported the use of the CIMT intervention in children with unilateral CP, with improvements noted at the ICF[2] levels of body structures and functions and activity.[37] Overall, the body of CIMT research showed an increased frequency of use of the involved upper extremity in participants with unilateral CP,[37] and in several studies, significant improvements in quality of movement were also documented.[38,40,42] However, based on the systematic review, it was not possible to identify the best CIMT method to use or the threshold for intensity of intervention that would constitute "an adequate dose" for improvement.[37] To add to this uncertainty, Islam et al[43] found no difference in positive outcomes of CIMT in individuals with CP based on their corticomotor projection patterns or characteristics of their brain lesions.

To explain, a lesion on one side of the brain may result in decreased formation of the contralateral pathways and, therefore, in a continuous use of ipsilateral corticospinal projections to the motor units of the affected upper extremity, while during typical development, these ipsilateral pathways usually retract in the first year of life.[43,44] Better hand function was documented in children with unilateral CP who had developed contralateral projection patterns, compared to those who had not.[44,45] Additionally, the location, type, and extent of brain lesions was shown to affect the motor function of the hand in this patient population.[46] However, in a study with 16 children aged 10 to 16 years who were diagnosed with unilateral CP, both of these factors were rendered irrelevant to CMIT outcomes based on the results of transcranial magnetic stimulation (TMS) used to examine the organization of the participants' motor cortex, and on magnetic resonance imaging (MRI) of their brain lesions.[43]

Eliasson et al[35] identified the existing gaps in information related to the CIMT application in children with unilateral CP and the most important priorities for future research in this area. The need to examine the effects of several factors on the success of CIMT was emphasized, including the child's age, the use of repeated CIMT intervention, and the dosing of structured practice.[35] Another direction of research suggested by a different group of authors was to investigate the efficacy of repetitive low-frequency TMS in combination with subsequent CIMT.[47] In a small RCT that involved 19 children with congenital hemiparesis aged 8 to 17 years, 8 of 10 participants in the TMS/CIMT group demonstrated improvement in hand function that was greater than the smallest detectable change, and only 2 of 9 participants in the sham TMS/CIMT group showed a similar result. Based on these findings, Gillick et al[47] recommended that research of this combined intervention move toward larger clinical trials, with the emphasis on determining the most appropriate patient characteristics, the optimal dosage of TMS, and the optimal amount of time between the TMS and CIMT.

ELECTRICAL STIMULATION

Electrical stimulation (ES) is an intervention strategy that triggers action potentials in nerve axons through depolarization of the axon membrane.[48] It can elicit skeletal muscle contraction when applied to a motor nerve that innervates the muscle.[48] Peripheral effects of ES on the musculoskeletal and neuromuscular systems, such as changes in spasticity, strength, muscle contraction patterns, or ROM were documented in published clinical studies.[48-51] ES may also have a central effect by contributing to neural reorganization of the brain or central nervous system (CNS) plasticity.[48] Based on a review of motor learning and ES literature, Merrill[48] proposed that, in order to trigger CNS plasticity mechanisms, the applied stimulation needs to be repetitive, task-specific, goal oriented, novel, challenging performance limits, and linked to feedback.

Two major types of ES described in literature, neuromuscular electrical stimulation or NMES, and threshold electrical stimulation or TES, are used in individuals with CP.[48,49] In NMES, electrical current is applied to the intramuscular branches of the nerve that supplies the targeted muscle through two surface electrodes placed on the skin.[49] To elicit a muscle contraction, the current needs to be of sufficient intensity.[49] Reed[52] described 2 strengthening mechanisms of NMES. The first mechanism, called *resistance overload*, is muscle hypertrophy that occurs when high-intensity stimulation is used, similar to the application of high-resistance isometric training that leads to increased cross-sectional area of the muscle and its strength.[49,52] The second mechanism is the selective recruitment of Type II (fast twitch) muscle fibers by NMES leading to selective strengthening of these fibers.[52] A subset of NMES that is applied to a muscle during its active contraction when a person is completing a functional task is known as *functional electrical stimulation* (FES).[49] TES is a different type of ES that is applied for 8 to 12 hours during sleep in the form of a low-level electrical stimulus that does not result in muscle contraction.[53] Pape[53] suggested that the TES mechanism of action leading to increased muscle bulk may be related to increased local blood flow that coincides with increased secretion of trophic hormones occurring during sleep.

Merrill[48] outlined the following clinical goals for the use of ES in children with CP:

- Reduce muscle stiffness, spasticity, and co-contraction of antagonist musculature
- Increase ROM and muscle strength
- Improve muscle contraction timing for coordinated movement

Specific strengthening objectives included increased recruitment of muscle fibers and improved gait.[48] In a review published by Kerr et al,[49] most studies of ES in children with CP used outcome measures that targeted body structures and functions and activity, while its possible effects on participation were not investigated.

Efficacy of ES was investigated in addressing upper and lower extremity ROM, strength, muscle tone, and motor function, including gait.[49-51,54-57] In an RCT conducted with 60 children with CP, age range 5 to 16 years, Kerr et al[55] examined the efficacy of NMES and TES used for bilateral quadriceps muscle strengthening, compared to a placebo. Both interventions were shown to be superior

TABLE 15-2

EXAMPLES OF UPPER EXTREMITY ELECTRICAL STIMULATION STUDIES CONDUCTED IN CHILDREN WITH UNILATERAL CEREBRAL PALSY

AUTHORS	STUDY DESIGN	INTERVENTION	PARTICIPANTS' MEAN AGE OR AGE RANGE	PARTICIPANTS' NUMBER	RESULTS
Kamper et al[50]	Repeated measures design	NMES to wrist flexor and extensor muscles	5-15 years	8	• Significant increase in AG wrist extension ROM • Significant increase in isometric wrist extension torque • No significant difference in spasticity and passive torque
Wright and Granat[51]	Repeated measures design	FES to wrist extensor muscles	10 years	8	• Significant improvement in hand function • Significant increase in active wrist extension ROM • Both observed at the end of treatment period and maintained at follow-up • No significant difference in wrist extension moment
Ozer et al[54]	Randomized repeated measures design	NMES to wrist extensors vs dynamic bracing vs NMES and dynamic bracing	3-18 years	24 (8 in each group)	• Significant improvements in grip strength, posture of the wrist and fingers, and UE function found only in the NMES/dynamic bracing group • These effects lasted only for 2 months after intervention was discontinued

Abbreviations: AG, against gravity; CP, cerebral palsy; FES, functional electrical stimulation; NMES, neuromuscular electrical stimulation; ROM, range of motion.

to the placebo in reducing the impact of disability on the participants and their families assessed using the Lifestyle Assessment Questionnaire—Cerebral Palsy (LAQ-CP).[58] However, because of the small sample size, positive changes observed for the mean peak torque and Gross Motor Function Measure (GMFM)[59] scores in the NMES and TES groups and a decrease in strength documented in the placebo group did not reach statistical significance.[55]

FES devices used to improve gait in this patient population will be discussed in Chapter 20. Cauraugh and Nalk[56] conducted a systematic review and a meta-analysis of the effects of ES on walking problems in children with CP and reported medium summary effect sizes that supported the use of ES to address gait-related alterations of body structures and functions and activity limitations. However, the authors reported a small number of published double-blind RCTs and pointed out the need to further investigate the effects of ES related to the age of participants, location and parameters of stimulation, and observed physiological responses.[56] In a later review, Wright et al[57] came to similar conclusions but also suggested that available evidence, although dominated by small studies, favored the use of NMES to address upper extremity impairments and function in children with CP.[57] Examples of such studies are provided in Table 15-2.[50,51,54]

The types of ES discussed previously use surface electrodes to deliver electrical current. While such a technique is noninvasive and can be applied by the child's caregiver, it has a number of disadvantages, including the following:

- The use of a relatively high intensity current that may lead to pain
- Lack of selectivity that may result in stimulation of muscles that were not initially targeted
- Difficulty providing stimulation to deep musculature
- Assistance required for donning and doffing ES equipment
- Challenges related to accurate electrode placement[48]

Merrill[48] described several types of implanted neurostimulation devices that may alleviate these problems by providing selective, lower intensity stimulation. One such device consists of implanted electrodes connected to an external pulse generator with percutaneous leads. Another, fully implanted system uses a central pulse generator connected by leads to several distributed electrodes. Both require surgical implantation, which is lengthy and, in case of full implantation, highly invasive. Furthermore, in both cases, additional surgeries may be required to replace any broken leads, and the risk of infection spread along the leads is another disadvantage of these ES systems.[48]

A different, wireless system, an implantable Radio Frequency Microstimulator (RFM) was developed by the Alfred Mann Foundation.[48] A minimally invasive surgery is needed to implant this device next to a motor point or a nerve, and the risk of infection is minimized since the system is wireless. However, external coils positioned on the patient's arm must be worn. The RFM has been used for upper extremity rehabilitation in patients who suffered a stroke but not in children with CP. Merill[48] proposed that an ES system for children with CP should include the following features:

- A portable controller that can be easily worn by the child
- A light-weight, compact trigger mechanism
- An easy access to the control switch provided to the child who then can stop stimulation if a muscle spasm occurs

The next generation of the RFM system, a Functional Electrical Stimulation Battery-Powered Microstimulator (FEBPM) is currently being developed to address the needs of children with CP.[48]

KINESIO AND FUNCTIONAL TAPING INTERVENTIONS

Many pediatric therapists use neuromuscular taping methods in their clinical practice.[60,61] One such method, Kinesio Taping (KT) is a technique in which a thin, latex-free, adhesive stretchable tape is applied to the child's skin.[60,62] The elastic properties of the tape have been compared to human skin because it can be stretched 40% to 60% from its initial length.[60] According to Yasukawa et al,[62] such elasticity and the proprioceptive feedback the tape provides may be the reasons for changes in function observed in patients for whom this intervention is being used. The proposed purposes of KT include addressing joint instability, ROM problems, muscle weakness or overuse, postural malalignment, pain, and inadequate subcutaneous blood flow or lymphatic circulation. Tape application and the amount of required pre-stretch vary depending on the position of a specific taping area and on the intervention goals.[62] In a functional MRI study, Callaghan et al[63] showed that patellar taping was capable of modulating brain activity when participants of their study repeatedly performed a proprioception task by moving their lower extremity to a target angle in the knee joint. da Costa et al[60] suggested that, similarly to the tape used in the study by Callaghan et al,[63] KT may also have modulation effects on brain activity, as the stimulation of cutaneous mechanoreceptors through tape application was observed to lead to improvements in muscle recruitment patterns and postural control.

In spite of its wide clinical application in a variety of patient populations, including in children with CP, KT efficacy research is limited.[61] Yasukawa et al[62] documented significant improvement in upper extremity function attributed to KT application in 15 children with disabilities. Farrell et al[64] described a child with CP who underwent a rehabilitation program that included KT and demonstrated improved functional mobility skills. da Costa et al[60] observed immediate positive effects of KT on the efficiency of the sit to stand transition, dynamic postural control, and dynamic functional balance, but not static balance, in 4 children with unilateral CP. Finally, in an RCT that compared the effects of KT and physical therapy to physical therapy alone, Şimşek et al[61] showed that KT did not have a direct effect on gross motor function or functional independence in children with CP, but helped improve their sitting posture. Overall, the level of evidence in support of the use of KT in children with CP is low.[61]

Another neuromuscular taping intervention termed functional taping (FT) combines the application of polyurethane foam and memory foam bands, inelastic tape, and silk and paper patches, to provide joint stability, improve ROM, facilitate more efficient movement patterns, and decrease muscle tone.[65,66] The use of FT may promote participation in peer activities as it allows the child to use regular clothes and shoes, compared to more bulky orthotic devices.[66] In two small studies conducted in children with unilateral CP, FT was shown to have positive effects on gross motor function, gait pattern and stability,[65] and upper extremity function.[66] An itchy rash is a possible side effect that can be prevented by adding cotton gauze for direct skin contact and by scheduling FT during cooler months of the year.[66]

PASSIVE STRETCHING

Physical therapists frequently use stretching interventions as a part of therapy programs for children and adults with CP to address the development of contractures.[67-69] Stretching intervention strategies may include passive stretching performed by the therapist or the child's caregiver; active stretching initiated and maintained by the child; proprioceptive neuromuscular facilitation (PNF) techniques, such as hold-relax or contract-relax; and sustained stretching of specific musculature achieved through positioning or the use of casts, splints, or orthoses.[69,70] The reader is referred to Chapter 20 for a detailed discussion of stretching orthotic intervention options.

In a survey study, Hadden and von Baeyer[71] found that 93% of parents who reported pain in their children identified stretching as a painful intervention, and the mean pain intensity associated with stretching was the highest. Another adverse effect of stretching was described by Chang et al,[72] who performed computerized tomography (CT) scans of the pelvis and the hip joint in children with CP, age range 4.5 to 9.6 years, at rest and during passive hamstring stretching. Passive stretching induced a 4.7% dynamic displacement of the femoral head on average, which ranged from -3.8% to 16.1% of the diameter of the femoral epiphysis (P < 0.001). Such displacement was significantly greater in the hips that, according to the resting images, had the migration percentage higher than 30%. The authors suggested that other stretching methods, rather than those that involve passive knee extension combined with hip flexion position, be used in children with known hip subluxation, especially when hip migration is greater than 30%.[72]

Multiple authors reported on the paucity of evidence in support of stretching interventions in patients with neurological dysfunction and questioned the quality of available research.[67-69] Based on their review of published literature, Wiart et al[69] were unable to reach any "strong conclusions" in regard to the efficacy of different types of stretching in children with CP. They agreed with Pin et al,[73] who conducted an earlier systematic review, and found that the small number of studies that examined passive stretching lacked methodological rigor and provided limited evidence on its benefits for improvement in joint ROM and reduction in spasticity in this patient population. Perhaps the strongest recommendation that came from this review was that sustained stretching through optimal day- and night-time positioning was preferred over short-duration manual stretching as it had a greater effect on ROM and muscle tone.[73]

It is important to note that in response to the review by Pin et al,[73] Gorter et al[70] warned against rejecting the use of stretching interventions based only on the paucity of relevant research because, according to Sackett et al,[74] in evidence-based practice, evidence derived from individual clinical expertise must be taken into consideration along with the available research evidence. Later, Wallen and Stewart[68] provided a similar warning. Gorter et al[70] recommended that stretching techniques and duration and frequency of their use be investigated further and in more rigorous studies, and proposed specific expertise-based stretching guidelines to be incorporated into clinical practice. According to these clinical guidelines, first, a thorough evaluation of the child needs to be conducted and appropriate goals set at all relevant ICF[2] levels, while taking into consideration the child's personal factors. After that, if ROM is considered to be an important variable in achieving the set goals, the most appropriate stretching strategy needs to be selected, based on whether the child can actively move the joint through the available range, can move it only partially, or has no active movement capability. With full active ROM, active stretching is recommended; active-assistive ROM exercise, PNF techniques, and sustained stretching can be used when only partial active movement is possible; and sustained stretching is suggested when the child is unable to actively move in the extremity joint.[70]

SOFT TISSUE MOBILIZATION

Soft tissue mobilization techniques, such as massage[75] and myofascial release,[76] are frequently used in pediatric clinical practice. Although some medical professionals think of massage as an alternative intervention, others no longer consider it complementary.[75] Massage can be defined as the manipulation of soft tissue for therapeutic purposes.[77] In a survey study of 104 families, 51% of respondents reported the use of massage for their children with CP.[75] Physical therapists administered massage in 49% of the cases. Other providers included massage therapists (23%) and the child's relatives (68%). The reported purposes of massage were relaxation; alleviation of pain, constipation, and agitation; and improvement of sleep and quality of life. Common reasons for discontinuing massage were the lack of time (46%), the lack of benefit from massage administration (11%), and cost (8%). Children with lower functional abilities and those whose mothers used massage themselves were most likely to be receiving this intervention on a regular basis.[75]

Evidence of efficacy of massage in children with CP is sparse.[3] In a study of 20 toddlers and preschoolers with CP, significant reduction in whole body and upper extremity spasticity; increased hip extension ROM; and improved developmental scores in cognitive, fine and gross motor, dressing, and social functioning areas were reported after massage intervention.[78] Another study examined the effects of Swedish massage on mechanical properties of calf muscle tissue in 5 adolescents with bilateral spastic CP.[79] Results revealed an inconsistent shortening or lengthening of spastic muscles in response to the massage intervention and decreased incidence of abnormal stretch reflexes recorded by electromyography (EMG) performed during stretching.[79] A Training and Support Program (TSP) that involved teaching basic massage skills implemented for parents of children with

CP was shown to positively affect parental mood and life satisfaction; reduce stress; and improve parental perceptions of their child's eating, sleeping, and mobility behaviors.[80] This program was also valued by the children who reported that they enjoyed relaxation provided by massage and appreciated its other benefits, including decreased pain and improvements in mobility and digestive functioning.[81]

Myofascial release is another form of soft tissue mobilization that targets muscle tissue and fascia.[76] It is "a hands-on soft tissue technique that facilitates a stretch into the restricted fascia."[82(p 232)] Myofascial release techniques are thought to restore the pliability of tightened or restricted fascia, in order to release the blood vessels, nerves, and other structures that are sensitive to pain, and to restore joint mobility and alignment.[82]

Research on the use of this intervention in children with CP is very limited. In a series of 6 case reports, a very modest decrease in muscle tone was documented in some of the described children.[76] Results of an RCT that included myofascial release as a part of osteopathic manipulative treatment (OMT) were more encouraging.[83] A statistically significant increase in the GMFM-88[59] and Functional Independence Measure for Children (WeeFIM)[84] mobility domain scores documented for the OMT group. However, whether myofascial release contributed to the overall functional improvement could not be discerned as other techniques were used together with this intervention as a part of the OMT.[83]

STRENGTH TRAINING

Contrary to the previously held view that strength training in individuals with CP is contraindicated because of its potential ability to increase spasticity, research showed that this assumption was wrong.[85-87] In fact, results of multiple studies revealed that strengthening exercise did not have any significant effects on spasticity.[85-87] Overall, few adverse effects of strength training were documented, including joint or muscle soreness[86] and detraining-related loss of strength observed a few weeks after the discontinuation of training programs.[86,87] Interestingly, Dodd et al[88] reported an unexpected finding of negative effects on self-concept in the areas of scholastic competence and social acceptance observed in children with CP who underwent a home-based progressive-resistive strengthening program. The authors cautioned against the generalization of these results to the whole population of children with CP because their study sample was relatively small.[88]

McNee et al[89] demonstrated that resistance training could lead to muscle hypertrophy, with a significant increase in muscle volume and strength documented in children with spastic CP. However, in their study of plantarflexor muscle strengthening, there was no significant concurrent increase in function. Nevertheless, the authors suggested that this intervention could still have a positive long-term effect on children with CP.[89] The ambulatory capacity in this patient population declines with age,[90,91] which, as proposed by McNee et al,[89] may be delayed by muscle conditioning. However, further research is needed to test this hypothesis.

Authors of 3 RCTs that compared lower extremity strengthening programs to traditional physical therapy reported varied effects on strength, gross motor function, mobility, and gait speed.[87,92,93] Lee et al[93] suggested that task-specific, closed chain, functional strength training may assist in carrying over the increase in strength to improvements in gross motor function, gait speed, and other gait parameters. Other researchers examined the effects of fitness programs that included cardiovascular and strength training components.[29-31,33] A systematic review of literature showed that there was evidence to support strength training as a part of exercise programs for children with CP, with progressive resistive exercise 3 times a week for at least 6 weeks shown to increase muscle force generation in these children.[29,85] However, there was insufficient published research to suggest that such mixed interventions may be beneficial in the areas of daily activity, self-competence, participation, or quality of life.[29]

Results of other systematic reviews that focused on strength training alone were also variable.[85,86,94] Dodd et al[85] and Mockford and Caulton[86] concluded that this intervention was effective in children and adolescents with CP, but their reviews included uncontrolled clinical trials.[95] Scianni et al,[94] who examined only RCTs, came to a conclusion that resistance training was not effective in this patient population. Verschuren et al[95] proposed that this controversy might be resolved by looking at specific strengthening protocols. While these authors acknowledged the need for further research to identify the optimal training parameters for children with CP of different age groups and functional levels, they also suggested that clinicians use the National Strength and Conditioning Association (NSCA) guidelines[96] when developing resistance training programs for their patients. Citing these guidelines[96] and other evidence, Verschuren et al[95] recommended that children and adolescents with CP may benefit from using the following:

- Single-joint resistance exercises as potentially more effective than multi-joint training because they are less likely to lead to compensations when significant muscle weakness is present

- Up to 3-minute long breaks between repetition sets, especially when the child is functioning at a lower level or is performing more complex exercises

- Strength intervention programs of sufficient intensity and at least 12 weeks long in order to achieve appropriate strengthening effects

Additional recommendations included reserving this type of intervention for older children and adolescents because of its complexity and the requirement of exerting a maximal effort, and using mental imagery, electrical stimulation, or biofeedback to enhance strength training in children who have greater difficulty generating a voluntary muscle contraction.[95]

TREADMILL TRAINING

Several treadmill training interventions used for children with disabilities, including CP, were investigated and described in research literature.[97-103] These interventions were partial body weight support (PBWS) treadmill training,[97-99] robotic-assisted treadmill training,[100] lower body positive pressure supported (LBPPS) treadmill training,[101] and treadmill training without body weight support.[102,103] Treadmill training interventions are aimed at attaining upright locomotion by providing the child with a task-specific repetitive training opportunity for practicing complete gait cycles.[97,99] The suggested theoretical explanation of this therapeutic strategy is that, as suggested by animal studies,[104,105] movement of the treadmill belt activates central pattern generators thought to be housed in the brain and spinal cord, which leads to the production of a coordinated stepping pattern.[98,99]

When a PBWS treadmill training method is used, the child wears a harness that takes on some of the body weight, thus reducing the effort required for upright locomotion.[1,99] The overhead harness system positioned over a treadmill provides postural stability, balance, and reduced lower extremity loading, and the therapist provides manual guidance for lower extremity movements while the child is ambulating at a set appropriate speed.[1,99] Robotic-assisted treadmill training described in a case report by Borggraefe et al[100] is another body-weight supported method that uses a pediatric Lokomat (Hocoma) device. The child dons a driven lower extremity gait orthosis that is positioned over a treadmill, and the orthosis moves at the velocity synchronized with that of the treadmill.[100] The LBPPS is yet another body-weight support system that includes an inflatable bag that encloses a treadmill.[101] The patient wears neoprene shorts that are attached to the bag, and the inflation of the bag is used to regulate the magnitude of the lifting force that reduces the lower extremity loading for upright locomotion.[101]

The effects of the body-weight supported methods of treadmill training were examined in a large number of studies conducted in children with a variety of motor disabilities, including ambulatory and non-ambulatory children with CP,[97-101,106] while treadmill training without PBWS was investigated in children with CP who functioned at GMFCS[34] levels I through III.[102,103] The latter was found to improve gross motor function and functional mobility in children who underwent lower extremity orthopedic surgeries.[102] It was also shown to be superior to an overground walking intervention in its effects on functional balance, mobility, performance, and overall gross motor function in children with CP, age range 3 to 12 years.[103]

In their overview of systematic reviews of treadmill interventions used in children with motor impairments, Zwicker et al[106] reported a low number of studies included in the reviews because of the low levels of evidence provided by the majority of published research. In addition, there were multiple discrepancies in the levels of evidence the authors of the systematic reviews[97-99,107,108] had assigned to the same studies. Furthermore, because of the differences in training parameters among the examined research reports, it was not possible to provide specific evidence-based recommendations for the amount of body-weight support, treadmill speed, frequency, duration, and intensity of intervention.[106] In their systematic review, Willoughby et al[97] offered an important consideration for clinicians in regard to the training parameters, and specifically, the need to match these parameters to the child's overall intervention goals. For example, when the child's goal is to increase the walking speed, it would be important to practice treadmill walking at increased speed as well.[97]

In spite of the problems revealed by several systematic reviews of literature,[97-99,107,108] a consensus was reached in regard to treadmill training being a safe intervention strategy for children with motor disorders. The encouraging results related to the body structures and functions and activity levels of ICF,[2] including improvements in gait parameters, 10-meter walk test and obtained GMFM[59] scores, especially for dimensions D and E, were also acknowledged.[106] However, all systematic reviews[97-99,107,108] indicated that the body of research was still insufficient to definitively confirm the positive effects of treadmill training on ambulation in children with CP, and there was a lack of evidence in support of participation benefits of treadmill interventions.[106] Therefore, several authors emphasized the need for large controlled clinical trials to address the identified deficiencies and to establish the optimal training parameters.[98,99]

HEALTH-RELATED FITNESS AND PHYSICAL ACTIVITY IN CHILDREN WITH CEREBRAL PALSY

Several interventions discussed in this chapter, including aquatic exercise, aerobic exercise, strength training, and treadmill training, target functional mobility and health-related fitness in individuals with CP. Verschuren et al[109] examined the available evidence in regard to long-term effects of these interventions on fitness in this patient population and came to the conclusion that it may be unrealistic to expect that children and adolescents with CP would be able to sustain daily moderate to vigorous physical activity. These authors suggested that it may be beneficial to look into reducing sedentary behaviors and increasing light physical activity performed throughout the day instead of exclusively targeting moderate to vigorous activity levels.[109]

The current definition of sedentary behavior includes 3 components: muscular inactivity, maintaining a sitting or reclining posture, and low energy expenditure (equal to or below 1.5 METs).[110-112] However, these may not be valid for individuals with CP who exert significant amounts of energy

TABLE 15-3
BARRIERS AND FACILITATORS FOR PARTICIPATION IN SPORT AND PHYSICAL FITNESS ACTIVITIES FOR CHILDREN AND ADULTS WITH DISABILITIES

BARRIERS	FACILITATORS
• Attitudes of people who are not disabled toward people with disabilities • Difficulty leading an active lifestyle • Emotional and psychological barriers • Lack of accessible environments, including sport and fitness programs • Lack of formal physical education programs, lack of movement in the classroom, and presence of other mobility restrictions in a school setting • Lack of information about available programs • Lack of interest • Lack of necessary components for participation in existing community fitness programs, including equipment, transportation, funding, and appropriate policies and procedures • Lack of time • Lack of trained staff • Need for assistance from caregivers • Parental stress related to lack of time and financial and psychological issues • Restrictions of physical disability	• Accessibility associated costs viewed as investments • Awareness and sensitivity of the public and facility owners to the needs of people with disabilities and their families • Availability of adaptive equipment in community facilitates • Availability of accessible parking spaces and accessible facility entrances • Consulting with people with disabilities when planning purchases of exercise equipment • Including accessibility into facility budgets and providing tax credits for updating facilities to make them accessible • Providing free facility passes to persons with disabilities to allow them to explore the facility benefits before becoming its members • Staff training and continuing education aimed at addressing accessibility issues • Supports that ensure a smooth transition from rehabilitation services to community programs (peer support, staff orientation, availability of physical and occupational therapists)
Compiled from Verschuren et al,[109] Fowler et al,[114] and Rimmer et al.[115]	

and use inefficient muscle co-activation strategies to maintain independent or even partially supported sitting positions.[109] Static standing also deserves special consideration. On the one hand, it is not considered a sedentary behavior in general population because it involves activation of many muscle groups in a human body.[113] On the other hand, it is not known whether muscular activity is present during supported standing in standing positioning devices that are frequently used by children with CP.[109] This foundational knowledge is critically needed in order to move toward feasible exercise interventions for individuals with CP and their families.[109]

As for the promotion of moderate to vigorous activity, several authors identified barriers to participation in sport and physical fitness programs for children and adults with disabilities, including CP.[109,114,115] These barriers[109,114,115] along with facilitators of participation identified by Rimmer et al[115] are listed in Table 15-3. It is important to note that in spite of the existing challenges, community-based fitness programs can be quite successful. Fragala-Pinkham

et al[116] reported on the implementation of a group fitness program for 28 children with disabilities that was based on a partnership between physical therapists and community centers. The fitness intervention program included warm-up, strength training, aerobic conditioning and cool-down components, and parental education in nutrition and wellness. Modifications to the program were implemented for children in wheelchairs. Although multiple falls during participation in the program activities were reported, none of them led to an injury. Overall, the program was shown to be safe. The mean rate of attendance was 75.3%, and significant improvements in all targeted clinical outcomes were reported, including functional mobility, muscle strength, energy expenditure, cardiorespiratory fitness, and flexibility. Implementation of similar fitness programs in other community settings may enhance participation of families of children with disabilities in health-related fitness activities.[116]

Complete video-based activities for Chapter 15 (see Activity Set 2 [activities 1, 3, and 4] and Activity Set 3 [activities 1, 3, and 4] on the book website).

REFERENCES

1. Stanger M, Oresic S. Rehabilitation approaches for children with cerebral palsy: overview. *J Child Neurol.* 2003;18(suppl 1):S79-S88.

2. World Health Organization. *International Classification of Functioning, Disability and Health.* Geneva, Switzerland: World Health Organization; 2001.

3. Franki I, Desloovere K, De Cat J, et al. The evidence-base for basic physical therapy techniques targeting lower limb function in children with cerebral palsy: a systematic review using the International Classification of Functioning, Disability and Health as a conceptual framework. *J Rehabil Med.* 2012;44(5):385-395.

4. Kelly M, Darrah J. Aquatic exercise for children with cerebral palsy. *Dev Med Child Neurol.* 2005;47(12):838-842.

5. Fragala-Pinkham MA, Dumas HM, Barlow CA, Pasternak A. An aquatic physical therapy program in a pediatric rehabilitation hospital: a case series. *Pediatr Phys Ther.* 2009;21(1):68-78.

6. Harris SR. Neurodevelopmental treatment approach for teaching swimming to cerebral palsied children. *Phys Ther.* 1978;58(8):979-983.

7. McManus BM, Kotelchuck M. The effect of aquatic therapy on functional mobility of infants and toddlers in early intervention. *Pediatr Phys Ther.* 2007;19(4):275-282.

8. Retarekar R, Fragala-Pinkham MA, Townsend EL. Effects of aquatic aerobic exercise for a child with cerebral palsy: single-subject design. *Pediatr Phys Ther.* 2009;21(4):336-344.

9. Fragala-Pinkham M, Haley SM, O'Neil ME. Group aquatic aerobic exercise for children with disabilities. *Dev Med Child Neurol.* 2008;50(11):822-827.

10. Ballaz L, Plamondon S, Lemay M. Group aquatic training improves gait efficiency in adolescents with cerebral palsy. *Disabil Rehabil.* 2011;33(17-18):1616-1624.

11. Oriel KN, Marchese VG, Shirk A, Wagner L, Young E, Miller L. The psychological benefits of an inclusive community-based aquatics program. *Pediatr Phys Ther.* 2012;24(4):361-367.

12. Kwon YH, Lee HY. Differences of respiratory function in children with spastic diplegic and hemiplegic cerebral palsy, compared with normally developing children. *J Pediatr Rehabil Med.* 2013;6(2):113-117.

13. Ersöz M, Selçuk B, Gündüz R, Kurtaran A, Akyüz M. Decreased chest mobility in children with cerebral palsy. *Turk J Pediatr.* 2006;48(4):344-350.

14. Toder DS. Respiratory problems in the adolescent with developmental delay. *Adolesc Med.* 2000;11(3):617-631.

15. Fitzgerald DA, Follett J, Van Asperen PP. Assessing and managing lung disease and sleep disordered breathing in children with cerebral palsy. *Paediatr Respir Rev.* 2009;10(1):18-24.

16. Finder JD. Airway clearance modalities in neuromuscular disease. *Paediatr Respir Rev.* 2010;11(1):31-34.

17. Yuan N, Kane P, Shelton K, Matel J, Becker BC, Moss RB. Safety, tolerability, and efficacy of high-frequency chest wall oscillation in pediatric patients with cerebral palsy and neuromuscular disease: an exploratory randomized controlled trial. *J Child Neurol.* 2010;25(7):815-821.

18. Rahlin M, Moerchen VA. Infants and children with cardiovascular and pulmonary dysfunction. In: Frownfelter D, Dean E, eds. *Cardiovascular and Pulmonary Physical Therapy: Evidence to Practice.* 5th ed. St, Louis, MO: Mosby, Inc.; 2012:600-624.

19. Button BM, Heine RG, Catto-Smith AG, Phelan PD, Olinsky A. Chest physiotherapy, gastro-oesophageal reflux, and arousal in infants with cystic fibrosis. *Arch Dis Child.* 2004;89(5):435-439.

20. Lannefors L, Button BM, McIlwaine M. Physiotherapy in infants and young children with cystic fibrosis: current practice and future developments. *J R Soc Med.* 2004;97(suppl 44):8-25.

21. Campanozzi A, Capano G, Miele E, et al. Impact of malnutrition on gastrointestinal disorders and gross motor abilities in children with cerebral palsy. *Brain Dev.* 2007;29(1):25-29.

22. Wang HY, Chen CC, Hsiao SF. Relationships between respiratory muscle strength and daily living function in children with cerebral palsy. *Res Dev Disabil.* 2012;33(4):1176-1182.

23. Portney LG, Watkins MP. Correlation. In: Portney LG, Watkins MP, eds. *Foundations of Clinical Research: Applications to Practice.* 3rd ed. Upper Saddle River, NJ: Pearson Education, Inc.; 2009:523-538.

24. Haley SM, Coster WJ, Ludlow LH, Haltiwanger JT, Andrellos PJ. *Pediatric Evaluation of Disability Inventory (PEDI).* Boston, MA: Trustees of Boston University; 1998.

25. Lee HY, Cha YJ, Kim K. The effect of feedback respiratory training on pulmonary function of children with cerebral palsy: a randomized controlled preliminary report. *Clin Rehabil.* 2014;28(10):965-971. doi: 10.1177/0269215513494876. Epub 2013 Jul 29.

26. Verschuren O, Takken T. Aerobic capacity in children and adolescents with cerebral palsy. *Res Dev Disabil.* 2010;31(6):1352-1357.

27. Rogers A, Furler B-L, Brinks S, Darrah J. A systematic review of the effectiveness of aerobic exercise interventions for children with cerebral palsy: an AACPDM evidence report. *Dev Med Child Neurol.* 2008;50(11):808-814.

28. Butler JM, Scianni A, Ada L. Effect of cardiorespiratory training on aerobic fitness and carryover to activity in children with cerebral palsy: a systematic review. *Int J Rehabil Res.* 2010;33(2):97-103.

29. Verschuren O, Ketelaar M, Takken T, Helders PJ, Gorter JW. Exercise programs for children with cerebral palsy. *Am J Phys Med Rehabil.* 2008;87(5):404-417.

30. Fowler EG, Knutson LM, DeMuth SK, et al. Pediatric endurance and limb strengthening for children with cerebral palsy (PEDALS) – a randomized controlled trial protocol for a stationary cycling intervention. *BMC Pediatrics.* 2007;7:14.

31. Fowler EG, Knutson LM, DeMuth SK, et al; for Physical Therapy Clinical Research Network (PTClinResNet). Pediatric endurance and limb strengthening (PEDALS) for children with cerebral palsy using stationary cycling: a randomized controlled trial. *Phys Ther.* 2010;90(3):367-381.

32. Nsenga AL, Shephard RJ, Ahmaidi S. Aerobic training in children with cerebral palsy. *Int J Sports Med.* 2013;34(6):533-537.

33. Verschuren O, Ketelaar M, Gorter JW, Helders PJ, Uiterwaal CS, Takken T. Exercise training program in children and adolescents with cerebral palsy: a randomized controlled trial. *Arch Pediatr Adolesc Med.* 2007;161(11):1075-1081.

34. Palisano RJ, Rosenbaum PL, Walter SD, Russell DJ, Wood EP, Galuppi BE. Development and reliability of a system to classify gross motor function in children with cerebral palsy. *Dev Med Child Neurol.* 1997;39(4):214-223.

35. Eliasson AC, Krumlinde-Sundholm L, Gordon AM, et al. Guidelines for future research in constraint-induced movement therapy for children with unilateral cerebral palsy: an expert consensus. *Dev Med Child Neurol.* 2014;56(2):125-137.

36. Taub E. Movement in nonhuman primates deprived of somatosensory feedback. *Ex Sport Sci Rev.* 1976;4:335-374.

37. Huang H, fetters L, Hale J, McBride A. Bound for success: a systematic review of constraint-induced movement therapy in children with cerebral palsy supports improved arm and hand use. *Phys Ther.* 2009;89(11):1126-1141.

38. Taub E, Ramey SL, DeLuca S, Echols K. Efficacy of constraint-induced movement therapy for children with cerebral palsy with asymmetric motor impairment. *Pediatrics.* 2004;113(2):305-312.

39. Gordon AM, Charles J, Wolf SL. Methods of constraint-induced movement therapy for children with hemiplegic cerebral palsy: development of a child-friendly intervention for improving upper-extremity function. *Arch Phys Med Rehabil.* 2005;86(4):837-844.

40. Eliasson AC, Krumlinde-Sundholm L, Shaw K, Wang C. Effects of constraint-induced movement therapy in young children with hemiplegic cerebral palsy: an adapted model. *Dev Med Child Neurol.* 2005;47(4):266-275.

41. Fergus A, Buckler J, Farrell J, Isley M, McFarland M, Riley B. Constraint-induced movement therapy for a child with hemiparesis: a case report. *Pediatr Phys Ther.* 2008;20(3):271-283.

42. Charles JR, Wolf SL, Schneider JA, Gordon AM. Efficacy of a child-friendly form of constraint-induced movement therapy in hemiplegic cerebral palsy: a randomized controlled trial. *Dev Med Child Neurol.* 2006;48(8):635-642.

43. Islam M, Nordstrand L, Holmström L, Kits A, Forssberg H, Eliasson AC. Is outcome of constraint-induced movement therapy in unilateral cerebral palsy dependent on corticomotor projection pattern and brain lesion characteristics? *Dev Med Child Neurol.* 2014;56(3):252-258.

44. Eyre JA, Smith M, Dabydeen L, et al. Is hemiplegic cerebral palsy equivalent to amblyopia of the corticospinal system? *Ann Neurol.* 2007;62(5):493-503.

45. Holmström L, Vollmer B, Tedroff K, et al. Hand function in relation to brain lesions and corticomotor-projection pattern in children with unilateral cerebral palsy. *Dev Med Child Neurol.* 2010;52(2):145-152.

46. Cioni G, Sales B, Paolicelli PB, Petacchi E, Scusa MF, Canapicchi R. MRI and clinical characteristics of children with hemiplegic cerebral palsy. *Neuropediatrics.* 1999;30(5):249-255.

47. Gillick BT, Krach LE, Feyma T, et al. Primed low-frequency repetitive transcranial magnetic stimulation and constraint-induced movement therapy in pediatric hemiparesis: a randomized controlled trial. *Dev Med Child Neurol.* 2014;56(1):44-52.

48. Merrill DR. Review of electrical stimulation in cerebral palsy and recommendations for future directions. *Dev Med Child Neurol.* 2009;51(suppl 4):154-165.

49. Kerr C, McDowell B, McDonough S. Electrical stimulation in cerebral palsy: a review of effects on strength and motor function. *Dev Med Child Neurol.* 2004;46(3):205-213.

50. Kamper DG, Yasukawa AM, Barrett KM, Gaebler-Spira DJ. Effects of neuromuscular electrical stimulation treatment of cerebral palsy on potential impairment mechanisms: a pilot study. *Pediatr Phys Ther.* 2006;18(1):31-38.

51. Wright PA, Granat MH. Therapeutic effects of functional electrical stimulation of the upper limb of eight children with cerebral palsy. *Dev Med Child Neurol.* 2000;42(11):724-727.

52. Reed, B. The physiology of neuromuscular electrical stimulation. *Pediatr Phys Ther.* 1997;9(3):96-102.

53. Pape K. Therapeutic electrical stimulation (TES) for the treatment of disuse muscle atrophy in cerebral palsy. *Pediatr Phys Ther.* 1997;9(3):110-112.

54. Ozer K, Chesher S, Scheker L. Neuromuscular electrical stimulation and dynamic bracing for the management of upper-extremity spasticity in children with cerebral palsy. *Dev Med Child Neurol.* 2006;48(7):559-563.

55. Kerr C, McDowell B, Cosgrove A, et al. Electrical Stimulation in cerebral palsy: a randomized controlled trial. *Dev Med Child Neurol.* 2006;48(11):870-876.

56. Cauraugh J, Nalk S. Children with cerebral palsy: a systematic review and meta-analysis on gait and electrical stimulation. *Clin Rehabil.* 2010;24(11):963-978.

57. Wright PA, Durham S, Ewins DJ, Swain ID. Neuromuscular electrical stimulation for children with cerebral palsy: a review. *Arch Dis Child.* 2012;97(4):364-371.

58. Mackie PC, Jessen EC, Jarvis SN. The lifestyle assessment questionnaire: an instrument to measure the impact of disability on the lives of children with cerebral palsy and their families. *Child Care Health Dev.* 1998;24(6):473-486.

59. Russell DJ, Rosenbaum PL, Avery LM, Lane M. *Gross Motor Function Measure (GMFM-66 & GMFM-88) User's Manual.* Lavenham, Suffolk: Mac Keith Press; 2002.

60. da Costa CS, Rodrigues FS, Leal FM, Rocha NA. Pilot study: investigating the effects of Kinesio Taping® on functional activities in children with cerebral palsy. *Dev Neurorehabil.* 2013;16(2):121-128.

61. Simsek TT, Türkücüoglu B, Çokal N, Üstünbas G, Simsek IE. The effects of Kinesio® taping on sitting posture, functional independence and gross motor function in children with cerebral palsy. *Disabil Rehabil.* 2011;33(21-22):2058-2063.

62. Yasukawa A, Patel P, Sisung C. Pilot study: investigating the effects of Kinesio Taping in an acute pediatric rehabilitation setting. *Am J Occup Ther.* 2006;60(1):104-110.

63. Callaghan MJ, McKie S, Richardson P, Oldham JA. Effects of patellar taping on brain activity during knee joint proprioception tests using functional magnetic resonance imaging. *Phys Ther.* 2012;92(6):821-830.

64. Farrell E, Naber E, Geigle P. Description of a multifaceted rehabilitation program including overground gait training for a child with cerebral palsy: as case report. *Physiother Theory Pract.* 2010;26(1):56-61.

65. Iosa M, Morrelli D, Nanni MV, et al. Functional taping: a promising technique for children with cerebral palsy. *Dev Med Child Neurol.* 2010;52(6):587-589.

66. Mazzone S, Serafini A, Iosa M, et al. Functional taping applied to upper limb of children with hemiplegic cerebral palsy: a pilot study. *Neuropediatrics.* 2011;42(6):249-253.

67. Katalinic AM, Harvey LA, Herbert RD. Effectiveness of stretch for the treatment and prevention of contractures in people with neurological conditions: a systematic review. *Phys Ther.* 2011;91(1):11-24.

68. Wallen M, Stewart K. The evidence for abandoning upper extremity limb stretch interventions in paediatric practice. *Dev Med Child Neurol.* 2013;55(3):208-209.

69. Wiart L, Darrah J, Kembhavi G. Stretching with children with cerebral palsy: what do we know and where are we going? *Pediatr Phys Ther.* 2008;20(2):173-178.

70. Gorter JW, Becher J, Oosterom I. 'To stretch or not to stretch in children with cerebral palsy'. *Dev Med Child Neurol.* 2007;49(10):797-800.

71. Hadden KL, von Baeyer CL. Pain in children with cerebral palsy: common triggers and expressive behaviors. *Pain.* 2002;99(1-2):281-288.

72. Chang CH, Chen YY, Wang CJ, Lee ZL, Kao H-K, Kuo KN. Dynamic displacement of the femoral head by hamstring stretching in children with cerebral palsy. *J Pediatr Orthop.* 2010;30(5):475-478.

73. Pin T, Dyke P, Chan M. The effectiveness of passive stretching in children with cerebral palsy. *Dev Med Child Neurol.* 2006;48(10):855-862.

74. Sackett DL, Rosenberg WM, Gray JA, Haynes RB, Richardson WS. Evidence based medicine: what it is and what it isn't. *BMJ.* 1996;312(7023):71-72.

75. Glew GM, Fan MY, Hagland S, Bjornson K, Beider S, McLaughlin JF. Survey of the use of massage for children with cerebral palsy. *Int J Ther Massage Bodywork.* 2010;3(4):10-15.

76. Whisler SL, Lang DM, Armstrong M, Vickers J, Qualls C, Feldman JS. Effects of myofascial release and other advanced myofascial therapies on children with cerebral palsy: six case reports. *Explore.* 2012;8(3):199-205.

77. Field TM. Massage therapy effects. *Am Psychol.* 1999;53(12):1270-1281.

78. Hernandez-Reif M, Field T, Largie S, et al. Cerebral palsy symptoms in children decreased following massage therapy. *Early Child Dev Care.* 2005;175(5):446-456.

79. Macgregor R, Campbell R, Gladden MH, Tennant N, Young D. Effects of massage on the mechanical behaviour of muscles in adolescents with spastic diplegia: a pilot study. *Dev Med Child Neurol.* 2007;49(3):187-191.

80. Barlow J, Powell L, Cheshire A. The Training and Support Programme (involving basic massage) for parents of children with cerebral palsy: an implementation study. *J Bodywork Mov Ther.* 2007;11(1):44-53.

81. Powell L, Cheshire A, Swaby L. Children's experiences of their participation in a training and support programme involving massage. *Complement Ther Clin Pract.* 2010;16(1):47-51.

82. Barnes MF. The basic science of myofascial release: morphologic change in connective tissue. *J Bodywork Mov Ther.* 1997;1(4):231-238.

83. Duncan B, McDonough-Means S, Worden K, Schnyer R, Andrews J, Meaney FJ. Effectiveness of osteopathy in the cranial field and myofascial release versus acupuncture as complementary treatment for children with spastic cerebral palsy: a pilot study. *J Am Osteopath Assoc.* 2008;108(1):559-570.

84. Granger CV, Hamilton BB, Kayton R. *Guide for the Use of the Functional Independence Measure (WeeFIM) of the Uniform Data Set for Medical Rehabilitation.* Buffalo, NY: Research Foundation, State University of New York; 1989.

85. Dodd KJ, Taylor NF, Damiano DL. A systematic review of the effectiveness of strength-training programs for people with cerebral palsy. *Arch Phys Med Rehabil.* 2002;83(8):1157-1164.

86. Mockford M, Caulton JM. Systematic review of progressive strength training in children and adolescents with cerebral palsy who are ambulatory. *Pediatr Phys Ther.* 2008;20(4):318-333.

87. Scholtes VA, Becher JG, Comuth A, Dekkers H, Van Dijk L, Dallmeijer AJ. Effectiveness of functional progressive resistance exercise strength training on muscle strength and mobility in children with cerebral palsy: a randomized controlled trial. *Dev Med Child Neurol.* 2010;52(6):e107-e113.

88. Dodd KJ, Taylor NF, Graham K. Strength training can have unexpected effects of the self-concept in children with cerebral palsy. *Pediatr Phys Ther.* 2004;16(2):99-105.

89. McNee AE, Gough M, Morrissey MC, Shortland AP. Increases in muscle volume after plantarflexor strength training in children with spastic cerebral palsy. *Dev Med Child Neurol.* 2009;51(6):429-435.

90. Bottos M, Feliciangeli A, Sciuto L, Gericke C, Vianello A. Functional status of adults with cerebral palsy and implications for treatment of children. *Dev Med Child Neurol.* 2001;43(8):516-528.

91. Bottos M, Gericke C. Ambulatory capacity in cerebral palsy: prognostic criteria and consequences for intervention. *Dev Med Child Neurol.* 2003;45(11):786-790.

92. Liao H-F, Liu Y-C, Liu W-Y, Lin Y-T. Effectiveness of loaded sit-to-stand resistance exercise for children with mild spastic diplegia: a randomized clinical trial. *Arch Phys Med Rehabil.* 2007;88(1):25-31.

93. Lee JH, Sung IY, Yoo JY. Therapeutic effects of strengthening exercise on gait function of cerebral palsy. *Disabil Rehabil.* 2008;30(19):1439-1444.

94. Scianni A, Butler JM, Ada L, Teixeira-Salmela LF. Muscle strengthening is not effective in children and adolescents with cerebral palsy: a systematic review. *Aust J Physiother.* 2009;55(2):81-87.

95. Verschuren O, Ada L, Maltais DB, Gorter JW, Scianni A, Ketelaar M. Muscle strengthening in children and adolescents with cerebral palsy: considerations for future resistance training protocols. *Phys Ther.* 2011;91(7):1130-1139.

96. Faigenbaum AD1, Kraemer WJ, Blimkie CJ, et al. Youth resistance training: updated position statement paper from the national strength and conditioning association. *J Strength Cond Res.* 2009;23(5 suppl):S60-S79.

97. Willoughby KL, Dodd KJ, Shields N. A systematic review of the effectiveness of treadmill training for children with cerebral palsy. *Disabil Rehabil.* 2009;31(24):1971-1979.

98. Damiano DL, DeJong SL. A systematic review of the effectiveness of treadmill training and body weight support in pediatric rehabilitation. *J Neurol Phys Ther.* 2009;33(1):27-44.

99. Mutlu A, Krosschell K, Gaebler Spira D. Treadmill training with partial body-weight support in children with cerebral palsy: a systematic review. *Dev Med Child Neurol.* 2009;51(4):268-275.

100. Borggraefe I, Meyer-Heim A, Kumar A, Schaefer JS, Berweck S, Heinen F. Improved gait parameters after robotic-assisted locomotor treadmill therapy in a 6-year-old child with cerebral palsy. *Mov Disord.* 2008;23(2):280-283.

101. Kurz MJ, Corr B, Stuberg W, Volkman KG, Smith N. Evaluation of lower body positive pressure supported treadmill training for children with cerebral palsy. *Pediatr Phys Ther.* 2011;23(3):232-239.

102. Grecco LA, de Freitas TB, Satie J, Bagne E, Oliveira CS, de Souza DR. Treadmill training following orthopedic surgery in lower limbs of children with cerebral palsy. *Pediatr Phys Ther.* 2013;25(2):187-192.

103. Grecco LA, Zanon N, Sampaio LM, Oliveira CS. A comparison of treadmill training and overground walking in ambulant children with cerebral palsy: randomized controlled clinical trial. *Clin Rehabil.* 2013;27(8):686-696.

104. Barbeau H, Rossignol S. Recovery of locomotion after chronic spinalization in the adult cat. *Brain Res.* 1987;412:84-95.

105. Barbeau H, McCrea DA, O'Donovan MJ, Rossignol S, Grill WM, Lemay MA. Tapping into spinal circuits to restore motor function. *Brain Res Rev.* 1999;30(1):27-51.

106. Zwicker JG, Mayson TA. Effectiveness of treadmill training in children with motor impairments: an overview of systematic reviews. *Pediatr Phys Ther.* 2010;22(4):361-377.

107. Fiss AC, Effgen SK. Outcomes for young children with disabilities associated with the use of partial, body-weight supported, treadmill training: an evidence-based review. *Phys Ther Rev.* 2006;11(3):179-189.

108. Mattern-Baxter K. Effects of partial body weight supported treadmill training on children with cerebral palsy. *Pediatr Phys Ther.* 2009;21(1):12-22.

109. Verschuren O, Darrah J, Novak I, Ketelaar M, Wiart L. Health-enhancing physical activity in children with cerebral palsy: more of the same is not enough. *Phys Ther.* 2014;94(2):297-305.

110. Ekblom-Bak E, Hellénius ML, Ekblom B. Are we facing a new paradigm of inactivity physiology? *Br J Sports Med.* 2010;44(12):834-835.

111. Yates T, Wilmot EG, Khunti K, Biddle S, Gorely T, Davies MJ. Stand up for your health: is it time to rethink the physical activity paradigm? *Diabetes Res Clin Pract.* 2011;93(2):292-294.

112. Tremblay MS, Colley RC, Saunders TJ, Healy GN, Owen N. Physiological and health implications of a sedentary lifestyle. *Appl Physiol Nutr Metab.* 2010;35(6):725-740.

113. Hamilton MT, Hamilton DG, Zderic TW. Role of low energy expenditure and sitting in obesity, metabolic syndrome, type 2 diabetes, and cardiovascular disease. *Diabetes.* 2007;56(11):2655-2667.

114. Fowler EG, Kolobe TH, Damiano DL, et al; Section on Pediatrics Research Summit Participants, Section on Pediatrics Research Committee Task Force. Promotion of physical fitness and prevention of secondary conditions for children with cerebral palsy: Section on Pediatrics Research Summit Proceedings. *Phys Ther.* 2007;87(11):1495-1510.

115. Rimmer JH, Riley B, Wang E, Rauworth A, Jurkowsky J. Physical activity participation among persons with disabilities. *Am J Prev Med.* 2004;26(5):419-425.

116. Fragala-Pinkham MA, Haley SM, Goodgold S. Evaluation of a community-based group fitness program for children with disabilities. *Pediatr Phys Ther.* 2006;18(2):159-167.

16

Complementary and Alternative Interventions

Before a practitioner uses or recommends any therapy, whether complementary or allopathic, evidence on its effectiveness, safety, costs, and utility should be published.

Gregory S. Liptak[1]

The National Center for Complementary and Alternative Medicine (NCCAM) website refers to *complementary and alternative medicine* (CAM) as health care practices and approaches that were developed and historically used outside the boundaries of conventional or mainstream medicine.[1-3] *Complementary* therapies are usually applied together or concurrently with interventions considered to be standard practice, while *alternative* approaches are supposed to be used instead of conventional therapy.[2] However, in reality, these 2 terms are often used interchangeably because most people do not completely discard mainstream interventions in favor of alternative medicine. Furthermore, it is not uncommon for clinicians who practice conventional therapies to combine them with CAM interventions.[2]

Because there is no cure available for children with cerebral palsy (CP), their parents frequently look for and consider CAM therapies hoping that they may help address the wide array of problems their children have.[1,4] It is imperative that health care professionals provide their patients' families with appropriate information on available intervention options.[1] In order to do that in an objective and unbiased way, therapists need to be equipped with the knowledge of the latest evidence that supports or refutes the effectiveness of these interventions in addressing the alterations of body structures and functions, activity limitations, and participation

restrictions in children and adults with disabilities, including CP.[1,3] Moreover, as suggested in the epigraph to this chapter, benefits, costs, and side effects of all therapeutic approaches and practices also need to be examined.[1]

The practitioners willingness to inform the caregivers of available evidence would potentially help them make informed decisions regarding their child's care and would also support building a trusting parent-therapist relationship.[1] On the other hand, the failure to counsel the family may lead to an inappropriate use of CAM interventions with potentially harmful consequences.[1]

Although such reasoning makes a lot of sense, the solution may not be that simple. To illustrate, let us consider the study by Willoughby et al,[4] who examined the effects of CAM on hip migration percentage in 23 children with CP. These children were followed for over 10 years after their families opted to use CAM approaches instead of preventive orthopedic surgeries. As a result, 19 of the 23 participants required reconstructive or salvage hip surgeries, and bilateral hip dislocation developed in one child whose parents continued to refuse surgical intervention. Furthermore, while none of the children with CP in the comparison group who underwent timely preventive orthopedic surgeries required a hip salvage procedure, children in the CAM group were twice as likely to need reconstructive or salvage surgeries to address the

Rahlin M. *Physical Therapy for Children With Cerebral Palsy: An Evidence-Based Approach (pp 263-270).*

progression of hip displacement accompanied by pain and deformity.[4] This example demonstrates the urgent need for further research of CAM approaches and for the development of more effective counseling strategies that would allow practitioners to assist their patients' parents in making sound decisions on the selection of best, evidence-based treatment options for their children.

Examples of CAM therapies include acupuncture, the Adeli suit, conductive education (CE), craniosacral therapy (CST), hippotherapy, hyperbaric oxygenation, and patterning, to name a few.[1,3] As discussed further in this chapter, evidence in their support varies in its amount, quality, and findings.[1,3]

ACUPUNCTURE

Acupuncture is an important part of traditional Chinese and overall East Asian Medicine.[5] It is thought to help restore the flow of energy (Qi) along 14 meridians of the human body if it is interrupted by the disease, and re-establish balance between yin and yang if it has been disrupted.[1,3,5] *Yin and yang* are basic opposite concepts or intuitions that complement each other and need to stay in harmony so that the state of health can be attained. To achieve a therapeutic effect, acupuncture needles are inserted into a number of specific points that connect the body into a matrix. According to the premises of traditional Chinese medicine, each point has a unique designation and affects either local symptoms of a disorder or the global balance of yin and yang. Usually, an acupuncture session involves the insertion of a combination of 5 to 15 fine needles in the designated points.[1,3,5]

The application of the needles may be combined with other therapies, such as traditional Chinese herbal treatments, massage, breathing techniques, and meditation.[5] Music[6] and electrical stimulation[7] have been also used in combination with acupuncture. The use of this modality to treat various disorders was extensively studied. It was found to be effective in alleviating nausea and vomiting in adults who underwent surgeries or chemotherapy, but its effects on pain related to a variety of conditions were not so clear-cut, and the lack of sound evidence was reported in other areas of its application.[5,8] Adverse effects of acupuncture reported in literature include bruising, broken or forgotten needles, infection, minor hemorrhage, pain, possible contact dermatitis, and transient hypotension.[1,3,5,9]

Although acupuncture has been widely used in children with CP and its efficacy has been examined in multiple studies, there is still insufficient evidence to suggest that it can be recommended as an effective intervention.[1,3,10,11] Many studies were conducted in China and published in Chinese language, although English language publications are also available.[1,3,7,10,12] The studies vary in rigor, methodological quality, and outcomes. For example, Svedberg et al[7] described positive effects of electroacupuncture on ankle range of motion (ROM) and spasticity in a 7-year-old child with unilateral spastic CP, while Duncan et al[11] reported

an unclear role of acupuncture administered in combination with intensive rehabilitation therapies to children with spastic CP in a randomized controlled trial (RCT). Results of a systematic review of RCTs indicated that some of the published acupuncture research was promising, but most studies were of low methodological quality.[10] Therefore, further, more rigorous research is needed to evaluate the efficacy of this intervention in children with CP.[10]

CONDUCTIVE EDUCATION

CE is a system of education for children and adults with disabilities due to central nervous system (CNS) damage that originated in the 1940s in Budapest, Hungary.[12,13] Its founder, Dr. András Petö, based this approach on the concept of *orthofunctioning*, which can be described as the ability to solve everyday problems imposed on the individual by biological and social demands of life in an active, independent, and motivated way. Orthofunctioning is the ultimate goal of CE. Dr. Mária Hári, who joined Dr. Petö as a medical student volunteer in 1945, continued his work and founded the András Petö Institute of Conductive Education in Budapest. The Institute provides a 4-year conductor training program, which emphasizes special education. Conductors select children for the CE program and develop individual and group curricula based on activities of daily living (ADLs), with children who have similar needs placed in the same groups.[12,13]

Principles of CE can be summarized as follows:

- CE approaches physical disabilities from an educational perspective.
- Children need to be encouraged to master their environment instead of trying to adapt the environment to their needs.
- CE takes an integrated approach to child development, including motor, cognitive, social, and academic skills.
- The child's ability to determine his or her own goals, combined with a high level of motivation, maximize learning and development.
- The emphasis of CE on functional skills and not on nonspecific exercise promotes independent learning.
- Conductors facilitate the learning process while teaching the child at the level appropriate for his or her development and personality.[12,13]

There are several unique features or *facilitations* of CE that are designed to increase the child's motivation.[12-14] *Physical guidance* or assistance is provided by the conductor, the child's parent, or an aide. Verbal guidance, termed *verbal* or *rhythmic intentions*, helps the child to anticipate what is to come next and to initiate and complete specific tasks. This guidance may be provided in the form of a rhyme or a song that the entire group of children recites or sings. *Daily schedule* includes normal daily routine activities performed by groups of children with similar individual needs, such as handwashing, eating, toileting, sitting, walking, and other ADLs.

TABLE 16-1

DIFFERENCES IN CONDUCTIVE EDUCATION PROGRAM INTENSITY, DURATION, AND PROVIDERS ACROSS STUDIES CONDUCTED IN FOUR DIFFERENT COUNTRIES

AUTHORS AND YEAR OF PUBLICATION	CE PROGRAM			
	Country	*Intensity*	*Duration*	*Providers*
Reddihough et al, 1998[14]	Australia	~3 hrs/week	6 months	Therapists and teachers, with Hungarian conductors consulting
Stiller et al, 2003[17]	United States	6 hrs/day 5 days/week	5 weeks	Petö Institute trained conductors, with PT students as aides
Blank et al, 2008[18]	Germany	7 hrs/day 5 days/week	3 blocks of 4 weeks over 9 months	Petö Institute trained conductors under periodic supervision of a Petö Institute director
Effgen & Chan, 2010[15]	Hong Kong	Full pre-school day 5 days/week	11 months	Interdisciplinary team of physical and occupational therapists and speech-language pathologists, with support of other staff and parents and periodic monitoring visits of Hungarian conductors

Abbreviations: CE, conductive education; hrs, hours; PT, physical therapy.

Task analysis and task series involve breaking down a functional objective into step-like elements that are practiced separately through movement and play in different positions within the context of a daily routine. This is followed by practicing the task series as a whole, thus achieving the objective at the level of *orthofunctioning*. The group is a major motivator for the child. It facilitates learning by helping children develop interpersonal relationships. Group participation encourages children to support and cheer for each other, which creates a positive environment for learning.[12-14] The use of wooden furniture of a unique design, such as ladder-back chairs and slatted plinths, is another characteristic feature of CE.[12,14] The use of other adaptive equipment is generally not encouraged but is allowed in many current CE programs.[1,12]

Costs of participation in CE programs vary, which is an important factor to consider when a family is exploring CAM interventions for their child.[1] When CE is provided in a school setting, there may be no additional cost involved,[15] while attending private programs may be associated with significant costs that may or may not be covered by the child's medical insurance and, in some instances, may be off-set by charitable donations.[16]

Typically, a CE program is scheduled for 6 hours per day, 5 days per week, but the overall length of the program may vary depending on its location.[17] At this time, CE programs are available in many countries.[12,17] Modifications to the intensity of intervention are frequently made, and professionals administering the programs also vary, all of which, unfortunately, complicates the comparison of outcomes across

different studies.[12,17] An evidence report published by the American Academy for Cerebral Palsy and Developmental Medicine (AACPDM) highlighted the need to standardize the parameters of CE in future research, including the content and intensity of intervention.[12] The use of small sample sizes, inclusion of children with varied ability levels, and the lack of consistency in involving conductors in CE programs across studies were identified as problematic.[12] Table 16-1 illustrates the differences in CE program intensity, duration, and providers in 4 published research reports.[14,15,17,18]

In their review of literature, Darrah et al[12] found conflicting evidence, with an equal number of statistically significant outcomes favoring the CE group and the control group obtained in the studies identified as the strongest. Because of the overall limited amount of research and its weak methodological quality, the authors of the AACPDM report found that the evidence in support or against the CE intervention was inconclusive.[12] Subsequently, other authors came to similar conclusions.[1,19,20] To illustrate, in an RCT by Reddihough,[14] children involved in CE and traditional programs showed comparable progress. Similarly, in a small study by Stiller et al,[17] there was no difference in outcome in 3 groups of children who received intensive conventional therapies, CE, and special education. However, within-group analysis revealed that only children in the intensive therapy group demonstrated significant gains in functional skills.[17] These findings brought up an important question: what matters more for children with CP, the intensity or method of intervention? This question will be discussed further in this chapter and also in Chapter 18.

CRANIOSACRAL THERAPY

CST is founded in the theory that a rhythm of flow of cerebrospinal fluid around the brain and spinal cord exists that can be subjectively detected by a trained practitioner and used for evaluation and treatment by means of gentle touch.[1,3,21-23] Another foundational element of CST is that the detection of this rhythm is possible because, despite of beliefs to the contrary, cranial sutures do not fully fuse in adulthood, which permits some mobility of cranial bones. Similarly, the mobility of the sacrum between the ilia also exists. The rhythm of the CSF flow, also termed *cranial rhythm* (CR), is transmitted to the moveable bone structures through mobile dural membranes that connect the cranium and the sacrum, and can be felt by a CST practitioner by placing his or hands on the patient's skull or ankles. Through palpation, the CR can be evaluated for its amplitude, frequency, regularity, symmetry, and quality, and the disruptions in the flow of CSF and associated restrictions in the tissues of the body can be corrected by the application of light touch that is thought to restore the alignment of the tissues leading to the alleviation or reduction in symptoms the patient is experiencing.[1,3,21-23]

This intervention has been used in patients with a variety of conditions and in children with disabilities, including CP, spina bifida, and other neurologic disorders.[1,3,22,24,25] Adverse effects of CST, such as vertigo, headache, possible seizure, and other symptoms, were reported only in 3 patients with traumatic brain injury,[26] and no side effects were reported in children with CP.[1,3] However, except for some anecdotal evidence,[25] there have been no sound published studies of the use of CST in this patient population.[1]

Over the years, multiple authors questioned the theoretical premises of CST and its practicality, both of which lack supporting scientific evidence.[1,3,23,24,27] The interexaminer reliability of measurement of CR rates was found to be "approximately zero,"[23] and results of a systematic review of literature showed that published CST efficacy studies had inadequate methodological quality.[24] Several authors concluded that the clinical use of CST cannot be supported until its theoretical assumptions and efficacy are adequately evaluated through properly designed research.[23,24,27]

DOMAN-DELACATO METHOD OR PATTERNING

In 1955, Glenn Doman founded the Institutes for the Achievement of Human Potential[28] that since then has been advocating patterning as a method of treatment for children with a variety of conditions that affect their brain, including autism, CP, Down syndrome, learning and intellectual disabilities, and others.[29,30] *Patterning* refers to a series of repetitive exercises that involve passive movement of the child's extremities and head in specific patterns performed by 3 to 5 adults at the same time.[31] These patterns are supposed to move the child through a "normal" developmental progression, with the idea that failure to complete any developmental stage would negatively affect the child's brain development and the stages that follow.[1,31] This method puts significant physical, financial, and emotional demands on the caregivers, who are warned that their child's gains will be lost if treatment is modified or interrupted.[31]

The American Academy of Pediatrics issued several policy statements that reviewed patterning as an intervention for children with neurologic disorders and cautioned against its use.[29,30] The reasons for such warnings were that this method was based on "oversimplified" theoretical concepts that were "inconsistent with accepted views of neurologic development,"[(p 1150)] and that the claims of its effectiveness were not substantiated by well-designed research.[30] Health care professionals must be aware of these findings and counsel their patients' families accordingly.[29,30]

EQUINE-ASSISTED THERAPIES

Equine-assisted therapies include hippotherapy and therapeutic horseback riding, both of which use horses and involve trained horse handlers and volunteer side-walkers, but differ in their purposes and are led by different professionals (Table 16-2).[32-37] The horse handlers lead the horse while the side-walkers provide assistance and guarding to the rider.[32-35] There are some similarities in activities used during therapeutic horseback riding lessons and hippotherapy sessions, which complicates making a distinction between the two.[32-35] Both interventions include placing the child on the horse in a variety of positions, transitioning between positions, and other activities that challenge the child's balance and head and trunk control, or address the ROM, strength, stability, and postural alignment needs.[32-35,38]

Besides these similarities, therapeutic horseback riding and hippotherapy produce similar physiological effects related to the reciprocal, 3-dimensional movement of the walking horse that is thought to simulate the movements of the pelvis observed during walking in people without disabilities.[34] In addition, both interventions target the rider's righting and equilibrium reactions and promote the development of anticipatory and reactive postural control by causing the displacement of the rider's center of mass (COM) through elicited changes in stride, velocity, and direction of the walking horse.[34]

The reported benefits of hippotherapy and therapeutic riding for children with movement disorders and, specifically, for those with CP include improvements in symmetry of hip adductor muscle activity[39]; head and trunk stability and functional reaching ability[40]; functional balance and performance of ADLs[38]; gait parameters[41] and pelvis, hip, and trunk motion during gait[42]; gross motor function[41,43]; perceived self-competence[43]; and, potentially, social and community participation.[1] Liptak[1] and Davis et al[44] listed such adverse effects of these interventions as falling from a horse, allergic reactions, and hip pain. According to a systematic review of

	TABLE 16-2	
DIFFERENCES BETWEEN HIPPOTHERAPY AND THERAPEUTIC HORSEBACK RIDING[32-37]		
COMPARISON CRITERIA	**THERAPEUTIC HORSEBACK RIDING**	**HIPPOTHERAPY**
Type of activity	Recreational sports activity that uses therapy-trained horses	Therapeutic activity in which the movement of a horse is used as an intervention strategy
Purposes/goals	Teach equestrian skills and offer recreational experience to people with special needs	Address alterations of structures and functions and improve functional skills in individuals with disabilities
Staff involved	Trained, non-therapist riding instructors with knowledge of disabilities of the riders and related safety precautions, and trained assistants (side-walkers)	Licensed health professionals, including physical and occupational therapists and therapist assistants, and speech-language pathologists and trained assistants (side-walkers)
Related professional organization	The Professional Association of Therapeutic Horsemanship International (PATH Intl)[a]	The American Hippotherapy Association (AHA)
[a] Formerly known as the North American Riding for the Handicapped Association (NARHA).		

literature, exclusion criteria for participant recruitment in equine-assisted therapies research were the inability to follow instructions; presence of uncontrollable seizures, severe agitation, or confusion; and such orthopedic problems as spinal instability or excessive scoliosis, kyphosis, or lordosis.[32]

Although positive effects of hippotherapy and therapeutic riding interventions in children with CP were reported in multiple studies, several systematic reviews of literature revealed that most of the published research used small sample sizes, combined equine-assisted therapies with other interventions, lacked control or randomization, and followed protocols that were inconsistent in duration and frequency of intervention.[32,34,45] Results of a well-designed RCT of therapeutic horseback riding conducted with ambulatory children with CP failed to demonstrate any significant effects of this intervention on the participants' health, quality of life, or gross motor function.[44] The authors suggested that the lack of responsiveness to change in the outcome measures they used might be one possible reason for such negative outcomes.[44] Overall, 4 systematic reviews of literature provided mixed results.[20,32,34,45] This indicated the need for large, well-designed RCTs with clearly described protocols that would use outcome measures sensitive to change in characteristics they assess, so that the earlier reported benefits of hippotherapy and therapeutic horseback riding in this patient population could be confirmed.[20,32,34,45]

HYPERBARIC OXYGEN THERAPY

Some conventional indications for hyperbaric oxygen therapy (HBOT) include decompression sickness, carbon monoxide poisoning, arterial gas embolism, and wound healing, for which this intervention is approved by the United States Food and Drug Administration.[46,47] However, it has been also used as a complementary treatment for people with neurologic conditions, including CP.[46-48] HBOT involves the administration of 100% oxygen delivered for inhalation in a hyperbaric chamber under pressure greater than 1 atmosphere.[47] The theory behind this intervention is that pressurized oxygen stimulates inactive brain cells located among other cells of the injured brain, leading to their recovery.[1,47,49]

Typically, pressures of 1.5 to 1.75 atmospheres are used in the hyperbaric chamber, and a course of treatment that costs thousands of dollars consists of 40 1-hour sessions administered once or twice daily, 5 to 6 days per week.[1,16] Adverse events associated with HBOT reported by several authors range from mild to life-threatening and may include ear problems, such as middle ear barotrauma, otitis, and pain[46,50]; myopia, pneumothorax, cough, and chest tightness[46]; aspiration[51]; seizures[46,47,51]; vomiting; and other problems.[50] Other potential risks listed in the literature are fire hazard and explosions associated with the use of oxygen.[1,46]

In spite of the high costs and adverse effects of HBOT documented in children with CP,[1,50,51] many families still frequently try this intervention in hope that it may help their children. However, a systematic review of literature demonstrated that observational research evidence in support of HBOT was lacking methodological quality, while evidence derived from 2 RCTs failed to show the HBOT superiority to mildly pressurized room air.[47,52-54] In addition, the information on adverse events associated with HBOT was found to be insufficient for making definitive conclusions in regard to its risks for children with CP.[47] For these reasons, HBOT cannot be recommended as an intervention of choice for children with CP.[47,52-54]

Suit Therapy

The Adeli suit was developed based on the Penguin Suit designed for Russian cosmonauts who used it in space flights to minimize such negative effects of weightlessness and hypokinesis as osteopenia and muscle atrophy.[1,55] The suit includes a vest, shorts, knee pads, and a system of elastic cords attached to a wide belt that is worn at the hips. The belt is connected to the child's shoes and knee pads, and a headpiece is available for children with insufficient head control.[1] The Adeli suit uses the method of *dynamic proprioceptive correction* with the elastic cords creating tension to provide resistance to movement and, thus, load the antigravity musculature and enhance proprioception.[1,55] This is thought to help decrease pathological synergies and normalize the afferent vestibulo-proprioceptive input into the CNS in children with CP, which, as suggested by Semenova,[55] may have a positive effect on the activity of the reticular formation and midbrain leading to improved cortical control of movement.

Initially, the Adeli suit therapy was available only in Europe, mainly Poland,[56] but patents for the suit equipment and methodology are now registered in multiple countries, including the United States,[1,57,58] where it is known as the *TheraSuit* (Therasuit LLC).[59,60] The suit therapy programs are usually intensive, with 0.5- to 4-hour sessions scheduled 5 to 6 days per week for 3 to 4 weeks and provided by physical therapists.[1,59-62] Massage, stretching, and sometimes strengthening exercises typically precede donning the suit, followed by vigorous therapeutic exercise, balance, coordination, and functional activities performed in the suit.[59-62] The reported adverse effects of suit therapy include mild to severe discomfort from suit wear,[60] fatigue, and lack of motivation.[62] Bar-Haim et al[61] reported on anecdotal evidence obtained from their study participants and their parents that indicated satisfaction with intensive intervention, and in a study by Bailes et al,[60] only 2 of 19 parents who filled out a satisfaction questionnaire stated that the intensity of therapy their children had received was excessive.

Investigations of efficacy of suit therapy vary in rigor, from case reports,[59] to a pretest–post-test single group design,[63] to RCTs.[60-62] Post-intervention improvements in gross motor[55,59-63] and self-care functional skills,[55,60] gait parameters,[59] mechanical efficiency of stair climbing,[61] and participation,[63] as well as decreased caregiver assistance needed for self-care activities[60] were reported. However, Christy et al,[63] who measured activity performance in a group of 17 ambulatory children with CP, documented no significant increase in daily walking amount and intensity after a 3-week suit therapy program. Furthermore, all RCTs failed to demonstrate the superiority of the suit therapy compared to neurodevelopmental treatment (NDT)[61,62,64,65] or a sham suit intervention,[60] which suggested that displayed improvements were most likely related to the intensity of therapy rather than a specific therapy approach. One exception was a report by Mahani et al,[62] which showed that using a modified intervention protocol for the Adeli suit therapy could produce significantly better results than the standard Adeli suit protocol and the NDT[64,65] intervention. The modified protocol included 1 hour of passive stretching activities and NDT followed by donning the suit, and another hour of goal-directed functional activities performed in the suit. These activities were selected based on the participants' preferences and abilities, which helped maintain their motivation.[62]

Summary and Clinical Implications

This chapter focused on complementary and alternative intervention methods that frequently attract the attention of parents of children with disabilities, including CP. Many of the interventions discussed in this chapter are intensive and may be costly, which may put significant demands on children and caregivers; some are associated with documented adverse effects; and, while research of a number of interventions has generated varied degrees of evidence in their support, others cannot be recommended.[1,16,17,20,31,50,51,59-62] The recommendations for use of specific interventions should be based on sound evidence of their efficacy and their risk-benefit, cost-benefit, and feasibility analyses.[1] For instance, the number, quality, and results of published studies show that clinical application of craniosacral therapy,[1,20,23,24,27] Doman-Delacato method or patterning,[1,29-31] and HBOT[1,20,47,50-54] is not supported by published research, while studies that investigated acupuncture,[1,7,10,11,20] hippotherapy,[1,20,32,34,44,45] conductive education,[12,19,20] and suit therapy[59-63] provide mixed results. In addition, conductive education and suit therapy literature suggests that therapy intensity as opposed to a specific intervention used may be the key factor in improvements documented in research participants,[17,60-62] which warrants further investigations. In the meantime, "doing no harm" is the main rule to follow when discussing CAM therapy recommendations with the families.[1]

References

1. Liptak GS. Complementary and alternative therapies for cerebral palsy. *Ment Retard Dev Disabil Res Rev.* 2005;11(2):156-63.

2. National Center for Complementary and Alternative Medicine. *CAM Basics: Complementary, Alternative, or Integrative Health: What's In a Name? NCCAM publication D347.* http://nccam.nih.gov/health/whatiscam. Published October 2008. Updated July 2014. Accessed July 31, 2014.

3. Oppenheim WL. Complementary and alternative methods in cerebral palsy. *Dev Med Child Neurol.* 2009;51(suppl 4):122-129.

4. Willoughby K, Jachno K, Ang SG, Thomason P, Graham HK. The impact of complementary and alternative medicine on hip development in children with cerebral palsy. *Dev Med Child Neurol.* 2013;55(5):472-479.

5. Kaptchuk TJ. Acupuncture: theory, efficacy, and practice. *Ann Intern Med.* 2002;136(5):374-383.

6. Yu HB, Liu YF, Wu LX. Acupuncture combined with music therapy for treatment of 30 cases of cerebral palsy. *J Tradit Chin Med.* 2009;29(4):243-248.

7. Svedberg L, Nordahl G, Lundberg T. Electro-acupuncture in a child with mild spastic hemiplegic cerebral palsy. *Dev Med Child Neurol.* 2003;45(7):503-504.

8. NIH Consensus Conference. Acupuncture. *JAMA.* 1998;280(17):1518-1524.

9. Yamashita H, Tsukayama H, Tanno Y, Nishijo K. Adverse events related to acupuncture. *JAMA.* 1998;280(18):1563-1564.

10. Zhang Y, Liu J, Wang J, He Q. Traditional Chinese medicine for treatment of cerebral palsy in children: a systematic review of randomized controlled trials. *J Altern Complement Med.* 2010;16(4):375-395.

11. Duncan B, Shen K, Zou LP, et al. Evaluating intense rehabilitative therapies with and without acupuncture for children with cerebral palsy: a randomized controlled trial. *Arch Phys Med Rehabil.* 2012;93(5):808-815.

12. Darrah J, Watkins B, Chen L, Bonin C. Conductive education intervention for children with cerebral palsy: an AACPDM evidence report. *Dev Med Child Neurol.* 2004;46(3):187-203.

13. Schenker R. Conductive education: history, definition, and basic concepts. Tsad Kadima. *The Association for Conductive Education in Israel.* http://www.tsadkadima.org.il/?CategoryID=186. Accessed August 3, 2014.

14. Reddihough DS, King J, Coleman G, Catanese T. Efficacy of programmes based on conductive education for young children with cerebral palsy. *Dev Med Child Neurol.* 1998;40(11):763-770.

15. Effgen SK, Chan L. Occurrence of gross motor behaviors and attainment of motor abilities in children with cerebral palsy participating in conductive education. *Physiother Theory Pract.* 2010;26(1):22-39.

16. 2016 Annual Fundraiser Northwest. *Center for Independence Through Conductive Education.* http://www.center-for-independence.org/fundraiser.html. Accessed February 13, 2016.

17. Stiller C, Marcoux BC, Olson RE. The effect of conductive education, intensive therapy, and special education services on motor skills in children with cerebral palsy. *Phys Occup Ther Pediatr.* 2003;23(3):31-50.

18. Blank R, von Kries R, Hesse S, von Voss H. Conductive education for children with cerebral palsy: effects on hand motor functions relevant to activities of daily living. *Arch Phys Med Rehabil.* 2008;89(2):251-259.

19. Anttila H, Suoranta J, Malmivaara A, Mäkelä M, Autti-Rämö I. Effectiveness of physiotherapy and conductive education interventions in children with cerebral palsy: a focused review. *Am J Phys Med Rehabil.* 2008;87(6):478-501.

20. Novak I, McIntyre S, Morgan C, et al. A systematic review of interventions for children with cerebral palsy: state of evidence. *Dev Med Child Neurol.* 2013;55(10):885-910.

21. Upledger JE. Craniosacral therapy. *Phys Ther.* 1995;75(4):328-329.

22. Hollenbery S, Dennis M. An introduction to craniosacral therapy. *Physiotherapy.* 1994;80(3):528-532.

23. Hartman SE, Norton JM. Interexaminer reliability and cranial osteopathy. *Sci Rev Altern Med.* 2002;6(1):23-34.

24. Green C, Martin CW, Bassett K, Kazanjian A. A systematic review of craniosacral therapy: biological plausibility, assessment reliability and clinical effectiveness. *Complement Ther Med.* 1999;7(4):201-207.

25. McManus V, Gliksten M. The use of CranioSacral therapy in a physically impaired population in a disability service in southern Ireland. *J Altern Complement Med.* 2007;13(9):929-930.

26. Greenman PE, McPartland JM. Cranial findings and iatrogenesis from craniosacral manipulation in patients with traumatic brain syndrome. *J Am Osteopath Assoc.* 1995;95(3):182-188;191-192.

27. Hartman SE, Norton JM. Craniosacral therapy is not medicine. *Phys Ther.* 2002;82(11):1146-1147.

28. About the Institutes. *The Institutes for the Achievement of Human Potential.* http://www.iahp.org/about-the-institutes/. Accessed August 7, 2014.

29. American Academy of Pediatrics Policy statement: the Doman-Delacato treatment of neurologically handicapped children. *Pediatrics.* 1982;70(5):810-812.

30. Ziring PR, Brazdziunas D, Cooley WC, et al. American Academy of Pediatrics. Committee on Children with Disabilities. The treatment of neurologically impaired children using patterning. *Pediatrics.* 1999;104(5):1149-1151.

31. Zigler E. A plea to end the use of the patterning treatment for retarded children. *Am J Orthopsychiatry.* 1981;51(3):388-390.

32. Tseng SH, Chen HC, Tam KW. Systematic review and meta-analysis of the effect of equine assisted activities and therapies on gross motor outcome in children with cerebral palsy. *Disabil Rehabil.* 2013;35(2):89-99.

33. Sterba JA, Rogers BT, France AP, Vokes DA. Horseback riding in children with cerebral palsy: effect on gross motor function. *Dev Med Child Neurol.* 2002;44(5):301-308.

34. Sterba JA. Does horseback riding therapy or therapist-directed hippotherapy rehabilitate children with cerebral palsy? *Dev Med Child Neurol.* 2007;49(1):68-73.

35. Casady RL, Nichols-Larsen DS. The effect of hippotherapy on ten children with cerebral palsy. *Pediatr Phys Ther.* 2004;16(3):165-172.

36. About PATH, Int. *The Professional Association of Therapeutic Horsemanship International.* http://www.pathintl.org/about-path-intl/about-path-intl. Accessed August 9, 2014.

37. Welcome to American Hippotherapy Association. *American Hippotherapy Association.* http://www.americanhippotherapyassociation.org/about-aha/about_aha/. Published 2010. Accessed August 9, 2014.

38. Silkwood-Sherer DJ, Killian CB, Long TM, Martin KS. Hippotherapy – an intervention to habilitate balance deficits in children with movement disorders: a clinical trial. *Phys Ther.* 2012;92(5):707-717.

39. McGibbons NH, Benda W, Duncan BR, Silkwood-Sherer D. Immediate and long-term effects of hippotherapy on symmetry of adductor muscle activity and functional ability in children with spastic cerebral palsy. *Arch Phys Med Rehabil.* 2009;90(6):966-974.

40. Shurltleff TL, Standeven JW, Engsberg JR. Changes in dynamic trunk/head stability and functional reach after hippotherapy. *Arch Phys Med Rehabil.* 2009;90(7):1185-1195.

41. Kwon JY, Chang HJ, Lee JY, Ha Y, Lee PK, Kim YH. Effects of hippotherapy on gait parameters in children with bilateral spastic cerebral palsy. *Arch Phys Med Rehabil.* 2011;92(5):774-779.

42. Encheff JL, Armstrong C, Masterson M, Fox C, Gribble P. Hippotherapy effects on trunk, pelvic, and hip motion during ambulation in children with neurological impairments. *Pediatr Phys Ther.* 2012;24(3):242-250.

43. Frank A, McCleskey S, Dole RL. Effect of hippotherapy on perceived self-competence and participation in a child with cerebral palsy. *Pediatr Phys Ther.* 2011;23(3):301-308.

44. Davis E, Davies B, Wolfe R, et al. A randomized controlled trial of the impact of therapeutic horseback riding on the quality of life, health and function of children with cerebral palsy. *Dev Med Child Neurol.* 2009;51(2):111-119.

45. Whalen CN, Case-Smith J. Therapeutic effects of horseback riding therapy on gross motor function in children with cerebral palsy: a systematic review. *Phys Occup Ther Pediatr.* 2012;32(3):229-242.

46. Leach RM, Rees PJ, Wilmshurst P. Hyperbaric oxygen therapy. *BMJ.* 1998;317(7166):1140-1143.

47. McDonagh MS, Carson S, Russman BS. Systematic review of hyperbaric oxygen therapy for children with cerebral palsy: the state of the evidence. *Dev Med Child Neurol.* 2007;49(12):942-947.

48. About us. *Hyperbaric Healing Institute.* http://www.oxygenunderpressure.com/hyperbaric-oxygen-therapy-in-kansas-city/. Accessed August 14, 2014.

49. Neubauer RA. Hyperbaric oxygenation for cerebral palsy. *Lancet.* 2001;357(9273):2052.

50. Muller-Bolla M, Collet JP, Ducruet T, Robinson A. Side effects of hyperbaric oxygen therapy in children with cerebral palsy. *Undersea Hyperb Med.* 2006;33(4):237-244.

51. Nuthall G, Seear M, Lepawsky M, et al. Hyperbaric oxygen therapy for cerebral palsy: two complications of treatment. *Pediatrics.* 2000;106(6):e80.

52. Collet JP, Vanasse M, Marois P, et al. Hyperbaric oxygen for children with cerebral palsy: a randomised multicentre trial. *Lancet.* 2001;357(9256):582-586.

53. Hardy P, Collet JP, Goldberg J, et al. Neuropsychological effects of hyperbaric oxygen therapy in cerebral palsy. *Dev Med Child Neurol.* 2002;44(7):436-446.

54. Lacey DJ, Stolfi A, Pilati LE. Effects of hyperbaric oxygen on motor function in children with cerebral palsy. *Ann Neurol.* 2012;72():695-703.

55. Semenova KA. Basis for a method of dynamic proprioceptive correction in the restorative treatment of patients with residual-stage infantile cerebral palsy. *Neurosci Behav Physiol.* 1997;27(6):639-43.

56. Euromed. Eurosuit methodology: proven, promising, intensive, complex treatment for cerebral palsy, spinal cord damage, locomotor dysfunctions. *Euromed.* http://locomotordysfunction.com/eurosuit/. Accessed February 13, 2016.

57. Adeli patents. *Adeli Method.* http://adeli.gr/adeli-patents_en.php. Accessed August 15, 2014.

58. Koscielny R, Koscielny I, inventors; Koscielny R, Koscielny I, assignees. Neurological motor therapy suit. US patent 7153246 B2. December 26, 2006.

59. Bailes AF, Greve K, Schmitt LC. Changes in two children with cerebral palsy after intensive suit therapy: a case report. *Pediatr Phys Ther.* 2010;22(1):76-85.

60. Bailes AF, Greve K, Burch CK, Reder R, Lin L, Huth MM. The effect of suit wear during an intensive therapy program in children with cerebral palsy. *Pediatr Phys Ther.* 2011;23(2):136-142.

61. Bar-Haim S, Harries N, Belokopytov M, et al. Comparison of efficacy of Adeli suit and neurodevelopmental treatments in children with cerebral palsy. *Dev Med Child Neurol.* 2006;48(5):325-330.

62. Mahani MK, Karimloo M, Amirsalari S. Effects of modified Adeli suit therapy on improvement of gross motor function in children with cerebral palsy. *Hong Kong J Occup Ther.* 2011;21:9-14.

63. Christy JB, Chapman CG, Murphy P. The effect of intense physical therapy for children with cerebral palsy. *J Pediatr Rehabil Med.* 2012;5(3):159-170.

64. Bobath K. *A Neurophysiological Basis for Treatment of Cerebral Palsy.* Lavenham, UK: Mac Keith Press; 1980.

65. Bobath K, Bobath B. The facilitation of normal postural reactions and movements in the treatment of cerebral palsy. *Physiotherapy.* 1964;50:246-262.

17

Significance of Manual Guidance in Pediatric Physical Therapy Practice

As empirical support continues to grow for the concept of grounded cognition and the theories that encompass it, it is clear that physical therapy interventions should be redesigned on the basis of these theories; redesigned interventions should replace more traditional, less effective interventions based on theories lacking support, such as those based primarily on maturation, reflex control and inhibition, and more passive experience.

Michele A. Lobo, Regina T. Harbourne, Stacey C. Dusing, and Sarah Westcott McCoy[1]

THE CONCEPT OF GROUNDED COGNITION

Advances in research on human development and learning have led to improved understanding of these processes.[1] Specifically, a convincing body of developmental research suggests that infants develop their cognitive abilities by interacting with objects and people during active exploration of the environment.[1-3] This means that cognition is embodied or grounded in perceptual-motor experiences.[1-3] The concept of grounded cognition is of great importance to pediatric physical therapists working with infants and children with movement disorders as they are in a unique position to make a difference in their patients' lives by providing them with effective interventions that enhance their global development.[1]

MANUAL GUIDANCE AS A FORM OF TOUCH

Infants' sensitivity and responses to touch are important for the development and regulation of their interactions with people.[4] Types and effects of therapeutic touch vary depending on specific interventions. Touch may have calming and comforting effects, such as in mother-infant skin-to-skin contact[5,6] or massage that produces relaxation and pain-reduction effects.[7] Passive stretching is another "passive" intervention that involves touch that often has an opposite effect on the child as its application may be associated with discomfort and pain.[8] Active-assistive exercise is a more "active" intervention that combines active movement produced by the patient with manual assistance provided by the therapist.[9] Touch or manual contact can be used to guard the patient for safety and to provide graded support or physical assistance.[10]

Finally, touch is an important component of a number of therapeutic approaches. Physical or manual guidance is a different form of touch, a type of augmented information that

Rahlin M. *Physical Therapy for Children With Cerebral Palsy: An Evidence-Based Approach (pp 271-274).*
© 2016 SLACK Incorporated.

serves to enhance the child's action in a specific situation.[11] Physical guidance constitutes an important part of a complementary intervention known as *conductive education*,[12,13] and manual guidance is a major component of neurodevelopmental treatment (NDT)[14-16] and Perception-Action (P-A)[17-19] therapeutic approaches (see Chapter 14 and Table 14-1).

CURRENT TRENDS IN PEDIATRIC PHYSICAL THERAPY PRACTICE

Current clinical practice in pediatric physical therapy can be characterized by varied opinions among clinicians on how to approach intervention for children with CP.[20] Historically, since the late 1940s through the beginning of this century, neurological rehabilitation was dominated by NDT, with parents actively seeking therapists trained or certified in this therapeutic approach. After evidence failed to show its superiority to other interventions, several common trends formed among pediatric clinicians. In a passionate editorial paper published in 2007, Damiano[20] described these trends as continued practice of the original NDT approach described by Bobath and Bobath[14,15]; practice of modified NDT while retaining its original name; and looking for interventions supported by solid research evidence. Damiano[20,21] listed strength resistance training[22-24] and treadmill training with and without partial body weight support (PBWS)[25-27] as activity-based intensive interventions supported by research. However, since then, the benefits of these interventions for activity and participation in individuals with CP have not been found so clear-cut as was originally thought[28-31] (see Chapter 15).

In the meantime, 2 other important trends not mentioned by Damiano[20] have evolved among therapists who favor evidence-based practice. One is a "hands-off approach" that involves therapeutic exercise, extensive caregiver education in functional activities, and the use of assistive technology for positioning and mobility. The "hands-off" intervention promotes the acquisition of such motor skills as upright sitting, standing, as well as supported, assisted, and, when possible, independent mobility. The coaching method in Early Intervention discussed in Chapter 12 is an example of such approach.[32]

The second, not as widely observed, trend involves the use of interventions that promote active exploration and problem solving on the part of the child, augmented with parent education and assistive technology that support these processes, thus advancing the development of grounded cognition or embodied mind.[1,2] In their recent perspective paper, Lobo et al[1] examined the concept of grounded cognition and argued that, based on related current research, early perceptual-motor experiences have a global effect on development and enhance learning and participation, and that delays in object interaction and exploratory abilities in sitting and during locomotion negatively affect cognitive performance and the ability to learn in infants and children with developmental disorders. Citing studies of interventions that were shown to improve the child's ability to interact with objects and advance the development of postural control in sitting and during locomotion,[19,29,33-35] these authors suggested that physical therapists should plan and structure interventions to include varied experiences that would allow infants and children to actively explore objects and events and interact with people, instead of focusing on having them learn motor skills "in isolation."[1] The child should be able to purposefully use the newly acquired behavior to further explore the world in real-life situations, thus leading to enhanced learning and participation.[1]

This trend differs sharply from the "hands-off" approach where adaptive equipment and extensive caregiver education are used to promote upright sitting, standing, and supported mobility *without* practicing active exploration and problem solving in challenging situations when external support may be absent or reduced as appropriate for the child's functional level. Adaptive equipment is frequently necessary to address a variety of activities of daily living, education, and transportation-related functional needs in children with movement disorders. However, research that examined the concept of embodied mind showed that active exploration and spontaneous movement opportunities are also necessary as they advance the development of both postural control and cognition.[1,2,36,37]

Harbourne[36,37] conducted several experiments that demonstrated that the development of sitting postural control and visual attention in young infants interact with each other, leading to a cognitive change. In these experiments, the duration of looking at an object, or *look time*, was used as a measure of the speed with which an infant extracts and processes visual information about that object. Results revealed the following:

- With the emergence of sitting postural control, look times decreased in both infants developing typically and infants with developmental delays.
- Infants with motor delays were found to have longer look times than infants developing typically.[36,37]
- Infants who displayed greater postural stability in sitting at any point of its development had shorter look times than those who had lower postural stability.[36]
- Infants developing typically who had insufficient sitting ability did not demonstrate shorter look times when provided with mechanical external support.[37]

These findings suggested that the use of static seating positioning devices widely recommended by physical and occupational therapists to improve function and visual attention in infants and children with movement disorders and developmental delays may not translate into immediate functional improvements.[36] Furthermore, active exploration of the child's environment and having opportunities to develop postural adjustments necessary for the acquisition of sitting postural control may be of utmost importance for the appropriate development of cognitive processing of visual information.[36,37] Thus, this research supported the concept of grounded cognition.[36]

MANUAL GUIDANCE AND GROUNDED COGNITION

So, how does manual guidance fit the picture of advancing the development of grounded cognition? As mentioned previously, manual guidance is a major component of the NDT[14-16] and P-A[17-19] therapeutic approaches. As described in Chapter 14, NDT uses manual guidance in the form of inhibition and facilitation techniques aimed at reducing abnormal tone and movement and promoting typical movement patterns.[15,16] Over the years, this intervention has been investigated in multiple studies. However, published research did not indicate that NDT could enhance development in other domains but motor.[38] In addition, according to a systematic review of literature sponsored by the American Academy of Cerebral Palsy and Developmental Medicine, evidence for qualitative effects of NDT on movement patterns and motor development was inconsistent across studies.[38] Furthermore, many studies failed to demonstrate the advantage of NDT over other treatment options,[38-41] which led to the conclusion of another systematic review of literature that this approach should be abandoned altogether.[41]

In the P-A approach, manual guidance avoids blocking or interrupting spontaneous movement (see Chapter 14).[17-19] The therapist does not guide the child's movement into a specific pattern.[17-19] Instead, light touch augments the natural forces experienced by the child by introducing a slight change in force distribution.[17-19,42] The therapist then examines the child's behavior for spontaneous initiation of purposeful movement.[17-19,42] Because the touch of the therapist's hands placed on the child's body is light and gentle, it fulfils another important function as the therapist is able to detect the child's movement intentions and actions, thus allowing for spontaneous movement to occur.[17-19]

Although the overall body of research on the efficacy of the P-A approach is much smaller than that on the efficacy of NDT, it provides promising results.[19,43] One possible reason for this is that manual guidance used in the P-A approach allows for child-produced, task-specific movement to occur throughout the session.[18,19] In a randomized controlled trial (RCT), the P-A approach was shown to be more effective than coaching in improving sitting postural control in infants with and at risk for CP.[19] Furthermore, an unintended result of this research was a qualitative improvement that was manifested in increased variability and complexity of sitting postural adjustment patterns in the P-A approach intervention group. This, in turn, led to a greater adaptability of movement as many of its participants learned to actively explore their environment by crawling. Perhaps linear and nonlinear measures used to evaluate the infants' postural control in this study[19] should be employed in a future RCT that can be designed to compare the effects of manual guidance in the NDT and P-A approach interventions in children with CP. This would provide objective quantitative data that would allow the researchers to compare the extent of qualitative changes in postural control[19] obtained by participants in 2 intervention groups.

In the meantime, it is important to note another, more recent RCT conducted by Harbourne et al[43] with 31 children with unilateral and bilateral CP, GMFCS levels I through III, age range 1 to 5 years. Its results demonstrated that the P-A approach was effective in enhancing sitting postural control in children with CP, with a concurrent improvement observed in cognitive and play skills. This indicated that improvement in sitting postural control leads to improvement in functional play and that the P-A approach intervention can positively affect other areas of development besides motor.[43]

The discussed research shows that, when applied appropriately, manual guidance can encourage spontaneous exploration, enhance postural control, and support cognitive development in children with CP.[19,43] As suggested by Lobo et al,[1] interventions that challenge children to explore their environment and move without extensive external support should not be overlooked. Such interventions have a potential to maximize the child's perceptual-motor abilities by providing opportunities for frequent interactions with people, objects, and events.[1] Manual guidance that possesses such qualities is one of these interventions that can be employed as a means to advance the development of grounded cognition.

CONCLUSIONS

The discussed evidence leads to a number of conclusions in regard to the significance of manual guidance in the pediatric physical therapy practice. First, heavy reliance on equipment with a disregard of the child's need for active spontaneous exploration needs to be re-evaluated. Clinicians cannot rely only on static supported postures to help infants develop active exploration strategies,[36] and children need to be challenged to find solutions to performing movement transitions and attaining postural stability to the best of their ability. Interventions such as resistance strength training and treadmill training have documented benefits for children with CP,[22-31] but they cannot serve as the only and primary solutions to all tasks these children face, including the development of grounded cognition that requires spontaneous movement and opportunities for problem solving.[1]

Furthermore, the trend to disregard manual guidance in current pediatric practice may lead to the loss of this important skill, especially if it disappears from physical therapy education. Therefore, skilled manual guidance needs to be increasingly taught to physical and occupational therapy students in entry-level professional programs and to experienced clinicians as a part of their continuing education. Finally, research studies need to be conducted to provide additional evidence of efficacy of manual guidance and to further confirm its importance for global development in children with movement disorders.

REFERENCES

1. Lobo MA, Harbourne RT, Dusing SC, Westcott McCoy S. Grounding early intervention: physical therapy cannot just be about motor skills anymore. *Phys Ther.* 2013;93(1):94-103.

2. Thelen E. Grounded in the world: developmental origins of the embodied mind. *Infancy.* 2000;1(1):3-28.

3. Gibson EJ. Exploratory behavior in the development of perceiving, acting, and the acquiring of knowledge. *Annu Rev Psychol.* 1988;39:1-41.

4. Fairhurst MT, Löken L, Grossmann T. Physiological and behavioral responses reveal 9-month-old infants' sensitivity to pleasant touch. *Psychol Sci.* 2014;25(5):1124-1131.

5. Ludington-Hoe SM, Ferreira C, Swinth J, Ceccardi JJ. Safe criteria and procedure for Kangaroo care with intubated preterm infants. *J Obstet Gynecol Neonatal Nurs.* 2003;32(5):579-588.

6. Rahlin M. Impaired ventilation, respiration/gas exchange and aerobic capacity/endurance associated with respiratory failure in the neonate. In: Frownfelter D, ed. *Cardiopulmonary Essentials: Preferred Physical Therapist Practice Patterns.* Thorofare, NJ: SLACK Incorporated; 2007:237-264.

7. Glew GM, Fan MY, Hagland S, Bjornson K, Beider S, McLaughlin JF. Survey of the use of massage for children with cerebral palsy. *Int J Ther Massage Bodywork.* 2010;3(4):10-15.

8. Hadden KL, von Baeyer CL. Pain in children with cerebral palsy: common triggers and expressive behaviors. *Pain.* 2002;99(1-2):281-288.

9. Kisner C, Colby LA. Range of motion. In: Kisner C, Colby LA, eds. *Therapeutic Exercise: Foundations and Techniques.* 5th ed. Philadelphia, PA: F.A. Davis Company; 2007:43-64.

10. Fairchild SL. Transfer activities. In: Fairchild SL, ed. *Pierson and Fairchild's Principles & Techniques of Patient Care.* 5th ed. St, Louis, MO: Saunders; 2013:169-211.

11. Valvano J, Rapport MJ. Activity-focused motor interventions for infants and young children with neurological conditions. *Infants Young Child.* 2006;19(4):292-307.

12. Darrah J, Watkins B, Chen L, Bonin C. Conductive education intervention for children with cerebral palsy: an AACPDM evidence report. *Dev Med Child Neurol.* 2004;46(3):187-203.

13. Schenker R. Conductive education: history, definition, and basic concepts. Tsad Kadima. *The Association for Conductive Education in Israel.* http://www.tsadkadima.org.il/?CategoryID=186. Accessed August 3, 2014.

14. Bobath K. *A Neurophysiological Basis for Treatment of Cerebral Palsy.* Lavenham, UK: Mac Keith Press; 1980.

15. Bobath K, Bobath B. The facilitation of normal postural reactions and movements in the treatment of cerebral palsy. *Physiotherapy.* 1964;50:246-262.

16. Howle J. *Neuro-Developmental Treatment Approach: Theoretical Foundations and Principles of Clinical Practice.* Laguna Beach, CA: NDTA; 2002.

17. Tscharnuter I. A new therapy approach to movement organization. *Phys Occup Ther Pediatr.* 1993;13:19-40.

18. Tscharnuter I. Clinical application of dynamic theory concepts according to Tscharnuter Akademie for Movement Organization (TAMO) therapy. *Pediatr Phys Ther.* 2002;14:29-37.

19. Harbourne RT, Willett S, Kyvelidou A, Deffeyes J, Stergiou N. A comparison of interventions for children with cerebral palsy to improve sitting postural control: a clinical trial. *Phys Ther.* 2010;90:1881-1898.

20. Damiano D. Pass the torch, please! *Dev Med Child Neurol.* 2007;49(10):723.

21. Damiano DL. Activity, activity, activity: rethinking our physical therapy approach to cerebral palsy. *Phys Ther.* 2006;86(11):1534-1540.

22. Andersson C, Grooten W, Hellsten M, Kaping K, Mattsson E. Adults with cerebral palsy: walking ability after progressive strength training. *Dev Med Child Neurol.* 2003;45(4):220-228.

23. Blundell SW, Shepherd RB, Dean CM, Adams RD, Cahill BM. Functional strength training in cerebral palsy: a pilot study of a group circuit training class for children aged 4-8 years. *Clin Rehabil.* 2003;17(1):48-57.

24. Dodd KJ, Taylor NF, Graham HK. A randomized clinical trial of strength training in young people with cerebral palsy. *Dev Med Child Neurol.* 2003;45(10):652-657.

25. Bodkin AW, Baxter RS, Heriza CB. Treadmill training for an infant born preterm with a grade III intraventricular hemorrhage. *Phys Ther.* 2003;83(12):107-118.

26. McNevin NH, Coraci L, Schafer J. Gait in adolescent cerebral palsy: the effect of partial unweighting. *Arch Phys Med Rehabil.* 2000;81(4):525-528.

27. Schindl MR, Forstner C, Kern H, Hesse S. Treadmill training with partial body weight support in nonambulatory patients with cerebral palsy. *Arch Phys Med Rehabil.* 2000;81(3):301-306.

28. Verschuren O, Ada L, Maltais DB, Gorter JW, Scianni A, Ketelaar M. Muscle strengthening in children and adolescents with cerebral palsy: considerations for future resistance training protocols. *Phys Ther.* 2011;91(7):1130-1139.

29. Damiano DL, DeJong SL. A systematic review of the effectiveness of treadmill training and body weight support in pediatric rehabilitation. *J Neurol Phys Ther.* 2009;33(1):27-44.

30. Mutlu A, Krosschell K, Gaebler Spira D. Treadmill training with partial body-weight support in children with cerebral palsy: a systematic review. *Dev Med Child Neurol.* 2009;51(4):268-275.

31. Zwicker JG, Mayson TA. Effectiveness of treadmill training in children with motor impairments: an overview of systematic reviews. *Pediatr Phys Ther.* 2010;22(4):361-377.

32. Chiarello, LA. Serving infants, toddlers, and their families: early intervention services under IDEA. In: Campbell SK, Palisano RJ, Orlin MN, eds. *Physical Therapy for Children.* 4th ed. St. Louis, MO: Saunders; 2012:944-967.

33. Lobo MA, Galloway JC. Postural and object-oriented experiences advance early reaching, object exploration, and means-end behavior. *Child Dev.* 2008;79(6):1869-1890.

34. Heathcock JC, Lobo MA, Galloway JC. Movement training advances the emergence of reaching in infants born at less than 33 weeks of gestational age: a randomized clinical trial. *Phys Ther.* 2008;88(3):310-322.

35. Ragonesi CB, Chen X, Agrawal S, Galloway JC. Power mobility and socialization in preschool: a case study of a child with cerebral palsy. *Pediatr Phys Ther.* 2010;22(3):322-329.

36. Harbourne RT. *The Embodied Mind in Early Development: Sitting Postural Control and Visual Attention in Infants with Typical Development and Infants with Delays* [dissertation]. Lincoln: University of Nebraska; 2009.

37. Harbourne RT, Ryallis B, Stergiou N. Sitting and looking: a comparison of stability and visual exploration in infants with typical development and infants with motor delay. *Phys Occup Ther Pediatr.* 2014;34(2):197-212.

38. Butler C, Darrah J. AACPDM evidence report: effects of neuro-developmental treatment (NDT) for cerebral palsy; 2001-2002. https://www.aacpdm.org/UserFiles/file/ndt-cp.pdf. Accessed February 13, 2016.

39. Fetters L, Kluzik J. Neurodevelopmental treatment versus practice for the treatment of children with spastic cerebral palsy. *Phys Ther.* 1996;76(4):346-358.

40. Bar-Haim S, Harries N, Belokopytov M, et al. Comparison of efficacy of Adeli suit and neurodevelopmental treatments in children with cerebral palsy. *Dev Med Child Neurol.* 2006;48(5):325-330.

41. Novak I, McIntyre S, Morgan C, et al. A systematic review of interventions for children with cerebral palsy: state of evidence. *Dev Med Child Neurol.* 2013;55(10):885-910.

42. Rahlin M. TAMO therapy as a major component of physical therapy intervention for an infant with congenital muscular torticollis: a case report. *Pediatr Phys Ther.* 2005;17(3):209-218.

43. Harbourne R, Willett SL, Ryalls B, Stergiou N. The use of stochastic noise during intervention to improve sitting postural control in children with cerebral palsy. In: Abstracts of Poster Presentations at the 2013 Combined Sections Meeting. *Pediatr Phys Ther.* 2013;25(1):105-106. Abstract.

18

Therapy Frequency, Duration, and Intensity Issues

Dosing represents a critical and pressing aspect of intervention that is central for treatment efficacy.

Thubi H.A. Kolobe, Jennifer Braswell Christy, Mary E. Gannotti, et al[1]

As research evidence demonstrates, infants who develop typically undertake massive amounts of daily practice when mastering such new skills as crawling and walking.[2-5] Specifically, they take approximately 3000 crawling steps over 5 hours of crawling experience per day, which corresponds to a distance equal to the length of 2 football fields.[2,3] Furthermore, after starting to walk, infants cover a distance greater than the length of 29 football fields and take approximately 9000 steps per day on average.[4,5] They practice walking on different surfaces, in different environments and situations, with frequent loss of balance that results in safe falls that occur 15 times per hour.[4,5]

The overwhelming evidence of enormous amounts of practice undertaken by infants with intact movement apparatus suggests that infants and children with movement disorders who have difficulties with postural control and independent mobility should require the same or even greater amounts of practice to overcome these difficulties and achieve their highest developmental potential. This hypothesis is supported by a growing body of research that examined intensive therapy schedules and interventions,[6,7] yet there appears to be a disconnect between evidence and clinical practice as practice seems to be lagging behind, with "traditional" interventions of low intensity still prevalent in the clinic.[6-8]

Ulrich[9] examined the issue of intensive intervention from the perspective of developmental theory, neuroscience, and clinical research. From a standpoint of the dynamic systems,[10,11] perception-action,[12,13] and neuronal group selection theories,[14,15] intensive interventions are supported by 5 principles:

1. Behavior results from self-organization of multiple subsystems of the human body around a specific task in a given environment.

2. Behavioral change occurs as the result of a continuously repeated perception-action loop that the person experiences within the context of the task and to the extent with which body capabilities are able to match the task demands.

3. Human brain has inherent redundancy in its pathways to allow for the performance of the same functional skill while using different neuronal connections.

4. All experiences build on one another, so even those that do not seem to matter at the first glance may produce an unexpected result.

5. The repeated perception-action loop has a significant impact on the nervous system, leading to a change in its organization.

Rahlin M. *Physical Therapy for Children With Cerebral Palsy:*
An Evidence-Based Approach (pp 275-282).

These principles highlight the importance of repetition, spontaneous movement, and active exploration in the developmental process.[9]

From a neuroscience perspective, neural recovery that engages the mechanisms of neuroplasticity after an injury to the developing brain requires significant amounts of practice as demonstrated by clinical research of intensive interventions conducted with children with cerebral palsy (CP).[9,16] The timing of intervention is extremely important for prevention of secondary and tertiary impairments related to insufficient activity that may lead to structural changes in muscle and bone and to changes in body composition.[9] Ulrich[9] proposed that, instead of waiting to provide intervention until the children fail to develop functional skills, therapists need to use intensive psychological, physical, and contextual strategies to engage them in spontaneous and repetitive physical activity. Current practice in early intervention when infants with or at risk for developmental disabilities receive on average 1 hour of physical therapy every 2 weeks needs to be re-examined. Nevertheless, dosing of intervention remains an under-researched area of practice for which consensus has not been reached.[9]

COMPLEXITY OF DECISION MAKING IN REGARD TO INTERVENTION PARAMETERS

Results of patient examination and evaluation lead to the development of goals that must be meaningful to the child and the family and need to address the child's activity and participation needs (see Chapter 11). Making the decision on the optimal frequency, duration, intensity, and type of intervention that will be used to achieve these goals comes next.[17] This is a complex process that has received significant attention in current literature.[1,18] *Frequency* is an intervention parameter defined as the number of sessions per a period of time, such as 1 day, 1 week, or 1 month.[1,18,19] *Duration* refers to the amount of time a therapy session lasts.[1,18,19] *Intensity* can be viewed from the perspective of a therapy schedule, which is a combination of intervention frequency and duration provided over a specific period of time.[7] If therapy is provided intermittently, then the duration of the *resting period* or a break between intervention bouts also needs to be identified.[7] Alternatively, *intensity* can be described as the number of repetitions per a unit of time or in terms of physiological costs of intervention that can be measured as the percentage of maximal heart rate, oxygen consumption, metabolic equivalents, or another method that determines the amount of work performed within a therapy session.[1,18,19] Finally, the *type* of intervention used during therapy sessions is another parameter related to dosing.[1,18,19]

Being able to establish the dosing parameters defined previously is critical for inducing clinically significant changes in the child's body structures and functions, activity, and participation.[1,18] However, the optimal and the minimal effective doses of intervention that would produce such changes in children with movement disorders, including CP, have not been determined, which has further implications for the development of health policy and reimbursement for therapy services.[18] The situation is further complicated by the existing variability in dosing among therapy settings that is frequently dictated by the current policy and system of reimbursement as described in Chapter 12.[20-23] This issue contributes to the previously mentioned disconnect between clinical practice and evidence that points to the benefits of intensive intervention.

MOUNTING RESEARCH EVIDENCE FOR THE EFFICACY OF INTENSIVE THERAPY SCHEDULES

Several research studies that examined the issue of optimal intervention parameters demonstrated a trend toward greater improvement in children with CP observed with intensive therapy when compared to traditional schedules.[7,24-27] Table 18-1 contains information on study designs, sample characteristics, and intervention schedules.[24-27] In a randomized controlled trial (RCT) conducted with children with moderate to severe CP, Bower et al[24] reported slightly greater benefits of a 2-week intensive physical therapy schedule compared to a conventional schedule. In another RCT, children with CP who functioned at the Gross Motor Function Classification System (GMFCS)[28] levels III through V were followed for 18 months.[25] Results of routine and intensive interventions were compared using the Gross Motor Function Measure (GMFM)[29] and the Gross Motor Performance Measure (GMPM).[30] Median amounts of physical therapy provided in the routine and intensive schedule groups are displayed in Table 18-1.[25] The investigators found no significant difference in GMFM[29] and GMPM[30] scores between the groups. Although a trend toward statistically significant improvement was documented in participants who received intensive therapy, this advantage was lost when these children returned to their traditional therapy schedules. Maintaining intensive therapy schedules for several months was found to be very demanding for the study participants, their parents, and therapists.[25]

Trahan and Malouin[26] conducted a multiple baseline design pilot study with 5 children with CP to compare intensive intermittent physical therapy to a conventional therapy schedule (see Table 18-1). Significantly increased GMFM[29] scores were reported during the intermittent intensive therapy phase in 3 of 5 study participants who tolerated this therapy schedule well and retained their gross motor skills during rest periods. These results suggested that routine intervention schedules commonly used by clinicians needed to be reconsidered as intermittent intensive therapy appeared to be optimal for this patient population and, at the same time, not as demanding as the previously described continuous intensive therapy.[25,26]

				INTERVENTION SCHEDULES	
AUTHORS	PUBLICATION YEAR	STUDY DESIGN	SAMPLE CHARACTERISTICS	*Traditional*	*Intensive*
Bower et al[24]	1996	RCT	44 children with moderate to severe bilateral CP Age range 3-11 years	1-3 hours of PT[a] over 2 weeks	6-10 hours of PT[a] over 2 weeks
Bower et al[25]	2001	RCT	56 children with CP GMFCS[28] levels III-V Age range 3-12 years	5 hours of PT[b] over 3 months	44 hours of PT[b] over 3 months
Trahan and Malouin[26]	2002	Multiple baseline design	5 children with CP GMFCS[28] levels IV-V Age range 10-37 months	2 PT sessions/week, 45 min/session over a baseline period of 8-20 weeks	4 PT sessions/week, 45 min/session over 4 weeks and rest period of 8 weeks, 2 cycles over 6 months
Shamir et al[27]	2012	Randomized controlled cross over study	10 children with CP, GMFCS[28] levels III-V Age range 12-22 months	1 PT session/week, 90 min/session over 8 weeks	4 PT sessions/week, 90 min/session over 1 week and rest period of 3 weeks, 2 cycles over 8 weeks

TABLE 18-1

RESEARCH DESIGNS, SAMPLE CHARACTERISTICS, AND INTERVENTION PARAMETERS IN STUDIES THAT COMPARED INTENSIVE AND TRADITIONAL THERAPY SCHEDULES USED IN CHILDREN WITH CEREBRAL PALSY

Abbreviations: CP, cerebral palsy; GMFCS, Gross Motor Function Classification System; min, minute; PT, physical therapy; RCT, randomized controlled trial.
[a] Mean number of hours was reported.
[b] Median number of hours was reported.

While Bower et al[24,25] enrolled children between 3 and 12 years of age in their 2 RCTs (see Table 18-1), Trahan and Malouin[26] conducted their research with infants and toddlers. Subsequently, Shamir et al[27] described a small randomized crossover study, in which they also enrolled infants and toddlers with CP, GMFCS[28] levels III through V. However, these investigators modified the intermittent intensive schedule proposed by Trahan and Malouin[26] to a 4-times-per-week regimen in week 1 followed by a 3-week rest period, and children in the control group were seen 1 time per week, with the physical therapy session duration set at 90 minutes. Results showed similar GMFM-88[29] scores in participants classified in GMFCS[28] levels III and IV in both groups, but a significantly greater improvement after intermittent intensive intervention compared to a traditional schedule was found in children classified in GMFCS[28] level V.[27]

Rahlin[7] applied available research evidence with a 4.5-year-old child with bilateral spastic CP, GMFCS[28] level III, and demonstrated that an intermittent intensive therapy schedule could be selected based on the child's individual characteristics and the wishes and concerns of the family. The child's parents expressed their interest in trying an intermittent intensive therapy schedule but were uncomfortable with the 8-week breaks between intensive intervention periods suggested by Trahan and Malouin.[26] They were concerned that it might not be possible for their daughter to retain her functional skills during such a long rest period. The decision in regard to her therapy schedule was reached in collaboration between the therapist and the parents. This child was seen 5 times per week for 60-minute physical therapy sessions over 2 weeks followed by a 2-week rest period, and this intervention cycle was repeated 3 times over a total of 3 months. The use of this intermittent intensive schedule resulted in the greatest mean increase in GMFM-66[29] scores compared to the preceding and following 3-month periods when traditional, twice per week therapy schedule was used. In addition, the child retained and further improved her skills during the rest periods.[7]

Although results of published studies point to the benefits of intensive and intermittent intensive therapy schedules,[7,24-27] they do not provide sufficient information to inform pediatric physical therapy practice in regard to what schedule or schedules would be most effective for children with CP of different age groups and GMFCS[28] levels. In addition, while mounting research evidence indicates that a variety of intensive interventions, from treadmill training[31,32] to virtual reality programs,[33] benefit this patient population, this information still appears to be insufficient to recommend one intensive intervention over others.[31,32,34-40] For example, 2 systematic reviews of literature discussed in Chapter 15 provided overall support for intensive treadmill training, but found that optimal parameters of this intervention had not been established.[31,32] Furthermore, in one study, partial body weight support treadmill training (PBWSTT) was shown to be as effective as intensive strengthening exercise for such important outcomes as satisfaction, goal attainment, participation, and quality of life, which suggested that the type of intervention used was not as important as its intensity.[34] Similarly, studies of various training protocols of constraint-induced movement therapy (CIMT) revealed its benefits for children with unilateral CP but also suggested that the intervention dose was more important for its success than a specific protocol.[35,36]

In their multiple baseline study, Trahan and Malouin[26] demonstrated the effectiveness of an intermittent intensive schedule of neurodevelopmental treatment (NDT), but as discussed in Chapter 16, Bar-Haim et al[37] showed that NDT was not superior to the use of the Adeli suit in improving gross motor functional skills in children with CP when these 2 interventions were administered using the same intensive protocol. Likewise, while a pretest–post-test single group design study demonstrated the effectiveness of an intensive TheraSuit program,[38] Bailes et al[39] reported no difference in functional improvement between the TheraSuit and sham suit groups when identical intensive protocols were applied to both interventions in an RCT. Similar conclusions in regard to intervention dosing were drawn from the results of an RCT that compared context therapy to a child-focused intervention (see Chapter 14 for information on context therapy).[40] Finally, intensive therapy schedules were shown to be effective when individual training was combined with group therapy[41] and when group therapy was used alone.[42]

Based on the available body of literature, it is fair to conclude that dosing parameters of frequency, duration, and intensity, and not the type of intervention or its individual or group mode of delivery, appear to be the most important agent of change and the driving force in achieving positive intervention outcomes in children with CP. This conclusion supports the premise previously discussed in this chapter that children with CP, same as children developing typically, need massive amounts of practice to learn, advance, and master their postural control and locomotor abilities.[2-5]

Emphasis on Activity

There is a staggering amount of accumulating evidence from current research literature in the areas of typical infant and child development and health, fitness, and intensive exercise interventions in children and adults with neurologic disorders, including CP.[43-45] This evidence suggests that

increasing motor activity is crucial for the prevention of alterations of body structures and functions; for the development and support of functional abilities; and for health promotion, community participation, and achievement of optimal quality of life in this patient population.[43-45] Therefore, in the last 20 years, moderate to vigorous activity has been increasingly emphasized as important for planning intervention.[43,45] Intensity of the child's participation in physical activities was found to be associated with improved parent- and self-reported perceptions of the child's physical and psychosocial well-being.[44] Additionally, results of a small qualitative study showed that an intensive physical therapy model applied in children with CP was perceived by parents and therapists as beneficial for participants' motor function, independence, confidence, community participation, and goal attainment.[46] However, intensive therapy was also found to be the source of stress and fatigue observed in children and acknowledged by parents and therapists.[46]

After examining the available body of research, Verschuren et al[45] concluded that being able to sustain daily moderate to vigorous physical activity may be an unrealistic expectation for children and adolescents with CP. These authors proposed reducing sedentary behaviors and increasing light physical activity performed by the child throughout the day as opposed to exclusively targeting moderate to vigorous activity levels.[45] This recommendation further highlights the need to identify the optimal frequency, duration, and intensity of activity required for individuals with CP[1,18] in order to help them achieve their highest potential in all areas of the International Classification of Functioning, Disability and Health (ICF).[47] As stated previously, decision making in regard to intervention parameters is a very complex process, affected by many factors, which will be discussed next.

Factors Affecting Decision Making in Regard to Intervention Parameters

The ICF Model[47] suggests that the relationship among its components determines one's current state of health, functioning, and disability. When planning intervention for children with CP, clinicians take into consideration a variety of factors. These include the following:

- Alterations in the child's body structures and functions, such as his or her primary and secondary impairments[48]
- Activity limitations related to the child's functional abilities, GMFCS[28] level, and his or her needs for equipment and environmental modifications[20,49]
- Participation restrictions that may but do not necessarily stem from the existing alterations in body structures and functions, and may often be related to a combination of contextual (environmental and personal) factors[47]

TABLE 18-2

ENVIRONMENTAL AND PERSONAL FACTORS AFFECTING DECISION MAKING IN REGARD TO THE SELECTION OF INTERVENTION PARAMETERS FOR CHILDREN WITH MOVEMENT DISORDERS, INCLUDING CEREBRAL PALSY[18,20,48-52]

ICF[47] CONTEXTUAL FACTORS	
Environmental	*Personal*
Community characteristics	Age
• Availability of health care services	Comorbidities
• Access to buildings, health care services, and recreational programs	Current potential for skill acquisition or regression
• Social support	Development
Family characteristics	Diagnosis
• Availability of time	Interests
• Compliance with recommendations	Motivation
• Education	Preferences for the following:
• Expectations	
• Home environment	• Activities
• Follow-through	• Participation
• Parental status (physical, psychosocial, and socioeconomic)	Prognosis
• Readiness for change	Readiness for change
• Structure and resources	Risk taking
• Support system	Satisfaction with the following:
• Type of health insurance	
Funding sources	• Activities
Health care services funding limitations related to the following:	• Care
• Health insurance coverage	• Level of participation
• Health policy	Temperament
Intervention approaches and options	
Amount of problem solving required from a licensed clinician	
Service delivery methods	
Social attitudes and environment	
Therapy practice setting	

Abbreviations: CP, cerebral palsy; ICF, International Classification of Functioning, Disability and Health.

Table 18-2, compiled from multiple sources, contains a number of contextual factors that, based on published literature, may play a role in the therapists' decision making in regard to the selection of intervention parameters for children with movement disorders, including CP.[18,20,48-52] In general, the environmental factors (eg, the living environment, societal entities, and the legal system) may affect the child's body structures and functions, activities, or participation in a positive or a negative way.[47] Similarly, the personal factors or one's set of specific inherent traits may play a positive or a negative role in the success or failure of therapeutic intervention.[47,53] Research suggests that environmental and personal factors may also account for the frequently observed phenomenon of a disconnect between the child's ability to perform a task during a therapy session (capacity) and the actual performance of the same task outside of the clinical situation.[18,53] Table 18-2 illustrates the complexity of the decision-making process on behalf of the therapist[18,20,48-52] that may be an important reason for the lack of translation of evidence on intensive interventions to pediatric physical therapy practice highlighted by several authors.[6-8] Some additional barriers to the implementation of intensive and intermittent intensive therapy in the clinic may include staffing issues and scheduling challenges.[7]

		TABLE 18-3	

RECOMMENDATIONS FOR FUTURE RESEARCH ON INTERVENTION DOSING PARAMETERS FOR CHILDREN WITH CEREBRAL PALSY[1,18]

STUDY CHARACTERISTICS	STUDY DESIGNS	SAMPLE CHARACTERISTICS	GENERAL RULES
Clinically feasible Collaborative Comparative Cost-effective Longitudinal Multicenter Safe Tolerable	Repeated measures rather than pretest–post-test designs PCTs rather than RCTs	Large Heterogeneous Recruited from varied settings Stratified by GMFCS[27] level and age	Start with establishing intervention effectiveness Next, identify the minimal intervention dose, change-inducing intervention components, and optimal intervention parameters Promote sustainability of intervention outcomes Define, assess, and analyze personal and environmental factors that affect the dose-response relationship Target the same outcomes in trials with similar goals

Abbreviations: GMFCS, Gross Motor Function Classification System; PCTs, practical clinical trials; RCTs, randomized clinical trials.[27]

WHERE DO WE GO FROM HERE?

An interdisciplinary research summit conducted by the American Physical Therapy Association (APTA) Section on Pediatrics in 2011 was aimed at advancing research and, subsequently, clinical practice in the area of intervention dosing for children with injured brain, including children with CP.[1] This summit generated recommendations for designing future studies in 3 major areas. The first group of clinical trials will identify minimal and optimal doses of intervention required to improve the upper extremity function. The second group will determine the optimal intervention dose that would lead to improvement of functional ambulation and help maintain it over time in children with CP classified in GMFCS[28] levels II and III. Finally, the third group will include longitudinal studies that will examine the relationship between service utilization and intervention outcomes.[1]

Earlier, Gannotti et al[18] proposed a multivariate path model that can be used in research to identify intervention dosing parameters and examine factors that affect dose-response relationships. The path model includes such components as the type of intervention used to address a specific ICF domain,[47] family and community characteristics, intervention dose, characteristics of the child, structural changes in body systems, and changes in both the child's functional capacity and his or her performance in real life situations.[18]

Table 18-3 provides a summary of recommendations for future research on intervention dosing parameters generated by the APTA Section of Pediatrics Research Summit III and implied by the path model.[1,18] It is interesting to note that Gannotti et al[18] recommended the use of practical clinical trials (PCTs) as a more cost-effective alternative to the use of RCTs. PCTs are designed to provide answers to important questions that would assist clinicians in decision making and to compare interventions of choice across a large number of health outcomes.[54] Such studies require large and diverse samples characterized by wide inclusion and narrow exclusion criteria and recruited from heterogeneous settings, which may be quite expensive.[54] At the same time, PCTs may be cost-effective because they allow for documentation of a wide variety of intervention attributes and contextual factors.[18,54]

Besides its application in research, the path model may also be helpful for clinicians; however, current evidence is insufficient in order to prioritize all of the factors that contribute to the decision-making processes related to physical therapy management of children with CP.[18] Until such evidence becomes available, clinicians are encouraged to consider the path model components while planning patient examination and evaluation, interpreting the evaluation findings, and planning intervention for these children.[18]

REFERENCES

1. Kolobe TH, Christy JB, Gannotti ME, et al and Research Summit III Participants. Research summit III proceedings on dosing in children with an injured brain or cerebral palsy: executive summary. *Phys Ther.* 2014;94(7):907-920.
2. Adolph KE. Learning to keep balance. In: Kail R, ed. *Advances in Child Development and Behavior, Vol. 30.* Amsterdam, Netherlands: Elsevier Science; 2002:1-30.
3. Adolph KE, Joh AS, Franchak JM, Ishak S, Gill SV. Flexibility in the development of action. In: Morsella E, Bargh J, Gollwitzer P, eds. *Oxford Handbook of Human Action.* New York, NY: Oxford University Press; 2009:399-426.
4. Adolph KE, Berger SE. Motor development. In: Damon W, Lerner R, Kuhn D, Siegler RS (eds). *Handbook of Child Psychology, Vol. 2: Cognition, Perception, and Language.* New York, NY: Wiley; 2006:161-213.

5. Adolph KE, Vereijken B, Shrout PE. What changes in infant walking and why. *Child Dev.* 2003;74:475-497.

6. Damiano DL. Rehabilitative therapies in cerebral palsy: the good, the not so good, and the possible. *J Child Neurol.* 2009;24(9):1200-1204.

7. Rahlin M. An individual intermittent intensive physical therapy schedule for a child with spastic quadriparesis. *Physiother Theory Pract.* 2011;27(7):512-520.

8. Chiarello LA, O'Neil M, Dichter CG, et al. Exploring physical therapy clinical decision making for children with spastic diplegia: survey of pediatric practice. *Pediatr Phys Ther.* 2005;17(1):46-54.

9. Ulrich BD. Opportunities for early intervention based on theory, basic neuroscience, and clinical science. *Phys Ther.* 2010;90(12):1868-1880.

10. Kelso JAS. *Dynamic Patterns: The Self-Organization of Brain and Behavior.* Cambridge, MA: The MIT Press; 1995.

11. Thelen E, Smith LB, eds. *A Dynamic Systems Approach to the Development of Cognition and Action.* Cambridge, MA: MIT Press; 1994.

12. Gibson JJ. *The Senses Considered as Perceptual Systems.* Boston, MA: Houghton Mifflin; 1966.

13. Gibson EJ. Exploratory behavior in the development of perceiving, acting, and the acquiring of knowledge. *Annu Rev Psychol.* 1988;39:1-41.

14. Edelman GM. *Neural Darwinism.* New York, NY: Basic Books; 1987.

15. Sporns O, Edelman G. Solving Bernstein's problem: a proposal for the development of coordinated movement by selection. *Child Dev.* 1993;64(4):960-981.

16. Hallett M. Neuroplasticity and rehabilitation. *J Rehabil Res Dev.* 2005;42:xvii-xxii.

17. O'Neil ME, Fragala-Pinkham MA, Westcott SL, et al. Physical therapy clinical management recommendations for children with cerebral palsy – spastic diplegia: achieving functional mobility outcomes. *Pediatr Phys Ther.* 2006;18(1):49-72.

18. Gannotti ME, Christy JB, Heathcock JC, Kolobe TH. A path model for evaluating dosing parameters for children with cerebral palsy. *Phys Ther.* 2014;94(3):411-421.

19. American College of Sports Medicine. General principles of exercise prescription. In: American College of Sports Medicine. *ACSM's Guidelines for Exercise Testing and Prescription.* 9th ed. Philadelphia, PA: Lippincott Williams and Wilkins; 2014:162-193.

20. Bailes AF, Succop P. Factors associated with physical therapy services received for individuals with cerebral palsy in an outpatient pediatric medical setting. *Phys Ther.* 2012;92(11):1411-1418.

21. Kleinert JO, Effgen SK. Early intervention. In: Effgen SK. *Meeting the Physical Therapy Needs of Children.* 2nd ed. Philadelphia, PA: F. A. Davis Company; 2012:475-493.

22. Chiarello, LA. Serving infants, toddlers, and their families: early intervention services under IDEA. In: Campbell SK, Palisano RJ, Orlin MN, eds. *Physical Therapy for Children.* 4th ed. St. Louis, MO: Saunders; 2012:944-967.

23. Effgen SK, Kaminker MK. The educational environment. In: Campbell SK, Palisano RJ, Orlin MN, eds. *Physical Therapy for Children.* 4th ed. St. Louis, MO: Saunders; 2012:968-1007.

24. Bower E, McLellan DL, Arney J, Campbell MJ. A randomized controlled trial of different intensities of physiotherapy and different goal-setting procedures in 44 children with cerebral palsy. *Dev Med Child Neurol.* 1996;38(3):226-237.

25. Bower E, Michell D, Burnett M, Campbell MJ, McLellan DL. Randomized controlled trial of physiotherapy in 56 children with cerebral palsy followed by 18 months. *Dev Med Child Neurol.* 2001;43(1):4-15.

26. Trahan J, Malouin F. Intermittent intensive physiotherapy in children with cerebral palsy: a pilot study. *Dev Med Child Neurol.* 2002;44(4):233-239.

27. Shamir M, Dickstein R, Tirosh E. Intensive intermittent physical therapy in infants with cerebral palsy: a randomized controlled pilot study. *Isr Med Assoc J.* 2012;14(12):737-741.

28. Palisano RJ, Rosenbaum PL, Walter SD, Russell DJ, Wood EP, Galuppi BE. Development and reliability of a system to classify gross motor function in children with cerebral palsy. *Dev Med Child Neurol.* 1997;39(4):214-223.

29. Russell DJ, Rosenbaum PL, Avery LM, Lane M. *Gross Motor Function Measure (GMFM-66 & GMFM-88) User's Manual.* Lavenham, Suffolk: Mac Keith Press; 2002.

30. Boyce W, Gowland C, Rosenbaum P, et al. *Gross Motor Performance Measure Manual.* Kingston, ON: Queen's University, School of Rehabilitation Therapy; 1998.

31. Damiano DL, DeJong SL. A systematic review of the effectiveness of treadmill training and body weight support in pediatric rehabilitation. *J Neurol Phys Ther.* 2009;33(1):27-44.

32. Mutlu A, Krosschell K, Gaebler Spira D. Treadmill training with partial body weight support in children with cerebral palsy: a systematic review. *Dev Med Child Neurol.* 2009;51(4):268-275.

33. Brien M, Sveistrup H. An intensive virtual reality program improves functional balance and mobility of adolescents with cerebral palsy. *Pediatr Phys Ther.* 2011;23(3):258-266.

34. Gates PE, Banks D, Johnston TE, et al. Randomized controlled trial assessing participation and quality of life in a supported speed treadmill training exercise program vs. strengthening program for children with cerebral palsy. *J Pediatr Rehabil Med.* 2012;5(2):75-88.

35. Klingels K, Feys H, Molenaers G, et al. Randomized trial of modified constraint-induced movement therapy with and without an intensive therapy program in children with unilateral cerebral palsy. *Neurorehabil Neural Repair.* 2013;27(9):799-807.

36. Gordon AM. To constrain or not to constrain, and other stories of intensive upper extremity training for children with unilateral cerebral palsy. *Dev Med Child Neurol.* 2011;53(suppl 4):56-61.

37. Bar-Haim S, Harries N, Belokopytov M, et al. Comparison of efficacy of Adeli suit and neurodevelopmental treatments in children with cerebral palsy. *Dev Med Child Neurol.* 2006;48(5):325-330.

38. Christy JB, Chapman CG, Murphy P. The effect of intense physical therapy for children with cerebral palsy. *J Pediatr Rehabil Med.* 2012;5(3):159-170.

39. Bailes AF, Greve K, Burch CK, Reder R, Lin L, Huth MM. The effect of suit wear during an intensive therapy program in children with cerebral palsy. *Pediatr Phys Ther.* 2011;23(2):136-142.

40. Law MC, Darrah J, Pollock N, et al. Focus on function: a cluster randomized controlled trial comparing child- versus context-focused intervention for young children with cerebral palsy. *Dev Med Child Neurol.* 2011;53(7):621-629.

41. Størvold GV, Jahnsen R. Intensive motor skills training program combining group and individual sessions for children with cerebral palsy. *Pediatr Phys Ther.* 2010;22:150-160.

42. Sorsdahl AB, Moe-Nilssen R, Kaale HK, Rieber J, Strand LI. Change in basic motor abilities, quality of movement and everyday activities following intensive, goal-directed, activity-focused physiotherapy in a group setting for children with cerebral palsy. *BMC Pediatr.* 2010;10:26.

43. Damiano DL. Activity, activity, activity: rethinking our physical therapy approach to cerebral palsy. *Phys Ther.* 2006;86(11):1534-1540.

44. Shikako-Thomas K, Dahan-Oliel D, Shevell M, et al. Play and be happy? Leisure participation and quality of life in school-aged children with cerebral palsy. *Int J Pediatr.* 2012;2012:387280. doi:10.1155/2012/387280.

45. Verschuren O, Darrah J, Novak I, Ketelaar M, Wiart L. Health-enhancing physical activity in children with cerebral palsy: more of the same is not enough. *Phys Ther.* 2014;94(2):297-305.

46. Christy JB, Saleem N, Turner PH, Wilson J. Parent and therapist perceptions of an intense model of physical therapy. *Pediatr Phys Ther.* 2010;22:207-213.

47. World Health Organization. *International Classification of Functioning, Disability and Health.* Geneva, Switzerland: World Health Organization; 2001.

48. Bartlett DJ, Palisano RJ. A multivariate model of determinants of motor change for children with cerebral palsy. *Phys Ther.* 2000;80(6):598-614.

49. Palisano RJ, Begnoche DM, Chiarello LA, Bartlett DJ, McCoy SW, Chang HJ. Amount and focus of physical therapy and occupational therapy for young children with cerebral palsy. *Phys Occup Ther Pediatr.* 2012;32(4):368-382.

50. Feldman DE, Swaine B, Gosselin J, Meshefedjian G, Grilli L. Is waiting for rehabilitation services associated with changes in function and quality of life in children with physical disabilities? *Phys Occup Ther Pediatr.* 2008;28(4):291-304.

51. Palisano RJ, Murr S. Intensity of therapy services: what are the considerations? *Phys Occup Ther Pediatr.* 2009;29(2):107-112.

52. Bailes AF, Reder R, Burch C. Development of guidelines for determining frequency of therapy services in a pediatric medical setting. *Pediatr Phys Ther.* 2008;20(2):194-198.

53. Wright FV, Rosenbaum PL, Goldsmith CH, Law M, Fehlings DL. How do changes in body functions and structures, activity, and participation relate in children with cerebral palsy? *Dev Med Child Neurol.* 2008;50(4):283-289.

54. Tunis SR, Stryer DB, Clancy CM. Practical clinical trials: increasing the value of clinical research for decision making in clinical and health policy. *JAMA.* 2003;290(12):1624-1632.

Section IV

QUESTIONS TO PONDER

1. If early intervention is aimed at promoting global development, how should the provision of these services be structured?

2. What are the barriers to increasing intervention frequency, duration, and intensity in early intervention and school settings, when indicated by the needs of the child?

3. What is the significance of therapy-related behavior for the success of intervention?

4. Can an intervention approach be effective if it is not supported by solid research evidence?

5. What are some possible reasons for the lack of research evidence in support of many intervention techniques used by physical therapists for children with CP?

6. Should physical therapists discard interventions that have limited research evidence available to support their efficacy? Please explain your answer.

7. What is the best strategy for designing training programs for children and adolescents with CP to address their fitness needs?

8. Based on the available research evidence, should manual guidance be employed as an intervention strategy in pediatric PT practice? Please explain your answer.

9. What are some of the strategies that can be employed to translate the available evidence on intensive interventions to pediatric PT practice, and what can be some of the barriers to implementation of such strategies?

10. What are some ways that physical therapists could incorporate motor learning concepts in the development and implementation of home exercise programs for children with CP in collaboration with their parents?

SUGGESTED QUESTIONS FOR FUTURE RESEARCH

1. What are the psychometric properties of sensory assessment techniques applied in children with CP?

2. What are the reliability estimates for the observation/movement activation/palpation method of manual muscle testing (MMT) in infants and toddlers with movement disorders?

3. What are the reliability estimates for the modified MMT scale in children who exhibit atypical movement patterns due to presence of spasticity?

(continued)

Section IV (continued)

SUGGESTED QUESTIONS FOR FUTURE RESEARCH (CONTINUED)

4. Are early intervention services provided using parent coaching as effective as the direct service model in promoting global development in infants and toddlers?

5. Do increased motivation and other positive therapy-related behaviors translate into improved long-term therapy outcomes?

6. Are behavior management techniques effective in improving therapy-related behavior and long-term therapy outcomes in children with developmental disabilities?

7. Which therapeutic approach is most effective in promoting global development in infants and toddlers with or at risk for developmental disability?

8. Which therapeutic approach is most effective in achieving activity performance and participation outcomes in children with CP?

9. What are the optimal parameters for cardiorespiratory endurance training programs to achieve the best outcomes for individuals with CP in the areas of activity performance, participation, and quality of life?

10. Can strength training delay the decline in ambulatory capacity in children, adolescents, and young adults with CP?

11. Is there a difference in the effects of manual guidance employed in the Neurodevelopmental Treatment and Perception-Action Approach interventions on variability, complexity, and adaptability of movement and postural control in children with CP?

12. What are the optimal intervention dosing parameters for children with CP, GMFCS[1] levels I through V, required to induce a minimal clinically important change in each of the areas of the International Classification of Functioning, Disability and Health (ICF)[2]?

13. What are the optimal intervention dosing parameters for children with CP, GMFCS[1] levels I through V, required to achieve their highest potential in each of the areas of the International Classification of Functioning, Disability and Health (ICF)[2]?

References

1. Palisano RJ, Rosenbaum PL, Walter SD, Russell DJ, Wood EP, Galuppi BE. Development and reliability of a system to classify gross motor function in children with cerebral palsy. *Dev Med Child Neurol.* 1997;39(4):214-223.
2. World Health Organization. *International Classification of Functioning, Disability and Health.* Geneva, Switzerland: World Health Organization; 2001.

Normal and Abnormal Gait Patterns and Current Evidence for Orthotic Management and Assistive Technology

19

Normal Gait Kinematics and Kinetics

Elaine Owen, MSc, SRP, MCSP, Clinical Specialist Physiotherapist

Understanding normal movement and having an appreciation of the underlying biomechanics is an essential prerequisite for successful rehabilitation. This chapter will describe and analyze normal standing, swaying, stepping, and full gait cycles (GCs) and their development in childhood. It will offer a new interpretation of the GC, one that is most helpful for the development of therapeutic strategies.

LANGUAGE AND DEFINITIONS FOR POSTURE AND GAIT

There have been many different terms and definitions used for descriptions of gait. This has contributed to some misinterpretations and inaccurate beliefs, so unambiguous language and definitions must be established.

Kinematic and Kinetic Analysis

Analysis of movement is normally divided into the 2 branches of *kinematics* and *kinetics*, followed by the analysis of their interaction. The following definitions refer to *a body*. In mechanics, this is defined as any object to which a force can be applied. In human movement analysis, the term *body* refers to the whole human body or individual parts of the body.

Kinematics is defined as the branch of mechanics concerned with the motion of a body. Kinematic analysis of human movement includes the motion of both joints and segments. Although modern analysis has mainly concentrated on joint kinematics alone, a full and meaningful understanding of normal standing and gait requires an understanding of both joint and segment kinematics, how they interact together, and with kinetics. *Kinetics* is defined as the branch of mechanics concerned with forces applied to a body. Kinetic analysis of human movement usually involves the analysis of forces, moments, and powers that are occurring around joints. It can also include the analysis of energy.

Movement analysis by the naked eye in real time may be flawed, so the development of advanced gait analysis equipment, which measures kinematics and kinetics in numerical values and produces informative graphs, has advanced our knowledge in this area. However, most clinicians do not currently have access to this equipment. Two simpler systems are now available: kinematic analysis from video cameras with real time, slow motion, freeze frame, and frame-by-frame advance facilities, and video vector gait analysis equipment. This produces an image of a major force occurring during gait, the *ground reaction force*, overlaid onto the video image to provide a combined kinematic and kinetic analysis.[1,2] This chapter contains selected still images of a GC from such a system.

Rahlin M. *Physical Therapy for Children With Cerebral Palsy: An Evidence-Based Approach* (pp 287-314).
© 2016 SLACK Incorporated.

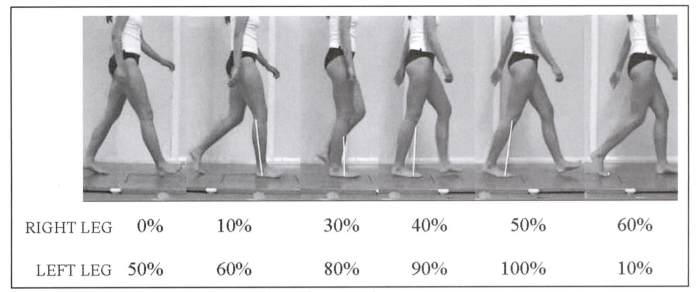

RIGHT LEG	0%	10%	30%	40%	50%	60%
LEFT LEG	50%	60%	80%	90%	100%	10%

Figure 19-1. Sagittal segment and joint kinematics, and kinetics during gait cycle.

The "-ions," "-ings," and "-ors" of Kinematic and Kinetic Language

Despite the volume of published normal gait data, there are some misunderstandings about the kinematics and kinetics that occur. Many of these have arisen because of the variety of language used and the lack of definitions for that language. This has resulted in some incorrect interpretations of normal gait, which have been translated into clinical practice. Some of this confusion seems to be because, with the emergence of complex gait analysis equipment, engineering language has been mixed with clinical language. Therefore, the literature on gait must be interpreted with a clear understanding of each author's definitions, which, unfortunately, are not always stated. It may be helpful to look at some of the terminology that gives rise to confusion, and then identify a clear definition for each term.

Some of the most confusing language has been generated due to the ill-defined use of the suffixes *-ion*, *-ing*, and *-or*. For example, most clinicians use the term *ankle plantarflexion* to describe the alignment or kinematics of the foot relative to the lower leg, or *shank*, as a position below the neutral or plantigrade position, which, in turn, is defined as the 90-degree alignment between the shank and the foot. However, in engineering science, the term *plantarflexion* may be used to describe the kinetic moment occurring at the ankle joint. An example of this is the use of the phrase *plantarflexion knee extension couple*.[3] In this phrase, the word *plantarflexion* is not referring to the alignment or kinematics of the ankle joint, it is referring to the internal moment at the ankle. Also, engineering science may use the term *plantarflexing* to indicate a change of direction of movement in the ankle joint, even when the ankle is remaining in dorsiflexion. For example, during the GC, the ankle joint dorsiflexes to 10 to

12 degrees by 40% GC (Figure 19-1). Ankle dorsiflexion then reduces to 7 degrees by 50% GC. This movement of a reduction in dorsiflexion has been referred to as a *plantarflexing* movement or even *plantarflexion*, even though there is no movement into plantarflexion occurring as defined previously. This description of ankle kinematics during GC seems to have led to a widely held belief that the ankle is in a kinematic position of plantarflexion in terminal stance, which is contrary to all of the published data on normal ankle kinematics.

For clarity, in this chapter, the following definitions of suffixes will be used:

- All words ending in an *-ion* will refer to the kinematics or movement of a joint.
- All words ending in an *-ing* will refer to the external moment about the joint.
- Finally, all words ending in an *-or* will refer to the internal moment about the joint.

Segment Lengths and Proportions

Normative data for segment lengths for all ages are well documented.[4] The normal adult human body has evolved into its current proportions.[5] Early bipedal hominids had short legs and long trunks. We have evolved to have longer legs and shorter trunks, for greater efficiency. We have also evolved segment lengths and proportions that produce the ability to be both stable in standing and mobile when walking, so when rehabilitating standing, stepping, and gait in children and adults, it is important to be cognizant of the body segment lengths and proportions required and to restore any inadequacies. The normalization of foot segment length and equalization of leg lengths in footwear and orthotic prescriptions is imperative. Table 19-1 documents the lower limb lengths and proportions for all age groups.

Table 19-1

Mean Height and Lower Limb Segment Lengths and Proportions for All Age Groups

AGE (YEARS)	HEIGHT (MM)	THIGH (MM)	SHANK (MM)	FOOT (MM)	WHOLE LEG (MM)	SH/TH (%)	F/TH (%)	F/SH (%)	F/LEG (%)
18-18.5	1718	417	406	252	823	97%	60%	62%	31%
17	1683	406	394	247	806	97%	61%	63%	31%
16	1685	409	404	249	813	99%	61%	62%	31%
15	1636	396	394	247	790	99%	62%	63%	31%
14	1594	388	384	244	772	99%	63%	64%	32%
13	1545	376	373	237	749	99%	63%	64%	32%
12	1486	363	364	232	727	100%	64%	64%	32%
11	1427	346	345	223	691	100%	64%	65%	32%
10	1376	328	327	216	655	100%	66%	66%	33%
9	1326	310	310	206	620	100%	66%	66%	33%
8	1264	292	292	197	584	100%	67%	67%	34%
7	1212	278	274	188	552	99%	68%	69%	34%
6	1145	257	257	176	514	100%	68%	68%	34%
5	1085	239	236	170	475	99%	71%	72%	36%
4	1014	218	216	160	434	99%	73%	74%	37%
2.5-3	934	195	193	147	388	99%	75%	76%	38%
20-23 mo	825			125					
16-19 mo	790			120					
12-15 mo	737			116					
9-11 mo	730			107					

Abbreviations: F/Leg, Foot to Leg; F/Sh, Foot to Shank; F/Th, Foot to Thigh; mo, months; Sh/Th, Shank to Thigh.

Thigh, shank, and foot measures from Tilley.[4] Proportions derived by Elaine Owen.

Alignment of Joints and Segments

The International Organization for Standardization provides the following definitions for the alignment of a joint or skeletal segment in ISO 8551:2003:

- The *alignment of a joint* is "the spatial relationship between the skeletal segments which comprise the joint."[6(p 1)]
- The *alignment of a skeletal segment* is "the spatial relationship between the ends of the segment."[6(p 1)]

Although not defined by the ISO, the nomenclature for joint alignments has a general international consensus. This is not the case for the nomenclature for the alignment of segments; however, a recent consensus has started to emerge.

The Alignment of a Joint

In order to define the alignment of any joint, the *line* of the segments that comprise the joint needs to be defined. For most segments, the line of the segment may seem obvious; for others, it may seem more complex (eg, the line of the pelvis segment). When an accurate measurement is needed, accurate definitions of the lines of the segments that comprise the joint are essential. Table 19-2 outlines the definitions of the lines of the segments that are used in gait analysis.[5,7,8]

The Alignment of a Segment

The definition of the alignment of a skeletal segment provided previously allows the alignment of any segment to be measured relative to any reference in space. When standing, stepping, and walking, we are trying to maintain postures against the force of gravity, which is acting vertically downward, and we often perform these activities on a horizontal surface, the horizontal being 90 degrees relative to the vertical. Therefore, it seems helpful to define the alignment of segments relative to the vertical and the horizontal.

TABLE 19-2

NOMENCLATURE FOR JOINT AND SEGMENT ALIGNMENT

JOINT OR SEGMENT	NOMENCLATURE			
	Alignment Definition	*Sagittal Plane*	*Coronal Plane*	*Transverse Plane*
Pelvis segment	Pelvis relative to spatial reference	*Pelvic Tilt (anterior/posterior)* Angle formed between the line joining the ASIS and PSIS and the horizon. Anterior tilt is "sacrum up."	*Pelvic Obliquity (up/down)* Angle formed between a line joining the 2 ASISs and the horizon	*Pelvic Rotation (fore/back)* Angle formed between the line joining the 2 ASISs and the line perpendicular to the direction of progression
Hip joint	Thigh relative to pelvis	*Flexion/Extension* Angle formed between the long axis of the thigh and the perpendicular to the line joining the ASIS to the PSIS	*Abduction/Adduction* Angle formed between the long axis of the thigh and a line perpendicular to the line joining the 2 ASISs	*Internal/External Rotation* Angle formed between the line bisecting the medial and lateral condyles of the femur and a line joining the ASISs
Thigh segment	Thigh relative to spatial reference	*Sagittal Thigh to Vertical Angle* The angle of the thigh relative to the vertical in the sagittal plane	*Coronal Thigh to Vertical Angle* The angle of the thigh relative to the vertical in the coronal plane	*Rotation* Angle formed by the line of the femur in the transverse plane and the direction of progression
Knee joint	Shank relative to thigh	*Flexion/Extension* Angle formed between the long axis of the thigh and the long axis of the shank	*Varus/Valgus* Angle formed between the long axis of the thigh and the long axis of the shank	*Rotation* Angle formed between the transverse line of the thigh and the transverse line of the tibia
Shank segment	Shank relative to spatial reference	*Sagittal Shank to Vertical Angle* The angle of the shank relative to the vertical in the sagittal plane	*Coronal Shank to Vertical Angle* The angle of the shank relative to the vertical in the coronal plane	*Rotation* Angle formed by the line of the tibia in the transverse plane and the direction of progression
Ankle joint	Foot relative to shank	*Dorsiflexion/Plantarflexion* Angle formed between the sagittal long axis of the shank and the plantar surface of the foot. *Plantigrade* is the term used for the neutral position.	*Inversion/Eversion* Angle formed between the coronal long axis of the shank and the long axis of calcaneus	*Abduction/Adduction* Angle between the long axis of the foot and the line perpendicular to the ankle joint axis
Ankle, subtalar and foot joints	Shank relative to foot and bones of the foot relative to each other	*Pronation/Supination* The subtalar, ankle, and foot joints are all uniaxial hinge joints. Their axes are oriented obliquely to all 3 cardinal planes. The movement about the axis is, therefore, triplanar for these joints. The triplanar movements of the ankle, subtalar, and foot joints are named supination and pronation. When analyzing supination and pronation, the movement can be observed from each of the 3 cardinal planes: sagittal, coronal, and transverse. The names of the movements observed in each plane are the same as for the ankle joint. Dorsiflexion, eversion, and abduction are components of pronation and plantarflexion, inversion, and adduction are components of supination.		

(continued)

TABLE 19-2 (CONTINUED)				
NOMENCLATURE FOR JOINT AND SEGMENT ALIGNMENT				
JOINT OR SEGMENT	**NOMENCLATURE**			
	Alignment Definition	*Sagittal Plane*	*Coronal Plane*	*Transverse Plane*
Foot segment	Foot relative to spatial reference	*Sagittal Foot to Horizontal Angle* Angle of the foot relative to the horizon	*Coronal Foot to Horizontal Angle* Angle of the foot relative to the horizon	*Foot Progression Angle* Angle between the long axis of the foot and the direction of progression
MTP joints	Toes relative to foot	*Flexion/Extension*	*Inversion/Eversion*	*Abduction/Adduction*
Abbreviations: ASIS, anterior superior iliac spine; MTP, metatarsophalangeal; PSIS, posterior superior iliac spine.				

Segment to Vertical and Segment to Horizontal Angles

The angle of any segment can be measured relative to the vertical or the horizontal (see Table 19-2). It can be assessed in static standing or during movement (eg, at intervals during GC). Until recently, a wide range of phrases and terminology was used to describe segment alignment angles. However, there is an emerging consensus, at least in relation to measures of the lower leg segment, or *shank*, relative to the vertical, that the angle should be described as the *segment to vertical angle*.[9,10] It would seem sensible to adopt similar terminology to describe the alignment of segments relative to the horizontal, the *segment to horizontal angle*. In the literature, the phrase *segment to vertical angle* is currently referring to the alignment in the sagittal plane, but it can also apply to measures in the coronal plane. Any measures should, therefore, be qualified by the plane in which the measurement is being taken. The *segment to vertical* or *segment to horizontal angles* are further defined by the actual segment being measured. Some examples would be *shank to vertical angle* in the sagittal plane, *foot to horizontal angle* in the sagittal plane, and *thigh to vertical angle* in the coronal plane. In deciding whether to describe the alignment of the segment relative to the vertical or horizontal, it is most intuitive to determine whether the segment is more closely aligned to the vertical or horizontal during the activities being analyzed, which for this chapter, are the activities of standing and walking. The head, trunk, thigh, and shank are more closely aligned to the vertical, and the pelvis and foot are more closely aligned to the horizontal. So we can measure the *head to vertical angle, trunk to vertical angle, pelvis to horizontal angle, thigh to vertical angle, shank to vertical angle,* and *foot to horizontal angle* in both the sagittal and coronal planes.

Consensus is also emerging for the preferred terminology to describe the actual segment alignment angles in the sagittal plane. Vertical alignment is described as just that. Measures of the segment relative to the vertical are described as being *inclined* if the segment is leaning forward from the vertical and *reclined* if it is leaning backward from the vertical.[9-12] Horizontal alignment is described as just that. For the

pelvis, its alignment relative to the horizontal in the sagittal plane is described as *anterior tilt* if the line of the pelvis is tilted downward anteriorly from the horizontal, and *posterior tilt* if it is tilted upward from the horizontal. The foot measures relative to the horizontal are described as *toe up* if the foot is orientated to a toe up position relative to the horizontal, and *heel up* if the foot is orientated to a heel up position relative to the horizontal.[13,14] All angles are measured in degrees from the vertical or horizontal, 0 degrees describing both the vertical and horizontal.

In order to measure the alignment of a segment, the *line of the segment* needs to be determined. These are defined in Table 19-2. The measurement of the shank alignment relative to the vertical in the sagittal plane will be one of the most used alignment measures in this and other chapters. The *sagittal shank to vertical angle* is the angle of the line of the shank relative to the vertical, measured in the sagittal plane and described in degrees from the vertical, vertical being 0 degrees.[10-12]

In a study by Owen[10,11,15] the sagittal line of the shank differed from the traditional measure of the knee joint center to the ankle joint center. Instead, a line along the anterior aspect of the tibia was assessed, as this is more easily used in clinical practice, especially when measuring alignments when the patient is wearing orthoses. It is the opinion of the author of this chapter that measures of the shank relative to the vertical using this method may differ only by 1 to 2 degrees from the traditional method.

Forces, Moments, and Powers

Force

Force is defined in Table 19-3.[5] When we are undertaking the activity of standing, our body weight is applying a force to the floor. In order to support the body, the floor has to provide an equal and opposite *reaction force*. If it is not strong enough to do that, we fall through the floor. The reaction force is usually called the *ground reaction force* (GRF) although *ground reaction* can suffice.[5,7]

TABLE 19-3		
FORCE, MOMENT, AND POWER		
VARIABLE	DEFINITION	MEASUREMENT UNIT
Force	Mass × acceleration	Newton
Moment arm	Perpendicular distance of the force from the axis of rotation, which in gait is the joint center	Meter
Moment	Force × moment arm	Newton Meter
Power	Moment × angular velocity	Newton Meter/sec

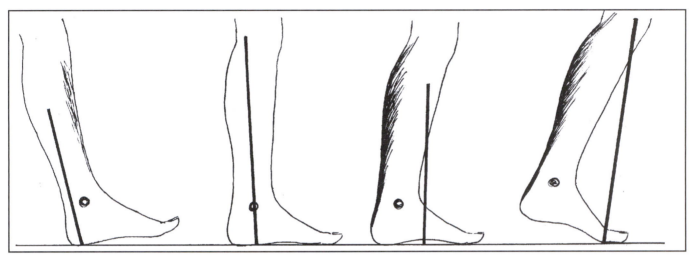

Figure 19-2. Internal and external moments occurring at the ankle joint at 4 points of the gait cycle.

Moment or Torque

When a force acts on a body, it may cause the body to turn about an axis. The "turning effect" is measured by calculating the *moment of force about the axis*. A moment is defined as "the product of the magnitude of the force and the perpendicular distance of the line of action of the force from the axis of rotation, the moment arm."[5(p 76)] The quantification of a moment is calculated by multiplying the magnitude of the force by the length of the moment arm (see Table 19-3).[5] The analysis of human body movement kinetics usually involves the estimation of internal and external moments. These need to be clearly differentiated and defined, and a clear nomenclature assigned to each type of moment.

External moments are moments created by forces external to the body, which in standing and walking is mainly the GRF, but other forces also play a part.[5,7,16,17] Using the suffix -ing will define a moment as being external (eg, *knee flexing moment*, *hip abducting moment*, and *ankle plantarflexing moment*).

Internal moments are moments created by forces internal to the body, which are mainly the forces created by musculotendinous units. Using the suffix -or will define a moment as being internal (eg, *knee flexor moment*, *hip abductor moment*, and *ankle plantarflexor moment*).

Power

Power in mechanics is defined as the rate at which a force does work, and it is calculated by multiplying the moment about a joint by the angular velocity of movement about the joint (see Table 19-3).[7,16,17] Power is different from strength.

Figure 19-2 illustrates the internal and external moments that occur at the ankle at 4 points of the GC. Both forces and moments are vectors that have a magnitude, a direction and a point of application (POA). When undertaking kinetic analysis, we need to be able to recognize normal and abnormal GRFs. The sagittal GRF of a normal adult GC can be seen in Figures 19-1 and 19-3. Observe that the POA remains at the foot, which is acting as the base of support (BOS) and moves along the foot during the GC. The magnitude of the GRF varies through the GC, with 2 peaks and a trough. The inclination of the GRF varies as well. Initially, it is leaning backward, then it becomes vertical and then it inclines forward. The GRF also varies its alignment relative to the ankle, knee, and hip joints, sometimes passing through the joint center and at other times, anteriorly or posteriorly, creating moment arms at the joints. Both, the quantity and moment arms of the GRF, vary throughout the GC.

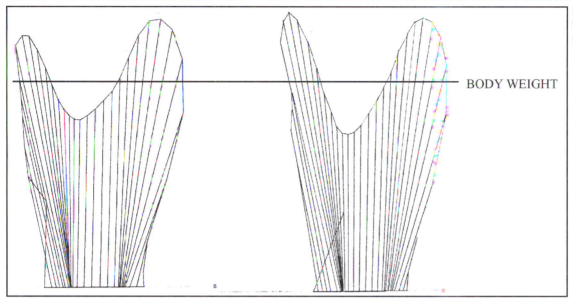

BODY WEIGHT

Figure 19-3. A "butterfly" diagram, sagittal plane.

Butterfly Diagrams

Figure 19-3 shows a sagittal plane "butterfly diagram," which displays a sequence of GRFs of a normal adult GC. The changes of POA along the foot and the magnitude and direction of the GRF are visible. The reason for the movement of the POA along the foot is obvious. Initial contact is made with the heel, the foot is then placed flat on the floor, and, by the middle of stance, body weight is equally distributed between the heel and the metatarsal heads, so the POA is in the middle of the foot (see Figures 19-1 and 19-3).[10] The heel then rises and the weight is taken on the metatarsophalangeal joints (MTPJs) and, later, the toes. The changes in the inclination of the vector are also relatively simple to explain. They are due to the anterior and posterior shear forces that occur during the GC, which are neutral when the vector is vertical, at 30% GC.[5,10,16]

There are controversies about why the magnitude of the GRF varies through stance, so a simplified explanation follows. The changing magnitude of the GRF largely relates to the movement of the body's center of mass (COM) combined with muscle activity that provides support to the limb and whole body during stance.[5,16] When we stand, the COM is relatively still and the height of the GRF represents body weight. Walking involves movement of the COM, and human walking has evolved to produce limited movement of the COM so that it only rises and falls 2 to 3 cm during a GC and is also constrained in the mediolateral direction.[5,13] When we accept weight onto the limb in early stance, the COM is dropping toward the floor and we are effectively heavier than body weight, so the GRF magnitude is greater than it is in standing. The stance limb has to produce sufficient support to prevent the COM from falling excessively downward, and once the weight has been accepted onto the stance limb, to move the COM upward again. By the middle of stance, the COM is accelerating upward and we are effectively lighter than body weight, so the GRF magnitude is smaller than it is in standing. Once the head and trunk move anteriorly to the supporting foot, the COM is accelerating downward again and we are again effectively heavier than our body weight, so the GRF magnitude is greater than it is in standing. The stance limb has to produce sufficient support to prevent the COM from falling too far.[5,16] It is important to note that children younger than 5 years of age do not reach values above their body weight for the second peak of the GRF, and even after age 5 years, they do not achieve them consistently, as detailed later in this chapter.

Moment Values and Directions

The value of a moment is calculated by multiplying the magnitude of the force by the length of the moment arm (see Table 19-3).[5] When a force passes directly through the joint center, no moment is created even if the force is very large. As soon as a moment arm is created, a moment is created.[5]

Moments are further defined by their direction, which describes the movement that would occur as a consequence of the moment.[17] Figure 19-4 illustrates the directions of the external moments that would be created by a GRF if it were acting with the illustrated moment arms. We have previously stated the importance of naming moments correctly, external moments having the convention that they end with an *-ing*. There is an exception to this rule as the coronal plane moments about the knee are usually named *varus* and *valgus*.[7]

Sagittal Plane

At the level of the hip, if the GRF action is anterior to the hip joint, an external hip flexing moment is created, and if it is acting posteriorly, an external hip extending moment is created (see Figure 19-4).[5,17] At the level of the knee, if the GRF action is anterior to the knee joint, an external knee extending moment is created, and if it is acting posteriorly, an external knee flexing moment is created. At the level of the ankle and foot, if the GRF action is anterior to the ankle or foot joints, an external dorsiflexing moment is created, and if it is acting posteriorly, an external plantarflexing moment is created.[5,17]

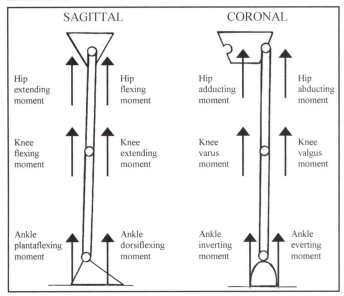

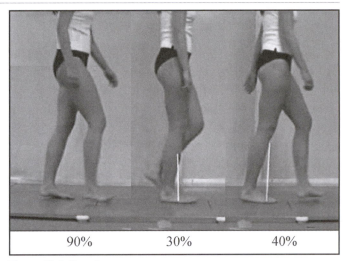

Figure 19-5. Stepping.

Figure 19-4. Directions of the external moments created by a GRF acting with the illustrated moment arms.

Coronal Plane

At the level of the hip, if the GRF action is medial to the hip joint, an external hip adducting moment is created, and if it is acting laterally, an external hip abducting moment is created (see Figure 19-4).[16] At the level of the knee, if the GRF action is medial to the knee joint, an external knee varus moment is created, and if it is acting laterally, an external knee valgus moment is created. At the level of the ankle and foot, if the GRF action is medial to the ankle or foot joints, an external inverting moment is created, and if it is acting laterally, an external everting moment is created.[17]

NORMAL STANDING, STEPPING, AND WALKING

Definitions

The International Classification of Functioning, Disability and Health (ICF)[18,19] classifies standing and walking as components of *Activity* and *Participation*. Chapter 4 of these ICF components, Mobility, provides definitions of standing and walking. Standing is categorized within *maintaining a body position*, d415, which is defined as "staying in the same position as required, such as remaining seated or remaining standing for work or for school."[18(p 135),19] Walking is categorized within *walking and moving*, and walking, d450, is defined as "moving along a surface on foot, step by step, so that one foot is always on the ground, such as when strolling, sauntering, walking forward, backward, sideways."[18(p 138),19] If 2 feet are off the ground, we are running or jumping.

To develop useful rehabilitation strategies, walking can be divided into *walking with full GCs* and *stepping*. As children, when developing walking skills, we first stand, then sway in standing, then step, and finally, develop walking with full GCs. The same process applies to habilitation or rehabilitation of walking; however, walking with full GCs may never be a possibility for some patients, so stepping is a safe and sustainable alternative walking style.

The term *gait cycle* was originally coined to describe the walking patterns of adults and the kinematics and kinetics that occur with mature stride lengths.[14] Normal adult human gait is described by anthropologists as *strider gait*, as we are the only species to have developed knee and hip extension in gait and the full terminal swing and terminal stance of a full GC, *the Big V* (see Figure 19-1, the first photo on the left). Strider gait is more efficient than the flexed gait of early hominids, and it is thought that it evolved to enable walking over long distances while carrying objects.[5]

The author of this chapter defines *stepping* as walking with an abbreviated GC, single stance finishing at 40% GC, and swing phase at 90% GC (Figure 19-5). It is different to strolling, which is slow walking with a full GC, including the terminal swing and heel strike, with short step lengths. In stepping, initial contact is with a horizontal foot, not the heel, and the shank is vertical. The stance limb then progresses until it achieves the kinematic and kinetic parameters of 40% GC, which are shank and thigh inclined, maximum stance phase knee extension and knee extending moments combined with almost maximum stance phase hip extension and hip extending moments (see Figure 19-5). The stance phase of stepping, as defined, would have some heel rise (see Figure 19-1), but in rehabilitation, it may be helpful in some circumstances to achieve stepping with the stance foot in full contact until the contralateral initial contact occurs.

Normal Gait

The normal gait of children and adults has been described in depth.[5,13,16,17,20-29] The first edition of *Human Walking* published in 1981,[13] is referenced because it is one of the few books to document segment kinematics. Sutherland et al[29-31] track the developmental changes in children from 1 to 7 years

TABLE 19-4

GAIT CYCLE SUBDIVISIONS

	GAIT CYCLE						
% GAIT CYCLE	0-10	10-30	30-50	50-60	60-73	73-86	86-100
PHASE	Stance				Swing		
SUBDIVISION	Loading Response	Midstance	Terminal Stance	Preswing	Initial Swing	Midswing	Terminal Swing

TABLE 19-5

DEFINITIONS AND TIMING OF TEMPORAL EVENTS IN THE STANCE PHASE OF GAIT

EVENT	DEFINITION	% GAIT CYCLE
Initial contact	The instant when the foot makes first contact with the ground	0
Foot flat	The first instance when the whole foot is flat on the ground	10
Temporal midstance	The instant when the head, trunk, and pelvis are directly over the supporting foot, which is at 50% of the time interval from initial contact to toe off	30
Heel off/heel rise	The instant when the heel leaves the ground	Just after 30
Contralateral initial contact	The instant when the contralateral foot makes contact with the ground	50
Toe off	The instant when the toe leaves the ground	60
Maximum knee extension	The instant in stance phase when maximum knee extension occurs	40
Maximum hip extension	The instant when maximum hip extension occurs	50

of age. All descriptions of normal gait are based on the analysis of a GC in each of the cardinal planes, sagittal, coronal, and transverse.[5,7,13,16]

Gait Cycle: Phases, Subdivisions, and Temporal Events

Human walking uses a repetitive sequence of lower limb motions, which seem complex but are, in fact, rather simple. During each stride, the limbs move through a GC, defined as the period from one *initial contact* of the foot to the next *initial contact* of the same foot. In order to make better sense of the kinematics and kinetics of the GC, authors have further divided it into phases and subdivisions.[13,16] Some have also described key temporal events, which occur at specific moments in the GC.[5,13,16] If a full sense of normal and abnormal gait patterns is to be established, it is essential to give equal importance to both the subdivisions and temporal events of the GC, and to understand how early authors chose these subdivisions and why they highlighted certain temporal events. It will also be helpful to expand current established interpretations of the GC, so that we have one that is most

meaningful for the rehabilitation of gait, standing, swaying, first steps, and stepping.

There are 2 phases to each GC: the stance phase, when the foot is in contact with the ground and the lower limb is supporting body weight, and the swing phase, when the foot is not in contact with the ground.[16] The GC subdivisions described by Perry[16] have been the most widely recognized over the recent decades (Table 19-4). They are sometimes referred to as the *Rancho Los Amigos* (RLA) *terms*. Temporal events of the stance phase occur at specific moments in the GC. They are discrete events, not subdivisions. The most commonly used terms in clinical practice are defined in Table 19-5, together with additional important temporal events.

A New Interpretation of the Gait Cycle

Perry[16] provided very meaningful subdivisions of the GC as she was mindful of both joint and segment kinematics. Some of the terminology used to name the stance phase subdivisions is not necessarily intuitive, so new subdivisions and nomenclatures have emerged. Zajac[32] and others use subdivisions termed *beginning stance* from 0 to 20% GC, *midstance* from 20 to 40% GC, and *late stance* from 40 to 60% GC.

	STANCE PHASE						
% GC	0-10%	10-20%	20-30%	30%	30-40%	40-50%	50-60%
RLA TERMINOLOGY PERRY[16]	Double support	Single support					Double support
	Loading response	Midstance			Terminal stance		Preswing
NEW TERMINOLOGY OWEN[11,12,34,35]	Entrance into midstance			Temporal midstance	Exit from midstance		
	Double support entry to temporal midstance	Single support entry to temporal midstance		Temporal midstance	Single support exit from temporal midstance		Double support exit from temporal midstance

TABLE 19-6

THE FIT OF NEW TERMINOLOGY SUGGESTED BY OWEN[11,12,34,35] WITH STANCE PHASE SUBDIVISIONS PROVIDED BY PERRY[16]

Abbreviations: GC, gait cycle; RLA, Rancho Los Amigos.

Baker[7] divides single stance into 3 subdivisions, called *early*, *middle*, and *late single stance*, to match the 3 swing phase subdivisions occurring at the same time. However, these new subdivisions do not divide stance phase into useful subdivisions for rehabilitation professionals as they do not coincide with key temporal events for segment and joint kinematics. To facilitate a better understanding of the GC, particularly so that improved rehabilitation strategies can be developed, a fresh look at the temporal events and additional naming of the subdivisions may help. Perry's subdivisions[16] remain the most helpful, especially if the segment kinematics and temporal events that created the subdivisions are given a greater emphasis.

Perry's stance phase subdivisions are related primarily to foot kinematics.[16] *Loading response* occurs from *initial contact* with a heel to *foot flat*; during *midstance*, the foot remains in full contact with the floor; the start of *terminal stance* sees the heel rise; and the end of *terminal stance* coincides with the contralateral *initial contact*. *Preswing* ends with *toe off*. The swing phase is divided largely by changes in the shank and thigh kinematics.[16]

Other temporal events are also important. *Temporal midstance* is a key event in the GC, and it occurs exactly in the middle of the stance phase, at 30% GC (see Figures 19-1 and 19-5).[33] At this instance, the head and trunk are positioned directly over the foot.[10,34] Prior to *temporal midstance*, the head and trunk are posterior to the supporting foot, and after *temporal midstance*, they are anterior to the supporting foot. There are also key kinetic features of *temporal midstance*, which will be discussed later. *Temporal midstance* is very akin to standing, a position from which we take our first steps in childhood and in rehabilitation.[10,34] First steps or stepping,

rather than walking, involve moving from a *temporal midstance* position while standing on 2 legs, through a partial terminal stance on the stance limb and a short swing phase in the swing limb. As walking skills develop, in both young children and those in rehabilitation, the full GC develops to include a full terminal stance and terminal swing, as detailed later in this chapter. The relevance and importance of *temporal midstance* will become clearer later in this chapter and also in a subsequent chapter relating to the biomechanical optimization of orthoses for the rehabilitation of standing, stepping, and gait.

Naming the GC around *temporal midstance* is more intuitive, especially for the development of rehabilitation strategies.[10-12,34,35] The proportion of the stance phase prior to *temporal midstance* can be described as *entrance to midstance*, and the proportion after *temporal midstance*, *exit from midstance*. As there are double and single support subdivisions of the GC both prior to and after *temporal midstance*, these subdivisions can be named *double support entry to midstance*, *single support entry to midstance*, *single support exit from midstance*, and *double support exit from midstance*.[32] The new terminology sits well within Perry's subdivisions of the stance phase of gait, but creates a new emphasis for the significance of *temporal midstance*, placing it "center stage" (Table 19-6).

Normal Gait Overview

Various authors teased out what they considered to be the most important qualities of normal walking. Perry[16] described 5 attributes or prerequisites for normal gait. These are stability in stance, foot clearance in swing, prepositioning of the foot for initial contact, adequate step length, and conservation of energy.[16] One attribute that contributes to the others is *stability in stance*. Kepple[36] described 5 major functions of the motor tasks used to transport the body in human gait. These included forward progression, which is the generation or maintenance of forward velocity; support of the upper body by preventing lower limb collapse during stance; balance of the body; control of foot trajectory during swing; and shock absorption.[36] All of these are important contributors to the production of normal gait and, in addition, we need to consider the accelerations and decelerations of segments and joints, pendular and ballistic movements, and the rhythms of gait.

While segment kinematics is of equal or greater importance to the understanding of gait, the major emphasis of gait analysis in recent decades was on joint kinematics.[3,8] The early pioneers of gait analysis did describe segment kinematics and made important inferences from their observations.[13] The current description of gait will give an equal emphasis to joint and segment kinematics.

When we observe segment kinematics through a whole GC, we see that the trunk translates forward in a vertical alignment with uniform angular velocity.[13,16,37] In stance, the shank and thigh segments always move in a clockwise direction, but not with a uniform angular velocity.[10,13,16,17,22,37-39] In the midstance subdivision, the angular velocity of the shank reduces, and the shank is almost stationary and in an inclined alignment at temporal midstance. The thigh segment has slower angular velocities in loading response and the latter part of terminal stance while its angular velocity is faster in midstance and early terminal stance.[10,13,16,17,22,37-39] The slowing of the angular velocity of the shank, coupled with its optimal inclined alignment at temporal midstance, facilitates thigh kinematics and the production of knee and hip extension and stabilizing extending moments during terminal stance.[10] The foot is horizontal and in full contact with the floor during the midstance subdivision. This is a stable alignment of the foot segment, which, when coupled with a virtually stationary shank at temporal midstance, provides a very stable distal BOS. The shank at this time is in a 10 to 12 degrees inclined alignment, which places the knee joint center over the center of the foot, a further contribution to stability at temporal midstance.[10-12] We must be aware that there is no place in the GC when both the shank and the thigh are vertical. The shank passes the vertical at approximately 10% GC, and the thigh at 30% GC. This is contrary to some traditional teaching, which states that the shank and the thigh are both vertical at temporal midstance.[10] This theory was established prior to objective segment data being available and, unfortunately, has persisted.

The increasing understanding of the importance of segment kinematics developed in recent years.[20-22,25,26,40-44] Recent investigators found that segment kinematics remain the same while walking both forward and backward.[37] This makes sense as when walking, we are essentially "stacking" the segments up against gravity in the most effective and efficient alignments. The interaction of the foot, shank, and thigh segments was studied, in both children and adults, so that the maturation of these interactions could be established.[23-26,40,44,45] The development of gait is discussed later. Segment kinematics was also central to the development of "roll over shapes," which are used to investigate normal barefoot walking, walking in footwear, and walking with orthoses and prostheses.[38,46-48]

A Video Vector Description of Normal Gait

This section will provide a video vector description of gait to which clinicians can easily refer when using video cameras or video vector systems for their gait analysis sessions. The phases, subdivisions, and temporal events of the GC are pictorially displayed (see Figure 19-1), and Tables 19-7 through 19-12 confirm the sagittal kinematics, kinetics, and muscle actions that are occurring. Because the analysis performed by these methods provides views in only the sagittal and coronal planes, the transverse plane and triplanar analyses have to be extrapolated from these 2 views and visual observations. These can be combined with clinical assessment measures and tracings of *foot progression angles* to make clinical judgements. The terms *temporal midstance*, *entry*, and *exit* are used, and the RLA equivalent terms are also provided.

Coronal Plane Kinematics, Kinetics, and Muscle Actions

There are only small joint and segment movements of the foot, ankle, shank, knee, hip, and pelvis in the coronal plane.[5,16,28] All are approximately 5 degrees. The GRF force remains medial to these joints throughout the stance phase, with small changes in moment arms. The moments are, therefore, constant external hip adducting moments, knee varus moments, and ankle and foot inverting moments. The hip abductor musculotendinous units (MTUs) have to create internal hip abductor moments to counteract the external hip adducting moment. Ligaments and MTUs counteract the external moments at the knee, ankle, and foot.[13,16]

Transverse Plane Kinematics, Kinetics, and Muscle Actions

Similar to the coronal plane, there are only small movements of joints and segments in the transverse plane of approximately 5 to 10 degrees at the foot, ankle, shank, knee, thigh, hip, and pelvis.[13,16] The foot, once in the full contact with the floor, from *foot flat* to *heel off*, has an alignment relative to the *line of progression*. This angle is called the *foot progression angle* and is measured between the *long axis of the foot*, usually defined as "a line from a bisect of the transverse view of the heel to between the second and third toes"[13(p 21)] and the *line of progression*, which is defined as "the line of travel in which the person is walking."[5(p 49)] The foot progression angle varies with age, becoming more externally rotated as children mature skeletally.[49] The external and internal moments are also small in the transverse plane.

Full descriptions of coronal and transverse kinematics and kinetics can be found elsewhere.[5,13,16,28]

	TABLE 19-7	
	SAGITTAL PLANE KINEMATICS, KINETICS, AND MUSCLE ACTIONS: STANCE PHASE SUBDIVISION, 0% TO 10% GAIT CYCLE	
	DOUBLE SUPPORT ENTRY TO TEMPORAL MIDSTANCE	
	RLA Loading Response	
	Temporal events occurring in the subdivision	
	Initial Contact 0% GC	
	Foot Flat 10% GC	
	Kinematics[a]	*Kinetics*
Head and trunk	Vertical	
Pelvis segment	Anterior tilt approximately 10	
Hip joint	Reducing flexion 35 to 30	GRF ANT to hip
		Flexing moment initially increasing and then decreasing
Thigh segment	Reducing recline 25 to 20	
Knee joint	Increasing flexion 5 to 15/20	GRF ANT to knee switching to POST to knee
	Dependent on gait velocity	Extending moment switching to flexing moment at 5% GC and then increasing flexing moment
Shank segment	Reducing recline 20 to 10/5	
Ankle joint	Plantigrade/5 plantarflexion to plantarflexion 5/10	GRF POST to ankle moving toward ankle joint
		Plantarflexing moment reducing to 0 by 10% GC
Foot segment	25 toe up to horizontal	GRF POA at heel at IC then moves along foot to 25% of foot length by 10% GC
MTP joints	25 extension to neutral'	
Muscle actions	The major hip extensors and hamstrings act concentrically to oppose the external hip flexing moment and stabilize the hip. The vasti act eccentrically to oppose the external knee flexing moment and provide controlled knee flexion. The rectus femoris is not acting at this time. The dorsiflexors act eccentrically to oppose the external ankle plantarflexing moment and produce controlled plantarflexion and lowering of the foot to the floor. The action of the dorsiflexors also pulls the shank forward to a less inclined position.	

Abbreviations: ANT, anterior to joint center; GC, gait cycle; GRF, ground reaction force; MTP, metatarsophalangeal; POA, point of application; POST, posterior to joint center; RLA, Rancho Los Amigos.

[a] Numbers (besides %) indicate degrees.

The Rockers of Gait

The term *rocker* or *rockers* is commonly used in descriptions of gait.[3,16,28,50] However, there has been increasing confusion as to what a *rocker* is, where the divisions between rockers occur, the kinematics and muscle actions that occur in each rocker, and the terminology used to describe them.[50] Reviewing the history of the rockers will help us understand how these confusions developed. It will also enable us to define and quantify them in a way that is most useful for developing rehabilitation strategies, orthoses, and prostheses.

The rockers of gait are illustrated in Figure 19-6. They were originally described by Perry[51] in 1974, and she attributed their purpose to the production of "tibial advancement"

during stance, an essential element in forward progression of the body during the GC. The rockers Perry[51] described involved both joints and segments, so her description included shank and foot segments, ankle and foot joints, and also muscle actions. When she first described the rockers of gait, she allocated them to just 3 of the RLA subdivisions of the GC: *loading response*, *midstance*, and *terminal stance*. No rocker was allocated to *preswing*, the fourth subdivision of stance. They were, therefore, attributed to only 50% of the GC. The rockers were given names, not numbers, with the exception of the first rocker. She described *initial* or *first rocker* as occurring during loading response, then the *mid-stance rocker* occurring during midstance, and finally, *terminal rocker* occurring during terminal stance. She later renamed

TABLE 19-8		
SAGITTAL PLANE KINEMATICS, KINETICS, AND MUSCLE ACTIONS: STANCE PHASE SUBDIVISION, 10% TO 30% GAIT CYCLE		
SINGLE SUPPORT ENTRY TO TEMPORAL MIDSTANCE		
RLA Mid Stance		
Temporal events occurring in the subdivision		
Foot Flat 10% GC		
Temporal Midstance 30% GC		
	Kinematics[a]	*Kinetics*
Head and trunk	Vertical	
Pelvis segment	Anterior tilt approximately 10	
Hip joint	Reducing flexion 30 to 5/10	GRF ANT to hip
		Reducing flexing moment
Thigh segment	20 reclined to vertical	
Knee joint	Reducing flexion 15/20 to 10	GRF POST to knee
		Reducing flexing moment
Shank segment	5/10 reclined to 10 inclined	
Ankle joint	5/10 plantarflexion to 10 dorsiflexion	GRF moving ANT to ankle
		Increasing ankle dorsiflexing moment
Foot segment	Horizontal	GRF POA moves along foot to 50% foot by 30% GC
MTP joints	Neutral	
Muscle actions	The major hip extensors and hamstring act concentrically to oppose the external hip flexing moment and reduce hip flexion. The vasti act concentrically to oppose the external knee flexing moment and reduce knee flexion. The rectus femoris is not acting at this time. Once the shank has passed vertical, the plantarflexors act eccentrically to oppose the external dorsiflexing moment and control the rate of shank inclination.	

Abbreviations: ANT, anterior; to joint center GC, gait cycle; GRF, ground reaction force; MTP, metatarsophalangeal; POA, point of application; POST, posterior to joint center; RLA, Rancho Los Amigos.

[a] Numbers (besides %) indicate degrees.

them, according to the pivot of each rocker: *heel rocker* during loading response, *ankle rocker* during midstance, and *forefoot rocker* during terminal stance. She also extended the description of the forefoot rocker to include preswing.[16]

It seems that the decision to extend the forefoot rocker to include both terminal stance and preswing was in response to debates at that time, and still ongoing, about the role of the calf muscle during the GC.[52] However, including both of these subdivisions in one rocker has led to a number of misunderstandings due to the lack of recognition of major differences in the kinematics and muscle actions occurring in terminal stance and preswing. Attributing different rocker mechanisms and names to each of the 4 subdivisions allows clarity to be restored (Table 19-13).[50] Perry also recently described a *toe-rocker*, which occurs in preswing.[28,53] This is helpful as it is not only a more accurate descriptor of the

fourth pivot but also differentiates the rockers occurring in terminal swing and preswing.

As gait analysis became less interested in the movement and function of segments and more oriented to the analysis of joint movement, the rockers of gait became reinterpreted as predominately relating to ankle joint kinematics and referred to as *first, second,* and *third ankle rockers*.[3] First rocker was described as the ankle joint plantarflexion that occurs during loading response, second rocker as the subsequent ankle joint dorsiflexion to its maximum at 40% to 45% GC in terminal stance, and third rocker as the ankle joint movement from the maximum dorsiflexion in terminal stance to maximum plantarflexion at the end of preswing. However, confining interpretation of the rockers to ankle joint kinematics alone presents a number of problems, as it does not recognize several significant factors.[50]

Table 19-9

Sagittal Plane Kinematics, Kinetics, and Muscle Actions: Stance Phase Temporal Event at 30% Gait Cycle

TEMPORAL MIDSTANCE

RLA Mid Stance Terminal Stance transition

	Kinematics[a]	Kinetics
		GRF is vertical, lower than body weight, at its lowest in GC "midstance trough"
Head and trunk	Vertical	
Pelvis segment	Anterior tilt approximately 10	
Hip joint	10 flexion	GRF vertical and aligned at hip joint Neutral moment
Thigh segment	Vertical	
Knee joint	10 flexion	GRF vertical and aligned at knee joint Neutral moment
Shank segment	10 inclined	
Ankle joint	10 dorsiflexion	GRF vertical and ANT to ankle Dorsiflexing moment
Foot segment	Horizontal	GRF POA at 50% foot length
MTP joints	Neutral	
Muscle actions	Once the external moments at the knee and hip have reduced to neutral moments, muscle actions are not required to stabilize these joints. The plantarflexors act to oppose the external dorsiflexing moment. They control the alignment and angular velocity of the shank, which is almost stationary at this time.	

Abbreviations: ANT, anterior to joint center; GC, gait cycle; GRF, ground reaction force; MTP, metatarsophalangeal; POA, point of application; RLA, Rancho Los Amigos

[a] Numbers (besides %) indicate degrees.

Figure 19-6. The 4-event model of the "Rockers of Gait." (Adapted with permission from Owen E. The importance of being earnest about shank and thigh kinematics especially when using ankle-foot orthoses. *Prosthet Orthot Int.* 2010;34(3):254-269. Copyright © 2010 by SAGE.)

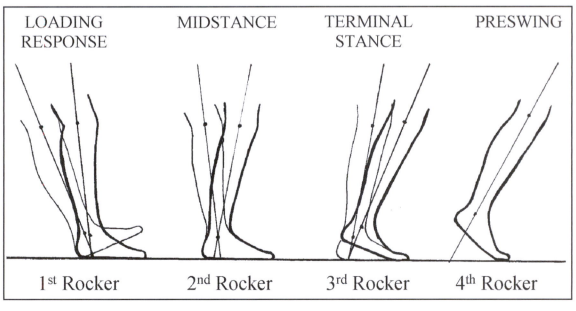

LOADING RESPONSE   MIDSTANCE   TERMINAL STANCE   PRESWING

1st Rocker   2nd Rocker   3rd Rocker   4th Rocker

TABLE 19-10

SAGITTAL PLANE KINEMATICS, KINETICS, AND MUSCLE ACTIONS: STANCE PHASE SUBDIVISION, 30% TO 50% GAIT CYCLE

SINGLE SUPPORT EXIT FROM TEMPORAL MIDSTANCE
RLA Terminal Stance
Temporal events occurring in the subdivision
Temporal Midstance at 30% GC
Maximum knee extension at 40% GC
Contralateral shank vertical at 40% GC
Maximum hip extension at 50% GC

	Kinematics[a]	Kinetics
Head and trunk	Vertical	
Pelvis segment	Anterior tilt approximately 10	
Hip joint	10 flexion to 10 extension	GRF increasing POST to hip
		Increasing hip extending moment
Thigh segment	Vertical 25 incline	
Knee joint	Reducing then increasing flexion 10 to 5 at 40% GC to 10 at 50% GC	GRF moves ANT to knee reaching patella by 40% GC
		It then returns to a less ANT position
		Increasing then decreasing knee extending moment
Shank segment	Increasing incline 10 to 25	
Ankle joint	Ankle remains in dorsiflexion	GRF increasing ANT to ankle
	It hardly moves and is quasi-stiff increasing then decreasing dorsiflexion 10 to 12 to 7 at 50% GC	Increasing dorsiflexing moment
Foot segment	Horizontal at 30% GC	GRF POA moves forward to MTP joints at 72% foot and remains there
	Heel rise at 31% GC	
	Heel up 20/25 at 50% GC	
MTP joints	Neutral to 20 extension	
Muscle actions	The hip and knee joints are now stabilized by external extending moments. The plantarflexors act to oppose the increasing external ankle dorsiflexing moment, creating "quasi-stiffness" at the ankle joint in dorsiflexion and heel rise. The plantarflexors act eccentrically through most of TST, controlling the rate of increasing dorsiflexion, then at 40-45% GC, their action changes to concentric to reduce ankle dorsiflexion.	

Abbreviations: ANT, anterior; to joint center GC, gait cycle; GRF, ground reaction force; MTP, metatarsophalangeal; PCA, point of application; POST, posterior to joint center; RLA, Rancho Los Amigos; TST, terminal stance.

[a] Numbers (besides %) indicate degrees.

Firstly, the original purpose of describing the rockers was to explain the mechanisms by which tibial advancement is produced.[51] It is not produced by the ankle joint movement alone. Foot segment and MTPJ kinematics are large contributors. Secondly, the original differentiation between the second and third rockers was heel rise.[16,51] This occurs at just after 30% GC at the start of terminal stance, the pivot transferring from the ankle to the forefoot.[14,16,54] The "ankle rockers model" ignores foot kinematics and has second rocker ending at 45% GC, which does not coincide with heel rise.[3,50] Thirdly, ankle joint kinematics is very different in terminal stance when compared to preswing in both position and speed of movement.[16,50,55] During terminal stance, the ankle is virtually locked, "quasi-stiff," in dorsiflexion. In preswing, the ankle joint moves very fast from a position of dorsiflexion to plantarflexion. The differences in ankle

TABLE 19-11

SAGITTAL PLANE KINEMATICS, KINETICS, AND MUSCLE ACTIONS: STANCE PHASE SUBDIVISION, 50% TO 60% GAIT CYCLE

DOUBLE SUPPORT EXIT FROM TEMPORAL MIDSTANCE

RLA Pre-Swing

Temporal events occurring in the subdivision
Maximum hip extension at 50% GC
Contralateral Initial Contact at 50% GC
Toe Off at 60% GC

	Kinematics[a]	Kinetics
Head and trunk	Vertical	
Pelvis segment	Anterior tilt approximately 10	
Hip joint	Reducing extension 10 to 5	GRF POST to hip moving toward hip
		Decreasing hip extending moment
Thigh segment	Reducing incline 25 to 10	
Knee joint	Increasing flexion 10 to 40	GRF switches from ANT to knee to POST to knee
		Knee extending moment switching to knee flexing moment
Shank segment	Increasing incline 25 to 45	
Ankle joint	7 dorsiflexion to plantigrade 55% GC to 20 plantarflexion 60% GC	GRF ANT to ankle
		Rapidly reducing ankle dorsiflexing moment
Foot segment	Heel up 20/25 to 70	GRF POA moves to toes
MTP joints	20 to 55 extension	
Muscle actions	The major hip flexors act concentrically to oppose the hip extending moment and to reduce hip extension. The rectus femoris acts proximally to assist the hip flexors, and distally it acts to oppose the external knee flexing moment and to control the rate of knee flexion. There is a debate about the actions of the plantarflexors in preswing. The emerging consensus is that the gastrocnemius MTU is passively shortening rather than actively shortening. It is acting as a spring, by the recoil of the previously stretched tendoachilles, once weight is transferred to the contralateral leg. The shortening of the MTU by the spring action moves the ankle rapidly from a position of dorsiflexion to plantarflexion and also flexes the knee.	

Abbreviations: ANT, anterior to joint center; GC, gait cycle; GRF, ground reaction force; MTP, metatarsophalangeal; MTU, musculotendinous unit; POST, posterior to joint center; RLA, Rancho Los Amigos.

[a] Numbers (besides %) indicate degrees.

kinematics need to be recognized, especially as the quasi-stiffness of the ankle joint in terminal stance is essential for the heel rise and for the ability to achieve maximum knee and hip extension in gait.

We can conclude that an "ankle rockers model" can be misleading and that a 3-event segment and joint model is inadequate.[50] These lead to erroneous understandings of gait and consequent inappropriate or suboptimal rehabilitation strategies. A 4-event model, which includes both joints and segments, is preferable.[50] It matches the 4 subdivisions of the GC that were originally determined by acknowledging significant temporal events in segment and joint kinematics, especially foot segment kinematics. Any model should include pivot points and the kinematics of all segments and joints involved. A 4-event model and a definition of the rockers have been proposed (see Table 19-13 and Figure 19-6).[10,50] The rockers are defined as "the mechanisms of the ankle and foot that produce shank kinematic during stance phase of the GC."[50(p S49)] First rocker uses a heel lever to move the foot to the floor, the angular velocity of the movement

TABLE 19-12

SAGITTAL PLANE KINEMATICS, KINETICS, AND MUSCLE ACTIONS: SWING PHASE SUBDIVISIONS, 60% TO 100% GAIT CYCLE

	SWING PHASE		
RLA Terminology	Initial Swing 60-73% GC	Mid Swing 73-87% GC	Terminal Swing 87-100% GC
		Kinematics[a]	
Head and trunk	Vertical	Vertical	Vertical
Pelvis segment	Anterior tilt approximately 10	Anterior tilt approximately 10	Anterior tilt approximately 10
Hip joint	5 extension to 20 flexion	20 to 35 flexion	35 flexion
Thigh segment	10 inclined to 10 reclined	10 reclined to 25 reclined	25 reclined
Knee joint	40 to 60 flexion	60 to 30 flexion	30 to 5 flexion
Shank segment	45 to 60 inclined	60 inclined to vertical	Vertical to 20 reclined
Ankle joint	20 plantarflexion to plantigrade	Plantigrade	Plantigrade
Foot segment	70 to 60 heel up	60 to horizontal	Horizontal to 20 toe up
MTP joints	Neutral	5 extension	5 to 25 extension
Muscle actions	Major hip flexors act concentrically to produce hip flexion. The rectus femoris acts proximally to assist the hip flexors, and distally it acts to control the rate of knee flexion. Ankle dorsiflexors act to bring the ankle to a neutral plantigrade position.	No muscle actions are required at the hip and knee as the movements occurring are largely ballistic. The ankle dorsiflexors act to support the weight of the foot and to hold the ankle at a neutral plantigrade position.	Major hip extensors and hamstrings act eccentrically or isometrically to prevent excessive flexion of the hip from the ballistic movement of the thigh. Hamstrings also act eccentrically to prevent excessive extension of the knee that may occur due to the ballistic movement of the shank on the thigh. The 3 vasti of the quadriceps act concentrically to facilitate the hamstrings action as hip extensors. The rectus femoris is not acting at this time. The dorsiflexors act isometrically to maintain the ankle plantigrade.

Abbreviations: GC, gait cycle; MTP, metatarsophalangeal; RLA, Rancho Los Amigos.

[a] Numbers (besides %) indicate degrees.

being controlled by the anterior tibial muscle actions, which also pull the shank forward to a less reclined or near vertical alignment by foot flat at 10% GC. In second rocker, the foot is in full contact with the floor, and tibial advancement occurs through dorsiflexion at the ankle joint, the calf muscles restraining the forward movement of the shank once it has passed vertical, and shank alignment becoming 10 to 12 degrees inclined and relatively stationary by temporal midstance at 30% GC.[50] Tibial advancement continues in third rocker by heel rise and MTPJ extension, the ankle joint being virtually locked in approximately 10 degrees dorsiflexion by calf muscle activity, quasi-stiffness of the ankle joint.[55] In fourth rocker, tibial advancement occurs by a combination of ankle joint motion, from dorsiflexion to plantarflexion, and MTPJ extension increasing heel rise.[50]

The importance of the rockers is that they dictate proximal kinematics and kinetics and are integral to the production of support, forward progression, stability, and mobility.[16] Distal segment kinematics is largely responsible for the overall kinematics and kinetics of standing, stepping, and gait. (Normal distal produces normal proximal and abnormal distal produces abnormal proximal.[10,11]) Understanding each of the rockers of gait and incorporating normal segment alignment strategies into all rehabilitation and orthotic interventions for standing, stepping and walking is essential.

	LR	**MST**	**TST**	**PSW**
Proposed Name	1st ROCKER	2nd ROCKER	3rd ROCKER	4th ROCKER
Pivot	Heel	Ankle	Forefoot/MTPJs	Forefoot/toes
Ankle Joint	Plantigrade to 5 degrees plantarflexion	5 degrees plantarflexion to 10 degrees dorsiflexion	Virtually locked in dorsiflexion 10 to 12 to 7 degrees	7 degrees dorsiflex to 20 degrees plantarflexion
MTPJs	Dorsiflex 25 to 0 degrees	0 to 0 degrees	0 degrees to dorsiflex 25 degrees	Dorsiflex 25 to 55 degrees
Shank Kinematics Degrees Relative to Vertical	20 to 5 degrees recline	5 degrees recline to 10 degrees incline	10 to 25 degrees Incline	25 to 50 degrees incline
Foot Kinematics	20 degrees toe up to horizontal	Horizontal	Horizontal to 20 degrees heel up	20 degrees heel up to 60 degrees heel up

TABLE 19-13

A FOUR EVENT MODEL OF THE ROCKERS OF GAIT PROPOSED BY OWEN

Abbreviations: LR, loading response; MST, midstance; MTPJs, metatarsophalangeal joints; PSW, preswing; TST, terminal stance.

Adapted from *Gait and Posture*, 30S, Owen E, How should we define the rockers of gait and are there three or four? 49. Copyright © (2009) with permission from Elsevier.

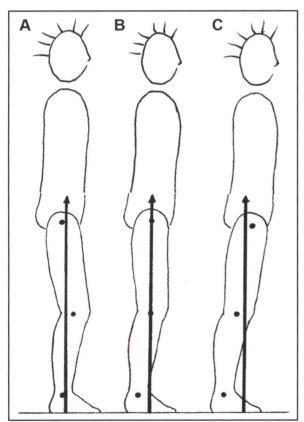

Figure 19-7. Optimal foot and shank alignment for anterior and posterior translation of a vertical trunk and switching of external moments at knee and hip joints. Each has the same alignment for foot, shank, and trunk: foot horizontal, shank to vertical angle 10 to 12 degrees inclined, trunk vertical. Thigh to vertical angle varies in each: (A) reclined, (B) vertical, and (C) inclined. Ground reaction force and resultant moments are also illustrated.

FROM "STABLE STANDING" TO "ROCK AND ROLL WALKING"

Previously in this chapter, standing, stepping, and walking were defined and the GC was interpreted in a new way. Temporal midstance was given center stage, the period of stance phase prior to *temporal midstance* was named *entrance to temporal midstance*, and the period after, *exit from temporal midstance*, or *entrance* and *exit* for short. The kinematics and kinetics of temporal midstance of a GC are akin to those of standing, and the periods just prior to and following temporal midstance are akin to swaying in standing. The difference in walking is that they are being achieved while weight bearing on just one leg.

Whether we are standing, swaying, stepping, or walking with a full GC, a common feature is that the HAT, which is the combined segments of the head, arms, trunk, and pelvis, is maintained in a vertical alignment in the sagittal plane (see Figures 19-1 and 19-7).[10,13,16] At temporal midstance, the HAT is directly over the foot, which is in full contact with the floor and is acting as the BOS. During *entrance*, the HAT is posterior to the foot, and during *exit*, anterior to the foot. Because the movements of the HAT in the 3 cardinal planes are very small and those of the lower limbs are large when walking, the HAT has been aptly called the *passenger unit*, and the combined segments of the lower limbs and pelvis, the *locomotor unit*.[16]

The distal segment alignments of the shank and foot will dictate the more proximal alignments of the thigh and the HAT.[10,11] Therefore, we need to examine which alignments create the conditions that make vertical translation of the HAT possible, and also how nonoptimal distal alignments can adversely influence proximal alignments. Examining the similarities between stable standing and temporal midstance and the conditions required for standing, stepping, and walking with full GCs not only improves our understanding of normal movements, but also helps develop rehabilitation strategies.

Stable Standing and Swaying

Figure 19-8 illustrates 9 standing conditions.[10,11] The segments have normal proportions. Each condition has a different combination of shank to vertical angle (SVA) and thigh to vertical angle (TVA). In all 9 conditions, the foot is aligned horizontally in full contact with the floor and is facing forward as in normal standing.[10,11]

The 3 SVA alignment conditions are as follows:

1. SVA 0 degrees or vertical that places the knee joint center directly over the ankle joint, which is one-quarter of the way along the foot
2. SVA 10 to 12 degrees inclined, which places the knee joint center over the middle of the foot and the patella over the MTPJs
3. SVA 20 degrees inclined, which places the patella over the end of the toes[10,11]

Combined with these 3 SVA alignments are 3 TVA alignments: reclined, vertical, and inclined. The resultant alignment of the HAT for each combination of SVA and TVA is also indicated. All 9 conditions in Figure 19-8 can be demonstrated by standing and adopting the 3 SVAs and in each SVA attempting to achieve a reclined, vertical, or inclined TVA.[10,11]

Rules of how distal segment alignments dictate proximal segment alignments become clear when we create Figure 19-8.[10,11] We discover that there is only one SVA alignment condition that will allow a thigh to become inclined—an essential condition for forward translation of a vertical HAT—and only one that will allow both forward and backward translation of a vertical HAT.[10,11] One reason for this is that to maintain balance in standing, the vertical projection of the COM must remain within the BOS, which in standing, is from mid-heel to MTPJs. Greatest stability is felt when the center of pressure (COP) is in the center of the BOS, rather than at the margins, and when it can freely move within the BOS.

A condition for translating a vertical HAT is that the TVA can become both inclined and reclined, and this is only possible in the SVA of 10 to 12 degrees incline condition.[10,11] With this SVA alignment, the thigh can move between vertical, inclined, and reclined TVA alignments and translate a vertical HAT. It is not possible to do this with either SVA

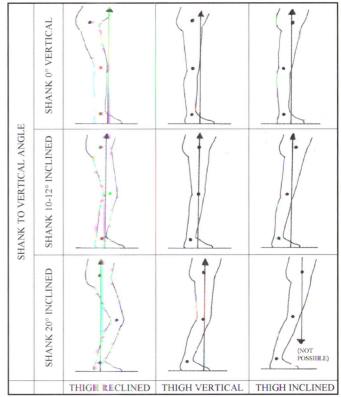

Figure 19-8. Nine conditions for foot, shank, and thigh alignments and resultant trunk, joint, and ground reaction force alignments. (Reprinted with permission from Owen E. The importance of being earnest about shank and thigh kinematics especially when using ankle-foot orthoses. *Prosthet Orthot Int.* 2010;34(3):254-269. Copyright © 2010 by SAGE.)

vertical or 20 degrees inclined. When the SVA is vertical, the thigh can only become inclined if the knees are able to hyperextend, which is undesirable. When the SVA is 20 degrees inclined, it is not possible to move the thigh to an inclined position as the COM would move outside the BOS. The thigh can move no further than a vertical alignment if the COM is to remain within the BOS. The TVA can become reclined in all 3 SVA alignment conditions. However, the HAT can only remain vertical with inclined SVAs. When the SVA is vertical and the TVA reclined, the HAT has to lean forward to maintain the COM within the BOS.[10,11]

The only SVA alignment condition in Figure 19-8 that allows forward and backward translation of a vertical trunk is 10 to 12 degrees incline.[10,11] It is likely that the range is 7 to 15 degrees incline with SVA 10 to 12 degrees incline being the optimal alignment.[11] Anthropometric measures of the length of the shank and foot mean that this alignment brings the knee joint center over the middle of the foot.[10,11] This provides a stable triangular distal base as the thigh moves from vertical to reclined and inclined alignments and translates a vertical HAT.[10,11]

Not only is the SVA of 10 to 12 degrees inclined the optimum SVA alignment condition that will allow forward translation of a vertical HAT, it is also the alignment that will allow the COP to remain easily within the BOS and allow moment switches from combined external extending moments at the hip and knee to combined external flexing moments at these joints, and vice versa.[10,11] First, let us look at how these alignments create stability through the positioning of the COM and COP in relation to the supporting foot and then the moments generated.

The position and movement of the COM dictates the position of the COP of the GRF on the foot, which is acting as the BOS.[17] When the SVA is 10 to 12 degrees inclined and the HAT and the thigh are vertical and aligned directly over the foot, the COM is in the middle of the BOS and standing is most stable. When the vertical HAT translates anteriorly and posteriorly, when swaying voluntarily or from disturbance, the COM can remain safely within the BOS as it moves forward and backward along the foot. The HAT has to translate a considerable distance anteriorly or posteriorly for the COP to reach the margins of the BOS.

The alignment of the segments in conjunction with the alignment of the GRF will determine the moment arms and moments generated at the ankle, knee, and hip. Figure 19-7 illustrates 3 scenarios: A, B, and C.[10,11] Video vector images of the same 3 scenarios, taken from a gait laboratory, are available.[10,11] In Figure 19-7B, when the HAT and thigh are vertically aligned and directly over the foot, the COP is in the middle of the foot and the GRF acts through the knee and hip joint centers, so the moments at the knee and hip are neutral. When the vertical HAT translates anteriorly and posteriorly (see Figure 19-7A and C), the COP moves to the anterior and posterior limits of the BOS. When the HAT translates posteriorly, the GRF is aligned posterior to the knee and anterior to the hip, creating destabilizing external flexing moments at the knee and hip, which have to be resisted by internal moments generated by muscles. When the vertical HAT translates anteriorly, the GRF is aligned anterior to the knee and posterior to the hip, creating stabilizing external extending knee and hip moments, with the generation of internal moments by muscles not being required. Stability at the knee and hip is, therefore, created by the optimal alignment of the segments, which, in turn, optimally positions the COM and GRF relative to the joints. There is, however, a large external ankle dorsiflexing moment, which has to be resisted by an internal ankle plantarflexor moment, created by calf muscle action, if the SVA is to be maintained at the optimal 10 to 12 degrees incline. SVAs greater than 20 degrees will not allow the thigh incline, anterior translation of the vertical HAT, and the creation of stabilizing external knee and hip extending moments to occur.[10,11]

Vertical SVA alignments have traditionally been used to achieve knee and hip extension in standing. However, it is physically challenging to align a vertical HAT over a vertical thigh and shank even for people with normal neurology.[11] It is possible to achieve this position, but it requires good strength and balance ability. This is because the ankle joint is positioned 25% along the length of the foot. To align the shank, thigh, and trunk vertically, the COP has to move to the posterior limit of the BOS at mid-heel. Consequently, standing becomes unstable and there is a high risk of falling backward. If a subject has poor balance and backward stepping reactions, it is not a position that is likely to be adopted. The safe option of forward trunk lean is chosen instead as this brings the COM over the middle of the BOS.[10,11,16]

Stable Stepping and Walking

Optimal distal segment alignments, to enable translation of a vertical HAT, are not only essential for stable standing, but also for stepping and walking with full GCs.[10,11,16] The ability to stand and sway with maximum stability and a vertical trunk involves maintenance of an optimally aligned distal base. At temporal midstance of both stepping and full GCs, conditions that are similar to those of stable standing apply. Stepping with maximum stability requires the additional skills of taking abbreviated *entrances* and *exits*, single stance ending at 40% GC, and swing at 90% GC. Walking with a full GC with maximum stability requires the skills to achieve temporal midstance and full *entrances* and *exits* and the *Big V* characteristic of strider gait.

One way to rehabilitate walking or teach first steps is to set the distal alignment conditions that are essential for standing and temporal midstance and then to incrementally increase skill level from swaying to small steps, larger steps, and, where possible, to the full GC of mature gait. These stages are appropriate for both rehabilitation and the development of gait in children. In essence, they progress from the conditions of "stable standing" to those of "rock and roll walking." The conditions for stable standing, stepping, and gait will now be fully described. A later chapter in this book uses algorithms to help determine the optimal orthosis designs that can be used to facilitate stable standing, stepping, and full GCs.

Conditions for Stable Standing, Stepping, and Full Gait Cycles

Conditions Required for Stable Standing

As shown in Box 19-1, condition 1 allows the foot to act as a stable and mobile BOS. Conditions 2 through 4 provide optimal segment proportions. Conditions 3 through 5 ensure that the heel and toe levers are of adequate length to produce optimum length of the BOS. Conditions 3 through 7 create the prerequisite kinematics and kinetics for conditions 8 through 11 to occur. All conditions were described in detail previously.

Conditions Required for Stable Stepping

The segment alignments of stepping create maximum stability while allowing some forward mobility. Conditions 1 through 11 for stable standing (see Box 19-1) are common to and provide the same effects as for stable stepping. There are additional conditions for stable stepping, including one

---

Box 19-1

Conditions for Stable Standing

1. Optimum tri-planar alignment of foot
2. Leg lengths equal or equalized
3. Feet correct length for height
4. Feet aligned such that they are approximate to the sagittal plane
5. Feet horizontal on the floor with both heel and forefoot contact
6. Shanks optimally aligned at SVA 10 to 12 degrees inclined
7. Shanks remaining still in their optimally aligned position
8. Thighs able to move from vertical to inclined and reclined positions
9. Trunk able to remain vertical and translate forward and backward
10. Centre of mass remains within the margins of the base of support
11. Body weight adequately supported

Box 19-2

Conditions for Stable Stepping

1-4. As for stable standing
5. Foot horizontal on the floor with both heel and forefoot contact for the majority or all of the activity. Keeping full foot contact provides the most stability. If the heel is to rise, then it will be late and shallow.
6. Stance shank optimally aligned at SVA 10 to 12 degrees inclined at temporal midstance.
7. Shanks remaining still in their optimally aligned position at temporal midstance. Prior to that, during the entrance, shank moving from vertical to 10 to 12 degrees inclined alignment. During the exit, if the heel rises, shank slightly increasing the inclined alignment.
8-11. As for stable standing.
12. The swing limb able to take a step equivalent to the length of the stance foot.

---

for the swing limb (Box 19-2). During stepping, the stance limb will effectively undertake the kinematics and kinetics of 10% to 40% of a GC. The swing phase will end at 90% of a GC, making initial contact with a vertical shank, a horizontal foot, and full foot contact, producing a very stable base on which to start the *entry*. The *exit* will have a shallow heel rise or, if the step is very short, there may be no heel rise. A reasonable step length can be achieved without any heel rise if the shank and thigh are inclined 10 to 12 degrees. These alignments, combined with the resulting GRF alignment, produce knee and hip extending moments and a very stable stance limb during the shortened exit.

Conditions Required for Stable Walking With Full Gait Cycles

The conditions for temporal midstance of the GC are common to those for stable standing (see Box 19-1). There are additional conditions for stance phase *entrance* and *exit* and also for the swing phase (Box 19-3). The conditions that are the same as those for stable standing and apply to stable walking create stability and the conditions for 8 through 11 to occur. The *entrances* and *exits* provide mobility combined with stability. The swing limb shank is reclined at initial contact, which increases stride length and positions the foot to make the initial contact with the heel so that the GC starts with a heel lever essential for first rocker. In the *single support exit from temporal mid-stance*, the quasi-stiffness of the ankle produces the heel rise.[16] This reduces the BOS but positions the POA of the GRF at the MTPJs, which is essential for the production of stabilizing external knee and hip extending moments in terminal stance. It also creates longer step and stride lengths. A full stride length with just 40% of the GC having only one leg in contact with the ground ensures the efficiency of gait.

Box 19-3

CONDITIONS FOR WALKING WITH FULL GAIT CYCLES

1-4.   As for stable standing
5.   Feet horizontal on the floor with both heel and forefoot contact for 10% to 30% GC and at temporal midstance. During the entrance, foot positioned toe up 25 degrees at initial contact moving to flat foot by 10% GC. During exit, heel rise occurring just after 30% GC and then heel up position increasing.
6.   Stance shank optimally aligned at 10 to 12 degrees inclined position at temporal midstance, 30% GC. Optimal alignments also during entrance and exit.
7.   Shanks remaining still in their optimally aligned position of SVA 10 to 12 degrees inclined at temporal midstance. During entrance, shank moving from a position of 20 degrees reclined at initial contact to 10 to 12 degrees inclined by 30% GC and slowing its forward angular velocity as temporal midstance is approached. During exit, shank moving to a position of 20 degrees inclined by 50% GC, the Big V, and 50 degrees inclined by 60% GC, toe off.
8.   Stance thigh able to move from a reclined position at initial contact to vertical position at temporal midstance and an inclined position during exit.
9.   Trunk able to remain vertical and translate forward.
10.   COM moving outside the BOS during the entrance and exits from temporal midstance.
11.   Body weight adequately supported.
12.   Swing limb able to take a full step length. Forty percent of the gait cycle will be spent in swing phase, 40% in single stance, and there will be 2 periods of double support, when both limbs are on the ground, 10% of the GC for each of these periods.

DEVELOPMENT OF GAIT

When analyzing walking in children, it is important to know when the various parameters mature to adult values and what their values are prior to maturation. Children start to walk independently in a bipedal fashion at about 1 year of age. Over the first few months and years, there is a rapid maturation that then continues at a slower pace. Sutherland[31] posed 3 questions:

1.   How does the gait of children differ from adults?
2.   When do children achieve an adult-like gait pattern?
3.   What are the factors controlling the maturation of gait?

At that time, the answers to the first 2 questions were already being clarified in regard to joint kinematics and kinetics, but understanding of the development of segment kinematics came much later. The third question is still debated, but most researchers believe that it is a combination of neurological maturation and experiential learning, which brings in the interaction and self-organization of multiple components.[25,26,45,56] Between age 1 and 3.5 to 4 years, there is evidence of influences on changes in gait parameters from both central nervous system maturation and skeletal growth. After age 4 years, changes in parameters are attributable to growth alone.[31]

When examining the development of walking, we will give equal emphasis to the kinematics of both segments and joints. Much is to be learned from segment analysis and the way in which children develop mature intersegmental coordination. Before looking at the objective data for the development of important parameters of normal mature adult walking patterns, it is worth studying the very early independent steps of toddlers. Many children with disabilities will never be able to achieve walking with full GCs, so these very early stages of development are crucial to our understanding.

We know that early steps are short with a wide base, that there is a high foot lift during swing, and the arms are held wide.[26,31,41,57] First steps combine some forward progression with elements of stepping in place, which has already been practiced by the infant prior to independent walking.[26,41,57] It was found that there was a similarity in the muscle actions and segmental kinematics of early toddler stepping and adult stepping in place, and also with adults moving slowly forward while performing stepping-in-place movements.[41,43,45] These adult movements and those of children taking early steps effectively represent an abbreviated mature GC, one with temporal midstance, a small portion of terminal stance, a part of midswing, and no terminal swing. As walking matures, a greater proportion of entry and exit of the GC develop and mature joint and segment kinematics emerge.[24,26,31]

Borghese and colleagues[22] demonstrated that, for a mature adult GC, when the alignments of the thigh, shank, and foot are plotted one vs the other, they describe a regular loop, which lies close to one plane. They called this the *rule of planar covariation* and argued that it represented a specific pattern of neural coordination of intersegmental kinematics, and that its development was functionally significant for the mechanical cost of walking.[22-24,58] These authors found that toddlers take their first unsupported steps with poorly coordinated lower limb segments, but that they develop rapidly and, by 6 weeks of walking practice, the intersegmental coordination is much improved, the segments now start to covary close to one plane, as in mature adult gait, and the trunk is stabilized.[23,24] By 18 months after the first steps, the shape of the intersegmental coordination pattern in that one plane almost resembles that of mature adult gait.[23,24] Newly walking infants have by this time undertaken considerable amounts of practice, likened to the schedules of elite athletes.[8,56]

Significantly, these investigators found that children first develop the ability to couple the kinematics of the 2 most distal segments: the shank and the foot.[23,24] They then develop the ability to couple the more proximal segments of the shank and the thigh, indicating that once the child starts walking unsupported, development is from distal to proximal in this regard.[23,24] This makes biomechanical sense. The foot is acting as the BOS and is the segment from which the GRF will originate. We know that the alignment of the shank when combined with that of the horizontal foot will dictate whether it is possible to incline a thigh and translate a vertical trunk.[10,11] We also know that the combined segments of the shank and the foot, when optimally aligned with the knee over the center of the foot, produce a very stable triangular BOS and the ability to balance.[10,11] The distal kinematics alignments will dictate the more proximal segment and joint kinematics and also kinetics, so organizing the distal segments optimally in the first instance would seem a sensible order of development. Understanding this concept is useful to rehabilitation strategies, and this will be explored in a later chapter.

Infants make initial contact with a high step, very flexed hip, flexed knee, vertical shank, and a horizontal foot.[23,24,29,59] There is no first flexion wave at the knee as the limb is already in a position equivalent to the end of loading response at initial contact. The full hip and knee extensions of terminal stance and terminal swing are not developed. Full GCs and the Big V will be apparent at age 2.5 years and will be fully developed by age 5.[23,24,29,59] Adult gait can be described as pendulum-like.[40] In early steps, the limbs do not behave as pendulums; this has to develop, and by the time of achieving the Big V, this feature of walking becomes mature.[40]

Time-Distance Parameters

Most time-distance parameters are related to musculoskeletal growth, so velocity, step length, and step frequency or cadence are not fully mature until the skeletal growth is completed.[29,31,60] Stride length is a consistent 76% of the child's height at a velocity of 1.04 meters per second regardless of age,[60] and there is a direct linear relationship between the step length and leg length in children of 1 to 7 years of age.[29] The step factor, which is step length divided by leg length, increases from ages 1 to 4 years, so both growth and maturation influence time-distance parameters between these ages.[31,61]

Single limb stance is a powerful indicator of the ability of the body to control body mass on one limb.[29] The ability to balance on one lower limb for 40% of a GC, 10% to 50% GC, is one of the markers of mature bipedal gait. This percentage of single stance is achieved in children by the age of 3.5 to 4 years.[29]

Kinematic and kinetic values will vary with speed, so when observing walking trials, comparisons should be made with normative data of the same speed.[13,62-65]

Kinematics

Children have greater inter-subject variability than adults, which decreases with age.[29,31] There are changes in a number of kinematic variables with age.[26,29,31] The dynamic joint angles mature up to age 3.5 to 4 years, which is also regarded as the time window for the completion of central nervous system maturation.[29,31] Gait kinematics then stabilize (Table 19-14).[31] In the coronal plane, pelvic obliquity is not apparent until 3 years of age.

Kinetics

As described in Table 19-14, the vertical force curves are not well developed in young children.[14,25,29,65-69] The first peak is apparent from age 1 year but only reaches body weight. It develops to become consistently above body weight by age 3.5 years. It occurs at 15% GC, as for adults. The mid-stance trough occurs at 30% GC at all ages, which is the same as for adults. Initially, it is shallow, developing into the more adult curve by age 3.5 years. The second vertical force peak occurs at 40% to 50% GC, as for adults.[29] Its value remains less than the first peak and body weight for some considerable years after the onset of walking.[29,31,66] It is well below body weight in children aged 2 years, then increases with age, but remains below body weight until age 5 to 7 years.[29] It can remain below body weight in 11% to 13% of children aged 6 to 8 years.[67] Sutherland[30] suggests that there is a maturation factor, relating to the action of the calf muscles in TST, which may be responsible for the lower values of second peak in younger children.

TABLE 19-14

DEVELOPMENT OF GAIT

PARAMETER	AGE OR AGE RANGE (YRS)												COMMENT
	1	1.5	2	2.5	3	3.5	4	5	6	7	8-12	>18	
FIVE IMPORTANT DETERMINANTS OF MATURE GAIT[29,30]													
Duration of single limb stance in a GC (%)		32	34	35		36			37	38		40	Rapid rate of change before 2.5 yrs
Velocity (cm/sec)	65	71	72	81	86	100	99	108	109	115		150	Rapid rate of change before 3.5 yrs
Cadence (steps/min)	180	171	156	156	154	160	152	153	146	145		113	Steady decrease with age
Step length (cm)	20	25	28	31	33	37	39	42	44	48		77	Rapid rate of change before 2.5 yrs
Pelvic span to ankle ratio	1.4	1.8		2.2		2.4							Rapid rate of change before 2.5 yrs
KINEMATICS													
Inter-segmental coordination maturity[23,24]	Poor	Poor		Full								Full	Development is distal to proximal. First couple foot/shank, then shank/thigh
Shank to vertical angle at initial contact[40] (degrees)	0	Reclined										20 Recl	When infants start walking, they do not have a terminal swing. Initial contact is with a vertical shank and horizontal foot. As a terminal swing develops, at initial contact the shank becomes reclined, with the foot *toe up,* and contact is with a heel.
Foot to horizontal angle at initial contact[40] (degrees)	0	Toe up										20 Toe Up	
Initial contact heel[29] (% of subjects)	30	100										100	
Opposite initial contact[29] (% GC)	50%											50%	Does not vary with age
Toe off[29] (% GC)	68%			66%	65%	64%				62%		60%	Time spent in "stance phase" reduces with age. Time spent in "double support" reduces with age. Time spent in single stance increases with age (see above).
Opposite toe off[29] (% GC)	18%			16%		14%		12%				10%	

(continued)

TABLE 19-14 (CONTINUED)

DEVELOPMENT OF GAIT

PARAMETER	AGE OR AGE RANGE (YRS)												COMMENT
	1	1.5	2	2.5	3	3.5	4	5	6	7	8-12	>18	
KINEMATICS													
Big V at 50% GC[29]	No			Yes								Yes	
Stance knee extension wave present[29] (% GC)	No		Poor		Yes 45%			Yes 40%				Yes 40%	"Maximum stance knee extension" and the "knee extension wave" are not fully developed until age 4 years.
Stance knee flexion wave present[29] (% subjects)	<50	75	92		100							Yes	If present at 1 year, it is small; it is not well developed until age 4 years.
Swing knee flexion wave present[29]	Yes											Yes	Slightly less in 1 year olds
Max hip extension[29] (degrees)	-10	-5	0									10	Occurs at 55% GC at age 1 year, then reduces to 50% GC by age 7 years
Max hip flexion[29] (degrees)	Midswing 45-50, Terminal Swing/Initial Contact 40-45											35	Excessive flexion in midswing and terminal swing, compared to adults
Reciprocal arm swing[29] (% of subjects)		65		90		98	100					100	
KINETICS: SAGITTAL VERTICAL FORCE													
Peak 1													
% body weight[29]	100					105			110			110-120	
Normalized for body weight (% body weight)[62,63,68]								120					Consistent for all ages walking at the same speed. Varies with speed at all ages, larger peak with increasing speed. Occurs at 12-16% GC at all ages
Normalized for body weight (% body weight)[69]									125				
% body weight[65]											95-115		Large variation with walking speed

(continued)

Table 19-14 (continued)

Development of Gait

PARAMETER	AGE OR AGE RANGE (YRS)												COMMENT
	1	1.5	2	2.5	3	3.5	4	5	6	7	8-12	>18	
KINETICS: SAGITTAL VERTICAL FORCE													
Midstance Trough													
% Body weight[29]		80						75				70-80	Trough less well developed in younger groups. Occurs at 30% GC at all ages
Normalized for body weight (% body weight)[62,63,68]								70					Consistent for all ages walking at same speed. Varies with speed at all ages, larger trough with increasing speed
Normalized for body weight (% body weight)[69]									54				
% Body weight[65]											75-95		Large variation with walking speed
Peak 2													
% Body weight[29]	90						95					110-120	Peak 2 less than Peak 1 but difference small by age 5-7 years. Occurs at 40-50% GC at all ages
Normalized for body weight (% body weight)[62,63,68]								110-120					Consistent for all ages
Normalized for body weight (% body weight)[69]									112				Consistent for all speeds
% Body weight[65]											95-105		Small variation with walking speed
Value (N/Kg)[66]					Less than Peak 1			16	12			0	Peak 2 less than Peak 1 at age 3-4 years
Does not exceed body weight[29,67] (% of subjects)	100												

Abbreviations: GC, gait cycle; Recl, reclined; Yrs, years.

REFERENCES

1. Stallard J. Assessment of the mechanical function of orthoses by force vector visualisation. *Physiotherapy.* 1987;73:398-402.

2. Tait JH, Rose GK. The real-time video vector display of ground reaction forces during ambulation. *J Med Eng Technol.* 1979;3:252-255.

3. Gage JR, ed. *The Treatment of Gait Problems in Cerebral Palsy. Clinics in Developmental Medicine, No. 164-165.* London, UK: Mac Keith Press; 2004:45.

4. Tilley AR. *The Measure of Man and Woman. Human Factors in Design.* New York, NY: John Wiley and Sons; 2002.

5. Rose J, Gamble JG, eds. *Human Walking.* 3rd ed. Philadelphia, PA: Lippincott Williams and Wilkins; 2006.

6. International Organization for Standardization. *ISO 8551 Prosthetics and Orthotics –Functional Deficiencies - Description of the Person to Be Treated with an Orthosis, Clinical Objectives of Treatment and Functional Requirements of the Orthosis.* Geneva: International Organization for Standardization; 2003.

7. Baker RW. *Measuring Walking: A Handbook of Clinical Gait Analysis.* London, UK: Wiley; 2013.

8. Ounpuu S, Gage JR, Davis RB. Three-dimensional lower extremity joint kinetics in normal paediatric gait. *J Pediatr Orthoped.* 1991;11:341-349.

9. Meadows CB, Bowers R, Owen E. Biomechanics of hip knee and ankle. In: Hsu JD, Michael J, Fisk J, eds. *AAOS Atlas of Orthoses and Assistive Devices.* Amsterdam, The Netherlands: Elsevier; 2008.

10. Owen E. The importance of being earnest about shank and thigh kinematics especially when using ankle-foot orthoses. *Prosthet Orthot Int.* 2010;34(3):254-269.

11. Owen E. *Shank Angle to Floor Measures and Tuning of Ankle-Foot Orthosis Footwear Combinations for Children with Cerebral Palsy, Spina Bifida and Other Conditions* [MSc Thesis]. Glasgow: University of Strathclyde; 2004.

12. Owen E. Tuning of ankle-foot orthosis combinations for children with cerebral palsy, spina bifida and other conditions. In: *Proceedings of ESMAC Seminar 2004.* Warsaw, Poland: European Society for Movement Analysis of Children and Adults; 2004.

13. Inman VT, Ralston HJ, Todd F. *Human Walking.* Baltimore, MD: Williams and Wilkins; 1981.

14. Murray MP. Gait as a total pattern of movement. *Am J Phys Med.* 1967;46(1):290-333.

15. Owen E. Shank angle to floor measures of tuned 'ankle-foot orthosis footwear combinations' used with children with cerebral palsy, spina bifida and other conditions. *Gait Posture.* 2002;16(suppl 1):S132-S133.

16. Perry J. *Gait Analysis: Normal and Pathological Function.* Thorofare, NJ: SLACK Incorporated; 1992.

17. Winter DA. *Biomechanics and Motor Control of Human Movement.* 2nd ed. New York, NY: John Wiley & Sons; 1990.

18. World Health Organization. *International Classification of Functioning, Disability and Health: ICF.* Geneva, Switzerland: World Health Organization; 2001.

19. World Health Organization. *International Classification of Functioning Disability and Health: Children and Youth Version: ICF-CY.* Geneva, Switzerland: World Health Organization: 2007.

20. Bianchi L, Angelini D, Orani GP, Lacquaniti F. Kinematic coordination in human gait: Relation to mechanical energy cost. *J Neurophysiol.* 1998;79(4):2155-2170.

21. Bianchi L, Angelini D, Lacquaniti F. Individual characteristics of human walking mechanics. *Eur J Physiol.* 1998;436(3):343-356.

22. Borghese NA, Bianchi L, Lacquaniti F. Kinematic determinants of human locomotion. *J Physiol.* 1996;494(3):863-879.

23. Cheron G, Bengoetxea A, Bouillot E, Lacquaniti F, Dan B. Early emergence of temporal co-ordination of lower limb segments elevation angles in human locomotion. *Neurosci Lett.* 2001;38(2):123-127.

24. Cheron G, Bouillot, Dan B, Bengoetxea A, Draye JP, Lacquaniti F. Development of a kinematic coordination pattern in toddler locomotion: planar covariation. *Exp Brain Res.* 2001;137:455-466.

25. Lacquaniti F, Ivanenko YP, Zago M. Patterned control of human locomotion. *J Physiol.* 2012;590(10):2189-2199.

26. Lacquaniti F, Ivanenko YP, Zago M. Development of human locomotion. *Curr Opin Neurobiol.* 2012;22(5):822-828.

27. McMahon TA. *Muscles, Reflexes and Locomotion.* Princeton, NJ: Princeton University Press; 1984.

28. Perry J. *Gait Analysis. Normal and Pathological Function.* 2nd ed. Thorofare, NJ: SLACK Incorporated; 2010.

29. Sutherland DH, Olshen RA, Biden EN, Wyatt MP. *The Development of Mature Walking. Clinics in Developmental Medicine. No. 104/105.* London, UK: Mac Keith Press; 1988.

30. Sutherland DH, Olshen R, Cooper L, Savio L-Y. The development of mature gait. *J Bone Joint Surg Am.* 1980;62(3):336-353.

31. Sutherland D. The development of mature gait. *Gait Posture.* 1997;6:163-170.

32. Zajac FE, Neptune RR, Kautz SA. Biomechanics and muscle coordination of human walking Part 2: Lessons from dynamical simulations and clinical implications. *Gait Posture.* 2003;17:1-17.

33. Gibson T, Jeffery RS, Bakheit MO. Comparison of three definitions of the mid-stance and mid-swing events of the gait cycle in children. *Disabil Rehabil.* 2006;28(10):625-628.

34. Owen E. From stable standing to rock and roll walking. Part 1. The importance of alignment, proportion and profiles. *APCP Journal.* 2014;5(1):7-18.

35. Owen E. A clinical algorithm for the design and tuning of ankle-foot orthosis footwear combinations (AFOFCs) based on shank kinematics. *Gait Posture.* 2005;22S:36–37.

36. Kepple TM, Siegel KL, Stanhope SJ. Relative contributions of the lower extremity joint moments to forward progression and support during gait. *Gait Posture.* 1997;6:1-8.

37. Grasso R, Bianchi L, Lacquaniti F. Motor patterns for human gait: Backward versus forward locomotion. *J Neurophysiol.* 1998;80(4):1868-1685.

38. Hansen AH, Childress DS, Knox EH. Roll-over shapes of human locomotor systems: effects of walking speed. *Clin Biomech.* 2004;19:407-414.

39. Pratt E, Durham S, Ewins D. Preliminary evidence for techniques used to optimally align (tune) fixed ankle-foot orthoses in children. *J Prosthet Orthot.* 2011;23(2):60-63.

40. Ivanenko YP, Dominici N, Cappellini G et al. Development of pendular mechanism and kinematic coordination from the first unsupported steps in toddlers. *J Exp Biol.* 2004;207:3787–3810.

41. Ivanenko YP, Domenici N, Cappellini G, Lacquaniti F. Kinematics in newly walking toddlers does not depend upon postural stability. *J Neurophysiol.* 2005;94:754-763.

42. Ivanenko YP, Cappellini G, Dominici N, et al. Modular control of limb movements during human locomotion. *J Neurosci.* 2007;27(41):11149–11161.

43. Ivanenko YP, d'Avella A, Poppele RE, Lacquaniti F. On the origin of planar covariation of elevation angles during human locomotion. *J Neurophysiol.* 2008;99:1890-1898.

44. Lacquaniti F, Ivanenko YP, Zago M. Kinematic control of walking. *Arch Ital Biol.* 2002:140(4):263-272.

45. Ivanenko YP, Domenici N, Lacquaniti F. Development of independent walking in toddlers. *Exerc Sport Sci Rev.* 2007;35(2):67-73.

46. Wang CC, Hansen AH. Response of able-bodied persons in changes to shoe rocker radius during walking: changes in ankle kinematics to maintain a consistent roll-over shape. *J Biomech.* 2010;43(12):2288-2293.

47. Hansen AH, Childress DS. Investigations of roll-over shape: implications for design, alignment, and evaluation of ankle-foot prostheses and orthoses. *Disabil Rehabil.* 2010;32(26):2201-2209.

48. Hansen AH, Meier MR. Roll-over shapes of the ankle-foot and knee-ankle-foot systems of able-bodied children. *Clin Biomech.* 2010;25:248-255.

49. Losel S, Burgess-Milliron MJ, Micheli LJ, Edington CJ. A simplified technique for determining foot progression angle in children 4 to 16 years of age. *J Pediatr Orthoped.* 1996;16(5):570-574.

50. Owen E. How should we define the rockers of gait and are there three or four? *Gait Posture.* 2009;30S:49.

51. Perry J. Kinesiology of lower extremity bracing. *Clin Orthop Relat Res.*1974;102:18-31.

52. Sutherland DH, Cooper L, Daniel D. The role of the ankle plantar flexors in normal walking. *J Bone Joint Surg Am.* 1980;62:354-363.

53. Perry J. Normal and pathological gait. In: Hsu JD, Michael JW, Fisk JR, eds. *American Academy of Orthopaedic Surgeons Atlas of Orthoses and Assistive Devices.* 4th ed. Philadelphia, PA: CV Mosby; 2008:61-82.

54. Singh HS. Pressure under the foot. *J Bone Joint Surg Br.* 1992;74-B(5):787.

55. Davis RB, DeLuca PA. Gait characterisation via dynamic joint stiffness. *Gait Posture.* 1996;4(3):224-231.

56. Adolph KE, Robinson SR. The road to walking: what learning to walk tells us about development. In: Zelazo P, ed. *Oxford Handbook of Developmental Psychology.* Vol. 1. New York, NY: Oxford University Press; 2013:403-443.

57. Ivanenko YP, Dominici N, Cappellini G, Poppele RE, Lacquaniti F. Changes in the spinal segmental motor output for stepping during development from infant to adult. *J Neurosci.* 2013;33(7):3025-3036.

58. Cheron G, Duvinage M, De Saedeleer C, et al. From spinal central pattern generators to cortical network: Integrated BCI for walking rehabilitation. *Neural Plast.* 2012;2012:375148. doi: 10.1155/2012/375148.

59. Statham L, Murray MP. Early walking patterns of normal children. *Clin Orthop Relat Res.* 1971;79:8-24.

60. Beck RJ, Andriacchi TP, Kuo KN, Fermier RW, Galante JO. Changes in the gait patterns of growing children. *J Bone Joint Surg Am.* 1981;63(9):1452-1457.

61. Scrutton D. Footprint sequences of normal children under 5 years old. *Dev Med Child Neurol.* 1969;11:44-53.

62. Stansfield BW, Hillman SJ, Hazlewood E, et al. Normalized speed, not age, characterizes ground reaction force patterns in 5- to 12-year-old children walking at self-selected speeds. *J Pediatr Orthoped.* 2001;21:395-402.

63. Stansfield BW, Hillman SJ, Hazlewood E, et al. Sagittal joint kinematics, moments, and powers are predominantly characterised by speed of progression, not age, in normal children. *J Pediatr Orthoped.* 2001;21:403-411.

64. Murray MP, Mollinger LA, Gardner GM, Sepic SB. Kinematic and EMG patterns during slow, free, and fast walking. *J Orthopaed Res.* 1984;2:272-280.

65. van der Linden ML, Kerr AM, Hazlewood ME, Hillman SJ, Robb JE. Kinematic and kinetic gait characteristics of normal children walking at a range of clinically relevant speeds. *J Pediatr Orthoped.* 2002;22:800-806.

66. Greer NL, Hamill J, Campbell KR. Dynamics of children's gait. *Hum Movement Sci.* 1989;8:465-480.

67. Mann AM, Loudon IR, Lawson AM, Robb JE, Meadows CB. Prospective study of gait maturation in normal children. *Gait Posture.* 1995;3(4):271-272.

68. Stansfield BW, Hillman SJ, Hazlewood E, et al. Normalization of gait data in children. *Gait Posture.* 2003;17:81-87.

69. White R, Agouris I, Selbie RD, Kirkpatrick M. The variability of force platform data in normal and cerebral palsy gait. *Clin Biomech.* 1999;14:185-192.

Common Approaches to Orthotic Management of the Lower Extremity, Trunk, and Upper Extremity

Donald McGovern, CPO, FAAOP and Mary Rahlin, PT, DHS, PCS

The International Classification of Functioning, Disability and Health (ICF) places the concept of disability on the same continuum as health.[1,2] The ICF Model[2] allows the physical therapist to use a strength-based approach to patient examination, evaluation, and development of the plan of care, which is compatible with the top-down approach to patient evaluation (see Chapter 11) and the participation-based approach to patient management (see Chapter 14) that employ a similar goal-oriented, family-centered, and collaborative philosophy.[3-5]

In their collaboration with the child, his or her orthotist, and family, the physical therapist who applies the ICF Model[2] to orthotic management should address the short- and long-term goals of the child and the family. The alterations in body structures and functions related to the aging process and similar issues, such as puberty-related growth, weight gain, or the development of bony deformities, should be taken into consideration when making decisions that would support the child's activity and participation goals. In addition, the therapist should consider the environmental and personal contextual factors that may help attain these goals. The ICF context for goals and outcomes of orthotic management is further discussed in Chapter 21.

The International Organization for Standardization (ISO)[6] defines orthosis as "an externally applied device used to modify the structural and functional characteristics of the neuromuscular and skeletal system."[(p 2)] According to the Merriam-Webster Dictionary,[7,8] orthotics refers to "a branch of mechanical and medical science that deals with the design and fitting" of orthoses, while an orthotic device is a "device (as a brace or a splint) for supporting, immobilizing, or treating muscles, joints, or skeletal parts which are weak, ineffective, deformed, or injured."

This chapter outlines common approaches to orthotic management of the alterations of body structures and functions observed in children and adults with cerebral palsy (CP), with the ultimate goal to address their activity and participation needs. Research evidence in support of clinical decision making for prescription, fabrication, and application of lower extremity (LE), upper extremity (UE), and spinal orthoses is discussed using the latest classification of CP presented in Chapter 3.[9]

LOWER EXTREMITY ORTHOSES FOR STANDING AND GAIT

Orthotic devices have been used for a very long time. Skeletons of ancient people have shown healed fractures in good alignment indicating a successful splint.[10] Culture, technology, and available materials have strong influences on the ability to change the shape of the body for fashion or healing. In the last century, the tradition of utilizing metal, leather, buckles, snaps, laces, and canvas[11,12] evolved toward plastics, Velcro, and carbon graphite. It has been noted in

Rahlin M. *Physical Therapy for Children With Cerebral Palsy: An Evidence-Based Approach* (pp 315-339).

clinical practice that the exuberance of new technology may overstep older valuable knowledge and leave it behind. In the field of contemporary orthotics, the symbiotic relationship of LE ambulatory aide devices and footwear has been often overlooked. With the advent of plastics, especially the low temperature plastics,[13] many providers of orthoses forgot the integral connection between the orthosis and the shoe. However, footwear does, indeed, matter.[14] It is important not only as the interface between the ground and the device that supports the mass above,[14] but also because its design can greatly contribute to the success of orthotic interventions (see Chapter 21).[15]

A plethora of orthotic interventions have been used to improve standing and ambulation in children with CP.[15-24] Clinically, the challenge is to apply the correct orthosis to meet the needs of the individual. To further complicate intervention choices, it is very likely that a single child may benefit from a variety of orthoses. Different activities often have different stability and mobility requirements, much like the general population has different footwear to correspond to a specific activity.[14] When applying orthotic interventions for standing and ambulation, one must consider the child's functional level, movement strategies, individual preferences, and body schema, as well as school, community, home, sports, and therapeutic activities.[25]

Common Orthotic Intervention Challenges

One aspect of traditional LE orthotic intervention rarely mentioned is the influence of one's philosophy of clinical treatment.[26] Practitioners adopt an orthotic approach often based on a concept that is attractive to one's focus. This may be crudely categorized as a division into 2 groups of clinicians: those influenced by the neuromuscular system focus and those who focus on the musculoskeletal system. As a result, in practice, a wide divergence of orthotic interventions is accepted or rejected depending on the philosophy of the clinic.[26] This discrepancy may be a major challenge for the orthotist and confusing for primary caregivers. It is common for the orthotist to receive very different prescriptions for children with very similar presentations who use very similar gait strategies. Current literature does not provide sound information for the referral sources to choose one orthotic device over another.[24,26] The review of published evidence shows that, when an orthosis is used in a study, its description in research reports is often inadequate and insufficient for replication.[17,27,28] This is now recognized by researchers and, hopefully, in forthcoming studies, this issue will be rectified. Clinicians will welcome this change because, at this time, most support the impetus toward the evidence-based practice.

One consistent practice in LE interventions that involve the ankle is the placement of the talocrural joint in a neutral alignment.[29] There is insufficient evidence for such ankle angle (AA) in an ankle-foot orthosis (AFO), and this approach may have detrimental effects on the musculoskeletal system. Often times, the AA of the AFO is placed in a neutral talocrural joint alignment[29] even though the child's ankle is plantarflexed because of muscle tightness, hypertonicity, spasticity, or dystonia, depending on the muscle tone abnormality. In a closed kinetic chain, the plantarflexed ankle placed in a neutral AA in the AFO induces dorsiflexion at the midtarsal joints and subtalar pronation to seat the foot within the AFO. This foot position is unstable and exacerbates pronation in gait, especially in the late stance phase as the body moves over the foot. The collapse at the midtarsal joints and calcaneal eversion lead to an inadequate lever arm, which cannot effectively support the body.[30] The drop of the midtarsal joints, combined with subtalar pronation, allows the talus to adduct and plantarflex, which has an internal rotation and forward inclination effect on the tibia.[31-33] If the knee joint does not absorb the resultant transverse moment of force, the internal rotation of the tibia and fibula will induce internal rotation of the hip.[33] Supination of the foot in a closed kinetic chain will have an opposite effect.[33]

The closed kinetic chain phenomena related to pronation or supination described previously may amplify proximal limitations. For example, in a child with CP, hypertonicity in the hip adductor and hamstring muscles may induce a valgus moment at the knee, which will result in excessive pronation.[34] This, in turn, will lead to internal tibial rotation and increase the valgus stress, which is likely to produce a valgus deformity of the developing knee. Another effect of the medial rotation of the hip that accompanies subtalar pronation may be to inhibit the developmental reduction in femoral anteversion.[34] If this condition persists, normal joint congruities will be altered according to the applied stresses.[30]

Fish and Nielsen[35] described 2 major deformity patterns coupled with pronation and supination, respectively. The term *internal rotary deformity* (IRD) is now commonly used in the field of orthotics[35] to describe the clinical observation of internal tibial rotation, genu valgum, hip internal rotation and adduction, anterior pelvic tilt, and increased lumbar lordosis induced by pronation. In the IRD situation,[35] as time progresses, the midtarsal joints collapse further as the largely unopposed powerful gastrocnemius muscle shortens and pulls the calcaneus into plantarflexion and valgus.[36] The plantarflexed calcaneus destabilizes the talus, which produces further midtarsal joint collapse with an increase in forefoot abduction creating a rocker bottom foot.[36] The term *external rotary deformity* (ERD), which is coupled with supination, is used to describe the effect opposite to that of the IRD.[35]

When the foot is enclosed in an orthosis, these undesirable consequences of pronation and supination lead to excessive pressure of the foot against the orthotic wall, which clinicians often note as a cause of discomfort and skin irritation for the wearer of the orthosis. Clinical experience has repeatedly shown that as the child ages, his or her mass and bony leverage increase the forces pressing the foot against the orthotic barrier. With the increase in pressure upon the foot, the individual rejects the orthosis, reduces ambulation, or utilizes comparatively more comfortable and, perhaps, more energy-consuming gait pattern. A decline in ambulation in children with CP with the present standard of care has been

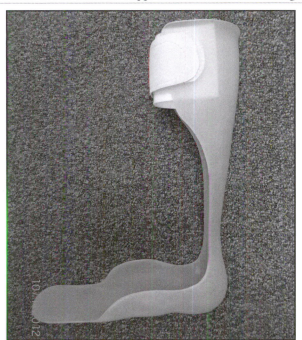

Figure 20-1. A polypropylene Posterior Leaf Spring AFO, custom fabricated from a cast.

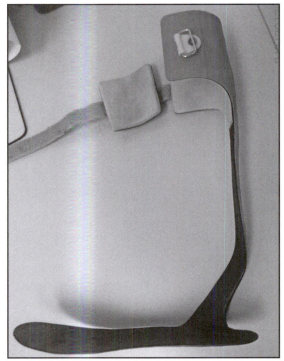

Figure 20-2. Medial view of a right Kinetic Research Advanced Carbon Fiber Noodle AFO with lateral strut, custom fabricated from a cast. The carbon fiber provides a lightweight material with spring characteristics which may yield some energy return. These can be prefabricated or custom made to measurement.

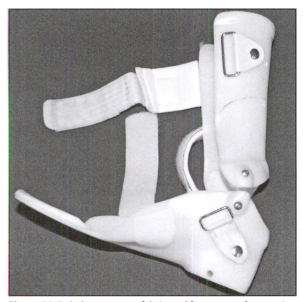

Figure 20-3. A short, custom fabricated from a cast, free motion articulated AFO with free plantarflexion and dorsiflexion, with dorsiflexion assist from the joint. Some practitioners prefer this design for mild dorsiflexor muscle weakness. The joints are Tamarack Flexure Joint Model 742, Dorsiflexion Assist hinges.

observed in practice and noted in the literature.[37,38] As a result, a growing number of experienced practitioners are utilizing a segmental kinematic approach to orthotic management for persons with CP and other physical challenges (see Chapter 21).[15]

The work by Rodda et al[39] offers a pragmatic approach to the discussion of clinically recognized gait patterns and possible orthotic interventions used with ambulatory children and adolescents with CP. It is necessary to note that while a gait pattern classification may be a useful clinical tool, it is usually inherently limited as it does not include every gait strategy that clinicians will see.[40,41] Table 20-1 contains the generally accepted gait descriptions, as well as orthotic interventions, dosage, and potential side effects.[39,42-44]

Management of Drop Foot Gait

Children and adults with unilateral CP may exhibit a drop foot gait pattern,[42] which is often managed with a dorsiflexion assist (DFA) AFO. A variety of DFA AFOs is available within the present orthotic armamentarium (see Table 20-1); from off-the-shelf polypropylene (PP) Posterior Leaf Spring (PLS) AFOs, to newer carbon graphite prefabricated anterior shell AFOs, to custom-molded AFOs made of PP (Figure 20-1) or carbon graphite (Figure 20-2). Newer, clinically considered interventions include neuroprostheses that utilize Functional Electrical Stimulation (FES) discussed later in this chapter.[45] Some clinicians prefer short, free motion, articulated, custom-molded AFOs with DFA joints for mild cases of drop foot (Figure 20-3). The need for foot control, function, weight, bulk, and expected daily wear will drive the decision regarding which of these devices will greater benefit the user.[29] In general, the greater the required foot control, the more customized the device. The cost of orthotic intervention will also influence these decisions,[29] otherwise, it would be very reasonable to recommend different orthoses for different purposes, just as the general population has a variety of footwear for a variety of activities.

TABLE 20-1

ORTHOTIC DEVICES COMMONLY USED TO ADDRESS DIFFERENT TYPES OF GAIT PATTERNS SEEN IN PERSONS WITH UNILATERAL SPASTIC CEREBRAL PALSY AND BILATERAL SPASTIC CEREBRAL PALSY (DIPLEGIA)ᵃ

GAIT PATTERN TYPE AND CHARACTERISTICS[39,42]	INTERVENTIONSᵇ	TYPICAL WEAR AS SEEN IN CLINICAL PRACTICEᶜ	SIDE EFFECTS
Drop Foot (unilateral CP): • Inadequate dorsiflexion in swing	Angle of the ankle set at neutral in the following: • SMO • PLS AFO • DFA, AAFO • PFS, FDF AAFO • Short, DFA AAFO • Prefabricated Carbon Graphite AFO • DFA Neuroprosthesis	Majority of walking time, except for the home or other safe environments where only short distances would be walked safely while barefoot	SMO does not provide mechanical advantage to the talocrural joint in the sagittal plane Decreased plantar proprioceptive input Possible disuse atrophy with an AFO[43,44]
True Equinus (from midstance to toe off): • Ankle is plantarflexed • Knee extends or hyperextends • Hip extends • Pelvis within normal range or slight anterior tilt	• UCBL • SMO Angle of the ankle set at neutral in the following: • PLS AFO • Free motion, DFA, AAFO • PFS, FDF AAFO • SAFO	Majority of walking time to improve gait pattern and muscle strength May choose not to use for climbing and sports activities	Skin breakdown issues, midtarsal joint destruction since talocrural joint cannot achieve a neutral position UCBL and SMO do not provide mechanical advantage for the talocrural joint in the sagittal plane Excessive supination, if present, often not addressed Decreased plantar proprioceptive input Excessive pressure on the forefoot, inadequate pressure on the heel
Jump (from midstance to toe off): • Ankle equinus • Knee and hip excessively flexed in early stance with later stance decreased flexion • Pelvis within normal range or anterior tilt	• UCBL • SMO Angle of the ankle set at neutral in the following: • PLS AFO • SAFO • PFS, FDF AAFO AAFO with limited ROM double-action joints, which may or may not have springs or elastomer mechanisms to resist dorsiflexion and plantarflexion	Majority of walking time to improve gait pattern and muscle strength May choose not to use for climbing and sports activities	Skin breakdown issues, midtarsal joint destruction since talocrural joint cannot maintain a neutral position Inadequate hip extension UCBL and SMO do not provide mechanical advantage for the talocrural joint in the sagittal plane Excessive supination, if present, often not addressed Decreased plantar proprioceptive input Excessive pressure on the forefoot, inadequate pressure on the heel Possible muscle disuse atrophy[43,44]

(continued)

TABLE 20-1 (CONTINUED)

ORTHOTIC DEVICES COMMONLY USED TO ADDRESS DIFFERENT TYPES OF GAIT PATTERNS SEEN IN PERSONS WITH UNILATERAL SPASTIC CEREBRAL PALSY AND BILATERAL SPASTIC CEREBRAL PALSY (DIPLEGIA)[a]

GAIT PATTERN TYPE AND CHARACTERISTICS[39,42]	INTERVENTIONS[b]	TYPICAL WEAR AS SEEN IN CLINICAL PRACTICE[c]	SIDE EFFECTS
Apparent Equinus (from midstance to toe off): • Ankle is plantigrade • Knee and hip flexion • Pelvis is in anterior tilt	• UCBL • SMO Angle of the ankle set at neutral in the following: • PLS • SAFO • PFS, FDF AAFO • GRAFO (FRAFO) AAFO with limited ROM double-action joints, which may or may not have springs or elastomer resistance mechanisms	Majority of walking time to improve gait pattern and muscle strength May choose not to use for climbing and sports activities	Skin issues, midfoot collapse UCBL and SMO do not provide mechanical advantage for the talocrural joint in sagittal plane Excessive supination, if present, is often not addressed Decreased plantar proprioceptive input Excessive pressure on the forefoot, inadequate pressure on the heel Possible muscle disuse atrophy[43,44]
Crouch (from midstance to toe off): • Ankle dorsiflexion • Knee and hip flexion • Pelvis may have posterior, normal or anterior tilt	Angle of the ankle set at neutral in the following: • SAFO ○ Anterior panel is sometimes added to the SAFO to increase the proximal lever arm resistance to excessive tibial incline • GRAFO (FRAFO) AFO with ROM double action joints to limit excessive tibial inclination. The joints may or may not have springs or elastomer resistance mechanisms	Majority of walking time to improve gait pattern and muscle strength May choose not to use for climbing and sports activities	Skin breakdown issues; midtarsal joint destruction since talocrural joint cannot maintain a neutral position Possible muscle disuse atrophy[43,44]

Abbreviations: AAFO, articulated AFO; AFO, ankle-foot orthosis; DFA, dorsiflexion assist; FDF, free dorsiflexion; GRAFO/FRAFO, ground/floor reaction AFO; IRD, internal rotary deformity; KAFO, knee-ankle-foot orthosis; PFS, plantarflexion stop; PLS, posterior leaf spring; ROM, range of motion; SAFO, solid AFO; SMO, supramalleolar orthosis; UCBL, University of California Biomechanics Laboratory orthosis.

a Many authors continue using the term *diplegia*, which implies greater involvement of lower than upper extremities in individuals with bilateral spastic CP.

b The above interventions have been seen clinically by the authors, but are not necessarily recommended. There is a paucity of published evidence-based information concerning the variety of interventions used for each gait strategy.

c There is a paucity of published evidence-based information concerning typical wear recommendations.

Gait pattern types and characteristics compiled from Rodda et al[39] and Rodda and Graham.[42]

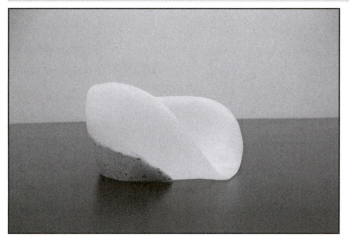

Figure 20-4. A Helfet heel cup with a thermocork post, custom fabricated from a cast. These are available premade and may be of use for very mild calcaneal valgus. The Helfet heel cup must be assessed in weight-bearing, and the resting calcaneus measured to assure the appropriate correction.

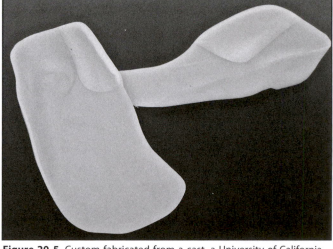

Figure 20-5. Custom fabricated from a cast, a University of California—Biomechanics Laboratory foot orthosis with extended lateral wall for control of foot abduction.

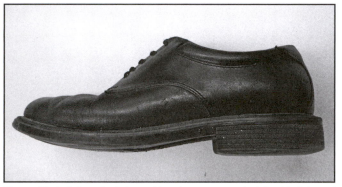

Figure 20-6. A tie oxford shoe with a three-quarter–inch heel height and a steel shank.

Clinicians must be cautious in their decision making in regard to the selection of orthotic intervention for a child with unilateral CP and drop foot gait. First, too often, the focus may be on the ankle muscle weakness without a close assessment of the entire affected side. Besides the drop foot, one must also consider pelvic alignment,[46] as well as hip and knee issues, which may require additional orthotic intervention. Clinical experience with the use of slow motion video in the observation of subtle gait disturbances has led to improved assessment capabilities,[42,47] which enhance the decision-making process. Second, the purported "uninvolved" side is, indeed, "involved" since the gait pattern is asymmetrical and a leg length discrepancy (LLD) may be present.[46] Therefore, the contralateral limb may sometimes also benefit from therapeutic and orthotic intervention. The LLD must be considered because it changes gait kinematics and kinetics.[46,48,49] A small amount of LLD (less than 2.5 cm) may be acceptable in the general population[50] but should be avoided in individuals with neuromotor disorders.[51] When the contralateral limb exhibits mild calcaneal eversion in weight-bearing, a Helfet heel cup[52-54] (Figure 20-4) or a flexible foot orthosis may suffice, but either device must be assessed in weight-bearing and the resting calcaneus measured to assure the appropriate correction. If more support is required, a custom-molded University of California—Biomechanics Laboratory (UCBL) device[55] is indicated (Figure 20-5).

The majority of the orthoses to follow in this section (see Table 20-1) will incorporate the footplate design features of the UCBL,[55] and those features will be reviewed as such. As indicated by its abbreviated name, the UCBL was first described at the University of California—Biomechanics Laboratory in 1967.[55] The trim lines encompassed the first and the fifth metatarsal heads; the height of the orthosis was just below the ankle and below the shoe height while maintaining a deep heel seat and encompassing the navicular.[55] It must be noted that the shoe style of 1967 would have been a tie oxford with a 0.75- to 1-inch heel height and a steel shank (Figure 20-6), which is very supportive by today's standards. The UCBL provides improved triplanar alignment with a medial arch support (to control pronation), calcaneal containment, and the lateral and medial walls.[55] In the case of calcaneal eversion, the lateral wall is extended to include the fifth metatarsal head and address foot abduction (see Figure 20-5). When excessive supination is observed, the arch support is lowered, and the medial wall is extended to include the first metatarsal head and address foot adduction (Figure 20-7). These characteristics should be incorporated into the LE orthoses described next to control excessive pronation or supination in a closed kinetic chain.

Management of True Equinus Gait

The true equinus gait pattern is defined as the ankle in plantarflexion, with gait compensations of full knee extension or hyperextension and normal hip and pelvic motion.[39] The gastrocnemius and soleus muscles are spastic and/or contracted, which limits the talocrural range of motion (ROM).[39] Traditionally, as shown in Table 20-1, orthotic intervention has placed the equinus foot in an AFO set at a neutral talocrural joint angle in a flexible, solid (Figure 20-8) or

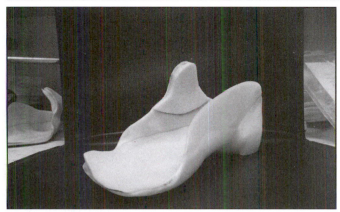

Figure 20-7. Custom fabricated from a cast, a UCBL orthosis with extended medial wall for control of foot adduction and lateral talar flange. UCBLs are commonly used to add stability to the subtalar and midtarsal joints. The trimlines should enclose the fifth metatarsophalangeal joint if the goal is to control the forefoot abduction.

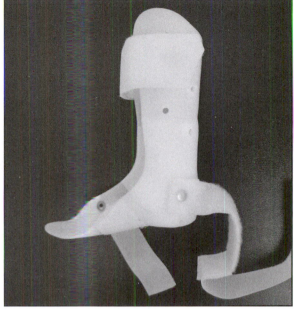

Figure 20-8. A solid AFO set at 90 degrees, custom fabricated from a cast.

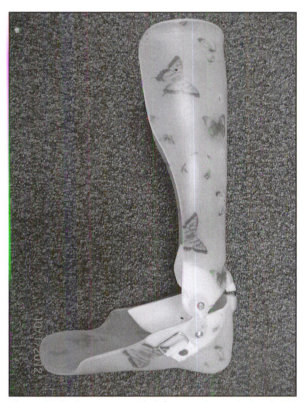

Figure 20-9. A custom-molded free motion articulated AFO with adjustable plantarflexion stop and free dorsiflexion with a dorsiflexion assist joint. The joints are Tamarack Flexure Joint Model 740, and the adjustable plantarflexion stop is an Otto Bock SNAPSTOP.

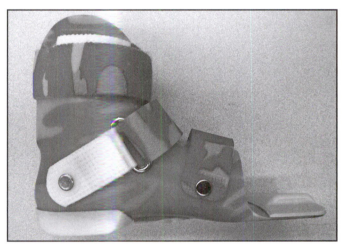

Figure 20-10. A supramalleolar orthosis (SMO). SMOs are often used to stabilize the subtalar and midtarsal joints but lend no structural support to the talocrural joint.

articulated system with free dorsiflexion and plantarflexion stop (Figure 20-9). Devices such as a UCBL[55] (see Figure 20-7) or a supramalleolar orthosis (SMO) (Figure 20-10) have also been prescribed, but these do not reduce the equinus structurally since they do not cross the ankle joint in the sagittal plane.[56] The reduction of plantarflexion in an AFO has been repeatedly shown to improve the equinus gait in individuals with CP,[24,56-60] but the orthotic intervention should also consider the need for the tibia to move from a reclined to inclined position in the stance phase of the gait cycle.[15] In a true equinus situation, the tibia cannot incline due to the lack of the ankle motion, nor will the plantarflexed foot fit well in a device set at a neutral AA, whether it is a PLS, a solid AFO (SAFO), or an articulated AFO with a plantarflexion stop (AAFO PFS). Common compensations within the traditional AFO include the midfoot collapse[61] and knee hyperextension, often with a forward torso lean. These problems tend to worsen with the use of the device and increase the need for more compensatory movement. Such complications have negative triplanar effects on proximal and distal structures as noted earlier.[24,30,33-35] An improved orthotic intervention would promote the forward progression of the tibia without causing distress to the distal and proximal structures. The next chapter addresses these concerns with a different approach to AFO design.[15]

Figure 20-11. Orthotic joints with elastomer bumpers. (A) An UltraFlex AFO with Adjustable Dynamic Response (ADR) Joints with anterior and posterior stops and anterior and posterior elastomer bumpers. (B) An Ultraflex ADR Joint with an elastomer bumper. (Reprinted with permission from UltraflexSystems, Inc.)

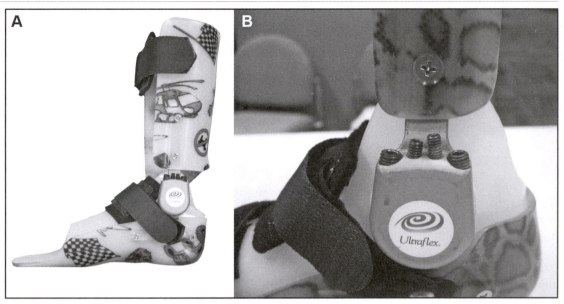

Management of Jump Gait

Similar to the true equinus gait, jump gait is also characterized by ankle plantarflexion, which is often exacerbated by spasticity of the hip flexors, hamstrings, and calf musculature.[39] The jump gait foot makes initial contact with the ground at the toes or forefoot, while the knee and hip are flexed. The ankle is plantarflexed from midstance to toe off, and the knee remains flexed until late stance when it moves into a relative extension position, without achieving its full range. The swing knee remains flexed, which leads to a short step length. Jump gait is often seen in children with bilateral CP with a greater involvement of LEs than UEs (diplegia).[39] This gait pattern is a very unstable mobility strategy. An assessment method that uses a slow motion video replay would show that the individual is moving one foot in front of the other with a burst of hip flexion as fast as possible to avoid a loss of balance. As observed clinically, the users of jump gait often find static, unsupported standing difficult. Jump gait is more prevalent in young children with diplegia, but this pattern tends to alter as the individual ages.[39,42]

Several orthotic interventions have been used in the clinic (see Table 20-1). The rationale for the selection of the UCBL and SMO options includes the child's ability to keep up with his or her peers and stay functional while the device provides some protection to the foot alignment.[29] The PLS AFO has been used with some success for foot control and mild knee control while the tibial progression over the foot is allowed.[22] The PLS, SAFO, and AAFO PFS often leave the child weight-bearing through the forefoot, with little influence on the position of the knee since the heel rarely makes contact with the ground. Compared with lower designs such as the UCBL and SMO, these higher designs may provide more protection to the LEs from rotary deformities, but research evidence in support of this notion is lacking. Orthotic joints with elastomer bumpers[62] (Figure 20-11) that resist excessive dorsiflexion and plantarflexion may provide greater adjustability to address the forces acting upon more proximal body segments. The elastomer bumpers are located within an orthotic joint[62] and become compressed as torque is applied in the closed kinetic chain. For example, the dorsiflexion bumper is compressed in terminal stance and resists the external dorsiflexion moment as the center of mass (COM) moves anteriorly to the ankle joint. It is not yet established that the use of these joints is an improvement compared to other orthotic interventions described earlier.

Management of Apparent Equinus Gait

The apparent equinus gait is characterized by an ankle with a normal open kinetic chain ROM and a neutral position in the closed chain, with the person bearing weight through the forefoot because of the hip and knee flexor contracture or tightness.[39,42] This alignment serves to maintain the COM over the base of support when the hip and knee are flexed.[39] It is not uncommon for the individuals who display this gait pattern to demonstrate jump gait at an earlier age.[39,42] Even though the ankle ROM allows dorsiflexion in an open kinetic chain, clinicians involved in the care of the child often observe that his or her previous history of jump or equinus gait often results in hypermobility of the foot, leading to excessive pronation or, less often, supination in the closed kinetic chain. Either position provides an unstable base and, therefore, the design of the foot section of the orthosis must yield more stability to address this problem.

Traditionally, a wide variety of orthotic interventions have been utilized for these purposes (see Table 20-1). The UCBL and SMO are sometimes used.[29] The structurally more supportive alternatives are PLS AFOs, SAFOs,[42,63-65] AAFO with PFS, and Ground Reaction AFOs (GRAFOs), also termed *Floor Reaction AFOs* (FRAFOs).[42,66] The GRAFOs provide a rigid footplate; the AFO section transfers the ground reaction force from the footplate to the anterior rigid plastic segment below the patella, which produces a knee extension moment[29]

(Figure 20-12). The proximal segment increases the lever arm length compared to the standard SAFO to address the increase in dorsiflexion moment at the ankle.[64] The GRAFO design can be used with hinges that limit dorsiflexion while plantarflexion is free.[24,64] It must be noted that the GRAFO may lose effectiveness in cases of significant external tibial torsion or if the foot is rotated away from the line of progression, leading to a considerable increase in foot angles.[66]

Management of Crouch Gait

Crouch gait is clinically recognized when the ankle is in dorsiflexion in stance, placing the entire foot on the floor with the knee and hip flexed.[39,42] The plantarflexors are usually overstretched and the foot is abducted.[42,67] Sutherland and Davids[67] report that the most common causes of crouch gait are hamstring contractures and the overlengthening of the triceps surae. According to Rodda et al,[39] crouch gait frequently results from an isolated surgical lengthening of the gastroc-soleus muscle group. Additionally, this pattern is seen in children with bilateral CP who have been ambulatory for a period of time.[39,68] Initially, these children often use one of the previously described mobility strategies,[39,68] but as their body mass increases, the tenuous compensations that appeared to be functional for them in the past are overcome by gravity, which pulls the LEs into a crouched posture. The orthoses that are most commonly used to address this problem are SAFOs[29,65] and GRAFOs[42,64-66] (see Table 20-1).

Functional Electrical Stimulation Devices Used to Improve Gait in Children With Cerebral Palsy

Functional electrical stimulation (FES) improves muscle function by applying electrical current to the muscle or nerve at the time the muscle is supposed to be active.[69-71] FES is a subset of neuromuscular electrical stimulation (NMES), which is generally used for muscle strengthening and for reduction of spasticity, often in the absence of a functional activity.[69-71] FES requires less intensive electrical stimulation since it amplifies the already existing muscle activation and is not intended to fatigue the muscle, as is the case with the NMES.[70,71] The FES devices are commonly referred to as *neuroprostheses*,[45,72] which may confuse the reader since, clinically, they function as orthoses and are often referred to as such in some of the literature.[73]

Liberson et al[74] published the first article using the FES concepts in 1961. The team used the FES system to correct the drop foot in adults with hemiparesis.[74] FES has been studied in the pediatric population including children with CP for some time, at least since the late 1990s.[69] Children with CP are especially arduous to study due to the heterogeneity of the involvement and differences in movement strategies.[69] This section is limited to the use of FES as an orthosis and as an alternative to an AFO that helps to clear the foot during the swing phase of gait.[45,75-73] FES has been used with children with CP to target various muscle groups, including

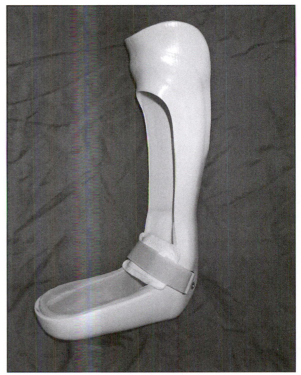

Figure 20-12. A ground reaction AFO (GRAFO) with an extended footplate for increased ground reaction leverage to resist dorsiflexion. The footplate is rounded to increase strength since laminate plastic tends to be more brittle than the more common polypropylene or copolymer.

the anterior tibialis, the gastrocnemius, the glutei, and the quadriceps and hamstring muscles.[70,71,79]

Description of Functional Electrical Stimulation Devices

FES uses electrodes placed on the skin to stimulate the motor nerve and elicit a muscle contraction.[72,75-79] Therefore, the peripheral nerve must be intact, and the FES is used for children and adults with an upper motor neuron lesion.[70,80,81] Three devices that are commercially available in the United States are listed in Table 20-2. They include the Ness L300 by Bioness Inc, the Odstock Drop Foot Stimulator (ODFS Pace) from Odstock Medical Limited, and the WalkAide from Innovative Neurotronics, Inc (Figure 20-13).[80-82] These devices stimulate the common peroneal nerve to activate the dorsiflexors and evertors of the ankle complex to address the drop foot problem.[77,80-82] The standard procedure is to place the first electrode over the common peroneal nerve, posterior and distal to the fibular head, and then place the second electrode over the tibialis anterior muscle.[72]

Benefits of Functional Electrical Stimulation Devices

Research conducted with adults with neurological disorders showed that compared to an AFO, FES devices allow greater ankle movement and enhanced proprioception, which are useful for postural control.[72,83] Other advantages may include improved knee and hip flexion in the swing

		TABLE 20-2	

COMMERCIALLY AVAILABLE FUNCTIONAL ELECTRICAL STIMULATION SYSTEMS FOR DROP FOOT THAT MAY BE USEFUL FOR CHILDREN AND ADULTS WITH CEREBRAL PALSY[a]

FEATURES	COMMERCIAL FES SYSTEMS		
	Ness L300[80]	ODFS Pace[81]	WalkAide[82]
Heel sensor	Yes	Yes	Yes
Tilt sensor	No	No	Yes
Electrodes and stimulator secured in a tibial cuff	Yes	No—customized suspension. Stimulator is clipped to waist belt or placed in a pocket	Yes
Pediatric cuff size	Smallest cuff size 9-inch circumference	A variety of suspension methods limited by clinician creativity	Yes
General contraindications[b]	Demand-type cardiac pacemaker, defibrillator, metallic or electrical implant		
	Electrodes must not be placed over the following:		
	• Areas of fracture or dislocation that would be negatively affected by movement induced by stimulation		
	• Broken, irritated, infected, or inflamed skin, rash, or blisters		
	• Malignant tumors		
	LE phlebitis, thrombophlebitis, or varicose veins		
	Seizure disorder or epilepsy		

Abbreviations: FES, functional electrical stimulation; LE, lower extremity; ODFS, Odstock Drop Foot Stimulator.

[a] This table is intended for a brief comparison of 3 clinically available FES units and is not meant to be all inclusive of every characteristic of the mentioned devices.

[b] General contraindications listed here are limited to those appropriate for children or adults with cerebral palsy. This combined list is not all inclusive of all contraindications, precautions, and warnings associated with each FES system.

Figure 20-13. A close-up of the WalkAide device attached to the lower leg of a child. (Reprinted with permission from Innovative Neurotronics, Inc.)

phase of gait,[72,84] prevention of muscle atrophy, and muscle re-education.[72,85] In addition, compared to an AFO, the FES units cover less skin, allow greater air circulation, and do not rely as much on the shoe wear; or, with the use of a tilt sensor, no shoes are required.[77] The tilt sensor is a switch sensitive to the inclination of the tibia and can be adjusted via a remote computer program. When the tibia is inclined in terminal stance, the tilt sensor activates the stimuli for swing; and at terminal swing or at initial contact, the tilt sensor ends the stimulation.[77,84] Furthermore, the FES units certainly do not require the individual to wear a larger shoe, which is usually needed when wearing an AFO.[84]

There is an indication that ankle dorsiflexion that occurs with electrical stimulation would sometimes carry over to gait in the absence of stimulation.[69,76,86,87] This has been observed for brief periods of time in both children and adults.[69,76,86,87] However, while research evidence shows that the use of an FES device, such as the WalkAide, improves ankle dorsiflexion during the swing phase of gait and at initial contact[88,89] and results in increased tibialis anterior muscle thickness,[90] it does not lead to a long-term improvement in ankle control during barefoot walking.[90] The latter finding indicates that a continued use of an FES device would be required to maintain improved ankle motion. In general, in most studies, the majority of participants accepted the FES device and chose to continue using it if it was made available.[44,76-78,86,88-90]

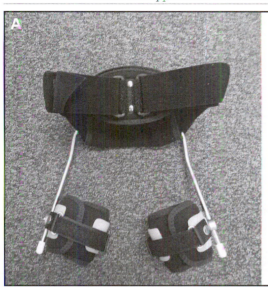
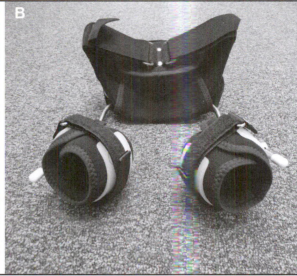

Figure 20-14. Standing, Walking and Sitting Hip orthosis by Allard USA, front view. (A) Hips extended for standing. (B) Hips flexed for sitting.

Issues to Consider

FES has many advantages compared to an AFO, yet it is not a common approach in the treatment of drop foot in children with CP[89] as it presents its own challenges. Clinical experience shows that an FES unit is approximately 3 times more expensive than an AFO; the electrode placement on the limb to elicit the desired response may be challenging when used on a daily basis; the electrodes must be replaced every 2 weeks; and they constitute a recurrent cost with the initial supply lasting approximately 6 months. The repeated use of the electrode may cause skin irritation.[45,77] The FES units may shift their position with activity, especially in children, and batteries lose their charge. Studies with children using the FES devices do not necessarily report uniform results, and the improvements observed may not be clinically significant.[87,91] It has been reported that FES is often not tolerated easily during a school day.[92] In addition, the daily use of FES requires regular follow up visits to ensure the effective use of the device, at least until the gait pattern has stabilized.[76]

Looking Forward

The clinical use of FES with children with CP is complicated but warrants further study.[69] Currently, establishing clinical guidelines would be difficult because of the lack of research evidence.[92] However, the results reported by Prosser et al[89] are promising as they showed a high rate of acceptance of the FES device, which was effective in controlling foot drop in 19 children with CP, Gross Motor Function Classification System (GMFCS)[93] levels I and II. Clinicians and researchers will continue looking into the use of FES as an orthotic device for children and adults with CP. Research that compared the use of an articulated AFO, an FES system, and a combination of these 2 interventions with adults with incomplete spinal cord injury showed the best results when the articulated AFO was used together with the FES system.[84] Such a combination has not been explored as an option for children with CP. The use of FES in conjunction with botulinum toxin A injections is also under investigation.[70]

Hip Orthoses for Gait

Ambulatory children with bilateral CP often have challenges in gait that arise from hip involvement.[94-102] The incidence of hip instability for children with unilateral or bilateral CP who walk by the age of 2.5 years is low.[103] Intoeing gait is frequently observed in this patient population,[97,104] reportedly in 66% to 70% of children with bilateral and 54% with unilateral involvement,[104] often related to a combination of the medial rotation of the hip and pelvis, internal tibial torsion, hind foot inversion, forefoot adduction, and spasticity.[96,97] Excessive internal rotation of the LE will make the foot progression difficult,[97] with increased tripping and falling.[102] Another hip difficulty is its excessive adduction, or scissoring, induced by the hypertonicity or spasticity of adductor muscles.[94,96] Both of these phenomena, the intoeing and scissoring, are significant barriers to energy conservation during gait.[94] Common surgical interventions to address rotational problems leading to hip instability were discussed in Chapter 8. Since the incidence of hip challenges rises with the GMFCS level,[100,101] which largely reflects the level of the child's functional ambulation,[93] one may hypothesize that functional ambulation may play a preventive role. If so, it may be possible that a conservative intervention, such as hip orthoses that aid the child's walking, may also play a role in improved hip development. A look at clinical practice and related research evidence is helpful in examining this hypothesis.

Current orthotic intervention includes the Standing, Walking and Sitting Hip (S.W.A.S.H.) orthosis by Allard USA (Figure 20-14). In gait, the S.W.A.S.H. brace does not address the transverse plane rotation, but it can be very useful in controlling the scissoring pattern and allowing one LE to progress past the other.[98] It can also alter the hip-pelvic relationship for sitting[98] to improve stability and ease bimanual UE task performance. The S.W.A.S.H. orthosis has a sophisticated design with multiple adjustment possibilities to maintain hip abduction and to customize the fit for a variety of

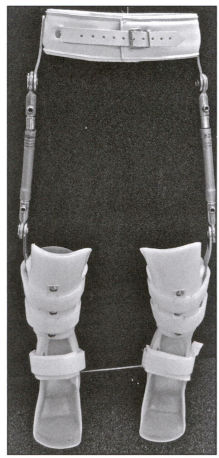

Figure 20-15. Bilateral Becker Torsion Splints attached to AFOs to reduce excessive transverse plane excessive rotation tendencies in the lower extremity. Absent from this photo is a Quick Disconnect component that may be used to detach the splints from the AFOs.

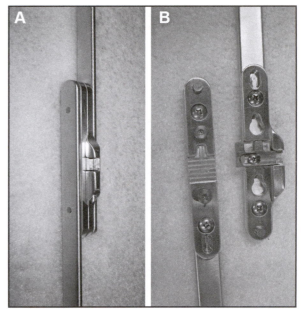

Figure 20-16. (A) Close view of a Quick Disconnect unit connected to upper and lower metal bars. The Quick Disconnect component allows for separation of one section of an orthosis from another for a variety of uses. If installed, this component can be used to separate the Becker Torsion Splints from the AFOs. (B) Close view of a Quick Disconnect unit separated to reveal the interlock mechanism.

hip joint presentations.[98] This device is generally worn over the child's clothes and adds bulk to the wearer. However, it is considered simple to don and doff[105] with Velcro pelvic section closures and adjustable Velcro thigh cuff snap closures (see Figure 20-14).

Several studies investigated the efficacy of the S.W.A.S.H. brace.[98,101,105,106] Graham et al[98] used this device in combination with botulinum toxin A injections to test their effects on hip stability in a randomized, controlled clinical trial (RCT), but their results did not support the hypothesis that this combined intervention would decrease the hip migration rate in children with spastic CP.[98,101] However, an earlier RCT demonstrated some functional advantage of such treatment approach for children classified in GMFCS levels II and III.[105] Another study used surface electromyography to alleviate a clinical concern that stretching imposed by the S.W.A.S.H. brace may increase hip adductor spasticity.[106] Results showed no significant difference in hip adductor muscle activity under sitting, standing, or walking conditions, with or without the brace, which also supported its continued clinical use.[106]

Torsional deformities of the LE observed in children with bilateral CP can be addressed by non-elastic bilateral Torsion Splints with a leather-covered metal pelvic belt and metal hip and knee joints, which are connected by torsion shafts and attached to AFOs (Figure 20-15). The Torsion Splints are custom fabricated from measurements by Becker Orthopedic. These are often referred to simply as twister cables. The portion attached to the AFO can be removable with the inclusion of a Quick Disconnect component (Figure 20-16). The twister cables will not alter the bone torsion, but can resist the stubborn internal rotation of the LE that inhibits foot progression[94] and may negatively affect participation. This type of orthotic intervention is generally regarded as a short-term solution for a child with significant torsional issues when one foot has substantial difficulty progressing past the other.[42] In the long term, transverse plane problems of this magnitude are commonly addressed by derotation osteotomy surgeries.[42,95]

UPPER EXTREMITY SEMI-RIGID ORTHOSES

According to the ICF model,[2] the UE can be assessed at several levels, including body functions and structures, as well as activity and participation.[107] The upper limb function is impaired in 50% to 80% of children with unilateral and bilateral CP.[108,109] UE deficits are observed during reaching activities and during grasping, manipulating,

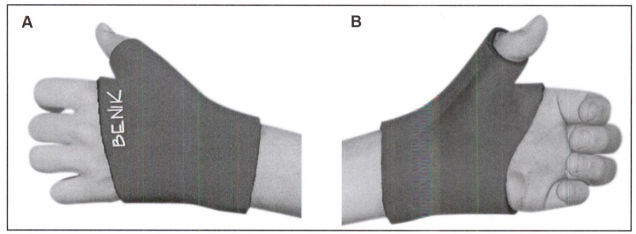

Figure 20-17. A neoprene HO with a thumb adduction post, from measurement or custom from measurement. The web space or thenar eminence can be reinforced with thermoplastic. This device will have little to no effect on the position of the wrist. (A) Dorsal view. (B) Palmar view. (Reprinted with permission from the Benik Corporation.)

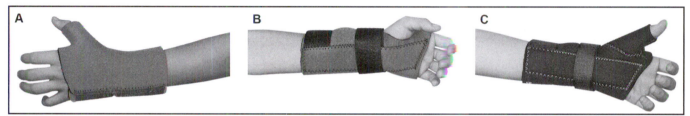

Figure 20-18. Several WHOs fabricated from measurement or custom from measurement. Additional thermoplastic can be added to address positioning requirements of the thumb and ulnar deviation. Several strapping configurations are also available. (A) A dorsal view of a neoprene WHO with a thumb post and wrist control. Excessive wrist flexion can be addressed by metal stays or heat moldable thermoplastic. (B) A palmar view of a neoprene WHO without a thumb post, with increased wrist control from metal stays on palmar and dorsal surfaces. (C) A palmar view of a neoprene WHO with thumb post and increased wrist control with metal stays on palmar and dorsal surfaces. (Reprinted with permission from the Benik Corporation.)

and releasing objects with the involved hand.[107] UE limitations greatly restrict participation in activities of daily living,[108,110-112] including self-care, play, school or work, and participation in leisure activities.[110] Disrupted sensory mechanisms and impaired muscle control compromise fine motor skills.[107,108,111,112] Hand movements in children and adults with CP are impeded by neuromuscular and musculoskeletal problems leading to contractures, deformities, and loss of force and function.[111] Bimanual tasks are especially challenging for affected UEs as they are the most difficult to execute.[108,109] According to published literature, spontaneous object manipulation during everyday life and outside of therapy sessions may be difficult for children with unilateral CP.[110] As the result, these children experience decreased performance in activities related to mobility, self-care, hygiene, play with their peers, and completion of school assignments. Other issues include the cosmetic appearance of the involved UE and pain.[108,113]

UE spasticity frequently leads to the development of stereotypical movement patterns that include medial rotation of the shoulder, a combination of elbow flexion and forearm pronation, wrist flexion combined with ulnar deviation, persistent thumb-in-palm position, and swan neck deformities of the fingers.[109,114,115] The thumb-in-palm position causes substantial difficulty for the functional hand use.[111,116] Improving the hand function for children and adults with

CP is a challenging and important goal,[117] consistent with the ICF framework.[2] Specific goals at the activity level may be related to the performance of manual tasks in such activities of daily living as play, eating, using a computer, and moving in home, school, and community environments in a power wheelchair. The child's goals of participation in favorite age-appropriate games, hobbies, school, and community activities or playing a favorite sport without pain, discomfort, or excessive fatigue related to the UE alignment can also be addressed by therapeutic intervention.

The use of UE orthoses is common in clinical practice, with reported goals at the body structure and function level of the ICF[2] that are related to achieving improvements in the arm and hand alignment, ROM, quality of movement, and functional use.[108] Although limited evidence supports the use of UE orthoses,[108,115,118-120] clinical experience suggests that orthotic devices may aid in preventing contractures and deformities,[109,110,118,120] and that supporting the wrist and thumb in a functional position may enhance the hand use.[108,118,120]

The 2 designs often used clinically include hand orthoses (HOs) (Figure 20-17) to maintain the web space, and wrist-hand orthoses (WHOs) to place the wrist in a functional position, with or without web space reinforcement (Figures 20-18 and 20-19). Louwers et al[110] found that a static wrist and thumb brace (see Figure 20-19) provided support to both

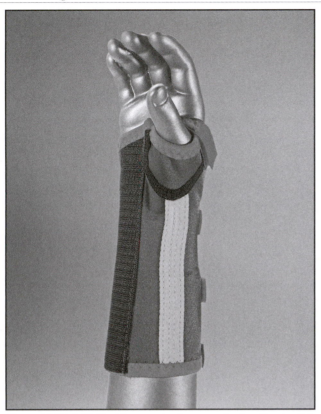

Figure 20-19. A WHO with a metal palmar stay for functional activities. (Reprinted with permission from Ottobock.)

the wrist and the carpometacarpal joints, which improved grasp, release, and bimanual function in 50% of the study sample of 25 children with unilateral CP. Barroso et al[111] reported improvements in overall hand function with the use of a WHO described as a wrist extending/thumb abduction (WETA) orthosis, which appeared very similar to the Benik BD-88 Option A sans the supportive wrist stay (see Figure 20-18A). Burtner et al[109] compared the use of static and dynamic spiral design WHOs with children with unilateral CP. The use of a dynamic spiral design yielded improved grip strength, dexterity, and normalized shoulder muscle activation compared to a static WHO.[109] Dynamic (spring torsion) splints have shown promise as an intervention for children with spastic CP.[109,113,121,122] These devices will be discussed further in the Stretching Orthoses section of this chapter.

Although UE orthoses are frequently used clinically, their application varies in this patient population.[123] Russo et al[123] reported poor compliance with UE orthoses, especially in older children with less involvement who had developed alternative functional methods to achieve specific tasks. Disturbed sensation is a noted challenge for children and adults with unilateral CP.[108,114] Clinical experience suggests that the reduction of sensory input by covering the hand with an orthosis may offset any benefit the device might offer. The review of the available literature shows that UE orthotic intervention is extremely challenging with insufficient evidence to guide the therapists in their decision-making process.

STRETCHING ORTHOSES

Spastic Muscle Considerations

Children and adults with CP often experience musculoskeletal challenges, such as weakness, reduced ROM, and contractures as secondary effects of the primary neurological pathology and abnormal muscle tone.[124-133] It is apparent that reduced ROM has a deleterious effect on posture, mobility, and overall activity.[124,125,130-132,134-137] Typically, the dysfunction of the spastic muscle progresses with time, further complicating these factors, resulting in pain and greater disability later in life.[136-138] A common therapeutic goal for children and adults with neurological dysfunction is to improve or maintain the ROM by stretching to enhance activity, prevent or reduce bone and joint deformities, and delay or eliminate the need for surgery.[124,130,135,136,139,140]

Structural and mechanical effects of spasticity on muscle tissue are poorly understood, but it has been demonstrated that spastic muscles differ from those with normal tone.[127,130,134,137,138,141-145] The reader is referred to Chapter 4 for a discussion of spastic muscle properties in children with CP. In general, the more spasticity a person has, the less motion he or she would actively perform, and the greater the likelihood of developing a contracture.[126,130,140] Spastic muscles that cross more than one joint, such as the gastrocnemius muscle, are often more prone to contractures than monoarticular muscles.[146] The reduced length of a muscle decreases both the available ROM in the joint and its strength.[125,134,146] Connective tissue shortening and relative increase in volume, as well as contracture-related bone and joint deformities are also observed.[140,146] Because of the negative effects of spasticity on muscles, bones, and joints, the goal of preventing the ROM deterioration is important if it is practical.[146] While many clinicians use passive stretching for these purposes, its benefits are still being debated.[130,133,135,137] The relevant published literature was discussed in Chapter 15.

Options for Orthotic Intervention

Many conservative interventions are traditionally used with the assumption that they will reduce joint limitations.[129,130,132,136,147-149] Along with daily stretching[129,130] serial casting,[147] positioning,[136,149] splinting,[147,150] and home exercise programs,[130,133] several types of UE and LE orthotic devices may be used for these purposes.[125] Generally, most stretching orthoses (SOs) for children and adults with CP are custom fabricated to allow for the ease of donning, decreased skin irritation, improved comfort, and proper joint alignment. Three main types of orthoses are commonly used clinically: static, adjustable static (often called *static dynamic*), and those with a torsion producing spring.[125,145] The term *dynamic orthoses* is frequently used to describe the devices that use a spring. In this chapter, the term *spring torsion* will be used instead as it seems to be more accurate in describing the action mechanism of this type of orthoses. Hopefully, this will lessen confusion when other dynamic devices are discussed.

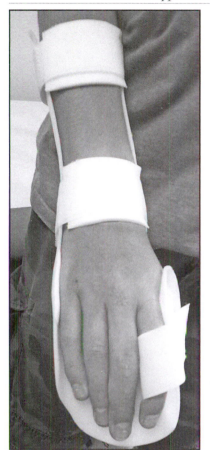

Figure 20-20. A Wrist-Hand-Finger Orthosis to prevent wrist flexion and ulnar deviation, custom fabricated from a patient model. A variety of strapping orientations can be used to address specific concerns. In this photo, the ulnar deviation correction was enhanced by a strap on just the index finger.

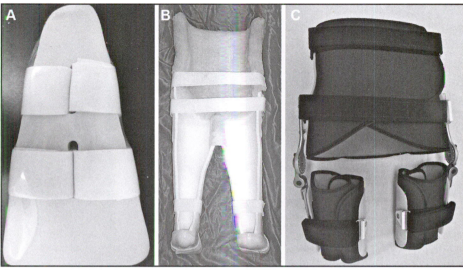

Figure 20-21. Hip abduction orthoses. (A) An off-the-shelf foam abduction wedge can be used to position the child's hips in mild abduction. These foam devices can be covered in moisture proof covers if the wearer is incontinent. (B) A total body orthosis, custom fabricated from a patient model. These were typically made to position the hips, knees, and ankles following a surgery before the off-the-shelf customizable devices became available. (C) A Maple Leaf Hip Abduction Orthosis by Becker Orthopedic. This device has static or adjustable static (pictured) sagittal and transverse hip joint range for greater hip abduction positioning; additional extensions that cross the knees are available.

Static devices are used on the UE and LE, most commonly as wrist-hand-finger orthoses (WHFOs) (Figure 20-20), hip abduction orthoses (Figure 20-21), or AFOs, usually to maintain a position, often postsurgically or following serial casting. The adjustable SOs can utilize a variety of joints, including turnbuckles, step lock, or ratchet joints (Figure 20-22), and free motion with dorsiflexion pull straps (Figure 20-23). The adjustment allows the mechanical joint to be altered, but once the position is changed, the joint is held statically. The adjustable SOs with metal joints usually have incremental changes of 6 to 10 degrees, which may or may not be congruent with the available anatomic joint range. This is usually managed by variable strap tightness that may be subject to inconsistent strap application, especially if the patient has multiple caretakers.

A spring torsion component of an SO provides constant torque, or rotation, around an axis.[125] This torque takes up the slack from the connective tissue creep, which makes the orthosis effective throughout the range for the full wear time (Figure 20-24A).[113,125] Orthoses with spring torsion components can be used for passive or active stretching

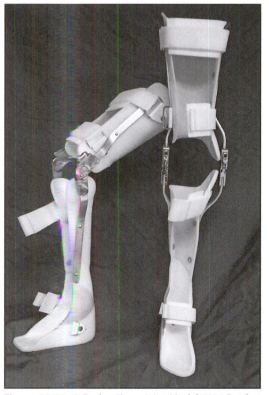

Figure 20-22. A Becker Knee Joint Model 1014 Ratchet Lock is one example of a joint with static adjustable positioning. The ratchet type generally has fairly large locking increments. Other designs utilize a clutch mechanism which allows one way motion in any increment, but prevents movement in the opposite direction.

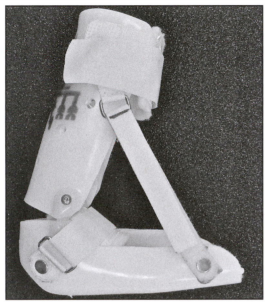

Figure 20-23. An AFO with an adjustable plantarflexion stop strap, custom fabricated from a patient model. These commonly address plantarflexor muscle tightness and must be used with another device to maintain the knee in a comfortable extension position. If the user is ambulatory, a nonslip plantar surface is necessary for shoeless walking.

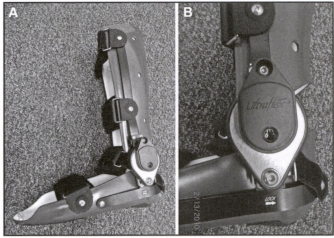

Figure 20-24. (A) An AFO with a spring torsion component that provides an adjustable torsion force, custom fabricated from a patient model. This is an Ultraflex AFO with a lateral power unit with adjustable tension that has dial locks on the medial and lateral sides of the ankle joint to set the limits on its ROM. (B) A closer view of the Ultraflex power unit. The visible zero is the tension calibration of the power unit; its settings vary from 0 to 7. The *LOCK* (in yellow) will eliminate all motion to facilitate independent donning and doffing.

Figure 20-25. Ultraflex orthoses custom fabricated from patient models. (A) An Ultraflex upper extremity orthosis with an adjustable spring torsion component at the elbow, a static adjustable forearm rotation section, and a static wrist-hand-finger section. A lateral power unit can apply adjustable tension at the joint, with the tension maintained throughout the ROM. This particular example has a dial lock on the lateral side to set the ROM limits. (B) An Ultraflex upper extremity orthosis with an adjustable spring torsion component at the wrist and a static hand-finger section. This particular example is a pediatric version, which has no dial lock to limit the affected range. (C) An Ultraflex hip orthosis with an adjustable spring torsion component placed between the thighs and static knee and ankle positioning. A power unit can apply adjustable tension against the hip adductors. This is a pediatric design that is donned one extremity at a time using a quick disconnect unit to ease the donning process for the caretakers. (D) An Ultraflex pediatric knee-ankle-foot orthosis (KAFO) with a spring torsion component that provides an adjustable stretching force at the knee. It has a lateral adjustable tension power unit and a quick disconnect assembly to detach the knee section from the static AFO, likely to improve the wear tolerance. (Reprinted with permission from Ultraflex Systems, Inc.)

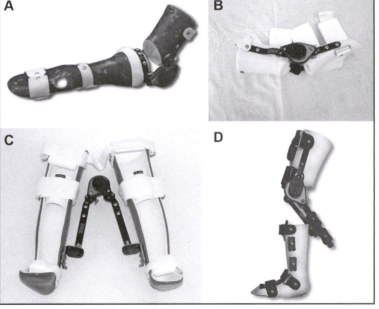

over longer periods of time than therapy allows, and can be removed for functional mobility activities.[125] These torsion units can be totally locked allowing no movement, stopped to prevent motion in one direction only, or stopped with tension to apply a continuous stretching force to the muscle while preventing excessive motion (Figure 20-24B). These custom devices are commonly applied to the elbow (Figure 20-25A), wrist (Figure 20-25B), hip (Figure 20-25C), knee (Figure 20-25D), and ankle joints (see Figure 20-24A). Separate joint lockouts eliminate the tension of the power unit torsion to ease donning and doffing, which improves

the user's independence. Custom SOs can be fabricated to address the alignment of two adjacent joints, such as the knee and the ankle (see Figure 20-25D) or the elbow and the wrist (see Figure 20-25A). However, one must be aware that the wearer may not tolerate the combined continuous stretching. Maintaining a single joint under continuous tension while the other joint is aligned in a static position may improve comfort. Devices that cover multiple joints can be fabricated with quick disconnect units that can be disassembled for the ease of donning and increased tolerance (see Figure 20-25D), but as observed clinically, they add bulk, cost, and weight.

So far, the length of daily wear time required to gain ROM or prevent its loss has not been established by solid evidence. In a single study of 10 children with CP using a specially designed apparatus, Tardieu et al[151] found it necessary to apply stretching for 6 hours per day to maintain the extensibility of the soleus muscle. The same report stipulated that this study outcome did not provide a standard of care for preventing contractures, and that the soleus findings might not carry over to other muscles.[151] The latter was supported by a number of authors, including, for example, Bromwich et al,[152] who obtained positive results using an orthosis for stretching for only 30 minutes per day, and Farmer et al,[145,153] who reported on the stretching benefits of 1-hour orthotic wear. Patient comfort and restrictions an orthosis may put on activities of daily living are other important considerations for clinical decision making regarding the SO wearing time.[145] Although SOs are often referred to as *night splints*, wearing them at night often disrupts sleep.[145] Therefore, it is important to discuss when and how long the SO should be worn by each individual patient.

It is common for children and adults with CP to have gastrocnemius muscles tightness, which is frequently addressed by the use of SOs.[137,145,146] The gastrocnemius is a biarticular muscle; this requires a device that addresses the knee and the ankle,[145] with additional attention given to the talocrural, subtalar, and midtarsal joints. The position of these joints within the device must be controlled so that the gastrocnemius bares the greatest tension and thus has the best opportunity for elongation. First, the knee must be kept in a consistent position near comfortable full extension.[137] Second, the subtalar and midtarsal joints must be aligned in a neutral position. As has been observed clinically, too often the joints stretched in devices aimed at affecting the talocrural joint ROM stretch the subtalar and midtarsal joints and do not address the knee position. Third, the heel must remain seated in the device.[151] A simple clinical method to monitor proper heel positioning is to have a 1- to 2.5-cm opening placed in the posterior-inferior section of the heel cup (Figure 20-26). This opening provides visual and tactile confirmation that the heel is well positioned, and promotes correct independent donning as noted by users of devices with such a feature. Some heel rise within the orthosis may be inevitable,[151] but no more than 6 mm is clinically acceptable.

Research Evidence

As noted by Wiart et al,[130] there is a lack of evidence to support stretching as an effective intervention to address the level of activity or participation in children with CP. Furthermore, without proper evidence, making a direct connection between changes at the level of body structures and functions, such as the ROM or muscle tone, and changes at the level of activity and participation, such as activities of daily living or classroom participation, is specifically discouraged by the ICF.[2,130] Of the research literature that supports stretching interventions, a sustained stretch appears preferable.[129,145]

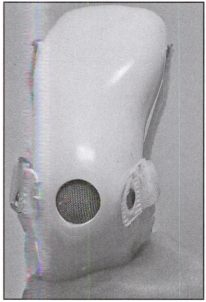

Figure 20-26. A common clinical issue is the difficulty determining the heel position in any stretching AFO. A generous hole at the heel is a simple remedy to validate correct heel contact within the AFO for caretakers or wearers.

Positive effects of the SO use in combination with botulinum toxin A injections[150] or NMES[113,121,122] were shown by several authors. Results of a study that examined the efficacy of static UE night splints demonstrated a long-term functional advantage in the group that used the splints over 6 months following a botulinum toxin A treatment, compared to the no splint use group.[150] Three studies reported positive changes in UE ROM,[113] spasticity,[121,122] grip strength,[121] and function[121,122] in children with CP from combining the use of NMES with spring torsion SOs. Each study employed a custom or off-the-shelf Ultraflex dynamic orthosis at the elbow and the wrist, or a different spring torsion method at the wrist, in conjunction with NMES that activated the antagonist extensor musculature for a limited time while the SO was worn.[113,121,122] Ozer et al[121] reported that significant effects of this combined intervention on UE strength, spasticity, and function were short-lived, which suggested the need for its continued use to maintain its benefits.

As for the LE, the use of a different, portable, intelligent ankle-stretching device, or intelligent stretcher (IS) that could be considered an elaborate orthosis or a robotic apparatus also showed some promising results.[131,132] The IS is a computer-aided machine driven by a servomotor that can stretch the musculotendinous unit safely and gradually for preset time periods that are simple to adjust. This device has passive-stretching and active-movement modes, and in the active movement mode, assistance or resistance can be provided. The child participates in computer games, which are controlled by ankle movements. Zhao et al[131,132] reported an increase in length and decrease in stiffness of gastrocnemius and soleus muscle fascicles in children with CP after a 6-week training period using this device.

Precautions and Contraindications for Stretching Orthoses

Clinical experience shows that SOs are not indicated for children and adults with CP who have rigid contractures, open wounds, moderate to severe dystonia, or athetosis. Those with absent or very limited sensation, limited cognition, or communication challenges must be monitored closely to avoid skin breakdown or unusual discomfort. Any device must be used judiciously to avoid skin irritation. In general, an SO will have abundant padding to avoid integumentary issues, but this adds to heat retention, which may be intolerable for some users.

Special caution must be taken when stretching the biarticular hamstring muscles.[154] As noted earlier, biarticular spastic muscles are more susceptible to shortening,[146] and preserving or recovering hamstring length is often an important rehabilitation goal.[154] Because manual passive hamstring stretching in a position of hip flexion may lead to a posterior hip subluxation in a child with decreased hip stability,[154] the use of an orthosis to address hamstring length limitations may be a better option.

Finally, research evidence and clinical experience agree that passive stretching causes pain.[130,133,140,155] In fact, Hadden and von Baeyer[155] found that parents rated manual stretching as the most intensely painful intervention their children with CP experienced. In light of this information, it is possible that SOs that offer a low-grade sustained stretch may be a more comfortable type of intervention than manual passive stretching; however, further evidence is needed to confirm this hypothesis. In the meantime, clinicians should approach each child individually in order to provide them with the most comfortable yet effective SO wear schedule.

SEMI-RIGID AND RIGID SPINAL ORTHOTIC INTERVENTIONS

The incidence of spinal deformities in children and adults with CP is higher than in the general population, ranging from 20% to 70%.[156-161] Such deformities may have very detrimental functional effects on crawling, sitting, and gait.[162] The most severe cases of scoliosis have been reported in persons with bilateral spastic CP who are bedridden, which indicates that gravity is not such a significant deforming force as the severity of the neurological impairment.[157-160,162-164] The curves are generally single (C-shaped) and long,[157-159,165] extend into the sacrum, and are associated with pelvic obliquity.[156,161,164,166-168] The scoliotic curves associated with spastic CP occur at early ages and will continue to progress beyond the skeletal maturity (see Chapter 4).[159,160,162,166,168]

A custom molded, total contact thoraco-lumbar-sacral orthosis (TLSO) is the orthotic treatment of choice for spinal deformities.[156,164,165,169,170] Several total contact designs are available to address specific alterations of body structures and functions, including truncal hypotonia, abdominal muscle weakness, decreased vital capacity of the lungs, and scoliotic and kyphotic curvatures of the spine observed in children and adults with CP (Table 20-3). The consensus in the literature reveals that orthotic intervention has no discernible effect on the progression of spinal curvatures in children with CP.[158,160,161,165,171] However, it is well accepted that the use of a TLSO will often assist in improving sitting balance, head and neck control, and UE function[158,160,162,164,165,169,170,172-174] and help with play, feeding, and transportation.[156] These findings provide indirect support for efficacy of spinal orthoses in addressing activity and participation goals for individuals with CP. However, further research is needed to establish a direct relationship between the use of the TLSO and the level of activity and participation (see Table 20-3).

Several authors reported positive physiological effects of spinal orthoses, including decreased energy consumption.[156,161] Some have speculated that lung capacity may be diminished while wearing a TLSO,[174] but subsequent studies demonstrated that a well-fitting TLSO had a positive effect on respiration.[162,165,170] A TLSO may assist in prevention of pulmonary and skin complications arising from large curves,[160] and may be a treatment of choice when other health complications place the individual at excessive risk for a spinal surgery.[165,170] In addition, it has been noted that, because of the development of spinal deformities, TLSO wear is sometimes required following a selective dorsal rhizotomy procedure.[161,175,176]

Thoraco-Lumbar-Sacral Orthosis Description and Fabrication

A custom TLSO made for children or adults with CP commonly consists of a foam lining with a plastic skeleton (Figure 20-27) or a foam lining with a full plastic cover[164,165] (Figure 20-28). The TLSO can have a posterior, anterior, or bivalve opening (see Figures 20-27 and 20-28). In the past, TLSOs were sometimes made of low temperature materials,[156] but these tended to lack durability. Some new low temperature materials that are available at this time may be helpful, but their use has not been reported in the construction of TLSOs for children or adults with CP.[177] A critical characteristic of the TLSO is the total contact fit that disperses forces evenly on the trunk surface.[164,165,178] However, the term *total contact* in relation to neuromuscular scoliosis must be understood in comparison to the TLSO used for children with idiopathic scoliosis, which applies specific points of pressure to correct the curve. A TLSO used for patients with neuromuscular scoliosis must provide pressure relief and must be made to alleviate potential skin integrity issues and support respiration. Soft TLSOs use a combination of soft and firm foams, with a plastic skeleton located outside or within the foam where more rigid support is required (see Table 20-3). This design is often well tolerated[169,170] because the edges of the plastic skeleton are

TABLE 20-3

ICF² MODEL-BASED CONSIDERATIONS FOR SPINAL ORTHOTIC INTERVENTIONS

EXAMPLES OF ULTIMATE ACTIVITY/PARTICIPATION GOALSª	ALTERATION OF BODY STRUCTURE AND FUNCTION	SUGGESTED INTERVENTION	TYPICAL WEAR RECOMMENDATIONS/ IMMEDIATE GOALS	SIDE EFFECTS[165,169]
Increase tolerance to the following daily activities without pain, discomfort, or excessive fatigue related to trunk alignment: • Sitting in a wheelchair/ positioning chair for meals, school work, and other functional activities • Transfers, standing, and walking activities • Self-care activities • Other activities of daily living Participate in favorite age-appropriate games, hobbies, and school and community events without pain, discomfort, or excessive fatigue related to trunk alignment, with some examples including the following: • Playing board games with siblings and/or friends • Participating in a church youth group • Practicing a favorite Paralympics sport • Participating in other relevant situations common for children and adults with and without disabilities	Hypotonia in trunk musculature	Soft TLSO		
	Abdominal muscle weakness	Soft TLSO		
	Decreased lung vital capacity	Custom molded, soft or rigid, bivalve or posterior open-ing TLSO with inferior costal margin relief and abdominal cut-out to relieve diaphragmatic compression, with or without elastic or equal abdominal support	Wear when upright[b] Support upright posture Independent sitting Free UEs for functional activities	Heat retention Pressure areas Gastrointestinal irritation Gastrostomy tube interference
	Thoracic kyphosis	Custom molded, total contact, rigid, bivalve or posterior opening TLSO		
	Scoliosis	Custom molded, total contact, rigid, bivalve or posterior open-ing TLSO with excellent pelvic containment, including greater trochanters		

Abbreviations: TLSO, Thoraco-Lumbar-Sacral Orthosis; UEs, upper extremities.

ª Further research into the efficacy of spinal orthoses is needed to support the use of this intervention in addressing the activity and participation-related goals.

b Based on clinical experience as evidence is not available.

covered with foam, which provides a gradual transition from the rigid surface of plastic to the skin, but with loss of support. Alternatively, a rigid design will have a soft lining fully covered with plastic (Figure 20-29); the advantage is greater support. Terjesen et al[165] reported good results with rigid plastic TLSOs made by skillful orthotists.

Side Effects of Thoraco-Lumbar-Sacral Orthosis Wear

Children and adults who wear TLSOs and their caretakers generally report concerns of heat retention (see Table 20-3). Ventilation holes combined with torso socks can mitigate

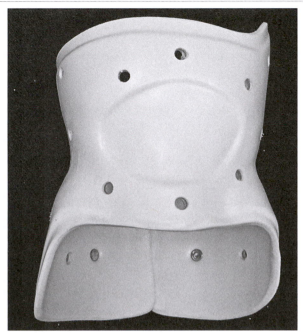

Figure 20-27. A "soft" TLSO with flexible abdominal area and ventilation holes, custom fabricated from a cast, posterior opening. The rigid plastic is sandwiched between the softer foam on the inside, and the stiffer foam on the outside. The soft edges or trim lines increase tolerance but diminish support.

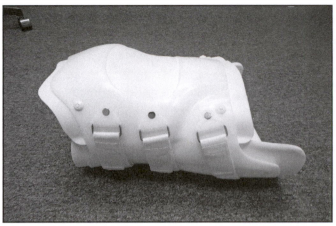

Figure 20-28. A bivalved "soft" TLSO, custom fabricated from a cast. The plastic is lined with two layers of foam. The inner layer is soft, the second layer is stiffer. The bivalve design has anterior and posterior sections; it is sometimes referred to as a *clam shell*. Some caretakers report this design is easier to don. The soft edges or trim lines increase tolerance but diminish support. The straps would be on both sides of the TLSO.

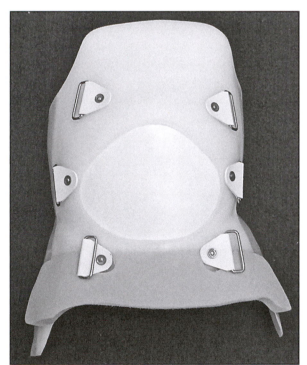

Figure 20-29. A custom fabricated from a cast, rigid, bivalved TLSO. This TLSO has padding on the inferior edge for comfort, since the rigid design does not have the soft edges of foam.

this phenomenon. Skin breakdown and patient intolerance are also common side effects of the TLSO wear.[165,169] Less common are gastrointestinal problems that may arise with the TLSO use.[165] Clinically, the first author of this chapter has received parental reports that their child would vomit after a meal if the TLSO is worn. In these cases, it was recommended that the device be removed for the meal and donned again 1 hour later.

THERATOGS AND LYCRA COMPRESSION GARMENTS

Besides rigid and semi-rigid orthoses, soft, elastic, and compressive materials are also used in clinical practice to address the child's posture, UE and LE alignment, movement, and gait. Examples of orthotic interventions constructed from such materials include TheraTogs,[179] Stabilizing Pressure Input Orthoses (SPIO),[180] and Dynamic Movement Orthoses (DMO).[181] TheraTogs is a system that combines undergarments made of a patented fabric and external elastic straps attached to the undergarments using Velcro closures.[179] This system creates a gentle but sustained stretching force that serves to realign the child's body to support his or her specific functional needs.[179] The SPIO garments are made of a Lycra fabric that has multidirectional stretch capabilities.[180] They are worn under the child's clothes and provide mild compression to the trunk or extremities that is thought to enhance proprioception and body awareness.[180] The DMO are a subgroup of dynamic elastomeric fabric orthoses, or DEFO, that are custom fabricated from a Lycra-based material and are designed to provide compressive and directional input to the child's extremities and trunk.[181] The proprioceptive input of the orthosis is delivered by its close fit while the resistance generated by extra layers of material is used to reinforce specific changes in posture and the direction of movement.[181]

Research evidence that supports these interventions varies in its volume and rigor. In 1997, Hylton and Allen[182] described the SPIO garment development, design and use.

However, the evidence that supports their clinical application is limited to case studies.[180,183,184] The efficacy of TheraTogs was investigated by several groups of researchers.[185-187] This orthotic system was shown to significantly increase the gluteus medius muscle activity in adult patients with hemiplegia following a unilateral stroke[185] and improve functional skills and kinetic and kinematic gait parameters in children with bilateral spastic CP, GMFCS levels I and III, when TheraTogs were worn.[186,187] However, these studies had small samples[185-187] and limited control for the investigator bias.[186,187] Furthermore, only one research report demonstrated a limited carry-over of the gains achieved with the garment wear to a no garment condition at follow-up.[186] The benefits of the TheraTog use described by parents of participants in that study included increased physical activity observed in their children who also exhibited increased confidence in their own physical abilities. The reported undesirable side effects of this intervention included difficulty toileting and dressing, and decreased tolerance to the garment wear in hot weather and during sports-related and gym activities.[186]

Several investigations addressed the efficacy of dynamic, Lycra-based, body, arm and leg splints.[181,188-191] In their study, Blair et al[188] found a Lycra-based UP suit to have immediate positive effects on posture and involuntary movement in children with CP while changes in functional skills varied. In a multiple single-subject research design, Matthews et al[191] examined the effects of DEFO leggings on walking ability in 8 children with bilateral spastic CP. Statistically significant improvements in gait velocity and performance consistency were demonstrated in 5 and 4 of 8 participants, respectively, as indicated by the 10-meter walking test results.[191] Finally, the RCT results reported by Elliott et al[189,190] included increased UE ROM and improved joint kinematics and fluency of movement after a 3-month Second Skin Lycra dynamic arm splint wear in children with CP, with the greatest improvement in movement fluency documented in those with dystonia. In addition, some carry-over of therapeutic effects on movement kinematics was observed immediately after the removal of the splint.[189] Small sample size and a short-lived or insufficient carry-over to a no splint condition were the limitations of the cited studies,[188-191] including the RCT.[189,190] Some of the reported undesirable effects of the splint wear included donning, doffing, and diapering difficulties, heat, cyanosis, respiratory compromise, and vomiting.[188,191]

This chapter explored a variety of orthotic interventions available to the clinician working with children and adults with CP for management of their UEs, LEs, and trunk. Clinical decision making related to the selection of appropriate orthoses for the needs of specific patients may be a daunting task as one must carefully consider multiple factors that play a role in their ability to achieve a desired level of activity and participation. The analysis of evidence related to the efficacy of specific orthotic devices should be an integral part of clinical reasoning underlying this important process.

REFERENCES

1. Kostanjsek N. Use of the International Classification of Functioning, Disability and Health (ICF) as a conceptual framework and common language for disability statistics and health information systems. *BMC Public Health.* 2011;11(suppl 4):53.

2. World Health Organization. *International Classification of Functioning, Disability and Health (ICF).* Geneva, Switzerland: World Health Organization; 2001.

3. Campbell PH. Evaluation and assessment in early intervention for infants and toddlers. *J Early Interv.* 1991;15:36-45.

4. Effgen SK. Serving the needs of children and their families. In: Effgen SK, ed. *Meeting the Physical Therapy Needs of Children.* 2nd ed. Philadelphia, PA: F. A. Davis Company; 2013:3-40.

5. Palisano R, Chiarello L, King G, Novak I, Stoner T, Fiss A. Participation-based therapy for children with physical disabilities. *Disabil Rehabil.* 34(12):1041-1052.

6. International Organization for Standardization, ISO 8549-1:1989. General terms for external limb prostheses and orthoses. In: *Prosthetics and Orthotics - Vocabulary.* Geneva, Switzerland: International Organization for Standardization; 1989.

7. Orthotics – definition and more from the Free Merriam-Webster Dictionary. *Merriam-Webster Online.* http://www.merriam-webster.com/dictionary/orthotics. Accessed February 18, 2013.

8. Orthotic – definition and more from the Free Merriam-Webster Dictionary. *Merriam-Webster Online.* http://www.merriam-webster.com/dictionary/orthotic. Accessed February 18, 2013.

9. Rosenbaum P, Paneth N, Leviton A, et al. A report: the definition and classification of cerebral palsy April 2006. *Dev Med Child Neurol.* 2007;49(s109):8-14. Erratum in: *Dev Med Child Neurol.* 2007;49(6):480.

10. Bunch WH. Introduction to orthotics. In: Bunch WH, Keagy R, Kritter AE, et al, eds. *Atlas of Orthotics.* 2nd ed. St. Louis, MO: Mosby Company; 1985:3-5.

11. Redford JB. Materials for Orthotics. In: Redford JB. *Orthotics Etcetera.* 3rd ed. Baltimore, MD: Williams & Wilkins; 1986:52-79.

12. Murphy EF, Burstein AE. Physical properties of materials, including solid mechanics. In: Bunch WH, Keagy R, Kritter AE, Kruger LM, Letts M, Lonstein JE, Marsolais EB, Matthews JG, Pedegana LR, eds. *Atlas of Orthotics: Biomechanical Principles and Application.* 2nd ed. St. Louis, MO: Mosby Company; 1985:6-33.

13. Kogler GF. Materials and technology. In: Lusardi MM, Nielsen CC, eds. *Orthotics and Prosthetics in Rehabilitation.* 2nd ed. St. Louis, MO: Elsevier Inc; 2007:15-34.

14. Bottomley JM. Footwear: foundation for lower extremity orthoses. In: Lusardi MM, Nielsen CC, eds. *Orthotics and Prosthetics in Rehabilitation.* 2nd ed. St. Louis, MO: Elsevier Inc.; 2007:155-175.

15. Owen E. The importance of being earnest about shank and thigh kinematics, especially when using ankle-foot orthoses. ISPO UK 2008 George Murdoch Prize Medal Essay and Lecture. *Prosthet Orthot Int.* 2010;34(3):254-269.

16. Smith PA, Hassani S, Graf A, Flanagan A, Reiners K, Kuo KN, Jae-Young R, Harris G. Brace evaluation in children with diplegic cerebral palsy with a jump gait pattern. *J Bone Joint Surg Am.* 2009;91:356-365.

17. Morris C. A review of the efficacy of lower-limb orthoses used for cerebral palsy. *Dev Med Child Neurol.* 2002;44(3):205-211.

18. Radtka SA, Skinner SR, Johanson ME. A comparison of gait with solid and hinged ankle-foot orthoses in children with spastic diplegic cerebral palsy. *Gait Posture.* 2005;21(3):303-310.

19. Brehm MA, Harlaar J, Schwartz M. Effect of ankle-foot orthoses on walking efficiency and gait in children with cerebral palsy. *J Rehabil Med.* 2008;40(7):529-534.

20. Balaban B, Yasar E, Dal U, Yazicioglu K, Mohur H, Kalyon TA. The effect of hinged ankle-foot orthosis on gait and energy expenditure in spastic hemiplegic cerebral palsy. *Disabil Rehabil.* 2007;29(2):139-144.

21. Buckon CE, Sienko Thomas S, Jakobson-Huston, Moor M, Sussman M, Aiona M. Comparison of three ankle–foot orthosis configurations for children with spastic diplegia. *Dev Med Child Neurol.* 2004;46(9):590-598.

22. Sienko-Thomas S, Buckon CE, Jakobson-Huston S, Sussman MD, Aiona MD. Stair locomotion in children with spastic hemiplegia: the impact of three different ankle foot orthosis (AFOs) configurations. *Gait Posture.* 2002;16(2):180-187.

23. Abel MF, Juhl GA, Vaughan CL, Damiano, DL. Gait assessment of fixed ankle-foot orthoses in children with spastic diplegia. *Arch Phys Med Rehabil.* 1998;79(2):126-133.

24. Morris C, Condie D, eds. Recent Developments in *Healthcare for Cerebral Palsy: Implications and Opportunities for Orthotics.* Copenhagen, Denmark: ISPO; 2009.

25. Hovorka CF, Geil MD, Lusardi MM. Principles influencing orthotic and prosthetic design: biomechanics, device-user interface, and related concepts. In: Lusardi MM, Nielsen CC, eds. *Orthotics and Prosthetics in Rehabilitation.* 2nd ed. St. Louis, MO: Elsevier Inc.; 2007:135-154.

26. Morris C, Newdick H, Johnson A. Variations in the orthotic management of cerebral palsy. *Child Health Care Dev.* 2002;28(2):139-147.

27. Ridgewell E, Dobson F, Bach T, Baker Richard. A systematic review to determine best practice reporting guidelines for AFO interventions in studies involving children with cerebral palsy. *Prosthet Orthot Int.* 2010;34(2):129-145.

28. Figueiredo EM, Ferreira GB, Moreira RCM, Kirkwood RN, Fetters L. Efficacy of ankle-foot orthoses on gait of children with cerebral palsy: systematic review of literature. *Pediatr Phys Ther.* 2008;20:207-223.

29. Lin RS. Ankle-foot orthoses. In: Lusardi MM, Nielsen CC, eds. *Orthotics and Prosthetics in Rehabilitation.* 2nd ed. St. Louis, MO: Elsevier Inc.; 2007:219-236.

30. Bernhardt DB. Prenatal and postnatal growth and development of the foot and ankle. *Phys Ther.* 1988;68:1831-1839.

31. Rose GK. Correction of the pronated foot. *J Bone Joint Surg Br.* 1962;44-B:642-647.

32. Sarrafian SK. Functional characteristics of the foot and plantar aponeurosis under tibiotalar loading. *Foot Ankle.* 1987;8:4-15.

33. Oatis CA. Biomechanics of the foot and ankle under static conditions. *Phys Ther.* 1988;68(12):1815-1821.

34. Tiberio D. Pathomechanics of structural foot deformities. *Phys Ther.* 1988;68(12):1840-1849.

35. Fish DJ, Nielsen JP. Clinical assessment of human gait. *J Pros Orthot.* 1993;5:39-50.

36. Owen E. The creation and prevention of fixed pronated/"rocker bottom" feet. In: *Advanced Paediatric Gait Analysis and Orthotic Management with AFO Footwear Combinations: A Segmental Kinematic Approach to Rehabilitation* [course manual]. Presented at: Rehabilitation Institute of Chicago, May 10-11, 2012; Chicago, IL.

37. Johnson DC, Damiano DL, Abel MF. The evolution of gait in childhood and adolescent cerebral palsy. *J Pediatr Orthop.* 1997;17(3):392-396.

38. Bell KJ, Ounpuu S, De Luca PA, Romness MJ. Natural progression of gait in children with cerebral palsy. *J Pediatr Orthop.* 2002;22(5):677-682.

39. Rodda JM, Graham HK, Carson L, Galea MP, Wolfe R. Sagittal gait patterns in spastic diplegia. *J Bone Joint Surg Br.* 2004; 86-B:251-258.

40. Dobson F, Morris ME, Baker R, Graham HK. Gait classification in children with cerebral palsy: a systematic review. *Gait Posture.* 2007;25(1):140-152.

41. Riad J, Haglund-Akerlind Y, Miller F. Classification of spastic hemiplegic cerebral palsy in children. *J Pediatr Orthop.* 2007;27(7):758-764.

42. Rodda J, Graham HK. Classification of gait patterns in spastic hemiplegia and spastic diplegia: a basis for a management algorithm. *Eur J Neurol.* 2001;8(suppl 5):98-108.

43. Costal RV, Rosa AA, Santana TA, Jorge LM, Corrêa FI, Corrêa JC, Oliveira CS. Analysis of electomyographic muscles activity of gait in healthy subjects with and without AFO developed for patients with hemiparesis. *Electromyogr Clin Neurophysiol.* 2010;50(6):295-301.

44. Geboers JF, Drost MR, Spaans F, Kuipers H, Seelen HA. Immediate and long-term effects of ankle-foot orthosis on muscle activity during walking: a randomized study of patients with unilateral foot drop. *Arch Phys Med Rehabil.* 2002;83(2):240-245.

45. Meilahn JR. Tolerability and effectiveness of a neuroprosthesis for the treatment of footdrop in pediatric patients with hemiparetic cerebral palsy. *PM R.* 2013;5(6):503-509. doi: 10.1016/j.pmrj.2012.11.005. Epub 2013 Jan 10.

46. Salazar-Torres JJ, McDowell BC, Kerr C, Cosgrove, AP. Pelvic kinematics and their relationship to gait type in hemiplegic cerebral palsy. *Gait Posture.* 2011;33(4):620-624.

47. Boyd RN, Graham HK. Objective measurement of clinical findings in the use of botulinum toxin type A for the management of children with cerebral palsy. *Eur J Neurol.* 1999;6(s 4):23-35.

48. Gurney B. Review: leg length discrepancy. *Gait Posture.* 2002;15:195-206.

49. Mahmood S, Huffman LK, Harris JG. Limb-length discrepancy as a cause of plantar fasciitis. *J Am Podiatr Med Assoc.* 2010;100(6):452-455.

50. Wills Jesse M, Leach J. Orthopedic conditions. In: Campbell SK, Palisano RJ, Orlin MN, eds. *Physical Therapy for Children.* 4th ed. St. Louis, MO: Saunders; 2012:414-452.

51. Owen E. Optimisation and normalisation of segment lengths (2) equalising leg lengths in AFOFCs. In: *Advanced Paediatric Gait Analysis and Orthotic Management with AFO Footwear Combinations: A Segmental Kinematic Approach to Rehabilitation* [course manual]. Presented at: Rehabilitation Institute of Chicago, May 10-11, 2012; Chicago, IL.

52. Helfet AJ. A new way of treating flat feet in children. *Lancet.* 1956;1:262-264.

53. Theologis TN, Gordon C, Benson MK. Heel seats and shoe wear. *J Pediatr Orthop.* 1994;14(6):760-762.

54. Bleck EE, Berzins UJ. Conservative management of pes valgus with plantar flexed talus, flexible. *Clin Orthop Relat Res.* 1977;(122):85-94.

55. Henderson WH, Campbell JW. UC-BL shoe insert casting and fabrication. *Bull Prosthet Res.* 1967;215-235.

56. Carlson WE, Vaughn CL, Damiano DL, Abel MF. Orthotic management of gait in spastic diplegia. *Am J Phys Med Rehabil.* 1997;76(3):219-225.

57. Crenshaw S, Herzog R, Castagno P, Richards J, Miller F, Michaloski G, Moran E. The efficacy of tone-reducing features in orthotics on the gait of children with spastic diplegic cerebral palsy. *J Pediatr Orthop.* 2000;20(2):210-216.

58. Rethlefsen S, Kay R, Dennis S, Forstein M, Tolo V. The effects of fixed and articulated ankle-foot orthoses on gait patterns in subjects with cerebral palsy. *J Pediatr Orthop.* 1999;19(4):470-474.

59. Brunner R, Meier G, Ruepp T. Comparison of a stiff and spring-type ankle-foot orthosis to improve gait in spastic hemiplegic children. *J Pediatr Orthop.* 1998;18(6):719-726.

60. Morris C, Bowers R, Ross K, Stevens P, Phillips D. Orthotic management of cerebral palsy: recommendations from a consensus conference. *NeuroRehabilitation.* 2011;28(1):37-46.

61. Bill M, McIntosh R, Myers P. A series of case studies on the effect of a midfoot control ankle foot orthosis in the prevention of unresolved pressure areas in children with cerebral palsy. *Prosthet Orthot Int.* 2001;25(3):246-250.

62. UltraSafeGait – Ultraflex. *Ultraflex*. http://www.ultraflexsystems.com/bracedesigns/PediGaitECE.htm. Accessed March 2, 2013.

63. Gage JR, Novacheck TF. An update on the treatment of gait problems in cerebral palsy. *J Pediatr Orthop B.* 2001;10(4):265-274.

64. Lucareli PBG, Lima MD, Lucarelli JG, Lima FP. Changes in joint kinematics in children with cerebral palsy while walking with and without a floor reaction ankle-foot orthosis. *Clinics (Sao Paulo)*. 2007;62(1):63-68.

65. Davids JR, Rowan F, Davis RB. Indications for orthoses to improve gait in children with cerebral palsy. *J Am Acad Orthop Surg*. 2007;15(3):178-188.

66. Rogozinski BM, Davids JR, MD, Davis RB, Jameson GG, MA, Blackhurst DW. The efficacy of the floor-reaction ankle-foot orthosis in children with cerebral palsy. *J Bone Joint Surg Am*. 2009;91(10):2440-2447.

67. Sutherland DH, Davids JR. Common gait abnormalities of the knee in cerebral palsy. *Clin Orthop Relat Res*. 1993;(288):139-147.

68. Vuillermin C, Rodda R, Rutz E, Shore BJ, Smith K, Graham HK. Severe crouch gait in spastic diplegia can be prevented. *J Bone Joint Surg Br*. 2011;93(12):1670-1675.

69. Cauraugh JH, Naik SK, Hsu WH, Coombes SA, Holt KG. Children with cerebral palsy: a systematic review and meta-analysis on gait and electrical stimulation. *Clin Rehabil*. 2010;24(11):963-978.

70. Seifart A, Unger M, Burger, M. Functional electrical stimulation to lower limb muscles after Botox in children with cerebral palsy. *Pediatr Phys Ther*. 2010;22(2):199-206.

71. Kerr C, McDowell B, McDonough S. Electrical stimulation in cerebral palsy: a review of effects on strength and motor function. *Dev Med Child Neurol*. 2004;46:205-213.

72. Ring H, Treger I, Gruendlinger L, Hausdorff J. Neuroprosthesis for footdrop compared with an ankle-foot orthosis: effects on postural control during walking. *J Stroke Cerebrovasc Dis*. 2009;18(1):41-47.

73. Carmick J. Letter to the editor. Lower extremity neuromuscular electrical stimulation. *Pediatr Phys Ther*. 2009;21(3):293-294.

74. Liberson WT, Holmquest HJ, Scot D, Dow M. Functional electrotherapy, stimulation of the peroneal nerve synchronized with the swing phase of the gait of hemiplegic patients. *Arch Phys Med Rehabil*. 1961;42:101-105.

75. Weber DJ, Chan KM, Loeb GE, et al. BIONic WalkAide for correcting foot drop. *IEEE Trans Neural Syst Rehabil Eng*. 2005;13(2):242-245.

76. Taylor P. The use of electrical stimulation for correction of dropped foot in subjects with upper motor neuron lesions. Paper presented at: RiMS meeting; February 7-8, 2003; Brussels, Belgum.

77. Stein RB, Chong S, Everaert DG, et al. A multicenter trial of a footdrop stimulator controlled by a tilt sensor. *Neurorehabil Neural Repair*. 2006;20(3):371-379.

78. Laufer Y, Hausdorff JM, Haim Ring H. Effects of a foot drop neuroprosthesis on functional abilities, social participation, and gait velocity. *Am J Phys Med Rehabil*. 2009;88(1):14-20.

79. van der Linden ML, Hazlewood ME, Hillman SJ, Robb JE. Functional electrical stimulation to the dorsiflexors and quadriceps in children with cerebral palsy. *Pediatr Phys Ther*. 2008;20(1):23-29.

80. Bioness® Ness L300 Foot Drop System. http://www.bioness.com/NewsMedia/Media_Gallery/L300/Bioness_L300_Foot_Drop_System_Overview.php. Accessed February 19, 2016.

81. Odstock® Medical FES. *National Clinical FES Centre*. http://www.salisburyfes.com/pdfs/products%20and%20services.PDF. Accessed March 7, 2013.

82. The WalkAide® System for Treatment of Foot Drop. http://www.walkaide.com/en-US/Pages/default.aspx. Accessed March 7, 2013.

83. Kottink AI, Oostendorp LJ, Buurke JH, Nene AV, Hermens HJ, IJzerman MJ. The orthotic effect of functional electrical stimulation on the improvement of walking in stroke patients with dropped foot: a systematic review. *Artif Organs*. 2004;28(6):577-586.

84. Kim CM, Eng JJ, Whittaker MW. Effects of a simple functional electric system and/or a hinged ankle-foot orthosis on walking in persons with incomplete spinal cord injury. *Arch Phys Med Rehabil*. 2004;85(10):1718-1723.

85. Alfieri V. Electrical stimulation for modulation of spasticity in hemiplegic and spinal cord injury subjects. *Neuromodulation*. 2001;4(2):85-92.

86. Taylor PN, Burridge JH, Dunkerley AL, et al. Clinical use of the Odstock dropped foot stimulator: its effect on the speed and effort of walking. *Arch Phys Med Rehabil*. 1999;80(12):1577-1583.

87. Postans NJ, Malcolm H Granat P. Effect of functional electrical stimulation, applied during walking, on gait in spastic cerebral palsy. *Dev Med Child Neurol*. 2005;47(1):46-52.

88. Durham S, Eve L, Stevens C, et al. Effect of functional electrical stimulation on asymmetries in gait of children with hemiplegic cerebral palsy. *Physiotherapy*. 2004;90:82-90.

89. Prosser LA, Curatalo LA, Alter KE, Damiano DL. Acceptability and potential effectiveness of a foot drop stimulator in children and adolescents with cerebral palsy. *Dev Med Child Neurol*. 2012;54(11):1044-1049.

90. Damiano DL, Prosser LA, Curatalo LA, Alter KE. Muscle plasticity and ankle control after repetitive use of a functional electrical stimulation device for foot drop in cerebral palsy. *Neurorehabil Neural Repair*. 2013;27(3):200-207.

91. Comeaux P, Patterson N, Rubin M, Meiner R. Effect of neuromuscular electrical stimulation during gait in children with cerebral palsy. *Pediatr Phys Ther*. 1997;9:103-109.

92. Wright P, Durham S, Ewins DJ, Swain ID. Neuromuscular electrical stimulation for children with cerebral palsy: a review. *Arch Dis Child*. 2012;97:364-371.

93. Palisano RJ, Rosenbaum PL, Walter SD, Russell DJ, Wood EP, Galuppi BE. Development and reliability of a system to classify gross motor function in children with cerebral palsy. *Dev Med Child Neurol*. 1997;39(4):214-223.

94. Hoffer M. Management of the hip in cerebral palsy. *J Bone Joint Surg Am*. 1986;68(4):629-631.

95. Brunner R, Krauspe R, Romkes J. Torsion deformities in the lower extremities in patients with infantile cerebral palsy: pathogenesis and therapy [abstract]. *Orthopade*. 2000;29(9):808-813. [Article in German]

96. Ekblom B, Mahr U. Effects of the hip abduction orthosis on muscle activity in children with cerebral palsy. *Physiother Theory Pract*. 2002;18:55-63.

97. Rethlefsen SA, Healy BS, Wren TA, Skaggs DL, Kay RM. Causes of intoeing gait in children with cerebral palsy. *J Bone Joint Surg Am*. 2006;88(10):2175-2180.

98. Graham HK, Boyd R, Carlin JB, et al. Does Botulinum Toxin A Combined with Bracing Prevent Hip Displacement in Children with Cerebral Palsy and "Hips at Risk"? *J Bone Joint Surg Am*. 2008;90(1):23-33.

99. Inan M, Altintas F, Duru I. The evaluation and management of rotational deformity in cerebral palsy. *Acta Orthop Traumatol Turc*. 2009;43(2):106-112.

100. Shore BJ, Yu X, Desai S, Selber P, Wolfe R, Graham HK. Adductor surgery to prevent hip displacement in children with cerebral palsy: the predictive role of the gross motor function classification system. *J Bone Joint Surg Am*. 2012;94(4):326-334.

101. Willoughby K, Ang SG, Thomason P, Graham HK. The impact of botulinum toxin A and abduction bracing on long-term hip development in children with cerebral palsy. *Dev Med Child Neurol*. 2012;54(8):743-747.

102. Rethlefsen SA, Kay RM. Transverse plane gait problems in children with cerebral palsy. *J Pediatr Orthop*. 2013;33(4):422-430.

103. Gordon GS, Simkiss DE. A systematic review of the evidence for hip surveillance in children with cerebral palsy. *J Bone Joint Surg Br*. 2006;88(11):1492-1496.

104. Wren TA, Rethlefsen S, Kay RM. Prevalence of specific gait abnormalities in children with cerebral palsy: influence of cerebral palsy subtype, age, and previous surgery. *J Pediatr Orthop*. 2005;25(1):79-83.

105. Boyd RN, Dobson F, Parrott J, et al. The effect of botulinum toxin type A and a variable hip abduction orthosis on gross motor function: a randomized controlled trial. *Eur J Neurol*. 2001;8(S5):109-119.

106. Embrey DG, Westcott SL. Effects of the standing walking and sitting hip orthosis in children with spastic cerebral palsy; surface electromyographic evidence. In: Abstracts of Platform Presentations for the 2006 Combined Sections Meeting. *Pediatr Phys Ther.* 2006;18(1):74-75. Abstract.

107. Klingels K, Jaspers E, Van de Winckel A, De Cock P, Molenaers G, Feys H. A systematic review of arm activity measures for children with hemiplegic cerebral palsy. *Clin Rehabil.* 2010;24(10):887-900.

108. Fedrizzi E, Pagliano E, Andreucci E, Oleari G. Hand function in children with hemiplegic cerebral palsy: prospective follow-up and functional outcome in adolescence. *Dev Med Child Neurol.* 2003;45(2):85-91.

109. Burtner PA, Poole JL, Torres T, et al. Effect of wrist hand splints on grip, pinch, manual dexterity, and muscle activation in children with spastic hemiplegia: a preliminary study. *J Hand Ther.* 2008;21(1):36-43.

110. Louwers AM, Meester-Delver A, Folmer K, Nolet FB, Beelen A. Immediate effect of a wrist and thumb brace on bimanual activities in children with hemiplegic cerebral palsy. *Dev Med Child Neurol.* 2011;53(4):321-326.

111. Barroso PN, Vecchio SD, Xavier YR, Sesselmann M, Araújo PA, Pinotti M. Improvement of hand function in children with cerebral palsy via an orthosis that provides wrist extension and thumb abduction. *Clin Biomech (Bristol, Avon).* 2011;26(9):937-943.

112. Klingels K, Feys H, De Wit L, et al. Arm and hand function in children with unilateral cerebral palsy: a one-year follow-up study. *Eur J Paediatr Neurol.* 2012;16(3):257-265.

113. Postans N, Wright P, Bromwich W, Wilkinson I, Farmer SE, Swain I. The combined effect of dynamic splinting and neuromuscular electrical stimulation in reducing wrist and elbow contractures in six children with cerebral palsy. *Prosthet Orthot Int.* 2010;34(1):10.

114. Koman LA, Gelberman RH, Toby EB, Poehling GG. Cerebral palsy management of the upper extremity. *Clin Orthop Relat Res.* 1990;(253):62-74.

115. Sköld A, Josephsson S, Eliasson AC. Performing bimanual activities: the experiences of young persons with hemiplegic cerebral palsy. *Am J Occup Ther.* 2004;58(4):416-425.

116. Goodman G, Bazyk S. The effects of a short thumb opponens splint on hand function in cerebral palsy: a single-subject study. *Am J Occup Ther.* 1991;45(8):726-731.

117. Exner CE, Bonder BR. Comparative effects of three hand splints on bilateral hand use, grasp, and arm-hand posture in hemiplegic children: a pilot study. *Occup Ther J Res.* 1983;3:75-92.

118. Reid DT, Sochaniwskyj A. Influences of a hand positioning device on upper-extremity control of children with cerebral palsy. *Int J Rehabil Res.* 1992;15(1):15-29.

119. Wright PA, Granat MH. Therapeutic effects of functional electrical stimulation of the upper limb of eight children with cerebral palsy. *Dev Med Child Neurol.* 2000;42(11):724-727.

120. Imms C. Bracing and splinting interventions in the upper limbs of people with cerebral palsy. *Dev Med Child Neurol.* 2011;53(4):293-4.

121. Ozer K, Chesher SP, Scheker LR. Neuromuscular electrical stimulation and dynamic bracing for the management of upper extremity spasticity in children with cerebral palsy. *Dev Med Child Neurol.* 2006;48(7):559-563.

122. Scheker L, Chesher S, Ramirez S. Neuromuscular electrical stimulation and dynamic bracing as a treatment for upper-extremity spasticity in children with cerebral palsy. *J Hand Surgery.* 1999;24(2):226-232.

123. Russo RN, Atkins R, Haan E, Crotty M. Upper limb orthoses and assistive technology utilization in children with hemiplegic cerebral palsy recruited from a population register. *Dev Neurorehabil.* 2009;12(2):92-99.

124. Anderson JP, Snow B, Dorey FJ, Kabo JM. Efficacy of soft splints in reducing severe knee-flexion contractures. *Dev Med Child Neurol.* 1988;30:502-508.

125. Farmer SE, James M. Contractures in orthopedic and neurological conditions: a review of causes and treatment. *Disabil Rehabil.* 2001;23(13):549-558.

126. Cadenhead SL, McEwen IR, Thompson DM. Effect of passive range of motion exercises on lower-extremity goniometric measurements of adults with cerebral palsy: a single-subject design. *Phys Ther.* 2002;82(7):658-669.

127. Lieber RL, Steinman S, Barash IA, Chambers H. Structural and functional changes in spastic skeletal muscle. *Muscle Nerve.* 2004;29(5):615-627.

128. Foran JR, Steinman S, Barash I, Chambers HG, Lieber RL. Structural and mechanical alterations in spastic skeletal muscle. *Dev Med Child Neurol.* 2005;47(10):713-717.

129. Pin T, Dyke P, Chan M. The effectiveness of passive stretching in children with cerebral palsy. *Dev Med Child Neurol.* 2006;48(10):855-862.

130. Wiart L, Darrah J, Kembhavi G. Stretching with children with cerebral palsy: what do we know and where are we going? *Pediatr Phys Ther.* 2008;20(2):173-178.

131. Zhao H, Wu Y, Liu J, Ren Y, Gaebler-Spira DJ, Zhang L. Changes of calf muscle-tendon properties due to stretching and active movement of children with cerebral palsy - a pilot study. *Conf Proc IEEE Eng Med Biol Soc.* 2009;2009:5287-5290.

132. Zhao H, Wu Y, Hwang M, Ren Y, Gao F, Gaebler-Spira D, Zhang L. Changes of calf muscle-tendon biomechanical properties induced by passive-stretching and active-movement training in children with cerebral palsy. *J Appl Physiol.* 2011;111(2):435-442.

133. Katalinic OM, Harvey LA, Herbert RD, Moseley AM, Lannin NA, Schurr K. Stretch for the treatment and prevention of contractures. *Cochrane Database Syst Rev.* 2010;(9):CD007455.

134. Lieber RL, Friden J. Spasticity causes a fundamental rearrangement of muscle-joint interaction. *Muscle Nerve.* 2002;25(2):265-270.

135. Harvey L, Herbert R, Crosbie J. Does stretching induce lasting increases in joint ROM? A systematic review. *Physiother Res Int.* 2002;7(1):1-13.

136. Gibson SK, Sprod JA, Maher CA. The use of standing frames for contracture management for non-mobile children with cerebral palsy. *Int J Rehabil Res.* 2009;32(4):316-323.

137. Maas JC, Dallmeijer AJ, Huijing PA, et al. Splint: efficacy of orthotic management in rest to prevent equinus in children with cerebral palsy, a randomised controlled trial. *BMC Pediatr.* 2012;12:38.

138. Booth CM, Cortina-Borja MJ, Theologis TN. Collagen accumulation in muscles of children with cerebral palsy and correlation with severe spasticity. *Dev Med Child Neurol.* 2001;43(5):314-320.

139. Flett PJ, Stern LM, Waddy H, TM Connell TM, JD Seeger JD, Gibbon SK. Botulinum toxin A versus fixed cast stretching for dynamic calf tightness in cerebral palsy. *J Paediatr Child Health.* 1999;35(1):71-77.

140. Holt S, Baagoe S, Lillelund F, Magnusson SP. Passive resistance of the hamstring muscles in children with severe multiple disabilities? *Dev Med Child Neurol.* 2000;42(8):541-544.

141. Mohagheghi AA, Khan T, Meadows TH, Giannikas K, Baltzopoulos V, Maganaris CN. In vivo gastrocnemius muscle fascicle length in children with and without diplegic cerebral palsy. *Dev Med Child Neurol.* 2008;50(1):44-50.

142. Barber L, Hastings-Ison T, Baker R, Barrett R, Lichtwark G. Medial gastrocnemius muscle volume and fascicle length in children aged 2 to 5 years with cerebral palsy. *Dev Med Child Neurol.* 2011;53(6):543-548.

143. Benard MR. *Analysis of 3-D Ultrasound of Calf Muscle Geometry in Children: Growth, Spasticity, Mechanisms and Treatment.* [PhD thesis]. Amsterdam, the Netherlands: VU University; 2011.

144. Smith LR, Lee KS, Ward SR, Chambers HG, Lieber RL. Hamstring contractures in children with spastic cerebral palsy result from a stiffer extracellular matrix and increased in vivo sarcomere length. *J Physiol.* 2011;589(Pt10):2625-2639.

145. Farmer SE, Woollam PJ, Patrick JH, Roberts AP, Bromwich W. Dynamic orthoses in the management of joint contracture. *J Bone Joint Surg (Br).* 2005;87(3):291-295.

146. Hof AL. Changes in muscles and tendons due to neural motor disorders: implications for therapeutic intervention. *Neural Plasiticity.* 2001;8(1-2):71-81.

147. Corry IS, Cosgrove, Duffy CM, McNeill S, Taylor TC, Graham HK. Botulinum toxin A compared with stretching casts in the treatment of spastic equinus: a randomised prospective trial. *J Pediatr Orthop.* 1998;18(3):304-311.

148. Wu YN, Hwang M, Ren Y, Gaebler-Spira D, Zhang LQ. Combined passive stretching and active movement rehabilitation of lower-limb impairments in children with cerebral palsy using a portable robot. *Neurorehabil Neural Repair.* 2011;25(4):378-385.

149. Helsel P, McGee J, Graveline C. Physical management of spasticity. *J Child Neurol.* 2001;16(1):24-30.

150. Kanellopoulos AD, Mavrogenis AF, Mitsiokapa EA, et al. Long lasting benefits following the combination of static night upper extremity splinting with botulinum toxin A injections in cerebral palsy children. *Eur J Phys Rehabil Med.* 2009;45(4):501-506.

151. Tardieu C, Lespargot A, Tabary C, Bret MD. For how long must the soleus muscle be stretched each day to prevent contracture? *Dev Med Child Neurol.* 1988;30(1):3-10.

152. Bromwich W, Farmer SE, Forward M, Roberts APR, Patrick JH. Mechanically applied stretch in the treatment of contractures: preliminary results [abstract]. *Physiotherapy.* 2002;88:55.

153. Farmer SE, James M. Contracture correction using mechanically applied torques: a report to the NHS Management Executive by Orthotic Research and Locomotor Assessment Unit, Oswestry, Shropshire and The Centre for Health Planning and Management, Keele University, Staffordshire;1997:23-27.

154. Chang CH, Chen YY, Wang CJ, Lee ZL, Kao H, Kuo KN. Dynamic displacement of the femoral head by hamstring stretching in children with cerebral palsy. *J Pediatr Orthop.* 2010;30(5):475-478.

155. Hadden KL, von Baeyer CL. Pain in children with cerebral palsy: common triggers and expressive behaviors. *Pain.* 2002;99(1-2):281-288.

156. Bunnell W, MacEwen GD. Non-operative treatment of scoliosis in cerebral palsy: preliminary report on the use of a plastic jacket. *Dev Med Child Neurol.* 1977;19(1):45-49.

157. Madigan RR, Wallace SL. Scoliosis in the institutionalized cerebral palsy population. *Spine.* 1981;6(6):583-590.

158. Miller A, Temple T, Miller F. Impact of orthoses on the rate of scoliosis progression in children with cerebral palsy. *J Pediatr Orthop.* 1996;16(3):332-335.

159. Saito N, Ebara S, Ohotsuka K, Kumeta H, Takaoka K. Natural history of scoliosis in spastic cerebral palsy. *Lancet.* 1998;351:1687-1692.

160. Thomson JD, Banta JV. Scoliosis in cerebral palsy: an overview and recent results. *J Pediatr Orthop B.* 2001;10(1):6-9.

161. Berven S, Bradford DS. Neuromuscular scoliosis: causes of deformity and principles for evaluation and management. *Semin Neurol.* 2002;22(2):167-178.

162. Kotwicki T, Jozwiak M. Conservative management of neuromuscular scoliosis: personal experience and review of literature. *Disabil Rehabil.* 2008;30(10):792-798.

163. Koop SE. Scoliosis in cerebral palsy. *Dev Med Child Neurol.* 2009;51(suppl 4):92-98.

164. Sarwark J, Sarwahi V. New strategies and decision making in the management of neuromuscular scoliosis. *Orthop Clin North Am.* 2007;38(4):485-496.

165. Terjesen T, Lange J, Steen H. Treatment of scoliosis with spinal bracing in quadriplegic cerebral palsy. *Dev Med Child Neurol.* 2000;42:448-454.

166. Imrie MN, Yaszay B. Management of spinal deformity in cerebral palsy. *Orthop Clin North Am.* 2010;41(4):531-547.

167. Senaran H, Shah SA, Glutting JJ, Dabney KW, Miller F. The associated effect of untreated unilateral hip dislocation in cerebral palsy scoliosis. *J Pediatr Orthop.* 2006;26(6):762-772.

168. McCarty R. Management of neuromuscular scoliosis. *Orthop Clin North Am.* 1999;30(3):435-449.

169. Letts M, Rathbone D, Yamashita T, Nichol B, Keeler A. Soft Boston orthosis in management of neuromuscular scoliosis: a preliminary report. *J Pediatr Orthop.* 1999;12(4):470-474.

170. Leopando MT, Moussavi Z, Holbrow J, Chernick V, Pasterkamp H, Rempel G. Effect of a soft Boston orthosis on pulmonary mechanics in severe cerebral palsy. *Pediatr Pulmonol.* 1999;28(1):53-58.

171. Yazici M, Senaran H. Cerebral palsy and spinal deformities. *Acta Orthop Traumatol Turc.* 2009;43(2):149-155.

172. Olafsson Y, Saraste H, Al-Dabbagh Z. Brace treatment in neuromuscular spine deformity. *J Pediatr Orthop.* 1999;19(3):376-379.

173. Morris C. Orthotic management of children with cerebral palsy. *JPO.* 2002;14(4):150-158.

174. Noble-Jamieson C M, Heckmatt JZ, Dubowitz V, Silverman M. Effects of posture and spinal bracing on respiratory function in neuromuscular disease. *Arch Dis Child.* 1986;61(2):178-181.

175. Johnson MB, Goldstein L, Thomas SS, Piatt J, Aiona M, Sussman M. Spinal deformity after selective dorsal rhizotomy in ambulatory patients with cerebral palsy. *J Pediatr Orthop.* 2004;24(5):529-536.

176. Golan JD, Hall JA, O'Gorman G, et al. Spinal deformities following selective dorsal rhizotomy. *J Neurosurg.* 2007;106(suppl 6):441-449.

177. Products. Allard USA. http://www.allardusa.com/frames/prod-frames.html. Accessed October 8, 2012.

178. Gavin TM. Fitting and fabrication of orthoses. In: Bunch WH, Patwardhan AG, eds. *Scoliosis: Making Clinical Decisions.* St. Louis, MO: CV Mosby; 1989:216-236.

179. What are Theratogs? Theratogs. http://theratogs.com/about/what-are-theratogs/. Accessed September 26, 2015.

180. SPIO®. http://www.spioworks.com. Accessed September 26, 2015.

181. Products – Dynamic Movement Orthotics. *DM Orthotics Ltd.* https://www.dmorthotics.com/products. Accessed September 26, 2015.

182. Hylton N, Allen C. The development and use of SPIO Lycra compression bracing in children with neuromotor deficits. *Pediatr Rehabil.* 1997;1(2):109-116.

183. Hylton N, Schoos KK. Deep pressure sensory input: SPIO flexible compression bracing. *NDTA Network.* January-February, 2007:8-12. http://www.spioworks.com/files/Deep%20Pressure%20Sensory%20Input%20Hylton%20Schoos.pdf. Accessed February 19, 2016.

184. Thorne T. Jumping for joy with SPIO and NDT strategies. *NDTA Network.* January-February, 2013:19-20.

185. Maguire C, Sieben JM, Frank M, Romkes J. Hip abductor control in walking following stroke – the immediate effect of canes, taping and TheraTogs on gait. *Clin Rehabil.* 2010;24(1):37-45.

186. Flanagan A, Krzak J, Peer M, Johnson P, Urban M. Evaluation of short-term intensive orthotic garment use in children with cerebral palsy. *Pediatr Phys Ther.* 2009;21(2):201-204.

187. Siracusa C, Taylor M, Geletka B, Overby A, Willan M. Effectiveness of a biomechanical intervention in children with spastic diplegia. In: Abstracts of Poster Presentations at the 2005 Combined Sections Meeting. *Pediatr Phys Ther.* 2005;17(1):83-84. Abstract.

188. Blair E, Ballantyne J, Horsman S, Chauvel P. A study of dynamic proximal stability splint in management of children with cerebral palsy. *Dev Med Child Neurol.* 1995;37(6):544-554.

189. Elliott CM, Reid SL, Alderson JA, Elliott BC. Lycra arm splints in conjunction with goal-directed training can improve movement in children with cerebral palsy. *NeuroRehabilitation.* 2011;28(1):47-54.

190. Elliott C, Reid S, Hamer P, Alderson J, Elliott B. Lycra® arm splints improve movement fluency in children with cerebral palsy. *Gait Posture.* 2011;33(2):214-219.

191. Matthews MJ, Watson M, Richardson B. Effects of dynamic elastomeric fabric orthoses on children with cerebral palsy. *Prosthet Orthot Int.* 2009;33(4):339-347.

21

Segmental Kinematic Approach to Orthotic Management
Ankle-Foot Orthosis/Footwear Combination

Elaine Owen, MSc, SRP, MCSP, Clinical Specialist Physiotherapist

This chapter will focus on how to best design, align, and tune orthoses in order to achieve activity and participation goals related to standing, stepping, and walking with full gait cycles, as well as goals related to structures and functions of the skeletal, musculotendinous, and neurological systems.[1-3] The content is highly applicable to all lower limb orthoses used for weight-bearing activities. It will, however, concentrate on ankle-foot orthoses (AFOs) or, more accurately, ankle-foot orthosis/footwear combinations (AFOFC). This is the term now used to describe the overall orthosis of an AFO and the accompanying footwear, as the footwear worn with any AFO is integral in determining the overall biomechanical control provided.[4-8] Describing the features of an orthosis in all 3 planes is essential, but this chapter concentrates on some key sagittal plane features. These will include principal alignments, proportions, and designs. To make full sense of this chapter, it is important to read Chapter 19 first.

DEFINITIONS AND INTERNATIONAL CLASSIFICATION OF FUNCTIONING, DISABILITY AND HEALTH CONTEXT

The International Organization for Standardization (ISO)[9,10] provides the following definitions:
- *Orthotics* is the "science and art involved in treating patients by the use of orthoses."[9(p 2)]

- An *ankle-foot orthosis* is an "*orthosis* that encompasses the ankle joint and the whole or part of the foot."[10(p 1)]

The definition of *orthotics* gives equal recognition to the art—the craftsmanship of making the optimal orthosis—and the science—the biomechanics and evidence base for orthotic interventions. The ISO[9,10] definition of *orthosis* provided in Chapter 20 also emphasizes that an orthosis has the potential to not only change the musculoskeletal system, but also the neuromuscular system. This is significant for all patients, but particularly for children who may have a primary neurological condition. While the primary neurological insult may be static, secondary skeletal and musculotendinous pathologies develop as the body grows and ages with the effects of neurology.[11] Children with neurological conditions show a wide variation in both their primary neurology and secondary changes. There is also primary and secondary heterogeneity of the group, with resulting complexity and uniqueness of the individual. Cerebral palsy (CP) is one such example. AFOs are commonly used for children with CP and other neurologic conditions.[12] For these conditions, there can be only a small tolerance of error away from the optimal orthosis design as small adjustments of even a few mm or degrees can make large differences to how orthoses perform.[4-8,13-19] Each orthosis must, therefore, be designed optimally for each patient and each limb. There is no other way of managing the heterogeneity of the group as a "one size fits all" approach to orthotic management does not produce effective results for this group of patients.

Rahlin M. *Physical Therapy for Children With Cerebral Palsy: An Evidence-Based Approach* (pp 341-370).
© 2016 SLACK Incorporated.

TABLE 21-1	

SUMMARY OF POSSIBLE GOALS AND OUTCOMES FOR ORTHOTIC MANAGEMENT
BASED ON AN "INSIDE-OUT" APPROACH AND THE
INTERNATIONAL CLASSIFICATION OF FUNCTIONING, DISABILITY AND HEALTH[1,2]

BONES, JOINTS, LIGAMENTS	MUSCULOTENDINOUS UNITS (MTUS) AND SKIN
BODY STRUCTURES & FUNCTION s7 Structures related to movement b2 Sensory functions and pain b7 Neuromusculoskeletal and movement-related functions	BODY STRUCTURES & FUNCTION s7 Structures related to movement s8 Skin and related structures b2 Sensory functions and pain b7 Neuromusculoskeletal and movement-related functions b8 Functions of skin and related structures
REDUCTION OF PAIN[a]	
To manage deformities that are preventable, reducible, irreducible but can be stabilized[a] *BONES/SEGMENTS* Maintain/encourage normal bony structure/growth Prevent/reduce abnormal bony structure/growth Stabilize abnormal bony structure Add length to a segment[a] Improve shape of a segment[a] *JOINTS* Optimize joint alignment appropriate for age Prevent/reduce/stabilize joint deformity[a] Maintain range of motion of a joint Increase range of motion, limit or prevent excessive motion of a joint[a] *LIGAMENTS* Prevent/reduce/stabilize ligamentous laxity Maintain optimal ligamentous length Prevent or minimize ligamentous shortening Normalize/optimize appropriate stretching of the joints during the gait cycle	To manage abnormal neuromuscular function including compensating for weak MTU actions and controlling effects of MTU hyperactivity[a] *MTU LENGTH* Obtain/maintain: optimum length of MTU; ratio of muscle to tendon; muscle belly extensibility; quality of muscle and tendon Normalize lengthening and shortening of MTUs in gait cycle *MTU TONE/STIFFNESS* Obtain/maintain normal or near normal muscle tone Minimize abnormal tone and normalize muscle tone during gait cycle Obtain optimal position of spastic catch *MTU STRENGTH* Obtain/maintain as near normal MTU strength as possible. During walking maximize use of muscle strength, and compensate for weak muscle actions *SELECTIVITY & TIMING* Obtain/maintain optimal selectivity and timing *INTEGRITY OF SKIN* Reduce/redistribute the load on tissues so as to protect tissues/promote healing[a]

[a] Denotes ISO 8551: 2003 Objective.[3]

(continued)

Opportunities to maximize standing and walking activities and prevent or reduce skeletal and musculotendinous pathologies are missed if orthoses are not optimized.[6,8,12,20] As with any other intervention, not only does the optimal *dosage* need to be determined, which in the case of an orthosis and footwear is their design, but also the *frequency* of administration.[12] It will only be possible to determine these once clear goals have been set for the desired outcomes of the orthotic intervention. The goals need to fulfill the expectations of the patient, carers, and clinicians.[21,22] A useful way to determine which goals to set and which might be a priority is to use the International Classification of Functioning, Disability and Health (ICF) model.[1,2] The aims and intended outcomes of orthotic interventions will relate to all aspects of the ICF: body structures and functions, activities, and participation.[1-3,22-24] For children, there will be short, medium, and very long-term goals. Table 21-1 outlines a summary of possible goals for orthotic management based on the ICF model[1,2] and an "Inside–Out" approach, which will be explained later in this chapter.

TABLE 21-1 (CONTINUED)	
SUMMARY OF POSSIBLE GOALS AND OUTCOMES FOR ORTHOTIC MANAGEMENT BASED ON AN "INSIDE-OUT" APPROACH AND THE INTERNATIONAL CLASSIFICATION OF FUNCTIONING, DISABILITY AND HEALTH[1,2]	
NEUROLOGICAL CONTROL AND DEVELOPMENT OF MOBILITY	**FUNCTIONING**
BODY STRUCTURES & FUNCTION	BODY STRUCTURES & FUNCTION
s1 Structures of the nervous system	b4 Functions of cardiovascular/respiratory
s7 Structures related to movement	ACTIVITIES & PARTICIPATION
b2 Sensory functions and pain	d1 Learning and applying knowledge
b7 Neuromusculoskeletal and movement-related functions	d4 Mobility
ACTIVITIES & PARTICIPATION	d5 Self care
d1 Learning and applying knowledge	d6 Domestic life
d4 Mobility	d8 Major life areas
	d9 Community, social, and civic life
REDUCTION OF PAIN[a]	
STANDING & WALKING	*MAINTAIN OR CHANGE BODY POSITION*
STEPPING & FULL GAIT CYCLES	*TRANSFERS[a]*
QUALITY & DEVELOPMENT	Obtain/maintain/improve sitting balance,[a] posture in sitting; standing balance,[a] posture in standing; ability to change position, pull to stand, kneel to stand, sit to stand,[a] stand to squat, bending down, step in place; transfer[a]
GAIT PATTERN	
KINEMATICS OF SEGMENTS & JOINTS	
Normalize/optimize the kinematics of segments and joints in standing, swaying, stepping in place, stepping, full gait cycles	
Obtain normal developmental order of segment kinematics acquisition- first learn to couple shank and foot and then learn to couple shank and thigh	*WALKING*
	Obtain/maintain/improve: walking ability in stepping, full gait cycles; gait efficiency, energy expenditure, endurance, distance, exercise tolerance; spatiotemporal measures, velocity, cadence, step/stride length
Obtain normal developmental order of joint kinematics acquisition	
KINETICS	
Normalize/optimize kinetics of standing, swaying, stepping in place, stepping, full gait cycles	*MOVING AROUND*
Prevent/reduce generation of abnormal moments when learning to stand, step and walk with full gait cycles	Obtain/maintain/improve ability to: walk within home, outside home, in other terrains and locations, short and long distances, on different surfaces, around obstacle; run; climb stairs; ride a toy, tricycle, bicycle; use mobility equipment or transportation
Obtain/maintain controlled rates of generation of normal/optimal moments	
MOTOR LEARNING	
Provide postural feedback[a]	*UPPER LIMB*
Facilitate motor learning by provision of normal or optimal postural feedback and from repetition of generation of normal kinematics and kinetics in standing, stepping, full gait cycles	Obtain/maintain/improve: Upper limb functions in sitting & standing; ability to carry, move and handle objects
	SELF CARE & DOMESTIC LIFE
	ACCESS TO EDUCATION, COMMUNITY, SOCIAL, AND CIVIC LIFE
	OTHER
	Cosmesis
[a] Denotes ISO 8551: 2003 Objective.[3]	

Biomechanical Optimization, Designing, Aligning, and Tuning

Much has been written about AFOs and footwear, but the literature does not demonstrate a comprehensive understanding of all aspects of AFO and footwear design.[4,6,8,12,25] As a consequence, many AFOFCs used in research trials have been suboptimally designed and aligned.[4,8,16,25,26] In addition, most have not been tuned to optimize their effect, which, unfortunately, makes much of the research invalid.[4,8,12,25] The terms *tuning, optimizing,* and *biomechanical optimization* have all been used to describe the process of selecting and adjusting the design and alignment of an AFOFC so that it will perform optimally.[8] There is a need to develop definitions as currently there are none that are agreed upon internationally. The following are of the author's choice. It is preferable to reserve the term *tuning* for the fine adjustments that are made to the design of the AFOFC during functional trials of activities such as standing or walking, and to use the term *biomechanical optimization* to encompass the whole process of designing, aligning, and tuning AFOFCs. The following definitions can then apply:

- *Biomechanical optimization of an AFOFC* is the process of designing, aligning, and tuning an orthosis in order to optimize its performance in the activity required (eg, standing, stepping, walking, or stair climbing).[8,27,28]
- *Tuning an AFOFC* is the process whereby fine adjustments are made to the design of the AFOFC in order to optimize its performance during the activity for which the AFOFC is intended to be used, such as standing, stepping, walking, and stair climbing.[4,8,27,28] Tuning can include adjustments to both alignments and designs of the AFOFC. The essence of tuning is that it is performed during practice trials of activities.

ISO 8549-1[9(p 4)] defines the alignment processes as follows:

- *Alignment*: "Establishment of the position in space of the components of the prosthesis or orthosis relative to each other and to the patient."
- *Static alignment*: "Process whereby the bench alignment is refined while the prosthesis or orthosis is worn by the stationary patient."
- *Dynamic alignment*: "Process whereby the alignment of the prosthesis or orthosis is optimized by using observations of the movement pattern of the patient."

The terms *tuning, optimization,* and *biomechanical optimization* have been used most often in regard to fixed ankle AFOFCs, but they can equally apply to flexible or hinged AFOFC designs (see Chapter 20), or any orthosis. Indeed, one of the first mentions of *fine tuning* referred to a flexible AFO.[29] All orthoses need to perform optimally and, to do so, they usually need adjustment of design.

There is now an emerging consensus that the tuning of AFOFCs should be integral to both research trials and clinical practice.[4,6,8,16,25] These reviews revealed that tuning has been referred to only sporadically in the literature. Its importance appears to have either not been understood or ignored. This is surprising if we consider that investigating suboptimal interventions in research or practicing suboptimally are not appropriate. It is less surprising if we consider that there are only a few studies that evaluated tuning of AFOFCs, some of which are unpublished[4,6,8,13,25]; that gait laboratories are usually necessary to detect the kinematic and kinetic changes that occur during tuning; and that there has been poor funding of this area of research. However, the studies that have been reported do suggest a positive effect of tuning, which has led to the recommendation that tuning AFOFCs is essential.[8,16] The author's center has enjoyed unusual routine clinical access to a "video vector gait laboratory" for nearly 20 years and has regularly tuned AFOFC prescriptions for a whole population of children.[30,31] We have been able to establish algorithms and indicative measures that can help make the process easier for researchers and clinicians who do not have kinetic facilities.

Alignment

This is one of the most important terms for orthotic management and rehabilitation, yet it has been much neglected. In recent decades, gait analysis and orthotic science have paid insufficient attention to the alignment of segments and mainly concentrated on the alignment of joints.[6] This has led to nonoptimal orthotic management and rehabilitation in both clinical practice and research.[12] ISO 8551:2003 provides definitions for the alignment of both joints and segments.[3] It is important that we return to giving equal emphasis to both of these alignments. Table 19-2 in Chapter 19 named and defined the alignments of the segments and joints of the body in each of the 3 cardinal planes. When describing any orthosis, the alignment of all of the segments and joints contained within the orthosis should be recorded. Some alignments are frequently described in the literature, others are not, and various and ambiguous terminology has been used, which has caused confusion.[4] Although not defined by ISO, a consensus has emerged for the terminology and definitions of 2 key sagittal alignments in an AFOFC[4-6,8,25,27,28]:

1. *Angle of the ankle in AFO* (AA-AFO) describes the sagittal alignment of the foot segment relative to the lower leg or shank segment within the AFO.[4] It is defined as the angle between the line of the shank relative to the lateral border of the foot, which is a line between the base of the heel pad to the most inferior point of the foot under the fifth metatarsal head. It is described in degrees of plantarflexion, dorsiflexion, or as plantigrade.[4]

2. The *shank to vertical angle (SVA) of the AFOFC* describes the alignment of the shank segment relative to the vertical when standing in the AFOFC.[4] It is defined as "the angle of the shank relative to a vertical to the horizontal surface when standing in the AFOFC with heels down and weight equally distributed between heel and toe."[4(p 2)] When measured in the sagittal plane, the SVA is described as inclined if the shank is leaning forward from the vertical and

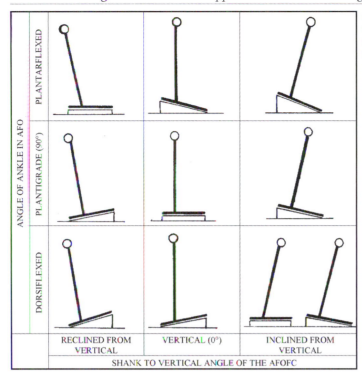

Figure 21-1. The relationship between and independence of the AA-AFO and SVA of the AFOFC. (Reprinted with permission from Owen E. The importance of being earnest about shank and thigh kinematics especially when using ankle-foot orthoses. *Prosthet Orthot Int.* 2010;34(3):254-269. Copyright © 2010 by SAGE.)

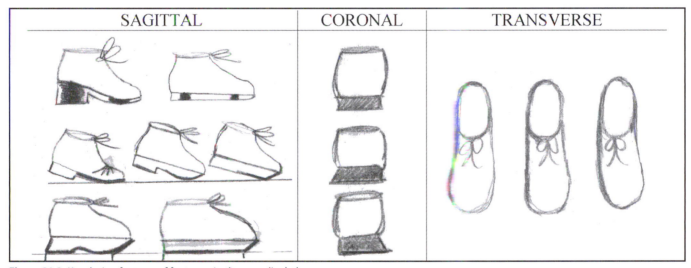

Figure 21-2. Key design features of footwear in three cardinal planes.

reclined if it is leaning backward from the vertical. It is described in degrees from the vertical, with 0 degrees designated as the vertical.[4] The SVA of an AFOFC is most commonly measured in the sagittal plane but may also be measured in the coronal plane.

Figure 21-1 illustrates the relationship between and independence of the AA-AFO and SVA of the AFOFC.[4,6] It is possible to achieve any SVA with any AA-AFO by varying the HSD (see definition later in this chapter). The history of orthotic literature is that only rarely have these 2 very different alignments been distinguished and regarded as independent of each other.[4,6,8,12,25] The existence of the SVA has been virtually ignored.[4,6] The confusion between the 2 alignments has been compounded by the fact that, in the early literature, they were initially given the same name. The term *dorsiflexed*

AFO, for example, could refer to either a dorsiflexed AA-AFO or an inclined SVA. The use of different nomenclature and the designation of the terms *dorsiflexion*, *plantarflexion*, and *plantigrade* to describe only the anatomical alignment, the AA-AFO, eliminates this confusion.[4,6]

Nomenclature and Definitions for Key Aspects of Footwear and Ankle-Foot Orthosis Designs

Figure 21-2 illustrates, in the 3 cardinal planes, some of the key design features that can be incorporated into footwear and that can be adjusted during the tuning process to optimize the AFOFC design. A few principal sagittal design features need to be defined: pitch, stiffness, and profiles.

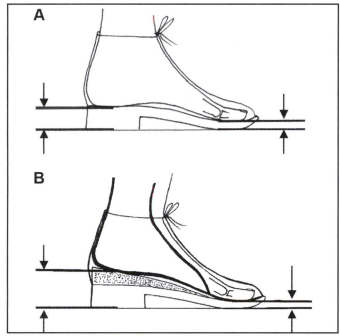

Figure 21-3. (A) Heel sole differential. (B) Final heel sole differential.

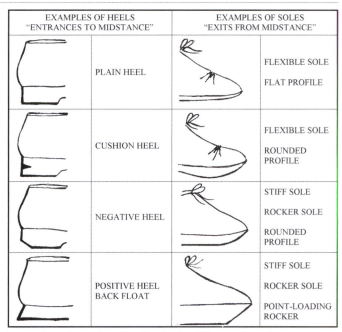

EXAMPLES OF HEELS "ENTRANCES TO MIDSTANCE"		EXAMPLES OF SOLES "EXITS FROM MIDSTANCE"	
	PLAIN HEEL		FLEXIBLE SOLE FLAT PROFILE
	CUSHION HEEL		FLEXIBLE SOLE ROUNDED PROFILE
	NEGATIVE HEEL		STIFF SOLE ROCKER SOLE ROUNDED PROFILE
	POSITIVE HEEL BACK FLOAT		STIFF SOLE ROCKER SOLE POINT-LOADING ROCKER

Figure 21-4. Examples of heel and sole stiffness and profile.

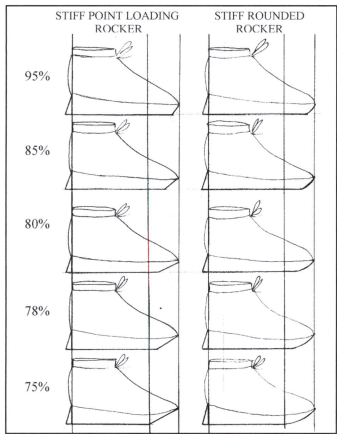

Figure 21-5. Position of the rocker along the length of footwear and toe spring angle.

Heel Sole Differential

The *heel sole differential* (HSD) describes the difference in height between the heel and the sole of the footwear, which is often referred to as the *pitch*. It is defined as the measured difference between the depth of the heel at the mid-heel and the depth of the sole at the metatarsal heads Figure 21-3A.[4,6] It is measured in cm or mm. It is different from *heel height* as that measurement only assesses the depth of the heel with no consideration of the depth of the sole of the footwear.

Final HSD is the sum of the HSD of the footwear and the thickness of any additions at the heel or sole (Figure 21-3B).[4,6] It is measured in cm or mm. The HSD or final HSD of an AFOFC needs to be maintained, so materials must be noncompressible.

Stiffness of the Heel and Sole

Stiffness refers to the ability of the material and design of the heel and sole of the footwear to resist bending.

Profile of the Heel and Sole

The profile of the heel or the sole is the shape of the sagittal view of the distal surface of the footwear.[4,6,27,28,32] Examples of a variety of heel and sole stiffness and profiles are illustrated in Figure 21-4 and their effects are described later. When footwear has a stiff sole and a rocker profile, the design of the sole is called a *rocker sole*.[32] Footwear with a flexible sole can also have a rounded profile, but it is not usually described as having a *rocker sole*. There are 2 main types of rocker sole: rounded rocker (RR) and point loading rocker (PLR).[32,33] They are differentiated by the acuteness of the angle where the sole profile diverts from the horizontal and often have a greater *toe spring angle*, which is the angle that the line of the rocker profile makes with the horizontal.[32] All rockers are also defined by their position along the length of the footwear, in absolute measures of cm, and also in percentage measures of the overall length of the footwear (eg, 75%, 85%) (Figure 21-5).[32,33]

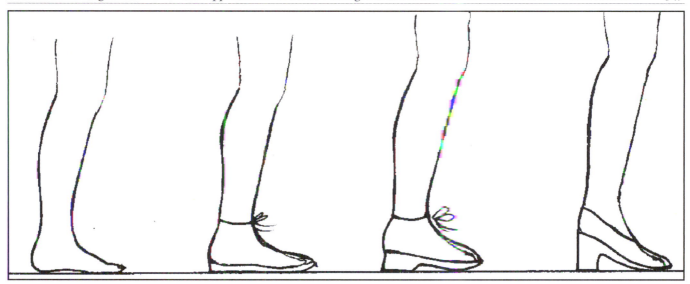

Figure 21-6. The relationship between the pitch of the footwear and the length of the effective foot.

The Actual Foot and the Effective Foot

The body has a foot segment at the end of each lower limb, the *actual foot*. Each limb segment has a length, and normative data for age are documented.[34] When walking in footwear, the footwear becomes the effective foot and the base of support (BOS), and it, too, will have a length.[27,28] When there is a *pitch* in the footwear, the *effective foot* is shorter than the actual foot, and as the *pitch* of the footwear increases, the *effective foot* becomes increasingly short (Figure 21-6).[4,6,27,28] Sometimes, the *actual foot* is shorter than the norm for the age, height, or lower limb length, so it usually needs to be normalized in an orthotic prescription by creating a longer *effective foot*.[27,28] This will also be the case if a normal length or a short foot is significantly plantarflexed in an orthosis.[4,6,27,28]

Stiffness of the Ankle-Foot Orthosis

Stiffness refers to the ability of the material and design to resist bending at the joints contained within the orthosis (eg, the ankle and metatarsophalangeal joints [MTPJs]).[35,36]

Application of the ICF Model for Determining Orthosis Designs

Table 21-1 outlines the major considerations we may take into account when choosing outcomes for the individual patient. The list can seem overwhelming, especially when working with the pediatric population for whom both short- and long-term goals are very important. An infant has 16 years of skeletal, muscular, and neurological growth and development ahead, so extraordinarily long-term goals have to be set. Dividing the lists into the ICF[1,2] domains simplifies the choices for both clinicians and patients, and for the short- and long-term goal setting. For example, for children, the development of a normal skeleton is extremely important, especially if surgery is to be avoided, but at the same time, the child has to be able to be a child and do activities appropriate for his or her age, and also to participate.[12,23] Usually, a

delicate balance of goals is required, and for children, this balance is constantly changing with age and development. Using the ICF model,[1,2] we can apply a simple "Inside-Out" approach to determine the desired goals and outcomes for each child.

Once a decision is made regarding which orthosis design can best meet the needs of the body structures and functions, it is possible to determine if that design would also meet the needs of activity and participation. If not, a compromise about where and when to use the orthosis can be made, and, if necessary, a choice can be made between the relative importance of activities and participation goals, and body structures and functions goals.

SHANK KINEMATICS AS A BASIS FOR GAIT CATEGORIZATION AND ORTHOTIC ALGORITHMS

It is possible to define and classify the characteristics of abnormal patterns of gait in a number of ways. Most often this has been done by joint kinematics or kinetics.[37-43] However, when trying to determine optimal orthotic prescriptions, a helpful way of defining and classifying gait is by segment kinematics, in particular, by the kinematics of the shank in the sagittal plane.[4,6] This is because, while all segment and joint abnormalities are important, correction of abnormal sagittal shank kinematics is the key to normalizing more proximal segment and joint kinematics and kinetics, as demonstrated in Chapter 19. Another primary goal of orthotic interventions is to restore or maintain normal sagittal foot kinematics. Once the foot and shank kinematics are normalized, it is possible to determine whether more proximal segment and joint deviations observed are of primary origin or whether they are secondary to distal segment deviations.

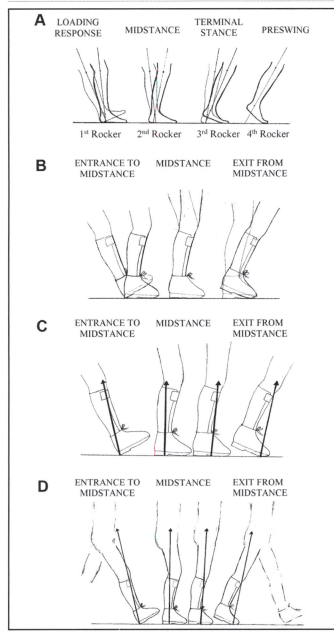

A LOADING RESPONSE   MIDSTANCE   TERMINAL STANCE   PRESWING

1st Rocker   2nd Rocker   3rd Rocker   4th Rocker

B ENTRANCE TO MIDSTANCE   MIDSTANCE   EXIT FROM MIDSTANCE

C ENTRANCE TO MIDSTANCE   MIDSTANCE   EXIT FROM MIDSTANCE

D ENTRANCE TO MIDSTANCE   MIDSTANCE   EXIT FROM MIDSTANCE

Figure 21-7. (A) The 4 rockers of barefoot gait. (B-D) Replicating normal foot, shank, thigh and trunk kinematics, and ground reaction force alignment with fixed ankle AFOFCs. (Adapted with permission from Owen E. The importance of being earnest about shank and thigh kinematics especially when using ankle-foot orthoses. *Prosthet Orthot Int.* 2010;34(3):254-269. Copyright © 2010 by SAGE.)

This chapter will present a categorization of gait and an algorithm for designing, aligning and tuning AFOFCs, based on shank kinematics.[4,6,44] If a patient presents with normal shank kinematics, the algorithm is still helpful. We need to understand how normal sagittal foot and shank kinematics can be created when fixing the ankle joint in AFOFCs, especially as there have been concerns in the literature that AFO designs that fix the ankle will prevent normal shank kinematics. Understanding that joint and segment movements are independent of each other helps us understand how it is possible to obtain normal foot and shank kinematics when using AFOFCs, even when the ankle and MTPJs are fixed.

Reviewing the 4 *rockers of gait*, especially the kinematics of the foot and shank during each of the rockers is helpful in understanding how normal foot and shank kinematics can be preserved when wearing footwear or AFOFCs (see Chapter 19). The rockers of normal barefoot gait were originally described by Perry in 1974.[45] While she initially used a 3-event model, a 4-event model is preferable if we are to fully understand gait and design optimal orthoses (see Table 19-13 for comparison).[46-48] The rockers have recently been defined as the "mechanisms of the ankle and foot that produce normal shank kinematics during stance phase."[46(p S49)] They are illustrated in Figure 21-7A and have been described in depth in Chapter 19. The rockers of barefoot gait are dependent on movement at both the ankle and MTPJs,[46,49] but if these joints are not able to move, it is still possible to produce normal shank kinematics if the correct footwear or orthosis design is used.

Let us look at how normal foot and shank kinematics are created when walking in footwear rather than barefoot. When walking in footwear with no HSD, the segment and joint kinematics will be the same as barefoot gait, as long as the sole is flexible to allow full MTPJ extension. Primitive footwear provided these conditions as it only consisted of material covering the sole of the foot. Gradually, footwear designs evolved to have a positive *pitch* or HSD, and varying designs of heels and soles emerged. We now have a vast variety of designs of footwear available, and the development of heel designs, flexible soles, stiff rockers, and "high heels" has become important in the modern market. When using footwear with a positive HSD, the base of the footwear becomes the *effective foot*.[4,6,27,28] The *effective foot* will undertake the normal foot kinematics while shank kinematics remains normal.[4,6,50,51] The adjustment to create normal segment kinematics is made by the ankle joint, which continues to produce movements similar to those for barefoot gait, but in a different range.[4,6,50-52] The most important kinematics for gait is segment kinematics, so joints adjust their kinematics to create normal segment kinematics.[50,51,53,54] When using footwear that has a stiff sole, a rocker profile must be incorporated into the design to enable the use of a simulated third and fourth rocker.[6,27,28,32] Wooden footwear and modern stiff rocker soles on fashion and trainer shoes are examples of this. The body usually adjusts to the footwear design, but if the footwear design does not enable normal foot and shank kinematics, it is uncomfortable or impossible to walk.

Let us now look at how normal foot and shank kinematics can be created when walking in AFOFCs. In abnormal patterns of gait, the segment and joint kinematics of some or all of the rockers may be insufficient or excessive.[4,6] An ideal orthotic design would correct the abnormal kinematics at both the ankle and MTPJs during each subdivision of the GC. Because of the different requirements of these joints during each of the four rockers, this is not yet easily possible, and compromises have to be made. For a number of reasons, we often have to fix the ankle joint and, sometimes, also the MTPJs. This prevents the use of anatomical rockers, so normal shank kinematics must be replicated by the use of simulated rockers created by the design of the footwear that is combined with the AFO.[4,6,27,28,44,55] Normal shank kinematics can be created by determining the optimal SVA alignment of the AFOFC and by optimizing the designs of the heel and sole of the footwear to facilitate the foot and shank kinematics required for entry to and exit from temporal midstance.[4,6,27,28,55] When using AFOFCs, the base of the footwear becomes the *effective foot*. Sole designs can vary the timing and rate of heel rise and consequent shank kinematics. Heel designs vary the rate of foot kinematics from heel strike to foot flat and, consequently, shank kinematics.[4,6,27,28]

The design of the AFOFC needs to create normal or most normal foot and shank kinematics, subsequent normal or most normal thigh kinematics, and knee and hip kinematics and kinetics.[6,27,28,55] There are 3 switches of moment direction at the knee during the stance phase (see Chapter 19). The first occurs during the entrance to temporal midstance, the second at about temporal midstance, and the third during double support exit. For children with disabilities, it is sometimes helpful to exaggerate the slowing of the angular velocity of the forward progression of the shank into temporal midstance, and maintain the shank in a still position at temporal midstance for longer than normal, in order to facilitate the ballistic movement of the thigh to an inclined position and the moment switching to external extending moments at the hip and knee.[27,28]

Categorization of Abnormal Gait Patterns

The gait of children with CP has usually been categorized by abnormality of joint kinematics, especially of the knee and ankle.[37-43,56] Four knee kinematic categories are commonly used. These are genu recurvatum or hyperextending knee, crouch knee, and jump knee in stance phase, and stiff knee gait in swing phase. In *hyperextending knee gait*, the knee hyperextends; in *crouch gait*, the knee is excessively flexed through midstance (MST) and terminal stance (TST); and in *jump gait*, it is excessively flexed in MST but recovers extension in TST.[39]

While joint kinematic categorization may be useful for determining some treatment options, it is not the most helpful for determining orthotic prescriptions. A categorization based on segment kinematics is more helpful, especially one based on shank segment kinematics.[4,6,44] This is because normalizing shank kinematics is essential for the normalization of segment and joint kinematics proximal to the shank and for the consequent normalization of joint kinematics and kinetics. Normalizing foot kinematics is, of course, also essential.

The normal shank kinematics of the GC produced by the rockers of gait was described in Chapter 19. The shank is reclined 20 degrees at initial contact; by temporal midstance it is 10 to 12 degrees inclined with a slowing of its angular velocity; by contralateral initial contact it is 20 degrees inclined; and by toe off, it is 50 degrees inclined. Children with CP most often have abnormal shank kinematics during part or all of the GC. The shank may be either

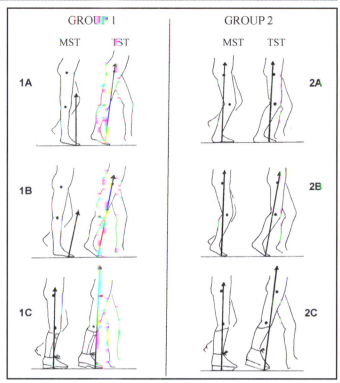

Figure 21-8. Categories of gait based on abnormality of stance phase shank kinematics. (Reprinted with permission from Owen E. The importance of being earnest about shank and thigh kinematics especially when using ankle-foot orthoses. *Prosthet Orthot Int*. 2010;34(3):254-269. Copyright © 2010 by SAGE.)

insufficiently or excessively inclined during MST and, possibly, TST (Figure 21-8). There are 2 subgroups in both of these main categories and some children have a combination of shank kinematic abnormality within a GC.[4,6] The abnormal shank kinematics is often combined with abnormal foot kinematics, but the categorization is largely by shank segment abnormality alone (see Figure 21-8 and Table 21-2).

Group 1: Insufficiently Inclined Shank Kinematics

For children who present with insufficiently inclined shank kinematics, the differentiation between the subgroups is that one group presents with *shank reversal* or *retrograde movement of the shank*, and the other group does not.[57,58] One reason for differentiating these 2 subgroups is that different AFOFC SVA alignments are required to optimize gait.[28]

Subgroup 1A

This subgroup has insufficiently inclined shanks but no shank reversal in MST. There is a vertical ground reaction force (GRF), which is excessively anteriorly aligned at the foot, knee, and hip.

Subgroup 1B

This subgroup has insufficiently inclined shank with shank reversal in MST. There is a forward leaning GRF in MST, which is excessively anteriorly aligned at the foot, knee, and hip.

TABLE 21-2			
CHARACTERISTICS OF ABNORMAL SHANK KINEMATICS IN CHILDREN WITH CEREBRAL PALSY			
INSUFFICIENT INCLINE	**KINEMATIC AND KINETIC CHARACTERISTICS**		**EXCESSIVE INCLINE**
Group 1A	Insufficiently inclined shanks in MST/TST. Excessively anteriorly aligned vertical GRF	Excessively inclined shanks in MST/TST. Foot horizontal in MST and no or poor heel rise in TST	Group 2A
Group 1B	Insufficiently inclined shanks in MST/TST with shank reversal. Excessively anteriorly aligned forward leaning GRF	Excessively inclined shanks in MST/TST. Foot heel up in MST and TST	Group 2B
NOTE: Some children may have normal shank kinematics combined with abnormal foot kinematics			
Abbreviations: GRF, ground reaction force; MST, midstance; TST, terminal stance;.			

Group 2: Excessively Inclined Shank Kinematics

For children who present with excessively inclined shank kinematics, the differentiation between the subgroups is that one group presents with the foot in full contact with the floor, and in the other group, there is contact only with the toe.

Subgroup 2A

This subgroup has excessively inclined shank kinematics. The foot is in full contact with the floor in MST and often also in TST. The GRF is excessively posteriorly aligned at the foot and knee.

Subgroup 2B

This subgroup has excessively inclined shank kinematics. The foot has only toe contact in MST and TST. The GRF is excessively anteriorly aligned at the foot in MST but excessively posteriorly aligned at the knee.

General Considerations

Group 1 is largely analogous to the category of hyperextending knee gait; however, knee hyperextension is often not present, and what is often observed as hyperextension by eye is, in fact, the shank reversal.[57] Group 2 is largely analogous to crouch gait. Jump knee gait is analogous to Group 2 in MST, but there is a recovery in TST. The GC starts with excessively inclined shanks and the foot in contact with the floor, but by TST, the kinematics and kinetics have recovered to normal, or sometimes, even to insufficient inclines.

Some children will present with normal shank kinematics but abnormal foot kinematics. The 3 algorithms presented in this chapter will be helpful when designing AFOFCs for these children. They can be used to facilitate designs that normalize foot kinematics while maintaining the normal shank kinematics and other segment and joint kinematics and kinetics. The identification of segment kinematics abnormality in some children may be obvious by visual observation of gait in real time, but it is far preferable to observe kinematics with slow motion video playback and, if possible, with a video and superimposed vector overlay.[59]

ORTHOTIC CONDITIONS FOR STABLE STANDING, STEPPING, AND GAIT—FROM STABLE STANDING TO ROCK AND ROLL WALKING

In Chapter 19, the kinematics and kinetics of normal standing, stepping, and gait were described and the GC was interpreted in a new way. When designing, aligning, and tuning AFOFCs for the activities of standing, swaying, stepping, and gait, we apply the principles of temporal midstance being center stage in the GC and akin to standing, and then divide the GC into temporal midstance, entrance to temporal midstance, and exit from temporal midstance as described in Chapter 19. To understand this section, it is essential to read Chapter 19 in full. In the current chapter, to delineate the difference between the terms *temporal midstance* and *midstance*, the abbreviation MST will be used only to designate the term *midstance* but not *temporal midstance*.

Orthotic designs must be determined according to the activity required when wearing the AFOFC.[21,22,60] Some AFOFC designs can make standing very stable, but if designs are too stable, they prevent the mobility required for walking and running.[28] One way to determine which designs may be optimal for each activity is to look at those that give most stability in standing and stepping, and then those required to optimize a full GC. We will concentrate initially on the sagittal plane and the conditions required for optimal segment alignment, segment proportion, and BOS.

The aim of biomechanical optimization of any orthosis is to provide an AFOFC that will normalize or most normalize segment and joint kinematics and kinetics of the required activity.[4,6,8,12,27,28] The optimal orthotic design for each leg of each individual will depend on their standing, stepping, and walking ability. Some patients are able to produce the necessary conditions for these activities with very little help from an orthosis, and others will need more biomechanical assistance. Some will not be able to get full benefit even with significant help from an AFOFC because, even if optimal conditions for stability and mobility are provided by the AFOFC, these patients will have additional significant problems, such as excessive joint stiffness or skeletal torsions, poor balance, or other additional disabilities. Some patients will require an assistive device to ambulate, but the same principles will apply for choosing optimal orthosis design.[27,28]

This chapter will present 3 clinical algorithms, all of which help determine the optimal orthotic design for each limb of each patient.[6,26-28,44] One of the algorithms determines whether a dorsiflexion free or a fixed ankle design is required, and the other 2 algorithms relate mainly to fixed ankle AFOs. There are, of course, many AFO designs, including free ankle designs, plantarflexion free and dorsiflexion stop designs, and designs with complex dorsiflexion and plantarflexion resist features, all of which have their place if the design matches the patient's needs.[21] Concentrating on fixed ankle designs in the first instance helps focus on the orthotic conditions that are required to normalize standing, stepping, and gait. If it is possible for the patient to achieve any of the conditions themselves, without biomechanical assistance from the orthosis, then, of course, their orthotic design should reflect this.

The following descriptions of the conditions required to achieve stable standing, stepping, and walking include principal alignments, principal proportions, and principal design features of AFOFCs.[44,61] The best order to describe the elements in orthotic designs that produce the necessary conditions is distal to proximal, as a stable distal BOS is essential for more proximal postural control, and distal conditions influence both distal and proximal kinematics and kinetics.[4-6,8,12,19,27,28,62]

There has been virtually no reference to equalizing and normalizing segment proportion in the literature, but this is essential for success of orthotic intervention.[27,28] Leg lengths must be equalized and foot lengths normalized. Sometimes, it is helpful to make the effective foot longer than it would be normally to increase the toe lever and induce greater stability.[27,28]

Orthotic Designs for Stable Standing, Stepping, and Walking With Full Gait Cycles

Orthotic designs for these activities need to follow the conditions discussed in detail in Chapter 19. This relationship is described in Boxes 21-1 through 21-5. As shown in Box 21-1, which describes conditions for stable standing, condition 1 allows the foot to act as a stable BOS; conditions 2 through 4 provide optimal segment proportion; conditions 3 through 5 ensure that heel and toe levers are of adequate length to produce the optimal length of the BOS; and conditions 3

through 7 create the prerequisite kinematics and kinetics for conditions 8 through 11 to occur.

The segment alignments of stepping create maximum stability while allowing some forward mobility. Stepping will usually be the mode of ambulation for patients who are unable to walk with full GCs and children who are developing first walking skills. Conditions 1 through 11 for stable standing listed in Box 21-2 apply only to the stance limb in stable stepping, with additional features shown for conditions 5 and 7. Condition 12 applies to the swing limb.

During stepping, the stance limb will undertake kinematics and kinetics similar to 10% to 40% of a full GC, and the swing limb to 90% of a GC as described in Chapter 19.[27,28] The initial contact will be with a vertical or near vertical shank and a horizontal or near horizontal foot, producing a very stable base on which to start the *entry*. The *exit* will have a shallow heel rise or, if the step is very short, no heel rise. A reasonable step length can be achieved without any heel rise if the shank and the thigh are inclined 10 to 12 degrees. These alignments combined with the resulting GRF alignment produce knee and hip extending moments and a very stable stance limb during the shortened *exit*. Stepping backward and forward with one limb, while maintaining a stable stance limb, provides good preparation for stepping.

When discussing orthotic designs for walking with full GCs, the conditions and orthotic designs for *temporal midstance* will first be considered, followed by those for the *entrance to temporal midstance* and *exit from temporal midstance* (see Boxes 21-3 through 21-5). The optimal orthotic design should, of course, be determined for each leg. As shown in Box 21-3, conditions 1 through 11 for stable standing apply to the stance limb in temporal midstance, with additional features for some of the conditions. Condition 12 applies to the swing limb. The kinematics of the foot and shank in first and second rockers of normal barefoot gait are combined in the *entrance* with an AFOFC (see Box 21-4). Patients will either be able to achieve a full or partial entrance into temporal midstance, dependent on their ability to achieve a full or partial terminal swing (TSW). A full *exit from temporal midstance* includes exit to 50% GC, when initial contact with the contra-lateral limb is made and the "Big V" is present (see Chapter 19 and Figure 19-1), and continues to 60% GC, toe off. Patients will either be able to achieve a full or partial *exit*, and the orthotic design will reflect the patient's need.

CLINICAL ALGORITHMS FOR DESIGNING, ALIGNING, AND TUNING ANKLE-FOOT ORTHOSIS/FOOTWEAR COMBINATIONS

Algorithms can simplify the process of clinical decision making in order to select optimal prescriptions. At least 30 sagittal, coronal, and transverse design variables may be included in an optimal prescription, and prescriptions may be different for each leg. Three algorithms have been

Box 21-1

ORTHOTIC DESIGNS FOR STABLE STANDING

1. Optimum tri-planar alignment of foot
2. Leg lengths equal or equalized
3. Effective feet correct length for height

   Some patients have short anatomical feet and some feet may become effectively short because of high arches, other clinical conditions or plantarflexion contractures requiring plantarflexed AA-AFO. It is essential for any orthotic prescription to create the correct length of effective foot for height. Sometimes, it may be helpful to make the feet longer than required for height, to increase the heel and toe levers.

4. Feet aligned so that they are approximate to the sagittal plane

   Some patients have FPAs that place the foot in an excessively in-turned or out-turned position and consequently, the length of the toe lever is lost. Where possible, the degree of excessive FPA needs to be minimized.

5. Effective feet horizontal on the floor with both heel and forefoot in contact.

   The actual foot may not be horizontal, but the effective foot is and will be providing the BOS. In order to place the effective foot flat on the floor, it is essential to have 2 optimal alignments in the AFOFC: the AA-AFO and the SVA of the AFOFC. The sole profile will also influence the ability of patients to stand with feet flat on the floor. Some patients will be able to maintain this position with footwear that has a negative heel and a flexible sole with a flat or rounded sole profile at 60% of the length of the footwear, which is a relatively unstable sole profile design, common in commercial footwear. Some will need plain heels and rocker positions of 75%, which places the rocker at the position of MTPJs in a normal foot, a more stable sole profile design. Others will need positive heels and a stiff rocker placed well forward of the anatomical MTPJs, a very stable sole profile design. The rocker position might be at 80% to 95% or even 100% to 110% of footwear length. This produces a very long and flat sole profile, with long heel and toe levers, which maintains the foot flat on the floor. For each patient, the optimal sole profile must be determined.

6. Shanks optimally aligned in an inclined position

   The optimal SVA alignment of the shank for normal barefoot standing is 10 to 12 degrees inclined, with a range of 7 to 15 degrees inclined. This condition places the knee joint over the center of the foot, producing a stable triangular distal BOS, and it also allows the thigh to move from a reclined to a vertical to an inclined position and forward translation of a vertical trunk while keeping the COM within the BOS. When using AFOFC interventions, optimal SVAs of the AFOFC will often be 10 to 12 degrees inclined, rarely less than 10 degrees inclined, and may be more than 15 degrees inclined. The reasons for this variety of SVAs will be explained later.

7. Shanks remaining still in their optimally aligned position.

   The same features for design of sole profiles which maintain the feet in full contact with the floor will also apply for maintaining SVAs still and optimally aligned. SVA alignment is lost if the heel is off the floor.

8. Thighs able to move from vertical to inclined and reclined positions

   The conditions that maintain the foot horizontal on the floor combined with the optimal AA-AFO and inclined SVA alignment in the AFOFC provide the conditions that allow the thigh to incline. However, for some patients, usually those with severe stiffness at the knees or hips, the degree of SVA incline necessary to allow the thigh to become vertical and inclined may be 20 degrees or more, which will bring the COM outside the BOS if the foot length is correct for the height. In these situations, stable standing can only be achieved with the use of foot lengths that are greater than the foot length normally required for height, or by the use of equipment or manual help (Figure 21-11). Footwear that is longer will need a stiff sole.

9. Trunk able to remain vertical and translate forward and backward

   The conditions that allow the thigh to move from reclined to vertical and inclined positions will produce this condition.

10. COM to remain within the margins of the BOS

    All the previous conditions will create this condition.

11. Body weight adequately supported

Abbreviations: AA-AFO, angle of the ankle in ankle-foot orthosis; AFOFC, ankle-foot orthosis/footwear combination; BOS, base of support; COM, center of mass; FPA, foot progression angle; MTPJs, metatarsophalangeal joints; SVA, shank to vertical angle.

Box 21-2

ORTHOTIC DESIGNS FOR STABLE STEPPING

1-4, 6, 8-11.   As for stable standing

5.   Effective foot horizontal on the floor with both heel and forefoot contact for the majority or all of the activity. Keeping full foot contact provides most stability. If the heel is to rise, then it will be late and shallow. If IC is with the heel, there will be a shallow toe up alignment.

7.   Shanks remaining still in their optimally aligned position at temporal MST. During the exit, if the heel rises, shank inclination increases slightly. During entrance, the shank to move from its vertical or near vertical alignment at IC to the optimized inclined SVA alignment of the AFOFC.

12.   The swing limb able to take a step equivalent to the length of the stance foot once stable conditions in the stance limb are established.

Abbreviations: AFOFC, ankle-foot orthosis/footwear combination; IC, initial contact; MST, midstance; SVA, shank to vertical angle.

Box 21-3

ORTHOTIC DESIGNS FOR FULL GAIT CYCLES, CONDITIONS FOR TEMPORAL MST, 30% GC

1-4, 6, 11.   As for standing

5.   As for standing, but if stiff rocker soles are used, the rocker position will not be more than 95%, as heel rise in exit must not be impeded.

7.   As for standing and in some circumstances, it is advantageous to maintain a stationary shank for a longer duration than would be expected in normal walking.

8-10.   Thigh and trunk vertical, COM over the center of the BOS.

12.   The swing limb is in mid-swing, with the knee joint positioned just anterior to the stance knee, and the heel and ankle joint are just posterior to the stance ankle. The foot is clear of the floor.

Abbreviations: BOS, base of support; COM, center of mass; MST, midstance.

Box 21-4

ORTHOTIC DESIGNS FOR FULL GAIT CYCLES, CONDITIONS FOR ENTRY TO TEMPORAL MIDSTANCE

1-4.   As for standing and temporal MST

5.   Initial contact with the heel of the effective foot and optimum angular velocity of the foot as it moves to "foot flat" Initial contact with a heel initiates a heel lever, which facilitates movement of the foot to the floor. In some prescriptions, the actual foot may not be "toe up" at IC, but the effective foot will be, and the effective foot will provide the *heel lever*. In order to make the IC with the heel, it is essential to have 2 optimal alignments in the AFOFC, the AA-AFO, and the SVA of the AFOFC. The stiffness and the profile of the footwear heel design increase or reduce the heel lever and consequently, influence the angular velocity of the foot segment during entrance.

6.   Optimal alignment of the shank
The degree of recline at IC will be influenced by the SVA and whether full or partial TSW has been achieved. By 20% to 30% GC, the whole foot to be in full contact with the floor and the shank to be optimally inclined for temporal MST.

7.   Shank to move with appropriate angular velocity
The stiffness and the profile of the footwear heel design not only influence the angular velocity of the foot, but also the shank during entrance.

8.   Thighs to move from reclined to vertical alignment

9.   Trunk to remain vertical and translate forward

10.   The COM will be outside the BOS at IC and move to a position within the BOS at MST.

11.   Body weight adequately supported

12.   Swing limb to achieve preswing and initial swing

Abbreviations: AA-AFO, angle of the ankle in the ankle-foot orthosis; AFOFC, ankle-foot orthosis/footwear combination; BOS, base of support; COM, center of mass; GC, gait cycle; IC, initial contact; MST, midstance; SVA, shank to vertical angle.

Box 21-5

Orthotic Designs for Full Gait Cycles, Conditions for Exit From Temporal Midstance

1-4.   As for standing and temporal MST. Foot alignment in the sagittal plane is important to optimize toe levers.

5.   Heel rise at optimum timing in GC and optimum angular velocity of the foot
The heel normally rises just after 30% GC. The stiffness and profile of the sole influence the length of the toe lever and, consequently, the timing and rate of heel rise. This, in turn, influences foot and shank kinematics and kinetics. Obtaining the optimal lengths of the effective foot and toe lever is crucial for exits. The rocker position will not be more than 95%, as heel rise has to occur during exit if a full or almost full GC is being achieved.

6.   Optimal alignment of the shank
At 30% GC, the SVA alignment will be optimal for temporal MST and then 25 degrees incline at 50% GC if a full TST is achieved, and 45 degrees at 60% GC, toe off.

7.   Shank to move with an optimal angular velocity
The "stiffening of the ankle" in TST of barefoot gait creates the necessary heel rise, from MTPJs extension, the consequent knee and hip extension, and knee and hip extending moments. An AFO can mimic the calf muscle activity to achieve this effect, and the rate of angular velocity of the shank during exit will be dictated by the design of the AFOFC at the MTPJs and of the sole of the footwear. In prescriptions with designs that are free at the MTPJs, both the flexibility of the AFO and footwear at the MTPJs will dictate shank kinematics. Some patients will need a fixed ankle combined with fixed MTPJs in an orthosis to achieve optimal exits from MST. When stiff soles are used, the position and type of rocker sole will be the determinants.

8.   Thighs able to move from an inclined position to a more inclined position
Inclined thighs and shanks will create maximum knee extension and knee extending moments at 40% GC, and maximum hip extension and hip extending moments at 50% GC.

9.   Trunk to remain vertical and translate forward

10.   The COM will move outside the BOS

11.   Body weight adequately supported

12.   Swing limb to achieve mid- and terminal swing

Abbreviations: AFO, ankle-foot orthosis; AFOFC, ankle-foot orthosis/footwear combination; BOS, base of support; COM, center of mass; GC, gait cycle; MST, midstance; MTPJs, metatarsophalangeal joints; SVA, shank to vertical angle; TST, terminal stance.

---

developed for the sagittal plane, with an understanding that considerations of the design in the coronal and transverse planes are equally important.[6,26-28,44,61] Sagittal design variables include details of which joints are fixed or free, the alignments of all the joints within the AFO, the overall SVA of the AFOFC, the stiffness of the AFO, the depth of the heel and sole of the footwear, the HSD of the footwear, the length of the heel and toe lever, the stiffness or flexibility of the sole and the heel, and the design profile of the heel and sole of the footwear, particularly the type and position of any rocker sole.[4,6-8,13,25-28,32,33,55,63-69]

Overview of the Algorithms

There are 3 algorithms: A, B, and C. The algorithm for designing, aligning, and tuning AFOFCs, Algorithm A (Figure 21-9), takes into account 2 major prerequisites for tuning AFOFCs, which are that both the ankle angle and AFO design must be optimal.[6,28,44] Initially, Algorithm A determines whether a hinged or a fixed ankle AFOFC would be optimal. A more comprehensive algorithm for this step is

presented and discussed later, Algorithm C.[26,28] Algorithm A then goes on to determine optimal designs for a fixed ankle AFO and accompanying footwear. Within Algorithm A, there is a stage where the optimal ankle angle must be determined, and for this, Algorithm B[6,27,28,61] (Figure 21-10) should be followed.

Algorithm A is based on the identification of abnormal shank kinematics in gait.[4,6,27,28,55] An assumption is made that the user understands that normal gait requires normal foot segment kinematics, and that it is the combination of normalized foot and shank kinematics that will allow for the normalization of more proximal joint and segment kinematics and kinetics. Normalizing shank kinematics alone will be less successful. The algorithm is primarily intended for tuning whole GCs but can also be used to determine optimal AFOFC designs for standing, swaying, stepping, and partial GCs.

Algorithm A first identifies children who may be suitable for a hinged or flexible AFO. For children who require a fixed ankle AFOFC, it has 2 main pathways. These are based on the presenting abnormality of stance phase shank

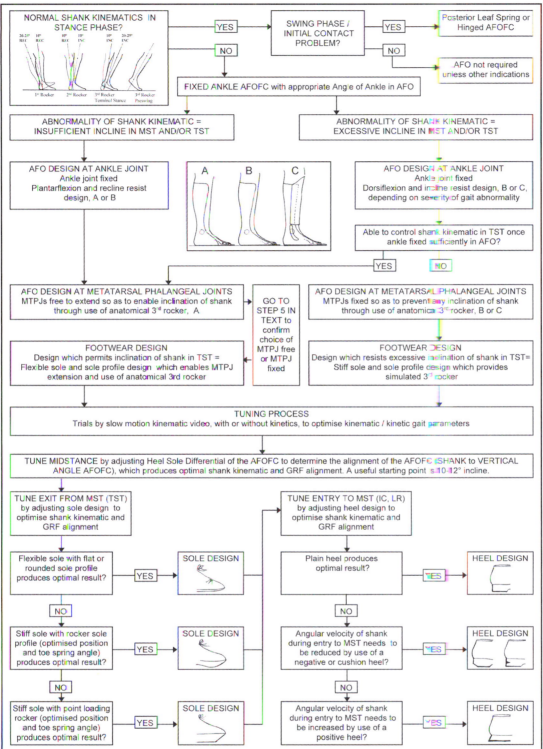

Figure 21-9. Algorithm A: designing, aligning and tuning AFOFCs. (Reprinted from *Gait and Posture*, 22S, Owen E, A clinical algorithm for the design and tuning of ankle-foot orthosis footwear combinations (AFOFCs) based on shank kinematics, 36-37. Copyright © (2005) with permission from Elsevier.)

kinematics observed in barefoot gait, which is either insufficient or excessive shank inclination in MST or TST. These were described previously. Some children present with normal shank kinematics but abnormal foot kinematics. The algorithm can also be helpful when designing fixed ankle AFOFCs for these children but would be used to facilitate designs that normalize foot kinematics while maintaining the normal shank kinematics.[44]

Following the categorization of gait, the algorithm determines the sagittal design of the AFO required for control of the ankle joint and shank segment for each category.[27,28] It guides the design required for control at the ankle joint and then the design required at the MTPJs.[27,28] The next stage in the algorithm is the tuning of the AFOFC, which is divided into 3 stages: tuning temporal midstance, exit from temporal midstance, and entrance to temporal midstance.[4-7,27,28,33,55]

Figure 21-10. Algorithm B: determining the optimal AA-AFO in fixed ankle AFOFCs. (Reprinted from *Gait and Posture*, 22S, Owen E, Proposed clinical algorithm for deciding the sagittal angle of the ankle in an ankle-foot orthosis footwear combination, 38-39. Copyright © (2005) with permission from Elsevier.)

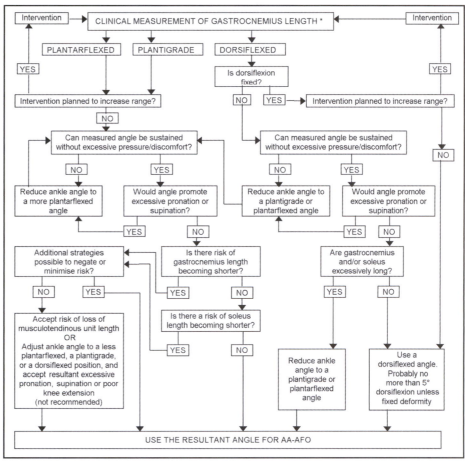

Three Algorithms Step by Step

In order to become confident in using the algorithms, it is easier to start by understanding how to design, align, and tune fixed ankle AFOFCS using Algorithm A and then review the other 2 algorithms.

Algorithm A: Designing, Aligning, and Tuning Ankle-Foot Orthosis/Footwear Combinations

Step 1: Identify Patients Who Require Fixed Ankle Ankle-Foot Orthosis/Footwear Combinations

Algorithm A has a simple approach to determining whether a fixed ankle AFO is the optimal design (see Figure 21-9).[44] It states that if shank kinematics in stance phase is abnormal, a fixed ankle AFO design is recommended.[44] This pathway came from many years of clinical experience of biomechanically optimizing AFOFC designs using a video vector gait laboratory. An extended algorithm for this decision gives a more complete picture and is discussed later, Algorithm C.[26,28]

Step 2: Determine the Optimal Ankle Alignment for the Fixed Ankle Ankle-Foot Orthosis

One principal prerequisite for successful tuning is to have the optimal AA-AFO. This decision has its own algorithm, Algorithm B (see Figure 21-10).[6,27,28,61]

Step 3: Identify the Abnormality of Shank Kinematics in Stance Phase

For children who have been identified as requiring a fixed ankle AFOFC, Algorithm A has 2 possible pathways (see Figure 21-9).[44] These are based on the presenting abnormality of stance phase shank kinematics observed in barefoot gait, described previously (see Figure 21-8 and Table 21-2).[6] For children who present with insufficiently inclined shanks, we need to follow the pathway on the left-hand side of the algorithm, and for those with excessively inclined shanks, we will follow that on the right (see Figure 21-9).[44] Some children will present with normal shank kinematics but abnormal foot kinematics. The identification of shank kinematics abnormality is best accomplished with a slow motion playback facility.[59]

Step 4: Identify the Design of Ankle-Foot Orthosis Required for Control of the Ankle and Shank in Stance Phase

Following the categorization of gait, the algorithm determines the sagittal design of the AFO (see Figure 21-9).[44] On the left-hand side of the algorithm, an AFO design that controls plantarflexion and insufficient incline is selected, design A or B.[70] Both these AFO designs provide the same control of the ankle joint. The difference between them is the design at the MTPJs, with design A being "MTPJ free" and design B "MTPJ fixed," a decision made at the next step.[44]

On the right-hand side of the algorithm,[44] an AFO design that controls dorsiflexion and excessive incline is selected, design B or C.[70] Designs B and C are different in that C has additional controls to prevent dorsiflexion and excessive incline. These are an anterior tibial shell and additional stiffness. An anterior tibial shell has greater control than a strap as the provided force is a greater distance from the ankle, creating a longer lever arm. An anterior tibial shell also spreads the load along the tibia and gives extra triplanar control of pronation and supination, if required. The extra stiffness at the ankle in design C is achieved by the choice of materials, depth at the ankle, use of ribs or carbons, and design of the "fit" about the ankle. An AFO designed to resist dorsiflexion in stance has to resist 100 Nm compared to 10 Nm resisting plantarflexion in swing.[70] So, for patients that need control of dorsiflexion, a substantial orthosis design is necessary. More control is required in a situation with greater gait deviation from normal, increased stiffness at hips and knees, calf weakness, or greater height and weight. However, an orthosis effective in controlling ankle joint dorsiflexion will only be effective in controlling excessive incline of the shank segment if it is coupled with the optimal design of footwear, Steps 6A, B, and C.[44]

Step 5: Identify the Design of Ankle-Foot Orthosis Required for Control of the Metatarsophalangeal Joints in Stance Phase

The algorithm is based on MTPJ designs needed to optimize gait, but there are additional reasons for selecting free or fixed designs at MTPJs.[44] Some patients will require an AFO design that allows the MTPJs to extend, an "MTPJ-free" design, A (see Figure 21-9).[44] This will be combined with footwear with a flexible sole to enable the use of the anatomical third rocker. This option is selected if the following occurs:

- The patient can obtain good kinematics and kinetics in TST once the ankle joint is fixed and the AA-AFO and SVA of the AFOFC are optimized.
- The MTPJs have full extension and there are no toe abnormalities requiring MTPJ fixation.
- The foot is not significantly short.
- There are no problems of forefoot adduction or abduction in the transverse plane which need control from a distal trimline on the medial or lateral wall of the AFO at the foot.[28]

Some patients will require an AFO design that prevents MTPJ extension, a "fixed MTPJ" design, B or C.[44] This disables the anatomical third rocker in order to create a more effective simulated third rocker in the AFOFC design. Whenever the MTPJs are fixed in the AFO, a rocker sole design on the footwear is essential to create the simulated third rocker.[28,32] This option is selected if the following occurs:

- There are poor hip and knee kinematics and kinetics in TST.
- The MTPJs do not have range to extend in gait or there are toe abnormalities requiring MTPJ fixation.

- The actual foot is significantly short and there is a need to create a longer effective foot. This requires MTPJ fixation combined with an optimized stiff rocker sole design.
- Control of forefoot adduction and/or abduction in the transverse plane requires trimlines of the medial and/or lateral walls of the foot to be distal to MTPJs.[28] This creates an "MTPJ-fixed" design.

The method for fixing the MTPJs in an AFO will depend on the severity of gait abnormality and the height and weight of the patient. Trimlines on the medial and lateral walls of the AFO at the foot can be brought distal to the MTPJs, and extra layers of material can be added to the base of the AFO to add extra stiffness. The MTPJs must be fixed at an optimal alignment, which is often 90 degrees to the shank. If the ankle is plantarflexed, this aligns the toes in extension, which is helpful for a pronating foot with poor arch development as it uses the windlass mechanism to encourage arch formation.

Step 6: Tuning Ankle-Foot Orthosis/Footwear Combinations for Stance Phase

Tuning, the process whereby fine adjustments are made to the design of the AFOFC in order to optimize its performance, can include adjustments to both design and alignments of the AFOFC.[20,27,28] The essence of tuning is that it is performed by the use of practice trials of activities.

When tuning full GCs, the process is divided into a sequence of 3 stages (see Figures 21-7 and 21-9).[4,6,7,27,28,44,55] Initially, temporal midstance is tuned by ascertaining the optimal SVA alignment of the AFOFC. This is followed by tuning the exit from temporal midstance by optimizing the design of the AFO at the MTPJs and sole of the footwear, and then by tuning the entrance to temporal midstance by optimizing the design of the heels. Adjusting the AFOFC design during the tuning process manipulates foot and shank kinematics and, consequently, more proximal segment and joint kinematics and kinetics. If tuning of temporal midstance cannot be achieved by simple adjustment of the SVA, then tuning the design of the footwear sole and heel is required. Entrance and exit then need to be reviewed.[4,6,7,27,28,44,55]

The algorithm can be used to tune AFOFC designs for standing, swaying, or stepping if the patient is not able to walk with full GCs or is using these activities in the rehabilitation process.[27,28] These activities may require slightly different prescriptions. Standing and swaying involves "temporal midstance tuning." For stepping, temporal midstance tuning and entrance and exit tuning are performed for an abbreviated GC, in which the stance phase will terminate at the equivalent of 40% GC and the swing phase will terminate at the equivalent of 90% GC.[27,28]

Step 6A: Tuning the Shank to Vertical Angle of the Ankle-Foot Orthosis/Footwear Combinations for Temporal Midstance

The kinematic and kinetic conditions that tuning is trying to create at temporal midstance were described previously in this chapter and also in Chapter 19. Adjusting the SVA of the AFOFC not only affects the quality of gait, but it can

TABLE 21-3

GUIDELINES FOR SELECTING THE OPTIMAL SHANK TO VERTICAL ANGLE FOR AN ANKLE-FOOT ORTHOSIS/FOOTWEAR COMBINATION			
INSUFFICIENT INCLINE	**GUIDELINE FOR OPTIMAL SVA OF THE AFOFC**		**EXCESSIVE INCLINE**
Group 1A	10 to 12 degrees inclined	10 to 12 degrees inclined	Group 2A or 2B and no excessive MTU or joint stiffness at hip or knee
Group 1B	12 to 15 degrees inclined	13 to 19 degrees inclined	Group 2A or 2B and excessive MTU or joint stiffness at hip or knee
Prerequisites for Successful SVA Optimization: Optimal AFO design Optimal AA-AFO Optimal leg and foot segment lengths Optimal heel and toe lever lengths			
To be effective, high SVAs for Group 2 require optimal toe lever lengths. It may be possible to use SVAs greater than 19 degrees incline, but only if the toe lever length is increased appropriately			

Abbreviations: AA-AFO, angle of the ankle in ankle-foot orthosis; AFO, ankle-foot orthosis; AFOFC, ankle-foot orthosis/ footwear combination; MTU, musculotendinous unit; SVA, shank to vertical angle of AFOFC.

also significantly change the child's standing balance ability and even make independent standing balance possible.[27,28] Tuning the SVA influences not only temporal midstance, but also the entrance and exit. When tuning temporal midstance, the SVA alignment of the AFOFC is adjusted until optimal kinematics and kinetics are produced in the required activity.[7,27,28,44] This process is called *dynamic alignment* (ISO 8549-1 1989).[9] Measuring the SVA of the AFOFC is performed in standing, and aligning the SVA in standing is called *static alignment* (ISO 8549-1 1989).[9]

The prerequisites for successful tuning of SVA alignments are optimal AA-AFO, optimal AFO design, and optimal segment proportions.[6,27,28,44] If these are optimal and temporal midstance tuning is not achieved with simple adjustment of the SVA, then 2 design options need to be reviewed: 1) the decision whether to leave free or fix the MTPJs; and 2) the design of the footwear sole or heel, and in particular, the sole design and the toe lever length.[44]

MEASURING THE SVA OF AN AFOFC

The SVA can be measured in a number of ways, from simple goniometers to complex inclinometers, directly or from a picture image. In our gait laboratory, we use the anterior border of the shank as the definition of the *line of the shank segment*. We have found this to be a simple and repeatable measure, especially as malleoli are often obscured by the AFOs and footwear. Also, children with disabilities can have abnormal tibial torsions, which may skew the measurement if using the usual method of defining the line of the shank segment as the knee joint center to ankle joint center.

The important rules for measurement of SVA alignment of the AFOFC are as follows:

- The foot is aligned in the sagittal plane, even if the patient does not normally stand with this posture.
- It is measured in standing with weight equally distributed between the heel and the sole.[4,27,28]

In a video vector gait laboratory, equal distribution of weight between heel and sole will be easily identified by the position of the point of application (POA) of the GRF. If measuring while the patient stands on a stool, check for equal weight distribution, both visually and manually.

ADJUSTING THE SVA OF AN AFOFC

If the SVA is insufficiently inclined, it is increased by increasing the HSD of the footwear by adding non-compressible wedges at the heel, on the inside or outside of the footwear, or both. If the SVA is excessively inclined, it is decreased by reducing the HSD, by decreasing the heel depth or increasing the sole depth (see Figures 21-3, 21-4, and 21-9).[4,6,27,28]

GUIDELINES FOR SUCCESSFUL AFOFC SVA ALIGNMENTS

There is a small window of optimal SVA alignments that are effective for standing, stepping, and gait. Within this window, each patient is sensitive to changes of alignment, especially if a neurological condition is present and the normal variety of compensations is not available.[4,7,13,27,28,55] Clinical experience indicates that there are different ranges of optimal SVA alignments for each of the gait categories. The optimal SVA for each patient seems to be dependent on 2 main factors: the primary neurology and the stiffness of the muscles and joints at the hip and knee in the sagittal plane. The guidelines shown in Table 21-3 were derived from an original study and clinical experience over 15 years of tuning AFOFCs in a video vector gait laboratory.[4,7] The study

	TABLE 21-4		

PUBLICATIONS DETAILING A RECOMMENDED OR OPTIMIZED SHANK TO VERTICAL ANGLE FOR FIXED ANKLE ANKLE-FOOT ORTHOSIS/FOOTWEAR COMBINATIONS

YEAR	AUTHOR(S)	SVA OF THE AFOFC	COMMENTS
1970	Jebsen et al[71]	10 degrees incline	Theoretical justification
1972	Glancy and Lindseth[72]	3 to 5 degrees incline	Visual gait analysis
1978	Fulford and Cairns[73]	Slight incline	Theoretical justification
1978	Simon et al[57]	10 to 15 degrees incline	SVA deducible from other data given in 1975 by Rosenthal et al[77]
			SVAs optimized on an inclined walkway
			Kinematic and kinetic gait analysis
1983	Nuzzo[64,65]	Knee cap over MTPJs	Theoretical justification from kinematic gait analysis
1984	Meadows[13]	4 to 17 degrees incline	SVAs deducible from other data given
			SVAs are best of selected SVA trials and may not be fully optimized
			Kinematic and kinetic gait analysis
1986	Nuzzo[74]	7 to 10 degrees incline	Theoretical justification and kinematic gait analysis
1990	Cusick[75]	5 degrees incline	Theoretical justification
1992	Hullin et al[76]	0 degrees with a rocker sole or 10 degrees incline without a rocker sole	SVAs deducible
			Two conditions trialed, SVA 0 degrees with rocker sole and SVA 10 degrees incline with no rocker sole
			Kinematic and kinetic gait analysis
2002	Owen[7]	7 to 15 degrees incline	SVAs tuned to optimal
		Mean 11.4 degrees incline	Kinematic and kinetic gait analysis
2009	Jagadamma et al[14]	10.8 degrees incline (SD 1.8)	SVAs are best of selected SVA trials and may not be fully optimized
			Kinematic and kinetic gait analysis
2010	Jagadamma et al[15]	14 degrees incline	SVA and sole design tuned to optimal
			Kinematic and kinetic gait analysis
			Single case study, adult with CVA[a]

Abbreviations: AFOFCs, ankle-foot orthosis/footwear combinations; CVA, cerebrovascular accident; MTPJs, metatarsophalangeal joints; SD, standard deviation; SVA, shank to vertical angle of AFOFC.

[a] Children were the participants in all but this study.

Adapted from Owen E. *Shank Angle to Floor Measures and Tuning of Ankle-Foot Orthosis Footwear Combinations for Children with Cerebral Palsy, Spina Bifida and Other Conditions* [MSc Thesis]. Glasgow: University of Strathclyde; 2004.

included a group of children with a variety of disabilities who walked independently without walking aids and functioned at the equivalent of GMFCS levels I and II for children with CP,[4,7] but the guidelines apply to all children who walk, including those who use assistive devices and function in GMFCS level III. The same SVA alignments will also usually apply for adults. Results of other studies concur with these guidelines (Table 21-4).[7,13-15,57,64,65,71-77]

In the study by Owen[4,6,7] that led to the development of the AFOFC SVA guidelines, children in Group 2A and 2B with no stiffness at the hips and knees had AFOFC SVA tuned to 7 to 12 degrees incline. However, experience following this data collection would suggest a range of 10 to 12 degrees incline as preferable for this group, with an occasional use of 9 degrees incline.[27,28] The change in practice is because we have improved the design of footwear for exit from temporal

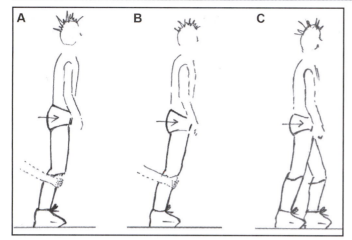

Figure 21-11. The relationship between the stiffness of knee and hip joints and the required SVA. (A-B) Aligning the SVA in standing. (C) Stepping with optimized SVA.

midstance. Children in Group 2A and 2B with significant stiffness at hips or knees from increased tone or joint contractures require AFOFC SVAs of 13 to 19 degrees inclined. The greater the stiffness, the greater SVA incline is required. The use of high SVAs for children with stiffness seems counterintuitive, but the increased incline of the SVA alignment facilitates the ability of the thigh to become vertical and inclined. This, in turn, facilitates the creation of knee and hip extending moments and knee and hip extension. Children who require SVA alignments above 15 degrees incline usually walk with assistive devices. These high SVA alignments require optimization of footwear designs, especially that of the toe levers, to be effective.[6,27,28,33] These groups of patients are often slow walkers or they may tire quickly. In these circumstances, it is often possible to judge which SVA may be optimal by standing trials, using the process of optimal aligning for standing, prior to attempting the walking trials. This is performed by determining in standing which SVA allows the thigh to become aligned vertical and inclined. The GRF can only create neutral knee and hip moments when the thigh is vertical and extending knee and hip moments when the thigh is inclined. The stiffer the patient's knee and hip joints, the greater the incline required (Figure 21-11).[27,28]

HISTORICAL PERSPECTIVE AND CURRENT EVIDENCE

Until recently, it has not been common practice to align the SVA of AFOFCs in the clinic or research trials.[4,12,20,25] If they were aligned, a "traditional" SVA was commonly used, which was a vertical or a few degrees inclined alignment, with 7 degrees often being considered the maximum incline that should be used.[8] However, once analyzed in gait laboratories, these values were found not to be optimal.[4,5,8,12,25] There is now an increasing understanding that the optimal SVA needs to be determined for each leg of each patient by means of tuning.[4,5,8,12,25]

There is limited research that provides guidelines for optimal AFOFC SVA alignments for children and adults (see Table 21-4).[7,13-15,57,64,65,71-77] Early guidelines were justified by a theoretical perspective or observational gait analysis

rather than from actual kinematic and kinetic tuning, and usually, just one AFOFC SVA alignment was suggested for all patients.[4] Only recently, evidence for optimal AFOFC SVA alignments emerged from gait laboratories.[4,6-8,15]

A review performed in 2004 revealed that only 9 of 312 papers stated the SVAs used or recommended an SVA alignment for AFOFCs.[4,13,57,64,65,71-76] It is interesting to note the dates of these 9 papers and to wonder why optimally aligning the SVA of AFOFCs became lost in clinical practice after the 1980s (see Table 21-4).[7,13-15,57,64,65,71-77] It may have been because of the move from leather and metal AFOs, which were attached to footwear, to plastic AFOs. Most of the 9 authors did not optimize the SVA by tuning in a gait laboratory as these were not readily available at the time.[4,13,27,57,64,65,71-77] The recommended and used SVA alignments came from clinical experience, theoretical kinematic justifications, novel approaches, or trials to measure the effects of varying the SVA.[4,13,27,57,64,65,71-77]

Jebsen et al,[71] writing the first paper on a polypropylene AFOFC, recommended an SVA of 10 degrees incline. Simon et al[57] used an inclined walkway to determine the optimal SVAs, which turned out to be 10 to 15 degrees inclined for a group of children with genu recurvatum. These authors then documented the positive short- and long-term effects by using a kinematic and kinetic gait lab.[57]

Other authors did use gait laboratories. Meadows[13] and Hullin et al[76] used kinematic and kinetic gait laboratories and, in their studies, they investigated the effects of a variety of SVAs on gait parameters, but not necessarily to full optimization. The most optimal SVA equivalents trialed by Meadows[13] were 4 to 17 degrees inclined. Hullin et al[76] recommended 10 degrees inclined SVA or 90 degrees combined with a rocker sole, after trialing these 2 prescriptions on a group of children with myelomeningocele. Nuzzo[74] recommended 7 to 10 degrees inclined SVA, based on a sound theoretical perspective. There was evidence of one case with the SVA being tuned kinematically. The findings of most of these 9 papers do concur with Owen.[4]

Owen[4,6,7] presented the first study to establish optimal SVA alignments using kinematic and kinetic gait analysis in a video vector gait laboratory, for a population of children with disabilities described previously. In that study, the AA-AFO was optimized using a clinical algorithm.[44] Full GCs were tuned, so the designs and alignments were optimized for entrance and exit, as well as for temporal midstance. One hundred and twelve AFOFCs were tuned, and the range of tuned SVAs for 112 legs of 74 children was 7 to 15 degrees inclined, mean 11.4 degrees inclined.[4,6,7]

Since the study by Owen,[4,6,7] there have been other studies published that used gait laboratories to optimize the SVA by tuning AFOFCs, but this has sometimes been done in isolation, without tuning the prescription for a full GC, so there may be a need to repeat these studies. However, the resultant tuned SVA alignments do concur with Owen (see Table 21-4).[4]

Jagadamma et al[14] (see Table 21-4) studied children with CP and a genu recurvatum gait who presented similar to children in Group 1 (see Table 21-3). These authors found that the untuned SVAs had a mean of 5.6 degrees inclined (SD 3), and the tuned SVAs, a mean of 10.8 degrees inclined (SD 1.8). In a later case study of a patient with stroke and genu recurvatum, Jagadamma et al[15] found the untuned SVA to be 0 degrees and the optimally tuned SVA to be 14 degrees inclined. In addition, for this patient, there was a need for a stiff rocker sole to tune the whole GC. McGovern and Boggs (September 23, 2010, oral and written personal communication) conducted an unpublished case series study of 18 patients with CP who had their AFOFCs tuned and found that the optimal SVAs ranged from 8 to 15 degrees inclined (Mean 11.7 degrees inclined). Pratt et al[78] undertook a study to investigate normative shank kinematics for 11 typically developing children aged 5 to 16 years. The authors demonstrated that at 30% GC, temporal midstance, the mean SVA for the group was 11.4 degrees inclined.[78] They concluded that these data supported the results reported by Owen.[7] More evidence for optimal SVA alignments for patients with a variety of gait disorders should now emerge as it has been recommended that all research investigating AFOFCs should always include the SVA alignment.[4,6,8,12,25]

Step 6B: Tuning Exit From Temporal Midstance

The kinematic and kinetic conditions that tuning is attempting to create in the exit from temporal midstance were described previously in this chapter and also in Chapter 19. A full exit from temporal midstance includes both single and double support exit. Single support exit occurs during TST, from 30% to 50% GC. At 50% GC, initial contact with the contralateral limb is made and the Big V is present. Double support exit or preswing occurs from 50% to 60% GC, ending with toe off. Some patients may not be able to achieve the full Big V, but the aim is to normalize this part of the GC as much as possible to gain the appropriate hip and knee joint extension and extending moments, as well as the consequent stabilities these bring to gait. Maximum knee extension and knee extending moment should occur at 40% GC, and maximum hip extension and hip extending moment, at 50% GC. Optimizing preswing also facilitates the swing phase.

Kinematics and kinetics are optimized by the choice of the AFOFC design. In normal barefoot gait, the quasi-stiffness of the ankle joint during TST is essential to achieve heel rise and knee and hip extension.[79,80] The fixed ankle in the AFOFC mimics the stiff ankle, and the timing and rate of heel rise will depend on the design of the AFOFC at the MTPJs and the sole of the footwear. These designs manipulate foot and shank kinematics and the position of the POA of the GRF, which consequently manipulates more proximal segment and joint kinematics and kinetics. The principal designs that are being manipulated are the length of the toe lever, the flexibility and stiffness of the AFO and footwear at the MTPJs, and the design profile of the footwear sole.[4,6,27,28,33]

THE LENGTH OF THE TOE LEVER AND THE TIMING OF HEEL RISE

Essential to optimizing exit is to have the optimal length of toe lever and effective foot.[4,6,27,28,33] Sole designs influence the length of the toe lever (see Figures 21-2, 21-4, and

21-5). This, in turn influences the timing of heel rise as well as the position of the GRF POA at the foot and its relation to knee and hip joints during exits. As discussed earlier in this chapter if, in any way, the actual foot is not able to provide the optimal toe lever, then a false longer foot needs to be created by the use of a stiff rocker sole. Sometimes, it is helpful to have a longer-than-normal foot length and toe lever for patients with stiffness at the knees and hips.[4,6,27,28,33]

The timing of heel rise dictates shank kinematics.[4,6,7,27,28,33] If heel rise occurs too late, the shank will become insufficiently inclined, with consequent knee hyperextension and excessive anterior pelvic tilt, and hip flexion may occur. If it occurs too early, the shank may become excessively inclined and knee and hip extension may be lost. Patients who find it difficult to achieve the hip and knee extension and extending moments in exits may benefit from a slightly later heel rise to provide more time for the thigh to become inclined and extending moments to be established. It is the amount of stiffness or flexibility of the footwear sole and the design of the sole profile that influence the timing of heel rise.[4,6,27,28,33]

FLEXIBLE OR STIFF AT MTPJS

Some patients will be able to achieve optimal heel rise and gait using their own MTPJ extension or anatomical third rocker, so they will need both an AFO and footwear that are flexible at the sole. Some will need a stiff rocker sole with optimized rocker position to achieve the optimal toe lever length and timing of heel rise. Some will need a stiff RR, some a stiff PLR, and all stiff rockers will need their position optimized.[6,27,28,32,33,44] The criteria that need to apply in selection of a flexible or a stiff design are listed under Step 5 of this algorithm.[44]

Stiff rocker soles may be used with AFOs that have flexibility at the MTPJ when the following conditions apply:

- Fixed MTPJs are required to gain control of gait kinematics and kinetics, but it is possible to fix the MTPJs with just a stiff sole on the footwear, which is usually only the case when the patient is a young child.
- No forefoot adductus or abductus is present that would require control by the distal trim of the medial or lateral wall of the AFO at MTPJs.[27,28]

If stiff rocker soles are to be effective, their position, design, and toe spring angle need to be optimized.[6,27,28,33,44,55]

OPTIMIZING THE POSITION OF THE ROCKER AND THE TOE LEVER LENGTH

Whether a rocker sole has a rounded design or a point loading design, the position of the rocker on the footwear will determine its effective toe lever (see Figures 21-4 and 21-5). The heel of the footwear cannot rise until the GRF POA reaches the rocker. The shorter the toe lever, the sooner in the GC the heel will rise. The longer the toe lever, the later the heel will rise in the GC. Extreme examples of this are "clown boots" or skis, where the very long toe lever prevents any heel rise.[73] The MTPJs on a normal foot are at 72% the length of the foot.[34] Some of the recommendations in the guidelines next, therefore, place the rocker in a position that creates a longer toe lever than that of a normal foot (Table 21-5).

TABLE 21-5

GENERAL GUIDELINES FOR SELECTING THE STIFF ROCKER POSITION IN PATIENTS WITH ABNORMAL SHANK KINEMATICS

INSUFFICIENT INCLINE		PROBABLE OPTIMAL RANGE FOR POSITION OF STIFF ROCKER		EXCESSIVE INCLINE
Group 1A	70% to 75%	75% to 95%		Group 2A
Group 1B	70% to 75%	85% to 95%		Group 2B
Prerequisites for Successful Optimization:				
Optimal AFO design				
Optimal AA-AFO				
Optimal leg and foot segment lengths				
Footwear with stiff soles				
Not all Group 1 and 2 patients will need stiff rocker soles (see text and algorithm).				
Other factors that determine rocker position, especially in Group 2, are step length, balance, and vision.				

Abbreviations: AA-AFO, angle of the ankle in ankle-foot orthosis; AFO, ankle-foot orthosis.

Before the rocker positions can be optimized, the patient must be provided with the optimum size of effective foot length by providing an AFOFC that has an optimal foot length for height (see Chapter 19, Table 19-1). If they have a small foot for height, the design of the AFOFC needs to create a longer effective foot. This is done by using a longer soleplate on the AFO and trimlines distal to MTPJs on the medial and lateral walls at the foot, and combining this with an optimized stiff rocker sole.

As shown in Table 21-5, for patients with insufficiently inclined shanks in TST and who need a stiff rocker, a position of 70% to 75% is usually sufficient to normalize shank kinematics and prevent knee hyperextension and excessive knee extending moments. If a rocker sole of less than 70% is used to control gait, it may make standing unstable, especially in children with disability. In this case, a compromise may be needed.

For patients with excessively inclined shanks in stepping and full GCs who need a stiff rocker, a position of 75% to 95% is usually sufficient to normalize shank kinematics. For standing only, a 100% or even 110% rocker can be used. When stepping, a 100% rocker could be used if only very short steps are required. If full or near full step lengths are required, then the heel has to be allowed to rise at the optimal percent of the GC. The position of the rocker can be optimized by walking trials.

The following further guidelines for rocker positions are suggested:

- If the patient has no or little stiffness at the knees and hips, a rocker within the range of 75% to 95% is usually optimum, the exact position depending on step

length. Short step lengths can be managed with a 95% rocker, but longer step lengths require the rocker to be at 75% to 85%

- If the patient has stiffness at the knees and hips, from joint stiffness or increased tone, a rocker at 85% to 95% is needed, the position depending on the degree of stiffness and the step length. Patients with very stiff hip and knee joints with short step lengths require a 90% to 95% rocker; patients with stiffness but normal or near normal step lengths require an 85% to 90% rocker.

OPTIMIZING ROCKER PROFILES—ROUNDED OR POINT LOADING

There are 2 stiff rocker sole profile designs, rounded and point loading (see Figures 21-4, 21-5, and 21-12A and B, respectively).[4,27,28,33,44,55,76] The following mechanisms will make any rocker profile effective. The first is the use of stiff materials. If the rocker is not stiff enough, its desired position cannot be maintained during gait. The second is the optimal position of the rocker described in the actual length along the footwear and as a percentage of the length of the footwear, as discussed previously. The third is a combined heel and sole unit, a wedge heel design, with a flat sole profile to the position required for the rocker, which improves the overall stiffness of the footwear sole.

PLR profiles have additional biomechanical controls compared to RR profiles.[27,28] Firstly, once heel rise occurs, the COP of the GRF is harnessed at the PLR and remains there until the most anterior aspect of the footwear makes contact with the floor, unlike an RR design when the GRF moves forward along the rocker (see Figure 21-12). The harnessing

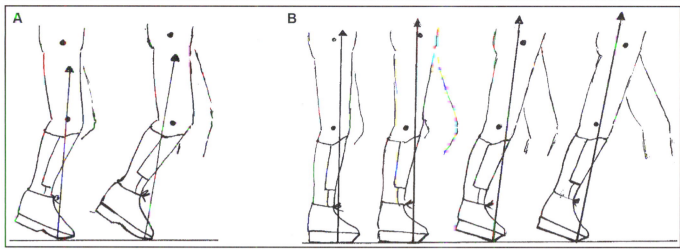

Figure 21-12. Effect of point loading rockers on kinematics and kinetics. (A) Rounded rocker sole profile. (B) Point loading rocker sole profile. (Reprinted from *Gait and Posture*, 20S, Owen E, The point of 'point-loading rockers' in ankle-foot orthosis footwear combinations used with children with cerebral palsy, spina bifida and other conditions, 586. Copyright © (2004) with permission from Elsevier.)

of the GRF at the floor facilitates the GRF alignment posterior to the hip and improved hip extending moments.[27,28,33] PLRs, therefore, add an additional biomechanical control when the gait abnormality in TST cannot be corrected with an optimized RR (see Figure 21-12).[33] Secondly, PLRs maintain their optimized position better than RRs, so gait control is maintained. PLRs are, therefore, used when RRs are not effective, when RRs will wear easily and become ineffective in a short time span, or when more control of standing, stepping, and gait is required. This is usually when there is poor knee and hip extension combined with poor knee and hip extending moments. PLRs provide exact control of standing, stepping, and gait, which creates the conditions for the "perfect practice" that is needed for motor learning. They are, therefore, useful in these situations at all ages, including the young children who are just starting to stand, step, and walk.

OPTIMIZING THE TOE SPRING ANGLE

For full GC step lengths, a toe spring angle (TSA) of 30 degrees is required. Less than a full GC step length requires a smaller TSA. The sole needs to be deep enough to ensure sufficient TSA. In a small study, the mean TSA was 33 degrees, range 18 to 50 degrees.[33] Rocker soles with TSA in excess of 30 degrees occurred by virtue of the position of the rocker on a deep sole.

ANGLED ROCKER SOLES ON FOOTWEAR FOR ROTATED FOOT PROGRESSION ANGLES

Rocker soles may need to be angled if the foot progression angle is significantly internally or externally rotated. This is essential when PLRs are used. RR soles may not always need to be angled. Angling the rocker on the footwear brings the line of the rocker 90 degrees to the line of progression and creates "effective MTPJs."[27,28]

Step 6C: Tuning Entrance to Temporal Midstance

The kinematic and kinetic conditions that tuning is trying to create in the entrance to temporal midstance were described previously in this chapter and also in Chapter 19.

When using a fixed ankle AFOFC, the kinematics of the foot and shank during first and second rockers of barefoot gait are combined. Patients will either be able to achieve a full or partial entrance into temporal midstance, depending on their ability to achieve a full or partial TSW. The degree of toe up at initial contact will depend on the SVA and on whether a full or partial TSW has been achieved (see Figures 21-7 and 21-13). As shown in Box 21-4, in some prescriptions, the actual foot may not be "toe up," but the effective foot will be, and it is the effective foot that provides the heel lever. For full GCs, initial contact with a heel is desirable as it initiates a heel lever, which facilitates movement of the foot to the floor and tibial progression. In order to make initial contact with the heel, it is essential to have 2 optimal alignments in the AFOFC, the AA-AFO, and the SVA of the AFOFC. The kinematics and kinetics are optimized by the choice of the footwear heel design, which manipulates foot and shank kinematics and consequently, more proximal segment and joint kinematics and kinetics.[4,27,28,44]

The principal designs that are being manipulated are the length of the heel lever, the flexibility or stiffness of the heel, and the design profile of the heel.[4,6,27,28,44] These design variables manipulate the length of the heel lever and, consequently, the position of the GRF POA and the moment arms created at the ankle, knee, and hip. These, in turn, influence the angular velocity of the foot and shank segments during entrance.[6,28,44,55,67-69,74] Patients may require negative, cushion, plain, or positive heels to normalize foot and shank kinematics (see Figures 21-4 and 21-13).[4,6,27,28,44,55] These increase or reduce the heel lever and, consequently, the angular velocity of the foot and shank segments.

Evidence for Motor Learning

Normalizing gait kinematics and kinetics by optimally designing, aligning and tuning the AFOFC may have a number of positive effects in all domains of the ICF[1,2] (see Table 21-1). In relation to neurological conditions, it is thought that there may be an important effect on motor

Figure 21-13. Biomechanical effect of negative, plain, and positive heels.

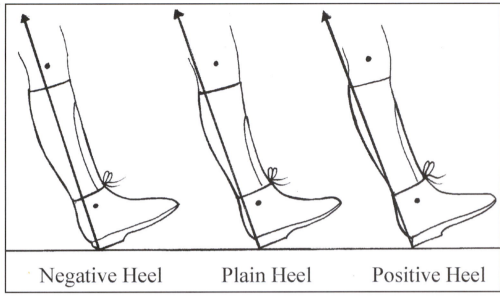

Negative Heel   Plain Heel   Positive Heel

learning when using tuned fixed ankle AFOFCs. In a previously mentioned study conducted in 1978, Simon et al[57] investigated the effects of fixed ankle AFOFCs on a group of 15 children with CP and genu recurvatum gait. Although not stated, the AFOFCs did have their SVAs tuned as the researchers determined the optimal alignment required to control the knee hyperextension for each child while using an inclined walkway (see Table 21-4). They found that, after 18 months of use, 3 of 15 children could stop wearing their AFOs as they had gained control of their knee kinematics. The authors did not postulate a reason for this outcome,[57] but the possibilities might have included lengthening of the calf muscle, reduced calf muscle stiffness, or strengthening of quadriceps muscles. Another explanation may be that the AFOFCs corrected the kinematics and kinetics of gait so accurately that there was a motor learning effect, or there might have been a combined effect of all these possibilities.

Another group also used fixed ankle AFOFCs with children with CP and an adult with a long-standing head injury.[80-82] The AFOFCs were kinematically and kinetically tuned in a video vector gait laboratory, at least for MST, by adjusting the AFOFC SVA, although no actual SVA measurements were taken. They, too, found improvements such that the patients could stop wearing AFOFCs or only use them intermittently and still maintain the quality of gait.[80-82] These authors did postulate a motor learning effect.[81-83]

It is likely that the outcomes described in these studies occurred due to a combination of motor learning, musculotendinous unit (MTU) lengthening, strengthening, and reductions in MTU stiffness. Whatever the mechanism, these results are enticing and more research is needed to conclude which or all of the possible effects determined the positive outcome. Certainly, walking in biomechanically optimized AFOFCs can produce the conditions required for the intensive "perfect practice" needed for motor learning to occur, for appropriate lengthening and shortening of MTUs during the activity, which may help maintain length and reduce stiffness

of MTUs, and also for strengthening, when MTUs are working against external moments. There is also other existing evidence for skill acquisition or motor learning in children with CP for interventions that introduce repetitive practice of the motor ability in the context of a functional activity.[12,84,85] Also, there is evidence from the treatment of other conditions that practice may increase skill acquisition, such as for treadmill training in children with Down syndrome.[86] These studies support the likelihood that effective amounts of practice with tuned AFOFCs may improve motor learning.

Algorithm B: Determining the Optimal Angle of the Ankle in Ankle-Foot Orthosis in Fixed Ankle Ankle-Foot Orthosis/Footwear Combinations

The sagittal angle of the ankle of the AFO describes the alignment of the foot segment relative to the shank segment within the AFO.[4,6,27,28] The optimal AA-AFO should be determined for each leg of each patient. We need to be conversant with the factors that might help us best determine this angle, which are the length and stiffness of MTUs and the desired triplanar skeletal alignment of the foot. The algorithm for determining the optimal AA-AFO (see Figure 21-10) gives consideration to all of these factors and any risks associated with the chosen alignments.[6,27,28,61]

Step 1: Assess Calf and Dorsiflexor Musculotendinous Unit Length

When assessing the calf MTU length for the AFOFCs that are only to be used with flexed knees, an assessment of soleus muscle length alone is sufficient. When AFOFCs are to be used in circumstances when the knee is in extension (eg, during standing or walking) the length of the gastrocnemius muscle should be taken into account.[6,12,27,28,61] Gastrocnemius is a tri-jointed MTU crossing the knee, ankle, and subtalar joints. Setting the AA-AFO without regard for the available gastrocnemius length will result in an insufficient length of this muscle being available to allow knee extension, or pronation or supination of the foot will occur to release the gastrocnemius length, or both of these scenarios will occur.[27,61] Neither one is desirable. They will compromise gait, prevent the optimal development of skeletal alignment of the foot, and prevent the MTU from being used at its optimal length. Some children with myelomeningocele and other rare disorders may have short dorsiflexor MTU length causing fixed dorsiflexion angles at the ankles. If this is the case, it is taken into account when determining the AA-AFO (see Figure 21-10).[6,27,28,61]

Step 2: Assess Calf and Dorsiflexor Musculotendinous Unit Stiffness

The overall calf MTU stiffness, which usually includes some hypertonia, will also determine if knees extend or if skeletal alignment of the foot is compromised when using AFOFCs.[6,27,28,61,87,88] Sanger[88] defines *hypertonia* as "abnormally increased resistance to externally imposed movement about a joint,"[(p e91)] excluding joint stiffness. The stiffness that is being felt can be a combination of stiffness caused by neurological deficits and stiffness within the MTU tissues themselves.[87-89] On clinical examination, the MTU length may be available, but the stiffness may be such that the AA-AFO has to be adjusted to obtain knee extension and maintain the skeletal alignment of the foot when walking. If the dorsiflexor MTU tone is high, this needs to be considered.[6,27,28,44]

Step 3: Assess Skeletal Alignment of the Foot

It is essential that children's feet develop to acquire optimal triplanar skeletal alignment. All feet, and children's feet in particular, will "escape" to triplanar pronation or supination in order to achieve greater degrees of dorsiflexion if there is an insufficient MTU length or excessive calf MTU stiffness.[11,90] Therefore, assessing the length and stiffness of calf MTUs in steps 1 and 2 is essential if the AA-AFO is to be set optimally for maintaining an optimal skeletal alignment of the foot. If the calf MTU is short or stiff, a neutral alignment of triplanar pronation or supination may only be achieved when the foot is optimally plantarflexed. Even when both of these MTU considerations are taken into account, some feet require additional plantarflexion to obtain the optimal triplanar alignment of the foot. Extending the toes, if appropriate, utilizes the "windlass mechanism" of the plantar aponeurosis to raise the arch.[91]

Step 4: Assess Risk to Musculotendinous Unit Shortening

Throughout the algorithm (see Figure 21-10) there are opportunities for non-AFOFC interventions, if desired.[61] An optimally designed and aligned AFOFC may be selected to increase the MTU length, reduce the MTU stiffness, and develop the optimal skeletal alignment of the foot.

To be able to determine whether intervention is needed to increase the calf MTU length, the normative data of MTU lengths for age are required. Reimers et al[92] documented the length of the triceps surae MTU measured as the angle of the lateral border of the foot relative to the axis of the lower leg.

This measurement was performed "with the knee extended and the hindfoot in a neutral position and the forefoot sufficiently adducted to bring the talus into a neutral position relative to the calcaneus."[92(p 71)] This angle was measured in 759 typically developing children. The proportion of children with one or both triceps surae muscles that would allow the feet to be brought only to a plantigrade position rose from 24% to 62% between the ages of 3 and 17 years. In 13% of adolescents, one or both ankles could only achieve 5 degrees plantarflexion. The researchers also found an association between a short triceps surae and pes planus in the older group.[92]

If the algorithm for determining the AA-AFO is followed (see Figure 21-10), a plantarflexed AA-AFO is the only recommendation when patients have a short or excessively stiff gastrocnemius muscle or a foot that will only align in neutral pronation/supination while in plantarflexion.[61] Any alternative would prevent the knee from extending or compromise the triplanar skeletal alignment of the foot. Compromising the foot has adverse consequences for the development of its normal skeletal structure, as well as for comfort and skin viability. As a consequence of the pronation or supination, foot progression angles may become excessively rotated, leading to reduced toe levers and adverse kinematics and kinetics at the knee and hip, and calf MTUs will not be optimally stretched.

Despite all of these good reasons to use a plantarflexed AA-AFO when it is deemed essential, until recently, there was a widely held view that aligning the ankle in plantarflexion in an AFO is not acceptable. This dominant view prevailed in the literature[4,12,16] with a notable exception when Nuzzo[63-65,74] expounded the use of plantarflexion where required and extolled its therapeutic effects. An exploration of the possible reasons why plantarflexed alignments of the ankle in the AFO were previously resisted may help understand why this opinion has been held and why it may now be abandoned. Firstly, there was a fear that using plantarflexed AA-AFO would always lead to a MTU shortening. The reality is that if the MTU is short enough to require a plantarflexed AA-AFO, there is no alternative, especially if knee extension is required. Knee extension is not only essential for normal standing and walking, but it also produces one of the main therapeutic effects on the MTU. This is allowing the MTU to stretch to its optimal length as the knee extends and the skeletal alignment of the foot is maintained, which can, in turn, maintain or increase the calf MTU length.[89] Additional strategies may be used to complement the AFOFCs with plantarflexed AA-AFO if the AFOFC intervention is not sufficiently successful in itself or if soleus length needs to be maintained.[6,27,28,44]

Secondly, previously, the AA-AFO and SVA were not well-differentiated and this, coupled with a belief that a vertical alignment of the SVA of the AFOFC is required for both standing and gait, led to a belief that a 90-degree AA-AFO was the only way to achieve a vertical SVA alignment.[6] It was not understood well enough that any SVA alignment could be achieved with any AA-AFO, and that inclined alignments of

Figure 21-14. Algorithm C: determining whether a dorsiflexion-free ankle-foot orthosis/footwear combinations may be appropriate.

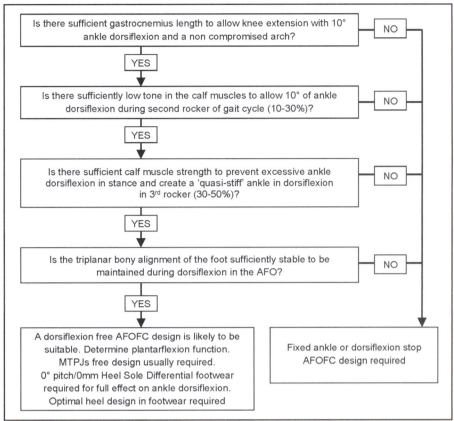

SVAs would offer the best chance of achieving optimal standing balance, kinematics, and kinetics in standing, stepping, and gait, especially with the knee and hip extension being an intervention goal.[4,6,27,28]

Leg lengths should be equalized in orthotic prescriptions, and using different AA-AFOs for each limb can often be a mechanism to achieve this effect fully or partially.[27,28] This is because the shorter leg is often more neurologically affected, so in this limb, the MTUs may be shorter or stiffer, or the skeletal alignment considerations may require a different AA-AFO compared to the less affected limb.

Algorithm C: Determining Whether a Dorsiflexion-Free Ankle-Foot Orthosis/Footwear Combinations May Be Appropriate

Some patients may meet the criteria to use a hinged, flexible, or posterior leaf spring AFO (see Chapter 20) rather than a fixed ankle design. These AFO designs are often "dorsiflexion free" and can be combined with a plantarfexion-free, resist or stop design. A common prescription is dorsiflexion-free, plantarflexion stop at 90 degrees. Algorithm C relates to an AFO design that allows free movement to dorsiflexion, defined as movement beyond neutral into dorsiflexion range (Figure 21-14).

In recent decades, the clinical community debated whether a fixed ankle AFO or a dorsiflexion-free design was "best," with strong opinions held in relation to children with CP.[12,17,93] There were a number of investigations of this question, but the research had numerous problems, particularly when related to gait.[12,17,26-28] First, research was often conducted to determine whether a fixed ankle or a hinged/dorsiflexion-free AFO design was optimal for diagnostic groups or categories. However, it is not possible to make global judgements. Children with CP have very heterogeneous presentations. In practice, a decision has to be made for each leg. Second, dorsiflexion-free AFOs were investigated with study subjects who had contraindications to their use. Third, the AFOFCs with dorsiflexion-free functions were coupled with fixed MTPJs, which might adversely affect ankle joint kinematics. Fourth, some of the literature contained statements that movement at the ankle joint is essential for gait and that ankle joints should not be fixed. This is incorrect. Segment kinematics dictate whether gait and activities can be normalized, not joint kinematics. Finally, some studies looked only at patient satisfaction, which is important but has to be balanced with the need to achieve other short- and long-term outcomes for children.[12,17,26-28]

The decision whether to fix an ankle joint, to prevent it moving from its set alignment, or to allow some or full movements to dorsiflexion and plantarflexion is multifaceted.[26,94] Algorithm A (see Figure 21-9) has a very simplistic approach, stating that a fixed ankle AFO design is recommended if shank kinematics in stance phase is abnormal.[44] This pathway came from years of clinical experience of biomechanically optimizing AFOFC designs in a gait laboratory. An extended algorithm, Algorithm C, is more helpful as it determines whether the patient has any contraindications to the use of a dorsiflexion-free AFOFC design in gait.[26-28]

Similar to the decision about the optimal AA-AFO alignment in a fixed ankle AFO, the decision is based on the calf MTU length, calf MTU stiffness, and triplanar skeletal alignment of the foot, with an additional consideration of the calf MTU strength. A simple algorithm can be created when these factors are related to a few key requirements of normal barefoot gait. These are summarized in Box 21-6.

Algorithm C Step by Step

Algorithm C determines whether there are any contraindications to the use of a dorsiflexion-free AFOFC required for walking.[27,28,44] If the answer to any of the questions is "no," a fixed ankle AFOFC is recommended.

Step 1: Assess Calf Musculotendinous Unit Length

This step asks if there is sufficient length of the soleus and gastrocnemius MTU to allow 10 degrees dorsiflexion at the ankle with the foot held in a neutral alignment of pronation/supination with an extended knee. This is the length of gastrocnemius muscle required for 40% GC. If the gastrocnemius length is insufficient, compensations will occur when walking. Either the ankle joint will not dorsiflex, negating the need for a dorsiflexion-free function in the AFO, or the dorsiflexion will not occur from sagittal ankle joint motion. It will occur from pronation or supination, or the ankle joint will dorsiflex, but the knee will not extend. Usually, deviations at both foot and knee occur.

Step 2: Assess Calf Musculotendinous Unit Stiffness

Having assessed that sufficient calf MTU length is available for the kinematics required at 40% GC, this step asks if there is sufficiently low tone in soleus and gastrocnemius MTU for those kinematics to occur. If the tone is such that it will prevent the dorsiflexion movement, the dorsiflexion-free function in the AFO design becomes superfluous in gait.

Step 3: Assess Calf Musculotendinous Unit Strength

This step asks if there is sufficient strength in the plantarflexor muscles to prevent excessive dorsiflexion at the ankle during second and third rockers. In second rocker,

the plantarflexors work eccentrically to control the rate and degree of dorsiflexion, and in third rocker, they hold the ankle in "quasi-stiff" dorsiflexion. The external dorsiflexing moments they are controlling are considerable, and if the plantarflexors have insufficient strength, the ankle will dorsiflex excessively and control of the knee and hip extension is lost.[70]

Step 4: Assess Skeletal Alignment of the Foot

The final step asks if it is possible to maintain the integrity of the arch appropriate for age with a dorsiflexion-free AFO design. This would mean that the foot, while the ankle is dorsiflexing in stance phase, would not excessively pronate or supinate within the AFO, as the triplanar controls in the AFO design are adequate to prevent this from happening.[90,95] Algorithm C summarizes the contraindications for dorsiflexion-free AFOFC designs (Box 21-7) and the advantages of fixed ankle AFOFCs (Box 21-8).

Dorsiflexion-free AFOs are often prescribed because it is felt that they are preferable to fixed ankle AFOFCs for functions other than gait, such as stair climbing or squatting to play or to pick things up from the floor. Traditionally, it has been felt that fixed ankle AFOFCs prevent these functions, but this may be because the SVA of fixed ankle AFOFCs has often

---

Box 21-8

ADVANTAGES OF FIXED ANKLE AFOFCS FOR GAIT

1. Gastrocnemius becomes a uni-jointed muscle and in TST, when it reaches its maximum length, this is akin to normal gait.
2. Gastrocnemius muscle lengthens and shortens more normally during the GC.
3. Potential for gastrocnemius muscle activation to be normalized
4. Improved control of foot and shank kinematics and GRF alignment in the GC
5. Triplanar control of pronation and supination

Abbreviations: AFOFCs, ankle-foot orthosis/footwear combinations; GC, gait cycle; GRF, ground reaction force; TST, terminal stance.

---

been aligned at or near vertical. Research shows that these alignments will not be optimal for standing, gait, or other functional activities (see Table 21-4).[7,13-15,57,64,65,71-76,96] SVAs of at least 10 degrees incline are needed to normalize gait, and these SVA alignments will place the knee over the middle of the foot while the foot is flat on the floor; and in this alignment, it is also possible to get up from a chair or the floor, squat, and climb stairs.

SUMMARY

This chapter has looked at designing, aligning, and tuning AFOFCs and their potential for improving body structures and functions, activities, and participation. The evidence for the efficacy of interventions for children with CP is showing positive effects for functional and task-oriented training, motor learning coaching, repetitions and practice, strengthening and lengthening of MTUs, and intensity of intervention.[12,85,97] Biomechanically optimized orthotic interventions prescribed at the optimum frequency of administration can provide all of these opportunities for "therapy while standing and walking." Obtaining evidence that may support the achievement of these outcomes is at an early stage of development. This is because research of this highly complex condition is difficult and requires studies into both short- and long-term outcomes. Research into interventions with orthoses is also difficult, as orthoses themselves are highly complex and have to be customized to be effective for the individual.[12,18]

Another problem for establishing an evidence base is that most research to date has not used optimally designed and aligned orthoses, and most have not been tuned to ensure they perform optimally.[4,6,8,12,25,26] Therefore, a great deal of work is needed, with great care taken over study design. All elements of the design and alignments need to be optimized to achieve optimal walking or other desired activities. When designing studies, rather than tuning one element in isolation, it is preferable to design and tune all elements of an AFOFC to optimum and then vary one element only. When tuning the AFOFC, it is also important to recognize

that walking cannot be observed accurately enough by eye.[59,98] Slow motion or frame-by-frame analysis is required to observe walking kinematics accurately and video vector analysis will improve confidence that the orthosis has been tuned optimally for both kinematics and kinetics, especially as the kinetics in some circumstances may not be suspected from the observed kinematics. Kinetics are required when there is a need to be confident that forces, moment arms, and moments have been optimized.[6,31,99]

We will finally be able to evaluate the effectiveness of AFOFC interventions in children with CP once sufficient research has been completed using AFOFCS that are kinematically and kinetically biomechanically optimized and all the possible outcomes have been considered. It will be interesting to review the literature once all of this has been achieved.

REFERENCES

1. World Health Organization. *International Classification of Functioning, Disability and Health: ICF*. Geneva, Switzerland: World Health Organization; 2001.
2. World Health Organization. *International Classification of Functioning Disability and Health: Children and Youth Version: ICF-CY*. Geneva, Switzerland: World Health Organization; 2007.
3. International Organization for Standardization. *ISO 8551 Prosthetics and Orthotics—Functional Deficiencies—Description of the Person to be Treated with an Orthosis, Clinical Objectives of Treatment and Functional Requirements of the Orthosis*. International Organization for Standardization; 2003.
4. Owen E. *Shank Angle to Floor Measures and Tuning of Ankle-Foot Orthosis Footwear Combinations for Children with Cerebral Palsy, Spina Bifida and Other Conditions* [MSc Thesis]. Glasgow: University of Strathclyde; 2004.
5. Meadows C, Bowers R, Owen E. Biomechanics of hip knee and ankle. In: Hsu J, Michael J, Fisk J, eds. *AAOS Atlas of Orthoses and Assistive Devices*. Amsterdam: Elsevier; 2008.
6. Owen E. The importance of being earnest about shank and thigh kinematics especially when using ankle-foot orthoses. *Prosthet Orthot Int*. 2010;34(3):254-269.
7. Owen E. Shank angle to floor measures of tuned 'ankle-foot orthosis footwear combinations' used with children with cerebral palsy, spina bifida and other conditions. *Gait Posture*. 2002;16(suppl 1):S132-S133.

8. Eddison N, Chockalingam N. The effect of tuning ankle foot orthoses-footwear combination on the gait parameters of children with cerebral palsy. *Prosthet Orthot Int.* 2013;37(2):95-107.

9. International Organization for Standardization. *ISO 8549-1:1989 Prosthetics and Orthotics—Vocabulary. Part 1—General Terms for External Limb Prostheses and Orthoses.* Geneva: International Organisation for Standardization; 2003.

10. International Organization for Standardization. *ISO 8549-3:1989 Prosthetics and orthotics—Vocabulary. Part 3—Terms Relating to External Orthoses.* Geneva: International Organisation for Standardization; 1989.

11. Bleck E. *Orthopaedic Management in Cerebral Palsy.* London, UK: Mac Keith Press; 1987.

12. Morris C, Condie D. *Recent Developments in Healthcare for Children with Cerebral Palsy: Implications and Opportunities for Orthotics.* International Society for Prosthetics and Orthotics, Consensus Conference; 2009.

13. Meadows C. *The Influence of Polypropylene Ankle-Foot Orthoses on the Gait of Cerebral Palsied Children.* [PhD Thesis]. Glasgow: University of Strathclyde; 1984.

14. Jagadamma K, Coutts F, Mercer T, et al. Effects of tuning of ankle foot orthoses-footwear combination using wedges on stance phase knee hyperextension in children with cerebral palsy—preliminary results. *Disabil Rehabil.* 2009;4(6):406-413.

15. Jagadamma K, Owen E, Coutts F, Herman J, Yirrel J, Linden Mvd. The effects of tuning an ankle-foot orthosis footwear combination on kinematics and kinetics of the knee joint of an adult with hemiplegia. *Prosthet Orthot Int.* 2010;34(3):270-276.

16. Bowers R, Ross K. A review of the effectiveness of lower limb orthoses in cerebral palsy. In: Morris C, Condie D, eds. *Recent Developments in Healthcare for Children with Cerebral Palsy: Implications and Opportunities for Orthotics.* International Society for Prosthetics and Orthotics, Consensus Conference; 2009.

17. Condie D, Meadows C. *Report of a Consensus Conference on the Lower Limb Orthotic Management of Cerebral Palsy.* International Society for Prosthetics and Orthotics; 1995.

18. Fatone S. Challenges in lower limb orthotic research. *Prosthet Orthot Int.* 2010;34(3):235-237.

19. Kerkum Y, Houdijk H, Brehm M, et al. The shank-to-vertical-angle as a parameter to evaluate tuning of ankle-foot orthoses. *Gait Posture.* 2015;42(3):269-274.

20. Eddison N, Chockalingam N, Osborne S. Ankle foot orthosis-footwear combination tuning: an investigation into common clinical practice in the United Kingdom. *Prosthet Orthot Int.* 2015;39(2):126-133. doi: 10.1177/0309364613516486. Epub 2014 Feb 24.

21. Harlaar J, Brehm M, Becher J, et al. Studies examining the efficacy of ankle foot orthoses should report activity level and mechanical evidence. *Prosthet Orthot Int.* 2010;34(3):327-335.

22. Brehm M, Bus S, Harlaar J, Nollet F. A candidate core set of outcome measures based on the international classification of functionning, disability and health for clinical studies on lower limb orthoses. *Prosthet Orthot Int.* 2011;35:269.

23. Majnemer A. *Measures for Children with Developmental Disabilities: An ICF-CY Approach.* London, UK: Mac Keith Press, Clinics in Developmental Medicine No. 194-195; 2012.

24. Schiariti V, Selb M, Cieza A, O'Donnell M. International Classification of Functioning, Disability and Health Core Sets for children and youth with cerebral palsy: a consensus meeting. *Dev Med Child Neurol.* 2015;57(2):149-158. doi: 10.1111/dmcn.12551. Epub 2014 Aug 6.

25. Ridgewell E, Dobson F, Bach T, Baker R. A systematic review to determine best practice reporting guidelines for AFO interventions in studies involving children with cerebral palsy. *Prosthet Orthot Int.* 2010;34(2):129-145.

26. Owen E. A proposed clinical algorithm for dorsiflexion free AFOFCs based on calf muscle length, strength, stiffness and skeletal alignment. Proceedings ISPO UK NMS Annual Scientific Meeting 2013. International Society for Prosthetics and Orthotics UKNMS; 2013.

27. Owen E. From stable standing to rock and roll walking. Part 1. The importance of alignment, proportion and profiles. *APCP J.* 2014;5(1):7-18.

28. Owen E. From stable standing to rock and roll walking. Part 2. Designing, aligning and tuning orthoses for standing, stepping and gait. *APCP J.* 2014;5(2):4-16.

29. Engen T. The TIRR polypropylene orthoses. *Orthotics Prosthet.* 1972;26(4):1-5.

30. Tait J, Rose G. The real-time video vector display of ground reaction forces during ambulation. *J Med Eng Technol.* 1979;3:252-255.

31. Stallard J. Assessment of the mechanical function of orthoses by force vector visualisation. *Physiotherapy.* 1987;73:398-402.

32. Hutchins S, Bowker P, Geary N, Richards J. The biomechanics and clinical efficacy of footwear adapted with rocker profiles – evidence in the literature. *The Foot.* 2009;19:165-170.

33. Owen E. The point of 'point-loading rockers' in ankle-foot orthosis footwear combinations used with children with cerebral palsy, spina bifida and other conditions. *Gait Posture.* 2004;20S:S86.

34. Tilley A. *The Measure of Man and Woman. Human Factors in Design.* New York, NY: John Wiley and Sons; 2002.

35. Convery P, Greig R, Ross R, Sockalingam S. A three centre study of the variability of ankle foot orthoses due to fabrication and grade of polypropylene. *Prosthet Orthot Int.* 2004;28:175-182.

36. Kobayashi T, Leung A, Hutchins S. Techniques to measure rigidity of ankle-foot orthosis: a review. *J Rehab Res Dev.* 2011;48(5):565-576.

37. Dobson F, Morris M, Baker R, Graham H. Gait classification in children with cerebral palsy: a systematic review. *Gait Posture.* 2007;25(1):140-152.

38. Winters T, Gage J, Hicks R. Gait patterns in spastic hemiplegia in children and young adults. *J Bone Joint Surg Am.* 1987;69A:437-441.

39. Sutherland D, Davids J. Common gait abnormalities of the knee in cerebral palsy. *Clin Orthop Relat Res.* 1993;288:139-147.

40. Hullin M, Robb J, IR L. Gait patterns in children with hemiplegic spastic cerebral palsy. *J Pediatr Orthoped.* 1996;5:247-251.

41. O'Byrne J, Jenkinson A, O'Brien T. Quantitative analysis and classification of gait patterns in cerebral palsy using a three-dimensional motion analyser. *J Child Neurol.* 1998;13(3):101-108.

42. Rodda J, Graham H. Classification of gait patterns in spastic hemiplegia and spastic diplegia: a basis for a management algorithm. *Eur J Neurol.* 2001;8:98-108.

43. Becher J. Pediatric rehabilitation in children with cerebral palsy: general management, classification of motor disorders. *J Prosthet Orthot.* 2002;14(4):143-149.

44. Owen E. A clinical algorithm for the design and tuning of ankle-foot orthosis footwear combinations (AFOFCs) based on shank kinematics. *Gait Posture.* 2005;22S:36-37.

45. Perry J. Kinesiology of lower extremity bracing. *Clin Orthop Relat Res.* 1974;102:18-31.

46. Owen E. How should we define the rockers of gait and are there three or four? *Gait Posture.* 2009;30S:49.

47. Perry J. Normal and pathological gait. In: Hsu J, Michael J, Fisk J, eds. *American Academy of Orthopaedic Surgeons Atlas of Orthoses and Assistive Devices.* 4th ed. Philadelphia: CV Mosby; 2008.

48. Perry J. *Gait Analysis. Normal and Pathological Function.* 2nd ed. Thorofare, NJ: SLACK Inc.; 2010.

49. Davis R, DeLuca P. Gait characterisation via dynamic joint stiffness. *Gait Posture.* 1996;4(3):224-231.

50. Hansen A, Childress D, Knox E. Roll-over shapes of human locomotor systems: effects of walking speed. *Clin Biomech.* 2004;19:407-414.

51. Hansen A, Childress D. Investigations of roll-over shape: implications for design, alignment, and evaluation of ankle-foot prostheses and orthoses. *Disabil Rehabil.* 2010;32(26):2201-2209.

52. Murray M. Gait as a total pattern of movement. *Am J Phys Med.* 1967;46(1):290-333.

53. Hansen A, Meier M. Roll-over shapes of the ankle-foot and knee-ankle-foot sytems of able-bodied children. *Clin Biomech.* 2010;25:248-255.

54. Wang C, Hansen A. Response of able-bodied persons to changes in shoe rocker radius during walking: changes in ankle kinematics to maintain a consistent roll-over shape. *J Biomech.* 2010;43(12):2288-2293.

55. Owen E. Tuning of ankle-foot orthosis combinations for children with cerebral palsy, spina bifida and other conditions. Proceedings of ESMAC Seminar 2004. Warsaw, Poland: European Society for Movement Analysis of Children and Adults; 2004.

56. Rodda J, Graham H, Carson L, Galea M, Wolfe R. Sagittal gait patterns in spastic diplegia. *J Bone Joint Surg Br.* 2004;86(2):251-258.

57. Simon S, Deutsch S, Nuzzo R, et al. Genu recurvatum in spastic cerebral palsy. Report on findings by gait analysis. *J Bone Joint Surg Am.* 1978;60(7):882-894.

58. Connelly P. Paradoxical movement of the tibia in patients with cerebral palsy. *Gait Posture.* 1999;10:59.

59. Baker R. *Measuring Walking: A Handbook of Clinical Gait Analysis.* London, UK: Wiley; 2013.

60. Hansen A, Wang C. Effective rocker shapes used by able-bodied persons for walking and fore-aft swaying: implications for design of ankle-foot prostheses. *Gait Posture.* 2010;32:181-184.

61. Owen E. Proposed clinical algorithm for deciding the sagittal angle of the ankle in an ankle-foot orthosis footwear combination. *Gait Posture.* 2005;22S:38-39.

62. Cook T, Cozzens B. The effects of heel height and ankle-foot-orthoses configuration on weight line location: a demonstration of principles. *Arch Phys Med Rehabil.* 1976;30:43-46.

63. Nuzzo R. Dynamic bracing: elastics for patients with cerebral palsy, muscular dystrophy and myelodysplasia. *Clin Orthop Relat Res.* 1980;148:263-273.

64. Nuzzo R. High-performance activity with below-knee cast treatment. Part 1: mechanics and demonstration. *Orthopedics.* 1983;6(6):713-723.

65. Nuzzo R. High-performance activity with below-knee cast treatment. Part 2: clinical application and the weak link hypothesis. *Orthopedics.* 1983;6(7):817-830.

66. Hullin M, Robb J. Biomechanical effects of rockers on walking in a plaster cast. *J Bone Joint Surg Br.* 1991;73(1):92-95.

67. Lehmann J, Warren C, deLateur B. A biomechanical evaluation of knee stability in below knee braces. *Arch Phys Med Rehabil.* 1970;51:688-695.

68. Weist D, Waters R, Bontrager E, Quigley M. The influence of heel design on a rigid ankle-foot orthosis. *Orthotics Prosthet.* 1979;33(4):3-10.

69. White F. Orthotics. In: Drennan J, ed. *The Child's Foot and Ankle.* New York, NY: Raven Press; 1992.

70. McHugh B. Analysis of body-device interface forces in the sagittal plane for patients wearing ankle-foot orthoses. *Prosthet Orthot Int.* 1999;23:75-81.

71. Jebsen R, Corcoran P, Simons B. Clinical experience with a plastic short leg brace. *Arch Phys Med Rehabil.* 1970;51:114-119.

72. Glancy J, Lindseth R. The polypropylene solid-ankle orthosis. *Orthot Prosthet.* 1972;26(1):14-26.

73. Fulford G, Cairns T. The problems associated with flail feet in children and their treatment with orthoses. *J Bone Joint Surg Br.* 1978;60(1):93-95.

74. Nuzzo R. A simple treatment of genu recurvatum in ataxic and athetoid cerebral palsy. *Orthopedics.* 1986;9(9):123-127.

75. Cusick B. *Progressive Casting and Splinting for Lower Extremity Deformities in Children with Neuromotor Dysfunction.* Tucson, AZ: Therapy Skill Builders; 1990.

76. Hullin M, Robb J, Loudon I. Ankle-foot orthosis function in low-level myelomeningocele. *J Pediatr Orthop.* 1992;12(4):518-521.

77. Rosenthal R, Deutsch S, Miller W, Schumann W, Hall J. A fixed-ankle, below-the-knee orthosis for the management of genu recurvatum in spastic cerebral palsy. *J Bone Joint Surg Am.* 1975;57:545-547.

78. Pratt E, Durham S, Ewins D. Preliminary evidence for techniques used to optimally align (tune) fixed ankle-foot orthoses in children. *J Prosthet Orthot.* 2011;23(2):60-63.

79. Perry J. *Gait Analysis. Normal and Pathological Function.* Thorofare, NJ: SLACK Incorporated; 1992.

80. Butler P, Nene A. The biomechanics of fixed ankle foot orthoses and their potential in the management of cerebral palsied children. *Physiotherapy.* 1991;77:81-88.

81. Butler P, Farmer S, Major R. Improvement in gait parameters following late intervention in traumatic brain injury: a long-term follow-up report of a single case. *Clin Rehabil.* 1997;11:220-226.

82. Butler P, Thompson N, Major R. Improvement in walking performance of children with cerebral palsy: preliminary results. *Dev Med Child Neurol.* 1992;34:567-576.

83. Butler P, Major R. The learning of motor control: biomechanical considerations. *Physiotherapy.* 1992;78(1):6-11.

84. Nascimento L, Gloria A, Habib E. Effects of constraint-induced movement therapy as a rehabilitation strategy for the affected upper limb of children with hemiparesis: systematic review of the literature. *Rev Bras Fisioter.* 2009;13(2):97-102.

85. Bar-Haim S, Harries N, Nammourah I, et al. Effectiveness of motor learning coaching in children with cerebral palsy: a randomized controlled trial. *Clin Rehabil.* 2010;24:1009-1020.

86. Ulrich D, Lloyd M, Tieman C, Looper J, Angulo-Barroso R. Effects of intensity of treadmill training on developmental outcomes and stepping in infants with Down syndrome: a randomized trial. *Phys Ther.* 2008;88(1):114-122.

87. Damiano D, Quinlivan J, Owen B, Payne P, Nelson K, Abel M. What does the Ashworth scale really measure and are instrumented measures more valid and precise? *Dev Med Child Neurol.* 2002;44(2):112-118.

88. Sanger T, Delgado M, Gaebler-Spira D, Hallet M, Mink J. Classification and definition of disorders causing hypertonia in childhood. *Pediatrics.* 2003;111(1):e89-e97.

89. Lieber R. *Skeletal Muscle Structure, Function, and Plasticity. The Physiological Basis of Rehabilitation.* 2nd ed. Baltimore, MD: Lippincott Williams and Wilkins; 2002.

90. Huijing P, Benard M, Harlaar J, Jaspers R, Becher J. Foot angle with tibia does not reflect ankle joint angle in spastic cerebral paresis: better estimator proposed. Presented at the ESMAC-SIAMOC Annual Scientific Meeting; September 29-October 3, 2014; Rome, Italy.

91. Hicks J. The mechanics of the foot II. The plantar aponeurosis and the arch. *J Anat.* 1954;88:25-30.

92. Reimers J, Pedersen B, Broderson A. Foot deformity and the length of the triceps surae in Danish children between 3 and 17 years old. *J Pediatr Orthop B.* 1995;4(1):71-73.

93. Neto H, Collange L, Galli M, Oliveira C. Comparison of articulated and rigid ankle-foot orthoses in children with cerebral palsy: a systematic review. *Pediatr Phys Ther.* 2012;24:308-312.

94. Vanderpool M, Collins S, Kuo A. Ankle fixation need not increase the energetic cost of human walking. *Gait Posture.* 2008;28:427-433.

95. Weber D. Use of the hinged AFO for children with spastic cerebral palsy and midfoot instability. *J Assoc Child Prosthet Orthot Clin.* 1991;25(4):61-65.

96. Malas B. The effect of ankle-foot orthoses on balance: a clinical perspective. *J Prosthet Orthot.* 2010;22(4S):24-33.

97. Novak I, McIntyre S, Morgan C, et al. A systematic review of interventions for children with cerebral palsy: state of the evidence. *Dev Med Child Neurol.* 2013;55(10):885-910.

98. Kawamura CM, de Morais Filho MC, Barreto MM, de Paula Asa SK, Juliano Y, Novo NF. Comparison between visual and three-dimensional gait analysis in patients with spastic cerebral palsy. *Gait Posture.* 2007;25(1):18-24.

99. Stallard J, Woollam PJ. Transportable two-dimensional gait assessment: routine service experience for orthotic provision. *Disabil Rehabil.* 2003;25(6):254-258.

22

Assistive Technology, With Emphasis on Positioning and Mobility Equipment

As one of the first rehabilitative specialists to provide services to children with disabilities and special health care needs, pediatric physical therapists are in an ideal position to recommend and implement the appropriate use of AT.

Toby M. Long and Debora F. Perry[1]

Assistive technology (AT) is a broad term that can be defined in several different ways.[1] Public Law (PL) 105-394, Assistive Technology Act of 1998,[2] defines AT as "technology designed to be utilized in an assistive technology device or assistive technology service."[(112STAT 3631)] According to this law, an *AT device* is "any item, piece of equipment, or product system, whether acquired commercially, modified, or customized, that is used to increase, maintain, or improve functional capabilities of individuals with disabilities,"[(112STAT 3631)] and *AT service* is "any service that directly assists an individual with a disability in the selection, acquisition, or use of an assistive technology device."[2(112STAT 3631-3632)] Based on these definitions, assistive devices, adaptive equipment, durable medical equipment, orthotics, prosthetics, and therapeutic equipment are terms that designate different types of AT.[1,2] These definitions also imply that, when a physical therapist as a member of an AT team completes an evaluation to determine the child's need for such technology, recommends a specific device, completes paperwork that assists the family in securing funding, fits the child with the device, and trains him or her in its use, all of these steps would constitute AT services.[1,2]

In this chapter, general AT categories, the AT team, and the roles of its members, including that of a physical therapist, will be described. In addition, relevant legislation, guidelines, and various other factors that affect the prescription and use of AT devices will be discussed and the AT evaluation process will be briefly outlined. The overall emphasis will be placed on the goals and evidence for use of positioning and mobility equipment by children with disabilities, and specifically, by children with cerebral palsy (CP).

ASSISTIVE TECHNOLOGY CATEGORIES, RELATED LEGISLATION, AND GUIDELINES

Examples of assistive devices include canes and crutches; positioning devices such as standing frames are adaptive standing devices; and gait trainers and wheelchairs are examples of durable medical equipment.1 Therapeutic equipment such as floor mats, balls, bolsters, wedges, stationary bicycles, treadmills, and other devices, some of which are shown in Figures 22-1 through 22-4, can be used both in the clinic and in the child's home for activities designed to improve his or her functional skills, thus fitting the legal definition of AT.[2] Orthoses used for standing and gait, upper extremity orthoses, stretching orthoses, and other orthotic devices were discussed in Chapters 20 and 21; and prosthetic interventions are beyond the scope of this text.

Rahlin M. *Physical Therapy for Children With Cerebral Palsy: An Evidence-Based Approach (pp 371-394).*

Figure 22-1. Therapy room in a pediatric clinic: mats used for safety and comfort during exercise and therapeutic activities; balls and bolsters used for strengthening, stretching and vestibular stimulation; cube chairs and adjustable bench used for sitting activities, balance training and practicing sit to stand transitions.

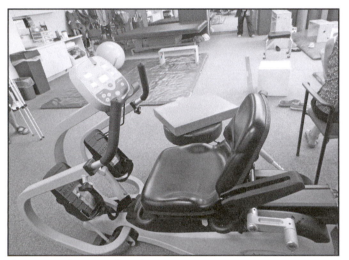

Figure 22-3. Stationary bicycle.

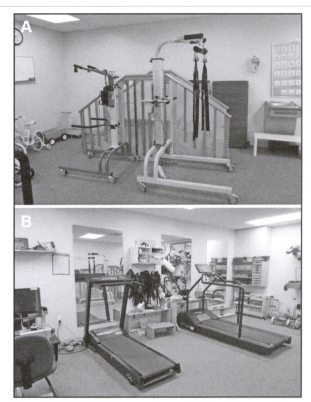

Figure 22-2. Gait training equipment. (A) A stair case and partial body weight support (PBWS) frames of different sizes. (B) Treadmills.

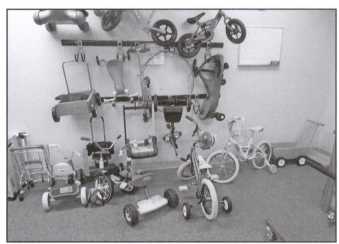

Figure 22-4. Tricycles, adaptive tricycles, bicycles with training wheels, wagons, scooters and scooter boards.

AT can be categorized in many different ways.[3-5] Table 22-1 contains general AT categories specified by the Rehabilitation Engineering and Assistive Technology Society of North America (RESNA),[5-9] with several examples provided per category. Some of the equipment listed in the table is shown in Figures 22-5 through 22-15. Because AT devices have been found to maintain appropriate postural alignment, enhance function, and facilitate performance of activities of daily living (ADLs) in individuals with disabilities,[1,2,10] federal legislation supports the use of AT by children and adults who have a need in such devices.[2,11-13] The relevant laws are listed and their significance is briefly described in Table 22-2.[2,11-13]

The American Academy of Pediatrics (AAP) is another entity that supports the use of AT for children with special health care needs (CSHCN) and, specifically, for transportation of these children in motor vehicles and on school buses.[14,15] In 1999, its Committee on Injury and Poison Prevention[14] published the guidelines for transporting children who have a tracheostomy, a spica cast, or muscle tone abnormalities, or exhibit behavioral problems. Another set of guidelines, this time for transporting CSHCN on a school bus, was published in 2001.[15] Health care professionals who work with children with disabilities, including physical therapists, should be aware of these guidelines and advise the families of these children accordingly, especially because, as shown by research, these guidelines are frequently not followed.[16] For example, O'Neil et al[16] reported that, in a study of 275 drivers who transported 294 CSHCN, 75.4% did so in AAP-recommended standard car safety seats, but only 26.8% of 280 assessed seats were used properly.

TABLE 22-1

GENERAL CATEGORIES OF ASSISTIVE TECHNOLOGY WITH EXAMPLES[5-9]

ASSISTIVE TECHNOLOGY CATEGORY[a]	EXAMPLES[b]
Access for Communication Systems and Computers	Direct selection: the child directly interacts with the device to make choices Indirect selection: the child uses a switch and an encoding system interfaced with a communication system or a computer Types of switches (activation methods) • Motion (mercury and infrared) • Photosensitive (blink) • Physioelectric (muscle tension and relaxation) • Pneumatic (sip and puff) • Pressure (application of pressure) • Sound (detection of sound)
Activities of daily living (Figures 22-5 through 22-7)	Adaptive bath and shower benches and chairs Adaptive kitchen equipment Adaptive toileting equipment Adaptive spoons and other utensils Grab bars, non-slip rugs, and other safety items
Assistive listening	Hearing aides Telecommunication device for the deaf (TDD) Visual signals
Augmentative communication	Aided[c] communication assistance systems • Communication boards, cards, wallets • Electronic "text-to speech" and voice output devices
Computer technology (Figures 22-8B and C)	Alternate keyboards and mouse access Voice recognition software
Environmental control	Electronic aides to daily living (environmental control units) for operating appliances, such as electric doors, lights, telephone, TV, etc, in different environments (home, school, work)
Mobility (Figures 22-8A and 24-9 through 22-12)	Adaptive strollers Assistive devices (walkers, crutches, canes) Gait trainers Manual wheelchairs Modified ride-on toy cars Powered scooters and wheelchairs Scooter boards
Positioning (Figures 22-13 through 22-15)	Recumbent (wedges, bolsters, sidelyers) Upright (adaptive seating and standing devices) • Feeding chairs • Positioning chairs • Standing frames

(continued)

TABLE 22-1 (CONTINUED)

GENERAL CATEGORIES OF ASSISTIVE TECHNOLOGY WITH EXAMPLES[5-9]

ASSISTIVE TECHNOLOGY CATEGORY[a]	EXAMPLES[b]
Recreation, leisure, and play	Adaptive playground equipment
	Adaptive toys
	Adaptive switches
	Computers
	Computer software
	Nonslip materials to stabilize toys on support surface
Visual technology	Auditory and tactile feedback toys
	Large print or Braille books
	Light-up toys
	Talking appliances

[a] Excludes orthotics and prosthetics

[b] Not all-inclusive

[c] Unaided communication assistance systems do not require equipment. Examples include gestures, vocalizations, sign language, etc.

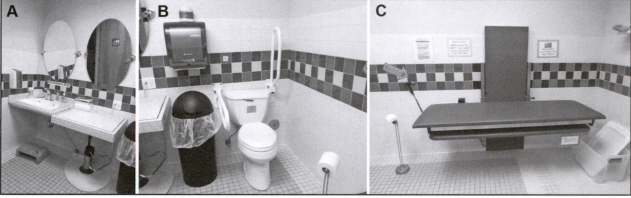

Figure 22-5. Adaptive bathroom. (A) Sink height adapted for wheelchair access; height-adjustable bathroom table. (B) Grab bars installed next to the toilet. (C) Adult-size height-adjustable changing table.

Figure 22-6. (A) A low-tech and low-cost shower bench constructed by the father of a young adult with cerebral palsy. (B) A flexible shower can be successfully used with this bench.

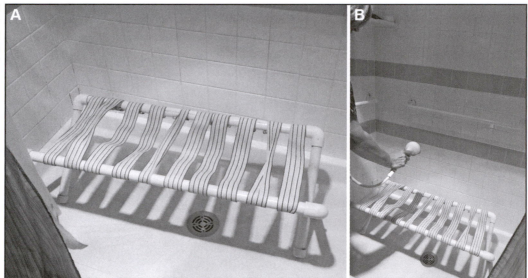

Figure 22-7. Adaptive kitchen. (A) Elevated dishwashing machine and sink with a wheelchair access capability. (B) Height-adjustable kitchen table.

Figure 22-8. An adult with cerebral palsy using assistive technology in her work place. (A) Head piece for telephone communication; power wheelchair for seating and mobility. (B) Adaptive computer keyboard. (C) Wrist and hand splint to assist with the use of the adaptive keyboard.

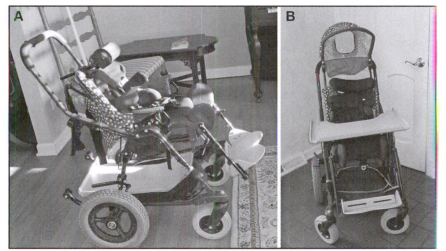

Figure 22-9. Adjustable adaptive stroller with the following features: (A) Tilt in space mechanism, headrest, lateral supports, hip supports, thigh supports, pelvic belt, arm rests, footplate, wheels, casters, and brake on the right. (B) Canopy, H-harness, and upper extremity support tray.

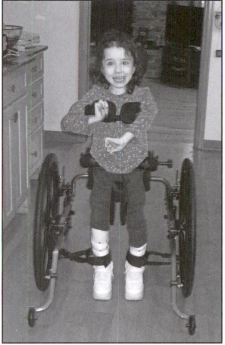

Figure 22-10. A child with cerebral palsy uses a KidWalk Mobility system that allows her to move close to objects and people and supports environmental exploration.

Figure 22-11. (A) A child with cerebral palsy in a manual wheelchair. (B) The same child during a power wheelchair evaluation.

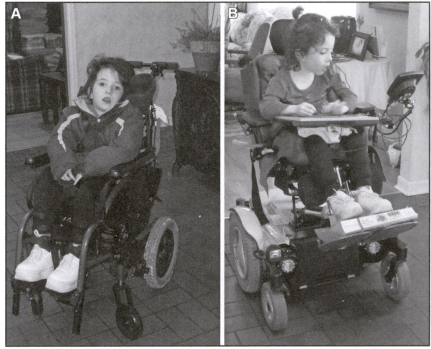

Figure 22-12. Custom-molded manual and power (on the left) wheelchairs with asymmetrically positioned headrests to accommodate for musculoskeletal deformities, shown in the home of an adult with cerebral palsy.

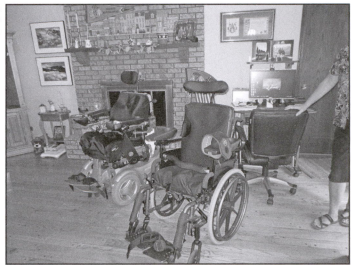

Figure 22-13. Proper adaptive seating positioning allows this girl to participate in a fun art activity and supports social interaction in a school setting.

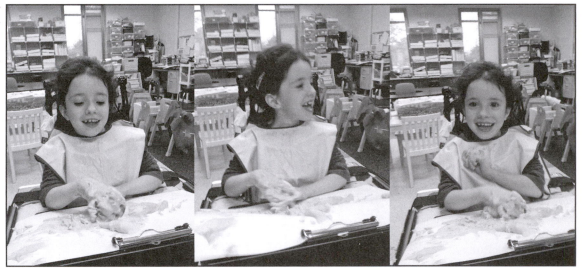

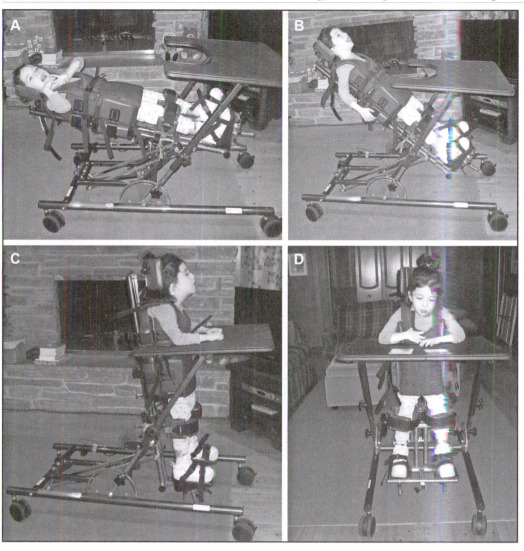

Figure 22-14. A child with CP uses a supine stander at home for upright positioning and weight-bearing through lower extremities. (A) Initial placement in the stander moved into a horizontal position. (B) The stander's angle-adjustable mechanism allows to gradually elevate the child from a horizontal position. (C) Slightly reclined positioning in the supine stander. (D) Completing an activity while positioned in a supine stander with the following features: a curved head rest; a chest support harness; a pelvic support harness; lateral trunk and hip positioning pads; an adjustable knee system with knee pads; adjustable footplates, heel loops and toe straps; and an upper extremity positioning tray.

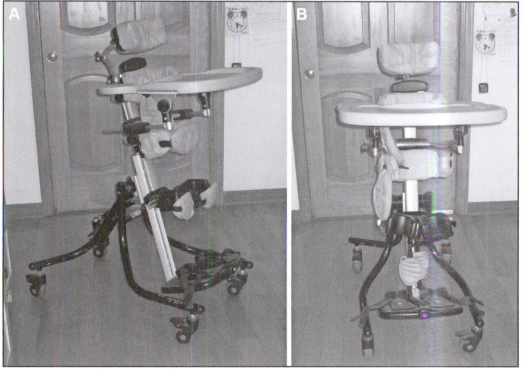

Figure 22-15. Leckey Squiggles Stander. (A) An oblique view featuring the following components: a contoured head rest; adjustable chest and pelvic lateral supports with harnesses and cushions; kneecups with knee pads; an adjustable footplate with sandals and sandal straps; and an upper extremity support tray. (B) A frontal view featuring unlocked chest and pelvic harness and knee pad straps.

TABLE 22-2

FEDERAL LEGISLATION THAT SUPPORTS THE PROVISION OF ASSISTIVE TECHNOLOGY SERVICES TO CHILDREN AND ADULTS WITH DISABILITIES IN THE UNITED STATES

YEAR	PUBLIC LAW	SIGNIFICANCE
1990	PL 101-336 The Americans with Disabilities Act[11]	Defined AT devices and AT services. Included provisions for reasonable accommodations for persons with disabilities, including AT, for accessibility and usability of public service and employment facilities
1998	PL 105-394 Assistive Technology Act[2]	Defined AT, AT device, and AT service and provided federal funding to increase public awareness of AT needs of individuals with disabilities and to promote and expand the AT use
2004	PL 108-364 Assistive Technology Act[12]	Amended PL 105-394 in support of continued and expanded comprehensive state-wide programs of technology assistance to individuals of disabilities of all ages through increased availability, access to, funding of, and training in use of AT devices and services
2004	PL 108-446 Individuals with Disabilities Education Improvement Act (IDEIA)[13]	Defined AT devices and services. Part B includes considerations in regard to the child's AT needs for the development, implementation, review, and revision of the child's IEP. AT devices and services are to be provided at no cost to the parents when AT needs are established and addressed by the IEP. Part C includes AT as an EI service, and the child's AT needs are addressed in the IFSP.

Abbreviations: AT, assistive technology; IEP, Individualized Education Program; IFSP, Individualized Family Service Plan; PL, public law.

ASSISTIVE TECHNOLOGY TEAM AND THE ROLES OF ITS MEMBERS, INCLUDING THE ROLES OF THE PHYSICAL THERAPIST

The *Guide to Physical Therapist Practice 3.0* (*Guide 3.0*) places prescription, application, and fabrication or modification of AT in the physical therapist's scope of practice[17]; entry-level Doctor of Physical Therapy (DPT) program curricula include AT-related content[18]; and AT training is supported by the American Physical Therapy Association (APTA).[1] However, results of a survey of 380 pediatric physical therapists published in 2008 revealed that respondents rated their AT training as "less than adequate" and reported insufficient confidence in their ability to deliver AT services to children with disabilities.[1] They commented on the paucity, low quality, and vendor bias of the available continuing education courses and expressed their interest in having access to affordable training that would cover AT evaluation procedures, specific AT devices, and obtaining AT funding. The preferred educational methods included person-to-person and group instruction.[1]

The need for additional, high-quality AT training is further supported by the fact that, although physicians are usually involved in AT-related decisions making, the majority of equipment used by children with disabilities is recommended by therapists.[19] In a survey study of 108 caregivers conducted

by Peredo et al,[19] only 15% of respondents reported that equipment for their children with disabilities was recommended by a physician alone; 76% stated that most commonly, physical and occupational therapists fulfilled this role; and in 17% of the cases, parents were the ones who initiated the process of obtaining equipment for their children. AT team members and their roles are described in Table 22-3.[8,20-30] As observed clinically, members' contributions to the team and their mutual respect and collaboration are crucial for the success of the AT intervention and may greatly affect its outcomes.

ASSISTIVE TECHNOLOGY UTILIZATION IN DIFFERENT SETTINGS AND FACTORS AFFECTING EQUIPMENT USE

Peredo et al[19] examined the use of AT devices among 108 children and adolescents with neurodevelopmental conditions, 48% of whom were diagnosed with CP. The survey used in this study focused on equipment other than wheelchairs. All participants combined owned 467 pieces of AT, which constituted greater than 4 different devices per child. Children with CP were found to use walkers, adaptive seating, and standing positioning services more frequently than participants with other disabilities. Eighty-seven percent of them used orthotic devices, 46% used adaptive seating,

TABLE 22-3

ASSISTIVE TECHNOLOGY TEAM MEMBERS AND THEIR RELATED ROLES

TEAM MEMBER	ROLES
AT or rehabilitation technology supplier or vendor[8]	Supplies positioning, seating, mobility, and other types of adaptive equipment to the child; may lend equipment to the child/family on a trial basis; provides information on available options and costs of the required device. Participates in assistive technology evaluations, delivers and adjusts equipment when necessary
Audiologist[20]	Performs hearing evaluation; suggests and provides appropriate intervention, when needed, including equipment necessary to support the child's ability to comprehend spoken language and to communicate with other people
AAC specialist[8,21,22]	A speech-language pathologist who provides AAC assessment, consultation, and intervention options to the child and family, when appropriate, from low-tech symbol charts to high-tech speech synthesizers
Education specialist or special educator[8]	A teacher who has a good knowledge of the child and who identifies specific classroom-related and educationally relevant demands that the child has difficulty meeting
Funding specialist[8]	A social worker or another health care provider with specific knowledge of AT funding sources, including public and private insurance, as well as charities and other organizations, who advises the team on obtaining funding for AT devices
Interface specialist[8]	An occupational therapist who identifies the best method for the child to access such AT equipment as AAC devices, computers, and environmental control units
Occupational therapist[23-25]	Evaluates the child's upper extremity function; ability to participate in ADLs; and the need for adaptive equipment, orthoses, and splints. Suggests and implements appropriate interventions, including AT fitting and training
Orthopedic surgeon[8,23,26]	Performs an examination of the child's bone and joint integrity and alignment; identifies, monitors, and addresses musculoskeletal deformities of the lower extremity and spine; and prescribes appropriate AT devices when necessary
Parent or family member[8]	Fulfills the spokesperson role for the child when necessary; provides information related to the previous and current use of AT and general history information; participates in AT evaluation and facilitates the child's AT use
Pediatrician[27,28]	Performs physical examination and neurological examination; generates referrals to rehabilitation professionals to address neuromotor deficits and developmental problems, and prescribes appropriate AT devices when necessary
Physiatrist[29]	Performs an evaluation of the child's physical function; identifies his or her rehabilitation needs; coordinates therapy services and communication between the rehabilitation specialists and the child's family; and prescribes appropriate AT devices when necessary
Physical therapist[23,24,30]	Evaluates the child's gross motor development and gross motor function, including posture, movement transitions, and mobility; cardiovascular and pulmonary function in relation to movement and position change; identifies the need for assistive devices, orthoses, and positioning and mobility equipment; and suggests and implements appropriate interventions, including AT fitting and training
Rehabilitation engineer[8]	An electrical or mechanical engineer who participates in AT evaluation for seating and positioning devices that require his or her expertise; is involved in problem solving related to the use of AT software; and fabricates non-standard parts for wheelchairs and other AT devices
Speech-language pathologist[20-24]	Evaluates the child's communication, speech and language skills, oral-motor function, and feeding; identifies the child's AAC needs; suggests and implements appropriate interventions, including AT, to address feeding and communication deficits; and trains communication partners

Abbreviations: AAC, Augmentative and Alternative Communication; AT, assistive technology.

42% had a bath chair and 27% had a stander. Walkers were used by 21%, and 19% owned AAC devices and gait trainers. It is interesting to note that 40% of the total study sample reported using AT devices at home while only 27% and 25% used them at home and at school or at home, at school, and in a therapy setting, respectively.[19]

Equipment utilization by setting in the previously mentioned study that was conducted in the United States[19] differed greatly from the results of research conducted in Taiwan and described by Huang et al.[31-33] The latter study examined the utilization of AT devices by 15 children with CP aged 8 to 15 years in their home and school settings. Results showed that children were much more likely to use their AT devices at school as compared to their homes. Specifically, 87.8% of available devices were used at school every day or 2 to 3 times per week, while only 39.5% were used with the same frequency at home.[31-33] Peredo et al[19] and Huang et al[31-33] listed several similar factors that contributed to the AT nonuse among the participants of their studies, including the child's refusal to use the device, difficulty fitting the device in the home, and insufficient parental education related to the child's equipment use.[19,31]

ASSISTIVE TECHNOLOGY EVALUATION

The AT evaluation is a complex process accomplished by the AT team, in which all members play their respective roles as described in Table 22-3.[8,20-30] Physical therapy examination and evaluation is an integral part of the AT evaluation when the child's needs for assistive devices, orthoses, and positioning and mobility equipment are assessed.[8,30] Components of physical therapy examination and relevant categories of examination procedures were discussed in Chapter 11. As shown in Table 11-1, the physical therapy examination should contain the assessment of all components of the International Classification of Functioning, Disability and Health (ICF),[34,35] which are also very relevant to the AT evaluation. When appropriate, the ICF components need to be assessed with and without the use of orthoses, adaptive equipment, and assistive devices (see Table 11-1). The environmental and personal factors outlined by the ICF model[34,35] also need to be assessed to determine how they may affect the use of AT.

A family-centered approach to the AT evaluation facilitates problem solving and decision making that have a potential to improve the quality of life for the child and the family through the use of AT.[10] Conducting assessment in natural environments in which the AT devices are or will be used help the team to make best recommendations that address the client's specific needs in performing functional tasks that are difficult or impossible to accomplish without AT.[7,8] The goals of an AT evaluation include the following:

- Assessment of the client's equipment needs in the environments is which he or she functions
- Reassessment of the current fit and the use of AT devices obtained previously

- Development of recommendations for obtaining specific equipment for initial use or to accommodate for the child's growth, for modifications to the device already in use, or for changing the device selection to a different model, if indicated

A detailed discussion of examination and evaluation procedures pertaining to specific AT categories is beyond the scope of this text and was presented elsewhere by a number of authors.[6-8,10]

To best fit the existing need, the selected AT device should match the client's capabilities and address his or her deficits in specific areas, which is achieved by examining available equipment options and their features.[6-8] Obtaining the recommended piece of equipment on a trial basis is often helpful as this allows the child to test it in a natural environment, further facilitates the selection of the best available option, and allows the therapist to justify that selection to the funding source.[7] Following the AT evaluation, a written report is completed, reviewed by the members of the team and submitted for funding. Typically, such report would contain the evaluation findings, recommendations for a specific device and its components, and a list of AT services the client will need. Once the device is obtained, the appropriate team member works with the client on learning how to use it in his or her daily routines.[7] Physical therapists frequently provide AT services to children with disabilities, including those with CP, to address their positioning and mobility needs.

GOALS AND EVIDENCE FOR USE OF POSITIONING AND MOBILITY EQUIPMENT

Examples of positioning and mobility devices were provided in Table 22-1 and presented in Figures 22-9 through 22-15. Goals for their use are summarized in Table 22-4.

Positioning Programs

Recumbent positioning programs are commonly used in daily management of children with disabilities and severely affected physical function, and also during a recovery period after children undergo orthopedic surgeries. Such programs involve placing the child in a supine, prone, or side-lying position with the use of adaptive equipment and rotating them among these positions.[7] Jones and Puddefoot[7] did not recommend using recumbent positions during the day because, usually, upright positioning is more conducive to social interactions. However, results of a school-based study demonstrated that 6- to 12-year-old students with severe disabilities and low communication levels were more likely to initiate interactions with others in a supine position on the mat without any equipment than when positioned in a side-lyer or sitting in a wheelchair.[36] Conversely, in a study with one adolescent and 4 adults with CP, multiple disabilities, and severe scoliosis, sitting and side-lying positions were found

TABLE 22-4

GOALS FOR USE OF POSITIONING AND MOBILITY EQUIPMENT

GENERAL GOALS	ASSISTIVE TECHNOLOGY CATEGORY	CATEGORY-SPECIFIC GOALS
Decrease atypical posturing Decrease fatigue Eliminate or correct flexible deformities or accommodate fixed deformities Enhance participation and social interactions Improve function	Positioning	Provide an alternative positioning option Provide comfort
Maintain proper skeletal alignment to the greatest extent possible Minimize the development of alterations in body structures and functions Provide sufficient support and stability for the desired activity	Mobility	Increase environmental exploration Increase activity Provide an alternative mobility option

to be better tolerated than supine positioning as indicated by changes in oxygen saturation, respiratory rate, and heart rate.[37] Finally, a sleep study of 10 children with CP classified in Gross Motor Function Classification System (GMFCS)[38] levels IV and V and aged 5 to 17 years showed that, compared to unsupported sleep, the use of positioning equipment at night time resulted in increased mean oxygen saturation in 3 participants while decreased oxygen saturation values were documented in 6 other children.[39]

The variability in research findings described previously[36,37,39] underscores the need for a thorough AT evaluation that considers individual characteristics of every child, adolescent, and adult with CP, and for performing a careful analysis of risks and benefits associated with equipment use when prescribing a specific AT device for a specific patient. It is important to remember that it may be impossible to make uniform recommendations for positioning across the entire population of patients with CP because of its significant heterogeneity. However, whenever possible, related research evidence should be an integral part of the decision-making process.

In a study of 246 children and adolescents with CP aged 14 months to 19 years, Porter et al[40] found an association between persistent asymmetrical posturing before the first birthday and the development of scoliosis, pelvic obliquity, windswept deformity, and hip subluxation or dislocation pattern later in life. Specifically, if the infant preferred head rotation to the right in a supine position or had a persistent preference for right side-lying, the postural deformity that developed was likely to include left scoliosis, pelvic obliquity with the left side lower than the right, lateral rotation of the right hip and subluxation or dislocation of the left hip. This finding highlighted the importance of appropriate positioning in early life for future postural development in children with CP.[40] Results of a prospective cohort study described by

Pountney et al[4] supported this conclusion. The use of positioning programs initiated before 18 months of age, including recumbent, sitting, and standing positioning devices or only 2 of these 3 types of equipment, was found to significantly decrease the likelihood of bilateral hip subluxation, the number of documented hip problems, and the need for orthotic intervention, botulinum toxin injections, or surgical intervention to address the alignment of the hips or spine in children with CP at the age of 5 years. Specifically, 87% of children in the positioning intervention group received no treatment for unilateral or bilateral hip problems compared to 48.5% of children in the historical control group.[41]

Programs that combine recumbent positioning at night and during naps with upright positioning during awake time should be initiated for children with bilateral CP in infancy, when abnormal posturing is observed, and continued and modified during childhood and adolescence, in the home and school settings.[7,42] Positioning interventions constitute a part of a postural management program that should be developed individually for each child depending on the GMFCS[38] level and should include such additional components as active exercise, individual therapy sessions, orthotics, and surgeries.[42] According to a consensus statement generated by a Mac Keith Multidisciplinary Meeting, for children classified in GMFCS[38] levels IV and V, recumbent positioning should be initiated shortly after birth, and seating and standing positioning should start at 6 and 12 months of age, respectively.[42] As discussed in Chapter 3, obtaining a diagnosis of CP is a complex task, which may take time.[30] However, as movement specialists, physical therapists can communicate their evaluation findings to other members of the interdisciplinary team working with the family and recommend appropriate positioning when an infant demonstrates atypical postures and movement, even before the diagnosis of CP is formally established.[30]

When the child is positioned upright, changing positions between sitting and standing is necessary in order to avoid the development of fatigue, pressure ulcers, joint contractures, and deformities, all of which may arise from maintaining the same position for an excessively prolonged period of time.[7] Maher et al[43] examined the implementation of postural management programs in Australian special schools and found that, while 93% of 43 surveyed therapists considered 3 to 4 daily position changes in a school setting optimal for nonambulatory children with CP, 77% of 18 surveyed teachers indicated that only 1 or 2 position changes would be optimal. The authors suggested that additional training for the teaching staff would be necessary to address this issue. Some of the facilitating factors in the implementation of postural management programs identified in this research were the availability of appropriate equipment; good communication among therapists, teachers, and families; staff knowledge, motivation, and skills; therapists' understanding of curricular, time availability, and staff constraint issues; and the use of written programs in staff instruction. Insufficient classroom space and curricular time; lack of collaboration among therapists, teaching staff, and families; lack of appropriate equipment; insufficient motivation, time, skill, and knowledge among teaching staff and their resistance to proposed changes were identified as the limiting factors.[43]

Standing Programs

Goals for use of positioning equipment listed in Table 22-4 are directly applicable to standing systems utilized for standing positioning programs in children with CP and other disabilities.[7,44] Standing programs provide an alternative positioning option for children with overall decreased mobility and an opportunity to bear weight through the lower extremities for those who are unable to stand on their own.[7] Supine, prone, and vertical standers; standing devices with a sit-to-stand mechanism; and power wheelchairs with a sit-to-stand option can all fulfil this function.[7,45] A variety of devices in each of these categories are available. For example, Figures 22-14A through D feature a child in a Superstand Multi-Position Standing System Manufactured by Prime Engineering, and Figures 22-15A and B show a Leckey Squiggles Stander the same child used earlier. Both of these devices can be adjusted from a supine to a vertical or a prone position and are designed to "grow" with the child.[46,47]

Because children with CP who are unable to stand unsupported often demonstrate decreased head and trunk control, vertical positioning may not be optimal for them, and tilting the standing frame slightly anteriorly or posteriorly may address this problem.[48] However, the use of a prone or a supine stander would also decrease the amount of weight-bearing through the child's lower extremities, with the angle of inclination from vertical serving as an important variable. In addition, support provided by positioning harnesses, straps, pads, and trays may further decrease the lower extremity weight-bearing load. Finally, the child's muscle tone and energy and fatigue levels also affect the amount of weight-bearing while using a standing device. In fact, in a study of 19 nonambulatory children with bilateral spastic CP aged 3 to 19 years, Herman et al[48] reported the amount of weight-bearing ranging from 23% to 102% of the participants' body weight. Physical therapists should be aware of this issue and attempt to position children for static standing in alignments maximally approximating vertical,[45,48,49] but without jeopardizing their functional abilities required for effective interactions with their environment.

As illustrated by Table 22-5, not all perceived benefits of standing programs are supported by research.[45,50-56] Furthermore, even when evidence is available, information on the dose-response relationship and minimal and optimal dosing parameters for standing programs that address specific outcome variables is still lacking.[45] However, the authors of a comprehensive systematic review published in 2013 concluded that the available evidence was sufficient to recommend the inclusion of a standing component into a 24-hour postural management program for children with disabilities who demonstrate decreased upright activity or are unable to walk or stand on their own.[45] This systematic review yielded evidence-based recommendations, which, combined with additional clinical considerations derived from published literature and the authors' personal expertise, are presented in Table 22-5.[45,50-56]

It is important to discuss several points highlighted in Table 22-5. First, when considering a standing program for a child with CP, besides bone mineral density (BMD), muscle tone, and range of motion (ROM) benefits, hip stability also needs to be taken into consideration.[45] While straddled weight-bearing through the lower extremities has been shown to decrease migration percentage or prevent its increase in children with CP,[49] the amount of hip abduction needs to be graded based on the child's tolerance that may vary depending on the amount of hip adductor spasticity or tightness.[45] Because concurrently with bilateral hip abduction and hip and knee extension need to be emphasized, it may not be possible to achieve the recommended 60-degree angle of total hip abduction for positioning in a standing frame (see Figure 22-14D). Paleg et al[45] recommended using the angle of 30 to 60 degrees as a guide; however, based on clinical experience of the author of this chapter, even 30 degrees of total bilateral hip abduction may not be achievable in some cases, and a combination of hip adductor and hamstring spasticity may create a valgus moment at the knee joints, causing significant discomfort for the child.

The second point that needs to be discussed in relation to Table 22-5 is the significance of whole body vibration (WBV) that can be introduced in conjunction with lower extremity weight-bearing.[45,56] This intervention may help increase muscle strength and BMD, as well as lead to functional improvements in children with CP.[45,53,56,57] In addition, the use of dynamic standers that intermittently and reciprocally load the lower extremities to simulate walking in nonambulatory children with CP has been shown to provide greater BMD-related benefits to these children compared to passive standers.[54,58] These findings support adding vibration and dynamic loading components to static standing to enhance its positive effects.[45,53-58]

TABLE 22-5

CLINICAL RECOMMENDATIONS FOR USE OF STANDING PROGRAMS FOR CHILDREN WITH DISABILITIES, INCLUDING CEREBRAL PALSY, TO ACHIEVE THEIR PERCEIVED AND REPORTED BENEFITS

PERCEIVED AND REPORTED BENEFITS[51-56]	ICF-CY[35] CATEGORIES/ SUBCATEGORIES	RECOMMENDATIONS FOR ACHIEVING THE LISTED BENEFITS[45]	EVIDENCE-BASED[45]	EXPERT OPINION-BASED[45]
Decreased spasticity	Body functions/ muscle tone b735	Standing for 30 to 45 minutes daily. The effect will only be temporary; therefore, follow up with walking or dressing to maximize benefits.	X	X
Enhanced pressure relief	Body structures/ skin and related structures s8103 – s8105	Avoid shear force during transfers. Perform skin inspection for excessive pressure that may be caused by prolonged sitting and frequently alternate sitting with supported standing for short periods of time. The child's buttocks and undergarments should be dry and clean during standing.		X
Improved alertness and academic performance	Body functions/ mental functions b110 – b139	Standing for a minimum of 30 minutes daily. A powered self-propelled stander or a powered wheelchair with a standing positioning option may enhance social interaction.	X	X
Improved bowel and bladder[a] function	Body functions/ digestive s-m and urinary s-m[a] b510 – b539 b610 – b639[a]	Use prone standers for reflux management while avoiding excessive pressure on the abdomen. Daily standing for 30 to 60 minutes may reduce bowel care time and use of suppositories.	X	X
Improved cardiovascular and pulmonary function	Body functions/ cardiovascular and respiratory s-ms b410 – b429 b440 – b449	Progress standing while carefully monitoring vital signs in a medically fragile child and interrupt the activity if physiological stability is compromised.		X
Increased joint ROM	Body functions/ neuromusculo-skeletal and move-ment-related b710 – b729	Daily standing for 45 to 60 minutes, with 60 minutes being optimal for ankle, knee, and hip ROM. To improve hip abduction ROM, gradually increase hip abduction over time to achieve 60 degrees, if possible.	X	X
Increased muscle strength	Body functions/ muscle power b730	Standing for 10 minutes twice daily in combination with WBV; or in a stander with LE flexion/extension option for LE strengthening; or in a stander with a self-propelling capability for UE and trunk strengthening.	X	X
Improved hip stability	Body structures/ hip stability s75001	Daily standing for 60 minutes with hips abducted to a total of 60 degrees while emphasizing hip and knee extension to neutral and fully loading the tibia and the femur.	X	X

(continued)

TABLE 22-5 (CONTINUED)				
CLINICAL RECOMMENDATIONS FOR USE OF STANDING PROGRAMS FOR CHILDREN WITH DISABILITIES, INCLUDING CEREBRAL PALSY, TO ACHIEVE THEIR PERCEIVED AND REPORTED BENEFITS				
PERCEIVED AND REPORTED BENEFITS[51-56]	**ICF-CY[35] CATEGORIES/ SUBCATEGORIES**	**RECOMMENDATIONS FOR ACHIEVING THE LISTED BENEFITS[45]**	**EVIDENCE-BASED[45]**	**EXPERT OPINION-BASED[45]**
Increased bone strength/BMD	Body structures/ bone S7400, s75000, s75010, s75020, s76001 – s76004	Standing 5 times per week for 60 to 90 minutes, distributed between the home and school settings. Continue with standing programs regardless of school breaks.	X	X
Improved gross motor function, gait parameters and education-related processes.	Activities and par-ticipation/mobility and major life areas d410 – d489 d810 – d859	Combining standing with WBV 5 times per week for 60 minutes may have a positive effect on function. Standing should be combined with participation in play, educational, or another meaningful activity and social interaction.	X	X

Abbreviations: BMD, bone mineral density; ICF-CY, International Classification of Functioning, Disability and Health: Children and Youth Version; LE, lower extremity; ROM, range of motion; s-m, system; UE, upper extremity; WBV, whole body vibration.

a No evidence in support of improved bladder function was reported.[45]

Data from Paleg et al.[45]

Finally, many recommendations that target different standing benefits included in Table 22-5 overlap in regard to the duration and frequency of standing.[45] Therefore, when developing a standing program for a specific child, the therapist needs to consider the primary reasons for incorporating this intervention in this child's postural management program to maximize its benefits for his or her body structures and functions, activity, and participation. Paleg et al[45] acknowledged that ideal standing programs with clear dose-response relationship guidelines were yet to be defined, and that definitive benefits of such programs for cardiovascular and pulmonary and digestive systems, as well as for the child's level of alertness and social participation were yet to be established through sound research.

In published literature, there is a paucity of information related to the effects of standing positioning programs on quality of life of children and adults with disabilities. One descriptive survey study was conducted in Sweden by Nordström et al.[59] Respondents were 319 persons with disabilities aged 2 to 86 years, including 149 with congenital disorders, such as CP, genetic syndromes, spina bifida, and other conditions. In that study, the following survey statements that addressed the participants' well-being and quality of life were rated the highest:

1. *Standing up gives a pleasant feeling in my body.*
2. *Standing up makes me feel healthier.*
3. *Standing up increases my quality of life.*

It is important to note that only 20% of respondents answered the survey questions themselves, while 33% required assistance, and 47% of all questionnaires were completed by others on the respondents' behalf.[59] Quality of life is a subjective construct and may be assessed differently by the person with disability and his or caregiver.[60-62] However, the median ratings of the 3 statements were between 6 and 9 out of 10 for all respondents, regardless of who filled out the questionnaire.[59] This finding suggested that the use of standing devices benefited the study participants by improving their perceived well-being and quality of life.[59]

Use of Standing Mobility and Assistive Devices

As discussed in Chapter 19, independent stepping is a skill that develops after the infant is able to stand unsupported and maintain balance during postural sway. Typically, walking develops after independent stepping; however, many children with CP are unable to progress to walking and use stepping as a method of upright locomotion. Goals of standing mobility devices are to provide an alternative mobility option to these children, to allow them to explore their environment in a standing position, and to increase their overall activity and participation (see Table 22-4).

Treadmills and body weight support harnesses that are used for partial body weight support (PBWS) treadmill training were described in Chapter 15. Other standing mobility devices include walking aides, such as gait trainers or support walkers, that are used by children who are unable to walk unsupported.[7,63-65] A multitude of such devices exist, with some of them, such as the Kaye Walker, requiring children to use their upper extremities to maintain an upright standing posture.[64,65] When this is the case, it is more appropriate to refer to these walking aides as *assistive devices*. Other support walkers, such as the Rifton Pacer Gait Trainer, provide forearm support to encourage upper extremity weight-bearing, accommodate elbow and wrist contractures, if present, and promote forward trunk lean and head control during supported standing and walking.[66] Finally, hands-free mobility in a supported standing position is provided by such devices as the KidWalk Mobility System[67] (see Figure 22-10) and the Hart Walker.[64,68] Such accessories as trunk prompts, forearm supports, pelvic seats or slings, and anti-scissoring systems are most commonly used to provide adequate support and alignment to the child's body for walking in a gait trainer.[63]

Low et al[63] surveyed 513 pediatric physical therapists about their use of support walkers for children with disabilities. The respondents worked in a variety of pediatric settings located in suburban, rural, and mixed geographic areas. Results showed that support walkers were most frequently recommended for children with spastic CP, followed by children with other types of CP, developmental delay, spina bifida, and other disorders. The respondents ranked muscle weakness and poor motor control, balance, posture, and endurance as the top 5 impairments they considered when selecting a specific device. The most important physiologic considerations were the child's hip development, respiratory and cardiovascular function, and bone density. The parental preference for a specific device was ranked as the most important family consideration in the selection process, and overall, 3 most important considerations for the selection of a specific device were the results of the child's clinical assessment, the time he or she could spent in the support walker, and current research evidence. However, in regard to the latter, Low et al[63] commented that the lack of evidence related to the effects of support walkers on gait and mobility was likely an impeding factor for clinical decision making related to the selection of the best device for a specific child.

The main benefits of support walkers reported by Low et al[63] were improved postural control and increased mobility and participation. Other reported benefits included improved bowel function, learning to take independent steps in the device, improved steering and continued use of the device at the end of the study.[64,69] However, no significant improvements in bone density or walking speed were reported.[64,69] Overall, evidence related to the effects of support walkers on mobility, ADLs, and participation in children with disabilities is very limited and further research is highly needed to support clinical decision making in regard to the selection of appropriate devices and to the development of mobility programs for these children. Studies comparing different types of gait trainers would assist in guiding the selection process.

Children with CP who require less support for maintaining a standing posture than that provided by gait trainers or support walkers with positioning accessories frequently use assistive devices, including anterior and posterior walkers, forearm crutches, and canes. Gait parameters in children with bilateral CP when using anterior and posterior walkers were compared in several small studies.[70-72] According to Greiner et al[70] and Park et al,[71] posterior walkers were found to provide greater benefits than anterior walkers, including decreased hip, knee, and trunk flexion during gait leading to an improved postural alignment; decreased oxygen consumption and oxygen cost; decreased double stance time; and increased step length and single support time. Mixed results were obtained in regard to walking velocity.[70,71] Mattsson and Andersson[72] reported no significant differences in oxygen cost, walking speed, or perceived exertion when children with CP walked with anterior and posterior walkers. However, most participants preferred using a posterior walker, which was consistent with lower perceived exertion scores obtained while walking with the preferred device.[72]

Most recently, Lephart et al[73] reported on estimates of energy expenditure in a child with CP, GMFCS[38] level III, who used a posterior walker and forearm crutches at school. Higher energy expenditure was found with the use of the posterior walker as indicated by a 47% higher energy expenditure index (EEI) obtained for walking with this device compared to walking with crutches. The authors recommended using the EEI as a reasonable and time-efficient measure when making decisions related to the selection of an assistive device for a specific student.[73] A more detailed discussion of the EEI that can be also termed the *physiological cost index* was provided in Chapter 11.[74]

Yeung et al[75] described another benefit of crutch walking, in this case in comparison to unsupported ambulation in children with bilateral spastic CP, age range 8 to 15 years. While gait speed and cadence were found to decrease and stride time to increase significantly when walking with one crutch, and changed even further when walking with 2 crutches, reduced activity of erector spinae musculature was registered using electromyography (EMG) under both crutch walking conditions. In addition, less extension of the lower trunk and greater amounts of anterior pelvic tilt during gait were documented when using crutches. The ground reaction force from the crutches was found to counteract the increased amplitude of pelvic motion in the sagittal plane, which would have generated a strong extensor muscle contraction during unsupported gait. The authors hypothesized that the reduction in muscle work during crutch use as opposed to unsupported walking may decrease stress on the back structures in ambulatory individuals with CP. This, in turn, may potentially have a positive effect on pain and gait deterioration related to the formation of a hyperlordosis associated with hip flexor contractures and tightness common in this patient population.[75]

Adaptive Seating

A variety of seating positioning devices is used for children with disabilities in their home and school settings, such as simple adaptations to home furniture, adaptive bath and toilet seats, floor sitters, contoured seat inserts, and adjustable positioning chairs.[76-79] Benefits of adaptive seating devices, seating systems, and their components were reported by many authors and included improvements in sitting posture, postural control, spinal alignment,[77-80] hip position,[81] upper extremity function,[78,80] performance of self-care and play activities,[83] and child and family functioning.[76,84] As shown in Figure 22-13, proper selection of adaptive seating and its components may support the child's participation in school activities and enhance social interaction.

Several systematic reviews of literature examined the effects of adaptive seating devices in children with CP.[78,82,85,86] The effects of such devices on upper extremity function, including reaching and grasping, were the focus of one review published in 2006.[82] All studies included in that review were conducted with a small number of subjects and varied in their rigor and methodology. Based on the available evidence, Stavness[82] was able to conclude that in order to promote upper extremity function in children with CP, the adaptive seating device should contain the following components:

- A neutral or a slightly forward tilted seat (range of 0 to 15 degrees)
- A hip belt
- An abduction orthosis
- Footrests
- A cut-out tray

However, the author cautioned that evidence in support of these recommendations lacked rigor and needed to be confirmed by further experimental research.[82] These recommendations were nearly identical to the sitting position described by Myhr and von Wendt,[87] who reported significant improvements in head and trunk control, foot control, and arm and hand function in their study participants with mild to severe CP when they were placed in what the authors termed a *functional sitting position* that included the above listed components.

The inconclusive nature of published literature in regard to the seat inclination angle was discussed by authors of 3 systematic reviews.[78,82,85] Although Stavness[82] and McNamara and Casey[85] found evidence for the use of anteriorly tilted seats, they suggested that an individual approach be used to select the most appropriate seat incline for each child with CP as opposed to issuing a blanket recommendation. Chung et al[78] commented on the varied methodological rigor and lack of standardization in classifying motor involvement of participants among the studies included in their systematic review published in 2008. In spite of a number of reports listing significant effects of different adaptive seating devices or their features on sitting posture or postural control, upper extremity function, ADLs, and social skills in children with CP, these authors found insufficient evidence to recommend one device over another or to propose a link between improvements in sitting postural control and functional skills.[78]

Michael et al[86] conducted another systematic review of literature to address the use of tilt-in-space seats in nonambulatory individuals with neuromotor disorders, including children with CP.[86] A tilt-in-space feature is frequently recommended for this patient population as a means to relieve pressure, increase sitting endurance, and improve head and trunk alignment. The authors, again, reported that, because of the inconsistencies in interventions, outcome measures, and clinical presentations of participants included in different studies, it was difficult to recommend specific seat tilt angles for children with CP.[86]

Authors of several research reports published more recently described study participants using the GMFCS[38] and the Manual Ability Classification System (MACS),[88] which made a difference for the external validity of results.[79,83,84] The outcome measures were also clearly described, which ensured the possibility of replication of these studies in future research. It is interesting to note that both studies used repeated measures as opposed to a 2-group experimental design.[79,83,84]

Cheng et al[79] reported on a randomized crossover repeated measures design that examined the effects of 2 sitting conditions (with and without lower body stabilization) and 3 writing tool configurations on posture in 14 children with CP, MACS[88] levels I through III, aged 7 to 17 years, when they were involved in a writing task. The researchers used still photography, an electrogoniometer, and surface EMG to assess the participants' postural alignment, vertical wrist deviation, and muscle activity, respectively. Results demonstrated that stable positioning of the child's lower body using a height-adjustable wooden chair with a pelvic belt and lower leg straps led to significant improvement in trunk posture, while the use of a pencil with a grip height of 2.8 cm or a biaxial pencil had significant positive effects on the head, trunk, and pelvic alignment during writing. However, no significant difference in the wrist inclination angle, writing-related muscle activity, or writing speed was found under different conditions in this study.[79]

Another repeated measures design research protocol included 30 parents of children with CP, age range 2 to 7 years, GMFCS[38] levels III and IV.[83,84] This study examined the effects of 2 adaptive seating devices—a floor sitter and an adaptive toilet seat—on the lives of children with CP and their families. A parent-report instrument, the Family Impact of Assistive Technology Scale (FIATS),[89,90] was a primary outcome measure in this research.[83] The FIATS contains 8 subscales that are used to assess such constructs as the child's autonomy and contentment, caregiver relief and effort, activity performance, family and social interaction, and caregiver supervision and safety.[83] Other outcome measures administered to the parents in this research were the Canadian Occupational Performance Measure (COPM)[90] and a home activity log.[84]

Results showed significant improvements in the lives of the children and their families and in satisfaction with and performance of self-care and play activities when the adaptive seating devices were introduced and used during a 6-week intervention period.[83,84] These effects were significantly reduced in response to the withdrawal of adaptive seating intervention in the second baseline period of the study. These results highlighted the significant role adaptive equipment played in the lives of children with CP and their families and also underscored the importance of a thorough AT evaluation of every child so that devices appropriate for his or her individual goals and needs could be recommended.[83,84]

Wheelchair Seating Systems

Goals for the use of wheelchair seating fit the general goal list provided in Table 22-4. It is especially important to keep in mind that the individuals who use wheelchairs as their primary mobility method spend a significant amount of time in these devices, and for many, the wheelchair is also used as the primary adaptive seating positioning device in their home, at school, and at work (see Figure 22-8A). In a study of 31 children with spastic, dyskinetic, and ataxic CP, age range 8 to 18 years, all participants used their wheelchairs at school and at home for a total of 11 hours per day.[92] Lacoste et al[92] surveyed therapists and parents of these children and found postural instability in the wheelchair in 87% of the participants despite of 65% to 100% of them using such wheelchair components as the anterior thoracic support, ankle support, armrests, footrests, head rest, lateral thoracic and pelvic or thigh supports, medial knee supports, and pelvic belt. The instability was manifested by the child sliding forward in the seat, with posterior pelvic tilt, pelvic obliquity, and pelvic rotation also observed. This usually occurred within the first 30 minutes of being positioned in the wheelchair and negatively affected the participants' ADL performance and sitting tolerance.[92]

A faulty sitting posture maintained over a prolonged period of time may lead to the development of secondary impairments, including musculoskeletal deformities, pressure ulcers, pain, cardiovascular and pulmonary problems, and functional difficulties.[92-95] Therefore, the goal of minimizing the development of alterations in body structures and functions becomes especially important and should guide the selection of the best wheelchair seating design for a specific patient. Pressure mapping by means of a sensor mat can be used to evaluate and monitor sitting posture in this patient population and to inform the seating design-related decision making.[93,94] Lampe and Mitternacht[94] developed an examination and intervention algorithm for children with scoliosis, pelvic obliquity, and windswept deformity, which includes measuring pressure distribution in the wheelchair seat while looking for values that would exceed critical pressure thresholds and/or indicate lateral pressure load asymmetry. Depending on the pressure distribution findings, the seat may need to be remolded, with subsequent immediate and follow-up pressure mapping performed to assess the results.[94] Apatsidis et al[95] used pressure mapping technology to assess four different materials used for custom-molded seating and found that foams were more effective than gels in providing lower peak-interface pressures and better pressure distribution. More recently, McDonald et al[96] demonstrated the usefulness of a pressure mapping system and an accelerometer in measuring skin interface pressure and postural adjustments, respectively, in children seated in a wheelchair. The authors suggested that such technology can guide decision making in this area of practice.[96]

Because of the high prevalence of scoliosis in nonambulatory individuals with bilateral spastic CP,[97,98] special attention needs to be paid to the configuration of wheelchair seating components so that the goal of maintaining proper skeletal alignment to the greatest possible extent (see Table 22-4) can be addressed. In a study of 16 children with bilateral spastic CP and neuromuscular scoliosis, age range 6.5 to 20.8 years, Holmes et al[80] found that a 3-point force system that consisted of lateral pads applied to the child's body was significantly more effective in achieving static correction of scoliotic curvatures than the use of lateral pelvic supports alone or with the addition of lateral thoracic supports applied at the same height. The authors reported that, in order to provide adequate load distribution in a 3-point force system, lateral pads needed to be highly adjustable and move in a mediolateral direction, as well as about the vertical and antero-posterior axes.[80]

Because postural alignment can be linked to pulmonary function, wheelchair positioning may impact the child's respiration.[99,100] Barks et al[99,100] evaluated the effects of 6 configurations of four different seating components on pulmonary function in children with CP, age range 5 to 10 years. The 6 separate seating conditions included upper extremity supports, lateral trunk supports, anterior pelvic belt, 30-degree posterior tilt in space, all components together, and no support. Although the mean total airway resistance was found to be the highest under the tilt-in-space condition and the lowest when the participants were provided with lateral trunk supports or upper extremity supports, the results failed to reach significance, most likely because only 8 participants completed the study. Therefore, while these findings provided foundation for future research, they could not be translated into clinical practice.[99,100]

Wheelchair Mobility

Children with CP classified in GMFCS[38] levels II through V use wheeled mobility to a greater or lesser extent, depending on their functional abilities. While it may be needed only on occasion or for long distance travel for children classified in GMFCS level II, children functioning in levels III through V increasing rely on this mobility mode.[38] Typically, adaptive strollers (see Figure 22-9) or companion wheelchairs (see Figure 22-11A), as well as powered mobility bases (see Figure 22-11B) are the main options available for this patient population. Manual wheelchairs are not widely used because of the upper extremity involvement and associated increase in energy expenditure documented in individuals with CP.[10] However, children classified in GMFCS level III may self-propel a manual chair for short distances.[38] Adaptive strollers and companion wheelchairs (see Figures 22-9 and 22-11A) are used for dependent transportation and, therefore, they are equipped with smaller size wheels than manual wheelchairs.[10] A stroller-like mobility base in combination with an adaptive seating system is frequently preferred by parents of young children who are not psychologically ready to consider a wheelchair as a viable option for addressing their child's mobility needs. Powered chairs, scooters, and similar devices are used for independent mobility.[10]

Selection of a mobility base for a child with CP is guided by a number of important factors. Besides the level of gross motor function and manual ability, motor planning, and perceptual-motor skills, independent wheelchair mobility requires sufficient cognitive abilities, such as memory, judgment, problem solving, and impulse control.[8] Vision and visual perception also play a role in being able to achieve independent wheeled mobility.[8] In addition, it is important to understand that, even when the child's level of physical and cognitive functioning allows him or her to become independent in propelling a manual or a power chair, the lack of motivation for or interest in doing so may lead to ordering a companion wheelchair as the only viable mobility option. That is why a trial session or a series of sessions should be incorporated in the wheelchair evaluation process.[7,10]

When powered mobility is considered, a child-size wheelchair and appropriate supports need to be provided to ensure adequate stability and comfort that would allow the child to operate this device to the best of his or her ability.[10] Additionally, the availability of several different wheelchair control options during a trial session may be crucial for success. Other important considerations in regard to power mobility include the availability of adequate space, accessibility of the child's home and other buildings where the wheelchair will be used, as well as its transportation and funding options.[10] Finally, training in the child's natural environments is required to master accurate and safe driving and to learn appropriate maneuvering skills.[7,10]

Evidence for Use of Powered Mobility

Independent powered mobility is widely used by individuals with disabilities across the life span, with advances in technology offering a multitude of options for the power base, seating, and control design, and for the overall maneuverability of the device.[10,101] Frank and Souza[101] reported on the results of a descriptive cross-sectional study of 544 individuals who received powered indoor and outdoor mobility devices through a regional organization funded by the UK National Health Service. Eighty-one percent of the wheelchair recipients had neurologic or neuromuscular conditions, of which 18.9% had CP and 16.4% had multiple sclerosis. Thirty-one percent (169 individuals), most of whom had CP or muscular dystrophy, received adaptive seating and 258 participants (90 with CP) obtained a tilt-in-space feature. Complex control systems provided to 52 wheelchair recipients included tray mounted controls; head, chin, or foot controls; light touch controls; and other features, such as nonstandard switches and control knobs, computer interfaces, and others.

Eleven participants with CP received tray-mounted controls and 6 used adaptive seating, tilt-in-space, and complex control technology.[101]

Types of Powered Mobility Devices

O'Shea and Bonfiglio[10] listed 3 main types of powered mobility devices: conventional designs that integrate the seat and the chassis, modular designs that consist of a separate seat and chassis, and 3- or 4-wheeled scooters. In addition, Huang and Galloway[9] introduced another powered mobility option—a modified toy car that can be used by a young child at home, at school, and in the clinic. While regular power chairs are large, heavy, and difficult to transport without an accessible van and require sufficient space for use in the child's home,[102] modified toy cars may provide a mobility option that overcomes all of these problems.[9] Huang and Galloway[9] suggested that the ride-on power toys can help children with mobility limitations to achieve the level of mobility enjoyed by children who develop typically, with a potential of also addressing their postural and motor limitations through enhanced seating, drive, and steering designs.

Postural Considerations and Developmental and Functional Outcomes

Berry et al[102] emphasized the importance of the opportunity to learn and develop self-esteem, which a powered mobility option may provide to a child with disability and which may outweigh the importance of symmetry and precise body alignment when seated in a wheelchair. Maintaining proper skeletal alignment to the greatest extent possible may assist in preventing the development of secondary impairments. However, a reasonable compromise may need to be achieved to address the child's motivation for learning to use a powered mobility device. For example, Huhn et al[103] reported on a case when offsetting the headrest position to accommodate the child's inability to sustain a midline head alignment decreased her frustration with the wheelchair driving task.

Liu et al[104] proposed a different solution to the postural asymmetry problem in children with bilateral CP by offering a bimanual interface for driving a power wheelchair, with gliding controls mounted on both sides of the mobility device as opposed to a unilateral joystick. In that study, all participants, including those with and without CP, achieved slower driving speeds when operating the bimanual interface compared to a joystick control. However, participants with CP displayed significantly greater frontal postural symmetry when using both hands to operate the wheelchair compared to the use of a unilateral joystick. It is common for a child with bilateral spastic CP to have more difficulty with object manipulation using the non-dominant hand as it is usually less functional. The authors reported that the bimanual interface encouraged simultaneous use of both hands, which helped decrease postural asymmetry in their study participants.[104]

For a very long time, powered mobility was the last possible option considered for children with movement disorders in order not to compromise their motor development and motivation for independent functioning.[10] Another reason for postponing powered mobility until adolescence was the notion that it was too difficult for young children to learn.[10] It is important to know that current research contradicts both of these assumptions.[105-112] Jones et al[105] conducted a pilot randomized controlled trial (RCT) with 28 children with severe motor impairments, including CP and other neurologic, neuromuscular, and genetic disorders, age range 14 to 30 months, who were receiving early intervention services. They were randomly assigned to 2 groups that did not differ in their baseline developmental and functional abilities, and children in the experimental group received a power wheelchair and power mobility training. Results showed significantly greater improvements in the experimental group compared to the control group on several outcome measures, including receptive communication, functional mobility skills, and caregiver assistance required for mobility and self-care.[105]

This and other studies demonstrated that infants as young as 7 to 14 months of age, as well as toddlers, preschoolers, and young children with CP and other movement disorders were able to learn powered mobility and use it to their advantage.[105-113] Positive outcomes, besides those reported by Jones et al,[105] included cognitive and language development exceeding that appropriate for the child's chronological age,[106] increased time spent on independent mobility throughout the day,[107] and increased functional independence and COPM[90] scores.[108] Furthermore, Guerette et al[109] reported improved parent-perceived positive social skills, such as understanding and getting along with others, expressing self in a positive way, and accepting rules; increased quantity of mobility activities in which children engaged during indoor play; and quality of interactive play outdoors. Other benefits described in research literature included increased parental acceptance of powered mobility from the beginning to the end of the study,[108] decreased parental stress, increased satisfaction with their child's play and social skills, and increased family social interactions when the wheelchair was delivered.[110]

Livingstone and Field[111] conducted a systematic review of literature that examined mobility outcomes related to the use of powered mobility in children with movement disorders from infancy through adolescence. This review revealed a significant amount of evidence in support of this intervention as a viable option for this patient population that can have positive effects on independent mobility; global development; and such ICF[34,35] categories as body functions, activities, and participation. However, most of that evidence came from descriptive research, with a very limited number of experimental studies published to date. The authors concluded that this area of study was "in its infancy."[p 954] Rigorous experimental research is required to determine the best strategies for power mobility training in children of different ages.[111]

Training Considerations

Powered mobility offers children and adults with severe physical disabilities an opportunity to experience independence denied to them by their bodies. However, learning to drive a power chair may be difficult and often requires hand-over-hand prompting and prolonged training.[114] In addition, not every child is capable of becoming proficient in this method of mobility because of physical or cognitive issues and because of the features of the device itself, driving as an activity, environmental factors, or a combination of some or all of the above.[115] The available body of literature suggests that early training may be advantageous for this patient population.[105-113]

Ragonesi et al[112,113] described a case of a 3-year-old child with bilateral spastic CP with an athetoid component who started using a powered mobility device in a preschool setting to enhance his mobility and socialization. While the child showed improvement in both of these areas when using the powered mobility device, his mobility and social interaction levels remained lower than observed in his peers.[112] However, participation in a short-term adult-directed "mobility and socialization" training program that included one-on-one instruction, supplemental group guidance, and environmental modifications appeared to have a positive impact on his social interactions, which exceeded that of "a comparison peer" developing typically.[113] Although after the training was over, the child reverted to a lower level of interaction, the authors were able to conclude that the training program they had developed was feasible for implementation in a preschool classroom setting. In addition, they suggested that a longer training program with a peer-mediated component may facilitate more independent peer interactions in young children, especially if powered mobility is introduced earlier than at the age of 3, to encourage the simultaneous development of mobility and socialization as is typically observed in infants and toddlers without disabilities.[113]

A subsequently published case report of an 11-month-old infant at risk for CP did show that, short-term, daily training that involved active exploration on the part of the child, combined with active participation of his parents in prompting assisted and independent mobility, led to the emergence of the initial ability to move the power chair.[107] This finding confirmed the need for further research to explore the benefits of early powered mobility training and the development of socialization in conjunction with mobility in infants and toddlers with movement disorders.[107]

Technological advances in the area of powered mobility have led to the development of new and exciting training options for children and adults not only with physical, but also cognitive impairments.[114,116-119] Several examples of training devices that incorporate advanced technology are provided, and their main features are listed in Table 22-6. Although tested on a small number of patients, the use of such technology has a potential to transform powered mobility training in persons with CP and other disabilities, which may have a significant positive impact on their independence and quality of life.[114,116-120]

An objective evaluation of powered mobility training needs, learning and outcomes is important for a number of reasons. It can help identify the wheelchair user's place on the learning continuum, assess his or her progress in training, and modify intervention and the environment in which

TABLE 22-6

EXAMPLES OF TECHNOLOGICALLY ADVANCED POWERED MOBILITY TRAINING DEVICES, THEIR DESCRIPTION, MAIN FEATURES, AND CAPABILITIES

DEVICE	DESCRIPTION/MAIN FEATURES	CAPABILITIES
Smart Wheelchair[116,117]	An augmentative mobility aid in the form of a platform that houses the user's own wheelchair. This device contains the following: • Collision sensors • Line follower sensor • Computerized control system	Stops automatically to avoid a collision Follows a path outlined on the floor As the navigation skills develop, training can be progressed to driving on collision sensors without the line follower function and eventually, to driving without collision sensors.
RObot-Assisted Learning for Young drivers (ROLY)[114]	A robotic wheelchair trainer, which is a prototype pediatric smart wheelchair that includes the following: • Webcam-based line follower function • Force-feedback joystick • Laser pointer	Self-steers following a line on the floor Provides tactile guidance to the child's hand placed on the joystick only when a steering error is detected Following the laser pointer light shone along the path outlined on the floor helps reduce the user's steering errors. As training progresses, the firmness of force feedback is faded to give the user more control while still limiting large errors.
Collaborative Wheelchair Assistant (CWA)[118,119]	A robotic wheelchair system with a regular power base and a joystick used to control the movement speed. Special features include the following: • Odometer and global positioning sensors • Joystick output routed through a laptop computer that processes the input received from the sensors and calculates the appropriate output in the form of path guidance	Does not move without the user's input The user controls the start and stop functions and movement velocity. The guidance system moves the device following a predesigned path, from the point of origin to the destination point, so no steering is required from the user. Operation modes include the following: • Free mode: no guidance provided • Guided mode: path guidance and steering back to the path when a deviation is detected • Flexible mode: allows for deviations from the preset path to avoid unforeseen obstacles or other interference while the user still feels the path guidance input

(continued)

training is provided.[121] Recently, Nilsson and Durkin[121] developed the Assessment of Learning Powered mobility (ALP) instrument, which can be applied with people across the life span, regardless of their developmental, functional, and cognitive level, with results independent from the person's age, culture, and previous experience, as well as from the environment in which he or she functions. The ALP Version 2.0 examines the occupational performance of the powered mobility user based on 5 categories: Level of Attention, Activity and Movement, Understanding the Tool Use, Expression and Emotions, and Interaction and Communication. This instrument covers the entire learning continuum and includes 8 phases of learning distributed over 3 stages. Phases 1 through 3 (*novice, curious novice,* and *beginner*) correspond to the *introvert stage* characterized by the exploration of functions; phases 4 and 5 (*advanced beginner* and *sophisticated beginner*) belong to the *transition stage* when function sequencing is explored; and phases 6 through 8 (*competent, proficient,* and *expert*) reflect the *extrovert stage* that involves exploring one's performance. The latter requires problem solving and judgment on the part of the user, which are exercised in relation to goal-directed powered mobility. The psychometric properties of the ALP instrument have not been examined, thus further research is required to establish its reliability and responsiveness to change.[121]

TABLE 22-6 (CONTINUED)

EXAMPLES OF TECHNOLOGICALLY ADVANCED POWERED MOBILITY TRAINING DEVICES, THEIR DESCRIPTION, MAIN FEATURES, AND CAPABILITIES

DEVICE	DESCRIPTION/MAIN FEATURES	CAPABILITIES
Intelligent wheelchair[120]	A powered wheelchair system equipped with the following: • Two computers • Planar laser as the main sensor • Odometer sensors • Wireless Ethernet card • User interface in the form of a touchscreen input device with visual display capability The navigation system includes the following: • The model builder that creates a model of the environment based on information received from the sensors and tracks the wheelchair location • The local planner that calculates the travel path that combines reaching the destination with avoiding unfavorable situations and obstacles	Minimizes the need for user input (after the user selects the final or intermediate destination point, the wheelchair safely travels to that location) Avoids obstacles detected by the laser sensor while navigating through unknown and dynamic environments Travel is not restricted by preset conditions. Training focuses on selection of appropriate intermediate destinations.

ACCESSIBLE HOME, ASSISTIVE TECHNOLOGY EQUIPMENT NEEDS, AND COSTS

The availability of physical space, presence or absence of indoor barriers, and appropriate environmental modifications can have a positive or a negative effect on the child's use of AT devices both at home and at school.[31-33] While the Americans with Disabilities Act[11] includes provisions that address the accessibility and usability of public service facilities (see Table 22-2), the burden of making a home accessible for a loved one with disability usually falls on that person's family.[122,123] Home modifications and adaptations required to make it accessible for a child with disability may be quite costly. In fact, in one study, median costs of home modifications were found to be the highest compared to the costs of all other items included in equipment purchases made by families of children with CP, GMFCS[38] levels III through V.[123]

The physical environment of a home can be defined as "the concrete physical dimensions of the home,"[(p 197)] including the outdoor environment in the home's immediate vicinity.[122] It is not uncommon for certain areas of a home to be more accessible to the child with mobility limitations than others. In a study of 82 children with CP, spina bifida, and muscular disease, Prellwitz and Skär[122] found the bathroom and the home entrance to be modified most frequently (in 32.5% and 26.8% of all cases, respectively), while only 3.2% of living rooms and 7.3% of hallways had modifications. It

is important to note that 33% of the children in this study reported problems with accessing different areas in their homes and 51% required assistance in the kitchen, which was not surprising, considering that kitchen modifications were completed only in 10% of the cases. In addition, stairs, thresholds, and inadequate ramps were reported to limit the participants' ability to access their home yard in 26% of the cases, while 22% required assistance to access the street immediately outside their homes because of similar problems, as well as because of such obstacles as heavy elevator doors, curbs, and ice or snow by the home entrance. The study participants expressed their wishes for further home modifications that included equipping all doors with automatic openers, installing a lift for their access to the first floor, lowering kitchen cabinets, and adding a gym area with a pool. For some of the children in this research, physical environmental barriers translated to decreased socialization with friends, which underscored the importance of home modifications as a factor that would support peer relationships in children with disabilities.[122]

Besides the costs of home modifications, families raising children with disabilities incur significant additional expenses related to AT purchases, as well as expenses that cover transportation, medical equipment, and home care.[123] At the same time, the child's and family's equipment needs are not always met. In one study, 46% of surveyed parents reported unmet needs in additional equipment, while 16% of those who did not purchase recommended equipment indicated having problems with referrals or insurance coverage.[19] Results of another survey study conducted with 29 families of children with

CP revealed the highest reported needs for positioning and mobility items, as well as for adapted toys and leisure equipment. In addition, greater equipment needs correlated with greater amounts of assistance the children needed in order to participate in recreation and play activities.[123] These findings highlighted the issue of financial burden faced by the families of children with complex disabilities, with funds often diverted from other areas of the family functioning.[123] This and other issues that impact the life-span care required by children and adults with CP will be discussed in the next chapter.

Complete video-based activities for Chapter 22 (see Activity Sets 2, 4, and 5 on the book website).

References

1. Long TM, Perry DF. Pediatric physical therapists' perceptions of their training in assistive technology. *Phys Ther.* 2008;88(5):629-639.
2. Pub L No 105-394, Assistive Technology Act of 1998, 112 Stat 3627-3662.
3. Assistive technology categories. *RehabTool.* http://www.rehabtool.com/at.html#categories. Updated March 22, 2004. Accessed January 14, 2015.
4. Categories of assistive technology. *Kids Together, Inc.* http://www.kidstogether.org/assistivetechnology/categoriesofAT.htm. Updated June 29, 2010. Accessed January 14, 2015.
5. RESNA Technical Assistance Project. *Assistive Technology and the Individualized Education Program (updated).* Washington, DC: RESNA Press, 1992.
6. Jones M, Puddefoot T. Assistive technology: augmentative, communication, and other technologies. In: Effgen SK. *Meeting the Physical Therapy Needs of Children.* 2nd ed. Philadelphia, PA: F.A. Davis Company; 2013:621-633.
7. Jones M, Puddefoot T. Assistive technology: positioning and mobility. In: Effgen SK. *Meeting the Physical Therapy Needs of Children.* 2nd ed. Philadelphia, PA: F.A. Davis Company; 2013:599-619.
8. Angelo J. *Assistive Technology.* Philadelphia, PA: F.A. Davis Company; 1997.
9. Huang HH, Galloway JC. Modified ride-on toy cars for early power mobility: a technical report. *Pediatr Phys Ther.* 2012;24(2):149-154.
10. O'Shea RK, Bonfiglio BS. Assistive technology. In: Campbell SK, Palisano RJ, Orlin MN, eds. *Physical Therapy for Children.* 4th ed. St. Louis, MO: Saunders; 2012: Chapter E4.
11. Pub L 101-336, Americans with Disabilities Act, 104 Stat 327-378.
12. Pub L 108-364, Assistive Technology Act of 2004, 188 Stat 1707-1737.
13. Pub L No 108-446, Individuals with Disabilities Education Improvement Act of 2004, 118 Stat 2647-2808.
14. Bull M, Agran P, Laraque D, et al. American Academy of Pediatrics. Committee on Injury and Poison Prevention. Transporting children with special health care needs. *Pediatrics.* 1999;104(4):988-992.
15. American Academy of Pediatrics: Committee on Injury and Poison Prevention. School bus transportation of children with special health care needs. *Pediatrics.* 2001;108(2):516-518.
16. O'Neil J, Yonkman J, Talty J, Bull MJ. Transporting children with special health care needs: comparing recommendations and practice. *Pediatrics.* 2009;124(2):596-603.
17. American Physical Therapy Association. *Guide to Physical Therapist Practice 3.0.* http://guidetoptpractice.apta.org/. Published August 2014. Accessed January 15, 2015.
18. American Physical Therapy Association. *A Normative Model of Physical Therapist Professional Education: Version 2004.* Alexandria, VA: American Physical Therapy Association; 2004.
19. Peredo DE, Davis BE, Norvell DC, Kelly PC. Medical equipment use in children with disabilities: a descriptive survey. *J Pediatr Rehabil Med.* 2010;3(4):259-267.
20. McLaughlin MR. Speech and language delay in children. *Am Fam Physician.* 2011;83(10):1183-1188.
21. Pennington L, Goldbart J, Marshall J. Speech and language therapy to improve the communication skills of children with cerebral palsy. *Cochrane Database Syst Rev.* 2004;(2):CD003466.
22. Light J, McNaughton D. Supporting the communication, language, and literacy development of children with complex communication needs: state of the science and future research priorities. *Assist Technol.* 2011;24(1):34-44.
23. Dodge NN. Cerebral palsy: medical aspects. *Pediatr Clin N Am.* 2008;55(5):1189-1207.
24. Aisen ML, Kerkovich D, Mast J, et al. Cerebral palsy: clinical care and neurological rehabilitation. *Lancet Neurol.* 2011;10(9):844-852.
25. Steultjens EM, Dekker J, Bouter LM, van de Nes JC, Lambregts BL, van den Ende CH. Occupational therapy for children with cerebral palsy: a systematic review. *Clin Rehabil.* 2004;18(1):1-14.
26. Morrell DS, Pearson M, Sauser DD. Progressive bone and joint abnormalities of the spine and lower extremities in cerebral palsy. *Radiographics.* 2002;22(2):257-268.
27. Fairhurst C. Cerebral palsy: the whys and hows. *Arch Dis Child Educ Pract Ed.* 2012;97(4):122-131.
28. Aneja S. Evaluation of a child with cerebral palsy. *Indian J Pediatr.* 2004;71(7):627-634.
29. Deon LL, Gaebler-Spira D. Assessment and treatment of movement disorders in children with cerebral palsy. *Orthop Clin N Am.* 2010;41(4):507-517.
30. Wright M, Wallman L. Cerebral palsy. In: Campbell SK, Palisano RJ, Orlin MN, eds. *Physical Therapy for Children.* 4th ed. St. Louis, MO: Saunders; 2012:577-627.
31. Huang IC, Sugden D, Beveridge S. Assistive devices and cerebral palsy: factors influencing the use of assistive devices at home by children with cerebral palsy. *Child Care Health Dev.* 2008;35(1):130-139.
32. Huang IC, Sugden D, Beveridge S. Assistive devices and cerebral palsy: factors influencing the use of assistive devices at school by children with cerebral palsy. *Child Care Health Dev.* 2009;35(5):698-708.
33. Huang IC, Sugden D, Beveridge S. Children's perceptions of their use of assistive devices in home and school settings. *Disabil Rehabil.* 2009;4(2):95-105.
34. World Health Organization. *International Classification of Functioning, Disability and Health.* Geneva, Switzerland: World Health Organization; 2001.
35. World Health Organization. *International Classification of Functioning, Disability and Health: Children and Youth Version.* Geneva, Switzerland: World Health Organization; 2007.
36. McEwen I. Assistive positioning as a control parameter of social-communicative interactions between students with profound multiple disabilities and classroom staff. *Phys Ther.* 1992;72(9):634-644.
37. Littleton SR, Heriza CB, Mullens PA, Moerchen VA, Bjornson K. Effects of positioning on respiratory measures in individuals with cerebral palsy and severe scoliosis. *Pediatr Phys Ther.* 2011;23(2):159-169.
38. Palisano RJ, Rosenbaum PL, Walter SD, Russell DJ, Wood EP, Galuppi BE. Development and reliability of a system to classify gross motor function in children with cerebral palsy. *Dev Med Child Neurol.* 1997;39(4):214-223.
39. Hill CM, Parker RC, Allen P, Paul A, Padoa KA. Sleep quality and respiratory function in children with severe cerebral palsy using night-time postural equipment: a pilot study. *Acta Paediatr.* 2009;98(11):1809-1814.
40. Porter D, Michael S, Kirkwood C. Is there a relationship between preferred posture and positioning in early life and the direction of subsequent asymmetrical postural deformity in non ambulant people with cerebral palsy? *Child Care Health Dev.* 2008;34(5):635-641.

41. Pountney TE, Mandy A, Green E, Gard PR. Hip subluxation and dislocation in cerebral palsy – a prospective study on the effectiveness of postural management programmes. *Physiother Res Int.* 2009;14(2):116-127.

42. Gericke T. Postural management for children with cerebral palsy: a consensus statement. *Dev Med Child Neurol.* 2006;48(4):244.

43. Maher CA, Evans KA, Sprod JA, Bostock SM. Factors influencing postural management for children with cerebral palsy in the special school setting. *Disabil Rehabil.* 2011;33(2):146-158.

44. Caulton JM, Ward KA, Alsop CW, Dunn G, Adams JE, Mughal MZ. A randomised controlled trial of standing programme on bone mineral density in non-ambulant children with cerebral palsy. *Arch Dis Child.* 2004;89(2):131-135.

45. Paleg GS, Smith BA, Glickman LB. Systematic review and evidence-based clinical recommendations for dosing of pediatric supported standing programs. *Pediatr Phys Ther.* 2013;25(3):232-247.

46. Superstand Pediatric Standing System. *Prime Engineering.* http://www.primeengineering.com/product_pages/superstand_youth.html. Published 2014. Accessed January 25, 2015.

47. Squiggles Stander. *Leckey.* http://www.leckey.com/products/squiggles-stander/. Accessed January 25, 2015.

48. Herman D, May R, Vogel L, Johnson J, Henderson RC. Quantifying weight-bearing by children with cerebral palsy while in passive standers. *Pediatr Phys Ther.* 2007;19(4):283-287.

49. Martinsson C, Himmelmann K. Effect of weight-bearing in abduction and extension on hip stability in children with cerebral palsy. *Pediatr Phys Ther.* 2011;23(2):150–157.

50. VanSant AF. Clinical guidelines and systematic reviews. *Pediatr Phys Ther.* 2013;25(3):231.

51. Taylor K. Factors affecting prescription and implementation of standing-frame programs by school-based physical therapists for children with impaired mobility. *Pediatr Phys Ther.* 2009;21(3):282-288.

52. Pin TW. Effectiveness of static weight-bearing exercises in children with cerebral palsy. *Pediatr Phys Ther.* 2007;19(1):62-73.

53. Glickman LB, Geigle PR, Paleg GS. A systematic review of supported standing programs. *J Pediatr Rehabil Med.* 2010;3(3):197-213.

54. Gudjonsdottir B, Stemmons Mercer V. Effects of a dynamic versus a static prone stander on bone mineral density and behavior in four children with cerebral palsy. *Pediatr Phys Ther.* 2002;14(1):38-46.

55. Salem Y, Lovelace-Chandler V, Zabel RJ, McMillan AG. Effects of prolonged standing on gait in children with spastic cerebral palsy. *Phys Occup Ther Pediatr.* 2010;30(1):54-65.

56. Stark C, Nikopoulou-Smyrni P, Stabrey A, Semler O, Schoenau E. Effect of a new physiotherapy concept on bone mineral density, muscle force and gross motor function in children with bilateral cerebral palsy. *J Musculoskelet Neuronal Interact.* 2010;10(2):151-158.

57. Ward K, Alsop C, Caulton J, Rubin C, Adams J, Mughal Z. Low magnitude mechanical loading is osteogenic in children with disabling conditions. *J Bone Miner Res.* 2004;19(3):360-369.

58. Damcott M, Blochlinger S, Foulds R. Effects of passive versus dynamic loading interventions on bone health in children who are nonambulatory. *Pediatr Phys Ther.* 2013;25(3):248-255.

59. Nordström B, Näslund A, Eriksson M, Nyberg L, Ekenberg L. The impact of supported standing on well-being and quality of life. *Physiother Can.* 2013;65(4):344-352.

60. Colver A. Quality of life and participation. *Dev Med Child Neurol.* 2009;51(8):656-659.

61. Zecovic B, Renwick R. Quality of life for children and adolescents with developmental disabilities: review of conceptual and methodological issues relevant to public policy. *Disabil Soc.* 2003;18:19-34.

62. Bjornson KF, McLaughlin JF. The measurement of health-related quality of life (HRQL) in children with cerebral palsy. *Eur J Neurol.* 2001;8(suppl 5):183-193.

63. Low SA, McCoy SW, Beling J, Adams J. Pediatric physical therapists' use of support walkers for children with disabilities: a nationwide survey. *Pediatr Phys Ther.* 2011;23(4):381-389.

64. Eisenberg S, Zuk L, Carmeli E, Katz-Leurer M. Contribution of stepping while standing to function and secondary conditions among children with cerebral palsy. *Pediatr Phys Ther.* 2009;21(1):79-85.

65. Walkers – posture control. *Kaye® Products, Inc.* http://kayeproducts.com/category/walkers-posture-control/. Accessed February 8, 2015.

66. Rifton Pacer gait trainers. *Rifton.* http://www.rifton.com/products/gait-trainers/pacer-gait-trainers?tab=accessories. Accessed February 8, 2015.

67. KidWalk Dynamic Mobility System. *Prime Engineering.* http://www.primeengineering.com/product_pages/kidwalk.html. Accessed February 8, 2015.

68. Hart Walker information. *MK II Hart Walker.* http://www.david-hartclinic.co.uk/. Accessed February 25, 2016.

69. Wright FV, Jutai JW. Evaluation of the longer-term use of the David Hart Walker Orthosis by children with cerebral palsy: a 3-year-prospective evaluation. *Disabil Rehabil Assist Technol.* 2006;1(3):155-166.

70. Greiner BM, Czerniecki JM, Deitz JC. Gait parameters of children with spastic diplegia: a comparison of effects of posterior and anterior walkers. *Arch Phys Med Rehabil.* 1993;74(4):381-384.

71. Park ES, Park CL, Kim JY. Comparison of anterior and posterior walkers with respect to gait parameters and energy expenditure of children with spastic diplegic cerebral palsy. *Yonsei Med J.* 2001;42:180-184.

72. Mattsson E, Andersson C. Oxygen cost, walking speed, and perceived exertion in children with cerebral palsy when walking with anterior and posterior walkers. *Dev Med Child Neurol.* 1997;39(1):671-676.

73. Lephart K, Utsey C, Wild DL, Fisher SR. Estimating energy expenditure for different assistive devices in the school setting. *Pediatr Phys Ther.* 2014;26(3):354-359.

74. Bratteby Tollerz LU, Olsson RM, Forslund AH, Norrlin SE. Reliability of energy cost calculations in children with cerebral palsy, cystic fibrosis and healthy controls. *Acta Paediatr.* 2011;100(12):1615-1620.

75. Yeung EH, Chow DH, Su IY. Kinematic and electromyographic studies on unaided, unilateral and bilateral crutch walking in adolescents with spastic diplegia. *Prosthet Orthot Int.* 2012;36(1):63-70.

76. Ryan SE, Sawatzky B, Campbell KA, et al. Functional outcomes associated with adaptive seating interventions in children and youth with wheeled mobility needs. *Arch Phys Med Rehabil.* 2014;95(5):825-831.

77. Washington K, Deitz JC, White OR, Schwartz IS. The effects of a contoured foam seat on postural alignment and upper-extremity function in infants with neuromotor impairments. *Phys Ther.* 2002;82(11):1064-1076.

78. Chung J, Evans J, Lee C, et al. Effectiveness of adaptive seating on sitting posture and postural control in children with cerebral palsy. *Pediatr Phys Ther.* 2008;20(4):303-317.

79. Cheng HY, Lien YJ, Yu YC, et al. The effect of lower body stabilization and different writing tools on writing biomechanics in children with cerebral palsy. *Res Dev Disabil.* 2013;34(4):1152-1159.

80. Holmes KJ, Michael SM, Thorpe SL, Solomonidis SE. Management of scoliosis with special seating for the non-ambulant spastic cerebral palsy population – a biomechanical study. *Clin Biomech.* 2003;18(6):480-487.

81. McDonald RL, Surtees R. Longitudinal study evaluating a seating system using a sacral pad and kneeblock for children with cerebral palsy. *Disabil Rehabil.* 2007;29(13):1041-1047.

82. Stavness C. The effect of positioning for children with cerebral palsy on upper extremity function: a review of evidence. *Phys Occup Ther Pediatr.* 2006;26(3):39-53.

83. Ryan SE, Campbell KA, Rigby PJ, Fishbein-Germon B, Hubley D, Chan B. The impact of adaptive seating devices on the lives of young children with cerebral palsy and their families. *Arch Phys Med Rehabil.* 2009;90(1):27-33.

84. Rigby PJ, Ryan SE, Campbell KA. Effect of adaptive seating devices on the activity performance of children with cerebral palsy. *Arch Phys Med Rehabil.* 2009;90(8):1389-1395.

85. McNamara L, Casey J. Seat inclinations affect the function of children with cerebral palsy: a review of the effects of different seat inclines. *Disabil Rehabil Assist Technol.* 2007;2(6):309-318.

86. Michael SM, Porter D, Pountney TE. Tilted seat position for non-ambulant individuals with neurological and neuromuscular impairment: a systematic review. *Clin Rehabil.* 2007;21(12):1063-1074.

87. Myhr U, von Wendt L. Improvement of functional sitting position for children with cerebral palsy. *Dev Med Child Neurol.* 1991;33(3):246-256.

88. Eliasson AC, Krumlinde-Sundholm L, Rösblad B, et al. The Manual Ability Classification System (MACS) for children with cerebral palsy: scale development and evidence of validity and reliability. *Dev Med Child Neurol.* 2006;48(7):549-554.

89. Ryan SE, Campbell KA, Rigby P, Germon B, Chan B, Hubley D. Development of the new Family Impact of Assistive Technology Scale. *Int J Rehabil Res.* 2006;29(3):195-200.

90. Ryan SE, Campbell KA, Rigby PJ. Reliability of the Family Impact of Assistive Technology Scale. *Arch Phys Med Rehabil.* 2007;88(11):1436-1440.

91. Law M, Baptiste S, Carswell A, McColl M, Polatajko H, Pollock N. *Canadian Occupational Performance Measure (COPM) Manual.* 4th ed. Toronto, Ontario: CAOT; 2005.

92. Lacoste M, Therrien M, Prince F. Stability of children with cerebral palsy in their wheelchair seating: perceptions of parents and therapists. *Disabil Rehabil Assist Technol.* 2009;4(3):143-150.

93. Fradet L, Tiernan J, McGrath M, Murray E, Braatz F, Wolf SI. The use of pressure mapping for seating posture characterization in children with cerebral palsy. *Disabil Rehabil Assist Technol.* 2011;6(1):47-56.

94. Lampe R, Mitternacht J. Correction versus bedding: wheelchair pressure distribution measurements in children with cerebral palsy. *J Child Orthop.* 2010;4(4):291-300.

95. Apatsidis DP, Solomonidis SE, Michael SM. Pressure distribution at the seating interface of custom-molded wheelchair seats: effect of various materials. *Arch Phys Med Rehabil.* 2002;83(8):1151-1156.

96. McDonald RL, Wilson GN, Molloy A, Franck LS. Feasibility of three electronic instruments in studying the benefits of adaptive seating. *Disabil Rehabil Assist Technol.* 2011;6(6):483-490.

97. Gudjonsdottir B, Stemmons Mercer V. Hip and spine in children with cerebral palsy: musculoskeletal development and clinical implications. *Pediatr Phys Ther.* 1997;9(4):179-185.

98. Morrell DS, Pearson M, Sauser DD. Progressive bone and joint abnormalities of the spine and lower extremities in cerebral palsy. *Radiographics.* 2002;22(2):257-268.

99. Barks L, Shaw P. Wheelchair positioning and breathing in children with cerebral palsy: study methods and lessons learned. *Rehabil Nurs.* 2011;36(4):146-152.

100. Barks L, Davenport P. Wheelchair components and pulmonary function in children with cerebral palsy. *Assist Technol.* 2012;24(2):78-86.

101. Frank AO, Souza LH. Recipients of electric-powered indoor/outdoor wheelchairs provided by a National Health Service: a cross-sectional study. *Arch Phys Med Rehabil.* 2013;94(12):2403-2409.

102. Berry ET, McLaurin SE, Sparling JW. Parent/caregiver perspectives on the use of power wheelchairs. *Pediatr Phys Ther.* 1996;8(4):146-150.

103. Huhn K, Guarrera-Bowlby P, Deutsch JE. The clinical decision-making process of prescribing power mobility for a child with cerebral palsy. *Pediatr Phys Ther.* 2007;19(3):254-260.

104. Liu WY, Chen FJ, Lin YH, Kuo CH, Lien HY, Yu YJ. Postural alignment in children with bilateral spastic cerebral palsy using a bimanual interface for powered wheelchair control. *J Rehabil Med.* 2014;46(1):39-44.

105. Jones MA, McEwen IR, Neas BR. Effects of power wheelchairs on the development and function of young children with severe motor impairments. *Pediatr Phys Ther.* 2012;24(2):131-140.

106. Lynch A, Ryu JC, Agrawal S, Galloway J. Power mobility training for a 7-month-old infant with spina bifida. *Pediatr Phys Ther.* 2009;21(4):362-368.

107. Ragonesi CB, Galloway JC. Short-term, early intensive power mobility training: case report of an infant at risk for cerebral palsy. *Pediatr Phys Ther.* 2012;24(2):141-148.

108. Bottos M, Bolcati C, Sciuto L, Ruggeri C, Feliciangeli A. Powered wheelchairs and independence in young children with tetraplegia. *Dev Med Child Neurol.* 2001;43(11):769-777.

109. Guerette P, Furumasu J, Tefft D. The positive effects of early powered mobility on children's psychosocial and play skills. *Assist Technol.* 2013;25(1):39-48.

110. Tefft D, Guerette P, Furumasu J. The impact of early powered mobility on parental stress, negative emotions, and family social interactions. *Phys Occup Ther Pediatr.* 2011;31(1):4-15.

111. Livingstone R, Field D. Systematic review of power mobility outcomes for infants, children and adolescents with mobility limitations. *Clin Rehabil.* 2014;28(10):954-964.

112. Ragonesi CB, Chen X, Agrawal S, Galloway JC. Power mobility and socialization in preschool: a case study of a child with cerebral palsy. *Pediatr Phys Ther.* 2010;22(3):322-329.

113. Ragonesi CB, Chen X, Agrawal S, Galloway JC. Power mobility and socialization in preschool: follow-up case study of a child with cerebral palsy. *Pediatr Phys Ther.* 2011;23(4):399-406.

114. Marchal-Crespo L, Furumasu J, Reinkensmeyer DJ. A robotic wheelchair trainer: design overview and a feasibility study. *J Neuroeng Rehabil.* 2010;7:40. doi:10.1186/1743-0003-7-40.

115. Field D. Powered mobility: a literature review illustrating the importance of a multifaceted approach. *Assist Technol.* 1999;11(1):20-33.

116. Nisbet P, Craig J, Odor P, Aitken S. "Smart" wheelchairs for mobility training. *Technol Disabil.* 1996;5:49-62.

117. McGarry S, Moir L, Girdler S. The Smart Wheelchair: is it an appropriate mobility training tool for children with physical disabilities? *Disabil Rehabil.* 2012;7(5):372-380.

118. Zeng Q, Teo CL, Rebsamen B, Burdet E. A collaborative wheelchair system. *IEEE Trans Neural Syst Rehabil Eng.* 2008;16(2):161-170.

119. Zeng Q, Burdet E, Leong C. Evaluation of a collaborative wheelchair system in cerebral palsy and traumatic brain injury users. *Neurorehabil Neural Repair.* 2009;23(5):494-504.

120. Montesano L, Diaz M, Bhaskar S, Minguez J. Towards an intelligent wheelchair system for users with cerebral palsy. *IEEE Trans Neural Syst Rehabil Eng.* 2010;18(2):193-202.

121. Nilsson L, Durkin J. assessment of learning powered mobility use – applying grounded theory to occupational performance. *J Rehabil Res Dev.* 2014;51(6):963-974.

122. Prellwitz M, Skär L. How children with restricted mobility perceive the accessibility and usability of their home environment. *Occup Ther Int.* 2006;13(4):193-206.

123. Bourke-Taylor H, Cotter C, Stephan R. Young children with cerebral palsy: families self-reported equipment needs and out-of-pocket expenditure. *Child Care Health Dev.* 2013;40(5):654-662.

Please see videos on the accompanying website at

www.healio.com/books/videosrahlin

Section V

QUESTIONS TO PONDER

1. How should physical therapists approach the selection of an optimal orthotic design for a specific child with insufficient evidence available to guide their decision-making process?

2. What are some of the reasons for decreased compliance with wearing lower extremity, upper extremity, and trunk orthoses in children with CP?

3. What strategies can be used to translate into clinical practice the research evidence related to the benefits of tuning ankle-foot orthoses/footwear combinations (AFOFCs) for children with CP and other movement disorders?

4. How should physical therapists address caregiver and school teacher education in appropriate positioning and position changes to achieve best possible outcomes for children with CP and other developmental disabilities?

5. Can the use of adaptive positioning devices be detrimental to the development of independent sitting postural control in infants and young children with and at risk for CP? Please explain your answer.

6. What are some of the challenges in determining the optimal seating positioning parameters for children with CP?

7. What are the barriers to a wider use of powered mobility among non-ambulatory children with disabilities?

SUGGESTED QUESTIONS FOR FUTURE RESEARCH

1. What is the optimal orthotic design for management of each of the gait types described by Rodda et al[1] and Rodda and Graham[2] in children with bilateral and unilateral CP?

2. What are the effects of the use of lower extremity orthoses of a specific design on activity, participation, and quality of life in children and adults with CP?

3. What is the optimal wear time for orthoses of a specific design to achieve best desired outcomes?

4. Is there a relationship between the use of positioning devices and quality of life in children and adults with CP?

5. What are the effects of ambulation with support walkers on daily activity, participation, and quality of life in children with CP and other movement disorders who are unable to stand and walk unsupported?

6. What are the effects of ambulation with different assistive devices on daily activity, participation, and quality of life in children and adults with CP classified in GMFCS[3] levels II and III?

7. What is the optimal number of position changes a non-ambulatory child with CP should undergo throughout the day to achieve best outcomes in the areas of body structures and functions, activity, participation, and quality of life?

8. What are the effects of early powered mobility on daily activity and social participation in young children with CP and other movement disorders?

9. What are the best strategies for power mobility training in children with movement disorders of different ages who do or do not have an intellectual disability that would significantly increase their independence and improve their quality of life?

References

1. Rodda JM, Graham HK, Carson L, Galea MP, Wolfe R. Sagittal gait patterns in spastic diplegia. *J Bone Joint Surg Br.* 2004; 86-B:251-258.
2. Rodda J, Graham HK. Classification of gait patterns in spastic hemiplegia and spastic diplegia: a basis for a management algorithm. *Eur J Neurol.* 2001;8(suppl 5):98-108.
3. Palisano RJ, Rosenbaum PL, Walter SD, Russell DJ, Wood EP, Galuppi BE. Development and reliability of a system to classify gross motor function in children with cerebral palsy. *Dev Med Child Neurol.* 1997;39(4):214-223.

Transition to Adulthood

23

Cerebral Palsy as a Life Span Condition

Cerebral palsy needs to be considered as a life-long condition,
requiring a life-span perspective in order to better organize optimal care.

Sander R. Hilberink, Marij E. Roebroeck, Wilbert Nieuwstraten et al[1]

Cerebral palsy (CP) is a condition that is perceived by many to be a disorder of childhood.[1] Pediatric physical therapists frequently see children with CP in a variety of settings. In fact, this is one of the most common diagnoses for which children are referred to rehabilitation professionals and the most common physical disability in children.[1,2] However, it is important to consider the increase in the life span of persons with many childhood-onset disabilities, including CP, observed in the past several decades, with a greater number of children surviving to adult age and requiring adult health care services.[3-6] This chapter will focus on such life-span issues as life expectancy; continuum and cost of care; availability and utilization of health care and rehabilitation services; caregiver burden; family needs for support and services; as well as the significance of sibling relationships, friendships, and social participation in the lives of people with CP.

SURVIVAL STATISTICS AND PROGNOSIS

According to the estimate provided by United Cerebral Palsy, approximately 764,000 children and adults in the United States have this condition.[4] Results of a large study conducted in California showed a trend for increased survival of individuals with CP through year 2010, with mortality in children declining at the rate of 2.5%, and in tube-fed adolescents and adults at 0.9% per year.[5] At the same time, no improvement was observed in the survival of people with CP aged 15 to 59 years who used oral feedings and people who were older than age 60 years, and, compared to general population, between 1983 and 2010, their mortality rates actually increased.[6] Brooks et al[6] provided probability estimates for survival of a 4-year-old child with CP to age 10, 15, 20, 25, and 30 years, as well as estimates of additional years of life expectancy for adolescents and adults, which factored in the individual's level of physical functioning and the feeding method. According to these estimates, a 4-year-old child with CP who is able to roll over but does not walk without assistance and is fed orally by others would have a 77% chance to live to age 30 years, and life expectancy for the same person at 30 years of age regardless of gender would be additional 19 + 1.2 years. For a specific individual with CP, the actual life expectancy may be higher or lower, depending on a variety of factors, but these data can be used as a good starting point for further development of the survival prognosis.[6] Because CP has effectively become a life-span condition,[1,3] such prognosis may play a very important role in life care planning that will be discussed next.[7]

Rahlin M. *Physical Therapy for Children With Cerebral Palsy:*
An Evidence-Based Approach (pp 399-416).
© 2016 SLACK Incorporated.

CONTINUUM AND COST OF CARE AND PLANNING CARE FOR LIFE

People with lifelong disabilities, such as CP, constitute a unique patient population that receives well-established habilitation services during childhood years in a variety of settings,[3] frequently starting with the Neonatal Intensive Care Units and proceeding to Early Intervention, schools, and outpatient clinics (see Chapter 12). Involvement of multiple body systems plays an important role in the complexity of care children and adolescents with CP require (see Chapter 4 for a detailed discussion of numerous issues related to all components of the International Classification of Functioning, Disability and Health [ICF][8,9] in this patient population). Secondary impairments that develop over time contribute to increased activity limitations and participation restrictions in individuals with childhood-onset disabilities.[3] Overall, physical and cognitive functional levels, along with environmental and personal factors, determine the prognosis for ambulation and mobility, employment, independent living, and social integration of people with CP (see Chapter 5). Therefore, addressing physical symptoms and cognitive deficits through early intervention and ensuring a subsequent continuation of services into adulthood may make a difference in these people's lives.[10]

Children with CP are seen by a number of pediatric specialists, including physicians, surgeons, rehabilitation professionals, and education specialists (see Chapter 6 and Table 6-1). However, in teenage years and young adulthood, the same patients and their families are suddenly faced with a shortage of health care providers who have the knowledge and expertise in treating adults with childhood-onset disabilities, including CP, myelomeningocele, genetic disorders, and others.[3] Many clinicians who work with adults in outpatient settings frequently lack sufficient understanding and knowledge of these conditions, their associated impairments and comorbidities, and appropriate ways they can be addressed through intervention. At the same time, pediatric therapists may have difficulty "letting go" of their aged pediatric clients and fail to facilitate their transition to adult-centered services, which often stems from the therapists' knowledge of and experience with challenges in finding providers who would be able to competently address their patients' unique needs. All of these issues result in decreased access to medical care and rehabilitation, complicate transitioning to adult health care and preventive services, and add to physical, medical, emotional, and financial challenges faced by individuals with life-long disabilities and their families.[3]

Orlin et al[3] who examined the role of the physical therapist in the continuum of care for people with childhood-onset disabilities recommended several strategies to improve the current situation. Among others, such strategies included opening niche physical therapy practices and modifying current adult-oriented practices to serve this patient population; ensuring physical accessibility of medical, rehabilitation, and fitness facilities to accommodate unique needs of such clients; and improving physical therapists' knowledge and competence in this area of practice through continuing education and inclusion of appropriate content into entry-level Doctor of Physical Therapy curricula.[3] Pediatric physical therapists have a unique opportunity to provide their insight, expertise, and anticipatory guidance to children and adolescents with life-long conditions and their families to address their future needs related to the development of secondary impairments, and to promote fitness and wellness across their life span.[3,11]

Because CP is a life-long condition that affects multiple body systems, it carries significant economic costs associated with the use of long-term services and supportive care.[12] Table 23-1 contains life-time costs data reported based on research conducted in 4 world countries.[12-15] While 3 of them considered direct and indirect economic costs,[12-14] the South Korean study focused on direct medical costs only.[15] Direct medical costs reported by all authors included medical visits, prescription drugs, hospitalizations, rehabilitation services, assistive devices, and long-term care costs.[12-15] As for direct nonmedical costs, estimates for the United States and China included vehicle and home modifications,[12,13] estimates for China and Denmark listed expenses associates with special education and developmental services,[13,14] and Danish estimates included additional social costs.[14] Finally, indirect costs listed for the United States, China, and Denmark referred to the loss of productivity related to premature mortality and increased morbidity that affected the ability to work, the work type, and the amount of work individuals with CP were able to perform.[12-14] In addition, estimates of indirect costs in China included a projected economic loss sustained by the patients' families.[13]

Interestingly, indirect costs were shown to be responsible for 81% of total lifetime costs of CP in the United States and 93% in China, in comparison to direct medical costs that constituted only 10% and 3%, respectively.[12,13] It is, therefore, appropriate to ask whether increasing direct medical costs by improving access to care[13] and providing optimally intensive therapeutic intervention to children and adults with CP (see Chapter 18) may be a solution for reducing the loss of productivity and decreasing the long-term economic burden of this condition.

Another possible solution was proposed in South Australia, which, in addition to other available means of disability support, would provide an annual "no-fault" life pension of AUD $10,000 to $50,000 for children included in the CP register.[16] According to the proposal, the exact pension amount would be dependent upon the level of disability and would be paid to the families that agree to wave civil litigation related to the diagnosis of CP.[16] As discussed in Chapter 3, despite a common perception that this diagnosis is linked to a perinatal brain injury, the complexity of interacting prenatal, perinatal, and postnatal factors in the infant's history frequently makes determining the causation and timing of the brain insult impossible.[17,18] Furthermore, in the majority of cases, neural injury leading to CP occurs in the prenatal period,[19]

TABLE 23-1				
ESTIMATED LIFETIME COSTS ASSOCIATED WITH THE DIAGNOSIS OF CEREBRAL PALSY IN SEVERAL WORLD COUNTRIES				
COUNTRY (PUBLICATION YEAR)	AUTHORS	SOURCE OF DATA	LIFETIME ESTIMATES (2003 US DOLLARS)	
			Average Total per Person	*For All Persons With CP*
United States (2004)	CDC[12]	Multiple national surveys and reports conducted/produced between years 1987 and 2000	921,000	11.5 billion
China (2008)	Wang et al[13]	Interviews with caregivers of 319 patients with CP conducted in 2004 in hospital located in 5 cities	67,044	2 to 4 billion
Denmark (2009)	Kruse et al[14]	Analysis of 2367 cases of individuals with CP from the Danish CP Register born between 1930 and 2000 and alive in 2000	969,500 (men)[a] 901,800 (women)[a]	—
South Korea (2011)	Park et al[15]	Information from the health insurance review and assessment service for years 2004-2008	26,383[b]	—
Abbreviations: CDC, Centers for Disease Control and Prevention; CP, cerebral palsy; US, United States.				
[a] Recalculated from euros based on 2003 exchange rate.				
[b] Includes only direct medical costs attributable to CP.				

which makes CP also largely impossible to prevent.[16,20] Nevertheless, litigation based on the assumption of a perinatal cause of CP is still a common practice in many countries.[16] According to MacLennan,[16] the proposed "no-fault" pension that would cost Australia AUD $93,000,000 annually can be funded by savings from medico-legal costs associated with CP litigation settlements.[16]

The issues of multisystem involvement, ongoing need for services, complexity of care, and costs associated with CP as a life-long condition bring about the necessity of life care planning.[7,21] Such planning is used as an effective method of case management in a variety of settings, as well as in litigation.[21] A life care plan is designed to address the person's needs for independence, appropriate health care services, equipment, and supplies that would support his or her quality of life, and to estimate related costs.[7,21] This document is based on a comprehensive assessment of a specific client and his or her needs, published evidence, and standards of practice.[21] Ideally, writing such a plan should be a collaborative process involving multiple professionals, and the plan should include specific goals related to prevention and rehabilitation that can be periodically updated. As rehabilitation professionals, physical therapists may be participating in the development of life care plans.[21] Major components of a life care plan are listed in Table 23-2.[7,21]

UTILIZATION OF HEALTH CARE SERVICES

Children With Developmental Disabilities, Including Cerebral Palsy

Health care utilization needs among children with developmental disabilities, including the use of the emergency room (ER), hospital, and physician services, was examined by a number of authors.[22-26] In a study based on the 2001 National Survey of Children with Special Health Care Needs (CSHCN), such needs and associated experiences were found to correlate with the degree of functional deficits exhibited by these children.[22] Additionally, children with greater functional limitations and their families were more likely to encounter delays in care, problems with referrals, unmet needs in services and their coordination, and overall dissatisfaction with services. Furthermore, caregivers of children with severe limitations encountered provider-related problems twice more frequently than those whose children did not have functional limitations. Such problems included inadequate listening skills, insufficient amount of time spent during visits, and failure to provide necessary information to and collaborate with the child's parents. The same group

TABLE 23-2

AREAS AND MAJOR COMPONENTS OF A LIFE CARE PLAN

AREA OF PLANNING	MAJOR COMPONENTS
Comprehensive assessment	Extent of physical, cognitive, or emotional deficits Sequelae of identified deficits Expected outcomes
Prognostic estimate	Prognosis for improvement in multiple functional areas Life expectancy
Long-term needs estimate	Adaptive equipment, assistive devices, and orthotics Education Fitness and wellness Home modifications, furniture, and supplies Home or institutional care Medical, surgical, and rehabilitative services Medications Supplies Transportation Vocational training
Cost estimate	For all components of long-term needs Total costs

Compiled from Katz and Johnson[7] and Johnson and Weed.[21]

of caregivers reported greater health insurance and financial difficulties, greater home care needs of their children, and greater impact of their child's disability on their ability to work, compared to caregivers of CSHCN without functional limitations.[22]

A subsequent National Survey of CSHCN conducted in 2005-2006 served as a foundation for another study that investigated the problem of higher utilization of ER visits among children with developmental disabilities compared to children developing typically.[23] Specifically, the relationship between the frequency of ER visits and the child's access to a patient-centered medical home (PCMH) was examined.[23] The PCMH is a concept related to the Affordable Care Act (ACA) that is currently being implemented in the United States.[27] Major attributes of a PCMH are summarized in Table 23-3.[27] Results showed that children whose caregivers reported 1 to 3 or more ER visits per year were significantly less likely than those who did not visit ER to receive ongoing, well-coordinated, comprehensive care through a medical home.[23] In addition, families of children who visited the ER 3 or more times within 1 year were significantly less likely to encounter a physician who would be a good listener, would be sensitive to the family's customs and values, and would partner with the parents in their child's care. The authors suggested that parental support provided by improvements in care coordination offered by a PCMH may help decrease ER

visits, which, in turn, would have a potential to lower health care costs and increase satisfaction with services.[23]

Because of their multisystem medical and surgical needs, children with CP, especially those with bilateral involvement, frequently require hospitalizations.[24] Burns et al[25] reported an increasing national trend in hospitalization rates among young children with complex medical conditions, with the relative complexity of hospitalized patients also increasing. However, there was no significant increase in hospitalizations observed among children with CP as a single diagnostic category.[25] Another study showed that the proportion of hospitalizations of children with neurologic disorders to all pediatric hospitalizations in the United States remained relatively stable over time.[26] Between 1997 and 2006, the proportion of such admissions to non-children's hospitals decreased by 0.5%, while the proportion of pediatric hospital admissions increased by 1.8%.[26]

Children With Complex Health Care Needs and Dependence on Technology

Hospitalized children with CP may be transferred to other health care facilities or referred to a home health care agency when discharged.[24] When such a discharge occurs, it is vital for the interdisciplinary team to address the child's ongoing needs by developing, implementing, and coordinating an

	TABLE 23-3

MAJOR ATTRIBUTES OF A PATIENT-CENTERED MEDICAL HOME AND THEIR CHARACTERISTICS[27]

ATTRIBUTE	CHARACTERISTICS
Comprehensive care	Accountable for addressing the majority of patients' needs in prevention and wellness and acute and chronic care
	Includes a large and diverse team of providers
	Use of virtual teams is possible
Patient-centered practice	Provides relationship-based primary health care that addresses the needs of the whole person
	Based on understanding of and respect for the patients' and their families' unique needs, values, preferences, and culture
	Supports patient/family autonomy in health care management and organization
	Views patients and families as partners in sharing information and planning care
Coordinated care	Care coordination across the health care system, covering specialty and hospital care, home health, community services, and supports
	Covers transitions between care sites
	Clear and open communication among all parties
Accessible services	Waiting times commensurate to the patient's level of need
	Improved hours of operation
	24/7 electronic and telephone access for team members
	Available alternative methods of communication
	Support for patient preferences in regard to the method of access to care
Quality and safety	Quality improvement through ongoing use of evidence-based medicine and clinical decision-support instruments
	Ongoing performance assessment and improvement
	Ongoing assessment of patient satisfaction and responsiveness to feedback
	Ongoing population health management practices
	Public sharing of obtained quality and safety data and improvement initiatives

appropriate plan of care.[28] This is especially true for those children who have complex health care needs and who are dependent on technology for maintenance of health and prevention of repeated hospitalizations. Such technology may include tracheostomy tubes, mechanical ventilation, oxygen, enteral feeding devices, intravenous catheters, and other similar equipment. In the past, when technology was needed, children remained hospitalized, but currently, they are frequently discharged home to continue complex medical interventions. Elias et al[28] published a 2-part report with clinical considerations for transitioning children and youth with complex conditions from the hospital to a home care environment and for caring for them at home. These considerations are briefly discussed next.

To transition a child to home care upon his or her discharge from the hospital, first a thorough evaluation of the child, the family, their home, and community is necessary in order to do the following:

- Determine whether caring for this child at home is feasible

- Identify the family needs, available resources, and preferences
- Assess the home environment for safety, structure, and accessibility
- Confirm the availability of appropriate community resources and supports[28]

The next step is to find a medical home for the child and the family, with the primary care physician willing and able to offer them the needed attention, support, knowledge, and care. A detailed plan is then developed, with a comprehensive list of medications, services, equipment, and supplies that will be needed upon discharge. Additional important steps are training the caregiver; arranging for home care, including nursing and developmental or educational services; identifying home care agencies that will provide equipment and supplies; and verifying insurance coverage, availability of additional coverage or benefits, and the family ability to finance the uncovered costs.[28]

To ensure success of home care upon the child's discharge from the hospital, basic medical and developmental issues need to be identified, with all involved parties having an understanding of the etiology of the child's condition so that appropriate care can be provided.[28] Assessment of adequacy of current services needs to be performed while keeping in mind the family strengths, problems, and ongoing changes, and while maintaining open communication between the family and service providers. Coordination of care through the child's medical home needs to be carefully arranged to ensure the appropriate frequency of follow-up visits with the primary care physician and specialists, and timely completion of all paperwork associated with obtaining necessary medications, equipment, and supplies. All necessary changes and financial issues need to be addressed so that all requirements are met in a safe, family-friendly, and effective manner.[28]

Youth and Adults With Cerebral Palsy

Adolescents, young adults, and adults with CP continue demonstrating complex health care issues that require access to specialty and hospital care.[3,29,30] However, the insufficient number of medical professionals who work in adult-oriented practices and have a good knowledge and understanding of the deficits and needs of aging populations of people with childhood-onset disabilities results in inadequate accessibility of medical office environments, problems with patient transfers and use of equipment, and ineffective communication.[3] Physical therapists with knowledge of this patient population have a unique opportunity to serve as a resource for primary care medical and dental professionals and advocate for changes to adult-oriented practices. Such changes may include restructuring office environments to allow for wheelchair access, installing electronic examination tables to support safe an efficient transfers, and allowing additional time for communication with patients who use augmentative communication devices.[3]

A unique issue that requires the attention of the medical community is the growth in the number of adults with childhood-onset conditions admitted to pediatric hospitals.[31,32] In 2002, Goodman et al[31] reported an increase in admission rates of patients aged 18 to 64 years to Child Health Corporation of America member hospitals between years 1994 and 1999. Among those patients, CP was 1 of the 4 most commonly encountered diagnoses.[31] A subsequent report for years 1999-2008 published in 2011 indicated that the number of adults hospitalized in pediatric hospitals continued to increase.[32] While the number of discharges and patient-days, as well as the amount of hospital charges for hospitalized children with CP, decreased significantly over time, there was a significant increase in these figures, with the exception of the incurred charges, reported for patients with CP aged 18 to 21 years and older. Furthermore, the documented growth in the overall number of patients between 18 and 21 years of age was disproportionate to the increase in the number of children hospitalized in pediatric hospitals.[32]

In their 2011 paper, Goodman et al[32] questioned whether pediatric hospitals should specialize in treatment of children or whether they should be admitting all patients with diseases originating in childhood. These hospitals are not designed to care for adult patients and lack adult-oriented ancillary supports. However, they are uniquely equipped to provide care for patients with childhood-onset disorders, including CP, with its heterogeneous presentation and complexity, which is less compatible with adult-oriented hospital environments. This issue needs to be resolved to ensure a successful transition to adulthood for individuals with childhood-onset disabilities.[32] Transition issues will be further discussed in Chapter 24.

Besides the need for inpatient care, adults with CP are in frequent need for community-based services and personal assistance with activities of daily living (ADLs).[33,34] Litigation brought in 1995 against Tommy Olmstead, the Georgia State Commissioner of Human Resources, on behalf of 2 women with mental illness and developmental disabilities, was seeking to allow them to be discharged from a psychiatric hospital in order to move into a community setting with available appropriate supports.[35] This litigation eventually led to a 1999 Supreme Court Olmstead Decision that established these women's right to obtain care in the most appropriate integrated setting.[36] This ruling directed an expansion of home- and community-based services (HCBS), which supported living accommodations for persons with disabilities in the least restrictive environments. Public entities must offer the HCBS if the following conditions are met:

- These services are appropriate.
- The person is not opposed to using community-based care.
- Such community services can be provided with reasonable accommodations.[36]

This ruling had a significant effect on state Medicaid programs and led to a number of initiatives to expand access to Medicaid-covered HCBS.[37]

Houtrow et al[33] examined the impact of one such initiative implemented in California on health care costs in a population of children and adults with CP. This Medicaid-funded In-Home Supportive Services (IHSS) initiative allows parents, relatives, and non-relative assistants to be paid for personal assistance services they provide to people with disabilities. Houtrow et al[33] analyzed data obtained in 2005 for 3193 individuals with CP younger than 65 years of age to determine whether allowing a family member to provide IHSS would increase health care costs related to additional ER visits and hospitalizations. Although the overall monthly health care expenditures for persons with CP were found to be approximately $1000 higher than for other recipients of IHSS, having parents as opposed to non-family members serve as IHSS providers made no difference in health care service utilization. These results supported paying patients' parents for the provision of personal assistance. If expanded nationally, such a service delivery model may greatly benefit people with disabilities and their families by maximizing their health, activity, and community participation and by addressing the current shortage in personal assistance workers across the United States.[33] In addition, this IHSS model may provide a helpful solution to financial problems and difficulty maintaining employment frequently faced by parents caring for their children with disabilities during childhood, adolescence, and young adulthood.[22,33]

UTILIZATION OF REHABILITATION SERVICES

Rehabilitation services typically include physical and occupational therapies and speech-language pathology (SLP) services.[38,39] Audiology, vision therapy, psychology, social work, and other services may be also included. When these therapies are provided to children with developmental disabilities with a goal to attain functional skills they never achieved before, such services are termed *habilitation* or *habilitative*.[40] The terms *rehabilitation* and *habilitation* services are frequently used interchangeably in published literature, with the term *rehabilitation* used most frequently.

Children with CP usually receive habilitation services in a variety of settings.[3] Begnoche et al[41] described the utilization of physical and occupational therapies and community recreation services among 399 toddlers and young children with CP whose parents were surveyed in the United States and Canada. Twenty-eight percent to 33% of the study participants received therapy services in several settings, with 94% and 86% receiving physical and occupational therapies, respectively, and 64% enrolled in community recreation programs. Therapy focus and amount differed depending on the Gross Motor Function Classification System (GMFCS)[42] levels, with activity emphasized for children classified in levels I through III and self-care for children in level I, compared to level V. The authors hypothesized that these differences might be associated with children with greater functional abilities having a greater potential for achieving independence, and with the related wishes of their parents. Children classified in level III were found to have the greatest number of minutes of physical therapy, and those in level V had the greatest amount of occupational therapy. Overall, children classified in GMFCS[42] level V received a greater number of physical therapy and occupational therapy minutes than those in level I, with children in the United States reported to receive more therapy than in Canada.[41]

While the demand for services increases with the severity of disability,[22] the amount and types of therapies children with CP receive varies among different settings (see Chapter 12) and, based on such factors as the governing laws,[43,44] the GMFCS[42] level, age, and insurance coverage.[45] For example, Bailes and Succop[45] reported that, in their outpatient hospital setting, children classified in GMFCS[42] level III received the greatest number of physical therapy units on average, and children functioning at levels II through IV had significantly greater amounts of therapy than those

functioning at level V. In addition, children aged 5 years and younger received more therapy than 12 to 18 year olds, and having private insurance coverage was associated with receiving a greater average number of physical therapy units than being covered by public insurance.[45]

Another study examined rehabilitation service utilization among 91 children of school age and 167 adolescents with CP living in Canada, including physical and occupational therapies, speech-language pathology, and psychological services.[38] Results showed that 84.6% of children and only 68.1% of adolescents were receiving at least one type of therapy, with school-based physical and occupational therapies being most common. A greater range of school-based service utilization was documented among children with greater motor deficits, activity limitations, and lower IQ, and an overall paucity of psychological services was reported, possibly leading to unmet social-emotional and behavioral needs. A decrease in direct services received in adolescence compared to childhood years was highlighted by this research.[38]

Moll and Cott[39] examined the same and other related issues in their qualitative study. These researchers interviewed 9 adults with CP who reported that, during their childhood, therapy services they received several times per week were aimed at normalizing their movement and learning to walk. However, although they made progress, their bodies continued looking different compared to children developing typically. The study participants expressed their regret about such significant emphasis placed on the normalization of their physical function, which, in their view, underestimated the importance of their psychological and social development and greatly contributed to the difficulties they encountered later in life. This approach seemed to overshadow the necessity of maintaining independence in ADLs in adolescence and adulthood and did not address learning to handle their declining functional skills, fatigue, and other problems associated with aging. At the same time, their access to rehabilitation services sharply decreased, which further contributed to their functional decline.[39]

The problems of decreased access to and utilization of rehabilitation services leading to unmet needs among young adults and adults with CP were reported in research literature that originated in a number of countries around the world.[1,46-48] Negative changes in physical function and unmet rehabilitation needs despite the presence of such symptoms as fatigue, pain, and joint deformities were reported in adults with CP.[1,46,47] Elrod and DeJong[48] highlighted medical insurance-related disparities in utilization of physical rehabilitation services by people with disabilities in the United States. Among 502 adults with CP, multiple sclerosis, and spinal cord injury, 53% reported unmet needs in this area, with those with Medicare and private insurance as opposed to Medicaid coverage, and those in worse health and with lower household income being less likely to participate in rehabilitation.[48]

Moll and Cott[39] suggested that the current system of service delivery and its organization may be an important factor that contributes to the difficulties experienced by adults

	TABLE 23-4

POSSIBLE CARE COORDINATOR ROLES AND RELATED TASKS OF A PHYSICAL THERAPIST WORKING WITH INDIVIDUALS WITH CHILDHOOD-ONSET DISABILITIES

CARE COORDINATION ROLE	TASKS
Primary care coordinator	Assume leadership in the care coordinator role, whole or partial
	Provide family-centered services
	Explore the availability of and refer the family to community resources
	Develop relationships with the family and providers
	Facilitate team work
	Develop a plan of care
	In states with direct access to PT, assume the role of a medical home provider to do the following:
	• Make appropriate referrals for medical and social services
	• Reduce barriers to obtaining necessary services
	• In outpatient settings, schedule regular well visits
	Serve as a service coordinator in EI in states where primary service providers typically assume this role

(continued)

with disabilities as they age, and that the lack of appropriate programs and services should be considered an economic and political problem. Greater financial and technological resources need to be allocated for rehabilitation programs that would serve the needs of this patient population in preventing and reducing secondary impairments and deterioration of physical function, maintaining functional independence across the life span, and improving quality of life.[39]

Another possible solution to reducing gaps in services may lie in improving care coordination.[28] McSpadden et al[49] described the gradual shift from medical to community-based services that occurred in recent decades. On the one hand, access to community-based services allowed families of CSHCN to obtain a greater number of necessary services and reduce their therapy-related travel. On the other hand, moving away from hospital-based care resulted in disordered and fragmented coordination of care, which, combined with poor communication among providers, led to gaps in services and to the care coordination role falling on the shoulders of family members. McSpadden et al[49] discussed the benefits of focused and competent care coordination and the potential care coordination roles that physical therapists may assume when working with CSHCN. These possible roles, including that of a primary care coordinator, member of a care coordination team, care coordination advocate, and researcher, are summarized in Table 23-4. This approach can be followed by clinicians working with children, young adults, and adults with disabilities, including CP.

CAREGIVER BURDEN

When their child is diagnosed with CP, parents and other family members have to adjust to this news and to the changes and challenges it brings into their everyday lives.[50] This process, together with the prospect and experience of caring for the child in the long term, has an impact on the parental psychological and physical health, social roles, employment, economic status, and overall quality of life.[50-52] Marital, parenting, and siblings roles may all be altered.[51] Juggling their roles as caregivers who manage their child's health and its complex issues that arise in the process with trying to attend to all other everyday roles and responsibilities may be a very daunting task for the parents.[53]

Psychological Health

Caregivers of children with CP report greater and more frequent distress and cognitive and emotional problems compared to caregivers in the general population[54] and have been found to have high depression rates (40% to 78%).[50,55-57] Parental feelings of anxiety, grief, and chronic sorrow have been also reported.[50,55,57,58] However, findings related to anxiety levels among caregivers of children with and without CP vary from no statistical difference[50,55] to significantly higher anxiety scores recorded in a group of mothers of children with CP.[57]

TABLE 23-4 (CONTINUED)	
POSSIBLE CARE COORDINATOR ROLES AND RELATED TASKS OF A PHYSICAL THERAPIST WORKING WITH INDIVIDUALS WITH CHILDHOOD-ONSET DISABILITIES	
CARE COORDINATION ROLE	**TASKS**
Member of a care coordination team	Assume the role of a member of an interprofessional team within a medical home by promoting fitness, wellness, and quality of life
	Provide consultations to and receive consultations from other providers within the medical home in regard to a variety of aspects of patient care
	Assist other team members in coordinating patient education, intervention, and support services
	Coordinate care between inpatient and school settings to ensure the following:
	• The patient's needs in ADLs, seating, and mobility equipment support his or her transition from the hospital to school environment
	• The family understands the differences between medical and school settings and is able to navigate both with confidence
	Play an informal role of an EI service coordinator by doing the following:
	• Providing appropriate referrals
	• Locating and initiating necessary services
	• Communicating with the medical team on behalf of the family and non-medical team members
	• Explaining medical information to the family and other non-medical team members
	• Developing questions to ask medical providers
	• Facilitating communication among team members
Care coordination advocate	Promote care coordination to the family, employer, and coworkers
	Provide information related to health care legislation and in support of care coordination needs to local, state, and national representatives
	Advocate for appropriate reimbursement for care coordination services
Researcher	Develop research proposals and conduct studies to examine the effects of care coordination on the following:
	• Access to rehabilitation services
	• Community participation
	• Employment outcomes
	• Health and wellness
	• Prevention of secondary impairments
	• Quality of life
	• Short- and long-term service outcomes
	Develop standardized outcome measures to assess effectiveness of care coordination

Abbreviations: ADLs, activities of daily living; EI, early intervention; PT, physical therapy.

Compiled from McSpadden et al.[49]

TABLE 23-5	
POSITIVE AND NEGATIVE PREDICTORS OF PSYCHOLOGICAL HEALTH IN CAREGIVERS OF CHILDREN WITH CEREBRAL PALSY REPORTED IN PUBLISHED LITERATURE	
POSITIVE PREDICTORS[50,51,53,57]	**NEGATIVE PREDICTORS**[50,51,53,54,56-58]
Availability of social support from extended family, friends, and neighbors	Child's speech problems
CHIP coping style 2[a]	CHIP coping style 2[a]
Fewer child behavior problems	Experiential avoidance
Higher levels of child's physical functioning as determined by the GMFCS level[b]	Greater disability demands
Higher levels of family functioning	Greater number of child behavior problems
Higher parental self-esteem and sense mastery	Higher level of caregiving stress
Lower caregiving demands	Low family income
Self-efficacy	Severe disability as determined by the GMFCS level[b]
Use of a greater number of stress management strategies	

Abbreviations: CHIP, Coping Health Inventory for Parents; GMFCS, Gross Motor Function Classification System.[42]

[a] Maintaining social support, self-esteem and psychological stability[59]; contradictory evidence obtained in 2 studies for this coping style[50,58]

[b] Yilmaz et al[57] reported a positive correlation between the GMFCS levels and maternal levels of depression and anxiety, while Unsal-Delialioglu et al[56] found no correlation between the child's GMFCS level and maternal depression.

Parents exhibit different levels of their ability to cope with adverse situations based on a multitude of factors, and not all families are affected equally.[50,51,53,58] Parental coping styles can be assessed using the Coping Health Inventory for Parents (CHIP) that is designed to evaluate the family's responses to the demands of managing chronic or serious illness of a child.[59,60] Its 3 scales represent the following 3 coping styles:

1. Maintaining family integration, cooperation, and an optimistic definition of the situation
2. Maintaining social support, self-esteem, and psychological stability
3. Understanding the medical situation through communication with other parents and consultation with medical staff[58-60]

The second of the CHIP[59] coping styles listed previously was found to be associated with variable outcomes related to parental psychological health.[50,58] Results of one study indicated that the use of this coping style, combined with experiential avoidance, was associated with such parental psychological symptoms as anxiety, depression, and stress.[58] Hayes et al[61] defined experiential avoidance as the attempts "to alter the form, frequency or situational sensitivity of private events even when doing so causes behavioral harm."[(p 7)] Such private events may include emotions, thoughts, sensations, and memories that the person finds uncomfortable and, thus, would like to avoid.[61,62] Unfortunately, as the result, the number of behaviors available to the person is reduced leading, in turn, to decreased functional and psychological

flexibility.[61,62] Whittingham et al[58] found that, in parents of children with CP, experiential avoidance uniquely predicted psychological symptoms of depression, anxiety, stress, and chronic sorrow. In addition, it predicted the parenting burden they experienced.[58]

While experiential avoidance was shown to negatively affect the caregivers,[58] self-efficacy was found to be a positive personal resource.[50] Guillamón et al[50] defined self-efficacy as "the sense of competence and personal control over the care situation,"[(p 1580)] which leads to the caregiver being able to ask for help, delegate tasks to others, or take time to rest when necessary. Considering this definition, it is not surprising that self-efficacy was found to be associated with lower anxiety scores and better psychological health.[50] Overall, as shown in Table 23-5, a variety of positive and negative factors may serve as predictors of psychological health in caregivers of children with CP.[50,51,53,54,56-58] Clinicians working with the families of these children need to be aware of such factors and take them into consideration when developing truly family-centered intervention plans that support the caregivers and lead to improved health outcomes not only for the children, but also for their parents.[53]

Physical Health

Besides psychological health, caring for a child with a disability may affect parental physical health.[53,54] Brehaut et al[54] demonstrated that caregivers of children with CP were more likely to experience pain and suffer from chronic physical problems than documented in the general population.

Reported conditions included back pain, migraine headaches, intestinal and stomach ulcers, asthma, and arthritis.[54] Higher levels of behavioral problems in children with CP were associated with lower levels of physical health.[53] Additionally, lower caregiving demands and higher levels of family functioning predicted better outcomes, while parental self-perception, stress management, gross family income, and the availability of social support had only indirect effects on the caregivers' physical health.[53]

Several authors identified maternal low back pain as a significant problem related to the child's non-ambulatory status, decreased overall mobility, and dependency in ADLs, as well as to significant barriers to mobility present in the home.[63,64] The needs for ergonomic training and home modifications were also highlighted.[63,64] Other musculoskeletal disorders reported in caregivers of children with CP included myofascial pain syndrome, fibromyalgia, and thoracic outlet syndrome.[65] The caregiving tasks of transfers and dressing were examined for actual and perceived exertion in another study.[66] Older age and greater physical size of the child or young adult with CP, older age of the caregiver, and higher heart rate and oxygen uptake measured at baseline were associated with higher levels of actual and perceived exertion reported during caregiving. Because physical strain may affect parental health, clinicians should assess the demands of caregiving-related tasks and suggest to the parents specific preventive measures and interventions that would reduce exertion while they care for their children.[66]

Financial Burden

Financial issues affecting families of people with disabilities should not be overlooked. Expenses that cover adaptive equipment and other assistive technology, medications, nursing and respite care, transportation, and home remodeling, especially when medical insurance coverage or support services are lacking, may create a significant financial strain.[51,52] Brehaut et al[54] reported lower income levels in caregivers of children with CP compared to the general population of caregivers, although their education levels were similar. In addition, parents, relatives, and foster parents caring for children with CP were found to be less likely to work full time or hold paid positions, and 37.2% of them reported caregiving being their main occupation. It is possible that their decreased ability to work related to the caregiving duties was, at least partially, responsible for increased financial burden the family experienced.[54]

Quality of Life

As discussed in Chapter 11, quality of life is a subjective multidimensional construct that encompasses the person's view of the place they have in the society, including the emotional, social, material, and physical well-being, as well as his or her self-esteem and self-determination.[67] Health-related quality of life (HRQL) is a part of quality of life that is in direct relationship with the person's health.[67] Results of several studies designed to assess parental HRQL showed that primary caregivers of children with CP had lower quality of life compared to those in the general population.[50,55,58] Specifically, physical functioning, vitality, emotional role, and general health were negatively affected,[68] and lower HRQL levels in the energy, emotional reactions, pain, physical activity, sleep, and social isolation domains were reported.[55] Additionally, Guillamón et al[50] found a significant relationship between parental self-efficacy and quality of life related to their physical health and satisfaction with interactions within their environment. This finding highlighted the importance of family-centered care, through which the caregivers' quality of life can be supported by fostering their self-efficacy.[50]

FAMILY NEEDS FOR SUPPORT AND SERVICES

The term *family-centered care* implies that the needs and priorities of the entire family, including the child, parents, siblings, extended family, and other family members involved in the care of the child, are taken into consideration when planning and providing services.[69,70] For example, parental needs for information change across the child's life span, from the initial knowledge required to understand their child's diagnosis, to short- and long-term prognosis and planning for the future.[70] Extended family members also need information that would help them understand the child's condition and its implications for his or her parents and siblings. Finally, as children with CP grow up, they need to have opportunities for learning about their diagnosis, asking questions and obtaining information that would assist them in understanding the implications of their disability.[70]

Family needs and priorities change based on the age, health, and functional status of the child and caregivers, and based on variations in family structure, dynamics, and environments.[69,70] Challenges in regard to service coordination, advocacy, and caregiving the family faces on a day-to-day basis also change over time.[69,70] This necessitates flexibility on the part of health care providers that, when not present, may lead to parental dissatisfaction with provided services.[70,71] Clinicians should be aware of this problem and must be ready to provide the families of their patients with much needed support.[70] Other sources of support and respite for the immediate family of a child with CP may include the extended family; work colleagues and friends of the child's parents; parents of other children with CP; as well as religious leaders, mentors, and leaders of extracurricular activities.[70]

Several groups of authors studied the needs for services and supports among families of children and adolescents with CP.[69,70,72] Table 23-6 contains data on family needs in the areas of financial assistance, information, services, and supports.[69,72] In their study conducted with 501 parents of children and youth with CP, Palisano et al[69] found that the child's GMFCS[42] level had a significant effect on the total number of family needs, which was the highest for parents of children

TABLE 23-6

FAMILY NEEDS FOR INFORMATION, SUPPORT, SERVICES, AND FINANCIAL ASSISTANCE

AREA OF NEED	SPECIFIC NEEDS
Financial assistance	Paying for child care, therapy, and other services
	Paying for equipment, toys, and home modifications
Information	Availability of activities meaningful to the child
	Current and future services
	Education and special education
	Planning for the child's future
Services	Community services as follows:
	• Centers equipped to provide leisure activities to children with disabilities
	• Entertainment and recreational activities
Supports	Equipment and modifications aimed to do the following:
	• Decrease caregiving demands
	• Support child's participation and independence
	Finding babysitting and respite care services
	Finding camps and leisure, recreational, and social activities in the community
	More personal time for parents
	Social and system supports, including the following:
	• Accessible leisure centers
	• Involvement of extended family in child care and transportation
	• Social networking

Data from Palisano et al[69] and Piškur et al.[72]

and youth classified in levels IV and V and the lowest for the parents of those in level I. Information related to current and future services, planning for the child's future, assistance with finding activities in the community, and more parental personal time were the needs reported most frequently.[69]

In a further examination of family needs, Almasri et al[73-75] identified the need profiles, determinants and predictors for families of children and youth with CP. This information is presented in Table 23-7.[73-75] In a total sample of parents and other family members of 579 children and youth with CP who filled out a modified Family Needs Survey[76] and a number of questionnaires, 51% had low family needs and 11% had high needs.[73] Families in the low needs cluster were found to have children who demonstrated better adaptive behaviors, and a large percent of families with children functioning at GMFCS[42] levels I and II (68% and 52%, respectively) had low needs. Families with low needs also reported higher household incomes, better family functioning, better access to services, and less involvement in service coordination for their children. For comparison, families in the high needs cluster had high and exceptionally high needs across the entire spectrum, which indicated that they would require a significant amount of support.[73]

The authors suggested that being aware of the family needs profile may be helpful for clinical decision making in regard to allocating resources and developing a plan of care in collaboration with the family.[73] Additionally, information on the determinants of family needs (see Table 23-7) can be used when planning and implementing intervention in the areas of the child's adaptive behavior and communication, family counseling, and when addressing the costs of necessary services and equipment.[74] Finally, knowledge of risk and protective factors (see Table 23-7) can be translated into providing need-based, family-centered services to children and youth with CP, which, in turn, may decrease the level of family needs.[75]

SIBLING RELATIONSHIPS AND FRIENDSHIPS ACROSS THE LIFE SPAN

Sibling Relationships

One area of family needs that requires separate attention is related to the impact of the child's disability on his or her

TABLE 23-7

AREAS, PROFILES, DETERMINANTS, AND PREDICTORS OF NEEDS FOR FAMILIES OF CHILDREN AND YOUTH WITH CEREBRAL PALSY

FAMILY NEEDS			
Areas[73-75]	Profiles[73]	Determinants[74]	Predictors[75]
1. Information related to child's health[a] 2. Financial and community resources[a,b] 3. Family functioning and supports[a,b] 4. Services[b]	*Cluster 1* Low needs in areas 1 through 3 *Cluster 2* High needs for information on the child's health to be able to explain his or her diagnosis to others and average needs in areas 2 and 3 *Cluster 3* Very high needs for financial and community resources and average needs in areas 1 and 3 *Cluster 4* Very high to exceptionally high needs in areas 1 through 3	*Child Characteristics* Associations found between the following: • Adaptive behavior and needs area 1 • GMFCS[42] level and needs area 2 • Communication problems and needs area 3 *Family Characteristics* Associations found between the following • Family relationships and needs areas 1 and 3 • Family income and needs area 2	*Risk Factor* GMFCS level predicted needs in areas 2 and 3 but not in area 4. *Protective Factors* • Strong family relationship predicted decreased needs in area 3. • Access to services predicted decreased needs in areas 2 and 3 • Parental perception of receiving respectful and supportive services and having services that meet the child's needs for participation predicted decreased needs in financial resources (area 2).

Abbreviations: GMFCS, Gross Motor Function Classification System[42]

[a] Relevant for profiles and determinants of needs[73,74]

[b] Relevant for predictors of needs[75]

siblings who may experience greater caregiving responsibilities earlier in life than typically observed and receive less attention from parents because of the overwhelming needs of their brother or sister with a disability.[51,70] Their expectations related to meeting their needs for comfort, transportation, family vacations, and overall care may also have to be adjusted.[70] Conversely, siblings of a child with CP may develop into more sensitive and caring individuals.[70]

Research that examines the psychosocial impact of having a sister or a brother with a disability on the sibling who develops typically may shed some light on how these relationships mold the siblings' views of each other and affect practical, social, and emotional support people without disabilities are willing and able to provide to their siblings with disabilities in their adult lives.[77] Most commonly, parents care for a child with a disability until and often after he or she reaches adulthood. However, as they age, physical aspects of care, such as transfers, showering, toileting, lifting, and feeding become more and more difficult for the parents, and adult siblings of people with disabilities may take over these responsibilities.[77]

Dew et al[77] conducted a review of literature to examine the development of sibling relationships over time, with a specific focus on the siblings of individuals with CP. The researchers found that 17 of 21 reviewed studies described sibling relationships in childhood, while only 4 focused on adults, and, therefore, there was insufficient information available in regard to the impact of childhood disability on adult sibling relationships. Furthermore, in the majority of childhood studies, mothers were the primary informants, and their reports seemed to be negatively biased, which was in contrast to the few studies in which the siblings' input was sought. The interviewed siblings were found to be more positive when describing their relationships with their brothers or sisters with disabilities.[77] Only in 2 of the examined studies did researchers obtain information from siblings who had a physical disability, and in both, siblings with and without disabilities viewed their relationships similarly.[77-79] As noted by Dew et al,[77] their review of literature highlighted feelings of love and solidarity between siblings with and without disabilities, with mostly positive accounts of family relationships and appreciation of their sisters and brothers with CP expressed by people without disabilities. However, this review did not find an answer to the question of what feelings individuals with disabilities may have about the transfer of the caregiving role from their parents to their siblings.[77]

A later study conducted by the same group of researchers examined relationships between adults and their siblings with CP who used augmentative and alternative communication (ACC).[80] Communication is an extremely important aspect of human interaction and, when it is impaired, the siblings' ability to understand their brothers and sisters with disabilities and interpret their communication to others may play a significant role in maintaining their quality of life after their parents are no longer able to provide them with support, advocate for them, and coordinate their services. Although this understanding develops during childhood and young children do not necessarily use AAC, the application of this communication method later in life may be very helpful for strengthening relationships between siblings with and without disabilities and for maintaining contact between them regardless of how far away they live from each other. Because siblings play greater and greater roles in the lives of their brothers and sisters with disabilities as they age, using effective communication strategies is essential for supporting their life-long relationships.[80]

Dew et al[77] highlighted the need for future longitudinal research of siblings with and without childhood-onset disabilities that would explore their relationships across the life span. Qualitative research would help clinicians understand the roles brothers and sisters with and without disabilities would like to play in each other's lives. Additionally, it would promote timely planning for the future and the development of services and policies that would support sibling relationships. Effective service planning would help persons with disabilities to live in the least restrictive environments in the community while their siblings assist them, when necessary, by managing their finances, providing emotional and social support, and participating in coordination of their care.[77]

Friendships and Their Significance for Social Participation

According to the federal law, whenever possible, children with disabilities are to be educated together with children developing typically (see Chapter 12).[81,82] Success of their classroom integration depends, in part, on whether children with disabilities are accepted by their peers.[83] Cunningham et al[84] demonstrated that, regardless of their gender, 6- to 12-year-old children with neurodevelopmental disorders, including CP, had fewer and lower quality friendships and saw their friends less frequently than their peers developing typically. The definition of *friendship quality* in that study included such characteristics of interactions with friends as to what extent they were able to get along and share things with each other, as well as how often a conflict occurred.[84]

In another study, boys and girls with disabilities were perceived differently by their peers.[85] Nadeau and Tessier[85] reported that, in their sample of school children aged 9 to 12 years, girls with CP, but not boys with the same condition, were found to have fewer friends and to be more isolated and victimized by other children than girls developing typically. It is interesting to note that, in an earlier study, Laws and Kelly[83]

highlighted another gender difference among children of the same age, this time, in regard to the attitudes of boys and girls without disabilities toward children with Down syndrome and children with CP. Overall, girls' attitudes toward physical disability were more positive than boys'. However, girls who were given information about Down syndrome exhibited significantly better attitudes toward intellectual disabilities, but the opposite was true in regard to their attitudes toward physical disabilities after being informed about CP. As for the boys, their attitudes toward both types of disability did not differ after they received such information.[83]

The varied results of discussed research[83-85] suggest that, in spite of available evidence, it may be difficult to generalize it to all children with and without disabilities and that, perhaps, the differences among the aims and methodologies used in different studies need to be closely examined in order to discern the reasons for the variability of results. Alternatively, when applying such evidence, the situation to which it is being applied needs to be evaluated for similarities with conditions under which the study was conducted. Regardless, based on published research, it is reasonable to conclude that friendships of children with CP are commonly affected by their disability to greater or lesser extent, with attitudes of children developing typically playing a major role in that outcome.[83-85]

Ability to communicate is another key variable in the development of friendships. In a small qualitative study, researchers interviewed 3 boys and 3 girls without disabilities, age range 7 to 14 years, about their friendships with children with CP who used AAC in the form of speech-generating devices (SGDs).[86] Participants had positive views of their friendships and reported that, through interactions with their classmates with CP, they were able to learn about different ways to communicate and develop a better understanding of body language and other means of nonverbal communication. In addition, results of this research highlighted a number of factors that helped initiate and maintain friendships between children with and without disabilities, and identified possible barriers to friendship quality and success, which are displayed in Table 23-8.[86]

Another important finding reported by Anderson et al[86] included increased disability awareness that might be attributed to friendships between children with and without CP. The authors listed such behaviors observed in the study participants as empathy and advocacy for inclusion of children with disabilities; commenting on the insufficient related knowledge among their classmates; linking this lack of knowledge to exclusion and bullying behaviors; and advocacy for including disability education in the curriculum as the means of instilling respect for their classmates with disabilities in children developing typically. At the same time, the researchers identified several behaviors that could lead to social experiences perceived by children with CP as negative. Such behaviors included "helping" friends with communication by typing messages in their SGDs, guessing what they were saying before they could express themselves fully, and expressing pity as opposed to empathy.[86] Some of the

TABLE 23-8	
SUPPORTING FACTORS AND BARRIERS TO FRIENDSHIP SUCCESS AND QUALITY BETWEEN CHILDREN WITH CEREBRAL PALSY WHO USE AUGMENTATIVE AND ALTERNATIVE COMMUNICATION AND CHILDREN WITHOUT DISABILITIES	
FACTORS SUPPORTING FRIENDSHIPS	**BARRIERS TO FRIENDSHIP SUCCESS AND QUALITY**
Children Developing Typically	*Setting-Related Barriers*
Alleviation of feeling of loneliness	Restricted access to play areas
Altruism	Separate break times
Attitudes toward disability	Visiting restrictions
Patience and understanding	*Person-Related Barriers*
Social-emotional needs	Being uncomfortable with friend's disability
Social values	High support needs of the child with CP
Children With CP Who Use AAC	Placing high expectations on friends without disabilities by appointing them as helpers
Engaging personality	*AAC-Use-Related Barrier*
Proficiency in sign language	Missing opportunities for conversations important for close friendships, including future careers, intimate relationships, and sexuality
Similar unique ability	
Other Factors	
External reinforcement by others	
Positive feedback from other people	

Abbreviations: AAC, augmentative and alternative communication; CP, cerebral palsy.

Data from Anderson et al.[86]

ways to address these issues may be providing children typically developing with appropriate information and informal training in communication with persons who use AAC, and offering positive comments in regard to proficiency in sign language and other skills or contributions to group exhibited by children with disabilities.[36,87]

In order to form friendships, children with disabilities need to participate in activities with their peers.[88] Palisano et al[88] reported greater social and community participation among youth with CP aged 13 to 21 years compared to children aged 6 to 12 years. The authors commented that this was consistent with developmental trends across the life span. All participants demonstrated the greatest involvement in skill-based and physical activities, and the lowest involvement in recreation. Participants classified in the GMFCS[42] level I performed the greatest percentage of activities with friends and other people as opposed to those in levels IV and V who were likely to be involved in the least percentage or no such activities. However, children and youth in the latter group were reported to spend the same percentage of time on activities performed outside their homes as those classified in level I, which, most likely, indicated the efforts of their families in encouraging such participation.[88]

In the same study,[88] higher functioning in the areas of sports, physical abilities, speech, and communication; being enrolled in a regular classroom as opposed to special

education; as well as the ability to find and engage in the desired activities determined greater participation with friends among youth with CP.[89] The authors suggested that physical therapists may help increase social participation of this group through the following:

- Collaborative goal setting to address the individual's physical, sports, and communication abilities
- Planning and encouraging engagement in meaningful recreational activities
- Developing interventions based on the analysis of skills required for participation in desired activities
- Removing barriers to participation through consulting, sharing information, and coordinating efforts with sports coaches, program instructors, and team members[89]

Another factor identified as important to social participation among youth with CP was their self-perceived competence as a friend, which was defined as the young person's view of his or her ability to make friends, interact with them, and help them when needed.[90] The reported number of activities performed with friends, but not how much they enjoyed them, correlated with the participants' level of self-perceived competence. The participants' gender, age, developmental problems, and level of gross motor function did not affect their self-perceived competence as friends in this research.[90]

Being able to develop life-long meaningful relationships and friendships is important for all humans as it supports their psychosocial well-being.[90] Therefore, physical therapists and other health professionals should promote engagement in sports and community recreation, peer mentoring, and educational experiences designed to enhance social participation among children and young adults with CP.[89,90] Effects of participation-based interventions on social participation and quality of life in this patient population needs to be examined through future research.[89]

Complete video-based activities for Chapter 23 (see Activity Set 6 [activities 1 through 3] on the book website).

REFERENCES

1. Hilberink SR, Roebroeck ME, Nieuwstraten W, Jalink L, Verheijden JM, Stam HJ. Health issues in young adults with cerebral palsy: towards a life-span perspective. *J Rehabil Med.* 2007;39(8):605-611.

2. Data & statistics for cerebral palsy. *Centers for Disease Control and Prevention.* http://www.cdc.gov/NCBDDD/cp/data.html. Updated December 27, 2013. Accessed December 27, 2014.

3. Orlin MN, Cicirello NA, O'Donnell AE, Doty AK. The continuum of care for individuals with lifelong disabilities: role of the physical therapist. Phys Ther. 2014;94(7):1043-1053.

4. Cerebral palsy fact sheet. *United Cerebral Palsy.* http://ucp.org/wp-content/uploads/2013/02/cp-fact-sheet.pdf. Accessed December 27, 2014.

5. Brooks JC, Strauss DJ, Shavelle RM, Tran LM, Rosenbloom L, Wu YW. Recent trends in cerebral palsy survival. Part I: period and cohort effects. *Dev Med Child Neurol.* 2014;56(11):1059-1064.

6. Brooks JC, Strauss DJ, Shavelle RM, Tran LM, Rosenbloom L, Wu YW. Recent trends in cerebral palsy survival. Part II: individual survival prognosis. *Dev Med Child Neurol.* 2014;56(11):1065-1071.

7. Katz RT, Johnson CB. Life care planning for the child with cerebral palsy. *Phys Med Rehabil Clin N Am.* 2013;24(3):491-505.

8. World Health Organization. *International Classification of Functioning, Disability and Health.* Geneva, Switzerland: World Health Organization; 2001.

9. World Health Organization. *International Classification of Functioning, Disability and Health: Children and Youth Version.* Geneva, Switzerland: World Health Organization; 2007.

10. Michelsen SI, Uldall P, Hansen T, Madsen M. Social integration of adults with cerebral palsy. *Dev Med Child Neurol.* 2006;48(8):643-649.

11. Horsman M, Suto M, Dudgeon B, Harris SR. Growing older with cerebral palsy: insiders' perspectives. *Pediatr Phys Ther.* 2010;22(3):296-303.

12. Centers for Disease Control and Prevention. Economic costs associated with mental retardation, cerebral palsy, hearing loss, and vision impairment – Unites States, 2003. *MMWR Morb Mortal Wkly Rep.* 2004;53(3):57-59.

13. Wang B, Chen Y, Zhang J, Li J, Guo Y, Hailey D. A preliminary study into the economic burden of cerebral palsy in China. *Health Policy.* 2008;87(2):223-234.

14. Kruse M, Michelsen SI, Flachs EM, Brønnum-Hansen H, Madsen M, Uldall P. Lifetime costs of cerebral palsy. *Dev Med Child Neurol.* 2009;51(8):622-628.

15. Park MS, Kim SJ, Chung CY, Kwon DG, Choi IH, Lee KM. Prevalence and lifetime healthcare cost of cerebral palsy in South Korea. *Health Policy.* 2011;100(2):234-238.

16. MacLennan AH. A 'no-fault' cerebral palsy pension scheme would benefit all Australians. *Aust N Z J Obstet Gynaecol.* 2011;51(6):479-484.

17. Rosenbaum P, Paneth N, Leviton A, et al. A report: the definition and classification of cerebral palsy April 2006. *Dev Med Child Neurol.* 2007;49(suppl 109):8-14. Erratum in: *Dev Med Child Neurol.* 2007;49(6):480.

18. Mantovani JF. Definition and classification of CP: medical-legal and service implications. *Dev Med Child Neurol.* 2007;49(suppl 109):42.

19. Reddihough DS, Collins KJ. The epidemiology and causes of cerebral palsy. *Aust J Physiother.* 2003;49:7-12.

20. MacLennan A. A template for defining a casual relation between acute intrapartum events and cerebral palsy: international consensus statement. *BMJ.* 1999;319:1054-1059.

21. Johnson CB, Weed RO. The life care planning process. *Phys Med Rehabil Clin N Am.* 2013;24(3):403-417.

22. Nageswaran S, Silver EJ, Stein RE. Association of functional limitation with health care needs and experiences of children with special health care needs. *Pediatrics.* 2008;121(5):994-1001.

23. Lin SC, Margolis B, Yu SM, Adirim TA. The role of medical home in emergency department use for children with developmental disabilities in the United States. *Pediatr Emerg Care.* 2014;30(8):534-539.

24. Murphy NA, Hoff C, Jorgensen T, Norlin C, Young PG. Costs and complications of hospitalizations for children with cerebral palsy. *Pediatr Rehabil.* 2006;9(1):47-52.

25. Burns KH, Casey PH, Lyle RE, Bird TM, Fussell JJ, Robbins JM. Increasing prevalence of medically complex children in US hospitals. *Pediatrics.* 2010;126(4):638-646.

26. Berry JG, Poduri A, Bonkowsky JL, et al. Trends in resource utilization by children with neurological impairment in the United States inpatient health care system: a repeat cross-sectional study. *PLoS Med.* 2012;9(1):e1001158. doi:10.1371/journal.pmed.1001158.

27. Patient Centered Medical Home Resource Center: defining medical home. *Agency for Healthcare Research and Quality.* http://pcmh.ahrq.gov/page/defining-pcmh. Accessed January 2, 2015.

28. Elias ER, Murphy NA; Council on Children with Disabilities. Home care of children and youth with complex health care needs and technology dependencies. *Pediatrics.* 2012;129(5):996-1005.

29. Young NL, Gilbert TK, McCormick A, et al. Youth and young adults with cerebral palsy: their use of physician and hospital services. *Arch Phys Med Rehabil.* 2007;88(6):696-702.

30. Young NL, Steele C, Fehlings D, Jutai J, Olmsted N, Williams JI. Use of health care among adults with chronic and complex physical disabilities of childhood. *Disabil Rehabil.* 2005;27(23):1455-1460.

31. Goodman DM, Mendez E, Throop C, Ogata ES. Adult survivors of pediatric illness: the impact on pediatric hospitals. *Pediatrics.* 2002;110(3):583-589.

32. Goodman DM, Hall M, Levin A, et al. Adults with chronic health conditions originating in childhood: inpatient experience in children's hospitals. *Pediatrics.* 2011;128(1):5-13.

33. Houtrow A, Kang T, Newcomer R. In-home supportive services for individuals with cerebral palsy in California. *J Pediatr Rehabil Med.* 2012;5(3):187-195.

34. Liptak GS. Health and well being of adults with cerebral palsy. *Curr Opin Neurol.* 2008;21(2):136-142.

35. Olmstead: community integration for everyone. *ADA.gov.* http://www.ada.gov/olmstead/olmstead_about.htm. Accessed January 4, 2015.

36. Olmstead v. L.C., 527 US 581 (1999). https://supreme.justia.com/cases/federal/us/527/581/case.html. Accessed January 4, 2015.

37. Ng T, Wong A, Harrington C. State Olmstead litigation and the Affordable Care Act. *J Soc Work Disabil Rehabil.* 2014;13(1-2):97-109.

38. Majnemer A, Shikako-Thomas K, Lach, L, et al; QUALA Group. Rehabilitation service utilization in children and youth with cerebral palsy. *Child Care Health Dev.* 2014;40(2):275-282.

39. Moll LR, Cott CA. The paradox of normalization through rehabilitation: growing up and growing older with cerebral palsy. *Disabil Rehabil.* 2013;35(15):1276-1283.

40. Coverage of habilitation services and devices in the Essential Benefits Package under the Affordable Care Act. *Association of University Centers on Disabilities.* http://www.aucd.org/docs/urc/TA%20Institute%202013/Habilitation%20White%20Paper%20(final)%20(D0391656)%20(3).pdf. Published October 25, 2011. Accessed February 26, 2016.

41. Begnoche DM, Wood A, Palisano RJ, Chiarello LA, Bartlett D, Chang HJ. Physical and occupational therapy services received by young children with cerebral palsy. In: Abstracts of Poster and Platform Presentations at the 2012 Combined Sections Meeting. *Pediatr Phys Ther.* 2012;24(1):97. Abstract.

42. Palisano RJ, Rosenbaum PL, Walter SD, Russell DJ, Wood EP, Galuppi BE. Development and reliability of a system to classify gross motor function in children with cerebral palsy. *Dev Med Child Neurol.* 1997;39(4):214-223.

43. Kleinert JO, Effgen SK. Early intervention. In: Effgen SK. *Meeting the Physical Therapy Needs of Children.* 2nd ed. Philadelphia, PA: F. A. Davis Company; 2012:475-493.

44. Effgen SK, Kaminker MK. The educational environment. In: Campbell SK, Palisano RJ, Orlin MN, eds. *Physical Therapy for Children.* 4th ed. St. Louis, MO: Saunders; 2012:968-1007.

45. Bailes AF, Succop P. Factors associated with physical therapy services received for individuals with cerebral palsy in an outpatient pediatric medical setting. *Phys Ther.* 2012;92(11):1411-1418.

46. Bottos M, Feliciangeli A, Scuito L, Gericke C, Vianello A. Functional status of adults with cerebral palsy and implications for treatment of children. *Dev Med Child Neurol.* 2001;43(8):516-528.

47. Neuwenhuijsen C, van der Laar Y, Donkervoort M, Nieuwstraten W, Roebroeck ME, Stam HJ. Unmet needs and health care utilization in young adults with cerebral palsy. *Disabil Rehabil.* 2008;30(17):1254-1262.

48. Elrod CS, DeJong G. Determinants of utilization of physical rehabilitation services for persons with chronic and disabling conditions: as exploratory study. *Arch Phys Med Rehabil.* 2008;89(1):114-120.

49. McSpadden C, Therrien M, McEwen IR. Care coordination for children with special health care needs and roles for physical therapists. *Pediatr Phys Ther.* 2012;24(1):70-77.

50. Guillamón N, Nieto R, Pousada M, et al. Quality of life and mental health among parents of children with cerebral palsy: the influence of self-efficacy and coping strategies. *J Clin Nurs.* 2013;22(11-12):1579-1590.

51. Hallum A. Disability and the transition to adulthood: issues for the disabled child, the family, and the pediatrician. *Curr Probl Pediatr.* 1995;25(1):12-50.

52. Glasscock R. A phenomenological study of the experience of being a mother of a child with cerebral palsy. *Pediatr Nurs.* 2000;26(4):407-410.

53. Raina P, O'Donnell M, Rosenbaum P, et al. The health and well-being of caregivers of children with cerebral palsy. *Pediatrics.* 2005;115(6):e626-e636.

54. Brehaut JC, Kohen DE, Raina P, et al. The health of primary caregivers of children with cerebral palsy: how does it compare with that of other Canadian caregivers? *Pediatrics.* 2004;114(2):e182-e191.

55. Ones K, Yilmaz E, Cetinkaya B, Caglar N. Assessment of the quality of life of mothers of children with cerebral palsy (primary caregivers). *Neurorehabil Neural Repair.* 2005;19(3):232-237.

56. Unsal-Delialioglu S, Kaya K, Ozel S, Gorgulu G. Depression in mothers of children with cerebral palsy and related factors in Turkey: a controlled study. *Int J Rehabil Res.* 2009;32(3):199-204.

57. Yilmaz H, Erkin G, Nalbant L. Depression and anxiety levels in mothers of children with cerebral palsy: a controlled study. *Eur J Phy Rehabil Med.* 2013;49(6):823-837.

58. Whittingham K, Wee D, Sanders MR, Boyd R. Predictors of psychological adjustment, experienced parenting burden and chronic sorrow symptoms in parents of children with cerebral palsy. *Child Care Health Dev.* 2013;39(3):366-373.

59. McCubbin HI, McCubbin MA, Patterson JM, Cauble AE, Wilson LR, Warwick W. CHIP - Coping Health Inventory for Parents: an assessment of parental coping patterns in the care of the chronically ill child. *J Marriage Fam.* 1983;45:359-370.

60. Coping Health Inventory for Parents. *American Psychological Association.* http://www.apa.org/pi/about/publications/caregivers/practice-settings/assessment/tools/coping-health.aspx. Accessed January 7, 2015.

61. Hayes SC, Luoma JB, Bond FW, Masuda A, Lillis J. Acceptance and commitment therapy: model, processes and outcomes. *Behav Res Ther.* 2006;44(1):1-25.

62. Hayes SC, Wilson KG, Gifford EV, Follette VM, Strosahl K. Experiential avoidance and behavioral disorders: a functional dimensional approach to diagnosis and treatment. *J Consult Clin Psychol.* 1996 64(6):1152-1168.

63. Tonga E, Düger T. Factors affecting low back pain in mothers who have disabled children. *J Back Musculoskelet Rehabil.* 2008;21(4):219-226.

64. Habib M, Khanam F, Moniruzzaman, Hafez A, Islam S. Prevalence of low back pain (LBP) and its effects on everyday life among female caregivers of children with cerebral palsy. *Ind J Physiother Occup Ther.* 2014;8(1):176-181.

65. Sharan D, Ajeesh PS, Rameshkumar R, Manjula M. Musculoskeletal disorders in caregivers of children with cerebral palsy following a multilevel surgery. *Work.* 2012; 41(suppl 1):1891-1895.

66. Andrews M, Bolt DM, Braun M, Benedict RE. Measuring exertion during caregiving of children and young adults with cerebral palsy who require assistance for mobility and self-care. *Phys Occup Ther Pediatr.* 2013;33(3):300-312.

67. Colver A. Quality of life and participation. *Dev Med Child Neurol.* 2009;51(8):656-659.

68. Tuna H, Ünalan H, Tuna F, Kokino S. Quality of life of primary caregivers of children with cerebral palsy: a controlled study with Short Form-36 questionnaire. *Dev Med Child Neurol.* 2004;46(9):647-648.

69. Palisano RJ, Almarsi N, Chiarello LA, Orlin MN, Bagley A, Maggs J. Family needs of parents of children and youth with cerebral palsy. *Child Care Health Dev.* 2010;36(1):85-92.

70. Reid A, Imrie H, Brouwer E, et al. "If I knew what I know now": parents' reflections on raising a child with cerebral palsy. *Phys Occup Ther Pediatr.* 2011;31(2):169-183.

71. Hummelinck A, Pollock K. Parents' information needs about the treatment of their chronically ill child: a qualitative study. *Patient Educ Couns.* 2006;62(2):228-234.

72. Piškur B, Beurskens AJ, Jongmans MJ, et al. Parents' actions, challenges, and needs while enabling participation of children with a physical disability: a scoping review. *BMC Pediatr.* 2012;12:177. doi:10.1186/1471-2431-12-177.

73. Almasri N, Palisano RJ, Dunst C, Chiarello LA, O'Neil ME, Polansky M. Profiles of family needs of children and youth with cerebral palsy. *Child Care Health Dev.* 2011;38(6):798-806.

74. Almasri NA, Palisano RJ, Dunst CJ, Chiarello LA, O'Neil ME, Polansky M. Determinants of needs of families of children and youth with cerebral palsy. *Child Health Care.* 2011;40(2):130-154.

75. Almasri NA, O'Neil M, Palisano RJ. Predictors of needs for families of children with cerebral palsy. *Disabil Rehabil.* 2014;36(3):210-219.

76. Bailey DB, Simeonsson RJ. Assessing needs of families with handicapped infants. *J Spec Educ.* 1988;22:117-127.

77. Dew A, Balandin S, Llewellyn G. The psychosocial impact on siblings of people with lifelong physical disability: a review of the literature. *J Dev Phys Disabil.* 2008;20:485-507.

78. Davis CS, Salkin KA. Sisters and friends: dialogue and multivocality in a relational model of sibling disability. *J Contemp Ethnogr.* 2005;34(2):206-234.

79. Magill-Evans J, Darrah J, Pain K, Adkins R, Kratochvil M. Are families with adolescents and young adults with cerebral palsy the same as other families? *Dev Med Child Neurol.* 2001;43(7):466-472.

80. Dew A, Balandin S, Llewellyn G. Using a life course approach to explore how the use of AAC impacts on adult sibling relationships. *Augment Altern Commun.* 27(4):245-255.

81. Pub L No 105-17, Individuals with Disabilities Education Act Amendments of 1997, 111 Stat 37-157.

82. Pub L No 108-446, Individuals with Disabilities Education Improvement Act of 2004, 118 Stat 2647-2808.

83. Laws G, Kelly E. The attitudes and friendship intentions of children in United Kingdom mainstream schools towards peers with physical and intellectual disabilities. *Int J Disabil Dev Educ.* 2005;52(2):79-99.

84. Cunningham SD, Thomas PD, Warschausky S. Gender differences in peer relations of children with neurodevelopmental conditions. *Rehabil Psychol.* 2007;52(3):331-337.

85. Nadeau L, Tessier R. Social adjustment of children with cerebral palsy in mainstream classes: peer perception. *Dev Med Child Neurol.* 2006;48(5):331-336.

86. Anderson K, Balandin S, Clendon S. "He cares about me and I care about him." Children's experiences of friendship with peers who use AAC. *Augment Altern Commun.* 2011;27(2):77-90.

87. Han J, Ostrosky MM, Diamond KE. Children's attitudes towards peers with disabilities: supporting positive attitude development. *Young Except Child.* 2006;10:2-11.

88. Palisano RJ, Kang LJ, Chiarello LA, Orlin M, Oeffinger D, Maggs J. Social and community participation of children and youth with cerebral palsy is associated with age and gross motor function classification. *Phys Ther.* 2009;89(12):1304-1314.

89. Kang LJ, Palisano RJ, Orlin MN, Chiarello LA, King GA, Polansky M. Determinants of social participation – with friends and others who are not family members – for youths with cerebral palsy. *Phys Ther.* 2010;90(12):1743-1757.

90. Kang LJ, Palisano RJ, King GA, Chiarello LA, Orlin MN, Polansky M. Social participation of youths with cerebral palsy differed based on their self-perceived competence as a friend. *Child Care Health Dev.* 2011;38(1):117-127.

Please see videos on the accompanying website at

www.healio.com/books/videosrahlin

24

Planning Transition to Adult Life

Donna Frownfelter, PT, DPT, MA, CCS, RRT, FCCP and Mary Rahlin, PT, DHS, PCS

For persons with disabilities, issues such as living independently, finding meaningful work,
and an accessible physical environment are more important than looking normal.

Johanna Darrah, Joyce Magill-Evans, and Robin Adkins[1]

Taking an active part in problem solving and decision making regarding life choices, including those related to rehabilitation, education, participation in society, and transition to adulthood, is important for young people with disabilities.[1,2] Transition planning generally begins in high school, at 14 to 16 years of age.[3] It is often an "unchartered experience" for the student, the family, teachers, and medical professionals.[4] Each transition planning needs to be individually tailored and person-centered, as each student's needs will be different. The process of transition is often not a smooth one as there are complex issues involved, such as ongoing medical and dental care, both for prevention and treatment; psychosocial support; postsecondary education opportunities; vocational possibilities; and independent living choices.[4,5]

TRANSITION-RELATED STRESSORS

As discussed in Chapter 23, children with complex needs usually have a multitude of intensive services, often in attempts at normalization of walking and functional activities.[5] However, it is commonly thought that in adolescence, they achieve their functional potential and there is not much more that can be done. This is unfortunate, considering that focusing on normalization of movement in earlier years often occurs "at the expense of learning to manage their bodies across the life course."[5(p 1276)]

Medical advances in the treatment of children with cerebral palsy (CP) are resulting in the expectation of a near normal life span.[6] However, while the adolescent moves toward adulthood, the availability of services decreases, which results in gaps in the continuity of care.[4,7] These gaps in the child's transition to adult services are associated with poor health outcomes.[6] Services that were available during childhood and adolescence are decreased, although CP is associated with a multitude of chronic issues and people with this condition will continue to need support and preventive medical care throughout their life span (see Chapter 23).[6]

Tsybina et al[6] reported on the Longitudinal Evaluation of Transition Services (LETS Study) and highlighted the need for new models of transition. These authors described a protocol for outcome evaluation of one such model that was aimed at maintaining the continuity of services between childhood and adulthood and at addressing a multitude of secondary outcomes related to the individual's health, well-being, and health care utilization, as well as to social participation and readiness for transition.[6]

Rahlin M. *Physical Therapy for Children With Cerebral Palsy:*
An Evidence-Based Approach (pp 417-431).
© 2016 SLACK Incorporated.

As discussed in Chapter 12, a Transition Individualized Education Program (IEP) is developed in the child's school setting at age 16 years.[8] During transition planning, new players come onto the IEP team, such as job coaches and agencies providing a variety of services, including potential housing, staffing for personal care assistance, and transportation.[9] For the family, this brings about the need to cope with new terms and new people, and often leads to confusion about what comes next. The roles of parents and their relationship to their young adult may need to be re-evaluated and often need to change during this period. This is difficult, especially for parents whose children have been very physically involved and dependent on them for their needs. Parents who have been very protective and have spent their lives caring for their children now face concerns regarding their son's or daughter's readiness for and ability to be independent, the resources their child is going to need, and how these resources will be provided.[9]

Individuals with CP have unique challenges in the transition process.[7] Besides the evaluation of the young adults' functional skills, it is important to find out what they want to achieve in their transition.[10] The greater the physical and cognitive needs, the more difficult the transition process becomes. Funding issues may be significant barriers to adult life with increased physical needs.[4] Furthermore, requiring assistance with mobility and self-care may be barriers to choices the young person may desire for education or vocation.[4,11]

Donkervoort et al[7] noted that 20% to 30% of young adults 16 to 20 years of age who did not have severe learning disabilities had restrictions in activities of daily living (ADLs), such as self-care, mobility, and nutrition, and also in social participation. Results of another study demonstrated that the young adults' social roles would vary depending on the type and severity of the person's impairment: the greater the severity, the less participation socially would be possible due to decreased opportunities available.[11] The ability to obtain post-secondary education was also decreased in young adults with significant physical limitations. These results suggested that services should be directed toward decreasing activity limitations and increasing educational opportunities to facilitate success in adult life and social roles.[11]

ISSUES IN ADOLESCENCE TO CONSIDER DURING TRANSITION

All adolescents have to cope with physical and emotional maturation issues.[12] However, in people with disabilities, adolescence is often prolonged. Hallum[13] listed 8 tasks of adolescence: separation from parents and individuation; development of relationships outside of one's family; acquisition of social skills; acceptance of responsibility for one's own decisions, behavior, and their consequences; development of appropriate responses to evaluation and feedback; acquisition

of personal identity and self-image; attainment of an adult sexual role; and establishment of vocational and career identity.[13] The application of these tasks to adolescents with disabilities is discussed next.

Separation from parents is a difficult step, especially if there has been much physical care required because of the individual being in a more dependent situation.[12,13] The person with a disability needs to move toward learning to make more choices and be responsible for his or her health care and daily activities, and the parents need to learn to "let go." This is difficult for both the parents and the young adult,[12,13] and, in addition to common issues in a typical parent/teen relationship, can prove to be a challenge in the transition. Young adults often do not fully understand the roles and responsibilities of being independent and have difficulty seeing the future as this is such a new territory for them.[13]

Developing relationships outside of the family needs to be intentional.[12,13] The student should be encouraged to get involved in after school and community activities, and explore other age-appropriate opportunities to interact socially.[12] This also may prove difficult because of transportation issues and needs for rest and position changes brought about by prolonged sitting in a wheelchair. As described by one parent interviewed by the first author of this chapter, her son would be willing to sacrifice comfort to be involved in a social activity and, as a result, would be exhausted. Clinicians need to promote awareness of CP being a lifespan issue in children with this condition and help them learn to "read" their bodies.[14] Ideally, this awareness would lead to their acceptance of age-related changes and to taking action by making appropriate adjustments to their daily routines. This, in turn, would help them improve their quality of life and remain more physically functional.[14]

Social skills usually develop in a context-specific manner by actually practicing social interactions in different environments.[12,13] Observing peer interactions, becoming involved in similar situations, and having access to positive role models of adults with disabilities may help adolescents with the same conditions develop an awareness of their own social roles.[4,12,13]

Typically, adolescents begin taking more responsibility by performing chores at home and acquiring part-time jobs, followed by exploring further employment opportunities.[12,13] Young adults with disabilities need to learn to make decisions in regard to their self-care and health care, such as what to wear and when to get up to be on time, or what medications need to be taken and at what times, and when they need to be reordered. When they are unable to accomplish specific tasks on their own, in order to become independent, they need to learn how to direct their care as well as possible so that they can assess their own needs and determine how they can direct the activity and participate in it as much as possible.[12,13]

Developing appropriate responses to evaluation and feedback involves self-awareness of one's own abilities and self-monitoring that allows the person to see how his or her behavior affects other people.[12] When children with disabilities are growing up, they are often given significant amounts of attention and positive affirmation for accomplishing small goals. With age, they need to become more aware of their abilities and develop an understanding of how their abilities match the available social and vocational opportunities.[12,13]

The acquisition of one's identity and self-image are important to all adolescents, and as they move toward adulthood, they need to learn to see themselves clearly, including both positive and negative aspects.[12,13] Peer groups can provide feedback and support. Self-esteem is developed as the person identifies their capabilities and goals.[13] Having a mentor that can help the adolescent in developing self-esteem may be a very valuable experience.[12,15]

Being able to acquire an adult sexual role is very important, however, many young adults with disabilities do not have the opportunity to develop dating relationships because of a number of factors, such as dependence on others for transportation, physical deficits, or the lack of accessible environments.[13,15,16] In a Dutch study of 74 young adults with CP, 73% of all participants had a romantic relationship in the past, but only 26% of them reported being in a current relationship compared to 91% and 63%, respectively, in a reference sample of young adults without disabilities. Positive factors that contributed to having romantic relationships were sexual esteem, self-esteem, and feeling competent in regard to self-efficacy.[16]

It is important for teachers and professionals who teach sex education to focus on people with disabilities and address such issues as self-esteem, safe sex, and personal hygiene, as well as physical challenges these people have.[13,16] Wiegerink et al[15] reported that being involved with a peer group activity and having social interactions were positive contributing factors to forming romantic relationships. Discussions conducted with families and young adults with CP by the first author of this chapter helped identify such positive factors for forming romantic relationships and dating as being able to talk with or confide in a mentor, as well as having a teacher's or parent's input. Some mentioned having dates arranged and opportunities for interaction encouraged. One interviewed mother shared information about a "dating club" that was a social event where dating was discussed and the environment was open and encouraging to help young adults meet and get to know each other, with an opportunity to date other young adults with disabilities facilitated by the group. However, this mother stated that despite these efforts, her son would much prefer to date a peer without disability.

Vocational choices and career identity are contemplated by all young people who are finishing high school.[13] However, many young adults with developmental disabilities have not had an opportunity to try different part-time jobs, have shadowing experiences, or explore areas of their interest.[12] Having access to positive role models and opportunities for observation and exploration of available choices while considering the young adult's abilities and interests may be very helpful.[13]

TRANSITION SERVICES

Transition planning is covered by federal law.[8,17] According to the Individuals with Disabilities Education Improvement Act of 2004, transition services are developed to assist the student in moving to areas of their interest and ability in post-secondary education, vocational training and jobs, therapy services for adults, as well as housing and community participation.[8] The focus is generally on the team's assessment of what is needed *for* the person while the student is often focused on what is important to him or her.[18] Both considerations are important to the development and implementation of a successful personal transition plan.[18]

Family Experiences With Transition

In a family-centered environment, since the birth of their child and beginning services, parents are encouraged to be involved and to assume an active role in rehabilitation decision making.[1] As a result, they become the decision makers for their child with input from professionals.[9] Now that the child becomes a young adult who is expected to participate and join in making decisions about the future, the situation is changing rapidly, and everyone in the family recognizes that. However, it may be difficult for the young adult to decide what to do and where to live because of a sense of learned helplessness that developed when others were making decisions for him or her. In addition, all parties, including parents, teachers, medical professionals, and the young adult, may not agree in their evaluation of his or her readiness for increased independence, decision making, and learning from own life experiences. It is difficult for parents to change their role and consider the separation from their child. There are also significant financial considerations involved if the young adult needs a high degree of personal care and supervision. Knowing how much they have been involved up to this point, it is hard to imagine that an agency staff could provide the same level of care the parents have given, and it is difficult for them to accept that they will have other people who are not their family members taking over their role.[9]

Darrah et al[1] reported that families of adolescents with CP appreciated people on the team who were caring and supportive. Small gestures and offering understanding of the difficulties they experienced were very helpful. However, the families often felt fatigued and reported that they needed to fight for their decisions and learn to "work the system." This process could become very tiring and, at times, the paperwork and bureaucracy made parents feel overwhelmed.[1] The first author of this chapter obtained similar information in her interviews with parents of young adults with CP. They reported that, during transition, large amounts of information could be communicated to them very rapidly, and the list of people that needed to be contacted and the number of decisions that needed to be made seemed to grow with each meeting. These parental accounts indicate that, because of the transitioning young adults' future health care and vocational needs, knowledge of the rights of people with disabilities is an urgent necessity for them and their parents.

Parents often need a clarification of information and paperwork given to them at the Transition IEP and follow-up meetings. Randolph[19] proposed that for any person, having access to information that is clear and easy to understand constitutes the first step to his or her empowerment. Parents are concerned about their child having provisions for health care, education, recreation, employment, transportation, and housing. During the transition, obtaining meaningful work and functioning in an accessible environment are more important goals to them than an elusive goal of "looking normal."[1] Now, as they transition to adulthood, they have to learn new strategies to address their medical, social, educational, employment, and leisure needs.[1] According to several authors, many young people with complex health issues have poor health and social outcomes following transition, which is important to consider when developing prevention programs and planning services for this population so that optimal functioning can be maintained over the life span.[20,21]

Role of the Physical Therapist

Rehabilitation professionals, including physical therapists, can play an integral role at this time by listening to the young adult and his or her parents who express their opinions and discuss their choices, and by helping them assess whether these choices are realistic.[22] The physical therapist may suggest specific adaptations that would facilitate success or offer another way to provide the family with an objective assessment of the situation.[22]

Another role of rehabilitation professionals is in helping the adolescents to develop self-awareness and learn to recognize the signals they receive from their bodies that indicate that they are fatigued or have increasing pain.[22] This, ideally, would carry over to the young adults being responsible for their own health care. If they find themselves in a situation when an activity proved to be "too much" for them so that they suffer fatigue and pain, they would need to reassess their actions and learn to plan, adapt, and prioritize their activities to incorporate rest and body position changes as necessary. They would need to learn when they have more energy and how to manage their time to be able to accomplish their daily routines with less fatigue, pain, and stiffness. It is important to prepare in advance by considering the energy demands for an activity and by planning it during a time that would be optimal for preventing excessive fatigue. Fatigue may be linked to poor sleep, inadequate activity level, poor balance, and spasticity, and these factors need to be understood by the young adult.[22]

Most teenagers do not think of planning their day or planning a week to complete specific activities and meet specific goals they set for themselves.[22] This usually comes later in adulthood, but according to published literature, adolescents with CP show a slow decline in gross motor performance, social function, and gait efficiency.[23] It is important for teenagers to be prepared for coping with these changes both physically and psychologically.[22] Some young adults report less fatigue when their full body weight is not required to complete an activity. Physical therapists can suggest such activities as aquatic therapy, including walking and swimming, so that exercise can be continued with less pain and fatigue.[22] In addition, rehabilitation professionals can help the young adults to assess their activities in order to identify possible reasons for increased fatigue or pain and then suggest effective changes or coping strategies.[22,23]

Physical activity has many important health benefits and has a positive association with quality of life and psychosocial well-being.[24,25] As people with CP age, they often become less active. Inactivity may result in decreased strength, contractures, pain, and decreased physical function. Young adults need to strive to maintain their best musculoskeletal function and a healthy lifestyle. Finding fun, enjoyable activities, and especially those that involve some social interaction, may motivate the person to continue with exercise over the life span.[24,25] Adaptive sports programs may be a helpful outlet depending on their availability and the interest of the individual.[26] Virtual reality games may be used in addition to outside activities and can provide enjoyable and challenging leisure experiences.[27] This intervention may have a role in improving self-esteem and developing a feeling of empowerment in this patient population.[27]

Vocational Choices and Employment

Prognosis for employment of people with CP was discussed in detail in Chapter 5, and positive and negative predictors of employment were summarized in Table 5-4. Local Vocational Rehabilitation offices (see Appendix) assist individuals with disabilities in their search for employment. For example, in the State of New York, the Office of Vocational and Educational Services for Individuals with Disabilities (VESID) provides services for youth of 14 years of age and older through the school system.[28,29] It may be helpful to invite vocational rehabilitation counselors into the transition planning meetings to assist in maximizing the students' employability. In addition, it is imperative to keep in mind that, although not every individual may desire employment, it nevertheless should be an important consideration in the transition planning.[30]

As discussed in conversations between the first author of this chapter and families of young adults with CP, health considerations and the person's level of disability also come into play when employment is considered. In general, the more physical needs the individual has and the more fatigue, pain, and spasticity he or she suffers, the more difficult the placement opportunity may be. Some individuals with poor hand function and upper extremity ability may find obtaining employment very difficult. Often, the job coaches who work with the transition teams try to fit the students with their existing contacts in the community, which at times, unfortunately, may be similar to putting a square peg in a round hole and may not be of interest to the student.

In an interview with a mother of a young adult age 30 years, she shared that it was a family decision for her son to leave high school at age 19 years rather than staying until he turns 21 when they were told that he would be unemployable. She stated that very little had been done and little adaptive technology used in his school setting to try any work formats for him. The job coach had him trying to shred paper, but with little supports provided and with poor hand function, he could not separate papers easily. Her son was frustrated and bored with the job given to him. Some other "jobs" he attempted at school, such as collecting attendance, could not translate into a possibility for future employment. This case demonstrates that, for persons with complex medical conditions, transition planning needs to be proactive, take into account possible health changes, and allow for a thorough assessment of needs for accommodation and adaptation.

As proposed by Marn and Koch,[12] in order to become self-advocates in finding employment, young adults need to learn their rights under Title I of the Americans with Disabilities Act (ADA).[31] They also need to learn to communicate clearly with potential employers by reporting their disability to them, identifying and requesting reasonable accommodations, and discussing options for the implementation of specific strategies for accommodation.[12,32] Many individuals did not have the knowledge of resource or support systems available to them on a long-term basis, nor are they able to recognize that their needs and supports may change over time.[12] Addressing this issue should become a more significant part of the transition team's responsibility.[12]

AVAILABILITY OF SERVICES IN ADULTHOOD

Medical Services

As discussed in Chapter 23, in the medical community, there is a general lack of expertise related to treating the aging population with a childhood onset disability.[6,33] While the care these individuals received during childhood and adolescence was interprofessional and specialized for their condition, in transition to adult care, they would find few specialists and many would not be skilled in the medical treatment of persons with CP.[6,33] This condition is associated with numerous comorbidities that need to be addressed, which highlights the need for individualized, holistic care that is person-centered, with both preventive and acute care focused on maintaining optimal health for the individual.[6]

Rehabilitation Services

Many young adults with developmental disabilities, including CP, do not have consistent access to rehabilitation services because of service availability issues and payment sources.[14] At times, some services may be available, but the locations may not be easy to access. As for their insurance

coverage, some individuals are covered by Medicaid, while others would continue with their parents' health insurance. In addition, children and young adults with childhood-onset disabilities may be able to obtain Supplemental Security Income and Medicare coverage.[34] Some parents continue paying privately for therapy services to try to prevent contractures, improve comfort level, and treat acute conditions in their adult children.

Community Services

Community services and resources available to persons with disabilities are variable from state to state and locally, and should be known to the transition team. It is important to keep this information updated. A list of community resources and their descriptions are provided in the Appendix to this chapter. Besides assistance received from the transition team, parents' networking can help identify other resources, and that is often where the best information may be found. As observed by the first author of this chapter, parents frequently form groups and explore possibilities that are "outside the box." There are groups working with microboards to identify opportunities and funding resources, as well as private organizations and partnerships available in the community. Some agencies have certain services they provide but may consider other services when approached. The person-centered plan must identify the needs and wants of the individual, which subsequently can be matched with the offerings available in the community, and the lack of availability can be also identified.[10,18]

Addressing the issue of payment and support is vital for success. The source of funding would depend on the State, and Federal funds are also available. The Prioritization for Urgency of Need for Services (PUNS),[35] Home and Community Based Services (HCBS),[36] and Community Integrated Living Arrangements (CILA)[37] are examples of state and federal entities that can be approached for assistance in the State of Illinois. Usually, a case manager is responsible for filing the paperwork for these services on behalf of the young adults. Yet, even if they are eligible, they must wait until their names are "pulled" and they are given the resources. In the first author's discussions with parents, they commented that this was "like winning the lottery."

Community support is very important for individuals with disabilities. Dawson and Liddicoat[38] described a unique camp program that could serve as a therapeutic intervention and a supportive community for campers of different ages with special needs. It was a very positive experience for the participants who had an opportunity to experience 1 week of independence. In addition, the parents had 1 week of respite and were able to feel comfortable letting go because of the availability of good medical and support services provided at the camp.[38]

College Education Issues

Post-secondary education opportunities available to young adults with disabilities may be limited depending on the person's physical needs, resources, and abilities.[11] Greater physical involvement may lead to decreased opportunities for continuing one's education.[11] Factors that need to be considered include transportation; building accessibility; and being able to take notes, write papers, keep up with class discussions, and manage health issues. It is not uncommon for the family to decide that, in spite of the young person's high intellectual capacity, college education may not be feasible for them because of significant physical and personal care needs and associated costs. (To illustrate this point, the reader is referred to the supplemental book materials for a recorded interview of an adult with CP and her parents.)

Independent Living

Prognosis for independent living was discussed in detail in Chapter 5, and related statistics were summarized in Table 5-5. Living options for adults with CP include continuing with the family home, supported living in the community, CILA, and independent living with a personal care assistant. For more complex medical needs, an Intermediate Care Facility for Persons with Developmental Disabilities (ICF/DD) or a nursing home setting can provide around-the-clock care. Rarely would any young adult with CP choose a nursing home, but as parents age and if resources are not available, this may, unfortunately, become a necessity. If the person's only resource is Public Aid, this would limit his or her placement to a Public Aid nursing home. A CILA placement for an adult with CP may be much more difficult than for persons with other developmental disabilities because of environmental accessibility and physical issues. Accessible and affordable private housing is rarely available, and many people with disabilities live on SSI benefits that would not cover their monthly rent.[4] The US Department of Housing and Urban Development (HUD) is working on increasing the availability of accessible housing for this population, but many challenges still remain in this area.[4]

Parents of young adults with CP shared with the first author of this chapter that they have been partnering with agencies to explore new housing options. For example, in a suburb of Chicago, Illinois, parents are buying into a condominium building in the town center. With direct access from the outside, elevators, and adaptations, they are creating an accessible, supportive environment with hopes of social and employment participation for their adult children. There will be a live-in couple or a family in residence to oversee the operations and tutors available who will work to meet the individual's needs and goals and train personal care attendants. The plan is to have 2 residents per each supported living condominium. Some unique arrangements that are contemplated may be a young adult with CP living with a person without disability who would act as a personal care assistant. Another option may be for the second young adult in the condo to be a person with disability but without significant physical challenges who may be able to provide some help, but in addition, a personal care assistant would come in to provide support.

The parents stated that they felt this would be a "synergistic" approach to independent living for their young adults with CP in the community where they were raised and have many connections. The people they went to school with are now owners of restaurants and businesses in the area and members of the chamber of commerce who can help make community decisions. The condominium building will be easily accessible and located in the downtown area where there are stores, restaurants, medical facilities, drug stores, entertainment, and possible employment where the person in a wheelchair does not need transportation. Of course, as parents noted, there will need to be more community education provided to ensure that these young people are accepted by the town residents without disabilities.

This is a pilot project that may become a model program for the future needs of people with significant physical challenges. It is important to understand that such undertaking may not be possible for every parent as purchasing a condo and also having to provide ongoing support through an agency is costly. The agencies are funded by state and federal money. The costs of such services have limited other, more "creative" independent living opportunities. However, as such model programs are initiated, data can be collected in terms of full community integration and participation of young adults with disabilities.

Ideally, independent living in a city center may allow more opportunities to exercise as there are gyms available that can be accessible for ongoing exercise and fitness. Physical activity may help prevent comorbidities and decrease a commonly observed decline in function.[4] Access to a gym setting provides opportunities for socialization and allows for participation in age-appropriate leisure activities with peers.[4,39] There is some evidence that strength training and exercise programs may provide fitness and ADL benefits to adults with CP and decrease their pain and fatigue levels.[40,41]

Another benefit of physical activity is its reported positive association with health-related quality of life and psychosocial participation.[24] As this population is at risk for inactivity, it is important to identify the level of exercise appropriate for each individual.[24] Physical therapists can help in the transition by providing ideas and instruction for using a gym and finding ways the young adults can participate. Ideally, it would be best for the physical therapist to take the young adult to the gym they would be using and evaluate the equipment, design the exercise routine, and identify key people or trainers that could help support and encourage the person's participation at the gym.

ADDITIONAL PARENTAL CONCERNS AS THEIR CHILD TURNS EIGHTEEN

Eighteen is considered the age of majority, at which time the young adult becomes responsible for his or her own decisions.[4] Parents who feel that their son or daughter is not ready for this responsibility or may need support in decision making can pursue means to protect and support their young adult through a variety of legal means. For example, they can seek a power of attorney or guardianship, either full, temporary, or limited to medical or financial decisions. Legal advice is suggested in pursuing these steps in the best interest of the young adult.[4] Establishing a Special Needs Trust[42] and planning for the future are recommended at this time as well. Identifying succession plans, such as who will be responsible for making decisions if something happens to the parent, and having the financial structure to provide the necessary care is essential. These concerns add to parental stress related to the transition planning.

FORMALIZING THE PERSON-CENTERED TRANSITION PLANNING

There have been efforts to formalize the transition planning and maximize the input of the transitioning individuals and their families. For example, in Illinois, the Ligas Person-Centered Transition Plan instrument was developed and is being used for these purposes. The reader is referred to the related links provided in the Appendix to this chapter, under Helpful Websites for Independent Living.[10] The transition plan is to be developed with the input from the young person, his or her family, the case management group, and, ultimately, the agency providing services.[10,18] This is a lengthy process that should be initiated while taking into account the interests, needs, and wants of the transitioning person.[10,18] Discussion topics include the young adults' considerations regarding their desire to move; where and with how many people they would like to live; what kind of food they like or any specific dietary issues they may have; as well as their preferences and arrangements for employment and community and leisure activities.[10] Of concern to the young adult is also a discussion of things that they dislike, such as loud noise, yelling, or a specific type of music; not being given time to transition to new activities; or other personal choices. In addition, special consideration is given to the person's needs related to mobility, use of adaptive equipment, physical assistance, medical and personal care, behavioral support, and other areas of functioning.[10]

Oertle and Trach[43] emphasized interagency collaboration as essential for the success of transition planning and implementation, and for the integration of youth with disabilities into the community.[43] As well-stated by Huang et al[30] who cited the work by Oertle and Trach,[43] "effective transition planning offers a natural structure for building important relationships between individuals with CP, their families, medical professionals, special educators and vocational rehabilitation counsellors."(p 1007)

SUMMARY

Person-centered transition planning needs to focus on the positive aspects of the young person's life and look at the possibility of what could be in their future as an adult.[18] It is essential for the pertinent discussions to cover the factors important to the transitioning person and his or her family. The young adult needs to be able to participate in the related meetings and provide personal input in regard to what he or she feels is important. The transition team members will offer information related to their assessment of the individual's skills, strengths, needs, interests, and aspirations. It is important that, together, they identify the supports that will be needed and resources that are available or, perhaps, could be developed. Identifying potential employment, leisure, and social opportunities is essential for full participation in life.[18]

The Illinois Department of Human Services website[18] offers the following summary statement that truly reflects the essence of transition planning:

In a nutshell, Person Centered Planning assists in identifying what is important to the individual whereas assessments identify what is important for the individual. For example, having a pet or a yard to enjoy may be important to the individual, whereas taking a needed medication is important for the individual. Support plans that include what is important to the individual have a far better chance of success than support plans that just include what is important for the individual.[18]

Complete video-based activities for Chapter 24 (see Activity Set 6 on the book website).

REFERENCES

1. Darrah J, Magill-Evans J, Adkins R. How well are we doing? Families of adolescents or young adults with cerebral palsy share their perceptions of service delivery. *Disabil Rehabil.* 2002;24(19):542-549.
2. Wright M, Wallman L. Cerebral palsy. In: Campbell SK, Palisano RJ, Orlin MN, eds. *Physical Therapy for Children.* 4th ed. St. Louis, MO: Saunders; 2012:577-627.
3. Effgen SK. Schools. In: Effgen SK. *Meeting the Physical Therapy Needs of Children.* 2nd ed. Philadelphia, PA: F.A. Davis Company; 2012:495-514.
4. Sobus KML, Karkos JB. Rehabilitation care and management for the individual with cerebral palsy, ages 13 through early adulthood. *Crit Rev Phys Rehabil Med.* 2009;21(2):117-165.
5. Moll LR, Cott CA. The paradox of normalization through rehabilitation: growing up and growing older with cerebral palsy. *Disabil Rehabil.* 2013;35(15):1276-1283.
6. Tsybina I, Kingsnorth S, Maxwell J, et al. Longitudinal Evaluation of Transition Services ("LETS Study"): Protocol for outcome evaluation. *BMC Pediatr.* 2012;12:51. doi: 10.1186/1471-2431-12-51.
7. Donkervoort M, Roebroeck M, Wiegerink D, van der Heijden-Maessen H, Stam H; Transition Research Group South West Netherlands. Determinants of functioning of adolescents and young adults with cerebral palsy. *Disabil Rehabil.* 2007;29(6):453-463.
8. Pub L No 108-446, Individuals with Disabilities Education Improvement Act of 2004, 118 Stat 2647-2808.

9. Magill-Evans J, Wiart L, Darrah J, Kratochvil M, Beginning the transition to adulthood: the experiences of six families with youths with cerebral palsy. *Phys Occup Ther Pediatr.* 2005;25(3):19-36.

10. LIGAS Transition Service Plan. *Illinois Department of Human Services.* http://www.dhs.state.il.us/onenetlibrary/12/documents/Forms/IL462-0159.pdf. Accessed January 31, 2015.

11. Van Naarden Braun K, Yeargin-Allsopp M, Lollar D. A multi-dimensional approach to the transition of children with developmental disabilities into young adulthood: The acquisition of adult social roles. *Disabil Rehabil.* 2006;28(15):915-928.

12. Marn LM, Koch LC. The major tasks of adolescence: Implications for transition planning with youths with cerebral palsy. *Work.* 1999;13(1):51-58.

13. Hallum A. Disability and the transition to adulthood: issues for the disabled child, the family, and the pediatrician. *Curr Probl Pediatr.* 1995;25(1):12-50.

14. Horsman M, Suto M, Dudgeon B, Harris SR. Growing older with cerebral palsy: insiders' perspectives. *Pediatr Phys Ther.* 2010;22(3):296-303.

15. Wiegerink, DJ, Roebroeck ME, Donkervoort M, Stam JH, Cohen-Kettenis PT. Social and sexual relationships of adolescents and young adults with cerebral palsy: a review. *Clin Rehabil.* 2006;20(12):1023-1031.

16. Wiegerink DJ, Henk J, Ketelaar M, Cohen-Kettenis P, Roebroeck ME. Personal and environmental factors contributing to participation in romantic relationship and sexual activity of young adults with cerebral palsy. *Disabil Rehabil.* 2012;34(17):1481-1487.

17. Pub L No 105-17, Individuals with Disabilities Education Act Amendments of 1997, 111 Stat 37-157.

18. Person-centered planning process. *Illinois Department of Human Services.* http://www.dhs.state.il.us/page.aspx?item=65954. Accessed February 2, 20015.

19. Randolph WA. Navigating the journey to empowerment. *Organizational Dynamics.* 24(4):19-32.

20. Colver AF, Merrick H, Deverill M, et al. Study protocol: longitudinal study of the transition of young people with complex health needs from child to adult health services. *BMC Public Health.* 2013;13:675. doi:10.1186/1471-2458-13-675.

21. van Staa AL, Jedeloo S, van Meeteren J, Latour JM. Crossing the transition chasm: experiences and recommendations for improving transitional care of young adults, parents and providers. *Child Care Health Dev.* 2011;37(6):821-832.

22. Brunton LK, Bartlett DJ. The bodily experience of cerebral palsy: a journey to self-awareness. *Disabil Rehabil.* 2013;35(23):1981–1990.

23. Kerr C, McDowell BC, Parkes J, Stevenson M, Cosgrove AP. Age-related changes in energy efficiency of gait, activity, and participation in children with cerebral palsy. *Dev Med Child Neurol.* 2011;53(1):61-67.

24. Thorpe D. The role of fitness in health and disease: status of adults with cerebral palsy. *Dev Med Child Neurol.* 2009;51(suppl 4):52-58.

25. Murphy KP. The adult with cerebral palsy. *Orthop Clin North Am.* 2010;41(4):595-605.

26. Groff DG, Lundberg NR, Zabriskie RB. Influence of adapted sport on quality of life: perceptions of athletes with cerebral palsy. *Disabil Rehabil.* 2009;31(4):318-326.

27. Weiss PL, Bialik P, Kizony R. Virtual reality provides leisure time opportunities for young adults with physical and intellectual disabilities. *Cyberpsychol Behav.* 2003;6(3):335-342.

28. Vocational and Educational Services for Individuals with Disabilities program information. *NYC.* http://www1.nyc.gov/nyc-resources/service/2696/vocational-and-educational-services-for-individuals-with-disabilities-program-information. Accessed February 1, 2015.

29. Vogtle LK. Employment outcomes for adults with cerebral palsy: an issue that needs to be addressed. *Dev Med Child Neurol.* 2013;55(11):973.

30. Huang IC, Holzbauer JJ, Lee EJ, Chronister J, Chan F, O'Neil J. Vocational rehabilitation services and employment outcomes for adults with cerebral palsy in the United States. *Dev Med Child Neurol.* 2013;55(11):1000-1008.

31. Pub L 101-336, Americans with Disabilities Act, 104 Stat 327-378.

32. A guide for people with disabilities seeking employment. *ADA.gov.* http://www.ada.gov/workta.htm. Updated October 9, 2008. Accessed February 1, 2015.

33. Orlin MN, Cicirello NA, O'Donnell AE, Doty AK. The continuum of care for individuals with lifelong disabilities: role of the physical therapist. *Phys Ther.* 2014;94(7):1043-1053.

34. Social security benefits for children with disabilities. Social Security Administration Publication No. 05-10026. http://www.ssa.gov/pubs/EN-05-10026.pdf. Published January 2014. Accessed February 1, 2015.

35. Understanding PUNS – DHS 4313. *Illinois Department of Human Services.* http://www.dhs.state.il.us/page.aspx?item=47620. Accessed February 1, 2015.

36. Home and Community Based Services. *Medicaid.gov.* http://www.medicaid.gov/Medicaid-CHIP-Program-Information/By-Topics/Long-Term-Services-and-Supports/Home-and-Community-Based-Services/Home-and-Community-Based-Services.html

37. Community Independent Living Arrangements (CILA). *Illinois Department of Human Services.* http://www.dhs.state.il.us/page.aspx?item=47487. Accessed February 1, 2015.

38. Dawson S, Liddicoat K. "Camp gives me hope": exploring the therapeutic use of community for adults with cerebral palsy. *Ther Recreation J.* 2009;43(4):9-24.

39. Boucher N, Dumas F, Maltais DB, Richards CL. The influence of selected personal and environmental factors on leisure activities in adults with cerebral palsy. *Disabil Rehabil.* 2010;32(16):1328-1338.

40. Taylor NF, Dodd KJ, Larkin H. Adults with cerebral palsy benefit from participating in a strength training programme at a community gymnasium. *Disabil Rehabil.* 2004;26(19):1128-1134.

41. Vogtle LK, Malone LA, Azyero A. Outcomes of an exercise program for pain and fatigue management in adults with cerebral palsy. *Disabil Rehabil.* 2014;36(10):818-825.

42. Lewis KM. Special Needs Trusts: the cornerstone of planning for beneficiaries with disabilities. *American Bar Association.* http://www.americanbar.org/content/dam/aba/publishing/rpte_ereport/te_lewis.authcheckdam.pdf. Published 2010. Accessed February 2, 2015.

43. Oertle KM, Trach JS. Interagency collaboration: the importance of rehabilitation professionals' involvement in transition. *J Rehabil.* 2007;73(3):36-44.

Please see videos on the accompanying website at

www.healio.com/books/videosrahlin

APPENDIX

RESOURCES FOR YOUNG ADULTS AND ADULTS WITH CEREBRAL PALSY AND OTHER DISABILITIES AND THEIR FAMILIES

ORGANIZATION	WEBSITE	BRIEF DESCRIPTION
		General Resources
MyChild	http://cerebralpalsy.org/about-mychild/	A national call center located in Novi, Michigan, that provides information on available resources and non-legal assistance related to home-, school-, and community-based care and other topics.
		Find Help and Services in Your Community
United Cerebral Palsy (UCP) – find local affiliates	http://ucp.org/findaffiliate/	UCP affiliates offer a variety of services, including assistive technology training, community living, early intervention services, employment, employment assistance and advocacy, housing, individual and family support, physical therapy, social and recreational programs, and state and local referrals. They advocate improvements in service provision and provide information and services to the community of people with developmental disabilities.
Centers for Independent Living	www.ilru.org/html/publications/directory/index.html	Directory of Centers for Independent Living (private, nonprofit corporations) that provide services to individuals with disabilities to maximize their independence and the accessibility of their local communities. These centers provide a variety of services, including advocacy, independent living training, information, peer counseling, and referrals.
Center for Parent Information and Resources	www.parentcenterhub.org/	Provides information to parents of children with disabilities ages birth to 26 years, including links to Parent Training and Information Centers by state, Resource Library for the Parent Center network, and numerous resources developed by the National Dissemination Center for Children with Disabilities.
Aging and Disability Resource Centers	www.adrc-tae.acl.gov/tiki-index.php?page=ADRCLocator	This is a listing of Aging and Disability Resource Centers that serve as single points of entry into the system of long-term supports and services for people with disabilities and older adults.
		Find Financial Assistance
United Cerebral Palsy (UCP) Elsie S. Bellows Fund	http://ucp.org/findaffiliat	A national program operated by UCP. It funds assistive technology equipment for people with disabilities. Individuals need to apply through their local UCP affiliate, which will submit an application to the UCP national office on their behalf. The Bellows Committee reviews the applications for funding.
State Assistive Technology Programs	www.resnaprojects.org/allcontacts/statewidecontacts.html	These are federally funded programs covered by the Assistive Technology Act. They promote the awareness of assistive technology devices and services and provide access to these services through funding and low interest loan programs to assist the device purchasing.
Social Security Disability Benefits	www.ssa.gov/disabilityssi/	Includes 2 programs of the Social Security Administration: the Supplemental Security Income (SSI) program and the Social Security disability insurance program. Information related to eligibility, application process, and claim denial appeal process if provided on the website

(continued)

426 Chapter 24

426

APPENDIX (CONTINUED)

RESOURCES FOR YOUNG ADULTS AND ADULTS WITH CEREBRAL PALSY AND OTHER DISABILITIES AND THEIR FAMILIES

ORGANIZATION	WEBSITE	BRIEF DESCRIPTION
Find Financial Assistance		
Centers for Medicaid and Medicare Services	www.cms.gov	Provides a wide range of information on Medicare and Medicaid services
Medicaid Waiver Programs	www.medicaid.gov/Medicaid-CHIP-Program-Information/By-Topics/Waivers/Waivers.html	State-based programs administered by the medicaid authority that may provide traditional medical and non-medical services
Benefits.Gov	www.benefits.gov	Provides citizens with online access to government assistance and benefits programs
Partnership for Prescription Assistance Programs	www.pparx.org	Assists the qualified individuals who do not have prescription drug coverage in obtaining the medicine they need free or nearly free of charge
NeedyMeds	www.needymeds.org/index.htm	A nonprofit organization that helps people find medication and disease-based assistance programs, free and low-cost clinics, and government programs that help cover health care-related costs
Laws and Advocacy		
ADA National Network	http://adata.org	Provides guidance, training, and information related to the Americans with Disabilities Act (ADA) and is designed to address the needs of individuals, businesses, and government at local, regional, and national levels through 10 Regional ADA National Network Centers
Protection and Advocacy for People with Disabilities Network	www.ndrn.org/en/about/paacap-network.html	A network of state protection and advocacy agencies mandated by federal government that functions to safeguard and advance the civil and human rights of persons with disabilities. Services include information and referral, investigations of complaints related to rights violations, as well as mediation, dispute resolution, and litigation.
American Bar Association on Mental and Physical Disability	www.americanbar.org/groups/disabilityrights.html	Is involved in activities and projects that address disability law and public policy, as well as the professional needs of law students and attorneys with disabilities

(continued)

APPENDIX (CONTINUED)

RESOURCES FOR YOUNG ADULTS AND ADULTS WITH CEREBRAL PALSY AND OTHER DISABILITIES AND THEIR FAMILIES

ORGANIZATION	WEBSITE	BRIEF DESCRIPTION
		Disability Publications
Ability Magazine	www.abilitymagazine.com	The focus of this magazine is health, disability, human potential, and ability levels
New Mobility	www.newmobility.com	A magazine for wheelchair users
Exceptional Parent	www.eparent.com	A magazine for parents of children and youth with disabilities
Disability Scoop	www.disabilityscoop.com/	A national news organization that reports on issues important for the developmental disability community, and specifically, people with autism, cerebral palsy, Down syndrome, and intellectual disabilities
E-Bility.com	www.e-bility.com	A website that offers information on resources, products, and services for people with disabilities, their families, and medical and other service providers
Mainstream Online	www.mainstream-mag.com/about-us	An online magazine "produced by, for, and about people with disabilities"
SpecialLiving	www.specialliving.com/	A magazine for people with mobility limitations that covers accessible housing, disability benefits, health and fitness, travel, and other issues
		For Job Seekers
EARNWorks: Job Seeker Tools and Resources	http://askearn.org/refdesk/FAQ/FAQ_Jobseekers	Provides information and resources that assist job seekers with disabilities in finding work
GettingHired.com	www.gettinghired.com	An Internet-based portal that serves job seekers with disabilities by connecting them to advocacy organizations, employers, and service providers
ABILITY JOBS	http://abilityjobs.com	Provides assistance with finding employment by posting resumes and job opportunities for people with disabilities
JobTIPS	www.do2learn.com/JobTIPS/index.html	A free program that assists people with disabilities in exploring their career interests, and seeking, obtaining, and successfully maintaining employment
DisAbledPerson.com	www.disabledperson.com	A free online job board that serves individuals with disabilities by connecting them to potential employers through posting resumes and job opportunities
Social Security Ticket to Work Site	www.ssa.gov/work/	Provides eligible Social Security beneficiaries with choices for receiving employment services, vocational rehabilitation, and other support services aimed at helping them achieve their work goals

(continued)

Appendix (continued)

Resources for Young Adults and Adults With Cerebral Palsy and Other Disabilities and Their Families

ORGANIZATION	WEBSITE	BRIEF DESCRIPTION
		For Job Seekers
Entrepreneurship for People with Disabilities	www.dol.gov/odep/pubs/misc/entrepre.htm	A fact sheet on entrepreneurship posted by the Office of Disability Employment Policy of the United States Department of Labor
The Abilities Fund	www.abilitiesfund.org	A nationwide nonprofit community developer and financial institution with an exclusive focus on expansion of entrepreneurial opportunities for individuals with disabilities by providing them with advisory supports, financial products, technical assistance services, and training
The US Office on Disability Employment Policy (ODEP)	www.dol.gov/odep/index.htm	Provides information on employment and disability; develops and affects the use of evidence-based disability employment policies and practices
Job Accommodation Network (JAN)	http://askjan.org/cgi-win/TypeQuery.exe?902	Provides contact information for state Vocational Rehabilitation (VR) agencies that provide counseling, education, medical, therapeutic, training, and other services for people with disabilities that help them prepare for work
Goodwill Industries International	www.goodwill.org/	A network of 165 independent, community-based Goodwills located in the United States and Canada that provides people with disabilities, those who have insufficient education and work experience, and those who have difficulty obtaining employment with customized job training, employment placement, and other services
National Center on Workforce and Disability/Adult (NCWD)	www.onestops.info/	Provides information, policy analysis, technical assistance, and training that help individuals with disabilities find work and advise employers on how to support employment of these individuals
SourceAmerica	www.sourceamerica.org/	A national nonprofit agency that secures federal contracts through the AbilityOne Program for its network of nonprofit community-based agencies to create employment opportunities for people with disabilities
The Employer Assistance and Resource Network (EARN)	http://askearn.org/	Provides free consulting services and resources to federal and private employers to support the recruitment, hiring, and retention of people with disabilities; connects employers with job seekers and provides online information and technical assistance that promote the workplace inclusion of employees with disabilities

(continued)

APPENDIX (CONTINUED)

RESOURCES FOR YOUNG ADULTS AND ADULTS WITH CEREBRAL PALSY AND OTHER DISABILITIES AND THEIR FAMILIES

ORGANIZATION	WEBSITE	BRIEF DESCRIPTION
		Health and Wellness Tips: Proper Nutrition
USDA Resource on Nutrition and Disability	http://snap.nal.usda.gov/professional-development-tools/hot-topics-z/nutrition-and-disability	Information and other valuable resources provided through Supplemental Nutrition Assistance program (SNAP) to educate individuals with disabilities about proper nutrition
National Center on Health, Physical Activity, and Disability	www.nchpad.org/Articles/12/Nutrition	Nutrition facts and recommendations for people with disabilities by specific diagnosis or health condition
		Health and Wellness Tips: Physical Activity
National Center on Health, Physical Activity, and Disability	www.nchpad.org	Provides factsheets and other helpful information on physical activity for individuals with disabilities, such as exercise guidelines, games, sports and recreational activities adapted for this population, as well as ways to find a certified inclusive fitness instructor and other resources
Disabled Sports USA	www.disabledsportsusa.org	A network of national sports rehabilitation programs, such as fitness and special sports events, summer and winter competitions, skiing, and water sports
Blaze Sports	www.blazesports.org	A network of community-based organizations and clubs that promotes healthy lifestyle and physical activity among children and adults with physical disabilities and provides them with opportunities to participate in competitive sports
Mobility International USA (MIUSA)	www.miusa.org	A nonprofit organization that offers international educational exchange programs, travel, placement in international work camps, international leadership training, and other opportunities for people with disabilities and others
		Health and Wellness Tips: Oral Health
Special Care Dentistry Association	www.scdaonline.org	An international organization of oral health professionals that serves to promote oral health and health care access for people with special needs through networking and education
Dental Lifeline Network	http://dentallifeline.org	A national nonprofit organization that provides access to dental care for people with disabilities, senior citizens, and medically fragile patients through a national network of direct service programs that involve volunteer dentists and laboratories
		For Home Modifications
Easter Seals Easy Access Housing for Easier Living Program	www.easterseals.com	Together with the CENTURY 21 System's Easy Access Housing for Easier Living Program, provides educational brochures, expert advice, and other resources for homeowners who would like to implement modifications to make their homes accessible or build a new accessible home

(continued)

APPENDIX (CONTINUED)

RESOURCES FOR YOUNG ADULTS AND ADULTS WITH CEREBRAL PALSY AND OTHER DISABILITIES AND THEIR FAMILIES

ORGANIZATION	WEBSITE	BRIEF DESCRIPTION
		For Home Modifications
Making Homes Accessible: Assistive Technology and Home Modifications	www.resnaprojects.org/nattap/goals/community/HMRG.htm	A resource guide that provides information on a variety of topics that cover home modifications and assistive technology
HomeMods.org	www.homemods.org	A website that promotes independent living for people across age groups and abilities and provides educational opportunities, training, and resources for professionals who are interested in delivering home modification services
		Assistive Technology
AbleData	www.abledata.com/	Provides information on assistive technology and rehabilitation equipment
Assistivetech.net National Public Website on Assistive Technology	http://assistivetech.net/	Provides information on assistive technology devices, services, and community resources through an online database that can be searched for by function, activity or vendor
Association on Higher Education and Disability (AHEAD)	www.ahead.org	An international and multicultural professional membership organization that promotes equal and full equal participation in higher education by personas with disabilities and supports the institutions and professionals committed to this mission through consultation, training, education, and publications
Division of Adult Education and Literacy	www2.ed.gov/about/offices/list/ovae/pi/AdultEd/disability.html	Supports a network of federal and state initiatives and programs available for people with disabilities through the Office of Career, Technical and Adult Education (OCTAE) of the US Department of Education
HEATH Resource Center	www.heath.gwu.edu	Provides information on post-secondary education, including adaptations, educational support services, opportunities at American campuses, policies, procedures, vocational-technical schools, and other post-secondary training institutions available for adults with disabilities
The DO-IT (Disabilities, Opportunities, Internetworking, and Technology) Center	wwww.washington.edu/doit/	Promotes participation in challenging academic programs and careers by individuals with disabilities in challenging academic programs and careers; provides information and resources and hosts projects for students with disabilities, as well as advocates, administrators, educators and employers
Online Colleges, College Scholarships and Degrees	www.college-scholarships.com/	A website that provides information on online colleges, degrees, financial aid, and scholarships, as well as articles for online students.

(continued)

APPENDIX (CONTINUED)

RESOURCES FOR YOUNG ADULTS AND ADULTS WITH CEREBRAL PALSY AND OTHER DISABILITIES AND THEIR FAMILIES

ORGANIZATION	WEBSITE	BRIEF DESCRIPTION
		Helpful Websites for Independent Living
Government Benefits	www.benefits.gov/	Helps people find government benefits for which they may be eligible using a free and confidential screening instrument
National Council on Independent Living (NCIL)	www.ncil.org/	A national organization that represents people with disabilities and such organizations as Centers for Independent Living and Statewide Independent Living Councils that advocate for the rights of individuals with disabilities in the United States
National Rehabilitation Information Center (NARIC)	www.naric.com/	Provides online disability- and rehabilitation-related information in a variety of areas, including independent living and community participation, as well as advocacy, assistive technology, benefits and financial assistance, education, employment, etc
Research and Training Center on Independent Living	http://rtcil.org/products	Produces and provides information on a variety of products that support independent living of people with disabilities
LCAS Transition Service Plan	www.dhs.state.il.us/onenetlibrary/12/documents/Forms/IL462-0159.pdf	An example of an instrument that is used to document individual needs and preferences of young adults with disabilities who wish to transition to community-based services or settings
Social Security Administration (SSA)	www.socialsecurity.gov/disability/ https://secure.ssa.gov/apps6z/FOLO/fo001.jsp	Provides cash benefits through the Social Security and Supplemental Security Income disability programs to qualified people with physical or mental disabilities. The amount of money and services received vary by state (use the second link to access the Social Security Online Office Locator)

Section VI

QUESTIONS TO PONDER

1. Can increasing direct medical costs be justified by possible long-term gains in productivity and quality of life of people with CP? Please explain your answer.

2. What are the reasons for decreased access to rehabilitation services experienced by young adults and adults with disabilities as they age? Is this a health care, economic, or political problem?

3. Besides those discussed in this text, what may be some other possible solutions to the problem of shortage of health care providers, including physical therapists, who can competently treat young adults and adults with developmental disabilities?

4. To follow up on the previous question, are there any incentives that may be developed to encourage physical therapists to consider specializing in this area of practice?

5. Is it appropriate to pay patients' parents for the provision of personal assistance duties? Please explain your answer.

6. What may be some underlying societal factors that determine the transition-related level of stress experienced by youth with disabilities and their parents and how can these factors be addressed?

SUGGESTED QUESTIONS FOR FUTURE RESEARCH

1. Would the implementation of optimally intensive therapy programs have a positive effect on indirect costs and overall economic burden of CP?

2. What effects does care coordination offered through a patient-centered medical home have on the number of emergency room visits, health care costs, and patient and family satisfaction?

3. Will an increase in utilization of rehabilitation services by adolescents and young adults with developmental disabilities result in improved quality of life in this patient population?

4. What is/are the optimal therapy delivery model(s), type(s), and intensity of intervention for adolescents, young adults, and adults with CP that would result in best outcomes in the areas of activity, participation, and quality of life?

5. Is there a relationship between family-centered care provided to children and youth with CP and health and health-related quality of life of their caregivers?

6. Considering the complexity of the issue of transition to adulthood, what are the best ways to investigate the determinants of success and outcomes of the transition process?

Financial Disclosures

Dr. Donna Frownfelter has no financial or proprietary interest in the materials presented herein.

Dr. Regina T. Harbourne has no financial or proprietary interest in the materials presented herein.

Dr. Roberta Henderson has no financial or proprietary interest in the materials presented herein.

Dr. Toby M. Long has no financial or proprietary interest in the materials presented herein.

Donald McGovern has no financial or proprietary interest in the materials presented herein.

Elaine Owen has no financial or proprietary interest in the materials presented herein.

Dr. Mary Rahlin has no financial or proprietary interest in the materials presented herein.

Dr. Wendy Rheault has no financial or proprietary interest in the materials presented herein.

Index

secondary variability, movement, 25-26
segmental fixation, 137
segments, in gait, 288-291, 297-303
seizures and epilepsy, 64-65, 67, 113-116
    intractable, 113
    prognosis in and social integration of people with, 95,97
    refractory, 113
    types of, 67
selective dorsal rhizotomy, 118, 120
selective motor control, 116
selective motor control (SMC) test, 187
self-organization, 15
sensation, vs. perception, 18-19
sensitivity, of standardized assessment instruments, 174
sensorimotor integration, problems with, 77
sensory systems
    alterations in in structures and function of, 65, 76-77
    medical and surgical management of, 152-153
sensory integrity, assessment of, 179
service delivery models, 207-221
    Apollo model, 219
    in Early Intervention, 212-213
    Life Needs Model of Pediatric Service Delivery, 219
    in a school setting, 216-218
sexual function and education, 419
shank kinematics, 290-291, 347-350
shank to vertical angle, of ankle-foot orthosis/footwear combination, 344-345, 357-364
shaping, in behavior management, 228-229
sharing, in interdisciplinary teams, 103-104
shoulder
    block to typical motor development, 33
    deformities of, 74, 135
shuttle run tests, 189-190
sialorrhea, 72, 121
sibling relationships, 410-414
single-event multilevel surgery (SEMLs), 129, 131-134, 137
sitting
    assistive technology for, 373, 375-376, 382, 385-387
    independent, in prognosis for ambulation, 88
sit-to-stand test, 188
six-minute walk test (6MWT), 194, 196
skills, hidden, 15
skin
    examination and evaluation of, 189-191
    medical and surgical management of, 151
    positioning for, 380-382
sleep disorders, 146-147
social integration, prognosis for, 95, 97
social participation, 412-414
soft tissue mobilization, 255-256
solid ankle-foot orthoses (SAFO), 318-319, 321-323
spasticity, 52, 53, 55
    assessment of, 177-179
    general movements, predictive of, 39

medical and surgical management of, 116-120
muscle weakness, associated with, 73
postural adjustments, in presence of, 69
stretching orthoses for management of, 328-332
special education, 213
Special Needs Trust, 423
specificity, of standardized assessment instruments, 174
speech deficits, 72, 121, 189, 412-413
spinal deformities, 76, 137-138. See also scoliosis
    evaluation of, 185
    orthotic management of, 332-334
    in seating system design, 387
spirometry, 189
spring torsion orthoses, 328-332
sprint tests, 196
stability, in walking, 70-71
Stabilizing Pressure Input Orthoses (SPIO), 334-335
Staheli test, 180-181
Standardized Walking Obstacle Course (SWOC), 194-196
standers and standing programs, 377, 382, 384-386
standing, 294
    frames for, 373, 377
    kinetics and kinematics of, 304-307
    orthotic management for, 315-326, 350-352
    programs of, 382-385
Standing, Walking and Sitting Hip (S.W.A.S.H.) orthosis, 325-326
stem cell therapies, 111-113
stepping, 15-16
    kinetics and kinematics of, 294, 306-307
    orthotic management for, 350-351, 353
stiffness, of orthoses and footwear heel and sole, 346-347
strength, deficits of, 73
strength testing, 185-188
strength training, 256
stressors, in transition to adult life, 417-418
stretching, passive, 255
stretching orthoses, 328-332
stretching velocities, in spasticity assessment, 177
suit therapy, 268
support walkers, 373, 375, 385
supramalleolar orthoses (SMO), 319, 321-322
"surrogate" strength assessment, 187
Surveillance of Cerebral Palsy in Europe classification of CP, 52
survival, of individuals with CP, 399
swallowing, disorders of, 72-73
S.W.A.S.H. (Standing, Walking and Sitting Hip) orthosis, 318-323
swaying, 305-306
swimming, 249-250
Synactive Theory of Development, 208

tactile deficits, 77
TAMO therapy, 234